Daniel S. Yeung   Zhi-Qiang Liu
Xi-Zhao Wang   Hong Yan (Eds.)

Advances in Machine Learning and Cybernetics

4th International Conference, ICMLC 2005
Guangzhou, China, August 18-21, 2005
Revised Selected Papers

Series Editors

Jaime G. Carbonell, Carnegie Mellon University, Pittsburgh, PA, USA
Jörg Siekmann, University of Saarland, Saarbrücken, Germany

Volume Editors

Daniel S. Yeung
Hong Kong Polytechnic University
Department of Computing
Hong Kong, China
E-mail: csdaniel@comp.polyu.edu.hk

Zhi-Qiang Liu
City University of Hong Kong
Department of Creative Media
Hong Kong, China
E-mail: zq.liu@cityu.edu.hk

Xi-Zhao Wang
Hebei University
Department of Mathematics and Computer Science
Baoding, China
E-mail: xizhaowang@ieee.org

Hong Yan
City University of Hong Kong
Department of Computer Science
Hong Kong, China
E-mail: h.yan@cityu.edu.hk

Library of Congress Control Number: 2006923359

CR Subject Classification (1998): I.2, F.4.1, F.1, F.2, G.3, I.2.3, I.4, I.5

LNCS Sublibrary: SL 7 – Artificial Intelligence

ISSN   0302-9743
ISBN-10   3-540-33584-6 Springer Berlin Heidelberg New York
ISBN-13   978-3-540-33584-9 Springer Berlin Heidelberg New York

This work is subject to copyright. All rights are reserved, whether the whole or part of the material is concerned, specifically the rights of translation, reprinting, re-use of illustrations, recitation, broadcasting, reproduction on microfilms or in any other way, and storage in data banks. Duplication of this publication or parts thereof is permitted only under the provisions of the German Copyright Law of September 9, 1965, in its current version, and permission for use must always be obtained from Springer. Violations are liable to prosecution under the German Copyright Law.

Springer is a part of Springer Science+Business Media

springer.com

© Springer-Verlag Berlin Heidelberg 2006
Printed in Germany

Typesetting: Camera-ready by author, data conversion by Scientific Publishing Services, Chennai, India
Printed on acid-free paper   SPIN: 11739685   06/3142   5 4 3 2 1 0

Preface

Machine learning and cybernetics play an important role in many modern electronic, computer and communications systems. Automated processing of information by these systems requires intelligent analysis of various types of data and optimal decision making. In recent years, we have witnessed a rapid expansion of research and development activities in machine learning and cybernetics. To provide opportunities for researchers in these areas to share their ideas and foster collaborations, the International Conference on Machines and Cybernetics (ICMLC) has been held annually since 2002. The conference series has achieved a great success in attracting a large number of paper submissions and participants and enabling fruitful exchanges among academic and industrial researchers and postgraduate students.

In 2005, the conference (ICMLC 2005) received 2461 full paper submissions and the Program Committee selected 1050 of them for presentation. It is especially encouraging that the conference is attracting more and more international attention. This year, there are contributions from 21 countries and 211 universities worldwide. Out of the 1050 papers presented at the conference, we selected 114 papers to be published in this volume of *Lecture Notes in Computer Science*.

The papers in this volume are divided into nine broad areas:

- Agents and distributed artificial intelligence
- Control
- Data mining and knowledge discovery
- Fuzzy information processing
- Learning and reasoning, machine learning applications
- Neural networks and statistical learning methods
- Pattern recognition
- Vision and image processing

In addition to new theoretical research results, such as on stability analysis of nonlinear control systems and innovative learning algorithms, the papers report a wide range of useful applications to biomedical engineering, commerce, database management, electronics, network security, transportation, etc.

We are grateful for the sponsorship of the conference from the IEEE Systems, Man and Cybernetics Society, Hong Kong Polytechnic University, Hebei University, South China University of Technology, Chongqing University, Sun Yat-sen University, the Harbin Institute of Technology and the International University in Germany. We would like to thank members of the ICMLC 2005 Advisory, Organizing and Program Committees for their hard work. We appreciate the help from Mrs. Inge Rogers, who arranged proofreading of the papers in this volume, and staff and students in our research groups, who provided a lot of assistance for the conference organization.

December 2005

YEUNG, Daniel
LIU, Zhiqiang
WANG, Xizhao
YAN, Hong

Organization

ICMLC 2005 Organization Committee

Honorary Conference Chairs

Hongrui Wang	China
Chung-Kwong Poon	Hong Kong, China
Yuanyuan Li	China
Daren Huang	China
Shuguo Wang	China
Xiaohong Li	China
Michael Smith	USA
William A. Gruver	Canada
Minghu Ha	China
Jan-Ming Ko	Hong Kong, China
Xinyi Peng	China
Yuantong Xu	China
Lichun Shu	China
Hongqing Zhang	China

Conference Chairs

Xizhao Wang	China
Daniel S. Yeung	Hong Kong, China
Ling Zhang	China
Jiwu Huang	China

Program Chairs

Michael Smith	USA
Donald Brown	USA
Xiaolong Wang	China

Publication Chairs

John W.T. Lee	Hong Kong, China

Invited Session Chair

Rocky Chang   Hong Kong, China

Tutorial Chair

Fang Yuan   China

Best Paper Award Chairs

Michael Smith	USA
James Kwok	Hong Kong, China
Hong Peng	China
Jiwu Huang	China

Local Arrangement Chairs

Guoqiang Han	China
Jiangqing Xi	China
Shenshan Qiu	China
Hongyang Chao	China
Jian Yin	China

Conference Secretaries

Qiang He	China
Wing W.Y. Ng	Hong Kong, China

Program Committee

Ashraf Abdelbar	Frederic Alexandre	P.E. Borne
Donald Brown	Patrick Chan	Huiyou Chang
Maiga Chang	Degang Chen	Ian Cloete
Robert I. Damper	Feiqi Deng	Maria Pia Fanti
Chun-Che Fung	Junbin Gao	Alessandro Giua
Colin Fyfe	Maozu Guo	William Gruver
Larry Hall	Qing He	T. Hegazy
Jiwu Huang	Deshuang Huang	Lahkmi Jain
Muder Jeng	Yunfei Jiang	Shuyuan Jin
Xiaoming Jin	Irwin King	Frank Klawonn
James Kwok	Loi-Lei Lai	Doo Yong Lee
John Lee	Jonathan Lee	Wing-Bun Lee

T.T. Lee
Kunlun Li
Da-Yin Liao
Zhi-Qiang Liu
Sadaaki Miyamoto
Wing Ng
Chaoyi Pang
Hong Peng
Tuan Pham
A.B. Rad
Daming Shi
Renming Song
Hideyuki Takagi
Ah-Chung Tsoi
Shengrui Wang
Zhenyu Wang
Kok-Wai Wong
Dit-Yan.Yeung
Leehter Yao
Xiaoqin Zeng
Guangquan Zhang

Chung-Lun Li
Jiuzhen Liang
Chin-Teng Lin
Vincenzo Loia
Jamshidi Mo
Duy Nguyen
Sulin Pang
Xinyi Peng
Robin Qiu
David Russell
Andrew Skabar
Jianbo Su
Y.Y. Tang
Defeng Wang
Shitong Wang
Qingshan Wei
Jitian Xiao
Jian Yin
Fang Yuan
Chengqi Zhang
Zhen Zhu

Fanchang Li
Yanchun Liang
Qing Liu
Ming Lu
Tadahiko Murata
Takehisa Onisawa
Zhi-Geng Pan
Yonghong Peng
Shenshan Qiu
Mika Sato
Wenhao Shu
Shunfeng Su
Eric Tsang
Dianhui Wang
Xiaolong Wang
Kit-Po Wong
Bugong Xu
Yang Yi
Ahmed Zobaa
Qilun Zheng

Sponsors

香港理工大學 THE HONG KONG POLYTECHNIC UNIVERSITY

HEBEI UNIVERSITY

International University in Germany

HARBIN INSTITUTE OF TECHNOLOGY

華南理工大學 South China University of Technology

SUN YAT-SEN UNIVERSITY

CHONGQING UNIVERSITY

Table of Contents

Agents and Distributed AI

Backward-Chaining Flexible Planning
  Li Xu, Wen-Xiang Gu, Xin-Mei Zhang 1

RRF: A Double-Layer Reputation Mechanism with Rating Reputation Considered
  Hang Guo, Ji Gao, Ping Xu 11

A Vickrey-Type Multi-attribute Auction Model
  Xiang Chen, Shan-li Hu 21

Strategy Coordination Approach for Safe Learning About Novel Filtering Strategies in Multi Agent Framework
  Sahin Albayrak, Dragan Milosevic 30

Modeling and Design of Agent Grid Based Open Decision Support System
  Jiayu Chi, Ling Sun, Xueguang Chen, Jinlong Zhang 43

Negotiating Agent: Concept, Architecture and Communication Model
  Mukun Cao, Yuqiang Feng, Yan Li, Chunyan Wang 53

Intelligent Control (I)

Particle Filter Method for a Centralized Multisensor System
  Wei Xiong, You He, Jing-wei Zhang 64

Design and Analysis of a Novel Load-Balancing Model Based on Mobile Agent
  Junfeng Tian, Yuling Liu, Xiaohui Yang, Ruizhong Du 70

Fuzzy Output Tracking Control and Its Application to Guidance Control for Lunar Gravity-Turn
  Pingyuan Cui, Junwei Sun, Fengqiu Liu 81

Motion Planning for Climbing Robot Based on Hybrid Navigation
  Yong Jiang, Hongguang Wang, Lijin Fang, Mingyang Zhao 91

Hierarchical Fuzzy Behavior-Based Control Method for Autonomous
Mobile Robot Navigation
    Shou-tao Li, Yuan-chun Li 101

Intelligent Control (II)

An LMI Approach to Robust Fault Detection Filter Design for
Uncertain State-Delayed Systems
    Hongru Wang, Changhong Wang, Huijun Gao 112

Input-to-State Stability Analysis of a Class of Interconnected Nonlinear
Systems
    Jia Wang, Xiaobei Wu, Zhiliang Xu 122

Construction and Simulation of the Movable Propeller Turbine Neural
Network Model
    Jiang Chang, Yan Peng 133

Research on the Control and Application of Chaos in an Electrical
System
    Zhao-ming Lei, Zuo-jun Liu, He-xu Sun, Hong-jun Chang 142

Data Mining and Knowledge Discovery (I)

Research and Application of Data Mining in Power Plant Process
Control and Optimization
    Jian-qiang Li, Cheng-lin Niu, Ji-zhen Liu, Luan-ying Zhang 149

Extended Negative Association Rules and the Corresponding Mining
Algorithm
    Min Gan, Mingyi Zhang, Shenwen Wang 159

An Ant Clustering Method for a Dynamic Database
    Ling Chen, Li Tu, Yixin Chen 169

An Efficient Algorithm for Incremental Mining of Sequential Patterns
    Jia-Dong Ren, Xiao-Lei Zhou 179

A Clustering Algorithm Based on Density Kernel Extension
    Wei-Di Dai, Pi-Lian He, Yue-Xian Hou, Xiao-Dong Kang 189

Associative Classification with Prediction Confidence
    Tien Dung Do, Siu Cheung Hui, Alvis C.M. Fong 199

Data Mining and Knowledge Discovery (II)

Exploring Query Matrix for Support Pattern Based Classification
Learning
Yiqiu Han, Wai Lam 209

From Clusters to Rules: A Hybrid Framework for Generalized Symbolic
Rule Induction
Qingshuang Jiang, Syed Sibte Raza Abidi 219

Trail-and-Error Approach for Determining the Number of Clusters
Haojun Sun, Mei Sun 229

Unifying Genetic Algorithm and Clustering Method for Recognizing
Activated fMRI Time Series
Lin Shi, Pheng Ann Heng, Tien-Tsin Wong 239

Repeating Pattern Discovery from Audio Stream
Zhen-Long Du, Xiao-Li Li 249

A Study on Information Extraction from PDF Files
Fang Yuan, Bo Liu, Ge Yu 258

Data Mining and Knowledge Discovery (III)

The Study of a Knowledge-Based Constraints Network System (KCNS)
for Concurrent Engineering
*Wei-ming Wang, Jie Hu, Fei Zhou, Da-yong Li, Xiang-jun Fu,
Ying-hong Peng* 268

Rule Induction for Complete Information Systems in Knowledge
Acquisition and Classification
Hong-Zhen Zheng, Dian-Hui Chu, De-Chen Zhan 278

A Method to Eliminate Incompatible Knowledge and Equivalence
Knowledge
Ping Guo, Li Fan, Lian Ye 285

Constructing Ontologies for Sharing Knowledge in Digital Archives
Yu-Liang Chi 295

A Similarity-Aware Multiagent-Based Web Content Management
Scheme
Jitian Xiao, Jun Wang 305

Information Assistant: An Initiative Topic Search Engine
*Xi-Dao Luan, Yu-Xiang Xie, Ling-Da Wu, Chi-Long Mao,
Song-Yang Lao* 315

Improving Retrieval Performance with the Combination of Thesauri
and Automatic Relevance Feedback
Mao-Zu Guo, Jian-Fu Li 322

Fuzzy Information Processing (I)

Choquet Integrals with Respect to Fuzzy Measure on Fuzzy σ–Algebra
Yan Huang, Congxin Wu 329

Robust H_∞ Control with Pole Placement Constraints for T-S Fuzzy
Systems
Liang He, Guang-Ren Duan 338

A Kind of Fuzzy Genetic Algorithm Based on Rule and Its Performance
Research
Fachao Li, Shuxin Luo, Lianqing Su 347

The Absolute Additivity and Fuzzy Additivity of Sugeno Integral
Congxin Wu, Liang Zhao 358

The Axiomatization for 0-Level Universal Logic
Yingcang Ma, Huacan He 367

Fuzzy Portfolio Selection Problems Based on Credibility Theory
Yanju Chen, Yan-Kui Liu, Junfen Chen 377

Fuzzy Information Processing (II)

Fuzzy Multiple Reference Models Adaptive Control Scheme Study
Zhicheng Ji, Rongjia Zhu, Yanxia Shen 387

Selection of Optimal Technological Innovation Projects Combining
Value Engineering with Fuzzy Synthetic Evaluation
Yuan-sheng Huang, Jun-hua Zhou, Jian-xun Qi 397

The Hierarchical Fuzzy Evaluation System and Its Application
Xiaoping Qiu, Yang Xu, Ming Jian, Haiming Li 407

A Solution to a System of Linear Equations with Fuzzy Numbers
Xingfang Zhang, Guangwu Meng 417

Evolutionary Synthesis of Micromachines Using Supervisory
Multiobjective Interactive Evolutionary Computation
  Raffi Kamalian, Ying Zhang, Hideyuki Takagi, Alice M. Agogino 428

Application of Weighted Ideal Point Method to
Environmental/Economic Load Dispatch
  Guo-li Zhang, Geng-yin Li, Hong Xie, Jian-wei Ma 438

Learning and Reasoning (I)

Reasoning the Spatiotemporal Relations Between Time Evolving
Indeterminate Regions
  Lei Bao, Xiao-Lin Qin, Jun Zhang, Qi-Yuan Li 448

Using Special Structured Fuzzy Measure to Represent Interaction
Among IF-THEN Rules
  Xi-Zhao Wang, Jun Shen 459

Novel Nonlinear Signals Separation of Optimized Entropy Based on
Adaptive Natural Gradient Learning
  Ren Ren, Jin Xu, Shihua Zhu, Danan Ren, Yongqiang Luo 467

Training Conditional Random Fields with Unlabeled Data and Limited
Number of Labeled Examples
  Tak-Lam Wong, Wai Lam 477

An Effective and Efficient Two Stage Algorithm for Global Optimization
  Yong-Jun Wang, Jiang-She Zhang, Yu-Fen Zhang 487

Learning and Reasoning (II)

Evolutionary Multi-objective Optimization Algorithm with Preference
for Mechanical Design
  Jianwei Wang, Jianming Zhang, Xiaopeng Wei 497

A New Adaptive Crossover Operator for the Preservation of Useful
Schemata
  Fan Li, Qi-He Liu, Fan Min, Guo-Wei Yang 507

Refinement of Fuzzy Production Rules by Using a Fuzzy-Neural
Approach
  Dong-mei Huang, Ming-hu Ha, Ya-min Li, Eric C.C. Tsang 517

A Particle Swarm Optimization-Based Approach to Tackling Simulation
Optimization of Stochastic, Large-Scale and Complex Systems
  Ming Lu, Da-peng Wu, Jian-ping Zhang 528

Combination of Multiple Nearest Neighbor Classifiers Based on Feature
Subset Clustering Method
  Li-Juan Wang, Qiang Hua, Xiao-Long Wang, Qing-Cai Chen 538

Learning and Reasoning (III)

A Statistical Confidence-Based Adaptive Nearest Neighbor Algorithm
for Pattern Classification
  Jigang Wang, Predrag Neskovic, Leon N. Cooper 548

Automatic 3D Motion Synthesis with Time-Striding Hidden Markov
Model
  Yi Wang, Zhi-qiang Liu, Li-zhu Zhou 558

Learning from an Incomplete Information System with
Continuous-Valued Attributes by a Rough Set Technique
  Eric C.C. Tsang, Suyun Zhao, Daniel S. Yeung, John W.T. Lee 568

Reduction of Attributes in Ordinal Decision Systems
  John W.T. Lee, Xizhao Wang, Jinfeng Wang 578

On the Local Reduction of Information System
  Degang Chen, Eric C.C. Tsang 588

Machine Learning Applications (I)

Spectral Analysis of Protein Sequences
  Tuan D. Pham 595

Volatility Patterns of Industrial Stock Price Indices in the Chinese
Stock Market
  Lan-Jun Lao 605

Data Migration in RAID Based on Stripe Unit Heat
  Yan Liu, Chang-Sheng Xie, Huai-yang Li, Zhen Zhao 614

Distribution Channel Coordination Through Penalty Schemes
  Quansheng Lei, Jian Chen 624

Automatic Keyphrases Extraction from Document Using Neural Network
Jiabing Wang, Hong Peng, Jing-song Hu 633

A Novel Fuzzy Anomaly Detection Method Based on Clonal Selection Clustering Algorithm
Fenghua Lang, Jian Li, Yixian Yang 642

Machine Learning Applications (II)

An Anti-worm with Balanced Tree Based Spreading Strategy
Yi-xuan Liu, Xiao-chun Yun, Bai-ling Wang, Hai-bin Sun 652

EFIS: Evolvable-Neural-Based Fuzzy Inference System and Its Application for Adaptive Network Anomaly Detection
Muhammad Fermi Pasha, Rahmat Budiarto, Mohammad Syukur, Masashi Yamada 662

Fast Detection of Worm Infection for Large-Scale Networks
Hui He, Mingzeng Hu, Weizhe Zhang, Hongli Zhang................ 672

Empirical Study on Fusion Methods Using Ensemble of RBFNN for Network Intrusion Detection
Aki P.F. Chan, Daniel S. Yeung, Eric C.C. Tsang, Wing W.Y. Ng 682

A Covariance Matrix Based Approach to Internet Anomaly Detection
Shuyuan Jin, Daniel So Yeung, Xizhao Wang, Eric C.C. Tsang 691

Use of Linguistic Features in Context-Sensitive Text Classification
Alex K.S. Wong, John W.T. Lee, Daniel S. Yeung 701

Machine Learning Applications (III)

Using Term Relationships in a Structured Document Retrieval Model Based on Influence Diagrams
Jian-min Xu, Shuang Zhao, Zhen-peng Liu, Bian-fang Chai 711

Kernel-Based Metric Adaptation with Pairwise Constraints
Hong Chang, Dit-Yan Yeung 721

Generating Personalized Answers by Constructing a Question Situation
Yanwen Wu, Zhenghong Wu, Yan Li, Jinling Li 731

A Multi-stage Chinese Collocation Extraction System
  Ruifeng Xu, Qin Lu 740

Monitoring Glaucomatous Progression: Classification of Visual Field
Measurements Using Stable Reference Data
  *Shuanghui Meng, Mihai Lazarescu, Jim Ivins,
  Andrew Turpin* 750

Neural Networks and Statistical Learning Methods (I)

A New Intelligent Diagnostic Method for Machine Maintenance
  Qianjin Guo, Haibin Yu, Aidong Xu 760

Prediction of Human Behaviour Using Artificial Neural Networks
  *Zhicheng Zhang, Frédéric Vanderhaegen,
  Patrick Millot* 770

Iterative Learning Controller for Trajectory Tracking Tasks Based on
Experience Database
  Xuesong Wang, Yuhu Cheng, Wei Sun 780

MGPC Based on Hopfield Network and Its Application in a Thermal
Power Unit Load System
  Peng Guo, Taihua Chang 790

Neural Networks and Statistical Learning Methods (II)

Solving the Minimum Crossing Number Problem Using an Improved
Artificial Neural Network
  Rong Long Wang, Kozo Okazaki 797

The Design of a Fuzzy-Neural Network for Ship Collision Avoidance
  Yu-Hong Liu, Xuan-Min Du, Shen-Hua Yang 804

A Genetic Algorithm-Based Neural Network Approach for Fault
Diagnosis in Hydraulic Servo-Valves
  Hao Huang, Kuisheng Chen, Liangcai Zeng 813

Sensitivity Analysis of Madalines to Weight Perturbation
  Yingfeng Wang, Xiaoqin Zeng, Daniel S. Yeung 822

Neural Networks and Statistical Learning Methods (III)

Fault Diagnosis for the Feedwater Heater System of a 300MW Coal-Fired Power Generating Unit Based on RBF Neural Network
    Liangyu Ma, Yongguang Ma, Jin Ma 832

The Application of Modified Hierarchy Genetic Algorithm Based on Adaptive Niches
    Wei-Min Qi, Qiao-ling Ji, Wei-You Cai 842

Construction of High Precision RBFNN with Low False Alarm for Detecting Flooding Based Denial of Service Attacks Using Stochastic Sensitivity Measure
    Wing W.Y. Ng, Aki P.F. Chan, Daniel S. Yeung,
    Eric C.C. Tsang 851

Context-Sensitive Kernel Functions: A Distance Function Viewpoint
    Bram Vanschoenwinkel, Feng Liu,
    Bernard Manderick 861

A Parallel Genetic Algorithm for Solving the Inverse Problem of Support Vector Machines
    Qiang He, Xizhao Wang, Junfen Chen,
    Leifan Yan 871

Neural Networks and Statistical Learning Methods (IV)

Short Term Load Forecasting Model Based on Support Vector Machine
    Dong-Xiao Niu, Qiang Wang, Jin-Chao Li 880

Evaluation of an Efficient Parallel Object Oriented Platform (EPOOP) for Control Intensive Intelligent Applications
    Chun Che Fung, Jia-Bin Li, Douglas G. Myers 889

Location of Tropical Cyclone Center with Intelligent Image Processing Technique
    Q.P. Zhang, L.L. Lai, W.C. Sun 898

A Hybrid Genetic Algorithm/Particle Swarm Approach for Evaluation of Power Flow in Electric Network
    T.O. Ting, K.P. Wong, C.Y. Chung 908

Pattern Recognition (I)

A Method to Construct the Mapping to the Feature Space for the Dot Product Kernels
Degang Chen, Qiang He, Chunru Dong, Xizhao Wang 918

An Edge Detection Method by Combining Fuzzy Logic and Neural Network
Rong Wang, Li-qun Gao, Shu Yang, Yu-hua Chai 930

Fast Face Detection Integrating Motion Energy into a Cascade-Structured Classifier
Yafeng Deng, Guangda Su, Jun Zhou, Bo Fu 938

Adaptive Online Multi-stroke Sketch Recognition Based on Hidden Markov Model
Zhengxing Sun, Wei Jiang, Jianyong Sun 948

To Diagnose a Slight and Incipient Fault in a Power Plant Thermal System Based on Symptom Zoom Technology and Fuzzy Pattern Recognition Method
Liangyu Ma, Jin Ma, Yongguang Ma, Bingshu Wang 958

Mandarin Voice Conversion Using Tone Codebook Mapping
Guoyu Zuo, Yao Chen, Xiaogang Ruan, Wenju Liu 965

Pattern Recognition (II)

Continuous Speech Recognition Based on ICA and Geometrical Learning
Hao Feng, Wenming Cao, Shoujue Wang 974

Underwater Target Recognition with Sonar Fingerprint
Jian Yuan, Guo-Hui Li 984

Multi-stream Articulator Model with Adaptive Reliability Measure for Audio Visual Speech Recognition
Lei Xie, Zhi-Qiang Liu 994

Optical Font Recognition of Chinese Characters Based on Texture Features
Ming-hu Ha, Xue-dong Tian 1005

Some Characteristics of Fuzzy Integrals as a Multiple Classifiers Fusion Method
Huimin Feng, Xuefei Li, Tiegang Fan, Yanju Chen 1014

Vision and Image Processing (I)

Error Concealment Based on Adaptive MRF-MAP Framework
Zhi-heng Zhou, Sheng-li Xie 1025

Spatial Video Watermarking Based on Stability of DC Coefficients
Tianhang Chen, Shaohui Liu, Hongxun Yao, Wen Gao 1033

A Learning-Based Spatial Processing Method for the Detection of Point Targets
Zhijun Liu, Xubang Shen, Hongshi Sang 1043

CTFDP: An Affine Invariant Method for Matching Contours
Hui-Xuan Tang, Hui Wei 1051

A De-noising Algorithm of Infrared Image Contrast Enhancement
Changjiang Zhang, Xiaodong Wang, Haoran Zhang 1060

Vision and Image Processing (II)

Speckle Suppressing Based on Fuzzy Generalized Morphological Filter
Lihui Jiang, Yanying Guo 1070

Research of Vehicle License Plate Location Algorithm Based on Color Features and Plate Processions
Yao-Quan Yang, Jie Bai, Rui-Li Tian, Na Liu 1077

Fast Measuring Particle Size by Using the Information of Particle Boundary and Shape
Weixing Wang 1086

A Statistical Image Fusion Scheme for Multi Focus Applications
Z.W. Liao, S.X. Hu, W.F. Chen, Y.Y. Tang, T.Z. Huang 1096

Author Index 1107

Backward-Chaining Flexible Planning

Li Xu, Wen-Xiang Gu, and Xin-Mei Zhang

School of Computer, Northeast Normal University, Changchun 130117, Jilin, China
{xul094, gwx, zhangxm372}@nenu.edu.cn

Abstract. Different from all other congeneric research carried out before, this paper pays attention to a kind of planning problem that is more complex than the classical ones under the flexible Graph-plan framework. We present a novel approach for flexible planning based on a two-stage paradigm of graph expansion and solution extraction, which provides a new perspective on the flexible planning problem. In contrast to existing methods, the algorithm adopts backward-chaining strategy to expand the planning graphs, takes into account users' requirement and taste, and finds a solution plan more suitable to the needs. Also, because of the wide application of intelligent planning, our research is very helpful in the development of robotology, natural language understanding, intelligent agents etc.

1 Introduction

Intelligent planning is an intersectional subject which deals with knowledge representation, data mining, human-machine interaction, non-monotone logic, cognition science and so on. Not only is its development of importance in artificial intelligence, but it will also fundamentally change the traditional way the human operates a computer. The research started in the 1950's. The problem solving system QA3[1] designed by Green in 1969 is considered to be the first intelligent planning system. The STRIPS[2] planner, designed by Fike and Nilsson in 1971, has historical significance in intelligent planning, in which knowledge representation and reasoning methods deeply affect later planning systems. But limited for objective conditions, the field was under the stagnant state at one time. It was not until the end of 1980's that the efficiency of planning systems in the field was improved greatly. The most remarkable approach was Graphplan developed by Blum and Furst. In their seminal paper[3,4] on the Graphplan system, they described a new plan generation algorithm based on planning graph, which was much faster than any other algorithms known at that time. It possesses some important properties, including: optimality in the number of actions and length of a synthesized plan; soundness and completeness; and polynomial time and space complexity of the creation of planning graph structure. Graphplan caused revolutionary progress in intelligent planning[5], and it started a whole series of research efforts that refined this approach by making it even more efficient and extending it to improve the quality of the plan. However, planning problems under Graphplan framework are cast in terms of imperative constraints that are either wholly satisfied or wholly violated. It is argued that this framework is too rigid to capture the full subtlety of many real problems. Hence, a new flexible planning problem is defined, which supports the soft constraints often found in reality. This paper just discusses this kind of complicated problem - flexible planning problems[6-8].

Flexible planning method, introduced by Miguel in 2000, has considered AI planning problems in terms of both the techniques to improve the efficiency of plan synthesis and the extension of the classical domain definition to support soft constraints. Some flexible problems in theory and in practice are international puzzles, but a lot of famous scholars home and abroad still devote themselves to the research. Many related papers have been published. Each of these papers has its merit, but they have a feature in common: expand the flexible planning graph forwards from the initial state to the goal set at first, and search a valid plan in the following. Different from all of these, this paper introduces a novel algorithm: adopting a backward-chaining strategy to expand the flexible planning graph from the goal set, then search a valid plan from the initial state. We call the algorithm backward-chaining flexible Graphplan algorithm (BCFGP), which improves the comprehensive quality of the problem solving in the artificial intelligence system plan. Unlike all other existing flexible Graphplan algorithms, our algorithm brings forward the method of flexible mutex inference backwards, avoids the process of satisfaction degree propagation, and guarantees to acquire a valid plan of the highest quality.

2 Definitions

Some already known definitions of the algorithm are presented here.

McDermott and James Hemdeler think a *plan* is devising the sequence of actions for an agent.[9] We generally think a *plan* is a sequence of sets of actions that will achieve the goals of a problem.

Interfere: two actions interfere with each other if one deletes a precondition or an effect of the other.

Valid plan: a valid plan for a planning problem consists of a set of actions and specified time steps in which each action is to be carried out. There will be actions at time step 1, actions at time step 2, and so forth. Several actions may be specified to occur at the same time step so long as they do not interfere with each other. A valid plan must make all the problem goals true at the last time step.

Satisfaction degree: L is composed of a finite number of membership degrees, $\{l_\bot, l_1, \ldots, l_\top\}$. The endpoints, $l_\bot \in L$ and $l_\top \in L$ respectively denote a complete lack of satisfaction and a complete satisfaction. The no-op action is a special case which has a satisfaction of $l_\top$. Satisfaction degrees are used to express how satisfactorily people carry out an action under the given preconditions.

Subjective degree of truth: K is composed of a finite number of membership degrees, $\{k_\bot, k_1, \ldots, k_\top\}$. Boolean propositions are captured at the endpoints of K, with $k_\bot \in K$ and $k_\top \in K$ indicating total falsehood and total truth respectively. Here, it is very natural and reasonable to apply a membership function in fuzzy mathematics to evaluate the subjective degree of truth of the flexible propositions.

Flexible propositions: A flexible proposition is described by a fuzzy relation[10], R, which is defined by a membership function μ_R (.) : $\varphi_1 \times \varphi_2 \times ... \times \varphi_j \to K$, where $\varphi_1 \times \varphi_2 \times ... \times \varphi_j$ is the Cartesian product of the subsets of Φ (the set of plan objects) allowable at this place in the proposition.

Flexible propositions are assigned subjective truth degrees. The flexible operators map from the space of flexible preconditions to a set of flexible effects and a satisfaction degree. Therefore, subjective knowledge can be utilized to entail inferences over preferred combinations of actions. Flexible propositions are very important because we can add the detail of problems and the subjective consciousness into them.

3 Limitations of Graphplan

In the real world, there exists a case that the users need a safe, satisfactory, high-quality plan without having to consider the complexity of the plan. Namely, they care how well the goal is achieved, not how to achieve it. In order to deal with this case, the planning algorithm must capture the detail of problems and some ideas of users. But the classical valid plan was weighed by its length, which don't take into account the user's requirement and taste. Furthermore, the practice has also proven that it has become increasingly clear that classical AI planning is insufficient to capture the full subtlety of many real world problems.

This section will analyze the reasons why the classical planning method exists some shortages. An illustrative example follows, derived from the logistics domain (see Fig.1).

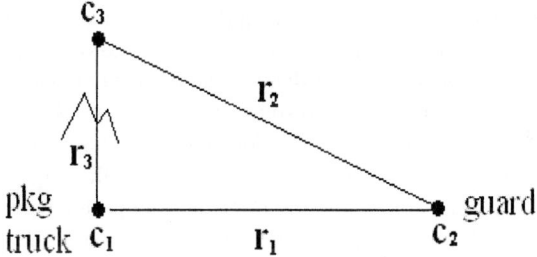

Fig. 1. An example of a flexible planning problem

In Fig. 1, c_i represent three cities, r_i represent three roads. The single goal of this problem is to transport pkg to c_3. There are three possible actions: *load, drive,* and *unload. Load-object* requires that object and truck be at the same place. *Unload-object* has a precondition - on object truck.

This problem has a valid plan apparently, that is {load-pkg, drive from c_1 to c_3, unload-pkg}. But now the problem becomes more complex. The problem is added much detail: firstly, we know the package is quite valuable; secondly, r_1 and r_2 are major roads and r_3 is a very unsafe track through the hills; Last, the goal of this problem is to transport pkg to c_3 safely, that is, we emphasize safety based on the original goal.

> Initial Conditions: (and(at truck c_1)(at pkg c_1)(at guard c_2)(connects r_1 c_1 c_2)(connects r_2 c_2 c_3)(connects r_3 c_1 c_3))
> Goal: (at pkg c_3)
> operator:
>   load
>   params: (?t truck)(?o pkg)(?o guard)(?c city)
>   : precondition(at ?t ?c)(at ?o ?c)
>   : effect(on ?o ?t)
>   drive
>   params: (?t truck)(?c city)(?d city)(?r road)
>   : precondition(at ?t ?c)(connects ?r ?c ?d)
>   : effect(at ?t ?d)
>   unload
>   params: (?t truck)(?o pkg)(?o guard)(?c city)
>   : precondition(at ?t ?c) (on ?o ?t)
>   : effect(at ?o ?c)

Fig. 2. STRIPS specification of the problem

Now, leaving the special knowledge alone, let us propose a solution for the problem. What should we do? At first, as far as the goal is concerned, it emphasizes safety not efficiency, so we should find the safest solution. It is {a.drive from c_1 to c_2, b.load-guard, c.drive from c_2 to c_1, d.load-pkg, e.drive from c_1 to c_2, f.drive from c_2 to c_3, g.unload-pkg}. The first three steps make *load-pkg* and *unload-pkg* go with a guard's protection, and the steps e and f avoid driving on r_3 that is a very unsafe track. This solution includes seven steps, four more than the classical one, but it considers the detail of the problem and the safety that is what the goal emphasizes.

Graphplan can-not acquire the 7-step solution, because it will end when it acquires a 3-step plan. This is attributed to its insufficiency to capture the total detail of the planning problem. The classical Graphplan is helpless in the large and complex real world problems, so a means of expressing priorities and preferences via flexible constraints is wanted. Flexible planning method emerges as the times require.

We can notice from the example above, that flexible planning method can synthesize the detail of problems and users' taste. It trades the compromise between plan length and satisfaction degree, and pays more attention to the quality of the plan.

4 Backward Mutex Inference and Satisfaction Degree Propagation

As is well known to us all, the two approaches of mutex inference and satisfaction degree propagation have a notable impact on the efficiency of the flexible Graphplan algorithm, and they are recognized as the emphasis and the difficulty in the flexible Graphplan algorithm by all. We pay enough attention to these problems in this paper as well.

4.1 Mutex Inference Backwards

We introduce the definition of mutex before showing the expansion algorithm.
Mutex: we define this relation recursively as follows (see Fig.3):
Two actions at level i are mutex if either

(a) *inconsistent effects*: the effect of one action is the negation of another action's effect, or
(b) *interference*: one action deletes the precondition of another, or
(c) *competing needs*: the actions have preconditions that are mutually exclusive at level i-1.

Two propositions at level i are mutex if one is the negation of the other, or if all ways of achieving the propositions (i.e. actions at level i-1) are pairwise mutex (*inconsistent support*).

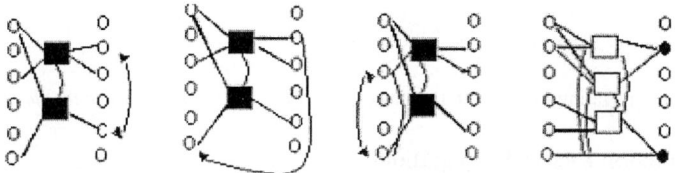

inconsistent effects   interference   competing needs   inconsistent support

Fig. 3. Graphical depiction of mutex definition (devised by David Smith). Circles denote propositions, squares represent actions, and thin, curved lines denote mutex relations. The first three parts illustrate deduction of an action-action mutex (between the dark boxes), and the last part depicts the discovery of mutex between propositions (the dark circles).

The algorithm needs to infer and propagate mutex backwards. A variation on this theme would involve doing the inference and propagation in the backward direction.
Reference[11] defines this relation recursively as follows:
Two actions are said to be backward mutex if:

(a) they are statically interfering, i.e. the effects of one violate the preconditions or "useful" effects (the effects of the action that are used to support propositions in the planning graph) of the other, or
(b) they have exactly the same set of useful effects, or
(c) the propositions supported by one action are pairwise mutex with the propositions supported by the other.

Two propositions are backward mutex if all the actions supported by one are pairwise mutex with all the actions supported by the other.
To illustrate this, consider the example shown in Fig. 4. Here, O_1 and O_2 are mutex since they are solely supporting p. This leads to a mutex relation between R and S (since they are supporting actions that are mutex). Finally, O_5 and O_7 are mutex since they are supporting mutex propositions.
The mutex definition is strengthened under flexible Graphplan framework by adding extra judgement conditions on the basis of the mutex definition under classical Graphplan framework.

Two flexible actions are also said to be mutex if:
One action has an effect proposition which expresses a different truth degree than for a proposition required as the precondition of the other.
Two flexible propositions are also said to be mutex if:
They express different truth degrees for the same core proposition.
The judgement methods are suitable for both forward flexible mutex and backward flexible mutex.

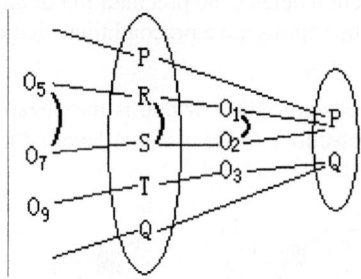

Fig. 4. Propagating mutexes in the backward direction (*mutexes shown as black links*)

4.2 Satisfaction Degree Propagation

Expanding the flexible planning graph needs to propagate satisfaction degrees of propositions and actions.

(1) The satisfaction degrees of propositions
Label proposition nodes with the highest satisfaction degree of those attached to all actions that assert it as an effect.
(2) The satisfaction degrees of actions

$$\text{Action satisfaction degree} = \min(\text{own satisfaction degree}, \min(\text{satisfaction degrees attached to each precondition})) \quad (1)$$

(3) The satisfaction degree of flexible plan

We can acquire the satisfaction degree of flexible plan by the satisfaction degree of actions and propositions. The satisfaction degree of a flexible plan is defined as the conjunctive combination of the satisfaction degrees of each action and each goal used in the plan. The conjunctive combination of two fuzzy relations, $Ri \otimes Rj$, is usually interpreted as the minimum membership value assigned by either relation. The quality of a plan is its satisfaction degree combined with its length, where the shorter of two plans with an equivalent satisfaction degree is better.

5 Description of BCFGP Algorithm

The BCFGP algorithm is composed of flexible planning graph expansion and solution extraction. The two parts will be carried out alternately. From the description below, we can find out the algorithm expands a planning graph from the goals with the highest satisfaction degree and avoids a complicated process of satisfaction degree propagation.

5.1 Graph Expansion

We introduce the flexible planning algorithm which adopts backward-chaining strategy to expand the planning graph from the goal set. The algorithm is described as follows:

(1) The construction of the proposition level at time step 1

All the goals are placed at the proposition level 1. Each proposition comes into being a node. Every goal is assigned the highest satisfaction degree.

(2) The construction of the action level at time step 1

For each clause of each flexible operator, if one of its effects is in the goal set, then instantiate it into action with the associated satisfaction degree in all possible ways. Let such actions whose associated satisfaction degree are more than or equal to those of goals form a set. Examine action-action mutex in the set. Connect the actions to their effects. If some goals can not find this kind of supporting action, replace the satisfaction degree of goals by the satisfaction degree less than and the closest to the current one in L. If such satisfaction degree is found, then carry out the algorithm once again. Else, the algorithm is over.

(3) The construction of the proposition level at time step i

The preconditions of the actions at time step i-1 just form the proposition level at time step i. Examine proposition-proposition mutex. Connect the actions to their preconditions. At this time, if all the propositions in the initial conditions appear and none of them are mutex, the algorithm is over. We can begin to carry out solution extraction.

(4) The construction of the action level at time step i

For each clause of each flexible operator, if one of its effects is in proposition level i, then instantiate it into action with the associated satisfaction degree in all possible ways. Let such actions whose associated satisfaction degrees are more than or equal to those of goals form a set. Examine action-action mutex in the set. Connect the actions to their effects. If some propositions can not find this kind of supporting action, replace the satisfaction degree of goals by the satisfaction degree less than and the closest to the current one in L. If such satisfaction degree is found, then carry out the algorithm once again. Else, the algorithm is over.

5.2 Solution Extraction

A main task is solution extraction in the planning problem. Every time the algorithm executes step (3) in Graphplan expansion, it examines whether at this time all the propositions in the initial conditions appear and none of them are mutex, if not, continue to expand the flexible planning graph. If it is true, we will begin to search a valid plan.

The basic idea of solution extraction is: judge whether there exists a valid plan, if not, the algorithm is over, otherwise, execute the valid plan extraction. We will follow up the way of searching the plan from initial conditions in the flexible planning graph. Firstly the initial conditions are viewed as a proposition set. Then we begin searching the valid plan, until finding it.

Choose a proposition in the proposition set. Look for an action, action1, which satisfies the following requirements: firstly, the action is at the same time step with the proposition; secondly, the preconditions of the action include the proposition; last, if there are many actions meeting the first two requirements, we should choose the one with the highest satisfaction degree. Then, choose another proposition in the set. Look for an action, action2, which satisfies the following requirements: firstly, the action is at the same time step with the proposition; secondly, the preconditions of the action include the proposition; thirdly, action1 and action2 must be guaranteed not to be mutex; last, if there are many actions meeting the first three requirements, we should choose the one with the highest satisfaction degree. If such action does not exist, the algorithm backtracks at once. Continue in this way, until we have found such an action for each proposition in the set and none of these actions are mutex. Let the effects of these actions comprise a proposition set. Carry out the above process until the proposition set is the superset of the goal set.

6 Advantages of the Algorithm

BCFGP is unaffected by irrelevant literals while FGP worsens in performance as the number of irrelevant literals in the initial state increases. And when initial state includes so many preconditions as to make the graph very wide, the algorithm is more predominant than FGP. Furthermore, the more irrelevant literals there are in the initial state and the wider the planning graph is, the more predominant our algorithm is. In addition, FGP has its special cases. If acquiring a valid plan with a low satisfaction degree, the algorithm will go on to expand the flexible planning graph to look for the valid plan with a higher satisfaction degree. Thus it will find a series of plans. But FGP searches a plan from the lowest satisfaction degree, which will lead to a large amount of backtracking. However, since BCFGP searches a plan from the highest satisfaction degree, it will avoid much unnecessary backtracking.

The cost of graph expansion can be reduced as follows. Consider the case where a plan with satisfaction degree l_i has been found. If $l_i < l_T$, FGP searches onwards in order to look for a plan with a higher satisfaction degree. However, there is no point in instantiating flexible operator clauses with a satisfaction degree less than or equal to l_i: A plan with this satisfaction degree has been found already - a longer plan with the same satisfaction degree is deemed to be of a lower quality. The conjunctive combination rule implemented via the *min* operator ensures that no plan of satisfaction degree l_j can contain an action of satisfaction degree l_i, where $l_i < l_j$. Hence, the completeness of the search is not affected by omitting such actions in later flexible planning graph layers. Our algorithm is suitable for the above pruning method, however, our algorithm searches a plan from the highest satisfaction degree, and it can make the pruning more extensive and faster.

7 Open Problems

To apply BCFGP to real world fields more effectively, we need to work on it further.

(1) One main limitation of BCFGP is that the problems handled by BCFGP are limited in STRIPS-like domain. It is an active research topic to extend action representations to ADL[12] and PDDL[13] domain.

(2) Nowadays, representative planners such as Blackbox[14], FF[15] are the combination of Graphplan and other planning methods. Similarly, we can combine BCFGP with other planning methods (such as the heuristic approach), explore the new algorithm and develop the planner with higher performance.

(3) Incorporate numerically weighed constraints into planning to give a quantitative means of distinguishing between different potential plans, as opposed to the qualitative methods in the paper.

(4) It is extremely useful to combine flexible planning with probabilistic planning.

(5) Explore an intelligent flexible planning algorithm that expands the flexible planning graph backwards from the goal set and forwards from the initial state at the same time.

(6) BCFGP is a general planning approach. How to add the domain-specific knowledge to certain domains, and to more effectively apply BCFGP to the real world is a significant future work.

8 Conclusions

In this paper, we perfect the strategy of reasoning flexible mutex backwards, avoid a complicated process of satisfaction degree expansion and introduce a novel flexible Graphplan algorithm. The algorithm has the following features: Solve the flexible planning problems quickly by adopting a back-chaining strategy to expand the planning graph and searching a valid plan from the initial conditions; pruning strategy utilizing satisfaction degrees speeds up the problem solving; ensure the acquisition of a valid plan of the highest quality. Also the problems handled by the algorithm are more complex than the classical ones and much closer to the real world.

Acknowledgements

The work described in this paper is sponsored in part by the National Nature Science Foundation of China grant 60473042 and 60573067. The authors are grateful to the anonymous reviewers for providing their detailed, thoughtful and helpful comments on improving the work presented here.

References

1. Green, C.: Application of theorem proving to problem solving. In: Proc.1st Int.Joint Conf.AI(1969)219-239
2. Fikes, R. Nilsson, N.: STRIPS: A new approach to the application of theorem proving to problem solving. Artificial Intelligence(1971)2: 189-208

3. Blum, A., Furst, M.: Fast planning through planning graph analysis. In:Proc.14th Int.Joint Conf.AI (1995)1636-1642
4. Blum, A., Furst, M.: Fast planning through Planning Graph analysis. J. Artificial Intelligence, 90(1--2):281—300 (1997)
5. Daniel S., Weld.: Recent Advances in AI Planning. Technical Report UW-CSE-98-10-01; In AI Magazine (1999)
6. Ian Miguel, Peter Jarvis, Qiang Shen.: Flexible Graphplan. In 14th European Conference on Artificial Intelligence (2000)
7. Ian Miguel, Qiang Shen.: Fuzzy rrDFGP and Planning. Artificial Intelligence 148□pages 11-52 (2003)
8. Ian Miguel. Dynamic flexible constraint satisfaction and its application to AI planning. Distinguished Dissertations (2004)
9. McDermott, D,et al.: Planning: What is, What it could be, An introduction to the Special Issue on Planning and Scheduling. Artificial Intelligence (1995)76:1-16
10. Pedrycz, W. , Gomide, F.: An Introduction to Fuzzy Sets: Analysis and Design. MIT Press(1999)
11. Kambhampati, R., Lambrecht, E., Parker, E.: Understanding and extending Graphplan. In Proc. 4th European Conference on Planning, Sept (1997)
12. Pednault E, P.: ADL: Exploring the middle ground between STRIPS and the situation calculus. In Proc. 1st International Conference(KR'89) (1989) pages 324-331
13. McDermott D, et al.: The PDDL Planning Domain Definition Language. The AIPS'98 Planning Competition Committee(1998)
14. Kaukz, H., Selman, B.: Blackbox: A new approach to the application of theorem proving to problem solving. In AIPS98 Workshop on Planning as Combinatorial Search, pages 58-60, June (1998)
15. Hoffmann, J., and Nebel, B.: The FF Planning System: Fast Plan Generation Through Heuristic Search. Journal of Artificial Intelligence Research (2001),14: pages 253-302

RRF: A Double-Layer Reputation Mechanism with Rating Reputation Considered

Hang Guo, Ji Gao, and Ping Xu

Institute of Artificial Intelligence, Zhejiang University,
Hangzhou 310027, China
gentleguoh@yeah.net, gentleguoh@sohu.com

Abstract. As reputation mechanism has been widely accepted and adopted to enhance trust in electronic communities, how to cope with the attack and disturbance problems on reputation mechanism, such as collusion, malicious or unfair rating, becomes a key challenge. This paper extends the normal mechanism, which mainly focuses on the trustworthiness of transactions, to a double-layer reputation mechanism, by distinguishing two type reputations: *capability reputation* and *rating reputation*. Based on the double-layer reputations, we present the *Rating Reputation Feedback* (RRF) mechanism to confront above problems. Basic concepts, key issues, instantiated sample and the effectiveness of RRF mechanism are discussed in the paper.

1 Introduction

Recently, the issues of trust and reputation mechanisms have attracted much attention in many areas, such as multi-agent systems, peer-to-peer systems, and e-commerce. In such areas, it is important for participants to estimate each other's trustworthiness in collaborations or trades. Reputation, which can be viewed as an aggregation of ratings of members in system, has been recognized as a key factor for successful electronic community[1]. Reputation mechanism has been viewed as an effective means to cope with cheat, fraud, and violation of commitment, elicit trustworthy behaviors, and promote trust between members.

Many reputation models and applicable systems have been proposed, and some applications are adopted and worked well in online marketplaces, such as Amazon, eBay and etc[1][2]. Although current reputation models and systems show quite good effectiveness in trust-enforcing, deterrent, and incentive mechanism to avoid cheats and frauds, some attack problems of reputation mechanism itself become key challenges. For example, some participants collude together to give high ratings to each other, or malicious agents report unfair ratings to disturb the reputation system. With usage of reputation mechanism, each one's profit is associated with its reputation, as well as its emulants'. Deliberate attacks or unintentional harmful ratings may lead to illegal benefit and systematic invalidation. Three representative sorts of these problems are *collusion*, *malicious or unfair rating*, and *insouciant rating*.

In this paper, we extend normal one-layer reputation mechanism, which only involves the trustworthiness of the transaction, to a novel double-layer mechanism to cope with above problems. We present the notion *rating reputation* to describe the trustworthiness of rating, distinguished from the reputation of the provision or transaction, called *capability reputation*. We propose the *Rating Reputation Feedback* (RRF) mechanism, essentially a double-layer reputation mechanism, based on the correlative integration of the capability reputation and rating reputation. RRF mechanism associates one's ratings with its rating reputation, continuously tuning the latter by feedbacks. Rating reputation reversely promotes the trustworthiness of ratings and deters the cheat or malicious report of ratings. It is more effective to cope with reputation attacks because many problems in this issue are caused by the malicious usage of ratings other than the low trustworthiness of business transactions.

In following sections, firstly we discuss works related to reputation mechanisms and present the position of this paper in section 2. Then, we propose the concept of double-layer reputations in section 3. We then show the definition of the RRF mechanism, an instance and its effectiveness, and some key challenge issues in section 4. Finally, we conclude in section 5.

2 Related Works

In the area of computing, the concept of reputation has been studied and applied to many areas, such as multi-agent systems[3], peer-to-peer systems[4][5], and electronic commerce[6][7]. Many reputation models and systems have been proposed or applied, such as SPORAS[8], REGRET[9], ROCQ[10], AFRAS[11], and etc. In practical applications of reputation mechanism, virtual marketplaces like Amazon and eBay are typical examples.

With reputation mechanism widely studied and its effectiveness on encouraging trustworthiness primarily proved, some weaknesses of tranditional reputation mechanism emerge and cause possible hazards. These problems, including collusion, malicious or unfair rating, and insouciant rating, have the characteristic that the participants does not mainly gain from deception of their capabilities or cheat of transactions, but benefit from cheat or disturbances of reputations. If reputations are not trustworthy, reputation mechanisms cannot play an effective role as expected, even quite the contrary. Some researches have paid attentions to some of these problems. Jurca[12] proposes an incentive compatible reputation mechanism, encouraging accurate ratings by positive reward. But it takes little consideration on intended attacks, and does not decrease the effect of repetitious attacks. Against unfair ratings, many researchers advocate to detect and eliminate them by filters[13][14]. They distinguish inaccurate ratings as the minority according to certain probabilistic hypothesis, or by some discrimination methods. However, the probabilistic or discrimination model hypothesis is strongly connected to specific situations. Moreover, this method may only decrease the negative effect of unfair ratings, but does not decrease malicious behaviors because malevolent recommenders are not punished.

Different from current approaches, this paper proposes two reputation layers: the capability reputation and the rating reputation. The former denotes the same meaning as the normal sense of the term "reputation". Additionally, we propose the concept rating reputation involved as the trustworthiness of ratings. Similar thinking has been implicated in some researches, such as the "credibility" in the ROCQ scheme[10], and the filtering algorithm in developed TRAVOS model[15]. But they mainly maintain the trustworthiness as private knowledge other than shared or reported properties of recommenders, and only use them as the weights in aggregation of ratings. Comparatively, the double-layer reputation architecture of RRF mechanism is more suitable for the determent of reputation attacks.

3 Double-Layer Reputations: Capability Reputation and Rating Reputation

Traditional trust problems in electronic communities are the cheats, frauds, and violations of commitment in cooperative or business transactions. For example, service providers declare mendacious capabilities to cheat, or sellers do not send the goods after receiving the money from buyers. As reputation mechanism being adopted as an effective method against these problems, some new problems of maliciously manipulating reputations emerge as hazards to reputation system. Following are some representative e-commerce scenarios of these problems:

Collusion:
(a) Sellers associate with some buyers to give itself highly positive ratings.
(b) Collusive sellers give highly positive ratings to each other by feigned trading and jointly increase their reputations.
(c) Sellers associate with some buyers to give low ratings to their contestants.

Malicious or unfair rating:
(d) Buyers purposely give extremely low or high rating about sellers.
(e) Honest buyer gives inaccurate ratings, due to its incorrect observation or limited rating capability.

Insouciant rating:
(d) Buyers have no interest to rate, ignoring it or giving random ratings.

Notice that this sort of problems is caused by the malicious manipulation or the inaccurate report of ratings, other than the low trustworthiness of service or transaction. A participant with high reliability of transactions does not certainly indicate high reliability of his ratings. Thus algorithms with only trustworthiness of services or transactions cannot effectively cope with this sort of problems. We propose that one's trustworthiness of rating should be distinguished from his trustworthiness of capability of completing certain transactions. We use two terms *capability reputation* and *rating reputation* to describe the distinguished two types of trustworthiness:

Definition 1. *Capability reputation*, is the trustworthiness degree of how an entity can complete tasks in e-service or commitments in transactions, and how much quality of provisions.

Definition 2. *Rating reputation*, is the trustworthiness degree of the accuracy of an entity's ratings about others. Its values are distinguished according to one's rating capability, rating motivation, and completeness of its observation. High rating reputation value denotes one's ratings are more likely accurate.

Capability reputation describes the degree in which we can trust one to give a good and reliable provision, while rating reputation indicates how trustful a recommender's ratings are. Although they are closely associated by decision and tuning relationships, capability reputation and rating reputation have many distinct properties. And they are computed by different algorithms and strategies in a reputation system. The confusion of these two reputations may lead to harmful impact to each other. For instance, the good records of one's sales may cover up its low accuracy of ratings.

Based on capability reputation and rating reputation, a *double-layer reputation architecture* can be built to enhance the trustworthiness of both transaction and rating, and adopted as a robust reputation system deterring the attacks and disturbances to reputation (Figure 1). In a service or business transaction, the provider's capability reputation decides the reliability of the completion and quality of the provision. After, the buyer reports a rating about the provider, according to the completion and quality of the provision. The capability reputation of the provider will be tuned by a compositive reference of buyer's ratings and their rating reputations. Furthermore, the recommender's rating reputation will be tuned according to the accuracy of his ratings. In this way, the impact of possibly harmful ratings from unreliable recommenders can be limited in the reputation computation, and inaccurate ratings will be punished by the decrease of rating trustworthiness and subsequent negative effects. Thus malicious manipulations and disturbances towards reputation can be minimized in such mechanism.

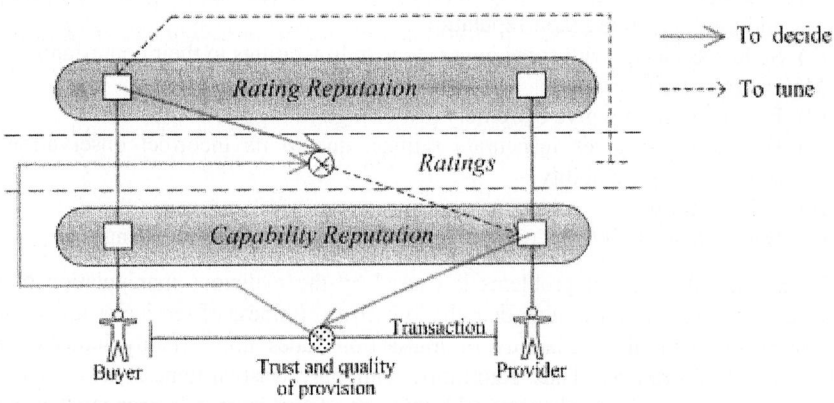

Fig. 1. Double-Layer Reputation Architecture

4 The Rating Reputation Feedback(RRF) Mechanism

Similar to the capability reputation, which is derived from the ratings of one's history transactions, rating reputation is evaluated by the accuracy of one's previous ratings. The judgment on the accuracy of a rating becomes a key factor in the design of double-layer reputation architecture. Under the assumption that most ratings about the same provision are close within a range referred to the actual completion and quality, we give the recommender whose rating is close to subsequent ratings about the same provision a higher positive tuning on his rating reputation, and vice versa. We propose a *rating reputation feedback (RRF) mechanism* in this approach (Figure 2). In RRF mechanism, one's rating reputation is continuously tuned by the distance between his ratings and feedbacks of others' ratings on the same service or goods. A similar rating feedback makes the rating reputation promoted, and a converse one decreases it. As the number of ratings increases, the tuning effect on the whole accords with the distance to the majority, which is seemed as the accurate value.

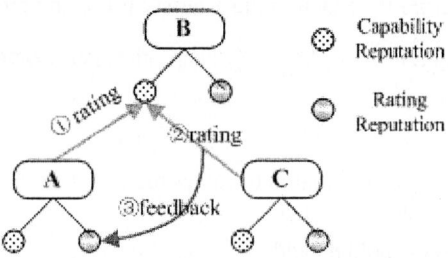

Fig. 2. Work Procedure of RRF Mechanism

4.1 Definition of RRF Mechanism

Before definition, we declare some notions and scenario assumptions. CR(x) and RR(x) respectively denote the capability reputation and rating reputation of member x. Let $Vr_k(A_i, A_j)$ be the rating reported by A_i about A_j as the k-th rating on the same type provision of A_j. In the mechanism, we assume that a transaction is a bilateral relationship, and only the buyer or consumer in a transaction need to report a rating about the provider. A bilateral rating situation can be extended similarly. After A_i reports a rating about A_j, its rating reputation will be continuously tuned by the feedbacks of subsequent ratings on the same type provision of A_j. We also assume that one's profit has a positive relationship with his capability reputation and rating reputation.

Definition 3. The *Rating Reputation Feedback (RRF) Mechanism*, is defined as a 7-tuple: (A_R, D_{CR}, D_{RR}, RT, I_R, g, h), in which

- A_R, is the set of members {A_i}, who has reputation property (CR(A_i), RR(A_i));
- D_{CR}, is the domain of the capability reputation values;
- D_{RR}, is the domain of the rating reputation values;
- RT, is the domain of the rating values;
- $I_R \subset D_{CR} \times D_{RR}$, is the set of the initial values of members' capability and rating reputation;
- $g : D_{CR} \rightarrow RT \times D_{RR} \times D_{CR}$, is a function to tune the capability reputation that

$$\Delta CR(A_s) = g(Vr(A_i, A_s), RR(A_i), CR(A_s)) \qquad (1)$$

which must satisfy following properties:

1) Higher value of $RR(A_i)$ has higher weight to affect $\Delta CR(A_s)$;

2) There exists a threshold r. If $RR(A_i) \leq r$, then $\Delta CR(A_s) = 0$.

- $h : D_{RR} \to RT \times RT \times D_{RR} \times D_{CR} \times \mathbf{R} \times D_{RR}$, is a function to tune the rating reputation according to the feedback rating, following that

$$\Delta RR(A_i) = h(Vr_{k1}(A_i, A_s), RR(A_i), Vr_{k2}(A_j, A_s), RR(A_j), CR(A_s), k_2) \quad (2)$$

in which $k_2 > k_1$, and the function must satisfy following properties:

3) Let $D = |Vr_{k1}(A_i, A_s) - Vr_{k2}(A_j, A_s)|$, keep other parameters in h constant, if $D_1 < D_2$, then

$$\Delta RR(A_i)_1 \geq \Delta RR(A_i)_2 .$$

It means A_i's rating reputation becomes higher when the feedback rating of A_j is closer to A_i, and vice versa.

4) There exist a threshold m, and

$$\begin{cases} \Delta RR(A_i) > 0, & \text{if } D < m; \\ \Delta RR(A_i) = 0, & \text{if } D = m; \\ \Delta RR(A_i) < 0, & \text{if } D > m. \end{cases}$$

In an RRF mechanism, its function g and h is the key factor to decide how the mechanism manipulates the capability reputation and rating reputation. They may be complex, involving complicated knowledge-based inference on rules, strategies, policies, etc. And they can also be simple functions, as what does in artificial neural networks. RRF mechanisms with different g and h exhibit different properties and functions.

4.2 A Primary Instance of RRF Mechanism and Its Effectiveness

To prove that the RRF mechanism can be implemented and has effectiveness on the solution to the reputation problems, we present a primary instance of RRF mechanism with simple linear and polynomial functions. In the sample, $D_{CR}, D_{RR} \in \mathbf{R}$, and $RT \in [-1,1]$. $Vr = 1$ means an extremely good remark, and $Vr = -1$ means the worst. A higher rating value denotes better remark. The functions g and h are defined as following:

$$g = \begin{cases} Vr(A_i, A_s) \cdot \dfrac{RR(A_i)}{Avr} & \text{if } RR(A_i) > 0 \\ 0 & \text{if } RR(A_i) \leq 0 \end{cases} \quad (3)$$

in which Avr denotes the average rating reputation, and

$$h = D^2 - 4D + 1.11 \quad (4)$$

where $D = |Vr_{k1}(A_i, A_s) - Vr_{k2}(A_j, A_s)| \in [0,2]$. Obviously, g and h satisfy the restrictions in definition 3, in which $r = 0$ and $m = 0.3$.

To observe the change of A_i's rating reputation caused by the rating $Vr_{k1}(A_i, A_s)$, the total change at the time when N ratings on the same provision have been reported after A_i is given by

$$\Delta RR(A_i) = \sum_{k2=k1+1}^{N} \left| Vr_{k1}(A_i, A_s) - Vr_{k2}(A_j, A_s) \right| \tag{5}$$

The ratings on the same product may have some distribution, because the product has its real quality to be observed by buyers. Assume ratings of the product have the normal distribution with a mean $\mu \in [-1,1]$, which can be seen as the most accurate rating value consistent to the quality of a provision, and a variance σ^2. Under this hypothesis, the expectation of the tuning by a feedback is given by

$$\int_{-1}^{1} ((Vr_0 - x)^2 - 4|Vr_0 - x| + 1.11) f(x) dx \tag{6}$$

where $f(x) = (\sigma\sqrt{2\pi})^{-1} e^{-(x-\mu)^2/2\sigma^2} + c$, and $Vr_0 = Vr_{k1}(A_i, A_s)$.

This RRF mechanism instance has following properties:

Property 1. The instance is incentive-compatible.

Proof: Consider the following function

$$I(y) = \int_{-1}^{1} ((y-x)^2 - 4|y-x| + 1.11) f(x) dx \tag{7}$$

$y \in [-1,1]$, which has its maximal value when $y = \mu$, and

$$\begin{cases} I(y_1) > I(y_2), \text{ if } y_2 > y_1 \geq \mu \\ I(y_1) > I(y_2), \text{ if } y_2 < y_1 \leq \mu. \end{cases}$$

That means a rating closer to μ will get a more positive tuning. However, μ is not a public value and cannot be obviously known. To chase the maximal profit, a recommender must try to report a more accurate rating. □

Property 2. Reporting an unfair or inaccurate rating, one's influence on reputation will be decreased.

Property 3. Effectiveness of continuous unfair ratings will be convergent in finite steps.

Proof: It takes some period of time to complete a transaction. Assume in every time unit, the malicious member A_0 continuously does a transaction and reports an unfair rating, and the provider to whom A_0 has rated before will complete a transaction, given a new rating. According to property 2, A_0's rating reputation will be tuned by a feedback as $I(Vr(A_0, A_k)) < c' < 0$. Let R_0 be the initial rating reputation value of A_0 at step 0. The rating reputation value of A_0 at step N, $RR(A_0)_N = R_0$ $+ \sum_{k=1}^{N} (\sum_{i=1}^{k} I(Vr_i(A_0, A_i))) < R_0 + (N^2+N)c'/2$. When $N > \sqrt{(c'-8R_0)/4c'} - 1/2$,

$RR(A_0)_N < R_0 + (N^2+N)c'/2 < 0$. That means the effectiveness of A0's ratings will be decreased to zero in finite steps. □

Property 4. Random rating makes one's rating reputation decreased.

Proof: The probabilistic density function of random rating is $f_2(x) = 1/2$, $x \in [-1,1]$. Following the function 7, the expectation of the rating reputation tuning caused by a random rating is

$$\int_{-1}^{1} \frac{1}{2} I(y) dy = \int_{-1}^{1} (-x^2 - 0.56) f(x) dx < 0$$

That means random rating makes one's rating reputation decreased. □

Properties 1 and 4 implicate the RRF mechanism instance can reduce the appearances of insouciant ratings, and properties 2 and 3 prove it can effectively cope with the attack and disturbance of malicious and unfair ratings. Furthermore, appropriate parameter configuration according to specific environment can show its capability of determent against collusion. Given the assumption that one's profit has a linear relationship with its capability and rating reputation, namely the profit function $p(A_s) = aCR(A_s) + bRR(A_s) + c$. And assume a collusion formation must satisfy the condition $Vr(A_i, A_s) > \mu + d$. If for $x \in [\mu + d, 1]$, $a \cdot g(x) + b \cdot I(x) \leq 0$, namely that the total profit of the beneficiary and the recommender is negative, the collusion will not be formed.

4.3 Challenges to Build an RRF Mechanism

To build an RRF mechanism, some challenges should be well solved. The key requirement of rating reputation is to benefit the accurate rating and punish the inaccurate one. However some problems may make this fair principle broken.

(1) *Quality variance.* The quality and trust of a provision may greatly change. Hence the subsequent ratings will be much different from the previous ones, and the latter ratings will be seemed as bad ones and tuned negatively by feedbacks. One solution to this problem is to make the weight of feedbacks attenuated when the interval between the initial rating and the feedback increases. After an appropriate period, the feedbacks related to an old rating make no more tuning.

(2) *Change insensitive.* One's trustworthiness of rating may change by some reason. However, the continuous accumulation of previous rating remarks will cover the recent change on the rating trustworthiness. The rating reputation must indicate both the history accumulation and recent change. It may take a trade-off on the sensitivity according to specific environment.

(3) *Feedback disturbance.* Although a bad or malicious rating from a member with low rating reputation affects little on the provider's capability reputation, it may disturb the previous recommenders' rating reputations as a feedback. Malicious members may use this deficiency to disturb the reputation system. Therefore, weight of rating reputation of the feedback may be taken into account in the tuning on rating reputation.

(4) *Hidden double-dealing.* Seller sells most products with high quality, but some products with low quality for benefit. The accurate negative reputation report from victim may be submerged, or be mistakenly regarded as unfair rating referred to the majority. The victim's rating reputation will be imposed unfairly negative tuning. This phenomenon may deter members from reporting actual observations.

5 Conclusions

As reputation mechanism is gradually accepted and adopted as an effective resolution to build trust system in electronic communities, some attack and trust problems of reputation mechanism itself, such as collusion, malicious or unfair rating, and insouciant rating, become possible hazards in application. The contribution of this paper is to extend normal one-layer reputation mechanism to a double-layer reputation mechanism, called Rating Reputation Feedback (RRF) mechanism, with two type reputations, the capability reputation and rating reputation, which respectively denotes the trustworthiness of one's capability and quality and that of one's rating. We propose that adding the rating reputation into reputation mechanism is more suitable to confront the attacks of reputation system, than only normal reputation itself. In future work, the problems of building a RRF system discussed in section 4.3 will be further studied. And the collective effect of RRF mechanism in electronic community platform will also be verified.

Acknowledgment

This work is supported by the Major State Basic Research Development Program of China under Grant No. 2003CB317000.

References

1. J. SABATER, C. SIERRA, "Review on Computational Trust and Reputation Models", In: Artificial Intelligence Review (2005) 24:33-60
2. Chrysanthos Dellarocas, "Analyzing the Economic Efficiency of eBay-like Online Reputation Reporting Mechanisms",In Proceedings of the 3rd ACM conference on Electronic Commerce(2001), pp 171-179
3. S.D.Ramchum, T.D.lluynh and N.R.Jennings, "Trust in Multi-Agent Systems", In: The Knowledge Engineering Review (2004) , Volume: 19(1)
4. Beng Chin Ooi, Chu Yee Liau, and Kian-Lee Tan, "Managing Trust in Peer-to-Peer Systems Using Reputation-Based Techniques",In: Proceedings of the WAIM 2003 (2003), LNCS 2762, pp2-12
5. Li Xiong and Ling Liu,"Building Trust in Decentralized Peer-to-Peer Electronic Communities" In Fifth International Conference on Electronic Commerce Research (2002), ACM Press.http://www.cc.gatech.edu/projects/disl/PeerTrust/pub/xiong02building.pdf.

6. C Dellarocas, "Self-Interest, Reciprocity, and Participation in Online Reputation systems" In Workshop in Information Systems and Economics 2003 (2004), http://ebusiness.mit.edu/research/papers/205_Dellarocas_EbayParticipation.pdf
7. C.Dellarocas, "The Digitization of Word of Mouth: Promise and Challenges of Online Feedback Mechanisms", In: Management Science (2003), Volume: 49(10), pp: 1407-1424
8. G. Zacharia,P. Maes, "Trust Management through Reputation Mechanisms", In: Applied Artificial Intelligence 14 (2000), pp 881–907.
9. J. SABATER, C. SIERRA, "Reputation and social network analysis in multiagent systems", Int. Joint Conf. on Autonomous Agents and Multiagent Systems (2002), pp 475–482
10. Anurag Garg, Roberto Battiti, Roberto Cascella, "Reputation management: experiments on the robustness of ROCQ", In Proceedings of Autonomous Decentralized Systems, ISADS 2005 (2005),pp 725-730
11. Javier Carbo, Jesus Garcia, and Jose M. Molina,"Subjective Trust Inferred by Kalman Filtering vs. a Fuzzy Reputation", In: ER Workshops 2004 (2004), LNCS 3289, pp. 496–505
12. R. Jurca and B. Faltings, "A Incentive Compatible Reputation Mechanism", In: *Proceeding of the IEEE International Conference on E-Commerce* (2003), pp: 285-292
13. A.Whitby, A. Josan and J.Indulska, "Filtering Out Unfair Ratings in Bayesian Reputation Systems", In: The Icfain Journal of Management Research (2005), Volume: 4(2), pp: 48-64
14. C.Dellarocas, "Immunizing Online Reputation Reporting Systems Against Unfair Ratings and Discriminatory Behavior", In: Proceedings of the 2nd ACM Conference on Electronic Commerce (2000), http://coof.ba.ttu.edu/zlin/readings/Chris-reputation.pdf
15. WTL Teacy, J Patel, NR Jennings, M Luck, "Coping with Inaccurate Reputation Sources: Experimental Analysis of a Probabilistic Trust Model", In Proceedings of Fourth International Joint Conference on Autonomous Agents and Multiagent Systems(2005), pp. 997-1004

A Vickrey-Type Multi-attribute Auction Model

Xiang Chen[1,2] and Shan-li Hu[1,2]

[1] Department of Computer Science and Techonoly,
Fuzhou University, Fuzhou, 350002, China
[2] Laboratory of Computer Science, Institute of Software,
Chinese Academy of Sciences, Bejing 100080, China
angus_cx@yahoo.com.cn, husl@fzu.edu.cn

Abstract. Internet auction is not only an integral part of Electronic Commerce but is also becoming a promising field for applying autonomous agents and multi-agent system (MAS) technologies. And auction, as an efficient resource allocation method, has an important role in MAS problems and as such is receiving increasing attention from scholars. This paper suggests a protocol (VAMA) and strategies for multi-attribute auction. Some useful properties such as strategy-proof are also proven. This paper also includes an analysis of the strategy of the buyer, and gives a decentralized mechanism for VAMA implementation as well as discussing some questions about VAMA. Finally, this protocol is compared with existing ones, improving on the work of Esther David etc.

1 Introduction

Recently, Internet auctions in open dynamic environment have been attracting more and more attention. Internet auction is not only an integral part of Electronic Commerce, but is also becoming a promising field for applying autonomous agents and multi-agent system (MAS) technologies [1,2].

Resource (resource here is general, including services, commodities, benefits and so on) allocation is an important question in MAS. In the Internet environment, a rational agent represents the intention of its master, whose goal is to maximize its benefit. When allocating a resource, the resource suppliers (sellers) expect to sell at the highest price possible, while the resource demanders (buyers) expect to buy at the lowest price possible. In this scenario, auction, as an efficient, operational method, can be used to allocate the resource in a fast, reasonable way. In coalition formation, coalition structure generation, allocating resources and tasks in the coalition, and dividing the revenue among agents are three interlaced activities [3]. Auction, as one of the efficient coordination mechanisms, can be used to allocate these+ resources (tasks, revenues etc.) In addition, in decentralized scheduling problems [4] and other MAS problems [5], auction plays an important role. Therefore, it has been gaining increasing attention recently.

In a classic auction, we determine the owner of some kind of resource according only to the price. However, resource has more than one attribute. For example, when assessing a task to be allocated, its properties may include the start time, the end time, the quality of its performance, and the price it commands, etc. Similarly, services' attributes may include the serviced time, the offered quality, etc. Therefore, a resource with more than one attribute is common and sometimes necessary. However, while multi-attribute resource should be a common phenomenon in auctions, it has been receiving decreasing levels of attention [6].

In this paper, we describe a multi-attribute auction model. Then, we study a Vickrey-type multi-attribute auction in detail. In the model, we use a scenario of government procurement, in which government as a resource demander is a public buyer while others who bid for the resource supplier are bidders or sellers. We study the auction with a single unit. And, intuitively, because the Internet environment seems virtual, it is more suitable for a sealed auction. So, we place the scenario in an Internet environment, where it is common that a buyer confronts multi sellers and determines who will be the supplier. In the model given by paper [7], attributes are limited to two and the evaluation function of a buyer and cost functions of sellers are limited accordingly. The number of attributes in the model developed in this paper has no limit to; furthermore, evaluation function and cost functions can be any function with its range real. Accordingly, this model is more general.

The remainder of this paper is organized as follows: In Section 2, we show the related works. In Section 3, we describe the model and some of its parameters. Detailed protocol and strategy are depicted in Section 4. After describing the protocol and some properties about it, we discuss the proposed protocol in Section 5. Finally, in Section 6, we present our conclusions.

2 Related Works

Auction is an efficient way to reach agreement among agents. There are several types of auctions, including English auction, Dutch auction, first-price sealed-bid auction, and second-price sealed-bid auction (Vickrey auction). In paper [7], Esther David etc studied the multi-attribute English auction and the first-price sealed-bid auction, giving the protocols and strategies accordingly. In paper [8] a strategy with a deadline is given, the attribute number of an item is 2, and the evaluation function of the buyer is the linear combination of the two attributes' reciprocal. In addition, the analysis about the strategies of the buyer and sellers is qualitative rather than strictly proven.

Bichler [9] carried out an experimental analysis of the main auctions. He found that the utility scores achieved in multi-attribute auctions were higher than those of single-attribute auctions in every tested auction. The experiment also showed that the second-price sealed-bid auction did better in impelling the sellers to give their dominant strategies. This is a good property enabling the buyer to acquire higher utility and is beneficial for a healthy market. In [10], M. Bichler etc. described an application of a multi-attribute auction. Unfortunately, there was no theoretical explanation.

Takayuki Suyama etc. [1] studied the combinatorial multi-attribute procurement auction, gave a model for combinatorial multi-attribute auction, developed a series of protocols and brought forward a notion of False-name Proof.

These works mainly involved some expansion on the classic auction scenario. However, they laid emphases on the utilities the buyers and sellers could get and had fewer discussions on a healthy market under certain protocols. More importantly, as to second-price sealed-bid protocol, there was no expansion for multi-attribute auction nor was there a theoretical analysis.

3 Model

Generally, an auction can be modeled as: M=<B,S,I,A,V,C,P,Sche>, in which,
- B is a set of buyers, B={$B_1,B_2,…,B_m$};
- S is a set of sellers, S={$S_1,S_2,…,S_n$};
- I is a set of items for selling, I = {$it_1,it_2,…,it_k$};
- A is a set of vectors, A = { $A_1, A_2,…, A_k$ };
- V is a set of the evaluation functions of buyers;
- C is the set of cost functions of sellers;
- P represents the protocols between buyers and sellers, which can be negotiated in advance; usually, one auction one protocol.
- Sche is the schemes of the bargain made between buyers and sellers in an auction.

This paper concentrates on the Vickrey-type multi-attribute auction, in which a buyer demands an item with certain properties and lots of sellers vie with each other to meet the demand, similar to a scenario of government procurement. In this case, the buyer is the auctioneer, and the sellers are the bidders. So, the general model degenerates to M=<b,S,it,A,V,C,P,Sche>, in which, B degenerates to b, since there is only one buyer; S remains the same, that is, a set of sellers; I degenerates to it, since there is only one item; particularly, A can now represent the attribute space with respect to item it. Suppose there are r kinds of attributes for item it: $a_1^{it},a_2^{it},…,a_r^{it}$; We can define: $A=A_1^{it} \times A_2^{it} \times … \times A_r^{it}$; in which A_i^{it} is the range of attribute a_i^{it} (i=1,2,…,r). V is now the evaluation function of b, while C is a set of functions for sellers' cost functions, so C_i represents the cost function of the seller S_i. An item can be described as <it,a>, in which a is the vector of the item's attributes, a∈A; In this paper, we discuss VAMA protocol; the P in the model refers to it. An elaboration will follow in Section 4. Sche represents the final striking scheme.

Judging a protocol, we may consider the following properties:

Strategy-proof: We can say a protocol is strategy proof or incentive compatible (or has a dominant strategy), if declaring the true evaluation value is an optimal strategy for each bidder regardless of the action of other bidders [1].

False-name-proof: In an Internet environment, users usually appear anonymously. This is one of the reasons we are interested in the sealed-bid auction. However, the participants, especially the bidders, can acquire two auctioning qualifications (usually two accounts in an Internet environment) through many other ways. Here, one of the qualifications can be thought of as a false name. It seems that the seller with two qualifications can win the auction more easily and gain an extra utility. But, in some protocols, the utility may decrease because of another name. Such protocols are called false-name proof [1].

Individual Rationality: In certain auction protocols, the utility for each rational agent/participant is non-negative; in these instances we can say the protocol has the property of individual rationality.

Pareto efficient: Utility is the common interesting topic among buyers and sellers. To a buyer, his/her utility is the price difference of evaluation value and the striking price. To a seller, his/her utility is the price difference of the cost and the protocol striking price (Please refer Section 4 for strict definition of striking price and protocol striking price). It is said that a protocol is Pareto efficient when the sum of all the participants' utilities is maximal in the dominant strategy.

Other properties about time are whether protocol can converge in a limited time, whether the item can be allocated or acquired efficiently or whether protocol is computable for a practical use. In addition to the market, we may consider whether the protocol is false-name proof or of benefit to a healthy market etc.

4 VAMA Protocol

4.1 VAMA Protocol (Vickrey-Type Auction for Multi-attribute)

Definition 1
Let PC_i represent the price concession of seller S_i and PC_i^m the maximal price concession.

Given a published evaluation function V of buyer and cost function C_i of seller S_i, we can define: $PC_i^m = \max_{a \in A}(V(a) - C_i(a)) = V(a_i^*) - C_i(a_i^*)$.

In which: $a_i^* = \arg\max_{a \in A}(V(a) - C_i(a))$; i.e., a_i^* is the dominant attribute vector of S_i with respect to the auctioned item, shortened as *dominant attribute*.

Definition 2
$SPC_i^m = \max(0, \max_{S_j \in S \text{ and } j \neq i}(PC_j^m))$
i.e., the non negative maximal price concession expect S_i.

Definition 3
According to the protocol, if the seller is suitable for reaching a bargain with, the seller/bidder is called *striking seller/bidder*. The attribute accordingly is called *striking attribute*; the bidding price accordingly is called *striking price*; and the scheme submitted is called *striking scheme*.

Definition 4
Different to striking price, for every seller, there is a *protocol striking price*:

$P_{i \text{ def}} = V(a_i^*) - SPC_i^m$; if P_i is the striking price and the price that the buyer finally pays, then for the price that buyer bargains with, we use P_i^* to denote. When the striking price is called *final striking price* and the attribute *final striking attribute*, the seller/bidder is called the *final striking seller/bidder*, and the scheme *final striking scheme*

VAMA protocol

1. The buyer gives the evaluation function V' (different from V);
2. Each bidder gives a sealed-bid SB_i ($SB_i \geq 0$);

3. Select a final striking bidder S_i in the striking sellers' set candidates (SB); if the set candidates (SB) is null, the auction fails;
4. Reach a bargain with S_i's protocol striking price.
   In which:
   $SB_{i\,def} = \max(PC_i^m, 0)$
   and candidates(SB) $_{def} = \{SB_i \mid SB_i = \max(SB_j)(j=1,2,...,n)$ and $SB_i > 0 (i=1,2,...,n)\}$

4.2 Some Properties

Property 1: This protocol is Strategy-proof
Proof:
   The utility for seller S_i is:
   $$U(S_i) = P_i - C_i = [V(a_i^*) - SPC_i^m] - C_i(a) = [V(a_i^*) - C_i(a)] - SPC_i^m$$
   Because the second term is independent of S_i, to maximize the utility, the seller should maximize the first item. That is, give his/her dominant attribute a_i^*. In other words, the strategy for S_i is to bid with his/her dominant attribute. Therefore, dominant strategies exist and the protocol is Strategy-proof.

Property 2: This protocol is False-name proof
Proof:
   Suppose S_i has a false name S_k, according to the definition above, we have:
   $P_k = V(a_k^*) - SPC_k^m$ and $U(S_k) = [V(a_k^*) - C_k(a_k^*)] - SPC_k^m$.
   According to the protocol, there is only one final striking seller, so, for S_i, he/she can only get utility $U(S_i)$ or $U(S_k)$. Suppose $U(S_i)$ will be acquired, will $U(S_i)$ be greater because of the existance of the false name S_k? In fact, it will not (Let's use SPC_i^{-km} representing the non negative maximal price concession except S_i when there is no false name S_k):
   $U(S_i) = [V(a_i^*) - C_i(a_i^*)] - SPC_i^m$
   $= [V(a_i^*) - C_i(a_i^*)] - \max(SPC_i^{-km}, PC_k^m) \leq [V(a_i^*) - C_i(a_i^*)] - SPC_i^{-km}$
   So, the seller S_i may get less if he/she bids with two accounts.

Property 3: The protocol is individual rationality
Proof:
   If candidates(SB) is null, then the utility for each seller is zero and the utility for the buyer is zero;
   Unless, according to the protocol and property 1, the candidates are in the set candidates (SB) and one of them reaches a bargain with the buyer at the dominant attribute price (or the protocol striking price) P_i, then the corresponding utility is:
   $U(S_i) = P_i - C_i = V(a_i^*) - C_i(a_i^*) - SPC_i^m = PC_i^m - SPC_i^m \geq 0$
   For other sellers, the utilities are zero. So, the sellers are all individual rationality.
   And the utility for the buyer is: $U(b) = V(a_i^*) - P_i^* = SPC_i^m \geq 0$.
   Therefore, the buyer is also acting rationally as an individual.

Property 4: If the buyer published the true evaluation function V, the protocol is Pareto efficient

Proof:

If auction fails, the total utility is zero;

Given the true evaluation function, suppose S_i is the final striking seller, and in this case, let's represent the total utility as $U(V)$, then:

$$U(V) = \sum U = \sum_{j=1}^{n} U(S_j) + U(b)$$
$$= (PC_i^m - SPC_i^m) + SPC_i^m = PC_i^m = \max_{a \in A}(V(a) - C_i(a))$$

If given the evaluation function V', in this case, supposing the striking attribute is a_i^*, and using $U(V')$ to represent the total utility, then:

$$U(V') = \sum U = \sum_{j=1}^{n} U(S_j) + U(b)$$
$$= (PC_i^m - SPC_i^m) + [V(a_i^*) - P_i^*] = (PC_i^m - SPC_i^m) + [V(a_i^*) - (V'(a_i^*) - SPC_i^m)]$$
$$= PC_i^m + [V(a_i^*) - V'(a_i^*)] = [V'(a_i^*) - C_i(a_i^*)] + [V(a_i^*) - V'(a_i^*)] = V(a_i^*) - C_i(a_i^*)$$
$$\leq \max_{a \in A}(V(a) - C_i(a))$$

We can see that, under dominant strategy, there is no greater utility than when the buyer gives the true evaluation function, i.e., if the buyer published the true evaluation function V, this protocol is Pareto efficient.

For this reason, we recommend the buyer give the true evaluation function. Then, the total utility achieves the maximum possible which is beneficial for a healthy market.

With respect to computation complexity and real time property, and according to the protocol, for the dominant strategy exists, to give the best option, sellers only need to calculate its maximal price concession. Therefore, this protocol is suitable for real time Internet auction.

5 Discussion and Comparisons

5.1 The Problem of Who Confirms the Striking Attribute

According to the proposed protocol, the buyer selects a striking seller in the candidates set of candidates(SB) while the striking attributes are in set:

$$\{x \mid x \in \arg\max_{a \in A}(V(a) - C_i(a)), i = 1, 2, \ldots, n\}$$

If the buyer selects one randomly, he/she in fact gives up the right of confirming an attribute vector. In some cases, it is not consistent with his/her benefit. Consider the following example:

Table 1. An example of VAMA auction

b	$V(a_1)=5.0$	$V(a_2)=3.0$	Bid	candidates(SB)
S_1	$C_1(a_1)=3.0$	$C_1(a_2)=0.5$	2.5	$\{S_1, S_2\}$
S_2	$C_2(a_1)=2.5$	$C_2(a_2)=2.0$	2.5	

This example illustrates simply an auction of a single item with two attribute vectors a_1, a_2, where there is one buyer b and two sellers S_1, S_2. According to the protocol, the buyer will select a striking seller randomly within $\{S_1,S_2\}$. In fact, commonly, the buyer may expect to make bargain with S_2, because that S_2 supplies an attribute vector a_1, which gives a higher value according to his/her evaluation function.

To fix this problem, we can expand the protocol by supplying the dominant attributes when sellers are bidding. That is, when bidding, the bidders should give $<SB_i,a_i>$ rather than SB_i. It is consistent with the market's rule of diversity of products and the subdivision of a market and so is beneficial for a healthy market.

5.2 The Problem of Dominant-Strategy for Buyer

In section 4.2, the property 1 shows that the dominant strategies exist for sellers. But, unfortunately for the buyer, there is no dominant strategy. Suppose the published evaluation function is V', while the true original evaluation function is V, then the utility of the buyer is:

$$U(b) = V(a_i^*) - P_i^* = V(a_i^*) - [V'(a_i^*) - SPC_i^m] = [V(a_i^*) - V'(a_i^*)] + SPC_i^m$$

It seems that when bargaining is finished, the buyer will get extra utility (the first item shows this), enabling an increase in the whole utility. In fact, function V and V' may not be linear, and the extra utility is not promised when considering the following example:

Table 2. A scenario of VAMA auction

b	$V(a_1)=5$	$V(a_2)=3$	Bid	Bid'
	$V'(a_1)=3$	$V'(a_2)=3.5$		
S_1	$C_1(a_1)=2.0$	$C_1(a_2)=2.0$	$<3.0,a_1>$	$<1.5,a_2>$
S_2	$C_2(a_1)=1.5$	$C_2(a_2)=2.0$	$<3.5,a_1>$	$<1.5,a_2>$
U			3.0	1.0

This scenario illustrates one situation when giving different evaluation functions of V and V'; the final striking bidders under the two functions are marked as italic, and the according utilities are shown in the last row.

From this scenario, we see that the utility becomes smaller when the buyer gives the evaluation function V'. We also see that finally, we get the item with an attribute vector a_2 as the result of the function V'; rather than a_1 which should be achieved when we give function V. In this case, it gives a wrong signal to the market. Furthermore, because of the buyer's disguise, the efforts to acquire the bias of buyers become wasted labor, and the sellers can't subdivide and locate the market precisely. This disturbs the order of a healthy market. For these reasons, we recommend that the buyer should give the true evaluation function – it is a good strategy for both the buyer and a healthy market and can be thought of as a hypo-optimal strategy.

5.3 Trust Problem in VAMA

From VAMA, we can see that it is an extension of Vickrey auction under multi-attribute, so, unavoidably, it inherits the disadvantages of Vickrey auction. A lying auctioneer [11] (the lying buyer in the government procurement scenario) may give a false SPC_i^m, so that he/she can get extra utility. In VAMA, there is no mechanism inhibiting this.

For this problem, we can introduce a mobile agent for a decentralized implementation of VAMA. That is, the agent represents the buyer and travels around sellers one by one in a random sequence where it compares the seller's PC_i^m with its carrying value then exchanges it so that it stores the bigger value. This distributing computation results in the agent returning with the biggest values and the striking seller obtaining a true SPC_i^m.

5.4 Tie Problem in VAMA

In an auction, when two bidders give an identical bid, a tie problem occurs. For an equal chance, who will be the final striking bidder? In our model, also, when the sellers give the same SB and attribute a (Table 2 is also an example for this), we should do something to assure equality.

Simply, we can ask the bidders who gave the striking bid for a second bid according to the VAMA protocol, under the condition that the restricted participants must now give an extra bid beyond the original.

5.5 Comparisons with Other Multi-attribute Auction Protocols

In [7] the selected models for first-price sealed-bid multi-attribute auction and English multi-attribute auction limited the number of attributes to two. Also, cost functions of sellers are a multiplication of the same function with the coefficient θ_i in tandem with S_i. The two assumptions simplify the auction model; enabling an optimal strategy for the buyer, but also bring it within the limitation of the two auction methods. In VAMA, there is the property of Strategy-proof, so the complexity of decision making for sellers is just equal to solving a maximum function. Obviously, the computing time needed is short. Also, it is a real-time auction. In English multi-attribute auction, the computing time is also limited in every circle, but the real-time property is worse because of multi circles; furthermore, it is easy to cause the false-name problems which are harmful to a healthy market. In first-price sealed-bid auction, the computation time is higher, and before making the decision, agents have to evaluate the cost functions of other sellers; the real time property is between English multi-attribute auction and VAMA auction. So, VAMA is more suitable for the real time network auction.

6 Conclusions

Aiming at multi-attribute auction, this paper gives a Vickrey-type multi-attribute auction model, and proposes a new protocol for multi-attribute auction, i.e., VAMA. Compared to the existing multi-attribute auction methods, the model of VAMA is more general and with a dominant strategy for sellers, also has the property of false-name proof. For a healthy market and long-term benefits, we recommend the buyer give the true valuation function, when the protocol has the property of Pareto-efficient. These characteristics are the improvements for existing multi-attribute auction methods.

Acknowledgements

The National Natural Science Foundation of China under Grant No.60373079, No.60573076 and the Foundation of the Computer Science Key Laboratory at the Software Institute in the China Science Academy under Grant No.SYSKF0505 support this research.

References

1. Takayuki and Suyama, Makoto Yokoo. Strategy/ False-name Proof Protocols for Combinatorial Multi-Attribute Procurement Auction. AAMAS'04, July 19-23, 2004, New York, New York, USA
2. M.Yokoo. Characterization of Strategy/False-name Proof Combinatorial Auction Protocols: Price-oriented, Rationing-free Protocol. In Proceedings of 19th International Joint Conference On Artificial Intelligence (IJCAI-2003),pages 733-739,2003
3. T.Sandholm, K. Larson, M. Andersson, O. Shehory, and F. Tohme. Coalition structure generation with worst case guarantees. Artificial Intelligence Journal, 1999
4. M Wellman, W. Walsh, P. Wurman,and J. MacKie-Mason. Auction protocols for decentralized scheduling. *Games and Economic Behavior*, 35:271–303, 2001
5. L Hunsberger and B. J. Grosz. A combinatorial auction for collaborative lanning. In Proc. 4th International Conference on Multi-Agent Systems (ICMAS-00), pages 151–158, 2000
6. D.C.Parkes and J.Kalagnanam. Multiattribute Reverse Auctions. Presented at AAAI, 2002
7. Esther David, Rina Azoulay-Schwartz, Sarit Kraus. An English Auction Protocol for Multi-Attribute Items. AMEC2002 52-68
8. Esther David, Rina Azoulay-Schwartz, Sarit Kraus. Bidders' Strategy for Automated Multi-Attribute sequential English Auction with a Deadline. In The Second International Joint Conference on Autonomous Agents and Multiagent systems, pages 457-464, 2003
9. M.Bichler. An Experimental Analysis of Multi-Attribute Auctions. Decision Support System, vol.28, 2000
10. M.Bichler and BidTaker. An Application of Multi-Attribute Auction Markets in Tourism. Presented and Wirtschaftsinformatik 2002, Augsburg, Germany , 2002
11. Sandholm, T. 2000. Issues in Computational Vickrey Auctions. International Journal of Electronic Commerce, 4(3), 107-129

Strategy Coordination Approach for Safe Learning About Novel Filtering Strategies in Multi Agent Framework

Sahin Albayrak and Dragan Milosevic

DAI-Labor, Technical University Berlin,
Salzufer 12, 10587 Berlin, Germany
{sahin, dragan}@dai-lab.de

Abstract. In commercial and information reach society, the properties of novel filtering strategies have to be explored without dramatically increasing response time while trying to combine them to effectively use available system resources. The major drawback of many existing systems, which try to make different synergies between filtering strategies, is usually concerned with not taking care of the availability of resources, being especially critical for the realisation of successful commercial deployments. The essence of a presented solution is both in the encapsulation of many known searching algorithms inside separate filtering agents, and in the integration of flexible resource aware coordination mechanisms into one manager agent. The flexibility of a realised coordination scheme in facilitating an easy integration of novel strategies is practically demonstrated in an intelligent personal information assistant (PIA). Experimental results, obtained during a 2 week internal PIA usage, show the elimination of jobs longer than 1000s together with an increase of up to 10% in a received feedback values.

1 Introduction

The astonishing human creativity has produced thousands of very different problems that require filtering capabilities to be somehow resolved. It is illogical to even hope that one single filtering algorithm will ever be so brilliant that it can be the best choice for fulfilling this huge variety of searching tasks. Hopefully, a fruitful history of filtering technologies has already brought many strategies [8][10][12][16][18][19][20][24] that are more or less suitable to be used in these different situations. One only needs a sophisticated reasoning that will be able to identify which particular strategy should be applied in a given situation to produce as good results as possible. There is an adventure behind since a particular strategy, being excellent in one situation, might be hardly applicable in yet another one. A system, tending to improve itself, should be thus careful while exploring the hidden capabilities of not known enough strategies.

To minimise a risk of choosing the inappropriate filtering strategy, many existing systems [15][22] usually combine only few well-known strategies in fixed static manners. One of used strategies is always a content-based filtering, which is a reasonable conventional decision, because all these systems are concerned with information retrieval. As an additional strategy, Letizia [14] and Amalthaea [17] utilise event based filtering for tracking users during browsing, PIAgent [13] applies neural networks for exploring users' needs, NewT [21] and PEA [23] use evolution strategies for adapting profiles, and FAB [5], P-Tango [7], TripMatcher [9] and many other systems deploy collaborative based filtering for exploring aspects that are only captured by humans.

According to the authors' best knowledge the most of the mentioned systems are tested in highly protected working conditions where the availability of resources is usually completely ignored. Although a particular strategy can be the best suited one for the assigned job, in the case where the needed system resource is highly loaded, that strategy will most probably have weak chances to successfully produce expected results. Self improving coordination approach [1][2] tries not selecting such a strategy for which the unfavourable resource situation exists, and to assign a job to a strategy that will produce results in a reasonable amount of time. This is simply achieved by estimating the current load of all relevant system resources before speculating how every available strategy is promising. A coordination scheme is named self improving, because of using a proportional selection [16], which gives chances to each strategy to be selected, and therefore exploring the unknown capabilities of novel strategies.

The drawback of this self improving coordination mechanism lies in its unfeasibility to provide any guaranties in the case where novel and not known enough strategies are asked to perform filtering. In highly dynamic conditions, every system should be able to evolve through an easy integration of novel filtering strategies, being better suited for resolving some particular types of problems. It will be wonderful when all nice properties of the coordination mechanism, which both takes care about resources while selecting a filtering strategy and tries to improve itself during runtime, can be preserved together with facilitating the integration of novel strategies. The way how this goal can be achieved will be the main topic of this paper, which is structured as follows. The next section illustrates these new coordination challenges in one scenario. The core contribution of this paper is then contained in the section, which presents the coordination approach, being quite flexible respecting the novel strategies. A paper is finished with sections where implementation and experimental result details are given.

2 Problem Description

The existence of many different strategies, making every searching problem solvable on many distinct ways, naturally imposes the challenge of either exploiting the already learnt properties of well known strategies or exploring the unknown, potentially promising, capabilities of novel ones. This challenge becomes even more severe when each few days a new strategy should be integrated. The exploration of unknown capabilities obviously has somehow to be performed without fatal errors by reason of not seriously destroying the confidence that users have into the deployed filtering engine.

A real environment, being the assumed playing ground for the coordination among available strategies, creates the yet another challenge that is contained in the highly changeable availability of needed system resources. It is far away of being truth that the load of system resources, such as CPU, database and memory, can be assumed to be static. On the other side, the existing strategies usually differ a lot concerning the requirements towards the needed resources. A selection of a strategy, for which not enough resources are available, is probably a bad move that will hardly provide good results within the assigned amount of time. The selection of strategies, which will perform the needed filtering activities, has by some means to take care both about available resources and about requirements of different strategies towards them.

Fig. 1a gives a scenario where a manager agent (M) has 4 filtering agents (F) on its disposal for resolving the assigned job. While each F has its own searching strategy, the burden of estimating a resource situation and choosing a responsible strategy is on M. The load of resources is on Fig. 1a represented as a number between zero and one, where a higher value means that the corresponding resource is more loaded.

To be able in a real-time environment, to choose in a long run for as many jobs as possible the most applicable solution, M estimates the availability of needed resources and evaluates the applicability of each available strategy. Together with these estimations and evaluation activities, M should try to learn about strengths and weaknesses of each available strategy, by analysing its behaviour in similar past situations. These estimation, evaluation, selection aspects will be analysed in the following section.

3 Approach

The authors' thoughts about the coordination, being naturally separated in the previous section on estimation, evaluation, selection and adaptation, are mainly concerned with the demands of a strategy towards different resources. Strategy, whose efficiency vitally depends on a currently highly loaded resource, will have weak chances to successfully work and to produce results in the reasonable amount of time. Such a strategy will probably produce perfect results after few hours or even days of filtering, but it is hardly possible and anyone will be patient enough to wait for them. It is probably much better to offer nearly perfect results that are obtained after a reasonable delay.

In [1] such a resource aware coordination is realised by describing each and every strategy by fitness values, which illustrates its requirements towards different system resources. Because central processor, database server and memory are found to be the most important filtering resources, CPU (F_{CPU}), database (F_{DB}) and memory (F_M) separate resource fitness values are introduced in a way that higher particular fitness value means that corresponding resource is needed in a smaller extent by a given strategy. While such a defined fitness values can be easily set for well known strategies, their initialisation is usually very problematic for novel filtering algorithms. Furthermore, fitness values can be unfortunately successfully adapted only by using the experience from jobs shorter than 10s [1]. The adaptation process from [1] additionally assumes a well formed community of strategies with correctly set fitness values, in order to be able to efficiently learn about novel strategies. These initialisation and adaptation problems obviously significantly reduce the flexibility regarding an integration of novel strategies with many hidden properties. Consequently, only the ability of a strategy to find accurate results will still be modelled by quality fitness F_Q as:

Def. 1. *Quality fitness* F_Q represents the level of users' satisfaction with that strategy in the past, where higher F_Q value corresponds to a more successful strategy [1][2].

An applicability of a particular strategy respecting available resources is illustrated through resource fitness F_R value, which is defined as:

Def. 2. *Resource fitness* F_R corresponds to the strategy ability to successfully work in a current runtime, where higher F_R means that a resource situation is more favourable for the particular strategy.

A fundamental difference between F_R and separate F_{CPU}, F_{DB}, F_M resource fitness value from [1] is in the computation of F_R on the flight, and thus no problematic initialisation and adaptation steps are anymore needed. The evaluation of F_R from the past experience is the cornerstone of this paper and it will be analysed in Section 3.2.

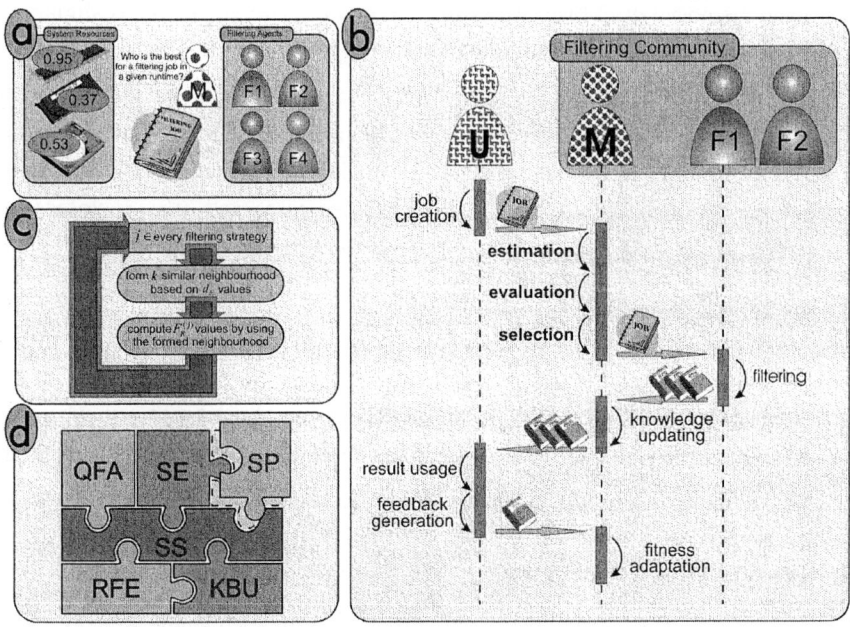

Fig. 1. (a) A coordination challenge (b) System architecture that illustrates communication between agents (c) Resource load fitness evaluation (d) Component structure of a manager

System architecture is given on Fig. 1b. *User agent* (U) is responsible for the creation of a filtering job by collecting the needed user preferences. It also knows how a user feedback can be first obtained and then forwarded to a manager agent. *Filtering agent* (F) encapsulates one particular strategy and it is always able to receive filtering jobs and to provide results after filtering has been finished. *Manager agent* (M) is the cornerstone that fulfils all coordination activities and ensures the satisfied quality of filtering services. M should be seen as the entity that performs estimation, evaluation, selection and adaptation coordination steps. After receiving a job from U, M will estimate the load of system resources, evaluate applicability of each strategy, and select one of them to which the actual job should be forwarded. As soon as the activated F has found results, they will be returned, via M, back to U. As the same time, M will adapt the knowledge that it possesses about the activated F based on the response time measurements. Finally, in the case of getting any relevance feedback from U, M will perform the adaptation of quality fitness, which may initially have a random value.

A concrete solution, showing how estimation, evaluation and selection steps will uncover the coordination mystery, will be described in following sub-sections. While knowledge updating is based on logging the duration, quality fitness adaptation uses the same technique as in [1][2], and thus these two steps will not be further analysed.

3.1 Strategy Evaluation

System runtime properties, being inside the scope of evaluation, are CPU (ω_{CPU}), DB (ω_{DB}) and memory (ω_M) load. An estimation of ω_{CPU}, ω_{DB} and ω_M is slightly different from [1], as found load values are bound to [0,1], which facilitates evaluation.

A CPU load is computed as $\omega_{CPU} = 1 - e^{-\beta_{CPU} t_{CPU}}$, where β_{CPU} is a tuning parameter and t_{CPU} is the time being needed for the computation of an algebraic expression, formed only in order to estimate a current CPU load. A higher CPU load naturally implies longer computation time t_{CPU}, $e^{-\beta_{CPU} t_{CPU}}$ decreases, and ω_{CPU} is closer to 1.

A DB load ω_{DB} is computed as $\omega_{DB} = 1 - e^{-\beta_{DB} t_{DB}}$, where again β_{DB} is a suitable tuning parameter and t_{DB} is the time being needed for the execution of a SQL query that is specially designed to estimate DB load. As a consequence of further loading DB, t_{DB} will increase, $e^{-\beta_{DB} t_{DB}}$ decreases, and that results in bigger ω_{DB} value.

A memory load $\omega_M = 1 - e^{-\beta_M s_M}$ reflects the amount of used memory, where β_M is a tuning parameter and s_M is the size of the currently used memory. It holds that more used memory s_M results in smaller $e^{-\beta_M s_M}$, and consequently in a larger ω_M.

3.2 Resource Fitness Evaluation

The resource fitness F_R value, representing the ability of each single strategy to efficiently exploit currently available resources, can be simply evaluated by analysing the behaviour of the corresponding strategy in the old runtime situations that are similar to the actual one. A cornerstone assumption is that the strategies with solid performances in similar runtime situations will hopefully be able to repeat such a good behaviour also in the future. It is therefore reasonable to assign to such strategies high F_R values, which will increase their chances to be selected to do the requested filtering.

Two main evaluation steps, being the formation of k-similar neighbourhood and F_R computation, are given on Fig. 1c. The former depends on the application of the appropriate distance function for finding k old runtime situations in which a particular strategy has been used and that are the most similar to an actual runtime. The latter will use the formed neighbourhood to assess how good a particular strategy can be in a current runtime. Both steps are repeated for each and every strategy, being the only way of getting the complete picture about the available filtering capabilities.

Finding k most similar old runtime situations is the known k-nearest neighbour search [12], performed on ω_{CPU}, ω_{DB} and ω_M attributes. By assuming that Euclidean distance $d_E(a,i)$ compares the actual runtime $a = (\omega_{CPU}^{(a)}, \omega_{DB}^{(a)}, \omega_M^{(a)})$ to any past runtime $i = (\omega_{CPU}^{(i)}, \omega_{DB}^{(i)}, \omega_M^{(i)})$, k runtime situations, having the smallest $d_E(a,i)$, will form a similar neighbourhood. The Euclidean distance $d_E(a,i)$ is defined as:

$$d_E(a,i) = \sqrt{\sum_{x \in \{CPU, DB, M\}} (\omega_x^{(a)} - \omega_x^{(i)})^2} \qquad (1)$$

The simple Euclidean distance is a good choice because all computations are performed in a very low dimensional space where all attributes ω_x have always defined values that are also already normalised to [0,1] in situation estimation (Section 3.1).

The resource fitness $F_R^{(j)}$, corresponding to a strategy j, is thus computed as:

$$F_R^{(j)} = \frac{1}{k} \sum_{i \in neighbourhood} s(a,i) e^{-\beta_t \frac{t_r^{(i)}}{avg(t_r)}} \qquad (2)$$

In (2), a summation is performed on found k neighbouring runtime situations that correspond to a strategy j. As the summation weight, a similarity $s(a,i)$ is used in order to ensure that a response time $t_r^{(i)}$ that corresponds to more similar old runtime situations, having smaller distance $d_E(a,i)$, has a greater influence on $F_R^{(j)}$ computation. A straightforward way to define such a similarity measure $s(a,i)$ is through:

$$s(a,i) = e^{-\beta_d \frac{d_E(a,i)}{avg(d_E)}} \qquad (3)$$

On the one side, a tuning parameter β_d, $\beta_d > 0$, controls a decay rate for $s(a,i)$ regarding a $d_E(a,i)$ grow. Larger β_d results that $s(a,i)$ drops faster when $d_E(a,i)$ increases, and reverse. Such $s(a,i)$ is actually ensuring that $F_R^{(j)}$ has small value for strategies that have not been used in similar runtime situations, being a sigh for a careful selection irrespective to $t_r^{(i)}$. On the other side, a larger $t_r^{(i)}$ results in smaller $e^{-t_r^{(i)}}$, and $F_R^{(j)}$ will be increased in a smaller extent. A parameter β_t, $\beta_t > 0$, controls the influence of t_r to F_R similarly as it was the case with β_d and $d_E(a,i)$. It holds that the small β_t decreases penalties that a strategy pays because of large t_r, and reverse.

The integration of $s(a,i)$ in (2) gives:

$$F_R^{(j)} = \frac{1}{k} \sum_{i \in \text{neighbourhood}} e^{-\left(\beta_d \frac{d_E(a,i)}{\text{avg}(d_E)} + \beta_t \frac{t_r^{(i)}}{\text{avg}(t_r)}\right)} \quad (4)$$

Both t_r and d_E are normalised by their average values $\text{avg}(t_r)$ and $\text{avg}(d_E)$ to eliminate the influence of different ranges of t_r and d_E. Therefore, the only weighting is performed through β_d and β_t parameters. The selection of values, assigned to β_d and β_t, defines that either good performances or the usage in similar past runtime situations has a priority while computing F_R. On the one hand, in the case where it is important that a particular strategy has been already used in the similar runtime situations while deciding about its new application, large β_d value ensures that all strategies with not similar enough runtime situations will pay large penalties and thus will have small F_R value. On the other hand, large β_t value will result that corresponding strategies with a bad performance and large t_r will have small F_R. Bad performances of a strategy, modelled through the large $t_r^{(i)}$, is an obvious sign that its selection is probably one bad move. Only strategies that are successfully used in similar runtime situations, will have small $t_r^{(i)}$ and large $s(a,i)$, which will finally result in large $F_R^{(j)}$.

Example 1. The cornerstone of this example is to illustrate how the resource fitness F_R values can be computed by using the data about the previous usage of the corresponding strategies. In the case where the actual runtime situation is $\omega_{CPU}^{(a)} = 0.38$, $\omega_{DB}^{(a)} = 0.83$ and $\omega_M^{(a)} = 0.15$, the found $F_R^{(j)}$, $j \in \{1,2,3\}$, values are given in Table 1. It is assumed that 3 available strategies have been used 5 $i \in \{1,...,5\}$, 7 $i \in \{6,...,12\}$ and 6 $i \in \{13,...,18\}$ times, respectively, and that for each usage both the corresponding runtime situation $\{\omega_{CPU}, \omega_{DB}, \omega_M\}$ and the measured response time t_r are known. Similarity $s(a,i)$ and $F_R^{(j)}$ are computed for both $(\beta_t, \beta_d) = (1,1)$ and $(\beta_t, \beta_d) = (1,2)$ to illustrate how the selection of weights β_t and β_d can significantly change the impression about every strategy. For each strategy $k = 3$ similar neighbourhoods are formed, and they are marked with a different cell filling. Larger neighbourhoods are not necessary because $s(a,i)$ will have small values for most participants in such neighbourhoods and they will consequently have very small influence on F_R value. The computed F_R values show that in both (β_t, β_d) configurations the most promising is the strategy $j = 3$, which had solid performances (small $t_r|_{j=3}$ values) in similar runtime situations. As far as strategies $j = 1$ and $j = 2$ are concerned, either a bad performance or a past usage in not similar runtime situations is responsible for small F_R values. On the one hand, strategy $j = 1$ has a bad $F_R^{(1)}$ because it has not been used in similar runtime ($s(a,i)|_{j=1}$ has very small values in the formed neighbourhood for the strategy $j=1$) and even its very good performances (very small $t_r|_{j=1}$) do not help. On the other hand, strategy $j=2$ also does not have remarkable $F_R^{(2)}$ value mostly because its very bad behaviour (very large $t_r|_{j=2}$) in a similar runtime.

The importance of β_t and β_d can be best assessed by the comparison of $F_R^{(1)}$ and $F_R^{(2)}$ for $(\beta_t,\beta_d)=(1,1)$ and $(\beta_t,\beta_d)=(1,2)$ configurations. In $(\beta_t,\beta_d)=(1,1)$, giving a priority neither to good performances nor to a usage in similar runtime situations, $j=1$ seams to be better than $j=2$ ($F_R^{(1)}|_{(\beta_t,\beta_d)=(1,1)}=15.8$ and $F_R^{(2)}|_{(\beta_t,\beta_d)=(1,1)}=9.7$). By increasing β_d, strategy $j=1$ starts to pay larger penalties of not being used in similar runtime situations. Therefore, in $(\beta_t,\beta_d)=(1,2)$, strategy $j=1$ is the least promising ($F_R^{(1)}|_{(\beta_t,\beta_d)=(1,2)}=4.5$ is almost two times smaller than $F_R^{(2)}|_{(\beta_t,\beta_d)=(1,2)}=8.3$).

Table 1. 18 runtime situations corresponding to three strategies for which $F_R^{(j)}$ is computed

j	i	ω_{CPU}	ω_{DB}	ω_M	t_r [s]	$d_E(a,i)$	$(\beta_t,\beta_d)=(1,1)$		$(\beta_t,\beta_d)=(1,2)$	
							$s(a,i)$	$F_R^{(j)}$	$s(a,i)$	$F_R^{(j)}$
1	1	0.83	0.21	0.75	13	0.973	10.81	15.8	1.17	4.5
	2	0.75	0.81	0.38	21	0.436	36.90		13.62	
	3	0.21	0.15	0.98	18	1.086	8.34		0.69	
	4	0.09	0.11	0.82	32	1.025	9.59		0.92	
	5	0.63	0.52	0.62	28	0.616	24.46		5.98	
2	6	0.78	0.38	0.54	14	0.717	19.40	9.7	3.76	8.3
	7	0.41	0.78	0.21	121	0.084	82.59		68.22	
	8	0.21	0.38	0.41	28	0.547	28.65		8.21	
	9	0.37	0.84	0.19	98	0.042	90.76		82.37	
	10	0.21	0.83	0.16	101	0.17	67.75		45.91	
	11	0.18	0.62	0.48	32	0.439	36.63		13.42	
	12	0.45	0.88	0.2	130	0.099	79.65		63.45	
3	13	0.41	0.78	0.21	32	0.083	82.59	46.2	68.22	40.1
	14	0.52	0.62	0.32	48	0.304	49.88		24.88	
	15	0.38	0.8	0.12	28	0.042	90.75		82.37	
	16	0.78	0.66	0.08	19	0.44	36.55		13.37	
	17	0.35	0.79	0.19	40	0.064	86.38		74.62	
	18	0.98	0.82	0.52	144	0.705	19.96		3.98	

3.3 Strategy Selection

A selection simulates the evolutionary process of a competition among strategies that are fighting for getting as many jobs as possible [16]. But, before a selection probability $P^{(i)}$ for a strategy i can be defined, a total fitness F_t, reflecting the demands of a strategy towards resources and its abilities to produce accurate results, is obtained as:

$$F_t = \alpha F_R + (1-\alpha) F_Q \qquad (5)$$

Parameter $\alpha \in [0,1]$ controls the influence of F_R and F_Q, where $\alpha = 1$ will lead to a pure resource based coordination. By using $F_t^{(i)}$ value, $P^{(i)}$, making the used selection to be nothing else than proportional or roulette wheel selection [16], is defined as:

$$P^{(i)} = F_t^{(i)} \left(\sum_{j=1}^{n} F_t^{(j)} \right)^{-1} \qquad (6)$$

Because ω_x parameters are from $[0,1]$, F_t value is bounded, and $P^{(i)}$ can be directly obtained by using F_t without any additional transformations, being applied in [1]. Although strategies with above F_t value will receive more attention, even the one with the worst F_t will have a chance to be selected and to improve its quality fitness.

4 Implementation

The manager agent is built out of components (Fig. 1d) in JIAC IV, being a serviceware framework for developing agent systems [11]. The *strategy selection* SS is a cornerstone component that takes care about which filtering strategies will be selected. While the evaluation functionality is integrated into *resource fitness evaluation* RFE component, *knowledge base updating* KBU takes care about the efficient storage and retrieval of the needed past experience. The *quality fitness adaptation* QFA and *situation estimation* SE facilitate an easy replacement of the algorithm that is used for estimating the current load of resources. Future plans are concerned with deploying advanced structures for performing knowledge updating in KBU, as well as with a usage of *situation prediction* SP component, which will most probably cooperate with SE to provide not only estimation but also the prediction of resource loads. A deeper analysis of both JIAC IV, as well as these shortly described components can be found in [3].

5 Experimental Results

The expected benefit of a presented fitness-less coordination scheme should be found both in its capability to be applied inside communities whose filtering agents cannot be easily described with separate resource fitness values and in its ability to eliminate long lasting jobs in the situation where novel strategies are regularly integrated. These aspects will be examined in a PIA environment [4], where PIA will be used because it currently supports almost 200 different web sources, grabs daily around 3 thousands semi-structured and unstructured articles, has more than 850 thousands pre-processed documents, and helps to 35 DAI Labor workers in their information retrieval activities.

5.1 Self Improving Versus Fitness-Less Coordination

To avoid a necessity to represent the runtime capabilities of strategies by the appropriate, specially defined, separate resource fitness values, as it has been done in [1], a flexible fitness-less coordination scheme is proposed in this paper. Although it is not difficult to set right fitness values to strategies for which it is well known how they depend on different available resources, it will be extraordinarily welcome to have a coordination approach that does not require sometimes problematic fitness value initialisation, and to assess its successfulness through a comparison with already proven self improving scheme [1], both in received user feedback and response time domains.

Starting from 15th of March 2005, the following 3 different coordination schemes were tested. The first two days PIA I was working with self improving coordination scheme that was based on completely randomly initialised fitness values. The next two days self improving coordination scheme was replaced in PIA II with in this paper presented fitness-less approach. Self improving coordination was again plugged in PIA III in the last two days of the experiment, but with the manually set initial fitness values that nearly correspond to the real capabilities of strategies. The obtained results are given in Table 2, where n_{fj} corresponds to the number of filtering jobs for which a feedback has been received, n_{lj} represents the number of long lasting jobs, having a duration of more than 1000s, $avg(d_{fj})$ is the average duration of jobs with feedback, and $avg(q_{fj})$ is the average received feedback value.

Table 2. Comparison of self improving coordination approach with in fitness-less scheme

	n_{fj}	n_{lj}	$avg(d_{fj})$ [s]	$avg(q_{fj})$ [%]
PIA I	42	2	83.7	53.8
PIA II	51	0	22.5	68.5
PIA III	49	0	19.2	73.2

The performed experiments have shown that self improving scheme is actually not managing to quickly repair the wrongly set fitness values, and consequently PIA I has both the lowest $avg(q_{fj})$ and the largest $avg(d_{fj})$. Completely opposite holds in the case where fitness values are not randomly set, i.e. PIA III is the absolute winner both in $avg(q_{fj})$ and $avg(d_{fj})$ domains. As far as fitness-less scheme is concerned, on the one side PIA II manages to significantly outperforms PIA I system and thus proves the assumption of being better choice when fitness values cannot be correctly initialised. On the other side, PIA II has produced for almost 5% smaller user satisfaction than PIA III together with more than 3s longer duration ($avg(d_{fj})|_{PIA\,II} = 22.5$ s and $avg(d_{fj})|_{PIA\,III} = 19.2$ s). The longer $avg(d_{fj})$ can be explained by very expensive on the flight computation of a resource fitness F_R that PIA II requires, whereas smaller user satisfaction shows that users are no ready to wait longer for getting results with a comparable usefulness. This experiment shows that fitness-less coordination scheme should be used instead of a self improving approach only in a case where many new strategies, for which only a pure random fitness initialisation is possible, are deployed.

5.2 Long Lasting Filtering Job Elimination

A trial to escape long lasting jobs, without limiting opportunities for the integration of novel strategies, was a main motivation for fundamentally changing strategy evaluation regarding to [1]. The following experiment is regularly integrating novel strategies and varying α in (5) to do comparisons in feedback and response time domains.

Starting from 29th of March till 11th of April 2005, each 2 days the inbuilt PIA coordination mechanism was changed by incrementing α value for 0.25, where on the beginning it was set $\alpha = 0$. To make tests as fair as possible, only working days are taken into account, being done because of the minor PIA usage during weekend days. The flexibility of the deployed coordination scheme to support novel strategies is checked by the automatic integration of one new strategy every 6 hours. The obtained results are given in Table 3, where the meaning of symbols is the same as in Table 2.

Table 3. Results of the internal usage of PIA that illustrate strengths and weaknesses of coordination algorithms, having different influence of resource and quality fitness (different α)

α	n_{fj}	n_{lj}	$avg(d_{fj})$ [s]	$avg(q_{fj})$ [%]
0	37	2	65.4	62.6
0.25	46	0	32.4	64.8
0.5	54	0	28.3	66.5
0.75	50	0	27.9	70.2
1	41	0	22.3	60.4

The results of this 10 day long experiments with different coordination mechanisms clearly show that the exclusion of a resource fitness component ($\alpha = 0$) potentially leads to the appearance of long lasting jobs, being the same conclusion as in [1]. In spite of frequent integrations of new strategies, taking care about resources ($\alpha > 0$) is managing to eliminate long lasting jobs. Because a user satisfaction is an imperative, setting $\alpha = 1$ seams as a bad choice by reason of having the lowest $avg(q_{fj})$, and an optimal solution is looked for $0 < \alpha < 1$. While $avg(d_{fj})$ is for $\alpha \in \{0.25, 0.5, 0.75\}$ comparable, the best $avg(q_{fj})$ is got for $\alpha = 0.75$. The increase of $avg(q_{fj})\big|_{\alpha=0.75}$ is almost 10%, when compared with $avg(q_{fj})\big|_{\alpha=1}$, whereas $avg(d_{fj})\big|_{\alpha=0.75}$ is for around 5s longer than $avg(d_{fj})\big|_{\alpha=1}$. Users are not ready to pay high price for the reduction of filtering time, and they are ready to wait little longer to get better recommendations.

6 Conclusion

The goal of this paper was to try to eliminate long lasting filtering jobs while integrating novel strategies and to pay as less as possible in a feedback domain. Although the first solutions for the evaluation of a resource fitness value are given, future work will optimise this activity by reason of avoiding a significant delay as a number of already processed jobs increases, which will reduce the scalability of this coordination scheme. The problem of not only estimating resources but also predicting their usability will be also taken into account. Even though, many things are still open, authors believe that this is the right way towards a comprehensive agent-based filtering framework.

Acknowledgement

Authors gratefully would like to thank to anonymous reviewers of the early version of this paper [3] for their insightful comments, which greatly helped to strengthen the article. Special thanks also go to other project team members mostly for realising GUI and extraction PIA sub-systems [4], and thus made feasible user evaluations.

References

1. Albayrak S., Milosevic D.: Self Improving Coordination in Multi Agent Filtering Framework. IEEE/WIC ACM Conference on IAT and WI, Beijing, China (2004) 239-245
2. Albayrak S., Milosevic D.: Multi-Domain Strategy Coordination Approach for Optimal Resource Usage in Agent Based Filtering Framework. WIAS, IOS Press (2005)(to appear)
3. Albayrak S., Milosevic D.: Flexible Strategy Coordination Approach for Supporting Resource Awareness in Multi Agent Filtering Framework. 4th Conference on Machine Learning and Cybernetics (ICMLC 2005), Guangzhou, China (2005) 5615-5623
4. Albayrak S., Wollny S., Varone N., Lommatzsch A., Milosevic D.: Agent Technology for Personalized Information Filtering: The PIA-System. 20th ACM Conference on Applied Computing, Santa Fe (2005) 54-59
5. Balabanovic M., Shoham Y., Fab: Content-Based Collaborative Recommendation. CACM, Vol. 40, No. 3 (1997) 66-72
6. Bäck T.: Selective Pressure in Evolutionary Algorithms: A Characterization of Selection Mechanisms. 1st IEEE Conference on Evolution Computation, New York (1994) 57-62
7. Claypool M., Gokhale A., Miranda T., Murnikov P., Netes D., Sartin N.: Combining Content-Based and Collaborative Filters in an Online Newspaper. ACM SIGIR Workshop on Recommender Systems, CA (1999)
8. Delgado J.: Agent Based Information Filtering and Recommender Systems. Ph.D. (2000)

9. Delgado J., Davidson R.: Knowledge Bases and User Profiling in Travel and Hospitality Recommender Systems. ENTER 2002, Innsbruck (2002) 1-16
10. Faloutsos C., Oard D.: A Survey of Information Retrieval and Filtering Methods. Technical Report (1995)
11. Fricke S., Bsufka K., Keiser J., Schmidt T., Sesseler R., Albayrak S.: Agent-Based Telematic Services and Telecom Applications. CACM, Vol. 44, No. 4 (2001) 43-48
12. Han J., Kamber M.: Data Mining: Concepts and Techniques. MK Publishers (2001)
13. Kuropka D., Serries T.: Personal Information Agent. Jahrestagung, (2001) 940-946
14. Lieberman H.: Letizia: An Agent That Assists Web Browsing. AI Conf., Montreal (1995)
15. Lieberman H, Neil V. D., Vivacqua A.: Let's Browse: A Collaborative Browsing Agent. Knowledge-Based Systems, Vol. 12, No. 8 (1999) 427–431
16. Michalewicz Z., Fogel D.: How to Solve It: Modern Heuristics. Springer-Verlag (2000)
17. Moukas A.: Amalthaea: Information Discovery and Filtering using a Multi agent Evolving Ecosystem. Application of Intelligent Agents & Multi-Agent Technology (1998)
18. Resnick P., Iacovou N., Suchak M., Ber gstrom P., Riedl J.: GroupLens: An open architecture for collaborative filtering of net news. ACM on Cooperative Work (1994) 175-186
19. Sarwar B., Karypis G., Konstan J., Riedl J.: Analysis of Recommendation Algorithms for E-Commerce", 2nd ACM Conference on Electronic Commerce, USA (2000) 158-167
20. Schafer B., Konstan J., Riedl J.: E-Commerce Recommendation Applications. Journal of Data Mining and Knowledge Discovery (2001) 115-153
21. Sheth B. D.: A Learning Approach to Personalized Information Filtering. M.Sc. (1994)
22. Thorsten J., Dayne F., Mitchell T.: WebWatcher: A Tour Guide for the World Wide Web. 15th Conf. on Artificial Intelligence (IJCAI), Nagoya, Japan (1997) 770-777
23. Winiwarter W.: PEA - A Personal Email Assistant with Evolutionary Adaptation. International Journal of Information Technology, Vol. 5, No. 1, 1999.
24. Young W. S., Zhang B. T.: A Reinforcement Learning Agent for Personalized Information Filtering. 5th Conf. on Intelligent User Interfaces, New Orleans, USA (2000) 248-251
25. Zhang B. T., Young W. S.: Personalized Web-Document Filtering Using Reinforcement Learning. Applied Artificial Intelligence, Vol. 15, No. 7 (2001) 665-685

Modeling and Design of Agent Grid Based Open Decision Support System

Jiayu Chi[1], Ling Sun[2], Xueguang Chen[3], and Jinlong Zhang[4]

[1] School of Business, Sun YAT-SAN University, 510275, P.R. China
[2] Lingnan College, Sun YAT-SAN University, 510275, P.R. China
[3] Institute of Systems Engineering, Huazhong University of Science and Technology, 430074, P.R. China
[4] Management College, Huazhong University of Science and Technology, 430074, P.R. China
chijiayu@tom.com

Abstract. Decision Support Systems (DSS) are computer-based information systems that help decision-makers solve half-structured or non-structured problems by using data and models. They are facing some serious problems in the heterogeneous, autonomic, dynamic and distributed decision support environment. As an advanced technology representing "the third Internet revolution", Grid brings about a lot of innovative ideas and technologies for the development of DSS. As an application of Grid in the field of DSS, this paper puts forward an improved model of Agent Grid Based DSS. A set of design methods of the system is discussed. With the National Economic Mobilization DSS as a practical case, we illustrate how the model works in practice.

1 Introduction

During the development history of DSS, computer technology, network technology, database technology, artificial intelligence and decision theory have made great impact on the theory of DSS. Nowadays, DSS can provide great support for the decision-makers, for it's more powerful in function, widely used on the Web, friendly in man-machine interface, and intelligent in operation. But there are still some serious problems that have limited the development of DSS. First, the existing DSS model and theory cannot direct the construction of DSS on the Internet environment effectively. They need further expansion to adapt to the great changes in content, form and methods of decision support. Second, there is no effective mechanism to publish, share and reuse decision support resources. Third, being deficient in openness, it is difficult to integrate new functions and link the other DSS, and it is necessary to establish protocols and standards for DSS. Finally, due to the modularization lever of DSS being very low, it is difficult to maintain DSS, and the upgrading cost of DSS is high.

Much research has been done to find a solution to these problems. Bhargava et al [1] put forward a new framework of electronic market for decision technologies named "Decision Net". The market provides decision technologies as user-based services rather than as products to the consumers. It is used to organize the consumers, the providers, as well as decision technologies. M.Goul et al [2] proposed a set of protocols for DSS deployment on the Internet called "Open-DSS protocol suite". Consumers and providers are connected via the open DSS protocols. Dong [3] proposed a framework for the architecture of a Web-based DSS Generator utilizing different software agents to enhance the functionalities of the existing DSS. Kwon [4] proposed an Open DSS based on Web in connection with Web technology and ontology metadata web services, in order to enhance the development and integration of the decision services. Sridhar [5] argued about the issues of DSS in the Intranet.

All of these studies are valuable to solve the problems stated above, but there are still many issues which need to be studied for the DSS on the Internet. Especially, as the scale of the Internet keeps growing, the efficient management and utilization of the resources become more challenging.

The development of DSS shows that every step forward of the network technology brings great influence to the concept, framework and function of DSS. Now, as an advanced technology representing "the third Internet revolution", Grid brings about many innovative ideas and technologies for the development of DSS. Grid appears as an effective technology coupling geographically distributed resources for solving large-scale problems in wide area network, which also support open standard and dynamic services. In addition, it provides highly intelligent communication between computers and humans. These characteristics are very suitable for the construction needs of the DSS platform. Grid will improve DSS greatly, and bring profound revolution to DSS theory and its application.

This article shows some research evolutions based on the work in reference [7], which put forward a framework of Grid Based Open DSS (GBODSS) and summarizes some basic characteristics of GBODSS. But the framework is not sufficient for a further study of GBODSS. In order to give a clearer picture of GBODSS and provide analysis and design methods and tools for GBODSS, this article introduces agent technologies into the research of GBODSS, and puts forward an improved model of Agent Grid Based Open DSS (AGBODSS).

2 MAS and Agent Grid

2.1 MAS and GBODSS

As a new research domain of DSS, GBODSS lacks suitable and effective theories, models and methods for its analysis, design, and development. It is necessary to introduce advanced thoughts and technologies from other relative subjects and domains into the GBODSS research. Multi-agent systems (MAS) technology seems to be a suitable candidate for the following reasons [8]:

1) The autonomy of individual agents enables each agent to encapsulate different problem-solving methods and domain models. Furthermore, the maintenance of this autonomy is often required by individual decision-makers in GBODSS.
2) The combination of responsive and proactive behavior enables the agent, acting as a node in a GBODSS, to respond appropriately to requests for information or to solve a problem and to manage on-going strategies in solving current problems

3) The ability to cooperate with other, similarly autonomous, agents and coordinate activity is critical in GBODSS. This is a core ability for agents designed to operate in the context of a multi-agent system.

Considering this correlation between the characteristics of GBODSS and MAS technologies, this paper proposes an approach to the modelling and construction of GBODSS based on an organization of agents. The Agent Grid system introduced below provides a solid supporting platform for the implementation of the modelling and design of GBODSS.

2.2 Agent Grid

The Agent Grid [9] is a proposed construct that is intended to support the rapid and dynamic configuration and creation of new functionality from existing software components and systems. It was first brought forward by the Defense Advanced Research Projects Agency (DARPA) in the Control of Agent Based Systems (CoABS) Program, in which the main aim was to enhance the interoperating, scalability and generalization of military information systems.

Manola views the Agent Grid from three different perspectives as below [9]:

1) Agent Grid should be considered as a collection of agent-related mechanisms and protocol.
2) Agent Grid should be considered as a framework for connecting agents and agent systems.
3) Agent Grid should be considered as model entities that might be used to model an organization chart, team or other ensemble.

These three views represent different aspects of the Agent Grid, and they can be valid simultaneously.

Agent Grid in CoABS program provides various Grid services to integrate all kinds of distributed and heterogeneous software components on the Internet such as objects, agents, legacy systems, and so on. These grid services include Registration Service, Logging Service, etc. Many other powerful grid services are under construction. All these grid services are elaborated in the references [10].

3 A Model of Agent Grid Based Open DSS (AGBODSS)

In an abstract sense, a Grid is fundamentally a mechanism/infrastructure that helps integrate resources. It can be divided into five layers by the resources integrated. Each layer provides management capabilities for the resources existing on it. These layers work together and coordinate with each other for the final application.

1) Computing layer, corresponding to the computing Grid.
2) Data and information layer, corresponding to the data and information Grid.
3) Service layer, including objects, services and legacy system.
4) Agent layer, namely the Agent Grid.
5) User layer.

In order to elaborate on the GBODSS, we have improved the model of the GBODSS in reference [7] based on the above Grid hierarchy framework. We have established an

Agent Grid based open DSS model (AGBODSS), as shown in Figure 1. The improved model can elaborate on the relationship between the components and layers of the GBODSS.

In the new model, a GBODSS can be looked as a problem-solving organization that is composed of decision-makers and their agents, which can make good use of the decision service and resources provided in diverse grid layers.

With practical problems in mind, the designer of the DSS can construct different DSS conveniently through a quick integration of the agents in the Agent Grid layer. The designer of the DSS needs firstly to design the organizational structure of the AGBODSS, and then choose suitable agents in the Agent Grid layer to play the roles in the AGBODSS.

The Agent Grid layer is the core of the AGBODSS model. On the one hand, it is the layer that interoperates directly with users. It includes agents and the agent systems that perform the main system functions and sub-functions. Moreover, it needs reliable interfaces for the users, to enable the users to utilize the resources in the Grid to solve their problems and so make the system integration easier. On the other hand, Agent Grid layer needs to connect the three Grid layers beneath it and manage the corresponding layers and resources. It facilitates the coordination between the different layers to accomplish concrete tasks.

The Agent Grid layer is composed of several registered agent groups and grid services, and each agent group is composed of some agents. The Agent Grid provides many services to support the management, interoperation and integration of the agents in this layer. Presently, the Agent Grid services include register service, brokerage service, logging service, security service and visualization service, etc. There will be many more powerful services in the Agent Grid in the future.

There are many kinds of agent in the Agent Grid, including entity agent, task agent, information agent, and resource management agent. Entity agent represents the entity in the real world (e.g. company or person) to utilize decision service on the Service Grid, and possesses limited decision-making capabilities. Task agent is a special kind of entity agent, which takes charge of carrying out the entire task. It decomposes the task into sub-tasks, assigns these sub-tasks to entity agents that take part in the decision, and integrates the decision results of these sub-tasks. Information agent can help find the required information in the Data and Information Grid by utilizing the query services provided by this Grid layer. Similarly, the resource management agent is used to acquire and coordinate the needed resource in the Computing Grid layers. Agents in the Agent Grid are divided into several agent groups according to their type and function, which facilitates the management and utilization of these agents.

The Service Grid layer is also very important in the architecture of AGBODSS. Decision resources, such as models and methods, can be encapsulated into decision services, which can be managed by the electronic market set up on the layer. The market can help to match the demand and supply of the decision resources by its competition mechanism and the services it provides, such as register service, query service, trade service, authentication service, etc. Agents in the Agent Grid layer can register and log in to the market to find and use the decision services in it.

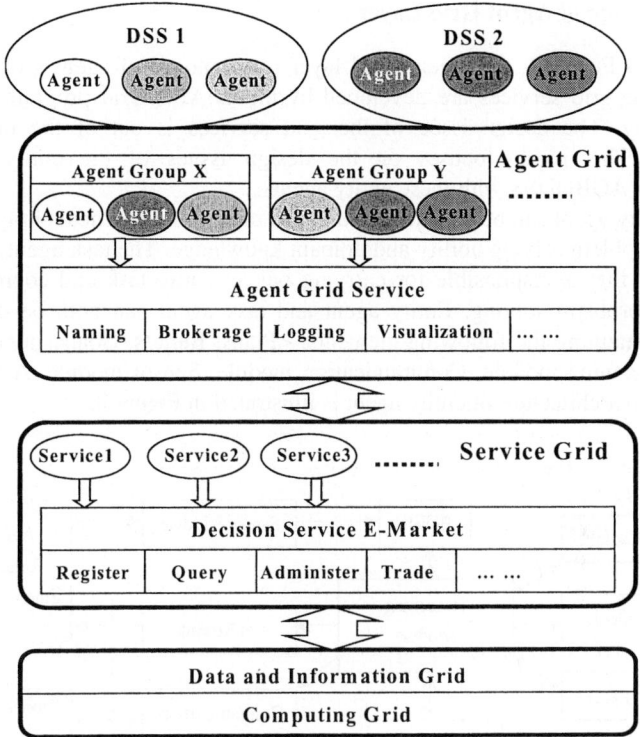

Fig. 1. Open DSS Model Based on the Agent Grid

The two bottom layers of the Grid stack are the basis of the AGBODSS, and can be considered to be the Grid infrastructure that can provide resource on the Grid. Heterogeneous resources in these layers can be fully utilized in a transparent way.

The AGBODSS model has many great advantages, such as outstanding intelligence, superior scalability, excellent adaptability to the changing circumstances and tasks, and excellent transparency of the heterogeneity of the low-level resources. These advantages ensure this AGBODSS model is suitable for the design and development of GBODSS.

4 The Design of AGBODSS

According to the AGBODSS model, the key issue to design an AGBODSS is the design of the Agent Grid layer, the design of the organizational structure of AGBODSS, and building GBODSS with the Agent Grid layer. We are not going to discuss the design issue of the three bottom layers of the Grid stack (the Computing Grid layer, the Data and Information Grid layer, the Service Grid layer).

4.1 The Design of Agent Grid Layer

As shown in Figure 1, the Agent Grid layer is composed of agent groups and grid services. The grid services are developed by the CoABS Grid program and can be used directly. The design issue of the grid services is out of the range of our discussion. This paper focuses on the design issues of the entity agent and constructing AGBODSS with these entity agents.

Each entity agent can be considered to be the model of a practical entity, which has a specific problem solving ability and domain knowledge. The task agent is a specific entity agent that is responsible for carrying out an entire task and coordinating the process of problem solving. Entity agent and task agent can both be defined as a structure containing the following elements: <Plans, Beliefs, Goals, Intentions, Data system, Reasoning module, Communication module, Sensor module, Act module >. The common architecture of entity agent is illustrated in Figure 2.

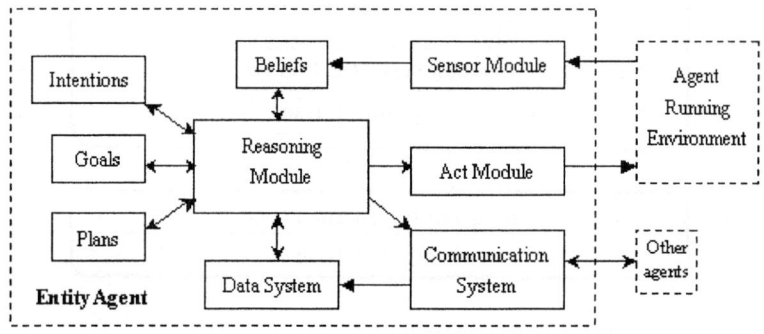

Fig. 2. Entity Agent Architecture

- **Reasoning module** is the central component of the entity agent architecture. It is responsible for the selection of the execution of plans and primitive intentions.
- **Plan** is a set of primitive problem-solving activities that can be executed by agents.
- **Intentions** are the instantiated procedures that are in the process of being executed.
- **Beliefs** are the agent's views of the state of the world.
- **Goals** are the states of affairs that the agent wishes to achieve.
- **Communication system** is responsible for communicating with other agents by the agent communication language (ACL).
- **Data system** is used to record the information that is produced during the cooperative problem solving process.
- **Act module** and **Sensor module** are used to interact with the environment.

The agents with similar task types should be aggregated into agent groups, which will facilitate the management and utilization of these agents. These agent groups can represent the practical teams or organizations in the real world and they can accomplish specific tasks by means of interoperation and negotiation.

4.2 The Design of the Organizational Structure of AGBODSS

Before constructing an AGBODSS, it is necessary to firstly design its organizational structure. Here, a role-based method that belongs to the organizational theory of MAS is used to design the organizational structure of AGBODSS.

Definition 1. The BNF definition of the organizational structure of AGBODSS is as follows:

    AGBODSS_Str   ::= < GOAL, ROLE, R_RELATION >
    GOAL   ::= { goal | goal $\in$ {$goal_1$, $goal_2$, …}}
    ROLE   ::= { role | role $\in$ { $role_1$, $role_2$, …}}
    R_RELATION   ::= { r_relation | r_relation $\in$ { $r\_relation_1$, $r\_relation_2$, …}}
      /*See note 1*/
    role   ::= < R_Goal, Plan_ABILITY, ACT_ABILITY, R_NORM>
    R_Goal   ::= { r_goal | r_goal $\in$ { r_goal_1, r_goal_2, …}}
    Plan_ABILITY   ::= { plan_ability | plan_ability $\in$ { $plan\_ability_1$, $plan\_ability_2$, …}}
    ACT_ABILITY   ::= { act | act $\in$ { act_1, act_2, …}}
    R_NORM   ::= < r_right, r_duty, r_interact >
    plan_ability::= < r_goal, r_plan >
    r_plan   ::= (act)*
      /* See note 2*/
    r_relation   ::= < REL_TYPE, $role_i$, [$role_i\_aspect_1$, [$role_i\_aspect_2$, [$role_i\_aspect_3$]]], $role_j$, [$role_j\_aspect_1$, [$role_j\_aspect_2$, [$role_j\_aspect_3$]]] >
    REL_TYPE   ::= {dep_act, contain, control, peer, friend, antag, contract, communicate, … }
      /* See note 3*/

Note 1: *GOAL* represents the decision problems required to be solved by AGBODSS. *ROLE is* the abstract of the function entities in AGBODSS

Note 2: *r_goal* represents the decision tasks the *role* is burdened with. *ACT_ABILITY* is a set of the actions that the *role* can take. *plan_ability* represents the the role can make (*r_plan*) for a *r_goal*. *r_plan* is a sequence of the role's action. *R_NORM* is a set of the role's action norm, which includes a set of the role's rights (r_right), a set of the role's duties (r_duty), a set of the role's interacting rules (r_interact).

Note 3: *r_relation* is a set of the relationship between the different roles. *REL_TYPE* is a set of the types of the *r_relation*, which includes action dependant relationship *(dep_act)*, contain relationship *(contain)*, control relationship *(control)*, peer relationship *(peer)*, friend relationship *(friend)*, antagonistic relationship *(antag)*, contract relationship *(contract)*, communication relationship *(communicate)*, etc.

Definition 2. The definition of *AGBODSS* can be proposed based on the definition of *AGBODSS_Str* as follows:

    AGBODSS   ::= < *AGBODSS_Str, AGENT, ASSIGN* >
    AGENT   ::= { *agent* | *agent* $\in$ { $agent_1$, $agent_2$, …}}
    ASSIGN   ::= { *assign* | *assign* $\in$ { $assign_1$, $assign_2$, …}}
    assign   ::= (*agent, role*)

AGBODSS has three basic elements: *AGBODSS_Str, AGENT and ASSIGN. AGENT* is the set of agents in the AGBODSS. *ASSIGN* is a set of role's assignments (*assign*) that links agents to roles.

Based on the definition of AGBODSS_Str, the following steps should be taken to design the organizational structure of AGBODSS:

1) Analyze the problem and task faced by the decision-makers, set up goals of the AGBODSS, and define decision support requirements.
2) Define the roles needed for these goals, imposing corresponding the responsibilities and rights on them and the relationship between them. The defined roles and their relationships compose the static structure of AGBODSS. Generally, there will be a leading role that is responsible for the whole task.
3) Define the dynamic action among the roles in the GBODSS, e.g. defining the agreement of the interaction and coordination among them, to get the dynamic structure of the AGBODSS.
4) Verify, optimize and revise the design of the organizational structure of AGBODSS.

4.3 Building AGBODSS with the Agent Grid Layer

AGBODSS is very similar to the concept of virtual organization. An AGBODSS can be considered as a new agent organization that is composed of agents from several different agent groups in the Agent Grid layer to accomplish specific tasks.

After the Agent Grid layer and the organizational structure of AGBODSS are designed, an AGBODSS can be conveniently constructed. The first work is to assign the roles in the organizational structure of AGBODSS to the entity agents in the Agent Grid layer. It is important that the leading role be assigned to a task agent. This step involves an iterative search of eligible agents that satisfy the requirements of the roles in previous steps. There are many methods for the matching of agents and their roles in the AGBODSS structure; these will be discussed in other papers.

With the above steps, a primitive AGBODSS has been built. But it still needs to be checked in a practical running situation. There will often be some iterative processes to go back to the previous steps in section 4.1 and section 4.2 which will require revision and adjustment.

5 A Case Study of AGBODSS

The modeling approach of the AGBODSS is a generic one with wide application. Taking the National Economy Mobilization DSS (NEM-DSS) as a practical case, we now elaborate on how to put AGBODSS into practice.

The National Economy Mobilization covers a range of government activity to schedule economic and social resources for emergent affairs. This paper uses the automobile mobilization as the example to analyze the application of the AGBODSS model. The aim of the NEM-DSS is to implement unified and effective management of automobile mobilization activities, including generating plans, simulating plans and executing plans. It can help managers increase the effectiveness of their decision-making.

The automobile mobilization involves several kinds of entity units, including component firms, assembly firms, transportation companies, warehouses and a mobilization command center. Each entity unit is an autonomic one that needs interoperation and negotiation to form a final plan that should be coordinated in its execution.

Based on the above analysis and design steps, we should first create an agent model for each entity involved in the automobile mobilization. The design for each entity agent includes its plans, competence, product model, inner spiritual states (e.g. beliefs, goals, intentions), communication module and reasoning module, etc. Components firm agent, assembly firm agent, transportation company agent, warehouse agent and mobilization command center agent are created at this stage. The agents can then be divided into several groups according to their task type. For example, several component firm agents can be put into a unified agent group and the same is true for other types of agents. These agent groups make up the Agent Grid layer.

The organizational structure of NEM-DSS should then be designed.

First, the roles in the mobilization need to be identified according to the requirement of the mobilization goal, including the roles of manufacturing, transportation, storage and command. And then the respective goals, responsibilities and rights of these roles and the relationships among them (such as controlling relationship, depending relationship, equal relationship, etc) should be designed. Undoubtedly, the commanding role is the leading role of the mobilization activities.

Second, the dynamic characteristics of the DSS need to be defined; these include the interaction activities between the roles, the message type, and the rules of coordination.

Finally, the automobile mobilization DSS can be constructed with the entity agents on the Agent Grid layer. Suitable entity agents should be assigned to the roles in the DSS. The mobilization command center agent acts in the commanding role, and it is the task agent that is to take charge of the mobilization activities. Other suitable agents play other roles according to their competence, reliability, and costs.

By now, a primitive AGBODSS has been built, but it may not be the final one, and needs to be revised and adjusted in practical use.

The AGBODSS has superior openness and excellent scalability. The entity agents can join and leave the AGBODSS dynamically according to the changing circumstances and tasks. The entity agents can sketch out mobilization plans through communication and negotiation, and they can coordinate to solve the problems in the execution of the plans. The AGBODSS can efficiently utilize all kinds of decision-making support services and resources on the Grid system.

Notably, the AGBODSS is of great value on the large-scale and distributed simulation of the mobilization plans, thus saving a lot of money and time that would otherwise be consumed in a practical mobilization exercise.

6 Summary and Prospect

This paper proposes an Agent Grid Based Open DSS model. The improved model can characterize the openness, dynamics and complexity of DSS in Grid circumstance. It effectively hides the heterogeneity of the resources with good intelligence, scalability and adaptability. With the National Economic Mobilization DSS as a practical case, the paper also illustrates how the model works in practice.

It also raises many problems about the AGBODSS, including performance assessment, the matching of the resource requests with the resources provided, the decision resource allocation and the application of AGBODSS in different fields; these are all the items for future research.

Acknowledgements

This work is supported by the National Nature Science Fund of China with the grant no. 60274065 and 70271031.

References

1. Bhargava H, Krishnan R, Mueller R. "Decision Support on Demand: On Emerging Electronic Markets for Decision Technologies", Decision Support System, Vol. 19, No. 3, pp. 193-214, 1997
2. Goul M, Philippakis A, Kiang M Y etc. "Requirements for the design of a protocol suite to automate DDS deployment on the World Wide Web: A client/server approach", Decision Support System, Vol. 19, No. 3, pp. 151-170, 1997.
3. DONG C J, LOO G S. "Flexible Web-Based Decision Support System Generator (FWDSSG) Utilising Software Agents", DEXA Workshop 2001, pp. 892-897, 2001
4. Kwon O B. "Meta Web Service: Building Web-based Open Decision Support System Based on Web Services", Expert Systems With Applications, Vol. 24, NO. 4, pp. 375-389, 2003
5. Sridhar S. "Decision Support Using the Intranet", Decision Support Systems, Vol. 23, No. 1, pp. 19-28, 1998
6. Foster I, Kesselman C, The Grid: Blueprint for a New Computing Infrastructure, 2nd ed., Morgan Kaufmann, San Fransisco, CA, 2003
7. Jiayu Chi, Xueguang Chen, Sun Ling. "A Study on the Framework of Grid Based Decision Support System", Proceedings of 2003 International Conference on Management Science & Engineering, Georgia, USA, pp. 45-49, 2003.
8. Chunhua Ju, Yun Ling, Timoth J. N., "Agent-Based and Software Composite DDSS", Proceedings of 36th International Conference on the Technology of Object-Oriented Languages and Systems, Xi'an, China, pp. 50-57, October, 2000
9. Manola F, Thompson C. "Characterizing the Agent Grid", http://www.objs.com/agility/tech-reports, 2001
10. Kettler B. "The CoABS Grid: Technical Vision", http://coabs.globalinfotek.com/public/downloads/Grid/documents/ Grid Vision Doc Draft 2-3 2001-09-30.doc, Sep. 2001.

Negotiating Agent: Concept, Architecture and Communication Model

Mukun Cao[1], Yuqiang Feng[1], Yan Li[1], and Chunyan Wang[2]

[1] Institute of Management Information System, Harbin Institute of Technology,
Heilongjiang 150001, China
{cameron, fengyq}@hit.edu.cn
[2] Beijing Institute of Information Control, Beijing 100037, China
wangchunyan@aerostrong.com.cn

Abstract. Traditional research in automated negotiation focuses on negotiation protocol and strategy. This paper studies automated negotiation from a new point, proposes a novel concept, namely negotiating agent, argues its significance in construction of automated negotiation system; designs its architecture, which can support both goal-directed reasoning and reactive response. In order to construct an interaction mechanism among negotiating agents, a communication model is proposed, in which the negotiation language used by agents is defined. Design of the communication model and the language has been attempted in such a way so as to provide general support for a wide variety of commercial negotiation circumstances, and therefore to be particularly suitable for electronic commerce. Finally, the design and expression of the negotiation ontology are discussed.

1 Introduction

Research in automated negotiation to date has been focused on the development of negotiation protocols and strategies [1]. For example, Jennings considered that automated negotiation research can be considered to deal with three broad topics, they are *negotiation protocols, negotiation objects* and *agents decision making models* [2]. Although there are many research achievements about protocols and strategies in the field of automated negotiation nowadays, realization and real application of automated negotiation system still has a long way to go. The reason is not just limited to the lack of research in negotiation protocol and strategies, but from the lack of research into negotiating agents. We consider that the research of negotiation protocols and strategies cannot answer the following three problems that must be solved properly when a practical automated negotiation system will be realized.

- Obviously, a run of negotiation protocol and strategy algorithm is heavily dependent on the construction of an agent. Especially, negotiation strategy can be regarded as a function module in agent's architecture. Then, how do the agents comply with certain protocols and execute certain strategies? Agent is a rational entity with Belief, Desire and Intention. In other words, how do the protocol and strategy take part in the BDI reasoning?

- Automated negotiation system is in essence a multi-agent system, whose run is heavily dependent on the communication between agents. Then, how does an automated negotiation system provide support for agents to communicate with each other? Everybody knows that negotiation is definitely a linguistic form. Then, what kind of language do the agents use when they are in a process of negotiation?
- Ultimate aim of researching automated negotiation is to realize a real and practicable automate negotiation system. Then, how to develop an automated negotiation system with existing software agent technology? This is the most fundamental problem when a practical automated negotiation system will be realized.

As a result, we consider that research of negotiation protocol and strategy cannot satisfy the whole requirements for realizing an automated negotiation system. Moreover, we draw the conclusion that analysis and design of negotiating agent should be regarded as a basic research element in the field. We call this kind of agent *Negotiating Agent*.

Negotiating agent is negotiation's executor, whose responsibility is to implement certain negotiation strategies complying with certain negotiation protocols. Negotiating agent has common features with the traditional agents. However, it has some special attributes; for example, it mainly uses *Speech Act* to interact with other agents and environment, simply because negotiation is a kind of linguistic behavior. Therefore, negotiating agent's concept shouldn't be replaced or covered up by traditional agent's concepts, but existing theory and technology of agent can be applied for research of negotiating agent.

A negotiating agent is analogous to a man in real negotiation. Negotiation cannot exist without men's participation. In the same way, automated negotiation cannot be divorced from the research of negotiating agent. Man in negotiation must know the negotiation's agenda (similar to negotiation protocol) and constitute strategy to be used in negotiation. Besides, he must study the opponent's character, preference and thought habit (similar to agent's mental states). Therefore, it can be seen from the real-world example that research of negotiating agent is necessary for automated negotiation.

Negotiating agent plays an important role in realization of automated negotiation system. Single agent is a basic element of multi-agent system. Negotiating agent provides the foundation for constructing multi-agent automated negotiation system; and it is a bridge between theoretical research and realization. Thus, we consider that the research of automated negotiation should be classified into three broad topics; they are *Negotiation Protocol*, *Negotiation Strategy* and *Negotiating Agent*.

The main aim of the work is to find a way to construct negotiating agent in automated negotiation. The research of negotiating agent includes negotiating agent's theoretical model, architecture and the method of communication between two or more negotiating agents. Recent theoretical work about agent has clarified the role of goals, intentions, and commitment in constraining the reasoning that an agent performs [3] [4], and has classified agent architecture into reactive system, real-time reasoning system and hybrid system. The hybrid agent has features in common with both reactive agent and real-time reasoning agent. For example, the PRS system [5] supports both the goal directed reasoning and the ability to react rapidly to the unanticipated changes in the environment. It has some features in common with the architecture described in this paper. However, these theories are quite general. Negotiating agent is a special kind of agent; its architecture must present its specific features. We propose negotiating agent architecture to satisfy the requirement.

Automated negotiation particularly depends on the interaction or communication between agents in open environments such as the Internet or the Semantic Web [6]. This paper proposes a negotiating agent communication model to solve the following problems:

- What kinds of language do the negotiating agents use when they are in a commercial negotiation process?
- How to express the negotiation language correctly and formally?

No one can ignore the fact that agents communicating in a common language will still be unable to understand each other if they use different vocabularies for representing shared domain concepts; that is *ontology*. So the sequential to be solved is:

- How to express the negotiation ontology?

The remainder of this paper is organized as follows. Section 2 describes the negotiating agent architecture. Section 3 describes the frame of the communication model for automated negotiation. Then, Section 4 discusses the negotiation language used by the agents during the negotiation process. Section 5 presents the design and expression of negotiation ontology which is an important component in the negotiation language. Finally, Section 6 draws conclusions and presents future work.

2 Negotiating Agent Architecture

Negotiating Agent Architecture (NAA) is designed for describing internal structure of negotiating agent. NAA is a kind of hybrid agent architecture (Figure 1). That means NAA has features coming from both BDI deliberative agent, which is based on goal directed reasoning, and reactive agent, which is controlled by reactive behavior. There has been some work in the design of agent architecture that attempts to integrate goal directed reasoning and reactive behavior. For example, the PRS interacts with the environment through four mechanisms: *sensors* and *monitor* (which are in charge of perception from the environment), *effectors* and *command generator* (which are used for acting on the environment) [9]. However, it is a common architecture for solving general problems in the field of reasoning systems and seems to be too complex for the applications of negotiation on-line. Since the negotiation is a kind of linguistic form, the NAA, different to traditional agent architecture, just needs a communication mechanism and a language generator for interaction with other agents. They are NAA's *communicator* and *speech-act planner*. In addition, NAA has a *reactive filter* for the purpose of increasing the system's capacity for reactivity.

Communicator is in charge of the agent's interaction with the environment, including other agents. It has the ability to process Agent Communication Language (ACL). It receives KQML messages about negotiation from the environment, and then parses them to get useful information for the agent to process. Finally, it sends KQML messages back to the environment.

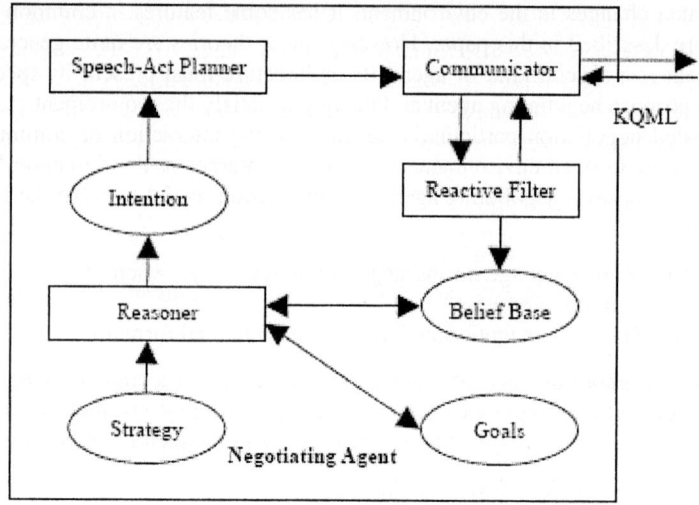

Fig. 1. Negotiating Agent Architecture (NAA)

Reactive Filter is a reactive mechanism, whose purpose is to provide an agent with fast, reactive capabilities for coping with events that are unnecessary or difficult for the reasoning mechanism to process. A typical event, for example, would be the wrong KQML message received by the *communicator*, which is always difficult to process by the *reasoner*. The *reactive filter* provides the agent with a series of *situation-reaction rules* for processing wrong messages, and for preventing other unpredictable situations. When a given rule is activated, an appropriate action is sent to the agent's communicator, which will send a responsive KQML message very quickly and directly to the environment. So, this mechanism guarantees a certain degree of reactivity.

Belief Base is a container for the current beliefs of the agent. Typically, beliefs include facts about static properties of the negotiating application domain, and beliefs acquired when the agent executes its reasoning. These will typically be conclusions about the current negotiation, and may change over time. The knowledge contained in the belief base is represented in first-order predicate calculus.

Goals are expressed as conditions over some interval of time, and are described by applying various temporal operators to state descriptions. This allows representation of a wide variety of goals, including goals for achieving maximum price, goals for shorter bargaining time and so on. A given speech-action or sequence of speech-actions, is said to be appropriate for achieving a given goal, if its theoretical execution results satisfy the goal description.

Strategy is a kind of knowledge about how to accomplish given goals or react to certain bids from other agents, and is presented by declarative procedure specifications. Each strategy consists of a *body*, which describes the algorism of the strategy, and a *condition* that specifies under what situations the strategy is applicable. Together, the condition and body express a declarative fact about the results and utility of performing certain negotiation strategies under certain conditions.

Intention structure is a data structure organizing all those strategies that the agent has chosen for execution, either immediately or at some later time. These adopted strategies are called intentions. The set of intentions comprising the intention structure form a partial ordering. An intention earlier in the ordering must be either realized or dropped (and thus disappear from the intention structure) before intentions appearing later in the ordering can be executed.

Reasoner runs the entire system. From a conceptual standpoint, it operates in a relatively simple way. At any particular time, when certain goals are active in the system and certain beliefs are held in the belief base, then a subset of strategies in the system will be invoked. One or more of these applicable strategies will then be chosen for execution and thus will be placed on the intention structure.

Speech-Act Planner is a language generator in NAA. No one can ignore the fact that the agent must select what it should say based on the relevance of the speech-act's expected outcome or rational effect of its goals. However, it cannot assume that the rational effect will necessarily result from sending random messages. The question then becomes which message or set of messages should be sent to another agent to assist or cause intention to be satisfied? If the agent is behaving in some reasonable sense, it will not send out a message whose effect will not satisfy the intention and hence achieve the goal. *Speech-Act Planner* is just such a mechanism, which can select appropriate *performatives* and form KQML messages according to the prospective rational effect of a certain intention. In other words, with the aid of the *speech-act planner*, the communicator has something to say.

3 Negotiating Agent Communication Model

Negotiating Agent Communication Model (NACM) is designed for describing two aspects of automated negotiation. One is the agents who participate in the automated negotiation. They are *Buyer Agents*, *Seller Agents* and *Facilitator* in the model. Another is communication language used by the agents. In order to describe what the agents should say in different circumstances, we define 6 meta-languages. They are *register*, *advertise*, *query*, *subscription*, *forward* and *negotiation*. However, NACM shouldn't be regarded as an agent interaction protocol, for there are many mature protocols which can be used nowadays. The main aim is to focus on an explicit definition of the language which the agents can use in any E-business oriented negotiation protocol.

At the moment, there are two main technological choices for building the agent communication model. One is Knowledge Query and Manipulation Language (KQML) [7], another is the Foundation for Intelligent Physical Agents (FIPA) specification [8]. KQML still suffers from poorly defined semantics. As a result, each of the many KQML implementations seems unique. This makes it difficult to communicate with other agents from heterogeneous systems. The FIPA specification, by contrast, attempts to formalize the semantics and provides a security model. However, in view of its recency, it has not been widely tested or adopted. As a result, it's not easy for the FIPA agent to find other agents with which to communicate. So we chose KQML for the communication model first, simply because of its current lead in market share.

KQML 97 [10] is a protocol for carrying and formatting messages based on speech acts theory. Unlike FIPA having comprehensive Interaction Protocols, ad hoc FIPA contract net and iterated contract net can be used directly in the negotiation system. There isn't any communication protocol defined in KSE's work, but KQML integrates a concept of *facilitator* [10], which refers to a class of agents who traffic in meta-knowledge about other agents, and provide communication services such as message forwarding and broadcasting, resource discovery, matchmaking and so on. Therefore, it is the main tool for users to construct their own interaction model. Figure 2 is the communication model based on KQML.

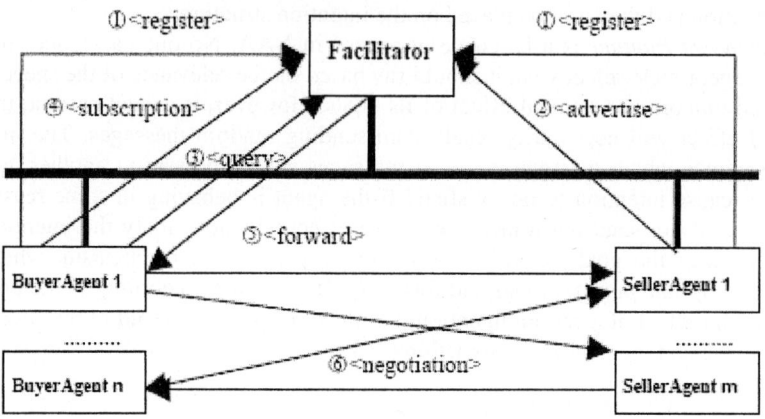

Fig. 2. Communication model in multi-agent automated negotiation system

A bargaining based on multi-agent automated negotiation must experience three stages. First, BuyerAgents and SellerAgents *register* on the Facilitator, which is set up by a third party, provide some basic private information, such as name, host's IP and port number; the Facilitator assigns an ID to them at a later stage. As an important step, the SellerAgents will *advertise* some product information to the facilitator who will help them *forward* the advertisement to BuyerAgents. Then, when a BuyerAgent wants something, it will *query* information from the Facilitator. If the Facilitator is ignorant of the product, the BuyerAgent will send a *subscription* to the Facilitator for further information. When the required information is available, the Facilitator will *forward* it to the claimer. Finally, a communication between the Buyer and Seller is constructed with the help of the Facilitator, and then direct *negotiation* can be implemented.

4 Negotiating Agent Communication Language

Automated negotiation relies on the idea that agents must use a shared format of communication in order to interact smoothly. In contemporary multi-agent negotiation systems, different formats of communication have been used in different systems.

Negotiating Agent: Concept, Architecture and Communication Model 59

However, in order to fully exploit the potential of open environments like the Internet, agents should use a united negotiating language which is most suitable to any type of negotiation in which they participate. In fact, there is currently no standard widely accepted specification for the language. Negotiating Agent Communication Language (NACL) aims to find an approach that permits agents to negotiate with most of the negotiation mechanisms. To do so, NACL is defined formally as the meta-negotiation language according to the KQML language specification, and expressed in BNF style as follows:

1) < register > ::= (register :sender < *Agent_name* > :receiver < *Facilitator_name* > [:reply-with < *ID* >] :language < *content_language_name* > :ontology *kqml-ontology* :content < *agent_information* >)

   Because the KQML does not limit the content language, which is used to express the knowledge delivered by KQML, so the *content language name* here refers to any kind of content expression language, e.g. KIF, LISP.

2) < advertisement > ::= (advertise :sender < *SellerAgent_name* > :receiver < *Facilitator_name* > :reply-with *ID* :language *KQML* :ontology *kqml-ontology* :content (stream-all :sender < *SellerAgent_name* > :receiver < *facilitator_name* > :in-reply-to *ID* :language < *content_language_name* > :ontology *negotiation-ontology* :content < *product_ information* >))

3) < query > ::= (recruit-one :sender < *BuyerAgent_name* > :receiver < *Facilitator_name* > :reply-with < *ID* > :language *KQML* :ontology < *kqml-ontology* > :content (ask-if :sender < *BuyerAgent_name* > :reply-with < *ID* > :language < *content_language_name* > :ontology *Negotiation* :content < *query_ content* >))

4) < subscription > ::= (subscribe :sender < *BuyerAgent_name* > :receiver < *Facilitator_name* > :reply-with < *ID* > :language *KQML* :ontology < *kqml-ontology* > :content (stream-all :sender < *BuyerAgent_name* > :receiver < *Facilitator* > :in-reply-to < *ID* > :language < *content_language_name* > :ontology *negotiation-ontology* :content < *subscription_ content* >))

5) < forward > ::= (forward :from < *BuyerAgent_name* > :to < *SellerAgent_name* > :sender < *Facilitator_name* > :receiver < *SellerAgent_name* > :reply-with < *ID* > :language *KQML* :ontology *kqml-ontology* :content (ask-if :sender < *BuyerAgent_name* > :receiver < *SellerAgent_name* > :in-reply-to < *ID* > :reply-with < *ID* > :language < *content_language_name* > :ontology *negotiation-ontology* :content < *product_ information* >))

6) When the agents don't have a learning function, and are just in a kind of simple interaction, the performative "tell" is enough. But in most cases, we always want the agent to have the ability to analyze the historical negotiating data, so the agent must have a Virtual Knowledge Base (VKB), *belief base* in NAA, to restore the data. So one round of negotiation means to "insert" a piece of "knowledge" into the agent's VKB. The negotiation can be expressed as:
   < negotiation > ::= < tell > | < insert >

   a) < tell > ::= (tell :sender < *Agent_name* > :receiver < *Agent_name* > :in-reply-to < *ID* > :reply-with < *ID* > :language < *content_language_name* > :ontology *negotiation-ontology* :content < *negotiation_ content* >)

b) < insert > ::= (insert :sender < *Agent_name* > :receiver < *Agent_name* > :in-reply-to < *ID* > :reply-with < *ID* > :language < *content_language_name* > :ontology *negotiation-ontology* :content < *negotiation_content* >)

Finally, we define two meta-language *fail* and *exception*, in order to process some exception cases. When one agent cannot handle messages from the other agents, or negotiation is broken, performative *sorry* can be used. Performative *error* is for other exceptions that the communicator cannot process.

7)   < fail > ::= (sorry :sender < *Agent_name* > | <*Facilitator_name*> :receiver < *Agent_name* > :in-reply-to < *ID* > :reply-with < *ID* >)
< exception > ::= (error :sender < *Agent_name* > | < *Facilitator_name* > :receiver < *Agent_name* > :in-reply-to < *ID* > :reply-with < *ID* >)

5 Automated Negotiation Ontology

As can be seen from the above, ontology is an important component in the communication language. Ontology is an agreement about a shared conceptualization, which includes frameworks for modeling domain knowledge and agreements about the representation of particular domain theories, often formally captured in some form of a semantic web. Its aim is to represent the shareable conceptual model in formalized specification [11].

There are two kinds of ontology in NACM, *kqml-ontology* and *negotiation-ontology*. Kqml ontology has been defined formally. We can find the OWL version from The DARPA Agent Markup Language web site. For example, the concept of "Agent" and "Facilitator" in kqml ontology can be expressed as: [12]

```
<owl: Class rdf: ID="Agent">
    <rdfs:comment>Agent</rdfs:comment>
    <rdfs: label>Agent</rdfs: label>
</owl:Class>

<owl: Class rdf: ID="Facilitator">
    <rdfs: comment>Facilitator</rdfs: comment>
    <rdfs: label>Facilitator</rdfs: label>
    <rdfs: subClassOf rdf: resource="#Agent" />
</owl: Class>
```

Negotiation ontology is based on the idea that there are some general concepts that are presented in any negotiation, and it is built on finding commonalities across different negotiation protocols. From an analysis of the classification framework illustrated in [13], the generic software framework for automated negotiation [14], and the work by Samir Aknine, Suzanne Pinson, and Melvin F. [15], we have identified the concepts and the relationships that are shared by most negotiation protocols. Figure 3 shows the negotiation ontology resulting from this merging process using an entity relationship model to represent concepts and relationships.

The ontology is defined in terms of the following concepts; each of them highlights a different aspect of a negotiation:

- *Negotiation protocol* defines a generic protocol defining the "rules of encounter" that are followed by negotiation participants during a negotiation process. The rules describe the conditions defining the interactions between agents and the deals that can be made[13];
- *Agent* describes a single agent or an organization of agents which participate in a negotiation. Several agents can negotiate, and they can play different roles in the negotiation;
- *Goods* describes the objects of the negotiation, that is the material or immaterial goods that are transferred once an agreement has been reached;
- *Negotiation rule* is a set of rules that govern a specific negotiation protocol. In the ontology this means that we identify a number of negotiation rules, and the way in which they are specified defines a specific negotiation protocol. This concept is specified by the different types of rules identified in [15];
- *Role* describes the role an agent or an organization of agents plays in the ontology. Role represents the participants in the negotiation rule. It is specified by the roles identified in [15].

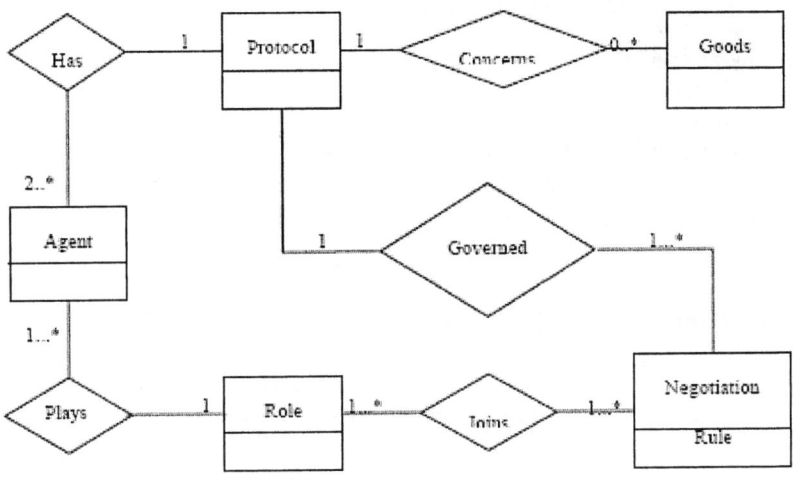

Fig. 3. ER model of the negotiation ontology

The relationships between the concepts are also defined to describe how the identified concepts interact to define the negotiation protocol domain. For example, a Protocol *Has* Agent which models the fact that at least two or more (2...*) agents interact in one negotiation protocol. That A Party *Plays* Role is modeling the fact that one agent can play a number of (1...*) different roles in the interaction. A protocol is also *governed by* a number of negotiation rules, and this aspect is also modeled by means of the relationship.

There are many tools and platforms for developing ontology. Ontolingua, as a part of KSE, is a famous project created by Stanford Knowledge Systems Laboratory. It makes use of the World Wide Web to enable wide access and provides users with the ability to publish, browse, create, and edit ontologies stored on an ontology server. We use ontolingua for defining the concepts in the negotiation ontology. For example, the concept *Agent* and relation *Has* can be expressed as: (We have not included the complete definition for reasons of space)

```
(Define-Frame Agent
  :Own-Slots(
     ( Arity 1 )
     (Documentation
         "Something or someone that can act on its own
         and produce changes in the world")
     (Instance-Of Class)
     (Subclass-Of)
     (Disjoint-Decomposition
         :Value (Setof Person Organization))
     (Subclass-Of Individual-Thing)
     (Superclass-Of Organization Person))
  :Template-Slots
     ((Name (Cardinality 1))))

(Define-Relation Has
   (?X ?Actor)
   "A mapping from anything to a name for that object.
   Note that ?x can have multiple names, so this is
   distinct from Name."
   :Axiom-Def
       (=> (= (actor ?X) ?Actor) (Has ?X ?Actor)))
```

6 Conclusions and Future Work

In this paper, a novel agent concept, namely negotiating agent, is established. On the basis of the theoretical model of negotiating agent, NAA and NACM defined above are explicit and formal specifications for the agents negotiating in an E-business environment; especially, NACM defines the negotiation language template shared among all agents formally and explicitly. The novelty of the communication model is twofold. In fact it is synthesis work in both agent communication technology and automated negotiation theory, which are important areas of e-business research. More importantly, NAA and NACM build the foundation for developing an automated negotiation system.

The approach we have presented in this paper is still at a very early stage, and there are a number of issues that need to be further investigated. One is how to perfect the negotiation ontology. Creating and expressing any size of ontology is difficult and time consuming work. We still need to investigate whether this negotiation ontology is sufficient to permit the necessary interaction or whether a different type of knowledge should be included in the ontology. Another aspect which we have disregarded in the paper but which we are planning to investigate is how to design an analogous negotiating model complying with FIPA specifications.

References

1. V. Tamma, M. Wooldridge, and I. Dickinson. An Ontology-based Approach to Automated Negotiation. In Proceedings of the Fourth International Workshop on Agent-Mediated Elctronic Commerce (AMEC-2002), Bologna, Italy, July 2002.
2. N. R. Jennings, P. Faratin, A. R. Lomuscio, S. Parsons, C. Sierra and M. Wooldridge. Automated negotiation: prospects, methods and challenges. Int. J. of Group Decision and Negotiation, (2001), 10(2): 199-215.
3. Paul R. Cohen and Hector J. Levesque. Intention is choice with commitment. Artificial Intelligent, (1990), 42(3): 213-261
4. Anand S. Rao and Michael P. Georgeff. Modeling rational agents within a BDI-architecture. In: Proceedings of the Second International Conference on Principles of Knowledge Representation and Reasoning, Boston, MA Morgan Kaufmann. (1991): 473-484
5. M. P. Georgeff and F. F. Ingrand. Research on procedural reasoning systems. Final Report, Phase 1, AI Center, SRI International, Menlo Park, Cal (1988)
6. S. Kraus. Strategic Negotiation in Multi-agent Environments. MIT Press: Cambridge, MA (2001)
7. Yannis Labrou and Tim Finin. A Proposal for a new KQML Specification. [online] http://www.cs.umbc.edu/kqml/papers. (1996)
8. FIPA (2000) Specification part 2-agent communication language. [online] http:// www.fipa.org/. (2002)
9. Georgeff, M. P. and Ingrand, F. F. Decision-making in an embedded reasoning system. In: Proceedings of the 11th International Joint Conference on Artificial Intelligence (IJCAI-89), Detroit, MI. Morgan Kaufmann. (1989) 972-978
10. Tim Finin, Jay Weber, James McGuire, Stuart Shapiro, Chris Beck. Specification of the KQML Agent Communication Language. [online] http://www.cs.umbc.edu/kqml/ papers. (1993)
11. Michael N. Huhns, Munindar P. Singh. Ontology for Agents. IEEE Internet Computing, December (1997) 81-83
12. Yisheng Dong, KQML ontology, [online] http://cse.seu.edu.cn/people/ysdong/kqml.owl. (2003)
13. C. Bartolini and C.P.N. Jennings. A generic software framework for automated network. Proceedings of the First International Conference on Autonomous Agent and Multi-Agent Systems (2002)
14. Alessio R. Lomuscio, Michael Wooldridge, and Nick R. Jennings. A classification scheme for negotiation in electronic commerce. Int. Journal of Group Decision and Negotiation, (2003), 12(1): 31–56.
15. Samir Aknine, Suzanne Pinson, and Melvin F. Shakun. An extended multi-agent negotiation protocol. International Journal on Autonomous Agents and Multi-agent Systems, (2004), 8(1): 5–45.

Particle Filter Method for a Centralized Multisensor System

Wei Xiong, You He, and Jing-wei Zhang

Research Institute of Information Fusion, Naval Aeronautical Engineering Institute,
264001 Yantai, China
xiongweimail@tom.com

Abstract. Multisensor state estimation is an important issue in multisensor data fusion. In order to solve the centralized multisensor state estimation problem of a non-Gaussian nonlinear system, the paper proposes a new multisensor sequential particle filter (MSPF). First, the general theoretical model of a centralized multisensor particle filter is obtained. Then, a sequential resampling method is proposed according to the characteristics of a centralized multisensor system. Last, a Monte Carlo simulation is used to analyze the performance of the method. The results of the simulation show that the new method can greatly improve the state estimation precision of a multisensor system. Moreover, it will gain more accuracy in estimation with an increase in sensor numbers.

1 Introduction

With the development of computer and communication technology, many kinds of multisensor systems, which are applied to more general environment (nonlinear/non-Gaussian), have appeared, including target tracking [1~4], mobile robotics [5], and navigation [6]. Accordingly, people begin to use more advanced methods, such as particle filtering, to obtain greater precision from the state estimation of the system.

Particle filter (PF) techniques have been a growing research area lately due to improved computer performance[3,7,8]. PF is a technique for implementing a recursive Bayesian filter using Monte Carlo simulations. The key idea[8] is to represent the required posterior density function by a set of random samples with associated weights and to then compute estimates based on these samples and weights. Compared to the other nonlinear filters, such as Extended Kalman filter (EKF) and Unscented Kalman filter (UKF), PF can cope with any nonlinear model without any limitations of linearization error and Gaussian noises assumption. Therefore, it can be used for the state estimation problem of non-Gaussian nonlinear systems.

Currently, there are few researchers who study multisensor particle filter technology. In [1], two different approaches have been developed for a distributed sensor system: a joint resampling scheme, and an individual resampling scheme. In [5], Matt et al. presented a selective communication scheme to solve the problem of decentralized sensor fusion with a distributed particle filter. However, these works are mostly focused on how to utilize certain schemes to solve the problem of multisensor particle filter, which cannot really be used as the theoretical model of multisensor particle filter. First, this paper presents the general theoretical model of centralized multisensor particle filter. Then, a sequential resampling method is proposed according to the characteristics of the centralized multisensor system.

2 System Description

The target dynamics are modeled as follows:

$$X_k = \mathbf{f}_k(X_{k-1}, V_{k-1}) \tag{1}$$

where $X_k \in R^{n_x}$ is the state vector at time k, $\{V_{k-1} \in R^{n_v}, k \in N\}$ is an i.i.d. process noise sequence, caused by disturbances and modelling errors, $\mathbf{f}_k : R^{n_x} \times R^{n_v} \to R^{n_x}$ is the nonlinear state transition function mapping the previous state and current control input to the current state, n_x, n_v are dimensions of the state and process noise vectors, respectively.

It is assumed that there are N disparate sensors. The measurement equation of every sensor is modeled as follows:

$$Z_k^i = \mathbf{h}_k^i(X_k, W_k^i) \tag{2}$$

where $Z_k^i \in R^{n_z}$ the observation vector of the i-th sensor at time k, $\{W_k^i \in R^{n_w}, i \in N\}$ is an i.i.d. measurement noise sequence, and is mutually independent with different sensor, n_z, n_w are dimensions of the measurement and measurement noise vectors, respectively, and $\mathbf{h}_k^i : R^{n_x} \times R^{n_w} \to R^{n_z}$ is a possibly nonlinear function of the i-th sensor.

3 Multisensor Sequential Particle Filter

3.1 The General Model of Multisensor Particle Filter

Let $\{X_{0:k}^i, q_k^i\}_{i=1}^{N_s}$ denote a random sample sequence that characterizes the posterior PDF $p(X_{0:k} | Z_{1:k}^1, \cdots, Z_{1:k}^N)$, where $X_{0:k}^i$ is a i-th sample with associated weight q_k^i, $Z_{1:k}^i, i = 1, \cdots, N$ is the set of all measurements of the i-th sensor up to time k, $X_{0:k} = \{X_j, j = 0, \cdots, k\}$ is the set of all states up to time k. The weights are normalized such that $\sum_i q_{k=1}^i = 1$. Then, the posterior density at k can be approximated as[3,8]

$$p(X_{0:k} | Z_{1:k}^1, \cdots, Z_{1:k}^N) \approx \sum_{i=1}^{N_s} q_k^i \delta(X_{0:k} - X_{0:k}^i) \tag{3}$$

In general, it is not possible to draw these samples directly from $p(X_{0:k} | Z_{1:k}^1, \cdots, Z_{1:k}^N)$. Instead, the samples are drawn from an importance density $\pi(X | Z)$ [3]. Then, the unnormalized weights in (3) are defined as follows[3]

$$\tilde{q}_k^i = \frac{p(Z_{1:k}^1,\cdots,Z_{1:k}^N \mid X_{0:k}^i)p(X_{0:k}^i)}{\pi(X_{0:k}^i \mid Z_{1:k}^1,\cdots,Z_{1:k}^N)} \tag{4}$$

If the important density is chosen to factor as

$$\pi(X_{0:k}^i \mid Z_{1:k}^1,\cdots,Z_{1:k}^N) = \pi(X_k^i \mid X_{0:k-1}^i,Z_{1:k}^1,\cdots,Z_{1:k}^N) \cdot \pi(X_{0:k-1}^i \mid Z_{1:k-1}^1,\cdots,Z_{1:k-1}^N) \tag{5}$$

then, substituting (5) into (4) yields

$$\begin{aligned}\tilde{q}_k^i &= \frac{p(Z_{1:k}^1,\cdots,Z_{1:k}^N \mid X_{0:k}^i)p(X_{0:k}^i)}{\pi(X_k^i \mid X_{0:k-1}^i,Z_{1:k}^1,\cdots,Z_{1:k}^N)} \times \frac{1}{\pi(X_{0:k-1}^i \mid Z_{1:k-1}^1,\cdots,Z_{1:k-1}^N)} \\ &= \frac{p(Z_k^1,\cdots,Z_k^N \mid X_k^i)p(X_k^i \mid X_{k-1}^i)}{\pi(X_k^i \mid X_{0:k-1}^i,Z_{1:k}^1,\cdots,Z_{1:k}^N)} \times \frac{p(Z_{1:k-1}^1,\cdots,Z_{1:k-1}^N \mid X_{0:k-1}^i)p(X_{0:k-1}^i)}{\pi(X_{0:k-1}^i \mid Z_{1:k-1}^1,\cdots,Z_{1:k-1}^N)} \\ &= \frac{p(Z_k^1,\cdots,Z_k^N \mid X_k^i)p(X_k^i \mid X_{k-1}^i)}{\pi(X_k^i \mid X_{0:k-1}^i,Z_{1:k}^1,\cdots,Z_{1:k}^N)} \cdot \tilde{q}_{k-1}^i\end{aligned} \tag{6}$$

According to [9], $p(Z_k^1,\cdots,Z_k^N \mid X_k^i)$ can be computed as follows

$$p(Z_k^1,\cdots,Z_k^N \mid X_k^i) = \prod_{j=1}^{N} p(Z_k^j \mid X_k^i) \tag{7}$$

Substituting (7) into (5) yields

$$\tilde{q}_k^i = \frac{\prod_{j=1}^{N} p(Z_k^j \mid X_k^i) p(X_k^i \mid X_{k-1}^i)}{\pi(X_k^i \mid X_{0:k-1}^i,Z_{1:k}^1,\cdots,Z_{1:k}^N)} \cdot \tilde{q}_{k-1}^i \tag{8}$$

In order to perform recursive Bayesian filtering, the importance density should only be dependent on the measurements and the states at time k-1. So,

$$\begin{aligned}\pi(X_k^i \mid X_{0:k-1}^i, Z_{1:k}^1,\cdots,Z_{1:k}^N) \\ = \pi(X_k^i \mid X_{k-1}^i, Z_k^1,\cdots,Z_k^N)\end{aligned} \tag{9}$$

Substituting (9) into (8) yields

$$\tilde{q}_k^i = \frac{\prod_{j=1}^{N} p(Z_k^j \mid X_k^i) p(X_k^i \mid X_{k-1}^i)}{\pi(X_k^i \mid X_{k-1}^i, Z_k^1,\cdots,Z_k^N)} \cdot \tilde{q}_{k-1}^i \tag{10}$$

A common problem with the particle filter is the degeneracy phenomenon[3,8] where, after a few iterations, all but one particle will have negligible weight. In order to reduce its occurrence, there are often two methods[3,8] employed, these being a good choice of importance density and use of resampling.

3.2 The Model of a Sequential Particle Filter

Let

$$\pi(X_k \mid X_{k-1}^i, Z_k^1,\cdots,Z_k^N) = p(X_k \mid X_{k-1}^i) \prod_{i=1}^{N-1} p(X_k \mid Z_k^i) \tag{11}$$

Then, a multisensor sequential particle filter (MSPF) can be expressed as follows.

A. Initialization: k=0
- FOR $i=1,\cdots,N_s$, draw the states (particles) X_0^i from the prior $p(X_0)$.

B. Sequential Importance Sampling: $k=1,2,\cdots$
  a) The first sample:
  - FOR $i=1,\cdots,N_s$
    - Draw $X_k^{i,1} \sim p(X_k | X_{k-1}^i)$
    - Calculate $\tilde{q}_k^1(i)$ according to the likelihood $p[Z_k^1 | X_k^{i,1}]$
  - FOR $i=1,\cdots,N_s$
    - Normalize: $q_k^1(i) = \dfrac{\tilde{q}_k^1(i)}{\sum_{i=1}^{N}\tilde{q}_k^1(i)}$
  - Resample using the methods of [3]

  b) Repeat step a) till the N-th sensor.
  - $X_k^{i,j}$ and $\tilde{q}_k^j(i)$ of the j-th ($j \leq N$) sample are calculated as follows:
    - Draw $X_k^{i,j} \sim p(X_k | X_{k-1}^{j-1})$
    - Calculate $\tilde{q}_k^j(i) = \tilde{q}_k^{j-1}(i) p[Z_k^j | X_k^{i,j}]$

  c) Output at time k: $\hat{X}_k = \dfrac{1}{N_s}\sum_{i=1}^{N_s} X_k^{i,N}$

4 Simulation

The simulations are referred to in [10]. There are three sensors, which are fixed in three platforms. All of these platforms move in the x-y plane according to the equations:

$$\begin{cases} x_i = -10000(6-i) + \Delta x \\ y_i = 4t + \Delta y \end{cases}, \quad i=1,2,3 \tag{12}$$

where Δx, Δy are mutually independent, zero-mean, white noise sequences with variances $r_x=1$ and $r_y=1$, respectively.

A target moves on the y-axis according to

$$X(k+1) = F(k)X(k) + \Gamma(k)V(k) \tag{13}$$

where

$$X(k) = \begin{bmatrix} y(k) \\ \dot{y}(k) \end{bmatrix}, \quad F(k) = \begin{bmatrix} 1 & T \\ 0 & 1 \end{bmatrix}, \quad \Gamma(k) = \begin{bmatrix} T^2/2 \\ T \end{bmatrix}$$

T is the time interval. $V(k)$ is zero-mean and white with variance $Q(k)=4$.

The i-th sensor measurement equation is

$$Z_i(k) = h_i(X(k)) + W_i(k) \tag{14}$$

$$h[\bullet] = \tan^{-1}\left(\frac{y - y_i}{x - x_i}\right) = \tan^{-1}\left(\frac{y - y_i}{-x_i}\right) \tag{15}$$

where $W_i(k)$ is zero-mean and white with variance $R(k)$, and is assumed to be independent of the platform perturbations and process noise.

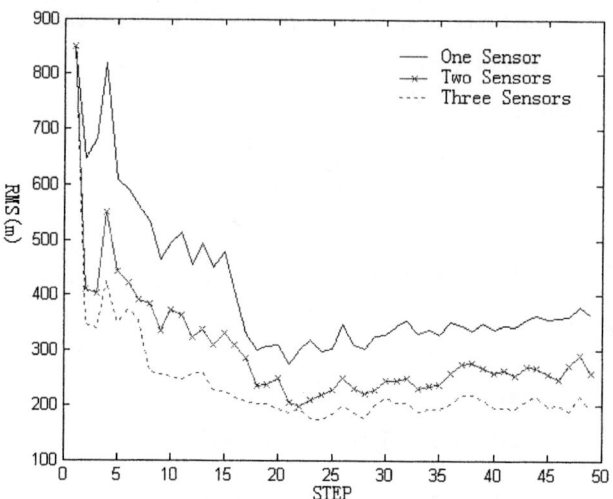

Fig. 1. RMS errors in position

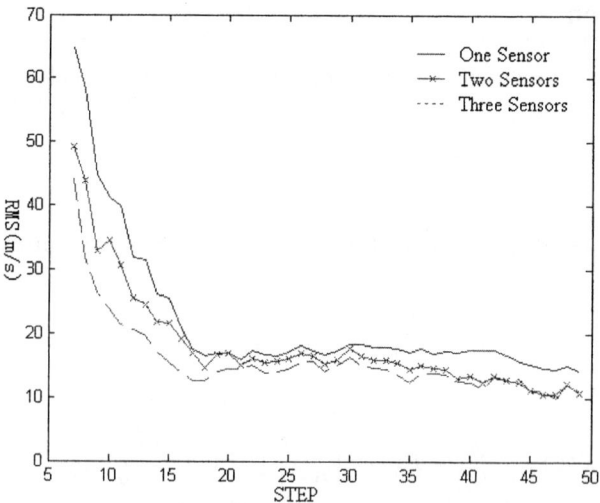

Fig. 2. RMS errors in velocity

In this case, the number of Monte Carlo runs is 50. The true initialization state of the target is $X(0) = [80,1]'$. In every run, the total simulation time is 50 steps, $T=2$s and the number of particles is 500.

Figs.1 and 2 show the simulation results, where three methods are used to track the target, as follows:

a) Only according to the measurements of the first sensor (one sensor),
b) According to the measurements of the first and second sensor (two sensors),
c) According to the measurements of all sensors (three sensors).

In this simulation, $R(k)=(1°)^2$, from Figs.1 and 2, it is shown that the new method can greatly improve the state estimation precision of a multisensor system. Moreover, it will deliver more accurate estimation with an increase in sensor numbers.

5 Conclusions

In order to solve the centralized multisensor state estimation problem of nonlinear non-Gaussian system, the paper proposes a new multisensor sequential particle filter. The results of the simulations show that the MSPF can increase the global estimation accuracy of a system. At the same time, the method can be easily implemented. With the development of computer performance, the computational complexity of the method will no longer prevent it from being applied to a variety of state estimation problems including multisensor navigation and multisensor tracking.

References

1. Ya Xue, Darryl Morrell: Target Tracking and Data Fusion using Multiple Adaptive Foveal Sensors. http://www.eas.asu.edu/~morrell/pubs/ IF2003.pdf (2004)
2. A.Farina, B.Ristic: Tracking a Ballistic Target: Comparison of several Nonlinear filters. Vol.38, No.3, IEEE Trans on AES (2002) 477–482
3. Shawn Michael Herman: A Particle Filtering Approach to Joint Passive Radar Tracking and Target Classification. University of Illinois (2002)
4. C.Hue, J.P.Le Cadre: Tracking Multiple Objects with Particle Filtering. Vol.38, No.3, IEEE Trans on AES (2002) 791–811
5. Matt Rosencrantz, Geoffrey Gordon, Sebastian Thrun: Decentralized sensor fusion with distributed particle filters. http://www-2.cs.cmu.edu/~ggordon/mrosen-ggordon-thrun.decentralzied.pdf (2004)
6. H.Carvalho, P.Del Moral: Optimal Nonlinear Filtering in GPS/INS Integration. Vol.33, No.3, IEEE Trans on AES (1997) 835–849
7. Gordon, N.J., Salmond: Novel Approach to Nonlinear/Non-Gaussian Baysian State Estimation. Pt.F.140, No.2, IEE-Proceedings (1993) 107–113
8. M.Sanjeev Arulampalam, Simon Maskell, Neil Gordon: a Tutorial on Particle Filters for Online Nonlinear/Non-Gaussian Bayesial Tracking. Vol.55, NO.2, IEEE Trans on AES (2002) 174–188
9. David A. Castanon, Demosthenis Teneketzis: Distributed Estimation Algorithms for Nonlinear Systems. Vol.Ac-30, No.5, IEEE Trans on AES (1985) 418–425
10. Bar-shalom,Y., Fortmann,T.E: Tracking and Data Association. New York, Academic press (1988)

Design and Analysis of a Novel Load-Balancing Model Based on Mobile Agent

Junfeng Tian, Yuling Liu, Xiaohui Yang, and Ruizhong Du

Institute of Computer Network Technology, Hebei University, Baoding 071002, P.R. China
{tjf, lyl, yxh, drzh}@mail.hbu.edu.cn

Abstract. Associating with the self-designed distributed database server system and studying the objective description and definition of load index, this paper proposes a three-level management framework of distributed redundant service system, introduces an active load-balancing idea into the system, and then presents the load-balancing model based on mobile agent. The performance of the system is finally analyzed. Compared with traditional distributed computing models, we conclude the novel model has lower cost, higher reliability, higher expandability, higher throughput, and higher efficiency.

1 Introduction

Distributed computing technology is one of the development potential of computer technology, and the Client/Server mode is becoming the mainstream of distributed computing technology gradually. However, the distributed computing environment with a single server is low in practicability and system performance. More research has focused on that a multi-server system with high-speed network offers redundant service. More and more distributed applications adopt redundant service to improve system performance and availability. Multi-server systems have good applied prospect in transaction processing, distributed database, web server, etc. Comparing with traditional mainframe systems, multi-server systems have lots of advantages such as lower price, higher reliability, higher expandability, higher throughput and plenty of system resources. But so far, the software technology applied in redundant service systems is laggard and the key technologies such as load-balancing strategies and error resilience are not mature.

Distributed database server system (DDSS) is a self-designed distributed information management system adopting the C/S mode, and it divides the database of system into a super-class database and a sub-class one based on data format. The super-class database contains the public and basic information, then it will be visited frequently even it is small. So it is located on the main server. Lots of special data are in the sub-class database. The structure model of the system is described as follows.

$Server::=<MS, SS>$, MS (*Main server*) is the set of main servers. SS (*Sub-Server*) is the set of sub-servers.

$MS = \{MS_i | 1 \leq i \leq 2\}$;

$MS_i:: = <Name, Database-Object, State>$;

$SS = \{SS_i | 1 \leq i \leq N-1\}$, N-1 is the number of the sub-servers which can work at the same time};

$SS_i ::= <Name, Database\text{-}Object, State>$, *Name* represents the only identification of a server, *Database-Object* is the identification of a database object, and *State* is the state of a server.

$Database\text{-}Object = \{DO_i | 1 \leq i \leq m\}$, m ($1 \leq m \leq N$) is the number of data objects. DO_1 is the invariable data object of the server, while DO_2, DO_3, ... , DO_m are the backup of the invariable data objects of the other servers.

$DO_i ::= <DO\text{-}Name, Attributes, Access>$. *DO-Name* is defined as its unique identification. *Attributes* are the properties of a data object. The information about the visited data object can be known from *Access*. *Access*=(0,1), 0 means the data object is not occupied and can be visited, and 1 shows it is busy and visitation is prevented.

State::=<0,1>, 0 means that the sub-server is offline or that the main server is copying. 1 shows the server is in the normal response state.

Request::=<REQ_1, REQ_2>, REQ_1 is the set of manipulation with writing property, such as modify, creation, delete and append. REQ_2 defines the set of manipulation with reading property, such as query and statistics.

Fig.1 shows the logical structure of DDSS.

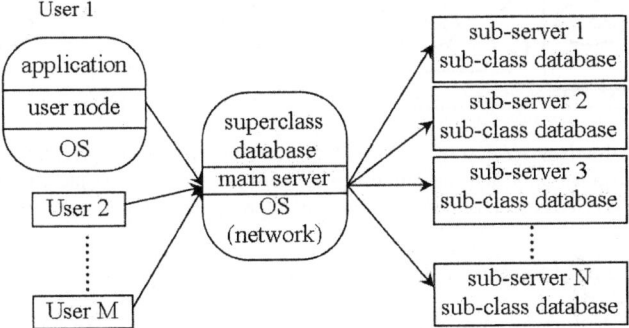

Fig. 1. The logical structure of DDSS. The black parts are the software running on each machine, including operating system, database management system and other applications used on each workstation individually. In the C/S mode, client runs the programs, which can illuminate its requests and transmits them to the main server.

Associating with DDSS, this paper applies mobile agent into distributed redundant service system and proposes an active load balancing manager model MMA (Object Manager-Mobile Agent-Server Agent) based on mobile agent. In addition, this paper studies and analyzes the definition of the load index that is the key problem of MMA.

2 Load-Balancing Model of DDSS

Distributed object technology is the integration of object technology and client/server computing mode in distributed computing environment, and it can effectively describe and solve such problems as redundant service definition and load-balancing [3]. Distributed objects encapsulate databases, events and methods together, provide uniform calling interface, and treat independent server resources in distributed computing environment as objects. Active objects are used for describing distributed computing environment. Active object can provide users with not only status information but also computing service, receive requests from clients, and call services of other objects.

Client and server can be classified according to requests: when an object sends requests to the others, it is client; when an object receives requests from the other objects, it becomes server. Thus we can abstract the client/server mode in DCS into relationship between requests and objects. As a result, the redundant service of DDSS is shown in Fig.2.

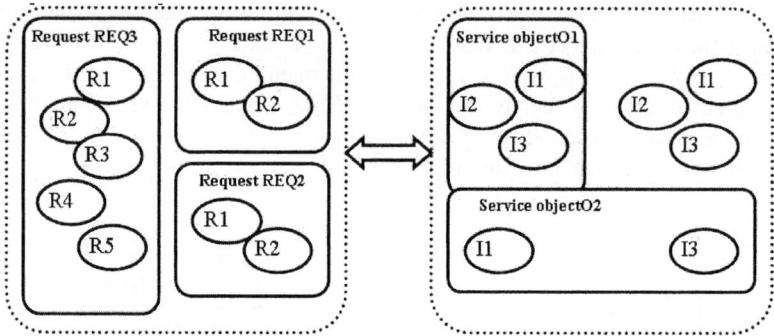

Fig. 2. The redundant service of DDSS. It is described as the displacement and schedule between the instance pool and the request pool, i.e. how to send a request to the instance of corresponding service object, or how to choose an appropriate instance to respond to a request.

2.1 Description of System Management Framework

Based on the discussion above, two types of resource objects can be abstracted from DDSS redundant service system: one is hardware resource (hosts), and another is software resource (service objects and instances). Furthermore, the management framework can be abstracted into a three-level management model, as shown in Fig.3.

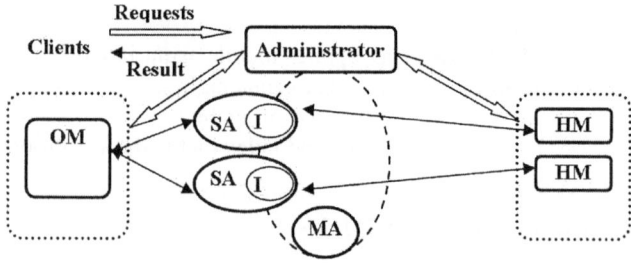

Fig. 3. Management framework of DDSS redundant service system, which consists of *Administrator, Managers, and Agents*

Administrator is the manager of all *Managers* in the system, responsible for collecting and maintaining global management information and global scheduling.

Manager consists of *OMs* (*Object Managers*) and *HMs* (*Host Managers*), which are managed by *Administrator,* and manage *Agent* at the same time. *OM* provides management interface for a kind of redundant service object and centrally manages the redundant service of a specified service class; *HM* stays at each host, providing management interface for it.

Agent is composed of *SAs (Server Agents)* and *MAs (Mobile Agents)*. *SA* adds a management interface to the service object instance, helping *Manager* to perform management functions; *MA* moves among the redundant service object instances according to some rules to collect load and status information of those instances it reached, and help *OM* to perform load-balancing cooperating with *SA* according to current situation of service object instances.

2.2 Load-Balancing Model Based on Mobile Agent

2.2.1 Mobile Agent

MA consists of three parts. The moving support module is responsible for identity authentication against *MA*, independent moving of *MA* and communication with its implementation environment. The method sets, namely, the task sets of *MA*, provide methods to collect current load and correlative status information of service object instance. The status sets contain the load and status information table of service object instances and the moving regulation of *MA* itself.

The life cycle of *MA* is divided into three stages: creation, running and elimination. The creation stage is performed by *OM*, whose main work is to build moving regulation; the running stage refers to the process that *MA* continuously migrates in a logical circle composed of a number of *SAs* and collects their load information; the elimination stage lasts from the moment when *MA* decides to return to *OM,* until it returns to *OM* and reports the load information to *OM*.

Each mobile agent entity is created by *OM*, and has its own migration regulation. The migration regulation depends on the following factors: the requested redundancy that the system permits at present, which determines the expected length of the migration regulation; and the current status of all service objects, which determines the actual length of the migration regulation.

If all the object instances of redundant service are heavily loaded, there is no object instance available for the redundant service, thus *OM* delays dispensing request and no MA is created. If there are enough underloaded service object instances, *OM* will queue object instances of the redundant service according to the values of load index and select n instances in best status to form the moving regulation of the corresponding MA entity together with *OM*. If MA entity meets with faults or invalid nodes during migration process, it can adjust the regulation and choose new target node automatically, and collect fault and invalidation information at the same time.

As described above, the requested redundancy n which system permits currently is the precondition to build MA's migration regulation. This paper adopts RoDO (Redundancy of Distributed Object) balancing model, which is based on PI

(Performance Index), to determine the instance redundancy of the service object. Its main idea [4] is as follows:

- From user's viewpoint, use average response time to the request to measure the performance of the system.
- Different penalty values are defined by the user against different response time: The shorter the response time, the lower the penalty value. Thus user's performance requirement can be effectively described and the system is accurately guided to carry out user's performance target.
- Define service object invalidation as the case that the response delay is ∞. Thus the penalty function can be expressed by a unified integration formula so that the balancing model of performance and usability is effectively simplified.

Based on the ideas above, the RoDO Model of the ith service is:

$$PI = \int_0^\infty w_i(t) P_i(t) dt = \int_0^{Td_i} w_i(t) P_i(t) dt + wf_i * F_i(u_i) \qquad (1)$$

where, $P_i(t)$ is the probability that the response time of the ith service request is t ($1 \leq i \leq M$) ; $w_i(t)$ is the penalty function that user defines according to the response time of the ith service request. OM inspects the invalidation of service object based on overtime mechanism. Td_i is the overtime time of service object i, namely the response time of the ith service request. If OM cannot receive the response result of transferred request in Td_i, we can think service object i invalid. wf_i is the penalty value that user defines when service object i is invalid. $F_i(u_i)$ is the function that the rate of invalidation of service object i against its instance redundancy u_i.

In redundant service system the functional relationship between the average response time of the ith service request and the count of redundant instance, namely instance redundancy u_i can be obtained according to experience formula, so the performance index PI can be expressed as a function of service instance redundancy u_i. From the design idea of RoDO model, we can conclude: the instance redundancy of the ith service is the count of instance that makes PI minimize.

2.2.2 Load-Balancing Model MMA
(1) Architecture of SA

The concrete task of *OM* is implemented by the cooperation of *MA* and *SA*, thus *SA* is not a simple service agent and its function should include: a management interface added on *OM* as to service object instance, periodically collects and calculates the load information of each instance; and an implementation environment for the visiting *MA*, includes receiving, initialization, localization and sending of *MA*.

SA has 5 layers. Network transfer protocol (NTP) layer provides interfaces to existing network communication protocol. *SA* can communicate with other *SAs*, and transferring and receiving of *MA* is carried on in NTP layer. Service layer builds running environment and security protection mechanism for *MA*, coordinating and supervising the implementation of each agent. Interface layer provides underlying interface for *MA* to communicate with the host and the other *MAs*. Language interpreter layer provides the support of the corresponding language interpreter in which *MA* is implemented. *Agent* application layer supports *MA* to perform its task of schedule.

(2) Definition of load index

Load index is usually defined as the criterion to measure the load of hosts and object instances. Therefore, accurately defining and describing load index is one of the key factors that affect the efficiency of load-balancing. All the traditional measure parameters describe and define the load state of hosts and instances with static targets, which cannot objectively reflect the load and its changing rules [3]. This paper objectively describes the load index of hosts and object instances by defining the concepts applicability to the load threshold and digestibility of the request.

Definition 1. The queue length of load queue is the count of requests, which the host and object instance are waiting for response. The queue length of instance Ins_L_i is the count of requests that queue at the ith instance waiting for response. The queue length of host $Load\_Queue$ is the sum of the count of the requests that queue on some host waiting for response. Hence,

$$Load\_Queue = \sum_{i=1}^{n} Ins\_L_i$$

Where n is the count of service instances on the host.

Definition 2. The dead zone is the alarming coverage in which the load index values mean that some hosts or instances are heavily loaded, which is determined by two parameters as below:

- Heavy load alarm line, which is the minimum of load queue length when hosts and instances are in heavy load. When load queue length is beyond it, the response time of requesting for service will obviously increase. They are respectively denoted as $Load\_Alarm$ and Ins_A_i.
- Overload alarm line, which is the maximum of load queue length that host and instances can support. When load queue length is beyond it, the response time of requesting for service will prolong infinitely. They are respectively denoted as $Load\_Died$ and Ins_D_i. Therefore the load queue length must be limited not to reach this value. Thus load threshold Max_Laod and Ins_Max_Li is defined:

$$Load\_Alarm \leq Max\_Laod < Load\_Died, \text{ and } Ins\_Ai \leq Ins\_Max\_Li < Ins\_Di$$

Definition 3. The digestibility of requesting service is the count of requests that are successfully carried out in one collecting cycle. If the load queue length of a host varies from $Load\_Queue_1$ to $Load\_Queue_2$, its digestibility is

$$P_r = (Load\_Queue_2 - Load\_Queue_1)/MAX(Load\_Queue_1, Load\_Queue_2)$$

Obviously, $0 \leq P_r \leq 1$ and $Pr>0$ indicates that the arrival velocity of service request is greater than that of fulfillment; $Pr<0$ indicates that the arrival velocity of service request is less than that of fulfillment. For object instance, it is denoted as Ins_Pr.

Definition 4. The load threshold applicability P_D indicates the degree to which current request queue approaches Max_Load. It is expressed as follows:

$$P_D = Load\_Queue/Max\_Load$$

Obviously, $0 \le P_D \le 1$, and greater P_D indicates the host is more heavily loaded. Accordingly, the applicability of instance is denoted as Ins_P_D.

Definition 5. The load index is the load status and changing trend of a host or an instance in the latest time slice. The less the load index, the lighter the load. It is shown as follows:

$$Load\_Index = k_1 \times (1-P_D) + k_2 \times P_r$$

$$Load\_Index = k_1 \times \frac{Max\_Load - Load\_Queue}{Max\_Load} + k_2 \times \frac{Load\_Queue_2 - Load\_Queue_1}{MAX(Load\_Queue_1, Load\_Queue_2)}$$

Where k_1, k_2 are adjustment coefficients. By experiment, when $k_1=0$ and $k_2=0.2$ Load_Index can reflect the load status more objectively. Accordingly, for instance it is Ins_Index.

To precisely define the load index of object instance on the host, host instance load index is introduced and defined as follows:

$$Ins\_Load\_Index = w_1 \times Load\_Index + w_2 \times Ins\_Index \qquad (2)$$

Where w_1, w_2 are distributing weight. By experiment, when $w_1=0.55$ and $w_2=0.45$, Ins_Load_Index can reflect the load status more objectively.

Definition 6. The light load threshold $Load\_Queue_0$ is the length of host load queue when the length of each instance load queue is 1, i.e. $Load\_Queue_0=n$. The light load threshold is introduced to meet the active load-balancing strategy.

All the parameters above are calculated and managed by *SA*. When *MA* traverses to the hosts, it takes them to *OM*.

(3) Collecting load information

The way of collecting load information is periodically pushing, which is fulfilled by the periodical self-duplication of *OM*. According to the difference among the execute time of different type of request, *OM* designs different duplication cycle, that is, the cycle of collecting load information, for each *MA*. When *MA* enters its life cycle, it will collect correlative information when it traverses a number of *SAs* participating in redundant service according to scheduled migration regulation. And it duplicates itself at the end of each collecting cycle and returns to *OM* with all collected information.

(4) Load-balancing Model MMA

In the load-balancing model of MMA, *OM*, *MA* and *SA* communicate with each other logically, which is shown in Fig.4. *OM* creates *MA*, initializes *MA* and takes *MA* back. *MA* participates in the load-balancing work according to scheduled migration regulation and method once entering its life cycle. *SA* provides environment for MA including receiving, initializing and localizing *MA* and providing methods for *MA*'s executing and migration. They cooperate to finish the task of load-balancing.

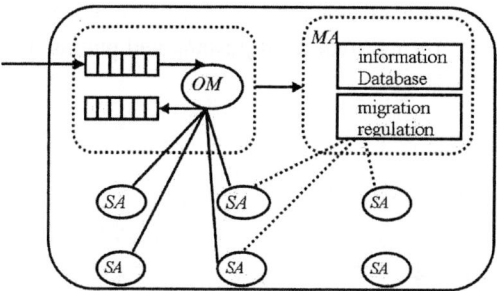

Fig. 4. The logical structure of the load-balancing model MMA. OM creates MA periodically, MA moves according to its migration regulation, collects load information of service object instance, and balances its load. Each MA entity records unique request identification. Only when a request has been executed and MA has checked all the SAs in the migration regulation, MA returns to OM with the latest load information, which refers to the end of its life cycle.

The load-balancing of whole system is realized from three aspects.

- When some kind of request arrives, *OM* queues in accordance to the load index *Ins_Load_Index* of the host instance object are recorded in the instance information table. Then n instances are chosen from the ordered instance table as the distributed request objects based on the permitted request redundancy n from the formula (1). At the same time, they form the migration regulation of *MA*.
- *MA* visits *SAs* in turn according to the migration regulation. When *MA* gets to *SA*, it collects current instance information, deletes completed request from current request queue of *SA* based on its visited instance objects and adjusts the current load of instance, which not only ensures the performance of system but also makes use of system resources greatly as well.
- The active load-balancing idea is introduced in this model as an effective supplement to ensure the efficiency of load-balancing. The active load-balancing strategy, driving receivers of load-balancing, does load-balancing manipulation in accordance to the load information in the part range of system, which has good extensibility and adapts the schedule of load-balancing well. Its idea is that the node with light load receives task from administrator not passively but actively.

When SA of one host finds the length of its load queue is shorter than that of the critical point (that is, $Load\_Queue \leq Load\_Queue_0$), it applies for load from *OM*, which avoids that the host with light load wastes time to wait for allocation of tasks.

3 Analysis of Load-Balancing Model in DDSS

3.1 Analysis of the Overhead of Load-Balancing

The overhead of load-balancing mainly comes from collecting information whose cost mainly depends on the overhead of network communication. So MMA will be compared with the traditional pushing and pulling operating mode based on the communication of network.

Supposing that the redundancy of the instance of the service object is k, the operation modes of MMA and traditional pushing and pulling are shown in Fig.5 and Fig.6 separately.

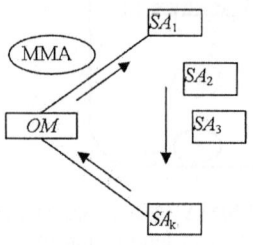

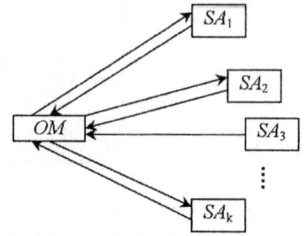

Fig. 5. Operation mode of MMA   **Fig. 6.** Operation mode of Pushing and Pulling

On the assumption that the communication overhead is equal between any two nodes, the communication cost of collecting all of the load information of SA under MMA mode is formulated as $CM = Cost \times (k+1)$ and the cost under pushing and pulling mode is $CP = Cost \times 2k$. Obviously, $CM \leq CP$.

By introducing *MA*, the distributed redundant service management system uses its mobility and intelligence to realize a flexible and effective load-balancing strategy. The strategy assigns the load-balancing work done by *OM* to the custom-built *MA* and *SA*, which decreases the work of *OM* and reduces the possibility that *OM* is the bottleneck greatly.

3.2 The Influence of the Definition of Load Index

Compared with other methods of definition, the load index from the formula (2) is an objective mode, which can reflect the load state of host and instance synthetically. The above conclusion can be drawn from the following forms.

(1) The load state of the host and instance including light load and heavy load is considered. The situation considering light load of instance neglecting heavy load when request is distributed is avoided.

For example, the length of the request queue of the host 1 ($Host_1$, Max_laod_1=30) increases from 13 to 15. And the length of the request queue of some instance i ($Ins\_Max\_L_i$=10, Ins_A_i=8) increases form 6 to 8. That is, it gets to the death domain. The length of the request queue of the host 2 ($Host_2$, Max_laod_1=30) increases from 15 to 17. And the length of the request queue of some instance j ($Ins\_Max\_L_j$=10, Ins_A_j=8) increases form 4 to 6. This instance is light load. The index of the instances loaded on the host is as follows.

HOST1: $Load\_Index_1 = 0.8 \times (30-15)/30 + 0.2 \times (15-13)/15 \approx 0.427$

               $Ins\_Index_1 = 0.8 \times (10-8)/10 + 0.2 \times (8-6)/8 = 0.21$

               $Ins\_Load\_Index_1 = 0.55 \times 0.427 + 0.45 \times 0.21 \approx 0.33$

HOST2: $Load\_Index_2 = 0.8 \times (30-17)/30 + 0.2 \times (17-15)/17 \approx 0.37$

               $Ins\_Index_2 = 0.8 \times (10-6)/10 + 0.2 \times (6-4)/6 \approx 0.227$

               $Ins\_Load\_Index_2 = 0.55 \times 0.37 + 0.45 \times 0.227 \approx 0.3$

The above formulas show $Ins\_Load\_Index_2 < Ins\_Load\_Index_1$. That is, though the load of $HOST_1$ is lighter than that of $HOST_2$, the request can't be sent to it, since the heavy load of the service object of $Host_1$. The result is our goal.

(2) The mode has intelligence, which analyzes the possible tendency of the load of host and instance and including gradual aggravation and gradual alleviation.

For example, the state of two hosts is light load and the lengths of their request queues are both 5. However, the length of host 1($Host_1$) reduces from 4 to 5 and that of host 2($Host_2$) increases from 3 to 5. Their thresholds of the load are both 10. Their load index is below from definition 5.

$$Load\_Index_1 = 0.8 \times (10-5)/10 + 0.2 \times (5-7)/7 \approx 0.34$$
$$Load\_Index_2 = 0.8 \times (10-5)/10 + 0.2 \times (5-3)/5 = 0.48$$

Though the queues of the two hosts have the same length, the length of the request queue of $HOST_1$ is shortened, which shows the tendency of the load is lightened. On the contrary, the load of $HOST_2$ is aggravated. So the new request will send to $HOST_1$, which is consistent with the result of calculation.

(3) The definitions of death domain, threshold and the critical point of light load not only are helpful to the description and analysis of the quantification of the load-balancing model, but also make the monitoring for the load change more sensitive and the control more easy.

3.3 Strategy of Active Load-Balancing

The strategy of active load-balancing has several merits. First, the exchange of load information isn't needed. Second, the nodes with light load, which reduce the burden of administrator and avoid the situation in which administrator becomes the bottleneck, do most of the work of load-balancing. Third, the disposal to the request of client can be parallelized, which significantly improves the average response speed of the system.

4 Conclusion

This paper proposes a 3-tier management framework of distributed redundant system associating with the self-designed distributed database server system, introduces an active load-balancing idea into the system studying the objective description and definition of load index, and establishes a load-balancing model based on mobile agent. The model has lots of advantages such as low cost, good intelligence, high efficiency, and objective and exact description of the load index etc.

References

1. Lei Yu, Zongkai Lin, Yuchai Guo, Shouxun Lin: Load-balancing and Fault-Tolerant Services in Multi-server System. Journal of System Simulation, Vol.13. (2001)325-328.
2. Junfeng Tian, Fengxian Wang: A Queue Mode of the Distributed Database System Based on the C/S Mode. Computer Engineering & Science, Vol.24. (2002)88-91.

3. Fang Qian, Peng Zou, Yu Chen, Jie Hung: A Redundant Server Mode Based on Distributed Objects. Journal of Computer Research & Development, Vol.36. (1999)1392–1393.
4. Fuxing Wang, Krithi Ramamritham: Determining Redundancy Levels for Fault Tolerant Real-time Systems. IEEE Trans. on Computers, (1995)292–301.
5. Huaping Chen, Yongchang Ji, Guoliang Chen: A Universal Mode of Distributed Dynamic Load-balancing. Journal of Software, Vol.44. (1998)25–29.
6. Yong Wang: Obtaining Information Based on Push Technology. Journal of the China Society for Scientific and Technical Information, Vol.19. (2000)363–368.

Fuzzy Output Tracking Control and Its Application to Guidance Control for Lunar Gravity-Turn

Pingyuan Cui[1], Junwei Sun[1], and Fengqiu Liu[2]

[1] Deep Space Exploration Research Center. Harbin Institute of Technology,
Harbin 150001, China
cui@astro.hit.edu.cn

[2] Department of Mathematics of Harbin University of Science and Technology,
Harbin 150018, China
liufengqiu2004@126.com

Abstract. A fuzzy observer-based mixed Parallel Distributed Compensation (PDC) fuzzy controller is utilized to generate guidance laws for lunar gravity-turn descent. First, the Takagi-Sugeno fuzzy model is employed to approximate the probe system. Next, based on the fuzzy model, a fuzzy observer-based mixed PDC fuzzy controller is discussed in accordance with the definition of stability in the sense of Lyapunov. Robust stability and disturbance rejection technique are also proposed in the following design of guidance control.

1 Introduction

The gravity-turn guidance descent, which has attracted a great deal of attention in recent years, is successfully applied to soft landing on the lunar surface and Martian surface [1, 2]. The linearization method is developed and a closed-loop guidance law can be realized. But the stability of guidance law is ignored [1]. The feedback linearization method is utilized to generate guidance laws to track desired height and velocity profiles respectively for lunar gravity-turn descent. The Lyapunov stability of the two following control systems is demonstrated in use of related theory of differential geometry [2]. However, robust stability and disturbance rejection are lacking.

In this paper, a fuzzy observe-based mixed PDC fuzzy controller simultaneously tracks the desired height, velocity, and local vertical for lunar gravity-turn descent. Moreover, the approximation error between Takagi-Sugeno fuzzy model and the probe system is considered. Disturbance rejection technique overrides the effect of the approximation error in fuzzy approximation procedure. A tracking guidance law design method, founded on fuzzy control, for the probe system is represented, which can guarantee control stability and robust stability based on the approximation error. The conclusions above can be solved efficiently by Linear Matrix Inequality(LMI).

The paper is organized as follows. The problem formulation is presented in Section 2. Section 3 discussed the guidance laws design and stability analysis.

Simulation is studied through guidance control of landing on the lunar surface in Section 4. Finally, the conclusions are drawn in Section 5.

2 Present the Problem

Consider the probe system of guidance control for lunar gravity-turn descent [2]

$$\dot{x}_1 = G\cos x_2 - Gu$$
$$\dot{x}_2 = -\frac{1}{x_1 + \tau} G\sin x_2 \qquad (*)$$
$$\dot{x}_3 = -x_1 \cos x_2$$
$$y = x$$

where $x = [x_1, x_2, x_3]^T$, x_1 denotes velocity, $x_2 (0 \leq x_2 < \pi/2)$ is the local vertical , x_3 is the height. $G = 1.63 m/s^2$ is the gravity constant on the lunar surface. u denotes the control input.

By define $z_1 = x_2$, $z_2 = \dfrac{1}{x_1 + \tau}$, $z_3 = \sin x_2$ and $z_4 = \cos x_2$. We obtain the Takagi-Sugeno fuzzy rules as follows:

IF z_1 is M_{i1} and z_2 is M_{i2} and z_3 is M_{i3} and z_4 is M_{i4}
THEN $\dot{x} = A_l x + Bu \qquad (l = 1, 2, \cdots, 16)$.

Here A_l and B are constant matrices which can be obtained. $M_{ij} (j = 1, 2, 3, 4; i = 1, 2, 3, 4)$ are membership functions [5].

In the next section, a tracking guidance law design method consisted of fuzzy observer-based mixed PDC fuzzy controller, for the probe system is presented. Stability, robust stability and disturbance rejection are discussed in detail.

3 Guidance Laws Design and Stability Analysis

3.1 Design of Augmented Takagi-Sugeno System

Consider a nonlinear system

$$\dot{x} = f(x) + g(x)u \qquad (1)$$
$$y = h(x) \qquad (2)$$

where $x(t) = [x_1(t), x_2(t), \cdots, x_n(t)]^T \in R^{n \times 1}$ denotes the state vector, $u(t) = [u_1(t), u_2(t), \cdots, u_n(t)]^T \in R^{m \times 1}$ denotes the control input, $f(x), g(x)$ and $h(x)$ are smooth functions, and $f(0) = 0$, $y(t) \in R^{p \times 1}$ is output of the system.

Our purpose is to design the output tracking controller such that $y(t) - \hat{y}(t) \to 0$ as $t \to \infty$, where $y(t)$ is output of the system and $\hat{y}(t)$ is objective output. As $y = h(x)$ is smooth function, if we design a state feedback controller and an observer, we always can construct a stabilizing output feedback controller.

According to (1) and (2), select the Takagi-Sugeno fuzzy rules as follows:

IF $z_1(t)$ is M_{i1} and $z_2(t)$ is M_{i2} and $\cdots$ and $z_r(t)$ is M_{ir}
THEN $\dot{x}(t) = A_i x(t) + B_i u(t)$
$$y(t) = C_i x(t) \qquad i = 1, 2, \cdots, l.$$

where M_{ij} are fuzzy sets, $A_i \in R^{n \times n}, B_i \in R^{n \times m}, C_i \in R^{p \times n}$ are constant matrices, l is the number of fuzzy rules, $z_1(t), \cdots, z_r(t)$ are premise variables. We set $z(t) = [z_1(t), \cdots, z_r(t)]$ and assume $z(t)$ is a given function. Then the state equations and the output are defined as follows:

$$\dot{x}(t) = \sum_{i=1}^{l} h_i(z(t))(A_i x(t) + B_i u(t)) \qquad (3)$$

$$y(t) = \sum_{i=1}^{l} h_i(z(t)) C_i x(t) \qquad (4)$$

where $\mu_k(z(t)) = \Pi_{j=1}^{r} M_{kj}(z_j(t))$, $h_i(z(t)) = \dfrac{\mu_k(z(t))}{\sum_{i=k}^{l} \mu_k(z(t))}$, $h_i(z(t)) \geq 0$ ($i = 1, 2, \cdots, l$) and $\sum_{i=1}^{l} h_i(z(t)) = 1$. System (1) and (2) can be rearranged as the following equivalent system:

$$\dot{x}(t) = \sum_{i=1}^{l} h_i(z(t))(A_i x(t) + B_i u(t)) + \Delta_x(t) \qquad (3')$$

$$y(t) = \sum_{i=1}^{l} h_i(z(t)) C_i x(t) + \Delta_y(t) \qquad (4')$$

where $\Delta_x(t) = f(x) + g(x)u - \sum_{i=1}^{l} h_i(z(t))(A_i x(t) + B_i u(t))$, $\Delta_y(t) = h(x) - \sum_{i=1}^{l} h_i(z(t)) C_i x(t)$. Assume that there exist $\alpha > 0$ and $\beta > 0$ such that

$$\Delta_x^T \Delta_x \leq \alpha^2 x^T x, \quad \Delta_y^T \Delta_y \leq \beta^2 x^T x \qquad (5)$$

Fuzzy observers are required to satisfy $e(t) = x(t) - \hat{x}(t) \to 0$ ($t \to \infty$), $\hat{x}(t)$ denotes the state vector estimated by a fuzzy observer, and $e(t)$ is error. This condition guarantees that the steady-state error $e(t)$ converges to 0. As in the case of controller design, the PDC concept is employed to arrive at the following fuzzy observer structure.

The fuzzy observer is represented as follows [5]:

$$\dot{\hat{x}}(t) = \sum_{i=1}^{l} h_i(z(t))[A_i \hat{x}(t) + B_i u(t) + L_i(y - \hat{y})] \qquad (6)$$

$$\hat{y}(t) = \sum_{i=1}^{l} h_i(z(t)) C_i \hat{x}(t) \qquad (7)$$

The designed fuzzy controller shares the same fuzzy sets with (3) and (4) in the premise parts. The PDC fuzzy controller is given as follows:

$$u(t) = \sum_{i=1}^{l} h_i(z(t)) F_i \hat{x}(t) \tag{8}$$

According to (3'),(4'),(6),(7), and (8), we have

$$\dot{x}(t) = \sum_{ij} h_{ij}(z(t)) \{(A_i + B_i F_j) x(t) - B_i F_j e(t)\} + \Delta_x(t) \tag{9}$$

$$\dot{e}(t) = \sum_{ij} h_{ij}(z(t))(A_i - L_i C_j) e(t) + \Delta_y(t) \tag{10}$$

where $\sum_{ij} h_{ij}(z(t)) = \sum_{i=1}^{l} \sum_{j=1}^{l} h_i(z(t)) h_j(z(t))$ and $X(t) = \begin{pmatrix} x(t) \\ e(t) \end{pmatrix}$, $\Delta_X = \begin{pmatrix} \Delta_x(t) \\ 0 \end{pmatrix}$, $\Delta_Y = \begin{pmatrix} 0 \\ \Delta_y(t) \end{pmatrix}$. Therefore, the augmented system including PDC fuzzy controller and observer are represented as follows:

$$\dot{X}(t) = \sum_{ij} h_{ij}(z(t)) S_{ij} X(t) + \Delta_X + \Delta_Y \tag{11}$$

where

$$S_{ij} = \begin{pmatrix} A_i + B_i F_j & -B_i F_j \\ 0 & A_i - L_i C_j \end{pmatrix} \tag{12}$$

3.2 Stability Analysis

In this subsection, we discuss the stability of the augmented system (11).

Theorem 1. *Suppose that there exists a common positive definite matrix P such that*

$$S_{ij}^T P + P S_{ij} + (\alpha^2 + \beta^2) I + 2PP < 0, \quad i,j = 1, 2, \cdots, l,$$

in which I is the identity matrix of appropriate dimension. Then the augmented system (11) is globally asymptotically stable.

Proof. Consider a candidate of Lyapunov function $V(X(t)) = X^T(t) P X(t)$, where $P > 0$. The time of derivative of $V(X(t))$ is

$$\dot{V}(X(t)) = \dot{X}^T(t) P X(t) + X^T(t) P \dot{X}(t) \tag{13}$$

By (11) and (13), we obtain

$$\dot{V}(X(t)) = \sum_{ij} h_{ij}(z(t)) X^T(t) [S_{ij}^T P + P S_{ij}] X(t)$$
$$+ X(t) P \Delta_X + \Delta_X^T P X(t) + \Delta_Y^T P X(t) + X(t) P \Delta_Y \tag{14}$$

and

$$\Delta = \Delta_X^T PX(t) + X(t)P\Delta_X + \Delta_Y^T PX(t) + X(t)P\Delta_Y$$
$$= -[\Delta_X - PX(t)]^T[\Delta_X - PX(t)] - [\Delta_Y - PX(t)]^T[\Delta_Y - PX(t)] + \Delta_X^T \Delta_X + \Delta_Y^T \Delta_Y + 2X^T(t)PPX(t)$$
$$\leq \Delta_X^T \Delta_X + \Delta_Y^T \Delta_Y + 2X^T(t)PPX(t) \qquad (15)$$

Using (15) in (14), we have
$$\dot{V}(X(t)) \leq \sum_{ij} h_{ij}(z(t))X^T(t)[S_{ij}^T P + PS_{ij} + (\alpha^2 + \beta^2)I + 2PP]X(t) \qquad \square$$

Particularly $\Delta_x = 0, \Delta_y = 0$, we obtain the following corollary:

Corollary 1. *If there exists a common positive definite matrix* $P = \begin{pmatrix} P_1 & 0 \\ 0 & P_2 \end{pmatrix}$ *such that* $\begin{bmatrix} \Phi_{ij} & \Psi_{ij} \\ \Psi_{ij}^T & \Upsilon_{ij} \end{bmatrix} < 0$, $(i,j = 1,2,\cdots,l)$. *Here,* $\Phi_{ij} = A_i R + R A_i^T + B_i M_j + M_j^T B_i^T$, $\Upsilon_{ij} = P_2 A_i + A_i^T P_2 - Q_i C_j - C_j^T Q_i^T$, $\Psi_{ij} = -B_i F_j - F_j^T B_i^T$, $R = P_1^{-1}$, $M_j = F_j R$, $Q_i = P_2 L_i$. *Then the augmented system (11) is globally asymptotically stable.*

3.3 Robust Stability

Robust stability for the uncertain fuzzy model of (1) and (2) is considered in this subsection. Suppose that there is no uncertainty in (2).

$$\dot{x}(t) = \sum_{i=1}^{l} h_i(z(t))[(A_i + \Delta A_i)x(t) + (B_i + \Delta B_i)u(t)] \qquad (16)$$

where $\Delta A_i, \Delta B_i$ are time-varying matrices with appropriate dimension, which represent parametric uncertainties in (16). As usual, we assume

$$[\Delta A_i, \ \Delta B_i] = D_i G_i(t)[E_{1i}, \ E_{2i}] \quad (i = 1,2,\cdots,l) \qquad (17)$$

and $G_i(t) : G_i^T(t)G_i(t) \leq I$, and denote

$$A_i + \Delta A_i = \overline{A}_i, \ B_i + \Delta B_i = \overline{B}_i. \qquad (18)$$

From (16) and (18), we obtain

$$\dot{x}(t) = \sum_{i=1}^{l} h_i(z(t))(\overline{A}_i x(t) + \overline{B}_i u(t)) \qquad (19)$$

Therefore, the augmented system (11) are represented as follows:

$$\dot{X}(t) = \sum_{ij} h_{ij}(z(t))\overline{S}_{ij} X(t) + \Delta_X + \Delta_Y \qquad (20')$$

where Δ_X and Δ_Y are the same as in (9) and

$$\overline{S}_{ij} = \begin{bmatrix} A_i + \overline{B}_i F_j & -\overline{B}_i F_j \\ 0 & A_i - L_i C_j \end{bmatrix} \quad (i,j = 1, 2, \cdots, l) \tag{20}$$

Lemma 1. *[3] Given constant matrices D and E, and a symmetric constant matrix S of appropriate dimension, the following inequality holds:*

$$S + DGE + E^T G^T D^T < 0$$

where G satisfies $G^T G \leq R$, if and only if for some $\varepsilon > 0$

$$S + \begin{bmatrix} \epsilon^{-1} E^T & \epsilon D \end{bmatrix} \begin{bmatrix} R & 0 \\ 0 & I \end{bmatrix} \begin{bmatrix} \epsilon^{-1} E \\ \epsilon D^T \end{bmatrix} < 0 \tag{21}$$

Theorem 2. *Suppose that there exist a common positive definite matrix P, F_j, L_i, and $\epsilon_{ij} > 0$ $(i,j = 1, 2, \cdots, l)$ such that*

$$\begin{bmatrix} \overline{S}_{ij}^T P + P \overline{S}_{ij} + (\alpha^2 + \beta^2) I + 2PP & \mathbf{E}_{ij}^T & PD_i \\ \mathbf{E}_{ij} & -\epsilon_{ij} I & 0 \\ D_i^T P & 0 & -\epsilon_{ij}^{-1} I \end{bmatrix} < 0$$

in which I is the identity matrix of appropriate dimension. And

$$\mathbf{E}_{ij} = \begin{bmatrix} E_{1i} + E_{2i} F_j & -E_{2i} F_j \\ 0 & E_{1i} \end{bmatrix}.$$

Then the augmented system described by (20') is globally asymptotically stable.

Proof. Consider a candidate of Lyapunov function $V(X(t)) = X^T(t) P X(t)$, where $P > 0$. From (14) and (15), we obtain

$$\dot{V}(X(t)) = \dot{X}^T(t) P X(t) + X^T(t) P \dot{X}(t)$$
$$\leq \sum_{ij} h_{ij}(z(t)) X^T(t) [(\overline{S}_{ij}^T P + P \overline{S}_{ij}) + (\alpha^2 + \beta^2) I + 2PP] X(t) \tag{22}$$

By (17),(18), and (20), we have

$$P \overline{S}_{ij} = P \begin{pmatrix} A_i + \Delta A_i + (B_i + \Delta B_i) F_j & -(B_i + \Delta B_i) F_j \\ 0 & A_i + \Delta A_i - L_i C_j \end{pmatrix}$$
$$= PS_{ij} + PD_i G_i(t) \begin{pmatrix} E_{1i} + E_{2i} F_j & -E_{2i} F_j \\ 0 & E_{1i} \end{pmatrix}$$

Therefore,

$$\dot{V}(X(t)) \leq \sum_{ij} h_{ij}(z(t)) X^T(t) \{ [S_{ij}^T P + PS_{ij} + (\alpha^2 + \beta^2) I$$
$$+ 2PP] + [\mathbf{E}_{ij}^T G_i^T(t)(PD_i)^T + (PD_i) G_i(t) \mathbf{E}_{ij}] \} X(t)$$

As $\dot{V}(X(t))$ is negative definite, the following matrix inequality satisfy:

$$S_{ij}^T P + PS_{ij} + (\alpha^2 + \beta^2)I + 2PP + \mathbf{E}_{ij}^T G_i^T(t)(PD_i)^T + (PD_i)G_i(t)\mathbf{E}_{ij} < 0. \tag{23}$$

By Lemma 1, the linear matrix inequality (23) for all $G_i(t)$ satisfying $G_i^T(t)G_i(t) \leq I$, if and only if there exist constant $\epsilon_{ij}^{1/2} > 0$ $(i,j = 1, 2, \cdots, l)$ such that

$$S_{ij}^T P + PS_{ij} + (\alpha^2 + \beta^2)I + 2PP + \begin{bmatrix} \epsilon_{ij}^{-1/2}\mathbf{E}_{ij}^T & \epsilon_{ij}^{1/2}PD_i \end{bmatrix} \begin{bmatrix} I & 0 \\ 0 & I \end{bmatrix} \begin{bmatrix} \epsilon_{ij}^{-1/2}\mathbf{E}_{ij} \\ \epsilon_{ij}^{1/2}D_i^T P \end{bmatrix}$$
$$= S_{ij}^T P + PS_{ij} + (\alpha^2 + \beta^2)I + 2PP + \begin{bmatrix} \mathbf{E}_{ij}^T & PD_i \end{bmatrix} \begin{bmatrix} \epsilon_{ij}^{-1}I & 0 \\ 0 & \epsilon_{ij}I \end{bmatrix} \begin{bmatrix} \mathbf{E}_{ij} \\ (PD_i)^T \end{bmatrix} < 0 \tag{24}$$

Applying Schur complement to (24),

$$\begin{bmatrix} S_{ij}^T P + PS_{ij} + (\alpha^2 + \beta^2)I + 2PP & \mathbf{E}_{ij}^T & PD_i \\ \mathbf{E}_{ij} & -\epsilon_{ij}I & 0 \\ D_i^T P & 0 & -\epsilon_{ij}^{-1}I \end{bmatrix} < 0 \qquad \square$$

3.4 Disturbance Rejection

Suppose $\triangle_y = 0$ and regard $\triangle_x$ as disturbance of (1). From (11) we have

$$\dot{X}(t) = \sum_{ij} h_{ij}(z(t))S_{ij}X(t) + \Delta_X \tag{25}$$

Still suppose (5), that is to say $\sup_{\Delta_x \neq 0} \frac{\|x(t)\|_2}{\|\Delta_x\|_2} \leq \frac{1}{\alpha}$. Hence, the disturbance rejection can be converted into the minimizing problem. By solving the minimizing problem, we obtain stabilizing PDC fuzzy controller and observer and consequently realize output tracking control.

Theorem 3. *If the following LMI (26) minimizing $1/\alpha^2$ are feasible,*

$$\min_{X(t), P, F_i, L_i} 1/\alpha$$
$$\text{subject to} \quad P > 0,$$

$$\begin{bmatrix} S_{ij}^T P + PS_{ij} + I & 0 \\ 0 & 1/\alpha^2 \end{bmatrix} < 0 \qquad i,j = 1, 2, \cdots, l. \tag{26}$$

the stable system (25) and maximal range of disturbance α are obtained.

Proof. Consider a candidate of Lyapunov function $V(X(t)) = X^T(t)PX(t)$, where $P > 0$, $\alpha > 0$. For any t and (25), we have

$$\dot{V}(X(t)) + X^T(t)X(t) - 1/\alpha^2 \Delta_X^T \Delta_X \leq 0 \tag{27}$$

Assume initial condition $X(0) = 0$ and integrate (27) from 0 to T, we get

$$V(X(T)) + \int_0^T \{(X^T(t)X(t)) - 1/\alpha^2 \Delta_X^T \Delta_X\} dt \leq 0 \tag{28}$$

Since $V(X(T)) > 0$, then $\int_0^T \{(X^T(t)X(t)) - 1/\alpha^2 \Delta_X^T \Delta_X\} dt \leq 0$, this implies $\sup_{\Delta_x \neq 0} \dfrac{\|x(t)\|_2}{\|\Delta_x\|_2} \leq \dfrac{1}{\alpha}$. Therefore, the stable system (25) and maximal range of disturbance α is obtained if (26) holds. Because of (20'), (27), and (5), we also have

$$\dot{X}^T(t)PX(t) + X^T(t)P\dot{X}(t) + X^T(t)X(t) - 1/\alpha^2 \Delta_X^T \Delta_X$$
$$= \sum_{ij} h_{ij}(z(t))(X^T(t) \ \Delta_X^T) \begin{pmatrix} S_{ij}^T P + PS_{ij} + I & 0 \\ 0 & -1/\alpha^2 \end{pmatrix} \begin{pmatrix} X(t) \\ \Delta_X \end{pmatrix}$$

Hence, the conclusion is obtained. □

Remark 1. Stabilizing state feedback PDC fuzzy controller u and coefficients L_i of observer are obtained, which results in the obtaining of the guidance law.

4 Simulation

Stability: Design stabilizing state feedback PDC fuzzy controller u and coefficients L_i of observer via subsection 3.1. Consequently lunar soft landing can be realized under the gravity-turn guidance law consisting of fuzzy observer-based mixed PDC fuzzy controller. Figure 1 depicts the simulation results. Find positive definite $P = diag(P_1, P_2)$ as follows:

$$P_1 = \begin{bmatrix} 0.1832 & 0.0067 & -0.0967 \\ 0.0067 & 0.7041 & -0.0090 \\ -0.0967 & -0.0090 & 0.4522 \end{bmatrix}, \quad P_2 = \begin{bmatrix} 1.1498 & -0.0000 & 0.0000 \\ -0.0000 & 1.1498 & 0.0000 \\ 0.0000 & 0.0000 & 1.1498 \end{bmatrix}$$

Robust stability: Where $G(t) = (0, 0, \cos(t))^T$, $D_l = diag(0.1, 0.1, 0.1)$, $E_{1l} = diag(0.11, 0.11, 0.11)$, $E_{2l} = 0$. Obviously, $G^T(t)G(t) \leq I$. By using Theorem 2, we obtain F_l, L_l, and uniform $\varepsilon = 0.2156$.

Disturbance rejection: According to the Theorem 3, we obtain the maximal range of disturbance $\max \alpha = 9.6696$, where $\Delta_x = (1, 0.1, -0.1)^T$. Then the stabilizing PDC fuzzy controller and observer can be obtained to arrive at our objective of tracking the desired height, velocity, and local vertical for lunar gravity-turn descent. Figure2 depicts the disturbance rejection simulation results.

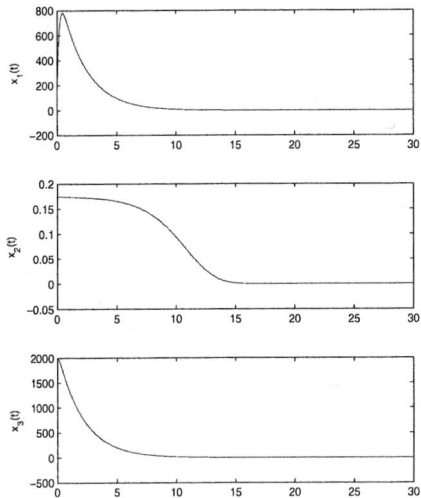

Fig. 1. Stability analysis simulation results

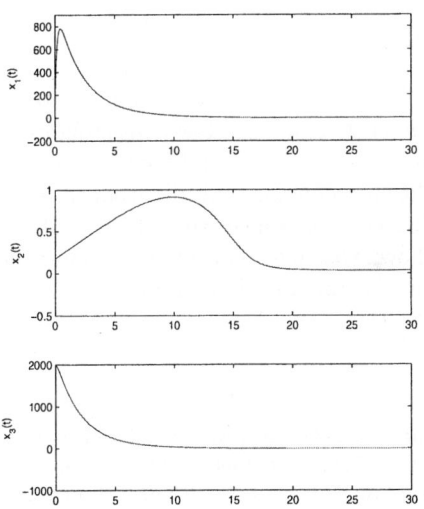

Fig. 2. Disturbance rejection simulation results

An example of the following guidance law is studied. The expected trajectory of landing on the lunar surface is

$$x_1 = \sqrt{2(u^* - 1)Gx_3} \qquad (29)$$

where $u^* = 1.45$, initial value $x_1(0) = 20$m/s, $x_2(0) = \pi/18$, and $x_3(0) = 2$km. Using $(*)$ in (29), the system (29) can track the trajectory of landing described by $(*)$. The simulation results are depicted in Figure 3.

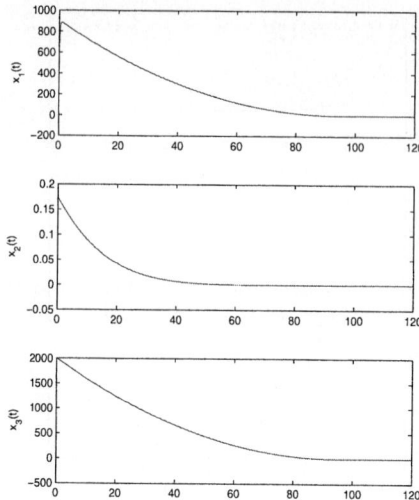

Fig. 3. An example simulation results

5 Conclusion

This paper introduces fuzzy output tracking control to the guidance control for lunar gravity-turn descent. Guidance law consisting of fuzzy observer-based mixed PDC fuzzy controller is discussed based on the Takagi-Sugeno fuzzy model. Robust stabilization technique and disturbance rejection are considered in the design of tracking control respectively. The results can be obtained by solving the LMI. It is shown that desired profiles tracking and lunar soft landing can be realized based on the guidance laws above.

References

1. Mcinnes C R. Nonlinear Transformation Methods for Gravity-turn Descent. Journal of Guidance, Control, and Dynamics, 1996,19(1):247-248.
2. Wang Dayi, Li Tieshou, Yan Hui, and Ma Xingrui. Guidandce Control for Lunar Gravity-Turn Descent. Chinese Space Science and Technology. 2000,10,17–29.
3. Ho. Jae. Lee, Jin. Bae. Park, and Guanrong Chen. Robust Fuzzy Control of Nonlinear Systems with Parametric Uncertainties. IEEE Transactions On Fuzzy Systems.2001, 9(2):369–379.
4. H. D.Tuan, P. Apkarian, T. Narikiyo, and Y. Yamamoto. Parameterized Linear Matrix Inequality Techniques in Fuzzy Control System Design. IEEE Transactions On Fuzzy Systems. 2001,9(2):324–332.
5. Kazuo Tanaka and Hua O. Wang. Fuzzy Control Systems Design and Analysis A Wiley-Interscience Publication 2001.

Motion Planning for Climbing Robot Based on Hybrid Navigation

Yong Jiang [1,2], Hongguang Wang [1,2], Lijin Fang [1], and Mingyang Zhao [1]

[1] Robotics Laboratory, Shenyang Institute of Automation, Chinese Academy of Sciences, 110016 Shenyang, China
[2] Graduate School of the Chinese Academy of Sciences, 100039 Beijing, China
jiangyong@sia.cn, hgwang@sia.cn, ljfang@sia.cn, myzhao@sia.cn

Abstract. In this paper, a motion planning method for autonomous control of a bipedal climbing robot based on hybrid navigation is presented. The algorithm of hybrid navigation blends the optimality of the trajectory planning with the capabilities in expressing knowledge and learning of the fuzzy neural network. The real task environment of the climbing robot is both known and dynamic. Therefore the trajectory planning is used to search roughly for the optimal trajectories which will lead towards the goal according to prior data. Meanwhile, by the process of the multi-sensor data fusion, the fuzzy neural network is employed in dealing efficiently with the uncertain and dynamic situations. The properties of motion planning based on the hybrid navigation are verified by the computer simulations and experiments.

1 Introduction

An important issue for an autonomous, intelligent robot system is to plan motions automatically without collision in an unknown and changing environment. The artificial potential field (APF) method provides simple and effective motion planning to solve this problem. However, the APF has a major disadvantage in that a local minimum of the potential function can trap a robot before it reaches its goal. Improvements in the APF method, such as the super quadratic potential [1], can avoid the local minimum but the calculation cost is increased because of the computational complexity. Also, the solutions employing different search techniques, including best-first [2] and constrained-motion [3], are usually unreliable for on-line purpose.

In real-time world systems, the sensor-based motion control becomes essential to deal with model uncertainties and unexpected obstacles [4]. In addition, the fuzzy neural networks (FNN), with the capabilities of expressing knowledge and learning, are widely applied to realize intelligent control in many areas [5], [6].

In this paper, a motion planning method based on hybrid navigation, which combines FNN and trajectory planning, is presented and applied to a bipedal climbing robot. The organization of the paper is as follows. Section 2 briefly describes the mechanical structure and the controller of the climbing robot. Section 3 develops a model of multi-sensor data fusion used practically in the control system. Section 4 presents the design of the five-layer FNN. Section 5 proposes a motion planning method based on hybrid navigation and analyses the results of simulations and experiments on the climbing robot. Finally, section 6 outlines the main conclusions of the work.

2 Bipedal Climbing Robot

2.1 Mechanical Structure

The mechanical structure of the climbing robot is designed as a bipedal robot with an under-actuated mechanism [7], which minimizes the number of motors without sacrificing mobility. As shown in Figure 1, motors 1 and 3 independently drive joints 1 and 5, respectively; thereby adjusting the tilt angle of the suction feet 1and 2 so that the robot can grip the surface firmly. Motor 2 is responsible for controlling joints 2, 3 and 4, separately. Joints 2 and 4 are revolute joints providing steering capability of the feet relative to the legs. Joint 3 represents the prismatic motion of the legs that allows the robot to expand and contract its legs. The under-actuated mechanism enables the robot to drive five joints using only three motors, thus reducing both the weight and the power consumption of the robot, achieving a good balance between compactness and maneuverability.

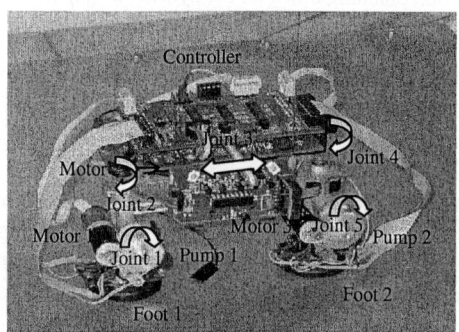

Fig. 1. Bipedal climbing robot

2.2 Controller

The controller of the bipedal climbing robot is composed of a CPU board and a driving board. On the CPU board, a TMS320F2812 digital signal processor (DSP) from Texas Instruments Inc. is used to build an embedded control system. The control-optimized peripherals such as PWM outputs, built-in quadrature encoder pulse (QEP) circuitry, capture units, A/D converter and digital I/O, make this DSP chip a desirable device to minimize the size, weight and battery capacity of the climbing robot. On the driving board, three quadruple half-H chips SN754410 are targeted to drive the servo motors and the pump motors.

3 Multi-sensor Data Fusion

Multi-sensor data fusion refers to the acquisition, processing and synergistic combination of information gathered by various knowledge sources and sensors to provide a better understanding of the phenomenon under consideration.

When moving in a dynamic and uncertain environment, the climbing robot can acquire the information of exterior and interior states for robot navigation by multiple sensors. A model of the multi-sensor data fusion is shown in Figure 2.

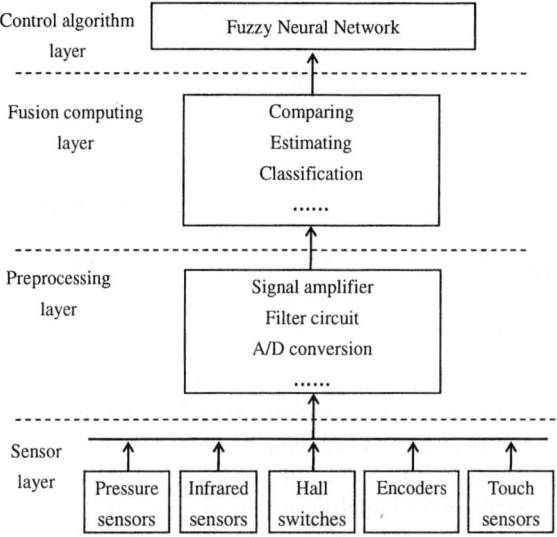

Fig. 2. Model for the data fusion process

The basic components of this model include a sensor layer, a preprocessing layer, and a fusion computing layer.

1) *Sensor layer*: The pressure sensors monitor the pressure level inside the two suction cups to ensure that the robot feet grip the object surface firmly and without leakage. The infrared sensors are used to measure the distance between the robot and the barriers. The Hall switches are installed on each leg to discriminate between different locomotion modes. The touch sensors affixed to the brim of the suction cups inspect tactile feedback. The encoders are responsible for detecting the movement position of each joint.
2) *Preprocessing layer*: The information from the sensor layer is modulated to suitable digital signals by such hardware circuits as amplifier, filter and A/D conversion, etc.
3) *Fusion computing layer*: As a core of the model, this layer includes special fusion rules. Fusion computing, such as comparing, estimating, classifying, etc, is based entirely on these rules.

4 Fuzzy Neural Network

A FNN with a five-layer structure is adopted in controlling the locomotion of the robot according to off-line learning and real-time sensors feedback.

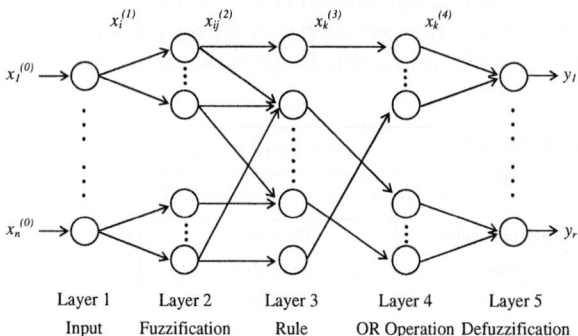

Fig. 4. Network structure of five-layered FNN

4.1 Network Structure

The proposed five-layer FNN is shown in Figure 4, which consists of input, fuzzification, rule, OR operation and defuzzification layers. It performs the multiple inputs and multiple outputs. Nodes in layer 1 are input nodes that transmit input signals directly to the next layer. Nodes in layer 2 are linguistic term nodes treated as membership functions to express the fuzzy linguistic variables. Each node in layer 3 is a rule node to represent the fuzzy rule. Each node in layer 4 represents a possible THEN part of the fuzzy rule. The nodes in layer 5 carry out the defuzzification to get crisp values for output variables.

1) Layer 1: Input layer transmits input vector $X = \left(x_1^{(0)} \quad x_2^{(0)} \quad \cdots \quad x_n^{(0)} \right)^T$ directly into the second layer. The ith node in this layer connects $x_i^{(0)}$ to $x_i^{(1)}$ ($i = 1, \cdots, n$), the ith output of layer 1. Each input variable $x_i^{(0)}$, as a fuzzy language variable, has m_i values. Let A_i^j ($j = 1, \cdots, m_i$) denote the jth language variable value of $x_i^{(0)}$.

2) Layer 2: The fuzzification layer transfers the crisp values to membership degrees through membership functions. The layer consists of the term nodes, such as NB, NM, NS, Z, PS, PM, PB, etc. The activation function in each node serves as a membership function. For each node in this layer, the input and output are represented in the form of Gaussian function (1), trapezium function (2) or Boolean function (3).

$$x_{ij}^{(2)} = e^{\frac{\left(x_i^{01} - c_{ij}\right)^2}{\sigma_{ij}^2}} \quad . \tag{1}$$

$$x_{ij}^{(2)} = \begin{cases} \dfrac{x_i^{(1)} - a}{b-a} & a \le x_i^{(1)} < b \\ 1 & b \le x_i^{(1)} \le c \\ \dfrac{d - x_i^{(1)}}{d-c} & c < x_i^{(1)} \le d \end{cases} . \tag{2}$$

$$x_{ij}^{(2)} = \begin{cases} 1 & x_i^{(1)} = x_0 \\ 0 & x_i^{(1)} \ne x_0 \end{cases} . \tag{3}$$

Here $i = 1, \cdots, n$, $j = 1, \cdots, m_i$, c_{ij} and σ_{ij} are the parameters of mean and standard deviation of the jth Gaussian membership function of $x_i^{(0)}$, respectively.

3) *Layer 3*: Each node in the rule layer represents a possible IF part of a fuzzy rule. The node in this layer performs fuzzy AND operation. The functions of the layer are

$$x_k^{(3)} = x_{1i_1}^{(2)} x_{2i_2}^{(2)} \cdots x_{ni_n}^{(2)} . \tag{4}$$

where $i_1 \in \{1, 2, \cdots, m_1\}$, $i_2 \in \{1, 2, \cdots, m_2\}$, $\cdots$, $i_n \in \{1, 2, \ldots, m_n\}$, $k = 1, \cdots, m$, $m = \prod_{i=1}^{n} m_i$. Thus, the output of node k in layer 3 is a product value of all input to this node.

4) *Layer 4*: This is the OR operation layer. Each node in it represents a possible THEN part of fuzzy rule. Fuzzy OR operation is performed. The nodes of Layers 3 and 4 are fully connected. The functions in this layer are

$$x_k^{(4)} = \dfrac{x_k^{(3)}}{\sum_{k=1}^{m} x_k^{(3)}} \qquad k = 1, \cdots, m . \tag{5}$$

5) *Layer 5*: The defuzzification layer, which performs the defuzzification of each node. The output signal can be evaluated as

$$y_l = \sum_{k=1}^{m} w_{kl} x_k^{(4)} \qquad k = 1, \cdots, m \quad l = 1, \cdots, r . \tag{6}$$

where w_{kl} is the connecting weight between the kth node in Layer 4 and the lth node in Layer 5.

4.2 Learning Parameters

All weights, except w_{kl} between Layers 4 and 5, are assigned to 1. The values c_{ij} and σ_{ij} are based on initial experiences and knowledge. The weights w_{kl} are updated to minimize the following error measure using the gradient descent learning algorithm

$$E = \frac{1}{2}\sum_{l=1}^{r}(y_{dl} - y_l)^2 . \qquad (7)$$

where y_{dl} and y_l is the desired and actual output, respectively. The updating process can be expressed as (8), where $0 < \beta \leq 1$ is the learning rate of the FNN.

$$w_{kl}(t+1) = w_{kl}(t) - \beta \frac{\partial E}{\partial w_{kl}} . \qquad (8)$$

5 Motion Planning

5.1 Hybrid Navigation

The navigation system, which has to decide at every given moment where to move next, taking into consideration all the a priori information on the environment, the sensory data and its knowledge of the current position and orientation as well as the goal position, is a vital part of the design for an autonomous robot [8], [9]. The methods for the navigation can be categorized as global if the algorithm relies mostly on a priori information or local if its decision is taken using mainly the current sensor data. Generally, a global algorithm can find optimal trajectories according to various optimality criteria. However, it is unable to deal properly with dynamic situations. Another disadvantage is the need to have detailed knowledge of the environment. On the contrary, a local algorithm is good at these challenges but can not guarantee an optimal result.

The task environment of the bipedal climbing robot, such as building, pipeline, etc, is both known and dynamic. In other words, we can obtain a priori data on the task environment, even when the uncertain and dynamic situations still exist. The solution presented here resolves this contradiction by using a hybrid navigation system composed of trajectory planning and FNN.

The composition and the functioning method of the hybrid navigation system are shown in Figure 5. The trajectory planning is used to roughly search the optimal trajectories based on a priori data. The FNN is employed in generating the movement control. According to the real-time sensor feedback, the FNN is responsible for dealing with the uncertain and dynamic situations. At the same time, the intercommunion between the trajectory planning and the FNN orients the search process.

5.2 Simulation and Experiment

In the simulations of the hybrid navigation to the bipedal climbing robot, the A^* algorithm is used for trajectory planning. The main idea of this algorithm is to try to continue the route from the intermediary state which seems to be the most favorable, taking into consideration not only the cost of the progress already made but also the estimate on the cost of the remaining part of the solution. Thereby, it can find the optimal route between an initial state and a goal state.

The membership functions of input and output variables to the FNN are shown in Figure 6. The inputs include *Touch Sensors (a), Pressure Sensor (b), Distance "L" (c)* and *Step Length (d)*. The outputs include *Suction Cup (e), Step Velocity (f)* and *Move Direction "MD" (g)*.

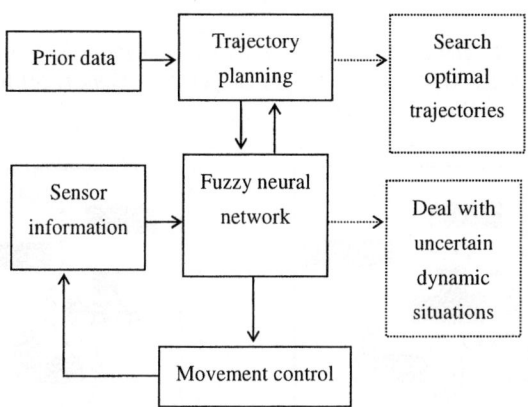

Fig. 5. Hybrid navigation system

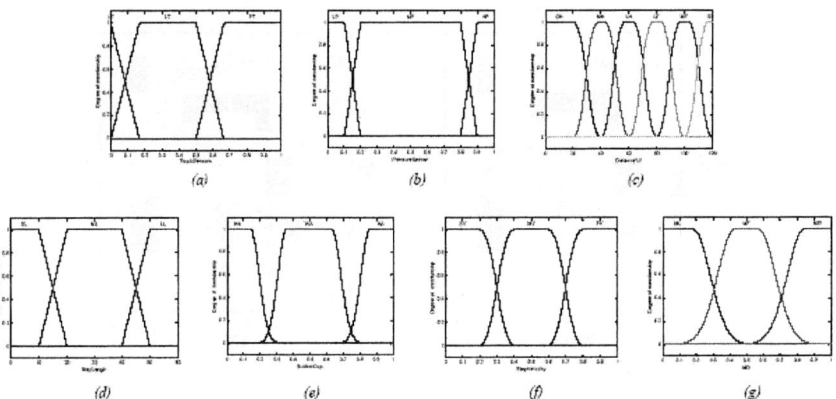

Fig. 6. Membership functions of input and output variables to FNN

The fuzzy rules are as follows.
  R_1: IF *"L" left* is GN and *"L" front* is GN THEN *"MD"* is MR.
  R_2: IF *"L" right* is GN and *"L" front* is GN THEN *"MD"* is ML.
  R_3: IF *"L" left* is MN and *"L" front* is GN THEN *"MD"* is MR.
  ......

Figure 7 presents the simulations of the FNN.

Some simulations are performed to compare the hybrid navigation with the APF algorithm, as in Figure 8.

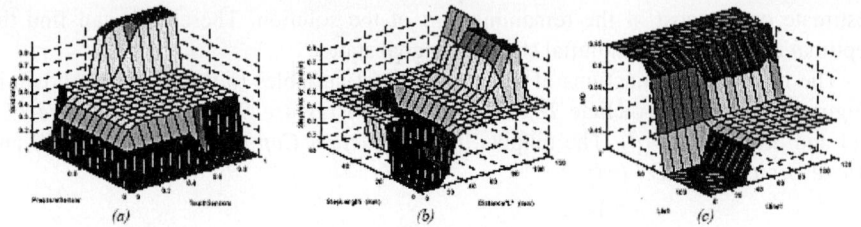

Fig. 7. Simulations of FNN *(a)* Inputs: *Touch Sensors* and *Pressure Sensor* Output: *Suction Cup (b)* Inputs: *Distance "L"* and *Step Length* Output: *Step Velocity (c)* Inputs: *"L" left* and *"L" front* Output: *Move Direction "MD"*

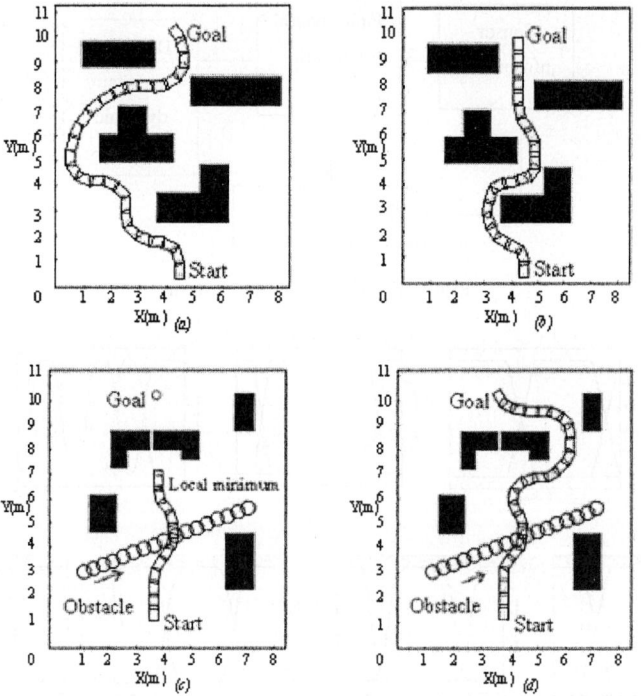

Fig. 8. Simulations of motion planning for the climbing robot *(a)* Motion planning by APF *(b)* Motion planning by hybrid navigation *(c)* Motion planning by APF *(d)* Motion planning by hybrid navigation

Figures 8*(a)* and 8*(b)* show that in the same environment without any local minimum of the potential function, the climbing robot can successfully reach the goal by either the APF algorithm or the hybrid navigation method. However, the lengths of the two routes in Figures 8*(a)* and 8*(b)* are unequal. The result by the hybrid navigation method is shorter than the one by the APF. In Figure 8*(c)*, the climbing robot is trapped by a local minimum of the potential function although it avoids the collision with a traveling obstacle after using the APF. Under the same conditions, Figure 8*(d)*

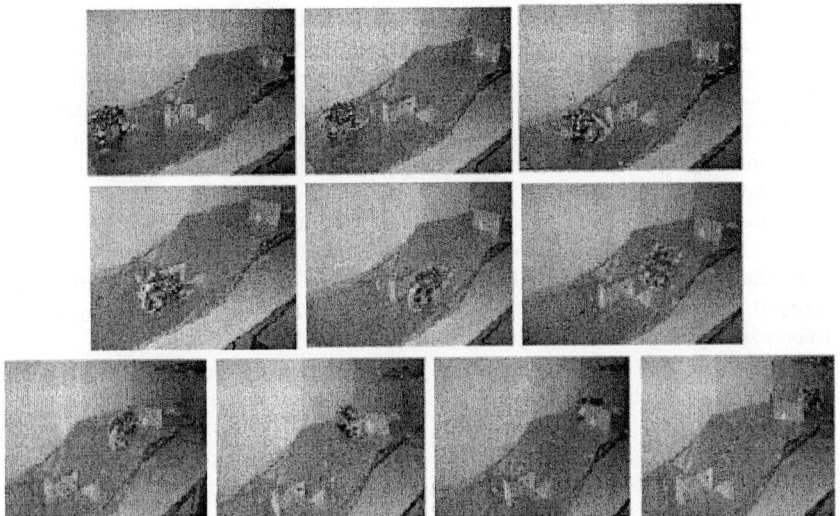

Fig. 9. Experimental result of the climbing robot

shows that the robot can not only avoid the collision with the traveling obstacle but also escape the local minimum using the hybrid navigation.

To further verify the effectiveness of the proposed method, a laboratory experiment has also been conducted to navigate the climbing robot on a special platform. There were two obstacles with a height of 100mm that the robot cannot step over in the experimental terrain. The positions of the starting point and target were inputted to the control system. Figure 9 shows the real photograph of the experimental climbing robot.

6 Conclusions

In this paper, a motion planning method based on hybrid navigation, which blends the optimality of the trajectory planning algorithm with the capabilities in expressing knowledge and learning of the FNN, is presented and applied to the autonomous navigation of the bipedal climbing robot. This navigation method not only makes good use of the prior data of the task environment, but also deals properly with uncertain and dynamic situations. Moreover, based on the multi-sensor data fusion, it is simple and efficient to solve the problem on the local minimum of the APF by this algorithm. The results of the simulations and experiments show that the hybrid navigation is valid for the real-time motion planning in both known and dynamic environments.

References

1. R. Volpe and P. K. Khosla, "Manipulator control with superquadratic artificial potential functions: Theory and experiments", IEEE Trans. Syst., Man, Cybern., vol. 20, pp. 1423-1436, Dec. 1990.
2. S. Sarkar, P. P. Chakrabarti and S. Ghose, "Learning while solving problems in best first search", IEEE Trans. Syst., Man, Cybern., vol. 28, pp. 534-541, Jul. 1998.

3. S. A. Masoud and A. A. Masoud, "Constrained motion control using vector potential fields", IEEE Trans. Syst., Man, Cybern., vol. 30, pp. 251-272, May 2000.
4. E. Freire, T. B. Filho, M. S. Filho and R. Carelli, "A New Mobile Robot Control Approach via Fusion of Control Signals", IEEE Trans. Syst., Man, Cybern., vol. 34, Feb. 2004.
5. L. H. Chen, C. H. Chiang, and J. Yuan, "New approach to adaptive control architecture based on fuzzy neural network and genetic algorithm", IEEE Int. Conf. Syst., Man, Cybern., vol. 1, pp. 347-352, 2001.
6. S. J. Huang and J. S. Lee, "A stable self-organizing fuzzy controller for robotic motion control", IEEE Trans. Ind. Electron., vol. 47, pp. 421-428, Apr. 2000.
7. J. Z. Xiao, Hans Dulimarta, N. Xi and R. L. Tummala, "Modeling and control of an under-actuated miniature crawler robot", Proc. of 2001 IEEE/RSJ Int. Conference on Intelligent Robots and Systems, IROS'01, Hawaii, USA, pp. 1546-1551, 2001.
8. C. H. Wang, T. C. Lin, T. T. Lee and H. L. Liu, "Adaptive hybrid intelligent control for uncertain nonlinear dynamical systems", IEEE Trans. Syst., Man, Cybern., vol. 32, pp. 583-597, Oct. 2002.
9. E. Zalama, J. Gomez, M. Paul and J. R. Peran, "Adaptive behavior navigation of a mobile robot", IEEE Trans. Syst., Man, Cybern., vol. 32, Jan. 2002.

Hierarchical Fuzzy Behavior-Based Control Method for Autonomous Mobile Robot Navigation

Shou-tao Li and Yuan-chun Li

Department of Control Science and Engineering, Jilin University,
Changchun 130025, China
list@jlu.edu.cn, liyc@email.jlu.edu.cn

Abstract. This paper proposes the core theoretical foundations on design of the Compound Zeno Behavior in hierarchical hybrid behaviors, including the definitions of different types of behaviors and some theorems. New hierarchical fuzzy behavior-based control architecture of an autonomous mobile robot using the information extracted from its sensors in unknown environments is presented. After that, the paper focuses on the coordination and fusion of the elementary behaviors, which are achieved by means of fuzzy reasoning scheme. Simulation results illustrate the effective performance of the control architecture.

1 Introduction

Autonomous navigation capability of a mobile robot is particularly important in unknown or unexplored environments where a priori map is unavailable. The goal of an autonomous mobile robot in an unknown environment is to navigate in real-time to a target from the start location by using the information extracted from its sensors. Behavior-based systems approach the autonomy question from the standpoint of collections of behaviors. A key issue of behavior-based control is how to efficiently coordinate or resolve conflicts and competition among different types of behaviors so as to achieve an effective performance. The wide range of possible behaviors demand that mobile robots have a behavior coordination mechanism (BCM) to provide the correct behavior in an unknown environment for any given situation.

There are two main BCMs now available; one is *Command Arbitration Mechanism* and the other is *Command Fusion Mechanism*. Arbitration Mechanism is to use multiple behaviors to generate several control suggestions, and select a more felicitous one based on the behavior's different priorities, which are designated in advance based on prior knowledge. We can get these examples from Brooks' *Subsumption Architecture*, which performs the behavior selection according to the state of the *Augmented Finite State Machines*[1]. Even though this approach is simple and effective under most situations, there is still a serious problem, which is demonstrated in [2]. *Command Fusion Mechanism* generates the overall linear velocity and angular speed control signals by fusing a set of behaviors to the robot actuators. There are several approaches, one of which allows control recommendations of different behaviors to be directly combined to form multiple control recommendations with different weights, from which a final control command is chosen[2]. Another method is hierarchical switching, in which the flexibility of fuzzy rules are used to perform the fusion operations. Fusion rules use sensor data, motivational state, or the value of the behavior outputs themselves to determine the appropriate weight for each behavior [3]. We can get several other ways to implement command fusion mechanism such as voting[4,5], superposition[6], decentralized information filter[7], fuzzy Logic[8,9], multiple objective optimization[10], and hybrid automaton [11].

The work given in this paper deals with the problem of the navigation of a mobile robot in unknown environments. This paper is organized as follows. In Section 2, we describe the control architecture based on hierarchical fuzzy behaviors. Section 3 addresses the core theoretical foundations of designing the Compound Zeno Behaviors. The designing of primitive behaviors and simulation experiment results are shown in Section 4 and 5, followed by discussions and conclusions in Section 6.

2 Hierarchical Behavior System

As we know, a behavior is a control law that satisfies a set of constraints to achieve and maintain a particular goal. Complex behaviors of the robot are generated by combining simple behaviors resulting from the interaction between the goals, the internal states and the environment. In this paper, we assume that the autonomous mobile robot does not have knowledge of the obstacles in the working environment, such as their positions, numbers, and size. In a totally unknown environment, the navigation is done completely in a reactive manner.

Figure 1 shows the hierarchical behavior system, which is composed of three kinds of hierarchical behaviors: Deterministic Behaviors, Zeno Behaviors and Compound Zeno Behaviors. As low-level behaviors, Deterministic Behaviors are achieved by special cells of the information sensor. Furthermore, Zeno Behaviors and Compound Zeno Behaviors, which are high-level behaviors, are composed of primitive Deterministic Behaviors. Hybrid Zeno Behavior System must guarantee the fulfillment of the high-level behaviors by selecting which primitive Deterministic Behavior should be activated at a given time depending on both the environment and the current goal. The contexts of applicability of certain behaviors are defined in the high control level by using a set of metarules. And the system must search for a safe path from an initial position to a final desired position. The hierarchy of the sensor-based behaviors is shown in Figure 1. For example, going to target, which is a high-level Zeno Behavior, is composed of Deterministic Behaviors such as Goto sub-goal, Go-Tangent, Follow-Wall, Follow-Corridor, Turn Left or Right corner, etc. The Deterministic Behaviors, which are in the lowest level, deal with the control of the robot motion, coupling sensors to actuators. Hybrid Zeno Behavior System is composed of several rule-based basic behaviors, which can be combined to generate a more complex observable behavior.

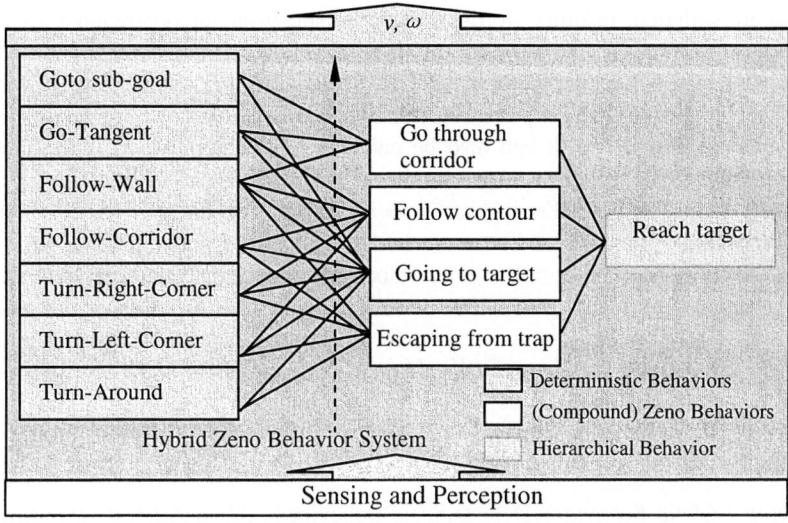

Fig. 1. Hybrid Zeno Behavior System

3 Hierarchical Behavior Theoretical Foundations

Let us consider the mobile robot located at a non-zero distance from a goal point (Goal) in a fixed Cartesian frame. Then the kinematics equations are:

$$\dot{x} = v \cos \varphi$$
$$\dot{y} = v \sin \varphi \quad (1)$$
$$\dot{\varphi} = \omega$$

Where v is the linear velocity vector and φ is measured with respect to the x-axis. The nonholonomic constraints kinematics can be written as Equation (2).

$$\dot{q} = S(q)u \quad (2)$$

with $q = \begin{bmatrix} x \\ y \\ \varphi \end{bmatrix}, u = \begin{bmatrix} v \\ \omega \end{bmatrix}$, and $S(q) = \begin{bmatrix} \cos(\varphi) & 0 \\ \sin(\varphi) & 0 \\ 0 & 1 \end{bmatrix}$.

Before explaining the design of each type of behavior, we will define the conceptual framework and give some definitions that are based on [11,12]. We assume that Euclidean spaces, R^n for $n \geq 0$, are given the Euclidean metric topology, where countable and finite sets are given the discrete topology (all subsets are open).

Definition 1 (Deterministic Behavior). A deterministic behavior is an on-line continuous controlling process which is produced by a behavior controller to act on the environment and internal state, when the environmental conditions Q_i, and internal state X_i are satisfied. In other words, a deterministic behavior is a reactive dynamic response procedure.

Consider DB_i as a convex collection $DB_i = \{Q_i, X_i, I_i, f_i, U_i, O_i\}$, where Q_i is the occurrence condition when a primitive behavior has been obtained actively by some environmental conditions. It can also be called behavior context. X_i is the internal state of the mobile robot, whose motion towards the *Goal* is governed by the combined action of both the angular velocity ω and the linear velocity v on the direction of one of the axes of frame attached to the robot. I_i is the initial condition of the mobile robot (i.e. the initial angular velocity ω, the initial linear velocity v, start point and goal point) during the finite sequence of the *i-th* intervals of the discrete transitions. And f_i is the kinematics system of a certain behavior, which input and output should satisfy, i.e. $\dot{X}_i = f_i(X_i, U_i)$. It corresponds to some fuzzy behavior controller and is assumed to be Lipschitz continuous in its second argument. U_i consists of the input of a behavior and the active condition. O_i is the output of a behavior.

Definition 2 (Zeno Behavior). Deterministic Behavior is called Zeno, if two primitive deterministic behaviors make an infinite number of discrete transitions in finite time. We can see from the definition that a zeno behavior is an emergence behavior in the system.

Definition 3 (Compound Zeno Behavior). Zeno Behavior is called compound, if more than two primitive behaviors join in the discrete transitions for infinite times in finite time. We can see from the definition that a compound zeno behavior is also an emergence behavior in the system.

Definition 4 (Hierarchical Hybrid Behavior). Hierarchical Hybrid Behavior is a behavior system network composed of a set of primitive behaviors. The activation of a primitive behavior is determined by the occurrence condition. The dynamic discrete transitions of the primitive behaviors are corresponding to the finite sequence of the hybrid behavior, which is in existence because the kinematics system of a certain primitive behavior is Lipschitz continuous. However, it is not unique because of the complex diversity of the finite sequence.

Theorem 1. Let Compound Zeno Behavior B_{CZ} be determined together by the kinematics system $f_i(X_{i(t)}, U_{i(t)})$ of certain primitive Deterministic Behaviors DB_i, and can be operated by operationality criterion in vectorial field, then B_{CZ}, which is a reacted dynamic response procedure, can be expressed by:

$$\dot{X}_{CZ(t)} = \sum_{i=1}^{N} a_{(t)}^i f_i(X_{i(t)}, U_{i(t)}) \qquad (3)$$

where $f_i(X_i(t), U_i(t)) \in R^n$, i=1,...,N, $\sum_{i=1}^{N} a_{(t)}^i = I$, $a_{(t)}^i \in diag(a_1(t), a_2(t),...,a_j(t),...,a_n(t))$, $a_j(t) \in [0,1]$, j=[1,2,...,n].

Proof. Let O_r^n be the neighboring region of $X_{CZ(t)} \in R^n$, and O_r^n is an open hypersphere whose radius is r (r is infinitesimal). Then $X_{i(t)}$ and $f_i(X_{i(t)}, U_{i(t)})$ (i=1,···,N) are in existence because the kinematics systems of certain primitive behaviors DB_i are Lipschitz continuous. And velocity field correspondence is $f_i(X_{i(t)}, U_{i(t)})$ (i=1,...,N), which are linear independent. So we can make a conclusion that in O_r^n, any velocity vector can be expressed by the convex topology sum of other velocity vectors (Equation (4)), which belong to the same vectorial field, because it is well known that any convex topology sum of convex collections belonging to the same convex collection, still belongs to the same convex collection.

$$\dot{X}_{CZ(t)} = \alpha^1_{(t)} f_1(X_{1(t)}, U_{1(t)}) + \alpha^2_{(t)} f_2(X_{2(t)}, U_{2(t)}) + \ldots$$
$$+ \alpha^N_{(t)} f_N(X_{N(t)}, U_{N(t)}) \qquad (4)$$
$$= \sum_{i=1}^{N} a^i_{(t)} f_i(X_{i(t)}, U_{i(t)})$$

where $\dot{X}_{CZ(t)} \in O_r^n$, and $\sum_{i=1}^{N} a^i_{(t)} = I$,

$a^i_{(t)} \in diag(a_1(t), a_2(t), \ldots, a_j(t), \ldots, a_n(t))$, $a_j(t) \in [0,1]$, j=[1,2,...,n].

Theorem 2: Where Compound Zeno Behavior B_{CZ} is determined together by the kinematics system $f_i(X_{i(t)}, U_{i(t)})$ of certain Deterministic Behaviors DB_i, and $\dot{X}_{i(t)} \in (a_-^n, a_+^n)$, $\ddot{X}_{i(t)} \in (b_-^n, b_+^n)$, $\sum_{i=1}^{N} a^i_{(t)} = I$, $\|\dot{\alpha}^i_{(t)}\| \leq \rho$, $\|\dot{\alpha}^j_{(t)}\| \leq \rho$ $\|f_i(X_{i(t)}, U_{i(t)}) - f_j(X_{j(t)}, U_{j(t)})\| \leq Q$,(i,j=1,...,N,N is the number of the primitive deterministic behaviors involved), then the kinematics system $X_{CZ(t)}$ of the Compound Zeno Behavior B_{CZ} must meet the Equations (5,6).

$$X_{CZ(t)} \in (a_-^n, a_+^n) \qquad (5)$$

$$\dot{X}_{CZ(t)} \in (b_-^n - (N-1)\rho Q, b_+^n + (N-1)\rho Q) \qquad (6)$$

Proof. Let $\dot{X}_{CZ(t)} \in O_r^n$, and O_r^n is an open hypersphere whose radius is r (r is infinitesimal). By straightforward calculation from Theorem 1, we know that $\dot{X}_{i(t)} \in (a_-^n, a_+^n)$, $\ddot{X}_{i(t)} \in (b_-^n, b_+^n)$ are all convex collections, and $\dot{X}_{CZ(t)} = \sum_{i=1}^{N} a^i_{(t)} f_i(X_{i(t)}, U_{i(t)})$, where $\sum_{i=1}^{N} a^i_{(t)} = I$,

$a^i_{(t)} \in diag(a_1(t), a_2(t), ..., a_j(t), ..., a_n(t))$, $a_j(t) \in [0,1]$, j=[1,2,...,n] , since $\dot{X}_{CZ(t)} \in O^n_r$, and it is well known that any convex topology sum of convex collections belonging to the same convex collection, still belongs to the same convex collection, we get $X_{CZ(t)} \in (a^n_-, a^n_+)$.

Consider $\dot{X}_{CZ(t)} = \sum_{i=1}^{N} a^i_{(t)} f_i(X_{i(t)}, U_{i(t)})$, therefore

$$\ddot{X}_{CZ(t)} = \sum_{i=1}^{N} \dot{a}^i_{(t)} f_i(X_{i(t)}, U_{i(t)}) + \sum_{i=1}^{N} a^i_{(t)} \dot{f}_i(X_{i(t)}, U_{i(t)}) \quad (7)$$

note that $\sum_{i=1}^{N} a^i_{(t)} = I$, so the right hand of the Equation (7) is :

$$= a^1_{(t)} f_1(X_{1(t)}, U_{1(t)}) + \sum_{i=2}^{N} \dot{a}^i_{(t)} f_i(X_{i(t)}, U_{i(t)}) + \sum_{i=1}^{N} a^i_{(t)} \dot{f}_i(X_{i(t)}, U_{i(t)})$$

$$= (1 - \sum_{i=2}^{N} a^i_{(t)})' f_1(X_{1(t)}, U_{1(t)}) + \sum_{i=2}^{N} \dot{a}^i_{(t)} f_i(X_{i(t)}, U_{i(t)}) + \sum_{i=1}^{N} a^i_{(t)} \dot{f}_i(X_{i(t)}, U_{i(t)})$$

$$= -\sum_{i=2}^{N} \dot{a}^i_{(t)} f_1(X_{1(t)}, U_{1(t)}) + \sum_{i=2}^{N} \dot{a}^i_{(t)} f_i(X_{i(t)}, U_{i(t)}) + \sum_{i=1}^{N} a^i_{(t)} \dot{f}_i(X_{i(t)}, U_{i(t)})$$

$$= \sum_{i=2}^{N} \dot{a}^i_{(t)} (f_i(X_{i(t)}, U_{i(t)}) - f_1(X_{1(t)}, U_{1(t)})) + \sum_{i=1}^{N} a^i_{(t)} \dot{f}_i(X_{i(t)}, U_{i(t)})$$

note that $\|f_i(X_{i(t)}, U_{i(t)}) - f_j(X_{j(t)}, U_{j(t)})\| \le Q$, and $\|\dot{a}^i_{(t)}\| \le \rho$, $\|\dot{a}^j_{(t)}\| \le \rho$, we can get that,

$$\ddot{X}_{CZ(t)} \le \sum_{i=2}^{N} \rho Q + \sum_{i=1}^{N} a^i_{(t)} \dot{f}_i(X_{i(t)}, U_{i(t)})$$

$$= (N-1)\rho Q + \sum_{i=1}^{N} a^i_{(t)} \dot{f}_i(X_{i(t)}, U_{i(t)})$$

$$\le (N-1)\rho Q + b^n_+$$

$$\ddot{X}_{CZ(t)} \ge -\sum_{i=2}^{N} \rho Q + \sum_{i=1}^{N} a^i_{(t)} \dot{f}_i(X_{i(t)}, U_{i(t)})$$

$$= -(N-1)\rho Q + \sum_{i=1}^{N} a^i_{(t)} \dot{f}_i(X_{i(t)}, U_{i(t)})$$

$$\ge -(N-1)\rho Q + b^n_-$$

i.e. $\dot{X}_{CZ(t)} \in (b^n_- - (N-1)\rho Q, b^n_+ + (N-1)\rho Q)$

4 Design of Primitive Deterministic Behaviors

The information provided by the sensors (depending on the kind of behavior) is fuzzified in several input variables that are used by the behaviors to compute their preferences among the control actions. The output of each fuzzy behavior in a robot-environment state is a fuzzy set $B_j(q, u)$(Equation (8)) derived from the fuzzy inference. Let q be the input array that defines the actual state and u the possible values in the output variable, for example the steering velocity, which shows the possible actions, then the fuzzy set B_j is given by Equation (8).

$$B_j(q,u) = \max_{1 \le i \le n} \min(Q_i(q), A_i(u)) \qquad (8)$$

Where $Q_i(q)$ is the truth value of the fuzzy proposition Q_i in the state q. A_i is a linguistic label of the consequent variable which represents a control action of the rule R_i of B_j.

R_i: IF Q_i;   THEN A_i;   i=1,...n; where n is the number of rules of B_j.

The design of a primitive Deterministic Behavior is actually the design of a fuzzy rules set and the definition of the shape of the linguistic variables membership functions of the fuzzy sets are collected in the rules. The primitive Deterministic Behaviors control blocks using the fuzzy rules consider two variables: translation velocity v and steering velocity ω. Therefore, each behavior has two rule bases: one to control the translation velocity v and another to control the steering velocity ω.

For the first behavior, *Goto sub-goal*, the input variables are translation velocity and steering angle to the goal. To perform the *Goto sub-goal* behavior, Angle variation (ω) will be NS if the Angle to goal (aG) is POS; and vice versa, until ω is equal to zero.

For the second behavior, *Go-Tangent*, the rule bases for *go towards obstacle tangent direction* are described here below:

(a) The rule base of the steering velocity control is shown in Table 1, which depends on the tangent angle of the obstacle (aO) and frontal obstacle distance (FD).
(b) For the translation velocity control, the rules are:
If v is HIGH and FD is {MEDIUM or NEAR}, then Δv is NM
If v is MEDIUM and FD is NEAR, then Δv is NS.

Table 1. Rules to control the steering velocity

	Go-Tangent behavior				Follow wall behavior			
FD aO	SMALL	MEDIUM	BIG	LD aLW	NEG	ZERO	POS
FAR	ZO	PS	PM	FAR	RM	RS	ZO
MEDIUM	PS	PM	PL	MEDIUM	RS	ZO	LS
NEAR	PM	PL	PL	NEAR	ZO	LS	LM

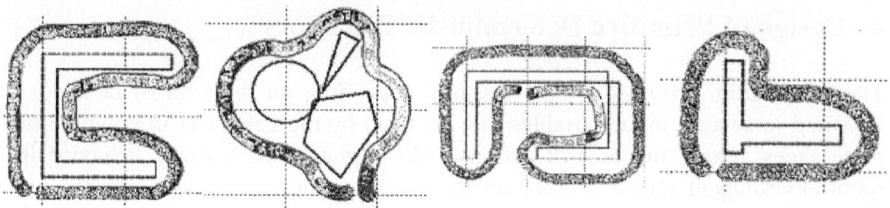

Fig. 2. Simulation results of the Following-Wall behavior in different environments

In the third behavior of *Following-Wall*, if the objective is to follow the left wall to a certain distance and the robot has to be aligned to the wall, then the input variables will be the current distance to the left wall (LD) and the angle to it (aLW). The rule bases are described here as below. The simulation result is shown in Figure 2.

(a) For the steering velocity control, which depends on LD (rows) and aLW (columns), the rule base is described in Table 1.
(b) For the translation velocity, the control rules are:
  If v is {MEDIUM or LOW} and LD is MEDIUM and aLW is ZERO, then Δv is PS.
  If v is HIGH and LD is {FAR or NEAR}, then Δv is NS.
  If v is HIGH and aLW is {POS or NEG}, then Δv is NS.

The other behaviors that should be performed in the same way will be skipped over here. Furthermore, the simulation task performed in the last chapter will only use the three primitive behaviors from the above paragraphs.

5 Simulation and Experiment Results

In order to test the performance of the control architecture designed and based on hierarchical behaviors, we have carried out different experimental tasks in simulation. The robot does not know the experiment environments except the coordinates of the initial and destination points. We have set the status of the first behavior *Goto subgoal* to be 1, and the second behavior *Follow-Wall* to be 2, the third one *Go-Tangent* to be 3. The navigation tasks require the mobile robot activate each of the behaviors separately in its own context of applicability.

The first navigation tasks that we have tested are showed in Figure 3. In the a) experiment, only the behavior *Follow-Wall* is active all the way. The positioning of the obstacles allows the robot to maintain a certain distance. We can see that a single deterministic behavior, *Follow-Wall*, cannot lead the robot to the goal. While in the experiment b), we can see that compound zeno behaviors are activated during the whole hybrid behavior. The robot begins to execute the zeno behaviors according to the current context of the robot. Figure 2 c) shows the state of the compound zeno behaviors during the different navigation phases in experiment b). At first, the robot moves towards the goal until it senses the unexpected obstacle, then it must move towards the tangent direction of the obstacle in order to avoid it. So activation of *Go-Tangent behavior* begins. Then in the next phase, the *Follow-Wall* behavior prefers to approach the obstacle while avoiding the obstacle. The zeno behaviors dominate the mobile robot alternatively, which lead the robot to move along the contour of the obstacle at a safe distance. After the triangle obstacle is detected, a similar procedure is executed. Finally, the robot arrives at the goal without collision with the obstacles. We can take the whole navigation sequence for a compound zeno behavior, and the zeno behavior may also affect the efficiency of the navigation.

Figure 4 shows a more complex navigation task. There are a lot of obstacles in the experiment, which is in three parts. The first one is a corridor, the second one is a "U" shaped object, and the third one is a clutter of obstacles. During the whole navigation, different zeno behaviors and compound zeno behaviors are activated. At the first navigation phase, the behavior *Goto sub-goal* leads the robot to approach the obstacle. While the robot approaches the wall, the second behavior, *Follow-Wall,* and the third behavior, *Go-Tangent,* are activated repetitiously. These are the behaviors that make the robot move into the corridor. After the robot enters the corridor, we can see that

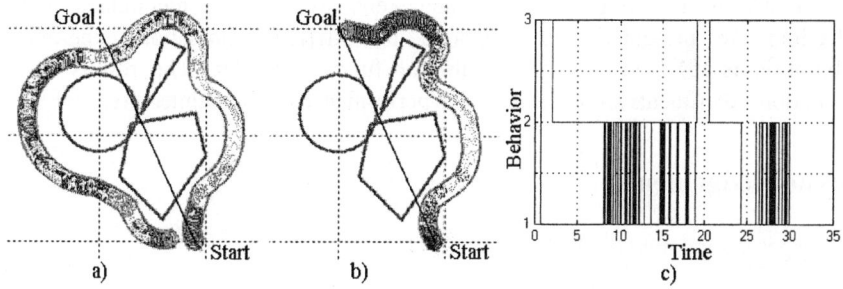

Fig. 3. Different navigation result of the deterministic behavior and hybrid behavior

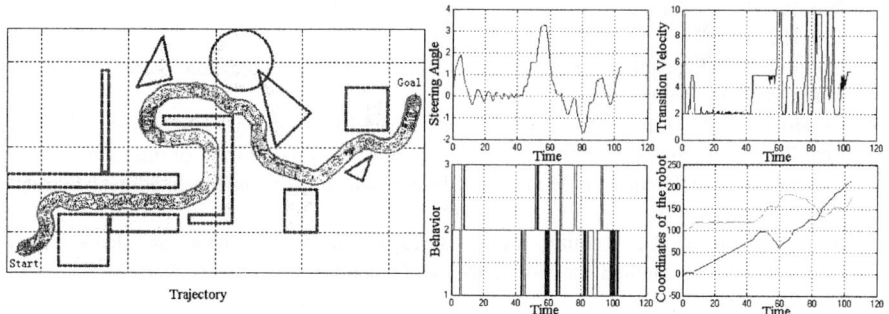

Fig. 4. Trajectory and Parameters of the Complex Experiment

only the *Follow-Wall* behavior controls it. When the robot is out of the corridor, the navigation goes to the second phase, because of the "U" shaped obstacle. Then a zeno behavior happens, which we call *Escaping from trap* behavior. Only two behaviors intervene in the zeno phenomenon. Before the robot goes out from the "U" shaped obstacle, the third phase of the navigation begins. We cannot give a clear boundary of the second and third phase of the navigation, because the zeno behavior has gradually changed into compound zeno behavior. Furthermore, in this phase of the navigation, the robot meets some cluttered obstacles, and another compound zeno behavior phenomenon named as *Follow contour* happens until the robot finds its way through the obstacles to arrive at the goal with smooth trajectories and without collision with any of the obstacles.

6 Conclusions

This work addresses the generation of complex hierarchical behaviors by the combination of simpler behaviors at the lowest level of a hybrid deliberative reactive architecture for mobile robot navigation. According to the proposed methodology for designing the elementary behaviors, fuzzy rules are used, which allow the linguistic descriptions of the control strategies to be easily understood. The core theoretical foundations of designing the Compound Zeno Behavior in hierarchical hybrid behaviors are presented and supported by different simulation experiments. Arbitration is resolved through the use of fuzzy metarules. The results of our simulation experiments show the effective performance of the architecture.

Acknowledgements

This paper is supported by the National 863 Project of China.

References

1. Brooks. R. A.: Intelligence without representation. Artificial Intelligence. 47 (1991) 139-159
2. Payton,D. W., Rosenblatt J. K. and Kersey D. M.: Plan guided reaction. IEEE Trans. Syst. Man Cyber. Vol. 20 (1990) 1370-1382
3. Goodridge, S. G., Luo, R. C., Michael, G. K.,: Multi-Layered Fuzzy Behavior Fusion for Real-Time Control of Systems with Many Sensors. Proceedings of the 1994 IEEE International Conference on Multisensor Fusion and Integration for Intelligent System, (1994) 272-279
4. John Y., Nathan P.,: A Fuzzy Logic Based Extension to Payton and Rosenblatt's Command Fusion Method for Mobile Robot Navigation. IEEE Trans. Syst. Man Cyber., Vol. 25 (1995) 971-978
5. Rosenblatt, J. K.: Utility Fusion: Map-Based Planning in a Behavior-Based System, In Field and Service Robotics,Springer-Verlag (1998)
6. Ye, C., Yung, N. H. C.: Vehicle Navigation Strategy based on Behavior Fusion. Proceedings of the IEEE International Conference on Systems, Man and Cybernetics, Vol. 4 (1997) 3698-3703
7. Freire, E. Bastos-Filho, T.: A New Mobile Robot Control Approach via Fusion of Control Signals. IEEE Trans. Syst. Man Cyber., Vol. 34 (2004) 419-429

8. Rusu, P., Petriu, E. M., Whalen, T. E., Cornell, A., Spoelder, H. J.W.: Behavior-Based Neuro-Fuzzy Controller for Mobile Robot Navigation. IEEE Instrumentation and Measurement Technology Conf. Anchorage, AK, USA(2002) 1617-1622
9. Shou Tao L., Yuan Chun L.: Autonomous Mobile Robot Control Algorithm Based on Hierarchical Fuzzy Behaviors in Unknown Environments, Journal of Jilin University Engineering and Technology Edition,Vol. 35. JiLin China (2005) 391-397
10. Payton, D, Estkowski, R., Howard, M.: Compound behaviors in pheromone robotics. Robotics and Autonomous Systems ,Vol. 44 (2003) 229-240.
11. Egerstedt, M.: Motion Planning and Control of Mobile Robots. Doctoral Thesis, Stockholm (2000)
12. He Hua J., Ping Yuan C., Gu Tao C.: Autonomous Behavior Agent-based Lunar Rover Motion Planning and Control. Conference on space navigation and astronautics, Harbin, China (2005) 48-58

An LMI Approach to Robust Fault Detection Filter Design for Uncertain State-Delayed Systems

Hongru Wang, Changhong Wang, and Huijun Gao

Harbin Institute of Technology, Science Park,
Space Control and Inertial Technology Research Centre,
P. O. Box 3015, 150001 Harbin, China
hitwan@126.com

Abstract. This contribution investigates the problem of robust fault detection and isolation for a class of state-delayed systems with norm-bounded uncertainties and unknown inputs. Attention is focused on formulating the design of robust fault detection filter as H_∞ filtering problem and designing the adaptive threshold. The existence condition of the above filters, which can guarantee the prescribed performance index, is established by means of linear matrix inequalities. A numerical example is employed to demonstrate the effectiveness of the proposed approach.

1 Introduction

The basic idea of model-based fault detection and isolation (FDI) is to construct the residual generator, then determine the evaluation function and the threshold. When the value of the evaluation function is greater than the prescribed threshold, an alarm of fault is generated. However, this approach is built upon a number of idealized assumptions, among them is that mathematical model must be a faithful replica of the plant dynamics. In practice, modeling errors and unknown inputs in complex engineering systems are unavoidable and can deteriorate fault detection and isolation system. As results, robustness issue plays an important role in the application of model-based FDI schemes and thus is receiving much attention in recent years (see, e.g., [1]-[8] and the references therein).

The robustness problem related to FDI is somewhat different from the robust control problem. Robustness in FDI problem should be considered in the context of high sensitivity of the fault detection and isolation systems to the faults even in the presence of modeling errors and external disturbances. Several major design methods of robust fault detection and isolation filter have been developed during the last decade. For example, unknown input observer [1], multi-objective optimization method [2], eigenstructure assignment [3], [4], parity spaces [5], adaptive observer [6], etc. Particularly, an H_∞ filtering formulation of robust FDI problem has been presented to solve robust FDI problem for uncertain LTI systems effectively [7], [8].

The existing methods of robust fault detection and isolation filter design, however, do not directly apply to state-delayed systems with norm-bounded. Since time delays usually result in unsatisfactory performance and are frequently a source of instability, their presence must be considered in realistic fault detection filter design [4], [6]. It turns out that the performance level guaranteed by robust fault detection and isolation filter design without considering time delays may collapse if the system actually exhibits non-negligible time delays. The robust fault detection and isolation problem for LTI systems with time-delays has been attracting increasing attention over the past few years. Specifically, the problem of fault detection for continuous-time systems with multiple state delays has been addressed by combining of using the left eigenstructure assignment and H_∞ optimization technique [4]. Jiang et al [6] deal with the nominal case fault identification without considering the influence of model uncertainty and unknown inputs. To the best of the author's knowledge, the problem of robust fault detection and isolation for a class of uncertain state-delayed systems has not been fully investigated.

The main focus of this contribution is to investigate the problem of robust fault detection and isolation for norm-bounded uncertain system with time-delay by extending robust H_∞ filter method of [9]. We construct the residual generator based on the full order filter. Attention is focused on formulating the design of robust fault detection and isolation filter as H_∞ filtering problem and designing the adaptive threshold. The objective is to make the difference between the residual and the fault as small as possible, and enhance the robustness to the unknown inputs and the control inputs in the presence of modeling errors. The sufficient condition for the existence of the above filters is established by means of LMIs. A numerical example is provided to demonstrate the feasibility of the proposed method.

2 Problem Formulation

Consider a class of uncertain systems with time-delay and unknown input as follows:

$$\dot{x}(t) = (A + \Delta A)x(t) + (A_d + \Delta A_d)x(t-\tau) + (B + \Delta B)u(t) + B_d d(t) + B_f f(t),$$
$$y(t) = Cx(t) + D_d d(t) + D_f f(t), \qquad (1)$$
$$x(0) = \phi(\theta), \ \theta \in [-\tau, \cdots, 0].$$

where $x(t) \in \mathrm{R}^n$ is the state, $u(t) \in \mathrm{R}^r$ is the control input, $d(t) \in \mathrm{R}^p$ is the unknown input, $f(t) \in \mathrm{R}^l$ is the fault to be detected, $y(t) \in \mathrm{R}^m$ is the measured output. $u(t)$, $d(t)$ and $f(t)$ are assumed to be L_2-norm bounded. $\phi(\theta)$ is a continuous initial vector function. ΔA, ΔA_d and ΔB are uncertain matrices but norm-bounded so that:

$$\Delta A = HF(t)E_1, \ \Delta A_d = HF(t)E_2, \ \Delta B = HF(t)E_3. \qquad (2)$$

where $F(t)$ is time-varying matrix and satisfies:

$$F^T(t)F(t) \le I . \qquad (3)$$

Throughout this paper, all matrices are assumed to be compatible if their dimensions are not explicitly stated, and the system (1) is asymptotically stable.

The problem of filter-based fault detection and isolation is to find an asymptotically stable filter as the residual generator, and then determine whether or not the faults occur by comparing the residual with the prescribed threshold.

For the system (1), construct the following fault detection filter (FDF):

$$\dot{x}_F(t) = A_F x_F(t) + B_F y(t),$$
$$r(t) = C_F x_F(t) + D_F y(t), \quad (4)$$
$$x_F(0) = 0$$

where $x_F(t) \in R^n$, $r(t) \in R^s$ is the so-called residual.

In order to enhance the sensitiveness of residual to fault as well as the robustness to control inputs, unknown inputs and model uncertainties, the fault is weighted as $\bar{f}(s) = Q(s)f(s)$, where $Q(s) \in RH_\infty$ is a given weighted function. The state-space realization of $\bar{f}(t)$ is shown as:

$$\dot{x}_Q(t) = A_Q x_Q(t) + B_Q f(t),$$
$$\bar{f}(t) = C_Q x_Q(t) + D_Q f(t), \quad (5)$$
$$x_Q(0) = 0.$$

where $x_Q(t) \in R^q$, $\bar{f}(t) \in R^s$, .

Augmenting the model of (1) to include the states of (4) and (5) and denoting $e(t) = r(t) - \bar{f}(t)$, we obtain the following dynamic system:

$$\dot{\xi}(t) = \bar{A}\xi(t) + \bar{A}_d \xi(t-d) + \bar{B} W(t),$$
$$e(t) = \bar{C}\xi(t) + \bar{D} W(t). \quad (6)$$

where $\xi(t) = [x^T(t) \ x_F^T(t) \ x_Q^T(t)]^T$, $W(t) = [u^T(t) \ d^T(t) \ f^T(t)]^T$,

$$\bar{A} = \begin{bmatrix} A + \Delta A & 0 & 0 \\ B_F C & A_F & 0 \\ 0 & 0 & A_Q \end{bmatrix}, \bar{A}_d = \begin{bmatrix} A_d + \Delta A_d & 0 & 0 \\ 0 & 0 & 0 \\ 0 & 0 & 0 \end{bmatrix}, \bar{B} = \begin{bmatrix} B + \Delta B & B_d & B_f \\ 0 & B_F D_d & B_F D_f \\ 0 & 0 & B_Q \end{bmatrix},$$

$$\bar{C} = \begin{bmatrix} D_F C & C_F & -C_Q \end{bmatrix}, \bar{D} = \begin{bmatrix} 0 & D_F D_d & D_F D_f - D_Q \end{bmatrix}.$$

Now the problem addressed in this paper can be stated as: to develop the robust fault detection and isolation filter of the form (4) for uncertain state-delayed continuous-time system such that the following two requirements are satisfied:

1. The augmented system (6) is asymptotically stable.
2. Under zero initial condition, the augmented system (6) guarantees the following H_∞ performance index for all nonzero $W \in L_2[0, \infty)$ and $\gamma > 0$:

$$\|e\|_2 < \gamma \|W\|_2 \quad (7)$$

where $\|e\|_2 = \left(\int_0^\infty e^T(t)e(t)dt \right)^{1/2}$, $\|W\|_2 = \left(\int_0^\infty W^T(t)W(t)dt \right)^{1/2}$.

After designing of FDF, the remaining important task is to evaluate the generated residual. One of the widely adopted approaches is to choose a so-called threshold J_{th} and, based on this, use the following logical relationship for fault detection.

$$\begin{aligned} J(r) > J_{th} &\Rightarrow \text{faults} \Rightarrow \text{alarm} \\ J(r) \leq J_{th} &\Rightarrow \text{no fault} \end{aligned} \tag{8}$$

where the residual evaluation function $J(r)$ is determined by

$$J(r) = \|r(t)\|_{2,T} = \left(\int_{t_0}^{t_0+T} r^T(t) r(t) dt \right)^{1/2}. \tag{9}$$

where t_0 is the initial evaluation time, T denotes the evaluation time window. The value of T is limited because an evaluation of the residual over the whole time range is impractical.

Remark 1. In the case of $\overline{f}(s) = Q(s)f(s)$, we call the optimization problem (7) the robust fault detection filter (RFDF) design problem, while the one with $\overline{f}(s) = f(s)$ the robust fault isolation (RFI) problem.

3 Design of Robust Fault Detection and Isolation Filters

In this section, an LMI approach is developed to solve the above-defined robust fault detection and isolation filter design problem. We introduce the two following Lemmas which are necessary to derive the main results.

Lemma 1. Suppose that D, E, $F(t)$ are compatible and $F^T(t)F(t) < I$, then there exits a scalar $\varepsilon > 0$ such that (10) holds.

$$DF(t)E + \left(DF(t)E\right)^T \leq \varepsilon DD^T + \varepsilon^{-1} E^T E. \tag{10}$$

Lemma 2. For a given scalar $\gamma > 0$ and all nonzero $W \in L_2[0, \infty)$, the augmented system (6) is asymptotically stable and satisfies (7) under zero initial condition if there exist symmetric positive definite matrices P and S such that (11) holds.

$$\Pi = \begin{bmatrix} \overline{A}^T P + P\overline{A}^T + S & P\overline{A}_d & P\overline{B} & \overline{C}^T \\ * & -S & 0 & 0 \\ * & * & -\gamma^2 I & \overline{D}^T \\ * & * & * & -I \end{bmatrix} < 0. \tag{11}$$

Proof. First, the global asymptotic stability of the augmented system (6) with $W(t) \equiv 0$ is established. For that, choose the Lyapunov functional

$$V\left(\xi_\theta(t)\right) = \xi^T(t) P \xi(t) + \int_{t-\tau}^{t} \xi^T(\alpha) S \xi(\alpha) d\alpha \tag{12}$$

where $\xi_\theta(t) = \xi(t+\theta)$, $\theta \subset [-\tau, 0]$.

Along the solution of (6) with $W(t) \equiv 0$ for any arbitrary initial condition, one has

$$\dot{V}(\xi_\theta(t)) = \dot{\xi}^T(t)P\xi(t) + \xi^T(t)P\dot{\xi}(t) + \xi^T(t)S\xi(t) - \xi^T(t-\tau)S\xi(t-\tau) \quad (13)$$

Using (6), (13) can be written in the following form:

$$\dot{V}(\xi_\theta(t)) = \begin{bmatrix} \xi^T(t) & \xi^T(t-\tau) \end{bmatrix} \Theta \begin{bmatrix} \xi(t) \\ \xi(t-\tau) \end{bmatrix}. \quad (14)$$

where $\Theta = \begin{bmatrix} \bar{A}^T P + P\bar{A}^T + S & P\bar{A}_d \\ * & -S \end{bmatrix}$.

It can be easily verified that (11) ensures that $\Theta < 0$. Therefore, from standard Lyapunov stability results, it can be concluded that the augmented system (6) is globally asymptotically stable.

To establish the performance for the augmented system (6), first notice that $\xi(t)$ tends to zero with $t \to \infty$ as (6) is globally asymptotically stable. Next, assuming zero initial conditions for the augmented system (6), the performance index

$$J \triangleq \int_0^\infty \left[e^T(t)e(t) - \gamma^2 W^T(t)W(t) \right] dt$$
$$= \int_0^\infty \left[e^T(t)e(t) - \gamma^2 W^T(t)W(t) + \dot{V}(\xi_\theta(t)) \right] dt + V(\xi_\theta(t))\big|_{t=0} - V(\xi_\theta(t))\big|_{t\to\infty} \quad (15)$$

Considering that $V(\xi_\theta(t))\big|_{t=0} = 0$ and $V(\xi_\theta(t))\big|_{t\to\infty} \to 0$, and using Schur complement, one can easily obtain that

$$J = \int_0^\infty \eta^T(t)\Pi\eta(t)dt. \quad (16)$$

where $\eta(t) = \begin{bmatrix} \xi^T(t) & \xi^T(t-\tau) & W^T(t) \end{bmatrix}^T$.

We can infer that $J < 0$ from (11), therefore (7) is obtained. The proof is completed.

Using Lemma 1, (17) is equivalent to (11).

$$\begin{bmatrix} \bar{A}_0^T P + P\bar{A}_0 + S + \varepsilon_1 \bar{E}_1^T \bar{E}_1 & P\bar{B}_0 & \bar{C}^T & P\bar{A}_{d0} & P\bar{H} & P\bar{H} & P\bar{H} \\ * & -\gamma^2 I + \varepsilon_3 \bar{E}_3^T \bar{E}_3 & \bar{D}^T & 0 & 0 & 0 & 0 \\ * & * & -I & 0 & 0 & 0 & 0 \\ * & * & * & -S + \varepsilon_2 \bar{E}_2^T \bar{E}_2 & 0 & 0 & 0 \\ * & * & * & * & -\varepsilon_1 I & 0 & 0 \\ * & * & * & * & * & -\varepsilon_2 I & 0 \\ * & * & * & * & * & * & -\varepsilon_3 I \end{bmatrix} < 0 \quad (17)$$

where $\bar{A}_0 = \begin{bmatrix} A & 0 & 0 \\ B_F C & A_F & 0 \\ 0 & 0 & A_Q \end{bmatrix}$, $\bar{A}_{d0} = \begin{bmatrix} A_d & 0 & 0 \\ 0 & 0 & 0 \\ 0 & 0 & 0 \end{bmatrix}$, $\bar{B}_0 = \begin{bmatrix} B & B_d & B_f \\ 0 & B_F D_d & B_F D_f \\ 0 & 0 & B_Q \end{bmatrix}$,

$$\bar{H} = \begin{bmatrix} H^T & 0 & 0 \end{bmatrix}^T, \ \bar{E}_1 = \begin{bmatrix} E_1 & 0 & 0 \end{bmatrix}, \ \bar{E}_2 = \begin{bmatrix} E_2 & 0 & 0 \end{bmatrix}, \ \bar{E}_3 = \begin{bmatrix} E_3 & 0 & 0 \end{bmatrix}.$$

P and S are selected as:

$$P = \begin{bmatrix} U & 0 \\ 0 & V \end{bmatrix}, \ S = \begin{bmatrix} \bar{S} & 0 \\ 0 & S_1 \end{bmatrix}. \tag{18}$$

where $U \in R^{2n \times 2n}$, $V \in R^{q \times q}$, $\bar{S} \in R^{2n \times 2n}$ and $S_1 \in R^{q \times q}$ are symmetric positive definite matrices.

Substituting (18) into (17), we can obtain that

$$\begin{bmatrix} \Omega & 0 & UB_0 & C_0^T & UA_{d0} & 0 & U\tilde{H} & U\tilde{H} & U\tilde{H} \\ * & A_Q^T V + VA_q & V\bar{B}_Q & -C_Q^T & 0 & 0 & 0 & 0 & 0 \\ * & * & -\gamma^2 I + \varepsilon_3 \bar{E}_3^T \bar{E}_3 & \bar{D}^T & 0 & 0 & 0 & 0 & 0 \\ * & * & * & -I & 0 & 0 & 0 & 0 & 0 \\ * & * & * & * & -\bar{S} + \varepsilon_2 \tilde{E}_2^T \tilde{E}_2 & 0 & 0 & 0 & 0 \\ * & * & * & * & * & -S_1 & 0 & 0 & 0 \\ * & * & * & * & * & * & -\varepsilon_1 I & 0 & 0 \\ * & * & * & * & * & * & * & -\varepsilon_2 I & 0 \\ * & * & * & * & * & * & * & * & -\varepsilon_3 I \end{bmatrix} < 0 \tag{19}$$

where $\Omega = A_0^T U + U A_0 + \bar{S} + \varepsilon_1 \tilde{E}_1^T \tilde{E}_1$, $\bar{B}_Q = \begin{bmatrix} 0 & 0 & B_Q \end{bmatrix}$, $C_0 = \begin{bmatrix} D_F C & C_F \end{bmatrix}$, $\tilde{E}_1 = \begin{bmatrix} E_1 & 0 \end{bmatrix}$,

$$A_0 = \begin{bmatrix} A & 0 \\ B_F C & A_F \end{bmatrix}, \ B_0 = \begin{bmatrix} B & B_d & B_f \\ 0 & B_F D_d & B_F D_f \end{bmatrix}, \ A_{d0} = \begin{bmatrix} A_d & 0 \\ 0 & 0 \end{bmatrix}, \ \tilde{H} = \begin{bmatrix} H \\ 0 \end{bmatrix}, \ \tilde{E}_2 = \begin{bmatrix} E_2 & 0 \end{bmatrix}.$$

Partitioning U and U^{-1} into the following matrices:

$$U = \begin{bmatrix} U_{11} & U_{12} \\ U_{12}^T & U_{22} \end{bmatrix}, \ Y = U^{-1} = \begin{bmatrix} Y_{11} & Y_{12} \\ Y_{12}^T & Y_{22} \end{bmatrix}$$

where $U_{11} \in R^{n \times n}$, $Y_{11} \in R^{n \times n}$.

Denote $J_Y = \begin{bmatrix} Y_{11} & I \\ Y_{12}^T & 0 \end{bmatrix}$, $J_U = \begin{bmatrix} I & U_{11} \\ 0 & U_{12}^T \end{bmatrix}$, $\bar{S} = \begin{bmatrix} S_2 & 0 \\ 0 & S_3 \end{bmatrix}$.

where $0 < S_2 = S_2^T \in R^{n \times n}$, $0 < S_3 = S_3^T \in R^{n \times n}$.

Performing congruence transformation to (19) by $\text{diag}\{J_Y, I, I, I, I, I, I, I, I\}$ and introducing a set of variables (20)

$$R = Y_{11}^{-1}, \ Z = U_{12} B_F, \ T = Y_{11}^T Y_{12} S_3 Y_{12}^T Y_{11}^{-1}, \ X = U_{11},$$
$$M = U_{12} A_F S_{12}^T S_{11}^{-1}, \ N = C_F S_{12}^T S_{11}^{-1}. \tag{20}$$

yield

$$\begin{bmatrix} \Xi_{11} & \Xi_{12} & 0 & RB & RB_d & RB_f & \Xi_{17} & RA_d & 0 & 0 & RH & RH & RH \\ * & \Xi_{22} & 0 & XB & \Xi_{25} & \Xi_{26} & CD_F^T & XA_d & 0 & 0 & XH & XH & XH \\ * & * & \Xi_{33} & 0 & 0 & VB_Q & -C_Q^T & 0 & 0 & 0 & 0 & 0 & 0 \\ * & * & * & \Xi_{44} & 0 & 0 & 0 & 0 & 0 & 0 & 0 & 0 & 0 \\ * & * & * & * & -\gamma^2 I & 0 & D_d^T D_F^T & 0 & 0 & 0 & 0 & 0 & 0 \\ * & * & * & * & * & -\gamma^2 I & D_f^T D_F^T - D_Q^T & 0 & 0 & 0 & 0 & 0 & 0 \\ * & * & * & * & * & * & -I & 0 & 0 & 0 & 0 & 0 & 0 \\ * & * & * & * & * & * & * & -S_2 + \varepsilon_2 E_2^T E_2 & 0 & 0 & 0 & 0 & 0 \\ * & * & * & * & * & * & * & * & -S_3 & 0 & 0 & 0 & 0 \\ * & * & * & * & * & * & * & * & * & -S_1 & 0 & 0 & 0 \\ * & * & * & * & * & * & * & * & * & * & -\varepsilon_1 I & 0 & 0 \\ * & * & * & * & * & * & * & * & * & * & * & -\varepsilon_2 I & 0 \\ * & * & * & * & * & * & * & * & * & * & * & * & -\varepsilon_3 I \end{bmatrix} < 0 \quad (21)$$

where

$\Xi_{11} = RA + A^T R + T + S_2 + \varepsilon_1 E_1^T E_1$, $\Xi_{17} = C^T D_F^T + N^T$, $\Xi_{33} = S_1 + A_Q^T V + VA_Q$

$\Xi_{12} = RA + A^T X + C^T Z^T + M^T + S_2 + \varepsilon_1 E_1^T E_1$, $\Xi_{25} = XB_d + ZD_d$, $\Xi_{26} = XB_f + ZD_f$,

$\Xi_{22} = XA + A^T X + ZC + C^T Z^T + S_2 + \varepsilon_1 E_1^T E_1$, $\Xi_{44} = -\gamma^2 I + \varepsilon_3 E_3^T E_3$.

U_{12} and Y_{12}^T are reversible because $UY = I$. Therefore

$$A_F = U_{12}^{-1} M Y_{11} (Y_{12}^T)^{-1}, \quad B_F = U_{12}^{-1} Z, \quad C_F = N Y_{11} (Y_{12}^T)^{-1}. \quad (22)$$

Substituting A_F, B_F, C_F and D_F into the transfer function of the fault detection filter (4) and performing some standard matrix manipulations, we can obtain

$$A_F = (R - X)^{-1} M, \quad B_F = (R - X)^{-1} Z, \quad C_F = N. \quad (23)$$

On the other hand, the positive definiteness of U and Schur complement give

$$X - R > 0. \quad (24)$$

Summarizing the above, we can obtain the sufficient condition for the existence of robust fault detection and isolation filter for uncertain state-delayed system, which is stated as Theorem 3.

Theorem 3. For a given scalar $\gamma > 0$, the augmented system (6) is asymptotically stable, and satisfies (7) under zero initial condition if there exist symmetric positive definite matrices R, X, V, T, S_1, S_2, S_3, matrices M, N, Z, D_F and scalars $\varepsilon_1 > 0$, $\varepsilon_2 > 0$, $\varepsilon_3 > 0$ such that (21) and (24) hold. Furthermore, the parameter matrices of admissible filter are given by (23).

The solution of RFI problem will be given in the following Theorem.

Theorem 4. Given scalar $\gamma > 0$, the RFI problem is solvable if there exist symmetric positive definite matrices R, X, V, T, S_1, S_2, general matrices M, N, Z, D_F and scalars $\varepsilon_1 > 0$, $\varepsilon_2 > 0$, $\varepsilon_3 > 0$ such that:

$$\begin{bmatrix} \Psi_{11} & \Psi_{12} & RB & RB_d & RB_f & \Psi_{16} & RA_d & 0 & RH & RH & RH \\ * & \Psi_{22} & XB & \Psi_{24} & \Psi_{25} & CD_F^T & XA_d & 0 & XH & XH & XH \\ * & * & \Psi_{33} & 0 & 0 & 0 & 0 & 0 & 0 & 0 & 0 \\ * & * & * & -\gamma^2 I & 0 & D_d^T D_F^T & 0 & 0 & 0 & 0 & 0 \\ * & * & * & * & -\gamma^2 I & D_f^T D_F^T & 0 & 0 & 0 & 0 & 0 \\ * & * & * & * & * & -I & 0 & 0 & 0 & 0 & 0 \\ * & * & * & * & * & * & -S_1 + \varepsilon_2 E_2^T E_2 & 0 & 0 & 0 & 0 \\ * & * & * & * & * & * & * & -S_2 & 0 & 0 & 0 \\ * & * & * & * & * & * & * & * & -\varepsilon_1 I & 0 & 0 \\ * & * & * & * & * & * & * & * & * & -\varepsilon_2 I & 0 \\ * & * & * & * & * & * & * & * & * & * & -\varepsilon_3 I \end{bmatrix} < 0 \quad (25)$$

$$X - R > 0 \quad (26)$$

where

$\Psi_{11} = RA + A^T R + T + S_1 + \varepsilon_1 E_1^T E_1$, $\Psi_{12} = RA + A^T X + C^T Z^T + M^T + S_1 + \varepsilon_1 E_1^T E_1$,
$\Psi_{16} = C^T D_F^T + N^T$, $\Psi_{22} = XA + A^T X + ZC + C^T Z^T + S_1 + \varepsilon_1 E_1^T E_1$,
$\Psi_{24} = XB_d + ZD_d$, $\Psi_{25} = XB_f + ZD_f$, $\Psi_{33} = -\gamma^2 I + \varepsilon_3 E_3^T E_3$.

The proof of Theorem 4 is similar to one of Theorem 3, therefore omitted.

4 Design of Adaptive Threshold

Consider the designed residual generation system

$$\begin{aligned} \dot{x}(t) &= (A + \Delta A)x(t) + (A_d + \Delta A_d)x(t-\tau) + (B + \Delta B)u(t) + B_d d(t) + B_f f(t), \\ \dot{x}_F(t) &= A_F x_F(t) + B_F C x(t) + B_F D_d d(t) + B_F D_f f(t), \\ r(t) &= D_F C x(t) + C_F x_F(t) + D_F D_d d(t) + D_F D_f f(t). \end{aligned} \quad (27)$$

By selecting (9) as the residual evaluation function, we have

$$\|r(t)\|_{2,T} = \|r_u(t) + r_d(t) + r_f(t)\|_{2,T} \quad (28)$$

where $r_u(t) \triangleq r(t)\big|_{d=0, f=0}$, $r_d(t) \triangleq r(t)\big|_{u=0, f=0}$, $r_f(t) \triangleq r(t)\big|_{u=0, d=0}$.

Moreover, the residual evaluation function with fault-free case can be written as $\|r_u + r_d\|_{2,T} \leq \|r_u\|_{2,T} + \|r_d\|_{2,T} \leq J_{th,u} + J_{th,d}$, where $J_{th,u} = \sup\|r_u\|_{2,T}$, $J_{th,d} = \sup\|r_d\|_{2,T}$.

We choose the threshold J_{th} as $J_{th} = J_{th,u} + J_{th,d}$, where $J_{th,d}$ is constant and can be evaluated off-line. The control input u is assumed to be known on-line and can be evaluated on-line by $J_{th,u} = \gamma_u \|u\|_{2,T}$, where $\gamma_u = \sup(\|r_u\|_{2,T}/\|u\|_{2,T})$ and can be determined by using Lemma 2. Under the assumption of $d \in L_2[0,\infty)$, we can further have $\sup\|r_d\|_{2,T} = M > 0$.

Therefore, the threshold can be determined by

$$J_{th} = M + \gamma_u \|u\|_{2,T} \, . \quad (29)$$

Note that the defined threshold consists of two parts: the constant part M and part $J_{th,u}$ which depends on the control input u and can be calculated on-line. Therefore, changing the control input u implies a new determination of the threshold. In this sense, the threshold is adaptive.

5 Numerical Example

Consider the following system governed by (1) with the parameters:

$$A = \begin{bmatrix} -8 & 1 \\ 0 & -10 \end{bmatrix},\ A_d = \begin{bmatrix} -1 & 0 \\ 0.8 & -1 \end{bmatrix},\ B_d = \begin{bmatrix} -0.1 \\ 0.1 \end{bmatrix},\ B = \begin{bmatrix} 1 \\ 1 \end{bmatrix},\ B_f = \begin{bmatrix} 1 \\ 1 \end{bmatrix},\ H = \begin{bmatrix} 0.1 \\ 0.1 \end{bmatrix},\ C = \begin{bmatrix} 1 & 1 \end{bmatrix},$$

$D_f = 1$, $D_d = 0.1$, $E_1 = [0.1\ 0.1]$, $E_2 = [0.1\ 0.1]$, $E_3 = 0.1$, $F(t) = \sin\theta, \theta = 30°$, $\tau = 2$.

Suppose that $A_Q = -5$, $B_Q = 5$, $C_Q = 1$, $D_Q = 0$. The unknown input $d(t)$ is supposed to be random noise whose amplitude is no more than 0.5. The control input $u(t)$ is taken as the unit step signal. The fault signal is simulated as a pulse of unit amplitude occurred from 5s to 15s and is zero otherwise.

By Theorem 3, we have the following parameters of the fault detection filter:

$$A_F = \begin{bmatrix} -9.6093 & 1.8493 \\ -1.0876 & -11.0486 \end{bmatrix},\ B_F = \begin{bmatrix} 0.9511 \\ 1.0295 \end{bmatrix},\ C_F = \begin{bmatrix} -0.4828 & -0.5221 \end{bmatrix},\ D_F = 0.5003,$$

$\gamma = 0.7212$, $\varepsilon_1 = 1.0655$, $\varepsilon_2 = 1.1080$, $\varepsilon_3 = 1.2776$.

By using Lemma 2, we have $\gamma_u = 0.2135$. Suppose the upper bound of $\|d\|_2$ is 0.2067, then the threshold can be determined as $J_{th} = 0.4909$. The simulation results indicate that the evaluation function $J(r) = 0.6230 > J_{th}$ when $T = 6$. This means that the appeared fault can be detected one second after its occurrence.

Fig. 1 shows the residual signal. It can be concluded that the residual is robust to unknown input, control input and modeling errors as well as sensitive to fault.

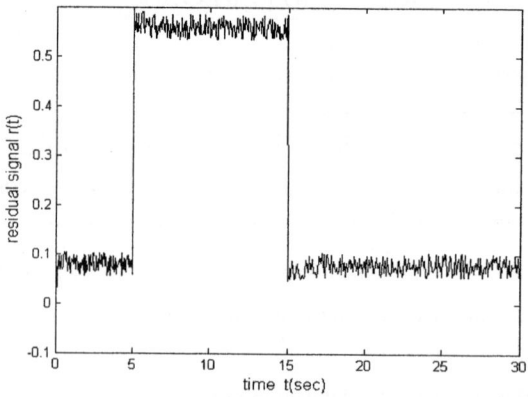

Fig. 1. Residual signal

6 Conclusion

In this paper, the solution to the problem of robust fault detection for a class of uncertain state-delayed systems is presented. We have reduced it to H_∞ filtering problem by using full order filter as the residual generator. The above filter design approach has been investigated in terms of LMIs. The fault detection filter has been designed by using the proposed method. The simulation result has shown the effectiveness and applicability of the obtained results.

References

1. Park, T., Lee, K.: Process fault isolation for linear systems with unknown inputs. IEE Proc. Control Theory and Application. 6 (2004) 720-726
2. Henry, D., Zolghadri, A.: Design of fault diagnosis filters: A multi-objective approach. Journal of the Franklin Institute. 342 (2005) 421-446
3. Patton, J., Chen, J.: On eigenvalue assignment for robust fault diagnosis. Int. J. Robust Nonlinear Control. 10 (2000) 1193-1208
4. Zhong, M. Y., Ding, S. X., Lam, J.: Fault Detection Filter Design for LTI System with Time Delays. Proceedings of the 42nd IEEE Conference on Decision and Control. Maui Hawaii USA (2003) 1467-1472
5. Gertler, J.: Fault detection and isolation using parity relations. Control Engineer Practice. 5 (1997) 653-661
6. Jiang, B., Ataroswiecki, M.: Fault identification for a class of time-delay systems. Proc. of the American Control Conference. Anchorage AK (2002) 2239-2244
7. Nobrega, E. G., Abdalla, M. O., Grigoriadis, K. M.: LMI-based filter design for fault detection and isolation. Proc. of the 39th conference on decision and control. Australia (2000) 4329-4334
8. Zhong, M. Y., Ding, S. X.: An LMI approach to design robust fault detection filter for uncertain LTI systems. Automatica. 3 (2003) : 543-550
9. Souza, C. E., Palhares, R. M., Peres, P. L. D.: Robust H_∞ filter design for uncertain linear systems with multiple time-varying state delays. IEEE Trans. On Signal Processing. 3 (2001) 569-576

Input-to-State Stability Analysis of a Class of Interconnected Nonlinear Systems

Jia Wang, Xiaobei Wu, and Zhiliang Xu

Department of Automation, Nanjing University of Science and Technology,
Nanjing, 210094 P.R.C
Nicole_wang@163.com, wuxb@mail.njust.edu.cn

Abstract. This paper proposes a new definition of string stability with bounded input from the input-to-state view. By viewing the interconnection as a kind of input to a subsystem, it specifies sufficient conditions of string stability for a class of directed circular interconnected nonlinear systems, which is based on the input-to-state stability analysis and singular perturbation theory. The proof is first conducted on a system with two subsystems, and then expanded to finite N subsystems. Furthermore, directed graph is used as an illustrative tool in this paper.

1 Introduction

Control of large-scale systems has gained renewed interest during the development of sensors, autonomous vehicle, and complicated modern manufacturing systems. Some of the large-scale systems are naturally interconnected systems, such as a team of autonomous vehicles or a sensor network, where a centralized control is impractical. Even though we can apply centralized control to other large-scale systems such as modern manufacturing systems, a decentralized control system is desired to enhance the robustness and decrease the cost and complexity of the controllers. This paper will focus on general interconnected systems.

A lot of work has been done to deal with the interconnections between subsystems in order to achieve good performance of the entire interconnected system, especially regarding stability issues. Both centralized and decentralized control have been applied to deal with interconnection. However, decentralized control is preferred due to its relatively simple control law, low cost and fault tolerance ability [1]. The pioneer work by Siljak [2] presents stability theorems of interconnected linear systems based on the structural information only. When the subsystems have nonlinear dynamics or the interconnected system is entered in a nonlinear fashion, the analysis and design problem becomes even more challenging, most of the research is focusing on some class of nonlinear system or nonlinear connection. Intelligent control has been used, such as fuzzy sets [3] and neural network [4], to achieve certain results. Adaptive control is applied for interconnected systems, where Lyapunov methodology is extensively utilized for the stability analysis and control design. Both state feedback [5–7] and output feedback control [8] are used.

Stability analysis is the essential problem in the design and analysis of control systems. Sontag proposed the ISS [9] in the 1980s, especially for nonlinear systems. A crude description of ISS is that for any bounded input, the state will be bounded. ISS analysis is more general in the sense that it takes care of the state bound of whole system under certain inputs. For instance, [10] and [11] study the ISS of affine systems and the corresponding Lyapunov function in this field. Sontag continued his work on the ISS of general nonlinear systems in [12]. More research focusing on the ISS of interconnected systems includes [13, 14].

Graph theory fits nicely in the analysis of interconnected systems, where the vertex denotes the states, inputs and outputs of a subsystem, and the edge denotes its interconnection. A directed graph of the interconnected system provides an alternative insight to the structure of the systems. Moreover, graph theory can be used to offer guidelines for partition and condensation of large-scale systems.

For certain systems, such as automated highway systems, string stability is of particular interest. It is the property of the vehicle string to attenuate disturbances as they propagate down the string. We can interpret the string stability to be a concept by which the error of state will be bounded or not as they propagate along the string. We can also see that the string stability mainly cares about the state of the systems and aims at suppressing error propagation. There are different definitions of the string stability, such as in context of vehicle following [15]; or in the sense of linear digital processors [16]; and also Lyapunov like definition [17]. The authors of [18] especially consider the LTI systems; while in [19] conditions where there are several formation leaders are studied. The concept of string stability is then expanded to mesh stability in [20], while mesh stability still has some limitations on formation translation. It is only used for the acyclic graph systems. In practical applications, sometimes we must consider the interaction between the subsystems and therefore cyclic graph system is often encountered.

In this paper, we will focus on the string stability of a class of interconnected nonlinear systems based on the ISS and singular perturbation, where we propose a new definition of string stability from the input-to-state view. The interconnection is treated as an input to the subsystems. This is different from the traditional view of interconnection as a disturbance to the subsystems. While identifying the ISS conditions of each subsystem, we extend the analysis to the entire interconnected system. This paper is organized as following: a problem statement is given in Section 2, and some preliminary results on ISS are also given. Sufficient conditions for string stability for two subsystems are presented in Section 3, and then we expand this work in Section 4 to a more complicated structure with finite N subsystems. Finally, Section 5 concludes the paper and outlines some future research directions.

2 Problem Statement

Consider the following autonomous interconnected system. First, we assume the interconnections between each subsystem are weak couplings and the interconnections just exist between the states of different subsystems and each subsystem is ISS. The dynamics of each nonlinear subsystem Σ_k is:

$$\dot{x}_k = f_k(x_1, \cdots x_{k-1}, x_k, x_{k+1}, \cdots x_N, u_k),$$

where $(k=1,\cdots N)$, N is the number of subsystems, $f_k: \mathbb{R}^{n_1} \times \mathbb{R}^{n_2} \times \cdots \times \mathbb{R}^{n_N} \times \mathbb{R}^{m_k} \to \mathbb{R}^{n_k}$ denotes the nonlinear dynamics, $x_k \in \mathbb{R}^{n_k}$ and $u_k \in \mathbb{R}^{m_k}$ are the state and input of the subsystem Σ_k. Without loss of generality, we can assume the origin of Σ_k is an isolated equilibrium point and f_k are locally Lipschitz in an open connected set which contains the origin. Let $x_j \in \mathbb{R}^{n_j}$ denote the state of subsystem Σ_j $(j=1,\cdots k-1, k+1, \cdots N)$. Let $x_j = h_{kj}(x_1, \cdots x_{j-1}, x_{j+1}, \cdots x_N)$ be an isolated root of equation $0 = f_j(x_1, \cdots x_n, 0)$ such that $h_{kj}(0) = 0$. Denote $y_{kj} = x_j - h_{kj}(x_1, \cdots x_{j-1}, x_{j+1}, \cdots x_N)$.

Now let the reduced system be:

$$\dot{x}_k = f_k(x_1, \cdots x_{k-1}, x_k, x_{k+1}, \cdots x_N, u_k) \tag{1}$$

and the boundary layer system:

$$\varepsilon_{kj} \dot{x}_j = f_j(x_1, \cdots x_{j-1}, h_{kj}, x_{j+1}, \cdots x_N, u_j) \tag{2}$$

be the singularly perturbed interconnected system, where ε_{kj} denotes a small positive weak coupling parameter that connects the subsystem Σ_j with the subsystem Σ_k.

For system (1) we use the following notation: $\|f_i(\cdot)\|_\infty$ denotes $\sup_{t>0} |f_i(t)|$, and $\|f_i(0)\|_\infty$ denotes $\sup_i |f_i(0)|$ and here we present the new definition of string stability.

Definition 1. *[String Stability with input]: The origin $x_i = 0$, $i \in N$ of (1) is of string stability with input if for any $e_1, e_2 > 0$, there exists a $\delta > 0$ such that $\|x_i(0)\|_\infty < \delta \Rightarrow \sup_i \|x_i(\cdot)\|_\infty < e_1$ given the input $\|u_i\| < e_2$.*

Now, we give some introduction of input-to-state stability (ISS), which will be used extensively in this paper. Consider the following system:

$$\dot{x} = f(x, u) \tag{3}$$

where $f: D \times D_u \to \mathbb{R}^n$ is locally Lipschitz in x and u. The sets D and D_u are defined by $D = \{x \in \mathbb{R}^n : \|x\| < r\}$, $D_u = \{u \in \mathbb{R}^m : \sup_{t>0} \|u(t)\| = \|u\|_{L_\infty} < r_u\}$.

Definition 2. *[Input-to-state stability [21]]: The system (3) is said to be input-to-state stable (ISS) if there exists a class KL function β and a class K function γ such that for any initial state $x(0)$ and any bounded input $u(t)$, the solution $x(t)$ exists for all $t \geq 0$ and satisfies $\|x(t)\| \leq \beta(\|x_0\|, t) + \gamma(\|u_T(\cdot)\|_{L_\infty})$, $0 \leq T \leq t$.*

Theorem 1. *[21]: A continuous function $V: D \to \mathbb{R}$ is an ISS Lyapunov function on D for the system (3) if and only if there exist class K function $\beta_1, \beta_2, \beta_3$ and σ such that the following two conditions are satisfied:*

$$\beta_1(\|x\|) \leq V(x(t)) \leq \beta_2(\|x\|) \quad \forall x \in D, t > 0 \tag{4}$$

$$\frac{\partial V}{\partial x} f(x,u) \leq -\beta_3(\|x\|) + \sigma(\|u\|) \quad \forall x \in D, u \in D_u \tag{5}$$

Function V is an ISS Lyapunov function if $D = \mathbb{R}^n, D_u = \mathbb{R}^m$ and $\beta_1, \beta_2, \beta_3$ and $\sigma \in K_\infty$. The existence of an ISS Lyapunov function is a sufficient and necessary condition for input-to-state stability [21].

3 String Stability of Two Interconnected Nonlinear Systems

The first result of string stability of an interconnected system is presented when N = 2, that is, we only have two subsystems and their interconnection exists only between the states.

Theorem 2. *For a weak perturbed interconnected directed circular graph system:*

$$\dot{x}_i = f(x_i, x_j, u_i) \tag{6}$$

$$\varepsilon \dot{x}_j = g(x_i, x_j, u_j) \tag{7}$$

where ε denotes a small positive weak coupling parameter, $x_i \in \mathbb{R}^{n_i}$, $x_j \in \mathbb{R}^{n_j}$, $u_i \in \mathbb{R}^{m_i}$, $u_j \in \mathbb{R}^{m_j}$. Assume the equilibrium point and the function f and g are globally Lipschitz in their arguments when both of the input u_1 and u_2 are zeros. Let $x_j = h_i(x_i)$ be the solution of $g(x_i, x_j, 0) = 0$, such that $h_i(0) = 0$. Let $y_i := x_j - h_i(x_i)$, $y_i \in \mathbb{R}^{n_j}$. The definition of h_j and y_j are also given as $y_j := x_i - h_j(x_j)$, $y_j \in \mathbb{R}^{n_i}$. And $\varepsilon \dot{x}_j = g(x_i, x_j, u_j)$ is called the boundary layer system, $\dot{x}_i = f(x_i, x_j, u_i)$ is called the reduced (unperturbed) systems.

If there exist positive constants, $\alpha_1, \delta_l, \delta_h, \delta_1, \delta_2 > 0$ and the following conditions are satisfied:

1) For each subsystem, there exists a Lyapunov function $V(x_k)$ ($k = i, j$) s.t. $\forall x_k \in \mathbb{R}^{n_k}$:

$$\left\| \frac{\partial V}{\partial x_k} \right\| \leq \alpha_1 \|x_k\| \tag{8}$$

2) For each subsystem, there exist a Lyapunov function $W(x_k, y_k)$ s.t. $\forall x_k \in \mathbb{R}^{n_k}$ $\forall y_k \in \mathbb{R}^{n_k}$:

$$\delta_l \|y_k\|^2 \leq W(x_k, y_k) \leq \delta_h \|y_k\|^2 \tag{9}$$

$$\frac{\partial W}{\partial y_k} g(x_k, y_k + h_k(x_k), 0) \leq -\delta_1 \|y_k\|^2 \tag{10}$$

$$\left\| \frac{\partial W}{\partial (x_k, y_k)} \right\| \leq \delta_2 \|x_k \quad y_k\| \tag{11}$$

And

$$\left(\frac{\partial W}{\partial x_k} - \frac{\partial W}{\partial y_k} \frac{\partial h_k}{\partial x_k} \right) f(x_k, y_k + h(x_k), 0) \leq \gamma_1 \|x_k\| \|y_k\| + \gamma_2 \|y_k\|^2 \tag{12}$$

with $\gamma_1 > 0$ and $\gamma_2 > 0$

3) There exists class KL function β and class K function γ, the input u_k of the system satisfies:

$$\|x_k(t)\| \leq \beta(\|x_k\|, t) + \gamma\left(\|u_k(\tau)\|_{L^\infty}\right) \quad \forall t \geq 0, \ 0 \leq \tau \leq t \tag{13}$$

Then there exists $\varepsilon^* > 0$ such that the perturbed system is exponentially stable for $\varepsilon < \varepsilon^*$. Both the states of interconnected system x_j and the states of reduced system x_i are bounded for small enough ε. These conditions ensure that when the two subsystems are viewed as the singular perturbations, they are string stable with bounded input.

Proof: The three conditions confirm that when the bounded input is considered the system states are still bounded. According to Definition 2, we can see that the reduced system is input-to-state stable because of Equation (13). Applying Theorem 1 an ISS Lyapunov function $V(x_i(t))$ can be found and there exist class K functions β_1, β_2, β_3 and σ such that conditions (4) and (5) are satisfied. So when the input u_i is zero we can find corresponding positive constants α_l, α_h and α_2 and satisfy:

$$\alpha_l \|x_i\|^2 \leq V(x_i) \leq \alpha_h \|x_i\|^2 \tag{14}$$

$$\frac{\partial V}{\partial x_i} f(x_i, h(x_i), 0) \leq -\alpha_2 \|x_i\|^2 \tag{15}$$

Combining equations (14), (15) with (8), these conditions assure that the reduced system is string stable and the equations (9)-(12) assure that the boundary layer system is string stable. From (8)-(12) and (14), (15), according to [22] we can conclude that there exists such $\varepsilon^* > 0$ that the perturbed directed acyclic system is string stable in sense of Lyapunov function (defined as [17]) for $\varepsilon < \varepsilon^*$.

Due to the weak interconnection between subsystems, we may view the different subsystems as perturbations to others. At the same time each perturbation should satisfy the reduced system condition 1) and 3). For instance, we conclude the string

Fig. 1. The interconnection of two subsystems

stability with input of the system Σ_i (satisfies condition 1) and 3)) with the singular perturbation Σ_j (satisfies condition 2)); and then similarly, when viewing subsystem Σ_i as the singular perturbation to Σ_j, the same result can be achieved for the Σ_i to satisfy the boundary layer system condition 2) for small enough ε.

Since the asymptotic stability of the origin of a system can not assure the input-to-state stability of the same system, we will consider the state bound with bounded input following [23].

The interconnection topology is defined using graph theoretic terminology (refer to Figure 1). Assume the interconnections are weak perturbed interconnection. Based on the ISS properties, according to (13) for different subsystems we can get

$$\|x_i(t)\| \le \beta_i(\|x_i(0)\|,t) + \gamma_{iu}(\sup\|u_i\|) + \gamma_{ix}(\sup\|x_j\|) \tag{16}$$

$$\|x_j(t)\| \le \beta_j(\|x_j(0)\|,t) + \gamma_{ju}(\sup\|u_j\|) + \gamma_{jx}(\sup\|x_i\|)$$

where β_i and β_j are class KL functions, γ_{iu}, γ_{ju}, γ_{ix} and γ_{jx} are class K functions.

Because each of the subsystems is ISS, for the whole system, let $\sup\|x_j\| \le M$. M is a positive constant, so rewrite (16) as:

$$\|x_i(t)\| \le \beta_i(\|x_i(0)\|,t) + \gamma_{iu}(\sup\|u_i\|) + \gamma_{ix}(M) \tag{17}$$

Then considering the interval $\left[\frac{t}{2},t\right]$, we can have:

$$\|x_i(t)\| \le \beta_i\left(\left\|x_i\left(\frac{t}{2}\right)\right\|,t\right) + \gamma_{iu}\left(\sup_{\left[\frac{t}{2},t\right]}\|u_i\|\right) + \gamma_{ix}(M) \tag{18}$$

$$\|x_j(t)\| \le \beta_j\left(\left\|x_j\left(\frac{t}{2}\right)\right\|,t\right) + \gamma_{ju}\left(\sup_{\left[\frac{t}{2},t\right]}\|u_j\|\right) + \gamma_{jx}\left(\sup_{\left[\frac{t}{2},t\right]}\|x_i\|\right) \tag{19}$$

Similarly, during the interval $\left[0,\frac{t}{2}\right]$, it becomes:

$$\left\|x_i\left(\frac{t}{2}\right)\right\| \le \beta_i\left(\|x_i(0)\|,\frac{t}{2}\right) + \gamma_{iu}\left(\sup_{\left[0,\frac{t}{2}\right]}\|u_i\|\right) + \gamma_{ix}(M) \tag{20}$$

$$\left\|x_j\left(\frac{t}{2}\right)\right\| \leq \beta_j\left(\|x_j(0)\|,\frac{t}{2}\right)+\gamma_{ju}\left(\sup_{\left[0,\frac{t}{2}\right]}\|u_j\|\right)+\gamma_{jx}\left(\sup_{\left[0,\frac{t}{2}\right]}\|x_i\|\right) \quad (21)$$

Now from the ISS of the Σ_i, we can have:

$$\sup_{\left[0,\frac{t}{2}\right]}\|x_i\| \leq \beta_i\left(\|x_i(0)\|,0\right)+\gamma_{iu}\left(\sup\|u_i\|\right)+\gamma_{ix}(M) \quad (22)$$

$$\sup_{\left[\frac{t}{2},t\right]}\|x_i\| \leq \beta_i\left(\|x_i(0)\|,\frac{t}{2}\right)+\gamma_{iu}\left(\sup\|u_i\|\right)+\gamma_{ix}(M) \quad (23)$$

Then substituting (21), (22) and (23) into (19) it follows that:

$$\|x_j(t)\| \leq \beta_j\left(\begin{pmatrix}\beta_j\left(\|x_j(0)\|,\frac{t}{2}\right)+\gamma_{ju}\left(\sup\|u_j\|\right)\\+\gamma_{jx}\left(\beta_i\left(\|x_i(0)\|,0\right)+\gamma_{iu}\left(\sup\|u_i\|\right)+\gamma_{ix}(M)\right)\end{pmatrix},t\right)$$
$$+\gamma_{ju}\left(\sup\|u_j\|\right)+\gamma_{jx}\left(\beta_i\left(\|x_i(0)\|,\frac{t}{2}\right)+\gamma_{iu}\left(\sup\|u_i\|\right)+\gamma_{ix}(M)\right) \quad (24)$$

Substituting (20) into (18), we can further obtain:

$$\|x_i(t)\| \leq \beta_i\left(\beta_i\left(\|x_i(0)\|,\frac{t}{2}\right)+\gamma_{iu}\left(\sup_{\left[0,\frac{t}{2}\right]}\|u_i\|\right)+\gamma_{ix}(M),t\right)+\gamma_{iu}\left(\sup_{\left[\frac{t}{2},t\right]}\|u_i\|\right)+\gamma_{ix}(M) \quad (25)$$

For any class K function χ and any nonnegative a and b we know the fact that $\chi(a+b) \leq \chi(2a)+\chi(2b)$. Let $x_l=(x_i,x_j)$, $u_l=(u_i,u_j)$ for the whole system, so there exists for the corresponding subsystem a class K Function γ_l and a class KL function β_l for the new combined subsystem Σ_l satisfying the following ISS condition:

$$\|x_l(t)\| \leq \beta_l\left(\|x(s)\|,t-s\right)+\gamma_l\left(\sup_{s\leq r\leq t}\|u_l(r)\|\right)$$

where

$$\beta_l = \beta_i\left(2\beta_i\left(r,\frac{t}{2}\right)\right)+\beta_j\left(2\beta_j\left(r,\frac{t}{2}\right)\right)+\beta_j\left(2\gamma_{jx}(r,0)\right)+\gamma_{jx}\left(2\beta_j\left(r,\frac{t}{2}\right)\right)$$

$$\gamma_l = \beta_i\left(2\gamma_{iu}(r)\right)+\beta_i\left(2\gamma_{ix}(r)\right)+\gamma_{iu}(r)+\gamma_{ix}(r)+\beta_j\left(2\gamma_{ju}(r)\right)$$
$$+\beta_j\left(2\gamma_{iu}(r)\right)+\beta_j\left(2\gamma_{ix}(r)\right)+\gamma_{ju}(r)+\gamma_{jx}\left(2\gamma_{iu}(r)\right)+\gamma_{jx}\left(2\gamma_{ix}(r)\right)$$

For $r \geq 0$, β_l is class KL function and γ_l is class K function, so we can confirm that the whole system is string stable with bounded input.

From Theorem 2 and the above analysis we can achieve sufficient conditions for string stability with bounded input of a weak interconnected directed circular graph system, that is: considering system (6) (7), the reduced systems should satisfy conditions (8) and (13); for the boundary layer system, it should satisfy conditions (9)-(12) when the directed graph is considered both the systems should satisfy all the conditions of Theorem 2 simultaneously and find the small enough ε.

4 Stability Analysis of Finite N-Interconnected Nonlinear Systems

Now we consider the interconnected system that has more than 2 subsystems. Since the number of subsystems is finite, for each one there exists both v_i and w_i simultaneously, so we can extend the results of string stable with input [24] to mesh or apply even more complicated interconnection between the subsystems (such as Figure 2) and the requirements are described as follows:

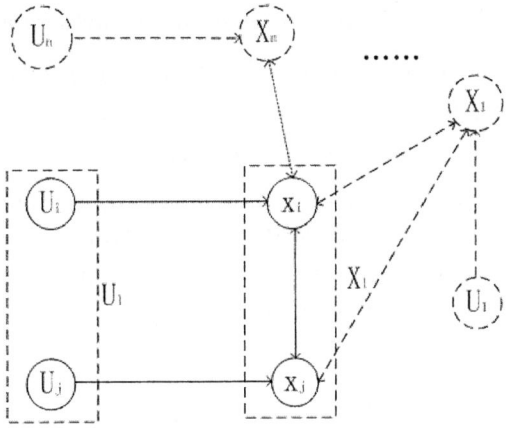

Fig. 2. The overall systems

Theorem 3. *Consider a weak interconnected system. For each subsystem Σ_k ($k = 1, \cdots N$), if there exist positive constants α_{1k}, α_{2k}, α_{3k}, α_{lk}, α_{hk}, δ_{lk}, δ_{hk}, and if the following conditions are satisfied:*

1) For each subsystem, there exists a Lyapunov function $V_k(x_k)$, $k = 1, \cdots N$, such that:

$$\alpha_{lk} \|x_k\|^2 \leq V_k(x_k) \leq \alpha_{hk} \|x_k\|^2 \qquad (26)$$

$$\frac{\partial V_k}{\partial x_k} f_k\left(x_1, \cdots x_{j-1}, h_{kj}(x_1, \cdots x_{j-1}, x_{j+1}, \cdots x_N), x_{j+1}, \cdots x_N, 0\right) \leq -\alpha_{1k} \|x_k\|^2 + \sum_{j=1, j \neq k}^{N} \alpha_{1kj} \|x_j\|^2 \qquad (27)$$

with $\alpha_{1kj} > 0$, $\alpha_{1k} > \dfrac{\alpha_{hk}}{\alpha_{lk}} \sum_{j=1}^{N} \alpha_{1kj}$ and

$$\left\| \dfrac{\partial V_k}{\partial x_k} \right\| \le \alpha_{2k} \|x_k\| \tag{28}$$

2) *There exists a Lyapunov function* $W_k(x_k, x_j)$ *such that:*

$$\delta_{lk} \|x_j\|^2 \le W_k(x_k, x_j) \le \delta_{hk} \|x_j\|^2 \tag{29}$$

$$\dfrac{\partial W_k}{\partial y_{kj}} f_j(x_1, \cdots x_{j-1}, y_{kj} + h_{kj}(x_1, \cdots x_{j-1}, x_{j+1}, \cdots x_N), x_{j+1}, \cdots x_N, 0) \le -\alpha_{3k} \|y_{kj}\|^2 \tag{30}$$

and positive constants, δ_{kx}, δ_{ky} *and* $\eta_{kN} \cdots \eta_{k1}$ *such that:*

$$\left\| \dfrac{\partial W_k}{\partial x_k} \right\| \le \delta_{kx} \|y_{kj}\|, \quad \left\| \dfrac{\partial W_k}{\partial y_{kj}} \right\| \le \delta_{ky} \|y_{kj}\|, \quad \left\| \dfrac{\partial h_{kj}}{\partial x_k} \right\| \le \eta_{kN}, \quad \cdots, \quad \left\| \dfrac{\partial h_{kj}}{\partial x_1} \right\| \le \eta_{k1}$$

Then, there exists $\varepsilon_{kj}^* > 0$ and the perturbed system is exponentially stable for $\varepsilon_{kj} < \varepsilon_{kj}^*$. According to [17, 20] the states of interconnected system are bounded for small enough ε_{kj}, both the states of the reduced system $x_k(t)$ $(k=1,\cdots N)$ and the states of the perturbation $x_j(t)$ are bounded. So when the subsystems $\Sigma_j (j=1,\cdots N)$ are viewed as singular perturbations, they are string stable with bounded input.

Proof: (Sketch of the proof) Since each subsystem is ISS, we can get (26),(27) when the interconnections are viewed as inputs to subsystem Σ_k $(k=1,\cdots N)$. When adding the input u_k, we can achieve: there exist class KL functions α_3 and class K function σ, and the input of each subsystem satisfies:

$$\dfrac{\partial V_k}{\partial x_k} f_k\left(x_1, \cdots x_{j-1}, h_{ij}\left(x_1, \cdots x_{j-1}, x_{j+1}, \cdots x_N\right), x_{j+1}, \cdots x_N, u_k\right)$$
$$\le -\alpha_3(\|x_k\|) + \sigma(\|u_k\|) + \sum_{j=1, j\ne k}^{N} \alpha_{1kj} \|x_j\|^2 \tag{31}$$

Condition 1) ensures the subsystems Σ_k $(k=1,\cdots N)$ are string stable in sense of Lyapunov when they are viewed as reduced subsystems. Then the condition 2) implies the following conditions:

$$\left(\dfrac{\partial W_k}{\partial x_k} - \dfrac{\partial W_k}{\partial y_k} \dfrac{\partial h_{kj}}{\partial x_k} \right) f_k\left(x_1, \cdots x_{j-1}, y_{ij} + h_{ij}\left(x_1, \cdots x_{j-1}, x_{j+1}, \cdots x_N\right), x_{j+1}, \cdots x_N, 0\right)$$
$$\le \delta_2 \|x_k\| \|y_{kj}\| + \delta \|y_{kj}\|^2 + \sum_{j=1, j\ne k}^{N} \delta_j \|x_j\|^2 \tag{32}$$

with $\delta > 0$, $\delta_j > 0$ and $\delta_2 > 0$. These conditions ensure the subsystems Σ_k $(k=1,\cdots N)$ are string stable in sense of Lyapunov when they are viewed as boundary layer systems.

When all the interconnected subsystems $\Sigma_1 \cdots \Sigma_N$ (Figure 2. the dashes) satisfy the conditions (26)-(32), the string stability with bound input of the entire system is assured. This conclusion can be deduced from the same analogy of Theorem 2. For example, consider the Σ_{i-1} as the perturbation to the Σ_l. If the Σ_l and Σ_{i-1} satisfy the conditions of Theorem 2, we can conclude that the interconnections between Σ_l and Σ_{i-1} are string stable with bounded input. So given countable interconnections between the subsystems, the entire system is string stable with bounded input.

5 Concluding Remarks

In this paper, we have presented the analysis of string stability of interconnected systems from the input to state view. The sufficient conditions of string stability for weak coupling directed circular interconnected systems are given. Moreover, we expand string stability to more complicated interconnected nonlinear systems. In future work, we will be further incorporating the graph theory into the research of string stability.

References

1. A. Ramakrishna, N. Viswanadham: Decentralized control of interconnected dynamical systems. IEEE Transactions on Automatic Control, Vol.27.(1982)159-164
2. D. D. Siljak: Decentralized Control of Complex Systems. Academic Press, Boston(1985)
3. B. S. Chen, C. H. Lee, Y. C. Chang: Tracking design of uncertain nonlinear SISO systems: adaptive fuzzy approach. IEEE Transactions on Fuzzy Systems, Vol.4.No.1.Feb.(1996)32-43
4. J. T. Spooner, K. M. Passino: Decentralized adaptive control of nonlinear systems using radial basis neural networks. IEEE Transactions on Automatic Control, Vol.44. No.11 (1999) 2050-2057
5. J. T. Spooner, K. M. Passino: Adaptive control of a class of decentralized nonlinear systems. IEEE Transactions on Automatic Control, Vol.41. No.2.(1996)280-284
6. D. T. Gavel, D. D. Siljak: Decentralized adaptive control: structural conditions for stability. IEEE Transactions On Automatic Control, Vol.34. No.4.(1989)413-426
7. L. Shi, S. K. Sigh: Decentralized adaptive controller design for large-scale systems with higher order uncertainties. IEEE Transactions on Automatic Control, Vol.AC-37. No.8. (1992) 1106-1118
8. Z. P. Jiang: Decentralized and adaptive nonlinear tracking of large-scale systems via output. IEEE Transactions on Automatic control, Vol.45. No.11.(2000)2122-2128
9. E. D. Sontag: Smooth stability implies coprime factorization. IEEE Transaction On Automatic Control, Vol.34. No.4.(1989)435-443
10. R. A. Freeman: Global internal stabilizability does not imply global external stabilizability for small sensor disturbances. IEEE Transactions on Automatic Control, Vol.40. No.12. (1995)2119-2122
11. M. Krstic,Z. H. Li: Inverse optimal design of input-to-state stabilizing nonlinear controllers. IEEE Transactions on Automatic Control, Vol.43. No.3.(1998)336-350
12. E. D Sontag: Further facts about input to state stabilization. IEEE Transactions on Automatic Control, Vol.35. No.4.(1990) 473-476
13. E. D. Sonag: On the input-to-state stability property. European Journal of Control, Vol.1. No.1. (1995)24-36

14. Z. P. Jiang, I. M. Y. Mareels: Small-gain control method for nonlinear cascaded systems with dynamic uncertainties. IEEE Transactions on Automatic Control, Vol.42. No.3. (1997)292-308
15. K. C. Chu: Decentralized control of high speed vehicle string. Transportation Research, Vol.8.(1974)361-383
16. S. S. L. Chang: Temporal stability of n-dimensional linear processors and its applications. IEEE Transactions on Circuits and Systems, Vol.CAS-27. No.8.(1980)716-719
17. D. Swaroop, J. K. Hedrick: String stability of interconnection systems. IEEE Trans.on Automatic Control, Vol.41. No.3. Mar. (1996)349-357.
18. S. Darbha: A note about the stability of string LTI systems. Journal of Dynamic Systems, Measurement and Control, Vol.124. No.3.(2002)472-475
19. J. K. Hedrick, M. Tomizuka, P. Varaiya: Control issues in automated highway systems. IEEE Control System Magazine, Vol.14. No.6.(1994)21-32
20. A. Pant, P. Seiler, K. Hedrick: Mesh stability of look-ahead interconnected systems. IEEE Transactions on Automatic Control, Vol.47. No.2.(2002)403-407
21. H. J. Marquez: Nonlinear Control Systems Analysis and Design, John Wiley & Sons. Hoboken, New Jersey,(2003)
22. P. Kokotovic, H. K. Hhalil, J. O'Reilly: Singular Perturbation Methods in Control: Analysis and Design. Academic, New York(1986)
23. H. K. Hhalil: Nonlilear Systems. Third Edition Prentice Hall, Upper Sadle River, New Jersey(2002)
24. Jia Wang, Xiaobei Wu, Zhiliang Xu: String Stability of a Class of Interconnected Nonlinear System from the Input to State View. 2005 International Conference on Machine learning and Cybernetics(2005)

Construction and Simulation of the Movable Propeller Turbine Neural Network Model

Jiang Chang[1] and Yan Peng[2]

[1] Department of Automation, Shenzhen Polytechnic, Shenzhen, 518055, China
changjiang@szpt.edu.cn
[2] Industry Center, Shenzhen Polytechnic, Shenzhen, 518055, China
5992507@oa.szpt.net

Abstract. Due to the difficulty in describing the nonlinear characteristics of a movable propeller turbine, this paper introduces the construction and simulation of the movable propeller turbine neural network model ZZ587. The convergence speed of the offline training is fast and the accuracy of the model is high when using the Levenberg-Marquardt algorithm. Matlab and Simulink are used for the nonlinear simulation of the movable propeller turbine neural network model ZZ587. The variability of the different inner parameters of the system and the turbine can be attained quickly and with integrity. It provides a good base for the research of control policy of the movable propeller turbine governing system.

1 Introduction

Movable propeller turbine governing system is a complex control system[1], and the digital simulation is an effective method to analyze its dynamic transition process. The accuracy of the movable propeller turbine model is the key to its nonlinear simulation[2]. The variety of movable propeller turbine moment and flow is difficult to describe by analysis equation. It is usually represented by a numerical table or curve based on the synthetic characteristic curve of the movable propeller turbine model. However, since the accuracy of the function relation represented by the curve or table is not high enough, the calculation is complicated. So, the reliability of the simulation result is affected because it is difficult to construct a relatively exact simulation model. The neural network can fully approximate any complex nonlinear system and study dynamic system behavior of any serious undetermined system. It has a high parallel calculation ability, strong robustness and fault tolerance[3]. Therefore, using the neural network is a very effective way to construct the nonlinear simulation model of a movable propeller turbine[4].

2 Construction of the Movable Propeller Turbine Neural Network

The movable propeller turbine neural network model ZZ587 includes the integrated characteristic neural network model NZZM, the coordinate characteristic neural network model NZZC and some other calculation blocks as shown in Fig.1.

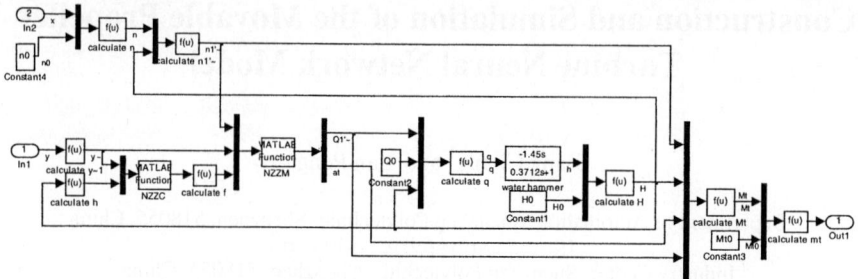

Fig. 1. The movable propeller turbine neural network model ZZ587

2.1 The Integrated Characteristic Neural Network Model NZZM

The nonlinear characteristic of a movable propeller turbine can be expressed by two equations as follows[5]:

$$M_t = M_t(H, n, \alpha, \varphi) \quad (1)$$

$$Q = Q(H, n, \alpha, \varphi) \quad (2)$$

In this equation, M_t is movable propeller turbine moment, Q is flow, H is water head, n is speed of rotation, α is guide vane opening, φ is vane corner.

The functions in equation (1) and (2) are nonlinear relations. The movable propeller turbine is nonlinear in essence. It is possible to describe the multivariable nonlinear characteristic of the movable propeller turbine using a neural network. The integrated characteristic neural network model NZZM can be constructed firstly.

The value η and $Q_1{'}$ under different values α, φ and $n_1{'}$ can be obtained from the integrated characteristic curve of the movable propeller turbine[6]. So the integrated characteristic neural network model NZZM uses the three-layered feed forward neural network where the inputs are guide vane opening α, vane corner φ and unit speed of rotation $n_1{'}$ and the outputs are efficient η and unit flow $Q_1{'}$. The structure of the integrated characteristic neural network model NZZM is shown in Fig.2.

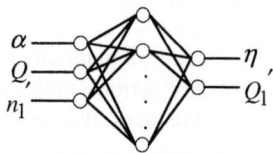

Fig. 2. The structure of the integrated characteristic neural network model NZZM

The Levenberg-Marquardt algorithm is used to train the above three-layer feed forward neural networks[7]. The Levenberg-Marquardt algorithm was designed to approach second-order training speed without having to compute the Hessian matrix. This algorithm appears to be the fastest method for training a moderate-sized feed forward neural network. It also has a very efficient MATLAB implementation.

The training samples of the integrated characteristic neural network model NZZM can be obtained from the integrated characteristic curve of the movable propeller turbine. However the small opening characteristic which is the key component of the digital simulation is usually lacking in the integrated characteristic curve. This part of the characteristic is often obtained by extension or interpolation of the big opening characteristic. The specific methods are graphical method, listing function interpolation method, approximation polynomial calculation method etc. The small opening characteristic is accurate when using the extension method with a control condition. The control point is no-load opening α_x. The compensation relation of no-load opening and small opening is shown in Fig.3.

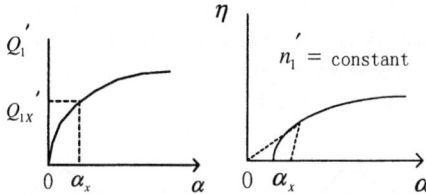

Fig. 3. The compensation relation

Fig.3 illustrates that the small opening characteristic of the movable propeller turbine is also nonlinear. So it is very suitable for compensating the small opening characteristic using feed forward neural network. The integrated characteristic neural network model NZZM can fully describe the efficient and flow characteristics of the movable propeller turbine under both big opening and small opening.

Thus the training samples of the integrated characteristic neural network model NZZM includes the big opening samples, control point extending to small opening and zero point. The big opening samples are the value η and Q_1' under different values α, φ and n_1' which are obtained from the integrated characteristic curve of the movable propeller turbine. The control point extending to the small opening can be obtained from the runaway characteristic and no-load characteristic of the movable propeller turbine. The runaway characteristic and no-load characteristic are also nonlinear so that the runaway characteristic neural network can be constructed.

2.2 The Runaway Characteristic Neural Network Model

It is possible for the hydrogenerator unit to suddenly throw away a whole load accidentally. If the governing mechanism moves into runaway mode at this time, then the guide vane can't close in time and the speed of rotation will increase incessantly until it reaches the highest possible value. This is called the runaway phenomenon of hydro turbine. The mode at this time is runaway mode and the highest speed of rotation is runaway speed of rotation. Obviously, the water moment is zero, the output power is zero and efficiency is also zero under runaway mode.

The no-load mode is the mode when the output power is zero under the rated speed of rotation. At this time, the water moment and the efficiency are zero. So we can say that the no-load mode is the mode when the runaway speed of rotation equals the rated speed of rotation. The runaway opening is no-load opening α_x at this point, and the flow under no-load mode is no-load flow Q_x.

Known from the no-load characteristic and runaway characteristic, the unit no-load flow Q_{1x}' and the efficient η are zero under unit rated speed of rotation n_{1r}', no-load opening α_x and vane corner φ. This is the control point extending to the small opening. The control point can be accurately and rapidly obtained from the runaway characteristic neural network of the movable propeller turbine.

The runaway characteristic neural network of the movable propeller turbine considers two situations of the runaway characteristic as follows:

1) Keep coordinate relation: The runaway speed of the rotation characteristic neural network is NZZNB. The inputs are unit runaway speed of rotation n_{1r}' and unit speed of rotation n_1' and the output is guide vane opening α. The runaway flow characteristic neural network is NZZQB. The inputs are guide vane opening α and unit speed of rotation n_1' and the output is the unit runaway flow Q_{1r}'. The structure of the NZZNB and NZZQB is shown in Fig.4.

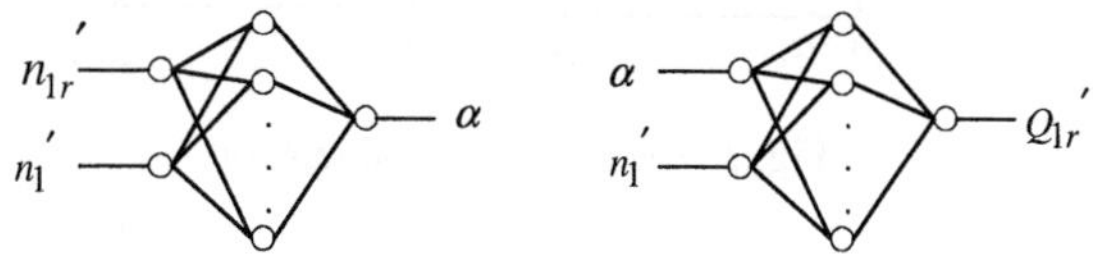

(a) NZZNB (b) NZZQB

Fig. 4. The structure of the runaway characteristic neural network model NZZNB and NZZQB

2) The coordinate relation is broken-down: The runaway speed of the rotation characteristic neural network is NZZN. The inputs are unit runaway speed of rotation n_{1r}' and vane corner φ and the output is guide vane opening α. The runaway flow characteristic neural network is NZZQ. The inputs are guide vane opening α and vane corner φ and the output is unit runaway flow Q_{1r}'. The structure of the NZZN and NZZQ is shown in Fig.5.

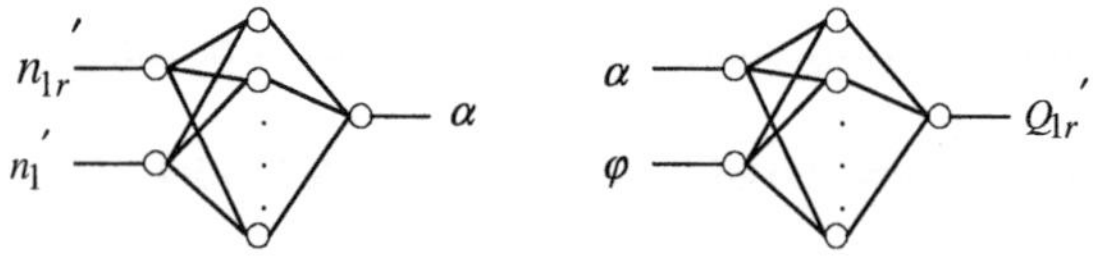

(a) NZZN (b) NZZQ

Fig. 5. The structure of the runaway characteristic neural network model NZZN and NZZQ

The runaway speed of rotation characteristic neural network of the movable propeller turbine is also trained using three-layered feed forward neural network and LM algorithm. After the neural network is trained, the no-load opening α_x can be obtained when the unit rated speed of rotation n_{1r}' obtained from Equation (3) is the input of neural network NZZNB (or NZZN). Then the no-load unit flow Q_{1x}' is obtained from neural network NZZQB (or NZZQ) and the no-load flow is obtained from equation (4).

$$n_{1r}' = n_r D_1 / \sqrt{H} \qquad (3)$$

$$Q_x = Q_{1x}' D_1^2 \sqrt{H} \qquad (4)$$

The training samples of the integrated characteristic neural network model NZZM are the control point $(n_{1r}', \alpha_x, \varphi \rightarrow Q_{1x}', 0)$ extending to the small opening obtained from the runaway characteristic neural network of the movable propeller turbine, zero point and big opening samples. After the NZZM is trained, the efficient η and the unit flow Q_1' can be obtained when the inputs are guide vane opening α, vane corner φ and unit speed of rotation n_1' no matter whether under big or small opening. The guide vane opening α and vane corner φ of the movable propeller turbine keep the coordinate relation. The nonlinear relation of the coordinate characteristic can also be described by neural network.

2.3 The Coordinate Characteristic Neural Network Model NZZC

The coordinate part of the movable propeller turbine governor carries the coordinate task governing the guide water machine and vane machine. Only under the coordinate mode can maximum efficiency of the hydro turbine unit be guaranteed, that is when the guide vane opening α and vane corner φ keep the best coordination.

Under the condition of certain water head, the coordinate relation curve of guide vane opening and vane corner is a single variable function. Strictly speaking, the coordinate relation of the movable propeller turbine is a nonlinear function with two variables such as:

$$\varphi = f(\alpha, h) \qquad (5)$$

The coordinate characteristic neural network model NZZC can be constructed according to the coordinate relation curve of the movable propeller turbine. NZZC is also trained by three-layered feed forward neural network and LM algorithm. The inputs of the NZZC are the guide vane opening α and relative working water h and the output is vane corner φ. The structure of the NZZC is shown in Fig.6.

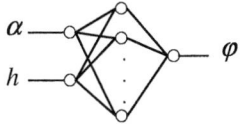

Fig. 6. The structure of the coordinate characteristic neural network model NZZC

3 Nonlinear Simulation

After the integrated characteristic neural network NZZM and the coordinate characteristic neural network NZZC of the hydroturbine ZZ587-LJ-330 are trained, they and some other calculation blocks consist of the movable propeller turbine neural network model ZZ587 shown in Fig.7.

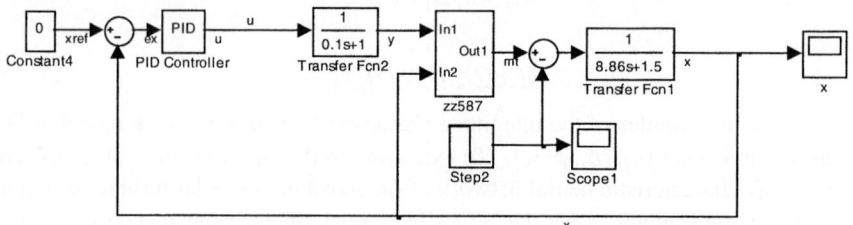

Fig. 7. The structure block diagram of the nonlinear simulation system

3.1 Construct and Train the Neural Network

There is a movable propeller turbine which type is ZZ587-LJ-330 in a certain hydroelectric power station. The relevant parameters are:

N_r=17.75MW H_r=28.5m n_r=214.3r/min
Q_r=71.1m/s D_1=4.1m T_a=8.86s T_w=1.45s

The samples of the runaway characteristic neural network model NZZN and NZZQ are obtained according to the runaway characteristic curve of hydroturbine ZZ587-LJ-330. The structure of the neural network NZZN is 2-10-1 and the structure of the neural network NZZQ is 2-8-1. The two neural networks are trained using LM algorithm and obtain a group of the optimal weight values respectively. So the no-load opening α_x and no-load flow Q_{1x}' which is the control point extending to the small opening under a different vane corner and rated unit speed of rotation are obtained.

The training samples of the neural network NZZM are the samples obtained from the integrated characteristic curve and control point. The structure of the neural network NZZM is 3-10-2. The integrated characteristic neural network NZZM of hydroturbine ZZ587-LJ-330 is obtained after being trained using LM algorithm. Its training process is shown in Fig.8.

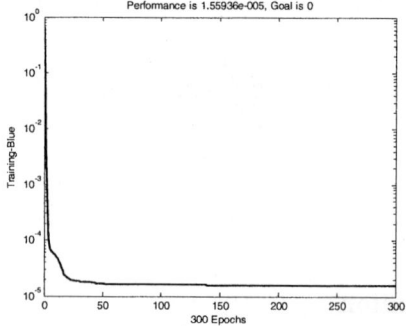

Fig. 8. The training process of NZZM

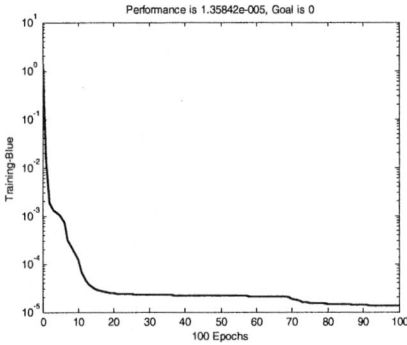

Fig. 9. The training process of NZZC

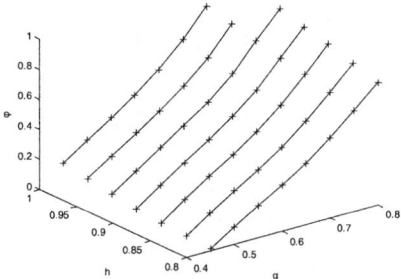

Fig. 10. The training result of NZZC

From Fig.8 we know that the convergence speed is fast and the accuracy of the model NZZM is high for using LM algorithm.

The training samples of the neural network NZZC are obtained from the coordinate curve of hydroturbine ZZ587-LJ-330. The structure of the neural network NZZC is 2-10-1. The training process of the coordinate characteristic neural network NZZC is shown in Fig.9. The coordinate characteristic curve obtained from the trained NZZC is shown in Fig.10.

In Fig.10, '+' expresses the training samples of the coordinate characteristic neural network NZZC. From Fig.9 and Fig.10 we know that the convergence speed is fast and the accuracy of the model NZZC is high from using the LM algorithm.

3.2 Nonlinear Simulation of the System

Given an initial mode of operation as: $\alpha_0=30$mm, $H_0=29$mm, $\varphi_0=10$mm, $\eta=0.818$, the ZZ587 is simulated under load disturbance using Simulink according to Fig.2[8]. The responding process curves are shown in Fig.11 when the rated load is suddenly decreased by 10% and $T_y=0.1$s. The parameters of the governor are: $K_I=0.4$, $K_P=2$, $K_D=2.4$.

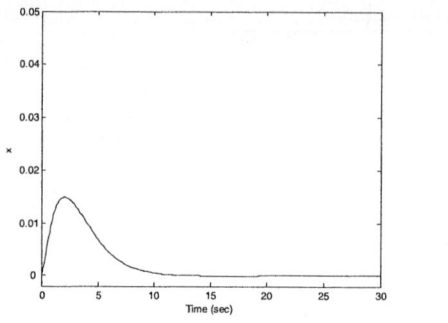
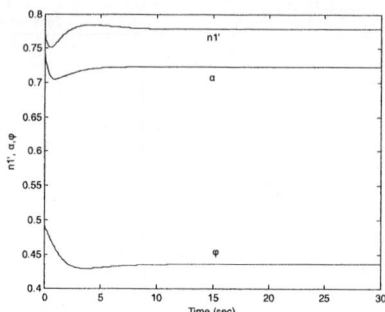

(a) The process curve of speed response

(b) The process curve of unit speed of rotation, guide vane opening and vane corner response

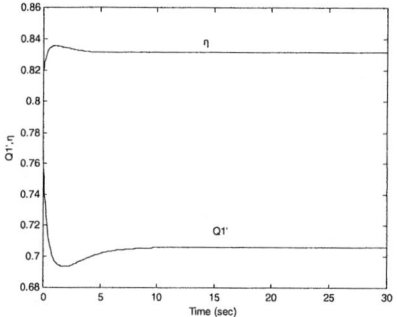

(c) The process curve of unit flow and efficiency response

(d) The process curve of relative moment response

Fig. 11. The responding process curves

4 Conclusions

Due to the nonlinear characteristic of the movable propeller turbine, the calculation of producing the model is very complex using traditional methods such as table, curve or polynomial. This paper takes advantage of the powerful nonlinear approximate ability of the feed forward neural network to construct the runaway characteristic neural network model, the integrated characteristic neural network model NZZM, the coordinate characteristic neural network mode NZZC and the movable propeller turbine neural network model ZZ587. The Levenberg-Marquardt algorithm is used to train the above neural networks. The simulation results show that the convergence speed of the offline training is fast and the accuracy of the model is high.

Big opening samples, zero point and the control point extending to small opening obtained from the runaway characteristic neural network are the training samples for the integrated characteristic neural network model NZZM of the movable propeller turbine. The NZZM can fully describe the efficiency and flow characteristic of the movable propeller turbine under both big opening and small opening. It simulates the real situation of the hydroelectric power station.

The movable propeller turbine governing system is simulated using Simulink of Matlab which is more simple and flexible than the simulation method of facing differential equations directly or by discrete link. The variability of the different inner parameters of the system and the turbine can be obtained quickly and with integrity. It provides a good base for the research of control policy of the movable propeller turbine governing system.

References

1. Zhuyi Shen: Hydroturbine Governing. Hydraulic and electric press, Beijing(1988)
2. Fangtong Xu and Zhixi Li: Computer simulation of hydroelectric power station. Hydraulic and electric press, Beijing(1994)
3. Li-cheng Jiao: Neural network system theory. Xian university of electronic science and technology press, Xian(1990)
4. Jiang Chang: Nolinear simulation of hydroturbine governing system based on neural network. 1996 IEEE International Conference on System, Man and Cybernetics(1996) 784-787
5. Chang-qi Zhang: Francis turbine principle and mathematical model. Huazhong Univesity of Science and Technology Press, Wuhan(1989)
6. Jiang Chang: The Research of Neural Network Theory and its Application on the Francis turbine Governing System. Dissertation of Doctor Degree. Wuhan University of Hydraulic and Electric Engineering, Wuhan(1997)
7. Jiang Chang, Zhi-huai Xiao, Shu-qing Wang: Neural network predict control for the hydroturbine generator set. The Second International Conference on Machine Learning and Cybernetics (ICMLC2003), Nov.2-5(2003)540-544
8. Dingyu Xue: Computer assist design-Matlab language and application. Tinghua university press, Beijing(1996)

Research on the Control and Application of Chaos in an Electrical System

Zhao-ming Lei, Zuo-jun Liu, He-xu Sun, and Hong-jun Chang

Institute of Automatics, Hebei University of Technology,
300130 Tianjin, China
LeiZhaoming@163.com

Abstract. Chaos and its application in an electrical system are studied in this paper. The simulation of chaos is presented. Some measures against the harm caused by chaos of ferroresonance are summarized. A utility scheme of chaos in the electrical system for steel smelting is proposed on the base of chaos controlling.

1 Introduction

In the past decades, chaos was misinterpreted in industrial practice: it was deemed a noise when the bounded range of chaotic behavior was narrow, whereas it was classified as an unstable phenomenon when the bounded range was wide. Since the late 1980s, chaos has been identified to be a real phenomenon in power electronics.

Ferroresonance is a complicated non-linear electrical phenomenon which can lead to dangerous over-voltage on electrical transformers, potential transformers (PT), and can sometimes result in the collapse of a large range of electrical networks. Ferroresonance occurs when a non-linear inductor, usually a transformer with a saturated magnetic core, is excited through a linear capacitor from a sinusoidal source, particularly in the presence of long lines or capacitive power cables [1][2]. It is usually initiated by a system disturbance of some form, such as the disconnection of transformer feeder lines or the opening of a circuit breaker in series with a voltage transformer. Although ferroresonance is by no means a widespread or dominant phenomenon, it is still necessary to research it deeply for the purposes of analyzing, controlling and utilizing.

Three types of ferroresonant behaviors in electrical systems are possible. These are fundamental frequency ferroresonance, sub-harmonic ferroresonance, and chaotic ferroresonance [3][4]. In the chaos of ferroresonance, oscillations appear to be random, and the transformer circuit shows universal chaotic behavior, being driven into chaos through a series of period doubling bifurcations [2][5][6]. In this paper, only the chaos phenomenon of ferroresonance in electrical power networks is discussed. In the second part of this paper, the chaotic characters of ferroresonance in electrical networks are presented. In the third part, the occurring conditions and performance of chaos in ferroresonance are analyzed and simulated. In the fourth part, some measures of limiting and controlling the chaos in electrical systems are summarized, and a scheme of chaos utility in the electrical system for steel smelting is proposed on the basis of chaos control.

2 Chaotic Characters in Ferroresonance

2.1 Chaos Circuits

The necessary condition of chaotic phenomenon occurring in a circuit or electrical power system is the existence of a non-linear negative resistance unit, for example, the Zener diode. As far as an electrical power system is concerned, a unit with non-linear negative resistance is indispensable for chaos. The transformer or potential transformer (PT) in electrical networks has a saturated magnetic core, and the inductive voltage UL would be equal to the capacitive UC with the increase of current as shown in Figure 1.

This equal point is the resonance point. However, the ΔU cannot be zero completely in practice, because power loss in the core and none sine wave in the windings. In this process, the voltage-current curve shows apparent non-linear negative resistance, so the occurrence of chaos in ferroresonance is possible when other conditions are satisfied.

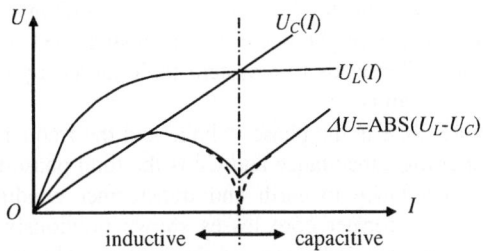

Fig. 1. Nonlinear negative resistance in saturated core

2.2 Strange Attractor and Spectrum

Chaos phenomenon is a special behavior in a non-linear dynamics system, while there is no condition for chaos in a linear system. Decades ago, the non-linear performance in an electrical power system was always simplified into a linear system for easier research.

However, there occurred some strange failures in ferroresonance, in which 25Hz and even 17Hz signals were found. This was unexplainable by linear or common non-linear theory, and only the chaotic theory in non-linear dynamics could give the answer. The conception and principles of strange attractor, spectrum and bifurcation provide a reasonable explanation for these behaviors.

2.3 Sensitivity to Initial Conditions

Chaos shows strong sensitivity to initial conditions. An effective way to eliminate ferroresonance in an electrical system is to shunt an adjustable inductor on the two open connectors of the secondary triangle winding on the three-phase five-core PT. Shortcutting a set of low power triangle windings on the main transformer at the possible time of ferroresonance is also effective. Compared to the high voltage and strong current, the trigging power is very small, even trivial, however, it limits the occurrence of chaos in ferroresonance. It presents strong sensitivity to the initial conditions and it is effective at utilizing this sensitivity to control the chaos in electrical systems.

3 Ferroresonance Simulation

3.1 Chaotic Ferroresonant Circuit

There are three standards for judging chaotic phenomenon; spectrum, Lyapunov exponents and fractal dimension. The chaos phenomenon can be identified with any one of these three conditions. In this paper, the first manner is used to judge the chaotic ferroresonance via simulation. If the solution or waveform of a system is continuous, then the system is in chaos state.

The basic chaotic ferroresonant circuit used in this paper is shown in Figure 2 [2][4]. The mathematic model would be built and simulated according to it to testify to chaos phenomenon. Figure 2a shows the circuit arrangement of a practical substation in the electrical power system. PT is a potential transformer isolated from sections of bus bars via disconnector DS2. CCB is the grading capacitance of circuit breaker CB. ferroresonance might occur upon closing DS1 with both the circuit breaker and DS2 open. This leads to a system fault caused by failure of the voltage transformer's primary winding.

As shown in Figure 2b, e is the phase voltage and the frequency ω is 50Hz. C1 is the circuit breaker grading capacitance and C2 is the total phase-to-earth capacitance, including bus bar capacitance to earth and transformer winding capacitance. The resistor R represents transformer core losses shown previously to be an important parameter in determining the behaviors of the system. The non-linear transformer magnetization curve is modeled by a single valued seventh order polynomial obtained from the measured transformer magnetization curve, as shown below.

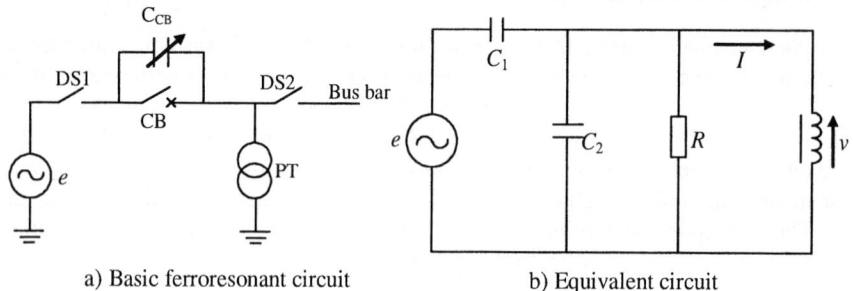

a) Basic ferroresonant circuit   b) Equivalent circuit

Fig. 2. Chaotic ferroresonant circuit

$$\begin{cases} v = \dfrac{d\phi}{dt} \\ I = a\phi + b\phi^7 \end{cases} \qquad (1)$$

where ϕ is transformer flux linkage. The mathematic model of the equivalent circuit is shown below.

$$\frac{1}{\omega}\cdot\frac{dv}{dt}+\frac{1}{q}v+\frac{a\phi+b\phi^7}{\omega(C_1+C_2)}=g\cdot\cos\omega t \quad (2)$$

where a is equal to 3.42, and b is equal to 0.41, the power supply frequency ω is 314, g and $1/q$ are the driving force amplitude and damping factor, respectively, which are given by

$$g=\sqrt{2}E\frac{C_1}{C_1+C_2} \quad (3)$$

$$\frac{1}{q}=\frac{1}{R\omega(C_1+C_2)} \quad (4)$$

So the behavior of a basic ferroresonant circuit in time domain can be described as equation (5)

$$\frac{1}{\omega}\cdot\ddot{\phi}+\frac{1}{q}\dot{\phi}+\frac{R}{q}(a\phi+b\phi^7)=g\cdot\cos\omega t \quad (5)$$

3.2 System Analysis

The simulation according to the circuit model is made in Matlab. As shown in Figure 3 and Table 1, different working states occur in various conditions. These are the normal state, the fundamental frequency ferroresonance, the subharmonic ferroresonance, and the chaotic ferroresonance, respectively. When the system comes into chaotic state, the transformer flux linkage is not in balance any more, and appears to be a random mass of activity. The circuit equations do not have the periodic solution, but a chaotic solution with continuous spectrum. Moreover, the practical data of the

Table 1. Different States of Ferroresonance

No.	R	Power loss in core	g	1/q	Transformer flux linkage	States
1	100MΩ	250W	2	10	Closed period orbit	Normal
2	210MΩ	120W	2	1	Distorted period orbit	Fundamental frequency ferroresonance
3	245.5MΩ	99W	2	0.007	Multi-orbit, period doubling bifurcations	Subharmonic ferroresonance
4	3500MΩ	8W	2	0.0007	Random chaotic oscillations	Chaotic ferroresonance

ferroresonance occurring in the electrical power system also shows 25Hz and 17Hz sine wave, which is 1/2 and 1/3 of the normal 50Hz frequency. So both the simulation and practical data prove the existence of chaos in ferroresonance.

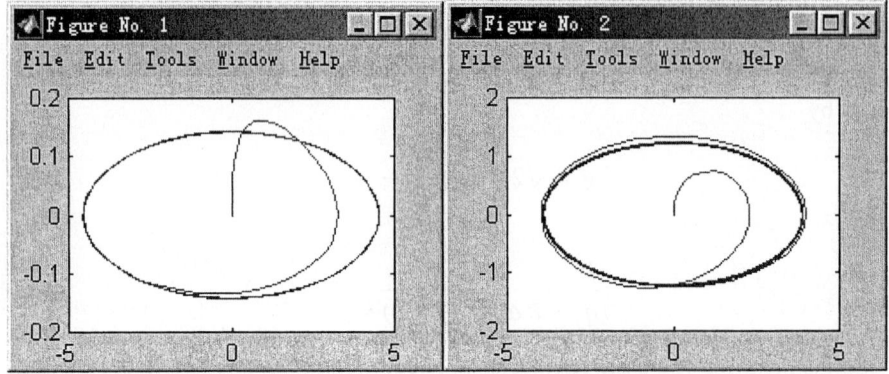

a) Normal status   b) Fundamental frequency ferroresonance

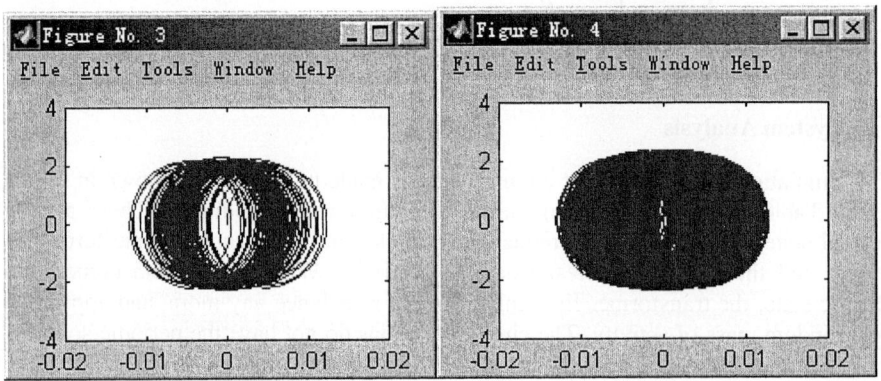

c) Subharmonic ferroresonance   d) Chaotic ferroresonance

Fig. 3. Simulation Results

4 Control and Utilization of Chaos in an Electrical System

4.1 Obviating Chaos

According to the theory of chaos control, many measures can be taken to eliminate the chaos in ferroresonance, such as OGY, feedback control, etc.

Utilizing sensitivity of chaos to initial conditions, the measures are shown as follows:

– shunting an adjustable inductor on the two open connectors of secondary triangle windings on the three-phase five-core PT ,

- shortcutting a set of low power triangle windings on the main transformer,
- temporarily grounding the neutral point of the transformer,
- any style files, templates, and special fonts you may have used,
- connecting damped resistance in a zero-sequence circuit.

It should also be noted that the special characters of chaos can provide a trigging signal for relay protection units, for example the 25Hz sine wave in the system.

4.2 Utilization of Chaos

Chaos was once misinterpreted as a harmful phenomenon. Later, chaos found great use in masking military communications and other fields. However, chaos and ferroresonance in power systems is still considered a harmful factor, and the attitude to it is still negative. The research on chaos mainly concentrates on obviating, not utilizing it. In philosophical opinions, there are advantages and disadvantages, good and bad aspects for everything. Chaos is no exception. According to the results of research in this field, chaos is not uncontrollable. As a result, the chaotic high over-voltage and strong current in ferroresonance could be utilized for some special purposes.

A scheme of chaos utility in the electrical system for steel smelting is presented below on the basis of chaos controlling. The traditional way for electrical smelting is via short circuit curl current. Great heat is produced in the short circuit for smelting metal. However, the short circuit process cannot be satisfied in many aspects, such as the response time, transient state and stability. While in chaotic circuit, a control order with small power can change different periodic orbits of the system in a stable way. These periodic orbits are a solution of system dynamics equations. The control of it needs only small, continuous signals. That is to say, the control of chaos is not like the control of a short circuit, in which always only two output orders, on and off, can be taken.

A chaotic steel-smelting furnace regulates its heating current according to the chaos control theory. The small change in initial conditions can drive the current into the desired state during a short transient process by using the sensitivity of chaos, while it would exhaust large quantities of power for controlling in a longer transient process in the traditional way. It is consistent with the basic idea of using weak electric signals to control the strong electrical actuators in computer control technology. On the contrary, in the traditional short circuit steel-smelting furnace, the heat is controlled in the way of pulse width modulation, which limits the performance of regulation. Chaotic high voltage generator can also be made in the use for verifying the quality of high voltage electrical apparatus in the manufacturing laboratory.

5 Conclusions

The chaos phenomenon caused by ferroresonance in power systems was misinterpreted for many years. However, following extensive research on the subject, it is now possible to control and utilize it in an active way. In this paper, on the basis of analyzing the chaos of ferroresonance in an electrical system, some measures on obviating and controlling chaos are summarized. The main contribution of this paper is the idea of a chaotic steel smelting furnace.

Acknowledgement

This work is supported by China Scholarship Council Fund (No.21813017) and Hebei Provincial Key Discipline of Control Theory and Control Engineering in Hebei University of Technology.

References

1. B. Zahawi: Chaos in ferroresonance winding voltage transformers, *IEE Proc-Sci. Technol*, vol.145, no.1, pp.45-51, 1998.
2. Z. Emin et al: Quantification of chaotic behaviour of ferroresonant voltage transformer circuits, IEEE Trans. on Circuits and Systems I: Fundamental Theory and Applications, vol.48 no.6, pp.757-760, 2001
3. A. Soudack: Ferroresonance in power system and chaos behavior, IEE Proc-Sci. Technol, vol.140, no.3, pp.16-22, 1993.
4. X. Yong: The simulation and analyze of ferroresonance in power networks, Electrical Information, vol.99, no.2, pp.14-17, 1999.
5. C.Y. Nie, L.Y. Zhang: Research on the chaos based on ferroresonance, Journal of Changchun University, vol.10, no.2, pp.45-49, 2000
6. X.M. Li: Research on ferroresonance in power system, Journal of Heilongjiang Automatic Technology, vol.18, no.3, pp.35-38, 1999
7. G.R. Wang et al: Control synchronization and application of chaos, Beijing, Defence Industry Press, 2001, Chap.7, pp.137-165.
8. J.H Chen et al: Experimental stabilization of chaos in voltage-mode DC drive system, IEEE Trans. on Circuits and Systems I: Fundamental Theory and Applications, vol.47 no.7, pp.1093-1095, 2000.

Research and Application of Data Mining in Power Plant Process Control and Optimization

Jian-qiang Li, Cheng-lin Niu, Ji-zhen Liu, and Luan-ying Zhang

Department of Automation, North China Electric Power University, Baoding 071003, China
{lijianqiang8, niuchenglin}@sohu.com

Abstract. As more and more real-time data is sent to databases by DAS, large amounts of data are accumulated in power plants. Abundant knowledge exists in historical data but it is hard to find and summarize this in a traditional way. This paper proposes a method of operation optimization based on data mining in a power plant. The basic structure of the operation optimization based on data mining is established and the improved fuzzy association rule mining is introduced to find the optimization values from the quantitative data in a power plant. Based on the historical data of a 300MW unit, the optimal values of the operating parameters are found by using data mining techniques. The optimal values are provided to guide the operation online and experiment results show that excellent performance is achieved in the power plant.

1 Introduction

Data mining, sometimes referred to as knowledge discovery from databases, is a non-trivial process of identifying implicit, valid, novel, potentially useful and ultimately understandable patterns in data. Data mining is used to improve decision-making ability, find regular patterns and predict future trends based on the archived data. Data mining is already widely used for commerce, finance, telecom and enterprise management. The researchers and engineers who have attempted to apply it to industrial monitoring and process control have achieved great success. McGreavy and Wang X Z used the KDD techniques to identify the status of the chemical industrial process in Britain [1]. Tony Ogilvie and B W Hogg put forward the idea of using data mining techniques [2] to establish the running and operating models in a power plant.

As the electricity industry develops, more and more real-time data is sent to databases by DAS and large amounts of data are accumulated. Abundant knowledge exists in historical data and it is hard to find and summarize this in a traditional way due to mass, high dimension and strong coupling of the data in the electric industrial process. Data mining technique provides a novel and effective method to help solve these difficulties. It can acquire useful knowledge and rules from the mass of data to provide better decision support and better adjustment guidance in industrial processes. It is significant to find knowledge and modes from historical data to improve the performance in power systems. This paper proposes a new method to improve the performance and efficiency of electricity industry processes by combining the data mining technique with operation optimization in a power plant.

2 The Basic Structure of Operation Optimization System Based on Data Mining

To keep the operating status optimized in an electric industrial process, two issues should be considered simultaneously: (1) The important process parameters must be controlled at high precision. (2) The optimization values must be properly decided. Generally, the advanced control techniques are partially emphasized, while the optimization target values are ignored. The improvement of the performance by feedback control can't exceed the condition decided by the target values. The optimization values reflect the reachable optimal parameters and status under a certain load, which is the basis for energy-loss and economical analysis. The decision regarding the optimization value is a very important question for operation optimization in a power plant and is decided by considering accuracy, real-time and feasibility [3]. Acquiring the optimization value from historical data by data mining technique is a novel and efficient method. It reflects the actual operating state and can be achieved in practice.

From the angle of data mining, the industrial process data in electricity production manifests stronger orderliness than the commercial process because the industrial process is less affected by uncertain factors. So we can design the artificial intelligence assistance system based on the results of data mining and make optimal options and decisions by computer to guide the industrial process. The operation optimization basic structure based on data mining is shown in Fig. 1.

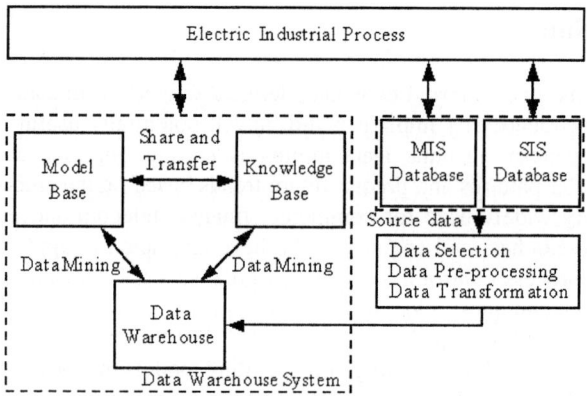

Fig. 1. The basic structure of the operation optimization system based on data mining

The architecture of operation optimization based on data mining includes three sub-parts: data warehouse, model base and knowledge base. The data warehouse is the base for data mining and decision-making and it collects data from MIS and SIS databases. The operation area is represented by several running models, which are obtained by data preprocessing, characteristic pick-up and clustering analysis. A series of dynamic models is established and the reasoning rules are formed. The real-time data is collected, preprocessed and identified. According to the results of identification and utilizing the knowledge and rules from previous data mining, the optimal model sets are obtained and used to guide the operation. The MB and KB systems store the algorithm and knowledge for advanced application that are retrieved by data mining. They have the self-study and self-organizing ability to work harmoniously together. The operator and manager can add or modify the model and knowledge to extend and perfect the function for all kinds of advanced applications.

3 Fuzzy Association Rule Mining

The goal of association rule mining is to discover important relations among items. Agrawal and his co-workers proposed Apriori algorithm based on the concept of large item sets to find association rules from transactions [4]. Apriori algorithm is used for mining Boolean association rules. Quantitative association rule mining involves separating the domain of quantitative attributes into intervals. The values of quantitative attributes were mapped to a set of contiguous integers, then the algorithm for finding Boolean association rules can be used on the transformed database to discover quantitative association rules [5][6]. However, distinct partition will exclude those potential elements which are neighboring the boundary.

To solve this problem, the fuzzy sets theory was introduced into the association rule mining process. The fuzzy concept is better than the partition method because fuzzy sets provide a smooth transition between members and non-members of a set. Therefore, we propose the use of fuzzy association rule mining to decide the operation optimization value in an electric industrial process.

3.1 Determining the Data Mining Target

Knowledge relevant to the object should be learned sufficiently before the data mining process commences. The coal consumption rate can reflect the economic performance in a power plant and is selected as the target of data mining. The parameter values that are relevant to the coal consumption rate are collected for the data mining process.

The economic operation of a unit is affected by many factors; for example the load, coal, equipment status and the operation level of the operators. In this paper the mainly controllable parameters related to the operation optimization are mined to find the optimization values. When the process parameters run at the optimization values, the coal consumption rate is minimized. The heat consumption is calculated according to the turbine power and the heat quantity and the boiler efficiency is calculated by the reverse-balance method. The coal consumption B_g (g / kW.h) is calculated as [7]:

$$B_g = \frac{H_{rt}}{29.31\eta\eta_0(1-\xi)} . \tag{1}$$

where H_{rt} is turbine heat consumption, kJ/(kW.h). η is boiler efficiency, %. η_0 is pipeline heat preservation efficiency, assigned to be 99%. ξ is electricity consumption, %. B_g is coal consumption, g /(kW.h) . The coal consumption B_g is the performance index to operation optimization. The aim of data mining is to acquire the quantitative association rules between parameter values and the optimal performance index.

3.2 Data Selection and Data Transformation

The running state in a power plant is often a dynamic process. When the unit state is far from the stable state, the performance index calculated from the process parameters cannot reflect the actual state of the unit [8]. So the data in the stable state is selected and analyzed when deciding the optimization values by data mining method. When the main steam pressure keeps stable for a period of time, the running state is defined to be a stable state because the main steam pressure is the most sensitive parameter to load change. The running state is stable when the variance of the main steam pressure $P_{main}^{(i)}$ is less than a certain threshold ξ in the time period $[t-d, t]$. The formula is as follows:

$$\sum_{i=t-d}^{t}(P_{main}^{(i)} - \bar{P}_{main})^2 < \xi . \tag{2}$$

where $\bar{P}_{main}$ is the average value of the main steam pressure $P_{main}^{(i)}$.

The data which satisfies the conditions mentioned above is selected, verified and transformed before data mining. The data is transformed into [0, 1]. The formula is

$$v'(i) = (v(i) - \min(v(i)))/(\max(v(i)) - \min(v(i))) . \tag{3}$$

where the minimum and maximum of v are calculated over a data aggregate or estimated by the domain expert. This data is expressed in the form of $<x, l, u>$. For example, the load is expressed by $<M_e, 0, 1>$, and the excess air ratio is expressed by $<a, 0, 1>$.

3.3 Improved Fuzzy Association Rule Mining Algorithm

In this paper the fuzzy sets theory was introduced into the association rule for mining quantitative data in the electricity industry. The proposed fuzzy mining algorithm first transforms each quantitative value into a fuzzy set using membership functions. The algorithm then calculates the scalar cardinality of each linguistic term on all the transaction data using the temporary set. The linguistic term with the maximum cardinality was used in later mining processes only, thus keeping the number of items the same as that of the original attributes. The mining process based on fuzzy counts is then performed to find fuzzy association rules [9]. In this paper the concept of interest is introduced to the fuzzy association rule mining to reduce invalid and redundant association rules. Interest is a judgment criterion to measure the novelty and importance of rules. The definition of interest is as follows.

$$Interest(X \Rightarrow Y) = \frac{1 - s(Y)}{[1 - s(X)] \times [1 - s(X \cup Y)]} . \tag{4}$$

where $s(X)$ is the support of item X. The association rule is more important and novel when the interest is higher.

The improved fuzzy association rule mining algorithm is described as follows.

Input: A body of n transaction data, each with m attribute values, a set of membership functions, a predefined minimum support value and a predefined confidence value. The p-th attribute in the j-th ($j=1, 2, ..., n$) transaction can be described by k membership functions $\mu_p^j(R_s^p)(s=1,2,...,k)$, $R_s^p(s=1,2,...,k)$ as a fuzzy set.

Output: A set of fuzzy association rules.

Step 1: Transform the quantitative value $t_p^j (p=1,2,...,m)$ of each transaction $T_j (j=1,2,...,n)$ in D into a fuzzy set f_p^j. t_p^j is described by fuzzy sets as:

$$f_p^j = \frac{\mu_p^j(R_1^p)}{R_1^p} + \frac{\mu_p^j(R_2^p)}{R_2^p} + ... + \frac{\mu_p^j(R_k^p)}{R_k^p} . \tag{5}$$

where $R_p^s(s=1,2,...,k)$ is p-th fuzzy region of attribute $T_j(j=1,2,...,n)$, and T_j is j-th transaction in D.

Step 2: Build a temporary set C_1 including all the pairs ($R_p^s, \mu_p^j(R_s^p)$) of data, where $p=1, 2, ..., m$, $s=1, 2, ..., k$. For each region R_p^s stored in C_1 calculate its scalar cardinality for all transactions:

$$weight_{p,s}^j = \frac{1}{n}\sum_{j=1}^{n}\mu_p^j(R_s^p) . \tag{6}$$

Step 3: Find $weight_p^{max} = \max_{s=1}^{k}(weight_{p,s}^j)$, for $p=1$ to m, where k is the number of fuzzy regions for transaction $T_j(j=1,2,...,n)$. $weight_p^{max}$ will be used to represent this attribute in later mining processes.

Step 4: Check whether the $weight_p^{max}$ of each $R_p^{max}(p=1,2,...,m)$ is larger than or equal to the predefined minimum support. If $R_p^{max}(p=1,2,...,m)$ is equal to or greater than the minimum support, insert it into the set of large 1 item sets (L_1). That is:

$$L_1 = \{R_p^{max} \mid weight_p^{max} \geq minsupport, 1 \leq p \leq m\} . \tag{7}$$

Step 5: Set $r=1$, where r is used to represent the number of items kept in the current large item sets.

Step 6: Generate the candidate set C_{r+1} from L_r. Restated, the algorithm joins L_r and L_r under the condition that $r-1$ items in the two items sets are the same and the other one is different. The item sets which have all their sub-r-item sets in L_r are put into C_{r+1}.

Step 7: Perform the following substeps for each newly formed $(r+1)$-item set $t = (t_1, t_2, ..., t_{r+1})$ in C_{r+1}:

(a) For each transaction T_j, calculate its fuzzy value on $t_\varepsilon (\varepsilon = 1, 2, ..., r+1)$ as:

$$\mu_{t_\varepsilon}^j = \mu_{p_1}^j (R_{p_1}^{\max}) \wedge \mu_{p_2}^j (R_{p_2}^{\max}) \wedge ... \wedge \mu_{p_{r+1}}^j (R_{p_{r+1}}^{\max}) . \tag{8}$$

where $j=1$ to n. If the minimum operator is used for the intersection, then:

$$\mu_{t_\varepsilon}^j = \min_{\varepsilon}^{r+1} \mu_{p_\varepsilon}^j (R_{p_\varepsilon}^{\max}) . \tag{9}$$

(b) Calculate $weight_{t_\varepsilon} = \frac{1}{n} \sum_{j=1}^{n} \mu_{t_\varepsilon}^j$ using C_{r+1}.

(c) If $weight_{t_\varepsilon}$ is larger than or equal to the predefined minimum support, put $t = (t_1, t_2, ..., t_{r+1})$ into L_{r+1}.

Step 8: If L_{r+1} is null, then perform the next step; otherwise, set $r=r+1$ and repeat Steps 6 to 8.

Step 9: Construct the association rules for all large q-item set t with items $(t_1, t_2, ..., t_q)$, $q \geq 2$ using the following substeps:

(a) Form all possible association rules as follows:

$$t_1 \wedge ... \wedge t_{k-1} \wedge t_{k+1} \wedge ... \wedge t_q \Rightarrow t_k, \quad k = 1, 2, ..., q . \tag{10}$$

(b) Calculate the confidence values of all association rules using:

$$\frac{\sum_{j=1}^{n} (\mu_{t_\varepsilon}^j)}{\sum_{j=1}^{n} (\mu_{t_1}^j \wedge ... \wedge \mu_{t_{k-1}}^j \wedge \mu_{t_{k+1}}^j \wedge ... \mu_{t_q}^j)} . \tag{11}$$

(c) Obtain the rules with confidence value larger than or equal to the predefined minimum confidence.

Step 10: Calculate the interest values of all association rules by formula (4). Output the rules that satisfy the requirements of interest.

After Step 10, the rules constructed are output and can act as the meta-knowledge for the given transaction. It is an expression based on reasoning and is easily understood.

4 The Application of Fuzzy Association Rule Mining in Operation Optimization

Based on the historical data of the 300MW unit in Zhangjiakou Power Plant, the typical parameters which are related to process optimization are analyzed. These parameters include load, main steam pressure, main steam temperature, re-heated temperature, feed water temperature, flue gas temperature, excess air ratio and so on. The quantitative association rules are acquired by analyzing the historical data. For example, $Load\ (L_1...L_n)$, $Parameters\ (P_1...P_n)$, $Parameters\ (T_1...T_m) \Rightarrow Coal\ consumption$ $(B_{g1}...B_{gn})$. In a given typical load range, the parameters related to a low coal consumption rate are chosen as optimization values to optimize the electric industrial process. The rule to determine the optimal parameter values is expressed as:

$$Load(L_1...L_n) \Rightarrow Parameter(P_1...P_n), Parameter(T_1...T_n)\ .$$

By this method, the optimal operation parameters are decided according to load and other related conditions. The optimal values achieved from data mining are attainable and can reflect the actual optimal state in operation.

According to the method mentioned above, the historical data from three recent months is analyzed. A total of 4,136 transactions of the operation parameters in a typical stable state are obtained. These transactions are standardized to the range [0, 1] by formula (3). The parameters in these transactions are separated into fuzzy sets by the membership function. The membership function of the parameters is shown in Fig. 2.

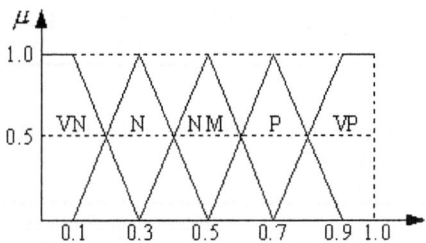

Fig. 2. The membership function

The gradient and distribution are determined according to the characteristic of the actual object. The minimum support is set at 30% and the minimum confidence is set at 75%. The improved fuzzy association rule mining algorithm is applied to find the optimization values of important procedure parameters.

Let's take the fuzzy mining process of excess air ratio and the flue gas temperature as an example. The records of excess air ratio and flue gas temperature are taken from historical data when the unit is in 300MW stable load. The data is then standardized and is mined by a fuzzy mining algorithm. The following rule is output:

$$<M_e, 1>, <B_g, 0.20, 0.30> \Rightarrow <\alpha, 0.30, 0.32>, <T_g, 0.64, 0.68>\quad (s=46\%, c=81\%)\ .$$

where M_e is load, B_g is coal consumption rate, a is excess air ratio and T_g is flue gas temperature. This rule has a support value of 46% and a confidence value of 81%. It satisfies the requirements of minimum support and minimum confidence. The interest requirement is also satisfied (*Interest*=2.1). The corresponding range is:

$$<M_e, 298, 300>, <B_g, 326, 330> \Rightarrow <\alpha, 1.290, 1.296>, <T_g, 145.6, 147.2>\quad (s=46\%, c=81\%)\ .$$

This rule means that when the load is in 100% load range (298MW~300MW) and the coal consumption is low (lower than 328g/kW.h), the optimal range of excess air ratio is 1.290~1.296 and that of flue gas temperature is 145.6~147.2 degrees centigrade. The midpoint of the interval can be adopted as the optimal point. Then the optimization value of excess air ratio a is 1.293 and that of the flue gas temperature is 146.4 degrees centigrade when the load is in the 100% load range. According to the method mentioned above, by utilizing the improved fuzzy association rule mining algorithm to mine the optimization value in a typical load range of 70%, 90% and 100%, a set of optimization values is obtained. The optimal values obtained from fuzzy data mining and the reference values obtained in the traditional way are listed in Table 1.

Table 1. The comparison of reference value and optimal value of a 300MW power unit

Parameters	210MW		270MW		300MW	
	Reference	Optimal	Reference	Optimal	Reference	Optimal
Main steam pressure MPa	12.96	13.24	16.67	16.66	16.67	16.71
Main steam temperature ℃	537.0	537.2	537.0	538.1	537.0	538.3
Reheat temperature ℃	537.0	535.4	537.0	537.4	537.0	537.8
Feed water temperature ℃	248.9	254.6	264.6	270.4	270.9	276.2
Flue gas temperature ℃	135.2	132.4	150.3	142.8	155.2	146.4
Excessive air ratio	1.450	1.482	1.354	1.321	1.328	1.293

Table 2. The comparison of experiment results between the data mining (DM) method and the traditional method (TM) under typical load ranges

Processing parameters	Experiment results comparison							
	TM	DM	TM	DM	TM	DM	TM	DM
Load (MW)	210.6	211.2	241.5	240.8	270.7	271.3	301.2	298.7
Feed water temperature (℃)	246.9	252.4	254.1	256.3	262.5	273.2	269.3	275.8
Flue gas temperature (℃)	136.1	134.2	145.4	138.5	151.6	142.4	156.8	147.2
Unburned carbon in fly dust (%)	4.02	3.45	3.85	3.34	3.54	3.07	4.16	3.62
Unburned carbon in slag (%)	5.13	5.21	5.42	4.42	4.11	3.12	4.48	3.25
Excess air ratio	1.448	1.481	1.402	1.396	1.351	1.317	1.334	1.294
Heat loss due to flue gas (%)	5.92	5.78	5.71	5.70	4.93	4.62	5.32	5.16
Unburned carbon loss (%)	1.68	1.49	1.53	1.47	1.51	1.42	1.76	1.54
Electricity consumption rate (%)	4.82	4.58	4.13	4.08	3.75	3.68	3.43	3.34
Boiler efficiency (%)	91.83	92.13	92.21	92.44	93.16	93.38	92.45	92.82
Coal consumption rate (g/kW.h)	351.5	350.1	346.2	345.3	338.6	336.2	332.4	330.7

Table 1 shows that the optimization values are close to the reference value, and the optimization values determined by data mining are inclined to reduce the coal consumption based on the theory analysis. The newly found rules and knowledge can be added to the model base or the knowledge base to optimize the industry process.

The optimization values are set online to examine the effects of optimization in Zhangjiakou Power Plant. The process parameters are optimized based on the results of the improved fuzzy association rule mining. The experiment results returned between traditional method (TM) and data mining (DM) method under different load ranges (70%, 80%, 90%, 100%) are shown in Table 2. It can be seen that the performance of the boiler improved noticeably. The average boiler efficiency improved by about 0.28% and the coal consumption reduced by about 1.6g/kW.h. The operation optimization based on data mining is an effective method to improve the efficiency in the power plant. The coal consumption and the emission of pollution also decreased greatly.

The optimal curves can be obtained by regression analysis of the optimization values that were determined by data mining. Taking the excess air ratio and the flue gas temperature as an example, the optimization value curves obtained by data mining and the reference value curves are shown in Fig. 3.

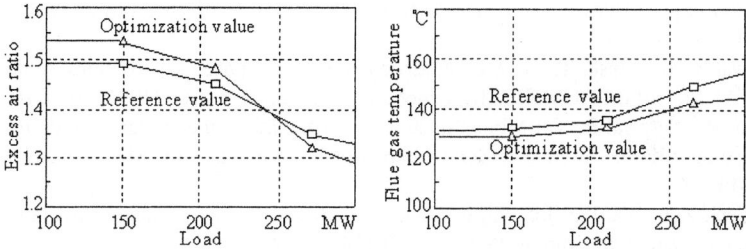

Fig. 3. The comparison of curves between optimization value and reference value of important controllable parameters

Fig. 3 shows that the optimization values of excess air ratio based on data mining are higher in low load range and lower in high load range than the reference values, with their values being close in 80% load. The higher excess air ratio is adopted in the lower load range for stable burning and safety, while the lower excess air ratio is adopted in higher load for reducing the heat loss in flue gas. The lower flue gas temperature is conducive to reducing heat loss and coal consumption. The optimal curves determined by data mining are inclined to improve the economic performance by theory analysis. Therefore, they can be used to guide the operation in industrial process.

5 Conclusion

The operation optimization is the main method to improve the performance in a power plant and the decision of optimization value is the key point in operation optimization. In this paper we proposed the process control and optimization based on data mining and applied the improved fuzzy association rule mining to find the optimization values in a power plant. The determination of optimization values based on data mining has several virtues over the traditional methods: (1) The optimization value can be dynamically regulated according to different decision requirements such as low coal consumption or low contamination emissions. (2) The target value which is determined from historical data is attainable and reasonable in practice. (3) The optimization value is presented in an interval, so the operator has more choices when optimizing the industrial process. Experimental results in a 300MW power plant show that the optimization value based on data mining performs very well and can be used to guide the operating process to achieve an efficient performance.

References

1. Wang X Z., A.: Automatic Classification for Mining Process Operational Data. Ind. Eng. Chem. Res, Vo37. (1998) 2215–2222
2. Tony Ogilvie., B W Hogg., C.: Use of data mining techniques in the performance monitoring and operation of a thermal power plant. IEEE Colloquium on Knowledge Discovery and Data Mining (1998)
3. Honghua Hu., Tinghui Huang., Weiguo Ai., A.: Study and determination of operation optimization target values of large size fossil-fired power unit. Electric Power, Vo37. (2004) 22–25
4. Agrawal R., Imielinski T., C.: Mining association rules between sets of items in large database [A]. Proc of the ACM SIGMOD conf on Management of data. (1993) 207–216
5. Srikant R., Agrawal R., C.: Mining quantitative association rules in large relational tables. Proceedings of the ACM SIGMOD International Conference on Management of Data. (1996) 1–12
6. XiaoFeng Zou., JianJian Lu., ZiLin Song., A.: Mining linguistic valued association rules. Journal of System Simulation, Vo14. (2002) 1130–1132
7. Fuguo Liu., Weidong Hao., Jianzhu Yang., A.: Economic analyze for utility boiler operated in different oxygen content outlet furnace and it's optimization. Proceedings of the CSEE. Vo23. (2003) 172–176
8. Fuguo Liu., A.: Performance characteristics identification and optimization of station boiler based on statistical analysis, Vo24. (2004) 477–494
9. T.P.Hong., C.S.Kuo., S.C.Chi.. A.: Mining association rules from quantitative data. Intelligent Data Analysis, Vo3. (1999) 363–376

Extended Negative Association Rules and the Corresponding Mining Algorithm

Min Gan[1], Mingyi Zhang[2], and Shenwen Wang[3]

[1] Department of Computer, Zhejiang Water Conservancy and Hydropower College,
310018 Hangzhou, Zhejiang, P.R. China
School of Computer Science and Engineering, Guizhou University,
550025 Guiyang, Guizhou, P.R. China
ganmin2008@163.com
[2] Guizhou Academy of Sciences,
550001 Guiyang, Guizhou, P.R. China
zhangmy045@hotmail.com
[3] School of Computer Science and Engineering, Guizhou University,
550025 Guiyang, Guizhou, P.R. China
wangshenwen@sina.com

Abstract. Recently, negative association rule mining has received some attention and proved to be useful. This paper proposes an extended form for negative association rules and defines extended negative association rules. Furthermore, a corresponding algorithm is devised for mining extended negative association rules. The extended form is more general and expressive than the three existing forms. The proposed mining algorithm overcomes some limitations of previous mining methods, and experimental results show that it is efficient on simple and sparse datasets when minimum support is high to some degree. Our work will extend related applications of negative association rules to a broader range.

1 Introduction

Association rule mining, as an important problem in data mining, was originally proposed in [1]. It is intended to discover implicit and interesting associations among data items in a dataset.

The originally proposed rules are positive association rules, which are implications of the form $X \rightarrow Y$, where $X, Y \subset I$ ($I = \{i_1, i_2, ..., i_m\}$, which is called a set of items). Most of the existing work has concentrated on positive association rules. Recently, mining for *negative* association rules has received some attention and proved to be useful.

1.1 Negative Association Rules

Logically speaking, a *negative association rule* is a rule with the connective "¬", which corresponds to the absence or negative attribute of an item or an itemset. For example, $a \wedge \neg b \wedge \neg(c \wedge d) \rightarrow e$ is a negative association rule. Negative association rules are introduced since there exist many cases where negative attributes of items or itemsets need to be considered in the real world.

1.2 Related Work

Negative correlation in association rules was first mentioned in [3]. Since then, to the best of our knowledge, three typical forms and three corresponding mining methods have been proposed. For convenience, we will denote the three forms by F_1, F_2, F_3, and the corresponding methods by M_1, M_2, M_3 respectively.

The first form F_1 [6] is defined as an implication of the form $X \not\rightarrow Y$, whose intuitive meaning is that $X \rightarrow Y$ does not hold. The basic idea is: if $\varepsilon p(Y|X)$ (*expected value*) is high to some degree, and $p(Y|X)$ (*actual value*) is significantly lower, then $X \not\rightarrow Y$ is an interesting negative rule. In M_1, the expected value is computed based on taxonomy.

The form F_2 [9,10] extends $X \rightarrow Y$ to four basic types: $X \rightarrow Y$, $X \rightarrow \neg Y$, $\neg X \rightarrow Y$ and $\neg X \rightarrow \neg Y$, where $X \rightarrow Y$ is a positive rule and the other three are negative rules. In M_2, rules are generated based on *observations*: if *minsup* is high, $sup(X \cup \neg Y) \geq minsup$ would mean that $sup(X \cup Y) \leq minsup$. Therefore, if *minsup* is high, negative rules are extracted from infrequent itemsets.

The form F_3 [7] can be represented as $X \wedge N \rightarrow c$, where $X \subset I$, $N \subset NI$, $c \in I$ or NI ($NI = \{\neg i_1, \neg i_2, ..., \neg i_m\}$). The essence of M_3 is to extend GRD (generalized rules discovery) approach [8] from generating positive rules to generating both positive rules and negative ones.

1.3 Motivation

We note that the three existing forms have some limitations. Obviously, F_1 is too vague to precisely describe the actual relationship between itemsets X and Y. Although F_2 and F_3 further refine F_1, they are not general enough. To sum up, none of the three forms can represent such a general form as: "$a \wedge \neg b \wedge \neg (c \wedge d) \rightarrow e \wedge \neg f \wedge \neg (g \wedge h \wedge i)$", which is sometimes used in cases in the real world.

One example is prevention or diagnosis of new infectious diseases such as SARS. Diagnosis of SARS is so complicated that, perhaps, we should consider three attributes (absence, presence and non-simultaneous presence) of symptoms to identify patients with SARS. In this case, the form of a rule may be:

$$s_1 \wedge ... \wedge s_i \wedge \neg s_j \wedge ... \wedge \neg s_{j+t} \wedge \neg(s_r \wedge s_{r+1}) \wedge ... \wedge \neg(s_{r+q} \wedge s_{r+q+1}) \rightarrow SARS \quad (1)$$

Another example is the analysis of certain chemical reactions. If we want to find out how a chemical compound is produced, we sometimes have to precisely consider conditions of reactions: what substances are present, what substances are absent and what substances are not simultaneously present.

To handle these cases, a *general form* for negative association rules should be proposed, and a corresponding mining algorithm should be devised. This is what this paper aims at. In addition, the proposed mining algorithm tries to overcome the limitations of the previous mining methods.

The rest of this paper is organized as follows. Section 2 defines an extended form for negative association rules and extended negative association rules. Section 3 proposes a corresponding mining algorithm. Experimental results are presented in Section 4. Section 5 contains our conclusion and future work.

2 Extended Negative Association Rules

This section proposes an extended form for negative association rules and defines extended negative association rules.

We observe that the general form mentioned above comprises *three basic components* as follows.

- a: Positive item, which denotes the presence of item a.
- $\neg b$: Negative item, which denotes the absence of item b.
- $\neg(c \wedge d)$: Negation of positive itemsets, which denotes the non-simultaneous presence of items c and d (Note: in this paper, $\neg(c \wedge d) = \neg(cd) = \neg\{c,d\}$).

Theoretically, a general form should permit the three basic components to occur in both the antecedent and the consequent of a negative rule. The extended form (EF) that we propose is such a form.

2.1 Concepts and Notation

In this study, the three basic components are referred to as a "pattern". Note that our use of pattern differs from that of the literature. A set of patterns is denoted by Pa ($Pa = I \cup NI \cup NS$), where I, NI and NS refer to the sets of the three basic components respectively. They are defined as:

- $I = \{i_1, i_2, ..., i_m\}(m = 1, 2, ...)$
- $NI = \{\neg i_1, \neg i_2, ..., \neg i_m\}(m = 1, 2, ...)$
- $NS = \{\neg X | X \subseteq I, |X| \geq 2\}$

Thus, *pattern* is the basic element of the EF that we propose.

A pattern p is frequent if a) $sup(p) \geq minsup$ and b) $1 - sup(p) \geq minsup$ if $p \in NI$ or $p \in NS$. $k - patternset$ is denoted by ps_k, which is defined as:

$$ps_k = \{\{p_1, ..., p_k\} | \forall i, j = 1, ..., k, p_i, p_j \in Pa, atoms(p_i) \cap atoms(p_j) = \emptyset\} \quad (2)$$

where $i \neq j$ and $atoms(p_i)$ is the set of atoms appearing in p_i. For example, if $p_i = \neg(c \wedge d)$, then $atoms(p_i) = \{c,d\}$. *Patternset* is denoted by ps ($ps = \cup_k ps_k$). Other related notations are defined as follows.

- PS (PS_k): a set of patternsets (k-patternsets)
- L (L_k): a set of frequent patternsets (k-patternsets)
- NSL: a set of frequent negations of positive itemsets
- PL (PL_k): a set of frequent positive itemsets (k-itemsets)
- NL_1: a set of frequent negative items ($NL_1 \subseteq NI$)

2.2 Definitions

Definition 1. *(EF) The extended form for negative association rules is an implication as follows:*

$$p_1 \wedge p_2 \wedge ... p_{n_1} \rightarrow q_1 \wedge q_2 \wedge ... q_{n_2} = \{p_1, p_2, ..., p_{n_1}\} \rightarrow \{q_1, q_2, ..., q_{n_2}\}$$

$$= Antecedent(Ant) \rightarrow Consequent(Cons) \quad (3)$$

where, $1 \leq n_1, n_2 < m$; $\forall i \in \{1, ..., n_1\}, p_i \in Pa$, $\forall j \in \{1, ..., n_2\}, q_j \in Pa$; $Ant \cup Cons \in PS_n$ ($n = n_1 + n_2$ is the size of the rule).

The form EF has the following five special cases:

- Case 1: $X \to Y$ when $Ant \subset I$, $Cons \subset I$
- Case 2: $X \to \neg Y$ when $Ant \subset I$, $Cons \in NS$ or NI
- Case 3: $\neg X \to Y$ when $Ant \in NS$ or NI, $Cons \subset I$
- Case 4: $\neg X \to \neg Y$ when $Ant \in NS$ or NI, $Cons \in NS$ or NI
- Case 5: $X \wedge N \to c$ when $Ant \subset (I \cup NI)$, $Cons \in I$ or NI.

Clearly, positive rules, F_1, F_2 and F_3 all fall within the special cases of EF.

Definition 2. *Rules of the form EF are called extended negative association rules (ENARs)*

Definition 3. *(An Interesting ENAR) Given minsup, mininterest and minconf, an extended negative association rule r: Ant $\to$ Cons is interesting iff*

1. $Ant \cup Cons \in L_n$
2. $interest(r) = sup(Ant \cup Cons) - sup(Ant)sup(Cons) \geq mininterest$
3. $conf(r) = [p(Cons|Ant) - p(Cons)]/[1 - p(Cons)] \geq minconf$

3 The Proposed Mining Algorithm

In this section, we propose an algorithm for mining extended negative association rules (AMENAR).

The main framework of AMENAR is Apriori-like [2], i.e., the mining problem is decomposed into two subproblems: a) Finding the set of frequent patternsets L; b) Generating all interesting ENARs from L. To avoid too many scans of the dataset, we select a highly compact data structure, Patricia trie [5], to represent dataset D, so that D fits in the main memory. Note that L_1 is the base for generating L. According to the definition of L_1, before L_1 is generated, the set of frequent positive itemsets, PL, must be found. The FP-growth algorithm [4] is used to find PL since it is an efficient FP-tree-based algorithm for generating frequent positive itemsets. Before moving on to the AMENAR algorithm, we review the Patricia trie roughly.

3.1 Patricia Trie

The Patricia trie [5] is a simple modification of the FP-tree [4] by combining unary branching nodes. The main reason for choosing the Patricia trie is that its high reduction ratio enables a moderate-sized dataset to fit in the main memory. It must be remarked that, in this study, we focus on only those cases where the Patricia trie fits in the main memory, and AMENAR is a memory-based algorithm.

Table 1. Dataset D and ordered frequent positive items

TID	Items bought	(Ordered) frequent positive items
01	f, d, b	b, f
02	a, b, c, f	b, c, a, f
03	b, e, f	b, f
04	a, f, c	c, a, f
05	f, b, c	b, c, f
06	c, a	c, a
07	a, c, b	b, c, a
08	c, e, a	c, a
09	d	
10	b	b

3.2 The AMENAR Algorithm

In AMENAR, all interesting ENARs are generated by the following four phases:

- Phase 1: Construct a Patricia trie for dataset D.
- Phase 2: Find the set of positive frequent itemsets PL by using the FP-growth algorithm; then generate the set of frequent 1-patternsets L_1.
- Phase 3: Starting from L_1, find the set of frequent k-patternsets L_k by using a strategy of candidate-generation-and-test iteratively ($L = \cup_k L_k$).
- Phase 4: Generate all interesting ENARs from L.

The four phases are illustrated by Example 1 below.

Example 1. Let dataset D be the first two columns of Table 1. Let $I = \{a, b, c, d, e, f\}$, $minsup = 0.4$, $mininterest = 0.1$, $minconf = 0.5$. We examine how AMENAR generates all interesting ENARs from D.

Phase 1. The Patricia trie is constructed as follows: a) Scan D once and collect the set of frequent positive items F, then sort F in support-descending order as $FList$; b) Scan D again and insert the ordered frequent positive items in each transaction into the Patricia trie. In this example, $FList = \{b : 6, c : 6, a : 5, f : 5\}$. The ordered frequent positive items are shown in the last column of Table 1, and the Patricia trie is shown in Fig.1.

Phase 2. First, find PL by using the FP-growth algorithm. After PL has been found, NL_1 and NSL can be generated directly according to their definitions. In this example, they are:

- $PL = \{\{b : 6\}, \{c : 6\}, \{a : 5\}, \{f : 5\}, \{(bf) : 4\}, \{(ca) : 5\}\}$
- $NL_1 = \{\{\neg b : 4\}, \{\neg c : 4\}, \{\neg a : 5\}, \{\neg f : 5\}\}$
- $NSL = \{\{\neg(bf) : 6\}, \{\neg(ca) : 5\}\}$
- $L_1 = PL_1 \cup NL_1 \cup NSL$

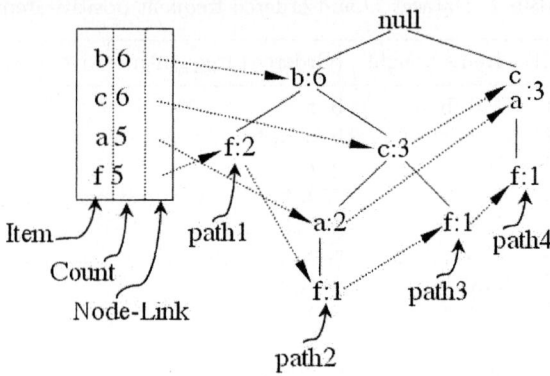

Fig. 1. Patricia trie for Dataset D

Phase 3. This phase implements two major operations: candidate-generation and test. For ensuring the correctness of the two operations, patterns are ordered according to $FList$.

In essence, the candidate-generation operation is a *join* operation, i.e., a set of candidate k-patternsets C_k is generated by joining L_{k-1} with L_{k-1}.

The *test* operation counts the support of each candidate as soon as a candidate c ($c \in C_k$) is generated. If the support is larger than $minsup$, then c is added to L_k, or else c is pruned. The key operation is the counting of support, which is illustrated by Example 2 below.

Example 2. Examine the dataset in Table 1 and the Patricia trie in Fig.1. Let $minsup = 0.3$, $l_1 = \{c, \neg b\}$, $l_2 = \{c, \neg(a \wedge f)\}$, $c' = l_1 \ join \ l_2 = \{c, \neg b, \neg (a \wedge f)\}$. $sup(l_1) = 0.3$, $sup(l_2) = 0.4$, $l_1, l_2 \in L_2$, $c' \in C_3$. We focus on the counting of $sup(c')$.

Note that $sup(c') = sup(l_1) - count(l)/10$, where $l = \{c, a, f, \neg b\}$. Now $count(l)$ needs to be counted. First, we introduce three notations: a) $I - P(l)$: part I of l; b) $NI - P(l)$: part NI of l; c) $NS - P(l)$: part NS of l. In this example, $I - P(l) = \{c, a, f\}$, $NI - P(l) = \{\neg b\}$, $NS - P(l) = \emptyset$. $Count(l)$ is counted as follows: choose the last element of $I - P(l)$ (denoted by $LastI - P(l)$), f, as a base, then travel each path (from the parent node of f to the root) to identify whether $l - \{f\}$ is on the path. If $l - \{f\}$ is on the path, then $f.num$ is added to $count(l)$. The paths are shown in Fig.1, where $path1 = \{b\}$, $path2 = \{a, c, b\}$, $path3 = \{c, b\}$, $path4 = \{a, c\}$. The $sup(c')$ is computed as follows.

$$count(l) = \sum_{i=1}^{4} count(pathi) = 0 + 0 + 0 + 1 = 1 \qquad (4)$$

$$sup(c') = 0.3 - 1/10 = 0.2 < minsup \qquad (5)$$

In addition, to avoid generating conflicting patternsets and too many candidates, two candidate-pruning strategies are implemented before $sup(c')$ is counted.

- Candidate-pruning1: A new candidate c' ($c' \in C_k$) is pruned if there exists an infrequent $(k-1)$-subset in c'.
- Candidate-pruning2: A new candidate c' ($c' \in C_k$) is pruned if it conflicts with an existing frequent patternset l ($l \in L_{k'}, k' = k$ or $k' = k - 1$), e.g., $c' = \{b, a, \neg d\}$, $l = \{b, a, d\}$, or $c' = \{b, c, f, \neg a\}$, $l = \{b, \neg a, \neg (c \wedge f)\}$.

Phase 4. This phase generates the ENARs that satisfy the constraints: $minsup$, $mininterest$ and $minconf$ from L. To avoid generating redundant rules, we consider two kinds of redundant rules and adopt two corresponding rule-pruning strategies, which are illustrated by Example 3 as follows.

Example 3. (adapted from [3]) Given a dataset D of 100 transactions, let $minsup = 0.2$, $mininterest = 0.13$, $minconf = 0.38$. We focus on the purchase of tea (t) and coffee (c). Their counts are shown in Table 2. Consider three negative rules: r_1: $\neg c \rightarrow t[0.42, 0.1384, 0.874]$, r_2: $\neg t \rightarrow c[0.34, 0.1384, 0.874]$ and r_3: $t \rightarrow \neg c[0.42, 0.1384, 0.386]$ (The three values behind each rule refer to $support$, $interest$ and $confidence$ of the rules respectively).

Table 2. Tea and coffee

	c	$\neg c$	$\sum_{row}$
t	22	42	64
$\neg t$	34	2	36
$\sum_{col}$	56	44	100

First, consider a pair of equivalent rules: r_1 and r_2. Logically, r_1 is equivalent to r_2, therefore the rule with lower support, r_2, can be pruned.

Second, consider a pair of reverse rules: r_1 and r_3. Clearly, the rule with lower confidence, r_3, can be pruned. Moreover, we observe that, in a pair of reverse rules, the rule with higher antecedent's support has lower confidence (the proof is omitted). The above pruning strategies are summarized as follows.

- Rule-pruning1: In a pair of equivalent rules, the rule with lower support is pruned.
- Rule-pruning2: In a pair of reverse rules, the rule whose antecedent has higher support is pruned.

We apply AMENAR, M_2 and M_3 to dataset D in example 1. The rules found by the three methods are compared in Table 3.

Remark 1. a) In Table 3, "Y" means the rule is included in the results; "N" means the rule can not be represented by the form; "$Miss$" means the rule is missed by the method, although it is an interesting rule by the definition; b) Redundant rules $r'_1 : \neg c \rightarrow \neg a$, $r''_1 : c \rightarrow a$ and $r'''_1 : \neg a \rightarrow \neg c$ are pruned in AMENAR; c) Some negative rules are missed in M_2 since the observations it is based on are inaccurate; d) M_1 is not included since it is dependent on taxonomy.

Table 3. Rules found by AMENAR, M_2 and M_3

AMENAR/EF	M_2/F_2	M_3/F_3
$r_1: a \rightarrow c$	$Y(r_1{'}, r_1{''}, r_1{'''})$	$Y(r_1{'}, r_1{''}, r_1{'''})$
$r_2: a \wedge \neg(b \wedge f) \rightarrow c$	N	N
$r_3: c \wedge \neg(b \wedge f) \rightarrow a$	N	N
$r_4: c \wedge a \rightarrow \neg(b \wedge f)$	$Miss$	N
$r_5: f \rightarrow b$	Y	Y
$r_6: \neg a \rightarrow b$	Y	Y
$r_7: \neg b \rightarrow \neg(b \wedge f)$	$Miss$	N

3.3 Advantages of AMENAR

Compared with M_1, M_2 and M_3, AMENAR has the following advantages:

- *Mining power:* a) As shown in Table 3, AMENAR is more powerful than M_2 and M_3, since it finds not just a subset but all interesting ENARs; b) Unlike M_1, AMENAR is independent on domain knowledge such as taxonomy.
- *Accuracy:* AMENAR is more accurate than M_2 and M_3 since a) it filters conflicting rules and two kinds of redundant rules; b) it will not miss rules.
- *Space efficiency:* a) Due to the high compactness of the Patricia trie, AMENAR has high space efficiency; b) The pruning strategies used in AMENAR further reduce the space cost.
- *Time efficiency:* a) I/O cost: only two scans of the dataset are required in AMENAR, while $(k+1)$ scans are required in the previous methods; b) The cost of generation and test: it is related to the characteristics of datasets. (In Section 4, the time efficiency will be analyzed further by experimental results).

4 Experimental Results

To study the effectiveness of the AMENAR algorithm, we have performed AMENAR, M_2 and M_3 on two synthetic datasets and compared their effectiveness.

4.1 Experiment Design and Environment

We use Visual C++ programming language to implement the algorithms. The algorithms are performed on a personal computer of an Intel Pentium processor with a clock rate of 2.6GHz and 512MB main memory.

4.2 Datasets

The experiments are conducted on two synthetic datasets: one is T10I4D100K, which is a simple and sparse dataset downloaded from [11], and the other is *Dtest*, which is a complex and dense dataset produced by a synthetic data generation program [2]. Table 4 shows the characteristics of the datasets.

Table 4. The characteristics of the datasets

Dataset	$|R|$	$|T|$	$|MaxFP|$	$|r|$
T10I4D100K	987	10	4	98376
$Dtest$	18490	43	10	87045

Remark 2. $|R|$: the number of items that occur in dataset D, $|R| = |I| = m$. $|T|$: the average number of items in each transaction. $|MaxFP|$: the size of maximal frequent positive itemsets. $|r|$: the number of transactions.

4.3 Experimental Results and Analysis

Figure 2 (a) shows the run time of the three algorithms on T10I4D100K with the variation of *minsup*. When *minsup* is lower than 2%, AMENAR is slower than M_2 and M_3. This is because when *minsup* is low, too many candidates are generated. When *minsup* is over 2%, AMENAR is more efficient than M_2 and M_3 since the number of candidates generated is not too large, and the main overhead is searching the Patricia trie in main memory for frequent patternsets.

Figure 2 (b) shows the run time on dataset *Dtest*. We see that AMENAR is not efficient on complex and dense datasets with too many items ($|R| = 18490$) and long frequent patternsets ($|MaxFP| = 10$), since too many frequent items are generated in Phase 2 and too many candidates are generated in Phase 3.

According to our experimental experience, AMENAR is efficient when a) $|PL_1|$ has a magnitude of $O(10^2)$; b) $|MaxFP| < 5$; c) *minsup* is high to some degree. Furthermore, the experimental results show that AMENAR has a linear scalability against the number of transactions.

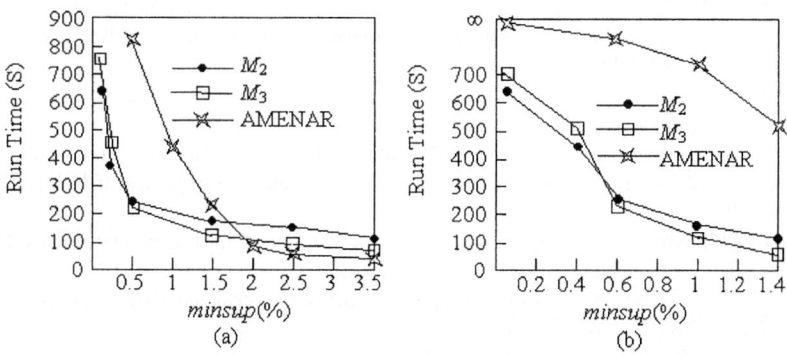

Fig. 2. (a) Run time on T10I4D100K (b) Run time on *Dtest*

5 Conclusions and Future Work

In this paper, we proposed an extended form for negative association rules and a corresponding mining algorithm AMENAR. The extended form is more expressive than the previous forms. The AMENAR algorithm is efficient on simple and sparse datasets, and has overcome some limitations of the previous methods.

Our work will extend related applications of negative association rules to a broader range, such as the prevention or diagnosis of some new infectious diseases and the analysis of some chemical reactions.

However, some problems remain unsolved in our current work. Furthermore, we intend to carry out the following work: first, we will improve the efficiency of AMENAR on complex and dense datasets and second, we will extend the form EF to quantitative, multilevel and multidimensional forms, and propose the corresponding mining methods.

Acknowledgements

We would like to thank Qiang Yang and Jiahuai You for their useful comments and suggestions. We would also like to thank Wu Chen and Yisong Wang for their helpful discussions.

References

1. R. Agrawal, T. Imielinski, A. Swami: Mining Association Rules between Sets of Items in Large Databases. Proceedings of the ACM SIGMOD Intl. Conf. on Management of Data (1993) 207-216
2. R. Agrawal, R. Srikant: Fast Algorithm for Mining Association Rules. Proceedings of VLDB (1994) 487-499
3. S. Brin, R. Motwani, C. Silverstein: Beyond Market Basket: Generalizing Association Rules to Correlations. Proceedings of the ACM SIGMOD (1997) 256-276
4. J. Han, J. Pei, Y. Yin, R. Mao: Mining Frequent Patterns Without Candidate Generation: A Frequent-pattern Tree Approach. Data Mining and Knowledge Discovery, Vol. 8 (2004) 53-87
5. A. Pietracaprina, D. Zandolin: Mining Frequent Itemsets Using Patricia Tries. Proceedings of IEEE FIMI (2003)
6. A. Savasere, E. Omiecinski and S. Navathe: Mining for Strong Negative Associations in a Large Database of Customer Transactions. Proceedings of ICDE (1998) 494-502
7. D.R. Thiruvady, G.I. Webb: Mining Negative Rules in Large Databases Using GRD. Proceedings of PAKDD (2004) 161-165
8. G.I. Webb, S. Zhang: Beyond Association Rules: Generalized Rule Discovery. Proceedings of KDD (2002) 14-17
9. X. Wu, C. Zhang, S. Zhang: Mining Both Positive and Negative Association Rules. Proceedings of ICML (2002) 658-665
10. X. Wu, C. Zhang, S. Zhang: Efficient Mining of Both Positive and Negative Association Rules. ACM Transactions on Information Systems. Vol. 22, No. 3 (2004) 381-405
11. Frequent Itemset Mining Dataset Repository, http://fimi.cs.helsinki.fi/data//

An Ant Clustering Method for a Dynamic Database

Ling Chen [1,2], Li Tu [1], and Yixin Chen [3]

[1] Department of Computer Science, Yangzhou University, Yangzhou 225009, China
[2] State Key Lab of Novel Software Tech, Nanjing University, Nanjing 210093, China
lchen@yzcn.net
[3] Department of Computer Science and Engineering, Washington University in St. Louis,
St. Louis, MO 63130, USA
chen@cse.wustl.edu

Abstract. We propose an adaptive ant colony data clustering algorithm for a dynamic database. The algorithm uses a digraph where the vertices represent the data to be clustered. The weight of the edge represents the acceptance rate between the two data connected by the edge. The pheromone on the edges is adaptively updated by the ants passing through it. Some edges with less pheromone are progressively removed under a list of thresholds in the process. Strong connected components of the final digraph are extracted as clusters. Experimental results on several real datasets and benchmarks indicate that the algorithm can find clusters more quickly and with better quality than K-means and LF. In addition, when the database is changed, the algorithm can dynamically modify the clusters accordingly to maintain its accuracy.

1 Introduction

Clustering aims to discover sensible organization of objects in a given dataset by identifying similarities as well as dissimilarities between objects. Without any prior knowledge, it classifies a mass of data into clusters which are clear in space partition outside and highly similar inside. Cluster analysis has found many extensive applications including classification of coals [1], toxicity testing [2], discovering of clusters in DNA nucleotides [3], etc.

Recently, inspired by the swarm intelligence [4-5] shown through the self-organizing behavior of social insects (e.g. birds, bee, fish, ants etc.), researchers created a new type of artificial ant to imitate the natural ants' behaviors, and named it artificial ant colony system. By simulating the ants' swarm intelligence, M. Dorigo et al. first advanced the ant colony optimization algorithm (ACO) [6-8] to solve several discrete optimization problems. In ACO, artificial ants are created to emulate the real ants in the process of seeking food and information exchange. The successful simulation has been applied to the traveling salesman problem (TSP) [9], system fault detection [10], sequential ordering [11], and other combinational optimization problems [12-13].

Researchers also have applied artificial ant colony to data clustering by simulating the behavior of ants' corpses piling. Deneubourg et al advanced a basic model (BM) [14] to explain the ants' corpses piling phenomenon and presented a clustering algorithm based on this model. By modifying BM algorithm, Lumer and Faieta [15] presented a formula to measure the similarity between two data objects and designed the LF algorithm for data clustering. In BM and LF, the ants consume large amounts of computation time and memory space since the data items cannot move directly and efficiently.

We propose an adaptive ant colony data clustering algorithm for a dynamic database. The algorithm uses a digraph where the vertices represent the data to be clustered and the weighted edges between the vertices represent the acceptance rate between the two data the algorithm connects. The ants travel in the digraph and update the pheromone on the edges as they pass through. Some edges with less pheromone are progressively removed under a list of thresholds in the process. Strong connected components of the final digraph are extracted as clusters. Experimental results on several real datasets and clustering benchmarks indicate that the algorithm is able to find clusters faster with better clustering quality and is easier to implement than K-means and LF. When the database is changed after inserting or deleting some records, the algorithm can dynamically modify the clustering accordingly to maintain its accuracy.

2 Ant Clustering with a Digraph

2.1 The Framework of the Algorithm Ant-Cluster

The framework of the proposed algorithm Ant-Cluster is as follows.

Algorithm 1. Ant-Cluster

```
1.  Initialize parameters; h=1;
2.  Initialize the pheromone digraph (V,E);
3.  Place ants at randomly selected data sites;
4.  while (iter-num<maxnum) do    // maxnum=500
5.      for each ant k do
6.          while not (∀ v∈ V have been visited) do
7.              Select the next edge in E to visit ac
                    cording to probability function p ;
8.          end do
9.      end for
10.     Update the pheromone on edges in E;
11.     if (iter-num%10==0) then
12.         for each edge(i,j) in E do
13.             if τ_{ij} < g_h  remove (i,j) from E;
14.         end for
15.         Adaptively update the value of α,β ;
16.         h=h+1;
17.     end if
18.     iter-num=iter-num+1;
19. end do
20. Compute the strong connected components of the final
       digraph to form the clusters.
```

2.2 The Acceptance Rate Between Data Objects

Line 2 in the algorithm constructs a weighted digraph where the weight of the edges is the acceptance rate between the two data it connects. The acceptance rate can be computed from the similarity between the data objects.

Definition 1. The Set of Data Items
We use $S = (O, A)$ to denote a set of n data items here

- $O = \{O_1, O_2, ...O_n\}$ represents the set of data objects,
- $A = \{A_1, A_2, ...A_r\}$ represents the attributes of data objects, where $\forall i, i \in (1,2,...n), \exists a_{ik}, k \in (1,2,...r)$ denotes the attribute A_k of O_i, therefore A_k could be denoted as a r-dimensional vector $(a_{i1}, a_{i2},...a_{ir})$, $i \in \{1,2,...n\}$.

Definition 2. The Difference between Data Items
The difference between two data items O_i and O_j is defined as:

$$dif(i, j) = \sum_{k=1}^{r} |a_{ik} - a_{jk}|, i, j = 1,2,...n . \qquad (2.1)$$

Definition 3. The Similarity between Data Items
For two data items O_i and O_j, we use $Sim(i, j)$ to denote their similarity:

$$Sim(i, j) = 1 - \frac{dif(i, j)}{\max dif} . \qquad (2.2)$$

Here, $\max dif = \max_{1 \le i, j \le n} dif(i, j)$ denotes the largest difference among the data items.

We use $avesim(i)$ and $\max sim(i)$ to denote the average and maximum similarity of O_i with all the other data items.

Definition 4. The Acceptance Rate
We use $accept(i, j)$ to denote the acceptance rate of data item O_i to O_j:

$$accept(i, j) = Sim(i, j) - \frac{1}{2}(avesim(i) + \max sim(i)) . \qquad (2.3)$$

The more similar two data objects are, then the greater the acceptance rates to each other will be. Where the value of $accept(i, j)$ is below zero, it will not be included in E. Using $accept(i, j)$ as the initial pheromone τ_{ij} of the edge (i,j), we can form a weighted digraph. The value of τ_{ij} will be updated in each step of clustering by the pheromone deposited by the ants passing this edge. The set of edges E will be updated in the process of the algorithm since some of the edges with pheromone less than a certain threshold can gradually be deleted from the graph.

In Ant-Cluster, the proposed initial pheromone values are set on the edges of the digraph, while in the traditional ant colony algorithm initial values of the pheromone at all edges are set as zero. This initial pheromone value of Ant-Cluster is very important for the ants' latter movements and for the efficiency of the algorithm's execution. It will help to update the digraph for the final clustering.

2.3 The Probability Function

In Ant-Cluster, artificial ants are used for visiting data items represented by the vertices in the digraph. A certain probability function is computed for the ant_k to select the next vertex, namely the next data object, to move to. To select the most similar data item, the ant on data item i should select the next data item j according to the following formula:

$$j = \begin{cases} \arg\max_{u \in allowed_k} \{[\tau_{iu}^{\alpha}(t)\eta_{iu}^{\beta}]\}, & \text{when } q \leq q_0 \\ \text{selected by probability } p_{ij}^{k}(t) & \text{otherwise} \end{cases} \quad (2.4)$$

where $allowed_k$ is the set of vertices that can be chosen by the k-th ant, and constant q_0 is a threshold for the vertex connected by the edge with the largest amount of pheromone to be chosen. In each iteration, a random number $q \in [0,1]$ is generated and compared with q_0. When $q > q_0$, data item j is chosen by the probability function defined as (2.5), otherwise the ant selects the vertex connected by the edge with the largest amount of pheromone.

$$p_{ij}^{k}(t) = \begin{cases} \dfrac{\tau_{ij}^{\alpha}(t)\eta_{ij}^{\beta}(t)}{\sum_{r \in allowed_k} \tau_{ir}^{\alpha}(t)\eta_{ir}^{\beta}(t)} & j \in allowed_k \\ 0 & \text{otherwise} \end{cases} \quad (2.5)$$

Here, we adopt the common probability formula form in ACO, but an adaptive strategy is applied on α and β which will be introduced in section 2.5.

2.4 Heuristic Function and Pheromone Updating

In (2.5), η_{ij} is the heuristic function which reflects the preference of the edge (i, j) to be selected by the ants. Obviously, the greater the similarity between the two connected data objects, the more preference the edge should receive. Therefore, η_{ij} is defined as:

$$\eta_{ij} = Sim(i, j) . \quad (2.6)$$

Different from pheromone τ_{ij}, η_{ij} is static and unidirectional heuristic information. After each iteration, line 10 in Ant-Cluster updates the pheromone of the edges on the paths the ants just passed through according to the following formula:

$$\tau_{ij}(t+1) = (1-\rho)\cdot \tau_{ij}(t) + \sum_{k=1}^{m} \Delta\tau_{ij}^{k} \quad . \tag{2.7}$$

In (2.7), $\rho \in (0,1)$ is a constant called coefficient of evaporation. At each iteration, the pheromone on each path will be evaporated by a rate of ρ. The increment of τ_{ij} by ant k is denoted as $\Delta\tau_{ij}^{k}$ and can be computed by (2.8) where Q is a constant.

$$\Delta\tau_{ij}^{k} = \begin{cases} Q\cdot Sim(i,j), & \text{if ant } k \text{ passes path } (i,j) \\ 0, & \text{otherwise} \end{cases} \tag{2.8}$$

It can be clearly seen from (2.8) that the more ants that pass through an edge, the more pheromone will be deposited on it, thus increasing the probability that it will be included in the same strong connected component of the weighted digraph constructed in the last part of the algorithm. Hence the two data items connected by this edge are more likely to be classified into one cluster.

2.5 Adaptively Update the Parameters α, β

In (2.5), α, β determine the relative influence of the trail strength τ_{ij} and the heuristic information η_{ij}. At the initial stage of the algorithm, the pheromone value on each edge is relatively small. To speed up the convergence, the ants should select the path mainly according to the heuristic information η_{ij}. Therefore, the value of β should be relatively large. After some iterations, the pheromone values on the edges are increased, their influence becoming more and more important. Therefore the value of α should be relatively large. Since the adjustment of the values of α and β should be based on the distribution of pheromone on the edges, in (2.9) we define τ_{ave} as the average amount of pheromone on the pheromone digraph and in (2.10) define ψ as the pheromone distributing weight to measure the distribution of pheromone on the graph.

$$\tau_{ave} = \frac{\sum_{(i,j)\in E} \tau_{ij}}{|E|} \quad . \tag{2.9}$$

$$\psi = \frac{1}{|E|}\left[\sum_{(i,j)\in E} (\tau_{ave} - \tau_{ij})^{2} \right]^{\frac{1}{2}} \quad . \tag{2.10}$$

Here E is the set of valid edges in the digraph.

Using the pheromone distributing weight ψ, the algorithm updates the value of α, β as follows:

$$\alpha = e^{-\psi}, \beta = \frac{1}{\alpha}.\tag{2.11}$$

The algorithm can accelerate the convergence and can also avoid local convergence and precocity by adjusting the value of α, β adaptively. Furthermore, since the amount of pheromone is an important measure for data clustering, the pheromone distributing weight ψ is also a critical factor in terminating the iterations of the algorithm.

3 Experiment Results

The algorithm Ant-Cluster is tested on Windows XP, P1.7G, Matlab 6.0 with the basic parameters set as $m=n/2$, $c=1$, $\rho=0.05$, $q_0=0.95$. We not only test on the ant-based clustering data benchmark but also on several real datasets. To compare the performance of our method with that of other clustering algorithms, we also test on these datasets using the K-means and LF algorithm.

3.1 Test on Ant Based Clustering Data Benchmark

We test a dataset with five data types, each of which consists of 10 two-dimensional data (x, y) which belong to five classes as shown in Figure 1. The five types of data (x, y) are [N(0.2,0.12),N(0.2,0.12)], [N(0.5,0.12),N(0.5,0.12)], [N(0.8,0.12), N(0.2,0.12)], [N(0.2,0.12),N(0.8,0.12)] and [N(0.8,0.12),N(0.8,0.12)] respectively, which obey normal distribution $N(u,\sigma^2)$.

The initial pheromone digraph of this dataset of 50 data items is shown in Fig. 2. Fig. 3 shows the modified pheromone digraph obtained after 60 iterations of Ant-Cluster.

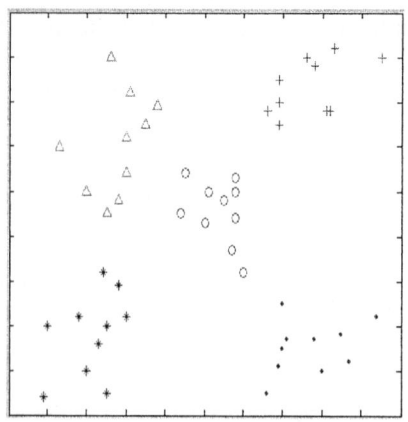

Fig. 1. The initial distribution of datasets

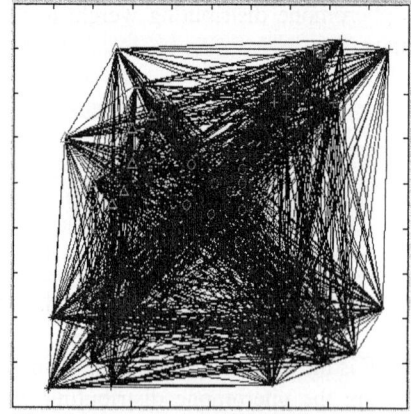

Fig. 2. The initial pheromone digraph

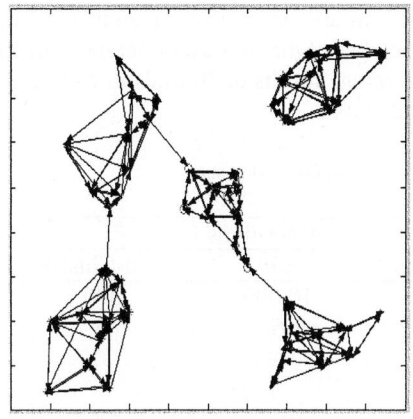 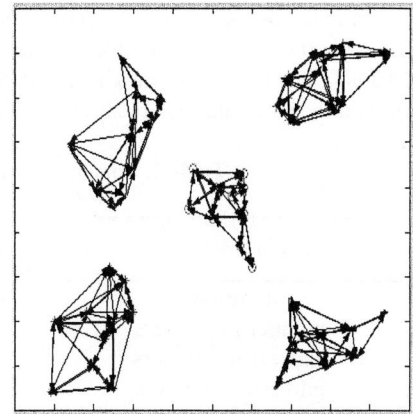

Fig. 3. The transferred pheromone digraph after 60 iterations

Fig. 4. The final clusters (strong connected components)

Five strong connected components of the transferred digraph are found as shown in Fig. 4. The final clusters are represented by these strong connected components.

Two more datasets which have 300 and 600 data items are also tested to compare the performance of Ant-Cluster with LF and K-means. Each dataset has two attributes and three classes where data items are generated at random in distributions of [N(0.3,0.12),N(0.3,0.12)], [N(0.8,0.12),N(0.3,0.12)] and [N(0.5,0.12),N(0.8,0.12)] respectively. Table 1 shows the average results of 50 trails on these two types of data using Ant-Cluster, LF and the classical K-means algorithm.

Table 1. The results of three algorithms on artificial studies

Clustering Algorithms	300 data items		600 data items	
	Error rate	Time cost(s)	Error rate	Time cost(s)
LF	0	135.08	1.98%	322.55
K-Means	0	112.30	2.57%	243.12
Ant-Cluster	0	53.27	0.38%	101.73

It can be clearly seen from Table 1 that although all the algorithms can get clusters on 300 data items without error, Ant-Cluster costs much less computational time than K-means and LF algorithm. For the test on 600 data items, Ant-Cluster performs much better than the other two methods in terms of error rate and time cost.

3.2 Test on Real Database Benchmarks

We also test on the real database benchmarks of Glass and Soybean (small) using Ant-Cluster, LF and K-means. Large numbers of experiment results show that the clustering results of Ant-Cluster after 500 iterations are mostly better than those of LF after 10,000 iterations. Therefore, we set the number of the maximum iterations of LF as 10,000, and those for Ant-Cluster as 500. Average results of 50 trials of each algorithm on the two datasets are shown in Tables 2 and 3.

Table 2. Comparison of the results on Glass datasets

Parameters	Algorithms		
	K-Means	LF	Ant-Cluster
iterations	k=6	10,000	500
number of clusters	6	6	6
max error numbers	17	14	11
min error numbers	9	7	6
average error numbers	12.15	10.31	7.82
average error rate	5.67%	4.68%	3.65%
time cost (s)	92.42	115.54	40.24

Table 3. Comparison of the results on Soybean datasets

Parameters	Algorithms		
	K-Means	LF	Ant-Cluster
iterations	k=4	10,000	500
number of clusters	4	4	4
max error numbers	5	7	2
min error numbers	0	1	0
average error numbers	2.48	3.21	0.78
Average error rate	5.27%	6.83%	1.66%
time cost (s)	29.37	38.25	9.33

From Tables 2 and 3, we can see that Ant-Cluster requires less iterations and hence less computation time than K-means and LF. The reason for low speed of LF algorithm is that it is very difficult for ants carrying an isolated data object to find a proper position to drop it. LF also lacks adaptive adjustment of parameters and can not speed up the process of clustering. The K-means algorithm has lower speed than Ant-Cluster because it is unsupervised and sensitive to the initialization. The tables also show that the error rates of Ant-Cluster are much lower than that of K-means and LF.

4 Maintaining the Clustering in a Dynamic Data Base

When a database is changed after inserting or deleting some records, the clustering should be dynamically modified accordingly to maintain its accuracy. In a large data base, adding or deleting a single record will not have much effect on the clustering; we do not re-cluster the database when only a single change occurs. Instead, we re-cluster the database when the number of such modifications exceeds a threshold *thresh*. To maintain the clustering, the digraph should be modified whenever a record is inserted or deleted. When a record is inserted, its distances to the other records are computed and it is assigned to a cluster where it has the least average distance to the other records. Then it is allocated into the digraph as a new vertex and the directed edges from it to the other vertices are also added. When a record is deleted, its vertex and the related edges are simply removed from the digraph. When the number of such changes exceeds the threshold *thresh*, we re-cluster the database on the modified digraph using the algorithm Ant-Cluster. Since in the digraph most of the vertices are properly clustered and the pheromone information on the edges is still useful, it takes little time to complete the re-clustering. Each time a new change occurs on the database, the following algorithm is executed where *change_num* is the number of changes on the database.

Algorithm 2. Modification

```
1.  if delete a record then
2.      Remove the vertex and related edges from the
            digraph;
3.  else if  insert a record then
4.      Compute its distances to the other records;
5.      Find  a cluster where it has the least average
            distance to the records;
6.      Add it into the digraph as a new vertex;
7.      Add the directed edges from the new vertex  to
            the other vertices;
7.  endif
8.  change_num=change_num+1;
9.  if change_num mod thresh=0 then
10.     Re-cluster the database by  Ant-Cluster;
11. endif.
```

5 Conclusion

In this paper, we propose an adaptive ant colony data clustering algorithm Ant-Cluster for a dynamic database. Different to other existing clustering algorithms, Ant-Cluster makes full use of the ant colony system to transform a weighted pheromone digraph and abstracts the strong connected components of the final digraph as the clusters. We proposed effective strategies for the ants selecting the edge, updating the pheromone, and adjusting the parameters adaptively to speed up the clustering procedure and to improve the clustering quality. Compared with K-means and LF algorithm, Ant-Cluster is direct, easy to implement, and self-adaptive. It produces higher quality clusters, and is much more computationally efficient than previous methods. In addition, when the database is changed, the algorithm can dynamically modify the clustering accordingly to maintain its accuracy.

Acknowledgement

This research was supported in part by the Chinese National Natural Science Foundation under grant No. 60473012, Chinese National Foundation for Science and

Technology Development under contract 2003BA614A-14, and Natural Science Foundation of Jiangsu Province under contract BK2005047.

References

1. Kaufman, L., Pierreux,A., Rousseuw, P., Derde, M.P., Detaecernier, M..R., Massart, D.L., Platbrood, G.: Clustering on a Microcomputer with an Application to the Classification of Coals, Analytica Chimica Acta, 153 (1983) 257–260.
2. Lawson, R.G., Jurs, P.C.: Cluster Analysis of Acrylates to Guide Sampling for Toxicity Testing. Journal of Chemical Information and Computer Science, 30 (1) (1990)137–144.
3. Beckers, M.L.M., Melssen, W.J., Buydens, L.M.C.: A self-organizing feature map for clustering nucleic acids. Application to a data matrix containing A-DNA and B-DNA dinucleotides. Comput. Chem., 21 (1997)377–390.
4. Kennedy, J., Eberhart, R.C.: Swarm Intelligence. Morgan Kaufmann Publishers, San Francisco CA (2001).
5. Bonabeau, E., Dorigo, M., Théraulaz, G.: Swarm Intelligence: From Natural to Artificial Systems. Santa Fe Institute in the Sciences of the Complexity. Oxford University Press, Oxford New York (1999).
6. Dorigo, M., Maniezzo, V., Colomi, A.: Ant system :Optimization by a colony of cooperating agents. IEEE Transactions on Systems, Man and Cybernetics-Part B, 26(1) (1996) 29–41.
7. Dorigo, M., Gambardella, L.M.: Ant colony system: a cooperative learning approach to the traveling salesman problem. IEEE Trans. On Evolutionary Computation, 1(1) (1997) 53–66.
8. Stutzle, T., Hoos, H.: MAX-MIN Ant systems. Future Generation Computer Sytems, 16(2000) 889–914.
9. Dorigo, M., Gambardella, L.M.: Ant colonies for the traveling salesman problem. BioSystems, 43(2) (1997) 73–81.
10. Chang, C.S., Tian, L., Wen, F.S.: A new approach to fault section in power systems using Ant System. Electric Power Systems Research, 49(1) (1999) 63–70.
11. Gambardella, L.M., Dorigo, M.: HAS-SOP: An Hybrid Ant System for the Sequential Ordering Problem. Tech. Rep. No. IDSIA 97-11, IDSIA, Lugano Switzerland (1997).
12. Kuntz, P., Layzell, P., Snyder, D.: A colony of ant-like agents for partitioning in VLSI technology. In: Husbands, P., Harvey, I.(eds.): Proceedings of the Fourth European Conference on Artificial Life, MIT Press, Cambridge MA (1997) 412–424.
13. Kuntz, P., Snyder, D.: New results on ant-based heuristic for highlighting the organization of large graphs. In: Proceedings of the 1999 Congress or Evolutionary Computation, IEEE Press, Piscataway NJ (1999) 1451–1458.
14. Deneubourg, J.L., Goss, S., Franks, N., Sendova-Franks, A., Detrain, C., Chretien, L.: The Dynamic of Collective Sorting Robot-like Ants and Ant-like Robots. In: Meyer, J.A., Wilson, S.W. (eds.): SAB'90-1st Conf. On Simulation of Adaptive Behavior: From Animals to Animats, Mit press, (1991) 356–365.
15. Lumer, E., Faieta, B.: Diversity and adaptation in populations of clustering ants. In: Meyer, J.A., Wilson, S.W. (eds.): Proceedings of the Third International Conference on Simulation of Adaptive Behavior: From Animates, Vol.3. MIT Press/ Bradford Books, Cambridge MA (1994) 501–508.

An Efficient Algorithm for Incremental Mining of Sequential Patterns

Jia-Dong Ren and Xiao-Lei Zhou

College of Information Science and Engineering, Yanshan University,
Qinhuangdao 066004, China
jdren@ysu.edu.cn, zxl8105230848@126.com

Abstract. Mining of sequential patterns is an important issue among the various data mining problems. The problem of incremental mining of sequential patterns deserves as much attention. In this paper, we consider the problem of the incremental updating of sequential pattern mining when some transactions and/or data sequences are deleted from the original sequence database. We present a new algorithm, called IU_D, for mining frequent sequences so as to make full use of information obtained during an earlier mining process for reducing the cost of finding new sequential patterns in the updated database. The results of our experiment show that the algorithm performs significantly faster than the naive approach of mining the entire updated database from scratch.

1 Introduction

Sequential patterns are often occurred patterns based on a time stamp or other sequences. Mining of sequential patterns is an important issue among the various data mining problems. The concept of sequential patterns was first introduced by R.Agrawal[1] in 1995, and it can be applied in many fields, such as transaction database analysis, web access logs, gene project, medicine and so on.

The problem of sequential pattern mining has been studied extensively. *Agrawal* and *Srikant* presented a generalized sequential pattern mining algorithm GSP[2], which follows the candidate generation and test philosophy. It starts with discovering frequent 1-sequences, and then generates candidate (k+1)-sequences from the sets of frequent k-sequences. Another algorithm, called SPIRIT[3], was presented by *Garofalakis*, and is based on regular expression constraints. The core of the algorithm is similar to *GSP*; the main difference is that the candidate generation must be restricted by constraints. Consequently, *Jia-Wei Han* presented Freespan[4] and Prefixspan[5] algorithms, which are based on projected databases, for mining sequential patterns. The algorithms apply a divide-and-conquer strategy, and generate many smaller projected databases of the sequence database, and then the frequent sequences are mined in each projected database by exploring local frequent patterns. However, none of this research deals with the incremental updating problem of sequential patterns.

In real applications, a sequence database is always updated with changing time. In this circumstance, a portion of the old sequential patterns may no longer satisfy the minimum support threshold. Meanwhile, some new sequential patterns may appear in the updated database. Therefore, there is a need to update and maintain the results of sequential pattern mining in time, so that the current database state can be reflected correctly. A naive approach is to re-run previously presented algorithms on the whole updated database from scratch. Clearly, this concept lacks efficiency in that it does not make use of the information obtained from prior mining processes. Many specialists and scholars working in the data mining community have presented various algorithms for the incremental mining of sequential patterns. An incremental maintenance technique of mining sequential patterns based on SPADE[6] was presented by *Zaki*. In this algorithm, all the frequent sequences and their negative borders build up a sequence lattice. When the incremental data arrives, the incremental parts are scanned and the sequence lattice is updated. Then, we can determine which parts of the original database should be scanned according to the sequence lattice. *Masseglia* presented ISE[7] algorithm for incremental and interactive sequence mining. The algorithm utilizes the results obtained from prior mining processes to generate a set of candidate sequences, which reduces the number of candidate sequences. Later, some researchers presented the FAST[8] algorithm for solving the maintenance problem of sequential pattern mining when the minimum support threshold changed and the sequence database didn't change.

So far, the researches on incremental mining of sequential patterns focus on two aspects: on the one hand, when new transactions and new data sequences are appended to the original database, how to deal with the incremental mining of sequential patterns; on the other hand, when the minimum support threshold changes, how to deal with the maintenance problem of sequential pattern mining. But in the fields of electronic commerce and web usage mining, we often delete information from a sequence database, in order to save storage space or because some information is no longer relative or become invalid.

In this paper, an algorithm called IU_D is presented to solve the problem of how to update discovered sequential patterns when some transactions and/or data sequences have previously been deleted from the original database. Our algorithm makes full use of the information obtained from prior mining processes, and stores the set of discovered frequent sequences in a database for further mining. It adopts a new candidate generation technique, which reduces the size of candidate sets to some extent.

The rest of the paper is organized as follows: In Section 2 we formulate the basic concept of sequential pattern mining and present the incremental mining problem of sequential patterns when a portion of the information is deleted from sequence databases. Section 3 presents the IU_D algorithm for the incremental mining problem of sequential patterns. The proposed algorithm is evaluated and exampled in Section 4. The experiment is described and evaluated in Section 5 and Section 6 concludes our study.

2 Statement of the Problem

2.1 Mining of Sequential Patterns

Let $I=\{i_1, i_2, \cdots, i_n\}$ be a set of all items. An *itemset* is a non-empty set of items. A sequence is an ordered list of itemsets. A sequence is denoted by $<s_1, s_2, \cdots, s_l>$, where s_j

is an itemset, i.e., $s_j \subseteq I$ for $1 \leq j \leq l$. s_j is also called an element of the sequence, and denoted as $(x_1x_2 \cdots x_m)$, where $x_k \in I$ for $1 \leq k \leq m$. For brevity, the brackets are omitted if an element has only one item. That is, element (x) is written as x. An item can occur once at the most in an element of a sequence, but can occur multiple times in different elements of a sequence. The number of instances of items in a sequence is called the length of the sequence. A sequence with length l is called an l-sequence. A sequence $a = \langle a_1, a_2, \cdots, a_n \rangle$ is called a subsequence of $b = \langle b_1, b_2, \ldots, b_m \rangle$ and b a super sequence of a, denoted as $a \subseteq b$, if there exist integers $1 \leq j_1 < j_2 < \cdots < j_n \leq m$ such that $a_1 \subseteq b_{j1}$, $a_2 \subseteq b_{j2}$, $\cdots$, $a_n \subseteq b_{jn}$. A sequence database D is a set of tuples $\langle sid, s \rangle$, where sid is a sequence-id and s is a sequence. A tuple $\langle sid, s \rangle$ is said to contain a sequence a, if a is a subsequence of s, i.e., $a \subseteq s$.

The support for a sequence is defined as the fraction of total data sequences that "contain" this sequence. A data sequence contains a sequence s if s is a subsequence of the data sequence.

Given a database DB of sequences, and some user specified minimum support m, a sequence is frequent if it is contained in at least m sequences in the database. The problem of sequential pattern mining is to find all the sequences whose support is greater than a specified minimum support m. Each of these represents a sequential pattern, also called a frequent sequence.

2.1 Incremental Mining of Sequential Patterns

Let DB be an original sequence database and s be the minimum support threshold. Let dd be the deleted sequence database (some deleted transactions and/or data sequences) and $U=DB-dd$ be the updated database after deleting dd. Let $\cup_k L_k$ be the set of frequent sequences in DB.

The incremental mining problem of sequential patterns is to find frequent sequences in U, denoted by LU, with respect to the same minimum support threshold, s. When the database is updated, the incremental mining technique must utilize previously found information ($\cup$k Lk) to avoid re-mining the whole updated database from scratch. The objective of incremental mining of sequential patterns is to respond to each mining quickly when we delete information from sequence databases, and to minimize the overall runtime for the whole process accordingly.

3 IU_D Algorithm

3.1 An Overview

Let DB be an original sequence database, s be the user specified minimum support threshold, D be the size of DB, $\cup_k L_k$ be the set of frequent k-sequences in DB, dd be the database consisting of deleted information ($dd \subset DB$) and d be the number of deleted data sequences in DB. The *support* of sequence x is denoted by $x.sup$. The updated sequence database is denoted by $DB-dd$.

When information is deleted from the database, the incremental updating problem of sequential patterns can be illustrated by the following two scenarios:

(1) Only some transactions (but not data sequences) are deleted from the sequence database, i.e. the minimum support count remains constant, but the database has changed.

Because some transactions are deleted, the support count of some sequences that contain these deleted items may diminish and not satisfy the minimum support count. They may become infrequent sequences. In this case, we can deal with it easily by deleting the infrequent sequences from the old set of sequential patterns. The method can be described as follows: Scanning the updated database DB-dd only once, we can obtain the support count of the sequences in $\cup kLk$. Then, infrequent sequences are filtered out from $\cup kLk$ and the frequent ones remain. In this case, it is obvious that we can obtain the set of new sequential patterns without any mining operations.

(2) Let us now consider the problem when some data sequences and some transactions are deleted from the original database. The size of the database will be reduced, which will result in a smaller minimum support count. That is to say, both the minimum support count and the database have changed (the minimum support count will be s*(D-d)). Now that some formerly frequent sequences have become infrequent ones, new frequent sequences may appear. Let DB and DB−dd be the original database and the updated database, respectively, $\cup k\ Lk$ and $\cup k\ Fk$ are the corresponding sets of frequent k-sequences, and C1 is the set of all the 1-sequences in DB.

For the case that the formerly frequent sequences become infrequent ones in DB−dd, we first scan the updated database DB−dd and obtain the new support count of the originally old frequent sequences in $\cup k\ Lk$. After that, the sequences that don't satisfy the new support count s*(D-d) will be filtered from $\cup k\ Lk$, and the frequent sequences will still be preserved. This case is the same as the abovementioned.

Sequences embedded in DB could become frequent since they have sufficient support. In order to find all new frequent sequences, we should first discover the candidate sets containing these new frequent sequences. This paper adopts a new candidate generation approach.

First, by scanning the updated sequence database $DB-dd$ once, we can count the support of the new candidate 1-sequences, denoted by NC_1, which are not contained in L_1. Obviously, the new set of candidate 1-sequences can be written as $NC_1=C_1-L_1$, thus the new frequent 1-sequences, denoted by NL_1, is $NL_1=\{x|x \in NC_1 \wedge x.sup\geq s*(D-d)\}$. The new frequent 1-sequences NL_1 and the originally old frequent 1-sequences L_1 make up all the frequent 1-sequences, denoted by F_1, in $DB-dd$, i.e. $F_1 = NL_1 \cup L_1$, obviously, $NL_1 \cap L_1 = \varnothing$ (here, L_1 is the set of frequent sequences which have been filtered out of infrequent sequences).

Let us now consider the problem of how to search for the set of frequent k-sequences L_k when $k \geq 2$. In order to improve the efficiency of incremental mining, we should try to reduce the number of candidate sequences. Take $k=2$ for example; because of $F_1 = NL_1 \cup L_1$ and $NL_1 \cap L_1 = \varnothing$, according to a basic Apriori[9] property: "Any subsequences of a frequent sequence must be frequent sequences." The new candidate 2-sequences NC_2 are generated by the sequences in NL_1 or are generated by a sequence from NL_1 and a sequence from L_1 (refer to the following function new_gen). (This part of NC_2 can be labeled as NC_k^2) Another part of NC_2 can be denoted by $C_2 - L_2$(labeled as NC_k^1). Here, C_2 is generated by the sequences in the updated L_1. It is obvious that the two parts of NC_2 (NC_k^1 and NC_k^2) are mutually exclusive. Scanning the updated database $DB - dd$ once for counting the support of the sequences in NC_2, and then choosing the frequent sequences, we can obtain the new frequent 2-sequences, denoted by NL_2. The updated sequential patterns are $F_2 = NL_2 \cup L_2$. When $k \geq 3$, we execute the above operations iteratively, until $F_{k-1} = \emptyset$.

3.2 The Updating Algorithm *IU_D*

Based on the above discussion, we shall now describe the *IU_D* algorithm.

```
Algorithm IU_D

Input: DB the original database, U_k L_k the set of frequent
k-sequences in DB, s user specified minimum support
threshold, D the size of DB, dd the deleted database, d the
number of deleted data-sequences, C_1 the set of all the
1-sequences in DB and n1 the length of the longest frequent
sequences in U_k L_k.

Output: The set U_k F_k of all frequent sequences in DB- dd.

Method:

//filter out the infrequent sequences in U_k L_k and preserve
the frequent ones

for (k=1; k≤n1; k++)

    L_k={x| x∈L_k and x.sup≥s*(D-d)};

endfor

//scan the updated database DB-dd once, count the support
of all the new candidate 1-sequences, denoted by NC_1, which
are not contained in L_1, and then find the new frequent
1-sequences NL_1

NC_1 = C_1 - L_1;

NL_1 = {x|x∈NC_1 ∧ x.sup≥s*(D-d)};

//the new frequent 1-sequences NL_1 and the originally old
frequent 1-sequences L_1 make up all the frequent 1-sequences
F_1

F_1 = NL_1 ∪ L_1;

//when k•2, the generation of new candidate k-sequences can
be considered as two parts: NC_k^1 and NC_k^2

k=2;
```

```
while F_{k-1} ≠ ∅ do
{
generate C_k from the frequent (k-1)-sequences in L_{k-1};
NC_k^1 = C_k - L_k;
NC_k^2 = new_gen(NL_{k-1}, L_{k-1});   //user-defined function
NC_k = NC_k^1 ∪ NC_k^2;
forall data sequences ds in database DB- dd do
   for each candidate sequence x∈NC_k do
      increase the support of x if x is contained in ds;
   endfor
endfor
NL_k = {x | x∈NC_k ∧ x.sup ≥ s*(D-d)};
F_k = NL_k ∪ L_k;
k++;
}
Answer = ∪_k F_k;
//user-defined function used to generate one part of the
new candidate sequences (NC_k^2)
new_gen(NL_{k-1}, L_{k-1})
{
generate T1 from the frequent (k-1)-sequences in NL_{k-1};
generate T2 from the frequent (k-1)-sequences p and q
(p∈NL_{k-1}, q∈L_{k-1});
NC_k^2 = T1 ∪ T2;
forall sequences S∈NC_k^2 do
   forall (k-1)-subsequences s' of S do
      if (s' ∉ NL_{k-1} ∪ L_{k-1}) or (s' ∈ L_{k-1})
         delete S from NC_k^2;
      endif;
   endfor;
endfor;
}
```

4 Example and Performance Analysis

Let us now consider the problem that occurs when a portion of information is deleted from the original sequence database (Table 1 and Table 2). Table 1 illustrates the original sequence database *DB* and Table 2 the deleted sequence database *dd*. We assume that the minimum support threshold is 50%. Now we show the mining process using the *IU_D* algorithm.

Consider the deleted database *dd* in Table 2; we can obtain the updated database $DB - dd$ illustrated by Table 3. A sequence is frequent in *DB* if it is contained in at least three data sequences in *DB*. In the original database *DB*, we can find the following frequent sequences: $L_1 = \{<a>, <b>, <c>, <d>, <e>\}$, $L_2 = \{<ab>, <ac>, <ad>, <(bc)>\}$ and $L_3 = \{<a(bc)>\}$. A sequence is frequent in the updated database $DB - dd$ if it is contained in at least two data sequences in $DB - dd$.

Table 1. An original sequence database (*DB*)

Sequence-id	Sequence
C1	<a(bc)e>
C2	<e(ab)(bc)dd>
C3	<(aef)(bc)dd>
C4	<adcb>
C5	<abc(ef)>

Table 2. A deleted sequence database (*dd*)

Sequence-id	Sequence
C2	<e(bc)>
C3	<dd>
C4	<adcb>
C5	<c>

Table 3. An updated database ($DB - dd$)

Sequence-id	Sequence
C1	<a(bc)e>
C2	<(ab)dd>
C3	<(aef)(bc)>
C5	<ab(ef)>

Here, some transactions and a data sequence are deleted from *DB*. For example, transactions (*e*) and (*bc*) are deleted from the second data sequence; (*d*) and (*d*)are deleted from the third data sequence, and the fourth data sequence is deleted from the original database. The mining processes of *IU_D* algorithm are performed as follows:

By scanning the updated database DB-dd only once, we find that <d> and <ad> in the old set of frequent sequences have become infrequent, so they have to be filtered out from $\cup_k L_k$. The updated $\cup_k L_k$ ={<a>, <b>, <c>, <e>, <ab>, <ac>, <(bc)>, <a(bc)>}. It is obvious that NC_1={<d>, <f>}, only <f> satisfies the minimum support count, i.e., 2, so NL_1={<f>}. All the frequent 1-sequences give that F_1= $NL_1 \cup L_1$={<a>, <b>, <c>, <e>,<f>}. From L_1, we can obtain that NC_2^1={<(ab)>, <(ac)>, <(ae)>, <ae>, ..., <(ce)>, <ce>}, and from L_1 and NL_1, calling the function *new_gen*, we can find that NC_2^2={<af>, <(af)>, ..., <ef>, <(ef)>, <ff>}. From NC_2^1 and NC_2^2, NL_2={<ae>, <be>, <(ef)>} can be obtained. All the frequent 2-sequences give that F_2= $NL_2 \cup L_2$={<ae>, <be>, <(ef)>, <ab>, <ac>, <(bc)>}. From NL_2 and L_2, we can obtain NC_3^2={<abe>}. From L_2, we can obtain $NC_3^1 = \emptyset$. So the new frequent 3-sequences NL_3 ={<abe>}. All the frequent 3-sequences in the updated database are F_3= $NL_3 \cup L_3$={<abe>, <a(bc)>}. After updating the database, all the frequent sequences in $DB - dd$ are $F_1 \cup F_2 \cup F_3$={<a>, <b>, <c>, <e>,<f>, <ae>, <be>, <(ef)>, <ab>, <ac>, <(bc)>, <abe>, <a(bc)>}. It should be noted that the results obtained by our approach are consistent with the results obtained by re-running the mining algorithm on the updated database from scratch.

When information is deleted from sequence databases, *IU_D* algorithm makes full use of the set of sequential patterns obtained from previous mining processes, which improves the mining efficiency and reduces the runtime. This can be evidenced by the following aspects:

(1) If only some transactions but not data sequences are deleted from the data sequences, we just scan the updated sequence database once and count the support of the sequences in $\cup_k L_k$, and then filter the infrequent sequences, preserving the frequent ones. No mining operation is required to obtain the new set of sequential patterns in this method. Obviously, this approach is much more efficient than the naive idea of re-running the sequential pattern mining algorithm from scratch.

(2) If some data sequences and some transactions are deleted from the original database, some new sequential patterns may appear. It should be noted that the minimum support count would become correspondingly smaller. In order to utilize the information obtained from the old sequential patterns to find the set of all the new sequential patterns, we use a new approach to generate all the candidate k-sequences, denoted by NC_k. NC_k can be divided into two parts (NC_k^1 and NC_k^2) in this approach:

On the one hand, the candidate k-sequences C_k generated by the sequences in the L_{k-1} may contain new frequent sequences. So, $NC_k^1 = C_k - L_k$. For example, in the third iteration in the above tables, there is only one candidate sequence generated, i.e. <abe>. If we use *GSP* algorithms to mine the updated data from scratch, there will be two candidate sequences, i.e., <abe> and <a(bc)>.

On the other hand, the new candidate k-sequences NCk2 are generated either by the sequences in NL_{k-1} or by a sequence from NL_{k-1} and a sequence from L_{k-1}.

Obviously, the number of the candidate sequences generated in our approach is much smaller than the one in the naive idea; therefore, the mining efficiency can be improved to some extent. But the approach still requires repeated scanning of the updated database, and, consequently, this should solve the problem.

5 Experiment Results

Our proposed algorithm was implemented in Java language on a Pentium IV-2.4G Windows-XP system with 512MB of main memory and JBuilder 8.0 as the Java execution environment. The dataset for our experiment was generated by the program developed by Agrawal and his co-worker[1]. 10,000 data sequences were generated at random. In our synthetic dataset, the number of items is set to 1,000. The average number of elements in a sequence is set to 8. The average number of items within elements is set to 8. The average length of maximal patterns is set to 8 and the average length of maximal frequent transactions is also set to 8. These values were chosen in order to follow closely the parameters usually chosen in other studies. After some transactions and sequences are randomly deleted from the initial synthetic dataset, we can obtain the updated dataset *Update_Dataset*.

First, we use GSP algorithm to mine sequential patterns with different minimum support thresholds on the initial synthetic dataset. Then, *IU_D* algorithm utilizes the results obtained in the first *GSP* mining processes to mine sequential patterns on the updated datasets. And *GSP* algorithm mines sequential patterns on the updated dataset from scratch with a corresponding minimum support threshold. Table 4 compares the relative performance of *IU_D* and *GSP* on the updated dataset *Update_Dataset* using corresponding minimum support thresholds.

Table 4. The runtime comparison of IU_D and GSP on the updated dataset *Update_Dataset*

Runtime (sec)	Minimum Support		
	0.10	0.15	0.20
GSP	3208	157	50
IU_D	646	98	32

From Table 4, it is easily seen that the runtime of the proposed algorithm *IU_D* is much less than that achieved by algorithm *GSP* on the updated dataset *Update_Dataset* for deletion of transactions and data sequences with a different minimum support threshold.

6 Conclusions

An important issue in data mining is to find the set of frequent sequences. The high cost of the process of finding sequential patterns requires deep research on incremental mining techniques of sequential patterns. In this paper, we discuss the problem of incremental mining of sequential patterns when some transactions and/or data sequences are deleted from an original database, and present the *IU_D* algorithm as a solution to the problem. Our algorithm adopts a new candidate generation approach and reduces the size of the candidate sequences set. Theory analysis and experiment results show that the algorithm has favorable performance.

Acknowledgements

The authors thank the reviewers' comments for improving the quality of the paper. This research has been supported partially by doctoral fund of Hebei province.

References

1. Agrawal, R., Srikant, R.: Mining sequential pattern, Proceedings of the 11th International Conference on Data Engineering (ICDE'95), Taipei, Taiwan, March (1995) 3-14
2. Srikant, R., Agrawal, R.: Mining sequential pattern: generalizations and performance improvements, Proceedings of the 5th International Conference on Extending Database Technology (EDBT'96), Avignon, France, (1996) 3-17
3. Garofalakis, M., Rastogi, R., Shim, K.: SPIRIT: Sequential pattern mining with regular expression constraints, Proceedings of the 25th International Conference on Very Large Databases (VLDB'99), (1999) 223-234
4. Han, J., Pei, J., Mortazavi-Asl, B.: FreeSpan: Frequent pattern-projected sequential pattern mining, Proceedings of the 6th International Conference on Knowledge Discovery and Data Mining (KDD'00), (2000) 355-359
5. Pei, J., Han, J., Mortazavi-Asl, B.: PrefixSpan: Mining sequential patterns efficiently by prefix-projected pattern growth, Proceedings of the 17th International Conference on Data Engineering (ICDE'01), (2001) 215-224
6. Zaki, M.: SPADE: An efficient algorithm for mining frequent sequences, Machine Learning Journal, Vol. 42, No.1, (2001) 31-60
7. Masseglia, F., Poncelet, P., Teisseire, M.: Incremental mining of sequential patterns in large databases, Actes des Jouenes Bases de Donnes Avances (BDA'00), Blois, France, 1999
8. Ouyang, W., Cai, Q.: An incremental updating techniques for discovering generalized sequential patterns, Journal of Software, Vol. 9, No. 10, (1998) 778-780
9. Agrawal, R., Imielinski, T., Swami, A.: Mining association rules between sets of items in large databases, Proceedings of the 1993 ACM SIGMOD Conference, Washington DC, USA, (1993) 207-216

A Clustering Algorithm Based on Density Kernel Extension

Wei-Di Dai[1], Pi-Lian He[1], Yue-Xian Hou[1], and Xiao-Dong Kang[2]

[1] Department of Computer Science and Technology, Tianjin University,
300072 Tianjin, China
Davidy@126.com, Plhe@tju.edu.cn, Yxhou@tju.edu.cn
[2] Department of Medical Image Tianjin Medical University,
300070 Tianjin, China
Kxd2004@eyou.com

Abstract. A new type of clustering algorithm called CADEKE is presented in this paper. CADEKE creates an extended density kernel structure for every cluster by using its neighborhood coefficient. Those unprocessed objects found in current kernel structure are added to extend the kernel structure until no new object is found. Each density kernel structure is regarded as one cluster. CADEKE requires only one input parameter as the initial radius of finding the density kernel and has no limitation on density threshold. Other characteristics include the capacity of discovering clusters with arbitrary shapes and processing the noise data. The results of our experiments demonstrate that CADEKE is significantly more accurate in discovering density-changeable clustering than the algorithm DBSCAN, and that CADEKE is less sensitive to input parameters.

1 Introduction

With the rapid increase of data production and storage, cluster analysis has become a key technique in data mining. It can be viewed as the process of grouping a set of physical or abstract objects into classes of similar objects. Clustering belongs to an unsupervised method and is mostly used to divide an unknowingly-distributed data set which has no transcendental knowledge or experiences and no class label attributes. Recently, density-based clustering methods [1], such as DENCLUE[2], DBSCAN[3], OPTICS[4] and DILC[5], have attracted extensive concern due to their capability for discovering clusters of arbitrary shapes in databases with noise.

DENCLUE is a clustering method based on a set of density distribution functions. The process of clustering depends on the identification of density attractors which are the local maxima of the sum of density influence functions from all data points. DENCLUE has effective clustering properties for data sets with large amounts of noise. However, the method is sensitive to input parameters and noise threshold.

DBSCAN, which requires two input parameters, namely radius of the ε-neighborhood and the minimum number of objects, can quickly discover different clusters of arbitrary shapes according to the connectivity of density. Actually, high-dimensional real data sets often have very skewed distributions such that DBSCAN's global density parameters may not characterize their intrinsic clustering structure. This causes sensitivity to the parameter values.

To avoid DBSCAN's global density parameters, OPTICS method computes an augmented cluster ordering which represents the density-based clustering structure of the data. Therefore, two values need to be saved for each object; core-distance and reachability-distance. OPTICS provides greater flexibility than the DBSCAN algorithm for discovering intrinsic structure by reason of its changeable radius of the ε-neighborhood and unchangeable minimum number of objects.

Density isoline clustering (DILC) starts from the density isoline figure of objects, and locates relatively dense regions. During the clustering process, the number of objects within the radius of the ε-neighborhood for each current object should be computed. DILC could be regarded as similar to algorithms based on an unchangeable radius of neighborhood and changeable minimum number of objects.

Density-based clustering methods mentioned above set two parameters: the radius of the neighborhood and the density threshold. These methods are put forward by three means: observing the density distribution by using an unchangeable radius of the neighborhood; investigating the changeability of the radius of the neighborhood; and adopting an unchangeable radius of the neighborhood and an unchangeable density threshold. The fixed input parameters put some constraint on algorithms and can't effectively reveal the true distribution of objects. A new kind of clustering algorithm called CADEKE (Clustering Algorithm based on Density Kernel Extension) is presented in this paper. CADEKE detects every density kernel object, which will be extended according to the local density's fluctuation until no new object is added, such that every generated tree structure is regarded as one cluster. On building the density tree, the radius of the neighborhood may increase to an inappropriate value from a low density region to a high density region. Our algorithm automatically computes the allowed maximum radius of the neighborhood by investigating the global density distribution of samples. The details of CADEKE are described in Section 2. Experimental results are presented in Section 3, followed by discussion. Finally, in Section 4, we present our conclusion and describe some topics for future work.

2 CADEKE Algorithm

2.1 Definitions

Definition 1. (point density) The number of objects within ε-neighborhood of a given object P is called the ε-neighborhood's density of object P, denoted by Density (P, ε).

Definition 2. (density kernel point) The object which is called density kernel object must have the maximal point density value in all unprocessed objects. Actually, the density kernel object denotes the root node of every cluster.

Definition 3. (neighborhood coefficient) If object Q is within the ε_p-neighborhood of object P, then the neighborhood coefficient of object Q is defined by:

$$\eta = \frac{\text{Density}(Q, \varepsilon_P)}{\text{Density}(P, \varepsilon_Q)} \tag{1}$$

Figure 1 shows how to compute the radius of a neighborhood. Following definition 1, Density(P, ε_P)=4, Density(A, ε_P)=2, Density(B, ε_P)=4, Density(D, ε_P)=5, then η_A =0.5, η_B =1, η_D =1.25. The radius of the neighborhood of Objects A, B and D can be calculated by the following expression:

$$\varepsilon_A = \eta_A \bullet \varepsilon_P = 0.5 \bullet \varepsilon_P$$
$$\varepsilon_B = \eta_B \bullet \varepsilon_P = \varepsilon_P$$
$$\varepsilon_D = \eta_D \bullet \varepsilon_P = 1.25 \bullet \varepsilon_P$$

The broken line in Figure 1 shows the calculated radius of the neighborhood of each object. Objects 1 and 2 are added into the neighborhood of Object D.

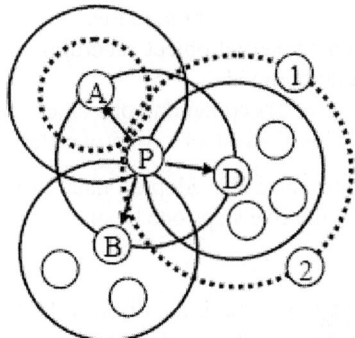

Fig. 1. Calculation of the radius of neighborhoods

2.2 Establishing Adjacency

For the purpose of making sure no object can be disposed of more than once, we establish the adjacent order of all objects by creating a density-based tree structure; the current object is regarded as the father node whose sons are other objects in the radius of its neighborhood. These sons on the same level rank from left to right according to the distance from their father. If a son node has several fathers, we choose the leftmost node as its father. By use of such transformation, a son's nodes' radius of neighborhood is computed only from its father node. Furthermore, the processed sequence of nodes is breadth-first.

As shown in Figure 2, Objects A, B and C are direct sons of Object P, and as |PA|<|PB|<|PC|, then Objects A, B, C are on the same level, and arranged by the distance |PA|, |PB| and |PC|. Object D exists in the neighborhood of Objects A and B, but A is at the left of B, so A is the father of D, not B.

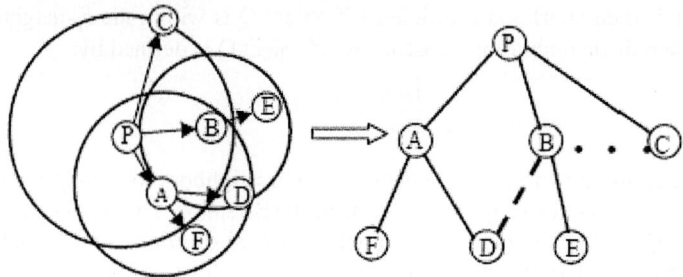

Fig. 2. Generation of tree structure

2.3 The Algorithm

In this section, we will present the details of CADEKE. This algorithm can be divided into five steps.

    Step 1: calculate the distance array Dist(i, j) among all objects.
    Step 2: calculate the allowed maximum radius of the neighborhood.
    Step 3: extend the density kernel object according to its dynamic generating radius of the neighborhood.
    Step 4: delete "noise" clusters containing one object or very few objects.
    Step 5: merge those "closer" clusters to improve clustering accuracy.

In the following, we introduce the adopted data structure while generating tree structure, and then describe the five steps one by one.

Data Structure
Each object has the same data structure: the distance from its father node; the identifier of itself; radius of neighborhood of its father node; and point density of its father node.

Calculating Dist (i, j)
Similarity matrix Dist(i, j) is computed from the distance function which is defined according to similarity. Its computational complexity is $O(n^2)$, where n is the number of objects. The other steps of CADEKE simply search this similarity matrix.

Calculating the Allowed Maximum Radius of the Neighborhood
This process is divided into three steps: first, search Dist(i, j) and compute point density of each object according to the radius of neighborhood, denoted by ε_0, where ε_0 is determined by users, and also taken as kernel objects' radius of neighborhood; second, rank objects with descending sequence by point density, recording corresponding identifiers into vector array Desc(n), and then compute median value of point density, denoted by Density(m, ε_m); and third, compute average value of point density, denoted by Density(Ave, ε_{Ave}), and adopt Density(m, ε_m) as the allowed maximum radius of the neighborhood:

$$\varepsilon_{max} = \varepsilon_0 \cdot \sqrt{\frac{Density(m,\varepsilon_m)}{Density(Ave,\varepsilon_{Ave})}} \quad (2)$$

Generating Tree Structure

Generating the tree structure is the main process of CADEKE algorithm, which is divided into two steps: sequentially set unprocessed objects in the array Desc(n) as density kernel points, then call the function "Searching_For_Sons" and iterate until no new object is added.

```
Creating_Tree_Structure(Desc(n),ε₀)
   Begin
      For i from 1 to n do
         If unprocessed(Desc(i))=TURE
            Step1: initialization of some parameters
            Step2: adding Desc(i)to the Queue of the
                   Current Cluster
            Step3: increasing length of the Queue by one
            Step4: Searching_For_Sons(Desc(i),ε₀);
         End If
      End For
   End

Searching_For_Sons(Desc(i),ε₀)
   Begin
      j=0;
      While j< QueueLength
         Step1: calculating the density of the object in
                the Queue sequentially according to its
                father's radius of neighborhoods
         Step2: calculating the ε_curr of the current point.
         Step3: set ε_curr to ε_max if ε_curr is larger than
                ε_max.
         Step4: adding unprocessed new sons of the current
                point to the Queue by the distance of the
                farther and the son in ascending way.
         Step5: set unprocessed sign to FALSE for each
                point which is added to the Queue.
         Step6: increasing length of the Queue
      End while
   End.
```

Fig. 3. Creating Tree Structure procedure

The procedure "Creating Tree Structure" creates a density tree through the function "Searching_For_Sons" by building a queue for each potential cluster. The function "Searching_For_Sons" sequentially sets objects into the queue as father nodes. The unprocessed son nodes will also be added into the queue. An unprocessed object with high point density is firstly set as the density kernel object of each potential cluster by reading array Desc(n).

Deleting Clusters Containing One Point or Very Few Points

The algorithm CADEKE has the capability of finding all potential clusters. However, some noise objects will be marked as clusters. For those clusters containing one point or very few points, the algorithm directly deletes them if users predefine a "noise" threshold.

Merging The Closest Clusters to Improve Clustering Accuracy

The reserved clusters will be merged into larger clusters according to the distance between density kernel points until termination conditions are satisfied. Although a larger input parameter could be predefined to avoid merging clusters, the number of clusters which satisfies users' requirements couldn't be achieve easily. The process of merging the closest clusters provides the flexibility of predefining the number of clusters, especially in the case of a small input parameter. The results of our experiments on a real document set show that CADEKE is significantly more accurate than DBSCAN.

Computational complexity. Suppose n is the number of objects with d dimension, and m is the number of density kernel points. In the previous step, the computational complexity of $Dist(i, j)$ is $O(n^2)$. Its computational time will be longer when d becomes larger. The other parts of our algorithm only index the distance array $Dist(i, j)$, without being affected by the number of dimensions. In computing the allowed max-radius of the neighborhood, a typical sorting algorithm has the computational complexity of $O(n \cdot \log n)$ when ranking objects according to point density. The computational complexity of merging clusters is $O(m^2)$. Therefore, the whole algorithm has the complexity of $O(n^2)+O(n \cdot \log n)+O(m^2)$. Generally speaking, $m<<n$ and $O(n \cdot \log n)$ could be ignored when n is larger, meaning the complexity of CADEKE is $O(n^2)$.

3 Performance Analysis

Four different test data sets are used to evaluate the performance of CADEKE. DB1 is the database3 used by DBSCAN; DB2 is the imitating data according to database2 in DBSCAN by Dr Jörg Sander; DB3 is generated randomly by obeying normal distribution; DB4 is the original document set *re0* from the website [6]. The programs, DBSCAN and CADEKE, are written in MatLab. All experiments have been run on a DELL 2600 server.

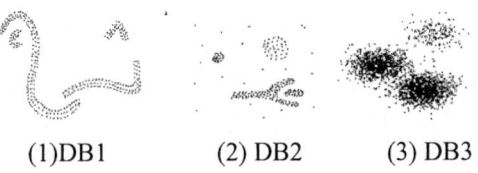

(1)DB1   (2) DB2   (3) DB3

Fig. 4. Data sets

3.1 Comparison of Clustering Accuracy

We compare CADEKE with the performance of DBSCAN for they are algorithms based on density. Figure 5 and Figure 6 show the clustering results of DBSCAN and CADEKE respectively.

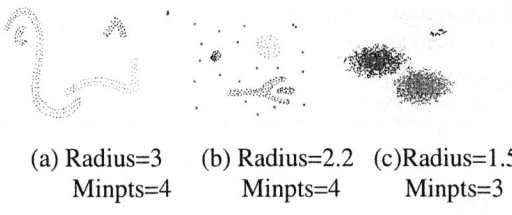

(a) Radius=3   (b) Radius=2.2   (c)Radius=1.5
    Minpts=4   Minpts=4   Minpts=3

Fig. 5. Clustering results of DBSCAN

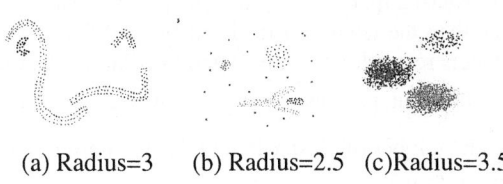

(a) Radius=3   (b) Radius=2.5   (c)Radius=3.5

Fig. 6. Clustering results of CADEKE

The experiments show that CADEKE delivers the same results as DBSCAN for data sets DB1and DB2, which have such features as existing obvious cluster boundary, a uniform distribution for each cluster, characterization by global parameters, arbitrary shapes for clusters, and noise data in DB2. For test data DB3, which has different density thresholds for clusters, DBSCAN is obviously unable to obtain satisfactory results. However CADEKE achieves optimized clustering qualities.

DB4 includes 1,054 documents classified into 13 clusters. Each document is viewed as one point in vector space mode. The similarity between two documents is calculated according to the cosine function [7]:

$$\cos(d_i, d_j) = \frac{d_i^t d_j}{\|d_i\| \|d_j\|} \quad (3)$$

In our experiments, F-measure is used to evaluate the result of the clustering qualities. Table 1 shows the main result on DB4.

The 3rd column reveals that CADEKE takes on the tendency of generating more small clusters with tight coupling before they are merged. This characteristic provides some flexibility for improving the clustering result. F-measure values on the 4th column display that our algorithm is more accurate than DBSCAN at a large range of parameter settings. For other document sets, CADEKE obtained similar results. Of course, adjustment of input parameters is needed for improving F-measure values.

Table 1. F-measure values on DB4 with different input parameters

algorithm	Input parameters	cluster number before merge	F-measure
DBSCAN	Radius=0.6 Minpts=6	12	0.317
	Radius=0.65 Minpts=6	9	0.332
	Radius=0.6 Minpts=5	14	0.313
CADEKE	Radius=0.85	9	0.330
	Radius=0.8	20	0.347
	Radius=0.75	22	0.268

3.2 Input Parameters

CADEKE requires only one input parameter for its initialization. Different input parameters affect the clustering qualities. Assume that P and Q are two clusters, and P is generated prior to Q, then the condition for identifying P from Q is: the minimal distance of any two objects respectively from P and Q is larger than the current object's radius of neighborhood, that is, $\min(|p_i q_j|) > \varepsilon_{p_i}$, where $p_i \in P$ (i=1,2,...m), $q_j \in Q$ (j=1,2,...n), m is the number of cluster P, and n is the number of cluster Q. Assume there is a path from p_0 to p_i: $p_0 \smallsetminus p_1 \smallsetminus p_2 \smallsetminus \ldots\ldots \smallsetminus p_i \smallsetminus \ldots\ldots$, p_0 is the root node of P, p_i is the current object, if the radius of the neighborhood along this path is no larger than the allowed maximum radius of neighborhood ε_{max}, then:

$$\varepsilon_{p_i} = \frac{Density(p_i, \varepsilon_{p_{i-1}})}{Density(p_{i-1}, \varepsilon_{p_{i-1}})} \times \frac{Density(p_{i-1}, \varepsilon_{p_{i-2}})}{Density(p_{i-2}, \varepsilon_{p_{i-2}})} \times \bullet\bullet\bullet \times \frac{Density(p_1, \varepsilon_{p_0})}{Density(p_0, \varepsilon_{p_0})} \times \varepsilon_{p_0}$$
$$= \frac{Density(p_i, \varepsilon_{p_{i-1}})}{Density(p_{i-1}, \varepsilon_{p_{i-1}})} \times \frac{Density(p_{i-1}, \varepsilon_{p_{i-2}})}{Density(p_{i-2}, \varepsilon_{p_{i-2}})} \times \bullet\bullet\bullet \times \frac{Density(p_1, \varepsilon_0)}{Density(p_0, \varepsilon_0)} \times \varepsilon_0 \quad (4)$$

The function above shows the radius of object p_i is relational to ε_0 and to the point density of all objects along this path, and then CADEKE has a wider range of parameter settings. The accuracy of CADEKE is determined by distribution of objects and the root node's radius of neighborhood. CADEKE achieves acceptable clusters when the root node's radius of neighborhood reveals distribution expressed by point density of objects.

3.2 Comparison of Effectiveness

We implemented CADEKE and DBSCAN based on generating array Dist(i,j) without adopting correlative optimizing techniques. The run time comparison of CADEKE and DBSCAN is show in Figure 7. Obviously, CADEKE spends more time in indexing the array Dist(i,j) than DBSCAN. Optimizing techniques are required when disposing of large amounts of data.

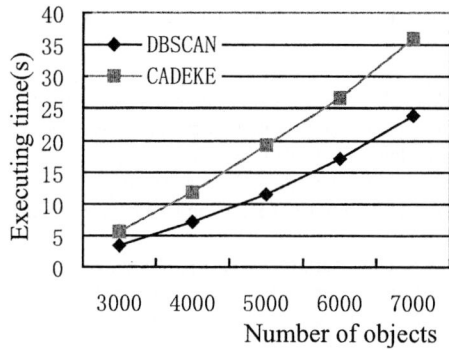

Fig. 7. Performance comparison

4 Conclusions

Most algorithms with global parameters can't effectively discover the true clustering structure due to deflective density distributions on real data sets. CADEKE computes the clustering radius of a current object according to the local density of its father. To establish father-son relations, we build a tree structure for every density kernel point in the clustering queue until no new object is added. CADEKE requires only one input parameter as its initial root nodes' radius of neighborhood, with the capability of discovering clusters of arbitrary shapes in databases with noise. The result of our experiments on synthetic data sets and real document sets demonstrates that CADEKE is significantly more accurate in discovering clusters and less sensitive to input parameters than the well-known algorithm DBSCAN.

Another important characteristic of CADEKE is to deal with different types of data sets by defining different "distances" for its similarity measure. Some optimizing techniques need to be taken when disposing of large scale data for its computational complexity of $O(n^2)$. Future research will consider how to reduce its computational complexity and how to get appropriate input parameters automatically on real data sets.

Acknowledgements

This work was supported by Science-Technology Development Project of Tianjin (04310941R) and Applied Basic Research Project of Tianjin (05YFJMJC11700). The authors wish to thank PH.D Ma Shuai from Peking University for providing test data DB1 and DB2.

References

1. Han JW, Kambr M: Data Mining Concepts and Techniques. Higher Education Press, Beijing(2001)
2. Alexander. Hinneburg, Daniel. A. Keim.: An efficient approach to clustering in large multimedia databases with noise. KDD'98, New York (1998) 58–65

3. Martin.Ester, Hans-Peter Kriegel, Jörg Sander, Xiaowei Xu: A Density-Based Algorithm for Discovering Clusters in Large Spatial Databases with Noise. KDD'96, Portland, OR (1996) 226–231
4. Mihael Ankerst, Markus M. Breunig, Hans-Peter Kriegel, Jörg Sander: OPTICS: Ordering Points To Identify the Clustering Structure. Proc.ACM SIGMOD'99 Int. Conf. On Management of Data, Philadelphia, PA(1999) 49–60
5. Zhao Yanchang, Xie Fan, Song Junde: DILC:A clustering Algorithm Based On Density-isoline. Journal of Beijing University of Posts and Telecommunication, Vol.25No.2, Beijing (2002) 8–13
6. Available on the WWW at URL http://www-users.cs.umn.edu/~karypis/cluto/download.html
7. Ying Zhao, George Karypis: Criterion Functions for Document Clustering: Experiment and analysis. Available at URL http://www-users.cs.umn.edu/~karypis/publications/Papers/

Associative Classification with Prediction Confidence

Tien Dung Do, Siu Cheung Hui, and Alvis C.M. Fong

School of Computer Engineering, Nanyang Technological University
Nanyang Avenue, Singapore
{pa0001852a, asschui, ascmfong}@ntu.edu.sg

Abstract. Associative classification which uses association rules for classification has achieved high accuracy in comparison with other classification approaches. However, the confidence measure which is conventionally used for selecting association rules for classification may not conform to the prediction accuracy of the rules. In this paper, we propose a measure called *prediction confidence* to measure the prediction accuracy of association rules. In addition, a probabilistic-based approach for estimating prediction confidence of association rules is given and its performance is evaluated. The use of prediction confidence helps improve the performance of associative classifiers.

1 Introduction

Associative classification (AC) uses association rules [1], which contain the relations between data items and its class labels, for predicting the class labels of unknown data samples [2]. The confidence value, which measures the degree of implication of association rules, is used as the goodness measure for selecting rules for classification. However, the confidence value of a rule does not imply directly to its prediction accuracy. The reason is that association rules are mined and measured based on the training set while the prediction is carried out on data samples of a test set. Thus, to classify a data sample, the association rules with the highest confidence values may not imply the best accuracy.

In this paper, we propose a measure called *prediction confidence* to measure the prediction accuracy of association rules. A probabilistic-based approach for estimating prediction confidence of association rules is presented and its performance is evaluated. The use of prediction confidence instead of the confidence measure helps select better association rules for AC. As a result, a more accurate associative classifier can be constructed using the prediction confidence measure.

2 Association Rules for Classification

An association rule R is an implication $X \Rightarrow Y$ occurring in a transactional database, where X and Y are sets of items or *itemsets* [1]. The *support* of the rule $supp(R)$ is the percentage of transactions containing X and Y with respect to the number of all transactions. The *confidence* of the rule $conf(R)$ is the percentage of transactions that contains Y among the transactions containing X. Association rule mining aims to generate all rules of which the support and confidence values are greater than or equal to the predefined support and confidence *thresholds* respectively.

Associative classification [2,3,4] uses association rules for classification. It generally consists of three major processes: rule generation, rule selection and classification. Firstly, in the *rule generation* process, a set of association rules is mined from a training dataset based on the support and confidence thresholds. Next, the *rule selection* process evaluates the set of association rules and selects a subset of rules, which gives the best classification accuracy, to form a classifier. Finally, in the *classification* process, new data samples in a test dataset are classified using the classifier.

The set of association rules is generated in the form of $iset \Rightarrow cl$ where *iset* is an itemset and *cl* is a class. These association rules are referred to as *class association rules* [2]. Let *RS* be the set of association rules selected from the rule selection process. In the classification process, to classify a test sample *d*, the rule $R: iset \Rightarrow cl$ in *RS* with the highest confidence value that *matches* with *d* (i.e. *d* contains *iset*) is selected. The test sample *d* is then assigned to class *cl* of *R* [2]. The AC approach is based mainly on the implication relationships of the association rules. The rule $iset \Rightarrow cl$ means that if a given test sample contains *iset*, then it will probably belong to class *cl*. The *confidence* measure, say 80%, guarantees the reliability of the classification decision. The test sample is classified into class *cl* as most of the transactions (80%) in the training dataset that contain *iset* fall into class *cl*.

The AC approach was first introduced in [2] with the Classification Based on Associations (CBA) algorithm. In [3], Liu *et al.* suggested the use of *multiple class support* thresholds that produce a more balanced numbers of association rules over different classes during the rule generation process. In [4], Li *et al.* used *multiple rules* instead of a single rule in the classification process. In this approach, all the rules that matched with a test sample are collected and grouped according to their class labels in order to classify the test sample. The test sample is then assigned to the class from the best group based on a statistical measure called $max\chi^2$. This multiple rule classification approach is similar to single rule classification in the sense that higher confidence rules are given higher weights in classifying unknown test samples.

3   Prediction Confidence

Let us consider the classification process in which association rules are used to classify test data samples. Let $R: iset \Rightarrow cl$ be a rule selected for the classification process. For a given test data sample *d*, if *d* matches with *R* (i.e. *d* contains itemset *iset*), then it will be predicted as belonging to class *cl* using *R*. Suppose there are *x* test samples containing *iset* and *y* test samples containing both *iset* and *cl* in the test set. The classification process, therefore, will predict correctly *y* among *x* test samples (i.e. *y/x*) using rule *R*. Thus the accuracy of the prediction is the confidence value of *R* in the test set. We call it as *prediction confidence*. The prediction confidence of a rule shows the accuracy when the rule is used to predict unknown test data samples.

Definition 3.1. *Prediction confidence* of an association rule is the average prediction accuracy when the association rule is used to predict the class labels of unknown data samples in associative classification.

Note that, the *confidence* value of a rule is conventionally counted from the training set. Given the sets of training data *TR* and test data *TS*, we denote the confidence of *R* as $conf_{TR}(R)$ and the prediction confidence of *R* as $conf_{TS}(R)$ (see Figure 1). Obviously, the prediction confidence should play a major role in selecting and ranking association rules for AC. A rule should be considered more important with higher weight than rules that have lower prediction confidence values during the classification process. Currently, the confidence measure is considered as the goodness measure of association rules in AC. Associative classification uses the confidence measure to generate and select rules, and to predict class labels for data samples.

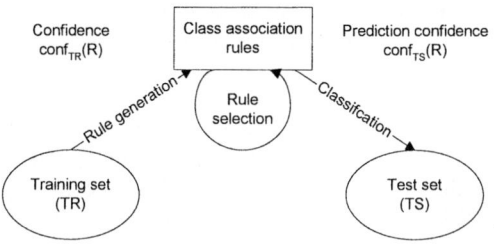

Fig. 1. Confidence and prediction confidence

In order to compute the prediction confidence, we examine the difference between confidence and prediction confidence. We refer the difference between confidence and prediction confidence of a rule *R* as *confidence decrease* (denoted as *decr(R)*) of *R*. The confidence decrease indicates the decrease in confidence of the same rule counted in the training set, from which the rules are mined, and the test set, to which the rules are applied for data prediction. Note that if a rule has prediction confidence higher than confidence, then the confidence decrease of the rule will be negative.

$$decr(R) = conf_{TR}(R) - conf_{TS}(R) \qquad (3.1)$$

We consider the following scenario of AC for a dataset *D* which is divided into the training set *TR* and test set *TS*. Let *N* and *n* be the numbers of data samples, *S* and *s* be the numbers of data samples containing *iset*, and *C* and *c* be the numbers of data samples containing both *iset* and *cl* respectively in *D* and *TR*. The other numbers of samples related to *R* that can be computed from *N*, *S*, *C*, *n*, *s* and *c* are shown in Table 1.

Table 1. Numbers of data samples related to rule R

R: iset $\Rightarrow$ cl	D	TR	TS
Number of samples	N	n	N-n
- containing iset	S	s	x = S-s
- containing both iset and cl	C	c	y = C-c
- containing iset but not cl	S-C	s-c	S-C-(s-c)
- not containing iset	N-S	n-s	N-S-(n-s)

We call s and c as the *support* and *confidence numbers* of rule R. They represent the absolute values of support and confidence of R on the training set. The confidence and prediction confidence values of R can be calculated as

$$conf_{TR}(R) = c/s \tag{3.2}$$

$$conf_{TS}(R) = (C-c)/(S-s) \tag{3.3}$$

The conditions for support and confidence numbers (i.e. s and c), and the number of training data samples (i.e. n) are listed below:

$$cond_1(s,c) = 1 \leq s \wedge s \leq S-1 \tag{3.4}$$
$$cond_2(s,c) = 0 \leq c \wedge c \leq C \wedge 0 \leq s-c \wedge s-c \leq S-C \tag{3.5}$$
$$cond(n) = 0 \leq n \wedge n \leq N \wedge 0 \leq n-s \wedge n-s \leq N-S \tag{3.6}$$
$$cond(s,c) = cond_1(s,c) \wedge cond_2(s,c) \tag{3.7}$$

The condition (3.4) ensures that rule R may play some roles in AC. The first expression (i.e. $1 \leq s$) means there is at least one data sample matching with R so that the rule may be generated during the rule generation process. The second expression (i.e. $s \leq S-1$) shows that there is at least one test sample matching with R so that it may be used in classifying data samples. The other conditions are implied from the fact that all the numbers in Table 1 must be non-negative. The conditions for s and c are combined to $cond(s,c)$ in (3.7). Here, the tight constraints for s, c and n are needed because we need them to examine all possible combinations of s, c and n subsequently.

Problem 3.1. Given an association rule R and a dataset D, determine the average value of confidence decrease of R when D is arbitrarily divided into training and test sets.

To obtain the confidence decrease value of rule R, we will examine all possible divisions of N data samples of dataset D into training set TR and test set TS. Each division of D corresponds to a combination of n data samples for TR and the remaining $N-n$ data samples for TS $(0 \leq n \leq N)$. For each combination, the confidence and prediction confidence are determined. The average value of confidence and prediction confidence are respectively the average values of the confidence and prediction confidence values of all possible combinations.

Given R and D, the numbers of data samples N, S and C can be obtained. For each combination of s, c and n, the number of different combinations of the training set TR can be calculated from (3.8). Here, n samples in TR include c out of C samples containing both *iset* and *cl*, $s-c$ out of $S-C$ samples containing *iset* but *cl*, and $n-s$ out of $N-S$ samples that do not contain *iset*. Then, for each pair of s and c, the number of different combinations of the training set TR can be computed from (3.9) using $comb(s,c,n)$ with all possible values of n satisfying the condition (3.6)

$$comb(s,c,n) = C_C^c \times C_{S-C}^{s-c} \times C_{N-S}^{n-s} \tag{3.8}$$

$$comb(s,c) = \sum_{cond(n)} comb(s,c,n) \tag{3.9}$$

Corresponding to each combination of n data samples in the training set, there will be one combination of $N-n$ data samples in the test set (i.e. the remaining $N-n$ data samples). For each combination, the confidence and prediction confidence values of R

can be calculated from s and c using the formulas in (3.2) and (3.3). Thus, the average values of confidence, prediction confidence and confidence decrease of rule R can be calculated as

$$conf_{TR}(S,C) = \frac{\sum_{cond(s,c)} comb(s,c) \times (\frac{c}{s})}{\sum_{cond(s,c)} comb(s,c)} \quad (3.10)$$

$$conf_{TS}(S,C) = \frac{\sum_{cond(s,c)} comb(s,c) \times (\frac{C-c}{S-s})}{\sum_{cond(s,c)} comb(s,c)} \quad (3.11)$$

$$decr(S,C) = \frac{\sum_{cond(s,c)} comb(s,c) \times (\frac{c}{s} - \frac{C-c}{S-s})}{\sum_{cond(s,c)} comb(s,c)} \quad (3.12)$$

Table 2 shows the values of the confidence decrease of rule R calculated using (3.12) with different values of S, C and N. The support and confidence numbers S and C are set such that $conf(R) = C/S = 80\%$. As shown in Table 2, the confidence decrease is very close to zero. It means that, in the classification process, if we arbitrarily choose a rule in RS (the set of rules of the classifier mentioned in section 2), the confidence and prediction values of the same rule will probably be the same.

Table 2. Average values of confidence decrease

	S=5, C=4	S=10, C=8	S=100, C=80
N = 100	-1.11E-16	3.33E-16	1.11E-16
N = 1000	-1.11E-16	-1.11E-16	-4.88E-15
N = 10000	2.22E-16	4.44E-16	-1.73E-14

In AC, however, rules contributing to the classification process depend on their confidence values. We refer the contribution or effect of a rule during the classification process as *classification weight* of the rule. In single rule classification, classification weight represents the probability with which if the rule matches with a data sample, then it is chosen for classifying the data sample. In multiple rule classification, the classification weight represents the weight of each rule when multiple rules matching with a data sample are used together to decide the class label for the data sample. For both cases of AC using single and multiple rules, the classification weight of a rule is proportional to its confidence value. In other words, the classification weight of a rule is a monotonic function $f(conf_{TR}(R))$ of its confidence value (i.e. $f(x) \geq f(y)$ for $x \geq y$). We call f as *classification weight function*. The classification weight function should also return a non-negative value that should not exceed 1 (i.e. with probability of 100% in single rule classification). Simple examples of classification weight function are $f(x) = x$ and $f(x) = x^2$.

Considering the classification weight, the average values of the confidence and prediction confidence of the rules used in classification are recalculated below:

$$conf_{TR}(S,C) = \frac{\sum_{cond(s,c)} comb(s,c) \times f(\frac{c}{s}) \times (\frac{c}{s})}{\sum_{cond(s,c)} comb(s,c) \times f(\frac{c}{s})} \quad (3.13)$$

$$conf_{TS}(S,C) = \frac{\sum_{cond(s,c)} comb(s,c) \times f(\frac{c}{s}) \times (\frac{C-c}{S-s})}{\sum_{cond(s,c)} comb(s,c) \times f(\frac{c}{s})} \quad (3.14)$$

$$decr(S,C) = \frac{\sum_{cond(s,c)} comb(s,c) \times f(\frac{c}{s}) \times (\frac{c}{s} - \frac{C-c}{S-s})}{\sum_{cond(s,c)} comb(s,c) \times f(\frac{c}{s})} \quad (3.15)$$

Note that $conf_{TR}(S,C)$ and $conf_{TS}(S,C)$ in (3.13) and (3.14) respectively are not purely the average confidence and prediction confidence values of the set of the selected rules. The frequencies of the rules that are used for classification are also included. Table 3 gives the confidence decrease of rule R with different values of N, S and C with the classification weight functions $f(x) = x$ and $f(x) = x^2$ using (3.15).

From Table 3, we have the following observations. Firstly, association rules used for the classification process have a positive confidence decrease. It means that prediction confidence has a smaller value than confidence. Secondly, confidence decrease depends on the support and confidence numbers. The confidence decrease is higher with a smaller support and confidence number. Thirdly, confidence decrease also depends on the classification weight function. For example, when $f(x) = x^2$, the confidence decrease is approximately 19.36% for $C = 4$, $S = 5$. It means that if a rule R with confidence value of 80% occurs only in 5 data samples of the dataset D, then the average prediction confidence value is only 80% - 19.36% = 60.6%. And with a considerable large support number, the confidence decrease will be closed to zero. And finally, confidence decrease is the same for different numbers of data samples (i.e. N). In other words, the confidence decrease depends on support number (i.e. S) rather than the support (i.e. S/N) of association rules. However, it is important to know that support is directly proportional to the support number for the same dataset.

Table 3. Average values of confidence decrease of classification rules

Classification weight function		$S=5, C=4$	$S=10, C=8$	$S=100, C=80$
$f(x)=x$	$N = 100$	12.15%	5.09%	0.41%
	$N = 1000$	12.15%	5.09%	0.41%
	$N = 10000$	12.15%	5.09%	0.41%
$f(x)=x^2$	$N = 100$	19.36%	9.44%	0.81%
	$N = 1000$	19.36%	9.44%	0.81%
	$N = 10000$	19.36%	9.44%	0.81%

4 Estimation of Prediction Confidence

Once the confidence decrease is determined, the prediction confidence value in the test set can be obtained from the confidence value in the training set using (3.1). However, there are still problems need to be resolved:

- The classification weight function (i.e. $f(x)$) has not been determined yet.
- In practical AC, we can only obtain the support and confidence values (i.e. s and c) for each rule in the training set. The whole dataset of N data samples with the support and confidence numbers of rule R (i.e. S and C) are unknown.
- The calculation of the confidence decrease is quite computationally expensive with huge numbers of possible combinations of data samples.

4.1 Determining Classification Weight Function

To determine the classification weight function, we use the following assumptions:

- *Rules are independent in matching with data samples.* That is, given a data sample d and two rules R_1 and R_2, the two events, R_1 matches with d and R_2 matches with d, are independent. Therefore,

$$P[R_1 \text{ match\_with } d \land R_2 \text{ match\_with } d]$$
$$= P[R_1 \text{ match\_with } d] \times P[R_1 \text{ match\_with } d] \quad (4.1)$$

- *Rule distribution is even.* For a data sample d, let $P(x,y)$ be the probability that there is at least a rule R matching with d, and R satisfies $x \leq conf(R)$ and $conf(R) < y$. With even distribution of rules we may imply $P(x_1,y_1) = P(x_2,y_2)$ for any x_1, y_1, x_2, y_2 such that $x_1 - y_1 = x_2 - y_2$. Now, let M be the $P(x,y)$ value in the range of 1% confidence difference such that $M = P(0,1\%)$. The value M is called the *matching factor*.

Let's consider a data sample d and a rule R with confidence value $x = conf_{TR}(R)$. From the assumption on even distribution of rules, the probability in which there is no rule with confidence value in a range of 1% confidence difference (e.g. [99%-100%]) matching with d is $1 - M$. From the assumption on rule independence, the probability with which there is no rule with confidence above x (i.e. from $100x\%$ to 100%) matching with d is $(1-M)^{100-100x}$. This is also the probability in the case of single rule classification, with which if R matches with d, then R is selected for classifying d (because there is no rule with confidence greater than the confidence value of R (i.e. x) matching with d). Therefore, the classification weight function can be defined as

$$f(x) = (1-M)^{100(1-x)} \quad (4.2)$$

4.2 Estimating Confidence Decrease and Prediction Confidence

In the previous section, we have estimated the classification weight function so that we can estimate the confidence decrease $decr(S,C)$ of rule R. Unfortunately, the estimation is based on the support and confidence numbers S and C counted in the dataset D. In practical AC, we can only obtain the support and confidence numbers s and c

counted from the training set *TR*. We denote $decr_{TR}(s,c)$ as the confidence decrease of R with the given support and confidence numbers s and c counted from the training set D_{TR}. Now we need to estimate $decr_{TR}(s,c)$ from $decr(S,C)$.

To estimate the confidence decrease we consider the leave-one-out cross validation in which the test set consists of only one data sample. Firstly, we calculate $decr(S,C)$. For leave-one-out test, the training set contains $n = N - 1$ data samples. Thus, from (3.6), the expression $n - s \leq N - S$ is equivalent to $N - 1 - s \leq N - S$ or $S - 1 \leq s$. From condition (3.4), we have $s \leq S - 1$. This means that $s = S - 1$. Similarly, from $s - c \leq S - C$, we imply $S - 1 - c \leq S - C$ or $C - 1 \leq c$. Thus we may imply that $c = C$ or $c = C - 1$. There are only two combinations of (s,c) which are $(S-1, C-1)$ and $(S-1, C)$:

$$comb(S-1, C-1) = C_C^{C-1} \times C_{S-C}^{S-1-(C-1)} \times C_{N-S}^{N-1-(S-1)} = C_C^{C-1} \times C_{S-C}^{S-C} \times C_{N-S}^{N-S} = C \quad (4.3)$$

$$comb(S-1, C) = C_C^{C} \times C_{S-C}^{S-1-C} \times C_{N-S}^{N-1-(S-1)} = C_C^{C} \times C_{S-C}^{S-C-1} \times C_{N-S}^{N-S} = S - C \quad (4.4)$$

The formula (3.15) can then be rewritten as

$$decr(S,C) = \frac{comb(S-1,C-1) \times f(\frac{C-1}{S-1}) \times (\frac{C-1}{S-1} - \frac{C-(C-1)}{S-(S-1)}) + comb(S-1,C) \times f(\frac{C}{S-1}) \times (\frac{C}{S-1} - \frac{C-C}{S-(S-1)})}{comb(S-1,C-1) \times f(\frac{C-1}{S-1}) + comb(S-1,C) \times f(\frac{C}{S-1})}$$

$$= \frac{C \times f(\frac{C-1}{S-1}) \times \frac{C-S}{S-1} + (S-C) \times f(\frac{C}{S-1}) \times \frac{C}{S-1}}{C \times f(\frac{C-1}{S-1}) + (S-C) \times f(\frac{C}{S-1})} = \frac{C \times (S-C)}{S-1} \times \frac{(f(\frac{C}{S-1}) - f(\frac{C-1}{S-1}))}{C \times f(\frac{C-1}{S-1}) + (S-C) \times f(\frac{C}{S-1})} \quad (4.5)$$

With a pair of S and C, the possible values of s and c are $(S-1, C-1)$ and $(S-1, C)$. In contrast, with a pair of s and c, the possible values of S and C are $(s+1, c+1)$ and $(s+1, c)$. Thus, with the support and confidence numbers s and c counting from the training dataset, the required $decr_{TR}(R)$ function can be estimated in between $decr(s+1,c+1)$ and $decr(s+1,c)$. We estimate $decr_{TR}(R)$ as the average value of $decr(s+1,c+1)$ and $decr(s+1,c)$:

$$decr_{TR}(s,c) = \frac{1}{2}[decr(s+1,c+1) + decr(s+1,c)] \quad (4.6)$$

The prediction confidence can then be obtained using the following formula:

$$conf_{TS}(s,c) = conf_{TR}(s,c) - decr_{TR}(s,c) \quad (4.7)$$

or

$$conf_{TS}(R) = conf_{TR}(R.s, R.c) - decr_{TR}(R.s, R.c) \quad (4.8)$$

Here, $R.s$ and $R.c$ represent the support and confidence numbers of rule R respectively.

5 Performance Evaluation

In this section, we have implemented a simple version of AC [2,3] denoted as AC-S for evaluating the effectiveness of the prediction confidence measure. The value of the prediction confidence measure is calculated from confidence decrease which is estimated using formula (4.8). AC-S consists of only two steps of AC, namely rule generation and classification. After the conventional rule generation process, the confidence values of the rules are replaced with the corresponding prediction confidence values. We use single rule classification in the classification process and there is no rule selection process.

The performance of popular AC approaches is obtained directly from [3,4] for comparison purposes. The approaches include Classification Based on Associations (CBA) algorithm [2], CBA(2) [3] and CMAR [4]. CBA(2) is an improved version of CBA with the use of multiple class support thresholds. CMAR is different from CBA in that it uses multiple rules instead of a single rule in the classification process.

Table 4. Experimental results in error rate

	CBA	CBA2	CMAR	AC-S	AC-S-Opt
1 anneal	3.6	2.1	2.7	4.8	3.8
2 australian	13.4	14.6	13.9	14.5	13.6
3 auto	27.2	19.9	21.9	22.9	22.0
4 breast-w	4.2	3.7	3.6	4.3	4.2
5 cleve	16.7	17.1	17.8	18.6	17.6
6 crx	14.1	14.6	15.1	14.8	13.9
7 diabetes	25.3	25.5	24.2	22.6	22.2
8 german	26.5	26.5	25.1	25.8	25.0
9 glass	27.4	26.1	29.9	26.1	25.1
10 heart	18.5	18.1	17.8	17.4	16.7
11 hepatitis	15.1	18.9	19.5	17.4	15.4
12 horse	18.7	17.6	17.4	17.1	16.9
13 hypo	1.7	1	1.6	1.2	0.9
14 ionosphere	8.2	7.7	8.5	7.4	7.4
15 iris	7.1	5.3	6	6.7	6.0
16 labor	17	13.7	10.3	11.0	9.0
17 led7	27.8	28.1	27.5	28.4	28.3
18 lymph	19.6	22.1	16.9	19.6	19.6
19 pima	27.6	27.1	24.9	23.3	21.9
20 sick	2.7	2.8	2.5	4.5	4.1
21 sonar	21.7	22.5	20.6	24.0	22.5
22 tac-toe	0.1	0.4	0.8	1.0	0.6
23 vehicle	31.3	31	31.2	35.1	34.9
24 waveform	20.6	20.3	16.8	17.4	17.3
25 wine	8.4	5	5	7.3	7.3
26 zoo	5.4	3.2	2.9	12.7	7.8
Average	15.77	15.19	14.78	15.61	14.77
Average of the first 20 datasets	16.12	15.63	15.36	15.42	14.68

The thresholds for mining association rules are set the same as the other approaches. The total minimum support is set to 1% and minimum confidence is set to 50%. AC-S has achieved good accuracy with the matching factor M set in the range [0 - 0.1]. The best value for M depends on the dataset. We have implemented AC-S with M setting to 0.04. The AC-S-Opt shows the best accuracy of AC-S with the optimal value of M in each dataset. The experiment is carried out using the same set of 26 datasets used in [2,3,4] which is obtained from the UCI Machine Learning Repository [5]. The discretization process, which discretizes continuous data into intervals and maps them into items, is performed using the Entropy method from [6].

Table 4 shows the performance results in error rate for the different approaches. The preliminary results have shown that the accuracy of AC-S is better than CBA but worse than CBA(2) and CMAR. For the first 20 datasets, AC-S is even better than CBA(2) and is comparable to CMAR. When obtaining the best performance with optimal matching factor for each dataset, the AC-S-Opt is similar to CMAR in the overall accuracy. The very simple but effective implementation of AC-S has shown the effectiveness of the proposed prediction confidence for associative classification.

6 Conclusion

Associative classification takes the advantage from association rule mining in extracting high quality rules that can accurately generalize a dataset. However, as association rules and classification are two different tasks, there is always a difference between the confidence of an association rule and its prediction capability for classification. In this paper, we have proposed a new measure called prediction confidence to measure the prediction accuracy of association rules. In addition, an effective probabilistic-based approach for estimating the prediction confidence measure has also been given and evaluated. Currently, we are investigating an approach for determining the most appropriate matching factor automatically for individual datasets in order to further improve the classification accuracy.

References

1. R. Agrawal and R. Srikant, "Fast algorithms for mining association rules", In Proc. of the 20th Int'l Conf. on Very Large Databases (VLDB '94), Santiago, Chile, pp. 487-499, June 1994.
2. B. Liu, W. Hsu and Y. Ma, "Integrating classification and association rule mining", In Proc. of the Fourth International Conference on Knowledge Discovery and Data Mining, pp. 80-86, New York, NY, 1998.
3. B. Liu, Y. Ma and C.K. Wong, "Classification Using Association Rules: Weaknesses and Enhancements". In Vipin Kumar et al., Data mining for scientific applications, 2001.
4. W. Li, J. Han, and J. Pei., "CMAR: Accurate and efficient classification based on multiple class-association rules", In Proc. of ICDM, 2001.
5. UCI Machine Learning Repository, Available online at <http://www.ics.uci.edu/~mlearn/MLRepository.html>.
6. R. Kohavi, G. John, R. Long, D. Manley, and K. Pfleger., "MLC++: A machine learning library in C++", In Tools with Artificial Intelligence, pp. 740-743. 1994.

Exploring Query Matrix for Support Pattern Based Classification Learning

Yiqiu Han and Wai Lam

Department of Systems Engineering and Engineering Management,
The Chinese University of Hong Kong,
Shatin, Hong Kong
{yqhan, wlam}@se.cuhk.edu.hk

Abstract. This paper explores the customized learning from specific to general for classification learning. Our novel learning framework called SUPE customizes its learning process to the instance to be classified called query instance. The data representation in SUPE is also customized to the query instance. Given a query instance, the training data is transformed into a query matrix, from which useful patterns are discovered for learning. The final prediction of the class label is performed by combining some statistics of the discovered useful patterns. We show that SUPE conducts the search from specific to general in a significantly reduced hypothesis space. The query matrix also facilitates the complicated operations in SUPE. The experimental results on benchmark data sets are encouraging.

1 Introduction

Common eager learning methods eagerly compile the training data into some concept descriptions. They attempt to seek a particular general hypothesis, which covers the entire instance space. On the contrary, customized learning, which is also called lazy learning in some literature, does not involve any model construction before it encounters the query instance, i.e., the instance to be classified. Our novel customized learning framework called SUpport Pattern lEarner (SUPE) tailors its learning process to different query instances, rather than partitioning the whole attribute space to obtain a global classifier such as a decision tree. In SUPE, The training data is also transformed into a binary matrix which is to be explored for useful patterns. SUPE makes use of Support Patterns (SPs), which are subsets of the query attributes as learning units. A SP is represented by a set of attribute values shared by the query instance and, potentially, some training instances [4, 5]. Another characteristic of SUPE is that it conducts learning from specific to general, as the contrary of many learning methods which conduct learning from general to specific. We will demonstrate that for learning scenarios with large hypothesis space and sparse training data, learning from specific to general is desirable. By learning from specific to general, SUPE can make use of the characteristics of the query instance to explore a focused hypothesis space during classification.

2 SUPE Framework

2.1 Query Matrix - A Customized Data Representation

Suppose the learning problem is defined on a class variable C and a finite set $F = \{F_i\}_{i=1}^n$ of random variables, i.e., attributes. Each attribute F_i can take on values from respective domains, denoted by $V(F_i)$. To simplify the discussion without loss of generality, we assume that the class variable C is a Boolean variable since a multi-class variable can be broken into a set of binary variables. The training data set is denoted by $D = \{d^j\}_{j=1}^m$. We use d_i^j to denote the value of the jth training instance on the ith attribute.

We consider a learning mechanism where each query instance can be handled independently in a "customized" learning process. In the learning process of a query instance, we propose to use a *query matrix* to represent the attributes and instances involved. Suppose there are m training instances and n attributes. Given the query instance $t = \{t_i\}_{i=1}^n$, we construct a $m \times n$ matrix:

$$A = (a_{ij})_{m \times n}, \tag{1}$$

where

$$\begin{aligned} a_{ij} &= 1, \quad \text{if } d_i^j = t_i, \\ &= 0, \quad \text{if } d_i^j \neq t_i \end{aligned} \tag{2}$$

Therefore, the query matrix A consists of n columns and m rows. Each column represents the corresponding attribute while each row represents a training instance. An element a_{ij} inside A is defined as "1" when the jth training instance shares the same value with the query instance on the ith attribute, and "0" if otherwise. This (0,1) matrix represents the relationship between attributes and instances for the learning customized to the query instance.

In the following discussion, we mainly focus on tackling discrete attribute values because continuous attribute values can be discretized before feeding into the learning model. We use the weather problem to demonstrate the concept of query matrix. Consider the attribute set $F = \{outlook, temperature, humidity, windy\}$ and the class label C defined on the value domain $\{yes, no\}$. The class attribute represents the fact that whether the weather condition is good for playing. The training data set consists of 14 instances, as shown in Figure 1. Consider the scenario of predicting the class label of two query instances, namely, $\{sunny, mild, normal, false\}$ and $\{overcast, cool, high, true\}$ under customized learning manner, two corresponding query matrices are then generated as shown in the bottom of Figure 1. Note that attribute and instance dimensions are not necessarily the same for different query matrices.

A query matrix is a binary relation over the training data set and the attribute set, but this relation is completely customized to the query instance. It can be viewed as the result of filtering the training instances with the query instance as a sifter. With the query matrix model of the training data and attribute values, the learning process can focus on local useful patterns and search more exhaustively to improve the classification performance.

All 14 training instances of the WEATHER problem

No.	Outlook	Temperature	Humidity	Windy	Play
1	sunny	hot	high	FALSE	No
2	sunny	hot	high	TRUE	No
3	overcast	hot	high	FALSE	Yes
4	rainy	mild	high	FALSE	Yes
5	rainy	cool	normal	FALSE	Yes
6	rainy	cool	normal	TRUE	No
7	overcast	cool	normal	TRUE	Yes
8	sunny	mild	high	FALSE	No
9	sunny	cool	normal	FALSE	Yes
10	rainy	mild	normal	FALSE	Yes
11	sunny	mild	normal	TRUE	Yes
12	overcast	mild	high	TRUE	Yes
13	overcast	hot	normal	FALSE	Yes
14	rainy	mild	high	TRUE	No

Query1	Outlook =sunny	Temp. =mild	Humidity =normal	Windy =false	Play=?	Query2	Outlook =overcast	Temp. =hot	Humidity =high	Windy =true	Play=?
	1	0	0	1	No		0	1	1	0	No
	1	0	0	0	No		0	1	1	1	No
	0	0	0	1	Yes		1	1	1	0	Yes
	0	1	0	1	Yes		0	0	1	0	Yes
	0	0	1	1	Yes		0	0	0	0	Yes
	0	0	1	0	No		0	0	0	1	No
	0	0	1	0	Yes		1	0	0	1	Yes
	0	1	0	1	No		0	0	1	0	No
	1	0	1	1	Yes		0	0	0	0	Yes
	0	1	1	1	Yes		0	0	0	0	Yes
	1	1	1	0	Yes		0	0	0	1	Yes
	0	1	0	0	Yes		1	0	1	1	Yes
	0	0	1	1	Yes		1	1	0	0	Yes
	0	1	0	0	No		0	1	1	1	No

Fig. 1. Example of two query matrices on the WEATHER problem

2.2 The Concept of Support Patterns

In the learning process of a query instance, we propose to use support patterns as the basic unit of learning. Generally, a *support pattern (SP)* can be viewed as a subset of the query instance. A query instance **t** is denoted by a full set of attribute values $\{t_1, \ldots, t_n\}$ where $t_i \in V(F_i)$. Therefore, a support pattern $\mathbf{A_t}$ for the query **t** can be viewed as a subset of the set $\{t_1, \ldots, t_n\}$. The cardinality of

A_t is denoted by $|A_t|$. Another requirement of a SP is that it must be supported by some training instances. A SP is *valid* when there are training instances matching with it. We denote the set of training instances that match with A_t by $I(A_t)$. If A_t is valid, then we have $|I(A_t)| > 0$. Given the query matrix for t, a valid SP is always associated with a sub-matrix. We are interested in those all-ones-sub-matrices, which represent useful SPs with all support instances sharing the same class label. Such a sub-matrix consists of an arbitrary subset of rows and columns of the query matrix, among which the permutation is allowed.

For example, suppose the query is to classify whether the weather is suitable for playing, given four attributes $\{outlook = sunny, temperature = mild, humidity = normal, windy = false\}$. Generally, the training data might only deliver a reliable pattern of a more general level, i.e., $\{sunny, ?, normal, ?\}$ is good for playing or not. These partially-specified attribute subsets are considered as SPs, if the corresponding support instance set is not empty. The subset relationship among SPs represents the "more-general-than" [9] relationship between their underlying concepts. Given two support patterns, namely, A_t and B_t, if $A_t \subseteq B_t$, then A_t is a *generalization* of B_t and B_t is a *specialization* of A_t. For instance, $\{sunny, ?, normal, false\}$ is a specialization of $\{sunny, ?, normal, ?\}$ while the latter is a generalization of the former. The "more-general-than" relationship between two SPs implies that $I(B_t) \subseteq I(A_t)$.

2.3 Reduced Hypothesis Space

In A SP in SUPE can be treated as a classification rule with the major class label among its support instances as the predictor. Because each attribute F_i can take on values in $V(F_i)$ or be missing in a classification rule, theoretically there are $\prod(|V(F_i)| + 1)$ rules to be explored. Even for the simplest case where all attributes are binary, $\prod(|V(F_i)| + 1)$ still equals 3^n where n is the number of attributes. In practice, it is difficult and usually infeasible to examine all potential rules, considering the large number of combinations of domain values.

A common technique in rule induction algorithms [2,10] is to search with the guide of heuristics. The Apriori Property, which means "nonempty subsets of a frequent item set must also be frequent.", helps to reduce the search space by pruning the infrequent item set. At each step, the heuristic looks no further than the next attribute to be selected, which is added into existing classification rules to produce new rules for verifying. As a consequence, the data space is recursively partitioned into a number of clusters. In contrast, our proposed SUPE framework utilizes the query instance and the training data to prune the hypothesis rule space, since each useful rule should be applicable to the query instance and supported by some training data. Moreover, the search sequence of SUPE is from specific to general. Each query or training instance is treated as the most specific classification rule, then it is generalized to produce more general rules. Since each instance containing n attribute values can be generalized to at most 2^n rules (including itself and the rule without antecedent), the rule space to be searched is significantly pruned.

It can be shown that maximal all-ones-sub-matrices of a query matrix D are one-to-one correspondence with fully connected sub-graphs of a bi-partite graph with the same binary adjacency matrix D. Therefore, it is a NP-complete problem since there are $(2^m - 1)(2^n - 1)$ sub-matrices available. However, since each given SP can only have one fixed set of support instances, there are $2^n - 1$ sub-matrices available for a query instance. It is the same as the maximal number of rules except for the removal of the non-antecedent rule. In real-world problems, $|V(F_i) + 1|$ is always no less than the minimum value 3. The number of attributes n might also be very large. Hence our customized learning method has advantages over common rule-based learning methods. More precisely, when $\prod(|V(F_i)| + 1)$ is very large and the training data is relatively sparse, SUPE will be more effective and efficient.

Moreover, since each useful rule should be supported by some training instances, all useful rules can be explored in handling all training instances separately as query instances. Suppose there are altogether e query instances to be classified and r training instances, the hypothesis rule space to be searched in SUPE is at most $2^n \min(r, e)$. Equation 3 shows the condition when our SUPE learning method can have significant computational advantages over common rule-based learning techniques.

$$2^n \min(r, e) << \prod(|V(F_i)| + 1) \qquad (3)$$

This condition can be easily met in practice because many real-world problems have a large attribute set with a relatively sparse training data set. Another simple but stricter condition is $3^n/2^n >> r$, assuming $e >> r$ and all attributes are simply binary. The data sets used for evaluation in Section 4 are selected according to this criterion.

Among all the SPs in the hypothesis space, only those supported by training data need to be considered, i.e., valid. Moreover, since we only consider patterns with sufficient support, only a small fraction of those SPs need to be processed. Therefore, the valid SPs to be processed is far less than $2^n \min(r, e)$. Consequently, we can develop pruning operations to discover valid SPs efficiently.

2.4 Searching from Specific to General

The search in our SUPE framework is conducted from specific to general. In contrast, common rule learning algorithms search for classification rules in a greedy manner, from general to specific [2,3,7]. Therefore, common rule-based learning algorithms can be viewed as conducting global "drill down" operations to produce more concrete rules from the current set of rules. Some techniques such as post-pruning or boosting are proposed to improve the performance and avoid overfitting [8,2]. Our method can be viewed as conducting "scroll up" operations from each training instance to produce more general concepts.

In common rule learning process, we need to find out a sequence of conditions or a sequence of attributes to discover a useful rule. Moreover, each selected attribute condition must obtain sufficient information gain value or similar kind of measures. However there might be no such sequences at all. If such a situation happens, that rule cannot be discovered via the common "drill-down" learning process. A typical scenarios is that the attribute with the largest information gain is not specified in the most useful rule. Then the partition of the attribute space will be deviated from that useful rule from the beginning. Returning to the weather problem described previously as an example, rule learning methods such as ID3 or J48, which search from general to specific, will return the result depicted as below:

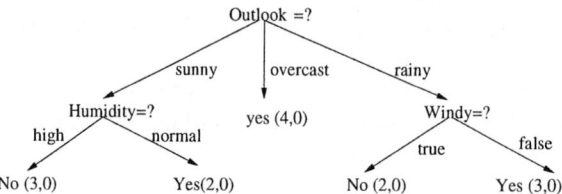

Fig. 2. Result of learning from general to specific on the Weather problem

However, the most useful SP in classifying the query $\{sunny, mild, normal, false\}$ is $\{?, ?, normal, false\}$. This rule is better than $\{sunny, ?, normal, ?\}$ because it has double support instances. Although these two SPs predict the same class label for the query, $\{?, ?, normal, false\}$ provides more reliability and confidence with the prediction. However, this better SP cannot be discovered via common searching from general to specific rule learning process. The reason is that the attribute "outlook", which attains the largest information gain and hence dominates the searching direction, is not specified in this useful SP.

In contrast, SUPE does not rely on such a sequence to discover useful SPs. SUPE can discover more useful and customized SPs (classification rules) for the query, such as $\{?, ?, normal, false\}$ in the above case. We introduce a search mechanism, which can be viewed as the inverse of Apriori Property. Suppose a user requires a useful support pattern to be with p or higher accuracy. If a support pattern can meet the requirement, all its specialized SPs are also very likely to have a high expected accuracy and the same majority class. In other words, the decision on a specific SP can be a reliable indicator of its general derivations, but not vice versa.

3 Exploring Query Matrix for Useful SPs

3.1 Selecting Useful SPs for Learning

In searching from specific to general, SUPE selects useful SPs, i.e., all-ones-sub-matrices in the query matrix. Suppose a SP A_t has x support training instances, i.e., $|I(A_t)| = x$, which is called frequency. Hence the corresponding all-ones-sub-matrix of A_t has x rows and $|A_t|$ columns. Among the x rows, y rows sharing the same majority class label is called majority count. Hence this SP becomes a sub-classifier whose prediction is the majority class label. y/x is called the majority rate of A_t. It can also be viewed as the empirical accuracy of classifying all rows of the corresponding sub-matrix. An ideal all-ones-sub-matrix for learning should have a large number of rows which all belong to the same class. Since the given query instance is a specialization of this SP, the query likely belongs to that class. We select those SPs which are reliable sub-classifiers with high empirical accuracy. Therefore, we are more interested in all-ones-sub-matrices with large number of rows and high majority rate. Moreover, the number of columns of the sub-matrix is also an indicator of the distance between the SP and the query instance, in terms of "more-general-than" relationship. In practice, a high majority rate and a high frequency are favorable.

We can explore all valid SPs efficiently, from the largest cardinality to the smallest cardinality, via scanning the training data. Suppose the largest cardinality among all SPs is k. The exploration starts with SPs with the largest cardinality k. They can be enumerated and explored directly by investigating all qualified training instances, i.e., sharing k attribute values with the query. Then all valid SPs with cardinality less than k can be exhaustively enumerated.

With the query matrix, operations on SPs are transformed into operations on a binary matrix. Each SP can be generated by filtering the original query matrix with a binary string as a bitwise-AND mask. Rows are ranked according to their number of ones, which indicates their similarities with the query. Thus at each step only a small fraction of rows needs to considered. The learning process usually completes after only examining those rows which have a large number of ones. For problems with large attribute dimensions but relatively sparse training data, our method has the capability of exploring all valid SPs exhaustively. Even for problems with both large attribute dimensions and large number of training instances, our method can still efficiently reduce the search space and discover useful SPs with the aid of a set of pruning rules as described in Section 3.2.

3.2 Discovery Process

The complete process of discovering useful SPs has several steps. First the training data is transformed into a binary matrix according to the query. All valid SPs are ranked and examined by scanning the rows of the query matrix. Then we use the selection metric to find useful valid SPs. If a SP is accepted as a good predictive sub-model, it will be selected as discovered knowledge. If a SP is rejected, it will be discarded. If a SP is neither selected nor discarded, it is then stored. The common subsets of stored SPs are used to generate new SPs which could not be explored directly from the training data. Finally the discovered SPs are combined to predict the query as described in Section 3.3.

Based on the "more-general-than" relationship, a pruning principle is utilized in the discovery process. Once a SP has been determined to be selected as useful or discarded as useless, all its generalizations have to be pruned. This pruning principle shows that SPs can be exploited by analyzing their relationship and observing their class distributions. The decision of selecting or discarding a particular SP will trigger a family of SPs to be pruned. These operations can significantly accelerate the searching for an appropriate set of useful SPs.

3.3 Combining Selected SPs for Classification

There are various ways to combine selected SPs for predicting the class label. A straightforward technique is to conduct a majority voting among the training instances associated with selected SPs. The class with the maximum sum of frequencies in all discovered SPs is the classification result of the query instance.

The output of SUPE is a weighted summary of the selected SPs. Common weighting schemes consider the TP/FP ratio of each applicable classification rule where TP is true positive and FP is false positive. The normalized form of $TP/(FP+g)$ is usually used as the weight of a rule in the final classification. In our SUPE method, we design a weighting scheme for selected SPs. Thus the weighted class frequencies of selected SPs can be combined to classify the query instance. The class label with the largest weighted sum of frequencies is assigned to the query instance. The weight $W(\mathbf{A_t})$ for a SP $\mathbf{A_t}$ is given as follows:

$$W(\mathbf{A_t}) = \frac{yE(|I(\emptyset)|)}{(x-y+g)E(|I(\mathbf{A_t})|)} \qquad (4)$$

where $E(|I(\emptyset)|)$ is the expectation of $|I(\emptyset)|$, $y/(x-y+g)$ is actually the empirical estimation of $TP/(FP+g)$. $E(|I(\emptyset)|)/E(|I(\mathbf{A_t})|)$ is introduced because we should take into account the expected frequency of $\mathbf{A_t}$. Intuitively, we should consider the similarity between a SP and the query instance in addition to considering the frequency x and the majority rate y/x. SPs with large cardinalities tend to have less support instances, but they are usually very close to the query instance. Their importance should be reflected despite their limited support instances. Therefore, we introduce the inversion of expected frequency as a weighting factor, which is defined as follows:

$$\frac{E(|I(\emptyset)|)}{E(|I(\mathbf{A_t})|)} \simeq \frac{\prod |V(F_i)|}{e^{\sum_i T_i(F_i) \ln |V(F_i)|}} \qquad (5)$$

The indicator variable $T_i(F_i)$ in Equation 5 equals 1 when $F_i \in \mathbf{A_t}$, otherwise it equals 0. $\prod |V(F_i)|/e^{\sum_i I_i(F_i) \ln |V(F_i)|}$ reflects the expected frequency ratio of training instances matching with $\mathbf{A_t}$, assuming that all data is evenly distributed over the attribute space.

4 Experimental Results

4.1 Benchmark Data Sets

To evaluate the classification performance of SUPE, we have conducted extensive experiments on a number of benchmark data sets from the UCI repository of machine learning database [1]. These data sets all satisfy $(3/2)^n/r > 1$, as discussed in Equation 3. They were collected from different real-world problems in various domains. We partitioned each data set into 10 even portions and then conducted 10-fold cross-validation. The performance is measured by the average classification accuracy (in percentage) of 10-fold cross-validation. In these experiments, we have also investigated the performance of kNN, Naive Bayesian, Lazy Bayesian Rule (LBR), SVM, and Decision Tree (J48) provided by Weka-3-2-6 machine learning software package, as mentioned in the previous section. All these models except for kNN use default settings. For kNN, we have conducted runs for $k = 1, 5,$ and 10. We reported the results for $k = 5$ because it achieves the best average classification accuracy among different k.

Table 1. Classification performance of SUPE and other classifiers on selected group of UCI data sets

Data Set	No. of Attr.(n)	No. of Classes	No. of Ins.(r)	$(3/2)^n/r$	SUPE	kNN	Naive Bayes	J48	SVM
Sonar	60	2	208	176771484.2	**87.0**	84.6	65.9	74.1	77.8
Annealing	39	5	898	5472.6	**99.0**	97.1	86.5	98.4	97.9
Ionosphere	34	2	351	2765.6	90.3	84.9	82.4	**90.9**	88.0
Kr-vs-Kp	36	2	3196	683.4	96.5	94.9	87.6	**99.5**	95.7
Hepatitis	19	2	155	14.3	**90.0**	85.8	83.8	79.4	85.8
Labor	16	2	57	11.5	**96.5**	86.0	94.7	78.7	92.7
Lymph	18	4	148	10.0	83.1	81.8	83.8	77.0	**86.5**
Zoo	17	7	101	9.8	**96.2**	95.1	95.2	92.1	92.1
Average					**92.3**	88.8	85.0	86.3	89.6

In Table 1, data sets are ranked in descending order of $(3/2)^n/r$. On this group of data sets, our SUPE method obtains the highest average accuracy 92.3% among all classifiers. In particular, on the data set of Sonar, which has an extremely large $(3/2)^n/r$, SUPE significantly outperforms other classifiers. As customized learning methods, SUPE and kNN perform similarly well on data sets such as Sonar and Zoo. On average, SUPE demonstrates advantages on data sets with high attribute dimension, taking the number of classes into consideration.

5 Conclusions and Future Work

This paper presents a novel customized algorithm called SUPE. To classify a query instance, SUPE constructs a query matrix to reduce the hypothesis space, and searches for useful local SPs from specific to general. The experimental results demonstrate that SUPE has a prominent learning performance. A promising future direction is to explore more sophisticated methods for exploring the query matrix. Moreover, we plan to develop a visualization platform for SUPE to facilitate interactive learning or online classification.

References

1. C. Blake, E. Keogh, and C. Merz. UCI repository of machine learning databases. http://www.ics.uci.edu/~ mlearn/MLRepository.html.
2. W. Cohen. Fast effective rule induction. In *Proceedings of the Twelfth International Conference on Machine Learning*, pages 115–123, 1995.
3. W. Cohen and Y. Singer. A simple, fast, and effective rule learner. In *Proceedings of the sixteenth national conference on Artificial intelligence and the eleventh Innovative applications of artificial intelligence conference innovative applications of artificial intelligence*, pages 335–342, 1999.
4. Y. Han and W. Lam. Lazy learning by scanning memory image lattice. In *Proceedings of the 2004 SIAM International Conference on Data Mining*, pages 407–423, 2004.
5. Y. Han and W. Lam. Lazy learning for classification based on query projections. In *Proceedings of the 2005 SIAM International Conference on Data Mining*, pages 227–238, 2005.
6. W. Lam and Y. Han. Automatice textual document categorization based on generalized instance sets and a metamodel. *IEEE Transactions on Pattern Analysis and Machine Intelligence*, 25(5):628–633, 2003.
7. W. Li, J. Han, and J. Pei. Accurate and efficient classification based on multiple class-association rules. In *Proceedings of the IEEE International Conference on Data Mining (ICDM)*, pages 369–376, 2001.
8. M. Mehta, J. Rissanen, and R. Agrawal. MDL-based decision tree pruning. In *Proceedings of the First International Conference on Knowledge Discovery and Data Mining (KDD'95)*, pages 216–221, 1995.
9. T. Mitchell. *Machine Learning*. McGraw Hill, 1997.
10. S. Weiss and N. Indurkhya. Lightweight rule induction. In *Proceedings of the International Conference on Machine Learning (ICML)*, pages 1135–1142. Morgan Kaufmann, 2000.

From Clusters to Rules: A Hybrid Framework for Generalized Symbolic Rule Induction

Qingshuang Jiang and Syed Sibte Raza Abidi

Faculty of Computer Science, Dalhousie University, Halifax, B3H 1W5, Canada
sraza@cs.dal.ca

Abstract. Rule induction is a data mining process for acquiring knowledge in terms of symbolic decision rules that explain the data in terms of causal relationship between conditional factors and a given decision/outcome. We present a Decision Rule Acquisition Workbench (DRAW) that discovers symbolic decision rules, in CNF form, from un-annotated data-sets. Our rule-induction strategy involves three phases: (a) conceptual clustering to cluster and generate a conceptual hierarchy of the data-set; (b) rough sets based rule induction algorithm to generate decision rules from the emergent data clusters; and (c) attribute oriented induction to generalize the derived decision rules to yield high-level decision rules and a minimal rule-set size. We evaluate DRAW with five standard machine learning datasets and apply to derive decision rules to understand optic nerve images in the realm of glaucoma decision support.

1 Introduction

All data mining endeavors assume that a data-set inherently embodies interesting patterns which are discoverable and potentially useful to the domain of its origin. The inherent patterns within a database can be discovered through a variety of data mining techniques and the discovered knowledge can be manifested in a variety of modalities, such as clusters, decision tree, prediction models symbolic rules and so on [1]. Discovering knowledge from un-annotated data—i.e. when the class label is not available—is a challenging task as the methods need to work without any a priori data discriminating information. Furthermore, it is of interest and practical use to acquire an objective and understandable description of the knowledge derived from un-annotated data—i.e. in terms of symbolic decision rules—to not only provide an opportunity for qualitative analysis of the data mining output, but also to get an understanding of intrinsic behavior of the data-set.

Rule induction is the process of acquiring knowledge (i.e. symbolic decision rules) from a number of specific 'examples' (i.e. the data-set), to explain the cause-and-effect relationship between conditional factors and a given decision/outcome. However, rule induction algorithms are supervised in nature and typically work on annotated data-sets, yet there is a case for interpreting un-annotated data-sets in terms of Conjunctive Normal Form (CNF) symbolic rules. This can be achieved by inductively clustering the data-sets and then explaining the intrinsic relationships between the attributes, that manifest as data clusters, in terms of symbolic decision rules [2].

In this paper we present a rule induction framework that discovers CNF decision rules from un-annotated data-sets. We use rough sets as the base rule-induction method, which has been successfully applied for this task [3]. Additionally, we present techniques to (a) reduce the size of the rule-set; and (b) to generalize the rules to high-level concepts. We present a hybrid rule-induction strategy that uses (i) conceptual clustering to cluster the un-annotated data-set (to acquire the underlying class information) and to generate a conceptual hierarchy that describes the data at different levels of abstraction [4]; (ii) rough sets based rule induction algorithm to generate decision rules from the emergent data clusters [5]; and (iii) attribute oriented induction in conjunction with the data's conceptual hierarchy to generalize the derived decision rules to high-level decision rules [6], and in the process minimizing the rule-set size without compromising classification accuracy. The rule induction framework is implemented in terms of *DRAW* (Decision Rule Acquisition Workbench), as shown in figure 1, and is evaluated with standard machine learning datasets.

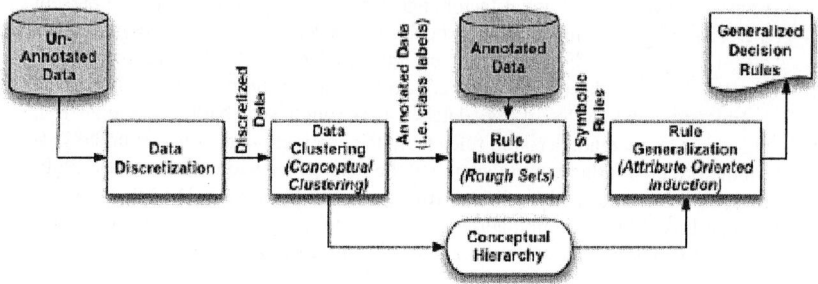

Fig. 1. The Functional Architecture of DRAW

We applied DRAW to derive decision rules for classifying *Confocal Scanning Laser Tomography* (CSLT) images of the optic disk for the diagnosis of glaucoma. The decision rules are expected to provide: (a) insight into the relationships between optic disk's shape features in relation to glaucoma damage; and (b) a description of five different classes (healthy, glaucoma, focal, senile, myopic damage) in terms of the features. The derived decision rules can be used for the classification of a new CSLT image—i.e. whether the patient is a normal or has a specific type of glaucoma.

2 Rule Induction and Rough Sets

Rule induction is an active machine learning research area with a wide variety of existing algorithms—to construct, classify and prune the rules—grounded in different theoretical principles [7]. Statistical methods, classified as classical and modern (such as Alloc 80, CASTLE, Naïve Bayes) methods, are based on linear discrimination and estimation of the joint distribution of the features within each class, respectively. Decision tree based rule induction methods, such as ID3, CART, C4.5 and CAL5, partitions the data points in terms of a tree structure such that the nodes are labeled as features and the edges as attribute values [8].

Rough sets provide an alternative method for rule induction due to their unique approach to handle inconsistencies in the input data. Rough set based data analysis involves the formulation of approximate concepts about the data based on available classification information [3, 9]. Functionally, rough sets based rule induction involves the formation of approximate concepts based on a minimum number of features—the approximate concepts, also called *dynamic reducts*, are capable of differentiating the various classes within the data. Rule induction involves the representation of dynamic reducts as succinct symbolic *if then* decision rules that potentially can inter-attribute dependencies and attribute significance and class information. There is no standard approach to rough set based rule induction, hence rough sets can be used at different stages a rule induction process. A number of rough set based rule induction approaches has been suggested such as *System LERS* [10]; *Discernibility matrix* [11] leading to a computational kernel of the system *Rosetta* [12]; *RoughDAS* [13] that allows users to specify conditions; rule induction framework, involving rule filtering methods, to generate cluster-defining rules [2]; and so on.

3 Our Rule Induction Approach

The featured work is an extension of the rule induction framework proposed by Abidi [2], in that we have introduced methods to generate generalized decision rules and to minimize the rule-set size. We discover symbolic rules from un-annotated datasets comprising an undifferentiated collection of continuous, discrete and nominal valued data-vectors $S = \{x_i : i \in [1, n]\}$, for which the classification attribute $c(x_i) = \alpha$ for $\alpha \in [1, k]$ is unknown [3]. We have developed a hybrid rule induction approach that dictates the systematic transformation of un-annotated data-sets to deductive symbolic rule-sets via a sequence of phases, as described below:

3.1 Phase 1 - Data Clustering and Conceptual Hierarchy Generation

Given an un-annotated dataset, the first step involves the unsupervised clustering of the data into k clusters in order to derive classification information that is required for subsequent rule induction. We have adapted *a Similarity Based Agglomerative Clustering* (SBAC) algorithm [4] that is based on a similarity measure from a biological taxonomy [14]. The clustering process is driven by two factors 1) the criterion function for evaluating the goodness of partition structure and 2) the control algorithm for generating the partition structure. The similarity measure regards a pair of objects *(i, j)* more similar than a second pair of objects *(l, m)* iff the object *i* and *j* exhibit a greater match in attribute values that are more uncommon in the population. This similarity measure can be conveniently coupled with a simple agglomerative control strategy that constructs a conceptual hierarchy, from which a distinct partition is extracted by a simple procedure that trades off distinctness for parsimony.

To derive the conceptual hierarchy, the original algorithm [4, 15] is modified as follows: (a) Each attribute of the data-set is applied the SBAC individually such that the similarity matrix is calculated based on the similarity measure among the values of each attribute instead of the combination of all the attributes; and (b) based on the similarity matrix of each attribute, the distinct values of an attribute are clustered agglomeratively such that a tree-like structure is formed, where the lowest level is made up of the distinct attribute values and the higher level is made up of clustered values which contain the values from lower level. The root of the conceptual hierarchy recursively contains all the distinct values of the attribute, which provides the most general attribute information (as shown in Table 1).

The outcome of phase I is two fold: (i) the data is partitioned into k number of data clusters; and (ii) a hierarchical concept tree is constructed to form the basis for attribute-oriented induction and the generalization of the cluster-defining symbolic rules.

Table 1. Conceptual hierarchy derived from the TGD data set. Attribute values are discretized into intervals. Intervals labeled by letters are at the higher level. Intervals labeled by numbers are on the lower level of the hierarchy and can be merged to form a more generalozed interval.

T3r (10)	Sthy (5)	Stri (6)	bTSH (3)	mTSH (10)
1 = [_ , 97) 2 = [97, 100) 3 = [100, 118) 4 = [118, 125) 5 = [125, _) a = [_ , 100) b = [100, 125) c = [125, _) e = [_ , 125) f = [125, _)	1 = [_ , 5.7) 2=[5.7, 14.2) 3 = [14.2, _) a = [_ , 14.2) b = [14.2, _)	1 = [_ , 1.25) 2 = [1.25, 3.65) 3 = [3.65, 3.95) 4 = [3.95, _) a = [_ , 3.65) b = [3.65, _)	1 = [_ , 4.30) 2 = [4.30, _) a = [_ , _)	1 = [_ , 0.35) 2 = [0.35, 0.65) 3 = [0.65, 7.25) 4 = [7.25, 10.5) 5 = [10.5, _) a = [_ , 0.65) b = [0.65, 10.5) c = [10.5, _) e = [_ , 10.5) f = [10.5, _)
tree: e→(a,b); a→(1,2,3); b→(4); f→c→5	tree: a→(1,2); b→3	tree: a→(1,2); b→(3,4)	tree: a→(1,2)	tree: e→(a,b); a→(1,2,3); b→(4); f→c→5

3.2 Phase 2 - Symbolic Rule Discovery

Given an annotated and discretized data-set together with the conceptual hierarchy that describes the characteristics of the data-set, the task in phase II is to generate a set of symbolic CNF rules that model the data-set in terms of class-membership principles and complex inter-relationships between the data attributes. In our work, we implemented a symbolic rule generation approach based on the Rough Set approximation [3, 9], as it provides a sound and interesting alternative to statistical and decision tree based rule induction methods. Our rule induction methodology is as follows:

Step 1: Dynamic Reducts Computation
We use *k-fold cross validation* to split the data-set into training and test sets. From the training data (for each fold), we compute multiple dynamic reduct sets, such that each reduct set is found through the identification of minimum attribute sets that are able to distinguish a data point from the rest of the data set. This is achieved via (a) *vertical reduction* whereby the redundant data objects are eliminated and (b) *horizontal reduction* whereby the redundant attributes are eliminated since logically duplicated

From Clusters to Rules: A Hybrid Framework for Generalized Symbolic Rule Induction

attributes cannot help distinguish a data point from the rest of the data set. At the completion of the reduction process we end up with a minimum set of attribute values that can distinguish any data point from rest of the data-set—i.e. a reduct set. Dynamic reducts are the reducts that have a high frequency of occurrence across all the available reduct-sets, and are of particular interest for rule generation purposes. The search for dynamic reducts is an NP-hard problem—the time complexity for finding the minimum attribute set increases exponentially with respect to the linear increase of the data set—and a genetic algorithm based reducts approximation method is used to compute the dynamic reducts [16, 17, 18].

Step 2: Symbolic Rule Generation via Dynamic Reducts

After computing the dynamic reducts we generate symbolic rules from them. Instead of using all the dynamic reducts to generate a large set of symbolic rules, we attempt to generate symbolic rules from the shortest possible length dynamic reducts; the rationale being that shorter length dynamic reducts have been shown to yield concise rule-sets that exhibit higher classification accuracy and generalization capabilities [2]. Our rule generation strategy therefore involves: (1) the selection of dynamic reducts that have a short length and (2) the generation of rules that satisfy a user-defined accuracy level. Our strategy for generating symbolic rules is as follows [2]:

Step 1 : Specify an acceptable minimum accuracy level for the rule set.
Step 2 : Find dynamic reducts from the sub-samples and place in set *DR*. Note that *DR* will comprise reducts with varying lengths.
Step 3 : From the reducts in *DR* determine the shortest reduct length (*SRL*).
Step 4 : From *DR*, collect all reducts that have a length equal to *SRL* and store them as set *SHRED*.
Step 5 : Generate symbolic rules from the reducts placed in *SHRED*.
Step 6 : Determine the overall accuracy of the generated rules with respect to the test data.
Step 7 : IF Overall accuracy of the generated rules is lower than the minimum accuracy level AND there exist reducts in the *DR* set with length > *SRL*
THEN Empty *SHRED* AND Update the value of *SRL* to the next highest reduct length in *DR* AND Repeat from step 6.
ELSE
Symbolic rules with the desired accuracy level cannot be generated.

3.3 Phase 3 – Rule-Set Generalization

Typically, The rule-set generated in phase II is quite large and might contain low quality rules, thereby compromising the classification efficiency of the classifier. In phase III, we attempt to minimize the rule-set size by generalizing the induced rules—i.e. a large number of low level concepts represented in the rules can be generalized to fewer higher-level concepts. The conceptual hierarchy derived in phase I is used to provide summarization of the induced rules by ignoring redundant differential at lower-levels. For rule generalization we have adapted a standard set-oriented induction method—called Attribute-Oriented Induction (AOI) [6]. We use the below four basic strategies for performing attribute-oriented induction on the rule set:

Strategy 1. (Concept tree ascension) If there exists a higher-level concept for an attribute value of a rule, the substitution of the value by its higher-level concept generalizes the rule. Ascending the tree one level at a time enforces minimal generalization as the substitution of an attribute value by its higher-level concept makes the rule cover more objects than the original one and thus generalizes the rule.

Strategy 2. (Vote propagation) The value of the vote for a rule is carried to its generalized rule, next the votes are accumulated when merging identical rules during generalization. The vote of each generalized rule registers the number of rules in the initial data relation generalized to the current one.

Strategy 3. (Threshold control on each attribute) If the number of distinct values of an attribute in the target class is larger than the generalization threshold value, generalization on this attribute is performed. The generalization threshold controls the maximum number of tuples of the target class in the final generalized relation.

Strategy 4. (Threshold control on generalized relations) If the number of rules of a generalized relation in the target class is larger than the generalization threshold value, further generalization on the relation is performed.

The AOI based rule generalization algorithm [6] is presented as follows:

Input: (i) A CNF rule set, (ii) the learning task, (iii) the (optional) preferred concept hierarchies, and (iv) the (optional) preferred form to express learning results (e.g., generalization *threshold*).
Output. A characteristic rule set generalized from the input rule set.
Method. Basic attribute-oriented induction consists of the following four steps:
Step 1. Collect the task-relevant data,
Step 2. Perform basic attribute-oriented induction
   begin {basic attribute-oriented induction}
      for each attribute Ai ($1 \leq i \leq n$, n = # of attributes) in the generalized relation GR **do**
         while number_of_distinct_values_in_Ai > threshold **do** {
            if no higher level concept in the concept hierarchy table for Ai
            then remove Ai
            else substitute Ai's by its corresponding minimal generalized concept;
            merge identical rules }
         while #_of_rules in GR > threshold **do** {
            selectively generalize attributes; merge identical rules }
   end.
Step 3. Simplify the generalized relation, and
Step 4. Transform the final relation into a logical rule.

4 Experimental Results

The experiments reported evaluate the final classification accuracy of rules discovered by DRAW, and also demonstrate the performance of the individual modules. Three experimental scenarios were performed, with standard data-sets, to demonstrate the performance of the various combinations of modules (as shown in Figure 1):

A). Rough set based rule induction (with class information) --> Decision rules

B). Conceptual Clustering (without class information) + Rough set based rule induction --> Decision rules
C). Conceptual Clustering (without class information) + Rough set based rule induction + Attribute-Oriented Induction --> Generalized decision rules

4.1 Classification Accuracy for Standard Data-Sets

Standard machine learning data-set—i.e. Thyroid gland data (TGD); Wisconsin Breast Cancer (WBC); Balance Scale Weight & Distance (BaS); Iris Plants Database (IRIS); Pima Indians Diabetes Database (Pima) were used for our evaluation. Table 2 shows the classification accuracy for the above experimental scenarios. Also, we compared the overall accuracy of our rules with rules derived from C4.5.

Table 2. Experimental results for scenarios A-C and the baseline C4.5 method

Data Sets	Accuracy				Sensitivity				Specificity			
	A	B	C	C4.5	A	B	C	C4.5	A	B	C	C4.5
TGD	0.88	0.89	0.84	0.93	0.97	0.93	0.87	0.97	0.92	0.96	0.95	0.97
WBC	0.93	0.90	0.93	0.92	0.97	0.91	0.96	0.98	0.96	0.99	0.97	0.98
BaS	0.62	0.57	0.64	0.64	0.76	0.75	0.73	0.79	0.82	0.76	0.89	0.79
Pima	0.87	0.89	0.85	0.92	0.94	0.95	0.86	0.96	0.93	0.93	0.99	0.96
IRIS	0.58	0.59	0.63	0.62	0.73	0.74	0.71	0.74	0.81	0.79	0.88	0.74

From the classification results the following was observed: (a) The overall classification accuracy offered by DRAW, for both annotated and un-annotated data-sets, is quite high and is comparable (in fact better in three cases) with the C4.5 method. The classification accuracy for scenario A is largely maintained throughout the subsequent stages of the process indicating the robustness of the rough set based rule-induction method. We conclude that our rough set based rule induction method amicably derives the underlying class structure from the data; (b) The classification accuracy for un-annotated data using SBAC conceptual clustering (scenario B) is comparable to both scenario A and C4.5, indicating the effectiveness of the conceptual clustering approach for rule induction for un-annotated data; (c) The classification accuracy for generalized rules (scenario C) is comparable to both scenario A and C4.5, indicating the effectiveness of the AOI method for rule generalization. Although no significant gain in the accuracy is noted for scenario C, yet the real impact of the AOI approach is noted in the minimization of the rule-set size without a discernable loss of classification accuracy; (d) Comparison of scenarios B & C indicate that the conceptual hierarchy derived in phase I is effective for AOI based rule generalization, and the generalized rules do not compromise the classification accuracy. This vindicates the role of the conceptual hierarchy and the AOI method for rule generalization.

4.1.2 Rule-Set Generalization
The application of the AOI based rule generalization method has reduced the rule-set size without compromising the classification (see table 3). Furthermore, different degrees of rule generalization takes place (as shown in table 4):

- Case 1 shows single-level generalization, where a single attribute mTSH is generalized at level 1 of the conceptual hierarchy as [1,2]-> a;
- Case 2, 3, 4 show multi-level generalization, where attribute mTSH is generalized at level 1 of the conceptual hierarchy as [1,2]-> a and [3,4]->b, the generalization goes on at the level 2 as [a,b] -> e, and continues until the root of the conceptual hierarchy tree is reached;
- Case 5 shows that generalization can be performed on more than 2 rules, the number of the rules can be generalized is determined by the number of children that belong to the same parent.

Table 3. Rule-set size comparison for the five different data-sets

Data Sets	Clustered Rough-Set Based Rules								Percentage Reduction
	Before AOI				After AOI				
	Acc	Sens	Spec	# of Rules	Acc	Sens	Spec	# of Rules	
TGD	0.892	0.927	0.962	67	0.836	0.875	0.955	52	22.39%
WBC	0.904	0.915	0.988	103	0.932	0.963	0.968	72	30.10%
BaS	0.573	0.749	0.765	217	0.645	0.728	0.886	194	10.60%
Pima	0.889	0.955	0.931	455	0.849	0.859	0.988	357	21.52%
IRIS	0.589	0.744	0.792	16	0.631	0.711	0.882	15	6.25%

Table 4. Different degrees of rule generalization achieved via AOI

Case	Decision Rule Before AOI	Decision Rule After AOI	Explanation
1	sthy(3) mTSH(1) -> 2 sthy(3) mTSH(2) -> 2	sthy(3) mTSH(a) -> 2	mTSH(1) and mTSH(2) generalized to mTSH(a)
2	t3r(3) mTSH(1) -> 1 t3r(3) mTSH(2) -> 1	t3r(3) mTSH(a) -> 1	mTSH(1) and mTSH(2) generalized to mTSH(a)
3	t3r(3) mTSH(3) -> 1 t3r(3) mTSH(4) -> 1	t3r(3) mTSH(b) -> 1	mTSH(3) and mTSH(4) generalized to mTSH(b)
4	t3r(3) mTSH(a) -> 1 t3r(3) mTSH(b) -> 1	t3r(3) mTSH(e) -> 1	mTSH(a) and mTSH(b) generalized to mTSH(e)
5	ucz(2) bn(1) ucp(4) -> 3 ucz(2) bn(2) ucp(4) -> 3 ucz(2) bn(4) ucp(4) -> 3	ucz(2) bn(a) ucp(4) -> 3	bn(1), bn(1)and bn(1) generalized to bn(a)

4.2 Real World Data Experiment

In our study, we extended our experiment to the medical domain. The *Confocal Scanning Laser Tomography* (CSLT) data set is used to analyze the damage to optic disks, typically in glaucoma patient. The data was collected at the Department of Ophthalmology of Dalhousie University. The CSLT data comprises 3574 visual field examinations with 17 morphological features for both normal and glaucomatous patients. The data has 5 classes. The features had continuous values and were normalized in the range [0, 1] with a linear transformation and discretized using Chi-2 method. The classification results (table 5) are promising as given the noise in the image capture procedure a classification accuracy of 70% was largely expected and achieved. A sample of the generalized rules is given in Table 6, showing the premise and the class.

Table 5. Classification results and rule-set size for the CSLT data-set

Scenario	Accuracy	Precision	Recall	Rule-Set Size
A	0.721	0.655	0.986	366
B	0.645	0.611	0.920	374
C	0.721	0.655	0.986	325

Table 6. Sample of decision rules derived from the CSLT data-set

Rule	Decision Rule Before AOI	Decision Rule After AOI	Explanation
1	CR_G(6) -> 4 CR_G(7) -> 4	CR_G(c) -> 4	CR_G(6) and CR_G(7) generalized to CR_G(c)
2	CR_TS(0) ST_NI(2) -> 1 CR_TS(1) ST_NI(2) -> 1	CR_TS(a) ST_NI(2) -> 1	CR_TS(0) and CR_TS(1) generalized to CR_TS(a)
3	CR_TS(2) ST_NI(2) -> 1 CR_TS(3) ST_NI(2) -> 1	CR_TS(b) ST_NI(2) -> 1	CR_TS(2) and CR_TS(3) generalized to CR_TS(b)
4	CR_TS(a) ST_NI(2) -> 1 CR_TS(b) ST_NI(2) -> 1	CR_TS(e) ST_NI(2) -> 1	CR_TS(a) and CR_TS(b) generalized to CR_TS(e)

5 Concluding Remarks

We have presented an interesting and efficient rule induction strategy that ensures the generation of complex and high-level decision rules for un-annotated data-sets. Rule granularity has been regarded as being an important factor in the comprehensibility of the discovered knowledge in terms of rules—longer and more specific rules do not necessarily provide better classification accuracy as compared to shorter and generalized rules. Hence, the need for more concise rules and smaller rule-sets. The rule induction strategy presented here allows for the generalization of rules whilst maintaining classification accuracy via the incorporation of attribute oriented induction—which integrates machine learning methodology with relational database operations—with rough sets based rule induction methods. The use of a conceptual hierarchy to describe the data is an interesting idea as it allows for viewing the data at different levels of abstraction, and enables the users to derive rules at a desired level of abstraction. We also will like to point out that the use of the base rough-sets method for rule induction does not impose any static statistical parameters or models upon the data, hence minimizing assumptions and allowing the data to represent itself.

In conclusion we will like to point out that the proposed sequential application of multiple data mining techniques—i.e. conceptual clustering, rough set based rule induction and attribute oriented induction—for symbolic rule generation, appears to be a pragmatic methodology for the intelligent analysis of un-annotated data-vectors.

Acknowledgements

This research is supported by a research grant from the Nova Scotia Health Research Foundation (NSHRF), Canada.

References

1. Fayyad, U.M., Piatetsky-Shapiro, G. & Smyth, P.: Knowledge Discovery and Data Mining: Towards a Unifying Framework. International Conference on Knowledge Discovery in Databases (1996), pp. 82-88.
2. Abidi, S.S.R., Hoe, K. M., Goh, A.: Analyzing Data Clusters: A Rough Set Approach to Extract Cluster Defining Symbolic Rules. In Hoffman F, Hand DJ, Adams N, Fisher D & Guimaraes G (Eds.) Lecture Notes in Computer Science 2189: Advances in Intelligent Data Analysis, Fourth International Conference of Intelligent Data Analysis, Cascais Portugal. Springer Verlag: Berlin, 2001. pp. 248-257.
3. Pawlak, Z.: Rough Sets. In: Lin T.Y., Cercone N. (eds.): Rough Sets and Data Mining: Analysis of Imprecise Data. Kluwer Academic Publishers, Dordrecht (1997) pp. 3-7.
4. Biswas, G., Weinberg, J., Li, C.: ITERATE: A Conceptual Clustering Method for Knowledge Discovery in Database. In Artificial Intelligence in the Petroleum Industry, B. Braunshweig and R. Day, Editors. Editions Techniq, chapter 3, pp. 111-139 (1995).
5. Slowinski K., Slowinski R., Stefanowski J.: Rough Sets Approach to Analysis of Data from Peritoneal Lavage in Acute Pancreatitis. Medical Informatics, vol. 13, pp. 143-159 (1988).
6. Han, J., Cai, Y. and Cercone, N.: Knowledge Discovery in Databases: An Attribute-Oriented Approach. In Proceedings of the 18th VLDB Conference, pp. 547-559, Vancouver, British Columbia, Canada (1992).
7. Shavlik J. W., Dietterich T.G.: Readings in Machine learning, Morgan Kaufman (1990).
8. Quinlan, R.: C4.5: Programs for Machine Learning. Morgan Kaufmann, California (1993).
9. Hu, X., Cercone, N.: Learning Maximal Generalized Decision Rules via Discretization, Generalization and Rough Set Feature Selection. Proc. 9th Int. Conf. on Tools with Artificial Intelligence (1997).
10. GrzymalaBusse J. W.: LERS A System for Learning from Examples Based on Rough Sets. In R. Slowinski, (ed.) Intelligent Decision Support, Kluwer Publishers, pp. 3-18 (1992).
11. Chan C.C., GrzymalaBusse J.W.: On the Two Local Inductive Algorithms: PRISM and LEM2. Foundations of Computing and Decision Sciences, vol. 19 (4), 185204 (1994).
12. Skowron A., Polkowski L.: Synthesis of Decision Systems from Data Tables. In Lin T.Y., Cecrone N.(ed.), Rough Sets and Data Mining, Kluwer Publishers, pp. 289-299 (1997).
13. Ohrn A., Komorowski J.: Diagnosing Acute Appendicitis with Very Simple Classification Rules. 3rd European Symposium on Principles and Practice of Knowledge Discovery in Databases, Prague, Czech Republic, LNAI 1704, Springer-Verlag, pp. 462-467.
14. Goodall, D.W. A New Similarity Index Based On Probability in *Biometrics*, Vol. 22, (1966), pp. 882-907.
15. Arabie P., Hubert L. J.: An Overview of Combinatorial Data Analysis. In Arabie P., Hubert L.J., Soete G.D. (eds) Clustering and Classification, World Scientific Publishing Co., NJ. (1996), pp. 5-63.
16. Bazan J. G.: Dynamic Reducts and Statistical Inference. Proc. 6th Int. Conf. on Information Processing and Management of Uncertainty in Knowledge-Based Systems (IPMIU'96). Vol. 3, Granada, Spain (1996) pp. 1147-1152.
17. Wróblewski, J.: Finding Minimal Reducts using Genetic Algorithms. Proc. 2nd Annual Joint Conf. on Information Sciences, Wrightsville Beach, NC. USA (1995) pp.186-189.
18. Komorowski J., Bjorvand A.T.: Practical Applications of Genetic Algorithms for Efficient Reduct Computation. Proc. of 15th IMACS World Congress on Scientific Computation, Modelling and Applied Mathematics, Berlin (1997).

Trail-and-Error Approach for Determining the Number of Clusters

Haojun Sun and Mei Sun

College of Mathematics and Computer Science, University of Hebei, Baoding Hebei,
071002, China
haojun.sun@mail.hbu.edu.cn, mei.sun@mail.hbu.edu.cn

Abstract. Automatically determining the number of clusters is an important issue in cluster analysis. In this paper, we explore "trial-and-error" approach to determining the number of clusters in a given data set. The fuzzy clustering algorithm, FCM, is selected as the basic "trial" algorithm and cluster validity optimization responses to the "error" procedure. To improve the computation speed, we propose two strategies, eliminating and splitting, which allow the FCM-based algorithms more efficient. To improve existing validity measures, we make use of a new validity function that fits particularly data sets containing overlapping clusters. Experimental results are given to illustrate the performance of the new algorithms.

1 Introduction

Cluster analysis is important issue in data mining. It groups a set of objects into classes or clusters so that objects within a cluster have high similarity, but are very dissimilar in different clusters. Clustering has its root in many fields, such as mathematics, computer science, statistics, biology, and economics. In different application domains, a variety of clustering techniques have been developed, depending on the methods used to represent data, the measures of similarity between data objects, and the techniques for grouping data objects into clusters. Cluster analysis plays an essential role in solving practical problems in such areas as financing, pattern recognition and image processing. Today, cluster analysis is a very active research area.

One of the major issues in cluster analysis is how to determine automatically the number of clusters in a given data set. An intuitive method is "trial-and-error" [1] approach. It pre-clusters the data set into c clusters, where c is a possible value of the number, and evaluate the result using a cluster validity index, which is related to cluster validation problem [2][3]. The pre-clustering often uses a basic clustering algorithm, such as the K-Means or FCM. The cluster validity index provides a numeric criterion for the possible number of clusters, c, by evaluating the clustering result. The optimal value of the index should be obtained at the true number of clusters.

In this paper, we present two new algorithms for automatic determination of the number of clusters. They are based on a basic clustering algorithm and a validity index. Among the clustering algorithms considered are K-Means, FCM and PCM [4] [5] as well as their variants. In this work, we are interested in FCM (Fuzzy C-Means) algorithm. This is motivated by the concept of fuzzy membership in this algorithm that enables the algorithm to effectively deal with outliers and to provide membership grading, which is very important in practice. The FCM is also one of the most widely used clustering algorithms. On the other hands, the choice of an appropriate validity index can have significant impact on the final number of clusters. Although, there are a lot of validity indices in the literature, our recent studies show that they do not perform well if clusters overlap. In this paper, we make use of our new index proposed recently [6]. The focus of this paper is to design efficient elimination and splitting strategies to be used with the basic clustering algorithm so that for each candidate number clusters, the clustering process can be performed starting from previously obtained clusters.

The paper is organized as follows. In section 2, we will present the pre-cluster algorithm, FCM algorithm. In section 3, we will illustrate the FCM-based "try-and-error" algorithm for determination of the number of clusters. In section 4, we will present the new algorithms, one is based on an elimination strategy and another one is based on a splitting strategy. We will also introduce our new validity function. Finally, in section 5, we present the experimental results.

2 Pre-cluster Algorithm

The FCM algorithm dates back to 1973. FCM-based algorithms are the most widely used fuzzy clustering algorithms in practice. The basic FCM algorithm can be formulated as follows:

$$\text{Minimize} \quad J_m(U,V,X) = \sum_{j=1}^{c}\sum_{i=1}^{n} (u_{ij})^m [d(x_j, v_i)] \quad (1)$$

where n is the total number of data in a given data set and c is the number of clusters; $X = \{x_1, x_2, \cdots, x_n\} \subset R^d$ and $V = \{v_1, v_2, \cdots, v_c\} \subset R^d$ are the given set of data and the set of cluster centers; $U = (u_{ki})_{n \times c}$ is a fuzzy partition matrix composed of the membership of each feature vector x_k in each cluster i. u_{ki} should satisfy $\sum_{i=1}^{c} u_{ki} = 1$ for $k = 1, 2, \cdots, n$ and $u_{ki} \geq 0$ for all $i = 1, 2, \cdots, c$ and $k = 1, 2, \cdots, n$. The exponent $m > 1$ is called fizzifier; $J_m(U,V,X)$ is a parameter which modifies the weighting effect of the membership value. Large m tends to result in approximately equal membership values u_{ki}, thus increasing the fuzziness of clusters. $d(x, y) = \|x - y\|$ ($x, y \in R^d$) is a distance function (for example, Euclidean distance). To minimize $J_m(U,V,X)$, the cluster centers (prototypes) v_i and the membership matrix U need to be computed according to the following iterative formula:

$$u_{ki} = \begin{cases} \left(\sum_{j=1}^{c} \left(\frac{\|x_k - v_i\|}{\|x_k - v_j\|} \right)^{\frac{2}{m-1}} \right)^{-1} & \text{if } \|x_k - v_j\| > 0, \forall j. \\ 1 & \text{if } \|x_k - v_i\| = 0 \\ 0 & \text{if } \exists j \neq i \|x_k - v_j\| = 0 \end{cases} \quad \begin{matrix} k=1,2,\cdots n \\ i=1,2,\cdots c \end{matrix} \quad (2)$$

$$v_i = \frac{\sum_{k=1}^{n} u_{ki}^m x_k}{\sum_{k=1}^{n} u_{ki}^m} \quad i=1,2,\cdots,c \quad (3)$$

The cluster centers v_i, $i = 1,2,\cdots,c$, are initialized by some method (for example, Random initialization and the initial elements of the membership matrix, u_{ki}, $k = 1,2,\cdots,n$, $i = 1,2,\cdots c$, are computed using Equation 2. To refine V and U, Equations 2 and 3 are used iteratively until the changes in V or U are sufficiently small. For final classification, the largest value of u_{ki}, $i = 1,2,\cdots c$ is selected to any x_k, and the corresponding i_0 identifies the cluster to which the x_k belongs. The basic Pre-cluster algorithm (FCM) is as follows:

Algo1: Pre-cluster algorithm (FCM Algorithm)
```
1.Input the number of clusters c, the fuzzifier m and the
  distance function ‖·‖ and threshold •>0.
2.Randomly initialize the cluster centers v_i^0 (i=1,2,···,c)
3.Calculate u_{ki}, k=1,2,···,n, i=1,2,···c using Equation 2.
4.Calculate v_i^1, i=1,2,···,c using Equation 3.
5.If max_{1≤i≤c}(‖v_i^0 - v_i^1‖/‖v_i^1‖) ≤ ε then go to Step 6; else let
  v_i^0 = v_i^1 (i=1,2,···,c) and go to Step 3.
6.Output the clustering results: cluster centers
  v_i^1, i=1,2,···,c •membership matrix U and, in some
  applications, the elements of each cluster i, i.e., all
  x_k such that u_{ki} > u_{kj} for all j ≠ i.
7.Stop.
```

3 Original Trial-and-Error Algorithm

The following algorithm indicates the principle of the original trial-and-error approach for automatically determining the number of clusters in a given data set. It applies the FCM clustering algorithm (**Algo1**) as the pre-clustering to the data set for $c = C_{min}, \cdots, C_{max}$ and chooses the best value of c based on a (cluster) validity criterion, $V_d(c)$, which evaluates the pre-cluster results. Here, C_{min} and C_{max} are predefined values that represent, respectively, the minimal and maximal numbers of clusters between which an optimal number is sought.

Algo2: FCM-based trial-and-error algorithm
```
1.Choose C_min and C_max.
2.For c = C_min to C_max:
   2.1. Initialize cluster centers (V) randomly;
   2.2. Apply the basic FCM algorithm to update the
        membership matrix (U) and the cluster centers (V);
   2.3. Test for convergence; if no, go to 2.2;
   2.4. Compute the validity value V_d(c);
```
3. Compute c_{Opt} such that the cluster validity function $V_d(c_{Opt})$ is optimal.
4. Stop.

Several techniques exist for initializing cluster centers (Step 2.1). Random initialization is often used because of its simplicity. Other initialization methods could be used in many cases. Recently, an empirical comparison of four initialization methods for the K-Means algorithm was reported in [7]. According to this study, random initialization is one of the best methods as it makes the K-Means algorithm more effective and less dependent on initial clustering and order of instances. Although it is not clear if these results can be generalized to the case of FCM, it is still reasonable to assume that random initialization is a good choice for **Algo2**.

4 The New Trial-and-Error Approach for Determining the Number of Clusters

In **Algo2**, we use random initialization at the beginning of each clustering phase. It is easy to imagine that re-initialization at each phase could be a source of computational inefficiency. Use of the clustering results obtained in previous phases may lead to a better initialization. We propose strategies that yield a new trial-and-error algorithm. In this section, we will explain the major steps of the algorithms in detail. Experimental results and discussion on the advantages of these algorithms will be given in the following section.

The **Trial-Error-Split Algorithm (TESA)** described below is called a splitting algorithm because it operates by splitting the "worst" cluster at each stage in testing the number of clusters c from C_{min} to C_{max}. The major differences between this algorithm and **Algo2** in the previous section lie in the initialization of cluster centers, the validity index used and the process for splitting "worst" clusters. The general strategy adopted for the new algorithm is as follows: at each step of the new algorithm (**TESA**), we identify the "worst" cluster and split it into two clusters while keeping the other c-1 clusters.

Algo3: TESA (Trial-Error-Split Algorithm)
```
1. Choose C_min and C_max.
2. Initialize C_min cluster centers (V).
3. For c = C_min to C_max:
   3.1. Apply the Algo1 to update the membership matrix
   (U) and the cluster centers (V);
   3.2. Test for convergence; if no, go to 3.1;
   3.3. Compute a validity value V_d(c);
   3.4. Compute a score S(i) for each cluster; split the
   worst cluster.
4. Compute c_f such that the cluster validity index
```
$V_d(c_f)$ is the optimal.

The general idea in the splitting algorithm **TESA** is to identify the "worst" cluster and split it, thus increasing the value of c by one. Our major contribution lies in the definition of the criterion for identifying the "worst" cluster. In this paper, we propose a "score" function $S(i)$ associated with each cluster i, as follows:

$$S(i) = \frac{\sum_{k=1}^{n} u_{ki}}{n_i} \quad (4)$$

here n_i is the number data in cluster i.

In general, if $S(i)$ is small, cluster i tends to contain a large number of data with low membership values. The lower the membership value, the farther the data is from its cluster center. Therefore, a small $S(i)$ means that cluster i is large in volume and sparse in distribution. On the other hand, a larger On the other hand, a larger $S(i)$ tends to mean that cluster i has a smaller number of elements and exerts a strong "attraction" on them. This is the reason we choose the cluster corresponding to the minimum of $S(i)$ as the candidate to split when the value of c is increased. Fig.1 illustrates the cluster i with larger $S(i)$. Fig.2 illustrate the cluster i with a small $S(i)$, the cross indicates the center of the cluster and the blue parts means the area with dense points.

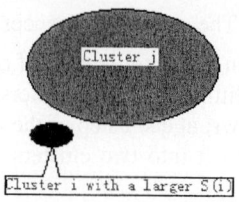 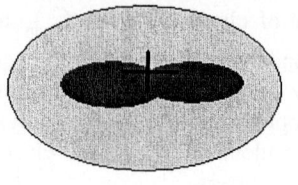

Fig. 1. Cluster with a larger $S(i)$ 　　**Fig. 2.** Cluster with a small $S(i)$

In order to split the cluster at Step 3.4 of **TESA**, we have adopted the "Greedy" technique [8]. The basic idea is first to select a data point within the cluster that is sufficiently far from the initial cluster center and also has a large number of data points nearby. This is the first center of the split. The initial cluster center has been used here as the competition center. After this step, we eliminate the initial center of the cluster and find the second center using the same method except that we use the first center as the competition center. After this step, we eliminate the initial center of the cluster and find the second center using the same method except that we use the first center as the competition center.

5 Cluster Validity Index

In our experiments, we found that currently used validity indices (e.g., partition coefficient, partition entropy, Xie's, FS validity, Rezaee's validity) behave poorly when clusters overlap. This motivated our search for an efficient validity index. In [6], we proposed a new validity index having the following form:

$$V_{WSJ}(c,U,V,X) = Scat(c) + \frac{Sep(c)}{Sep(C_{max})} \tag{5}$$

Here the compactness of the computed clusters is defined as $Scat(c) = \dfrac{\frac{1}{c}\sum_{i=1}^{c}\|\sigma(v_i)\|}{\sigma(X)}$,

where $\sigma(X) = \{\sigma(X)^1, \sigma(X)^2, \cdots, \sigma(X)^d\}$, $\sigma(v_i) = \{\sigma(v_i)^1, \sigma(v_i)^2, \cdots, \sigma(v_i)^d\}$,

$\sigma(X)^p = \frac{1}{n}\sum_{k=1}^{n}(x_k^p - \overline{x}^p)^2$ 　　 $\sigma(v_i)^p = \frac{1}{n}\sum_{k=1}^{n}u_{ki}(x_k^p - \overline{v_i}^p)^2$ (p=1,2,...,d), and

$\overline{x} = \frac{1}{n}\sum_{k=1}^{n}x_k$. On the other hand, $Sep(c) = \dfrac{D_{max}^2}{D_{min}^2}\sum_{i=1}^{c}\left(\sum_{j=1}^{c}\|v_i - v_j\|^2\right)^{-1}$, where $D_{min} = \min\limits_{i\neq j}\|v_i - v_j\|$ and $D_{max} = \max\limits_{i,j}\|v_i - v_j\|$ represents separations between clusters.

The cluster number that minimizes V_{WSJ} is considered to be the optimal value for the number of clusters present in the data set. This index has proved to be particularly efficient in dealing with overlapping clusters (see [6] for more details). Concerning the experiments reported here, V_{WSJ} is used in all of **Algo2** and **TESA**.

6 Experimental Results

In this section, we show the performance of the new algorithms on several real data sets. Among the test data sets, we have used the public data sets X_{30} and IRIS, a number of generated data sets with overlapping clusters and a high dimensional data set from G5. There are two aspects of performance to be considered here. One concerns the ability of the new algorithm to find the exact number of clusters. The other one concerns the computational efficiency of the new algorithms. For the first aspect, we have obtained similar results with any of the three algorithms to those reported in our previous paper [6]. In other words, the new algorithm (**TESA**) perform similarly as **Algo2**, i.e. they find very accurately the true number of clusters for each of the test data sets with V_{WSJ} as validity index. Furthermore, they produce almost the same cluster centers when the number of clusters tested are close to the true number of clusters. Our extensive experiments have shown that the use of V_{WSJ} as validity index is the major factor to guarantee the accuracy of the number of clusters determined. This extends the conclusions made in our previous paper [6], in which the experimental results were obtained only from **Algo2** (with different validity indices). Therefore, the elimination and splitting strategies used in **TESA** do an efficient job to circumscribe the search space of the trial-and-error algorithm.

In the follows, we will focus on the computational efficiency of the new algorithms as well as on the accuracy of cluster centers obtained. In comparing **TESA** with **Algo2**, we are particularly interested in reduction in the number of iterations for each subsequent value of c tested. We will also compare the cluster centers obtained at the optimal number of clusters (c_{Opt}) with the true centers of clusters when they are known. We report here test results on three data sets.

In all experiments, the fuzzifier m in the algorithm was set to 2, the test for convergence in the basic FCM algorithm (**Algo1**) was performed using $\varepsilon = 0.001$, and the distance function $\|\cdot\|$ was defined as Euclidean distance. Choosing the best range of the number of clusters is a difficult problem. Here we adopted Bezdek's suggestion: $C_{min} = 2$ and $C_{max} = \sqrt{n}$ [9]. Initialization of cluster centers in **TESA** (step 2) and **Algo2** (step2.1) used the random procedure. In order to decrease the effect of random initialization in each algorithm, we run each algorithm 20 times and record the average number of iterations for each c and the CPU time.

6.1 Tests on Data Set X_{30} and IRIS

Test results on the public domain data sets X_{30}, which has three clusters and a total of 30 data points, and IRIS [10], which has three clusters and a total of 150 data points were reported here. The Tables 1 and 2 give the true cluster centers in each data set and the computed cluster centers by **TESA**. Figure 3 and 4 show the average number of iterations that **Algo2** and **TESA** need for each value of c and for each test set. The last column on these figures shows also the real (average) CPU time taken by each algorithm.

Table 1. Comparison between the true centers and obtained centers by **TESA** on X_{30}

	True centers	Obtained centers	Error
Cluster1	(1.77, 2.22)	(1.771, 2.221)	(0.001, 0.001)
Cluster2	(11.27, 12.05)	(11.287, 12.053)	(0.018, 0.003)
Cluster3	(5.39, 6.07)	(5.392, 6.074)	(0.002, 0.004)

Table 2. Comparison between the true centers and obtained centers by **TESA** on IRIS

	True centers	Obtained centers	Error
Cluster1	(6.59, 2.97, 5.55, 2.03)	(6.77, 3.05, 5.64, 2.05)	(0.18, 0.02, 0.09, 0.02)
Cluster2	(5.00, 3.42, 1.47, 0.24)	(5.00, 3.40, 1.49, 0.25)	(0, -0.02, 0.02, 0.01)
Cluster3	(5.92, 2.77, 4.26, 1.33)	(5.87, 2.76, 4.36, 1.40)	(-0.05, -0.01, 0.1, 0.07)

From these results and from the results on similar small size data sets, we could make following conclusions:

– The cluster centers computed by **TESA** are accurate for small data sets containing less than several hundred data points (which is the case for most public domain data sets). Even when there are overlapping clusters, which is the case of IRIS data set, the new algorithms is still able to produce very good estimates. However, it is difficult to carry out these comparisons on real large data sets because the information required for the comparison such as the true number of clusters and true cluster centers is often not available.
– In terms of computational efficiency, **TESA** needs, in general, less number of iterations than **Algo2**.
– It is easy to understand that the number of iterations for each value of c tends to be small when c is close to the true number of clusters. When the value of c moves away from the true number of clusters, **TESA** tend to have a more brutal increase in the number of iterations. Another very interesting property of the algorithm is that the number of iterations is very stable for each value of c. The good property that could be useful if we want to develop a strategy to further limit the search range of c.

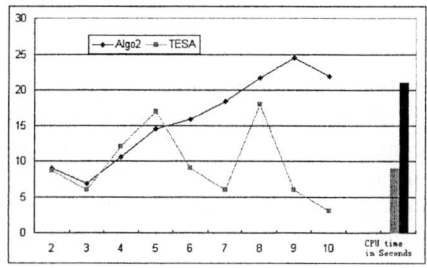

Fig. 3. Comparison of the number of iteration of Algo2 and TESA on the data set X_{30}

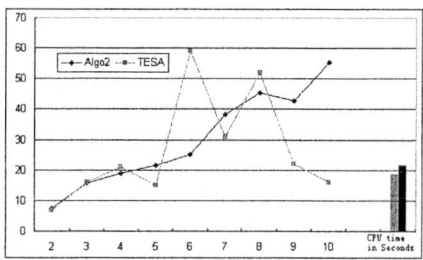

Fig. 4 Comparison of the number of iteration of Algo2 and TESA on the data set IRIS

6.2 Test on Generation 5 Data Set

To further illustrate the computational efficiency of the proposed algorithm, we report here experiments on a real data set from Generation 5 (G5). The data set contains 10,000 data points and each point has 22 variables. We do not know exactly the number of clusters. The number is estimated to be between 4 and 8. The three algorithms **Algo2** and **TESA** conclude that the number of cluster is 5, which is acceptable. The number of iterations that **Algo2** and **TESA** need for each value of c is shown in Figure 5. This is a more convincing example that **Algo2** needs more iterations than **TESA**. For the CPU time, **TESA** is about 50\% faster than **Algo2**. We are obtained constantly similar results with data sets of about same size.

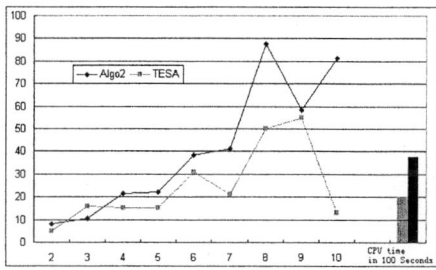

Fig. 5. Comparison of the number of iteration of Algo2 and TESA on the data set of G5

7 Conclusion

The major achievements of this paper are an improved FCM-based algorithm for determining the number of clusters. The new algorithm has been tested on many data sets, of which some contain strong overlapping clusters. The results obtained have shown several clear advantages over other FCM-based algorithms, which benefits from the use of a new validity index and strategies to better initialize the cluster centers. We are currently working on integration of these algorithms into a data mining system.

References

1. A.K. Jain and R.C. Dubes, "Algorithms for Clustering Data. NJ: Prentice-Hall", Englewood Cliffs, 1988.
2. M. Rezae, B. Letlieveldt, and J. Reiber, "A new cluster validity index for the fuzzy c-means," Pattern Recognition Letters, vol. 19, pp. 237-246, 1998
3. H. Rhee and K. Oh, "A Validity Measure for Fuzzy Clustering and Its Use in Selecting Optimal Number of Clusters," in Proceedings of IEEE, pp. 1020-1025, 1996.
4. J. Bezdek, "Fuzzy mathematics in pattern classification." Ph.D. Dissertation, Cornell University, 1973.
5. R. Krishnapuram and J. Keller, "A possibilistic approach to clustering," Fuzzy Systems, vol. 1, pp. 98-109, May 1993.
6. H. Sun, S. Wang, and Q. Jiang, "A new validation index for determining the number of clusters in a data set," in Proceedings of IJCNN, (Washington DC., USA), pp. 1852-1857, July 2001.
7. J. Pena, J. Lozano, and P. Larranaga, "An empirical comparison of four initialization methods for the k-means algorithm," Pattern Recognition Letters, vol. 20, pp. 1027-1040, 1999.
8. T. Gonzalez, \Clustering to Minimize and Maximum Intercluster Distance," Theoretical Computer Science, vol. 38, pp. 293-306, 1985.
9. J. Bezdek, "Chapter F6: Pattern Recognition in Handbook of Fuzzy Computation," IOP Publishing Ltd, 1998.
10. N. Pal and J. Bezdek, "On Cluster Validity for the Fuzzy C-Means Model," *IEEE Trans. On Fuzzy Systems*, vol. 3, no. 3, pp. 370-390, 1995.

Unifying Genetic Algorithm and Clustering Method for Recognizing Activated fMRI Time Series

Lin Shi, Pheng Ann Heng, and Tien-Tsin Wong

Department of Computer Science and Engineering,
The Chinese University of Hong Kong, Shatin, NT, Hong Kong
{lshi, pheng, ttwong}@cse.cuhk.edu.hk

Abstract. In order to get more reliable activation detection result in functional MRI data, we attempt to bring together the advantages of the genetic algorithm, which is deterministic and able to escape from the local optimal solution, and the K-means clustering, which is fast. Thus a novel clustering approach, namely the genetic K-means algorithm, is proposed to detect fMRI activation. It is more likely to find a global optimal solution to the K-means clustering, and is independent of the initial assignments of the cluster centroids. The experimental results show that the proposed method recognizes fMRI activation regions with higher accuracy than ordinary K-means clustering.

1 Introduction

Based on the blood oxygen level-dependent (BOLD) principle, functional magnetic resonance imaging (fMRI) has become one of the typical tools in the neurological disease diagnosis and human brain research. Because of the low signal-to-noise ratio (SNR), the complexity of noise sources, and the diversity in experiment design, detecting activated regions in fMRI still remains challenging. The fMRI dataset is a 4-dimensional dataset, which is not only composed of spatial correlation, but also sharing temporal relationship.

The existing activation detection methods can be roughly categorized into two families, *hypothesis-based* and *exploratory* approaches. The hypothesis-based methods parametrically fit a prior model (e.g. general linear model [1]) to the data. A representative of this category is the statistical parametric mapping (SPM) [2]. Exploratory approaches, on the other hand, aim at revealing the activation information in fMRI data content without prior knowledge. Principal component analysis (PCA) [2], independent component analysis (ICA) [3], and clustering methods are examples of this category.

The most popular clustering method to analyze the fMRI data is the fuzzy K-means algorithm, the fuzzy version of the simple and popular clustering algorithm, K-means algorithm. K-means algorithm is based on a simple iterative scheme for finding a locally optimal solution, and thus may converge to a suboptimal partition. This algorithm starts with a randomly initialization of centroids, and iteratively generates new sets of centroids using the existing centroids with very simple steps.

The basic idea of applying genetic algorithm to clustering is to simulate the evolution process in nature and evolve clustering solutions from one generation to the next. In contrast to the K-means algorithm, which might converge to a local optimum, the genetic clustering algorithm is insensitive to the initial assignment and always converges to the global optimum eventually [4] [5]. In this paper, we apply the genetic K-means algorithm to cluster the fMRI time series, which is expected to converge to the global optimal clustering solution with higher detection accuracy.

2 Method

2.1 Framework

Fig. 1 gives the framework of fMRI clustering via genetic K-means algorithm. The first phase is the fMRI data preprocessing. The raw fMRI slices are first spatially and temporally aligned. Then the time series are normalized and detrended so that the resultant data only reflects the variation. Finally, the size of the dataset is reduced by removing the voxels that are definitely not activated voxels based on their correlation coefficient with the stimulation.

The second phase is the clustering of the time series by genetic K-means algorithm. It consists of an initialization step, where the initial population P_0 is generated. Then the genetic operators, namely the selection, mutation and K-means operators, are applied to evolve the next generation P_{i+1}. This evolution is performed until a termination condition is satisfied. The clustering result

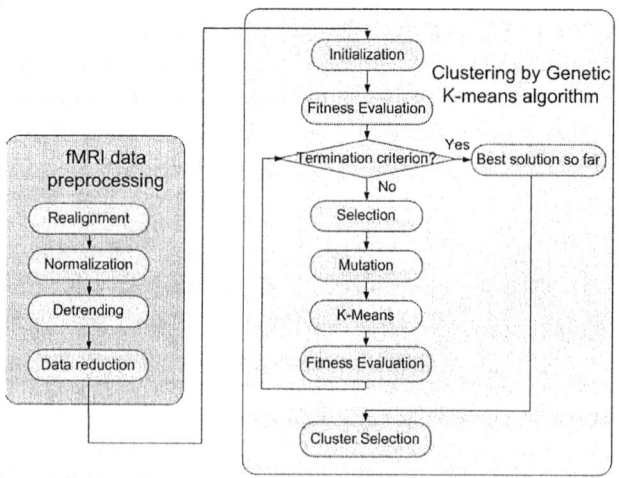

Fig. 1. Framework of fMRI time series clustering via genetic K-means algorithm

is considered to be a proper partition that distinguishes the activated voxels from the non-activated ones. The cluster whose centroid has larger correlation coefficients with the stimulation paradigm is selected as the activated cluster.

2.2 Chromosome Encoding

Suppose the fMRI dataset consists of N patterns, which corresponds to the N time series. Each pattern is a D dimensional vector representing D intensity values recorded on D time points respectively. The goal of the genetic K-means algorithm is to partition the N patterns into K groups, such that the total within cluster square error ($TWCSE$) is minimized. The $TWCSE$ is defined as follows:

$$TWCSE = \sum_{k=1}^{K} \sum_{X_i \in C_k} \|X_i - z_k\|^2$$

where C_k represents the kth cluster. Let $X_1, X_2, \cdots, X_N$ be the N samples, and X_{id} denotes the intensity of time series X_i in time point d. Each partition is represented by a string, a sequence of numbers $a_1 a_2 \cdots a_N$, where a_i is the index of the cluster that sample X_i belongs in this partition. a_i is also called an *allele*. The centroid of cluster C_k is calculated by $z_k = \frac{\sum_{X_i \in C_k} X_i}{|C_k|}$, where $|C_k|$ denotes the cardinality of C_k. The genetic K-means algorithm maintains a population of coded solutions. Each solution is called a chromosome, coded by a string $a_1 a_2 \cdots a_N$ of length N, where a_i takes a value from $\{1, 2, \cdots, K\}$ representing the cluster index to which the corresponding pattern belongs. For example, $a_1 a_2 a_3 a_4 a_5 = $ "11221" encodes a partition of 5 patterns where X_1, X_2, and X_5 belong to cluster 1, and X_3 and X_4 belong to cluster 2.

Given a partition $S_i = a_1 \cdots a_N$, let $e(S_i)$ be the number of non-empty clusters in S_i divided by K. $e(S_i)$ is called the legality ratio. We say chromosome S_i is legal if $e(S_i)$ is equal to 1, and illegal otherwise. Hence, an illegal chromosome represents a partition in which some clusters are empty. For example, given $K = 3$, the string $a_1 a_2 a_3 a_4 a_5 = $ "11222" is illegal since cluster 3 is empty.

2.3 Fitness Function

The fitness value of each solution in the current population is defined as its merit to survive in the next generation. In the context of fMRI time series clustering, since our aim is to partition the time series patterns into K clusters according to their similarities, it is natural to minimize the $TWCSE$. Partition with smaller $TWCSE$ should have higher probability to survive and should be assigned with greater fitness value. As we do not expect to see the partition that contains empty cluster, illegal chromosomes are less preferred and deserve lower fitness values. Thus, the fitness value for chromosome S_i is defined as

$$F(S_i) = \begin{cases} 1.5 \times TWCSE_{max} - TWCSE(S_i) & \text{if } S_i \text{ is legal} \\ e(S_i) \times F_{min} & \text{otherwise} \end{cases} \quad (1)$$

Note that $TWCSE_{max}$ is the maximal $TWCSE$ value in previous generations, F_{min} is the smallest fitness value of the legal strings in the current population if they exist, otherwise F_{min} is defined as 1. This definition simply implies that a solution with a smaller $TWCSE$ should have a greater fitness value and has a higher probability to survive. Illegal solutions are allowed to survive too but with lower fitness values.

2.4 Genetic K-Means Algorithm

The pseudocode of genetic K-means algorithm is presented as follows.

Genetic K-Means Algorithm
Input:
   Population size: N
   Mutation probability: p_m
   Maximum number of generation: MAX_GEN
Output: Solution chromosome: s^*

Initialize the population P;
$s^* = S_1$ (the first chromosome in population P);
for $gNo = 1$ to MAX_GEN
   Calculate the fitness values for chromosomes in P;
   $S_i = selection(S_i)$;
   for $i = 1$ to N, $S_i = Mutation(S_i)$;
   for $i = 1$ to N, $S_i = K\text{-}Means(S_i)$;
   $s =$ chromosome in P that has the highest fitness value;
   if $(F(s^*) < F(s))$ $s^* = s$;
end
output s^*;

Selection Operator. The probability of each chromosome S_i in the previous generation to be selected is as follows

$$p(S_i) = \frac{F(S_i)}{\sum_{j=1}^{N} F(S_i)} \quad (2)$$

Here, $F(S_i)$ is the fitness value of chromosome S_i in the current population, as have been defined in 2.3. We use the roulette wheel strategy for this random selection.

Mutation Operator. The mutation operator changes an allele a_j in a chromosome S_i to a new value a'_j with probability p_m, where p_m is called the *mutation probability* and can be specified by the user. The mutation probability is preferred to be small because high values may lead to oscillating behavior of the algorithm. In order to generate an offspring superior to their parents, to facilitate the algorithm escape from the local optimum, and to redirect the algorithm toward the global optimum solution, the mutation operator is designed in the following way.

The mutation operator mutates a_j to a'_j for all $j = 1, \cdots, N$ in the same run. a'_j is selected randomly from $(1, \cdots, K)$ with the probability $(p_1, \cdots, p_K)$, where p_k is computed as

$$p_k = \frac{\alpha \times D_{max}(X_\ell) - D(X_\ell, z_k) + \beta}{\sum_{k=1}^{K}(\alpha \times D_{max}(X_\ell) - D(X_\ell, z_k) + \beta)} \tag{3}$$

Note that $D(X_\ell, z_k)$ is the Euclidean distance between the pattern X_ℓ and the centroid z_k of the kth cluster. And $D_{max}(X_\ell) = \max D(X_\ell, z_k)$. $D(X_\ell, z_k)$ is defined as zero if cluster C_k is empty. α and β are the user specified parameters, where $\beta \neq 0$ is introduced in order to avoid divide-by-zero error in the case that all patterns are equal and are assigned to the same cluster in the solution. In this definition, we allow illegal chromosomes and have the following considerations. Firstly, each cluster may be randomly reassigned with a probability. Secondly, the probability of changing allele value a_j to a cluster number k is greater if it is closer to the centroid of cluster C_k. Thirdly, the empty cluster can be viewed as the closest cluster.

K-Means Operator. Simply utilizing the mutation operators may take more time to converge, because the initial assignments are arbitrary and the subsequent changes of the assignments are probabilistic. We adopt the K-means operator after mutation, which has the advantage of converging very fast.

Assume a chromosome in the current population P is S_i. The K-means operator consists of two steps:

1. Recalculate the cluster centroids using $z_k = \frac{\sum_{X_\ell \in C_k} X_\ell}{|C_k|}$.
2. Reassign each data point to the cluster with the nearest cluster centroid, i.e. $a'_j = \arg \min_k \{D(X_\ell, C_k)\}$.

Note that we define $D(X_\ell, C_k) = \infty$ if the kth cluster is empty. And the purpose of this definition is to avoid assigning all patterns to empty clusters. Illegal string will still remain illegal after performing K-means operator.

In our experiments, the values of the above parameters are: population size N is 50, the number of generations MAX_GEN is 50, mutation probability p_m is 0.005, and coefficients α and β are 1.5 and 0.5 respectively.

3 Experiments and Result

3.1 Data Preprocessing

Realignment. We use the SPM99 software (http://www.fil.ion.ucl.ac.uk/spm/software/spm99/) to perform the data realignment in this work.

Normalization and Detrending. We first normalize the fMRI time series by subtracting the mean value for each of the time series, and adjust the variance of each time course to be one. The spline detrending method is applied to remove the baseline drift [6].

Data Reduction. If we take all time-varying signals as the data input into the clustering procedure, serious problems would occur. As "activated" voxels are only a small fraction of the whole brain voxels, the potential clusters would be ill-balanced, so the K-means clustering could generate inaccurate outcomes. Moreover, the large number of data brings unnecessary computational burden in the clustering. Noting these facts, we use the F-test [7] to remove time courses that definitely will not be considered as "activated" [8].

3.2 Phantom Data

We construct the phantom dataset via simulating a single time-varying slice of fMRI data that contains 79×95 voxels. The length of each time series is 200. The baseline image is the average of slice No.30 in the preprocessed auditory dataset described in subsection 3.3. According to [9], the BOLD response $b(t)$ can be modeled by

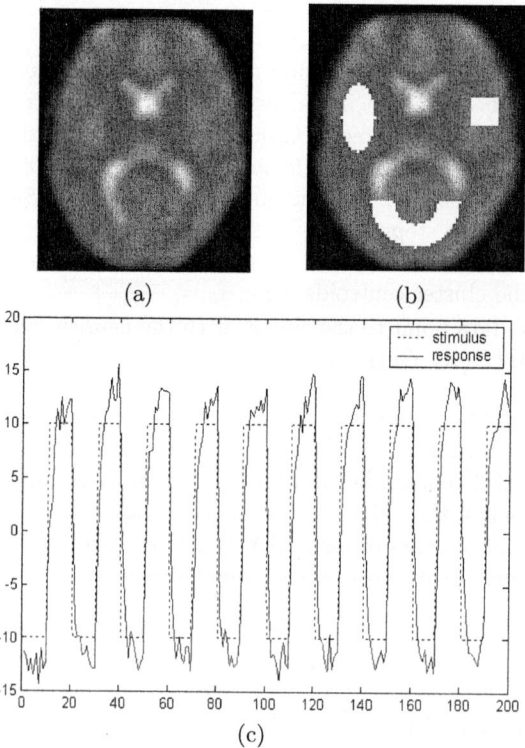

Fig. 2. Phantom dataset (a) baseline slice (b) spatial layout of the artificial activation regions (c) artificial response and the stimulus for reference

$$h_a(t) = \left(1 - e^{-\frac{1}{t_a}}\right)^2 (t+1)e^{-\frac{t}{t_a}}$$
$$h_b(t) = \left(1 - e^{-\frac{1}{t_b}}\right)^2 e^{-\frac{t}{t_b}}$$
$$b(t) = c_a(h_a * s)(t - t_0) + c_b(h_b * s)(t - t_0) + c_c(h_a * s)(t - t_0)(h_b * s)(t - t_0)$$

where $s(t)$ represents the stimulus paradigm.

Three activation areas are generated with the same activation pattern, i.e. with the same setting of the parameters: $c_a = 0.6$, $c_b = 0.02$, $c_c = 0.2$, $t_a = 1$, $t_b = 10$, $t_0 = 2$. The baseline slice is shown in Fig. 2(a). The spatial layout of the artificial activation regions are given in Fig. 2(b). And the stimulus paradigm (dash line) and the simulated BOLD response in the activated areas (solid line) are plotted in Fig 2(c). Then we add onto all the voxels the additive white Gaussian noise with intensities proportional to the baseline voxel intensities, thus simulate noise conditions with various Contrast-to-Noise Ratio (CNR).

Fig. 3 shows the activated voxels detected by K-means (b) and genetic K-means (c) respectively. As the genetic K-means algorithm converges to the

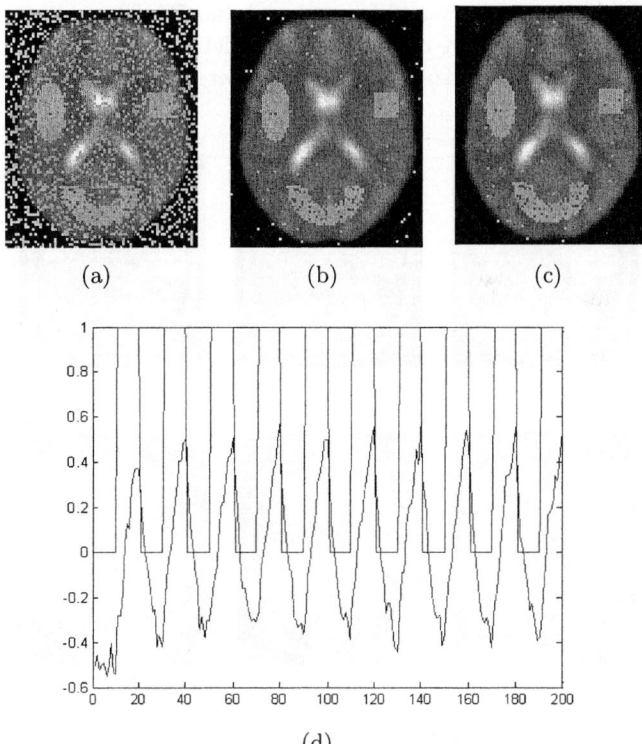

Fig. 3. The activation detection results on phantom fMRI dataset (a) the result after data reduction (b) activation detected by K-means (c) activation detected by genetic K-means (d) the average variation pattern detected by genetic K-means

global minimum instead of the local minimum, its result with less isolated voxels compared with that of K-means algorithm.

3.3 Real fMRI Data

We also test our method on a real fMRI dataset acquired from the Wellcome Department of Cognitive Neurology with permission from the Functional Imaging Laboratory. The experiment was conducted to measure the activation in the subjects brain when given an auditory bi-syllabic stimulation. This whole brain BOLD/EPI data was acquired with a modified 2-T SIEMENS scanner and the TR is set to 7 sec. The spatial resolution of the volume data is $64 \times 64 \times 64$, and the size of the voxel is $3mm \times 3mm \times 3mm$. In the experiment, the subject is given a boxcar stimulation: first begin with rest, and switch between rest (6 scans, last for 42 sec) and stimulation (6 scans, last for 42 sec). By discarding the first few scans, the total 96 scans acquired are reduced to 84 scans.

We also test the performance of our method on this in vivo dataset, and the detection results are superimposed onto the corresponding anatomical MRI dataset. Fig. 4 shows resultant activated voxels on the 31th, 32th and 33th slices by K-means and genetic K-means respectively. All the results cover the Brodmanns area (BA) 42 (primary auditory cortex) and BA 22 (auditory associated area). However, the genetic K-means algorithm detected more continuous "activated" regions, i.e. with less isolated voxels compared to the K-means clustering.

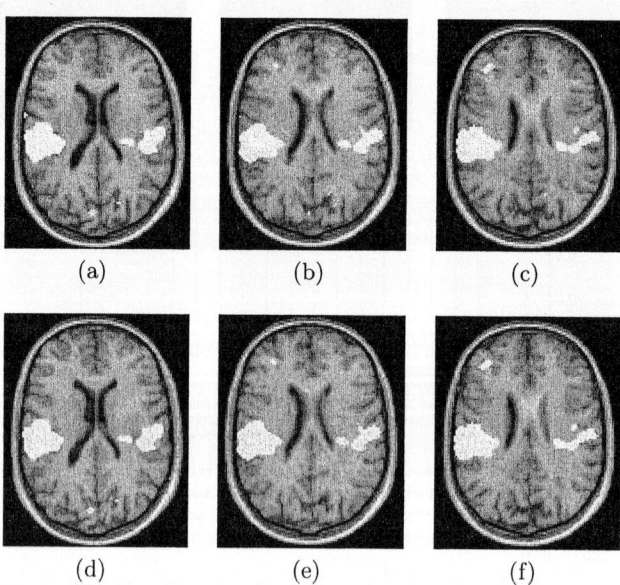

Fig. 4. The "activated" clusters detected by K-means and genetic K-means algorithms. (a), (b), and (c) show the result from K-means algorithm on the 31~33th slices of the real fMRI dataset; (d), (e), and (f) are the result from genetic K-means algorithm on the 31~33th slices of the real fMRI dataset. Note that all the results are superimposed onto the corresponding anatomical MRI slices.

3.4 Statistical Results

In Fig. 5(a), we find that the $TWCSE$ almost remains unchanged after the number of iteration is equal to or above 7. We define the misclassification ratio to be the number of misclassified voxels (time series) divided by the total number of voxels (time series). We record the misclassification ratio of ordinary K-means algorithm and genetic K-means algorithm under different CNR values, which is shown in Fig. 5(b). From this experiment, we can find that the genetic K-means algorithm detects activated voxels with higher accuracy than ordinary K-means algorithm under various noise conditions.

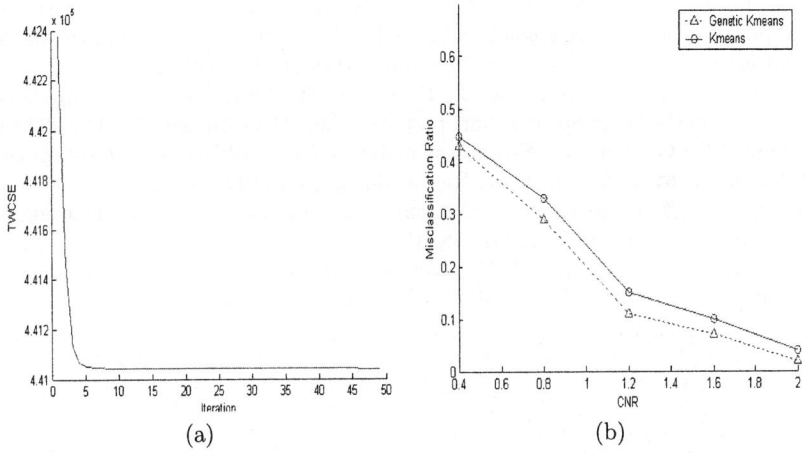

Fig. 5. (a) The value of $TWCSE$ in different iteration (b) The misclassification ratios on phantom dataset under different CNR values

4 Conclusion

In this paper, a genetic version of the K-means algorithm is utilized to cluster the fMRI time series so that the activated voxels can be detected. This genetic K-means algorithm is able to converge to the global optimal clustering solution and thus is more reliable than the K-means algorithm. The experiments show the effectiveness of this clustering method on the phantom fMRI dataset as well as the *in vivo* fMRI dataset.

Acknowledgment

This work was supported by a grant from the Research Grants Council of the Hong Kong Special Administrative Region, China (Project No. CUHK4223/04E)

References

1. Bandettini, P.A., Jesmanowicz, A., Wong, E.C., Hyde, J.S.: Processing strategies for time-course data sets in functional mri of the human brain. Magn Reson Med **30** (1993) 161–173
2. Sychra, J.J., Bandettini, P.A., Bhattacharya, N., Lin, Q.: Synthetic images by subspace transforms. i. principal components images and related filters. Med Phys **21** (1994) 193–201
3. Mckeown, M.J., Makeig, S., Brown, G.G., Jung, T.P., Kindermann, S.S., Bell, A.J., Sejnowski, T.J.: Analysis of fmri data by blind separation into independent spatial components. Hum Brain Mapp. **6** (1998) 160–188
4. Krishna, K., Murty, M.: Genetic k-means algorithm. IEEE Trans. on Systems, Man and Cyber. Part B:Cybernetics **29** (1999) 433C439
5. Lu, Y., Lu, S., Fotouhi, F., Deng, Y., Brown, S.: Fast genetic k-means algorithm and its application in gene expression data analysis. Technical Report TR-DB-06-2003 (2003) http://www.cs.wayne.edu/ luyi/publication/tr0603.pdf
6. Tanabe, J., Miller, D., Tregellas, J., Freedman, R., Meyer, F.G.: Comparison of detrending methods for optimal fmri preprocessing. NeuroImage **15** (2002) 902–907
7. Ardekani, B.A., Kanno, I.: Statistical methods for detecting activated regions in functional mri of the brain. Magn Reson Imaging **16** (1998) 1217C1225
8. Goutte, C., Toft, P., Rostrup, E., Nielsen, F.A., Hansen, L.K.: On clustering fmri time series. NeuroImage **9** (1999) 298–310
9. Purdon, P., Solo, V., Brown, E.M., Weisskoff, R.: Functional mri signal modeling with spatial and temporal correlations. NeuroImage **14** (2001) 912–923

Repeating Pattern Discovery from Audio Stream

Zhen-Long Du[1,2] and Xiao-Li Li[1]

[1] Lanzhou University of Technology, Lanzhou, 730050, P.R. China
duzhl-cad@263.net, lixiaoli@lut.cn
[2] State Key Lab of CAD&CG, Zhejiang University,
Hangzhou 310058, P.R. China
duzhl@cad.zju.edu.cn

Abstract. In this paper, an effective method to discover repeating pattern from audio is proposed. Since the previous feature extraction methods are usually process monophony audio, for extracting more descriptive features from polyphony audio, Gabor filters bank is introduced. Meanwhile the measure criteria is suggested for qualitatively and quantitatively weighting the discernibility of extracted features. In addition, the presented algorithm is based on the incremental match and has time complexity $O(nlog(n))$. Experimental evaluations show that our proposed method could extract complete and meaningful repeating patterns from polyphony audio.

1 Introduction

With the advance of digitizing technique, more and more media archives are produced. In these archives, huge exploitable information is contained. Thus a method which can quickly index media archives is urgent to people's usage. In this paper, we only focus on audio media. The involved repeating pattern [1] in audio, which is often used by music composers to express one specific theme, is important in many applications, such as audio analysis, audio thumbnail [2], audio summarization, and audio retrieval. In the paper, a method for discovering audio repeating pattern is presented, which is an extension of Hsu's method[7]. Meanwhile, Gabor filters bank is exploited for extracting audio features from spectrogram. The proposed approach could find out the repeating pattern from polyphonic audio.

How to extract audio features is crucial to audio process, and the number of dominant features is often related with audio characteristics. Gu and Zhang [3] employed the eigen-decomposition method to extract dominant feature vectors, but the prior threshold is set for weighting the importance of eigen-vector. Gu's approach may cause different frames to be with unequal size of vector, moreover, the threshold setting depends on the audio type.

Audio feature extracted by the existing methods could not fully represent the audio content. According to the audio constitution, audio could be categorized two classes: monophony and polyphony. Audio sung by single musical instrument belongs to the monophony type, and the polyphony consists of many monophonys. In monophony processing, MFCC (Mel Frequency Cepstral Coefficients) [2,5] is widely used, and it is sufficient for most cases. However, MFCC is prone to vary when arrangements of accompaniments or melody are changed after repetition, which might lead to undesired results. Gabor filters bank [4] is broadly used in image processing, it can capture more thorough features than conventional filter. Wolfe [4] ever applied Gabor wavelet to construct the optimal audio dictionary. In this paper we extract audio feature from the spectrogram by Gabor filters bank.

The rest of the paper is organized as follows. In the following section, we discuss how to make use of spectrogram and design Gabor filters bank. In section 3, we present the algorithm of repeating pattern finding. In section 4 some experiment evaluations are exhibited, and the last one is the conclusion.

2 Spectrogram and Gabor Filters Bank Design

In this section, we discuss why we choose spectrogram, and how to design Gabor filters bank.

2.1 Spectrogram

Spectrogram is a three-dimensional (time, frequency, intensity) representation of acoustic signal. It depicts the time-frequency distribution of audio with an easy interpretation manner, as the illustration of Fig. 1(b). Based on the spectrogram, it is readily to find out some acoustic features, so we employ it for discovering repeating pattern from audio. The spectrogram construction is composed of two procedures: firstly transforming the signal from temporal domain to frequency domain by STFT (Short Time Fourier Transform); then, uniformly sampling in temporal domain and exponentially sampling in frequency domain from the transformed signal. In Fig. 1(b), it displays the spectrogram of *welcome*-the starting music of Windows 2000, the sidebar(Fig. 1(c)) gives the color plate used in spectrogram. We easily observe that many small patches with similar color appear more than once in different frequency band (horizontal and vertical axes of the spectrogram represent time t and frequency f, respectively), these repetitive patches are the repeating pattern which we will find.

MFCC is widely used for speech recognition as well as audio classification. In Fig. 1(a), it illustrates six MFCC coefficients. From them, it is difficult to tell where the location of repeating pattern is. Comparing with MFCC, spectrogram is more suitable for finding repeating pattern.

We conclude the characteristics of MFCC and spectrogram, and state as follows.

1. MFCC and spectrogram are results of spectral-decomposition. The decomposition is based on DCT (discrete cosine transform) transformation.

2. MFCC and spectrogram are all the results of non-linear sample in frequency domain. This kind of sampling technique is even suitable for human auditory system.

3. Spectrogram is more intuitive than MFCC in the representation form.

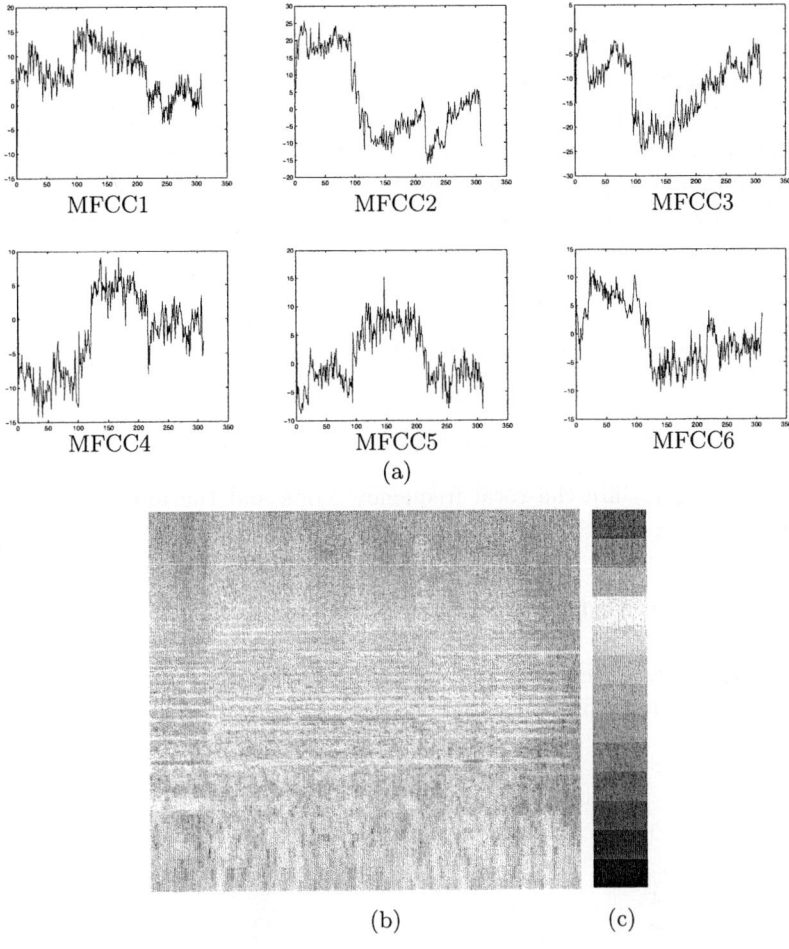

Fig. 1. MFCC and Spectrogram

Essentially speaking, it is hard to say which kind of representation is better. We are in favor of choosing spectrogram because it can represent the characteristics of all frequency bands in one figure, and facilitate us to thoroughly grasp the audio essence.

2.2 Gabor Filters Bank

Individual two dimensional Gabor filter is sinusoidally modulated Gaussian function, Gabor filters bank consists of Gabor filter with different scales and orientations. Gabor filter is the elliptic gaussian function, hence it bears the anisotropy property. In implementation each Gabor filter is positioned at different location, therefore, the output presents local characteristic, not like FFT transformation, whose output is global. The Gabor filters bank is defined as that:

$$G_{ij}(\omega_t, \omega_F) = G(\omega_t - \omega_{t_i}^0, \omega_F - \omega_{F_j}^0) \qquad (1)$$

where

$$G(\omega_t, \omega_F) = \exp(\frac{-\omega_t^2}{2\sigma_{t_i}^2}) \exp(\frac{-\omega_F^2}{2\sigma_{F_j}^2})$$

with $1 \leq i \leq M$ and $1 \leq j \leq N$, M and N are the number of scales and orientations, respectively. And t and F denote time and frequency. Each Gabor filter is determined by an unique quadruple $(\sigma_{t_i}, \omega_{t_i}^0, \sigma_{F_j}, \omega_{F_j}^0)$, the filter location is decided by $\omega_{t_i}^0$ and $\omega_{F_j}^0$, and the shape by σ_{t_i} and σ_{F_j}. The evaluation of quadruple is given below:

$$\sigma_{t_i} = \pi/2N$$
$$\omega_{t_i}^0 = 2\sigma_{t_i}(i-1)$$
$$\sigma_{F_j} = 2^{j-1}\sigma$$
$$\omega_{F_j}^0 = \omega_{min} + \{1 + 3(2^{j-1} - 1)\}\sigma$$

where σ and ω_{min} are the total frequency scope and the minimal frequency, respectively.

3 Repeating Pattern Finding by Correlation Matrix

In this section, we discuss how to exploit the filtered output of Gabor filters bank for finding repeating pattern.

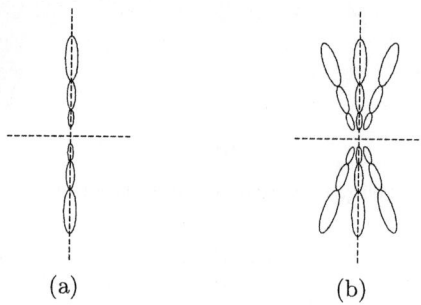

Fig. 2. Configuration of Gabor Filters Bank

At any location (t, f) of spectrogram, we employ Gabor filters bank to extract audio features $A = [g_1, g_2, \ldots, g_{MN}]$, each item of which corresponds to one filtered output of Gabor filters bank.

3.1 Audio Frame Feature

Individual audio frame feature is drawn from the Gabor filter output within one frame. The Gabor filter result at any location could be evaluated according to the discussions in subsection 2.2 and 3.1. Direct exploitation these feature causes heavy computation, so it is need to cluster them into a representative feature for a frame.

Let $\mathcal{A} = [A_1^T, A_2^T, \ldots, A_\mathcal{S}^T]$ be the frame matrix, the subscript $\mathcal{S}$ is the total sample number of a frame, it is set to 256 × 15 in most cases. Each column component of $\mathcal{A}$ is composed of the filter output of the same time. We employ SVD method to evaluate the eigen-vector $\Lambda = [\lambda_1, \lambda_2, \ldots, \lambda_\mathcal{K}]$ of $\mathcal{A}$, and use Λ as audio frame feature. $\mathcal{K}$ is the number of frame feature.

3.2 Construction of Correlation Matrix

For any two audio frames U and V, their corresponding eigen-values are Λ_U and Λ_V. We apply L_2 norm to weight the frame discernibility. The audio frame discernibility d between any two frames U and V is defined as follows:

$$d(\Lambda_U, \Lambda_V) = L_2(\Lambda_U, \Lambda_V) \qquad (2)$$

Discernibility Matrix D is employed for weighing the similarity of all frames, and every entry of D corresponds to the discernibility of two frames, as illustrated by Table 1. Due to the existence of noise, in practise, it is hard to find two pairs of frames with absolutely equal frame discernibility, for example, $d(\Lambda_P, \Lambda_Q){=}d(\Lambda_U, \Lambda_V)$, thus we introduce the coherence criteria to evaluate the frame similarity, which includes the qualitative measure and quantitative measure. The qualitative measure is used for varying trend judgement, such as increase or decrease, while the quantitative measure is for equal/unequal determination. Pairs of frames satisfying the qualitative and quantitative measures are considered to gratify the coherence criteria. Such Sequences of frames are regarded as the repeating pattern.

3.3 Repeating Pattern Finding

In this section, we present an incremental repeating pattern finding algorithm, which estimates the current repetitive pattern length depending on the combination of previous result and current status. Our proposed algorithm is much similar to Hsu's proposed [6], but with some modifications. The problem of repeating pattern finding is essential a repetitive substring-finding. For a frame set A with T elements, if A contains n substrings SP. The possible substring number of A is $T + (T - 1) + \ldots + 1$. If the length of substring SP is n, the needed comparison times is $O(T \times n)$. Moreover, the procedure to decide the appearing frequency of SP in A also needs $O(T \times n)$. So the time complexity of substring-finding algorithm is $O(n^4)$. For a audio with 100 frames, it will need $O(10^8)$ comparisons. The heavily computational cost makes the repeating pattern finding from long duration audio becomes impossible. In the paper the time complexity of proposed algorithm is $O(n \log(n))$. All repeating patterns and their appearing frequencies are found from the correlation matrix. We build a set called the candidate set (denoted CS) to record the repeating patterns and their appearing frequencies, each element in in the candidate set CS is an

Table 1. Discernibility Matrix: D

A	A_1	A_2	A_3	A_4	A_5	A_6	A_7	A_8	A_9	A_{10}
A_1	0	30	35	31	31	40	33	45	56	39
A_2	30	0	14	31	18	30	35	51	62	41
A_3	35	14	0	13	17	31	41	61	30	20
A_4	31	31	13	0	13	30	39	37	17	18
A_5	31	18	11	13	0	11	11	13	41	51
A_6	40	11	31	11	11	0	41	19	11	31
A_7	33	43	41	31	11	41	0	13	15	21
A_8	45	51	61	37	13	19	13	0	16	25
A_9	56	62	30	17	41	11	15	16	0	49
A_{10}	39	41	20	18	51	31	21	25	49	0

triple with form (*pattern*, *rep_count*, *sub_count*), where *pattern*, *rep_count* and *sub_count* are used to represent a repeating pattern, its appearing frequency and the number of the repeating pattern being a substring of the other repeating patterns, respectively. We take an example to illustrate the role of *sub_count*. For two extracted patterns $(A_4A_5A_6, 3, 2)$ and $(A_5A_6, 1, 1)$, A_5A_6 is the substring of $A_4A_5A_6$, because the *sub_count* of first pattern is greater than the *sub_count* of second pattern, the second pattern would not be included in the final result.

The correlation matrix T serves as an auxiliary means to decide which patterns should be selected to insert **CS**. For the discernibility matrix is symmetric, the finding of repeating pattern only operate in upper/lower-triangular correlation matrix. The determination of each element relates to the element along primary diagonal, for example, $T_{(i+1,j+1)}$ is set to nonzero value only $T_{(i,j)} = 1$ or $T_{(i,j)} > 1$ holds.

(1) $1 < \forall i \leq S$ and $1 \leq j \leq S$

(2) $D_{(i,j)} = D_{(i-1,j)}$

(3) $D_{(i+1,j+1)} = D_{(i,j+1)}$

(4) $D_{(i,j)} < D_{(i-1,j)}$ and $\frac{\min(D_{(i,j)}, D_{(i-1,j)})}{\max(D_{(i,j)}, D_{(i-1,j)})} > \eta$

(5) $D_{(i,j)} > D_{(i-1,j)}$ and $\frac{\min(D_{(i,j)}, D_{(i-1,j)})}{\max(D_{(i,j)}, D_{(i-1,j)})} > \eta$

(6) $D_{(i+1,j+1)} < D_{(i,j+1)}$ and $\frac{\min(D_{(i+1,j+1)}, D_{(i,j+1)})}{\max(D_{(i+1,j+1)}, D_{(i,j+1)})} > \eta$

(7) $D_{(i+1,j+1)} > D_{(i,j+1)}$ and $\frac{\min(D_{(i+1,j+1)}, D_{(i,j+1)})}{\max(D_{(i+1,j+1)}, D_{(i,j+1)})} > \eta$

Based on the above conditions, the below rules are used for setting the value of $T_{(i,j)}$ or $T_{(i+1,j+1)}$

Table 2. Correlation Matrix: T

A	A_1	A_2	A_3	A_4	A_5	A_6	A_7	A_8	A_9	A_{10}
A_1	–	0	0	0	0	0	0	0	0	0
A_2		–	0	1	0	0	1	0	0	1
A_3			–	0	2	1	0	0	0	0
A_4				–	0	3	1	0	0	0
A_5					–	0	0	0	0	0
A_6						–	0	0	0	0
A_7							–	0	0	0
A_8								–	0	0
A_9									–	0
A_{10}										–

Rule 1: If one of (2), (4) or (5) holds, and $T_{(i-1,j-1)} = 0$, then set $T_{(i,j)} = 1$.

Rule 2: (2) and (3) hold, $T_{(i,j)}$ is set to $T_{(i-1,j-1)} + 1$.

Rule 3: (6) holds after (2) or (4) holds, $T_{(i,j)}$ is set to $T_{(i-1,j-1)} + 1$.

Rule 4: (7) holds after (2) or (5) holds, $T_{(i,j)}$ is set to $T_{(i-1,j-1)} + 1$.

Applying above rules to the data in Table 1, we can draw out $CS = (A_4 A_5 A_6, 3, 1)$, $(A_7, 1, 0)$, $(A_{10}, 1, 0)$, $(A_6 A_7, 2, 1)$ as the repeating pattern, which is illustrated by Table 2.

4 Experiments Evaluation

We devise three experiments to evaluate the completeness of extracted pattern by the proposed algorithm. The evaluations are carried out by audio retrieval experiments. For objective evaluating the index result, we define the indexing accuracy to be the ratio of the number of accurately indexing frames to the total frame number. The first experiment is for comparing the completeness of the found patterns by MFCC and Gabor filters bank. The found repeating patterns are used for indexing, the source from which patterns are extracted are clipped into many clips with varied length. For the same test audio data, the indexing accuracy by Gabor filters bank is always higher than one by MFCC. The More frames are used for finding pattern, the more higher the indexing accuracy becomes, as the illustration in Figure 3(a). The second experiment is for evaluating the influence of clip length on the index result. The preparation of experiment is similar to experiment 1, but when one round of indexing is finished, all test data are recliped with different length. From the experiment results, we found that when the length of clip is small, the indexing accuracy is low, the indexing accuracy increases with the length increase of audio clip, when the length of clip reaches a certain threshold, the indexing accuracy keeps

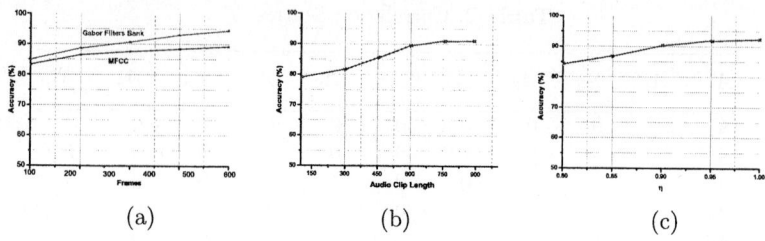

Fig. 3. Some Evaluation Results

nearly constant, as the illustration in Figure 3(b). The third experiment is for testing the influence of η to pattern discovering. The initial value of η is assigned to 0.8, the maximal value is assigned to 1. The indexing accuracy increases as η becomes large, but the indexing accuracy increases minor when η is greater than 0.9, as illustration in Figure 3(c), because two frames are much similar when η is greater than 0.9.

5 Conclusion

Audio is an important source for people to acquire knowledge, and it is becoming indispensable in everyday life. Such audio as classical and pop music, contains repeating pattern, which is helpful for people to quickly comprehend and memorize the melody. In the paper we propose a new method to extract audio features by employing Gabor filters bank, which could deal with polyphony audio. By exploited the extracted features, the repeating pattern is then discovered. In the content-based audio retrieval evaluations, we found that Gabor filter bank has stronger feature extraction ability than MFCC, especially for polyphony audio. Moreover, the repeating pattern could be finished in less than ten seconds, which shows its feasibility for practical use. In future, we would investigate how to apply the extracted features to more audio applications.

References

1. L. Lu, M. Wang, H.-J. Zhang, Repeating pattern discovery and structure analysis from acoustic music data. Workshop on Multimedia Information Retrieval 2004, pp.275-282, 2004.
2. L. Lu, W. Liu, H.-J. Zhang, Audio Textures: theory and applications. IEEE Trans. on Speech and Audio Processing, vol. 12, no. 2, pp. 156-167, March, 2004.
3. J. Gu, L. Lu, R. Cai, H.-J. Zhang et al, Dominant feature vectors based audio similarity measure. In Proc. of Pacific-Rim Conference on Multimedia (PCM) 2004, 2:890-897, 2004.
4. P.J. Wolfe, S.J. Godsill, A Gabor regression scheme for audio signal analysis. In Proc. of the IEEE Workshop on Applications of Signal Processing to Audio and Acoustics, 2003.

5. Z. Xiong, R. Radhakrishnan, A. Divakaran, T.S. Huang, Comparing MFCC and MPEG-7 audio features for feature extraction, maximum likelihood HMM and entropic prior HMM for sports audio classification. In Proc. of ICME'2003, vol. 3, pp.401-404, July 2003.
6. J.L. Hsu, C.C. Liu, A.L.P. Chen, Discovering non-trivial repeating patterns in music data. IEEE Trans. on Multimedia, vol. 3, no. 3, pp.311-325, 2001.
7. J.L. Hsu, C.C. Liu, A.L.P. Chen, Efficient repeating pattern finding in music databases, In Proc. of the ACM Int'l Conf. on Information and Knowledge Management (ACM CIKM'1998), pp.281-288, 1998
8. Y. Rubner, C. Tomasi, Coalescing texture descriptors, In Proc. of ARPA Image Understanding Workshop, 1996.

A Study on Information Extraction from PDF Files

Fang Yuan[1,2], Bo Liu[1], and Ge Yu[2]

[1] College of Mathematics and Computer Science,
Hebei University, Baoding, Hebei, 071002 P.R. China
[2] College of Information Science and Engineering,
Northeastern University, Shenyang, Liaoning, 110004 P.R. China
yuanfang@mail.hbu.edu.cn

Abstract. Portable Document Format (PDF) is increasingly being recognized as a common format of electronic documents. The prerequisite to management and indexing of PDF files is to extract information from them. This paper describes an approach for extracting information from PDF files. The key idea is to transform the text information parsed from PDF files into semi-structured information by injecting additional uniform tags. An extensible rule set is built on tags and other knowledge. Guided by the rules, one pattern matching algorithm based on a tree model is applied to obtain the necessary information. A further experiment proved that this method was effective.

1 Introduction

With the development of information technology and the wide spread use of the Internet, a large number of electronic documents are stored in Portable Document Format (PDF) files. How to manage and search available PDF files efficiently and quickly has become a problem which needs to be solved urgently.

The first step to solving this problem is to extract information from PDF files in which the end-users are interested. This is just one of the major researching fields of Information Extraction (IE). The process of IE could be simply described as the information extraction from a data source based on a set of pre-defined rules (or templates). The rule set is constructed manually or learned from training data and subsequently modified. Many different IE approaches have been introduced. For example, STALKER [1] is a kind of hierarchical information extraction method. It divides extracted data into certain levels, with the content of lower levels being more specific and concrete than higher levels. Another method, $CCWRAP_{LR}$ [2] divides data into tuples, and each tuple contains specific attributes. The main task of the information extraction algorithm is to find out the symbol of both the left side and right side of each attribute. By improving these two methods, HPIE [3] and MKIE [4] take charge of some additional confirmed knowledge before extracting.

However, all of the above methods focus on semi-structured data; for example, web pages. So we can't apply these methods to PDF files directly because the information extracted from PDF files is stored in free-form text. In this paper we adopt a method called "tag injection", which means we insert format information in the form of tags

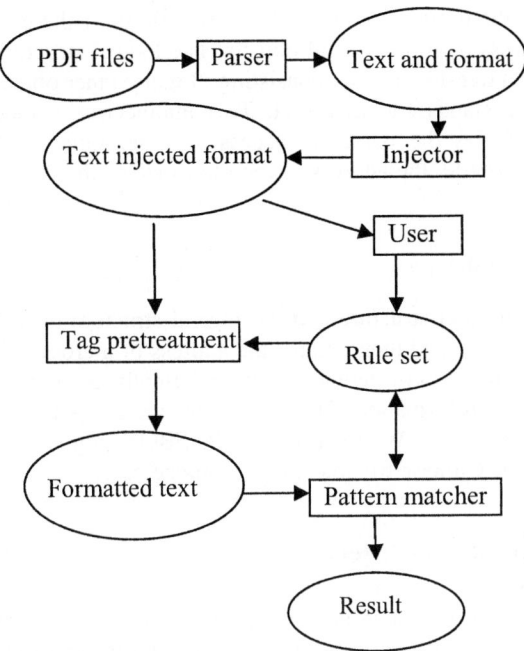

Fig. 1. Process of IE of PDF files

into text files, to transform text into a kind of document-like semi-structured data. The whole process of IE is shown as Figure 1 (the ellipse stands for data and the rectangle stands for functional module).

The organization of the paper is as follows: Section 2 describes the PDF files parser. Section 3 describes the tag injector. Following is a discussion of the rule set in Section 4, then tag preprocessor and pattern matcher are described in Section 5 and Section 6 respectively. We describe some experiments we performed to validate our proposed algorithm in Section 7 and give the conclusions in Section 8.

2 Construction of PDF Files Parser

PDF files make use of inner objects to describe information such as text, image, table and so on. The organization [5] of inner objects is defined by file structure and document structure of PDF files. The file structure is equal to the physical structure and the document structure is equal to the logical structure.

2.1 Structure of PDF Files

The physical structure [5] of PDF Files usually consists of header, body, cross-reference table and trailer. Header includes version number. Body is the main part of a PDF file and it is coded with a certain format. A cross-reference table is similar to an address table of inner objects. It records each inner object and its offset address.

When it comes to the trailer, it records the start address of the cross-reference table and the offset address of some special objects. The logical structure [5] of PDF files can be depicted as a tree-like model, consisting of many inner objects. Each node that belongs to the tree stands for an object. To combine tree a model with a cross-reference table, enables the parser to access arbitrary objects of the file. As an entrance to the whole file, the address of the root node of the tree is recorded as part of the trailer.

2.2 Parser of PDF Files

According to the physical structure and the logical structure of a PDF file, a parser firstly locates the trailer, and then obtains the address of a cross-reference table. Furthermore, it parses the cross-reference table and finally accesses each node of the tree-like model to get information. These functions are implemented by a PDF class library named PDFBOX [6]. We modified the PDFBOX to give it a fully compatible ability to interpret the Chinese (double-word) characters.

3 Construction of Tag Injector

In PDF files, text information is not organized by rows but by the coordinates of every character. So it is necessary to arrange characters in paragraphs by referring to their coordinate information before inserting tags.

To insert tags, three problems need to be solved. The first one is to decide the insertion position; the second one is deciding how to present the tags and the last one is deciding the content of the tags. The injector inserts tags into text when a format change happens. Therefore, we can preserve the format information of original documents and minimize the amount of tags. The format change can be regarded as font change, font size change and empty row. Especially, empty row indicates that the spacing between two close rows is more than one row. For instance, empty row usually exists between title and straight matter.

To summarize the type of format change, the corresponding tag is defined as follows:

<SC
BR (TRUE/FALSE) FS (BEFORE-AFTER/NONE) FN (BEFORE-AFTER/NONE)
/SC>

where "<SC" and "/SC>" respectively denote the start point and the end point of one tag; "BR", "FS" and "FN", three optional attributes of a tag, respectively denoting the empty row, font size and font name; "TRUE/FALSE" means "has" or "has not" an empty row; "BEFORE-AFTER" means the change in values from one character to another; and "NONE" means non-change. For the value of font size, the system just selects its true value; on the other hand, because there are various fonts, recording all of them will complicate tag formatting. As a solution, the system just generalizes all of the fonts to bold fonts, italic fonts and unknown fonts, which are separately denoted by "BOLD", "ITALIC" and "UNKNOWN".

The relationship between every pair of tags can be defined as either symmetrical tags or consentaneous tags. Pairs of symmetrical tags have the same attributes and their attribute value is represented symmetrically. An example is shown as follows:

<SC FS(15-18) FN(BOLD- UNKNOWN) /SC>
<SC FS(18-15) FN(UNKNOWN -BOLD) /SC>

Pairs of consentaneous tags have the same attributes and their attribute value is represented consentaneously. Actually, they are the same tags. An example is shown as follows:

<SC FS(18-15) FN(BOLD- UNKNOWN) /SC>
<SC FS(18-15) FN(BOLD-UNKNOWN) /SC>

The text and format information are outputted by the parser, and then inputted into the tag injector which inserts a tag into every format change position.

4 Rule Set

The whole process of information extraction is rules-guided. So the rule set is one of the core constituents of our system.

4.1 Components of the Rule Set

The rule set consists of four essential components:

- *Restricted word set* contains the words which have obvious semantic information.
- *Rule set about formatted document* contains rules that are used to extract information from files.
- *Rule set about a single tag* contains rules that are used to find out other tags which are symmetrical or consentaneous to a given tag or a rule.
- *Rule set about a pair of tags* contains rules that are used to find out other tag pairs which match with a given tag pair or a rule.

We describe these components in detail below:

Restricted Word Set. The words belonging to a restricted word set have obvious semantic information that will not be changed in different files ready for extraction. For example, in many papers, "Abstract" and "Keywords" are usually used as the identifiers of the content of abstract and keywords, so "Abstract" and "Keywords" could be added to a restricted word set. This set is pre-defined and updated in a later process of IE.

Rule Set About Formatted Documents. Rules belonging to this set are used to extract information from formatted documents. These rules consist of attribute pairs and each pair contains a text block number and its semantic information. In the last process of IE (as Figure 1 shows), the pattern matcher, guided by rules in the set, obtains meaningful text blocks then arranges them as output.

Rule Set About a Single Tag. The function of the rules in this set is to identify symmetrical tags or consentaneous tags. Additionally, all the rules belonging to the set are generalized rules. For example, the following two tags are considered as rigorous symmetry because any level of generalized rule will consider them to be symmetrical.

<SC BS (TRUE) FS (15-18) FN (UNKNOWN-BOLD) /SC>
<SC BS (TRUE) FS (18-15) FN (BOLD-UNKNOWN) /SC>

From two tags mentioned above, we can see that both of them contain an empty row, and the appearance of font change and font size change are symmetrical. If we want to identify approximate symmetrical tags, the corresponding rule should be generalized. The higher the level of a generalized rule, the more tags it will match.

To figure out the order of generalization, the priority of the three attributes, "BS", "FS", and "FN" should be determined first. The complete generalized rules belonging to each level are shown as Table 1.

Table 1. Table of generalized rules

Level	Rule
1	<BR(TRUE) FS FN(True Name)>
2	<BR(TRUE) FS FN>
3	<BR(TRUE) FS(I/D) FN>
4	<BR(TRUE) FS>
5	<BR(TRUE) FS(I/D) > <BR(TRUE) FN >
6	<BR(TRUE)>
7	<FS FN(True Name)>
8	<FS FN>
9	<FS(I/D) FN>
10	<FS> <FN(True Name)>
11	<FS(I/D)> <FN>
12	< >

The first level of matching rule (<BR (TRUE) FS FN(True Name)>) is the most rigorous. It requires font name and font size to be symmetrical or consentaneous in value. Compared with the first level, the third level requires font size to be symmetrical or consentaneous in trend but not in value (the increase or decrease of font size is written in "I" and "D" respectively in short) and font name must be symmetrical or consentaneous about its abstract name ("BOLD", "ITALIC" and "UNKNOWN"), but not its true name. The final level matches all the tags.

Based on the generalized rules, we define two types of operation on rules; they are intersection (denoted by symbol ∩) and union (denoted by symbol ∪). The intersection of two rules is equal to the rule which has the lower generalizing level and the union of two rules is equal to the rule which has the higher generalizing level. If two rules have the same generalizing level, the intersection of them is equal to the intersection of their attributes; similarly, the union of them is equal to the union of their attributes. Some examples of rules' operation are shown in Table 2.

Table 2. Some examples of rules' operation

Rule	Rule	Operation	Result
<BR(TRUE)FS(I/D) >	<BR(TRUE) FN >	∪	<BR(TRUE) FS(I/D) FN>
<BR(TRUE)FS(I/D) >	<BR(TRUE) FN >	∩	<BR(TRUE) >
<BR(TRUE) FS>	<FS(I/D)>	∪	<BR(TRUE)FS>
<BR(TRUE) FS>	<FS(I/D)>	∩	<FS(I/D)>

Table 3. Some examples of rule of tag

Tag	Rule of tag
<SC BS(TRUE) FS(15-18) FN(UNKNOWN-BOLD) /SC>	<BR(TRUE) FS(I/D) FN>
<SCBS(TRUE) FS(DECREASE)) /SC>	<BR(TRUE) FS(I/D)>

We also define the concept of rule of tag. The rule of a tag means a rule which matches the given tag perfectly. Some examples are shown in Table 3.

Rule Set About a Pair of Tags. The rules belonging to the set focus not only on the tag pair but also the content that is located between the two tags. The content could be expressed as a character set or as words in a restricted word set, or even other tags, but it is usually characters. A complete rule could be declared as:

$$<BR\ (TRUE)\ FS\ (I) > [Character\ Set]\ <BR\ (TRUE)\ FS\ (D) >$$

When we need to calculate the intersection or union of two rules, we could apply computation criterions mentioned before. The only difference is that we need to calculate the intersection or union of two character sets additionally.

4.2 Building a Rule Set

The establishment of a rule set is carried out under the user's instruction. Before building and processing, we need a training set consisting of some texts that have been injected with tags by the system. The user then needs to label auxiliary information such as restricted words, the extraction rules of documents, starting tag, ending tag, redundant tag pairs on texts. Regarding this information, the system separately executes the following processes:

To the restricted words and extraction rules of documents, the system inserts these rules directly to an update restricted words set and document extraction rules set.

To the tag pairs, the system uses the operation mentioned before to update the tag pairs rule set. First, the system gathers the rule of each pair of tags, and then makes a union operation between the rule that is ready to be inserted and the corresponding rule that already exists in the set. At the same time, the system must make sure that the result of the union operation will not contradict any other labeled text in the training set. If not, the system will consider these as new rules and insert them into a rule set.

5 The Process of Tag Preprocessor

According to the corresponding rules, the main task of a tag preprocessor is to locate the start tag and the end tag, eliminate the redundant tags, and then output a kind of list-like structure as Figure 2 shows. The performance of the preprocessor relies on the robustness of the rule set.

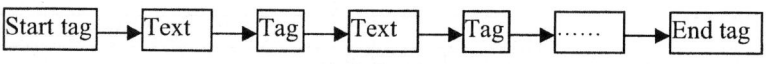

Fig. 2. A list of formatted text

Guided by the rule set about tags, the first task of tag pretreatment is to eliminate any redundant symmetrical tag. This type of tag is useless and will disturb the accuracy of the information extracted. The system can locate these tags based on rules which specify the useful information needed to be extracted and the redundant tags can then be neglected.

The rule set about tags is also used to locate the start tag and end tag of the list of formatted text. The content that is before the start tag and after the end tag will be neglected. One problem which should be noticed is that the priority of restricted words is higher than the tags' priority. For example, if the content between two tags that are labeled as end tags is one of restricted words, the system will record it, and then once the system searches this word in other formatted text, it will stop extraction no matter whether the tag behind the word is an end tag or not.

6 Construction of Pattern Matcher

The pattern matcher receives preprocessed formatted text, and then searches the matching pattern from a pattern set. If it finds one it will continually search corresponding rules from the rule set and output the result at the end.

The pattern set is organized as a kind of tree-like model. There are two types of nodes in the model. One is normal node which contains information ready to be extracted; another is restricted word node which contains the restricted words. Tags are stored by the edges of the tree. The whole process of matching is to find the longest path started by the root node that matches the list of formatted text as input data.

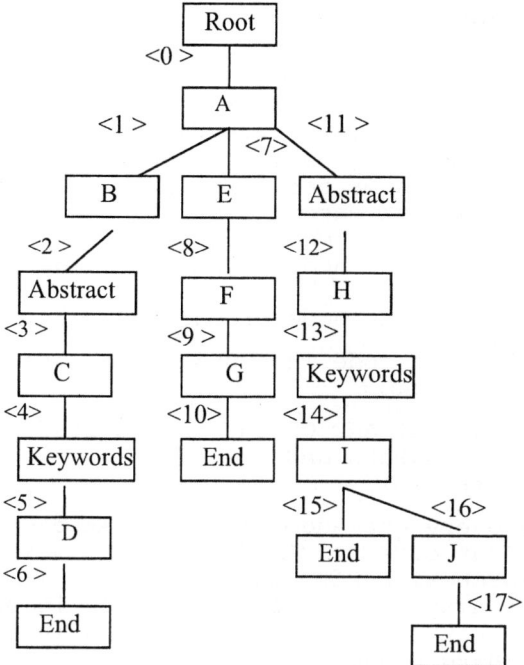

Fig. 3. Tree-like model

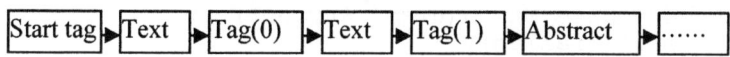

Fig. 4. An Example list of formatted text

Figure 3 shows a simple model of a pattern set which consists of four training files. The training task is supposed to extract information from papers.

All the nodes and edges of the tree are numbered, and the nodes which contain "Abstract" and "Keywords" are nodes of restricted word nodes. The pattern matcher uses the rules of judging consentaneous tags to find the longest path that is consentaneous with the input text. It should be noted that the priority of the node of restricted words is higher than that of the tags.

For example, a list of formatted text is shown as Figure 4. It supposes that "tag(0)" is consentaneous with "<0>". When the pattern matcher separately matches "tag (1)" with "<1>", "<7>" and "<11>", the next node of "<11>" is just the same as the next node of input text (Both their contents are "Abstract"), so it will choose the path along the "<11>" to continue to match. Once the process of matching has failed, the matcher will insert the rest of the list of text into a false matching position on the tree. For example, the embranchment of "I" results from false matching. The system will create new rules of extraction whenever the false matching happens to satisfy the false documents.

6.1 Matching Algorithm

The matching algorithm is shown as follows:

```
Match (PMTree,Doc,CPath,MaxPath,CTNode,CPNode)
  /*PMTree,a tree-like model of pattern set.
  Doc, a list of formatted text.
  CPath, the current matching path.
  MaxPath, the longest matching path.
  CTNode, the current node of PMTree ready to be
  matched.
  CPNode, the current node of Doc ready to be matched.*/

  If CPNode is end node Then update MaxPath and CPath.
     Return (success);

  If CTNode is leaf AND CPnode is not leaf
    Then update MaxPath and CPath.
       Return (failed);

  Searching every out-edge, named as TArc of CTNode
  PArc = an out-edge of CPNode
  If TArc match with PArc then
     CPNode = next node that use PArc as in edge;
     CTNode = next node that use TArc as in edge;
     Update MaxPath and CurrentPath;
     Match (PMTree, Doc,CPath,MaxPath,CTNode,CPNode)

     If TArc and PArc are not matching
     then update MaxPath and CurrentPath
       Return(failed).
```

7 Result of the Experiments

The experiment data consists of 240 papers that come from 163 publishers after 2003. The task of information extraction is to obtain the title, author, address, abstract, keywords and the class number from these papers. The result is shown in Table 4. For validating the effect of the training data on the result of the experiment, we randomly selected 120 papers from the 200 papers mentioned above as training data and let the other 80 papers be used as testing data. This result is also shown in Table 4. Therefore, from Table 4, we could conclude that with an increase in the amount of training data, the accuracy of information extraction will increase correspondingly.

Table 4. Result of experiment

Training data	Testing data	Correct extraction	Accuracy
40 papers	200 papers	179 papers	89.5%
120 papers	80 papers	74 papers	92.5%

8 Conclusions

The result of our experiments proved that our new method is effective. Our work provides a foundation for managing and searching through large amounts of PDF files. Future work is focused on modifying the PDF parser and improving its compatibility while also optimizing the matching algorithm to achieve higher accuracy.

Acknowledgements

This work is partially sponsored by the Research Plan of Education Office of Hebei Province (2004406) and the National Research Foundation for the Doctoral Program of Higher Education of China (20030145029).

References

1. Ion Muslea, Steve Minton, and Craig A. Knoblock: Hierarchical approach to wrapper induction, Proceedings of the Third International Conference on Autonomous Agents, Seattle, WA1999, 221-227
2. Nicholas Kushmerick. Wrapper Induction: Efficiency and expressiveness, Artificial Intelligence, 2000(118): 15-68
3. Ming Zhu, Jun Wang, Junpu Wang. Multiple Record Extraction from HTML Page Based On Hierarchical Pattern, Computer Engineering, 2001, 27(9): 40-42
4. Ming Zhu, Yun Huang, Qingsheng Cai. Information Extraction From Web Pages Based On Multi-Knowledge, Mini-Micro System, 2001, 22(9): 1058-1061
5. Adobe Systems Incorporated. Adobe Portable Document Format Version 1.4, American Addison Wesley, 2001
6. Ben Litchfield PDFBOX[CP] http://sourceforge.net/projects/pdfbox/

The Study of a Knowledge-Based Constraints Network System (KCNS) for Concurrent Engineering

Wei-ming Wang, Jie Hu, Fei Zhou, Da-yong Li,
Xiang-jun Fu, and Ying-hong Peng

School of Mechanical Engineering, Shanghai Jiao Tong University,
Shanghai 200030, P.R. China
wangweiming@sjtu.edu.cn

Abstract. This research article demonstrates the use of a constraints network for modeling the knowledge which is necessary for concurrent product design. A Knowledge-based Constraints Network System (KCNS) has been developed to maintain design consistency and to support the selection of appropriate design parameter intervals. A data-mining algorithm named fuzzy-rough algorithm is developed to acquire the knowledge level constraints from the numerical simulation. The method integrated Case Based Reasoning (CBR) and Rule Based Reasoning (RBR) with interval consistency algorithm is adopted to predict the potential conflicts and to specify the interval of design parameters. The design example of a crank connecting link in a V6 engine shows the validity of the system.

1 Introduction

Concurrent Engineering (CE) as a philosophy aims to address the consideration of different life cycle issues of a product in the early stages of the design process. There are many constraints related to part features, feature-process relations, assembly dimension, tolerance and implicit knowledge in concurrent product development [1]. Such constraints in a design process form a network of interconnected variables known as a constraints network, which is a fairly recent development. Young and O'Grady have thoroughly investigated constraints network for concurrent design, and have developed several applicable constraints systems such as Saturn, Jupiter, and Spark [2].

Recently, CAE technology, especially numerical simulation, has become the third mode of science complementing theory and experiments in concurrent product design [3]. The massive amount of simulation result data implies much useful knowledge. Extracting the implicit knowledge as knowledge level constraints from simulation results is a very meaningful procedure. However, modeling of knowledge level constraints network has not yet been fully addressed. At the same time, KBE is widely used in the engineering area, which integrates artificial intelligence with CAX systems. KDD can acquire implicit and useful knowledge in large-scale data sets and has made great success in commercial areas. It has expanded to engineering disciplines, but in here it is very different to KDD as used in the commercial areas.

To achieve an effective management of constraints, an efficient and timely communication network system should be provided within different design areas. Such a system should include a strategy for conflict resolution to avoid disagreements within the different activities or areas. Young proposed a reduction algorithm for qualitative constraints networks that can describe the effect of disturbances from one variable on the other variables [4]. However, for some changes such as the addition of a new constraint, all of the relations between variables must be manually recalculated. Therefore, the static algorithm cannot adapt to concurrent product development.

This paper describes a Knowledge-based Constraints Network System (KCNS) for concurrent product design using a combination of both mathematic methods and knowledge-based engineering (KBE) techniques. With the proposed method, the system can combine the quantitative computation of feasible solution spaces with the rules from simulation and designers' expertise to determine design variables. Section 2 describes the model of the KCNS. Section 3 introduces a data-mining algorithm named fuzzy-rough algorithm to acquire the knowledge level constraints from the numerical simulation result. Section 4 introduces the method integrated CBR and RBR with interval consistency algorithm to predict the potential conflicts and specify the interval of design parameters. Section 5 illustrates the design of a crank connecting link in a V6 engine using the proposed method. Section 6 concludes the paper.

2 Knowledge-Based Constraints Network System (KCNS)

2.1 System Model of KCNS

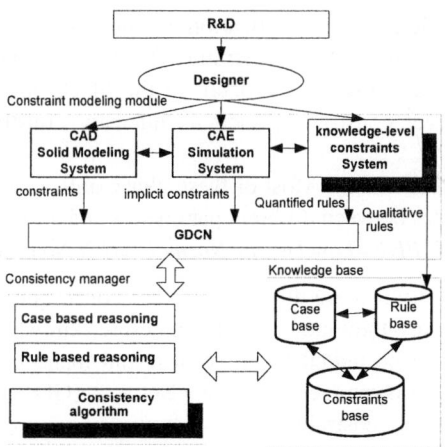

Fig. 1. Architecture of KCNS

The proposed system model of KCNS embodies a CAD solid modeling system, a CAE simulation system, knowledge-level constraints system, consistency manager system, and various knowledge bases. The architecture of the knowledge-based constraints network system (KCNS) is shown in Figure 1.

(1) Constraints modeling module: The module is used to model design parameters and requirements about various life-cycle issues. Constraints are also collected from

different sources such as the CAD system, CAE system and appropriate experts. The constraints modeling module is linked to the consistency manager module.

(2) Consistency manager module: It detects conflicts, and gives warnings and explanations to the users, and finally applies a suitable strategy (Case Based Reasoning - CBR, Rule Based Reasoning - RBR, or consistency algorithm) for solving conflicts. It makes sure that design consistency is in the constraints network and design output.

(3) Knowledge base: Knowledge base includes case base, rule base and constraints base.

2.2 Constraints in the KCNS

There are several variables in the product development including symbol variable, logic variable, fuzzy variable, disperse variable, continuous variable and vector etc. Constraints in the product development can be separated into the following four types according to the representation:

1. Equation constraints. In these constraints, the relation between the variables is expressed by equalities, inequalities and ordinary differential equation constraints, such as: L2=2*L1, L3>=L1+2*L2. Most of these constraints are geometry level, including the constraints between the parts attributes: assembly dimension, tolerance etc.

2. Qualitative constraints. Relation between the variables is expressed qualitatively, such as: type of oil pump = "point blank". Most of these constraints are product level constraints, describing the general specification of a product.

3. Implicit constraints: black box constraints. There are certain relations between input and output, without knowing the detail in the black box. Most of these constraints are domain level constraints, such as intensity constraints, dynamic constraints etc.

4. Knowledge level constraints: Most of these constraints are expert knowledge and the various inference rules between different parameters and attributes during the design process. For example, *IF BHF=Low Depth=Normal THEN No crack No wrinkle.*

Knowledge level constraints are different to other constraints, but only in the their existent form and the way they are applied. Therefore, knowledge level constraints and other constraints can be united to be defined and managed by the hybrid constraints based Generalized Dynamic Constraints Network (GDCN).

During knowledge level constraints, such as "*IF $x_1 \leq x \leq x_2, y \leq y_1,$ THEN $z_1 \leq z \leq z_2,$*" denotes quantified rules with the option of numerical explanation, for example *IF $5 \leq d \leq 25,$ THEN $d_k = 4 + 0.52(d-5)$*. Such as "*IF a AND b, THEN c*" denotes qualitative rules of reasoning, for example *IF BHF=Low Depth=Normal THEN No crack No wrinkle*. Quantified rules are added to the GDCN for perfecting the constraints network. Qualitative rules are added to the rules base for conflict resolution.

Knowledge level constraints often hide in the bottom data. They can not be mined and obtained through general methods. So developing effective acquisition methods of knowledge level constraints is the key to modeling a generalized dynamic constraints network.

3 Acquisition of Knowledge Level Constraints

We have some achievement in the fields of equation constraints, qualitative constraints and implicit constraints [5]. The discovery process of knowledge level constraints from CAE result is proposed as shown in Figure 2.

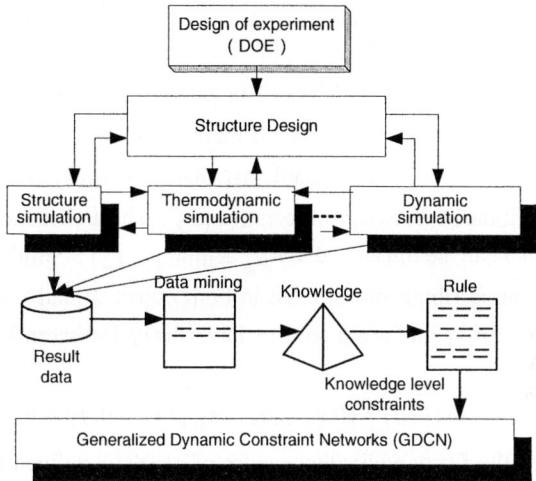

Fig. 2. Discovery processes of knowledge level constraints from CAE simulation data

First, to study the relation between the design parameters and the product's performance, DOE technology is used. The design structure is adjusted according to the experiment data. The simulation programs evaluate the performance of corresponding domains based on the adjusted design structure, such as dynamic domain, thermodynamic domain, structure mechanics domain, etc. The simulation result data is used as the data source for knowledge level constraints discovery.

The second step is data mining, an iterative process including five basic steps: domain understanding, data selection and integration, data pre-processing, rule induction, knowledge evaluation and interpretation. Production rules are selected as the knowledge level constraints.

The third step of the process is the knowledge level constraints management. The knowledge level constraints in the form of rules are added to the generalized dynamic constraints network (GDCN).

3.1 Acquisition Algorithm

The rough-set theory (RST) proposed by Pawlak has been used widely in knowledge reasoning and knowledge acquisition. Since the basic RST algorithm can only handle nominal features in a decision table, most prior studies have only shown how binary or crisp training data may be handled [6]. In this study, an improved algorithm named fuzzy-rough sets algorithm is developed by integrating fuzzy set theory with rough set theory. It can act as the DM algorithm in knowledge level constraints discovery from numerical simulation result data.

By introducing fuzzy indiscernibility relation to replace the equivalence relation in basic RST, information processing scope can be extended greatly. Also, the generated knowledge is nearer to natural language.

A decision table is $S = (U, A \cup \{d\})$. If V_a is composed of quantitative value, the value on attribute $a \in A$ can be catalogued into several fuzzy sets described by natural language such as "low", "normal", or "high" etc. Assume that the set L_a of linguistic terms of attribute a is $\{l_1^a, l_2^a, ..., l_{|L_a|}^a\}$. Object x belongs to the l-th fuzzy set with fuzzy function f_{al}^x. For any two objects x and y, if there exists linguistic term l of attribute α satisfying $f_{al}^x > 0$ and $f_{al}^y > 0$, it is said that there are fuzzy indiscernibility relations on single attribute B between objects x and y. The indiscernibility degree on the linguistic term l can be measured by $\mu_{al} = \min(f_{al}^x, f_{al}^y)$. Similarly, if the same linguistic terms of an attribute subset exist in both object x and y with membership values larger than zero, x and y are said to have fuzzy indiscernibility relations on attribute subset B.

$$IND'(B) = \{((x,y), \mu_B) : \forall_{a \in B} (f_{al}^x > 0, f_{al}^y > 0)\} \qquad (1)$$

$[x]_{IND'(B)}$ denotes the fuzzy equivalence class of $IND'(B)$ defined by x. Thus fuzzy lower approximation and fuzzy upper approximation of subset X in U are defined as follows:

$$\underline{B'}(X) = \{[x]_{IND'(B)}, \mu_B(x) : x \in U, [x]_{IND'(B)} \subseteq X\} \qquad (2)$$

$$\overline{B'}(X) = \{([x]_{IND'(B)}, \mu_B(x)) : x \in U, [x]_{IND'(B)} \cap X \neq \Phi\} \qquad (3)$$

By computing $\underline{B'}(C_k)$ and $\overline{B'}(C_k)$ $(1 \leq k \leq r(d))$, certain possible rules can be induced respectively. Also, the member value μ_B can be viewed as the rule's efficiency measurement. This helps rule selection and sorting in knowledge reasoning. The mined rule set is usually redundant. Therefore, rule refinement must be made before use.

4 Consistency Manager

While the system carries out various constraints such as equation constraints, qualitative constraints, implicit constraints and knowledge level constraints, a huge amount of information is accessed and shared in the knowledge base.

Procedure rule-reasoning (frame, slot):
```
BEGIN
     Calling the center reasoning module
   REPEAT
      Taking out a conflict resolution rule R_i ;
      Matching R_i ;
    IF (matching successfully)
```

```
        THEN executing rule conclusion;
          ELSE continue;
          IF (conflict solved successfully)
             THEN stopping rule reasoning;
               ELSE extending rules;
               IF (no rules can be used)
                  THEN stopping rule reasoning;
   UNTIL no rule could be matched;
END
```

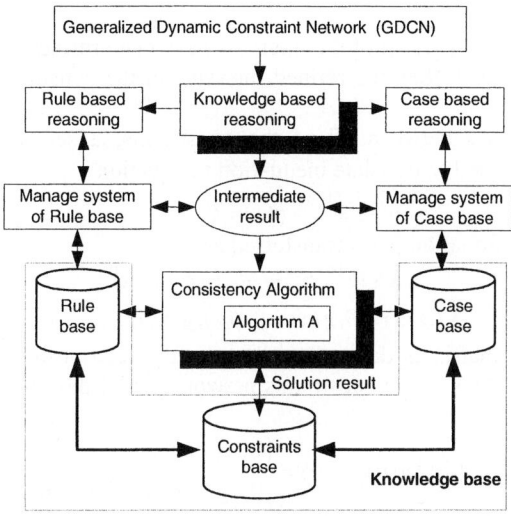

Fig. 3. Consistency manager system integrated CBR and RBR with consistency algorithm

Figure 3 shows details of the process of conflict resolution in the consistency manager system integrated with CBR and RBR and with consistency algorithm. The consistency manager system detects violation, and sends a message to a method slot, which carries a knowledge-based reasoning subsystem or consistency algorithm module for conflict resolution. Conflicts are treated by the knowledge-based reasoning subsystem first. If this subsystem can handle the conflict, Rule Based Reasoning (RBR) or Case Based Reasoning (CBR) will be called to deal with the conflict; else conflicts will be transported to the consistency algorithm module. In the consistency algorithm module, consistency algorithm is presented to determine the interval of design parameters as the last step. After successful solution, cases and rules obtained during the solution process are added to the case base and rule base individually for perfecting the knowledge base.

Definition 1, Conflict: If all intervals in vector $[x^L, x^U]$ are empty after being refined using the algorithm in Equation (1), the present constraints network model contains a conflict, which means that no solution exists in the present constraints network model and the design is unfeasible.

Definition 2, Algorithm A : The Algorithm A can be expressed as
$$x \in [x^{L0}, x^{U0}] \xrightarrow{A} x \in [x^L, x^U]$$
$$s.t. \begin{cases} g(x) = 0, g(x) = [g_1(x), g_2(x), ... g_l(x)]^T \\ h(x) \leq 0, h(x) = [h_1(x), h_2(x), ... h_m(x)]^T \end{cases} \quad (4)$$

where, $x \in R^n$ is nth dimensional design parameter vector, g, h are equation and inequation constraints function for parameter, $[x^{L0}, x^{U0}]$ is the original evaluated intervals of parameter, $[x^L, x^U]$ consistent intervals filtered by consistency algorithm which are correspondent to the given design goals.

Definition 3, Consistency: If all of the intervals have been refined using Algorithm A and no conflict is found, then the refined intervals in the constraints network model achieve consistency.

To keep uniformity between all of the constraints, a secondary variable vector $\theta \in R^q (\theta \geq 0)$ is added to translate inequation to equation:
$$h(x) \leq 0 \Rightarrow h(x) + \theta = 0 \quad (5)$$

By Equation (5), Equation (4) is transferred as:
$$x \in [x^{L0}, x^{U0}] \xrightarrow{A} x \in [x^L, x^U]$$
$$s.t. g(x) = 0, g(x) = [g_1(x), g_2(x), ... g_{l+m}(x)]^T \quad (6)$$

The relationship matrix is defined to describe the relationship between the constraints and the variables in the constraints network model described in Equation (6), and is defined as:
$$G = \{g(ij)\} \; g(ij) = \begin{cases} 1, & g_i \text{ contains } x_j \\ 0, & g_i \text{ does not contains } x_j \end{cases} \quad (7)$$

Where $1 \leq i \leq l+m$, $1 \leq j \leq k+m$. In addition, we define two secondary vectors:
$$p_c = [p_c(1), p_c(k+m)]$$
$$p_c(\lambda) = \begin{cases} 1, & \lambda = c \\ 0, & \lambda \neq c \end{cases} \quad c = 1, 2, ..., k+m \quad (8)$$
$$q_r = [q_r(1), q_r(2), ..., q_r(k+m)]^T \quad (9)$$

Making $p_i G q \neq 0$ for every j gives the solution functions of constraints g_j in Equation (6) which are $x(j) = g_i^j(x_1, ..., x_{j+1}, ..., x_{k+m})$.

Where g_i^j is actually the projection of constraints g_i on variable $x(j)$, $1 \leq j \leq k+m$.

The paper uses a consistency algorithm to solve the interval problem described by Equation (6). The consistency algorithm uses the following notations:

Algorithm A :
  Procedure LabelResolve (In $\{C = [g_i^j], x = 0, y = [x^{L0}, x^{U0}]\}$
```
BEGIN
     WHILE ( y≠x ) DO
          x = y
               FOR j=1 to k+m
```

```
            FOR i=1 to l+m
               IF ( p_iGq_j ≠ 0 )
```
$$y_i = g_i^j(x)$$
```
               ENDIF
               IF y_i == {null set}
                  Show conflict message
                  Exit
               ENDIF
            END FOR
         END FOR
ENDWHILE
END
END Procedure
```

5 Design Example

As an example, the crank and connecting rod design of one V6 engine is used to show the validity of knowledge-based constraints network system (KCNS) in the concurrent design. Population parameters of the engine:

- number of cylinders(n) : 6 cylinders
- firing order (n_ingite) : 1-4-2-6-3-5
- balance layout (f_balwt) : 1-3-6-7-10-12
- number of revolutions per minute (rpm) : 3000rpm
- material of connecting rod: 40Mn2S

The multi-body dynamics software package (ADAMS) is selected as a simulation tool.

The parameters of interest in design are the mass of the connecting rod (mass), the length of the plug between the basic shaft and the connecting rod (length), the diameter of the plug between the basic shaft and the connecting rod (diameter). They are denoted by a0, a1, and a2 individually. The force of the crankshaft (force) is a goal attribute. An experiment design method called Orthogonal Latin Square is adopted. The simulations are carried out 64 times with various design parameters.

According to the proposed method of knowledge level constraints acquisition, 16 quantified rules are discovered. For example a2=0 =>a3=2 expresses IF diameter <=20(mm) THEN force>34110(N); a2=1 =>a3=0, expresses IF 20(mm)<diameter<=20.1(mm), THEN force<=34108(N).

14 qualitative rules are discovered. For example IF Mass=Low AND Length=Normal AND Diameter=High THEN No Crack. It means that when the mass of the connecting rod is low and the length of the plug between the basic shaft and the connecting rod is normal, and the diameter of the plug between the basic shaft and the connecting rod is low, then there is no cracking occurring in the crankshaft.

All the constraints of crank and connecting rod design which are considered during the entire design process are listed in Table 1.

Table 1. Design constraints

Constraints Name	Constraints Expression	Responsibility
Reciprocate inertia force of con-rod	$P_{cl} = -mca$	Mechanical design team
Velocity of piston	$v = r*\omega*\sin(\alpha+\beta)/\cos\alpha$	Mechanical design team
Palstance of con-rod	$=\omega*\lambda*\cos\alpha/(1-\lambda^2*\sin^2\alpha)^{1/2}$	Mechanical design team
Allowable fatigue stress	$\sigma_{max} \leq \sigma_u/[n]$	Mechanical design team
Deformation of stiffness	$\Delta R_{max} < D_1/2 \;\; \Delta r_{max} < D_2/2$	Mechanical design team
Boundary constraints	$R_1 - d > 0 \;\; R_2 - D > 0$	Mechanical design team
Implicit constraints	$f_1(x) = 34647 - 837.88x_1 + 13.96x_2$ $-16.84x_3 + 3.37x_1x_2 + 37.35x_2x_3 - 1.669x_1x_3$	CAE team
Knowledge level constraints	IF 20(mm)<diameter<=20.1(mm), THEN force<=34108(N)	CAE&KBE team
Knowledge level constraints	IF Mass=Low Length=Normal Diameter=Low THEN No crack	CAE&KBE team

Table 2 lists the consistency results caused by an engineering change in the design process. The input of the constraints network is in the form of design parameter intervals which given by the designers from their experience. The output is the filtered design intervals in which conflict parameters have been removed. In Table 2, the upper and lower estimate limits are, respectively, x^{L0} and x^{U0}. After being refined, they are identified as x^L and x^U as in (6).

Table 2. consistency result of constraints

Name	(x^{U0})	(x^{U0})	(x^U)	(x^L)
$D(mm)$	65.00	75.00	68.00	73.50
$m(kg)$	0.59	0.63	0.60	0.61
$L(mm)$	50.00	60.00	55.37	56.45
$D_1(mm)$	15.50	23.60	18.90	20.08
$B(mm)$	40.90	52.50	46.40	47.08
$D_2(mm)$	24.50	36.80	28.40	30.05
$d_m(mm)$	53.00	71.25	56.20	58.03
$R_1(mm)$	7.80	10.50	9.30	10.02
$R_2(mm)$	58.00	68.00	60.10	62.05

When the design was completed, the consistency design intervals were: $L \in [55.37, 56.45]$, $m \in [0.60, 0.61]$, $D_2 \in [18.90, 20.08]$

The crankshaft design is a typical concurrent design problem. The current method achieves a satisfactory solution for the parameter. The method described in this paper was used to develop a concurrent and collaborative design system using visual.NET, which is now running in an engine design project.

6 Conclusions

This paper describes a knowledge-based constraints network system for concurrent product design. First, a data-mining algorithm named fuzzy-rough algorithm is developed to acquire knowledge level constraints. Then, the method integrated CBR and RBR with interval consistency algorithm is adopted to refine the intervals. Finally, the method is demonstrated by the design of a crank connecting link in a V6 engine. As initial results obtained from the examples are promising, using these methods could lead to a significant reduction in future production costs and time.

Acknowledgements

This paper is supported by the National Natural Science Foundation of China (No. 60304015 and 50575142), Natural Science Foundation of Shanghai, China (No. 04ZR14081) and the Science & Technology Commission of Shanghai Municipality (No. 04dz11009 and No. 04JC14050).

References

1. G. L. Xiong, T. Q. "Chang, Coordination model for the concurrent engineering product development process", High Technol. Lett., Vol 4, No2, pp.1-8,1998.
2. Guangleng Xiong, Tao Li, " Robust Design Based on Constraints Networks" IEEE Transaction on systems, man, and cybernetics-PART A: system and human, Vol 32, No 5, pp.596-604, September 2002
3. Bernhard Mitschang, "Data propagation as an enabling technology for collaboration and cooperative information systems", Computers in Industry,Vol 52, pp.59–69, 2003
4. RE Young, A Greef, and P. O'Grady, An artificial intelligence-based constraints network system for concurrent engineering, Int. J. Prod. Res., vol. 30, no. 7, pp.1715–1735,1992
5. Jie Hu, Guangleng Xiong, Z. Wu , "A variational geometric constraints network for a tolerance types specification", Int J Adv Manuf Technol. Vol 24, pp.214–222 ,2004
6. Zdzislaw Pawlak, Andrzej Skowron, "Rough Set Rudiments", Bulletin of International Rough Set Society, Vol 3, No. 4, pp. 181-185, 1999.

Rule Induction for Complete Information Systems in Knowledge Acquisition and Classification

Hong-Zhen Zheng[1], Dian-Hui Chu[1], and De-Chen Zhan[2]

[1] Department of Computer Science & Technology, Harbin Institute of
Technology at Weihai, 264209, China
hithongzhen@163.com
[2] Department of Computer Science & Technology, Harbin Institute of Technology,
Harbin, China
dechen@hit.edu.cn

Abstract. This paper proposes a modified rule generation (MRG) algorithm and rule induction prototype(RGRIP). It can help the decision-maker predict the outcomes of new cases effectively. Not only MRG algorithm provides a very fast and effective way to generate a minimal set of rule reducts from which "certain" rules can be induced, but also produces as a byproduct a revised decision tabel T from which "possible" rules could be conveniently induced. Then, combining the MRG algorithm with the rule induction schemes, we proposed a rule generation and rule induction prototype(RGRIP) that can automatically generate a minimal set of reducts and induce all certain rules as well as possible rule with all their plausibility indices. In term of ability to deal with uncertainty and inconsistency in the data set, RGRIP approach appears simplicity and conciseness in the process of its usage. The approach is efficient and effective in dealing with large data sets.

1 Introduction

In recent years, although many inductive learning techniques have been developed, most of them focus on inducing classification rules by using decision tree learning techniques or by using concepts of set theory[1,2,3,4], which require training data to be consistent and complete. These approaches, however, cannot deal with very large datasets.

Most rough set-based classification and rule induction approaches analyze decision rules from lower and upper approximations of the data sets. After we classify objects with similar properties or decision features into approximation sets, we still need to induce decision rules from the approximation sets. The lower approximation set produces"certain"rules, while the upper approximation set generates "possible"rules. This direct method of rule induction becomes impractical when the data set is really large.

In this paper we proposed a modified rule generation algorithm(MRG) to generate a minimal set of rule reducts. Each rule reduct represents a unique decision rule. It is very expedient to induce rules from the minimal set of rule reducts. The proposed

MRG algorithm helps ease this burden greatly. Not only it provides a very fast and effective way to generate a minimal set of rule reducts from which "certain"rules can be induced, it also produces as a by product a revised decision table from which "possible"rules could be conveniently induced with "plausibility" indices.

2 Rough Sets

The rough set methodology is a series of logic reasoning procedures by analysing decision tables. The set of attributes include several condition attributes and one or more decision attribute. From the decision table, the rough set theory utilizes the concept of indiscerniblity to clarify equivalent classes and to compute a minimal set of significant attributes(ruduct).

Most rough sets-based rule induction techniques employ two basic concepts:lower and upper approximations of a set. A lower approximation means the elements that certainly belong to the set, and the upper approximaton denotes the elements possibly belong to the set.

Let A be a set of condition attributes used to desvribe objects in U and R be a sub sets of A that we wish to investigate as a possible identifier or classifier of X. R can be used to define "indifference"or "indiscernible"classes of U,denoted $Ind(R)$, in the sense that elements of U x and $y \in Ind(R)$ if and only if x and y are indiscernible by the value of condition attributes R.Finallywe donote elementary set with respect to R containing object x in U as $[x]_{IND(R)}$ or $R(x)$.

We define a lower approximation LX_R and upper approximation UX_R of the set X with respect to the set of condition attributes R as follows:

$$LX_R = \{x_i \in U \mid [x_i]_{ind(R)} \subset X\} \qquad (1)$$

$$UX_R = \{x_i \in U \mid [x_i]_{ind(R)} \cap X \neq \phi\} \qquad (2)$$

3 Rule Induction for Complete Information System

3.1 An Reduct Generation Algorithm(RG)

In the real world, data sets are very large. We need a systematic procedure to compute all possible rule-reducts. A reduct generation algorithm based on the developments in Pawlak[4] will be present next.The RG algorithm is as follows:

```
Step1 Initialize object number i=1, feature number j=1;
Step2 Seletc feature j=1~n, for all k≠i, if a_ij ≠ a_kj or
      a_ij=a_kj ∧ d_i=d_k then a_ij can generate r-reducts. If
      all found, go to Step3;
Step3 Set i=i+1. If all objects have been considered,
      go to Step 4; Otherwise, go to Step2;
Step4 Select two feature and go to Step2, until all n-1
      features r-reducts have been considered.
```

RG algorithm, which produces a very efficient scheme for generating all possible reducts with minimal set of attributes. However, the proposed RG algorithm although can generate all possible rule-reducts, in general will not generate a minimal set of rule reducts. Some generated rule-reducts are rule- overlapped and cannot uniquely represent decision rules. If we can erase all redundant r-reducts, then we chan achieve a minimal set of r-reducts, from which a useful and complete set of decision rules can be easily induced. However, removing all the redundant reducts from a rule reduct table generated by the RG algorithm is time consuming and impractical. It is the main objective of this section to propose a modified RG algorithm that can produce a minimum set of ruducts "directly".

3.2 Modified Rule Generation Algorithm

As we have already mentioned in Rough set, indiscernibility is an equivalence relation between objects having the same condition attribute values C. For every subset of attributes $R \subseteq A$, the reduced decision table U/R or $U/Ind(R)$ contains several equivalence classed of condition attributes. From the reduced decision table,the RG algorithm generates a set of R-reducts for every decision class using a minimal number of condition attributes.

The main idea of the RG algorithm is based on what Pawlak [4] calls "simplitication fo decision tables". It utilizes relation between objects in indiscernibility sets to produce reducts.

we give the following key results that will be useful in modifying RG algorithm to genetate only a minimum set of r-reducts. To be sure, we again define a redundant r-reduct as one which produces exactly the same decision rule as same other r-reducts which have a smaller set attributes.

Lemma 1. Each one-feature r-reduct is in a minimal form. That is,there is no redundant one-feature r-reduct.

It is clear from *Lemma 1* that redundant reducts will only involve reducts with two or more features. Clearly "redundant" higher- order reducts can always be constructed from lower-order reducts.

Proposition 1. Non-redundant higher-order reducts can be constructed if those and only those combinations,each one forming a lower-order reduct, are removed from further consideration in forming higher-order reducts[5].

Now we give modified RG algorithm as follows:

```
Step1 Arrange input data according to the value of
decision attribute.

Step2 Initialize object number i=1, the number of
attribute in reduct r=1.

Step3 Scan row i from column j=1. If a_ij ≠ "*", go to
step 4, otherwise go to step 5.

Step4 For all k≠i, if a_ij≠a_kj or a_ij=a_kj ∧ d_i=d_k, then aij
can produce r-reduct. It all columns j=1,…,n have been
scanned, go to step5. Otherwise, go back to step 3 to
scan the next column j=j+1.
```

Step5 Set *j=i+1*, go to *step 3*, until all objects have been considered. Go to *step 6* after all objects have been considered.

Step6 Based on the objects which have the same corresponding feature value, revise the decision table *T* by replacing the value of $a_{ij} \neq$ "*x*" used to form the corresponding 1-attribute reduct by "***". Go to *step 7*.

Step7 Based on the revised decision tabel T, begian indentifying higher-order reducts by setting *r=r+1*. If *r=m*, stop.otherwise set *i=1* and go to *step 8*.

Stept8 Scan row *i* to identify *r* eligible attribute *Fj1,…Fjr* along with *aij1,…,aijr* to form an r-attribute reduct. If such an eligible set{ *aij1,…,aijr* } exists, go to *step9*. otherwise goto *step 10*.

Step9 For all $k \neq i$, if $a_{ij} \neq a_{kj}$ for at least one $j=j_1,…j_r$ or $a_{ij}=a_{kj}$ for j= $j_1,…j_r \wedge d_i=d_k$, then{ *aij1,…,aijr* } forms an r-attribute reduct. Based on the objects which have the same corresponding eligible set, each *aij1,…,aijr* is then marked by the same symble such as "**r*" to identify that the combination { *aij1,…,aijr* } has been used to form an r-reduct and the combination shoud not be used to form any part of any further reduct. Return to *step8*.

Step 10 Set i=i+1. if i>* of objects in U, go to *step 7*.otherwise go to *step 7*.

The key different between the RG and MRG algorith is that MRG contains two-level mechanisms. The first accomplished reduct generation by using the RG algorithm (*step2-5*), whereas the second updates the decision table by removing or marking the feature values that have been used to define lower-order reducts(*step6-10*). By removing all a_{ij}'s corresponding to one-attribute reducts and by considering only eligible combinations of higher-order reducts, MRG algorithm achieves both data reduction and minimal sets of rule reduct generation.

4 Rule-Reduct Generation and Rule Induction Prototype

In the previous section, we proposed a modified rule generation algorithm(MRG) to generate a minimal set of rule reducts. Each rule reduct represents a unique decision rule. It is very expedient to induce rule rules from the minimal set of rule ruducts. We summarize the necessary result and observation below:

4.1 Representation of a "certain" Rule by an r-Reduct

Proposition 2: Each r-reduct from the minimal set generated by the MRG algorithm corresponds to a "certain" decision rule.

Proof: By construction, each r-feature reduct, $r=1,2,......,n$, corresponding to an object i and the set of features $R=\{j_1,......,j_r\}$ is formed by the MRG method if and only if for each object $k \neq i$ in the data set U.

(1) $a_{kj} \neq a_{ij}$ for at least one $j \in R$.
(2) $a_{kj} = a_{ij}$ for all $j \in R$. and $d_k = d_l$

Both (1) and (2) together imply that $[i]_{IND(R)}$, the elementary set of R in U that containing object I, is a subset of $[i]_{di}$, i,e,

$$[i]_{IND(R)} \subseteq [i]_{di}$$

Thus by definition, R defines a lower approximation of the set $X=\{k \in U | d_k = d_i\}$ and the corresponding rule "If $F_j = a_{kj}, j \in R$, then $d_k = d_i$" represent a "certain" rule.

4.2 Generation of "possible" Rules with "plausibility" Indices

In using the MRG algorithm, a revised decision table T produced consists of two types of entries:

(1) entry a_{ij} that is permanently replaced by "*" or "marked" by a symbol as part of combination that makes up a higher-order reduct.
(2) Entry a_{ij} that is unchanged from the original entry.

The type(1) is used to form r-reducts, which in turn a yield a set of certain rules. The type (2) can be used to generate "possible" rules along with their associated "plausibility" indices as follows:

By examining entries in the revised decision table T that are not change to "*", we can generate one-feature "possible" rules and compute their plausibility indices as follows:

```
Step1: start with i=1 and j=i

Step2: if aij="*" •go to step 4.Otherwise, establish a
"possible" rule "if Fj=aij  then output feature d=di"
and calculate the associated plausibility index as
```

$$\frac{\text{\# of objects k with } a_{kj} = a_{ij} \text{ and } d = d_i}{\text{\# of objects k with } a_{kj} = a_{ij}}$$

Each time a possible rule is formed all a_{ij} and $a_{kj} = a_{ij}$ should be replace by "*".

```
Step3: Set j=j+1. If j> of condition features in the
data set, go to step4. Otherwise go to step2.

Step4: Set j=j+1.If i># of objects in the data set,
stop. Otherwise go to step 2.
```

At the end of the above task, we should have a newly revised decision table T that is ready for generating non-redundant higher-order possible rules using the following steps:

```
Step1: Start with i=1 and r=1;

Step2: Find and eligible r-member   subset of features
   (i.e find R(j_1,......,j_r) ⊆ {1,.....,N}).If no  eligible R
   exists, go to step4. Otherwise, establish a "possible
```

"rule: "If $F_j=a_{ij}, j \in R$, then output feature $d=d_i$" and calculate the plausibility index as:

$$\frac{\text{\# of objects k with } a_{kj}=a_{ij} \text{ for all } j \in R \text{ and } d=d_i}{\text{\# of objects k with } a_{kj}=a_{ij} \text{ for all } j \in R}$$

Step3: Each time a "possible" rule in step2 above is formed all a_{ij}, $j \in R$ and all $a_{kj}=a_{ij}$, $j \in R$ and $k \neq i$ should be replaced by a marker to indicate its use in forming an r-reduct possible rule. Then go to step 2.

Step 4: Set i=i+1. If i># of objects in the data set, stop. Otherwise go to step 2.

4.3 A Rule Generation and Rule Induction Prototype

Combining the MRG algorithm with the above rule induction schemes, we proposed a rule generation and rule induction prototype(RGRIP) that can automatically generate a minimal set of reducts and induce all certain rules as well as possible rule with all their plausibility indices as shown in Fugure4.1.

The first step of RGRIP is to transfer the data set into a decision table T. This generally involes data cleaning to eliminate obvious redundant or superfluous data

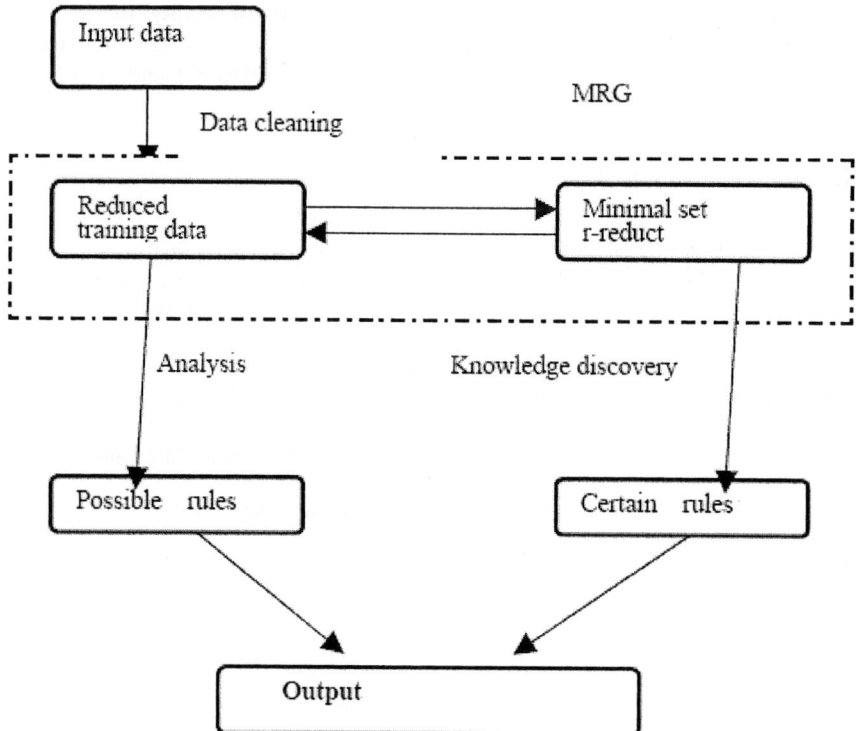

Fig. 1. The Mechanism of RGRIP

that may exist in a typical real world data set. The main step of RGRIP is to use MRG to generate a minimal set of rule-reducts and revise the training data set iteratively. All certain rule are then deduced directly from the minimal set of rule reducts. And all possible rules along with their plausibility indices are then deduced from the revised decision table.

5 Conclusion

First, we proposed a modified MRG algorithm to generate a minimal set of rule reducts directly and efficiently. MRG algorithm achieves both data reduction and minimal sets of rule reduct generation.The key different between the RG and MRG algorith is that MRG contains two-level mechanisms.The drawbacks of the RG algorithm is that it contains redundant and repeated reducts, which cannot provide wider pictures for predicting outcomes. Furthermore , when the lower dimension reducts fail to predict the new case, the MRG algorithm can tell us when to stop due to no higher order reducts are existed. Whereas MRG algorithm can help the decision-maker predict the outcomes of new cases effectively.

Then, Combining the MRG algorithm with the rule induction schemes, we proposed a rule generation and rule induction prototype(RGRIP) that can automatically generate a minimal set of reducts and induce all certain rules as well as possible rule with all their plausibility indices.In term of ability to deal with uncertainty and inconsistency in the data set, RGRIP approach appears simplicity and conciseness in the process of its usage. The approach is efficient and effective in dealing with large data sets.

References

1. Quinlan, J.R.(1986). Induction of decision tree.Machine learning 1:81-106.
2. Grzymala-Busse J.W.(1992)"LERS-A system for learning from example based on rough sets"Intelligent decision support:hand book of applications and advances of the rough set theory. Kluwer,3-18.
3. Khoo,L.P. ; Tor,S.B.;Zhai,L.Y.,"Rough-Set-based Approach to Classification and Rule INduction"International Journal of Advanced Manufacturing Technology, Sroiger- verlag, 1999. 15,438-444.
4. Pawlak,Z., "Rough Sets":Theoretical Aspects of Reasoning About Data,Kluwer,Boston. 1991.
5. Jia-Yuarn Guo, "Rough Set-Based Approach to Data Mining", 2003. IEEE

A Method to Eliminate Incompatible Knowledge and Equivalence Knowledge

Ping Guo, Li Fan, and Lian Ye

School of Computer Science, Chongqing University, Chongqing, 400044, China
guoping@cqu.edu.cn

Abstract. Knowledge base is the foundation of intelligent systems. It is very important to insure the consistency and non-redundancy of knowledge in a knowledge base. Due to the variety of exterior knowledge sources, it is necessary to eliminate incompatible knowledge and equivalence knowledge in the process of knowledge integration. In this paper, we research a strategy to eliminate incompatible knowledge and equivalence knowledge in knowledge integration based on equivalence classification, and so present a new knowledge integration algorithm which is effective in improving the efficiency of knowledge integration.

1 Introduction

Knowledge base is widely applied in expert systems and intelligent information systems. These systems require consistent, complete and unambiguous knowledge, and the convenience to use and maintenance the knowledge base. As much knowledge in knowledge base (especially, domain knowledge) is derived from different experts and exterior environments in the domain, there exists, therefore, redundant, conclusive, and indeed incompatible knowledge. For example, the knowledge of a diagnostic expert system is often distributed among groups of experts in correlative domains rather than being available for elicitation from a single expert. There may exist different diagnoses and treatments for the same symptom from different experts, and as such there may also exist redundancy, subsumption and contradiction as a consequence of integrating the knowledge too simply. The purpose of knowledge integration is to eliminate the redundancy, subsumption and contradiction.

Knowledge integration has been widely researched. Gaines and Shaw[1], Baral, Kraus and Minker[2] researched integrated techniques of multiple knowledge. Medsker, Tan and Turban[3] mention that integrating multiple knowledge sources is a multi-objective optimization problem, for which, due to the large search space, it is very difficult to find an optimal solution.

Wang, Hong and Tesng[5,6,7] propose the knowledge-integration strategies based on genetic algorithm (GA) at the rule-set level in a distributed-knowledge environment. The proposed knowledge integration consists of two phases: knowledge encoding and knowledge integration. In the first phase, the knowledge from different knowledge sources is transformed into centralized inner representation, and then encoded as a fixed-length bit string. In the second phase, the bit strings combined together thus form an initial knowledge population for genetic operation. The genetic process runs generation after generation until certain criteria (such as convergence of fitness values) have been met. The integrated knowledge base can be obtained by decoding the last population obtained. In [8], they add the knowledge precision procedure into the second phase. The quality of knowledge base can be improved even further with the interaction of experts.

In our view, the automatic knowledge-integration procedure could improve the construction of knowledge base, but the interaction with experts can slow the construction of a knowledge base, and add new inconsistencies, and even contradictions into the knowledge base. In this paper, we research the incompatible knowledge elimination approach in knowledge integration based on rough set theory, and give the approach to eliminate equivalence knowledge in knowledge base based on equivalence classification, then present a new knowledge-integration algorithm. The remainder of this paper is organized as follows: stipulate the centralized representation patterns based on whole dictionary in Section 2. In Section 3, the knowledge base is divided into non-incompatible knowledge set and possible incompatible knowledge set based on RS theory. In Section 4, the contradiction elimination approach and strategy in incompatible knowledge set is discussed, and it is proven that the knowledge set obtained is non-contradiction. In Section 5, a method to eliminate equivalence knowledge based on equivalence classification is presented. A new knowledge-integration algorithm is shown in Section 6. Conclusions are given in Section 7.

2 Uniform Representation Form for Knowledge

Knowledge integration is to bring together the knowledge or knowledge base from different sources and different representational forms, and to engender a logically centralized representation form for the knowledge, so that the knowledge in the knowledge base after integration is consistent, compatible and non-redundant. It should be convenient to use and maintenance such a knowledge base.

However, the greatest difficulty in knowledge integration is that the knowledge from different knowledge sources may have different forms of representation. They are shown as: (1) the same concepts expressed by different vocabularies; (2) similar vocabularies expressing different concepts; (3) uncertain natural language arousing uncertain concepts; (4) each expert has a different understanding and expression of the same knowledge. The representational differences bring difficulty in consistency detection, contradiction elimination and redundancy elimination of knowledge. So, we establish the centralized representation form for knowledge first. The steps are as follows:

(1) Establish whole centralized dictionary.
(2) Use production to represent the knowledge needed to integrate.

Dictionary is the set of conception, and it gives the consistency all knowledge needs to integrate effectively. It unifies the useable concepts in knowledge representation. Thus, it stipulates the diction of knowledge representation, and eliminates the uncertain knowledge representation caused by understanding, semantics and pragmatics etc. The dictionary is denoted as V.

It's well known that production is one of the most important representation forms, such as formula (1).

$$r: p \rightarrow q \tag{1}$$

There, p is the logic precondition and q is the logic conclusion of knowledge r respectively; they are denoted as pre(r) and con(r).

Using production, the knowledge u_i, which is needed to integrate in knowledge set $U=\{ u_i \}$, can be expressed as follows:

$$u_i: p_{i1} \wedge p_{i2} \wedge \ldots \wedge p_{in} \rightarrow q_i \tag{2}$$

There, $p_{ij} \in V$ or $\neg p_{ij} \in V$, $1 \leq j \leq n$; $q_i \in V \cup \{true, false\}$ or $\neg q_i \in V \cup \{true, false\}$.

Formula (2) is the centralized representation form for knowledge.

3 Knowledge Classification Based on RS

The set of formula (2) constructs a decision-making table on U. In this section, we will use RS theory to classify U. We construct the relation R in knowledge set U as follows:

$$R: u_i R u_j \Leftrightarrow \text{logic precondition of } u_i = \text{logic precondition of } u_j \ \forall u_i, u_j \in U \tag{3}$$

That is, relation R exists between u_i and u_j iff logic precondition of u_i and u_j are the same.

That R is an equivalence relation on U can be proved. The equivalence class obtained by equivalence relation R on U is denoted as U_R.

The set composed of knowledge logic conclusion in U is denoted as Q:

$$Q = \{ con(u_i) \mid u_i \in U \}$$

The subset U_i of U can be defined by knowledge logic conclusion Q:

$$U_i = U(u_i) = \{ u_j | u_j \in U, q_j = q_i, con(u_j) = con(u_i) \} \tag{4}$$

Obviously, there is $U = \cup U_i$ and if $U_l \neq U_m$ then $U_l \cap U_m = \emptyset$.

Therefore, some definitions are given as follows:

Definition 1. Suppose subset $U_i \subset U$,

$$\underline{Apr}_R(U_i) = \{ u | u \in x \ \& \ x \in U_R \ \& \ x \subset U_i \}$$

$$\overline{Apr}_R(U_i) = \{ u | u \in x \ \& \ x \in U_R \ \& \ x \cap U_i \neq \emptyset \}$$

Called lower-approximation set and upper-approximation set of U_i based on equivalence relation R, respectively, we mark the symbol:

$$\underline{Apr}_R(U) = \bigcup_i \underline{Apr}_R(U_i) \tag{5}$$

Definition 2. Suppose subset $U_i \subset U$,

$$BND_R(U_i) = \overline{Apr}_R(U_i) - \underline{Apr}_R(U_i)$$

Called boundary set of U_i based on equivalence relation R, we mark the symbol:

$$BND_R(U) = \bigcup_i BND_R(U_i) \tag{6}$$

Definition 3 is given as follows in order to eliminate the possible contradiction in knowledge of U:

Definition 3. $\forall u_j, u_k \in U$, if $per(u_j) = per(u_k)$ and $con(u_j) \neq con(u_k)$, we called u_j is inconsistent with u_k.

Using the lower-approximation set and boundary set of U_i, we can obtain Theorem 1.

Theorem 1. The knowledge in $\underline{Apr}_R(U_i)$ is non-contradiction, and the knowledge in $\underline{Apr}_R(U)$ is non-contradiction.

Proof: divide two steps to prove.

(1) To prove the knowledge in $\underline{Apr}_R(U_i)$ is non-contradiction.

For $\forall u_j, u_k \in \underline{Apr}_R(U_i)$, by definition 1, $u_j, u_k \in U_i \subset U$, so $con(u_j) = con(u_k)$. There are two instances:

① when u_j, u_k belongs to the same equivalence class of U_R, $per(u_j) = per(u_k)$, so u_j is consistent with u_k.

② when u_j, u_k belongs to different equivalence classes of U_R, $per(u_j) \neq per(u_k)$, so u_j is consistent with u_k.

Therefore, the knowledge in $\underline{Apr}_R(U_i)$ is non-contradiction.

(2) To prove the knowledge in $\underline{Apr}_R(U)$ is non-contradiction.

Obviously, proof is only needed when $U_l \neq U_m$, the knowledge in $\underline{Apr}_R(U_l)$ is consistent with the knowledge in $\underline{Apr}_R(U_m)$.

Applying negative approach for proof: suppose $u_j \in \underline{Apr}_R(U_l)$ contradicts $u_k \in \underline{Apr}_R(U_m)$, referring to Definition 3, there is $per(u_j) = per(u_k)$ and $con(u_j) \neq con(u_k)$. According to $u_j \in \underline{Apr}_R(U_l)$, $u_k \in \underline{Apr}_R(U_m)$ and the definition of lower-approximation set, there are:

$$\exists x \in U_R \ \& \ u_j \in x \ \& \ x \subset U_l$$

$$\exists y \in U_R \ \& \ u_k \in y \ \& \ y \subset U_m$$

Considering the supposition $per(u_j) = per(u_k)$, that is, u_j and u_k belong to the same equivalence class, we have:

$$x = y$$

so,

$$u_j \in x \subset U_l \cap U_m$$

which is incompatible with $U_l \neq U_m$ because when $U_l \neq U_m$, $U_l \cap U_m = \emptyset$.
As summarized above, the theorem is correct. [♦]
Considering the relation between $\overline{Apr}_R(U)$ and $BND_R(U)$, we have Theorem 2.

Theorem 2. The knowledge in $\overline{Apr}_R(U)$ and $BND_R(U)$ is non-contradiction.

Proof:
Applying the negative approach for proof: suppose $u_j \in \overline{Apr}_R(U)$ contradicts $u_k \in BND_R(U)$, referring to Definition 3, there is $per(u_j) = per(u_k)$ and $con(u_j) \neq con(u_k)$. That is, u_j and u_k have the same logic preconditions and different logic conclusions.
On the one hand, due to $per(u_j) = per(u_k)$, then $\exists x \in U_R$, there is $: u_j \in x$ & $u_k \in x$.
On the other hand, due to $u_j \in \overline{Apr}_R(U)$, then $\exists U_l$, there is $u_j \in \overline{Apr}_R(U_l)$. Furthermore, we have:

$$\exists y \in U_R \ \& \ u_j \in y \ \& \ y \subset U_l$$

Therefore, $u_j \in x$, $u_j \in y$, and x, y are equivalence classes in U_R, there is $x = y$. This is,

$$u_j, u_k \in x \subset U_l$$

so

$$con(u_j) = con(u_k)$$

which contradicts $con(u_j) \neq con(u_k)$.
Therefore, u_j doesn't contradict u_k. That is, the knowledge in $\overline{Apr}_R(U)$ is consistent with the knowledge in $BND_R(U)$ [♦]
Furthermore, we can prove: $\forall U_l, U_m$,

$$BND_R(U_l) \cap \overline{Apr}_R(U_l) = \emptyset$$

$$\overline{Apr}_R(U_l) \cap \overline{Apr}_R(U_m) = \emptyset$$

$$BND_R(U_l) \cap \overline{Apr}_R(U_m) = \emptyset$$

Hence,

$$U = \bigcup_i \overline{Apr}_R(U_i) = \bigcup_i (BND_R(U_i) \cup \overline{Apr}_R(U_i)) \tag{7}$$
$$= \bigcup_i BND_R(U_i) \cup \bigcup_i \overline{Apr}_R(U_i)) = BND_R(U) \cup \overline{Apr}_R(U)$$

According to Theorem 1, Theorem 2 and Formula (7), we have: Theorem 3. If there is contradiction in U, it's inevitable that the knowledge in $BND_R(U)$ is contradictive.
From Theorem 3, for eliminating the incompatible knowledge in U, we only need to eliminate the incompatible knowledge in $BND_R(U)$.

4 Eliminating Incompatible Knowledge

There has been much research to eliminate incompatible knowledge in a knowledge base, and many strategies have been presented. For example, genetic algorithm in [5,6,7,8] is used to eliminate incompatible knowledge. In this paper, a test dataset is introduced to eliminate the contradiction of knowledge in $BND_R(U)$.

Definition 4. Assume the test object set Ω. That object $o \in \Omega$ is correctly predicted by knowledge u_i which means the logic precondition of u_i is satisfied with o and the logic conclusion of u_i is consistent with the conclusion of o. Denote the object set correctly predicted by u_i as Ω_{u_i}. That object o is wrongly predicted by knowledge u_i meaning the logic precondition of u_i is satisfied with o but the logic conclusion of u_i is inconsistent with the conclusion of o. Denote the object set wrongly predicted by u_i as $\bar{\Omega}_{u_i}$.

By using test object set Ω, calculate the object set Ω_{u_i} correctly predicted and the object set $\bar{\Omega}_{u_i}$ wrongly predicted by each item of knowledge u_i in $BND_R(U)$, and calculate the following parameters:

$$A(u_i) = \begin{cases} 0 & |\Omega_{u_i}| + |\bar{\Omega}_{u_i}| = 0 \\ \dfrac{|\Omega_{u_i}|}{|\Omega_{u_i}| + |\bar{\Omega}_{u_i}|} & |\Omega_{u_i}| + |\bar{\Omega}_{u_i}| \neq 0 \end{cases} \tag{8}$$

$$E(u_i) = \sum_{o \in \Omega} \frac{\Phi(u_i, o)}{\sum_{u \in BND_R(U)} \Phi(u, o)} \tag{9}$$

Therefore,

$$\Phi(v, o) = \begin{cases} 1 & \text{test object } o \text{ is correctly predicted by knowledge } v \\ 0 & \text{otherwise} \end{cases}$$

$$C(u_i) = \frac{|\Omega_{u_i}| + |\bar{\Omega}_{u_i}|}{|\Omega|} \tag{10}$$

The calculated result of Formula (8), (9) and (10) is called accuracy, utility and coverage of u_i, respectively. For every knowledge base, high accuracy, utility, and coverage are desired, but these cannot usually be satisfied at the same time. Calculate the following integrative criterion:

$$f(u_i) = A(u_i) * E(u_i) * C(u_i) \tag{11}$$

The strategy for eliminating incompatible knowledge in $BND_R(U)$ by calculating the result of formula (11) is shown in the following steps:

(1) The calculated results of Formula (11) are sorted in descending order.
(2) for $\forall u_i, u_j \in BND_R(U)$ {
   if $(pre(u_i) = pre(u_j))$ and $(con(u_i) \neq con(u_j))$ then
      if $f(u_i) \geq f(u_j)$ then $BND_R(U) \leftarrow BND_R(U) - \{u_j\}$
      else $BND_R(U) \leftarrow BND_R(U) - \{u_i\}$
   }

After eliminating incompatible knowledge in $BND_R(U)$, we obtain the result set denoted as $\underline{BND_R(U)}$, then denote:

$$\underline{U} = \underline{Apr_R(U)} \cup \underline{BND_R(U)} \tag{12}$$

We can obtain:

Theorem 4. The knowledge in $\underline{U}$ is non-contradiction.

Proof:

$\forall u_j, u_k \in \underline{U}$, there are three cases as follows:

① $u_j, u_k \in \underline{Apr_R(U)}$, by Theorem 1, u_j is consistent with u_k.
② $u_j \in \underline{Apr(U)}$, $u_k \in \underline{BND_R(U)}$, because of $\underline{BND_R(U)} \subset BND_R(U)$ and Theorem 2, u_j is consistent with u_k.
③ $u_j, u_k \in \underline{BND(U)}$. u_j is consistent with u_k according to the construction procedure of $\underline{BND(U)}$

Summarized above, the theorem is correct. [♦]

5 Eliminating Equivalence Knowledge in a Knowledge Base

Here, we discuss the method to eliminate equivalence knowledge in $\underline{U}$ based on equivalence class.

Definition 5. $u_j, u_k \in \underline{U}$, if:

$$per(u_j) = per(u_k) \ \& \ con(u_j) = con(u_k)$$

u_j and u_k are called equivalence knowledge.

Obviously, saving all equivalence knowledge in a knowledge base is insignificant for the application of a knowledge base; we can save only one piece of knowledge and eliminate the other knowledge.

Similar to Formula (3), the equivalence relation R' in $\underline{U}$ is defined as:

$$R': u_i R' u_j \Leftrightarrow pre(u_i) = pre(u_j) \ \forall u_i, u_j \in \underline{U}$$

The equivalence class obtained by equivalence relation R' on $\underline{U}$ is denoted as $U_{R'}$.

Theorem 5. $\forall x \in \underline{U_R}$, if $|x|>1$, the knowledge in x is equivalence.

Proof:

Due to $|x|>1$, $\forall u_j, u_k \in x$, we have:

$$per(u_j) = per(u_k)$$

and the knowledge in $\underline{U}$ is consistent, so,

$$con(u_j) = con(u_k)$$

Therefore, u_j and u_k are equivalence knowledge. [♦]

Furthermore, we can prove:

Theorem 6. $\forall x, y \in \underline{U_R}$, if $x \neq y$, the knowledge in x is not equivalent to the knowledge in y.

According to Theorem 5 and Theorem 6, each equivalence class of $\underline{U}_R$ can eliminate redundant equivalence knowledge by saving only one piece of knowledge. This process can be judged by the logic precondition of knowledge as follows:

for $\forall u_j, u_k \in \underline{U}$ if $pre(u_j) = pre(u_k)$ then $\underline{U} \leftarrow \underline{U} - \{u_k\}$

Through the process of elimination, there is no equivalence knowledge in $\underline{U}$.

6 Knowledge-Integration Algorithm

According to research conclusions from Section 2 to Section 5, the algorithm KBI_EIK&RK, which is applied to eliminate incompatible knowledge and equivalence knowledge in the process of knowledge integration, is shown as follows:

Algorithm KBI_EIK&RK;
```
  Input: Knowledge base B_i from a different knowledge
         source, test object set Ω;
  Output: Integration knowledge base B;
  Steps:

   (1) Building whole dictionary V;
   (2) According to V, create knowledge set U as For-
       mula (2) to code all knowledge in ∪B_i ;
   (3) For U, create equivalence classification U_R in U as
       Formula (3);
   (4) For U, create subset set {U_i} of U as Formula (4);
   (5) For each U_i ∈U, calculate Apr_R(U_i) and BND_R(U_i);
   (6) Calculate
```
$$\underline{Apr}_R(U) = \bigcup_i \underline{Apr}_R(U_i) \,;$$

$$BND_R(U) = \bigcup_i BND_R(U_i) \,;$$

```
   (7) For each u_i ∈ BND_R(U), Calculate:
       f(u_i)=A(u_i)*E(u_i)*C(u_i) as Formula (11);
   (8) Sort {f(u_i)} in descending order;
   (9) For each u_i, u_j∈ BND_R(U),
         If u_i and u_j are incompatible then {
           If f(u_i) ≥ f(u_j) then BND_R(U)← BND_R(U) -{u_j};
           else BND_R(U)← BND_R(U) -{u_i};
         }
  (10) U ← Apr_R(U) ∪ BND_R(U) ;
  (11) For each u_i , u_j∈ U, if pre(u_i)=pre(u_j) then U ←
       U -{u_j};
  (12) Return U.
```

By the Theorem 4,5,6, algorithm KBI_EIK&RK is correct. The time complexity of KBI_EIK&RK is $O(|U|^2 + |BND_R(U)| \times |\Omega|)$ can be proved.

7 Conclusions

One of the pivotal problems in knowledge-integration research is how to eliminate the incompatible knowledge and redundant knowledge from a knowledge base. In this paper, the knowledge in knowledge base is divided into two types by RS theory: non-incompatible knowledge set and possible incompatible knowledge set. For each item of knowledge in a possible incompatible knowledge set, calculating the accuracy, utility and coverage of test data provides a feasible approach to eliminating incompatible knowledge. For the knowledge base, which has eliminated the incompatible knowledge, we give the method to eliminate equivalence knowledge through distinguishing the logic precondition of knowledge based on the equivalence classification.

The research in this paper indicates that it is an effective method to divide the knowledge base to be integrated into a non-incompatible knowledge set and a possible incompatible knowledge set for knowledge integration. The paper presents a new algorithm to eliminate incompatible knowledge and redundant knowledge in a knowledge base. On the one hand, our knowledge-integration approach takes less processing time than some other previous knowledge-integration approaches. On the other hand, if we combine our research with GA, select boundary set $BND_R(U)$ obtained by RS classification as initial population instead of the whole knowledge base U (which is effective to reduce the scale of genetic initial population and to improve the efficiency of genetic operation), we can prove, when the conclusion set of genetic operation is a non-incompatible knowledge set, that the union of the set and lower-approximation set $\underline{Apr}_R(U)$ of RS classification is a non-incompatible knowledge set too.

Acknowledgements

This research was supported by the National Natural Science Foundation of China, NO. 50378093.

References

1. Gaines, B. R., & Shaw, M. L. (1993). Eliciting knowledge and transferring it effectively to a knowledge-based system. IEEE Transaction on Knowledge and Data Engineering, 5 (1), 4–14.
2. Baral, C., Kraus, S., & Minker, J. (1991). Combining multiple knowledge bases. IEEE Transactions on Knowledge and Data Engineering, 3 (2), 208–220.
3. Yuan, Y., & Zhuang, H. (1996). A genetic algorithm for generating fuzzy classification rules. Fuzzy Sets and Systems, 84, 1–19.
4. Medsker, L., Tan, M., & Turban, E. (1995). Knowledge acquisition from multiple experts: problems and issues. Expert Systems with Applica-tions, 9 (1), 35–40.
5. Wang, C. H., Hong, T. P., & Tseng, S. S. (1997). Knowledge integration by genetic algorithms. Proceedings of the Seventh International Fuzzy Systems Association World Congress, 2, 404–408.
6. Wang, C. H., Hong, T. P., & Tseng, S. S. (1998). A genetic fuzzy-knowledge integration framework. The Seventh International Conference of Fuzzy Systems, 1194–1199.
7. Wang, C. H., Hong, T. P., & Tseng, S. S. (2000). Integrating membership functions and fuzzy rule sets from multiple knowledge sources, Fuzzy Sets and Systems, 112, 141–154.

8. Wang, C. H., Hong, T. P., & Tseng, S. S. (2000). A Genetics-Based Approach to Knowledge Integration and Refinement. Journal of Information Science and Engineering, 17, 85-94.
9. Mathias,K.E.&Whity,L.D.(1994),Transforming the Search Spacs with Gray Coding, Proc. of the 1st IEEE Intl. Conf. On Evolutionary Computation,Orlando,Florid,USA,IEEE Press,519-542.
10. Wang, C. H., Hong, T. P., & Tseng, S. S. (2000). A Coverage-based Genetic Knowledge-integration strategy, Experty Systems with Applications,19(2000),9-17.

Constructing Ontologies for Sharing Knowledge in Digital Archives

Yu-Liang Chi

Department of Management Information System, Chung Yuan Christian University,
200 Chung Pei Rd., Chung-Li, 32023 Taiwan, R.O.C
maxchi@cycu.edu.tw

Abstract. This study describes the building of ontologies to enhance current digital museum archives. Ontologies are employed to move the service level from information to knowledge retrieval. This study concentrates on a design procedure that exploits Formal Concept Analysis (FCA) to obtain conceptual structures, and Description Logic (DL) to denote concept relations in logic expressions. The empirical findings reveal that development procedures help guide ontology builders to build ontological knowledge bases step by step. Furthermore, the knowledge extraction is helpful and connectable for builders and other tools.

1 Introduction

The digital archives project has been established in the National Museum of Natural Science (NMNS) in Taiwan. This project is designed for devising various domains of natural science, such as zoology, botany, geology and anthropology. Although the content can be manually represented using a query or through metadata schemas or hyperlinks, this study argues that the digital archive is a promising model for providing "knowledge". Restated, the usability of the current NMNS focuses only on providing explicit and static information. The current systems are thus inadequate for supporting advanced knowledge engineering, such as knowledge inference processes.

Digital museums apply information technology to establish online services that users can access without requiring their physical presence. Some challenges facing current information systems have to be considered to enable knowledge reuse and sharing for the public. Ontology is an approach utilized in knowledge management to create well defined knowledge bases [2], [13]. Ontology need to be built in a systematic, granular fashion, because large gaps exist between cognitions of the real world and conceptual structures of ontology, a development of construction is required [16]. Therefore, this study has the following objectives: (1) to design an approach for efficiently identifying ontological conceptual structures, and (2) designing a means to assist knowledge representation using a logic-based language. To achieve these aims, this study examined existing extraction approaches, surveyed corresponding tools, and made necessary revisions.

This study employs formal concept analysis (FCA) to recognize concepts and determine their hierarchical relationships. To simplify the application of description logic (DL), this study proposes several DL models for developers. The empirical feedback demonstrates that FCA is valuable when constructing conceptual structures in ontology. Additionally, developers do not need much design time or mathematical skill to apply DL models.

2 Ontology and XML-Based Ontology Languages

Ontologies have long been adopted to express shared understanding of information by human beings. Gruber defined ontology as "*a specification of a conceptualization*" [7]. A conceptualization is an abstract, simplified view of the world for representation. That is, the ontology is a formal description of the concepts, attributes and relationships involved in building a common understanding for cognitions of real world events [2], [17]. The knowledge base community employs ontological approaches by defining a set of terminologies, the universe of discourses and axioms [9]. Consequently, ontology is valuable for defining the common vocabulary used to represent shared knowledge [8]. Wide agreement exists that developers employing ontology-based systems must concentrating on specific domain problems and provide common understandings of individual concepts. However, challenges exist in eliciting cognition from the real world and thus designing concepts of ontology.

XML technology has recently been introduced for data exchange and system development in various application fields. Ontology research uses XML to construct building and schema bases for ontological development languages. Moreover, many XML-based ontology editing tools have been developed [3], [10]. Two ontology languages, DAML+OIL and OWL, are described below:

DARPA Agent Markup Language (DAML). Since 2000, DAML (DARPA Agent Markup Language) has been developed as an extension to XML and RDF. The recent release of DAML plus Ontology Interchange Language (OIL) provides a rich set of constructs for building ontologies and marking up information to make it machine readable and understandable [5], [14]. More details of DAML+OIL can be found at http://www.daml.org.

Ontology Web Language (OWL). OWL is the newest XML-based ontological language to be developed by the W3C. OWL inherits most features from DAML+OIL, and has now become an official and formal standard. According to the OWL specifications, the standard has three increasingly expressive sublanguages for various levels of usability [12]: OWL-Lite is designed for a classification hierarchy and straightforward constraint features; OWL-DL supports users who want the maximum expressiveness while retaining computational completeness and decidability, and OWL-Full has useful computational properties for reasoning systems with maximum expressiveness, but without computational guarantees. Further background on OWL can be found at http://www.w3c.org/2004/owl.

3 Ontology Concepts Recognized by the Formal Concept Analysis

To establish an ontology concept framework and discover hierarchical structures among concepts, this study applies formal concept analysis (FCA) approach. FCA was originally a data analysis method based on lexical and hierarchical problems [9], and categorizes elements as formal objects and formal attributes. The sets of formal objects and attributes, together with their relationship with each other, form a "formal context". When the relationships in a pair of formal objects and attributes can not be increased, the pair is closed and further called a "formal concept". Concept lattices comprise the set of concepts of a formal context and the hierarchical relations among the concepts [11]. More detailed descriptions of FCA can be found in [6].

Table 1. An example of vascular plants in lattice context

	Seed	Fern seed	Herb	Arborous	Angiospermae	Gymnospermae
Pinacene	X			X		X
Thelypteridaceae	X			X	X	
Aceraceae		X	X			
Araceae	X		X			

According to FCA theory[6], the formal context of concepts *(K)* can be denoted as *K= (G, M, I)*. The objects *(G)* include *{Pinacene, Thelypteridaceae, Aceraceae, Araceae}*, while the attributes *(M)* include *{Seed, Fern seed, Herb, and arborous, Angiospermae, Gymnospermae}*. Table 1 presents the objects on the left hand side and the attributes on the top. The symbol X denotes a binary relation between an object and its attribute. For instance, the object "Pinacene" has the attribute "Seed".

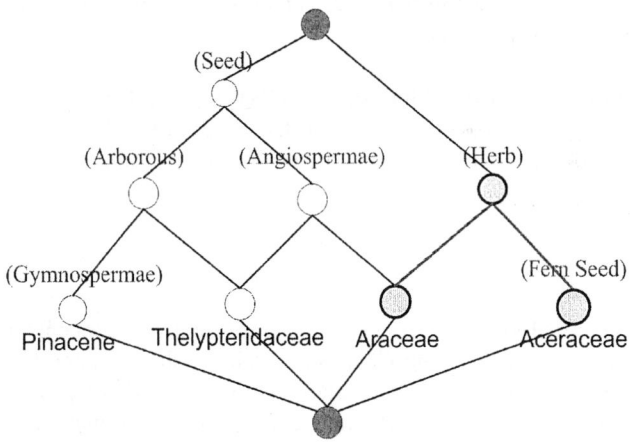

Fig. 1. An example of vascular plants analyzed by FCA and demonstrated in the line diagram. The attribute tag is above the node, and the object tag is below the node.

A line diagram visually represents the FCA formal context. The line diagram in Fig. 1 consists of nodes, lines and the tags of all objects (denoted below the node) as well as attributes (denoted above the node) of the given context. The line diagram depicts the dependency relationships among formal concepts. A formal concept can be defined as {(objects set), (attributes set)}. For instance, the formal concept *{(ϕ), (Herb)}* is attached to a node above the *{(Araceae), (Herb, Seed, Arborous)}* and *{(Aceraceae), (Herb, Fern Seed)}* nodes. Each node below its super-node, indicates a "super-sub" relationship in terms of the "is-a" hierarchical conceptual clustering. Hence, FCA is a helpful technique for determining stable dependency relationships among concepts.

4 Knowledge Representation: Using Description Logic

Knowledge representation represents expertise into information systems with specific formats. The description logic (DL) is a describable fragment consisting of classes, properties and logical notations that express attribute or class relations [1]. DL has been widely employed as a representation format by various ontology development approaches including OIL and OWL [4]. To facilitate the inference capability, this study utilizes OWL-DL as the knowledge representation. A description logic reasoner can calculate a subsumption hierarchy of all named concepts. A concept is categorized into the defined ($\equiv$) or primitive ($\sqsubseteq$) class. Every description is primitive, that is, with at least one set of necessary conditions, by default. Conversely, a class is defined if it has descriptions and sufficient conditions. The difference between the primitive and defined class is that the defined class can be equally bi-directional. In the expression $C \equiv D$, if an instance is a member of the concept D then it must fulfill a member of concept C. An instance in a primitive class is not equally bi-directional. The following DL models are proposed to help developers define proper logic expressions.

The Complement Concept Model: Let $C(x)$ represent a concept comprising relationship $R_{(x)}$ and two concepts, $C(x)'$ and $C(x)''$. Both $C(x)'$ and $C(x)''$ can be any concepts related to $C(x)$. The CComplement denotes a complementary concept of $C(x)$, and is marked by the complement symbol ($\neg$).

$$C(x) = (C(x)' \ R_{(x)} \ C(x)'') \tag{1}$$
$$C_{Complement}(x) \equiv \neg C(x)$$

The New Concept Model: Let $C(x)$ and $C(y)$ represent two concepts. Concept $C(x)$ comprises two concepts $C(x)'$ and $C(x)''$ and a relationship $R_{(x)}$, and $C(y)$ consists of two concepts $C(y)'$ and $C(y)''$ and a relationship $R_{(y)}$. Both $C(x)$ and $C(y)$ can be replaced by their complements. A new concept Cnew signature is defined as follows.

$$C(x) = (C(x)' \ R_{(x)} \ C(x)'') \text{ or } C_{Complement}(x) \tag{2}$$
$$C(y) = (C(y)' \ R_{(y)} \ C(y)'') \text{ or } C_{Complement}(y)$$
$$C_{new} \sqsubseteq C(x) \ R_{(x,y)} \ C(y)$$

To define detailed semantic of concepts, DL applies property restrictions for precisely description, such as quantifier, cardinality and assigned value.

Table 2. Let C and D denote two concepts respectively. Table 2 lists the basic description logic axioms used to describe relationships between ontology concepts.

Axiom	Notation	Implication
$C \sqsubseteq D$	subClassOf	The former concept C is the subclass of the later concept D.
$C \sqcap D$	intersectionOf	Anything is concept C that is also Concept D.
$C \sqcup D$	unionOf	Anything that is either concept C or concept D.
$\neg D$	complementOf	Anything that is not concept D.

The Quantifier Restriction Model: The quantifier restriction comprises a quantifier $R_{(x)}$, a property $P(x)$ and a filler $C(x)$ (which can be a concept or concepts combination). Two quantifiers, existential ($\exists$) and universal ($\forall$), are frequently employed to represent the amount. The signature of a new concept C_{new} can be written as

$$C_{new} \sqsubseteq {}_{R(x)} P(x) \, C(x) \quad (3)$$

The Cardinality Restriction Model: The cardinality restriction comprises a property $P(x)$, a quantifier $R_{(x)}$ and a numeral number. Three cardinalities are applied to represent at most ($\geq$), the exactly ($=$), and at least ($\leq$). The signature of a new concept C_{new} can be expressed as

$$C_{new} \sqsubseteq P(x) \, {}_{R(x)} \text{Numeral} \quad (4)$$

The Value Restriction Model: The value restriction comprises a property $P(x)$, a value quantifier ($\ni$) and an instance. The signature of a new concept C_{new} can be expressed as

$$C_{new} \sqsubseteq P(x) \ni I(x) \quad (5)$$

Let C and D denote two concepts. Table 3 summarizes the property restriction constructors, axioms and their meanings.

Table 3. Basic description logic axioms used in defining restrictions of ontological properties

Axiom	Notation	Description
$\exists C$	at least	At least something from concept C.
$\forall C$	all things	All things from concept C.
$C \geq 2$	at least (value)	There must be at least 2 concept C.
$C \leq 2$	at most (value)	There must be at most 2 concept C.
$C = 2$	at exactly (value)	There must be at exactly 2 concept C.
$\exists n$	has value	A property *hasthing* has value *true*.

The above models help address most cases when defining ontological concepts. However, some exceptions, such as the disjoint and inverse axioms, require further supporting supplements. Disjoint concepts are concepts that do not belong to each other, and therefore conflict with each other. The inverse property gives related concepts or individuals a bi-direction relationship. For instance, if $C\ hasValue\ D$ denotes a DL expression, where C and D represent two classes, then the inverse property of the DL expression is given by $D\ isValue\ C$.

5 An Example

5.1 Create Vascular Plant Ontology

This study utilizes Protégé and relevant supporting tools to establish ontological knowledge bases. Protégé is an integrated development tool providing simple customizable editor and implementation functions. Protégé serves as a common architecture allowing plug-ins of extensible applications plug-in and providing add-on functionality [12], [15]. The protégé plug-in allows developers to manipulate and visualize OWL classes and their properties, such as reasoning engines. Racer is a reasoner that enables inference functionalities by calculating the concept definitions defined using description logic. Hence, these supporting tools provide synergy to help create an ontological knowledge base.

This study created the vascular plant ontology, based on Protégé, to illustrate the usability of ontological knowledge bases. A retrieval system programmed using the work was employed to query knowledge semantically. To elicit concepts efficiently from knowledge and create an ontological structure, both knowledge engineers and experts were trained to use formal concept analysis to extract cognitions into ontological concept structures, as depicted in the tree view in the left window of Fig. 2. The next step, after establishing the conceptual structures, is to provide formal definitions, using description logic, to describe each part. For instance, the asserted conditions window in the middle-bottom part of Fig. 2 describes the "Rhododendron". The following expressions are partial definitions of the "Rhododendron":

1. Rhododendron ⊑ NamedPlant
2. Rhododendron ⊑ ∃hasFlower((Flower ⊓ (∃hasCorolla CampanulateCorolla))⊔ TubularCorolla ⊔ (Funnelform-Corolla⊓ (∃hasInflorescence Raceme)) ⊔ CompoundRaceme)
3. Rhododendron ⊑ ∃hasFruit(Fruit ⊓ (∃hasSeed Seed)⊓ (∃hasCotyledon EvenCotyledon))
4. Rhododendron ⊑ ∃hasLeaf((Leaf ⊓ (∃hasShapeOfLeaf EllipticalLeaf))⊔ LanceolateLeaf ⊔ DeltoidLeaf ⊔ (ObovateLeaf⊓ (∃hasShapeOfLeaf Entiremargin)))
5. Rhododendron ⊑ ∃hasRoot MycorrhizaRoot
6. Rhododendron ⊑ ∃hasStem ErectStem
7. Rhododendron ⊑ ∃hasVascular Vascular

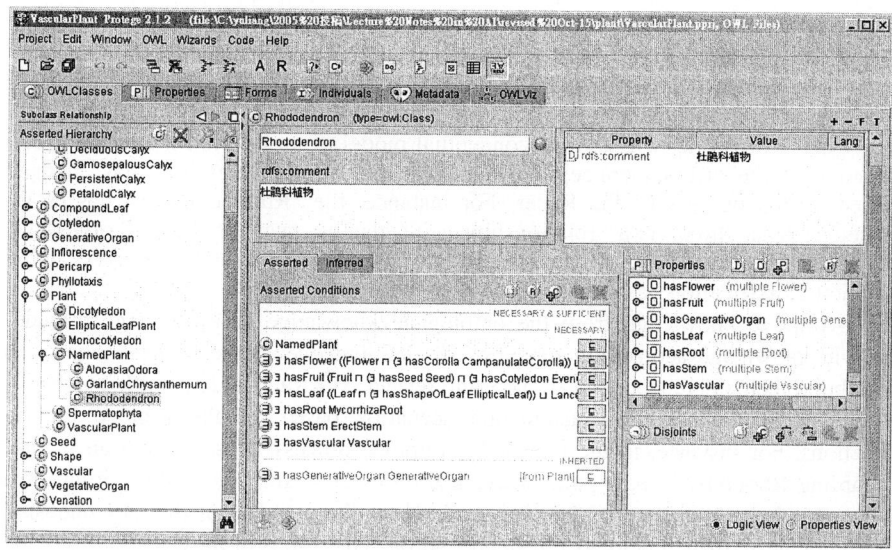

Fig. 2. A screen shot of building vascular ontology using a Protégé editor. The asserted conditions window demonstrates the DL expressions of the "Rhododendron" concept (class).

Each DL expressions can be associated with several items including notations, properties and fillers. The filler can be a class, a set of classes, or a combination of another DL expression. For instance, if the "Rhododendron" has a feature of erect steam, then this feature can be described using an existential notation ($\exists$), a property (*hasStem*) and the filler (*erectStem*). The DL expression is therefore defined as $\exists hasStem\ (erectSteam)$. The asserted conditions have two different categories, necessary ($\sqsubseteq$) and necessary & sufficient ($\equiv$). The necessary expressions represent a subsumption relationship, and the necessary & sufficient expressions represent a bidirectional equivalent relationship. In this example, the "Rhododendron" only indicates necessary expressions.

The OWL plugin provides integrated capability to description logic reasoner such as Jess, Clips and Racer. This study utilizes the Racer to exploit inference functionalities, such as consistency checking and taxonomy classifying. The consistency checking validates each class definition. Any inconsistency signifies that the ontology has logic issue and can not be classified correctly. Therefore, the user has to change the asserted conditions. The taxonomic classification is determined according to asserted conditions based on DL, generating an inferred hierarchy including both asserted and inferred classes.

5.2 Knowledge Inference and Retrieval

The protégé platform can integrate description logic reasoner engine, such as Jess, Clips and Racer. This study uses the Racer as a DL reasoner. The Racer provides several functionalities, such as consistency checking and taxonomic classification for basic inference process. The consistency checking validates each class definition. If any inconsistency occurs, then the ontology has a logic issue and can not be classified accurately. Designers must then modify definitions in the ontology, such as asserted conditions. The taxonomic classification is conducted according to asserted conditions to generate an inferred hierarchy, which includes both asserted and inferred classes.

Figure 3 illustrates a graphical conceptual model of an inferred hierarchy. Compared with the original conceptual hierarchy, the inferred hierarchy has changed based on the process of the Racer. For instance, the "Rhododendron" has established at least three "is-a" relationships with classes, such as the "Dicotyledon", "EllipticalLeafPlant" and "Spermatophyta". Therefore, a reasoner derives more implicit classification based on asserted conditions.

To retrieve knowledge from the ontological knowledge bases, Protégé provides built-in knowledge acquisition functions by defining query criteria. Developers can also build their inference applications using related API, such as Jena API. This study designs several knowledge acquisition scenarios based on the protégé built-in functions. For instance, in the knowledge retrieval process, a user makes an inquiry regarding Rhododendron, a pink flower and an erect steam. The system produces a recommended Rhododendron list. Figure 4 shows the outcome of the user choosing "Dendrocharis", which belongs to Rhododendron. The results of most sections provide general information regarding plant characteristics. Meanwhile, the "has image" section displays two URLs of images located in a mirror site of the NMNS content management system. Two images are obtained and displayed in different windows.

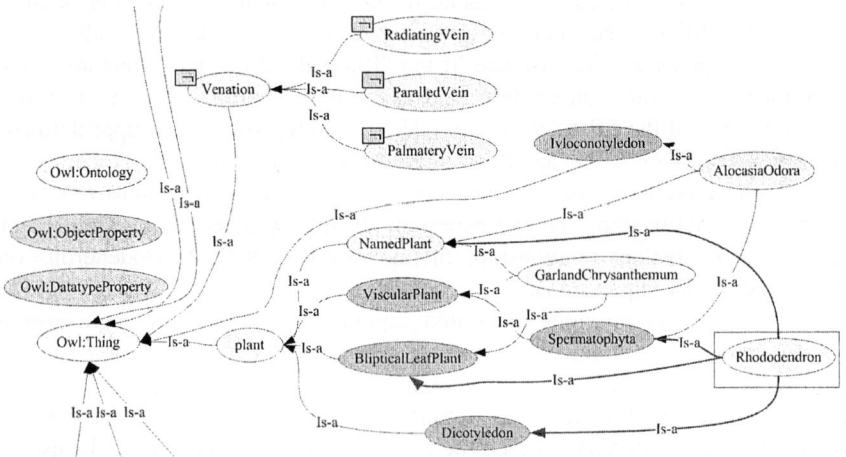

Fig. 3. Inferred conceptual hierarchy of vascular plant ontology emphasizes derived implicit relations. This shows several new "is-a" relations (thick line) from the "Rhododendron" class.

6 Conclusion

Figure 4 looks like a standard Web page that can be published by any author who fills out proper data. However, the value of this study lies in demonstrating that the digital archives of NMNS can be promoted as knowledge sources, and can be reused by the public in the future. Conventional approaches may only provide system integration rather than infer their contents in knowledge layers. That is, knowledge sharing involves not only system connection but also the participation of knowledge inference mechanisms. The following empirical conclusions related to development techniques can be drawn. First, the formal concept analysis (FCA) can be employed as a knowledge acquisition approach to acquire concepts and attributes from expertise. Second, the OWL-DL can be employed as a knowledge representation language that provides formal logic expressions to describe knowledge concepts. Consequently, this study indicates that ontological techniques have excellent knowledge-building potential. Future studies should be undertaken to construct related ontologies and further cooperate with other ontological knowledge bases.

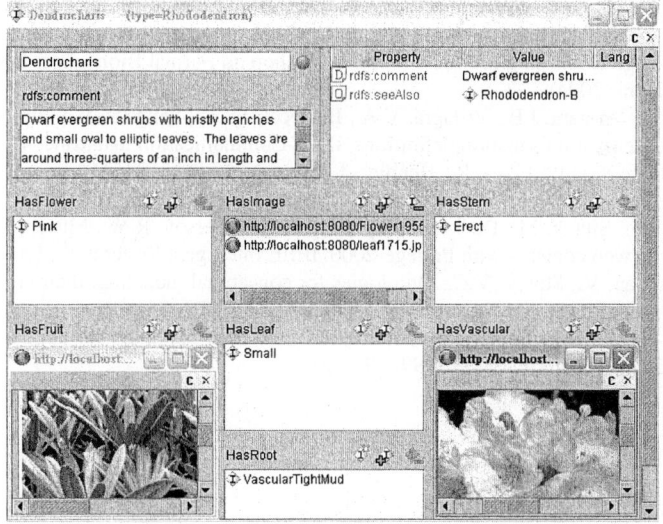

Fig. 4. General information of "Dendrocharis" is retrieved from Protégé query functions. Two images in different windows are pasted in the bottom of this figure.

References

1. Baader, F., Calvanese, D., McGuinness, D., Nardi, D. and Parel-Schneider, P. (eds.): The Description Logic Handbook. Cambridge University Press, Cambridge, UK (2003)
2. Chandrasekaran, B., Josephson, J.R., Benjamins, V.R.: What are ontologies, and why do we need them? IEEE Intelligent Systems 14 (1999) 20-26
3. Decker, S., Melnik, S., Harmelen, F.V., Fensel, D., Klein, M., Broekstra, J., Erdmann, M., Horrocks, I.: The Semantic Web: The Roles of XML and RDF. IEEE Internet Computing 4 (2000) 63-74
4. Diego, C., Giacomo, G.D., Lenzerini, M.: Description Logics: Foundations for Class-based Knowledge Representation," Proc. of the IEEE Sym. on Logic in Computer Science (2002) 359-370

5. Dieter, V. Horrocks, I. Harmelen, F.V. McGuinness, D. Patel-Schneider, P.E.: OIL: ontology infrastructure to enable the semantic Web. IEEE Intelligent System 16 (2001) 38-45
6. Ganter, B., Wille, R.: Formal Concept Analysis: Mathematical Foundations. 1st edn. Springer-Verlag, Berlin Heidelberg New York (1997)
7. Gruber, T.R.: A translation approach to portable ontologies. Knowledge Acquisition 5 (1993) 199-220
8. Gruninger, M., Atefi, K., Fox, M.S.: Ontologies to support process integration in enterprise engineering. Computational and Mathematical Organization Theory, 6 (2000) 381-394
9. Guarino, N.: Formal ontology, conceptual analysis and knowledge representation. Int. J. Human-Computer Studies 43 (1995) 625-640.
10. Horrocks, I. Patel-Schneider, P.F., Harmelen, F.V.: From SHIQ and RDF to OWL: the making of a Web Ontology Language. Web Semantics: science, services and agents on the WWW 1 (2003) 7-26
11. Jiang, G., Ogasawara, K., Endoh, A., Sakurai, T.: Context-based Ontology Building Support in Clinical Domains using Formal Concept Analysis. J. of Medical Informatics 71 (2003)71-81
12. Knublauch, H., Dameron, O., Musen, M.A.: Weaving the biomedical semantic Web with the Protégé OWL plugin. Proc. 1st Int. Workshop on Formal Biomedical Knowledge Representation (2004)
13. López de Vergara, J.E., Villagrá, V.A., Berrocal, J.: Applying the Web ontology language to management information definitions. IEEE Communication magazine, 42 (2004) 68-74
14. McGuinness, D.L., Fikes, R., Hendler, J., Stein, L.A.: DAML+OIL: an ontology language for the Semantic Web. IEEE Intelligent Systems 17 (2002) 72-80
15. Noy, N.F., Sintek, M., Decker, S., Crubezy, M., Fergerson, R.W., Musen, M.A.: Creating semantic web contents with Protege-2000. IEEE Intelligent Systems, 16 (2001) 60-71
16. Sugumaran, V., Storey, V.C.: Ontologies for conceptual modeling: their creation, use, and management. Data and Knowledge Engineering 42 (2002) 251-271
17. Uschold, M., Grueninger, M.: Ontologies: principles, methods and applications. Knowledge Engineering Review 11 (1996) 93-155

A Similarity-Aware Multiagent-Based Web Content Management Scheme

Jitian Xiao[1] and Jun Wang[2,1]

[1] School of Computer and Information Science,
Edith Cowan University, 2 Bradford Street,
Mount Lawley, WA 6050, Australia
j.xiao@ecu.edu.au

[2] School of Computer Science and Engineering,
Wenzhou University, Wenzhou,
Zhejiang 325027, China
j.wang@ecu.edu.au

Abstract. This paper presents a similarity-aware multiagent-based web content management scheme. Based on a set of similarity measures that assess similarities between web documents, we propose a similarity-aware multi-cache architecture, in which the cached web documents are organized into a number of sub-caches according to their content similarity. A predictor is then developed to predict the cached documents a user might access next. Once a pre-fetching plan was formed, a set of agents are employed to work together for pre-fetching document between proxy caches and browsing clients. Preliminary experiments have shown that our predictor offers superior performance when compared with some existing prediction algorithms.

1 Introduction

Web content management is intended to reduce network traffic, server load and user-perceived retrieval latency [1]. Web content caching, in its various forms, is seen as a set of techniques based upon historical analysis and/or projection, to alleviate the effects of server bottlenecks and the vagaries of network traffic volume, thereby reducing latency experienced by a server, user or by client programs. Traditional caching, at its basic level, locally stores recently requested pages so they do not have to be retrieved subsequently every time each is accessed. In brief, recently requested pages or files are held, or cached, on a local, or less remote, server in anticipation that they will be accessed again by clients. Such caching does much to reduce repeat network traffic. Clearly, though, newly requested documents will never be contained in such a cache. Pre-fetching is an active technique that attempts to guess those documents that are likely to be requested when a page leading to them is accessed - success of this technique is measured as a "hit-ratio". However, in such guessing, there is a need for an effective balance to be achieved between user comfort and computational overheads - the extremes are: too little effort applied, resulting in too many on-demand-fetches, while too much effort results in too many pre-fetches. The consequence of either is that of slower response to a user.

Previous work by Xiao *et al* [2] in developing pre-fetching predictions between caching proxies and browsing clients was based on measures of similarity between web users established that pre-fetching is capable of increasing the hit-ratio. Xiao's work further established that organisation of the cache affects opportunities for successful pre-fetching. In this position paper we describe a means of similarity based content management to improve the relative performance of pre-fetching techniques based upon document similarity detection.

Pre-fetch caching in the context of this study will be based upon similarity detection and involve four phases. Similarities will be sought from previously cached documents employing several concurrently applied, but differing, algorithms to detect equivalences of, e.g. broad-content or keywords, images and picture-titles and links contained within pages under scrutiny. Similarities between web-pages, having been detected, will then be ranked for candidature to be fetched in anticipation of a user's intentions. Following the ranking exercise, content settings may be realized for sub-caches and pre-fetching may then proceed.

The rest of the paper is organized as follows. Section 2 defines the similarity measures. In Section 3, we propose a similarity based web cache architecture. Section 4 presents the similarity-aware multiagent-based web document pre-fetching scheme, and Section 5 concludes the paper.

2   Similarity Measurement and Detection

Generally, the exercise of measuring similarities among documents follows two main streams: one uses a single relationship between documents or data objects while the other uses multiple relationships. Early research used a single relationship to measure the similarity of data objects. In the original *vector space model* (VSM) [3], "terms" (e.g. key words or stems) were used to characterize queries and documents, yielding a document-term relationship matrix to compute similarities among terms and documents by taking the inner product of the two corresponding row or column vectors. Dice, Jaccard and Cosine [4] used such document-term relationships to measure the similarity of documents for retrieval and clustering purposes. Deerwester and Dumais [5][6] saw that a document might not be well represented by its contained keywords and developed a Latent Semantic Index (LSI). In this, they apply a *singular value decomposition* (SVD) method to map the document-term matrix into some lower dimensional matrix where each dimension associates with a hidden "concept", where any similarity of text objects (documents and queries) is measured by relationships to those "concepts" rather than the keywords they contained.

With the advent of Word Wide Web, relationships with document objects, e.g. their hyperlink relationships, were used to derive similarity; a mechanism employed by both Dean [7] and Kleinberg [8] to discover similar web pages. Further, Larson [9] and Pitknow [10] applied co-citation to a hyperlink structure to measure any similarity of two web pages. Xiao *et al* [2] employed user-document access relationships to cluster users of similar interests. Flesca [11] proposed a method to measure the similarity of two documents that represents the current and the previous version of monitored pages for effective web change detection. The approaches introduced above all relied upon a single relationship to measure any similarity of data objects. However, such approaches may run into serious problems when applications require accurate similarity e.g. where multiple types of data objects and relationships must be handled in an integrated manner. Accordingly, in the extended VSM [12], feature vectors of data objects were augmented by adding attributes from objects of other related spaces. Similarity computation is then obtained from calculation on these enhanced feature vectors. The extended feature vectors were used for document search [13] or clustering purposes [14]. Racchio [15] and Ide [16] expanded the query vector using those frequently-used terms appearing in the foremost documents retrieved by a query to improve search effectiveness. Similarly, Brauen [17] modified document vectors by related query terms.

Recently, it has been tried to calculate the similarity of two data objects based upon any similarity of their related data objects. Raghavan and Sever [18] tried to measure the similarity of two queries by correspondences found in their respective search lists. Beeferman and Berger [19] clustered queries using the similarity of both their selected web pages and cluster web pages based upon similarities of the queries that lead to the selection of those web pages. Both [20] and [21] calculated the query similarity based on both the query contents similarity and the similarity of the documents that were retrieved by the queries.

In this paper we define similarity measures of web documents for effective web document caching and pre-fetching. To pre-fetch documents that are of similar topic to the document a user is currently viewing, we need to derive the similarity of contents of web documents, ignoring any structural elements, e.g. HTML formatting. For efficacy of on-line pre-fetching, we propose different levels of similarity measures to capture levels of similarity between web documents. Consider a search of scientific papers over the web. A keyword based search usually returns a list of documents containing some or all of the given keywords. The matched keywords in the returned documents may appear in the title, keywords section, or other parts. Title/author-based searches follow similar principles. However, when a user is viewing a document and wishes to search for documents of similar topic, then the matching strategy may be quite different because the words to be matched may be related rather than explicitly stated. In our study, similarities between text documents are measured based on topics, page titles, keywords or page contents or combinations thereof. Compared with a keyword-based similarity measure, a content-based similarity is complicated by the need for special techniques, e.g., from the area of information retrieval [13]. However, any computation of similarity still needs to be completed within a reasonable time limit.

2.1 Document Model

To calculate similarities among web documents, we use a model based on the document model representation in [11], wherein structured web documents are represented as unordered labeled trees. That is, we consider containment rather than order of appearance of words within a document. However, our model differs from that in [11] in two ways: first, we don't consider the HTML formatting elements and, second, we consider a document's structure to be based on sectional elements, e.g. Abstract and subsections, while their work specifies texts in terms of pairs of start and end tags, e.g., <table> ... </table>, <ul>... </ul>.

In the resultant tree, each non-leaf node corresponds to a subsection of the document (e.g. characterizing the title of the subsection), except that the root-node might also contain a set of *keywords*, a list of *authors*, a string for *title*, or/and a set of words comprising the *abstract*. Each leaf node corresponds to the text of that (sub)section. Notably, such a structure allows us to determine sectional similarities between particular elements such as titles; between the various contents, and, implicitly, between the structures of compared documents. In brief, then, a document tree is an unordered tree wherein each node is characterized by an associated set of type-value pairs.

Given a document tree T, of root r, with a node n_r we may represent a sub-tree of T rooted at n_r as $T(n_r)$. We define a set of functions, each characterizing some element, on the document tree: *keyword(r)*, *title(r)*, *authors(r)*, *abstract(r)* and *text(r)*. For a document tree rooted at r, *keyword(r)*=$\{s \mid s$ is a keyword contained in the keyword section of $r\}$. The *title(r)*, *authors(r)* and *abstract(r)* can be defined similarly. If $n_1, n_2, \ldots, n_k$ are child nodes of r, then

$$text(r) = \begin{cases} title(r) \cup \cup_{i=1}^{k}\{s \mid s \in text(n_i)\} & \textit{if r is a non-leaf node}, \text{with} \\ & \textit{children } n_1, \ldots, n_k \\ \{s \mid s \textit{ is a word in leaf}(T(r))\} & \textit{if r is a leaf node of T} \end{cases}$$

Essentially *text(r)* is a set of words contained in the various strings associated with nodes of the (sub-)tree rooted at r. Note that text(r) is defined recursively.

Our similarity calculation algorithm works on this tree structure by exploiting the information contained in individual nodes and the whole tree. Observe that each node keeps track of its level in the tree, its content and the content of its child nodes.

2.2 Levels of Document Similarity Measures

Levels of document similarity measures are defined by making use of the text extracted from elements of document (sub-)trees. To compute the similarities efficiently, the measures must be normalized, allowing the comparison of pairs of documents and the selection of different levels of elements/components. Given two document trees T_1 and T_2, and two nodes $r_1 \in T_1$ and $r_2 \in T_2$, define

$$intersect(w(r_1), w(r_2)) = \frac{w(r_1) \cap w(r_2)}{w(r_1) \cup \cap w(r_2)} \qquad (1)$$

where *w(r)* is a set of strings associated with nodes of the (sub-)tree rooted at r. The function $intersect(w(r_1), w(r_2))$ returns the percentage of the number of common words divided by the number of all words that appear in both $w(r_1)$ and $w(r_2)$. Clearly, $intersect(w(r_1), w(r_2)) \leq 1$, while equality exists when $w(r_1) = w(r_2)$.

For two document trees rooted at r_1 and r_2, respectively, similarities of keyword, title and abstract may be defined by the formulae (2) through (4):

$$SIM_{KB}(r_1, r_2) = intersect(keyword(r_1), keyword(r_2)) \qquad (2)$$
$$SIM_{TB}(r_1, r_2) = intersect(title(r_1), title(r_2)) \qquad (3)$$
$$SIM_{AB}(r_1, r_2) = intersect(abstract(r_1), abstract(r_2)) \qquad (4)$$

while the content-based similarity is defined as

$$SIM_{CB}(r_1, r_2) = intersect(w(r_1), w(r_2)) \qquad (5)$$

where $w(r_i) = text(r_i) \cup keywords(r_i) \cup abstract(r_i), 1 \leq i \leq 2$.

In most cases, the higher a word occurrence in a document, the closer that word relates to the theme of the document and this may be used as a measure of similarity. Let $wt_r(s)$ be the number of appearances of the word s in document represented by r, then the intersect function can be defined as

$$intersect_{wt}(w(r_1), w(r_2)) = \frac{\sum_{s \in w(r_1) \cap w(r_2)} min\{wt_{r_1}(s), wt_{r_2}(s_2)\}}{\frac{1}{2} \sum_{s \in w(r_1) \cup w(r_2)} |wt_{r_1}(s) + wt_{r_2}(s)|} \qquad (6)$$

Based on this function, the weighted similarity measures $SIM_{KB}()$, $SIM_{TB}()$, $SIM_{AB}()$ and $SIM_{CB}()$ defined in (2) through (5) above can all be re-defined by replacing $intersect()$ with $intersect_{wt}()$.

2.3 Data Pre-processing

To calculate similarities among documents, a text filter was developed to extract meaningful words from related sections of a document, and count them per section. The method is described briefly below:

In the text filter, raw text is first parsed into generalized words, called *tokens*. Tokens include meaningful strings, abbreviations, punctuation and other specialized symbols that have been derived from the structure found in the document's sections. For example, while typical words such as "web" and "page" are taken as tokens, the punctuation mark "$" and the URL "www.ecu.edu.au" are also tokens. However, digits and others insignificant words, e.g. pronouns and prepositions, are not treated as tokens.

For each section, the text filter produces a list of *(token, c(token))* pairs, where *c(token)* is the count of that token within the section - in effect, a *bag-of-words* basis for our representation. Note that for brevity of the token list and subsequent comparison, each word is reduced to its stem (e.g., *server* and *service* into *serve*). While the unordered bag-of-words model will not suffice for linguistic analysis, we assume it captures most of the information needed for calculating similarities using formula (2) through to (5).

3 Similarity-Aware Web Content Management

The basic idea of web-caching is to reduce network traffic load and reduce retrieval latency by holding recent requested documents at the proxy caches so that they do not have to be fully retrieved upon identical request.

Document similarity information is fundamental to effective caching and prefetching, yet it has never been incorporated directly in cache replacement algorithms. Rather, other properties of the request stream (e.g., document size and access frequency etc.), being easier to capture on-line, are used to infer similarity, and hence driven cache replacement policies. In this section, we propose a similarity-based multi-cache web content management scheme and on-line algorithm to capture and maintain an apposite similarity profile of documents requested through a caching proxy and describe a novel cache replacement policy using such information to support the similarity-aware pre-fetching.

3.1 The Caching Architecture

We now present a similarity-based multi-cache web content management scheme. There are four major components: *central router, similarity profiles (SP), sub-caches*, and *document allocator*. Of these, the central router is pivotal in controlling and coordinating the other components.

Before configuring the multi-cache web content management scheme, we first cluster documents in cache based on the similarity measures introduced in (2) to (6), and determine the number of themes, N, of the documents. For each theme/cluster, a number of *stems* relating to it were chosen (e.g., by looking at all stems produced by the text filter when SP vectors were computed). Then the cache is divided into $N+1$ sub-caches. Each of the first N sub-caches stores documents of one particular theme, and the last sub-cache stores other documents not belonging to any of the N themes. In this way, we ensure that similarities among documents in any sub-cache are relatively higher, while relegating those among documents across sub-caches.

The SP comprises N two-dimensional arrays $A_i(*, *)$, $i=1, 2, , N$, of which each corresponds to one of the first N sub-caches. For each document j in sub-cache i, SP counts the number of occurrences of the stems that relate to the theme of the sub-cache, storing the numbers in vector $A_i(j,*)$. This information is useful when performing similarity-aware pre-fetching from the sub-cache to a client. For each theme, we limit the number of stems to be 100.

A sub-cache is an independent cache that has its own cache space, contents and replacement policy. Since documents in a same sub-cache are usually of similar theme, simpler replacement policies, e.g. LRU, LFU and FIFO, may be applied.

The sub-cache allocator assesses comprehensively a candidate set of evictions selected by sub-caches, with possible results of: re-caching, eviction or probation. Of these, re-caching and eviction are instantaneous, while a probation document will be held by the allocator in its own space pending a final decision.

3.2 Algorithm Framework of Similarity-Aware Content Management (SACM)

A request for a document d invokes the SACM algorithm to action as follows: an instance of d is sought in an in-cache index; if d is already cached (i.e., cache *hit*) and still *fresh* its containing sub-cache is noted whereupon d will be returned to the requesting client. If the instance of d is not fresh, then re-cache from an origin server, updating related parameters such as SP vectors. For a cache *miss*, the request for d will be forwarded to the origin server and a resultant downloaded document d_{new} is returned to the client. Based on the content of d_{new}, a SP vector will be calculated to determine a sub-cache c_d in which d_{new} is to be cached. Where there is insufficient space for d_{new}, then sub cache c_d makes room according to its eviction (e.g. LRU, LFU) and/or space sharing policies. The document allocator of c_d will then assess and purge any eviction candidates.

The central router mediates between cooperating sub-caches. Although a document may be cached "conceptually" in several sub-caches in terms of sub-cache document allocator evaluation, only one object copy will be maintained.

4 Web Document Pre-fetching

In this section, we focus on pre-fetching between caching proxies and browsing clients in idle periods of their network links when a current web document is read by a user. If the proxy can predict those cached documents a user might access next, the idle periods may be used to push them to the user, or to have the browser/client pull them. Since the proxy only initiates pre-fetches for documents in its caches, there is no extra internet traffic increase.

4.1 Multiagent-Based Similarity-Aware Pre-fetching

An agent is a software entity that carries out some set of operations on behalf of a client/program with some degree of independence or autonomy [22]. In this study, we employ both proxy-side and client-side agents that exchange messages using a predefined protocol for actualizing similarity detection, document prediction, network traffic monitoring and proxy-client coordination intentions during the document pre-fetching process where they negotiate to reach the most probable solution.

In the similarity-aware web document pre-fetching process, three activities crucial. they are: (i) identifying similarities between documents in the proxy cache and the document a user is viewing; (ii) predicting documents that a client is most likely to access next; and (iii) monitoring idle network periods to pre-fetch the documents. These activities are carried out by multi-agent interaction, and are briefly described as below:

The *Client Agent* (CA) plays the role of a client. It delivers a pre-fetching request to the *Coordination Agent*. Upon receipt of an initial pre-fetching plan (i.e., a list of candidate documents to be pre-fetched) from the CoA, it modifies the plan by removing the candidates that were hit by its local cache, and then returns the modified plan to the CoA for final pre-fetching.

By its name, *Coordination Agent* (CoA) is responsible for receiving the pre-fetching requests from clients, and coordinates among agents such as similarity detection agent (SDA), access pattern matching agent (PMA), pre-fetching agent (PFA) and network traffic monitoring agent (TMA), for document pre-fetching process. Through the interaction between the agents and the client in the architecture, the detailed job of the CoA involves following steps: (i) receive pre-fetching requests from CAs; (ii) invoke SDA to identify a set of cached documents (in one or more sub-caches) whose similarities with the document the client is viewing surpass certain threshold; (iii) invoke PMA to assess and identify a set of users' past (historical) access patterns that could be referenced for prediction of future access of the client; (iv) upon receipt of the responses from steps (ii) and (iii), assign a process that calls PFA to produce an initial pre-fetch plan (e.g., a list of candidate documents for pre-fetching); (v) send the initial pre-fetch plan to the

CA to determine which in-list candidates should not be pre-fetched due to local cache hit; and (vi) upon receipt of the modified pre-fetch plan from a CA, assign the plan to a TMA for document pre-fetching.

4.2 Pre-fetching Prediction

We propose two agent-based algorithms to guide similarity-aware pre-fetching from proxy caches to clients. The first one is a pure similarity-based pre-fetching predictor which considers only those documents whose similarities with the document in viewing surpass a certain threshold. The second algorithm (i.e., similarity-aware pre-fetching) combines the prediction by partial matching (PPM) method [1] and the pure similarity-based pre-fetching strategies. These algorithms are the main functionalities and behaviour of PFAs, and are addressed in the next two sections.

4.3 Similarity-Based Pre-fetching Predictor

The similarity-based PFA predicts the next k documents in the proxy cache based on document similarities. With the support of the similarity-aware web cache architecture, the PFA works based on a very simple rule. Suppose a client is viewing a document, say d (at this time, a copy of d must be cached in a certain sub-cache, say c_i, or being held by the allocator). When a pre-fetching request is received, the CoA invokes a SDA which computes the similarities between d and those documents in sub-cache c_i by referencing the similarity information in i_{th} SP. No documents in other sub-caches are considered because of their low similarities with d. Then the predictor simply chooses k documents whose similarities with d are among the top k highest ones. These k documents, together with those cached pages to which hyperlinks exist from d, will form an initial pre-fetching plan and be returned to CoA for possible pre-fetching.

4.4 Similarity-Aware Pre-fetching Predictor

The PPM [1] essentially predicts the next l requests on the past m accesses of a user, limiting candidates by an access probability threshold t. The performance metrics of the algorithm depend on the (m, l, t) configurations. However, the algorithm uses patterns observed from all users' references to predict a particular user's behaviour. Referencing too many contexts makes the prediction inaccurate, inefficient and unwieldy.

Our previous work [2] extended the PPM algorithm by referencing only those access patterns from a small group of other users exhibiting high similarities in their past access patterns to predict a current user's next access. The number of times the algorithm can make prediction is reduced because of the smaller sample size, but the hit ratio of the pre-fetching increases because more related access patterns are referenced. We call the method *pattern-similarity based* PPM (or *ps*PPM).

To be more similarity-aware, we now modify PPM and *ps*PPM by replacing the access threshold t with s, where s is the similarity threshold between the document to be pre-fetched and the document the client is viewing. Thus the new algorithm has the following parameters:

- r: the number of users whose access patterns are referenced to predict future accesses of the current user.
- m: the number of past accesses that are used to predict future ones. We call m the *prefix depth*.
- l: the number of steps that the algorithm tries to predict into the future.
- s: the similarity threshold used to weed out candidate document. Only those documents whose similarity with the viewing document is greater than s, where $0 \leq s \leq 1$, is considered for pre-fetching.

Suppose a user u is viewing a document d. When a pre-fetching request is received, the CoA invokes a PMA to assess and identify a set of r users' access patterns of relatively high similarities with u (sorted in descending order). For $l>1$, not only the immediate next request, but the next few requests after an URL are also considered for potential pre-fetching. For example, if $l=2$, the PFA predicts both the immediate next and its successor for the user. If $m>1$, more contexts of the r users' past accesses are referenced for the purpose of improving the accuracy of the prediction.

The PFA maintains a data structure that tracks the sequence of URLs for every user. For prediction, the past reference, the past two references, and up to the past m references are matched against the collection of succession to the users' past access patterns to produce a list of URLs for the next l steps. If a longer match sequence can be found from the other r users' patterns, the next URL to the longest match is also taken as a potential document to be accessed next by the user. The outcome of each prediction is a list of candidate documents, ordered by their similarities with d. For those candidate documents with the same similarity value, the URL matched with longer prefix is put first in the list.

We conducted two series of preliminary simulations. The first series of simulations is to demonstrate the capability of our similarity measures for document comparison to determine the document themes (or clusters). Using the obtained similarity information, our second series of simulations demonstrates the improvement in prediction accuracy (and thus hit rate) of the pre-fetching between caching proxies and browsing users using our similarity-based/aware predictors and the multiagent-based document pre-fetching mechanism. The preliminary results indicate that our predictor is capable of practical prediction for web document pre-fetching in the sense that an improvement of the order of 10% over traditional PPM has been achieved. We intend to perform more extensive simulations on real Web log data, of which the results will be published in the future.

5 Conclusions

This paper proposed a similarity-aware agent-based web content management scheme. We presented the web-caching architecture and developed similarity-aware predictors for web document pre-fetching between proxy caches and browsing clients. Preliminary simulations have shown that our predictor is capable of practical prediction for web document pre-fetching in the sense that it may predict more accurately and effectively than the traditional PPM does by only referencing a reduced set of users' past access patterns.

References

1. Fan, L., Cao P., Lin W. and Jacobson Q., Web Prefetching between Low-Bandwidth Client and Proxies: Potential and Performance, SIGMETRICS'99, 1999.
2. Xiao, J., Zhang, Y., Jia, X., and T. Li. Measuring Similarity of Interests for Clustering Web-Users. Proceedings of the 12th Australian Database Conference 2001 (ADC'2001). Gold Coast, Australia, 107-114, 2001.
3. Salton. G., Automatic Information Organization and Retrieval. McGraw-Hill, 1968.
4. Rasmussen, E., Clustering algorithms. Information Retrieval: Data Structure and Algorithms. Prentice Hall, 419-442, 1992.
5. Deerwester, S., Dumais, S.T., Landauer, T.K., Furnas, G.W., and Harshman., R.A., Indexing by Latent Semantics Analysis, Journal of the Society for Information Science, 41(6), 391-407.
6. Dumais, S.T., Furnas, G.W., Landauer, T.K., and Deerwester, S., Using Latent Semantic Analysis to Improve Information Retrieval, Proceedings of the CHI'88: Conference on Human Factors in Computing Systems, New York, ACM, 281-285.
7. Dean, J., and Henzinger, M.R., finding Related Pages in the World-Wide Web. Proceedings of the 8th International Conference on World Wide Web, 1999.
8. Kleinberg, J.M., Authoritative Sources in a Hyperlinked Environment, J. of the ACM (JACM), 46(5). 604-632.
9. Larson, R.R., Bibliometrics of the World-Wide Web: An Exploratory Analysis of the Intellectual Structure of Cyberspace. Proceedings of the Annual Meeting of the American Society for Information Science, Baltimore, Maryland, 1996.
10. Pitkow, J. and Pirolli, P., Life, Death, and Lawfulness on the Electronic Frontier. Proceedings of the Conference on Human Factors in Computing Systems, Atlanta, Georgia, 1997.
11. Flesca, S. and Masciari, E. Efficient and Effective Web Change Detection, Data and Knowledge Engineering, Elsevier, 2003.
12. Fox, E., Extending the Boolean and Vector Space Models on Information Retrieval with P-Norm Queries and Multiple Concepts Types. Cornell University Dissertation.
13. Shaw, J.A., and Fox E.A., Combination of Multiple Searches. Proceedings of the 3rd Text Retrieval Conference (TREC-3), 1994, 105.
14. Chakrabarti, S., Dom, B.E., Kumar, S.R, Raghavan, P., Rajagopalan, S., Tomkins, A., Gibson, D. and Kleinberg, J.M., Mining the Web's Link Structure, IEEE Computer, 32 (8). 60-67.
15. Rocchio, J.J. and McGill, M.J., Relevance Feedback in Information Retrieval. Prentice-Hall Inc., Englewood Cliff, NJ, 1997.
16. Ide, E., New Experiments in Relevance Feedback, Prentice-Hall, 1971.
17. Brauen, T., Document Vector Modification, Prentice-Hall Inc., Englewood Cliff, New Jersey, 1971.
18. Popescul, A., Flake, G., Lawrence, S., Ungar, L.H., and Gile, C.L., Clustering and Identifying Temporal Trends in Document Database. Proceedings of the IEEE advances in Digital Libraries, Washington, 2000.
19. Beefermand, D., Berger, A., Agglomerative clustering of a search engine query log. Proceedings of the sixth ACM SIGKDD International Conference on Knowledge Discovery and Data Mining, Boston, MA, 407-415, 2000.
20. Wen, J.R., Nie, J.Y., and Zhang, H.J., Query Clustering Using User Logs., ACM Transactions on Information Systems (TOIS), 20(1), 59-81, 2002.
21. Su, Z., Yang, Q, Zhang, H.J., Xu, X., and Hu, Y., Correlation-Based Document Clustering Using Web Logs. Proceedings of the 34th Hawaii International Conference on System Science, Hawaii, USA, 2001.
22. Bradshaw, J.M., Software Agents. San Francisco, CA, USA: AAAI Press/MIT Press, 1997.

Information Assistant: An Initiative Topic Search Engine

Xi-Dao Luan, Yu-Xiang Xie, Ling-Da Wu, Chi-Long Mao, and Song-Yang Lao

Centre for Multimedia Technology, National
University of Defense Technology, Changsha, 410073, China
yxxie@nudt.edu.cn, wld@nudt.edu.cn

Abstract. The problems of information overload with the use of search engines and the temporal efficiency loss of the indexed data have been significant barriers in the further development of the Internet. In this paper, a new knowledge based initiative topic search engine called *Information Assistant* is designed and realized. It breaks through the traditional passive service style of the search engine, and solves the problem of topic information collection and downloading from the Internet. Its design, which is based on the knowledge base, raises the precision and the recall of the information retrieved. It also probes into the works of the structure and content mining of web pages. Experiments prove the efficiency of the search engine.

1 Introduction

With the development of the Internet, research on the search engine has thrived in recent years [1]. Although search engines have solved some problems of information retrieval from the Internet [2-4], additional problems appear, such as information overload. The work efficiency reduces to some extent when there is too much information retrieved, as users cannot quickly target useful information accurately.

There are hundreds of different search engines. Though dissimilar to each other in realization, they include five basic parts, namely: spider, analyzer, indexer, searcher and user interface (Ref. Fig. 1).

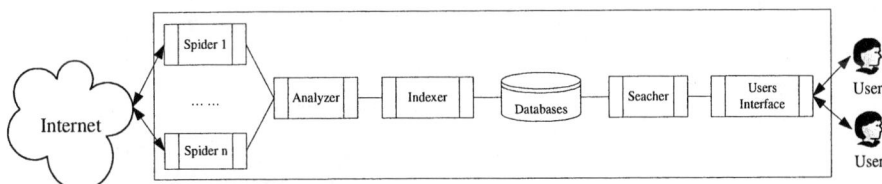

Fig. 1. The structure of a search engine

The workflow of most search engines is as follows:

- the search engine collects web pages automatically by use of a spider
- after the analyzer disposes of unnecessary data, the indexer indexes the retained data
- the searcher responds to the users' queries
- after matching the queries and sorting the results, the final results are returned to the users.

As we can see, most search engines know little of the users' needs until they submit their queries, and the indexes restrict the final results. Though many new techniques have been investigated to improve the performance of the search engine, such as the agent-based search engine [5] proposed in recent years, the working style of these search engines is still passive.

In general, there are some problems still to be solved. First, most search engines have tried to index as many websites as possible to satisfy their users. The result is an increase in recall, but with a corresponding decrease in precision. However, the aim of the users is to find the exact information with the least cost. So, the traditional passive service style cannot meet users' rigorous needs. Second, the data indexed by the search engines cannot keep up with the updating frequency of the Internet. Therefore, it cannot be assured that the collected information is the most recent. Third, as we sometimes need to gather information about a topic on a large scale automatically, it is not wise to browse all the retrieved pages one by one. Fourth, it is very difficult for a user to find and collect information from a website which has not had a search interface.

2 Initiative Topic Search Engine - IA

To solve the above problems, we propose an initiative topic search engine called IA, which is the short name of Information Assistant. It is based on the knowledge base; the

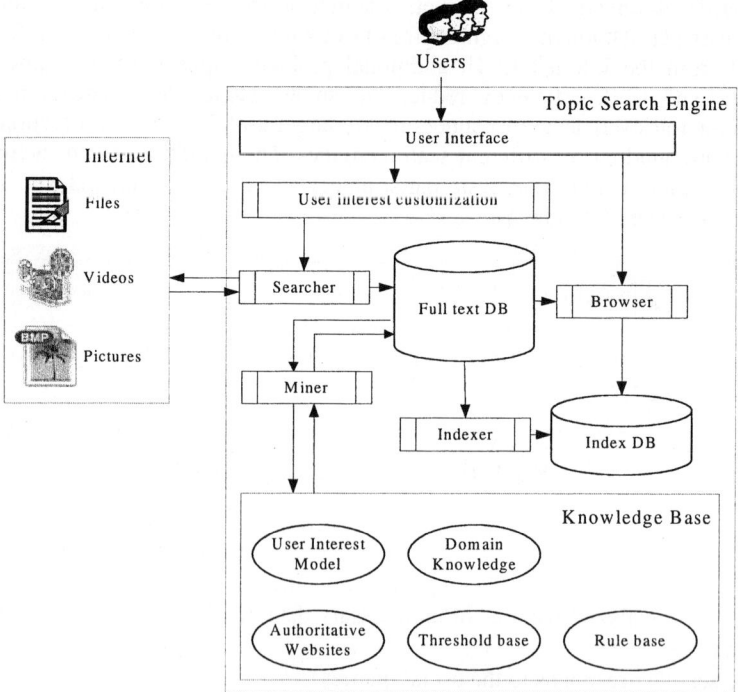

Fig. 2. The framework of IA

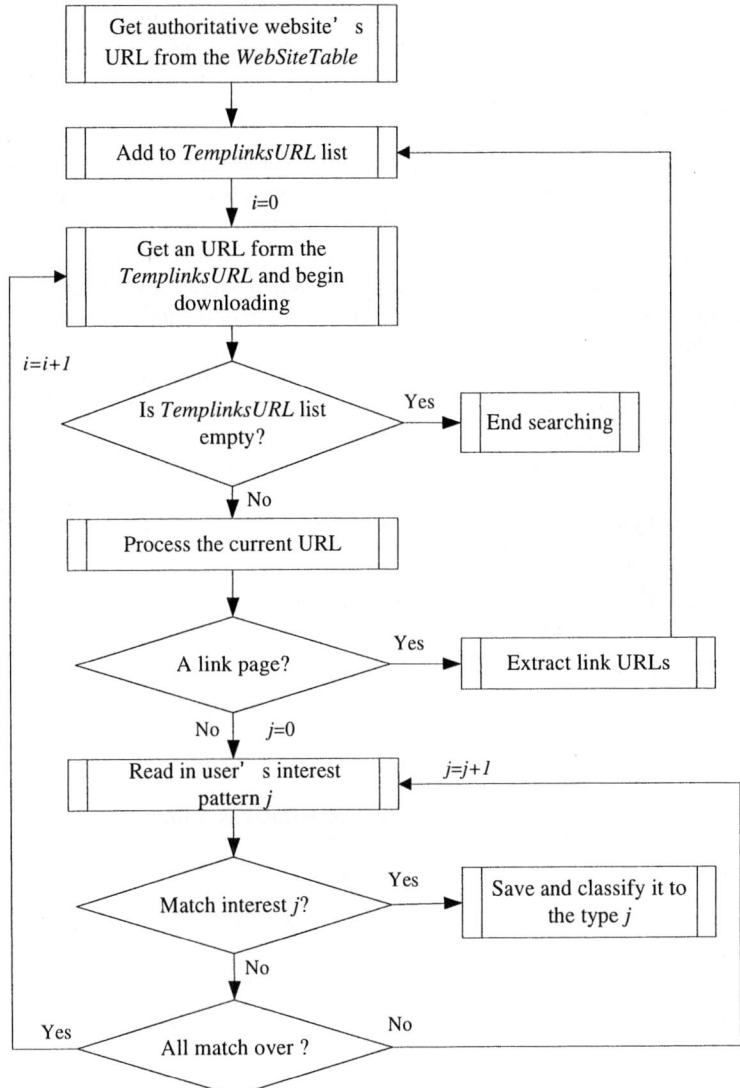

Fig. 3. The flowchart of initiative topic engine IA

user defines the topics, the authoritative websites and the information to be collected, including pictures and videos. At the same time, a flexible interface is provided for the user's browsing use and for retrieval of the downloaded information.

2.1 Framework of IA

The framework of IA is shown in Fig. 2. It includes knowledge base, spider, miner, indexer, searcher, full text database and index database. The knowledge base is important to the search engine, which includes a user interest model base, a domain knowledge base, a rule base, an authoritative websites base and a threshold base, etc.

2.2 Flowchart of IA

The flowchart of IA is shown in Fig. 3. After defining the authoritative websites and the user's interests, the spider searches the data in the websites in accordance with the user's need. WebSiteTable is a table keeping authoritative websites that are defined by the user or are selected from the knowledge base. TemplinksURL is a table of URLs that have not been analyzed. The downloaded documents and files are saved in the full text database with their classification sign. With the help of the indexer and the searcher interface, the user can retrieve and browse the downloaded information. While keywords are easy to use and would not miss the relative information, we adopt keyword vector to describe the user's interests.

Supposing that for topic T, for example the recent Iraq War, the keywords $K1, K2, \ldots, Kn$ are defined to describe T. The length of keywords $K1, K2, \ldots, Kn$ is $l_1, l_2, \ldots, l_n$, and the frequency of the keywords is $f_1, f_2, \ldots, f_n$, while the number of the file D's characters is L.

The weight of keyword Ki is w_i, which is defined as follows:

$$w_i = \begin{cases} \dfrac{1}{2^i}, 1 \leq i < n, n > 1 \\ \dfrac{1}{2^{i-1}}, i = n \text{ or } n = 1 \end{cases} \quad (1)$$

The relevancy of the file D and the topic T is defined as follows:

$$Sim(T, D) = \left(\dfrac{\sum_{i=1}^{n} f_i * l_i * w_i}{L} \right) * f_1 * f_2 \quad (2)$$

If $Sim(T, D) = 0$, then we can see that the file D is irrelevant with the topic T, and this file can be rejected.

3 Mining Module of IA

The mining process will begin when the collected information exceeds the amount of predefined information in the knowledge base. The mining module of IA includes the following:

3.1 Authoritative Websites Mining

An authoritative website [6] can ensure the authority and the precision of the information on the website. This is important for the collection of topic information. By use of the mining techniques [7], new authoritative websites can be found and added to the table TemplinksURL, thus the scope of the retrieved information is expanded.

3.2 Structure and Content Mining

To find relevant pictures and videos requires the structure mining of websites [8-10]. The mining procedure is as follows:

Step1: Judge whether the HTML page is a link page by the threshold K in the threshold base. If it is a link page, then extract its links and add them to the TemplinksURL table. Otherwise, it must be a content page, then judge whether or not it is relevant to the user's interests and executed the structure mining in the next step.

The judging method is as follows:
Supposing the average length of the links in the HTML page D is $Am(D)$,

$$Am(D) = \frac{Length(D)}{NumberofHyperlink(D)} \quad (3)$$

If $NumberofHyperlink(D) \geq 0$ and $Am(D) \leq K$ then
    Mark the page as a link page;
Else
    Mark the page as a content page.

$NumberofHyperlink(D)$ is the number of links in the HTML page D, and $Length(D)$ is the number of characters in the page D.

Step2: For content pages, which satisfy the condition of $K_1 \leq Am(D) \leq K_2$ and belong to the same website, discover structures of the website pages and obtain the content of those pages, where $K1$ and $K2$ are thresholds in the database.

Step3: Discover and filter pictures and videos in the content part of a page to obtain relevant pictures and videos.

Step4: Discover useful patterns in these pictures and videos, such as maps.

4 Experiment Results

The experiment is carried out on the website with the URL of http://zbkj.gfkd.mtn. The website is an authoritative news website on the All-Army Public Data Exchange Network of the Chinese People's Liberation Army (PLA), and its structure and service style is very similar to those news websites on the Internet. Table 1 shows the user's defined topics and key phrases.

Table 1. News topics and their key phrases

Topic name	Key phrases
Iraq War	Bush, Baghdad, White House…
Korea Crisis	Pyongyang, nucleus, White House, …

From the beginning to the end of the process, meaning that all web pages in the website have been analyzed, search engine IA runs for 2,543 seconds, analyzes 2,647 web pages, processes 37,649 URLs, and collects 182,314K byte of data. The results are shown in Table 2.

Table 2. Experiment result

Information Type	Number	quality (K Byte)	Precision	Recall
HTML pages	128	212	89.84%	100%
PDF files	27	10,927	81.49%	100%
Pictures	94	1,748	88.29%	100%
Videos	8	169,427	75%	100%

From Table 2, we can see that the precision of the collection of HTML files is fairly high, while the precision of the collection of videos and PDF files is somewhat lower. After analysis, we find that the reason is the editor's inexact description of these files. The average precision is 83.66% when the recall is 100%.

Our initiative topic search engine has the following advantages:

- It is fast, accurate and comprehensive in collecting information because of its scheme based on knowledge. It uses key phrases to express users' queries, which is convenient and in accordance with users' customs. It is also easy to realize and seldom needs training.
- It supports the downloading and processing of many topics at the same time. By using the structure and content mining method, it can complete the task of collecting different types of information such as HTML pages, PDF files, pictures and videos.
- It has achieved good results in the area of retrieval precision. When the recall is 100%, the average retrieval precision of our initiative topic search engine is 83.66%.

The shortcomings of search engine IA are as follows:

- It is more dependent on the user's topic description and the authoritative websites in the knowledge base. If the information on the authoritative websites is not updated in time or not relevant to the user's needs, the search engine may not get perfect results.
- The query results depend on the correct expression of the user's interests. In the user interest model, the condition of $Sim(T,D) \neq 0$ means that the first and second key phrases should give expression to the main meaning of the topic.

5 Conclusions

In general, our proposed initiative topic engine has the following advantages:

- first, it is initiative, which reflects the user's interests in a more friendly manner and means it can obtain acceptable results in retrieval precision
- second, it can complete the tasks of collecting, classifying and downloading multi-topics at the same time, in a manner superior to other search engines

- third, it can ensure the authority of the collected information and the real time processing of the information
- fourth, it is expandable.

There is much work to do in the future. We will further investigate some aspects, such as the filtering of similar web pages, the discovering of authoritative websites and useful pictures, and some specific information services, such as the analyzing of news and stocks.

References

1. Fredirik Espinnoza, Kristina Hook. An interactive WWW interface to an adaptive information system. In: Proceedings of the Reality of Intelligent Interface Technology Workshop. Massachusetts: User Modeling Inc. 1997.
2. Jorng-Tzong Horng, Ching-Chang Yeh,Applying genetic algorithms to query optimization in document retrieval,Information processing & management, 2000, 36(5):737~759.
3. Michael J Pazzani,Representation of electronic mail filtering profiles: A user study. Proceedings of the 2000 international conference on intelligent user interfaces, 2000:202~206.
4. Schapire.R, Singer,Y. BoosTexter: A boosting-based system for text categorization, Machine Learning, 2000,39(2/3):135~168.
5. T Kurki, S Jokela, R Sulonen, M Turpeinen,Agents in delivering personalized content based on semantic metadata,In Proc.1999 AAAI Spring Sympposium Workshop on Intelligent Agents in Cyberspace, Stanford, USA, 1999:84~93.
6. J.M.Kleinberg and A. Tomkins, Application of linear algebra in information retrieval and hypertext analysis, Proc. Of 18th ACM Symp. Principles of Database Systems (PODS), 185-193,Philadelphia, PA, May 1999.
7. Jiawei Han, Micheline Kamber,Data Mining: Concepts and Techniques, San Mateo, CA:Morgan Kaufmann Publishers, Inc., 2001.
8. S.Chakrabarti, B.E. Dom, S.R. Kumar,P.Raghavan, S. Rajagopalan, A. Tomkins, D. Gibaon, and J.M. Kleinberg. Mining the web's link structure. COMPUTER, 32:60-67,1999.
9. K.Wang, S.Zhou,and S.C.Liew, Building hierarchical classifiers using class proximity, Proc. Of 1999 Int.Conf. Very Large Data Bases (VLDB'99), 363-374,Edinburgh, UK, Sept.1999.
10. Cooley R, Srivastava J. Data Preparation for Mining World Wide Web Browsing Patterns,Journal of Knowledge and Information Systems: 1999,1(1): 17~24.

Improving Retrieval Performance with the Combination of Thesauri and Automatic Relevance Feedback

Mao-Zu Guo and Jian-Fu Li

School of Computer Science and Technology,
Harbin Institute of Technology, Harbin 150001, China
maozuguo@hit.edu.cn

Abstract. The ever growing popularity of the Internet as a source of information, coupled with the accompanying growth in the number of documents available through the World Wide Web, is leading to an increasing demand for more efficient and accurate information retrieval tools. One of the fundamental problems in information retrieval is word mismatch. Expanding a user's query with related words can improve the search performance, but the finding and using of related words is still an open problem. On the basis of previous approaches to query expansion, this paper proposes a new approach to query expansion that combines two popular traditional methods—thesauri and automatic relevance feedback. According to theoretical analysis and experiments, the new approach can effectively improve the web retrieval performance and out-performs the optimized conventional expansion approaches.

1 Introduction

The ever growing popularity of the Internet as a source of information, coupled with the accompanying growth in the number of documents available through the World Wide Web, is leading to an increasing demand for more efficient and accurate information retrieval tools. One of the fundamental problems information retrieval(IR) fails is word mismatch, which occurs when the author of a document and the user of an information retrieval system use different words to describe the same concept [1], [2]. Usually, valuable information is mixed with many irrelevant documents. The problem is best illustrated by through the scenario of information search on the Web, where the queries are usually of two words long and a large number of "hit" documents are returned to the user. Part of the reason comes from the inherent ambiguity of word in natural language. Another part is the difference of interpretation for a query. That is, given the same query expression by different users, due to different backgrounds and experiences of different users, the information inquired could be different.

With the explosive growth of information in Internet, the word mismatch problem becomes more significant as observed by Furnas [3] in a more general context. In his experiments, two users using the same term to describe an object is less than 20% of the time. Particularly, the problem is more severe for short casual queries than for long elaborate queries because as queries get longer, there is more chance of some important words co-occurring in the query and the relevant documents. Unfortunately, short queries are becoming increasingly common in retrieval applications, especially with the advent of the World Wide Web (WWW). Nowadays, the ubiquity of word mismatch has become the bottleneck to improve the performance of information retrieval systems. Addressing the word mismatch problem has become an increasingly important research topic in IR.

Query expansion [4] is a technique utilized within IR to remedy this problem. A query is expanded by adding other terms closely related to the original query terms. In the last decades of years, a wide range of methods for query expansion have been proposed, from manual techniques such as thesauri to automatic techniques such as automatic relevance feedback. These methods have shown effective on different extent in improving the performance of IR system, but they are still far from being satisfactory. On basis of the analysis of the traditional approaches to query expansion, this paper proposes an alternative approach to query expansion, which is an integration of thesauri with automatic relevance feedback. The scheme is effective for query expansion for web retrieval: in terms of theoretical analysis and experimentation, the new approach can improve IR effectiveness and out-performs the optimized, conventional expansion approaches.

The remainder of the article is organized as follows. Section 2 reviews existing techniques and points out their advantages and disadvantages. Section 3 details the new approach to query expansion and analyzes the new approach in theory. Section 4 compares the new approach with traditional expansion methods through experiments and concludes the work.

2 The Analysis of Traditional Query Expansion Methods

Currently, the most generally accepted approaches to query expansion include thesauri and relevance feedback techniques. In this section, each approach is briefly explained.

2.1 Thesauri

A "thesaurus" is defined as a dictionary of synonyms and related words. In most situations, thesauri are used to improve retrieval performance by expanding queries with words that are related to the original keywords [5]. After a user submits his query to information retrieval system, the system can automatically consults the thesaurus and displays all the terms related to original the query to the use for selecting. The user can select some of the related terms to refine the query or not select any term. Then the refined query is resubmitted to the system again, and several documents are retrieved as a result of the refined query retrieval.

In the information research systems based on thesauri, the thesauri are built in advance, every time to expand query is only to search the thesauri for terms related to queries, which is very simple and fast.

However, the approaches based on thesauri still have some drawbacks: first, since thesauri are built manually by linguist and domain experts, manual thesauri are often too broad or too narrow. For example, a general-purpose dictionary might contain too many synonyms for a word while a medical thesaurus can consist of thousands of groups of related medical terms but nothing outside its domain. Second, building a manual thesaurus is usually time-consuming even in a narrow domain because the knowledge of a whole domain has to be reviewed. Third, the structure of manual thesaurus depends on some people, which is very subjective. Duo to different backgrounds and experiences of different people, there is no a criterion to built thesauri. If a user is not familiar with the structure of the thesaurus in use, it is very difficult for the user to select appropriate terms to expand query. Finally, in order to adapt to the change of domain knowledge, the experts must often update thesauri, and even sometimes the updating even means reforming of the whole thesaurus which can not be completed only by people.

2.2 Relevance Feedback

Relevance feedback [6], [7] is a cyclic process (as shown in Figure 1) whereby the user feeds back into the system decisions on the relevance of retrieved documents and the system then uses these evaluations to automatically modify the retrieval process [3]. The main idea consists of choosing important terms in relevant documents, and of enhancing the weight of these terms in a new query formulation. Analogously, terms included in previously retrieved irrelevant documents could be deemphasized in any future query formulation. The effect of such a query modification process is to "move" the query in the direction of the relevant items and away from the irrelevant ones, in the expectation of retrieving more wanted and fewer non-wanted items in a later search. Relevance feedback has shown to be effective to expand query and has been being improved continuously. Currently, according to the way how to get the relevance of documents, relevance feedback can fall into two categories: manual relevance feedback and automatic relevance feedback.

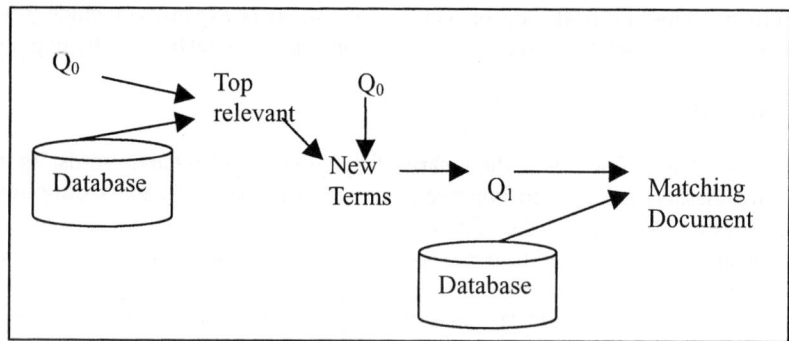

Fig. 1. The architecture of relevance feedback

In the manual relevance feedback [8], relevance is conceptualized as the "users' decision to accept or reject information retrieved from an information system" [6]. That is, the relevance is depends on user's assessment. Manual relevance feedback has been shown to be quite effective, but the limitations of the approach have been widely recognized by the information research community. In a call for papers for a workshop on relevance feedback in information research hosted by the Department of Computer Science of the University of Glasgow, some of the problems were highlighted: it requires users to take a great deal of time to read every retrieved documents and tell the system that which documents are relevant and which documents are not relevant, which puts burden on users and often irritates users. Furthermore, if the user is not familiar with the vocabulary of a document collection, it is difficult to obtain good expansion terms, unless the system can suggest terms to the user.

More recently, search improvements are being achieved without users' intervention, that is, automatic relevance feedback. Unlike manual relevance feedback, in the automatic relevance feedback, just as its name implies, system can automatically assess the relevance of originally retrieved documents but not depends on users. The main idea of the approach is based on the assumption that the top-n (fox example the top-20) originally retrieved documents are relevant. Then the additional terms are selected using statistical heuristics from the top-n documents. A great improvement to manual relevance feedback of automatic relevance feedback is that the users are not needed to spend a great deal time in reading every retrieved documents and assessing the relevance. In this information research based on automatic relevance feedback, the users can concentrate on searching information and the assessment of document relevance is completed by system, which lightens down the burden of users and improves the objectivity of system. Again, there are many experiments showed that the method can improve search effectiveness [8]. But, the automatic relevance feedback is not perfect, and it also has some limitations. The main drawback is that there is a reasonable amount of computation that takes place after the user submits a query, which is a great problem for interactive systems.

In conclusion, the approaches based on relevance feedback or ones based on thesaurus have been shown be effective in improving the performance of information retrieval. However, both of them have disadvantages and are far from being satisfactory. To improve IR effectiveness further, the paper combines the two approaches and proposes a new approach.

3 The Combination of Thesauri and Automatic Relevance Feedback

As above, query expansion based on thesauri is simple and fast. But the building, maintenance and updating of thesauri are time-consuming and it is difficult for manual thesauri to include all new information in time. In relevance feedback, additional terms comes directly from documents, which avoid the problems caused by untimely updating. However, due to the requirement of users' intervention, manual relevance feedback can refine queries comparatively exactly, but it puts burden on users, which most users are unwilling to accept or they are not able to complete. On the assumption that the top-n retrieved documents are relevant, automatic relevance feedback has been shown to be quite effective in improving the information retrieval effectiveness without the intervention of people, however the main drawback of the method is that there is a reasonable amount of computation that takes place after the user submits a query, which is a great problem for interactive systems. To improve the performance of query expansion further, the paper propose a new approach (as shown in figure 2) which holds the advantages of the query expansion based on thesauri and based on automatic

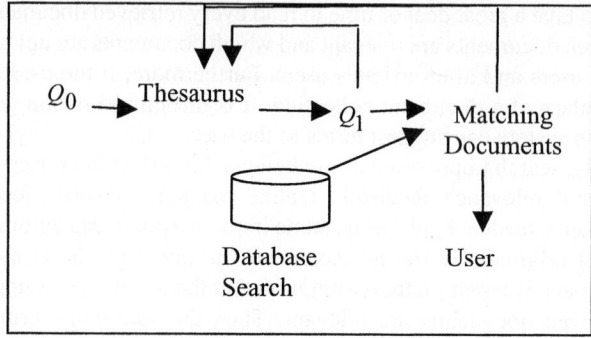

Fig. 2. The architecture of the new approach to query expansion

relevance and out-performs any of the two approaches. In this section, the new approach will be detailed.

From the architecture of the new approach to query expansion, it can be seen that this approach is based on thesauri which holds the advantages of simplicity and speediness, but the new approach is different from manual thesaurus, the thesaurus in the approach is automatically updated by automatic relevance feedback which avoids the disadvantages of general thesaurus.

The steps of the new approach are as follows:

Step 1: A user submits a query Q_0 to the IR system.

Step2: Through the mechanism of thesaurus, a list of terms related to the keywords in Q_0 are displayed, the user can select some words from the list to refine Q_0. The Q_0 can be expanded into Q_1.

Step3: The expanded query Q_1 is run to search database to find matching documents.

Step4: The matching documents sorted by relevance are sent to the user.

Step5: The system further analyzes the retrieved documents and Q_1 to optimize the thesaurus.

From the process of the new approach, the advantages of the new approaches can be seen:

(1) Query expansion in this approach is simple and fast.

From the whole architecture, the approach is based on thesauri. Every time to expand query, the system can automatically consults the thesaurus and display all the terms related to the query to the user for selecting.

(2) The thesaurus is automatically updated.

Unlike manual thesaurus, the updating of the thesaurus in the new approach can be automatically updated by analyzing current matching documents and the expanded query, without the intervention of human which avoid the problems caused by untimely updating.

(3) The structure of the thesaurus is more logical.

In manual thesaurus, the structure depends on some managers, which is very subjective. By using the matching documents and the users' feedback information to update the thesaurus, the structure of the thesaurus becomes fit for the recognition rules of human and terms are extracted from documents, which make the structure of the thesauri in the new approach is logical.

(4) The time to retrieve is reduced.

At present, query expansion based on relevance feedback often spends some time in expanding query. The time can be fall into two parts. The first part of time is used to execute the original search and get retrieved documents; the second part of time is spent in analyzing the retrieved documents, from which some terms can be extracted. Moreover, the amount of computation of the analysis of the retrieved documents is very great. So the second part of time will be very long which results that the whole search process is time-consuming. In the new approach, the analysis of the retrieved documents, which the amount of computation is very great, is a background process and can not affect search process. To users, the system simply is based on thesaurus which is very fast. When related documents are returned to users, the search process ends. To users, the whole search process need only a few seconds. On the other hand, the system still goes further on analyzing the documents to update the thesaurus. Although the analysis is time-consuming, it has been set as a background process which can not affect the speed of whole system.

4 Experiments and Conclusions

The paper proposed a new approach to query expansion. The underlying idea is that the approaches based on thesauri and the ones based on automatic relevance feedback has different characteristics. Therefore, their combination can provide a valuable approach to query expansion and further improve retrieval performance. In terms of theoretical analysis, the new approach has been shown great improvement in both speed and quality over traditional methods of query expansion as above.

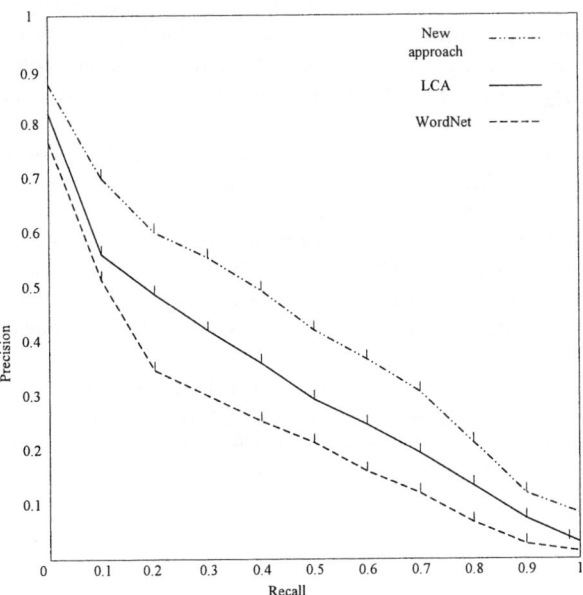

Fig. 3. Comparison of performance of the WordNet, LCA and the new approach

In order to validate the validity of the new approach in terms of experiments, the WordNet [10] and the Local Context Analysis (LCA) [11], one of most popular automatic relevance feedback at present are combined. From the result of experiments (as shown in figure 3), the use of the new approach gives better retrieval results than just using WordNet and LCA respectively.

Acknowledgements

The work was supported by the National 863Hi-tech Project of China under Grant No.2003AA118030 and the Natural Science Foundation of Heilongjiang Province under Grant No.F2004-16.

References

1. Mei Kobayashi, Koichi Takeda: Information on retrieval on the web. ACM Computing Survey, Vol. 32, No. 2, (2000) 328-354,.
2. Nekrestyanov I.S., Panteleeva N.V.: Text Rrtrieval Systems for The Web. Programming and Computer Software, Vol. 28, No. 4, (2002) 207-225
3. Furnas: Information Retrieval Using a Singular Value Decomposition Model of Latent Semantic Structure. Proceeding of the 11th International Conference on Research and Development in Information Retrieval, New York (1998) 465–480
4. Chung Young Mee, Lee Jae Yun: Optimization of Some Factors Affecting The Performance of Query Expansion. Information Processing and Management, Vol. 40, No. 6, (2004) 891-917
5. Fang Sheng, Xien Fan, Gary Thomas. A Knowledge-Based Approach to Effective Document Retrieval. Journal of Systems Integration, Vol. 10, No. 2, (2001) 411-436
6. Buckley. C. and Salton. G.: The Effect of Adding Relevance Information in a Relevance Feedback Environment. Proceedings of the 17th Annual International ACM-SIGIR Conference on Research and Development in Information Retrieval, London, 1994 (2-300)
7. Kazem Taghva, Julie Borsack, Thomas Nartker and Allen Condit: The Role of Manually-Assigned Keywords in Query Expansion. Information Processing and Management, Vol. 40, No. 3, (2004) 41-458
8. Ekmekcioglu: Effectiveness of Query Expansion in Ranked-Output Document Retrieval Systems. Journal of Information Service, Vol. 18, No. 2, (1992) 139-147
9. Shu-Sheng Liaw, Hsiu-Mei Huang: An Investigation of User Attitudes toward Search Engines as an Information Retrieval Tool. Computers in Human Bebavior, Vol. 19, No. 2, (2002) 751-765
10. Dan Moldovan, Adrian Novischi: Word Sense Disambiguation of WordNet Glosses. Computer Speech and Language, Vol. 18, No. 3, (2004) 301-317
11. Jinxi XU, W. Bruce Croft: Improving The Effectiveness of Information Retrieval with Local Context Analysis. ACM Transactions on Information Systems, Vol 18, No. 1, (2000) 79-112

Choquet Integrals with Respect to Fuzzy Measure on Fuzzy σ-Algebra

Yan Huang and Congxin Wu

Harbin Institute of Technology,
Harbin 150001, P.R. China
huangyan15@hit.edu.cn

Abstract. In this paper a new kind of Choquet integral with respect to fuzzy measure on fuzzy σ-algebra is introduced, and some elementary properties of this kind of Choquet integral are studied. Convergence theorems for sequences of Choquet integrals are shown. A transformation theorem is given, which reveals the relation between this kind of Choquet integral on fuzzy sets and the Choquet integral on classical crisp sets. Finally, a new set function defined by this kind of Choquet integral is discussed. This new set function preserves many structural characteristics of the original set function.

1 Introduction

The Choquet integral with respect to fuzzy measure on classical σ-algebra was proposed by Murofushi and Sugeno [1]. It was introduced by Choquet [2] in potential theory with the concept of capacity. This kind of non-additive fuzzy integral is a generalization of the classical Lebesgue integral and has been applied to many fields. It has been used in the areas of image processing, pattern recognition, information fusion and data mining [3, 4, 5, 6], and has been used for economic theory [7, 8], in the context of fuzzy measure theory [9, 10, 11, 12]. Another kind of important fuzzy integral is the Sugeno integral, which was originally introduced by Sugeno [13]. These two famous fuzzy integrals mentioned above, Choquet integral and Sugeno integral, are all defined on classical crisp sets. Wang and Qiao [14, 15] generalized Sugeno integral on fuzzy sets. Similarly, in this paper we establish a theory of Choquet integrals with respect to fuzzy measure on fuzzy σ-algebra of fuzzy sets, i.e., we generalize Choquet integrals on fuzzy sets.

This paper is organized as follows. Section 2 presents some concepts for preparation. Section 3 defines the Choquet integral with respect to fuzzy measure on fuzzy σ-algebra and shows the basic properties. Section 4 gives a transformation theorem which reveals the relation between the Choquet integral on fuzzy sets and the Choquet integral on crisp sets. Section 5 investigates the convergence for sequences of Choquet integrals. As an application of Choquet integrals Section 6 defines a new set function which preserves many structural characteristics of the original set function. Section 7 concludes this paper.

2 Preliminaries

In the paper the following concepts and notations will be used. $R^+ = [0, \infty]$ denotes the set of extended nonnegative real numbers. Let X be a nonempty set, $\mathcal{F}(X) = \{\tilde{A} \mid \tilde{A} : X \to [0,1]\}$ be the class of all fuzzy subsets of X.

Definition 1. [14, 15] A fuzzy σ-algebra $\tilde{\mathcal{F}}$ is a nonempty subclass of $\mathcal{F}(X)$ with the properties:

1. $X, \phi \in \tilde{\mathcal{F}}$;
2. If $\tilde{A} \in \tilde{\mathcal{F}}$, then $\tilde{A}^c \in \tilde{\mathcal{F}}$;
3. If $\{\tilde{A}_n\} \subset \tilde{\mathcal{F}}$, then $\cup_{n=1}^{\infty} \tilde{A}_n \in \tilde{\mathcal{F}}$.

Evidently, an arbitrary classical σ-algebra must be a fuzzy σ-algebra. In this paper, $\tilde{\mathcal{F}}$ shall always denote a fuzzy σ-algebra.

Definition 2. [14, 15] Let $\tilde{\mu} : \tilde{\mathcal{F}} \to [0, \infty]$ be a set function. $\tilde{\mu}$ is called a fuzzy measure if it satisfies the following conditions:

1. $\tilde{\mu}(\phi) = 0$;
2. $\tilde{\mu}(\tilde{A}) \leqslant \tilde{\mu}(\tilde{B})$ whenever $\tilde{A} \subset \tilde{B}$, $\tilde{A}, \tilde{B} \in \tilde{\mathcal{F}}$ (monotonicity);
3. $\tilde{\mu}(\cup_{n=1}^{\infty} \tilde{A}_n) = \lim_n \tilde{\mu}(\tilde{A}_n)$ whenever $\tilde{A}_n \subset \tilde{A}_{n+1}$, $\tilde{A}_n \in \tilde{\mathcal{F}}$, $n \in N$ (continuity from below);
4. $\tilde{\mu}(\cap_{n=1}^{\infty} \tilde{A}_n) = \lim_n \tilde{\mu}(\tilde{A}_n)$ whenever $\tilde{A}_n \supset \tilde{A}_{n+1}$, $\tilde{A}_n \in \tilde{\mathcal{F}}$, $n \in N$ and $\tilde{\mu}(\tilde{A}_{n_0}) < \infty$ for some $n_0 \in N$ (continuity from above).

Remark 1. '$\subset$', '$\cup$', '$\cap$', '^{c}' used in Definition 1 and Definition 2 represent inclusion, union, intersection and complement for fuzzy sets respectively.

A function $f : X \to [0, \infty]$ is said to be measurable if

$$f_\alpha = \{x \in X \mid f(x) \geqslant \alpha\} \in \tilde{\mathcal{F}} \text{ for any } \alpha \geqslant 0.$$

For convenience, let $M^+ = \{f : X \to [0, \infty] \mid f \text{ is measurable}\}$. Obviously, $f \in M^+$ if and only if $f_{\bar{\alpha}} = \{x \in X \mid f(x) > \alpha\} \in \tilde{\mathcal{F}}$ for any $\alpha \geqslant 0$.

Definition 3. $\tilde{\mu} : \tilde{\mathcal{F}} \to [0, \infty]$ is called crisp null-subtractive, if $\tilde{\mu}(\tilde{A} \cap B^c) = \tilde{\mu}(\tilde{A})$ whenever $\tilde{A} \in \tilde{\mathcal{F}}$, crisp set $B \in \tilde{\mathcal{F}}$ and $\tilde{\mu}(B) = 0$; $\tilde{\mu}$ is called superadditive if $\tilde{\mu}(\tilde{A} \cup \tilde{B}) \geqslant \tilde{\mu}(\tilde{A}) + \tilde{\mu}(\tilde{B})$ whenever $\tilde{A}, \tilde{B} \in \tilde{\mathcal{F}}$, $\tilde{A} \cap \tilde{B} = \phi$; $\tilde{\mu}$ is called fuzzy multiplicative if $\tilde{\mu}(\tilde{A} \cap \tilde{B}) = \tilde{\mu}(\tilde{A}) \wedge \tilde{\mu}(\tilde{B})$ whenever $\tilde{A}, \tilde{B} \in \tilde{\mathcal{F}}$.

Proposition 1. $\tilde{\mu} : \tilde{\mathcal{F}} \to [0, \infty]$ *is called crisp null-subtractive if and only if* $\tilde{\mu}(\tilde{A} \cup B) = \tilde{\mu}(\tilde{A})$ *whenever* $\tilde{A} \in \tilde{\mathcal{F}}$, *crisp set* $B \in \tilde{\mathcal{F}}$ *and* $\tilde{\mu}(B) = 0$.

Definition 4. [14] $\tilde{\mu} : \tilde{\mathcal{F}} \to [0, \infty]$ is subadditive if $\tilde{\mu}(\tilde{A} \cup \tilde{B}) \leqslant \tilde{\mu}(\tilde{A}) + \tilde{\mu}(\tilde{B})$ whenever $\tilde{A}, \tilde{B} \in \tilde{\mathcal{F}}$; $\tilde{\mu}$ is autocontinuous from above (or from below) if $\tilde{\mu}(\tilde{B} \cup \tilde{A}_n) \to \tilde{\mu}(\tilde{B})$ (or $\tilde{\mu}(\tilde{B} \cap \tilde{A}_n^c) \to \tilde{\mu}(\tilde{B})$, respectively) whenever $\{\tilde{A}_n\} \subset \tilde{\mathcal{F}}$, $\tilde{B} \in \tilde{\mathcal{F}}$, and $\tilde{\mu}(\tilde{A}_n) \to 0$.

Definition 5. Let $\{f, f_n\} \subset M^+$, $\tilde{A} \in \tilde{\mathcal{F}}$, $H = \{x \in X \mid f_n(x) \to f(x)\}$ and $D = \{x \in X \mid f_1(x) = f_2(x)\}$.

1. [14]If $\tilde{A} \subset H$, then we say f_n converges to f everywhere on $\tilde{A}$, and denote it by $f_n \to f$ on $\tilde{A}$.
2. [14]If for any given $\varepsilon > 0$, we have $\tilde{\mu}(\tilde{A} \cap \{\mid f_n - f \mid \geqslant \varepsilon\}) \to 0$ when $n \to \infty$, then we say f_n converges in fuzzy measure $\tilde{\mu}$ to f on $\tilde{A}$, and denote it by $f_n \xrightarrow{\tilde{\mu}} f$ on $\tilde{A}$;
3. If there exists a crisp set $E \in \tilde{\mathcal{F}}$, $\tilde{\mu}(E) = 0$ and $\tilde{A} \cap E^c \subset D$, then we say f_1 is equal to f_2 almost everywhere on $\tilde{A}$, and denote it by $f_1 = f_2$ a.e. on $\tilde{A}$.

Definition 6. [10, 16]Let $f, g \in M^+$, we say f and g are comonotonic if $f(x) < f(x') \Rightarrow g(x) \leqslant g(x')$ for $x, x' \in X$.

3 Choquet Integrals on Fuzzy Sets

When $\tilde{\mu}$ is a fuzzy measure on $\tilde{\mathcal{F}}$, the triple $(X, \tilde{\mathcal{F}}, \tilde{\mu})$ is called a fuzzy measure space. Throughout this paper, unless otherwise stated, the following are discussed on the fuzzy measure space $(X, \tilde{\mathcal{F}}, \tilde{\mu})$.

Definition 7. Let $f \in M^+$ and $\tilde{A} \in \tilde{\mathcal{F}}$. Then the Choquet integral of f on a fuzzy set $\tilde{A}$ is defined as

$$(c)\int_{\tilde{A}} f d\tilde{\mu} = \int_0^\infty \tilde{\mu}(\tilde{A} \cap f_\alpha) d\alpha.$$

Remark 2. Definition 7 is a generalization of the well known definition of the Choquet integral with respect to fuzzy measure on classical σ-algabara to fuzzy σ-algabara, i.e., a generalization of the Choquet integral on classical crisp sets to fuzzy sets. That is to say, we define the Choquet integral on fuzzy sets.

Next we give an equivalent definition of the Choquet integral on fuzzy sets.

Proposition 2. *Let $f \in M^+$ and $\tilde{A} \in \tilde{\mathcal{F}}$, then $(c)\int_{\tilde{A}} f d\tilde{\mu} = \int_0^\infty \tilde{\mu}(\tilde{A} \cap f_{\tilde{\alpha}}) d\alpha$.*

Proposition 3. *The Choquet integrals on fuzzy sets have the following properties.*

1. *If $\tilde{\mu}(\tilde{A}) = 0$, then $(c)\int_{\tilde{A}} f d\tilde{\mu} = 0$;*
2. *$\tilde{\mu}(\tilde{A} \cap \{x \mid f(x) \neq 0\}) = 0 \Leftrightarrow (c)\int_{\tilde{A}} f d\tilde{\mu} = 0$;*
3. *If $\tilde{\mu}_1 \leqslant \tilde{\mu}_2$, then $(c)\int_{\tilde{A}} f d\tilde{\mu}_1 \leqslant (c)\int_{\tilde{A}} f d\tilde{\mu}_2$, where $\tilde{\mu}_1 \leqslant \tilde{\mu}_2$ if and only if $\tilde{\mu}_1(\tilde{A}) \leqslant \tilde{\mu}_2(\tilde{A})$ for any $\tilde{A} \in \tilde{\mathcal{F}}$;*
4. *If $f_1 \leqslant f_2$ on X, then $(c)\int_{\tilde{A}} f_1 d\tilde{\mu} \leqslant (c)\int_{\tilde{A}} f_2 d\tilde{\mu}$;*
5. *If $\tilde{A} \subset \tilde{B}$, then $(c)\int_{\tilde{A}} f d\tilde{\mu} \leqslant (c)\int_{\tilde{B}} f d\tilde{\mu}$;*
6. *$(c)\int_{\tilde{A}}(a + f) d\tilde{\mu} = a \cdot \tilde{\mu}(\tilde{A}) + (c)\int_{\tilde{A}} f d\tilde{\mu}$ $(a \geqslant 0)$;*
7. *$(c)\int_{\tilde{A}} a \cdot f d\tilde{\mu} = a \cdot (c)\int_{\tilde{A}} f d\tilde{\mu}$ $(a \geqslant 0)$;*

8. $(c)\int_{\tilde{A}} fd(a\tilde{\mu}_1+b\tilde{\mu}_2) = a \cdot (c)\int_{\tilde{A}} fd\tilde{\mu}_1 + b \cdot (c)\int_{\tilde{A}} fd\tilde{\mu}_2$ for $a,b \geqslant 0$ and $\tilde{A} \in \tilde{\mathcal{F}}$, where $(a\tilde{\mu}_1+b\tilde{\mu}_2)(B) = a \cdot \tilde{\mu}_1(B) + b \cdot \tilde{\mu}_2(B)$ for any $B \in \tilde{\mathcal{F}}$.

Theorem 1. *For any $\{f,g\} \subset M^+$ and $\tilde{A} \in \tilde{\mathcal{F}}$, $f = g$ a.e. on $\tilde{A}$ implies $(c)\int_{\tilde{A}} fd\tilde{\mu} = (c)\int_{\tilde{A}} gd\tilde{\mu}$ if and only if $\tilde{\mu}$ is crisp null-subtractive.*

Proof. Sufficiency: Let $D = \{x \in X \mid f(x) = g(x)\}$. Since $f = g$ a.e. on $\tilde{A}$, there exists a crisp set $E \in \tilde{\mathcal{F}}$, $\tilde{\mu}(E) = 0$ and $\tilde{A} \cap E^c \subset D$. By $g_\alpha \supset f_\alpha \cap D$ for $\alpha \geqslant 0$, we have $\tilde{A} \cap g_\alpha \supset \tilde{A} \cap f_\alpha \cap D \supset \tilde{A} \cap E^c \cap f_\alpha$. It follows from the monotonicity and crisp null-subtraction of $\tilde{\mu}$ that $\tilde{\mu}(\tilde{A} \cap g_\alpha) \geqslant \tilde{\mu}(\tilde{A} \cap f_\alpha)$. Hence $(c)\int_{\tilde{A}} gd\tilde{\mu} \geqslant (c)\int_{\tilde{A}} fd\tilde{\mu}$. Similarly, we have $(c)\int_{\tilde{A}} fd\tilde{\mu} \geqslant (c)\int_{\tilde{A}} gd\tilde{\mu}$.
Necessity: Otherwise, there exist $\tilde{A} \in \tilde{\mathcal{F}}$, a crisp set $B \in \tilde{\mathcal{F}}$ and $\tilde{\mu}(B) = 0$ such that $\tilde{\mu}(\tilde{A}) > \tilde{\mu}(\tilde{A} \cap B^c)$. Let $f(x) = \chi_{supp\tilde{A}}(x)$ and $g(x) = \chi_{supp(\tilde{A} \cap B^c)}(x)$ (where $supp\tilde{A}$ denotes the support set of $\tilde{A}$, i.e. $supp\tilde{A} = \{x \in X \mid \tilde{A}(x) > 0\}$ and $\chi_{supp\tilde{A}}$ denotes the characteristic function of $supp\tilde{A}$). Clearly, $supp(\tilde{A} \cap B^c) \subset \{x \in X \mid f(x) = g(x)\}$ and $f = g$ a.e. on $\tilde{A}$. By the hypothesis we obtain $\tilde{\mu}(\tilde{A}) = \tilde{\mu}(\tilde{A} \cap supp\tilde{A}) = (c)\int_{\tilde{A}} fd\tilde{\mu} = (c)\int_{\tilde{A}} gd\tilde{\mu} = \tilde{\mu}(\tilde{A} \cap supp(\tilde{A} \cap B^c)) = \tilde{\mu}(\tilde{A} \cap B^c)$, and this is a contradiction. □

4 Transformation Theorem

Let $\mathcal{F} = \{E \mid E \text{ is a crisp set in } \tilde{\mathcal{F}}\}$. It is clear that $\mathcal{F}$ is a classical σ-algebra, $\mathcal{F} \subset \tilde{\mathcal{F}}$ and all functions in M^+ are measurable on $\mathcal{F}$.

s is called a simple function on $\mathcal{F}$, if there exist $E_1, E_2, \cdots, E_n \in \mathcal{F}$ (where $E_i \neq \phi$, $i = 1,2,\cdots,n$, $E_i \cap E_j = \phi$, $i \neq j$, $\cup_{i=1}^n E_i = X$) and real numbers $\alpha_1, \alpha_2, \cdots, \alpha_n \in [0,\infty)$ (where $\alpha_i \neq \alpha_j$, $i \neq j$) such that $s = \sum_{i=1}^n \alpha_i \chi_{E_i}$. Clearly $s \in M^+$.

Theorem 2. [15] *For any given $\tilde{A} \in \tilde{\mathcal{F}}$, define $\mu(E) = \tilde{\mu}(\tilde{A} \cap E)$ for any $E \in \mathcal{F}$, then μ is a fuzzy measure on $(X,\mathcal{F})$, it is called the fuzzy measure induced by $\tilde{\mu}$ and $\tilde{A}$.*

From this theorem, we can easily obtain the following transformation theorem.

Theorem 3. (transformation theorem) *Let $f \in M^+$, $\tilde{A} \in \tilde{\mathcal{F}}$ and μ be the fuzzy measure in Theorem 2. Then*

$$(c)\int_{\tilde{A} \cap E} fd\tilde{\mu} = (c)\int_E fd\mu \text{ whenever } E \in \mathcal{F},$$

where $(c)\int_E fd\mu = \int_0^\infty \mu(E \cap f_\alpha)d\alpha$ is the Choquet integral on a crisp set E. Particularly, $(c)\int_{\tilde{A}} fd\tilde{\mu} = (c)\int_X fd\mu$.

By Theorem 3 and the known Choquet integration for crisp sets we have the following propositions.

Proposition 4. *Let $f \in M^+$, $\tilde{A} \in \tilde{\mathcal{F}}$ and μ be the fuzzy measure induced by $\tilde{\mu}$ and $\tilde{A}$. Then $(c)\int_{\tilde{A}} fd\tilde{\mu} = \sup\{(c)\int_X gd\mu \mid g \leqslant f, g \text{ is a simple function on } \mathcal{F}\}$.*

Proposition 5. *For any given $\tilde{A} \in \tilde{\mathcal{F}}$, the following statements are equivalent:*

1. $(c)\int_{\tilde{A}}(f\vee g)d\tilde{\mu}+(c)\int_{\tilde{A}}(f\wedge g)d\tilde{\mu}\leqslant (c)\int_{\tilde{A}}fd\tilde{\mu}+(c)\int_{\tilde{A}}gd\tilde{\mu}$ *for any $f,g\in M^+$;*
2. $(c)\int_{\tilde{A}}(f+g)d\tilde{\mu}\leqslant (c)\int_{\tilde{A}}fd\tilde{\mu}+(c)\int_{\tilde{A}}gd\tilde{\mu}$ *for any $f,g\in M^+$;*
3. $\mu(B_1\cup B_2)+\mu(B_1\cap B_2)\leqslant \mu(B_1)+\mu(B_2)$ *for any crisp sets $B_1, B_2 \in \mathcal{F}$, where μ is the fuzzy measure induced by $\tilde{\mu}$ and $\tilde{A}$.*

Similarly, we replace all "$\leqslant$" by "$\geqslant$", and the conclusion is still true.

Proposition 6. *Let $f,g \in M^+$. If f and g are comonotonic, then*

$$(c)\int_{\tilde{A}}(f+g)d\tilde{\mu} = (c)\int_{\tilde{A}}fd\tilde{\mu} + (c)\int_{\tilde{A}}gd\tilde{\mu}$$

for any $\tilde{A} \in \tilde{\mathcal{F}}$.

5 Convergence Theorems

Convergence properties are basic to the study of fuzzy measure and integral. In this section, we show several necessary and sufficient conditions of convergence for sequences of Choquet integrals on fuzzy sets.

By Proposition 4.5. in [14] we can further get the following theorem.

Theorem 4. *Let $\{f_n, f\} \subset M^+$, $\tilde{A} \in \tilde{\mathcal{F}}$.*

1. *For any $f_n \uparrow$ on X and $f_n \to f$ on $\tilde{A}$, we have $(c)\int_{\tilde{A}}f_n d\tilde{\mu} \uparrow (c)\int_{\tilde{A}}fd\tilde{\mu}$;*
2. *For any $f_n \downarrow$ on X and $f_n \to f$ on $\tilde{A}$ with $(c)\int_{\tilde{A}}f_{n_0}d\tilde{\mu} < \infty$ for some $n_0 \in N$, we have $(c)\int_{\tilde{A}}f_n d\tilde{\mu} \downarrow (c)\int_{\tilde{A}}fd\tilde{\mu}$.*

Remark 3. The condition of "$(c)\int_{\tilde{A}}f_{n_0}d\tilde{\mu} < \infty$ for some $n_0 \in N$" is inevitable in Theorem 4, as we show in the following example.

Example 1. Let $X = [0, \infty)$, $\tilde{\mathcal{F}}$ be the class of all Lebesgue measurable sets on X and $\tilde{\mu}$ be Lebesgue measure. Clearly $\tilde{\mu}$ is a fuzzy measure on $(X, \tilde{\mathcal{F}})$. Let $f_n(x) = \chi_{\{0\}\cup(n,\infty)}(x)$ and $f(x) = \chi_{\{0\}}(x)$. Then $f_n \downarrow f$ on X and $(c)\int_X f_n d\tilde{\mu} = \infty, n = 1, 2, \cdots$. But $(c)\int_X fd\tilde{\mu} = 0$.

Definition 8. *Let $\tilde{\mu}_n, \tilde{\mu} : \tilde{\mathcal{F}} \to [0, \infty]$ be fuzzy measures.*

1. *$\tilde{\mu}_n \uparrow \tilde{\mu}$ if and only if $\tilde{\mu}_n(\tilde{A}) \uparrow \tilde{\mu}(\tilde{A})$ for any $\tilde{A} \in \tilde{\mathcal{F}}$;*
2. *$\tilde{\mu}_n \downarrow \tilde{\mu}$ if and only if for any $\tilde{A} \in \tilde{\mathcal{F}}$ with $\tilde{\mu}_{n_0}(\tilde{A}) < \infty$ for some $n_0 \in N$ we have $\tilde{\mu}_n(\tilde{A}) \downarrow \tilde{\mu}(\tilde{A})$;*
3. *$\tilde{\mu}_n \to \tilde{\mu}$ if and only if for any $\tilde{A} \in \tilde{\mathcal{F}}$ we have $\tilde{\mu}_n(\tilde{A}) \to \tilde{\mu}(\tilde{A})$.*

Theorem 5. *Let $\tilde{\mu}_n, \tilde{\mu} : \tilde{\mathcal{F}} \to [0, \infty]$ be fuzzy measures. Then*

1. *For any $f \in M^+$ and $\tilde{A} \in \tilde{\mathcal{F}}$ we have $(c)\int_{\tilde{A}}fd\tilde{\mu}_n \uparrow (c)\int_{\tilde{A}}fd\tilde{\mu}$ if and only if $\tilde{\mu}_n \uparrow \tilde{\mu}$;*

2. For any $f \in M^+$ and $\tilde{A} \in \tilde{\mathcal{F}}$ with $(c)\int_{\tilde{A}} f d\tilde{\mu}_{n_0} < \infty$ for some $n_0 \in N$ we have $(c)\int_{\tilde{A}} f d\tilde{\mu}_n \downarrow (c)\int_{\tilde{A}} f d\tilde{\mu}$ if and only if $\tilde{\mu}_n \downarrow \tilde{\mu}$.

Proof. 1. Sufficiency: $\tilde{\mu}_n \uparrow \tilde{\mu} \Rightarrow \tilde{\mu}_n(\tilde{A} \cap f_\alpha) \uparrow \tilde{\mu}(\tilde{A} \cap f_\alpha)$ for any $\tilde{A} \in \tilde{\mathcal{F}}, \alpha \geqslant 0$

$$\Rightarrow (c)\int_{\tilde{A}} f d\tilde{\mu}_n = \int_0^\infty \tilde{\mu}_n(\tilde{A} \cap f_\alpha) d\alpha \uparrow \int_0^\infty \tilde{\mu}(\tilde{A} \cap f_\alpha) d\alpha = (c)\int_{\tilde{A}} f d\tilde{\mu}.$$

Necessity: For any $\tilde{A} \in \tilde{\mathcal{F}}$, let $f(x) = \chi_{supp\tilde{A}}(x)$, then $\tilde{\mu}_n(\tilde{A}) = (c)\int_{\tilde{A}} f d\tilde{\mu}_n \uparrow (c)\int_{\tilde{A}} f d\tilde{\mu} = \tilde{\mu}(\tilde{A})$.

2. Sufficiency: Since $(c)\int_{\tilde{A}} f d\tilde{\mu}_{n_0} = \int_0^\infty \tilde{\mu}_{n_0}(\tilde{A} \cap f_\alpha) d\alpha < \infty$ for some $n_0 \in N$, we have $\tilde{\mu}_{n_0}(\tilde{A} \cap f_\alpha) < \infty$ for any $\alpha > 0$. By Definition 8(2), we get $\tilde{\mu}_n(\tilde{A} \cap f_\alpha) \downarrow \tilde{\mu}(\tilde{A} \cap f_\alpha)$ for any $\alpha > 0$. Hence we have $(c)\int_{\tilde{A}} f d\tilde{\mu}_n \downarrow (c)\int_{\tilde{A}} f d\tilde{\mu}$. Necessity: For any $\tilde{A} \in \tilde{\mathcal{F}}$ with $\tilde{\mu}_{n_0}(\tilde{A}) < \infty$ for some $n_0 \in N$, let $f(x) = \chi_{supp\tilde{A}}(x)$, then $(c)\int_{\tilde{A}} f d\tilde{\mu}_{n_0} = \tilde{\mu}_{n_0}(\tilde{A}) < \infty$. By the hypothesis we have $\tilde{\mu}_n(\tilde{A}) = (c)\int_{\tilde{A}} f d\tilde{\mu}_n \downarrow (c)\int_{\tilde{A}} f d\tilde{\mu} = \tilde{\mu}(\tilde{A})$. □

Theorem 6. *Let $\tilde{\mu}_n, \tilde{\mu}, \tilde{v} : \tilde{\mathcal{F}} \to [0, \infty]$ be fuzzy measures, $\tilde{A} \in \tilde{\mathcal{F}}$ and $f \in M^+$. If $\tilde{\mu}_n \to \tilde{\mu}$ and $\tilde{\mu}_n \leqslant \tilde{v}$ with $(c)\int_{\tilde{A}} f d\tilde{v} < \infty$, then $(c)\int_{\tilde{A}} f d\tilde{\mu}_n \to (c)\int_{\tilde{A}} f d\tilde{\mu}$.*

Definition 9. [12] *Let $\{f_n, f\} \subset M^+$ and $\tilde{A} \in \tilde{\mathcal{F}}$, sequence $\{f_n\}$ is said to mean converge to f on $\tilde{A}$, if $\lim_{n \to \infty}(c)\int_{\tilde{A}} |f_n - f| d\tilde{\mu} = 0$, and denoted by $f_n \overset{m.}{\to} f$ on $\tilde{A}$.*

By transformation theorem and the results given in [12], we can prove the following convergence theorems.

Theorem 7. *Let $\{f_n, f\} \subset M^+$ and $\tilde{A} \in \tilde{\mathcal{F}}$, then $f_n \overset{m.}{\to} f$ on $\tilde{A}$ implies $f_n \overset{\tilde{\mu}}{\to} f$ on $\tilde{A}$.*

Theorem 8. *For any given $\tilde{A} \in \tilde{\mathcal{F}}$, if $(c)\int_{\tilde{A}} f_n d\tilde{\mu} \to (c)\int_{\tilde{A}} f d\tilde{\mu}$ whenever $\{f_n, f\} \subset M^+$ and $f_n \overset{\tilde{\mu}}{\to} f$ on $\tilde{A}$, then μ is autocontinuous, where μ is the fuzzy measure induced by $\tilde{\mu}$ and $\tilde{A}$.*

Definition 10. *Let $\{f_n\} \subset M^+$ and $\tilde{A} \in \tilde{\mathcal{F}}$, sequence $\{f_n\}$ is called equi-integrable on $\tilde{A}$ if for any given $\varepsilon > 0$, there exists $M(\varepsilon) > 0$ such that $(c)\int_{\tilde{A}} f_n d\tilde{\mu} \leqslant \int_0^M \tilde{\mu}(\tilde{A} \cap f_\alpha^n) d\alpha + \varepsilon$ for all $n = 1, 2, \cdots$, where $f_\alpha^n = \{x \mid f_n(x) \geqslant \alpha\}, \alpha \geqslant 0$.*

Theorem 9. *Let $\tilde{A} \in \tilde{\mathcal{F}}$, $\tilde{\mu}(\tilde{A}) < \infty$, and μ be the fuzzy measure induced by $\tilde{\mu}$ and $\tilde{A}$. If μ is autocontinuous, then $(c)\int_{\tilde{A}} f_n d\tilde{\mu} \to (c)\int_{\tilde{A}} f d\tilde{\mu}$ whenever $\{f_n, f\} \subset M^+$, $f_n \overset{\tilde{\mu}}{\to} f$ on $\tilde{A}$ and f_n is equi-integrable on $\tilde{A}$ with $(c)\int_{\tilde{A}} f d\tilde{\mu} < \infty$.*

By Theorem 8 and Theorem 9 we obtain the following corollary.

Corollary 1. *Let $\tilde{A} \in \tilde{\mathcal{F}}$, $\tilde{\mu}(\tilde{A}) < \infty$ and μ be the fuzzy measure induced by $\tilde{\mu}$ and $\tilde{A}$. μ is autocontinuous if and only if $(c)\int_{\tilde{A}} f_n d\tilde{\mu} \to (c)\int_{\tilde{A}} f d\tilde{\mu}$ whenever $\{f_n, f\} \subset M^+$, $f_n \overset{\tilde{\mu}}{\to} f$ on $\tilde{A}$ and f_n is equi-integrable on $\tilde{A}$ with $(c)\int_{\tilde{A}} f d\tilde{\mu} < \infty$.*

6 Set Function Defined by Choquet Integrals on Fuzzy Sets

In this section let $(X, \tilde{\mathcal{F}}, \tilde{\mu})$ be a fuzzy measure space and $f \in M^+$. A set function $\tilde{\nu}$ on $\tilde{\mathcal{F}}$ is defined by

$$\tilde{\nu}(\tilde{E}) = (c)\int_{\tilde{E}} f d\tilde{\mu} \quad (\tilde{E} \in \tilde{\mathcal{F}}).$$

This new set function $\tilde{\nu}$ preserves many structural characteristics of the original set function $\tilde{\mu}$, which is demonstrated by the following theorems.

Theorem 10. *$\tilde{\nu}$ is a fuzzy measure on $(X, \tilde{\mathcal{F}})$.*

Proof. We only prove the continuity from above of $\tilde{\nu}$. For any $\{\tilde{A}_n\} \subset \tilde{\mathcal{F}}$, $\tilde{A}_n \downarrow \tilde{A} \in \tilde{\mathcal{F}}$ with $\tilde{\nu}(\tilde{A}_{n_0}) < \infty$ for some $n_0 \in N$. Since $\tilde{\nu}(\tilde{A}_{n_0}) = \int_0^\infty \tilde{\mu}(\tilde{A}_{n_0} \cap f_\alpha)d\alpha < \infty$, we have $\tilde{\mu}(\tilde{A}_{n_0} \cap f_\alpha) < \infty$ for any $\alpha > 0$. By using the continuity from above of $\tilde{\mu}$, we have

$$\tilde{\mu}(\tilde{A}_n \cap f_\alpha) \downarrow \tilde{\mu}(\tilde{A} \cap f_\alpha) \quad \forall \alpha > 0.$$

Since $\tilde{\mu}(\tilde{A}_n \cap f_\alpha) \leqslant \tilde{\mu}(\tilde{A}_{n_0} \cap f_\alpha)$ $(n \geqslant n_0)$, it follows from the dominated convergence theorem of Lebesgue integral that

$$\tilde{\nu}(\tilde{A}_n) = \int_0^\infty \tilde{\mu}(\tilde{A}_n \cap f_\alpha)d\alpha \to \int_0^\infty \tilde{\mu}(\tilde{A} \cap f_\alpha)d\alpha = \tilde{\nu}(\tilde{A}).$$

Hence $\tilde{\nu}$ is continuous from above. □

Theorem 11.
1. *If $\tilde{\mu}$ is crisp null-subtractive, then so is $\tilde{\nu}$;*
2. *If $\tilde{\mu}$ is subadditive, then so is $\tilde{\nu}$;*
3. *If $\tilde{\mu}$ is superadditive, then so is $\tilde{\nu}$;*
4. *If $\tilde{\mu}$ is autocontinuous from below, then so is $\tilde{\nu}$;*
5. *If $\tilde{\mu}$ is autocontinuous from above with $\tilde{\nu}(X) < \infty$, then so is $\tilde{\nu}$;*
6. *If $\tilde{\mu}$ is fuzzy multiplicative, then so is $\tilde{\nu}$.*

Proof. We only prove 6. For any given $\tilde{A}, \tilde{B} \in \tilde{\mathcal{F}}$, we consider the following two cases:

(i) If $\tilde{\mu}(\tilde{A} \cap f_\alpha) = \tilde{\mu}(\tilde{B} \cap f_\alpha)$ for any $\alpha > 0$, then $\tilde{\nu}(\tilde{A}) = \tilde{\nu}(\tilde{B})$. Thus

$$\tilde{\nu}(\tilde{A} \cap \tilde{B}) = \int_0^\infty \tilde{\mu}((\tilde{A} \cap \tilde{B}) \cap f_\alpha)d\alpha = \int_0^\infty \tilde{\mu}(\tilde{A} \cap f_\alpha)d\alpha = \tilde{\nu}(\tilde{A}) \wedge \tilde{\nu}(\tilde{B}).$$

(ii) If $\tilde{\mu}(\tilde{A} \cap f_\alpha) \neq \tilde{\mu}(\tilde{B} \cap f_\alpha)$ for some $\alpha > 0$, without loss of generality, we may assume that $\tilde{\mu}(\tilde{A} \cap f_\alpha) > \tilde{\mu}(\tilde{B} \cap f_\alpha)$ for some $\alpha > 0$, then we affirm $\tilde{\mu}(\tilde{A} \cap f_\alpha) \geqslant \tilde{\mu}(\tilde{B} \cap f_\alpha)$ for any $\alpha > 0$. Otherwise, there exists some $\beta > 0$ such that $\tilde{\mu}(\tilde{A} \cap f_\beta) < \tilde{\mu}(\tilde{B} \cap f_\beta)$. There are two cases:
(a) If $0 < \alpha < \beta$, then $\tilde{\mu}(\tilde{B} \cap f_\alpha) \geqslant \tilde{\mu}(\tilde{B} \cap f_\beta)$. It follows from fuzzy multiplicativity of $\tilde{\mu}$ that $\tilde{\mu}((\tilde{A} \cap f_\alpha) \cap (\tilde{B} \cap f_\beta)) = \tilde{\mu}(\tilde{B} \cap f_\beta)$ and $\tilde{\mu}((\tilde{B} \cap f_\alpha) \cap (\tilde{A} \cap f_\beta)) = \tilde{\mu}(\tilde{A} \cap f_\beta)$. However, $\tilde{\mu}((\tilde{A} \cap f_\alpha) \cap (\tilde{B} \cap f_\beta)) = \tilde{\mu}((\tilde{B} \cap f_\alpha) \cap (\tilde{A} \cap f_\beta))$, that is $\tilde{\mu}(\tilde{B} \cap f_\beta) = \tilde{\mu}(\tilde{A} \cap f_\beta)$, it is a contradiction.

(b) If $0 < \beta < \alpha$, then $\tilde{\mu}(\tilde{A} \cap f_\alpha) \leq \tilde{\mu}(\tilde{A} \cap f_\beta)$. It follows from fuzzy multiplicativity of $\tilde{\mu}$ that $\tilde{\mu}((\tilde{A} \cap f_\alpha) \cap (\tilde{B} \cap f_\beta)) = \tilde{\mu}(\tilde{A} \cap f_\alpha)$ and $\tilde{\mu}((\tilde{B} \cap f_\alpha) \cap (\tilde{A} \cap f_\beta)) = \tilde{\mu}(\tilde{B} \cap f_\alpha)$. However, $\tilde{\mu}((\tilde{A} \cap f_\alpha) \cap (\tilde{B} \cap f_\beta)) = \tilde{\mu}((\tilde{B} \cap f_\alpha) \cap (\tilde{A} \cap f_\beta))$, that is $\tilde{\mu}(\tilde{A} \cap f_\alpha) = \tilde{\mu}(\tilde{B} \cap f_\alpha)$, it is a contradiction. Hence, by (a) and (b) we obtain $\tilde{\mu}(\tilde{A} \cap f_\alpha) \geq \tilde{\mu}(\tilde{B} \cap f_\alpha)$ for any $\alpha > 0$. Thus

$$\tilde{\nu}(\tilde{A}) = \int_0^\infty \tilde{\mu}(\tilde{A} \cap f_\alpha) d\alpha \geq \int_0^\infty \tilde{\mu}(\tilde{B} \cap f_\alpha) d\alpha = \tilde{\nu}(\tilde{B})$$

and $\tilde{\nu}(\tilde{A} \cap \tilde{B}) = \int_0^\infty \tilde{\mu}((\tilde{A} \cap \tilde{B}) \cap f_\alpha) d\alpha = \int_0^\infty (\tilde{\mu}(\tilde{A} \cap f_\alpha) \wedge \tilde{\mu}(\tilde{B} \cap f_\alpha)) d\alpha$

$$= \int_0^\infty \tilde{\mu}(\tilde{B} \cap f_\alpha) d\alpha = \tilde{\nu}(\tilde{B}) = \tilde{\nu}(\tilde{A}) \wedge \tilde{\nu}(\tilde{B}).$$

It follows from (i) and (ii) that $\tilde{\nu}$ is fuzzy multiplicative. □

7 Conclusion

This paper introduces a new kind of Choquet integral with respect to fuzzy measure on fuzzy σ–algebra, obtains basic properties and convergence theorems, and defines a new set function by using this kind of Choquet integral. This new set function preserves the following structural characteristics of the original set function: crisp null-subtractivity, subadditivity, superadditivity, autocontinuity from below (or from above), and fuzzy multiplicativity. Furthermore, by transformation theorem some results of this kind of Choquet integral can be obtained directly or indirectly from the well known Choquet integration for crisp sets.

Acknowledgements

The work in this paper is supported by the National Natural Science Foundation of China (Grant No. 10571035).

References

1. Murofushi, T., Sugeno, M.: An interpretation of fuzzy measures and the Choquet integral as an integral with respect to a fuzzy measure. Fuzzy Sets and Systems **29** (1989) 201-227
2. Choquet, G.: Theory of capacities. Ann. Inst. Fourier **5** (1955) 131-295
3. Grabisch, M., Murofushi, T., Sugeno M.(Eds.): Fuzzy Measures and Integrals: Theory and Applications. Physica-Verlag. Heidelberg (2000)
4. Leung, K., Wong, M., Lam, W., Wang, Z., Xu, K.: Learning nonlinear multiregression networks based on evolutionary computation. IEEE Trans. Syst. Man. Cybern. **32** (2002) 630-644
5. Xu, K., Wang, Z., Heng, P., Leung, K.: Classification by nonlinear integral projections. IEEE Trans. Fuzzy Systems **11** (2003) 187-201

6. Hocaoglu, A. K., Gader, P. D.: Domain learning using Choquet integral-based morphological shared weight neural networks. Image and Vision Computing **21** (2003) 663–673
7. Denneberg, D.: Conditional expectation for monotone measures, the discrete case. Journal of Mathematical Economics **37** (2002) 105-121
8. De Waegenaere, A., Kast, R., Lapied, A.: Choquet pricing and equilibrium. Insurance: Mathematics and Economics **32** (2003) 359-370
9. Bolaños, M.J. et al.: Convergence properties of the monotone expectation and its application to the extension of fuzzy measures. Fuzzy Sets and Systems **33** (1989) 201-212
10. Narukawa, Y., Murofushi, T.: Conditions for Choquet integral representation of the comonotonically additive and monotone functional. J. Math. Anal. Appl. **282** (2003) 201-211
11. Wang, Z., Klir, G.J., Wang, W.: Monotone set functions defined by Choquet integral. Fuzzy Sets and Systems **81** (1996) 241-250
12. Wang, Z.: Convergence theorems for sequences of Choquet integrals. Int. J. General Systems **26** (1997) 133-143
13. Sugeno, M.: The theory of fuzzy integral and its applications. Ph.D Dissertation. Tokyo Institute of Technology (1974)
14. Qiao, Z.: On fuzzy measure and fuzzy integral on fuzzy set. Fuzzy Sets and Systems **37** (1990) 77-92
15. Wang, Z., Qiao, Z.: Transformation theorems for fuzzy integrals on fuzzy sets. Fuzzy Sets and Systems **34** (1990) 355-364
16. Pap, E.: Null-Additive Set Functions. Kluwer Academic. Dordrecht (1995)

Robust H_∞ Control with Pole Placement Constraints for T-S Fuzzy Systems

Liang He[1] and Guang-Ren Duan[2]

[1] Center for Control Theory and Guidance Technology,
Harbin Institute of Technology,
P. O. Box 416, Harbin, 150001, P.R. China
cctgt@hit.edu.cn, grduan@iee.org

Abstract. This paper addresses the problem of designing a robust fuzzy controller for a class of uncertain fuzzy system with H_∞ optimization and D-stability constraints on the closed-loop pole locations. Takagi and Sugeno (T-S) fuzzy models are used for the uncertain nonlinear systems. By utilizing the concept of the so-called parallel distributed compensation (PDC) method, solutions to the problem are derived in terms of a family of linear matrix inequalities and are numerically tractable via LMI techniques.

1 Introduction

During the last few years, a number of papers have been presented to deal with the problem of systematic analysis and design of fuzzy logic controllers for fuzzy dynamic systems (see [1]-[4] for example). The design method can be mainly stated as follows: to represent a nonlinear system in a family of local linear models smoothly connected through fuzzy membership functions such that the control law for each local model can be designed by using linear control system theory, and then to construct a global controller from the local controllers in such a way that global stability of the closed-loop fuzzy control system is guaranteed.

There has been a flurry of activity in multi-objective control since the LMI technique was systematically introduced in [5]; there are, however, few publications about this topic in fuzzy control. In [6], the synthesis of stability with pole placement in a circular region is presented. Fuzzy pole placement blended with H_∞ disturbance attenuation for a class of uncertain nonlinear systems is considered in [7], and the uncertainties are supposed to be norm bounded.

This paper concerns the H_∞ control problem with pole placement constraints for systems described by T-S models with linear fractional uncertainties. By using the so-called parallel distributed compensation method (see [8]) and LMI technique, a global fuzzy controller is designed to guarantee the closed-loop system with two mentioned objectives and derived by the numerical solutions of a set of coupled LMIs.

The notations used throughout this paper are fairly standard. The superscripts 'T' and '-1' stand for the matrix transposition and inverse respectively, I_k is the

$k \times k$ identity matrix, R^n denotes the n-dimensional Euclidean space, $R^{m \times n}$ is the set of all $m \times n$ real matrices, Her(A) is a shorthand notation for $A + A^T$, '$\otimes$' is the Kronecker product, and the notation $P > 0$ means that P is a symmetric and positive definite matrix. In addition, we use '*' as an ellipsis for the terms that are introduced by symmetry.

2 Problem Formulation

The following uncertain nonlinear system can be used to represent a class of complex multi-input and multi-output systems with both fuzzy inference rules and local analytic linear models.

Plant Rule i :

IF $z_1(t)$ is M_{i1} and $\cdots$ $z_n(t)$ is M_{in}

Then
$$\begin{cases} \dot{x}(t) = (A_i + \Delta A_i)x(t) + (B_{1i} + \Delta B_{1i})u(t) + (B_{2i} + \Delta B_{2i})w(t) \\ z(t) = (C_i + \Delta C_i)x(t) + (D_{1i} + \Delta D_{1i})u(t) + (D_{2i} + \Delta D_{2i})w(t) \end{cases}, \quad (1)$$

where $x(t) \in R^n$, $u(t) \in R^m$, $w(t) \in R^p$ and $z(t) \in R^q$ are the state vector, control input vector, disturbance input vector and the controlled output vector, respectively; $z_i(t)$, $i = 1, 2, \cdots, n$ are ancestor variables of rules, M_{ij} is the fuzzy set, r is the number of IF-THEN rules; A_i, B_{1i}, B_{2i}, C_i, D_{1i} and D_{2i} are real known matrices with appropriate dimensions, and ΔA_i, ΔB_{1i}, ΔB_{2i}, ΔC_i, ΔD_{1i} and ΔD_{2i} represent the time-varying parameter uncertainties satisfying the following assumption.

Assumption 1. The parameter uncertainties are linear fractional uncertainties and structured:

$$\begin{bmatrix} \Delta A_i & \Delta B_{1i} & \Delta B_{2i} \\ \Delta C_i & \Delta D_{1i} & \Delta D_{2i} \end{bmatrix} = \begin{bmatrix} H_1 \\ H_2 \end{bmatrix} \Delta(\zeta) [E_{1i} \ E_{2i} \ E_{3i}], \quad (2)$$

$$\Delta(\zeta) = F(\zeta)[I - JF(\zeta)]^{-1}, \quad (3)$$

$$I - J^T J > 0, \quad (4)$$

where H_1, H_2, E_{1i}, E_{2i}, E_{3i}, $i = 1, 2, \cdots, n$ and J are known real matrices with appropriate dimensions. The uncertain matrices $F(\zeta)$ satisfy:

$$F(\xi) \in \Omega := \{F(\xi) \mid F^T F \leq I, \forall \xi, F(\xi) \text{ is Lesbesgue measurable}\}. \quad (5)$$

Remark 1. This kind of fractional uncertainty represents a wide variety of uncertainties. The norm-bounded parameter uncertainty and the positive-real uncertainty are its special cases.

By using a center-average defuzzifer, the fuzzy model (1) can be inferred as follows:

$$\begin{cases} \dot{x}(t) = \sum_{i=1}^{r} h_i(Z(t))\{(A+\Delta A_i)x(t)+(B_{1i}+\Delta B_{1i})u(t)+(B_{2i}+\Delta B_{2i})w(t)\} \\ z(t) = \sum_{i=1}^{r} h_i(Z(t))\{(C+\Delta C_i)x(t)+(D_{1i}+\Delta D_{1i})u(t)+(D_{2i}+\Delta D_{2i})w(t)\} \end{cases}, \quad (6)$$

where $Z(t) = (z_1(t), z_2(t), \cdots, z_n(t))$, $\sum_{i=1}^{r} h_i(Z(t)) = 1$.

In virtue of the PDC method, we consider following state feedback control law,
Control Rule i:
IF $z_1(t)$ is M_{i1} and $\cdots$ $z_n(t)$ is M_{in}
Then $u(t) = K_i x(t)$, $i = 1, 2, \cdots, r$ (7)

The global fuzzy controller is:

$$u(t) = \sum_{i=1}^{r} h_i(Z(t))K_i x(t), \quad (8)$$

To simplify the representation, we ignore the time dependence of the variables. From (6) and (8), the closed-loop system becomes

$$\begin{cases} \dot{x}(t) = \tilde{A}x(t) + \tilde{B}w(t) \\ z(t) = \tilde{C}x(t) + \tilde{D}w(t) \end{cases}, \quad (9)$$

here:

$$\begin{bmatrix} \tilde{A} & \tilde{B} \\ \tilde{C} & \tilde{D} \end{bmatrix} = \begin{bmatrix} \bar{A} & B_w \\ \bar{C} & D_w \end{bmatrix} + \begin{bmatrix} B_p \\ D_p \end{bmatrix} \Delta(\xi) \begin{bmatrix} C_q & D_{qw} \end{bmatrix}. \quad (10)$$

$$\bar{A} = \sum_{i=1}^{r}\sum_{j=1}^{r} h_i(Z(t))h_j(Z(t))[A_i + B_{1i}K_j], \quad B_p = \sum_{i=1}^{r} h_i(Z(t))H_1,$$

$$C_q = \sum_{i=1}^{r}\sum_{j=1}^{r} h_i(Z(t))h_j(Z(t))[E_{1i} + E_{2i}K_j], \quad B_w = \sum_{i=1}^{r} h_i(Z(t))B_{2i},$$

$$\bar{C} = \sum_{i=1}^{r}\sum_{j=1}^{r} h_i(Z(t))h_j(Z(t))[C_i + D_{1i}K_j], \quad D_p = \sum_{i=1}^{r} h_i(Z(t))H_2,$$

$$D_{qw} = \sum_{i=1}^{r} h_i(Z(t))E_{3i}, \quad D_w = \sum_{i=1}^{r} h_i(Z(t))D_{2i}.$$

The definition of the L_2 gain of the system (9) is denoted by

$$\|T_{zw}\|_\infty = \sup_{\|w\|_2 \neq 0} \frac{\|z\|_2}{\|w\|_2}, \quad (11)$$

where T_{zw} denotes the transfer function from w to z, the L_2 norm of u is $\|u\|_2^2 = \int_0^\infty u^T u\, dt$, and the supremum is taken over all nonzero trajectories of the system (9), starting from $x(0) = 0$. Consider a candidate of Lyapunov function $V(x(t)) = x(t)^T Px(t)$, where $P > 0$. Given a prescribed positive scalar γ, then the uncertain fuzzy system (9) is said to be quadratically stable with $\|T_{zw}\|_\infty < \gamma$ if for all t, the Lyapunov derivative satisfies:

$$\frac{dV(x)}{dt} + z^T z - \gamma^2 w^T w < 0 \tag{12}$$

for all trajectories of system (9).

Generally, H_∞-norm does not directly deal with the transient response of the closed-loop systems. In contrast, the transient responses are most easily tuned in terms of pole location; hence, we consider placing the eigenvalues in a prescribed subregion (D) in the complex left half plane to prevent fast controller dynamics and to achieve desired transient behavior.

Definition 1. A subset D of the complex plane is called an LMI region if there exist a symmetric matrix $L \in R^{m \times m}$ and a matrix $M \in R^{m \times m}$ such that

$$D = \{z = x + jy \in C : f_D(z) = L + Mz + M^T \bar{z} < 0\}. \tag{13}$$

Definition 2. Given any LMI region D defined by (13), a real matrix A is called D-stable, i.e., has all its eigenvalues in the LMI region D, if and only if there exists a matrix $X > 0$ such that

$$M_D(A, X) := L \otimes X + M \otimes (AX) + M^T \otimes (AX)^T < 0. \tag{14}$$

Based on the above preparations, the following multi-objective control synthesis is proposed.

Problem RFHD. Given the uncertain system (1), a prescribed LMI domain and the perturbation matrices satisfying Assumption 1, determine the global fuzzy controller (8) such that the resulting closed-loop system (9) is robust D-stable and possesses H_∞ performance.

3 Main Results

In order to solve problem RFHD, we introduce two lemmas in advance.

Lemma 1. Given matrices M, Γ and Ξ of appropriate dimensions with $M = M^T$, then

$$M + \Gamma \Delta(\xi) \Xi + \Xi^T \Delta^T(\xi) \Gamma^T < 0 \tag{15}$$

for any $\Delta(\xi)$ satisfying (3)-(5), if and only if there exists a scalar $\delta > 0$, such that

$$\begin{bmatrix} M & \Xi^T & \delta \Gamma \\ \Xi & -\delta I & \delta J \\ \delta \Gamma^T & \delta J^T & -\delta I \end{bmatrix} < 0, \tag{16}$$

Remark 2. Lemma 1 is directly derived from the result proposed in paper [9] by using Schur complementary lemma and variable transformation. Let $\Delta(\xi) = \bar{\Delta}^T(\xi)$, $J = \bar{J}^T$, and $F(\xi) = \bar{F}^T(\xi)$, it is easy to verify that $\bar{\Delta}(\xi) = [I - \bar{F}(\xi)\bar{J}]^{-1}\bar{F}(\xi)$ with $\bar{F}(\xi)\bar{F}^T(\xi) \leq I$ and $I - \bar{J}\bar{J}^T > 0$. In this case, Lemma 1 is equivalent to the result proposed in [10].

Lemma 2. From the results in [11], the properties of Kronecker product are formulated as:

$$(X \otimes Y)(U \otimes V) = XU \otimes YV, \text{ if } XU \text{ and } YV \text{ exist},$$
$$(X \otimes Y)^T = X^T \otimes Y^T, (X \otimes Y)^{-1} = X^{-1} \otimes Y^{-1}, 1 \otimes A = A,$$
$$(X+Y) \otimes (U+V) = X \otimes U + X \otimes V + Y \otimes U + Y \otimes V.$$

We easily have the fact that:
$$I \otimes X \geq I \otimes Y, \text{ if } X \geq Y.$$

Based on the above preliminaries, the following theorems are proposed.

Theorem 1. Given the fuzzy control system (9), let $\gamma > 0$ be given, then the H_∞-norm of T_{zw} does not exceed γ if and only if there exist a matrix $X > 0$, a scalar $\delta > 0$ such that:

$$\begin{bmatrix} \bar{A}X + X\bar{A}^T & * & * & * & * \\ \bar{B}_w^T & -\gamma I & * & * & * \\ \bar{C}X & \bar{D}_w & -\gamma I & * & * \\ C_q X & D_{qw} & 0 & -\delta I & * \\ \delta B_p^T & 0 & \delta D_p^T & \delta J^T & -\delta I \end{bmatrix} < 0, \qquad (17)$$

Proof. In virtue of (12), calculate the derivative of $V(x)$ along all the trajectories of (9), it yields:

$$\begin{aligned} \Psi &:= \dot{V}(x) + z^T z - \gamma^2 w^T w \\ &= \text{Her}[x^T P\dot{x}] + [\tilde{C}x + \tilde{D}w]^T[\tilde{C}x + \tilde{D}w] - \gamma^2 w^T w \\ &= \text{Her}[x^T P(\tilde{A}x + \tilde{B}w)] + [\tilde{C}x + \tilde{D}w]^T[\tilde{C}x + \tilde{D}w] - \gamma^2 w^T w \\ &:= \varphi^T \Pi \varphi \end{aligned} \qquad (18)$$

where:

$$\varphi(t) := \begin{bmatrix} x^T & w^T \end{bmatrix}^T, \quad \Pi = \begin{bmatrix} \tilde{A}^T P + P\tilde{A} + \tilde{C}^T\tilde{C} & P\tilde{B} + \tilde{C}^T\tilde{D} \\ \tilde{B}^T P + \tilde{D}^T\tilde{C} & -\gamma^2 I + \tilde{D}^T\tilde{D} \end{bmatrix}.$$

Using the Schur complementary lemma and some variable transformations, $\Psi < 0$ if and only if there exists a matrix $X > 0$ such that

$$\begin{bmatrix} \tilde{A}X + X\tilde{A}^T & \tilde{B} & X\tilde{C}^T \\ \tilde{B}^T & -\gamma I & \tilde{D}^T \\ \tilde{C}X & \tilde{D} & -\gamma I \end{bmatrix} < 0. \qquad (19)$$

Note the representations in (10), denote:

$$M = \begin{bmatrix} \bar{A}X + X\bar{A}^T & * & * \\ B_w^T & -\gamma I & * \\ \bar{C}X & D_w & -\gamma I \end{bmatrix}, \Gamma = \begin{bmatrix} B_p \\ 0 \\ D_p \end{bmatrix}, \Xi = \begin{bmatrix} C_q X & D_{qw} & 0 \end{bmatrix}$$

Inequality (19) can be rewritten as:

$$M + \Gamma \Delta(\xi)\Xi + \Xi^T \Delta^T(\xi)\Gamma^T < 0. \quad (20)$$

From Lemma 1, (17) is directly obtained.

Theorem 2. Given an LMI region represented by L and M, the closed-loop system (9) is D-stable if there exist a matrix $X > 0$ and a matrix G such that:

$$\begin{bmatrix} M_D & * & * \\ M_2 \otimes C_q X & -G \otimes I & * \\ GM_1 \otimes B_p^T & G \otimes J^T & -G \otimes I \end{bmatrix} < 0. \quad (21)$$

where $M_D = L \otimes X + M \otimes (\bar{A}X) + M^T \otimes (\bar{A}X)^T$, $M_1^T M_2 = M$. M_1 and M_2 are full-column rank (can be obtained from the SVD of M).

Proof. By Definition 2, the closed-loop system (9) is D-stable with $w \equiv 0$ against all admissible uncertainties if for all t, there exists an $X > 0$ satisfying:

$$\Lambda_D(\tilde{A}(t), X) = L \otimes X + M \otimes (\tilde{A}(t)X) + M^T \otimes (\tilde{A}(t)X)^T < 0. \quad (22)$$

Denote $M_D = L \otimes X + M \otimes (\bar{A}X) + M^T \otimes (\bar{A}X)^T$, we get:

$$\Lambda_D(\tilde{A}(t), X) = M_D + \text{Her}[M_1^T M_2 \otimes B_p F(I - JF)^{-1} C_q X]$$
$$= M_D + \text{Her}\{[M_1^T \otimes (B_p F(I - JF)^{-1})][M_2 \otimes (C_q X)]\}$$

thus, (22) holds if for any vector $v \neq 0$ and admissible F, there holds

$$vM_D v^T + 2v[M_1^T \otimes (B_p F(I - JF)^{-1})][M_2 \otimes (C_q X)]v^T < 0. \quad (23)$$

for any fixed v, (23) holds if and only if for any

$$p \in S_v = \{v[M_1^T \otimes B_p F(I - JF)^{-1}] : F^T F \leq I\},$$

there holds

$$vM_D v^T + 2p[M_2 \otimes (C_q X)]v^T < 0. \quad (24)$$

Notice that $p = v[M_1^T \otimes B_p F(I - JF)^{-1}]$ is the unique solution to the equation $p = q(I_k \otimes F)$, where $q = [p(I_k \otimes J) + v(M_1^T \otimes B_p)]$, S_v is simplified as:

$$S_v = \{p : p = q(I_k \otimes F) : F^T F \leq I\}$$

for any $G \in R^{k \times k} > 0$, we have:

$$q(G \otimes I)q^T - p(G \otimes I)p^T$$
$$= q(G \otimes I)q^T - q(I_k \otimes F)(G \otimes I)(I_k \otimes F^T)q^T.$$
$$= q[G \otimes (I - FF^T)]q^T \geq 0$$

Thus, a sufficient condition for (23) is, while $q(G \otimes I)q^{\mathrm{T}} - p(G \otimes I)p^{\mathrm{T}} \geq 0$, there holds:

$$vM_D v^{\mathrm{T}} + 2p[M_2 \otimes (C_q X)]v^{\mathrm{T}} < 0. \quad (25)$$

which means if

$$[v \ p]\left(\begin{bmatrix} M_1^{\mathrm{T}} \otimes B_p \\ I \otimes J \end{bmatrix}(G \otimes I)\begin{bmatrix} M_1 \otimes B_p^{\mathrm{T}} & I \otimes J^{\mathrm{T}} \end{bmatrix} + \begin{bmatrix} 0 & 0 \\ 0 & -G \otimes I \end{bmatrix}\right)\begin{bmatrix} v^{\mathrm{T}} \\ p^{\mathrm{T}} \end{bmatrix} \geq 0$$

is satisfied, there holds:

$$[v \ p]\begin{bmatrix} M_D & (M_2 \otimes C_q X)^{\mathrm{T}} \\ M_2 \otimes C_q X & 0 \end{bmatrix}\begin{bmatrix} v^{\mathrm{T}} \\ p^{\mathrm{T}} \end{bmatrix} < 0. \quad (26)$$

In virtue of the S-procedure, the above condition is equivalent to the following inequality constraint:

$$\left(\begin{bmatrix} M_1^{\mathrm{T}} \otimes B_p \\ I \otimes J \end{bmatrix}(G \otimes I)\begin{bmatrix} M_1 \otimes B_p^{\mathrm{T}} & I \otimes J^{\mathrm{T}} \end{bmatrix} + \begin{bmatrix} 0 & 0 \\ 0 & -G \otimes I \end{bmatrix}\right) + \begin{bmatrix} M_D & (M_2 \otimes C_q X)^{\mathrm{T}} \\ M_2 \otimes C_q X & 0 \end{bmatrix} < 0. \quad (27)$$

Using the Schur complementary lemma, (21) is obtained.

Remark 3. Theorem 2 is *almost* a dual form of the result proposed in [12].

Based on the above two theorems, the main result for the multi-objective control synthesis to Problem RFHD is summarized in the following theorem.

Theorem 3. Consider the uncertain system (1), there exists a robust fuzzy controller (8) such that the closed-loop system (9) is D-stable with $\|T_{zw}\|_\infty < \gamma$ for all admissible uncertainties, if there exist common matrices $X > 0$, G, a positive scalar δ and matrices Y_i, $i = 1, 2, \cdots, r$, satisfying following LMIs:

$$\Phi_{ii} < 0, \Psi_{ii} < 0, \ i = 1, 2, \cdots, r, \quad (28)$$

$$\Phi_{ij} + \Phi_{ji} < 0, \Psi_{ij} + \Psi_{ji} < 0, \ i < j \leq r, \quad (29)$$

where

$$\Phi_{ij} = \begin{bmatrix} A_i X + B_{1i} Y_j + (A_i X + B_{1i} Y_j)^{\mathrm{T}} & * & * & * & * \\ B_{2i}^{\mathrm{T}} & -\gamma I & * & * & * \\ C_i X + D_{1i} Y_j & D_{2i} & -\gamma I & * & * \\ E_{1i} X + E_{2i} Y_j & E_{3i} & 0 & -\delta I & * \\ \delta H_1^{\mathrm{T}} & 0 & \delta H_2^{\mathrm{T}} & \delta J^{\mathrm{T}} & -\delta I \end{bmatrix},$$

and

$$\Psi_{ij} = \begin{bmatrix} \tilde{M}_D & * & * \\ M_2 \otimes (E_{1i} X + E_{2i} Y_j) & -G \otimes I & * \\ G M_1 \otimes H_1^{\mathrm{T}} & G \otimes J^{\mathrm{T}} & -G \otimes I \end{bmatrix},$$

here:

$$\tilde{M}_D = L \otimes X + M \otimes (A_i X + B_{1i} Y_j) + M^T \otimes (A_i X + B_{1i} Y_j)^T.$$

Furthermore, the state feedback gains are given by:

$$K_i = Y_i X^{-1}, \ i = 1, 2, \cdots, r. \tag{30}$$

Proof. The inequalities (17) and (21) are equivalent to

$$\sum_{i=1}^{r}\sum_{j=1}^{r} h_i(Z(t))h_j(Z(t)) \begin{bmatrix} \vec{A}X + X\vec{A}^T & * & * & * & * \\ B_{2i}^T & -\gamma I & * & * & * \\ \vec{C}X & D_{2i} & -\gamma I & * & * \\ \vec{C}_q X & E_{3i} & 0 & -\delta I & * \\ \delta H_1^T & 0 & \delta H_2^T & \delta J^T & -\delta I \end{bmatrix} < 0 \tag{31}$$

and

$$\sum_{i=1}^{r}\sum_{j=1}^{r} h_i(Z(t))h_j(Z(t)) \begin{bmatrix} \vec{M}_D & * & * \\ M_2 \otimes \vec{C}_q X & -G \otimes I & * \\ GM_1 \otimes H_1^T & G \otimes J^T & -G \otimes I \end{bmatrix} < 0 \tag{32}$$

where $\vec{A} = A_i + B_{1i} K_j$, $\vec{C} = C_i + D_{1i} K_j$, $\vec{C}_q = E_{1i} + E_{2i} K_j$ and
$\vec{M}_D = L \otimes X + M \otimes (\vec{A}X) + M^T \otimes (\vec{A}X)^T$.

Denote:

$$Y_i = K_i X, \ i = 1, 2, \cdots, r, \tag{33}$$

then it can be easily shown that (31) and (32) are equivalent to the following conditions:

$$\sum_{i=1}^{r} h_i(Z(t))h_j(Z(t))\Phi_{ii} + \sum_{i<j} h_i(Z(t))h_j(Z(t))[\Phi_{ij} + \Phi_{ji}] < 0 \tag{34}$$

and

$$\sum_{i=1}^{r} h_i(Z(t))h_j(Z(t))\Psi_{ii} + \sum_{i<j} h_i(Z(t))h_j(Z(t))[\Psi_{ij} + \Psi_{ji}] < 0 \tag{35}$$

respectively. Hence, if conditions (28) and (29) are satisfied for all i, j, then (34) and (35) are satisfied. Furthermore, from (33), we have $K_i = Y_i X^{-1}$.

Remark 4. The result of Theorem 3 can be directly applicable to the H_∞ optimization with domain pole placement constraint. Specifically, solving the LMI problem

  Minimize γ over the variables X, Y_i, G and δ
  Subject to LMIs (28) and (29)

yields the smallest γ. This gives an upper estimate of the H_∞ performance under the pole placement constraints.

4 Conclusion

In the paper, we developed a robust fuzzy controller design method for uncertain nonlinear systems described by T-S models. Based on the notation of D-stability and an L_2 norm bound, sufficient conditions to solve the robust H_∞ control blended with D-stability problem have been obtained and solutions were formulated in terms of LMIs. Moreover, a procedure was given to select an optimal fuzzy controller in the sense of minimizing the upper bound of H_∞ performance index under D-stability constraint.

References

1. Lee, K. R., Jeung, E. T., Park, H. B.: Robust H_∞ control for uncertain nonlinear via feedback: an LMI approach. Fuzzy Sets Syst. No. 120 (2001) 123-134
2. Sing, K. N., Wudhichai, A.: H_∞ Filtering for Fuzzy Dynamical Systems With D Stability Constraints. IEEE Trans. on Circ. and Syst. Vol. 50, No. 11, (2003) 1503-1508
3. Ma, G. F., Shi, Z., Zhu, L. K., Liu, Y. Q.: Robust analysis of fuzzy guaranteed cost control for a class of time-delay systems with uncertain parameters. Proc. of the Int. Conf. on Machine Learning and Cybernetics. (2004) 471-474
4. Lo, J. C., Lin, Y. T.: State feedback via circle criterion for fuzzy systems subject to input saturations. Proc. of Int. Conf. on Networking Sensing & Control. (2004) 920-925
5. Boyd, S., Ghaoui, L. E., Feron E., Balakrishnan, V.: Linear Matrix Inequalities in System and Control Theory. SIAM. Philadephia PA, (1994)
6. Hong, S. K., Nam, Y.: Stable fuzzy control system design with pole-placement constraint: an LMI approach. Computers in Industry. Vol. 51, (2003) 1-11
7. Fei, L.: Fuzzy pole placement design with H_∞ disturbance attenuation for uncertain nonlinear systems. Proc. of IEEE Conf. on Contr. Appl. Vol. 1, (2003) 23-25
8. Sugeno, S., Kang, T.: Fuzzy Modeling and Control of Multilayer Incinerator. Fuzzy Sets Syst. No.18, (1986) 329-346
9. Xie, L.: Output feedback H_∞ control of systems with parameter uncertainty. Int J Control. Vol.63, No.4, (1996) 741-750
10. Zhou, S. S, Lam, J., Xu, S. Y.: Robust H_∞ control for discrete-time polytopic uncertain systems with linear fractional vertices. Journal of Control Theory and Applications. Vol.2, No.1, (2004) 75-81
11. Graham, A.: Kronecker product and Matrix Calculus with Applications. Chichseter, U.K., Ellis Horwood, (1981)
12. Yu, L.: Robust control, a Linear Matrix Inequality approach. Tsinghua University Press, (2002)

A Kind of Fuzzy Genetic Algorithm Based on Rule and Its Performance Research

Fachao Li[1], Shuxin Luo[2], and Lianqing Su[2]

[1] College of Economics and Management, Hebei University of Science and Technology,
Shijiazhuang, 050018, P.R. China
lifachao@tsinghua.org.cn
[2] College of Science, Hebei University of Science and Technology,
Shijiazhuang, 050018, P.R. China
{lianqing_su, luosx}@hebust.edu.cn

Abstract. Ranking fuzzy information has been becoming the key issue in solving uncertainty optimization problems. Credibility being not embodied, it becomes powerless for both the order relation based on level cuts and the order relation determined by centralized quantification to play their key part in ranking fuzzy information under certain consciousness. In this paper, we introduce the concept of location values of fuzzy numbers with a rule pool and develop a new way to rank fuzzy numbers. We give the further descriptions of the location values by using coincidence degrees of fuzzy numbers with a rule pool. Composite quantifica-tion technique is used for processing fuzzy information. Moreover, we present a numerical model for computing location values and coincidence degrees. Furthermore, we propose a kind of fuzzy genetic algorithm based on rules, BR-FGA, by using the location values and coincidence degrees of fuzzy numbers with rules, and its performance is then considered with two illustrative examples.

1 Introduction

Evolutionary algorithms and fuzzy techniques have been proven to be powerful in intelligent computations. Combining both strengths together is essential for many actual domains such as optimization problems in complex systems, artificial intelligence and computer techniques.

In 1965, fuzzy sets, put forward by Zadeh[1], made it possible to describe uncertain information. In 1973, Holland[2] developed the genetic algorithm (GA) based on the natural evolution principle of living things. Although fuzzy techniques and evolutionary computation can be regarded as the two main components of the soft computing, they lack of consistency theoretically. As known, GA can be applied to optimize the shape and parameters of the membership function of a fuzzy set and fuzzy techniques are also setting their foot in genetic computing, but there are few results involving the essential combination of the two.

For evolutionary computations, current theoretical researches mainly focus on the improvement of accuracy, convergence and precocity of the computing and the extension of the function[3-5], which are all based on the simple genetic algorithm proposed by Holland. All these results start with a fitness function, which is used to evaluate the fitness of an individual to the environment. More precisely speaking, the selection probability is based on the fitness of the individuals only, according to which reproducing process, and then the crossover and mutation processes may go But for practical problems with uncertainty, it is impossible to determine exactly the fitness of an individual. So the reproducing process must be distorted, which will then affect the succeeding steps. The uncertainty engaged in evolutionary computation comes mainly from the environments, the fitness values of the individuals will change as the environments change, which will then affect the computing result. This important issue has already attracted the attention of many scholars.

Fuzzy number theory is commonly used to describe the uncertainty contained in practical problems. Its applications involve many domains such as fuzzy control, fuzzy optimization, fuzzy programming, etc.[6-10]. In these application domains, it is often necessary to compare different fuzzy numbers. So a suitable order relation on the fuzzy number space is always the main concern for many scholars. In 1981, Goetschel & Voxman[11] discussed the topological structure of fuzzy numbers and presented the representation theorem in the interval form of fuzzy numbers, by which some kinds of fuzzy programming or fuzzy optimization problems can be transformed into classical ones at certain levels [12-15]. But in most situations, fuzzy information should be taken as a whole, so the order structure of fuzzy numbers should be consi-dered. Although some theoretical results about the order structure of fuzzy numbers have been given[16-20], all these disregarded credibility, which make it difficult to rank fuzzy information under certain consciousness for fuzzy rules.

All the analyses above show that ranking fuzzy numbers rationally is still the key point in the uncertainty evolutionary computation. This paper focus on this aspect and the main works are organized as follows: In Section 2, a ranking approach for fuzzy numbers is proposed based on the concept of a rule pool; In Section 3, the corresponding numerical computing model is given. In Section 4, by using the loca-tion values and coincidence degrees of fuzzy numbers with rules, we propose a kind of fuzzy genetic algorithm based on rule, BR-FGA, and then analyze its performance with two illustrative examples.

In what follows, let R be the real number field, $\mathcal{F}(R)$ the family of all fuzzy sets on R, and $I(R)$ the class of all closed intervals on R. For $A \in \mathcal{F}(R)$, let $A(x)$ be the membership function of A, $A_\lambda = \{x \mid A(x) \geq \lambda\}$ the λ-cuts of A.

2 Location Values and Coincidence Degrees of Fuzzy Numbers Based on a Rule Pool

Definition 1[11, 21]. $A \in \mathcal{F}(R)$ is called a fuzzy number if $A_1 \neq \phi$, $A_\lambda \in I(R)$ for each $\lambda \in (0,1]$ and $\text{supp}A = \{x \mid A(x) > 0\}$ is bounded. The class of all fuzzy numbers is called fuzzy number space, and denoted by E^1.

For convenience, we denote the closure of suppA by A_0 and the singular set $\{a\}$ of real number a by $[a, a]$. Clearly, $A \in E^1$ implies that $A_0 \in I(R)$. Let $A = (b; [a, c])$ denote the triangular fuzzy number with its membership function as

$$A(x) = \begin{cases} (x-a)/(b-a) & \text{if } a \le x \le b \\ (x-a)/(b-a) & \text{if } b \le x \le c \\ 0 & \text{otherwise} \end{cases} \quad (1)$$

Obviously, for $A = (b; [a, c])$, we have $A_\lambda = [a + (b-a)\lambda, c - (c-b)\lambda]$ for each $\lambda \in [0, 1]$, and $A_0 = [a, c]$, $A_1 = \{b\}$.

Definition 2. For $A, B \in E^1$, say B the t-translation about A (here, t is a real number), and written as $B = t \oplus A$, if $B(x) = A(x-t)$ for all $x \in R$. Furthermore,

$$\mathcal{R}(A) = \{t \oplus A \mid -\infty < t < +\infty\} \quad (2)$$

is called a complete rule pool of A, and A the rule basis of $\mathcal{R}(A)$.

Remark 1. Since $0 \oplus A = A$ and $t_1 \oplus (t_2 \oplus A) = (t_1 + t_2) \oplus A$, then for two arbitrary rule bases $A^{(1)}$ and $A^{(2)}$, $\mathcal{R}(A^{(1)}) = \mathcal{R}(A^{(2)})$ implies that there exists a real number $t \in R$ such that $A^{(2)} = t \oplus A^{(1)}$, which indicates that $\mathcal{R}(A) = \mathcal{R}(t \oplus A)$. For convenience, we might as well take the rule basis A, a fuzzy number such that 0 is the center point of A_1, as the standard rule basis.

Theorem 1. Let D be the metric on E^1, $\mathcal{R}(A)$ be a given rule pool and $B \in E^1$. Set $G(t) = D(t \oplus A, B)$, then

1) $G(t)$ is uniformly continuous on $(-\infty, +\infty)$ and $\lim_{t \to \infty} G(t) = +\infty$;

2) There exist $t_1, t_2 \in R$ with $t_1 \le t_2$ such that $G(t)$ is monotone decreasing on $(-\infty, t_1]$, and monotone increasing on $[t_2, +\infty)$.

Theorem 1 is the immediate deduction of the properties of metric (see [21]).

From Theorem 1 we see that the minimum value of $D(t \oplus A, B)$ must be attaina-ble on $(-\infty, +\infty)$ for any given $B \in E^1$. But there may be more than one minimum value point, or precisely, many rules in $\mathcal{R}(A)$ may have the same distance to B.

Definition 3. Let A be a rule basis, D the metric on E^1 and $B \in E^1$. We say B coincide with the rule $t_0 \oplus A$, written as $B \tilde{\in} t_0 \oplus A$, if $D(t_0 \oplus A, B) = \min_{t \in R} D(t \oplus A, B)$. Denote

$$B_A = B_A^{\sup} = \max\{t_0 \mid B \tilde{\in} t_0 \oplus A\} \quad (3)$$

$$\delta(B_A) = [1 + (B_A^{\sup} - B_A^{\inf})]^{-1} \quad (4)$$

then B_A is said to be the location value of B with respect to the rule basis A, and $\delta(B_A)$ the sensitivity of B with respect to the rule basis A.

Remark 2. For a given rule basis A, we can define the following order relation "$\leq$" on $\mathcal{R}(A)$ by $t_1 \oplus A \leq t_2 \oplus A$ if and only if $t_1 \leq t_2$. If t is regarded as the representative value of the rule $t \oplus A$, B_A will then be the representative value of the rule in the pool $\mathcal{R}(A)$ that most approximate to B. Hence the order relation between fuzzy numbers could be constituted utilizing the order relation on $\mathcal{R}(A)$.

Definition 4. Let A be a given rule basis, D the metric on E^1 and $B \in E^1$. Then

$$CD_A(B) = \left(1 + [D(B_A \oplus A, B)]^\alpha\right)^{-1} \tag{5}$$

is called the coincidence degree of B with $\mathcal{R}(A)$. Here, $\alpha \in [0,1]$ can be viewed as an adjustment parameter.

Obviously, both $\delta(B_A)$ and $CD_A(B)$ rely on B, the rule pool $\mathcal{R}(A)$ and the metric D, but not on the choice of the rule basis A. $\delta(B_A)$ can express the characteristic of the relative membership between B and the rule pool $\mathcal{R}(A)$. $CD_A(B)$ can be regarded as a quantitative index representing the coincidence degree of B with $\mathcal{R}(A)$. It is easy to see that $CD_A(B) = 1 \Leftrightarrow B \in \mathcal{R}(A)$.

To sum up, B_A can be viewed as an index reflecting the global position of B in the pool $\mathcal{R}(A)$, while $CD_A(B)$ and $\delta(B_A)$ can be viewed as assistant indexes for further description about B_A, which describe the relations between B and the pool $\mathcal{R}(A)$ from different sides. Accordingly, the ordered numbers $(B_A, CD_A(B), \delta(B_A))$ can be thought of as the composite quantification for the position of B in $\mathcal{R}(A)$. In practical applications, the composite quantification can be processed synthetically according to different decision consciousness.

3 Numerical Model Computing Location Values

For a given rule pool $\mathcal{R}(A)$ and $B \in E^1$, it is difficult to determine the exact position B_A by the definition of B_A. We could follow the following steps to compute B_A, and then $\delta(B_A)$, $CD_A(B)$.

Step1. Select a layer classification parameter N and a translation step-length parameter Δt;

Step2. Compute λ_i – cuts $A_{\lambda_i} = [\underline{a}(\lambda_i), \overline{a}(\lambda_i)]$, here $\lambda_i = i/N$, $i = 0, 1, 2, \cdots, N$;

Step3. Set $t_0 = \underline{b}(0) - m(A_0)$, $K = \text{int}(1 + [m(A_0) + m(B_0)]/\Delta t)$ and $t_k = t_0 + k\Delta t$, $k = 0, 1, \cdots, K$, calculate the following quantities in turn:

$$\Sigma(t_k) = \sum_{i=1}^{N} [|t_k + \overline{a}(\lambda_i) - \overline{b}(\lambda_i)| + |t_k + \underline{a}(\lambda_i) - \underline{b}(\lambda_i)|], \quad \Sigma_{\min} = \min_{0 \leq k \leq K} \Sigma(t_k),$$

$$t_{\min} = \min\{t_j \mid \Sigma(t_j) = \min_{0 \leq k \leq K} \Sigma(t_k)\}, \quad t_{\max} = \max\{t_j \mid \Sigma(t_j) = \min_{0 \leq k \leq K} \Sigma(t_k)\};$$

Step4. Compute $CD_A^*(B) = [1 + (\Delta t \cdot \Sigma_{\min})^\alpha]^{-1}$, $\delta^*(B_A) = [1 + (t_{\max} - t_{\min})]^{-1}$;

Step5. Output $(B_A, CD_A(B), \delta(B_A)) = (t_{\max}, CD_A^*(B), \delta^*(B_A))$.

Here, $A_\lambda = [\underline{a}(\lambda), \overline{a}(\lambda)]$ and $B_\lambda = [\underline{b}(\lambda), \overline{b}(\lambda)]$ are the $\lambda-$ cuts of A and B, respectively.

Sum up all the above, we can obtain a numerical model about location values and coincidence degrees (all the notations are as above):

$$\begin{cases} (A; B; N; \Delta t) \\ CD_A^*(B) = [1 + (\Delta t \cdot \Sigma_{min})^\alpha]^{-1} \\ t_{min} = \min\left\{t_j \mid \Sigma(t_j) = \min_{0 \le k \le K} \Sigma(t_k)\right\} \\ t_{max} = \max\left\{t_j \mid \Sigma(t_j) = \min_{0 \le k \le K} \Sigma(t_k)\right\} \\ \delta^*(B_A) = [1 + (t_{max} - t_{min})]^{-1} \end{cases} \quad (6)$$

We can prove that $(t_{max}, CD_A^*(B), \delta^*(B_A))$ strictly approximate $(B_A, CD_A(B), \delta(B_A))$ as $\Delta t \to 0, N \to \infty$, which will be considered in another paper.

4 Fuzzy Genetic Algorithm Based on Rule

For uncertainty evolutionary computation, the following three types of fitness function are often encountered:

Type1 The variables are real, but the operational coefficients are fuzzy;
Type2 The variables are fuzzy, but the operational coefficients are real;
Type3 Both the variables and the operational coefficients are fuzzy.

These three types of optimization problems cannot be solved by using existing genetic algorithms because of the powerless of them in the aspect of processing the fuzziness contained in the fitness function. Considering the shortcomings of current fuzzy order structures, we present an approach to rank fuzzy information under a certain rule, which will be some effective in solving the above problems.

Generally, a fuzzy variable can be transformed into a module with special structure using the structure characteristic of a fuzzy number and then the genetic operation could be carried out, which is not further discussed here. In the sequel, we will establish a kind of fuzzy genetic algorithm only for *Type1* by using the composite quantification technique.

4.1 Selection Operator in Uncertainty Evolutionary Mechanism

Let S be the individual space, S^M the population space, $\vec{X}(n) = \{X_1, X_2, \cdots, X_M\} = \{X_1(n), X_2(n), \cdots, X_M(n)\}$ the nth generation population in the evolution process. f denotes the fuzzy fitness function, a mapping from the individual space S to $E^1(+) = \{A \in E^1 \mid A_0 \subset [0, +\infty)\}$. T_s denotes the selection operator, a mapping from the population space S^M to the matrix space S^2. With the help of location values and coincidence degrees of fuzzy numbers, we can give the following steps to determine the selection operator T_s:

Step1. Determine location values $[f(X_k)]_A$ and coincidence degrees $CD_A(f(X_k))$ of fuzzy fitness values $f(X_k), k = 1, 2, \cdots, M$ with rule pool $\mathcal{R}(A)$;

Step2. Determine composite effect quantifications of $f(X_k)$:
$$[f^*(X_k)]_A = [f(X_k)]_A \cdot [CD_A(f(X_k))]^\theta, \ k=1, 2, \cdots, M,$$
here, $\theta \in [0, \infty)$ is the coincidence effect parameter;

Step3. Set $P\{T_s(\vec{X}(n)) = X_k\} = [f^*(X_k)]_A (\sum_{i=1}^N [f^*(X_i)]_A)^{-1}$, and
$$P\{T_s(\vec{X}(n)) = \{X_i, X_j\}\} = P\{T_s(\vec{X}(n)) = X_i\} \cdot P\{T_s(\vec{X}(n)) = X_j\}. \tag{7}$$

4.2 Structure of BR-FGA

For uncertainty evolutionary computation like *Type1*, if the solution is coded with *l*-bits based on the set $\{0,1\}$, or $S = \{0, 1\}^l$, the selection operator T_s is taken as in equ. (7), the mutation operator T_m follows the way that the values of every genes of an individual are independently mutated according to the probability p_m, and the crossover operator T_c is taken to be one-point crossover, randomized one-point crossover, or randomized uniform crossover etc., then the population genetic sequence $\{X(n)\}_{n=0}^\infty$, which is defined by

$$\vec{X}(n+1) = \{X_k(n+1) = T_m \circ T_c \circ T_s(\vec{X}(n)), k = 1, 2, \cdots, M\}, \tag{8}$$

possesses similar properties to existing genetic algorithms with real type of fitness values. It is easy to show that if the optimum individual is always kept down to the next generation, then $\{X(n)\}_{n=0}^\infty$ satisfies the following properties:

1) The population state space is finite;
2) Sequence $\{X(n)\}_{n=0}^\infty$ must be a homogenous finite Markov chain. And for $0 < p_m < 1$, $\{X(n)\}_{n=0}^\infty$ will also become aperiodic and irreducible, hence there must be a stationary distribution for $\{X(n)\}_{n=0}^\infty$ independent of $\vec{X}(0)$, the initial population.

In order to distinguish with other algorithms, the algorithm defined by equ. (8) will be called fuzzy genetic algorithm based on rules, or briefly, BR-FGA.

4.3 Examples

There are various kinds of uncertain information in real life, so different types of uncertainty optimizations should be considered. In business, managers expect to employ as few employees as possible under certain regular production condition; In selecting basketball players, coaches always choose a tall individual with strong body and moderate form; and so on. Among these optimizations, "regular pro-duction condition" and "strong body and moderate form" are all fuzzy rules. In order to solve these optimization problems, one needs to consider uncertainty optimization based on rules. The key point is to optimize the objective value in the rule pool by synthesizing all the factors. We proceed with two examples to illustrate the applica-tion of BR-FGA in solving these optimization problems.

For convenience, in the following two examples, we will apply the following genetic operating mechanism: Individuals are coded with 16-bits binary system, the size of population is selected as $M = 40$, the selection operator T_s is taken as in equ. (8), the crossover operator T_c is taken to be one-point crossover and the mutation operator T_m is taken as the way of mutating bit by bit. In addition, optimum keeping technique is applied in the genetic process, and we stop when the variance of individual fitness is less than 10^{-6} the algorithm.

Example 1. Let $A = (0; [-1, 2])$. For rule pool $\mathcal{R}(A)$, determine the maximum value of fuzzy value function $f(x_1, x_2) = (x_1 x_2) \cdot A_1$, where $A_1 = (5; [3, 8])$, $-3 \leq x_i \leq 3$ ($i = 1, 2$). It is necessary to determine the optimal location of $f(x_1, x_2)$ with the rule pool $\mathcal{R}(A)$ as the criterion. Existing genetic algorithms can't help with this problem because of their ineffectiveness to fuzzy fitness values. Considering the discussions above and Model (6), if we employ location values and coincidence degrees to describe fuzzy fitness values, this optimization problem can be solved by genetic algorithm under certain consciousness. The operating steps are presented as follows:

1) Select a layer classification parameter N, a translation step-length parameter Δt, and a vision parameter α for fuzzy information;
2) Determine the synthetic effect location value $F(x_1, x_2)$ of $f(x_1, x_2)$;
3) Select parameters M, p_c and p_m involved in the genetic mechanism;
4) Construct the genetic sequence according to (8).

Following the above steps, for objective function $\max F(x_1, x_2) = B_A \cdot CD_A(B)$, $-3 \leq x_i \leq 3$ ($i = 1, 2$), where $B = (x_1 x_2) \cdot A_1$, if the parameters are selected as: $\alpha = 0.1$, $N = 10$, $\Delta t = 0.1$, $p_c = 0.6$, and $p_m = 0.001$, we obtain the convergence curves for objective function, location values and coincidence degrees of fuzzy optimization function as shown in Fig.1, Fig.2 and Fig.3, respectively.

Example 2. Let $A = (0; [-1, 2])$. For rule pool $\mathcal{R}(A)$, determine the maximum value of fuzzy value function $f(x_1, x_2, x_3) = x_1^2 \cdot A_1 + (x_2 x_3) \cdot A_2$, $0 \leq x_i \leq 3, i = 1, 2, 3$, where $A_1 = (5; [3, 6])$, $A_2 = (6; [5.5, 9])$.

Similar to Example 1, for objective function $\max F(x_1, x_2, x_3) = B_A \cdot CD_A(B)$, $0 \leq x_i \leq 3$, $i = 1, 2, 3$, where $B = x_1^2 \cdot A_1 + (x_2 x_3) \cdot A_2$, if the parameters are selected as: $\alpha = 0.1$, $N = 10$, $\Delta t = 0.1$, $p_c = 0.6$ and $p_m = 0.001$, we obtain the convergence curves for objective function, location values and coincidence degrees of fuzzy optimization function as shown in Fig.4, Fig.5 and Fig.6, respectively.

Setting the adjustment parameter $\alpha = 0.1$, the layer classification parameter $N = 10$, and the step-length parameter $\Delta t = 0.1$ for different mutation probability p_m and different crossover probability p_c, we have tested independently 200 times using MATLAB 6.5 in a 500MHZ computer and gave the solutions of Examples 1 and Examples 2 respectively. At last, average generation numbers $\bar{k}$ to the optimum (or satisfied) solution with the above BR-FGA were obtained, which are listed in Table 1 and Table 2 respectively. In addition, the distributions of the number of convergence generation (for parameters $p_c = 0.7$, $p_m = 0.0001$) are illustrated in Fig.7 and Fig.8.

Table 1. Comparison of average numbers of convergence generations in Example 1

p_m	0.01	0.01	0.01	0.005	0.005	0.005	0.001	0.001	0.001	0.0001	0.0001	0.0001
p_c	0.6	0.7	0.8	0.6	0.7	0.8	0.6	0.7	0.8	0.6	0.7	0.8
$\bar{k}$	20.04	21.12	21	17.37	18.13	18.19	15.28	15.65	14.90	14.90	14.87	15.08

Table 2. Comparison of average numbers of convergence generations in Example 2

p_m	0.01	0.01	0.01	0.005	0.005	0.005	0.001	0.001	0.001	0.0001	0.0001	0.0001
p_c	0.6	0.7	0.8	0.6	0.7	0.8	0.6	0.7	0.8	0.6	0.7	0.8
$\bar{k}$	24.37	25.57	25.43	21.64	21.93	20.49	16.58	16.74	16.94	15.76	15.93	15.91

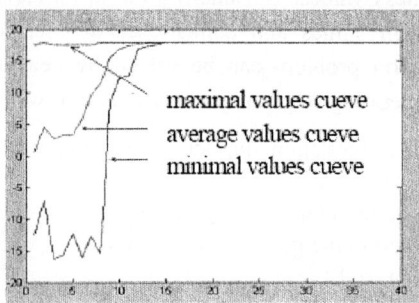

Fig. 1. Convergence curves for objective function in Example 1

Fig. 2. Convergence curves for location values in Example 1

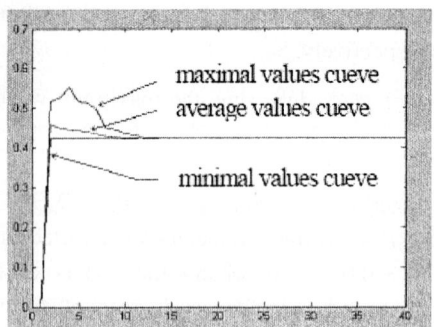
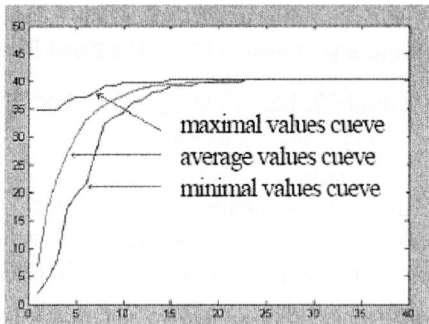

Fig. 3. Convergence curves for coincidence degrees in Example 1

Fig. 4. Convergence curves for objective function in Example 2

One may notice that, in order to obtain the optimal solution for Examples 4.1 & 4.2, 15 with 20 generations operated average running times are about 47 & 65 seconds, respectively. All these testing results and the characteristics of the convergence curves show that uncertainty optimizations could be solved effectively using BR-FGA technique, and the corresponding convergence speed will also be fast. In the testing process, we also find that the computing results tend to be almost changeless with the layer classification parameter N getting large and the step-length parameter Δt getting small. Of course, good effect relies on the appropriate selection of parameters. N is suggested to be selected between 10 and 20 while Δt between 0.05 and 0.1.

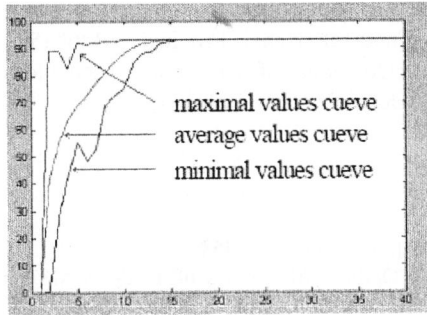

Fig. 5. Convergence curve for location values in Example 2

Fig. 6. Convergence curve for coincidence degrees in Example 2

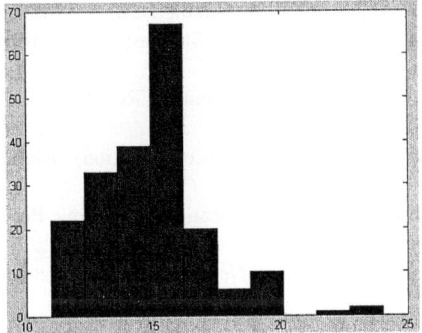 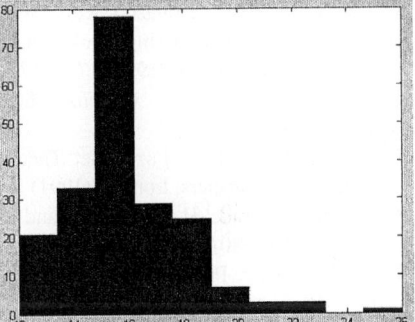

Fig. 7. Distribution of the number of convergence generation in Example 1

Fig. 8. Distribution of the number of convergence generation in Example 2

Noticing the structure of BR-FGA, we can see that when the rule basis is selected as a real-type fuzzy number and the fitness function is taken as a real function, our BR-FGA will be identical to the ordinary genetic algorithms, which indicates that BR-FGA indeed extend existing algorithms. Besides, for the same type of fuzzy optimization, different solutions may be obtained by BR-FGA for different rule bases or differ-ent processing techniques for fuzzy information, which indicates that BR-FGA can reflect the decision consciousness to a certain extent, and then differs intrinsically from existing genetic algorithms.

All the above show that BR-FGA can not only overcome the shortcoming of being powerless to process uncertain information for existing genetic algorithms, but also converges more rapidly. But these analyses and testing results cannot completely reflect the intrinsic performance of BR-FGA, which will be further discussed in another paper.

Acknowledgement

This work is supported by the Ph. D. Fund of Hebei Province (B2004509, 05547004D-2) and the Science Fund of Hebei University of Science and Technology (QD200314) and the Natural Science Fund of Hebei Province (603384).

References

1. Zadeh, L. A.: Fuzzy Sets. Information and Control 8 (1965) 338–353
2. Holland, J. H.: Genetic Algorithms and the Optimal Allocations of Trials. SIAMJ of Computing 2 (1973) 8–105
3. Grefenstette, J.J.: Optimization of Control Parameters for Genetic Algorithms. IEEE Trans. Syst. Man and Cybernetics 16 (1986) 122–128
4. Srinivas, M., Patnaik, L. M.: Adaptive Probabilities of Crossover and Mutation in Genetic Algorithms. IEEE Trans. Syst. Man and Cybernetics 24(1994) 656–667
5. Dae-Yeong Jeno, Dongsoo Kim, Song-Yop Hahn, et al: Optimum Design of Linear Synchronous Motor Using Evolutionary Strategy Combined with Stochastic FEM. IEEE Trans. on Magnetic 35(1999) 1734–1737
6. Li Hong-Xing, Yen, V. C.: Fuzzy Sets and Fuzzy Decision-Making. CRC Press, Boca Raton (1995)
7. Zimmermann, H. J.: Fuzzy Set Theory and Its Applications (Second Edition). Kluwer Academic Publishers, London (1991)
8. Dubois, D., Prade, H.: Fuzzy Sets and Systems–Theory and Applications. Academic Press, New York (1980)
9. Li Hong-Xing, Philip Chen, C. L., Han–Pang Huang: Fuzzy Neural Intelligent Systems. CRC Press, Boca Raton (2001)
10. Chen Shi-Jay, Chen Shyi-Ming: Fuzzy Risk Analysis Based on Similarity Measures of Generalized Fuzzy Numbers. IEEE Trans. on Fuzzy Systems 11(2003) 45–56
11. Goetschel, R., Voxman, W.: Topological Properties of Fuzzy Number. Fuzzy Sets and Systems 10 (1983) 87–99
12. Tong Shaocheng: Interval Number and Fuzzy Number Linear Programming. Fuzzy Sets and Systems 66 (1994) 301–306
13. Kuwano, H.: On the Fuzzy Multi-objective Linear Programming Problem: Goal Programming Approach. Fuzzy Sets and Systems 82 (1996) 57–64
14. Liu Baoding: Fuzzy Random Chance Constrained Programming. IEEE Trans. on Fuzzy Systems 9 (2001) 713–720
15. Kassem, M. A. E., Ammar, E. I.: Stability of Multi-objective Nonlinear Programming Problem with Fuzzy Parameters in the Constraints. Fuzzy Sets and Systems 29 (1989) 315–326
16. Lee, S., Olson, D.: Comparison Fuzzy Number Based on the Probability Measure of Fuzzy Events. Operation Research 15 (1988) 887–896

17. Liou, T., Wang, M.: Ranking Fuzzy Numbers with Integral Value. Fuzzy Sets and Systems 50 (1992) 247–255
18. Zhang Kunlun, Kaofu Hirota: On Fuzzy Number-Lattice $(\tilde{R}, \leq)$. Fuzzy Sets and Systems 92 (1997) 113–122
19. Liu Min, Li Fachao, Wu Cheng: The Order Structure of Fuzzy Numbers Based on the Level Characteristic and Its Application in Optimization Problems. Science in China (Series F) 45 (2002) 433-441
20. Lee-Kwang, H., Jee-Hyong Lee: A Method for Ranking Fuzzy Numbers and Its Application to Decision-making. IEEE Trans. on Fuzzy Systems 7 (1999) 677–685
21. Liu Min, Li Fachao, Wu Cheng: Fuzzy Metric Based on the Distance Function of Plane and Its Application in Optimal Scheduling Problems. Science in China (Series F) 46 (2003) 210-224

The Absolute Additivity and Fuzzy Additivity of Sugeno Integral

Congxin Wu and Liang Zhao

Department of Mathematics, Harbin Institute of Technology,
Harbin, 150001, China
zhaoliang170@yahoo.com.cn

Abstract. In this paper, based on the foundation of the discussion of the Sugeno integral for real functions which was presented by Wu Congxin and Mamadou in 2003, we introduce and consider the concept of the absolute additivity of the Sugeno integral for real functions. We also discuss the fuzzy additivity of the Sugeno integral for real functions. For these two kinds of additivity, we obtain two necessary and sufficient conditions, a sufficient condition, a necessary condition and several counter examples.

1 Introduction

It is well known that the theory of fuzzy integral for nonnegative functions was firstly introduced by Sugeno [1] in 1974 and then by Ralescu and Adams [2] in 1980. Fuzzy integral theory is an important part of fuzzy analysis and has been applied widely and deeply in many areas of science and technology such as control theory, computer science, economics etc. We can find the development of fuzzy integral in recent monographs [3-5].

In 2003, using a similar method for the extension of the classical Lebesgue integral from nonnegative functions to real functions, Wu and Mamadou [6] extended the Sugeno integral to the case of real functions and investigated the corresponding properties. We focus on presenting the characterization of the absolute integrability of Sugeno integral for real functions, which is a basic topic for each kind of nonlinear integral. In fact, Sipos [7], Marinova [8], Kolesarova [9], Narukawa, Murofushi and Sugeno [10] also used this traditional method to research the other fuzzy integral for real functions.

Since the various additivities for any type of integral are important, in this paper we will discuss two kinds of additivity of Sugeno integral for real functions. First, in the discussion of absolute integrability of Sugeno integral for real functions in [6], it is natural to define the absolute additivity of Sugeno integral for real functions by means that for any $f \in L^1(\mu)$ always implies $|f| \in L^1(\mu)$ and

$$(s)\int_\Omega |f| d\mu = (s)\int_\Omega f^+ d\mu + (s)\int_\Omega f^- d\mu$$

Section 3 of this paper gives the characterizations of absolute superadditivity and absolute additivity of Sugeno integral for real functions. Section 4 generalizes the fuzzy superadditivity of Sugeno integral in [3] to the case of real functions and provides a counter example to show that the sufficient condition of fuzzy additivity of Sugeno integral in [12] cannot be generalized to the case of real functions.

2 Preliminaries

First, we recall some definitions which will be used for this work.

Definition 1. [3,4] Let Ω be a nonempty set, Σ be a classical $\sigma-$algebra on Ω and $\mu: \Omega \to [0,+\infty]$. If μ satisfies the following conditions:

1. $\mu(\phi) = 0$ (ϕ is the empty set);
2. if $A, B \in \Sigma$ and $A \subset B$, then
$$\mu(A) \leq \mu(B);$$
3. if $\{A_n\}_{n=1}^{\infty} \subset \Sigma$ and $A_1 \subset A_2 \subset \cdots$, then
$$\mu\left(\bigcup_{n=1}^{\infty} A_n\right) = \lim_{n \to \infty} \mu(A_n);$$
4. if $\{A_n\}_{n=1}^{\infty} \subset \Sigma$, $A_1 \subset A_2 \subset \cdots$ and there exists a positive integer n_0 such that $\mu(A_{n_0}) < \infty$, then
$$\mu\left(\bigcup_{n=1}^{\infty} A_n\right) = \lim_{n \to \infty} \mu(A_n),$$

then we say that μ is a fuzzy measure and (Ω, Σ, μ) is a fuzzy measure space.

Definition 2. [3,4] Let (Ω, Σ, μ) be a fuzzy measure space, $f: \Omega \to [-\infty,+\infty]$ be an extended real-valued function on Ω. Then f is a $\mu-$measurable function if :
$$N_\alpha(f) = \{x \in \Omega: f(x) \geq \alpha\} \in \Sigma$$
for all $\alpha \in (-\infty, +\infty)$.

Definition 3. [3,4] Let (Ω, Σ, μ) be a fuzzy measure space, $f: \Omega \to [0,+\infty]$ be a $\mu-$ measurable function and $A \in \Sigma$. Then the Sugeno integral (in short $(s)-$ integral) on A is defined by:
$$(s)\int_A f d\mu = \bigvee_{\alpha > 0} \alpha(\wedge \mu(N_\alpha(f) \cap A))$$
where $\vee = \sup$ and $\wedge = \inf$. And we say that f is $(s)-$integrable on A if $(s)\int_A f d\mu < \infty$.

Definition 4. [6] Let (Ω, Σ, μ) be a fuzzy measure space, $f: \Omega \to [-\infty, +\infty]$ be $\mu-$ measurable and

$$f^+(x) = f(x) \vee 0, \ f^-(x) = (-f(x)) \vee 0$$

for all $x \in \Omega$.

Clearly, f^+ and f^- are also $\mu-$ measurable and $f(x) = f^+(x) - f^-(x)$ for all $x \in \Omega$. If f^+ and f^- are also $(s)-$ integrable on $A \in \Sigma$, then we say that f is $(s)-$ integrable on A and define:

$$(s)\int_A f d\mu = (s)\int_A f^+ d\mu - (s)\int_A f^- d\mu$$

and denote:

$$L^1(\mu) = \{f: \Omega \to [-\infty, \infty]: f \text{ is } (s)- \text{ integrable on } \Omega\}$$

Definition 5. Let (Ω, Σ, μ) be a fuzzy measure space. If for any $f \in L^1(\mu)$ we have $|f| \in L^1(\mu)$ and:

$$(s)\int_\Omega |f| d\mu = (s)\int_\Omega f^+ d\mu - (s)\int_\Omega f^- d\mu$$

then we say that the Sugeno integral for real functions has absolute additivity. The definition of superadditivity is similitude.

We will also be using some notations for a fuzzy measure space (Ω, Σ, μ).

(i) (Null-additivity) [3,4]. For any $A, B \in \Sigma$ with $A \cap B = \phi$ and $\mu(B) = 0$, we have

$$\mu(A \cup B) = \mu(A)$$

(ii) (Subadditivity) [3,4]. For any $A, B \in \Sigma$ and $A \cap B = \phi$, we have

$$\mu(A \cup B) \leq \mu(A) + \mu(B)$$

(iii) For any $A, B \in \Sigma$ with $A \cap B = \phi$ and $\mu(A \cup B) = \infty$, we have

$$\mu(A \cup B) \leq \mu(A) + \mu(B)$$

(iv) For any $A, B \in \Sigma$ with $A \cap B = \phi$, we have

$$\mu(A) = 0 \text{ or } \mu(B) = 0$$

(v) There does not exist $A, B \in \Sigma$ with $A \cap B = \phi$ such that

$$\mu(A) = \mu(B) = \infty$$

(vi) [11] For any $A \in \Sigma$ we have:

$$\mu(A) = 0 \text{ or } \mu(A) = \mu(\Omega)$$

(vii) (Countable additivity) For any $\{A_n\}_{n=1}^\infty \subset \Sigma$ with $A_i \cap A_j = \phi$ for all $i \neq j$, we have

$$\mu\left(\bigcup_{n=1}^\infty A_n\right) = \sum_{n=1}^\infty \mu(A_n)$$

(viii) (Fuzzy additivity) [12] For any $A, B \subset \Sigma$ we have
$$\mu(A \cup B) = \mu(A) \vee \mu(B)$$

3 Absolute Additivity of Sugeno Integral for Real Functions

Theorem 1. (The necessary condition of absolute superadditivity) Let (Ω, Σ, μ) be a fuzzy measure space. Then the absolute superadditivity of Sugeno integral for any $f \in L^1(\mu)$ implies that μ satisfies the condition (v).

Proof. If fuzzy measure μ does not satisfies (v), then $A_0, B_0 \in \Sigma$ exist with $A_0 \cap B_0 = \phi$ such that $\mu(A_0) = \mu(B_0) = \infty$ (so that $\mu(A_0 \cup B_0) = \infty$)
Define:
$$f(x) = \begin{cases} 1, & \text{if } x \in A_0 \\ -1, & \text{if } x \in B_0 \\ 0, & \text{if } x \in \Omega \setminus (A_0 \cup B_0) \end{cases}$$

Then $f^+(x) = \chi_{A_0}(x)$, $f^-(x) = \chi_{B_0}(x)$, $|f|(x) = \chi_{A_0 \cup B_0}(x)$ for all x and
$$(s)\int_\Omega |f| d\mu = (s)\int_\Omega f^+ d\mu = (s)\int_\Omega f^- d\mu = 1,$$
where χ_A is the characteristic function of $A \in \Sigma$. Therefore:
$$(s)\int_\Omega |f| d\mu \geq (s)\int_\Omega f^+ d\mu + (s)\int_\Omega f^- d\mu$$
does not hold, it is a contradiction.

Theorem 2. (Absolute superadditivity) Let (Ω, Σ, μ) be a fuzzy measure space such that μ satisfies the condition (v). Then for any $f \in L^1(\mu)$, we have $|f| \in L^1(\mu)$ and:
$$(s)\int_\Omega f d\mu \geq (s)\int_\Omega f^+ d\mu + (s)\int_\Omega f^- d\mu ;$$
if and only if μ satisfies conditions (iii) and (iv).

Proof. Sufficiency: If $f \in L^1(\mu)$, then by [6] Theorem 3.1 we know that condition (iii) implies $|f| \in L^1(\mu)$.
Let:
$$A = \{x \in \Omega : f(x) > 0\}, B = \{x \in \Omega : f(x) < 0\}$$
then clearly, $A, B \in \Sigma$ and $A \cap B = \phi$.
By condition (v), we must have $\mu(A) < \infty$ or $\mu(B) < \infty$.

By condition (iv), we may assume $\mu(A) = 0$, so that:
$$(s)\int_\Omega f^+ d\mu = (s)\int_A f^+ d\mu = 0$$

Hence, we obtain:
$$(s)\int_\Omega |f| d\mu = (s)\int_{A\cup B} |f| d\mu \geq (s)\int_B |f| d\mu$$
$$= (s)\int_B f^- d\mu = (s)\int_\Omega f^- d\mu$$
$$= (s)\int_\Omega f^+ d\mu + (s)\int_\Omega f^- d\mu$$

Necessity: Suppose there were $A_0, B_0 \in \Sigma$ with $A_0 \cap B_0 = \phi$ such that
$$\alpha_0 = \mu(A_0) \wedge \mu(B_0) > 0$$

Note that $\mu(A_0 \cup B_0) \geq \alpha_0$ and by the condition (v), $\alpha_0 < \infty$.

Define:
$$f_0(x) = \alpha_0 \chi_{A_0}(x) - \alpha_0 \chi_{B_0}(x) \text{ for all } x \in \Omega$$

Then:
$$f_0^+(x) = \alpha_0 \chi_{A_0}(x), f_0^-(x) = \alpha_0 \chi_{B_0}(x), |f_0|(x) = \alpha_0 \chi_{A_0 \cup B_0}(x) \text{ for all}$$
$$x \in \Omega$$

Hence
$$(s)\int_\Omega |f| d\mu = \alpha_0 \wedge \mu(A_0 \cup B_0) = \alpha_0 < 2\alpha_0$$
$$= \alpha_0 \wedge \mu(A_0) + \alpha_0 \wedge \mu(B_0)$$
$$= (s)\int_\Omega f^+ d\mu + (s)\int_\Omega f^- d\mu$$

This is a contradiction. Therefore, μ satisfies the condition (iv).

Moreover, by [6] Theorem 3.1 we know that μ also satisfies condition (iii).

Theorem 3. (Absolute additivity) Let (Ω, Σ, μ) be a fuzzy measure space such that μ satisfies condition (v). Then the following statements are equivalent:

(1) Sugeno integral for real functions is absolutely additive;
(2) μ satisfies the conditions (ii) and (iv);
(3) μ satisfies the conditions (vii) and (iv);
(4) μ satisfies the conditions (i) and (iv);
(5) μ satisfies the conditions (vi) and (vii).

Remark 1. In general, under the conditions (iv) and (v), we can obtain
$$(s)\int_\Omega |f| d\mu \geq (s)\int_\Omega f^+ d\mu + (s)\int_\Omega f^- d\mu$$

for $f \in L^1(\mu)$, but may not obtain $|f| \in L^1(\mu)$, basically because, it is not absolutely superadditive.

Example 1. Let $\Omega = \{a,b\}$, $\Sigma = P(\Omega)$ be the class of all subsets of Ω and

$$\mu(A) = \begin{cases} 0, & \text{if } A = \emptyset, \{b\} \\ 1, & \text{if } A = \{a\} \\ \infty, & \text{if } A = \Omega \end{cases}$$

Evidently, (Ω, Σ, μ) is a fuzzy measure space and μ satisfies conditions (iv) and (v), but μ does not satisfy condition (iii).

Define:

$$f(x) = \begin{cases} \infty, & \text{if } x = a \\ -\infty, & \text{if } x = b \end{cases}$$

Then for any $x \in \Omega$,

$$f^+(x) = \begin{cases} \infty, & \text{if } x = a \\ 0, & \text{if } x = b \end{cases}, \quad f^-(x) = \begin{cases} 0, & \text{if } x = a \\ \infty, & \text{if } x = b \end{cases}$$

$$|f|(x) = \infty.$$

Since

$$(s)\int_\Omega |f|\, d\mu = \mu(\Omega) = \infty,$$

$$(s)\int_\Omega f^+\, d\mu = \mu(\{a\}) = 1,$$

$$(s)\int_\Omega f^-\, d\mu = \mu(\{b\}) = 0,$$

we have $|f| \notin L^1(\mu)$ and $f^+, f^- \in L^1(\mu)$ so that $f \in L^1(\mu)$ and

$$(s)\int_\Omega |f|\, d\mu > (s)\int_\Omega f^+\, d\mu + (s)\int_\Omega f^-\, d\mu.$$

4 Fuzzy Additivity of Sugeno Integral for Real Functions

The following theorem shows that the fuzzy superadditivity of Sugeno integral for nonnegative functions [3,4] can be extended to the case of real functions.

Theorem 4. For any $f, g \in L^1(\mu)$, we have

$$(s)\int_\Omega f \vee g\, d\mu \geq (s)\int_\Omega f\, d\mu \vee (s)\int_\Omega g\, d\mu$$

Proof. Let:

$$E_1 = \{x \in \Omega : f(x) \geq 0, g(x) \geq 0\}, \quad E_2 = \{x \in \Omega : f(x) \geq 0, g(x) < 0\}$$
$$E_3 = \{x \in \Omega : f(x) < 0, g(x) \geq 0\}, \quad E_4 = \{x \in \Omega : f(x) < 0, g(x) < 0\}$$

Then we have:
$$(f \vee g)^+(x) = \begin{cases} f^+(x) \vee g^+(x), & (x \in E_1) \\ f^+(x), & (x \in E_2) \\ g^+(x), & (x \in E_3) \\ 0, & (x \in E_4) \end{cases},$$

$$(f \vee g)^-(x) = \begin{cases} 0, & (x \in E_1) \\ 0, & (x \in E_2) \\ 0, & (x \in E_3) \\ f^-(x) \wedge g^-(x), & (x \in E_4) \end{cases}$$

It follows that:
$$(s)\int_\Omega f \vee g \, d\mu = (s)\int_\Omega (f \vee g)^+ \, d\mu - (s)\int_\Omega (f \vee g)^- \, d\mu$$
$$= \bigvee_{\alpha>0} \alpha \wedge \mu\big((N_\alpha(f^+ \vee g^+) \cap E_1) \cup (N_\alpha(f^+) \cap E_2)$$
$$\cup (N_\alpha(g^+) \cap E_3)\big) - \bigvee_{\alpha>0} \alpha \wedge \mu(N_\alpha(f^- \wedge g^-) \cap E_4)$$

Notice that:
$$N_\alpha(f^+ \vee g^+) \cap E_1 = (N_\alpha(f^+) \cap E_1) \cup (N_\alpha(g^+) \cap E_1)$$
$$N_\alpha(f^- \wedge g^-) \cap E_4 = (N_\alpha(f^-) \cap E_4) \cap (N_\alpha(g^-) \cap E_4)$$

We obtain:
$$(s)\int_\Omega f \vee g \, d\mu \geq \bigvee_{\alpha>0} \alpha \wedge \mu\big((N_\alpha(f^+) \cap E_1) \cup (N_\alpha(f^+) \cap E_2)\big)$$
$$- \bigvee_{\alpha>0} \alpha \wedge \mu\big((N_\alpha(f^-) \cap E_3) \cap (N_\alpha(f^-) \cap E_4)\big),$$
$$= (s)\int_\Omega f^+ \, d\mu - (s)\int_\Omega f^- \, d\mu = (s)\int_\Omega f \, d\mu$$
$$(s)\int_\Omega f \vee g \, d\mu \geq \bigvee_{\alpha>0} \alpha \wedge \mu\big((N_\alpha(g^+) \cap E_1) \cup (N_\alpha(g^+) \cap E_3)\big)$$
$$- \bigvee_{\alpha>0} \alpha \wedge \mu\big((N_\alpha(g^-) \cap E_2) \cup (N_\alpha(g^-) \cap E_4)\big)$$
$$= (s)\int_\Omega g^+ \, d\mu - (s)\int_\Omega g^- \, d\mu = (s)\int_\Omega g \, d\mu$$

So that:
$$(s)\int_\Omega f \vee g \, d\mu \geq (s)\int_\Omega f \, d\mu \vee (s)\int_\Omega g \, d\mu$$

Remark 2. We point out that even for nonnegative $f, g \in L^1(\mu)$ we may not have $f \vee g \in L^1(\mu)$.

Example 2. Let $\Omega = \{a,b\}$, and:

$$\mu(A) = \begin{cases} 0, & \text{if } A = \phi, \{a\}, \{b\} \\ \infty, & \text{if } A = \Omega \end{cases}$$

Define:

$$f(x) = \begin{cases} 0, & \text{if } x = a \\ \infty, & \text{if } x = b \end{cases}, g(x) = \begin{cases} \infty, & \text{if } x = a \\ 0, & \text{if } x = b \end{cases},$$

then $f(x) \vee g(x) = \infty$ for all $x \in \Omega$ and:

$$(s)\int_\Omega f(x)d\mu = \mu(\{b\}) = 0,$$
$$(s)\int_\Omega g(x)d\mu = \mu(\{a\}) = 0,$$
$$(s)\int_\Omega f \vee g\, d\mu = \mu(\Omega) = \infty$$

so that $f, g \in L^1(\mu)$, but $f \vee g \notin L^1(\mu)$.

Remark 3. We cannot extend the Wangs' conclusion in [12], i.e. condition (viii) implies the fuzzy additivity of Sugeno integral for nonnegative functions to the case of real functions.

Example 3. Let $\Omega = \{a,b,c,d\}$, $\Sigma = P(\Omega)$ and

$$\mu(A) = \begin{cases} 0, & \text{if } A = \phi \\ 1, & \text{if } A = \{d\} \\ 2, & \text{otherwise} \end{cases}$$

We can easily see that (Ω, Σ, μ) is a fuzzy measure space and μ satisfies condition (viii).

Define:

$$f(x) = \begin{cases} 1, & \text{if } x = a \\ 1, & \text{if } x = b \\ -2, & \text{if } x = c \\ -1, & \text{if } x = d \end{cases}, g(x) = \begin{cases} 1, & \text{if } x = a \\ -2, & \text{if } x = b \\ 1, & \text{if } x = c \\ -1, & \text{if } x = d \end{cases}$$

Then for each $x \in \Omega$:

$$(f \vee g)^+(x) = \chi_{\{a,b,c\}}(x), (f \vee g)^-(x) = \chi_{\{d\}}(x)$$
$$f^+(x) = \chi_{\{a,b\}}(x), g^+(x) = \chi_{\{a,c\}}(x),$$

$$f^-(x) = \begin{cases} 0, & \text{if } x = a,b \\ 2, & \text{if } x = c \\ 1, & \text{if } x = d \end{cases}, g^-(x) = \begin{cases} 0, & \text{if } x = a,c \\ 2, & \text{if } x = b \\ 1, & \text{if } x = d \end{cases}$$

Therefore:
$$(s)\int_\Omega f \vee g\, d\mu = 1 \wedge \mu(\{a,b,c\}) - 1 \wedge \mu(\{d\}) = 1 \wedge 2 - 1 \wedge 1 = 0,$$
$$(s)\int_\Omega f\, d\mu = 1 \wedge \mu(\{a,b\}) - \left(\bigvee_{1\geq\alpha>0} \alpha \wedge \mu(\{c,d\})\right) \vee \left(\bigvee_{2\geq\alpha>1} \alpha \wedge \mu(\{c\})\right)$$
$$= 1 \wedge 2 - 1 \vee 2 = -1,$$
$$(s)\int_\Omega g\, d\mu = 1 \wedge \mu(\{a,c\}) - \left(\bigvee_{1\geq\alpha>0} \alpha \wedge \mu(\{b,d\})\right) \vee \left(\bigvee_{2\geq\alpha>1} \alpha \wedge \mu(\{b\})\right)$$
$$= 1 \wedge 2 - 1 \vee 2 = -1$$

so that:
$$(s)\int_\Omega f \vee g\, d\mu \neq (s)\int_\Omega f\, d\mu \vee (s)\int_\Omega g\, d\mu$$

5 Conclusion

This paper introduces the concept of the absolute additivity of the Sugeno integral for real functions, and discuss the fuzzy additivity of the Sugeno integral for real functions. For these two kinds of additivity, two necessary and sufficient conditions, a sufficient condition, a necessary condition and several counter examples are presented.

Acknowledgement

Supported by Natural Science Foundation of China (10571035)

References

1. Sugeno, M.: Theory of fuzzy integral and its application. Ph. D. Thesis. Tokyo Institute of Technology (1974)
2. Ralescu, D., Adams, G.: The fuzzy integral. J. Math. Anal. Appl. 75 (1980) 562-570
3. Wang, Z., Klir, G. J.: Fuzzy Measure Theory. Plenum Press. New York (1992)
4. Pap, E.: Null-Additive Set Functions. Kluwer. Dordecht. The Netherlands (1995)
5. Grabisch, M., Murofushi, T., Sugeno, M.(Eds.): Fuzzy Measures and Integral: Theory and Applications. Physica-Verlag. Heideberg (2000)
6. Wu, C., Mamadou, T.: An extension on Sugeno integral. Fuzzy Sets and Systems 138 (2003) 537-550
7. Sipos, J.: Integral with respect to a pre-measure. Math. Slovaca 29 (1979) 141-155
8. Marinova, I.: Integration with respect to a ⊕measure. Math. Slovaca 36 (1986) 15-24
9. Kolesarova, A.: Integration of real functions with respect to a ⊕ measure. Math. Slovaca 46 (1996) 41-52
10. Narukawa, Y., Murofushi, T., Sugeno, M.: Extension and representation of comonotonically additive functionals. Fuzzy Sets and Systems 121 (2000) 217-226
11. Klement, E. P., Ralescu, D. A.: Nonlinearity of the fuzzy integral. Fuzzy sets and systems 11 (1983) 309-315
12. Wang, Z., Leung, K., Wang, J.: Determining nonnegative monotone set function based on Sugeno's integral: an application of genetic algorithms. Fuzzy Sets and Systems 112 (2000) 155-164

The Axiomatization for 0-Level Universal Logic

Yingcang Ma[1,2] and Huacan He[2]

[1] College of Science,
Xi' an University of Engineering Science and Technology,
Xi'an 710048, China
mayingcang@263.net
[2] School of Computer Science,
Northwestern Polytechnical University,
Xi' an 710072, China
hehuac@nwpu.edu.cn

Abstract. The aim of this paper is the partial axiomatization for 0-level universal logic. Firstly, a propositional calculus formal deductive system $UL_{he(0,1]}$ of 0-level universal logic is built up, and the corresponding algebra $L\Pi G$ is introduced. Then we prove the system $UL_{he(0,1]}$ is sound and complete with respect to the 0-level continuous universal AND operators on [0, 1]. Lastly, three extension logics of $UL_{he(0,1]}$ are also introduced.

1 Introduction

How to deal with various uncertainties and evolution have been critical issues for further development of AI. The well-developed mathematical logic is too rigid and it can only solve certainty problems. Therefore non-classical logic and modern logic develop rapidly, for example fuzzy logic (FL) and universal logic (UL).

In recent years considerable progress has been made in logical foundations of fuzzy logic, (See [2,3,4,5,9,10,11,18]). Some well-known logic systems have been built up, such as the basic logic (BL) introduced by Hajek; the monoidal t-norm based logic (MTL) introduced by Esteva and Godo; a formal deductive system L^* introduced by Wang (see [14,15,16,17]), and so on.

UL[6] was proposed by Huacan He in 2001. In the recent years, the study of UL semantics has acquired significant development (see [1,6,7,8,12,13]), but the study of UL axiomatization is in the pilot study. In this paper we will propose a propositional calculus formal system $UL_{he(0,1]}$ of 0-level UL, and its completeness will be proven.

The paper is organized as follows. After this introduction, Section 2 contains necessary background knowledge about BL and UL. In Section 3 the propositional calculus formal deductive system $UL_{he(0,1]}$ is built up. The soundness theorem and some other theorems of $UL_{he(0,1]}$ are proven. In Section 4 we prove the system $UL_{he(0,1]}$ is complete with respect to the 0-level continuous universal AND operators on [0,1]. In Section 5 some extension logics of $UL_{he(0,1]}$ are introduced. The final section offers the conclusions.

2 Preliminaries

In this section we summarize the basic notions and results from BL and UL that will be used throughout this paper.

2.1 The Basic Fuzzy Logic BL and BL-Algebra

The language of the basic logic BL is based on two basic connectives $\rightarrow$ and $\&$ and one truth constant $\bar{0}$. Further connectives are defined as follows:

$\varphi \wedge \psi$ is $\varphi \& (\varphi \rightarrow \psi)$; $\varphi \vee \psi$ is $((\varphi \rightarrow \psi) \rightarrow \psi) \wedge ((\psi \rightarrow \varphi) \rightarrow \varphi)$;
$\neg \varphi$ is $\varphi \rightarrow \bar{0}$; $\varphi \equiv \psi$ is $(\varphi \rightarrow \psi) \& (\psi \rightarrow \varphi)$.

The following formulas are the axioms of BL:

(A1) $(\varphi \rightarrow \psi) \rightarrow ((\psi \rightarrow \chi) \rightarrow (\varphi \rightarrow \chi))$
(A2) $(\varphi \& \psi) \rightarrow \varphi$
(A3) $(\varphi \& \psi) \rightarrow (\psi \& \varphi)$
(A4) $\varphi \& (\varphi \rightarrow \psi) \rightarrow (\psi \& (\psi \rightarrow \varphi))$
(A5a) $(\varphi \rightarrow (\psi \rightarrow \chi)) \rightarrow ((\varphi \& \psi) \rightarrow \chi)$
(A5b) $((\varphi \& \psi) \rightarrow \chi) \rightarrow (\varphi \rightarrow (\psi \rightarrow \chi))$
(A6) $((\varphi \rightarrow \psi) \rightarrow \chi) \rightarrow (((\psi \rightarrow \varphi) \rightarrow \chi) \rightarrow \chi)$
(A7) $\bar{0} \rightarrow \varphi$

The deduction rule of BL is modus ponens.

It has been shown that the well-known Lukasiewicz logic is the extension of BL by the axiom: (Ł) $\neg \neg \varphi \rightarrow \varphi$, and product logic is just the extension of BL by the following two axioms:

(Π1) $\neg \neg \chi \rightarrow (((\varphi \& \chi) \rightarrow (\psi \& \chi)) \rightarrow (\varphi \rightarrow \psi))$, and (Π2) $\varphi \wedge \neg \varphi \rightarrow \bar{0}$.

Finally, Gödel logic is the extension of BL by the axiom: (G) $\varphi \rightarrow (\varphi \& \varphi)$.

A BL-algebra is an algebra $L = (L, \cap, \cup, *, \Rightarrow, 0, 1)$ with four binary operations and two constants such that

1. $(L, \cap, \cup, 0, 1)$ is a lattice with the greatest element 1 and the least element 0 (with respect to the lattice ordering $\leq$),
2. $(L, *, 1)$ is a commutative semigroup with the unit element 1, i.e. $*$ is commutative, associative and $1 * x = x$ for all x,
3. The following conditions hold for all x, y, z:

(a) $z \leq (x \Rightarrow y)$ iff $x * z \leq y$; (b) $x \cap y = x * (x \Rightarrow y)$; (c) $(x \Rightarrow y) \cup (y \Rightarrow x) = 1$.

Defining $\neg x = (x \Rightarrow 0)$. MV-algebras are BL-algebras satisfying: $\neg \neg x = x$. Product algebras are BL-algebras satisfying: $x \cap \neg x = 0$ and $(\neg \neg z \Rightarrow ((x * z \Rightarrow y * z) \Rightarrow (x \Rightarrow y))) = 1$. G-algebras are BL-algebras satisfying: $x * x = x$.

Let us denote by $Ł$, $Π$, and G, Lukasiewicz, Product, and Gödel logic, respectively, and, as usual, let us denote by standard MV-algebra (Product algebra, G-algebra respectively) the BL-chain on [0,1] defined by the Lukasiewicz t-norm (product t-norms or min t-norm, respectively). The standard completeness results of $Ł$, $Π$, and G that is the completeness with respect to their corresponding standard algebras.

2.2 UL and 0-Level Universal Operations

UL thinks that all things in the world are correlative, that is, they are either mutually exclusive or mutually consistent, and we call this kind of relation generalized correlation. Any two propositions have generalized correlation. The degree of general correlation can be described quantitatively by the coefficient of the generalized correlation $h \in [0,1]$: If we define the h of operator $T(a,b)$ as the ratio between the volume of $T(a,b)$ and the volume of maximal operator, then $h = 1$ means the maximal attractive state; $h = 0.75$ means independency correlative state; $h = 0.5$ means neutral state; $h = 0$ means maximal exclusive state. The 0-level universal AND operators and 0-level universal implication operators are defined as:

0-level universal AND operators are mapping: $T : [0,1] \times [0,1] \to [0,1]$, $T(x, y, h) = \Gamma^1[(x^m + y^m - 1)^{1/m}]$, which is usually denoted by $\wedge_h$; the real number m has relation with the coefficient of generalized correlation h as:

$$m = (3 - 4h)/(4h(1 - h)) . \qquad (1)$$

$h \in [0,1]$, $m \in R$. And $\Gamma^1[x]$ denotes x is restricted in $[0,1]$, if $x > 1$ then its value will be 1, if $x < 0$, its value will be 0.

0-level universal IMPLICATION operators are mapping: $I : [0,1] \times [0,1] \to [0,1]$,

$$I(x, y, h) = ite\{1 \mid x \leq y; 0 \mid m \leq 0 \text{ and } y = 0; \quad \Gamma^1[(1 - x^m + y^m)^{1/m}]\},$$

which is usually denoted by $\Rightarrow_h$. In the above equation with m and h is the same as (1). In the above the $ite\{a \mid b; c\}$ denotes that the value is a if b is true, otherwise c.

Remark 1. If h does not equal 0, the 0-level universal AND operators are continuous and for the same h, 0- universal IMPLICATION operators and 0-level universal AND operators are an adjoint pair. So we don't discuss when h=0.

3 0-Level UL System: $UL_{h \in (0,1]}$

If we fix $h \in (0, 1]$, we fix a propositional calculus $PC(h)$: $\wedge_h$ is taken for the truth function of the conjunction &, the residuum $\Rightarrow_h$ of $\wedge_h$ becomes the truth function of the implication $\to$. In more detail, we have the following:

Definition 1. The propositional calculus $PC(h)$ given by h has propositional variables $p_1, p_2, \cdots$, connective &, $\to$ and the constant $\overline{0}$ for 0. Formulas are defined in the obvious way: each propositional variable is a formula; $\bar{0}$ is a formula; if φ,ψ are formulas, then $\varphi\&\psi, \varphi\to\psi$ are formulas. Further connective variables are defined as follows:

$\varphi\wedge\psi$ is $\varphi\&(\varphi\to\psi)$; $\varphi\vee\psi$ is $((\varphi\to\psi)\to\psi)\wedge(\psi\to\varphi)\to\varphi)$,

$\neg\varphi$ is $\varphi\to\bar{0}$; $\varphi\equiv\psi$ is $(\varphi\to\psi)\&(\psi\to\varphi)$.

An evaluation of propositional variables is a mapping v assigning to each propositional variable p its truth value $v(p)\in[0,1]$. This extends uniquely to the evaluation of all formulas as follows:

$v(\bar{0})=0$; $v(\varphi\to\psi)=(v(\varphi)\Rightarrow_h v(\psi))$; $v(\varphi\&\psi)=(v(\varphi)\wedge_h v(\psi))$.

That is, an evaluation of $PC(h)$ is a ($\wedge_h, \to_h$)-type homomorphism from $PC(h)$ to $[0,1]$. All valuations $v: PC(h)\to[0,1]$ are denoted by Ω. It is clear that:

$v(\phi\wedge\psi)=\min(v(\varphi),v(\psi))=\wedge_1(v(\varphi),v(\psi))$, $v(\varphi\vee\psi)=\max(v(\varphi),v(\psi))$.

Definition 2. A formula φ is a 1-tautology of $PC(h)$ if $v(\varphi)=1$ for each evaluation $v\in\Omega$.

In the following we are going to choose some formulas that are 1-tautology of each $PC(h)$ for our axioms and develop a logic that is common base of all the logics $PC(h)$.

Definition 3. Axioms of the system $UL_{he(0,1]}$ are those of BL plus :

$(\textit{Ł}\Pi G)$: $(\varphi\to\varphi\&\psi)\to((\varphi\to\bar{0})\vee\psi\vee((\varphi\to\varphi\&\varphi)\wedge(\psi\to\psi\&\psi)))$

The deduction rule of $UL_{he(0,1]}$ is modus ponens.

Remark 2. The axioms of system $UL_{he(0,1]}$ are similar to the axioms of logic $\textit{Ł}\Pi G$ in [2], but their semantics are different.

We can define the concepts such as proof, theorem, deduction from a formula set Γ, Γ-consequence in the system $UL_{he(0,1]}$. $\Gamma\vdash\varphi$ denotes that φ is provable in the theory. $\vdash\varphi$ denotes that φ is a theorem of system $UL_{he(0,1]}$. $\vDash\varphi$ denotes that φ is a 1-tautology of each $PC(h)$. $\Gamma\vDash\varphi$ denotes that φ is a 1-tautology of each $PC(h)$ whenever $v(\Gamma)\subseteq 1$.

Proposition 1. The hypothetical syllogism holds, i.e. let $\Gamma=\{\varphi\to\psi,\psi\to\chi\}$, then $\Gamma\vdash\varphi\to\chi$.

Proposition 2. The following formulas are the theorems of the system $UL_{he(0,1]}$:

(T1) $\varphi\to(\psi\to\varphi)$

(T2) $(\varphi\to(\psi\to\chi))\to(\psi\to(\varphi\to\chi))$

(T3) $\varphi\to\varphi$

(T4) $(\psi\to\chi)\to(\varphi\&\psi\to\varphi\&\chi)$

(T5) $(\psi\to\chi)\to((\varphi\to\psi)\to(\varphi\to\chi))$

(T6) $(\psi \to \chi) \vdash (\varphi \to \psi) \to (\varphi \to \chi)$

(T7) $(\varphi \to \psi) \vdash (\psi \to \chi) \to (\varphi \to \chi)$

For brevity, we omit the proofs of the above two propositions.

Theorem 1. (Soundness) All axioms of $UL_{h\in(0,1]}$ are 1-tautology in each $PC(h)$. If φ and $\varphi \to \psi$ are 1-tautology of $PC(h)$, then ψ is also a 1-tautology of $PC(h)$. Consequently, each formula provable in $UL_{h\in(0,1]}$ is a 1-tautology of each $PC(h)$, i.e. $\Gamma \vdash \varphi$, then $\Gamma \vDash \varphi$.

Proof. It is clear that the the evaluation of $PC(h)$ is a part of the evaluation of $PC(\star)$, where $\star$ is a fixed continuous t-norm, and (A1)-(A7) are 1-tautologies in each $PC(\star)$, then (A1)-(A7) are 1-tautologies in each $PC(h)$. For ($Ł\Pi G$), if $h=1$, we have $v((\varphi \to \varphi \& \psi) \to ((\varphi \to \overline{0}) \vee \psi \vee ((\varphi \to \varphi \& \varphi) \wedge (\psi \to \psi \& \psi)))) = (v(\varphi) \to_1 v(\varphi) \& v(\psi)) \to_1 ((v(\varphi) \to_1 0) \vee v(\psi) \vee ((v(\varphi) \to_1 v(\varphi)) \& v(\varphi)) \wedge (v(\psi) \to_1 v(\psi))$. $\& v(\psi)))) = 1$ The similar proof for others $h \in (0,1)$. For modus ponens observe that if $x=1$ and $x \to_h = 1$, then necessarily $y=1$.

Definition 4. Let $\varphi, \psi \in PC(h)$, if $\vdash \varphi \to \psi$ and $\psi \to \varphi$, we say that φ and ψ is provable equivalence, and denote $\varphi \sim \psi$.

Proposition 3. The provable equivalence is an equivalence relation on $PC(h)$.

Proposition 4. The provable equivalence is a congruence relation on $PC(h)$, i.e.
(1) If $\varphi \sim \psi$ and $\chi \sim \omega$, then $\varphi \& \chi \sim \psi \& \omega$.
(2) If $\varphi \sim \psi$ and $\chi \sim \omega$, then $\varphi \to \chi \sim \psi \to \omega$.

Proof. (1) If $\varphi \sim \psi$ and $\chi \sim \omega$, then $\chi \& \varphi \to \chi \& \psi$ by $\varphi \to \psi$, (T4) and MP rule. Using (A3) and HS rule we get $\varphi \& \chi \to \psi \& \chi$. On the other hand, by $\chi \to \omega$,(T4) and MP rule we have $\psi \& \chi \to \psi \& \omega$. Hence, $\varphi \& \chi \to \psi \& \omega$ from HS rule. By the same method we can prove that $\psi \& \omega \to \varphi \& \chi$. Then, $\varphi \& \chi \sim \psi \& \omega$.
(2) If $\varphi \sim \psi$ and $\chi \sim \omega$, then $(\varphi \to \chi) \to (\varphi \to \omega)$ by $\chi \to \omega$ and left-isotonic rule (T6). According to $B \to_p A$ and right-antitonic rule (T7), we get $(\varphi \to \omega) \to (\psi \to \omega)$. Therefore, $(\varphi \to \chi) \to (\psi \to \omega)$ from HS rule. By the same way, we can prove that $(\psi \to \omega) \to (\varphi \to \chi)$ .Then, $\varphi \to \chi \sim \psi \to \omega$.

4 The $Ł\Pi G$ Algebra and the Completeness of $UL_{h\in(0,1]}$

Definition 5. A $Ł\Pi G$ algebra is a BL-algebra in which the identity
$(x \Rightarrow x * y) \Rightarrow ((x \Rightarrow 0) \cup y \cup ((x \Rightarrow x * x) \cap (y \Rightarrow y * y))) = 1$ is valid.

Example. (1) MV-algebra, Product algebra and G-algebra are $Ł\Pi G$ algebra.

(2) For each $h \in (0,1]$, $([0,1], \min, \max, \wedge_h, \Rightarrow_h, 0, 1)$ which is called $Ł\Pi G$ unit interval is a linear ordering $Ł\Pi G$ algebra with its standard linear ordering.

Definition 6. Let L be a $Ł\Pi G$ algebra. In an analogy, we define an L-evaluation of propositional variables to be any mapping v assigning to each propositional variables p an element $v(p)$ of L. This extends on L as truth function, i.e. $v(\overline{0}) = 0$, $v(\varphi \rightarrow \psi) = (v(\varphi) \Rightarrow v(\psi))$, $v(\varphi \& \psi) = (v(\varphi) * v(\psi))$, and hence $v(\phi \wedge \psi) = (v(\varphi) \cap v(\psi))$, $v(\varphi \vee \psi) = (v(\varphi) \cup v(\psi))$, $v(\neg \varphi) = (v(\varphi) \Rightarrow 0)$.
All L-evaluations $v: PC(h) \rightarrow L$ are denoted by $\Omega(L)$. If $\forall v \in \Omega(L)$, $v(\varphi) = 1$, then φ is called an L-tautology. denoted by $\vDash_L \varphi$. $\Gamma \vDash_L \varphi$ denotes that φ is an L-tautology whenever $v(\Gamma) \subseteq 1$.

Theorem 2. (L-soundness) The system $UL_{h \in (0,1]}$ is sound with respect to $Ł\Pi G$-tautologies: if φ is provable in $UL_{h \in (0,1]}$, then φ is an L-tautology for each $Ł\Pi G$ algebra L. More generally, if Γ is a theory over the system $UL_{h \in (0,1]}$ and Γ proves φ, then, for each $Ł\Pi G$ algebra L and each L-tautology of v of propositional variables assigning the value 1 to all the axioms of Γ we have $v(\varphi) = 1$.

Proof. Soundness of axioms is straightforward from the definition of $Ł\Pi G$ algebra. If $\Gamma \vdash \varphi$, then φ is a axiom, or $\varphi \in \Gamma$, or φ is obtained from ψ and $\psi \rightarrow \varphi$ by MP, where ψ and $\psi \rightarrow \varphi$ are Γ-consequence, and $v(\psi) = v(\psi \rightarrow \varphi) = 1$. If φ is a axiom, or $\varphi \in \Gamma$, then $v(\varphi) = 1$. If φ is obtained from ψ and $\psi \rightarrow \varphi$ by MP, then $v(\varphi) \geq v(\psi) * (v(\psi) \Rightarrow v(\varphi)) = v(\psi) * (v(\psi \rightarrow \varphi)) = 1$, hence $v(\varphi) = 1$.

Definition 7. Let Γ be a fixed theory over $UL_{h \in (0,1]}$. For each formula φ, let $[\varphi]_\Gamma$ be the set of all formulas ψ such that $\Gamma \vdash \varphi \equiv \psi$ (formulas Γ-provably equivalent to φ). L_Γ is the set of all the classes $[\varphi]_\Gamma$. We can give the following definitions:
$0 = [\overline{0}]_\Gamma$; $1 = [\overline{1}]_\Gamma$; $[\varphi]_\Gamma * [\psi]_\Gamma = [\varphi \& \psi]_\Gamma$; $[\varphi]_\Gamma \Rightarrow [\psi]_\Gamma = [\varphi \rightarrow \psi]_\Gamma$,
$[\varphi]_\Gamma \cap [\psi]_\Gamma = [\varphi \wedge \psi]_\Gamma$; $[\varphi]_\Gamma \cup [\psi]_\Gamma = [\varphi \vee \psi]_\Gamma$.

Definition 8. Let L be a $Ł\Pi G$ algebra. A filter on L is a non-empty set $F \subseteq L$ such that for each $x, y \in L$, $a \in F$ and $b \in F$ implies $a * b \in F$, $a \in F$ and $a \leq b$ implies $b \in F$. F is a prime filter if F is a filter and for all $a, b \in L$, $(a \Rightarrow b) \in F$ or $b \Rightarrow a \in F$.

Proposition 5. Let L be a $Ł\Pi G$ algebra and let F be a filter.

1 The relation $a \sim_F$ iff $(a \Rightarrow b) \in F$ and $b \Rightarrow a \in F$, is a congruence relation over a $Ł\Pi G$ algebra.
2 The quotient of L by $\sim_F$ is a $Ł\Pi G$ algebra
3 The quotient algebra is linearly ordered iff F is a prime filter.

Proof. Being a $Ł\Pi G$ algebra is a BL-algebra plus the identity
$$(x \Rightarrow x*y) \Rightarrow ((x \Rightarrow 0) \cup y \cup ((x \Rightarrow x*x) \cap (y \Rightarrow y*y))) = 1,$$
so the proofs are analogous to those for BL-algebras.

Proposition 6. Let L be a $Ł\Pi G$ algebra and let $a \in L$, $a \neq 1$. Then there is a prime filter F on L not containing a.

Proof. There are filters not containing a, e.g. $F_0 = \{1\}$. We can show that the smallest filter containing F as a subset and z as an element is
$$F' = \{x \in L \mid \exists y \in F, \exists n \in N, y*z^n \leq x\}.$$

Indeed, if $F'' \supseteq F$ is a filter and $z \in F$ then for each $y \in F$ and $n \in N$, $y*z^n \in F''$; on the other hand, F' itself is a filter since it is obviously closed under $*$ and contains with each z all $z' \geq z$. any filter not containing a and $b,c \in L$ are such that $b \Rightarrow c \notin F$ and $c \Rightarrow b \notin F$, then there is the filter F'.

Thus assume $b,c \in L$, s.t. $b \Rightarrow c \notin F$ and $c \Rightarrow b \notin F$, let
$$F_1 = \{x \in L \mid \exists y \in F, \exists n \in N, y*(b \Rightarrow c)^n \leq x\},$$
$$F_2 = \{x \in L \mid \exists y \in F, \exists n \in N, y*(c \Rightarrow b)^n \leq x\}.$$

From above let F_1, F_2 be the smallest filters containing F as a subset and $b \Rightarrow c$, $c \Rightarrow b$ respectively as an element.

We claim that $a \notin F_1$ or $a \notin F_2$. Assume the contrary; then for some $y \in F$, and natural n, $y*(b \Rightarrow c) \leq a$ and $y*(c \Rightarrow b) \leq a$, thus $a \geq y*(b \Rightarrow c) \cup y*(c \Rightarrow b) = y*((b \Rightarrow c)^n \cup (c \Rightarrow c)^n) = y*1 = y$, thus $a \in F$, a contradiction. Thus, $a \notin F_1$ or $a \notin F_2$.

Now if L is countable, then we may arrange all pairs (b,c) from L^2 into a sequence $\{(b_n, c_n) \mid n \in N\}$, put $F_0 = \{1\}$ and having constructed F_n such that $a \notin F_n$ we take $F_{n+1} \supseteq F_n$ such that $a \notin F_{n+1}$ according to our construction; if possible we take F_{n+1} such that $(b_n \Rightarrow c_n) \in F_{n+1}$. Our desired prime filter is the union $\cup_n F_n$.

If L is uncountable, then one has to use the axiom of choice and work similarly with a transfinite sequence of filters.

Proposition 7. Each $Ł\Pi G$ algebra is a subalgebra of the direct product of a system of linearly ordered $Ł\Pi G$ algebra.

Proof. Let $A = \{F \mid F \text{ is a prime filter on } L\}$, then $A \neq \emptyset$. For $F \in A$ let $L_F = L/F$ and let $L^* = \prod_{F \in A} L_F$. L^* is the direct product of linearly ordered $Ł\Pi G$ algebra $\{L_F \mid F \in A\}$. We may prove that the mapping $i: L \rightarrow L^*, x \rightarrow ([x]_F)_{F \in A}$ is an embedding from L to L^*.

Clearly this embedding preserves operations; it remains to show that it is one-one. $\forall x, y \in L$ and $x \neq y$, without loss of generality, we assume $x \not\leq y$, then $(x \Rightarrow y) \neq 1$.

There exists a prime filter F on L such that $x \Rightarrow y \notin F$ by proposition 6, thus $[x]_F \not\leq [y]_F$ in L/F, hence $[x]_F \neq [y]_F$, i.e. $i(x) \neq i(y)$.

Proposition 8. [2] The logic $Ł\Pi G$ proves φ iff φ is a tautology in each of the standard MV, product and G algebras.

From remark 2, we can obtain the following theorem directly.

Theorem 3. The system $UL_{h\in(0,1]}$ proves φ iff φ is a tautology in each of the standard MV, product and G algebras.

Theorem 4. φ is a tautology in each of the $Ł\Pi G$ unit interval iff φ is a tautology in each of the standard MV, product and G algebras.

Proof. Because $([0,1], \min, \max, \wedge_{0.5}, \Rightarrow_{0.5}, 0, 1)$ is just standard MV-algebra, $([0,1], \min, \max, \wedge_{0.75}, \Rightarrow_{0.75}, 0, 1)$ is just standard product algebra, $([0,1], \min, \max, \wedge_1, \Rightarrow_1, 0, 1)$ is just standard G-algebra, then the necessity is obvious. Because for each $h \in (0, 0.75)$, $([0,1], \min, \max, \wedge_h, \Rightarrow_h, 0, 1)$ is MV-algebra, for each $h \in (0.75, 1)$, $([0,1], \min, \max, \wedge_h, \Rightarrow_h, 0, 1)$ is product algebra, for $h = 1$, $([0,1], \min, \max, \wedge_h, \Rightarrow_h, 0, 1)$ is G-algebra, then from the completeness of MV, product and G algebras, the sufficient condition also holds.

Theorem 5. (Completeness) The system $UL_{h\in(0,1]}$ is complete, i.e. If $\vDash \varphi$, then $\vdash \varphi$. In more detail, for each formula φ, the following are equivalent:

(1) φ is provable in $UL_{h\in(0,1]}$, i.e. $\vdash \varphi$,

(2) φ is an L-tautology for each $Ł\Pi G$-algebra L,

(3) φ is an L-tautology for each linearly ordered $Ł\Pi G$-algebra L,

(4) φ is a tautology for each $Ł\Pi G$ unit interval, i.e. $\vDash \varphi$.

Proof. The implications from (1) to (2) is soundness, (2) to (3) and (3) to (4) are trivial to verify. From the above two theorems we can get (4) $\Rightarrow$ (1) directly.

5 Some Extension Logics of $UL_{h\in(0,1]}$

According to the same method for $h \in (0,1]$, we can also build up the systems $UL_{h\in(0,1)}$, $UL_{h\in[0.75,1]}$ and $UL_{h\in(0,0.75)\cup 1}$ if we fix $h \in (0,1)$, $h \in [0.75, 1]$ and $h \in (0, 0.75) \cup 1$ respectively in $PC(h)$. We can get the following.

Definition 9. Axioms of the the system $UL_{h\in(0,1)}$ are those of $UL_{h\in(0,1]}$ plus

$$(Ł\Pi) \quad (\varphi \to (\varphi \& \psi)) \to ((\varphi \to \bar{0}) \vee \psi).$$

The deduction rule of $UL_{h\in(0,1)}$ is modus ponens.

Definition 10. Axioms of the the system $UL_{h\in[0.75,1]}$ are those of $UL_{h\in(0,1)}$ plus

$$(\Pi G)\ (\varphi \wedge (\varphi \to \bar{0})) \to \bar{0}.$$

The deduction rule of $UL_{h\in[0.75,1]}$ is modus ponens.

Definition 11. Axioms of the the system $UL_{h\in(0,0.75)\cup 1}$ are those of $UL_{h\in(0,1)}$ plus

$$(ŁG)\ (((\varphi \to \bar{0}) \to \bar{0}) \to \varphi) \vee (\varphi \to (\varphi \& \varphi)).$$

The deduction rule of $UL_{h\in(0,0.75)\cup 1}$ is modus ponens.

Theorem 6. (Soundness) (i) $UL_{h\in(0,1)}$ is soundness, i.e. each formula provable in $UL_{h\in(0,1)}$ is a 1-tautology of each $PC(h)$ ($h\in(0,1)$), i.e. if $\vdash \varphi$, then $\vDash \varphi$.

(ii) $UL_{h\in[0.75,1]}$ is soundness, i.e. each formula provable in $UL_{h\in[0.75,1]}$ is a 1-tautology of each $PC(h)$ ($h\in[0.75,1]$), i.e. if $\vdash \varphi$, then $\vDash \varphi$.

(iii) $UL_{h\in(0,0.75)\cup 1}$ is soundness, i.e. each formula provable in $UL_{h\in(0,0.75)\cup 1}$ is a 1-tautology of each $PC(h)$ ($h\in(0,0.75)\cup 1$), i.e. if $\vdash \varphi$, then $\vDash \varphi$.

Theorem 7. (Completeness) (i) The system $UL_{h\in(0,1)}$ is complete, i.e. If φ is a tautology for each $PC(h)$($h\in(0,1)$), then φ is provable in $UL_{h\in(0,1)}$, i.e. If $\vDash \varphi$, then $\vdash \varphi$.

(ii) The system $UL_{h\in[0.75,1]}$ is complete, i.e. If φ is a tautology for each $PC(h)$($h\in[0.75,1]$), then φ is provable in $UL_{h\in[0.75,1]}$, i.e. If $\vDash \varphi$, then $\vdash \varphi$.

(iii) The system $UL_{h\in(0,0.75)\cup 1}$ is complete, i.e. If φ is a tautology for each $PC(h)$($h\in(0,0.75)\cup 1$), then φ is provable in $UL_{h\in(0,0.75)\cup 1}$, i.e. If $\vDash \varphi$, then $\vdash \varphi$.

6 Conclusion

In this paper a propositional calculus formal deductive system $UL_{h\in(0,1)}$ of 0-level universal logic is built up. The soundness theorem and some other theorems of $UL_{h\in(0,1)}$ are proven. Moreover, we prove the system $UL_{h\in(0,1)}$ is complete with respect to the 0-level continuous universal AND operators on [0,1]. Three extension logics of $UL_{h\in(0,1)}$ are also introduced.

References

1. Z.C.Chen, H.C.He, M.Y.Mao. Correlation Reasoning of Complex System Based on Universal Logic. IEEE Proceedings of 2003 ICMLC, Xi'an, pp. 1831-1835, 2003
2. R.Cignoli, F.Esteva, L.Godo, A.Torrens, Basic fuzzy logic is the logic of continuous t-norms and their residua, Soft computing, Vol.4, pp.106-112, 2000
3. F.Esteva, L.Godo, Monoidal t-normbased logic:towards a logic for left-continous t- norms. Fuzzy Sets and Systems, Vol.124, 2001,pp.271--288
4. P. Hajek, Metamathematics of Fuzzy Logic, Kluwer Academic Publishers, Dordrecht/ London, 1998

5. P. Hajek, Basic fuzzy logic and BL-algebras, Soft computing, Vol.2, pp.124-128, 1998
6. Huacan He et al, Universal Logic Principle, Science Press (in Chinese), Beijing, 2001
7. Huacan He, Yonghuai Liu, Daqing He, Generalized Logic in Experience Thinking. Sciences in China (Series E) ,Vol.26 , pp.72–78,1996
8. Huacan He, Lirong Ai, H. Wang, Uncertainties and the flexible logics. Proceedings of 2003 ICMLC Vol.26, 2003, pp.72--78
9. U.Hohle, Commutative, residuated l-monoids, in: Non-Classical Logics and Their Applications to Fuzzy Subsets, U.Hohle and E. P. Klement (eds.), Kluwer Academic Publishers, Dordrecht/London, pp.53--106, 1995
10. R.Horčík, P.Cintula, Product Lukasiewicz Logic, Mathematical Logic, Vol.43, pp. 477--503, 2004
11. E.P.Klement, et al, Triangular Norms. Kluwer Academic Publishers, Dordrecht/London, 2000
12. Y.C.Ma, H.C.He. Triple-I algorithm on a kind of residuated lattice. Computer Science, Vol.31, 2004, pp: 127--129
13. Y.C.Ma, H.C.He. The BP Algorithm of Fuzzy Reasoning Based on UL. Research Progress in Fuzzy Logic and Computational Intelligence ---Proceedings of 2005 National Joint Conference on Fuzzy Logic and Computational Intelligence, Shenzhen, pp. 281-284, April 2005
14. D.W.Pei, G.J.Wang, The completeness and applications of the formal system L*. Science in China (Series F) Vol.45, pp.40--50, 2002
15. G.J.Wang, Non-classical Mathematical Logic and Approximate Reasoning, Science Press(in Chinese), Beijing, 2000
16. G.J.Wang, On the Logic Foundation of Fuzzy Reasoning. Information Sciences, Vol.117, pp.47–88, 1999
17. G.J.Wang, The full implication triple I method for fuzzy reasoning. Sciences in China (Series E), Vol.29, pp.43--53, 1999
18. S.M.Wang, B.S.Wang, D.W. Pei, A fuzzy logic for an ordinal sum t-norm, Fuzzy Sets and Systems, Vol.149, pp.297-307, 2005

Fuzzy Portfolio Selection Problems Based on Credibility Theory

Yanju Chen, Yan-Kui Liu, and Junfen Chen

College of Mathematics and Computer Science, Hebei University
Baoding 071002, Hebei, China
{yanjuchen, yliu}@mail.hbu.edu.cn

Abstract. We first deduce the variance formulas of normal, triangular and trapezoidal fuzzy variables in credibility theory. Then two classes of fuzzy portfolio selection models are built based on credibility measure, the expected value and variance of a fuzzy variable. To solve the proposed models, a genetic algorithm is employed. Finally, two numerical examples are provided for the proposed portfolio selection models to test the designed algorithm.

1 Introduction

Markowitz [12][13] applied probability theory to the portfolio selection problem and proposed the famous mean-variance model. He considered return rates of individual bonds as random variables. In the mean-variance model, the expected value and variance of the return rate were taken as the investment return and risk, respectively. Since then, a large number of portfolio selection models have been proposed [1][7][14][17]. In all these models, the return rates of bonds have been treated as random variables and the portfolio selection problem has been formulated as a stochastic programming problem for a long time. On the other hand, based on possibility theory [4][18], a lot of researchers such as Carlsson, Fullér and Majlender [2], Inuiguchi and Tanino [6], Tanaka, Guo and Türksen [16] and León, Liern and Vercher [8] have devoted their efforts to the fuzzy portfolio selection problem. It is known that an investor will decide the investment proportion to each investment type according to the return rate of each investment type. But the investor cannot know the exact return rate in the decision-making stage. In order to estimate the return rate, the investor will take experts' knowledge into account. To that end, a fuzzy variable is an appropriate tool. So it is reasonable to treat the return rate of the investment type as a fuzzy variable. As a consequence, the portfolio selection problem is formulated as a fuzzy programming problem. Since experts' knowledge is very valuable in a decision-making process, fuzzy portfolio selection models are useful in real investment problems. Traditionally, possibility measure is regarded as the counterpart of probability measure and is widely used in literature. However, it is the credibility measure [10] that plays the role of probability measure in fuzzy decision systems. Consequently, a new theory, called credibility theory, has been developed by the motivation of the facts in [11]. Credibility measure is nonadditive and is employed to measure the degree to which a fuzzy event holds. Based on credibility measure, Liu and Liu [10] also defined the expected value and variance of a fuzzy variable. This paper will give the variance formulas of three common fuzzy variables, and employ credibility theory to study portfolio selection problems. In our portfolio selection models, we treat the return rate as a fuzzy variable, and use the expected value and variance [10] of a fuzzy variable to characterize the return and risk of the investment.

The rest of the paper is organized as follows. Section 2 introduces the calculating formulas of the variances of three common fuzzy variables in credibility theory. In Section 3, we will give the portfolio selection models based on credibility measure, the expected value and variance of a fuzzy variable. A genetic algorithm to solve the portfolio selection problem is described in Section 4, and two numerical examples are also provided in this section. Finally, a brief summary is given in Section 5.

2 Several Useful Variance Formulas

Let ξ be a fuzzy variable with possibility distribution $\mu : R \to [0, 1]$. A fuzzy variable is said to be normal if there exists a real number r such that $\mu(r) = 1$. In this paper, we always assume that the fuzzy variables are normal.

Let r be a real number. It is well known that the possibility of the event $\{\xi \geq r\}$ is defined by

$$\mathrm{Pos}\{\xi \geq r\} = \sup_{u \geq r} \mu(u), \qquad (1)$$

and the necessity of the event $\{\xi \geq r\}$ is defined by

$$\mathrm{Nec}\{\xi \geq r\} = 1 - \mathrm{Pos}\{\xi < r\}. \qquad (2)$$

Definition 1 ([10]). *Let ξ be a fuzzy variable. For any $r \in \Re$, the credibility of the fuzzy event $\{\xi \geq r\}$ is defined as*

$$\mathrm{Cr}\{\xi \geq r\} = \frac{1}{2}(1 + \mathrm{Pos}\{\xi \geq r\} - \mathrm{Pos}\{\xi < r\}). \qquad (3)$$

Definition 2 ([10]). *Let ξ be a fuzzy variable. The expected value of ξ is defined as*

$$E[\xi] = \int_0^\infty \mathrm{Cr}\{\xi \geq r\}dr - \int_{-\infty}^0 \mathrm{Cr}\{\xi \leq r\}dr. \qquad (4)$$

If $\xi = n(m, \sigma)$ denotes a normal fuzzy variable with possibility distribution

$$\mu(r) = \exp\left(\frac{-(r-m)^2}{2\sigma^2}\right), \qquad (5)$$

then the expected value of ξ is $E[\xi] = m$.

If $\xi = (r_0, \alpha, \beta)$ is a triangular fuzzy variable with center r_0, left-width $\alpha > 0$ and right-width $\beta > 0$, and possibility distribution

$$\mu(r) = \begin{cases} \frac{r-r_0+\alpha}{\alpha}, & \text{if } r_0 - \alpha \leq r \leq r_0 \\ \frac{r_0+\beta-r}{\beta}, & \text{if } r_0 \leq r \leq r_0 + \beta \\ 0, & \text{otherwise,} \end{cases} \qquad (6)$$

then the expected value of ξ is $E[\xi] = \frac{1}{4}(4r_0 - \alpha + \beta)$.

If $\xi = (r_1, r_2, \alpha, \beta)$ is a trapezoidal fuzzy variable with left-width $\alpha > 0$ and right-width $\beta > 0$, and possibility distribution

$$\mu(r) = \begin{cases} \frac{r-r_1+\alpha}{\alpha}, & \text{if } r_1 - \alpha \leq r \leq r_1 \\ 1, & \text{if } r_1 \leq r \leq r_2 \\ \frac{r_2+\beta-r}{\beta}, & \text{if } r_2 \leq r \leq r_2 + \beta \\ 0, & \text{otherwise,} \end{cases} \qquad (7)$$

then $E[\xi] = \frac{1}{4}(2r_1 + 2r_2 - \alpha + \beta)$.

Definition 3 ([10]). *Let ξ be a normalized fuzzy variable with finite expected value. The variance of ξ is defined as*

$$V[\xi] = E[(\xi - E[\xi])^2]. \qquad (8)$$

For the variances of normal, triangular and trapezoidal fuzzy variables, we have the following results:

Proposition 1. *If $\xi = n(m, \sigma)$ is a normal fuzzy variable with possibility distribution $\mu(r) = \exp(\frac{-(r-m)^2}{2\sigma^2})$, then $V[\xi] = \sigma^2$.*

Proof. We have $E[\xi] = m$ based on Definition 2. In addition, for any $r \geq 0$, since

$$\text{Pos}\{(\xi - m)^2 = r\} = \text{Pos}(\{\xi - m = \sqrt{r}\} \cup \{\xi - m = -\sqrt{r}\})$$
$$= \text{Pos}\{\xi - m = \sqrt{r}\} \vee \text{Pos}\{\xi - m = -\sqrt{r}\}, \qquad (9)$$

we have

$$\text{Pos}\{(\xi - m)^2 \geq r\} = \exp\left(\frac{-r}{2\sigma^2}\right)$$

and

$$\text{Cr}\{(\xi - m)^2 \geq r\} = \frac{1}{2}\exp\left(\frac{-r}{2\sigma^2}\right).$$

As a consequence,

$$V[\xi] = E[(\xi - m)^2] = \int_0^\infty \text{Cr}\{(\xi - m)^2 \geq r\}dr = \sigma^2.$$

The proof is complete. □

Proposition 2. If $\xi = (r_0, \alpha, \beta)$ is a triangular fuzzy variable, then

$$V[\xi] = \begin{cases} \frac{33\alpha^3 + 11\alpha\beta^2 + 21\alpha^2\beta - \beta^3}{384\alpha}, & \alpha > \beta \\ \frac{\alpha^2}{6}, & \alpha = \beta \\ \frac{33\beta^3 + 11\alpha^2\beta + 21\alpha\beta^2 - \alpha^3}{384\beta}, & \alpha < \beta. \end{cases} \quad (10)$$

Proof. Let $m = E[\xi]$. In the case of $\alpha = \beta$, by (9) we have

$$\text{Pos}\{(\xi - m)^2 \geq r\} = \begin{cases} \frac{\beta - \sqrt{r}}{\beta}, & 0 \leq r \leq \beta^2 \\ 0, & \beta^2 \leq r, \end{cases}$$

$$\text{Cr}\{(\xi - m)^2 \geq r\} = \begin{cases} \frac{\beta - \sqrt{r}}{2\beta}, & 0 \leq r \leq \beta^2 \\ 0, & \beta^2 \leq r, \end{cases}$$

$$V[\xi] = E[(\xi - m)^2] = \int_0^\infty \text{Cr}\{(\xi - m)^2 \geq r\} dr = \frac{\alpha^2}{6}.$$

In the case of $\alpha > \beta$, we have

$$\text{Pos}\{(\xi - m)^2 \geq r\} = \begin{cases} 1, & 0 \leq r \leq (r_0 - m)^2 \\ \frac{r_0 + \beta - m - \sqrt{r}}{\beta}, & (r_0 - m)^2 \leq r \leq r_s \\ \frac{-\sqrt{r} - (r_0 - \alpha - m)}{\alpha}, & r_s \leq r \leq (r_0 - \alpha - m)^2 \\ 0, & (r_0 - \alpha - m)^2 \leq r, \end{cases}$$

$$\text{Cr}\{(\xi - m)^2 \geq r\} = \begin{cases} 1 - \frac{\sqrt{r} - (r_0 - \alpha - m)}{2\alpha}, & 0 \leq r \leq (r_0 - m)^2 \\ \frac{r_0 + \beta - m - \sqrt{r}}{2\beta}, & (r_0 - m)^2 \leq r \leq r_s \\ \frac{-\sqrt{r} - (r_0 - \alpha - m)}{2\alpha}, & r_s \leq r \leq (r_0 - \alpha - m)^2 \\ 0, & (r_0 - \alpha - m)^2 \leq r, \end{cases}$$

where $r_s = \frac{(\alpha + \beta)^2}{16}$. As a consequence,

$$V[\xi] = E[(\xi - m)^2] = \int_0^\infty \text{Cr}\{(\xi - m)^2 \geq r\} dr = \frac{33\alpha^3 + 11\alpha\beta^2 + 21\alpha^2\beta - \beta^3}{384\alpha}.$$

In the case of $\alpha < \beta$, we have

$$\text{Pos}\{(\xi - m)^2 \geq r\} = \begin{cases} 1, & 0 \leq r \leq (r_0 - m)^2 \\ \frac{-\sqrt{r} - (r_0 - \alpha - m)}{\alpha}, & (r_0 - m)^2 \leq r \leq r_s \\ \frac{r_0 + \beta - m - \sqrt{r}}{\beta}, & r_s \leq r \leq (r_0 + \beta - m)^2 \\ 0, & (r_0 + \beta - m)^2 \leq r, \end{cases}$$

$$\text{Cr}\{(\xi - m)^2 \geq r\} = \begin{cases} 1 - \frac{r_0 + \beta - m + \sqrt{r}}{2\beta}, & 0 \leq r \leq (r_0 - m)^2 \\ \frac{-\sqrt{r} - (r_0 - \alpha - m)}{2\alpha}, & (r_0 - m)^2 \leq r \leq r_s \\ \frac{r_0 + \beta - m - \sqrt{r}}{2\beta}, & r_s \leq r \leq (r_0 + \beta - m)^2 \\ 0, & (r_0 + \beta - m)^2 \leq r. \end{cases}$$

Therefore, we have

$$V[\xi] = E[(\xi - m)^2] = \int_0^\infty \mathrm{Cr}\{(\xi - m)^2 \geq r\}dr = \frac{33\beta^3 + 11\alpha^2\beta + 21\alpha\beta^2 - \alpha^3}{384\beta}.$$

The proof is complete. □

Proposition 3. *Let $\xi = (r_1, r_2, \alpha, \beta)$ be a trapezoidal fuzzy variable with expected value m. Then*
(1) If $\alpha = \beta$, then

$$V[\xi] = \frac{3(r_2 - r_1 + \beta)^2 + \beta^2}{24}. \qquad (11)$$

(2) If $\alpha > \beta$, then

$$V[\xi] = \begin{cases} \frac{1}{6}[-\frac{(r_2-m)^3}{\beta} - \frac{(r_1-\alpha-m)^3}{\alpha} \\ \quad + \frac{(\alpha r_2 + \beta r_1 - m(\alpha+\beta))^3}{\alpha\beta(\alpha-\beta)^2}], & \text{if } r_1 - m < 0 \\ \frac{1}{6}[\frac{(r_1-m)^3}{\alpha} - \frac{(r_2-m)^3}{\beta} - \frac{(r_1-\alpha-m)^3}{\alpha} \\ \quad + \frac{(\alpha r_2 + \beta r_1 - m(\alpha+\beta))^3}{\alpha\beta(\alpha-\beta)^2}], & \text{if } r_1 - m \geq 0. \end{cases} \qquad (12)$$

(3) If $\alpha < \beta$, then

$$V[\xi] = \begin{cases} \frac{1}{6}[\frac{(r_1-m)^3}{\alpha} + \frac{(r_2+\beta-m)^3}{\beta} \\ \quad - \frac{(\alpha r_2 + \beta r_1 - m(\alpha+\beta))^3}{\alpha\beta(\alpha-\beta)^2}], & \text{if } r_2 - m > 0 \\ \frac{1}{6}[\frac{(r_1-m)^3}{\alpha} + \frac{(r_2+\beta-m)^3}{\beta} - \frac{(r_2-m)^3}{\beta} \\ \quad - \frac{(\alpha r_2 + \beta r_1 - m(\alpha+\beta))^3}{\alpha\beta(\alpha-\beta)^2}], & \text{if } r_2 - m \leq 0. \end{cases} \qquad (13)$$

Proof. We only prove the assertions (1) and (2). The third can be proved similarly.
(1) If $\alpha = \beta$, then we have

$$\mathrm{Cr}\{(\xi - m)^2 \geq r\} = \begin{cases} \frac{1}{2}, & 0 \leq r \leq (r_2 - m)^2 \\ \frac{r_2 + \beta - m - \sqrt{r}}{2\beta}, & (r_2 - m)^2 \leq r \leq (r_2 + \beta - m)^2 \\ 0, & (r_2 + \beta - m)^2 \leq r. \end{cases}$$

So

$$V[\xi] = E[(\xi - m)^2] = \int_0^\infty \mathrm{Cr}\{(\xi - m)^2 \geq r\}dr = \frac{3(r_2 - r_1 + \beta)^2 + \beta^2}{24}.$$

(2) Let $\alpha > \beta$. If $r_1 - m < 0$, then we have

$$\mathrm{Cr}\{(\xi - m)^2 \geq r\} = \begin{cases} \frac{1}{2}, & 0 \leq r \leq (r_2 - m)^2 \\ \frac{r_2 + \beta - m - \sqrt{r}}{2\beta}, & (r_2 - m)^2 \leq r \leq r_s \\ \frac{-\sqrt{r}-(r_1-\alpha-m)}{2\alpha}, & r_s \leq r \leq (r_1 - \alpha - m)^2 \\ 0, & (r_1 - \alpha - m)^2 \leq r, \end{cases}$$

where $r_s = (\frac{\alpha r_2 + \beta r_1 - m\alpha - m\beta}{\alpha - \beta})^2$. As a consequence,

$$V[\xi] = E[(\xi - m)^2] = \int_0^\infty \mathrm{Cr}\{(\xi - m)^2 \geq r\} dr$$

$$= \frac{1}{6}[-\frac{(r_2 - m)^3}{\beta} - \frac{(r_1 - \alpha - m)^3}{\alpha} + \frac{(\alpha r_2 + \beta r_1 - m(\alpha + \beta))^3}{\alpha\beta(\alpha - \beta)^2}].$$

If $r_1 - m \geq 0$, then we have

$$\mathrm{Cr}\{(\xi - m)^2 \geq r\} = \begin{cases} 1 - \frac{\sqrt{r} - (r_1 - \alpha - m)}{2\alpha}, & 0 \leq r \leq (r_1 - m)^2 \\ \frac{1}{2}, & (r_1 - m)^2 \leq r \leq (r_2 - m)^2 \\ \frac{r_2 + \beta - m - \sqrt{r}}{2\beta}, & (r_2 - m)^2 \leq r \leq r_s \\ \frac{-\sqrt{r} - (r_1 - \alpha - m)}{2\alpha}, & r_s \leq r \leq (r_1 - \alpha - m)^2 \\ 0, & (r_1 - \alpha - m)^2 \leq r. \end{cases}$$

Therefore, we have

$$V[\xi] = E[(\xi - m)^2] = \int_0^\infty \mathrm{Cr}\{(\xi - m)^2 \geq r\} dr$$

$$= \frac{1}{6}[\frac{(r_1 - m)^3}{\alpha} - \frac{(r_2 - m)^3}{\beta} - \frac{(r_1 - \alpha - m)^3}{\alpha} + \frac{(\alpha r_2 + \beta r_1 - m(\alpha + \beta))^3}{\alpha\beta(\alpha - \beta)^2}].$$

The proof is complete. □

In the following sections, these formulas will be used to solve portfolio selection problems.

3 Formulation of Portfolio Selection Problem

In a fuzzy decision system, fuzzy portfolio selection problem can be described as follows. Assume that an investor wants to allocate his wealth of one unit among n investment types. Each investment type is characterized by a fuzzy return and thus its risk is measured by the variance of the fuzzy return. The objective of the investor is to find the proportions of his wealth to be invested in each investment type in order to get a desired portfolio selection.

In this section, we will give two types of portfolio selection problem in fuzzy decision systems under two different optimization decision criteria.

First, following the idea of the mean-variance model, we use the expected value of the return rate to quantify the investment return, and the variance of the return rate to characterize the investment risk. If the return rate is treated as a normal (triangular or trapezoidal) fuzzy variable, then we can obtain the expected value and variance of the return rate by using the formulas given in Section 2.

If an investor wants to maximize the return and minimize the risk simultaneously, then the portfolio selection problem may be formulated as the following bi-objective programming problem:

$$\begin{cases} \max & E[\sum_{i=1}^{n} \xi_i x_i] \\ \min & V[\sum_{i=1}^{n} \xi_i x_i] \\ \text{s.t.} & \sum_{i=1}^{n} x_i = 1, \\ & x_i \geq 0, i = 1, 2, \cdots, n \end{cases} \quad (14)$$

where ξ_i is the return rate of the i-th investment type and assumed to be a fuzzy variable, and x_i is the decision variable which shows the investment proportion to the i-th investment type.

Although this model reflects all investors' investment expectations, it describes only an ideal result which can not be realized in a real investment environment. That is to say we can not find a decision which is suitable for the investor to minimize the risk and maximize the return simultaneously. Furthermore, instead of a single optimal solution, we usually obtain the Pareto-optimal solutions [3] of the above model. For this case, the investor can use many different multiobjective optimization methods such as the weighting method, the constraint method and goal programming [15]. In this section, we adopt the weighting method to turn the above model into the following single objective model:

$$\begin{cases} \max & \omega E[\sum_{i=1}^{n} \xi_i x_i] - (1-\omega) V[\sum_{i=1}^{n} \xi_i x_i] \\ \text{s.t.} & \sum_{i=1}^{n} x_i = 1, \\ & x_i \geq 0, i = 1, 2, \cdots, n \end{cases} \quad (15)$$

where the weighting coefficient $\omega \in [0,1]$ denotes the degree that the investor is willing to burden risk. The greater ω is, the higher degree the investor is willing to burden risk. When $\omega = 1$, the investor will ignore the risk, when $\omega = 0$, the investor will be extremely conservative.

Second, suppose that an investor has invested his money in some investment types. If the return on other investment types is higher than the investor's chosen types, the investor may regret his choices. Since we cannot know the return rate in the decision-making stage, any investment decision may bring regret to the investor. If the investor is interested in minimizing the pessimistic value to the regret, then the portfolio selection problem can be built as the following chance-constrained programming [9]:

$$\begin{cases} \min & \bar{r} \\ \text{s.t.} & \text{Cr}\{r(\sum_{i=1}^{n} \xi_i x_i) \leq \bar{r}\} \geq \alpha, \\ & \sum_{i=1}^{n} x_i = 1, \\ & x_i \geq 0, i = 1, 2, \cdots, n \end{cases} \quad (16)$$

where $r(\sum_{i=1}^{n} \xi_i x_i)$ is the regret which can be quantified by many different ways (see [6]), $\alpha \in (0,1]$ is a prescribed confidence level, and $\bar{r}$ is the α-pessimistic value to the regret $r(\sum_{i=1}^{n} \xi_i x_i)$.

4 Genetic Algorithm and Numerical Examples

In this section, we will use genetic algorithm to solve fuzzy portfolio selection problems. Genetic algorithm is a type of stochastic search method based on the mechanics of natural selection and natural genetics. Genetic algorithm has demonstrated considerable success in providing good solutions to many complex optimization problems. For detailed discussion about the genetic algorithm, the interested readers may refer to [5]. The genetic algorithm procedure is described as follows:

Step 1. Initialize pop-size chromosomes at random.
Step 2. Update the chromosomes by crossover and mutation operations.
Step 3. Calculate the objective values for all chromosomes.
Step 4. Compute the fitness of each chromosome according to the objective values.
Step 5. Select the chromosomes by spinning the roulette wheel.
Step 6. Repeat the second to fifth steps for a given number of cycles.
Step 7. Report the best chromosome as the optimal solution.

We now solve two numerical examples by genetic algorithm described above with the following parameters: the population size is 30, the probability of crossover is 0.3, and the probability of mutation is 0.2.

Example 1. Consider the following fuzzy portfolio selection model:

$$\begin{cases} \max & \omega E[\sum_{i=1}^{5} \xi_i x_i] - (1-\omega)V[\sum_{i=1}^{5} \xi_i x_i] \\ \text{s.t.} & \sum_{i=1}^{5} x_i = 1, \\ & x_i \geq 0, i = 1, 2, \cdots, 5, \end{cases} \qquad (17)$$

where $\xi_1 = n(0.26, 0.1170)$, $\xi_2 = n(0.23, 0.0977)$, $\xi_3 = n(0.21, 0.0977)$, $\xi_4 = n(0.16, 0.0818)$ and $\xi_5 = n(0.06, 0.06)$ are normal fuzzy variables.

Since $\xi_i, i = 1, \cdots, 5$ are normal fuzzy variables, $\sum_{i=1}^{5} \xi_i x_i$ is also a normal fuzzy variable, and we can calculate $E[\sum_{i=1}^{5} \xi_i x_i]$ and $V[\sum_{i=1}^{5} \xi_i x_i]$ by the formulas given in Section 2. For different values of ω, 500 generations of genetic algorithm provides the following results:

Table 1.

ω	$(x_1, x_2, x_3, x_4, x_5)$	E	V
0	(0,0,0,0,1)	0.06	0.0036
0.2	(0.9186,0.0813,0,0,0)	0.2576	0.0133
0.5	(0.9763,0.0233,0.0004,0,0)	0.2593	0.0136
0.8	(0.9994,0.0005,0.0001,0.0001,0)	0.26	0.0137
1	(0.9630,0.0369,0.0001,0,0)	0.2589	0.0135

From the distribution of $\xi_i (i = 1, \cdots, 5)$, we know that $V[\xi_i] > V[\xi_j]$ ($i < j$) and $E[\xi_i] > E[\xi_j]$ ($i < j$). Since $\omega = 0$ implies that the investor is very conservative, the solution suggests an investment in the fifth type of investment whose risk is the least and so is more suitable for the conservative investor. When the investor is willing to take more risk ($\omega > 0$), the solutions suggest the investments in the first type whose expected return is the largest.

Example 2. Consider the following fuzzy portfolio selection model:

$$\begin{cases} \min \bar{r} \\ \text{s.t.} \quad \text{Cr}\{r(\sum_{i=1}^{5} \xi_i x_i) \leq \bar{r}\} \geq \alpha, \\ \sum_{i=1}^{5} x_i = 1, \\ x_i \geq 0, i = 1, 2, \cdots, 5, \end{cases} \quad (18)$$

where $\xi_i, i = 1, \cdots, 5$ are the same fuzzy variables as in Example 1.

Let $r(\sum_{i=1}^{5} \xi_i x_i) = \max_i\{\xi_i - \sum_{i=1}^{5} \xi_i x_i, \ i = 1, 2, \cdots, 5\}$. Note that minimizing $\bar{r}$ is equivalent to minimizing $\xi_i - \sum_{i=1}^{5} \xi_i x_i, i = 1, 2, \cdots, 5$, simultaneously; no matter which investment types have the best return, we have the least regret if $\bar{r}$ is minimized. For $\alpha = 0.9$ and $\alpha = 0.95$, we run the genetic algorithm 500 generations, and get the results reported in Table 2.

Table 2.

α	$(x_1, x_2, x_3, x_4, x_5)$	$\bar{r}$
0.9	(0.4136,0.3065,0.2495,0.0304,0)	0.2513
0.95	(0.3898,0.2970,0.2556,0.0576,0)	0.3066

From the results we can see that two distributive investment solutions to the portfolio selection model (18) are obtained.

5 Concluding Remarks

The major results can be summarized as the following three aspects:

(i) The variance formulas of normal, triangular and trapezoidal fuzzy variables were given.
(ii) Two kinds of fuzzy portfolio selection models were proposed based on credibility theory.
(iii) Two numerical examples were provided, and the second example illustrated that the model based on "the minimize regret criterion" can derive distributive investment solutions.

Acknowledgments

This work was supported by the National Natural Science Foundation of China Grant 70571021, and the Natural Science Foundation of Hebei Province Grant A2005000087.

References

1. Arenas Parra, M., Bilbao Terol, A., Rodríguez Uría, M. V.: A Fuzzy Goal Programming Approach to Portfolio Selection. European Journal of Operational Research **133** (2001) 287–297
2. Carlsson, C., Fullér, R., Majlender, P.: A Possibilistic Approach to Selecting Portfolios with Highest Utility Score. Fuzzy Sets Syst. **131** (2002) 13–21

3. Cohon, J. L.: Multiobjective Programming and Planning. Academic Press, New York (1978)
4. Dubois, D., Prade, H.: Possibility Theory. Plenum Press, New York (1988)
5. Gen, M., Cheng, R.: Genetic Algorithms and Engineering Design. Wiley, New York (1997)
6. Inuiguchi, M., Tanino, T.: Portfolio Selection under Independent Possibilistic Information. Fuzzy Sets Syst. **115** (2000) 83–92
7. Konno, H., Yamazaki, H.: Mean-Absolute Deviation Portfolio Optimization Model and Its Application to TOKYO Stock Market. Management Science **37** (1991) 519–531
8. León, T., Liern, V., Vercher, E.: Viability of Infeasible Portfolio Selection Problems: a Fuzzy Approach. European Journal of Operational Research **139** (2002) 178–189
9. Liu, B., Iwamura, K.: Chance-Constrained Programming with Fuzzy Parameters. Fuzzy Sets Syst. **94** (1998) 227–237
10. Liu, B., Liu, Y.-K.: Expected Value of Fuzzy Variable and Fuzzy Expected Value Models. IEEE Trans. Fuzzy Syst. **10** (2002) 445-450
11. Liu, B.: Uncertain Theory: An Introduction to its Axiomatic Foundations. Springer-Verlag, Berlin (2004)
12. Markowitz, H. M.: Portfolio Selection. Journal of Finance **7** (1952) 77–91
13. Markowitz, H. M.: Portfolio Selection: Efficient Diversification of Investments. Wiley, New York (1959)
14. Sharp, W. F.: A Simplified Model for Portfolio Analysis. Management Science **9** (1963) 277–293
15. Steuer, R. E.: Multiple Criteria Optimization: Theory, Computation, and Application. Wiley, New York (1986)
16. Tanaka, H., Guo, P., Burhan Türksen, I.: Portfolio Selection Based on Fuzzy Probabilities and Possibility Distributions. Fuzzy Sets Syst. **111** (2000) 387–397
17. Xia, Y., Liu, B., Wang, S., Lai, K. K.: A Model for Portfolio Selection with Order of Expected Return. Computers & Operations Research **27** (2000) 409–422
18. Zadeh, L. A. Fuzzy Sets as a Basis for a Theory of Possibility. Fuzzy Sets Syst. **1** (1978) 3–28

Fuzzy Multiple Reference Models Adaptive Control Scheme Study

Zhicheng Ji, Rongjia Zhu, and Yanxia Shen

Institute of Electrical Automatic,
Control Science and Engineering Research Center,
Southern Yangtze University, Jiangsu, Wuxi, 214036, China
zcji@sytu.edu.cn, wxzzrrjj@163.com

Abstract. A new method of fuzzy multiple reference models adaptive control (FMRMAC) for dealing with significant and unpredictable system parameter variations is presented. In this method, a suitable reference model is chosen by parameters estimation and fuzzy rules when changes occurred to the original model parameters. A successful application to the speed servo system of a dynamic model of a Brushless DC motor (BLDCM) shows this method works well with high dynamic performance under the condition of command speed change and load torque disturbance, so the applicability and validity of FMRMAC in pa-rameters variation system accommodation control was proven.

1 Introduction

Most industrial systems are non-linear with strong coupling and multiple states. Under the disturbance of noise, imprecise modeling and time-varying target, the systems usually have some uncertainties. Usually the adaptive control theory is a very useful way for handing these cases and the reference model adaptive control method (MRAC) is especially effective when the objective is to track the output with a command or trajectory. Much research using this approach has been performed, and provides better results than the conventional PI controller [13]. However, when there is a sudden change in the system parameters, due to the target changing or inter-nal/external disturbance, such dynamic controllers fail to perform the given performance criteria and will even make the system unstable [4]. Therefore, Narendra [5] introduced the concept of multiple reference models, but how to choose a suitable model is the focus of our studies.

In 1965, the fuzzy theory was proposed by Zadeh. Due to its simplicity in dealing with complex processes, it has been used as a highly effective way to optimize the settlement of complicated problems in many fields [6]. Fuzzy logic rules are the algorithms for synthesizing the linguistic control protocol of the experience of the skilled human operator. In the past, more attention had been paid to the application of the fuzzy theory to optimize the controller than to fuzzy classification and fuzzy selection. In fact, fuzzy logic rules have a strong ability to sort through different situations of a system and to choose the most appropriate control strategy [7].

In this paper, we propose a new method which combines the fuzzy selection with multiple reference models adaptive control and we have named it fuzzy multiple reference models adaptive control method (FMRMAC). In this method, a novel multiple input indirect adaptive algorithm is given, the fuzzy rules are designed to classify the system situation and choose properly the model which is to be the reference model. A mathematical model of BLDCM is used for testing the FMRMAC system with MATLAB. The simulation results show this method has a strong ability to adapt the conversion between high speed and low speed, or load torque alteration.

The paper is organized as follows. In Section 2, the structure of the control system is proposed. Section 3 is devoted to the description of the FMRMAC approach. A simulation example is given in Section 4. Finally, some concluding remarks are drawn in Section 5.

2 Structure of the Control System

The fuzzy multiple reference models adaptive control system is shown in Figure 1, including its five parts: indirect adaptive algorithm, controller, plant, multiple reference models, and fuzzy selection mechanism. The solid line shows the adaptive control layer, and the dotted line shows the intelligent adjustment layer. The plant auxiliary parameters and system input signal are utilized as the inputs of the fuzzy system, and with the choosing of a reference model by fuzzy logic rules, the output of the plant is made to track the reference model.

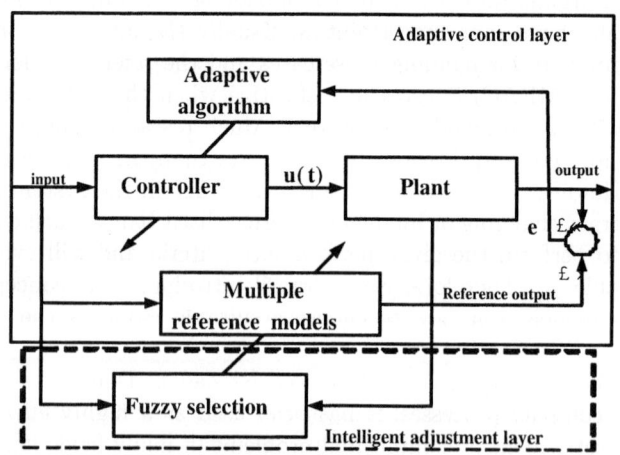

Fig. 1. Fuzzy multiple reference models adaptive control system

3 The FMRMAC Approach

3.1 Indirect Model Reference Adaptive Control

Consider a system described by a non-linear input-output model of the form:

$$A(q^{-1})y(n) = q^{-d_1}B(q^{-1})u(n) + q^{-d_2}C(q^{-1})v(n) + L(q^{-1})\Xi(n) \quad (1)$$

where:
$$A(q^{-1}) = 1 + a_1 q^{-1} + \cdots + a_{na} q^{-na},$$
$$B(q^{-1}) = b_0 + b_1 q^{-1} + \cdots + b_{nb} q^{-nb}, b_0 \neq 0$$
$$C(q^{-1}) = c_0 + c_1 q^{-1} + \cdots + c_{nc} q^{-nc}, c_0 \neq 0$$
$$L(q^{-1}) = 1 + l_1 q^{-1} + \cdots + l_{nl} q^{-nl}$$

q^{-1} is the backward shift operator, and we have $q^{-m}x(n) = x(n-m)$, $y(n)$ is the measurable output, $u(n)$ and $v(n)$ are control inputs, $\Xi(n)$ is assumed as the white noise with zero mean and its variance is σ^2. $d_1 \geq 1$ and $d_2 \geq 1$ are integers representing the plant time delay.

Choose the reference model of the form:

$$D(q^{-1})y_m(n) = q^{-d_1}E(q^{-1})u_m(n) + q^{-d_2}F(q^{-1})v_m(n)$$

Where $D(\cdot) E(\cdot) F(\cdot)$ are the matrix polynomials of backward shift operator q^{-1}. In case of $\Xi \equiv 0$, defining $\eta(n) = y(n) - y_m(n)$, the control objectives are achieved if the following equation holds:

$$D_1(q^{-1})\eta(n+1) = 0 \quad (2)$$

Using the well-known Bezout identity:

$$D_1(q^{-1}) = A(q^{-1})D(q^{-1}) + q^{-1}R(q^{-1}) \quad (3)$$

where:
$$S(q^{-1}) = 1 + s_1 q^{-1} + \cdots + s_{ns} q^{-ns}$$
$$R(q^{-1}) = r_0 + r_1 q^{-1} + \cdots + r_{nr} q^{-nr}$$

Introducing (3) into (2), it can be formulated that:

$$D_1(q^{-1})\eta(n+1) = q^{-d_1+1}B(q^{-1})S(q^{-1})u(n) + q^{-d_2+1}C(q^{-1})S(q^{-1})v(n)$$
$$+ R(q^{-1})y(n) - D_1(q^{-1})y_m(n+1) \quad (4)$$

Given $d_1 \leq d(2)$, and define $\tau = d_2 - d_1$, multiplying the factor q^{d_1-1} at both sides of (4), gives:

$$B(q^{-1})S(q^{-1})u(n) + C(q^{-1})S(q^{-1})v(n-\tau) + R(q^{-1})y(n+d_1-1)$$
$$- D_1(q^{-1})y_m(n+d_1) = 0 \quad (5)$$

From (5), we have:

$$u(t) = \frac{1}{b_0}[-B_s(q^{-1})u(n-1) - C_s(q^{-1})v(n-\tau) - R(q^{-1})y(n+d_1-1)$$
$$+ D_1(q^{-1})y_m(n+D_1)]$$
$$= \frac{1}{b_0}[D_1(q^{-1})y_m(n+d1) - P^T \Phi(n)]$$

Where $P^T = [b_0 s_1 + b_1, b_1 s_1 + b_0 s_2 + b_2, \cdots, c_0 s_1 + c_1, c_1 s_1 + c_0 s_2 + c_2, \cdots, r_0, \cdots, r_{nr}]$, $\Phi^T(n) = [u(n-1), \cdots, u(n-ns-nb), v(n-\tau), \cdots, v(n-\tau-ns-nc), y(n+d_1-1), \cdots, y(n+d_1-nr-1)]$, and using the reference model output $y_m(n+i), i = 1, \cdots, d_1 - 1$ to replace the future output of plant $y(n+i)$:

$$\hat{\Phi}^T(n) = [u(n-1), \cdots, u(n-ns-nb), v(n-\tau), \cdots, v(n-\tau-ns-nc),$$
$$y_m(n+d_1-1), \cdots, y_m(n+1), y(n), \cdots, y(n+d_1-nr-1)]$$

Now, one of the system inputs is generated as follows:

$$u(n) = \frac{1}{b_0}[D_1(q^{-1})y_m(n+d_1) - P^T \hat{\Phi}(n)] \quad (6)$$

Multiplying the factor q^{d_2-1} at both sides of (4), we get:

$$B(q^{-1})S(q^{-1})u(n+\tau) + C(q^{-1})S(q^{-1})v(n) + R(q^{-1})y(n+d_2-1)$$
$$- D_1(q^{-1})y_m(n+d_2) = 0 \quad (7)$$

$$v(n) = \frac{1}{c_0}[-C_s(q^{-1})v(n-1) - B_s(q^{-1})u(n+\tau) - R(q^{-1})y(n+d_2-1)$$
$$+ D_1(q^{-1})y_m(n+d_2)]$$
$$= \frac{1}{c_0}[D_1(q^{-1})y_m(n+d_2) - \overline{P}^T \overline{\Phi}(n)]$$

where $\overline{P}^T = [c_0 s_1 + c_1, c_1 s_1 + c_0 s_2 + c_2, \cdots, b_0 s_1 + b_1, b_1 s_1 + b_0 s_2 + b_2, \cdots, r_0, \cdots, r_{nr}]$ $\overline{\Phi}^T(n) = [v(n-1), \cdots, v(n-ns-nc), u(n+\tau), \cdots, u(n+\tau-ns-nb), y(n+d_2-1), \cdots, y(n+d_2-nr-1)]$, and using the reference model output $y_m(n+i), i = 1, \cdots, d_2 - 1$ to replace the future output of plant $y(n+i)$, also considering at time n, the controller output values $[u(n+1), \cdots, u(n+\tau)]$ do not exist yet, we have to use the $u(n)$ to approximate to them. Define $\widehat{\overline{\Phi}}^T(n) = [v(n-1), \cdots, v(n-ns-nb), u(n), \cdots, u(n-1), \cdots, u(u+\tau-ns-nb), y_m(n+d_2-1), \cdots, y_m(n+1), y(n), \cdots, y(n+d_2-nr-1)]$, then:

$$v(n) = \frac{1}{c_0}[D_1(q^{-1})y_m(n+d_2) - \overline{P}^T \widehat{\overline{\Phi}}(n)] \quad (8)$$

From (6) and (8), it can be seen that the controller output depends on the output of the reference model. If a suitable reference model in different situations is chosen, the performance of the system can be improved.

3.2 Parameter Estimation

The recursive least-squares algorithm is adopted in this paper for parameters prediction. Introducing the filtered operator, let:

$$\tilde{\eta} = D_1(q^{-1})\eta(n)$$

$$\tilde{y}(n) = D_1(q^{-1})y(n)$$

$$\tilde{y}_m(n) = D_1(q^{-1})y_m(n)$$

$$\tilde{\Xi}(n) = S(q^{-1})L(q^{-1})\Xi(n)$$

Notice 1. The filter operator introduced to deal with the noise only makes form changes on the output of plant and reference model, and has no influence on these in the real system.

Considering the noise, the equation (4) can be written as:

$$\tilde{\eta}(n+1) = \varphi^T m(n) - \tilde{y}_m(n+1) + \tilde{\Xi}(n+1) \tag{9}$$

where:

$$m^T(n) = [u(n-d_1), \cdots, u(n-d_1-ns-nb), v(n-d_2), \cdots,$$
$$v(n-d_2-ns-nc), y(n-1), \cdots, y(n-nr)]$$

$$\varphi^T = [b_0, b_0 s_1 + b_1, \cdots, b_{nb} s_{ns}, c_0, c_0 s_1 + c_1, \cdots, c_{nc} s_{ns}, r_0, \cdots, r_{nr}]$$

From (9), we can obtain:

$$\tilde{y}(n+1) = \varphi^T m(n) + \tilde{\Xi}(n+1) \tag{10}$$

Then, we can get the formula of unbiased and minimum variance estimation:

$$\hat{\varphi}(n+1) = \hat{\varphi}(n) + \Gamma(n+1)[\tilde{y}(n+1) - \hat{\varphi}^T(n)m(n)]$$

$$\Gamma(n+1) = P(n)m(n)[m^T(n)P(n)m(n) + \overline{\sigma}^2]^{-1}$$

$$P(n+1) = P(n) - \Gamma(n+1)m(n)P(n)$$

where $\Gamma(n) = [m^T(n)m(n)]^{-1}$ is covariance function, and $\overline{\sigma}^2 = (1+\sum_{i=1}^{ns} s_i^2)\sigma^2$.

3.3 Structure of Reference Model

Choosing a discrete objective with dual inputs as reference model:

$$D(q^{-1})y_m(n) = q^{-d_1} E(q^{-1})u_m(n) + q^{-d_2} F(q^{-1})v_m(n) \tag{11}$$

And (11) can be rewritten as:

$$y_m(n) = q^{-d_1} \frac{E(q^{-1})}{D(q^{-1})} u_m(n) + q^{-d_2} \frac{F(q^{-1})}{D(q^{-1})} v_m(n) \tag{12}$$

From (12), the model construction parameters be described as:

$$\tilde{\theta} = \begin{bmatrix} e_0 & \cdots & e_{ne} & f_0 & \cdots & f_{nf} & 1 & \cdots & d_{nd} \end{bmatrix}^T \quad (13)$$

The vector $\tilde{\theta}$ was used to describe the dynamic characteristics of the system. If set to the fixed values, they will represent a single reference model. On the other hand, if different values are chosen for them on line, this means the poles and zeros of the system have changed, and different reference models are given, i.e., multiple reference models.

3.4 Fuzzy Classification and Fuzzy Selection

In this paper, the parameters changing space S are regarded as the universe of discourse U (U can be discrete or continued aggregate). According to the states of the system, the universe of discourse can be separate into several subspaces $\{A_i\}, i = 1, 2, \cdots, n$. For every reference model, there exists a subspace in the finite reference model ranges which fully determines the plant parametric change. This concept is outlined in Figure 2.

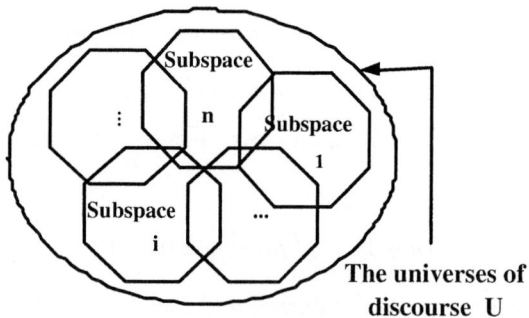

Fig. 2. Domain of subspaces with parametric transformation

Using Gauss function as membership function, then the membership function of the fuzzy subset $\{A_i\}$ with center c_i can be described as:

$$O_i(X_k) = exp(-\frac{\parallel X_k - c_i \parallel^2}{2\xi_i^2})$$

Where $\parallel \cdot \parallel$ is Euclidean norm. X_k is the kth input of universe of discourse. ξ_i is the width of subset $\{A_i\}$.

The multiple reference models describe the desired input/output properties of the closed-loop plant for different environment conditions. Consider a fuzzy system output denoted by a function $f(X)$:

$$f(X) = \frac{\sum_{i=1}^{n} r_i \mu_i}{\sum_{i=1}^{n} \mu_i} \quad (14)$$

Where n is the number of fuzzy logic rules. Assuming that this fuzzy system is constructed in such a way that the $\sum_{i=1}^{n} \mu_i \neq 0$ for every relevant auxiliary state and the system input, then (14) can be rewritten in the following form [8]:

$$f(X) = M^T \theta \qquad (15)$$

where:

$$M^T = \begin{bmatrix} r_1 & r_2 & \cdots & r_n \end{bmatrix}$$

is input vector, and $\theta = \dfrac{[\mu_1 \cdots \mu_n]}{\sum_{i=1}^{n} \mu_i}$ is the vector of membership functions. Then the fuzzy linguistic rules base involved in the FMRMAC system can be summarized as:

Rule i,

If x_1 is $\widetilde{M}_{i1}$ $\cdots$ and x_n is $\widetilde{M}_{in}$
Then r_i is $\begin{bmatrix} r_i^1 & r_i^2 & \cdots & r_i^m \end{bmatrix}^T$, $m = ne + nf + nd + 2$

As the rank of the polynomial is known, we can adjust the poles and the zeros of the reference model:

$$\widetilde{\theta}^* = \hbar \cdot f(X) \cdot \widetilde{\theta} \qquad (16)$$

where $\hbar$ is the operator factor, $\widetilde{\theta}$ is the structure parameter of the reference model, and the $\widetilde{\theta}^*$ denotes the modified parameters.

4 Simulation

To test the accuracy of the controllers, two kinds of methods (MRAC and FM-RMAC) were applied to speed servo system of BLDC [10]. The parameters are: DC voltage $U = 36V$, resistance of stator phase winding $R = 5\Omega$, self-inductances of the stator respectively $L = 0.002H$, mutual inductances of stator respectively $M = -0.0067H$, moment of inertia $J = 0.003 kg \cdot m$, rated speed $n = 2500 r/min$, number of pole pairs $n_p = 1$.

As shown in Figure 3, a case study was performed to show the effect of changing the system conditions on the different controller performances. Under

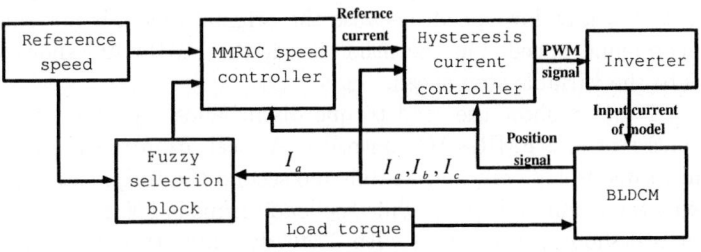

Fig. 3. BLDC control system in Matlab/Simulink

Table 1. Fuzzy rule base

Reference input	Stator current of phase A				
	VS	S	M	L	VL
VS	VS	VS	S	M	L
S	VS	S	M	M	L
M	S	M	L	L	VL
L	M	S	M	L	VL
VL	VL	L	VL	VL	VL

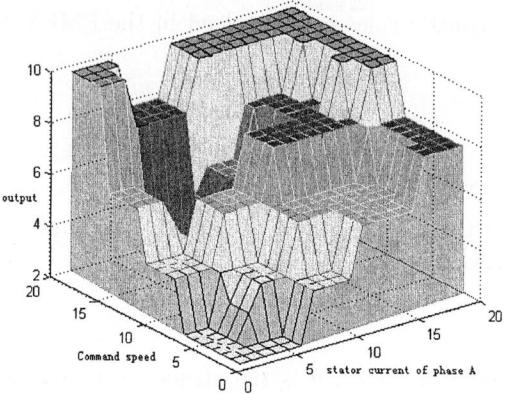

Fig. 4. Ratiocination space of fuzzy selection

the tremendous changes of command speed ($1800r/min$-$130r/min$) and the load torque disturbance ($1N{\cdot}m$ -$5N{\cdot}m$), two methods were compared with each other. The fuzzy rules of FMRMAC are presented in Table 1, and the Ratiocination space of membership function is shown in Figure 4. The input and output of the fuzzy selection can be adjusted to normalize the universes of discourse for some certain ranges. Here, inputs are normalized to $[0, 20]$, and outputs are normalized to $[2, 10]$.

The speed response using MRAC and FMRMAC controller respectively are shown in Figures 5 and 6, where the command speed is a step function, the initial speed is $1800r/min$, and at time 0.5 second, the command speed reduce to $130r/min$. As shown in the figures, the MRAC behave well at high speed, but failed to track at low speed, because the original model is not suitable for the new command speed. On the other hand, the FMRMAC showed perfect responses to the variable step speed.

Figures 7 and 8 show the load torque disturbance rejection capability by MRAC controller and FMRMAC controller. As seen from the Figures 7 and 8 the initial torque is $1N \cdot m$, and at time 0.6 second the torque adds to $5N \cdot m$. For tracking the command speed while the load torque is $1N \cdot m$, the MRAC has significant overshoot and emerges with a steady-state error. Compared to the simulation results of MRAC, FMRMAC performs much better showing almost no speed change when the load torque is disturbed.

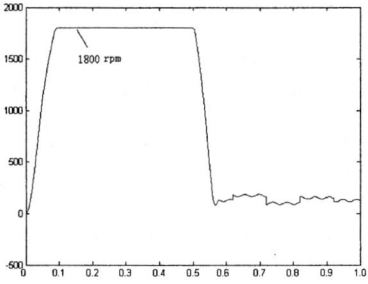 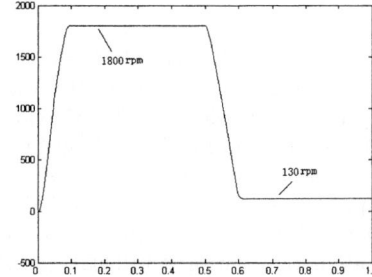

Fig. 5. Speed tracking performance-MRAC (Command speed: 1800r/min-130r/min)

Fig. 6. Speed tracking performance-FMRMAC (Command speed: 1800r/min-130r/min)

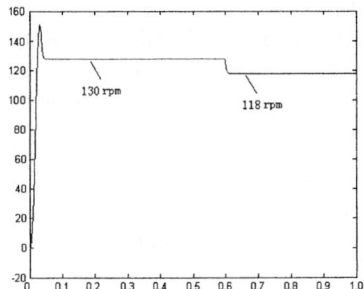 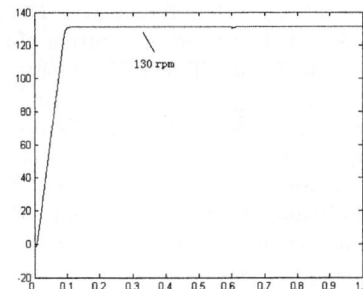

Fig. 7. Speed tracking performance-MRAC (Load torque:1Nm-5Nm)

Fig. 8. Speed tracking performance-FMRMAC (Load torque:1Nm-5Nm)

The simulation results show that the FMRMAC has much better performance in terms of overshoot and steady-state error than the conventional MRAC when the command speed undergoes tremendous changes or the load torque is disturbed.

5 Conclusion

In this article, a novel fuzzy multiple reference model adaptive control method for the different system operating region is presented. With the parameters prediction adaptive algorithm, this method chooses the suitable reference model by fuzzy logic rules to achieve improved performance. A successful application of the FMRMAC algorithm for BLDC has been given, and an outstanding advantage of the FMRMAC algorithm is that the closed-loop system performance can be guaranteed even when significant and unpredictable plant parameter variations occur. Some remarks are given to explain the obtained results, and to point out the limitations that the calculation of this method will have for complex models.

References

1. Michael A.D., Rosen I.G.: Variable structure model reference adaptive control of parabolic distributed parameter systems. Proceeding of the American Control Conference, Anchorage. (2002) 4371–4376
2. Mitsuru K., Masayoshi T.: Model reference adaptive control of linear systems with input saturation. Proceeding of the 2004 IEEE International Conference on Control Application, Taipei, Taiwan. (2004) 1318–1323
3. Daniel E.M.: A new approach to model reference adaptive control. IEEE Trans. Automatic Control. **48** (2003) 743–757
4. Alvaro K., Ramon R., Liu H., et.al.: Multivariable adaptive control using high-frequency gain matrix factorization. IEEE Trans. Automatic Control. **49** (2004) 1152–1157
5. Narendra K., Balakrishnan J.: Adaptive control using multiple models. IEEE Trans. Automatic Control. **42** (1997) 171–187
6. Yinsong Wang, Wulin Liu: A kind of PID-typed fuzzy neural network controller. Journal of System Simulation. **15** (2003) 389–392
7. Sukumar K.: A new generation of adaptive control: an intelligent supervisory approach. Toledo, Toledo University. (2004)
8. Sukumar K., Adel A.G., Khalid S.A.: A fuzzy multiple reference model adaptive control scheme for flexible link robotic manipulator. Proceeding of the 2004 IEEE International Conference on Computational Intelligence for Measurement Systems and Applications, Boston. (2004) 162–167
9. Bo Zhang, Zhong Li, Zongyuan Mao: Mathematical model of permanent-magnet synchronous motors and its fuzzy modeling. Control theory and application. **19** (2002) 841–844
10. Zhicheng Ji, Yanxia Shen and Jianguo Jiang: A novel method for modeling and simulation of BLDC system based on Matlab. Journal of System Simulation. **15** (2003) 1745–1749

Selection of Optimal Technological Innovation Projects Combining Value Engineering with Fuzzy Synthetic Evaluation

Yuan-sheng Huang, Jun-hua Zhou, and Jian-xun Qi

Department of Economy and Management,
North China Electric Power University,
071003 Baoding, China
hys2656@yahoo.com.cn

Abstract. Value engineering is introduced into a selection of optimal technological innovation projects. The function and cost factors of a project have been analyzed from the viewpoint of the whole enterprise, and new index systems of evaluation on the project are constructed. Since many factors influence the success of a technological innovation project in direct ways or in potential indirect ways, it is difficult to find a common appraisal method to achieve a satisfactory and effective scientific result. Therefore, multistage fuzzy synthetic evaluation is adopted. In addition, this novel method can be programmed to be used in similar fields, so it is of high practicability.

1 Introduction

In the face of a fierce competitive market, strengthening technological innovation strategy has already become the inevitable choice in enterprise development. If an enterprise never innovates, it will be eliminated through market competition; once an enterprise's technological innovation succeeds, the competitive power of the enterprise will be greatly promoted; once it fails, the enterprise will face high risks. So, how to appraise innovation projects completely and choose the optimal one scientifically in an enterprise's technological innovation has been the focus that the theory circle and enterprise operators have paid close attention to [1-4]. In past research, diversified analytical methods have been proposed. Here, value engineering is introduced into the optimization of technological innovation projects: the function or benefit, which results from one technological innovation project, is analyzed from the viewpoint of the whole enterprise; at the same time the project's expenses, opportunity cost and risks are also considered. In addition, the purpose of value engineering lies in promotion of the object's value. To a certain degree, it accords with the goal that a technological innovation project pursues. Therefore, this paper places emphasis on factor analysis based on value engineering and the application of fuzzy synthetic evaluation in the optimization of technological innovation projects.

2 Principle of Value Engineering

Value engineering (VE), also called value analysis, was proposed by the American engineer, L. D. Miles, in the 1940s. It has since been widely used in various fields now.

As a method of technical economic analysis, value engineering can be formulated as:

$$Value = Fuction\Big/Cost \tag{1}$$

In the equation, Value means the ratio between the total function and the total cost of the object; Function means the attribute that a certain demand can be satisfied; Cost means all expenses to realize all functions of the object.

From the above definition, using VE to appraise and choose technological innovation projects has unique advantages, because an enterprise usually faces a lot of project alternatives while implementing technological innovation strategy and these can bring different functions to the enterprise at different costs. For optimization of the projects, VE is a very suitable means of technological analysis.

However, examples of Chinese and foreign enterprises' technological innovations prove that there exit some factors influencing the success of the projects directly, and other ones doing so potentially indirectly. Thus, merely adopting VE to evaluate technological innovation projects means it is usually difficult to get the appropriate objective and overall result. For this reason, the application of VE in the evaluation of the innovation project is limited. So this paper puts forward using fuzzy synthetic evaluation theory to analyze different technological innovation projects. In fact, this method overcomes the above limitations.

3 Establishment of Evaluation Index Systems Based on VE

3.1 Analysis of the Factors Influencing the Success of a Technological Innovation Project

An enterprise's implementation of a technological innovation strategy, in essence, is the embodiment of the strategic objective that the enterprise pursues continuous benefit and maintains sound development. As a kind of strategic decision-making, the selection of innovation projects generally needs to consider various factors synthetically and analyze their influences on the implementation of the projects carefully. In references [3~5], these factors have been analyzed roundly, but this paper generalizes the factors as three aspects:

(1) Influence of an enterprise's environment on an innovation project. Any technological innovation project must take into account whether it can suit national macroscopic policies and legal systems. In addition, it also needs to consider the development state of the same trade, impact of scientific and technological progress, possible reaction of rivals, analysis of market prospect, rivals' competitive products, market situation and economic strength of rivals, and consumer acceptance of the new product, etc. All these factors influence the success of the technological innovation project directly.

(2) State analysis of an innovation project itself. In choosing technological innovation projects, the success possibilities and risk factors of the projects must

be fully considered; namely, whether the innovation project is ripe technically; whether the technology involved is adequately advanced; whether or not the project is too complicated; whether personnel meet the project's research and development demand; whether there are adequate funds to implement the project; whether correlative technologies are easy to obtain; whether the supply of key resources is stable; and whether the R&D period of the project is too long to enter the market in time, etc.

(3) Strategic objectives of an enterprise and condition of an innovation project implementation. This mainly includes the factors as follows: the R&D strength of the enterprise, the enterprise's staff quality, expenses of talent introduction and staff training, enterprise's financial state, opportunity cost, adaptive capacity of the existing equipment, funds required for changing equipment and introducing new technology, production cost of the innovation project, cost risk in initial low scale, the enterprise's marketing ability, the expenses of exploiting the product market.

3.2 Index System of the Project's Function Factors

Based on the above analysis of the factors influencing a technological innovation project, the function factors can be distinguished according to their influence, such as bringing economic benefits to the enterprise, promoting the enterprise's competitive power, enriching the product structure and so on. With the method of AHP, the evaluation index system of function factors is set up. (See Fig. 1.)

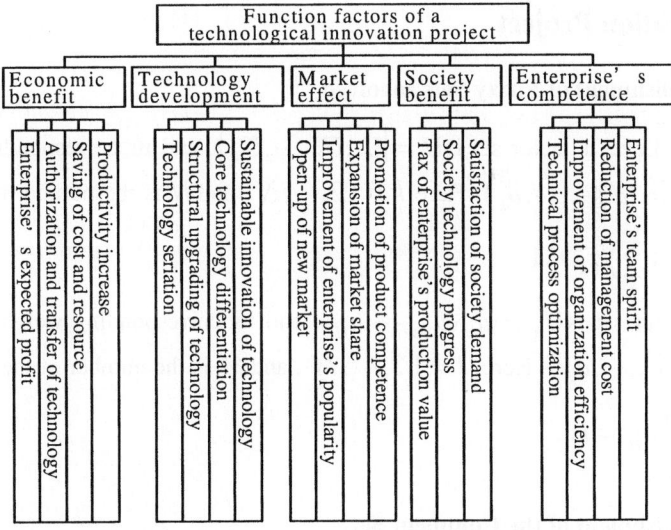

Fig. 1. Function factors of an innovation project

3.3 Index System of the Project's Cost Factors

Analogously, according to the enterprise's expenses and risks in technological innovation, the cost factors can also be distinguished. With AHP, the evaluation index system of cost factors is set up. (See Fig. 2.)

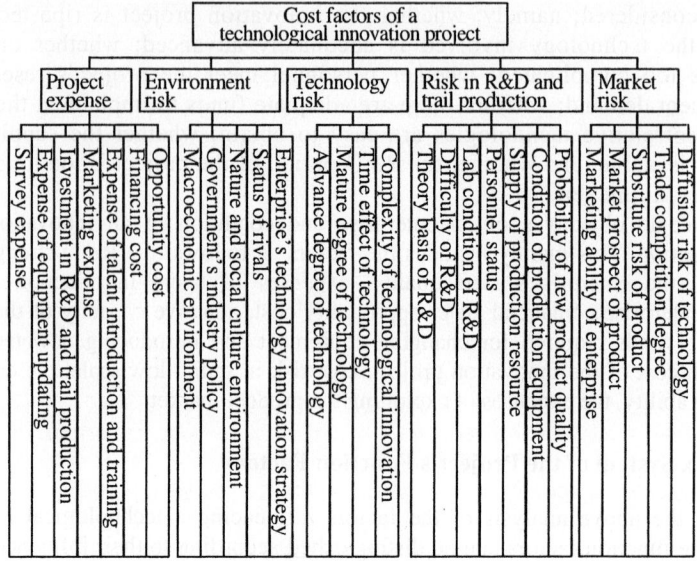

Fig. 2. Cost factors of an innovation project

4 Multistage Fuzzy Synthetic Evaluation of a Technological Innovation Project

4.1 Establishment of Fuzzy Sets Involved

Definition: Level 1 factor set is $U = \{U_1, U_2, \cdots, U_k\}$, and its corresponding weight vector is $A = (a_1, a_2, \cdots, a_k)$. Here, $k = 1, 2, \cdots, N$, and N is the number of the sub-index of U; $\sum_{k=1}^{N} a_k = 1$.

Level 2 factor set is $U_k = \{u_{k1}, u_{k2}, \cdots, u_{kl}\}$, and its corresponding weight vector is $A_k = (a_{k1}, a_{k2}, \cdots, a_{kl})$. Here, $l = 1, 2, \cdots, M$, and M is the number of the sub-index of U_k; $\sum_{l=1}^{M} a_{kl} = 1$.

4.2 Establishment of the Comment Set

Considering the operation and precision of evaluating practical problems, a five level comment set is adopted, which is $V = \{v_1, v_2, v_3, v_4, v_5\}$, and its corresponding comment grades are as follows: v_1 is the "worst" grade; v_2 is a "bad" grade; v_3 is a "neutral" grade; v_4 is a "good" grade; v_5 is the "best" grade.

4.3 Calculating Weight Vectors of Factor Sets

In fuzzy synthetic evaluation, weight allocation of the indexes has much influence on the evaluation result, and even affects the selection result of the projects directly. So it is important to determine the weight vectors accurately, objectively. This paper introduces the method of analytical hierarchy process (AHP) and its application in Matlab6.x to calculate weight vector.

AHP is a multigoal decision-making method which combines qualitative analysis and quantitative analysis. The main calculation process is as follows:

Step 1. Ask all members of the expert panel to write down the relative degree of importance between every two factors in each factor set, and then develop fuzzy judgement matrixes.

Step 2. Calculate the weight vector of each judgement matrix with the eigenvector method, and carry out a consistency check on these matrixes to accept or reject for them;

Step 3. Use geometrically weighted arithmetic to compute the weight vectors of the judgement matrix group in terms of multiperson and single rule; and,

Step 4. Work out the final weight vectors of all factor sets. By utilizing the powerful matrix function of the software Matlab6.x program, the calculation of a judgement matrix's maximal eigenvalue and corresponding eigenvector are greatly simplified. For example, build up the M-file briefly in the editor of Matlab 6.1. See Fig. 3.

```
clear all; clc;
R=[r11,r12,...,r1k;...;ri1,ri2,...,rik];      %input judgement matrix of the factor set
[a,b]=eig(R)                                   %compute eigenvector of R
n=input('Please input the row number of judgement matrix');
defult_CR=input('Please input the defult value of CR');
defult_RI=(0 0 0.58 0.9 1.12 1.24 1.32 1.41 1.45 1.49 1.52 1.54)
CI=(b(1,1)-n)/(n-1);RI=defult_RI(1,n);CR=CI/RI  %carry on consistency check
If CR<defult_CR
W=a(:,1)/sum(a(:,1))                            %carry on normalization
else; 'Consistency check is not passed'
end
```

Fig. 3. Example of M-file for computing eigenvector

Finally, the weight vector W is obtained after computation.

4.4 Determining Fuzzy Judgement Matrixes of Factor Sets

4.4.1 Determining Single Factor Judgement of a Quantificational Index

According to the above comment set, consult the experts repeatedly to determine five rational ranges of each quantificational index value, which corresponds to the five grades of the comment set. The division basis can refer to the enterprise's actual ability and the standard of congener technological innovation projects in the same trade, etc. As for a positive correlation index, suppose that five ranges of the value of

u_{ki} ($i = 1,2,\cdots,l$), which corresponds to five grades of the comment set, are respectively as follows: $(-\infty,\alpha_2),(\alpha_1,\alpha_3),(\alpha_2,\alpha_4),(\alpha_3,\alpha_5),(\alpha_4,+\infty)$, and then the trigonometric membership function is constructed:

$$r_{v_1}(u_{ki}) = \begin{cases} 1, & u_{ki} \leq \alpha_1 \\ (u_{ki} - \alpha_2)/(\alpha_1 - \alpha_2), & \alpha_1 \leq u_{ki} \leq \alpha_2 \\ 0, & others \end{cases}$$

$$r_{v_2}(u_{ki}) = \begin{cases} (u_{ki} - \alpha_1)/(\alpha_2 - \alpha_1), & \alpha_1 \leq u_{ki} \leq \alpha_2 \\ (u_{ki} - \alpha_3)/(\alpha_2 - \alpha_3), & \alpha_2 \leq u_{ki} \leq \alpha_3 \\ 0, & others \end{cases}$$

$$r_{v_3}(u_{ki}) = \begin{cases} (u_{ki} - \alpha_2)/(\alpha_3 - \alpha_2), & \alpha_2 \leq u_{ki} \leq \alpha_3 \\ (u_{ki} - \alpha_4)/(\alpha_3 - \alpha_4), & \alpha_3 \leq u_{ki} \leq \alpha_4 \\ 0, & others \end{cases} \quad (2)$$

$$r_{v_4}(u_{ki}) = \begin{cases} (u_{ki} - \alpha_3)/(\alpha_4 - \alpha_3), & \alpha_3 \leq u_{ki} \leq \alpha_4 \\ (u_{ki} - \alpha_5)/(\alpha_4 - \alpha_5), & \alpha_4 \leq u_{ki} \leq \alpha_5 \\ 0, & others \end{cases}$$

$$r_{v_5}(u_{ki}) = \begin{cases} 1, & u_{ki} \geq \alpha_5 \\ (u_{ki} - \alpha_4)/(\alpha_5 - \alpha_4), & \alpha_4 \leq u_{ki} \leq \alpha_5 \\ 0, & others \end{cases}$$

Here, with different quantificational indexes, the value of $\alpha_m (m = 1,...,5)$ is also different. The curve graph of the trigonometric membership function is displayed in Fig. 4.

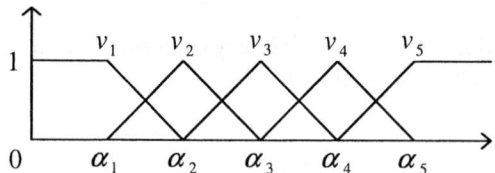

Fig. 4. Curve graph of trigonometric membership function

So, according to the value of the quantificational index u_{ki}, its single factor judgement can be calculated:

$$\left(r_{v_1}(u_{ki}), r_{v_2}(u_{ki}), r_{v_3}(u_{ki}), r_{v_4}(u_{ki}), r_{v_5}(u_{ki})\right)$$

In addition, as for a negative correlation index, such as quantificational indexes in cost factors, five grades of the comment set are just the reverse of a positive correlation index; namely, $(-\infty,\alpha_2)$, (α_1,α_3), (α_2,α_4), (α_3,α_5), $(\alpha_4,+\infty)$

corresponds to the grades v_5, v_4, v_3, v_2, v_1 respectively. Its trigonometric membership function and curve graph transform in the same way.

4.4.2 Determining Single Factor Judgement of a Qualitative Index

First, let the experts determine the comment criteria according to the information of how technological innovation projects fit with the enterprise's actual situation and the feature of each technological innovation project itself. Then, use a fuzzy statistical method to calculate the single factor judgement of qualitative indexes; that is to say, let all members of the expert panel classify u_{ki} ($i = 1, 2, \cdots, l$) in the factor set U_k. Then, gathering the result, count the frequency $W_{ki}^{(m)}$ that u_{ki} belongs to the grade $v_m (m = 1,2,3,4,5)$ in V, and so $r_{v_m}(u_{ki})$ can be calculated:

$$r_{v_m}(u_{ki}) = W_{ki}^{(m)} \Big/ T \tag{3}$$

In this equation, $r_{v_m}(u_{ki})$ means the membership degree or the membership function; T means the number of experts.

Thus, single factor judgement of the index u_{ki} is:

$$\left(r_{v_1}(u_{ki}), r_{v_2}(u_{ki}), r_{v_3}(u_{ki}), r_{v_4}(u_{ki}), r_{v_5}(u_{ki})\right)$$

4.4.3 Calculating Fuzzy Judgement Matrix of the Factor Set U_k

After calculating the single factor judgement of all indexes in the factor set U_k, arrange them to form $l \times 5$ matrix, which is a fuzzy judgement matrix of U_k:

$$R_k = \begin{bmatrix} r_{k1,1} & r_{k1,2} & r_{k1,3} & r_{k1,4} & r_{k1,5} \\ r_{k2,1} & r_{k2,2} & r_{k2,3} & r_{k2,4} & r_{k2,5} \\ \vdots & \vdots & \vdots & \vdots & \vdots \\ r_{kl,1} & r_{kl,2} & r_{kl,3} & r_{kl,4} & r_{kl,5} \end{bmatrix}$$

Here, $r_{ki,j}(i = 1, 2, \cdots, l; j = 1,2,3,4,5; k = 1,2,\cdots,N)$ is a single factor judgement of the index u_{ki}.

4.5 Multistage Fuzzy Synthetic Evaluation

4.5.1 Fuzzy Synthetic Evaluation of Level 2 Index

With fuzzy weighted averaging operator $M(\bullet, \oplus)$, carry out a matrix synthetic operation on the fuzzy judgement matrix R_k and its weight vector $A_k = (a_{k1}, a_{k2}, \cdots, a_{kl})$. Thus, the membership vector of U_k to V is computed:

$$\tilde{B}_k = A_k \circ R_k = (a_{k1}, a_{k2}, \cdots, a_{kl}) \circ \begin{bmatrix} a_{k1,1} & a_{k1,2} & a_{k1,3} & a_{k1,4} & a_{k1,5} \\ a_{k2,1} & a_{k2,2} & a_{k2,3} & a_{k2,4} & a_{k2,5} \\ \vdots & \vdots & \vdots & & \vdots \\ a_{kl,1} & a_{kl,2} & a_{kl,3} & a_{kl,4} & a_{kl,5} \end{bmatrix} = (b_{k1}, b_{k2}, \cdots, b_{k5}) \quad (4)$$

Here, fuzzy subset $\tilde{B}_k = (b_{k1}, b_{k2}, \cdots, b_{k5}), (k = 1, 2, \cdots, N)$ is also the result of the fuzzy synthetic evaluation of the Level 2 index U_k.

4.5.2 Fuzzy Synthetic Evaluation of Level 1 Index
With the fuzzy subset $\tilde{B}_k \ (k = 1, 2, \cdots, N)$, fuzzy judgement matrix of the factor set U is obtained:

$$R = \begin{bmatrix} \tilde{B}_1 \\ \tilde{B}_2 \\ \vdots \\ \tilde{B}_k \end{bmatrix} = \begin{bmatrix} b_{11} & b_{12} & b_{13} & b_{14} & b_{15} \\ b_{21} & b_{22} & b_{23} & b_{24} & b_{25} \\ \vdots & \vdots & \vdots & \vdots & \vdots \\ b_{k1} & b_{k2} & b_{k3} & b_{k4} & b_{k5} \end{bmatrix}$$

In the same way, with the operator $M \ (\bullet, \oplus)$, carry out a matrix synthetic operation on fuzzy judgement matrix R and its weight vector $A = (a_1, a_2, \cdots, a_k)$. Thus, the membership vector of U to V is computed:

$$\tilde{B} = A \circ R = (a_1, a_2, \cdots, a_k) \circ \begin{bmatrix} b_{11} & b_{12} & b_{13} & b_{14} & b_{15} \\ b_{21} & b_{22} & b_{23} & b_{24} & b_{25} \\ \vdots & \vdots & \vdots & & \vdots \\ b_{k1} & b_{k2} & b_{k3} & b_{k4} & b_{k5} \end{bmatrix} = (b_1, b_2, \cdots, b_5) \quad (5)$$

When $\sum_{n=1}^{5} b_n \neq 1$, carry on normalization; namely, set $b_n^* = b_n / \sum_{n=1}^{5} b_n$ and compute:

$$\tilde{B}^* = (b_1^*, b_2^*, \cdots, b_5^*)$$

$\tilde{B}^*$ is the fuzzy evaluation result of Level 1 index U.

4.6 Evaluation Result of a Technological Innovation Project
After the above fuzzy synthetic evaluation of a technological innovation project's function factors, the result can be obtained:

$$\tilde{B} = (b_1, b_2, b_3, b_4, b_5)$$

In order to compare different projects and derive more convenient calculation, transform the result into the number value type. After consulting the experts, set each comment $v_m (m=1,2,3,4,5)$ that corresponds to a weight value $f_m (m=1,2,3,4,5)$, which denotes the importance of this comment grade. So, the result becomes:

$$F = \tilde{B}(f_1, f_2, f_3, f_4, f_5)^T \tag{6}$$

Similarly, as for the project's cost factors, the evaluation result can be obtained:

$$B' = (b_1', b_2', b_3', b_4', b_5')$$

Remember that these are negative correlation indexes. Therefore, when transforming into the number value type, the weight value, corresponding to each comment, should be different depending on the function factors. Then the result becomes:

$$C = \tilde{B}'(f_1', f_2', f_3', f_4', f_5')^T \tag{7}$$

Ultimately, put F and C into Formula (1), and so the "value" of the technological innovation project is:

$$V = \frac{F}{C} = \frac{\tilde{B}(f_1, f_2, f_3, f_4, f_5)^T}{\tilde{B}'(f_1', f_2', f_3', f_4', f_5')^T} \tag{8}$$

4.7 Optimality Analysis of Evaluation Result in Terms of "Value"

The detailed analysis includes: first, with the above-mentioned fuzzy analysis principle, the evaluation results of all technological innovation project alternatives are worked out. The results are ranked from large to small. The greater the "value" of a project is, the more attention we should pay to it in the selection of the projects. Undoubtedly, this selection method offers a scientific basis for the enterprise's decision-making.

Secondly, VE aims at the promotion of an object's value. Introducing VE into the evaluation of innovation projects is simply for analyzing different projects' function and cost characteristics in the view of "value". Namely, compare the situation of the function and the cost of the projects, analyze their difference, and find key factors to influencing function and controlling cost. Obviously, this analysis is highly useful to improve function, reduce cost and control risks in the future project implementation, management and control, so it is very important. And the optimality analysis in terms of "value" is the essence of this paper.

5 Conclusions

(1) The purpose of VE lies in the promotion of the object's value; at the same time, technological innovation is just the activity of creating greater value at certain cost.

So, to a certain extent, VE has offered a suitable approach to analyze a technological innovation project.

(2) Considering that many factors influence the success of a technological innovation project in direct or potentially indirect ways, using a common method to appraise the project makes it difficult to obtain the appropriate objective and scientific result. Here, fuzzy synthetic evaluation is a kind of comparatively ideal method; with it, more extensive appraisal on the project can be obtained.

(3) This paper combines VE with a fuzzy analytical method to select optimal technological innovation projects, because it overcomes the limitation of common methods and obtains very effective results. In similar fields, the method has extensive reference value. In addition, the above selection method can also be realized with computer programming. Therefore, it has very high practicability.

References

1. Pan Peng, Qing Yang: Evaluation Criterion of Technology Selection. Science & Technology Progress and Policy, Vol 16, No. 1. Jan. (1999) 28-29
2. Dongbo Hu: Application of Value Engineering in Enterprise's Technological Innovation. Science & Technology Progress and Policy, Vol 18, No. 6. Jun. (2001) 70-72
3. Xiaobing Liu: Application of Analyzing Enterprise's Technological Innovation with Value Engineering. Scientific Management Research, Vol 21, No.1. Jan. (2003) 16-18
4. Jin Chen, Peng Shang: Strategic Management of Product Innovation Projects. Science & Technology Progress and Policy, Vol 20, No. 4. Apr. (2003) 23-25
5. Keyuan Xie: Risk of Technological Innovation. Science & Technology Publishing House, Shijiazhuang, China (2003)
6. Jingwen Zhang, Yu Xu, Guorong Cai: Comparative Study on Risk Assessing Methods of the High-tech Project Investment", R&D Management, Vol 16, No.2. Apr. (2004) 39-45
7. Yuhua Li, Hongwen Lang: Reseach on Fuzzy Overall Evaluation Model for Investment Risks in High-tech Projects. Journal Harbin Univ. Sci. & Tech., Vol 9, No. 1. Feb. (2004) 72-75
8. Weimin Xiang, Mei Feng: Fuzzy Synthetic Evaluation of the Risks of Technology Innovation for Enterprises. Journal of Chongqing University, Vol 26, No. 12. Dec. (2003) 142-144

The Hierarchical Fuzzy Evaluation System and Its Application

Xiaoping Qiu [1,2], Yang Xu [2], Ming Jian [1], and Haiming Li [2,3]

[1] School of Economics and Management, Southwest Jiaotong University,
Chengdu (610031), Sichuan, P.R. China
[2] Intelligent Control Development Center, Southwest Jiaotong University,
Chengdu (610031), Sichuan, P.R. China
[3] School of Information and Engineering, Zhejiang Forestry University,
Lin'an, Hangzhou (311300), Zhejiang, P.R. China
qxp@home.swjtu.edu.cn

Abstract. The hierarchical fuzzy evaluation system (HFES) and its application in intelligent workflow management system (IWfMS) are discussed in this paper. First, the definition of HFES is discussed, including the definitions of the evaluation items and the relationships among them, based on the five common operations. Second, the running algorithms of the HFES are introduced to compute the values of those evaluation items and the result of the HFES. Subsequently, the application of the HFES in the IWfMS is presented in detail including the cooperating model. The experiments are carried out and the results show that the HFES is effective.

1 Introduction

Evaluation plays an important role in management [1,2]. With it, we can find out the current status (the profit, the loss, etc.) of our business and analyze the relationship between the status and our objectives [3]. Based on the analyzed results, the corresponding methods are proposed and adopted. Usually, the evaluation system has many evaluation items and the hierarchical frame is its common frame [4], in which we can organize the evaluation items conveniently.

Fuzzy information exists in evaluation procedure [5–7], and fuzzy theory is used as a powerful method for evaluation [8–10]. If we take an evaluation item as one fuzzy proposition in a fuzzy logic system, the evaluation system can be transferred into a fuzzy formula. For one evaluation object, each fuzzy proposition assigns one value and the evaluation result of the object is the value of the corresponding fuzzy formula. In [11, 12], we have achieved the classical logic formula computing method integrated with neural networks [13–15], meaning that the fuzzy formulae can all be processed by computer instead of by hand.

At the same time, with the development of the information society, computers are important to our life and works. So the evaluation system should be designed with this in mind. As we know, workflow technology is one of the support technologies of information systems.

Workflow technology has developed rapidly since the 1990s, giving us new ideas on how to better manage information [16]. In order to further satisfy user requirements, intelligent workflow management system (abbr. IWfMS) was proposed [17, 18]. As many information systems are designed based on the workflow technology, the evaluation method for work needs to be updated with those environments and this is the focus of our work in this paper.

The hierarchical fuzzy evaluation system (abbr. HFES) and its application in this IWfMS is discussed in this paper. Based on the database technology, the HFES is constructed like the IWfMS, by which the information of the HFES is saved for writing and reading. The conjunctive method operating between the HFES and the IWfMS is that the HFES refers to the IWfMS when constructing the HFES and specifies the data source (dynamic SQL statement managing the data in the IWfMS) of each evaluation item in the HFES.

In our HFES, five common operations are concerned including the conjunctive operation, the disjunctive operation, the negative operation, the lattice-value implicative operation and the weighted averaging operation. All these operations are unitary or binary operations and their attributes can be saved in a uniform format. The relationships among the evaluation items are defined after the definition of the evaluation items in the HFES.

Our paper is organized as follows. First, we discuss the definition of the evaluation system including the evaluation items' storage, then the relationships among the evaluation items are presented in the next section. The two main algorithms are presented in Section 3. Subsequently, the connection model and works between the HFES and the IWfMS are introduced in Section 4 and the experiment is carried out in Section 5. We present our conclusion in Section 6.

2 The Definition of HFES

First, the methods to construct HFES are introduced. In this section, the top-down definition of the evaluation items and the bottom-up definition of the relationships among those items are discussed based on database technology.

2.1 The Attributes of the Evaluation Items

To ensure an accurate definition, the attributes of the evaluation items first need to be identified. As a feasible method, the hierarchical frame can be represented by the code of the evaluation items. At the same time, the layer number and the length of each layer's code must be specified. We suppose that the layer number is N and the maximum length of each layer's code is k. The main attributes of the items are listed in Table 1.

Table 1. The attributes of the evaluation items

Attributes	Type	Length	Primary Key
Own no.	VarChar	$N \times k$	Yes
Layer no.	Integer	Default	No
Parent no.	VarChar	$(N-1) \times k$	No
Name	VarChar	20	No
Data source	VarChar	100	No
Value	Decimal	5, 3	No

In Table 1, the primary key in the evaluation items table (EIT) is 'Own no.' field, which is derived from the 'Parent no.' (see Table 3). The 'Parent no.' of the root evaluation item is '0'. So, conveniently, the hierarchical frame of the evaluation system can be saved in the EIT. It should be noted that the field 'Data source' is used to connect IWfMS through the dynamic SQL statements. Obviously, the definition of HFES must start with the root item and the children items are defined after the definition of their parent items.

2.2 The Relationships Among the Evaluation Items

Usually, the relationships among the evaluation items in HFES are formed from the following five common operations.

1) The fuzzy conjunction operation:

$$a \wedge b = \min(a, b) \tag{1}$$

2) The fuzzy disjunction operation:

$$a \vee b = \max(a, b) \tag{2}$$

3) The fuzzy negative operation:

$$\sim a = 1 - a \tag{3}$$

4) The lattice-value implication operation [19]:

$$a \rightarrow b = \min(1, 1 - a + b) \tag{4}$$

5) The weighted averaging operation [20, 21]:

$$a \lozenge_\alpha b = a \times \alpha + (1 - \alpha) \times b \tag{5}$$

in which α is the weight of a and $1 - \alpha$ is the weight of b.

The weighted averaging operation is a common operation in the existing evaluation system. Also, the weighted averaging operation of the n (> 1) evaluation items can be transferred into $n - 1$ binary operation 'W-AVG'.

For example, if we have four evaluation items, a, b, c and d with the corresponding weights, 0.2, 0.3, 0.3 and 0.2, the weighted averaging operation will be used three time as follows (this work can be finished by a special module in the program, usually to three decimal places):

$$\begin{aligned} &0.2\,a + 0.3\,b + 0.3\,c + 0.2\,d \\ &= 0.8 \times (0.625 \times (0.4\,a + 0.6\,b) + 0.375\,c) + 0.2\,d \\ &= ((a \lozenge_{0.4} b) \lozenge_{0.625} c) \lozenge_{0.8} d \end{aligned} \tag{6}$$

Therefore, the definition of the relationships is based on the operations, which only require one or two input items. In the bottom-up definition, we start with the endmost evaluation items (located in the lowest layer). The value of the parent item is defined by the operation of its children items. Obviously, each item can only be calculated once.

With the unitary operation and the binary operations above, the relationships can be easily saved in the uniform table named as IRT. The attributes of the relationships (operations) needed to be saved are listed in Table 2.

Table 2. The attributes of the item's relationships

Attributes	Type	Length	Primary Key
Sequence no.	Integer	Default	Yes
1st input	VarChar	$N \times k$	No
2nd input	VarChar	$N \times k$	No
Unit type	VarChar	5	No
Output	Decimal	5, 3	No

The 2nd input is null for the negative operation. The operation type is filled with the first letter of the operation, conjunction (C), disjunction (D), negation (N) and implication (I), the α (expressed as a string) of the weight averaging operation.

If the evaluation items are defined, they can't be chosen again. But the system will generate a special code (or sequence no.) for their result. If all the child items are defined, the system will prompt that their parent item is satisfactory and can be chosen in the following steps.

3 The Main Algorithms in HFES

Corresponding to the definitions of the HFES, there are two main algorithms when the HFES runs. The values of the endmost evaluation items (saved in the EIT table) must be figured out first. Then the bottom-up computing algorithm runs based on the relationships among the evaluation items (saved in the IRT table).

3.1 The Values of the Endmost Evaluation Items

In order to get the values of the endmost evaluation items with the selected object(s), we should input the values manually or first connect to the relative database of IS. The algorithm operates each record in the EIT table (with SQL statements here). The input parameter is the ID(s) of the selected object(s). The algorithm is:

```
1 i = 1;
2 Get the 'Own no.' field of the i-th record;
3 Judge whether the 'Own no.' appears in 'Parent no.'
  field through the whole table;
  3.1 If no, go to 7;
  3.2 If yes, get the SQL statement in the 'Data source'
      field of the i-th record;
4 Input the ID of the select object into SQL statement;
5 Execute the dynamic SQL and save the result into the
  'Value' field of the i-th record;
6 i = i + 1, go to 2;
7 The algorithm is over.
```

Notes and Comments: For one selected object, the algorithm should be executed once. The following computing algorithm runs based on the results here.

3.2 The Bottom-Up Computing Algorithm

After the above algorithm runs, the computing algorithm for the HFES should be executed. Refer to similar finished works in [11, 22].

In order to refer to the computed result (Output)s in IRT, the primary key 'Sequence no.' must be written with a constant length in either the '1st input' field or the '2nd input' field. The special letter is placed in front of the 'Sequence no.' to distinguish it from the 'Own no.' of the evaluation item. Here, the format 'Axx' is used, in which 'xx' represents the 'Sequence no.' with the constant length 2. For example, 'A05' indicates the 'Output' field of the record whose 'Sequence no.' is equal to 5.

```
1 Judge the definition (formula) of the HFES - is it cor-
  rect? If yes, go to 2; otherwise, the algorithm prompts
  for the relative information and terminates.
2 i = 1, sort the IRT with 'Sequence no. Ascending';
3 Get the '1st input' field, '2nd input' field and 'Opera-
  tion type' field of the i-th record, then save them
  into sa, sb and t respectively;
4 Judge Left(sa, 1) = 'A'? If yes, j = integer(Right(sa,
  2)), get the 'Output' field of the j-th from IRT; oth-
  erwise, get the 'Value' field corresponding to sa from
  EIT; save the return valve in the variable a;
5 Judge Left(sb, 1) = 'A'? If yes, j = integer(Right(sb,
  2)), get the 'Output' field of the j-th from IRT; oth-
  erwise, else get the 'Value' field corresponding to sb
  from EIT; save the return valve in the variable b;
6 Compute the 'Output' field of the j-th record under the
  following six different conditions:
  6.1 If IsNumber(t) = true, compute with the weighted
      averaging operation:           c = Dec(t) × a
      + (1 - Dec(t)) × b.
  6.2 If t = 'C', compute with the fuzzy conjunctive op-
      eration: c = min (a, b);
  6.3 If t = 'D', compute with the fuzzy disjunctive op-
      eration: c = max (a, b);
  6.4 If t = 'N', compute with the fuzzy negative opera-
      tion: c = 1 - a;
  6.5 If t = 'I', compute with the implicative operation:
      c = min (1, 1 - a + b);
  6.6 If t = 'E', no computation is needed;
7 Write c into the 'Output' field of the j-th record;
8 i = i + 1, go to 3;
9 Output the 'Output' field of the aftermost record.
```

Notes and Comments: In this algorithm above, i) *Left*(*sa*, 1) is used to get the first character in the string *sa* from left to right, *Right*(*sa*, 2) the two characters from right to left. ii) *IsNumber*(*t*) is used to judge whether the string *t* is converted from a number or not.

As to the weighted averaging operation, the result of the judgment is true. The function $Dec(t)$ is used to converted to a decimal for calculation purposes. iii) In Step 6.6, the letter 'E' is the first character of 'Equal', which is used to combine the value of the parent and the results of the children based on their relationships.

The two main algorithms above run in turn, so the conclusion below is obtained.

Proposition 1. *The definitions of the hierarchical evaluation system are correct if and only if the algorithm terminates at Step 9.*

The definitions of the hierarchical evaluation system are incorrect if and only if the algorithm terminates at Step 1.

Proposition 2. *The computational complexity of the algorithms is $O(n)$.*

4 Application in IWfMS

The connection model between HFES and IWfMS is shown in Fig 1. There are three steps to connect HFES and IWfMS when constructing including a), b) and c). The first two steps are used to establish the hierarchical frame of the evaluation system, which is explained in the two sections above, and they also need to refer to the IWfMS corresponding to the evaluation requirements and the management information system.

In the third step c), the data source of each evaluation item needs to specify the necessary dynamic SQL statements with the variables corresponding to the organization of the information in the IWfMS. At the beginning of the evaluation procedure, the necessary parameters should be specified, too, such as the weights when the weighted averaging operation is used. The operational relationships among the items above are shown as the hollow wide arrows in Figure 1.

When the fuzzy evaluation system runs, the solid thin arrows are used to express the operational relationships of those works in italic format. When we select the

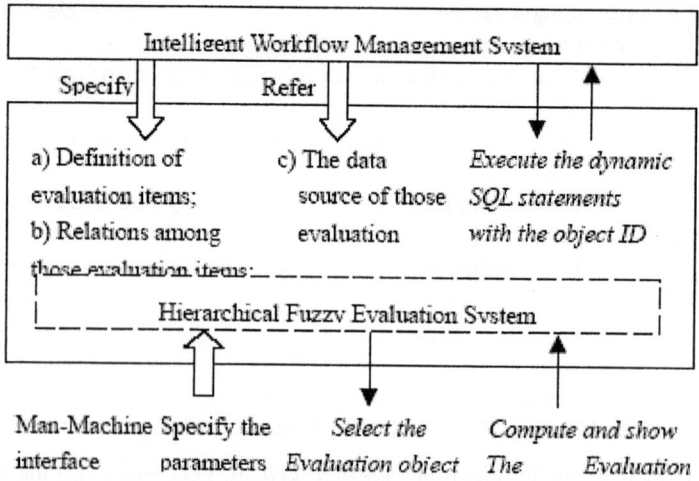

Fig. 1. The connection model between HFES and IWfMS

evaluation object(s), the system first replaces the variable of the dynamic SQL statements with the ID(s) of the evaluation object(s). Then the dynamic SQL statements are executed in the IWfMS and the results are returned. So we can achieve the evaluation results after the HFES's computing.

5 Experiment

Suppose we have a hierarchical evaluation frame in IWfMS as in Figure 2, which has three layers and nine endmost evaluation items corresponding to three parent evaluation items in the second layer respectively.

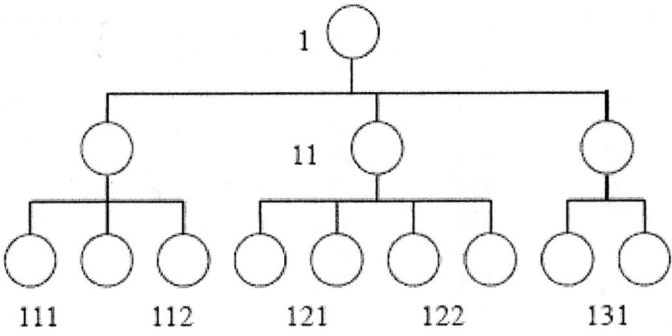

Fig. 2. The example

Taking the code with square brackets as its corresponding fuzzy proposition, the attributes of the evaluation items are list in Table 3, in which only the endmost evaluation items have the corresponding values. Those values are obtained by executing the corresponding dynamic SQL statements.

Table 3. The attributes of the evaluation items

Own no.	Layer no.	Parent no.	Value
[1]	1	0	Null
[11]	2	1	Null
[12]	2	1	Null
[13]	2	1	Null
[111]	3	11	0.60
[112]	3	11	0.70
[113]	3	11	0.90
[121]	3	12	0.85
[122]	3	12	0.65
[123]	3	12	0.80
[124]	3	12	0.55
[131]	3	13	0.35
[132]	3	13	0.85

Then the relative operations among those evaluation items are listed as follows:

[11] = ([111] ∨ [112]) → [113]
[12] = ([121] ∧ [122]) ∨ ([123] ∧ [124])
[13] = (~ [131]) ∨ [132]
[1] = 0.6 × [11] + 0.3 × [12] + 0.1 × [13]
     = 0.6 × [11] + 0.4 × (0.75 × [12] + 0.25 × [13])

Accordingly, the IRT of the example is as shown in Table 4, in which the attributes of all the relationships in the HFES are listed.

Table 4. The attributes of the items' relationships

Sequence no.	1st input	2nd input	Operation type	Output
1	111	112	D	0.60
2	A01	113	I	1.00
3	A02	11	E	1.00
4	121	122	C	0.85
5	123	124	C	0.80
6	A04	A05	D	0.80
7	A06	12	E	0.80
8	131	Null	N	0.65
9	A08	132	D	0.65
10	A09	13	E	0.65
11	A10	12	0.75	0.7625
12	A11	11	0.40	0.905
13	A12	1	E	0.905

As we have the values of the evaluation items in the EIT, the output of the evaluation system is equal to the practical result, 0.905, which shows the HFES is effective.

6 Conclusion

In this paper, the HFES is discussed in detail. In our following work, this method can be used to evaluate more objects, such as the activity in the workflow process. Meanwhile, applying the linguistic value to the hierarchical evaluation system is also an important direction [23]. Furthermore, the persons in any organization working with the IWfMS are also hierarchical, then the research to combine these two hierarchical frames is a challenge to us.

Acknowledgements

This research is supported by two National Natural Science Foundations of China (Grant No. : 60474022 & 70502025), the key project of Sichuan province (Grant No.:

04GG010-006-3) and the plan project of Zhejiang province in China (Grant No.: 2005C31005).

References

1. Tsai, H.C., Hsiao, S.W.: Evaluation of alternatives for product customization using fuzzy logic. Information Science 158 (2004) 233–262
2. Sadiq, R., Al-Zahrani, M.A., Sheikh, A.K., Husain, T., Farooq, S.: Performance evaluation of slow sand filters using fuzzy rule-based modelling. Environmental Modelling & Software 19 (2004) 507–515
3. Luis M., Liu J., Yang J., Francisco H.: A multigranular hierarchical linguistic model for design evaluation based on safety and cost analysis. International Journal of Intelligent System 22 (2005) 1161-1194
4. Shieha J.S., Linkensb D.A., Asbury A.J.: A hierarchical system of on-line advisory for monitoring and controlling the depth of anaesthesia using self-organizing fuzzy logic. Engineering Applications of Artificial Intelligence. 18 (2005) 307–316
5. Hsu, H.M., Chen, C.T.: Aggregation of fuzzy opinions under group decision making. Fuzzy Sets and Systems 79 (1996) 279–285
6. Samarasooriya, V.N.S., Varshney, P.K.: A fuzzy modeling approach to decision fusion under uncertainty. Fuzzy Sets and Systems 114 (2000) 59–69
7. Choi, D.Y.: A new aggregation method in a fuzzy environment. Decision Support System 25 (1999) 39–51
8. So, S.S., Cha, S.D., Kwon, Y.R.: Empirical evaluation of a fuzzy logic-based software quality prediction model. Fuzzy Sets and Systems 127 (2002) 199–208
9. Jaber, J.O., Mamlook, R., Awad, W.: Evaluation of energy conservation programs in residential sector using fuzzy logic methodology. Energy Policy 33 (2005) 1329–1338
10. Berenji H.R., Khedkar P.S.: Using fuzzy logic for performance evaluation in reinforcement learning. International Journal of Approximate Reasoning 18 (1998) 131–144
11. Li, H., Xu, Y.: Dynamic neural networks for logic formulae computing. Proc. 8th international conference on information processing 1 (2001) 1530–1535
12. Qiu X., Min L., Li H., Xu Y.: The classical logic formula computing based on dynamic neural networks, Journal of Wuhan University of Technology (Transportation Science and Engineering), 27 (2003) 750–753
13. Jouseau, E., Dorizzi, B.: Neural networks and fuzzy data fusion - Application to an on-line and real time vehicle detection system. Pattern Recognition Letters 20 (1999) 97–107
14. Nikravesh, M., Aminzadeh, F.: Mining and fusion of petroleum data with fuzzy logic and neural network agents. Journal of Petroleum Science and Engineering 29 (2001) 221–238
15. Salido, J.M.F., Murakami, S.: Rough set analysis of a general type of fuzzy data using transitive aggregations of fuzzy similarity relations. Fuzzy Sets and Systems 139 (2003) 635–660
16. Ferreira, D.M.R. Ferreira J.J.P.: Developing a reusable workflow engine. Journal of Systems Architecture 50 (2004) 309–324
17. Mahling, D.E., Craven, N., Croft, W.B.: From office automation to intelligent workflow systems. IEEE Intelligent System 10 (1995) 41–47
18. Moreno, M.D.R., Kearney, P.: Integrating AI planning techniques with workflow management system. Journal of Knowledge-base System 15 (2002) 285–291
19. Xu Y., Ruan D., Qin K., Liu J.: Lattice-valued logic, Springer, 2003

20. Yager, R.R.: Families of OWA operators. Fuzzy Sets and Systems 59 (1993) 125–148
21. Yager, R.R.: Quantifier guided aggregation using OWA operators. Internat. J. Intell. Systems 11 (1996) 49–73
22. Qiu X., Li H., Jian M., Xu Y.: The Fuzzy Hierarchical Evaluation System in Intelligent Workflow Management System. Proc. 2005 International Conference on Machine Learning and Cybernetics 5 (2005) 2676–2680
23. Ghyym, S.H.: A semi-linguistic fuzzy approach to multi-actor decision-making: application to aggregation of experts' judgments. Annals of Nuclear Energy 26 (1999) 1097–1112

A Solution to a System of Linear Equations with Fuzzy Numbers

Xingfang Zhang and Guangwu Meng

School of Mathematics System Science,
Liaocheng University,
Shandong 252059, P.R. China
zxf@lctu.edu.cn

Abstract. The concepts and solutions to a system of linear equations of interval numbers have been discussed previously. In this paper, we will extend the concepts and solutions to from the system of interval numbers to the system of fuzzy numbers. The basic properties of the system of linear equations with fuzzy numbers are discussed.

1 Introduction

In this paper, we will introduce the concept of a system of linear equations with fuzzy numbers. It first can be converted into the system of linear equations with interval numbers, and then the solution can be addressed by the approach given in [1]. However, such solution may have bad properties and depiction. Therefore, based on some underlying concepts of interval numbers, this paper first extends the system to the fuzzy number and then gives an improvement of the solution to the fuzzy numbers system of linear equations.

2 Systems of Linear Equations of Interval Numbers[1]

In this paper, the set of real numbers is denoted by R, the interval number $[a,b]$ $(a \leq b, a,b \in R)$ and is written as $\begin{bmatrix} b \\ a \end{bmatrix}$, and the following symbols will be used:

$$[R] = \{ \begin{bmatrix} b \\ a \end{bmatrix} : a \leq b, a,b \in R \},$$

$$[R]^n = \{ (\begin{bmatrix} y_1 \\ x_1 \end{bmatrix}, \begin{bmatrix} y_2 \\ x_2 \end{bmatrix}, ..., \begin{bmatrix} y_n \\ x_n \end{bmatrix}) : \begin{bmatrix} y_i \\ x_i \end{bmatrix} \in [R], i = 1,2,...n \}$$

$$[R]^n = \{ (\begin{bmatrix} y_1 \\ x_1 \end{bmatrix}, \begin{bmatrix} y_2 \\ x_2 \end{bmatrix}, ..., \begin{bmatrix} y_n \\ x_n \end{bmatrix}) : \begin{bmatrix} y_i \\ x_i \end{bmatrix} \in [R], i = 1,2,...n \},$$

$$[R^+] = \{\begin{bmatrix} b \\ a \end{bmatrix} : 0 \leq a \leq b, a,b \in R\}, \quad [R^-] = \{\begin{bmatrix} b \\ a \end{bmatrix} : a \leq b \leq 0, a,b \in R\},$$

$$[R^{-,+}] = \{\begin{bmatrix} b \\ a \end{bmatrix} : a < 0, b > 0, a,b \in R\}$$

Definition 2.1[2]. We call product $A_1 \times A_2 \times \cdots \times A_n, A_i \in \{[R^+],[R^-],[R^{-,+}]\}$, $i=1,2,\cdots,n$ as the branch of $[R]^n$.

Definition 2.2[3]. We call:

$$\begin{cases} \begin{bmatrix} b_{11} \\ a_{11} \end{bmatrix}\begin{bmatrix} y_1 \\ x_1 \end{bmatrix} + \begin{bmatrix} b_{12} \\ a_{12} \end{bmatrix}\begin{bmatrix} y_2 \\ x_2 \end{bmatrix} + \cdots + \begin{bmatrix} b_{1n} \\ a_{1n} \end{bmatrix}\begin{bmatrix} y_n \\ x_n \end{bmatrix} = \begin{bmatrix} d_1 \\ c_1 \end{bmatrix} \\ \begin{bmatrix} b_{21} \\ a_{21} \end{bmatrix}\begin{bmatrix} y_1 \\ x_1 \end{bmatrix} + \begin{bmatrix} b_{22} \\ a_{22} \end{bmatrix}\begin{bmatrix} y_2 \\ x_2 \end{bmatrix} + \cdots + \begin{bmatrix} b_{2n} \\ a_{2n} \end{bmatrix}\begin{bmatrix} y_n \\ x_n \end{bmatrix} = \begin{bmatrix} d_2 \\ c_2 \end{bmatrix} \\ \cdots \\ \begin{bmatrix} b_{s1} \\ a_{s1} \end{bmatrix}\begin{bmatrix} y_1 \\ x_1 \end{bmatrix} + \begin{bmatrix} b_{s2} \\ a_{s2} \end{bmatrix}\begin{bmatrix} y_2 \\ x_2 \end{bmatrix} + \cdots + \begin{bmatrix} b_{sn} \\ a_{sn} \end{bmatrix}\begin{bmatrix} y_n \\ x_n \end{bmatrix} = \begin{bmatrix} d_s \\ c_s \end{bmatrix} \end{cases} \quad (1)$$

the system of linear equations of interval numbers, and it may be denoted by SLEI, and:

$$\begin{bmatrix} y_j \\ x_j \end{bmatrix}, \begin{bmatrix} b_{ij} \\ a_{ij} \end{bmatrix}, \begin{bmatrix} d_i \\ c_i \end{bmatrix}, i=1,2,\ldots,s, j=1,2,\ldots,n$$

are called interval numbers, variable interval numbers, coefficient and interval constant terms, respectively.

Definition 2.3. Let B be a branch set of $[R]^n$. If there exists:

$$(\begin{bmatrix} y_1 \\ x_1 \end{bmatrix}, \begin{bmatrix} y_2 \\ x_2 \end{bmatrix}, \ldots, \begin{bmatrix} y_n \\ x_n \end{bmatrix}) \in B$$

such that it is a solution of SLEI (1), then we say SLEI(1) has its solution in B; otherwise we conclude that SLEI (1) has no solution in B.

Remark 2.4. From Theorem 1.3, by determining the signs of x_i and y_i in variable $\begin{bmatrix} y_i \\ x_i \end{bmatrix}$, we can obtain only the result of $\begin{bmatrix} b_i \\ a_i \end{bmatrix}\begin{bmatrix} y_i \\ x_i \end{bmatrix}$. This is the background to the introduction of Theorem 1.6.

The proof of the following theorem are all omitted.

Theorem 2.5. Let B be a branch set of $[R]^n$. For each $(\begin{bmatrix} y_1 \\ x_1 \end{bmatrix}, \begin{bmatrix} y_2 \\ x_2 \end{bmatrix}, \ldots, \begin{bmatrix} y_n \\ x_n \end{bmatrix}) \in B$, there exists $i \in \{1,2,\ldots s\}$ and

$$a_1 \in \begin{bmatrix} b_{i1} \\ a_{i1} \end{bmatrix}, a_2 \in \begin{bmatrix} b_{i2} \\ a_{i2} \end{bmatrix}, \ldots, a_n \in \begin{bmatrix} b_{in} \\ a_{in} \end{bmatrix}$$

and

$$x_1' \in \begin{bmatrix} y_1 \\ x_1 \end{bmatrix}, x_2' \in \begin{bmatrix} y_2 \\ x_2 \end{bmatrix}, \ldots, x_n' \in \begin{bmatrix} y_n \\ x_n \end{bmatrix}$$

such that $a_1 x_1' + a_2 x_2' + \cdots + a_n x_n' \notin \begin{bmatrix} d_i \\ c_i \end{bmatrix}$, then SELI (1) has no solution in B.

Suppose that B is a branch set of $[R]^n$. Let us find the solution of SELI (1) in B. From SELI (1) we get:

$$D = \begin{bmatrix} \begin{bmatrix} b_{11} \\ a_{11} \end{bmatrix} & \begin{bmatrix} b_{12} \\ a_{12} \end{bmatrix} & \cdots & \begin{bmatrix} b_{1n} \\ a_{1n} \end{bmatrix} & \begin{bmatrix} d_1 \\ c_1 \end{bmatrix} \\ \begin{bmatrix} b_{21} \\ a_{21} \end{bmatrix} & \begin{bmatrix} b_{22} \\ a_{22} \end{bmatrix} & \cdots & \begin{bmatrix} b_{2n} \\ a_{2n} \end{bmatrix} & \begin{bmatrix} d_2 \\ c_2 \end{bmatrix} \\ \cdots & \cdots & \cdots & \cdots & \cdots \\ \begin{bmatrix} b_{s1} \\ a_{s1} \end{bmatrix} & \begin{bmatrix} b_{s2} \\ a_{s2} \end{bmatrix} & \cdots & \begin{bmatrix} b_{sn} \\ a_{sn} \end{bmatrix} & \begin{bmatrix} d_s \\ c_s \end{bmatrix} \end{bmatrix},$$

This is called the interval augmented matrix of (1). In $\begin{bmatrix} y_i \\ x_i \end{bmatrix}$ the signs of x_i and y_i are ensured by B, and we have:

$$\begin{bmatrix} b_{ij} \\ a_{ij} \end{bmatrix} \begin{bmatrix} y_j \\ x_j \end{bmatrix} = \begin{bmatrix} r_{ij1} x_j + r_{ij2} y_j \\ r_{ij3} x_j + r_{ij4} y_j \end{bmatrix}, i = 1, 2, \ldots s, j = 1, 2, \ldots, n.,$$

where

$$r_{ijk} \in \{a_{ij}, b_{ij}, 0\}, i = 1, 2, \ldots s, j = 1, \ldots, n, , k = 1, 2, 3, 4.$$

Now we construct a new matrix as follows:

$$D_B = \begin{bmatrix} \begin{bmatrix} r_{1111} & r_{112} \\ r_{113} & r_{114} \end{bmatrix} & \begin{bmatrix} r_{121} & r_{122} \\ r_{123} & r_{124} \end{bmatrix} & \cdots & \begin{bmatrix} r_{1n1} & r_{1n2} \\ r_{1n3} & r_{1n4} \end{bmatrix} & \begin{bmatrix} d_1 \\ c_1 \end{bmatrix} \\ \begin{bmatrix} r_{211} & r_{212} \\ r_{213} & r_{214} \end{bmatrix} & \begin{bmatrix} r_{221} & r_{222} \\ r_{223} & r_{224} \end{bmatrix} & \cdots & \begin{bmatrix} r_{2n1} & r_{2n2} \\ r_{2n3} & r_{2n4} \end{bmatrix} & \begin{bmatrix} d_2 \\ c_2 \end{bmatrix} \\ \cdots & \cdots & \cdots & \cdots & \cdots \\ \begin{bmatrix} r_{s11} & r_{s12} \\ r_{s13} & r_{s14} \end{bmatrix} & \begin{bmatrix} r_{s21} & r_{s22} \\ r_{s23} & r_{s24} \end{bmatrix} & \cdots & \begin{bmatrix} r_{sn1} & r_{sn2} \\ r_{sn3} & r_{sn4} \end{bmatrix} & \begin{bmatrix} d_s \\ c_s \end{bmatrix} \end{bmatrix},$$

We call this a transition matrix of SELI(1) in correlation to the branch set B.

Furthermore, we can obtain a white matrix:

$$D_B^* = \begin{bmatrix} r_{111} & r_{112} & r_{121} & r_{122} & \cdots & r_{1s1} & r_{1s2} & d_1 \\ r_{113} & r_{114} & r_{123} & r_{124} & \cdots & r_{1n3} & r_{1n4} & c_1 \\ \cdots & \cdots & \cdots & \cdots & & \cdots & & \\ r_{s11} & r_{s12} & r_{s21} & r_{s22} & \cdots & r_{sn1} & r_{sn2} & d_s \\ r_{s13} & r_{s14} & r_{s23} & r_{s24} & \cdots & r_{sn3} & r_{sn4} & c_s \end{bmatrix},$$

This is called a white dependent matrix of SELI(1) in correlation to the branch set B.

Let us take D_B^* as an augmented matrix and construct a system of linear equations:

$$\begin{cases} r_{111}x_1 + r_{112}y_1 + r_{121}x_2 + r_{122}y_2 + \cdots + r_{1n1}x_n + r_{1n2}y_n = d_1 \\ r_{113}x_1 + r_{114}y_1 + r_{123}x_2 + r_{124}y_2 + \cdots + r_{1n3}x_n + r_{1n4}y_4 = c_1 \\ \cdots \quad \cdots \quad \cdots \quad \cdots \quad \cdots \quad \cdots \\ r_{s11}x_1 + r_{s12}y_1 + r_{s21}x_2 + r_{s22}x_2 + \cdots + r_{sn1}x_n + r_{sn2}y_n = d_s \\ r_{s13}x_1 + r_{s14}y_1 + r_{s23}x_2 + r_{s24}y_2 + \cdots + r_{sn3}x_n + r_{sn4}y_n = c_s \end{cases} \quad (2)$$

This is called a system of white linear equations (SWLE) in correlation to SELI(1).

Theorem 2.6. Let B be a branch set o $[R]^n$ and suppos that ($x_{10}, y_{10}, x_{20}, y_{20}, \ldots, x_{n0}, y_{n0}$) is a solution of SWLE (2). Then

$$\vec{\otimes} = (\begin{bmatrix} y_{10} \\ x_{10} \end{bmatrix}, \begin{bmatrix} y_{20} \\ x_{20} \end{bmatrix}, \ldots, \begin{bmatrix} y_{n0} \\ x_{n0} \end{bmatrix})$$

is the solution of SELI(1) in B if $\vec{\otimes} \in B$ 4

3 System of Linear Equation of Fuzzy Numbers

In this paper, we only discuss that fuzzy numbe [3] $A^{(m)}[a,b]$ ($A(a) = A(b) = 0, A(m) = 1$) are continuous on close interval.

We will introduce the concept system of linear equation of fuzzy numbers, and give solving its method based on simplification of operations of addition, subtraction, multiplication and division on fuzzy numbers [4].

Definition 3.1. Let fuzzy number $A^{\lambda(m)}[a,b]$. If the membership function of the fuzzy number $A[a,b]$ is continuous and austerely monotone on $[a,m]$ and $[m,b]$, respectively, then it is called an austerely monotone continuous fuzzy number.

Definition 3.2. We call:

$$\begin{cases} A_{11}^{(m_{11})}[a_{11},b_{11}]X_1[x_1,y_1] + A_{12}^{(m_{12})}[a_{12},b_{12}]X_2[x_2,y_2] \\ + \cdots A_{1n}^{(m_{1n})}[a_{1n},b_{1n}]X_n[x_n,y_n] = C_1^{(l_1)}[c_1,d_1] \\ A_{21}^{(m_{21})}[a_{21},b_{21}]X_1[x_1,y_1] + A_{22}^{(m_{22})}[a_{22},b_{22}]X_2[x_2,y_2] \\ + \cdots + A_{2n}^{(m_{2n})}[a_{2n},b_{2n}]X_n[x_n,y_n] = C_2^{(l_2)}[c_2,d_2] \\ \cdots\cdots\cdots\cdots\cdots\cdots\cdots\cdots\cdots\cdots\cdots\cdots \\ \cdots\cdots\cdots\cdots\cdots\cdots\cdots\cdots\cdots\cdots\cdots\cdots \\ A_{s1}^{(m_{s1})}[a_{n1},b_{n1}]X_1[x_1,y_1] + A_{s2}^{(m_{s2})}[a_{n2},b_{n2}]X_2[x_2,y_2] \\ + \cdots A_{sn}^{(m_{sn})}[a_{nn},y_{nn}]X_n[x_n,y_n] = C_s^{(l_s)}[c_s,d_s] \end{cases}$$

as n unknown in the system of linear equations of fuzzy numbers, it may be denoted by SLEF, and the fuzzy numbers $X_j[x_j,y_j], A_{ij}[a_{ij},b_{ij}], C_i[c_i,d_i]$, ($i=1,2,\ldots,n, j=1,2,\ldots,s$) are called fuzzy numbers variable, fuzzy numbers coefficient and fuzzy constant terms, respectively.

We first discuss the circs of $s = n = 1$.

Theorem 3.3. Let SLEF

$$A^{(m)}[a,b] \times X[x,y] = B^{(n)}[e,f] \quad (\#),$$

where $A^{(m)}[a,b]$ and $B^{(n)}[e,f]$ ($a \neq 0$ or $b \neq 0, m \neq 0$) are all austerely monotone continuous fuzzy numbers.

If $X[x,y]$ is the solution of (#), then:

(1) $[x,y]$ is the solution of linear equation $[a,b] \times [x,y] = [e,f]$;

(2) 1^0 $X(\dfrac{n}{m}) = 1$.

If $x < \dfrac{n}{m} < y$, then $X(x) = X(y) = 0$; If $x = \dfrac{n}{m}$, then $X(x) = 1$;

If $y = \dfrac{n}{m}$, then $X(y) = 1$;

2^0 $\forall x_t \in (x, \dfrac{n}{m}) \cup (\dfrac{n}{m}, y)$, only there exists (a_t, e_t), $a_t \in [a,b]$, $e_t \in [e,f]$ such that $a_t \times x_t = e$ and $A(a_t) = B(e_t)$, so that $X(x_t) = A(a_t)$.

Proof. (1) and (2) 1^0 are apparent. We prove (2) 2^0. For $x_t \in (x, \frac{n}{m})$ (Proof of $x_t \in (\frac{n}{m}, y)$ is similar to it), if $[a,m] \times [x, \frac{n}{m}] = [e,n]$ (Rest circs are similar to it).

Let $F(a_t) = B(a_t x_t) - A(a_t)$, $a_t \in [a,m]$, such that $F(a_t)$ are austerely monotone continuous on $[a,m]$, and

$$F(ax_t) = B(ax_t) - A(a) = B(ax_t) - 0 \geq 0,$$
$$F(mx_t) = B(mx_t) - A(m) = B(ax_t) - 1 \leq 0,$$

By zero theorem, so that only there exists $a_t \in [a,m]$ such that $F(a_t) = B(a_t x_t) - A(a_t) = 0$ so that there exists only (a_t, e_t), $a_t \in [a,b], e_t \in [e,f]$ such that $a_t \times x_t = e$ and $A(a_t) = B(e_t)$. Therefore, $X(x_t) = A(a_t)$.

We secondly discuss the circs of $s = n = 2$.

Theorem 3.4. Let binary SLEF

$$\begin{cases} A_{11}^{(m_{11})}[a_{11},b_{11}]X_1[x_1,y_1] + A_{12}^{(m_{12})}[a_{12},b_{12}]X_2[x_2,y_2] \\ = C_1^{(n_1)}[c_1,d_1] \\ A_{12}^{(m_{21})}[a_{21},b_{21}]X_1[x_1,y_1] + A_{22}^{(m_{22})}[a_{22},b_{22}]X_2[x_2,y_2] \\ = C_2^{(n_2)}[c_2,d_2] \end{cases} \quad (*)$$

If $(X_1[x_1,y_1], X_2[x_2,y_2])$ is the solution of (*), then
(1) $[x_1,y_1],[x_2,y_2])$ is the solution of SLEI

$$\begin{cases} [a_{11},b_{11}][x_1,y_1] + [a_{12},b_{12}][x_2,y_2] = [c_1,d_1] \\ [a_{21},b_{21}][x_1,y_1] + [a_{22},b_{22}][x_2,y_2] = [c_2,d_2] \end{cases}$$

(2) $\forall \lambda \in [0\ 1]$, let λ-cross section of fuzzy number $A_{ij}^{(m_{ij})}$ ($i = 1,2, j = 1,2$) are $[a_{ij\lambda}, b_{ij\lambda}]$ ($i = 1,2, j = 1,2$) respectively, λ-cross section of fuzzy numbers C_i^i ($i = 1,2$) are $[c_{i\lambda}, d_{i\lambda}]$ respectively, and if that $([x_{1\lambda}, y_{1\lambda}],[x_{2\lambda}, y_{2\lambda}])$ is the solution of SLEI

$$\begin{cases} [a_{11\lambda},b_{11\lambda}][x_{1\lambda},y_{1\lambda}]+[a_{12\lambda},b_{12\lambda}][x_{2\lambda},y_{2\lambda}]=[c_{1\lambda},d_{1\lambda}] \\ [a_{21\lambda},b_{21\lambda}][x_{1\lambda},y_{1\lambda}]+[a_{22\lambda},b_{22\lambda}][x_{2\lambda},y_{2\lambda}]=[c_{2\lambda},d_{2\lambda}] \end{cases}$$

then

$$X_1(x_{1\lambda})=X_1(y_{1\lambda})=X_2(x_{2\lambda})=X_2(y_{2\lambda})=\lambda.$$

Especially, if $(z_1,z_2)(z_1 \in [x_1,y_1], z_2 \in [x_2,y_2])$ is the solution of

$$\begin{cases} m_{11}z_1 + m_{12}z_2 = n_1 \\ m_{21}z_1 + m_{22}z_2 = n_2 \end{cases}$$

then $X_1(z_1)=X_2(z_2)=1$, $X_1(x_1)=X_1(y_1)=X_2(x_2)=X_2(y_2)=0$.

Proof. By simplified four arithmetic operations [4,5] of fuzzy numbers, this conclusion is evident.

Theorem 3.5. To find all the solutions of SLEF

$$\begin{cases} A^{(2)}{}_{11}[1,4]X_1[x_1,y_1]+A^{(1)}{}_{12}[0,3]X_2[x_2,y_2] \\ =C^{(6)}{}_1[1,25] \\ A^{(1)}{}_{21}[0,2]]X_1[x_1,y_1]+A^{(3)}{}_{22}[1,5]]X_2[x_2,y_2] \\ =C^{(8)}{}_2[1,23] \end{cases}$$

where

$$A_{11}^{(2)}(x) = \begin{cases} x-1 & x\in [0,1] \\ \dfrac{1}{-2}(x-4) & x\in (2,4] \end{cases},$$

$$A_{12}^{(1)}(x) = \begin{cases} x & x\in [0,1] \\ \dfrac{1}{-2}(x-3) & x\in (1,3] \end{cases},$$

$$A_{21}^{(1)}(x) = \begin{cases} x & x\in [0,1] \\ -(x-2) & x\in (1,2] \end{cases}$$

$$A_{22}^{(3)}(x) = \begin{cases} \dfrac{1}{2}(x-1) & x\in [1,3] \\ \dfrac{1}{-2}(x-5) & x\in (3,5] \end{cases}$$

$$C_1^{(6)}(x) = \begin{cases} \dfrac{1}{5}(x-1) & x \in [1,6] \\ \dfrac{1}{-19}(x-25) & x \in (6,25] \end{cases},$$

$$C_2^{(8)}(x) = \begin{cases} \dfrac{1}{7}(x-1) & x \in [1,8] \\ \dfrac{1}{-15}(x-23) & x \in (8,23] \end{cases}$$

1^0 First to find all the solutions of SLEI

$$\begin{cases} \begin{bmatrix} 4 \\ 1 \end{bmatrix} \begin{bmatrix} y_1 \\ x_1 \end{bmatrix} + \begin{bmatrix} 3 \\ 0 \end{bmatrix} \begin{bmatrix} y_2 \\ x_2 \end{bmatrix} = \begin{bmatrix} 25 \\ 1 \end{bmatrix} \\ \begin{bmatrix} 2 \\ 0 \end{bmatrix} \begin{bmatrix} y_1 \\ x_1 \end{bmatrix} + \begin{bmatrix} 5 \\ 1 \end{bmatrix} \begin{bmatrix} y_2 \\ x_2 \end{bmatrix} = \begin{bmatrix} 23 \\ 1 \end{bmatrix} \end{cases} \quad (3.1)$$

In $[R^+] \times [R^+]$, $\vec{\otimes} = (\begin{bmatrix} 4 \\ 1 \end{bmatrix}, \begin{bmatrix} 3 \\ 1 \end{bmatrix})$ is the solution of (3.1). Apparently, no solution exists in the rest of the branch set of $[R]^2$

2^0 $X_1(2) = Y_1(2) = 1, X_1(1) = Y_1(4) = X_2(1) = Y_2(3) = 0$.
$\forall \lambda : 0 < \lambda < 1$, have

$$\begin{cases} [\lambda+1, 4-2\lambda].[x_{1\lambda}, y_{1\lambda}] + [\lambda, 3-2\lambda].[x_{2\lambda}, y_{2\lambda}] \\ = [5\lambda+1, 25-19\lambda] \\ [\lambda, 2-\lambda].[x_{1\lambda}, y_{1\lambda}] + [1+2\lambda].[1+2\lambda].[5-2\lambda].[x_{2\lambda}, y_{2\lambda}] \\ = [7\lambda+1, 23-15\lambda] \end{cases}$$

then

$$\begin{cases} (\lambda^2 + 3\lambda + 1)x_{2\lambda} = 2\lambda^2 + 7\lambda + 1 & (1) \\ x_{1\lambda} = -2\lambda + (1+\lambda)x_{2\lambda} & (2) \\ (7-4\lambda)y_{2\lambda} = -4\lambda^2 - 9\lambda + 21 & (3) \\ y_{1\lambda} = 1 - 2\lambda + y_{2\lambda} & (4) \end{cases}$$

so that $\lambda = \dfrac{7 - 3x_{2\lambda} - \sqrt{(5x_{2\lambda}^2 - 30x_{2\lambda} + 41)}}{2(x_{2\lambda} - 2)}$, $x_{2\lambda_0} = 1$, $\lambda_0 = 0$. and

$$\lambda = \frac{9-4y_{2\lambda}+\sqrt{(4y_{2\lambda}-9)^2+16(21-7y_{2\lambda})}}{-8}$$

by $y_{2\lambda_0}=3$, $\lambda_0=0$.

Therefore, the fuzzy number

$$X_2[1,3] = \begin{cases} \dfrac{7-3x-\sqrt{5x^2-30x+41}}{2(x-2)} & x\in[1,2] \\ \dfrac{9-4x+\sqrt{(4x-9)^2+16(21-7x)}}{-8} & x\in(2,3] \end{cases}.$$

To find $X_1[1,4]$ from it (omit).

In a general way, we have arrived at:

Theorem 3.6. Let SLEF (*)

$$\begin{cases} A_{11}^{(m_{11})}[a_{11},b_{11}]X_1[x_1,y_1]+A_{12}^{(m_{12})}[a_{12},b_{12}]X_2[x_2,y_2] \\ +\cdots A_{1n}^{(m_{1n})}[a_{1n},b_{1n}]X_n[x_n,y_n]=C_1^{(l_1)}[c_1,d_1] \\ A_{21}^{(m_{21})}[a_{21},b_{21}]X_1[x_1,y_1]+A_{22}^{(m_{22})}[a_{22},b_{22}]X_2[x_2,y_2] \\ +\cdots+A_{2n}^{(m_{2n})}[a_{2n},b_{2n}]X_n[x_n,y_n]=C_2^{(l_2)}[c_2,d_2] \\ \cdots\cdots\cdots\cdots\cdots\cdots\cdots\cdots\cdots\cdots\cdots\cdots\cdots \\ \cdots\cdots\cdots\cdots\cdots\cdots\cdots\cdots\cdots\cdots\cdots\cdots\cdots \\ A_{s1}^{(m_{s1})}[a_{n1},b_{n1}]X_1[x_1,y_1]+A_{s2}^{(m_{s2})}[a_{n2},b_{n2}]X_2[x_2,y_2] \\ +\cdots A_{sn}^{(m_{sn})}[a_{nn},y_{nn}]X_n[x_n,y_n]=C_s^{(l_s)}[c_s,d_s] \end{cases}$$

where $X_1[x_1,y_1], X_2[x_2,y_2],..,X_n[x_n,y_n]$ is variable respectively.

If $(X_1[x_1,y_1], X_2[x_2,y_2],..,X_n[x_n,y_n])$ is the solution of (*), then

(1) $([x_1,y_1],[x_2,y_2],..,[x_n,y_n])$ is the solution of SLEI by

$$\begin{cases} \begin{bmatrix} b_{11} \\ a_{11} \end{bmatrix}\begin{bmatrix} y_1 \\ x_1 \end{bmatrix}+\begin{bmatrix} b_{12} \\ a_{12} \end{bmatrix}\begin{bmatrix} y_2 \\ x_2 \end{bmatrix}+\cdots+\begin{bmatrix} b_{1n} \\ a_{1n} \end{bmatrix}\begin{bmatrix} y_n \\ x_n \end{bmatrix}=\begin{bmatrix} d_1 \\ c_1 \end{bmatrix} \\ \begin{bmatrix} b_{21} \\ a_{21} \end{bmatrix}\begin{bmatrix} y_1 \\ x_1 \end{bmatrix}+\begin{bmatrix} b_{22} \\ a_{22} \end{bmatrix}\begin{bmatrix} y_2 \\ x_2 \end{bmatrix}+\cdots\begin{bmatrix} b_{2n} \\ a_{2n} \end{bmatrix}\begin{bmatrix} y_n \\ x_n \end{bmatrix}=\begin{bmatrix} d_2 \\ c_2 \end{bmatrix}; \\ \cdots\cdots\cdots\cdots\cdots\cdots\cdots\cdots\cdots\cdots\cdots \\ \begin{bmatrix} b_{s1} \\ a_{s1} \end{bmatrix}\begin{bmatrix} y_1 \\ x_1 \end{bmatrix}+\begin{bmatrix} b_{s2} \\ a_{s2} \end{bmatrix}\begin{bmatrix} y_2 \\ x_2 \end{bmatrix}+\cdots+\begin{bmatrix} b_{sn} \\ a_{sn} \end{bmatrix}\begin{bmatrix} y_n \\ x_n \end{bmatrix}=\begin{bmatrix} d_s \\ c_s \end{bmatrix} \end{cases}$$

(2) $\forall \lambda \in [0\ 1]$, let λ - cross section of fuzzy number $A_{ij}^{(m_{ij})}$ ($i=1,2,...,s, j=1,2,...,n$) are $[a_{ij\lambda}, b_{ij\lambda}](i=1,2,...,s, j=1,2,...,n)$ respectively, and λ cross section of fuzzy numbers C_i^i ($i=1,2,...s$) are $[c_{i\lambda}, d_{i\lambda}]$ ($i=1,2,...,s$) respectively, and if $([x_{1\lambda}, y_{1\lambda}], [x_{2\lambda}, y_{2\lambda}], ..., [x_{n\lambda}, y_{n\lambda}])$ is the solution of SLEI

$$\begin{cases} [a_{11\lambda}, b_{11\lambda}][x_{1\lambda}, y_{1\lambda}] + [a_{12\lambda}, b_{12\lambda}][x_{2\lambda}, y_{2\lambda}] \\ + \cdots + [a_{1n\lambda}, b_{1n\lambda}][x_{n\lambda}, y_{n\lambda}] = [c_{1\lambda}, d_{1\lambda}] \\ [a_{21\lambda}, b_{21\lambda}][x_{1\lambda}, y_{1\lambda}] + [a_{22\lambda}, b_{22\lambda}][x_{2\lambda}, y_{2\lambda}] \\ + \cdots + [a_{2n\lambda}, b_{n\lambda}][x_{n\lambda}, y_{n\lambda}] = [c_{2\lambda}, d_{2\lambda}] \\ \cdots\cdots\cdots\cdots\cdots\cdots\cdots\cdots \\ \cdots\cdots\cdots\cdots\cdots\cdots\cdots\cdots \\ [a_{s1\lambda}, b_{s1\lambda}][x_{1\lambda}, y_{1\lambda}] + [a_{s2\lambda}, b_{s2\lambda}][x_{2\lambda}, y_{2\lambda}] \\ + \cdots + [a_{sn\lambda}, b_{sn\lambda}][x_{n\lambda}, y_{n\lambda}] = [c_{n\lambda}, y_{n\lambda}] \end{cases}$$

Then

$$X_1(x_{1\lambda}) = X_1(y_{1\lambda}) = X_2(x_{2\lambda}) = X_2(y_{2\lambda})$$
$$= \cdots = X_n(x_{n\lambda}) = X_n(y_{n\lambda}) = \lambda$$

especially, if $(z_1, z_2, ...z_n)$ $(z_1 \in [x_1, y_1], z_2 \in [x_2, y_2], ..., z_n \in [x_n, y_n])$ is the solution of

$$\begin{cases} m_{11}z_1 + m_{12}z_2 + ... + m_{1n}z_n = l_1 \\ m_{21}z_1 + m_{22}z_2 + ... + m_{2n}z_n = l_2 \\ \cdot\ \ \cdot\ \ \cdot\ \ \cdot\ \ \cdot\ \ \cdot\ \ \cdot\ \ \cdot\ \ \cdot \\ m_{s1}z_1 + m_{s2}z_2 + ... + m_{sn}z_n = l_s \end{cases}$$

then

$$X_1(z_1) = X_2(z_2) = ... = X_n(z_n) = 1$$

$$X_1(x_1) = X_1(y_1) = X_2(x_2) = X_2(y_2)$$
$$= ... = X_n(x_1) = X_n(y_n) = 0.$$

4 Conclusion

In this paper, we first have improved the existed method for solving the system of linear equation of interval numbers. We have presented a concept of a system of linear equation of fuzzy numbers and given an approach to its solution. The future work will include the simplified representation of the solution.

Acknowledgements

We acknowledge with thanks the anonymous referees and the editors for their valuable comments and proofreading, which have led to a substantial improvement of this paper. This research is supported by the fund of Shandong Natural Science.

References

1. Zhang Xingfang.: A kind of system grey linear equations and the solution of its matrix. The journal of grey system 1.2:2(1990),119-129
2. The property of four arithmetic operation of fuzzy numbers and linear equation of fuzzy number. Proceedings of 2003 IEEE International Conference on Machine Learning and Cybernetics, pp2669-2671..
3. Li HongXing , Wang PeiZhuang.: Fuzzy mathematics, Beijing National Defense Industry Publishing Company (in Chinese), 1993.
4. Zhang Xingfang.: The simplification of addition and subtraction operations of fuzzy numbers . The Journal of Fuzzy Math.4(2002),959-968

Evolutionary Synthesis of Micromachines Using Supervisory Multiobjective Interactive Evolutionary Computation

Raffi Kamalian[1], Ying Zhang[2], Hideyuki Takagi[1], and Alice M. Agogino[2]

[1] Faculty of Design, Kyushu University,
Fukuoka 815-8540, Japan
{raffi, takagi}@design.kyushu-u.ac.jp
[2] BEST Lab, 6102 Etcheverry Hall, University of California, Berkeley,
CA 94720, USA
{yzh, agogino}@berkeley.edu

Abstract. A novel method of Interactive Evolutionary Computation (IEC) for the design of microelectromechanical systems (MEMS) is presented. As the main limitation of IEC is human fatigue, an alternate implementation that requires a reduced amount of human interaction is proposed. The method is applied to a multi-objective genetic algorithm, with the human in a supervisory role, providing evaluation only every n^{th}-generation. Human interaction is applied to the evolution process by means of Pareto-rank shifting for the fitness calculation used in selection. The results of a test on 13 users shows that this IEC method can produce statistically significant better MEMS resonators than fully automated non-interactive evolutionary approaches.

1 Introduction

In this paper we present a new method of synthesis utilizing human interaction to augment the use of evolutionary computation to generate resonating microelectromechanical systems (MEMS). MEMS, also known as Micromachines are electromechanical mechanisms and transducers created using IC microfabrication techniques. In this paper we use the example application of the design of a resonating mass, a simple MEMS example that can be extended to the design of MEMS-based RF filters or inertial sensors.

1.1 MEMS Evolutionary Synthesis

An evolutionary MEMS synthesis tool has been presented in [1], [2]. A multi-objective genetic algorithm (MOGA)[3], as well as simulated annealing (SA) [4] have been used as an evolutionary computation method for the design of a variety of MEMS test applications, including the design of electrostatic actuators [5],[6], accelerometers and vibrating rate gyroscopes [7].

A MEMS simulator is used by the evolutionary algorithm to predict the performance of the candidate design. Unfortunately to remain tractable for the evolutionary process, simplified, reduced order modelling tools can not predict the sensitivity of a design to fabrication uncertainty and do not include the effects of certain design features on performance. A fabrication and characterization study (Fig. 1) has shown that these sensitivities can dramatically affect the quality of the solutions generated. Many of these potential problems are clearly visible to a human user visually observing the design layout, but they would be difficult, if not impossible, to mathematically model and simulate in software and incorporate into a flexible MEMS synthesis program. A human's opinion, based on their experience, expert domain knowledge or simple preference can not be easily coded into a numerical fitness function. Therefore we developed a human-interactive MEMS design tool to allow the inclusion of this human knowledge.

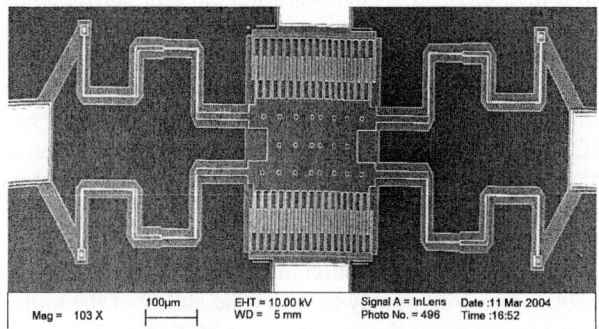

Fig. 1. Example of resonating micromachine design generated by our MOGA tool that has been fabricated and characterized. The center mass is approximately 0.2mm wide.

1.2 Interactive Evolutionary Computation

Interactive Evolutionary Computation (IEC) is a method for optimizing a system using subjective human evaluation as part of the optimization process. It is well suited for optimizing systems whose evaluation criteria are preferential or subjective, such as graphics, music and design, and systems that can be evaluated based on expert's domain knowledge. Fields in which this technology has been applied includes graphic arts and animation, 3-D CG lighting, music, editorial design, industrial design, facial image generation, speech and image processing, hearing aid fitting, virtual reality, media database retrieval, data mining, control and robotics, food industry, geophysics, education, entertainment, social system, and others [8].

In [9], an initial method of using IEC to further hone MEMS designs generated by a MOGA was presented. In this case output from the automated MOGA tool was used to draw the initial designs for IEC. This allowed the human user to further evolve the output into designs that better met their expert opinions and goals. A single objective genetic algorithm used the user's evaluation for fitness ranking. A user study presented shows that the combination of the automated and human interactive can produce better designs than by simple automated evolutionary synthesis alone. A simple example of a human's evaluation of two MEMS resonating mass designs can be seen in Fig. 2.

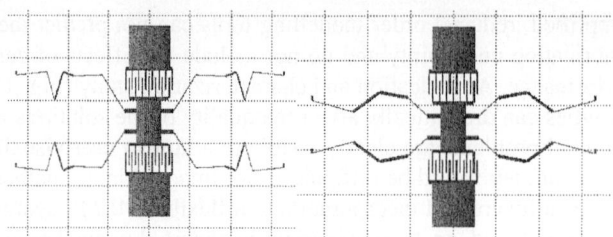

Fig. 2. (a) left: MEMS resonator design produced by Non-interactive MOGA, given a poor score by a user due to potential stress concentrations in the legs. (b) right: High scoring MOGA+IEC design generated by the same user, free of perceived negative traits.

One of the limitations of IEC that does not exist in conventional, non-interactive EC, is that the humans evaluating the fitness of designs suffer from fatigue, and therefore we would like to search out new methods of better matching the capabilities of the human and the computer to exploit their strengths and minimize their weaknesses.

Based on the observations of the user study, presented in [10], we developed a new version of EC with human interaction. This new implementation differs in that the human's participation is more in a supervisory role, utilizing the tireless computation power of computer but still allowing the human to input their expert knowledge and visual perception of a design when desired.

In this paper we present a description of the new interactive EC tool for MEMS, as well as the results from a user study to verify the ability of the tools to produce better output, compared to our original non-interactive MOGA tool.

2 Alternate MEMS IEC Implementation

The original IEC MEMS synthesis, as presented in [9], used a population size of 27, and evaluated up to 10 generations. A human evaluated each individual of each generation based on the layout as well as the performance predicted by a simulator tool. The score given ranged from 1 to 5 and was selected by the user by a mouse click (see Fig. 3 for user interface). The human user generated a single subjective score based on his/her opinion of the shape as well as the performance in four objectives, in essence mentally computing a weighting function to generate a score with a range of 1 to 5.

A user study of 11 test subjects showed that IEC produced statistically significant better results than non-interactive evolutionary synthesis. With up to 270 human evaluations required, human fatigue was a concern and limited the number of generations the evolution could continue.

In our original user study, we identified two interesting types of reactions from the human when scoring the individuals via IEC. When humans detected design features they did not like they generally immediately scored that design very low regardless of the objective performance of that individual. This situation can be described as a human-applied constraint violation, or as the human attempting to screen the population by culling (or 'killing off') designs of which they disapprove.

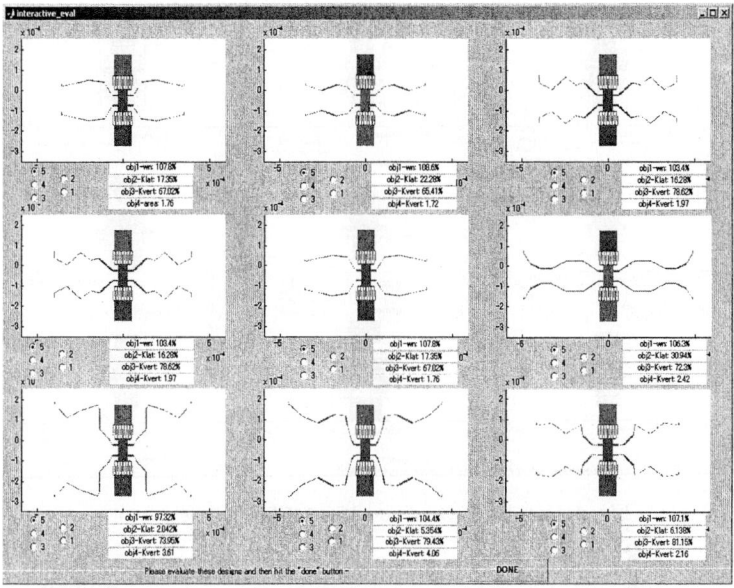

Fig. 3. User interface of original IEC MEMS synthesis tool

The second type of behavior was the opposite, where a design feature of interest prompted the human to score a design highly despite poor performance in the objective space. In a normal GA, this design would not be likely to pass along its features to subsequent generations, but IEC allows the human to give it a 'stay of execution', so that its features are allowed to propagate to future generations of the design.

2.1 Improved IEC Approach

We chose to build upon these observations to create a version of IEC where the human's interactions are limited to these two types of action. We developed an interface (see Fig. 4) where the human can chose to give either a *promote* (positive) or *demote* (negative) reaction to each design presented. This human evaluation is then used to shift the ranking of the design accordingly. Our MOGA implementation uses Pareto ranking to handle multiobjectives, which is then used by a roulette wheel function for selection for genetic operations. Therefore the human interaction is used to adjust the Pareto ranking of a design (upwards or downwards). The default choice is to not take any action for a design, leaving its Pareto ranking unaltered.

In practice this means a design not on the Pareto frontier may be artificially promoted to the Pareto dominant set by the human, which will allow it to be passed to the next generation by elitism, and make it much more likely to be chosen as a parent for crossover. Likewise a Pareto frontier design might be demoted to a lower rank by the human, making it less likely to pass along its traits in the future.

It should be noted that as we are adjusting the Pareto ranking, which is used for roulette wheel (probabilistic) selection, the human's actions differ slightly from a

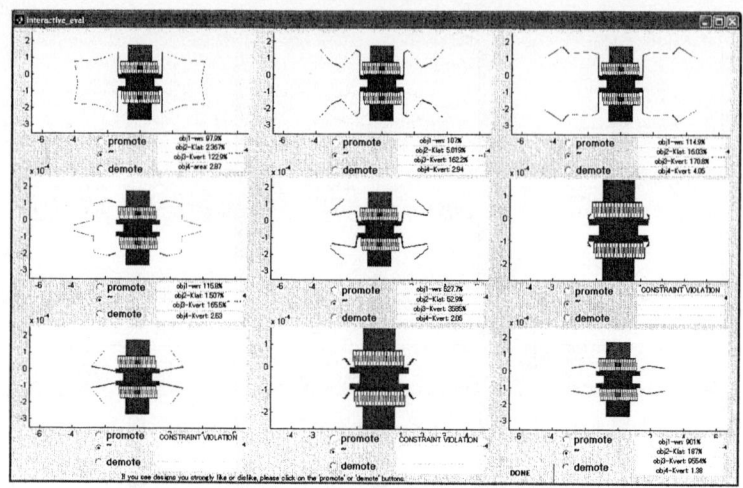

Fig. 4. User interface of new IEC MEMS synthesis tool

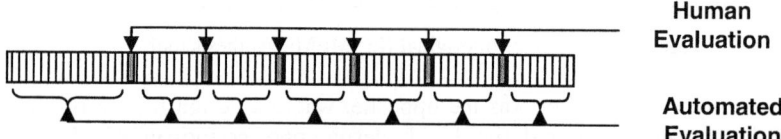

Human Evaluation

Automated Evaluation

Fig. 5. Schematic of interspresed human interaction in automated evolutionary synthesis

simple absolute screening approach. It should also be noted that the human's interaction can be applied as little or as much as desired. Generally we find that users have a strong opinion (positive or negative) only a relatively small percentage of the time. Therefore this approach requires less activity (through scoring via the graphical user interface (GUI)) than the previous IEC MEMS tool.

This method is also unique in that it combines IEC with multiobjective GA. With few exceptions, [8],[11] most IEC applications are limited to single objective optimization problem, this implementation allows a human to interact with a MOGA without needing to combine objectives into a weighted sum (either explicitly via a formula or implicitly within the user's head).

Another unique aspect of our proposed alternate method is that the level of human interaction is flexible; if the human were to not score any designs, the tool becomes identical to the automated MOGA, using the unmodified Pareto ranking. In this respect, we have chosen a method where the human interaction for evaluation occurs only every n^{th}-generation (see Fig. 5). Automated evolution with occasional human 'review' combines the tirelessness and speed of the computer with the more 'expensive' (in terms of time and fatigue) opinion of the human.

The time and attention required by the human is further reduced by not displaying physically invalid designs in the interactive phase. As much as half of the population at any given point may violate a validity constraint such as those introduced to remove designs that are not physically realizable in the MEMS fabrication environment (e.g., no crossing of legs, minimum distances between parts, etc.) By removing these designs from human consideration, they can focus their attention exclusively on meaningful designs, delaying the onset of fatigue. In practical terms, this means the user's effort can be focused on producing more better designs rather than being expended looking at invalid designs.

3 Experiment

To verify the success of the tool, we performed a user test of 13 student volunteers using the tool. The design of a symmetric, four legged resonating mass was used as a test problem. Four objective goals are set for the synthesis: ω_t (10,000Hz), area (minimized), lateral stiffness (100 N/m) and vertical stiffness (0.5 N/m). The problem formulation, geometrical bounds, constraints and objectives are identical to those used in [7],[9],[12].

Table 1. Settings for improved IEC user test

Property	Setting
Population Size	80
Generations	80
Interval for human interaction	Every 10th generations
Starting point for human interaction	20th generation
Total number of human interaction generations	6 (20,30,40, 50,60,70th generations)

3.1 User Test Setup

The settings and parameters for the Interactive evolutionary implementation used in this paper are presented in Table 1. The human evaluation phase occurs 6 times over the course of the 80 generation test. As our initial population is randomly generated from scratch, human interaction is not initiated until the 20th generation to give the GA the opportunity to first converge towards the objective goals before the human expertise is applied. Each generation of human interaction, approximately five screens worth of designs (up to 9 designs per screen) are displayed, for a total of approximately 300 designs presented to the human throughout the course of the synthesis, of which the human may only actually chose to adjust the ranking of a fraction of these.

3.2 MEMS Synthesis Quality Metric

Design synthesis [13] relies on the ability to accurately predict in advance the performance of a proposed design. Through a study of MEMS synthesis designs fabricated and characterized, we have found that certain types of design features lead to inaccurate predictions using the tractable MEMS simulation tools capable of being used in an evolutionary computation algorithm at the present time.

The characterization test of fabricated evolutionary synthesis output reveals two important factors that dramatically impact the accuracy of some of the designs generated [7]. When fabricated, these designs' performance differ dramatically from the predicted performance in the most critical objective, the resonant frequency. These designs are susceptible to one or both of two phenomenon - simulator deficiencies and fabrication variation.

Finite Element Modeling (FEM) has the ability to very accurately predict the performance of a resonating mass, but requires a significant time to simulate. We therefore use a simplified nodal analysis-based simulator, which also has the benefit of easier integration with our discretized component-based evolutionary encoding. The open source simulation tool SUGAR [14] is used as the evaluation engine, but it lacks the ability to accurately model the end conditions of beam elements. This leads to a loss of accuracy in certain geometrical configurations (such as thin-thick junctions at acute angles).

Likewise, the presence of uncharacterized process variation can dramatically impact the performance of a design when fabricated. Currently in most MEMS foundries, there is no characterization or prediction of the level of residual stress that exists in material layers. This residual stress can dramatically impact the resonant frequency for certain geometrical configurations as well (such as designs with a very high lateral stiffness, large anchor width, etc).

In [12] a performance metric for these two deficiencies was presented. The first was a 'simulation error percentage', the percentage difference between the frequency predicted by SUGAR and that predicted by the FEM tool ANSYS. The second metric was 'fabrication error percentage', the percent change in the frequency with and without a typical amount of compressive residual stress included. (Note, a 5 MPa compressive stress was used for this study). This percentage is equivalent to the sensitivity of a particular design to the presence of residual stress. For more information on these metrics and their sources, please refer to [12].

The goal of the user study of our new IEC tool is to test whether the IEC output has a lower amount of simulation error on average than that of the automated MOGA. We also would like to show that IEC has less sensitivity to residual stress, (which is generated in the fabrication process) than the automated designs. The absolute magnitude of these numbers is not important, rather we focus on their relative improvement and statistical variation.

An analysis of variance (ANOVA) test [15] is used to measure the level amount of variation between two groups and tell us if it is statistically significant. This test is applied to compare the two groups of designs for each of the two metrics to tell if there is a significant difference between the two methods

3.3 Results

Employing a similar testing strategy as [10] and [12], we take the best two designs produced by each synthesis run that are within 500 Hz of the goal of 10 kHz. Each of these is evaluated in SUGAR, and the FEM tool ANSYS. The simulator error percentage and fabrication error percentage are calculated. These results are compared to the results of 10 runs of the automated synthesis program - identical settings and code, except no human interaction is used.

The average error as well as the standard deviation is presented in Table 2. In the case of both metrics, the IEC results perform better (have less sensitivity to these factors) than the automated version. The standard deviation amongst the human inter

Table 2. Comparison of results of improved IEC user test and automated EC for 4-objective MEMS resonator test problem. The IEC method presented in this paper performs better than the baseline, non-interactive EC method for both metrics.

	Improved IEC (26 designs)	Automated EC(20 designs)
Simulator Error Percentage		
Average	0.3%	3.3%
Std. dev	4.7%	2.7%
ANOVA P-value	P=0.016 (98% significance)	
Fabrication Error Percentage		
Average	58%	73%
Std. dev	15%	23%
ANOVA P-value	P=0.014 (98% significance)	

action results is higher for the simulator error, which can possibly be attributed to the difference in the quality of the interaction by the various users in the study. Whereas the automated synthesis tool is generally more consistent from run to run, despite producing less desirable designs. The results of the ANOVA test are also presented in Table 2. They confirm that there is a statistically significant difference in the quality of output for both factors.

As user fatigue is difficult to quantify, we can not make conclusions about the success of this system compared to our previous IEC MEMS program or other implementations of IEC in terms of user fatigue. However a general idea of fatigue can be drawn by looking at the number of actions required to execute the synthesis run (in this case mouse clicks on radio buttons in the graphical user interface).

In the new IEC implementation, the user need only act approximately 60-90 times per synthesis run (although our observation is that some users actually score much more than this at their choice). Even for a user who rates more than a few designs per screen, this compares well against the 240-270 actions required in the previous IEC implementation presented in [9]. Similarly the average time required for one run of the IEC presented in this paper is shorter than the time required for the previous implementation, approximately 45 minutes per user versus one hour per user, respectively.

4 Conclusion / Future Work

This work presents an initial trial of a new implementation of human interaction for evolutionary MEMS design synthesis. Our user study shows that the quality of the output is superior to the output of a non-interactive evolutionary design program.

More testing to directly compare the performance of this new IEC to the previous IEC implementation is needed before the benefits of the alternate methods can be fully gauged; this requires another user study that compares the performance of two methods analytically. The challenge is to develop a fair test that can compare the quality of the output produced by the two methods when they require an equivalent amount of effort (fatigue) from the human, or to compare the amount of effort required to produce the equivalent quality output. We would then validate the results of this study by fabricating and characterizing the output produced by this implementation and comparing the real world performance with other designs generated by other interactive and non-interactive synthesis implementations.

Finally, we intend to apply this method to the design of other MEMS devices, such as MEMS inertial sensors. Additionally it would be interesting to apply this method to the device or layout design in other engineering domains as well, such as the design of circuits, building structures, HVAC, etc.

A promising extension of this method is to include a human predictor to either assist or partially replace the human interaction. For example a neural network could be trained either before or during evolution to predict which designs might warrant a 'promote' or 'demote' score. This predictor could anticipate the users preferences for all the designs in the IEC UI; the user need only review these predictions and correct any mistakes. This could further reduce the amount of physical and mental effort required, allowing for larger population sizes or more generations of evolution. An alternate approach utilizes a neural network to evaluate a much larger population on behalf of the user, while the user only occasionally provides a small amount of additional evaluation to improve the training of the neural network. We are currently investigating these approaches and testing their implementation for application to MEMS synthesis.

Acknowledgements

This research was conducted, in part, through NSF grant CCR-DES/CC-0306557. Any opinions, findings, and conclusions or recommendations expressed in this material are those of the authors and do not necessarily reflect the views of the National Science Foundation.

References

1. Zhou, N., Zhu, B., Agogino, A. M. and Pister, K. S. J.: Evolutionary Synthesis of MEMS MicroElectronicMechanical Systems Design, Intelligent Engineering System through Artificial Neural Networks Proceedings of the Artificial Neural Networks in Engineering (ANNIE2001), (2001) 197-202
2. Zhou, N., Agogino, A. M., and Pister, K. S. J.: Automated Design Synthesis for Micro-Electro-Mechanical Systems (MEMS), Proceedings of ASME Design Automation Conference, (2002)
3. Goldberg, D. E.: Genetic Algorithms in Search, Optimization and Machine Learning, Addison-Wesley Longman, Boston, MA, (1989)
4. van Laarhoven, P. J. M., Aarts, E. H. L.: Simulated Annealing: Theory and Applications, Reidel Publishing, Dordrecht, Holland, (1987)
5. Zhou, N.: Simulation and Synthesis of Microelectromechanical Systems, Doctoral Thesis, UC Berkeley, (2002)
6. Kamalian, R., Zhou, N., Agogino, A.M.: A Comparison of MEMS Synthesis Techniques, Proceedings of the 1st Pacific Rim Workshop on Transducers and Micro/Nano Technologies, Xiamen, China, (2002), 239-242
7. Kamalian, R.: Evolutionary Synthesis of MEMS, Doctoral Thesis, UC Berkeley, (2004)

8. Takagi, H.: Interactive Evolutionary Computation: Fusion of the Capacities of EC Optimization and Human Evaluation, Proceedings of the IEEE, vol. 89, no. 9, (2001), 1275-1296
9. Kamalian, R., Takagi, H., Agogino, A.M.: Optimized Design of MEMS by Evolutionary Multi-objective Optimization with Interactive Evolutionary Computation, Proceedings of GECCO 2004, Genetic and Evolutionary Computation Conference, (2004), 1030-1041
10. Kamalian, R., Takagi, H., Agogino, A.M.: The Role Of Constraints and Human Interaction in Evolving MEMS Designs: Microresonator Case Study, Proceedings of DETC'04, ASME 2004 Design Engineering Technical Conference, Salt Lake City, UT, (2004)
11. Singh, A., Minsker, B. S., Takagi, H.: Interactive Genetic Algorithms for Inverse Groundwater Modeling, American Society of Civil Engineers (ASCE) Environmental & Water Resources Institute (EWRI) World Water & Environmental Resources Congress 2005, Anchorage, AK, (2005)
12. Kamalian, R., Agogino, A.M.: Improving Evolutionary Synthesis of MEMS through Fabrication and Testing Feedback, IEEE SMC 2005, IEEE Conference on Systems, Man and Cybernetics, (2005)
13. Antonsson, E. K., Cagan, J. (eds): Formal Engineering Design Synthesis, Cambridge University Press, Cambridge, (2001)
14. SUGAR: Simulation Research for MEMS, http://bsac.eecs.berkeley.edu/cadtools/sugar/sugar/
15. ANOVA: ANalysis Of VAriance between groups, http://www.physics.csbsju.edu/stats/anova.html

Application of Weighted Ideal Point Method to Environmental/Economic Load Dispatch

Guo-li Zhang[1], Geng-yin Li[1], Hong Xie[2], and Jian-wei Ma[1]

[1] Department of Applied Mathematics,
North China Electric Power University,
071003 Baoding, China
{zhangguoli, ligy}@ncepu.edu.cn,
majianweima@sina.com
[2] Department of Electronic Engineering,
Shanghai Maritime University,
200135 Shanghai, China
xiehong_hzh@sohu.com

Abstract. This paper proposes a novel environmental/economic load dispatch model by considering the fuel cost and emission functions with uncertain coefficients and the constraints of a ramp rate. The uncertain coefficients are represented by fuzzy numbers, and the model is known as fuzzy dynamic environmental/economic load dispatch (FDEELD) model. A novel weighted ideal point method (WIPM) is developed to solve the FDEELD problem. The FDEELD problem is first converted into a single objective fuzzy nonlinear programming by using the WIPM. A hybrid evolutionary algorithm with quasi-simplex techniques is then used to solve the corresponding single objective optimization problem. A method of disposing constraint and a fuzzy number ranking method are also applied to compare fuzzy weighted objective function values of different points. Experimental results show that FDEELD model is more practical; the algorithm and techniques proposed are efficient to solve FDEELD problems.

1 Introduction

The conventional economic dispatch problem mainly concerns the minimization of operating cost subject to diverse constraints in terms of units and systems. However, the environmental pollution problem caused by generation has been detected in recent years. A variety of feasible strategies [1-3] have been proposed to reduce atmospheric emissions. These include installation of pollutant cleaning equipment, switching to low emission fuels,replacing the aged fuel-burners and generator units, and emission dispatching. The literature [3] referred the first three options should be the long-term ones, the emission dispatching option is an attractive short-term alternative. In fact, the first three options should be determined by the generation companies, but not by the regulatory authorities, especially in the circumstances of power market. Thus, the desired long-term target is to reduce the emission of harmful gases, in other words, the emission of harmful gases by generation should be curtailed in accordance with laws and regulations. Therefore, the environmental/ economic load dispatch problem considering emission of harmful gases is a kernel issue in power markets.

However, in previous environmental/economic load dispatch models [1-6], the uncertainties of fuel cost and emission functions were not considered. In this paper, we consider fuel cost and emission functions with uncertainty coefficients, and propose a novel environmental/economic load dispatch model. In the model, the uncertain coefficients of the fuel cost and emission functions are represented by fuzzy numbers, and the model is therefore called fuzzy dynamic environmental/economic load dispatch (FDEELD) model. A novel weighted ideal point method is presented to solve the FDEELD problem. In the WIPM, the FDEELD problem is converted into a single objective fuzzy nonlinear programming problem. Solving the single objective problem contributes not only to obtaining Pareto optimal solution, but also to predicting the magnitude of the effects of the set of weights on each objective function value. A hybrid evolutionary algorithm with quasi-simplex techniques is used to seek the single objective optimization problem resulting from the WIPM. A method of disposing constraint and a fuzzy number ranking method are applied to compare fuzzy weighted objective function values of different points.

The structure of the rest of this paper is arranged as follows. The FDEELD model is proposed in Section 2 by describing the coefficients of fuel cost and emission functions as fuzzy numbers. A weighted ideal point method (WIPM), a hybrid evolutionary algorithm, a method of disposing constraint, and a fuzzy number ranking method to solve the FDEELD problem are applied and developed in Section 3. The experimental results are given in Section 4. Conclusions are presented in Section 5.

2 Fuzzy Dynamic Environmental/Economic Load Dispatch Model

The basic structure of power market in the literatures [7-9] consists of Power Exchange (PX) and Independent System Operator (ISO). In this structure, the PX takes charge of spot trade, and then economic load dispatch is its main task. On the other hand, the ISO takes the responsibilities for network security and auxiliary service etc. Therefore, in the load dispatch model, the network constraints and spinning reserve etc. can be neglected, but the ramp rate limit must be considered to assure the optimum solution. Considering the uncertainties of the coefficients of fuel cost and emission functions, it is not precise to describe these coefficients as destinies. To guarantee the accuracy of the fuel cost and emission functions, these coefficients take the forms of fuzzy numbers. Based on the analysis above, the FDEELD model can be described as follows:

$$\begin{cases} \min f = \sum_{t=1}^{T}\sum_{j=1}^{N}(\tilde{a}_j + \tilde{b}_j P_j(t) + \tilde{c}_j P_j^2(t)) \\ \min e = \sum_{t=1}^{T}\sum_{j=1}^{N}(\tilde{\alpha}_j + \tilde{\beta}_j P_j(t) + \tilde{\gamma}_j P_j^2(t)) \\ \sum_{j=1}^{N} P_j(t) = P_D(t) + P_L(t) \\ P_{jlow}(t) \leq P_j(t) \leq P_{jhigh}(t) \end{cases} \quad (1)$$

where T is the number of hours for the time horizon; N is the total number of committed units; $P_j(t)$ is the power output for the thermal unit j during the hour t; f is the fuel cost function of unit j, $\tilde{a}_j, \tilde{b}_j, \tilde{c}_j$ are the fuzzy coefficients, e is the emission function of unit j, $\tilde{\alpha}_j, \tilde{\beta}_j, \tilde{\gamma}_j$ are the fuzzy coefficients, $P_{j\min}$ is the minimum output of the unit j, $P_{j\max}$ is the maximum output of the unit j, $P_D(t)$ is the load demand at time interval t, $P_L(t)$ is the network loss at time interval t, D_j is the down ramp rate limit of the unit j, R_j is the up ramp rate limit of the unit j and

$$P_{jlow}(t) = Max\{P_{j\min}, P_j(t-1) - D_j\} \tag{2}$$

$$P_{jhigh}(t) = Min\{P_{j\max}, P_j(t-1) + R_j\} \tag{3}$$

3 Weighted Ideal Point Method and Hybrid Evolutionary Algorithm

3.1 Weighing Ideal Point Method

It is well known that both the weighted method and the reference point method are effective that contribute to Pareto optimal solution of multi-objective nonlinear programming problems. Strictly speaking, the weights represent only the relative importance of different objectives functions; it is hard to know the effect of the setof weights on each objective function value. The reference point method is a relatively practical interactive approach to multi-objective optimization problems that introduces the concept of a reference point suggested by the decision maker, which presents in some the desired values of the objective functions. It is very hard to determine weights and reference points in application, besides the interactive approach increases heavily computing burden. This paper proposes a new weighted ideal point method that needs no alternation and can predict the magnitude of the effect of the set of weights on each objective function value.

The general nonlinear programming problem can be formulated as the following:

$$\min_{x \in S} f(x) = (f_1(x), f_2(x), \cdots, f_k(x)) \tag{4}$$

where $f_1(x), \cdots, f_k(x)$ are k distinct objective functions and S is the constrained set defined by

$$S = \{x \in R^n \mid g_j(x) \leq 0, j = 1, \cdots, m\} \tag{5}$$

In this paper, we propose a weighted ideal point method (WIPM) as follows:

$$g(x) = w_1 \left(\frac{f_1 - f_1^{\min}}{f_1^{\min}}\right)^2 + \cdots + w_k \left(\frac{f_k - f_k^{\min}}{f_k^{\min}}\right)^2 \tag{6}$$

where $f_i^{\min} = \min_{x \in S} f_i(x)$, $i = 1, \cdots, k$. the vector $f^{\min} = (f_1^{\min}, \cdots, f_k^{\min})$ is so-called ideal or utopia point, $w = (w_1, \ldots, w_k)$ is weight vector, where $\sum_{i=1}^{k} w_i = 1$, and $w_i > 0, i = 1, \ldots, k$.

The Pareto optimal solution of the problem (4) can be obtained by solving the single objective optimization problem below

$$\min_{x \in S} g(x) \tag{7}$$

The model (7) is different with the general weighted method or reference point method. Because the different objective function values in (4) can be greatly different, it is hard to make clear the effect quantities of the weights to each objective function value. In model (7), $\frac{f_i - f_i^{\min}}{f_i^{\min}}$ converts every objective into the same magnitude level, we can therefore predict the effect quantities of the weights to the objectives. For example, if $w_1 = 3w_2$, $\frac{f_2^* - f_2^{\min}}{f_2^{\min}} \approx 3 \frac{f_1^* - f_1^{\min}}{f_1^{\min}}$, where $f_i^* = f_i(x^*)$, $i = 1, 2$, x^* is the optimal solution of the problem (7). In other words, the weights of WIPM reflect the trade-off rate information in the objective functions.

When the coefficients are fuzzy numbers in the objective function, we also use the model (7) to convert the problem (4) into the corresponding single objective fuzzy optimization problem.

3.2 Quasi-simplex Techniques

To solve the single objective problem (7), the quasi-simplex techniques are introduced in this section. Simplex is one of the widely accepted conventional direct search methods [10]. A simplex in an n-dimensional space is defined by a convex polyhedron that consists of $n+1$ vertices, which are not in the same hyper-plane. Assume that there are $n+1$ points in the n-dimensional space, denoted by x_i respectively and the objective function values over these points are denoted by f_i, $i = 1, 2, \ldots, n+1$, respectively. The worst and the best points in terms of function values are denoted by x^H and x^B, respectively. Two potential optimal search directions in generating prospective offspring are considered in the quasi-simplex techniques. One direction is the worst-opposite direction which is used in the conventional simplex techniques, and the other is the best-forward direction which is a ray from the centroid of a polyhedron whose vertexes are all the points but the best one towards the best point of the simplex. Along the worst-opposite direction, four prospective individuals will be generated by using the reflection, expansion and compression operations, respectively, and can be determined by the following formula

$$x = x^C + \alpha(x^C - x^H) \qquad (8)$$

where x^C is the centroid and can be calculated by

$$x^C = \left[\left(\sum_{i=1}^{n+1} x^i\right) - x^H\right]\bigg/ n \qquad (9)$$

α is a coefficient whose value determines the position of a potential better point along this direction, such as α=1 for the reflection point x^R, α >1 for the expansion points x^E, -1 < α < 0 and 0 < α < 1 for the compression points x^M and x^N, respectively.

Along the best-forward direction, using the following formula (10), four individuals x^e, x^r, x^m and x^n will be calculated by the operations that are similar to the expansion, reflection, and compression operations used in the conventional simplex method

$$x = x^B + \beta(x^B - x^D) \qquad (10)$$

where x^D denotes the centroid of the polyhedron whose vertexes are all the points but the best point and can be calculated by the following formula

$$x^D = \left(\left(\sum_{i=1}^{n+1} x^i\right) - x^B\right)\bigg/ n \qquad (11)$$

β is a coefficient whose value determines the position of calculated point on the best-forward line. The four prospective points along the best-forward direction have values corresponding to β >1, β=1, -1 < β < 0 and 0 < β < 1, respectively.

3.3 The Method of Disposing Constraint

To solve the single objective constrained optimization problem, the common practice method is to use the Lagrange Relaxation method to construct a penalty function. However penalty factor is hard to determine in application. A method of disposing constraint is given below. Define the extent of constraints violation as follow:

$$v(g) = \max\{0, P_{jlow}(t) - P_j(t)\} + \max\{0, P_j(t) - P_{jhigh}(t)\} \qquad (12)$$

Where g represents the objective function obtained by WIPM from model (1).

In the algorithm proposed, selection operation and quasi-simplex techniques need individuals order relation.

Give below individuals order by using values of function g and values of the $v(g)$:

(1) if $v[g(x)] = v[g(y)]$, then

$$x \prec y \Leftrightarrow g(x) \leq g(y) \qquad (13)$$

(2) if $v[g(x)] \neq v[g(y)]$, then

$$x \prec y \Leftrightarrow v[g(x)] \leq v[g(y)] \qquad (14)$$

where x and y are two individuals of the population.

3.4 Fuzzy Number Ranking Method

In solving the single objective problem (7), we do not convert the problem (7) into non-fuzzy programming problem by using α-level set [11], but directly compare the fuzzy function values by using fuzzy number order. Different methods for ranking fuzzy numbers have been suggested [12-14]. The definition below comes from Lee and Li [12].

Definition 3.1. Let $\tilde{a}, \tilde{b} \in F(R)$ be two fuzzy numbers, and the definition of ranking two fuzzy numbers is as follows:

$$\tilde{a} \leq \tilde{b} \text{ if } m(\tilde{a}) < m(\tilde{b}) \text{ or } m(\tilde{a}) = m(\tilde{b}) \text{ and } \sigma(\tilde{a}) \geq \sigma(\tilde{b}) \qquad (15)$$

where $m(\tilde{a})$ and $\sigma(\tilde{a})$ are mean and standard deviation of the fuzzy number $\tilde{a}$, respectively, $s(\tilde{a}) = \{x \mid \tilde{a}(x) > 0\}$ is the support of fuzzy number $\tilde{a}$.

For triangular fuzzy number $\tilde{a} = (l, m, n)$

$$m(\tilde{a}) = \frac{1}{3}(l + m + n) \qquad (16)$$

$$\sigma(\tilde{a}) = \frac{1}{18}(l^2 + m^2 + n^2 - lm - ln - mn) \qquad (17)$$

3.5 Weighted Ideal Point Method and Hybrid Evolutionary Algorithm

Combining the previous WIPM with the quasi-simplex techniques, the method of disposing constraint, the fuzzy number ranking method and an evolutionary algorithm, we propose a new weighted ideal method and hybrid evolutionary algorithm (WIEA), the basic steps as follows:

Step1: Convert problem (4) into the problem (7) by WIPM;
Step2: For the problem (7), initialize a population of size $\mu = K(n+1)$;
Step3: Evaluate the fitness value for each individual x_i of the population based on the objective function value $g(x_i)$ and $v[g(x_i)]$;
Step4: Subdivide the population into K subpopulations;
Step5: For each subpopulation, create offspring by Gaussian mutation, Cauchy mutation and quasi-simplex techniques in parallel. In order to increase subpopulation varieties, select the best point as offspring from the points obtained by the equation (8) and (10), the rest offspring of subpopulation are created by Gaussian mutation and Cauchy mutation; i.e.,

$$x_{i-g,j} = x_{ij} + \eta_{ij} N_j(0,1) \qquad (18)$$

$$x_{i-c,j} = x_{ij} + \eta_{ij} \delta_j(0,1) \qquad (19)$$

$$\eta_{ij}' = \eta_{ij} \exp(\tau' N(0,1) + \tau N_j(0,1)) \qquad (20)$$

where x_{ij} is the j–th components of the parent x_i, $x_{i-g,j}$ and $x_{i-c,j}$ represent the j–th components of the offspring generated from the Gaussian and the Cauchy mutations, the factors τ and τ' are commonly set to be $\left(\sqrt{2\sqrt{n}}\right)^{-1}$ and $\left(\sqrt{2n}\right)^{-1}$ respectively; $N(0,1)$, $N_j(0,1)$ denote a normally distributed random number with mean 0 and standard deviation 1, respectively, and δ_j is a Cauchy random variable.

Step6: Sort the union of parents and offspring in the ascending order according to their fitness by using the method of disposing constraint and the fuzzy number ranking method previously mentioned.
Step7: For each subpopulation, select the top n+1 individuals out from the union of parents and offspring, and unite all individuals selected to be the parents of next generation.
Step8: Stop if the halting criterion is satisfied, otherwise, return to Step 3.

4 Experiment Study

To validate the model (1), the FDEELD is converted into the single objective optimization problem by WIPM. Because the single objective optimization problem obtained is high-dimension constrained nonlinear optimization one, nobody knows where the global minimum point is. In order to demonstrate the effectiveness of the proposed algorithms, the mean and standard deviation of fuzzy fuel cost, fuzzy emission and fuzzy total cost corresponding to the optimal outputs are significant and convincing. In addition, in order to compare the magnitude of effect of the set of weights on fuzzy fuel cost and fuzzy emission, we calculate 3 group results for 3 different weights. Table 4 lists the means and standard deviations of fuzzy fuel cost, fuzzy emission and fuzzy total cost for 10 the results obtained by the proposed algorithm running independently 10 times.

4.1 Test Data

Table 1. Limits of units output and ramp rate

Unit No.	P_{min}	P_{max}	D_j	R_j	Unit No.	P_{min}	P_{max}	D_j	R_j
1	10	125	30	20	4	35	210	40	30
2	10	150	30	20	5	130	325	60	40
3	35	225	40	30	6	125	315	60	40

Where the unit of P_{min} and P_{max} are MW, the unit D_j and R_j are MW/h.

Table 2. Fuzzy coefficients of fuel cost and emission functions

Unit No	a_0	a_1	a_2	α_0	α_1	α_2
1	734.0948	756.79886	775.71883	13.5821	13.85932	14.13651
2	437.7853	451.32513	462.60826	13.5821	13.85932	14.13651
3	1023.747	1049.9977	1070.9976	39.4615	40.26690	41.07224
4	1212.442	1243.5311	1268.4017	39.4615	40.26690	41.07224
5	1625.398	1658.5696	1683.4481	42.0376	42.89553	43.75344
6	1329.526	1356.6592	1377.0090	42.0376	42.89553	43.75344

Unit No.	b_0	b_1	b_2	β_0	β_1	β_2
1	37.46062	38.53973	39.46468	0.32015	0.32767	0.33422
2	44.86670	46.15916	47.26698	0.32015	0.32767	0.33422
3	39.38673	40.39665	41.20458	-0.55642	-0.54551	-0.53460
4	37.34789	38.30553	39.07164	-0.55642	-0.54551	-0.53460
5	35.60126	36.32782	36.90907	-0.52138	-0.51116	-0.50094
6	37.50500	38.27041	38.88274	-0.52138	-0.51116	-0.50094

Unit No.	c_0	c_1	c_2	γ_0	γ_1	γ_2
1	0.14866	0.15247	0.1556718	0.00411	0.00419	0.00427
2	0.10322	0.10587	0.1080932	0.00411	0.00419	0.00427
3	0.02747	0.02803	0.0285345	0.00669	0.00683	0.00697
4	0.03476	0.03546	0.0360982	0.00669	0.00683	0.00697
5	0.02075	0.02111	0.0214266	0.00452	0.00461	0.00470
6	0.01768	0.01799	0.0182598	0.00452	0.00461	0.00470

Table 3. Load demands

T	1	2	3	4	5	6	7	8	9	10	11	12
D	520	500	500	510	560	630	700	750	760	800	780	740
T	13	14	15	16	17	18	19	20	21	22	23	24
D	720	720	760	800	850	880	900	870	780	710	650	560

where T is the time interval, D is the corresponding load demand.

4.2 Test Results

Table 4. Comparisons of the results obtained with different weights

(w_1, w_2)	MFC	STDEV-FC	MEC	STDEV-EC	MTC	STDEV-TC
(0.3,0.7)	854984.9	229.24	11412.73	38.74	866234	201.55
	874417	251.14	11947.76	39.83	886199	221.18
	890110.4	271.91	12463.23	40.95	902405.6	240.32
(0.5,0.5)	854826.9	199.91	11423.23	53.49	866150.6	183.15
	874163.9	217.78	11993.81	54.89	886047.5	195.74
	889776.3	236	12537.37	56.28	902194.8	209.86
(0.7,0.3)	854737.9	236.1	11487.18	48.88	866314.2	232.67
	874099.5	249.51	12022.18	49.91	886185.9	242.58
	889731.5	263.89	12539.55	50.92	902313.6	253.23

where MFC, MEC, MTC represent the means of the fuel cost, the emission, the total fuel cost and emission for 10 the results obtained by the proposed algorithm running independently 10 times, respectively; STDEV-FC, STDEV-EC and STDEV-TC are the corresponding standard deviations.

Obviously, the standard deviations of each result are all very small. So the results are reasonable. It can be seen that the fuel costs decrease and the emissions increase when the weight of the fuel cost increases.

5 Conclusions

A new dynamic environmental/economic load dispatch model considering the uncertainties of coefficients of fuel cost and emission functions is proposed. The WIEA is developed to solve the FDEELD problem. FDDELD problem is fuzzy multi-objective nonlinear programming problem. In this paper, we do not use the traditional Maximum satisfaction factor method and the concepts of the λ-level set that convert the problem to several non-fuzzy programming problems, but directly optimize the objective value by the fuzzy number ranking method that can avoid the possibility of losing some useful information by getting λ-level set in the beginning. Meanwhile, decision makers are likely to get some important information from the fuzzy objective value. The method has the following advantages:

(1) The fuel cost and emission coefficients presented by fuzzy numbers can lead to more accurate model.
(2) The fuzzy minimum tells not only the approximate fuel cost and emission but also the diversity degree of the minimal fuel cost and emission.
(3) The obtained optimum solution is steady and trusty, because we choose the solution of minimum dispersivity when many solutions have approximately the same total cost.

References

1. Abido, M. A., "Environmental/economic power dispatch using multiobjective evolutionary algorithms", IEEE Transactions on Power Systems, Vol. 18, Issue 4, pp. 1529-1537, Nov (2003).
2. Venkatesh, P., Gnanadass, R, Padhy, N.P., "Comparison and application of evolutionary programming techniques to combined economic emission dispatch with line flow constraints", IEEE Transactions on Power Systems, Vol. 18, Issue 2, pp. 688-697, May (2003).
3. Rughooputh, H. C. S., Ah King, R. T. F., "Environmental/economic dispatch of thermal units using an elitist multiobjective evolutionary algorithm", Industrial Technology, 2003 IEEE International Conference on, Vol. 1, pp. 48-53, Dec. (2003).
4. Kiyota, T., Tsuji, Y., Kondo, E., "Unsatisfying functions and multiobjective fuzzy satisfaction design using genetic algorithms", IEEE Transactions on Systems, Man and Cybernetics, Part B, Vol. 33, Issue 6, pp. 889-897, Dec. (2003).
5. Kit Po Wang, Yuryevich, J., "Evolutionary programming based algorithm for environmentally constrained economic dispatch", IEEE Transactions on Power Systems, Vol. 13, Issue 2, pp. 301-306, May (1998).
6. Chao-Ming Huang, Hong-Tzer Yang, Ching-Lien Huang, "Bi-objective power dispatch using fuzzy satisfaction-maximizing decision approach", IEEE Transactions on Power Systems, Vol. 12, Issue 4, pp. 1715-1721, Nov. (1997).
7. David Watts, Paulo Atienza, Hugh Rudnick, "Application of the Power Exchange-Independent System Operator Model in Chile", Power Engineering Society Summer Meeting, 2002 IEEE, Vol. 3, pp. 1392-1396, July (2002).
8. Fushuan Wen, A.K.David, "Coordination of bidding strategies in day-ahead energy and spinning reserve markets", International Journal of Electrical Power & Energy Systems, Vol. 24, Issue 4, pp. 251-261, May (2002).
9. Farrokh Albuyeh, Ziad Alaywan, "California ISO formation and implementation", IEEE Computer Applications in Power, Vol. 12, Issue 4, pp. 30-34, (1999).
10. Nelder. J. A., Mead. R., "A simplex method for function minimization", the computer Journal, 5, (1965).
11. Guangquan Zhang, Yong-Hong Wu, M. Remias, Jie Lu "Formulation of fuzzy linear programming problems as four-objective constrained optimization problems", Applied Mathematics and Computation, Vol. 139, Issues 2-3, pp. 383-399, July (2003).
12. Lee. E. S., Li. R. L., "Comparison of fuzzy numbers based on the probability measure of fuzzy events", Comput. Math. Appl. 15, pp. 887- 896. 15, (1988).
13. Ching-Hsue Cheng, "A new approach for ranking fuzzy numbers by distance method, Fuzzy Sets and Systems", Vol 95, Issue 3, pp. 307-317, May (1998).
14. Liem Tran, Lucien Duckstein, "Comparison of fuzzy numbers using a fuzzy distance measure", Fuzzy Sets and Systems, Vol. 130, Issue 3, pp. 331-341, September (2002).

Reasoning the Spatiotemporal Relations Between Time Evolving Indeterminate Regions

Lei Bao[1,2], Xiao-Lin Qin[1], Jun Zhang[1], and Qi-Yuan Li[2]

[1] College of Information Science and Technology, Nanjing University of Aeronautics and Astronautics, 210016, Nanjing
[2] College of Electronics Engineering, Navy University of Engineering, 430033, Wuhan
{blnj2000, qinxcs}@nuaa.edu.cn

Abstract. Temporal and spatial reasoning are two important parts of Artificial Intelligence and they have important applications in the fields of GIS (geographic information system), Spatiotemporal Database, CAD/CAM etc. The development of temporal reasoning and spatial reasoning includes three aspects: Ontology, representation models and reasoning methods. This paper checks the correspondence between spatiotemporal relations and the 3D topological relations and presents a relation analysis model for indeterminate evolving 2D regions. It extends the 2D Egg/Yolk model into the third dimension that can describe the approximate topological relations for indeterminate evolving regions. The result is a collection of relation clusters that have different spatiotemporal natures.

1 Introduction

The topic of spatiotemporal reasoning is a new area of research. Related research includes spatiotemporal ontology, spatiotemporal relationship representation models and spatiotemporal reasoning methods. Formal works on the relationship representation model are based on an assumption that all the objects are determinate. But the spatiotemporal objects in the world around us can't be measured exactly. Objects do not have crisp boundaries, relationships among them can not be precisely defined, and measurements of objects' positions have errors. To survive in the complex spatiotemporal reality, we need sophisticated analysis on the uncertain spatiotemporal relation models, which are essential for spatiotemporal reasoning research.

In this paper, we present a model for the approximate spatiotemporal relationships between indeterminate 2D evolving objects. Our goal is to extend the indeterminate 2d spatial topological relations model to spatiotemporal dimension and provide a set of J.E.P.D. (Joint Exclusive and Pairwise Disjoint) basic topological relations for uncertain spatiotemporal objects. The remaining sections are organized as follows: Section 2 introduces the related works, including indeterminate spatial topological relations models and crisp spatiotemporal reasoning issues. Section 3 presents the idea of extending a 2d indeterminate spatial topological relations model to spatiotemporal space. Section 4 examines the correspondence between indeterminate spatiotemporal relations and 3D topological relations. Section 5 gives a comparison to related works.

2 Related Work

Recently, in the area of uncertain spatial reasoning, several contributions[1][2] have already provided topological relationship models for uncertain spatial reasoning by extending topological relations with fuzzy logic or probability functions. Furthermore, the model of approximate relations presented in reference[3] assumes that all uncertain spatial objects have a broad boundary and extended the 9-intersection model to represent their topological relations. The model, called Egg/Yolk[4], which is based on the RCC model, can also gives J.E.P.D. basic relations. The Cone-Based model[5], Projection-Based model[5] and Double-Cross model[6] also provided us with the orientation relations analysis between point objects, while the work of Goyal and Egenhofer presented their "Orientation Relation Matrix"[7] for all the spatial data types.

For spatiotemporal reasoning, the most popular approach is to combine a temporal logic T with a spatial logic S to get the spatiotemporal result, such as the F.O.S.T. spatiotemporal logic provided by Wolter[8], the 2D spatiotemporal logic P.S.T.L. by Bennett[9]. Muller's[11] extension on Asher's spatial logic[10] also gives a spatiotemporal model which has stronger reasoning ability. Another approach is the algebraical approach, including Medak's "lifestyles" approach[12], Viqueira's "quantum" model[13] and Claramunt's extension[14] to Ladkin algebra[15].Other works focused on the relation model for certain applications. Muller presented a qualitative relation model[16], which defines six basic spatiotemporal relations: leave, reach, collide, inner, outer, intersect. Erwig uses spatiotemporal predicates in the formal representation of spatiotemporal topological relations[17], which are basic functions defined on spatiotemporal abstract data types.

From related works, we noticed that the area of formal definition on the indeterminate topological relations between uncertain spatiotemporal objects remains untouched. The continuity and infinity of time and the interaction of spatial indeterminacy with temporal indeterminacy makes it difficult to represent indeterminate spatiotemporal objects. The lack of indeterminate spatiotemporal representation models further hindered the research on the analysis of topological relations between them. In 2002, E.Tossebro and M.Nygard presented a formal definition on indeterminate spatiotemporal objects[18]. Based on this representation model and the related indeterminate spatial relations research we can give the formal analysis of indeterminate topological relations between uncertain evolving objects.

3 Extending 2d Egg/Yolk Model to 3D Space

The formal definition of indeterminate spatiotemporal regions is their abstract data type, which can be defined as a function from time to spatial region:

$$TG_A : time \xrightarrow{indeterminate} G_A.$$

G_A is the indeterminate spatial data type of regions, the indeterminacy not only exists in G_A, but also exists in the functions itself. TG_A is not a certain function, but a band of functions that can express the relationship of time to a spatial region approximately.

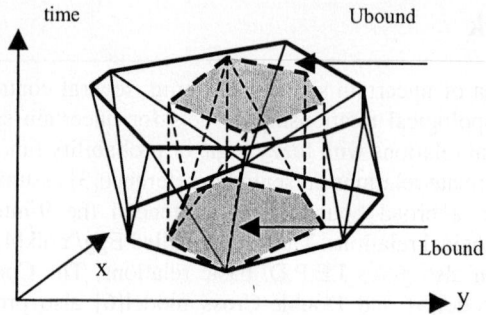

Fig. 1. An indeterminate moving region during one time period

The discrete implementation of indeterminate spatiotemporal type TG_A is based on the slice of time periods. As shown in **Figure 1**, for an indeterminate moving region, time is sliced into many sections, each section is called a unit and all the units are organized by an A.V.L. tree[18]. In each unit, the development of moving objects can be expressed by a pair of simple functions, usually the linear approximation[18], a fixed value, or more complicate grey models[19]. When spatial indeterminacy and temporal indeterminacy affect each other, the calculation of these functions includes some merging and morphing algorithms, which we will not discuss in this paper due to the length limit.

The Egg/Yolk model or Extended Egg/Yolk model presented in [4] uses pairs of RCC regions to describe indeterminate regions G_A. The topological relations between indeterminate region A and B can be classified by the RCC-5 relations between their "Egg" and "Yolk", which can be defined as a certain matrix pattern:

$$\begin{bmatrix} R(y(A), y(B)) & R(y(A), e(B)) \\ R(e(A), y(B)) & R(e(A), e(B)) \end{bmatrix}$$

$y(A)$ is the yolk of A, $e(A)$ is the egg of A. R is RCC-5 relations, including relations **DR, PO, PP, EQ** and **PPI**, shown in **Figure 2**.

From the Egg/Yolk model, for 2D indeterminate regions, we can obtain 46 basic relations which are J.E.P.D.

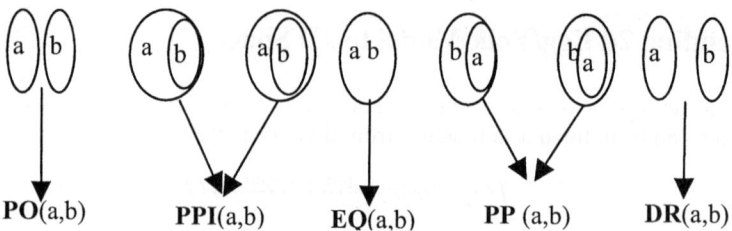

Fig. 2. rcc-5 relations of regions

Fig 2 conceptualizes TG_A as pairs of exact spatiotemporal objects, which can be visualized as purely geometric 3d volumes when the time axis is regarded as a third geometric dimension. The Egg/Yolk model is dimension extensible, the RCC regions can be either 2D or 3D, so the relations between 3D indeterminate volumes have the same collection of JEPD topological relations; note that the two volumes must have the same dimension. In [17], Erwig has proven the spatiotemporal space and the 3d geometric space to be homeomorphic and topologically equivalent, so 3D topological relations can be used to describe the spatiotemporal relations between indeterminate evolving regions. For example, indeterminate 3D topological relations *possibly overlap (A,B)* can describe the condition that *A,B* sometimes possibly intersect each other, as shown in **Figure 3**.

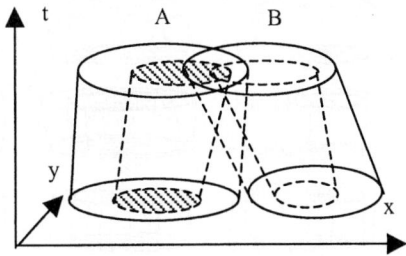

Fig. 3. Possibly overlap ↔ sometime possibly intersect

4 Correspondence Between Approximate Spatiotemporal Relations and Indeterminate 3D Topological Relations

Using the dimensional extensibility, we get 46 basic relations between 3D volume pairs, which inherited the J.E.P.D. characteristics from the 2D Egg/Yolk model, shown in **Figure 4**.

The spatiotemporal space defined by Erwig is homeomorphic and topologically equivalent to 3D geometric space. The relations between 3D volume pairs can be used to describe spatiotemporal relations between indeterminate evolving regions. But while the spatiotemporal relations do have their temporal nature, there will be problems when directly using 3d topological relations to describe spatiotemporal relations, especially when the indeterminacy is concerned.

In **Figure 5**, under each of the two conditions, evolving regions *A* and *B* have the same topological relation, but their spatiotemporal relation is certainly different.

Now we need an assumption that can simplify the problems and eliminate some meaningless topological relations derived from the different time spans between indeterminate evolving regions.

Assumption: when we discuss the spatiotemporal relations between two indeterminate evolving regions *A* and *B*, we are interested in the evolving regions which are of the same time span and in any time instant *t* during their time span, the snapshot of *A* and *B* at *t* has a non-empty yolk:

$$\forall t \in timespan(A) \cap timespan(B), yolk(ut(A,t)) \neq \emptyset, yolk(ut(B,t)) \neq \emptyset$$

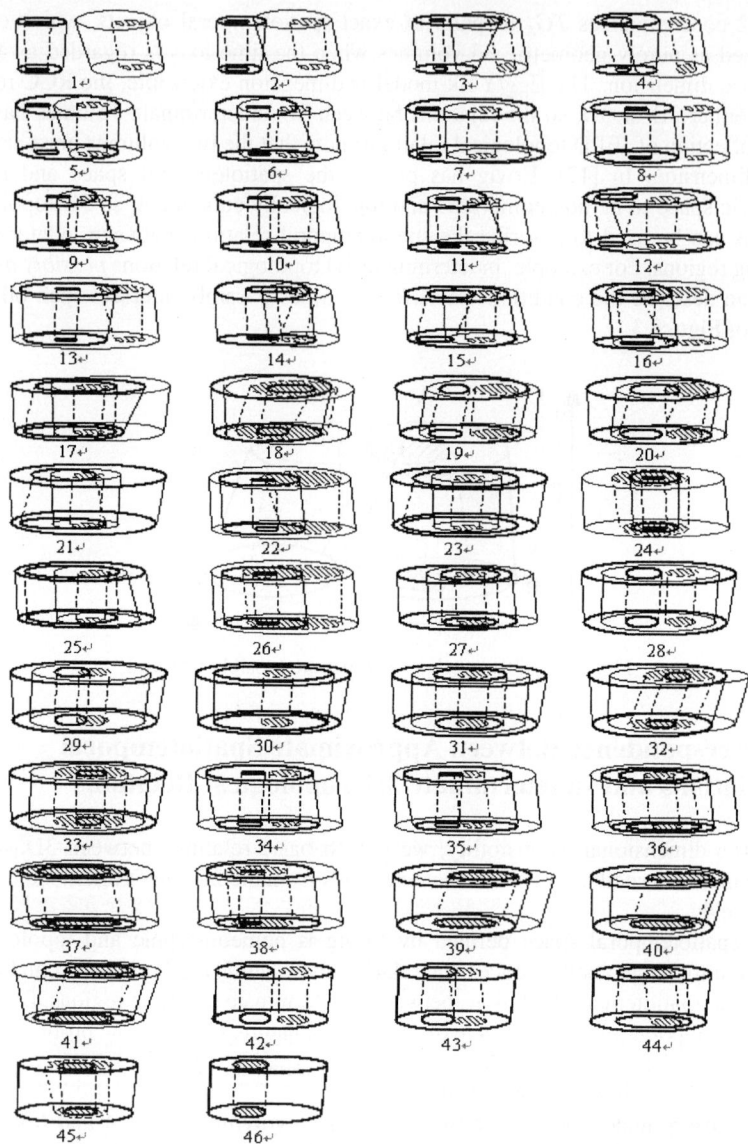

Fig. 4. Basic relations between 3D volumes pairs

Predicate *at* returns the snapshots of spatiotemporal objects at a given time.

As shown in **Figure 6,** two common indeterminate evolving regions can be sliced into several parts, while the sliced parts between *t1*, *t2* and *t3* conform to our assumption.

Another problem will arise when we use 3d topological relation to describe spatiotemporal relations, that is, some spatiotemporal relations require that topological relations remain valid throughout the whole time span of objects, while 3d topological predicates are not restricted to being valid on the whole coordinate of time dimension.

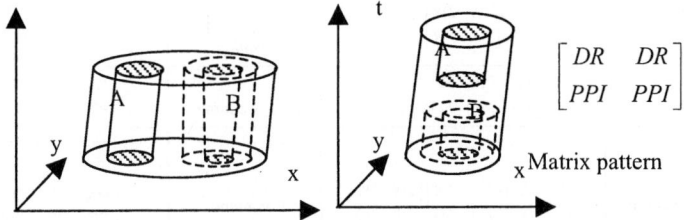

Fig. 5. Different spatiotemporal relations with the same topological relation

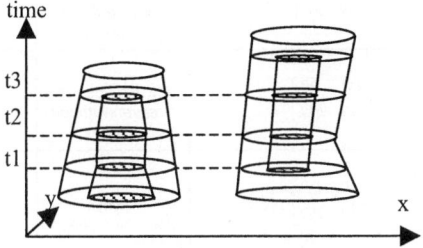

Fig. 6. Slicing of time

To distinguish these different conditions, we introduce the key words *sometimes* and *always*,

Sometimes $R(A,B) \Leftrightarrow \exists t \in \text{timespan}(A) \cap \text{timespan}(B), R(at(A,t), at(B,t))$,
Always $R(A,B) \Leftrightarrow \forall t \in \text{timespan}(A) \cap \text{timespan}(B), R(at(A,t), at(B,t))$

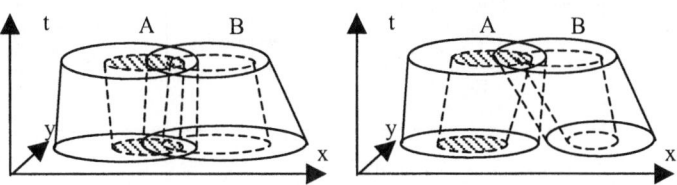

Fig. 7a. Always possibly overlap **Fig. 7b.** Sometimes possibly overlap

Figure 7 illustrates the difference between *always possibly overlap* and *sometimes possibly overlap*.

By using these two key words *Always* and *Sometimes*, the relations clusters of the 2d Egg/Yolk model should be further examined and regrouped. The correspondence

Table 1. The relation clusters between indeterminate time evolving 2d regions

Cluster name	Matrix pattern	Cluster name	Matrix pattern
Always disjoint	$\begin{bmatrix} DR & DR \\ DR & DR \end{bmatrix}$	Sometimes overlap	$\begin{bmatrix} PO & PO \\ PO & PO \end{bmatrix}$
Always inside	$\begin{bmatrix} PP & PP \\ PP & PP \end{bmatrix} \begin{bmatrix} PP & PP \\ EQ & PP \end{bmatrix}$	Always contains	$\begin{bmatrix} PPI & PPI \\ PPI & PPI \end{bmatrix} \begin{bmatrix} PPI & EQ \\ PPI & PPI \end{bmatrix}$
Sometimes possibly meet	$\begin{bmatrix} DR & DR \\ DR & PO \end{bmatrix} \begin{bmatrix} DR & DR \\ PO & PO \end{bmatrix} \begin{bmatrix} DR & PO \\ DR & PO \end{bmatrix}$	Sometimes possibly overlap	$\begin{bmatrix} DR & PO \\ PO & PO \end{bmatrix} \begin{bmatrix} DR & PP \\ DR & PO \end{bmatrix}$ $\begin{bmatrix} DR & PP \\ PO & PO \end{bmatrix} \begin{bmatrix} DR & DR \\ PPI & PO \end{bmatrix}$ $\begin{bmatrix} DR & PO \\ PPI & PO \end{bmatrix}$
Always Coveredbyboundary	$\begin{bmatrix} DR & PP \\ DR & PP \end{bmatrix}$	Always Possibly coveredbyboundary	$\begin{bmatrix} DR & PP \\ PO & PP \end{bmatrix}$
Always coverswithboundary	$\begin{bmatrix} DR & DR \\ PPI & PPI \end{bmatrix}$	Always Possibly coverswithboundary	$\begin{bmatrix} DR & PO \\ PPI & PPI \end{bmatrix}$
Sometimes boundaryoverlap	$\begin{bmatrix} DR & PP \\ PP & PO \end{bmatrix}$	Always boundaryoverlap	$\begin{bmatrix} DR & PP \\ PPI & PPI \end{bmatrix} \begin{bmatrix} DR & PPI \\ PP & PPI \end{bmatrix}$ $\begin{bmatrix} DR & PP \\ PPI & EQ \end{bmatrix}$
Sometimes strongoverlap	$\begin{bmatrix} PO & PP \\ PPI & PO \end{bmatrix} \begin{bmatrix} PO & PP \\ PPI & PP \end{bmatrix} \begin{bmatrix} PO & PP \\ PPI & PPI \end{bmatrix}$ $\begin{bmatrix} PO & PP \\ PPI & EQ \end{bmatrix} \begin{bmatrix} PPI & PP \\ PPI & PO \end{bmatrix} \begin{bmatrix} PP & PP \\ PPI & PO \end{bmatrix}$	Always StrongOverlap	$\begin{bmatrix} EQ & PP \\ PPI & PO \end{bmatrix}$
Sometimes nearlycoverdby	$\begin{bmatrix} PO & PP \\ PO & PO \end{bmatrix} \begin{bmatrix} PO & PP \\ PO & PP \end{bmatrix}$	Always nearlycoverdby	$\begin{bmatrix} PP & PP \\ PO & PP \end{bmatrix} \begin{bmatrix} PP & PP \\ PO & PO \end{bmatrix}$
Sometimes nearlycovers	$\begin{bmatrix} PO & PO \\ PPI & PO \end{bmatrix} \begin{bmatrix} PO & PO \\ PPI & PPI \end{bmatrix}$	Always nearlycovers	$\begin{bmatrix} PPI & PO \\ PPI & PPI \end{bmatrix} \begin{bmatrix} PPI & PO \\ PPI & PO \end{bmatrix}$
Always nearlyfill	$\begin{bmatrix} PP & PP \\ PPI & PP \end{bmatrix} \begin{bmatrix} PP & PP \\ PPI & PPI \end{bmatrix} \begin{bmatrix} PP & PP \\ PPI & EQ \end{bmatrix}$ $\begin{bmatrix} EQ & PP \\ PPI & PPI \end{bmatrix}$	Always nearlyfilledby	$\begin{bmatrix} EQ & PP \\ PPI & PP \end{bmatrix} \begin{bmatrix} PPI & PP \\ PPI & PPI \end{bmatrix}$ $\begin{bmatrix} PPI & PP \\ PPI & PP \end{bmatrix} \begin{bmatrix} PPI & PP \\ PPI & EQ \end{bmatrix}$
Always equal	$\begin{bmatrix} EQ & PP \\ PPI & EQ \end{bmatrix}$		

between 3D topological RCC relations and these two keywords can be described in 5 lemmas as follows:

Lemma 1 $DR^{3d} \leftrightarrow$ *always disjoint*
Lemma 2 $PO^{3d} \leftrightarrow$ *sometimes overlap*
Lemma 3 $PP^{3d} \leftrightarrow$ *always inside*
Lemma 4 $EQ^{3d} \leftrightarrow$ *always equal*
Lemma 5 $PPI^{3d} \leftrightarrow$ *always Contain*

We only provide proof for **Lemma 1** due to the length limit of this paper:

Proof for Lemma 1. For $\mathbf{DR}^{3d}(A,B)$, let $Z = \{z \in IR \mid \exists x, y \in IR : (x, y, z \in A \cap B)\}$, if $\mathbf{DR}^{3d}(A,B)$ holds, then for each $z \in Z$, *disjoint* holds for those regions obtained as cuts parallel to the plane from A and B. Interval Z can be mapped to a time interval T, and for all times $t \in T$, disjoint holds for $at(A,t)$ and $at(B,t)$. For all $z \notin Z$, predicate *disjoint* can not hold. Consequently, for all $t \notin T$, predicate disjoint can hold for $at(A,t)$ and $at(B,t)$, so disjoint always holds, and vice versa.

By using these lemmas, the 46 basic topological relations can be grouped into spatiotemporal relations clusters which have different spatiotemporal natures. The 21 relation clusters named and corresponding matrix patterns are listed in Table 1.

The clustering of these relations and the neighborhood graph of clusters is shown in **Figure 8**.

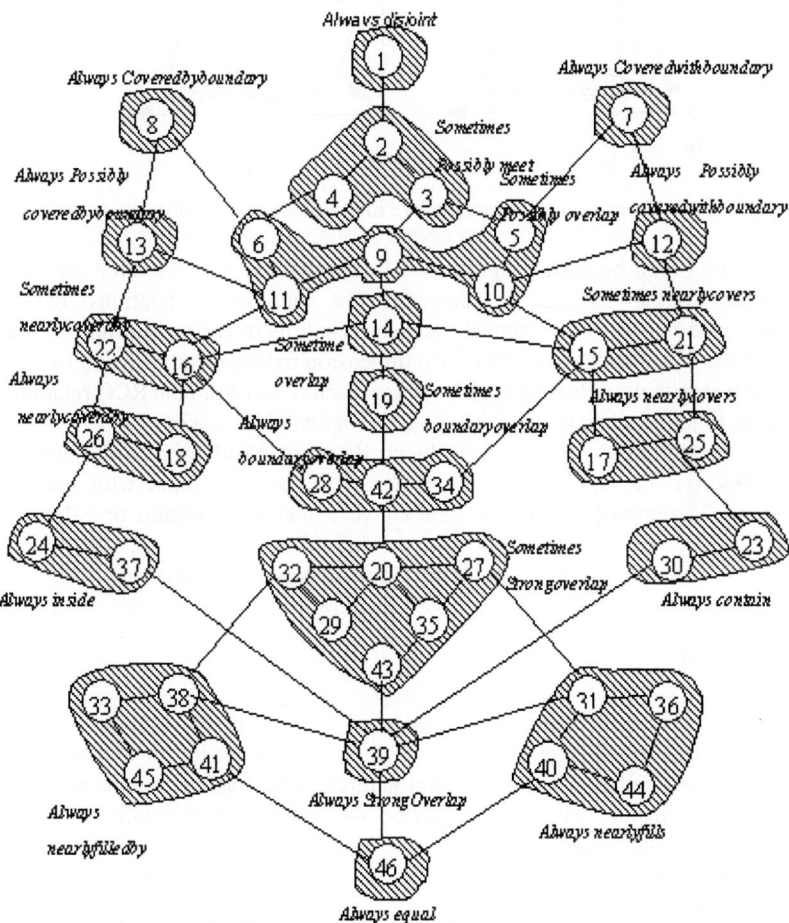

Fig. 8. Neighborhood graph of relation clusters

5 Comparison to Related Works

The area of research that is relevant to the model presented in this paper is the topological relation model of spatial objects[3][4]. Our model is based on the 2D indeterminate topological model presented in reference [4]. The main difference between our work and that model is that we extended it to the third dimension and paid more attention to the temporal nature of spatiotemporal relations.

Figure 9 shows two relations groups, *Sometimes nearlycoveredby* and *Always nearlycoveredby,* and their matrix pattern. In the 2D version model, these 2 relations are grouped into one relation cluster, but for spatiotemporal relations, they are different.

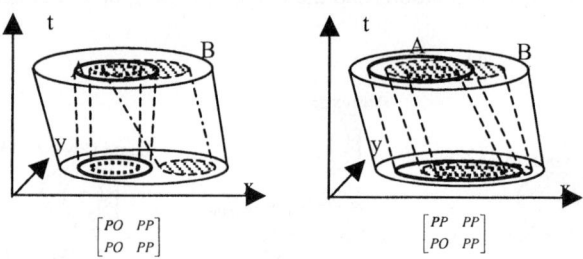

Fig. 9.(a) Sometimes nearlycoveredby   **Fig. 9. (b)** Always nearlycoveredby

Clementini's broad boundary region model extended the 9-intersection model for indeterminate spatial regions to describe the topological relations between indeterminate 2d regions and obtained the same result as reference [9] did. We have noticed that the 9-intersection model is also dimension extensible and is also fit for 3d volumes. The reason we chose the Egg/Yolk approach is that from the RCC relations it can be easier to judge when to use the keywords *sometimes* or *always*.

Another relevant area is the moving objects database. Wolfson provided four key words to describe the uncertain relations between moving points with uncertain positions and 2d regions[20], but he didn't give a formal definition or calculation methods of these relations. While following the definition of our model, one can judge certain spatiotemporal relations from the RCC relations between crisp volumes.

6 Conclusion

In this paper, we extended the Egg/Yolk model to the third dimension; the result is a collection of basic topological relations which is jointly exclusive and pair wise disjoint. From their different spatiotemporal natures, these basic relations are further grouped into 21 clusters which can describe the indeterminate relations between indeterminate evolving regions.

The novel findings are:

(1) A formal definition of topological relations between indeterminate spatiotemporal objects.

(2) We checks the correspondence between relations of 3d indeterminate objects and relations of indeterminate spatiotemporal objects and provides some restrictions to make the 3d relation model fit for spatiotemporal objects.

Issues still to be investigated include:

(1) Topological relations between complex objects and objects which have different dimensions, or indeterminate moving points, for instance.
(2) Fast algorithms for the computation of matrix elements.

Acknowledgements

This work was supported by the grant of National Nature Science Foundation of China (69973032) and the grant of State Nature Science Foundation of JiangSu (BK2001045).

References

1. Schneider, M.: Finite resolution crisp and fuzzy spatial objects. Proceedings of the 9th International Symposium on Spatial Data Handling. Beijing: International Geographical Union (2000) 3-17
2. Winter, S.: Uncertainty of topological relations in GIS. Proceedings of ISPRS Commission III Symposium: Spatial Information from Digital Photogrammetry and Computer Vision. Bellingham (1994)924-930
3. Clementini,E. Felice,D.: Approximate topological relations. International Journal of Approximate Reasoning, Vol 16 No. 2(1997)173-204.
4. Cohn AG, Gotts NM: The 'Egg-Yolk' representation of regions with indeterminate boundaries. In: Burrough PA, Frank AU, eds. Geographic Objects with Indeterminate Boundaries. London: Taylor & Francis(1996)171-187.
5. Andrew UF. Qualitative spatial reasoning about cardinal directions. Proc. of the 7th Austrian Conf. on Artificial Intelligence. Baltimore(1991) 157~167
6. Christian F. Using orientation information for qualitative spatial reasoning. Proc. of the Int'l Conf. on GIS. Berlin: Springer-Verlag(1992)162-178
7. Roop G, Egenhofer MJ. Similarity of Cardinal Directions. Advances in Spatial and Temporal Databases. Redondo Beach: Springer-Verlag(2001) 36-55
8. Wolter F, Zakharyaschev M. Qualitative spatio-temporal representation and reasoning: A computational perspective. Exploring Artificial Intelligence in the New Millenium. San Francisco(2002) 175-216
9. Bennett B, Cohn G, Wolter F, Zakharyaschev M. Multi-Dimensional modal logic as a framework for spatio-temporal reasoning. Applied Intelligence, Vol 3, No. 4(2002) 239-251
10. Asher N, Vieu L. Towards a geometry of common sense: A semantics and a complete axiomatisation of mereotopology. Proc. of the 14th Int'l Joint Conf. on Artificial Intelligence. Montréal(1995)846-852
11. Muller. Topological spatio-temporal reasoning and representation. Computational Intelligence, Vol 18, No. 3(2002)420-450
12. Medak D. Lifestyles—A paradigm for the description of spatiotemporal databases [Ph.D. Thesis]. Vienna: Technical University Vienna(1999)
13. Viqueira JRR. Relational algebra for spatio-temporal data management. Proc. of the EDBT 2000 Ph.D. Workshop. Konstanz (2000)235-243

14. Claramunt C. Extending Ladkin's algebra on non-convex intervals towards an algebra on union-of regions. Proc. of the 8th ACM Symp. on GIS. Washington(2000) 9-14
15. Ladkin PB. The logic of time representation [Ph.D. Thesis]. Berkekey: University of California at Berkeley(1987)
16. Muller: A qualitative theory of motion based on spatio-temporal primitives. Proc. of the 6th Int'l Conf. on Knowledge Representation and Reasoning. Trento(1998)131-143
17. Erwig M., Schneider M.: Spatio-Temporal predicates. IEEE Trans. on Knowledge and Data Engineering, Vol 14, No. 4(2002)881~901
18. Tossebro E.,Nygard M.: Uncertainty in Spatiotemporal Databases. In Proc. 2nd Biennial Int. Conference on Advances in Information Systems,(2002)43-53
19. Bao Lei, Qin Xiao-Lin: The Overview of Grey Spatiotemporal Data Types. 2nd Asian Workshop on Foundations of Software. Nanjing(2003)53~57
20. Wolfson O.: Querying the Uncertain Position of Moving Objects. Temporal Databases: Research and Practice. Springer Verlag LNCS 1399(1998)

Using Special Structured Fuzzy Measure to Represent Interaction Among IF-THEN Rules

Xi-Zhao Wang and Jun Shen

Machine Learning Center, Faculty of Mathematics and Computer Science,
Hebei University, Baoding, 071002, China
wangxz@mail.hbu.edu.cn, shenjun79225@126.com

Abstract. When fuzzy IF-THEN rules are used to approximate reasoning, interaction exists among rules. Handling the interaction based on a non-integral can lead to an improvement of reasoning accuracy but the determination of non-linear integral usually needs to solve a linear programming problem with too many parameters when the rules are a little many. That is, the number of parameters increases exponentially with the number of rules. This paper proposes a new approach to denoting the interaction by a 2-additive fuzzy measure which replaces the general set function of the old non-linear integral approach. The number of parameters determined in the new approach is greatly less than the number of parameters in the old approach. Compared with the old approach, the new one has a little loss of accuracy but the new approach reduces the number of parameters from an exponential to polynomial quantity.

1 Introduction

Fuzzy IF-THEN rules are widely used in expert systems to represent fuzzy and uncertain concepts. Given a set of FPRs and an observed fact, FPR reasoning is used to draw an approximate conclusion by matching the observed fact against the set of FPRs. Many researchers have investigated this fundamental issue in fuzzy reasoning ([1-6]).

It is important to find the interaction among rules. Interaction can help domain experts discover new knowledge existing among rules. With respect to a given consequent, knowing and modelling the enhancing or resisting effect among rules learned from data is helpful to maintain the rule base. By discovering the interaction among the rules and then applying it to fuzzy reasoning, it is expected to improve the reasoning accuracy. In [1], we can see the WFPR (Weighted Fuzzy Production Rule) fails to apply to such a situation that interaction exists among the rules. In order to handle this situation, the authors propose to use a non-linear integral tool. The interaction among the rules is considered as the non-additive set function, and the classification is computed by using the integral model. Such a handling of interaction in fuzzy IF-THEN rule reasoning can lead to a well understanding of the rule base, and also can lead to an improvement of reasoning accuracy.

Reference [1] investigates how to determine from the given data the non-additive set function which cannot be specified by domain experts. The main problem of the proposed approach to interaction handling is too many parameters when the number of the rules increases. The approach is not appropriate in many situations due to the exponentially increasing complexity. In order to solving this problem, we could consider the special structured fuzzy measure to replace the general set function. There are many fuzzy measures that have the special structure, for example, the belief fuzzy measure, the plausibility fuzzy measure, λ – fuzzy measure, 2-additive fuzzy measure and so on. In [8, 9], the authors once used genetic algorithms to determine the λ – fuzzy measure. In this paper, we propose using 2-additive fuzzy measure to represent the interaction among the rules such that the representation parameters can be reduced greatly. The parameter reduction is at the cost of some loss of accuracy.

2 Background on Fuzzy Measures and Integrals

2.1 Fuzzy Measures

Definition 1. A fuzzy measure μ defined on X is a set function $\mu : p(X) \to [0,1]$, satisfying the following axioms:

(1) $\mu(\emptyset) = 0, \mu(X) = 1$

(2) $A \subseteq B \Rightarrow \mu(A) \leq \mu(B)$

A fuzzy measure can be additive, supper-additive, or sub-additive. Let $X = \{R_1, R_2, \cdots, R_n\}$ be a set of rules with the same consequent. We regard A, B as two subsets of rules. $\mu(A)$ is the importance of the subset A. The additive means that there is no interaction among two subsets; the sub-additive and super-additive mean that there exists interaction. The sub-additive indicates that the two sets of rules are resisting each other; super-additive means that the two sets of rules are enhancing each other.

2.2 k-Additive Fuzzy Measures

Definition 2. A Pseudo-Boolean function is a real valued function $f : \{0,1\}^n \to \Re$.

A fuzzy measure can be viewed as a particular case of the pseudo-Boolean function, defined for any $A \subset X$, such that A is equivalent to a $\{x_1, x_2, ..., x_l\}$ in $\{0,1\}^l$, where $x_i = 1$ if $i \in A$. It can be shown that any pseudo-Boolean can be expressed as a multi-linear polynomial in L variables, that is $f(x) = \sum_{T \subset L} \left\{ a(T) \prod_{i \in T} x_i \right\}$

with $a(T) \in R$ and $x \in \{0,1\}^l$. The coefficients $a(T), T \subset X$ can be interpreted as the Mobius transform of a set function. We note $\mu_i = a_i$, $\mu_i = \mu(\{i\}), a_i = a(\{i\})$.

Definition 3. A fuzzy measure μ defined on X is said to be k-order additive if its corresponding Pseudo-Boolean function is a multi-linear polynomial of degree k, i.e., $a(T)=0$, $\forall T$ such that $|T|>K$, and there exits at least one T of k elements such that $a(T)\neq 0$.

For any $K \subset X$ and $|K|\geq 2$, with $x_i=1$ if $i\in K$, $x_i=0$ otherwise. The 2-additive fuzzy measure is defined by: $\mu(K)=\sum_{i=1}^{n}a_i x_i + \sum_{\{i,j\}\subseteq X}a_{ij}x_i x_j$. The fact that $\mu_i = a_i$ for all i, we can get the following expression:

$$\mu_{ij}=\mu(\{x_i,x_j\})=a_i+a_j+a_{ij}=\mu_i+\mu_j+a_{ij}.$$

The general formula for 2-additive fuzzy measure is

$$\mu(K)=\sum_{i\in K}a_i + \sum_{\{i,j\}\subseteq K}a_{ij} = \sum_{\{i,j\}\subseteq K}\mu_{ij}-(|K|-2)\sum_{i\in K}\mu_i$$

for any $K\subset X$ and $|K|\geq 2$. For example

$$\mu_{ijk}=\mu(\{x_i,x_j,x_k\})=\mu_i+\mu_j+\mu_k+a_{ij}+a_{ik}+a_{jk}.$$

The 2-additive fuzzy measure is determined by the coefficients μ_i and μ_{ij}, only $L(L+1)/2$ coefficients μ_i and μ_{ij} have to be determined from training data. The coefficients for all other subsets $K\subset X$ and $|K|\geq 2$ are calculated from μ_i and μ_{ij}. In order to obtain a monotonic fuzzy measure, the coefficients μ_i and μ_{ij} must satisfy particular conditions. The monotonicity which constraints on the coefficients of the 2-additive fuzzy measure can be formulated as follows:

$$\sum_{j\in K}\mu_{ij}-\sum_{j\in K}\mu_j-(L-2)\mu_i\geq 0, \forall i\in X, K\subseteq X\setminus\{i\} \quad (1)$$

where $|X|\models L$, to obtain a fuzzy measure normalized to the interval $[0,1]$, the coefficients μ_i and μ_{ij} must also satisfy the normalization condition, for $k=2$, we have $\mu(X)=\sum_{i\in X}\mu_i + \sum_{\{i,j\}\subseteq X}a_{ij}=1$.

In order to ensure the monotonicity and normalization, 2-additive fuzzy measure satisfies constrains:

$$a(\emptyset)=0,$$

$$\sum_{i\in L}a_i + \sum_{\{i,j\}\subseteq L}a_{ij}=1, a_i\geq 0, \forall i\in L,$$

$$a_i + \sum_{j\in T}a_{ij}\geq 0, \forall i\in L, \forall T\subseteq L\setminus\{i\}.$$

The concept of 2-additive fuzzy measure provides a trade-off between richness and complexity of fuzzy measure.

2.3 Fuzzy Integral

Fuzzy integral is a type of integrals of a real function with respect to a fuzzy measure. There have been several definitions of fuzzy integrals. We restrict our discussion here to the Choquet integral.

Definition 4. Let $X = \{x_1, x_2, ..., x_n\}$, μ be a fuzzy measure defined on the power of X, f be a function from X to $[0,1]$. The Choquet integral of f with respect to μ is defined by

$$(C)\int_X f d\mu = C_\mu(f(x_1),...,f(x_n)) = \sum_{i=1}^n \left(f(x_{(i)}) - f(x_{(i-1)})\right)\mu(A_i)$$

where the subscript (i) indicates that the indices have been permuted so that $0 \le f(x_{(1)}) \le ... f(x_{(n)}) \le 1$, also $A_i = (x_{(1)},...,x_{(n)})$, and $f(x_0) = 0$.

3 Using 2-Additive Fuzzy Measure to Represent Interaction Among Rules

Yeung et al. determined the set function by solving a linear programming problem in [1]. The main problem of the proposed approach to interaction is too many parameters when the number of rules increases. At this stage, the approach is not yet appropriate for many cases due to the exponential complexity. Actually, it is not feasible to implement in the real world. In this paper we propose to use 2-additive fuzzy measure to replace the general set function for the interaction handling. In [1], the number of the parameters of a set function is $2^m + 2^{M-m} - 2$. If we use 2-additive fuzzy measure instead of the set function, we only need to determine $m \times (m+1)/2 + (M-m) \times (M-m+1)/2$ parameters.

Let us recall in detail the question given in [1]. Suppose that, using some learning techniques, we have already extracted M fuzzy rules from the N examples. The FPR form is IF (attribute-value) THEN (Class), where the class is either C1 or C2. The extracted M rules are categorized into two groups, $S_1 = \{R_i, i=1,2,...,m\}$ and $S_2 = \{R_i, i=m+1, m+2,..., M\}$, one leading to the consequent C1 and the other leading to C2. The N examples are also classified into two parts, as follows: $T_1 = \{e_i, i=1,2,...,n\}$ and $T_2 = \{e_i, i=n+1, n+2,...N\}$. The actual classification of the examples within T_1 is C1, and within T_2 is C2. Noting the definitions of S_1, S_2 and T_1, T_2, we hope that the following inequalities hold: $x_{i1} > x_{i2}$ for $i=1,2,...,n$, $x_{i1} < x_{i2}$ for $i = n+1, n+2,..., N$.

We may numerically determine the fuzzy measure which is unknown by using the optimisation criterion of reasoning accuracy. Let μ_1, μ_2 be two set functions defined on $S_1 = \{R_i, i=1,2,...,m\}$ and $S_2 = \{R_i, i=m+1, m+2,...,M\}$.

Suppose that matching degree functions of e_i matching S_1 and S_2 are

$$f_{i1} = \left(SM_i^{(1)}, SM_i^{(2)}, \ldots SM_i^{(n)}\right) \text{ and } f_{i2} = \left(SM_i^{(m+1)}, SM_i^{(m+2)}, \ldots SM_i^{(M)}\right),$$

where $SM_i^{(j)}$ is the result of e^i matching the j-th rule R_j $(i=1,2,\ldots,N; j=1,2,\ldots,M)$
then $x_{i1} = (C)\int_{S_1} f_{i1} d\mu_1$ and $x_{i2} = (C)\int_{S_2} f_{i2} d\mu_2$.

Therefore we have the following inequalities:

$$(C)\int_{S_1} f_{i1} d\mu_1 > (C)\int_{S_2} f_{i2} d\mu_2 \text{ for } i=1,2,\ldots,n,$$

$$(C)\int_{S_1} f_{i1} d\mu_1 < (C)\int_{S_2} f_{i2} d\mu_2 \text{ for } i=n+1,n+2,\ldots,N,$$

subject to $0 \leq \mu_1, \mu_2 \leq 1$.

If we use 2-additive fuzzy measure instead of the set function in [1], the problem of solving the inequalities (13)-(16) in [1] can be transformed into the following linear programming problem (2).

Minimize: $\xi_1 + \xi_2 + \ldots + \xi_n$

Subject to
$$\sum_{i=1}^{m}\sum_{j=i}^{m} b_{ij}^k a_{ij} + \sum_{i=m+1}^{M}\sum_{j=i}^{M} b_{ij}^k a_{ij} + \xi_k > 0 \quad K=1,2,\ldots N \quad (2)$$

$$\sum_{i \in L_1} a_{ii} + \sum_{\{i,j\} \subseteq L_1} a_{ij} = 1 \quad L_1 = \{1,2,\ldots,m\};$$

$$\sum_{i \in L_2} a_{ii} + \sum_{\{i,j\} \subseteq L_2} a_{ij} = 1 \quad L_2 = \{m+1, m+2, \ldots, M\};$$

$a_{ii} \geq 0 \quad \forall i \in L_1, \forall i \in L_2;$

$a_{ii} + \sum_{j \in T_1} a_{ij} \geq 0 \quad \forall i \in L_1, \forall T_1 \subseteq L_1 \setminus \{i\};$

$a_{ii} + \sum_{j \in T_2} a_{ij} \geq 0 \quad \forall i \in L_2, \forall T_2 \subseteq L_2 \setminus \{i\};$

$\xi_i > 0 \quad i=1,2,\ldots N$

where a_{ii} is the measure of R_i, μ_{ij} is the measure of $\{R_i, R_j\}$,

$$L_1 = \{1,2,\ldots,m\}, L_2 = \{m+1, m+2, \ldots M\} \quad \mu_i = a_i = a_{ii},$$
$$\mu_{ij} = a_i + a_j + a_{ij} = a_{ii} + a_{jj} + a_{ij}.$$

In this section, with respect to our particular issues of handling interaction among rules, we only need to determine the values of μ_i and μ_{ij}, that is a_{ii} and a_{ij}. Once we determined the value of a_{ii} and a_{ij}, the other value of the composed rules can be expressed by a_{ii} and a_{ij}. The details about no interaction case are presented in [1].

When we use 2-additive fuzzy measure to replace the set function, the advantage is that the number of parameters is reduced from an exponential to polynomial quantity with the increasing number of rules; the disadvantage is that the accuracy may be lower than the set function. Because 2-additive fuzzy measure satisfies monotocinity, it only considers the enhancing-effect as the interaction exists among rules, but the resisting-effect cannot be considered. The set function not only expresses the enhancing-effect but also resisting-effect properly, but it has too much computational complexity.

4 Experimental Simulation

We chose 5 widely used machine learning classification problems to verify advantages of our method. The five databases employed for experiments are obtained from [7]. We conduct our experiments as follows. Each database is randomly split into two parts. One part is used for training while the remaining is used for testing.

Table 1. The comparative of the reasoning accuracy of globally weighted, the set function, 2-additive fuzzy measure

Database	Globally weighted		The set function		2-additive fuzzy measure	
	Training accuracy	Testing accuracy	Training accuracy	Testing accuracy	Training accuracy	Testing accuracy
Glass Identification	60%	58.47%	70.47%	61.54%	66.67%	60%
Pima India diabetes	75.06%	73.6%	78.4%	74.46%	77.47%	74.03%
Rice taste	84.9%	84.4%	86.3%	87.5%	84.9%	87.5%
Mango	70.96%	72%	71.55%	72%	72.41%	72%
Wine	95.97%	77.78%	95.97%	79.63%	95.97%	77.78%

From Table1, we can summarize the following experimental conclusion:

1) To a certain degree, the amount of training and testing accuracy improvement depends on the concrete structure of database.

2) Of the five databases, the accuracy of using 2-additive fuzzy measure to represent the interaction is between the weighted fuzzy reasoning and reasoning based on the set function.

3) In Table 1, the Mango leaf data's testing accuracy is almost same in three methods. This implies that the rules extracted from the database have not interactive effect. Wine data shows that the learning accuracy does not improve significantly. This implies that the rules extracted from the databases have little interactive effect. In these

situations the handling of interaction among rules can be replaced with handling based on weights.

4) From Rice Taste and Glass Identification databases, we can see that the interaction exists among the rules and the accuracy of using 2-additive fuzzy measure to represent the interaction is between the weighted fuzzy reasoning and the reasoning based on the set function.

From Table 1, we see that the interaction can be ignored in some databases. We also see that 2-additive fuzzy measure can replace the set function in some cases and to some extent.

5 Conclusions

The number of the determined parameters by using a set function is too large when there are many rules. It is not feasible to implement in the real world. This paper proposes using 2-additive fuzzy measure to replace the set function for the interaction handling. The main advantage is that the parameters can be reduced greatly. The disadvantage is that the reasoning accuracy of using the 2-additive to represent the interaction is little lower than using the set function in some cases. To balance the complexity (i.e., the number of parameters to be determined) and the reasoning accuracy, this paper seems to have given an appropriate trade-off by replacing the general set function with the 2-additive fuzzy measure.

Acknowledgement

This research is supported by the National Natural Science Foundation of China (NSFC 60473045 / 60573069); the Natural Science Foundation of Hebei Province (603137).

References

1. Daniel Yeung, Xi-Zhao Wang, Handling Interaction in Fuzzy Production Rule Reasoning, IEEE Transactions on Systems, Man and Cybernetics, Part B: Cybernetics, Volume: 34, No.5, October 2004, pp. 1-9
2. M. Grabisch, The representation of importance and interaction of features by fuzzy measures, Pattern Recognition Letters., vol.17,pp.567-575,1996.
3. D.S.Yeung and E.C.C.Tsang, A comparative study on similarity based fuzzy reasoning methods, IEEE Trans, Systems, Man, Cybernetics, part B, vol.27, pp. 216-227, Apr. 1997.
4. D.S.Yeung and E.C.C.Tsang, A multilevel weighted fuzzy reasoning algorithm for expert systems, IEEE Transactions on System. Man and Cybernetics, vol. 28, pp.149-158, Apr. 1998.
5. D. S. Yeung and E. C. C. Tsang, Weighted fuzzy production rules, Fuzzy Sets and Systems, vol. 88, No 3, pp. 299-313, 1997
6. Shyi-Ming Chen, Weighted Fuzzy Reasoning Using Weighted Fuzzy Petri Nets, IEEE Transactions on Knowledge and Data Engineering, Volume: 14, No.2, March/April 2002, pp. 386-397

7. UCI Repository of Machine Learning Databases and Domain Theories[Online]. Available: ftp://ftp.ics.uci.edu/pub/machine-learningdatabases
8. W. Wang, Z. Wang, and G. J. Klir, "Genetic algorithms for determining fuzzy measure from data," J. Intell. Fuzzy System, vol. 6, no. 2, pp.171–183, 1998.
9. Z. Wang, K.-S. Leung, and J. Wang, "A genetic algorithm for determining nonadditive set functions in information fusion," Fuzzy Sets Systems, vol. 102, no. 3, pp. 463–469, 1999.

Novel Nonlinear Signals Separation of Optimized Entropy Based on Adaptive Natural Gradient Learning

Ren Ren[1,2], Jin Xu[3], Shihua Zhu[1], Danan Ren[4], and Yongqiang Luo[1]

[1] School of Electronic & Information Engineering, Xian Jiao Tong University,
Xi'an 710049, P.R. China
[2] Department of Physics, Xian Jiao Tong University, Xi'an 710049, P.R. China
[3] Institute of Biomedical Engineering, Xian Jiao Tong University, Xi'an 710049, P.R. China
[4] Department of Mathematics, Northwest University, Xi'an 710069, P.R. China
renr01@sohu.com

Abstract. Without knowing the signal probability distribution and channel, novel blind source separation (BSS) of singular value decomposition (SVD) with adaptive minimizing mutual information is proposed to extract mixed signals. Adaptive natural gradient decent algorithm attains fast convergence speed and reliability. We focus on applying cost function BSS and SVD to achieve the solution of decomposition signals. The results indicate that the SVD combining minimizing mutual information can predict the extent of mixed signal and searching direction. The simulation illustrates that the method improves the performance, convergence and reliability. The different results can be attained by distinctive nonlinear function. The algorithm of adaptive changing de-mixed function is a better way to break through the limitation of nonlinear BSS.

1 Introduction

In recent years, there are few important topics of research and developments in blind signal processing areas, especially remote sensing, communication, data mining, neural network, biomedical engineering, radar, image processing and speech sounds. Blind source separation consists of on-line and non-line algorithm, whole blind source and semi blind source separation. Independent component analysis (ICA), adaptive filter analysis and maximizing entropy estimation are the main ideas of this subject. Now, ICA research in these areas is a fascinating blend of heuristic theories of blind source separation.

The blind algorithm needn't know the channel information and source signals. Because of not using any training sequence, the system saves precious channel bands and improves the information transmission efficiency. But the OFDM system makes out the signals by utilizing redundant information produced by cycle prefix and correlated information of receiver signals. The defects are that OFDM has a long time convergence and requires high SNR. Using all kinds of prior information, semi-blind adopts the known signals training sequence and estimating the source data in a semi-blind way. In the light of data, the system estimates the channel to improve the estimated signals precision by stepwise recursion. Using few signals, the estimated error reduces.

In wireless communication information processing, a linear or non-linear transform is designed to solve the decomposed problem. The maximizing entropy and ICA utilize statistically independent components to separate source signal from the mixture of independent sources by optimizing some criteria. The mixture data of receiver can be decomposed into useful signal subspace and noise subspace using standard techniques like robust PCA, SVD and nonlinear adaptive filtering.

Herelt and Jutten began BSS research early. Burel proposed symplectic nonlinear analysis to recover the independent component using neural network in 1996. The group of Pajunen, Hyvarinen and Karhunen adopted a self-organization map to extract the source signals, but the network algorithm complexity goes up with exponential form. Cardoso solved BSS using polynomial functions. Bell and Comon use the method of sigmoid functions. Amari was interested in the development of biologically plausible neural network models with unsupervised learning which can separate and extract the useful signal from mixed biomedical source signals disturbed by interference and noise. Another group of researchers is interested in using the blind method of digital communication system, such as MIMO equalizers/ filters, combiners of inter symbol interference (ISI), multi-path interferences, adjacent and cochannel channel interferences (ACI and CCI)[1,2,5,10,11,12,13,14].

2 Blind Signal Separation

The model of blind subspace separation can be given in the following form: supposing that a transmitter is permuted by a column vector, the signals adapt expression of mixing dictionary. The source signals are n-dimensional vector $S=[S_0, S_1, S_2......S_{n-1}]^T$ and vector forms N×1 matrix. Here we have two types of interference. The first kind is the adjacent channel interference of which output is a mixture signal of transmitter source. The second is so called "inner noise" produced by inter symbol interference and some primary sources that can't be observed directly, but contained in the observations. $S_i=[f(i, 0), f(i,1), f(i,2), ..., f(i,M-1)]^T$, wireless channel matrix H is M×N real matrix. Formally the model can be written as follows; a received m-dimensional vector of signal X(k) is a mixture of source signal plus observation errors.

$$x(k) = Hs(k) + n(k) \qquad (1)$$

Where K=0,1,2,...... is a discrete-time index; $x(k)=[x_0,x_1,x_2,......,x_{m-1}]^T$ is a m-dimensional vector of receiver signal; n(k) is m-dimensional vector of additive Gaussian white noise.

From the matrix, if R is the rank of m×n real matrix and real symmetry square matrix H, eigenvalue are λ_i (i=1,2, 3,..., R, R<min[m,n]). Supposed that eigen vectors satisfy orthogonal generalized condition, it means that source signals have equalizing value zero and variance one. $[\lambda_1 \lambda_2 ..... \lambda_{R-1}]$ eigenvalue are arranged as $\lambda_1 \geq \lambda_2 \geq ... \geq \lambda_R$.

The mixed signal is an observed vector of x(k) with noise and channel interference. Therefore, the mathematics model of separation subspace can be expressed:

$$x(k) = Hs(k) \quad k=1,2,3,... \qquad (2)$$

Because a wireless channel has non-linear properties, we cannot decompose the independent source signal from the mixture matrix unless source signals have independent restrain. When the mixture of non-linear function isn't limited, mixture signals only solved by independent or uncorrelated properties don't ensure decomposition of any information from source signals. Hence, we suppose the signal separated process course as following.

3 De-mixing Model and Maximizing Entropy

Considering the mixture output is $x(t) = f(As(t))$ according to non-linear properties, Let $g(x(t)+\theta) = f^{-1}(x(t))$ and

$$y(t) = A^{-1}g(x(t)+\theta) \quad (3)$$

where f(·) generally is an unknown non-linear function, and supposing that $H \in R^{m \times n}$ is non-singular mixing matrix. The model of the system can be assumed as shown in Fig 1 [6,7,8,9].

Fig. 1. Mixing and separation system structure

When $g(x(t)+\theta) = f^{-1}(x(t))$, $W = A^{-1}$, then
$$y = Wg(x(t)+\theta)$$
$$= A^{-1}g(x(t)+\theta)$$
$$= A^{-1}f^{-1}(x(t)) = s(t)$$

For an diagonal matrix Λ and permutation of matrix P,
$$W = \Lambda P A^{-1}$$
$$y = Wg(x(t)+\theta)x(t)$$
$$= \Lambda P A^{-1}g(x(t)+\theta)f(As(t))$$
$$= \Lambda P s(t)$$

Here the signal source vector estimation is $y(t)=[y(0),y(1),y(2),\ldots,y(N-1)]^T \in R^N$. According to the blind source separation based on nonlinear wireless channel and nonlinear mixture, the source signal matrix first deals with linear mixture, then is processed by non–linear mixture. So the separation ways of blind signal must be first shifted by non-linear inverse transformation g(.) or $f^{-1}(.)$. Furthermore, signal vector v(t) is solved by linear transform W or A^{-1} as shown in Fig1.

Let λ_i is the eigenvalue of R-dimension vector, corresponding none zero eigen vectors v_i (i=1,2,3,...,R).

Supposing that U_i, V_i put in order of column to form matrix 1×m and matrix 1×n. It is given by

$$U = [u_1, u_2, ..., u_R, u_{R+1}, u_{R+2}, ..., u_m]$$
$$V = [v_1, v_2, ..., v_R, v_{R+1}, v_{R+2}, ..., v_n]$$

Let us make the eigenvalue λ_i of matrix H in order of reducing, adding zero to form matrix m×n. The number of row of zero vectors is m-R, and the number of column of zero vectors is n-R

$$\Lambda = \text{diag}(\lambda_1, \lambda_2, ..., \lambda_R)$$

$$\Lambda = \begin{bmatrix} \lambda_1 & & & & 0 \\ & \lambda_2 & & & \\ & & ... & & 0 \\ 0 & & & \lambda_R & \\ & & 0 & & 0 \end{bmatrix}$$

From matrix theory of eigen vectors, eigenvalue can be defined as follows.

$$HH^T u_i = \lambda_i u_i$$
$$H^T H v_i = \lambda_i v_i$$

Then the result is, $HH^T U = U\Lambda^{\frac{1}{2}}[\Lambda^{\frac{1}{2}}]^T$, $H^T V = V[\Lambda^{\frac{1}{2}}]^T \Lambda^{\frac{1}{2}}$

Because that U and V are real symmetry square matrix, $U^T = U^{-1}$,

$$HH^T = U\Lambda^{\frac{1}{2}}[\Lambda^{\frac{1}{2}}]^T U^T$$
$$HH^T = V[\Lambda^{\frac{1}{2}}]^T \Lambda^{\frac{1}{2}} V^T$$

$$H = U\Lambda^{\frac{1}{2}} V^T \qquad (4)$$

Let the right expression (4) is expanded

$$H = \sum_{i=1}^{R} \lambda_i^{\frac{1}{2}} u_i v_i^T \qquad (5)$$

Where $\lambda_i^{\frac{1}{2}}$ is the singular value of channel responses matrix H, it is decomposed by the way of singular value decomposition.

The above singular value decomposition (SVD) can separate the mixture source signals to apply in recovering source signals.

When the number of transmitter vectors n is smaller than the number of receiver signals m, n<m, the matrix H is an orthogonal and can be decomposed and applied to recover the information of source signals. The vector $u_i v_i^T$ is the base of high

dimension. Each transmitter source signal can be expressed by base vector. We use recursion weight to adapted to the singular value and convergence gradient.

It can be seen that, singular value decomposition procedure actually is an orthogonal transform process. Utilizing statistically independent properties of transmitter signals and supposing that transmitter signals are synchronised, we don't use the parameter of channel and only take advantage of orthogonal statistically independent properties to identify the source signal subspace. Final, mixture signal space separation can be identified by SVD and ICA from blind spaces to recover transmitter signals.

If m>n the number of receivers is more than the number of transmitters, linear equation system number is more than the unknown number of signals. The equation is called over-determined. If the order of column matrix H is N, H^TH is m×n square matrix; and H^TH is full rank which the rank of equation is n. the result is $(H^TH)^{-1}H^TH = E_n$.

However, problems in practice are often that, when the number of transmitter signals n is more than the number of receiver signals m, it is difficult in recovering the source signals because that observed signal number is not enough to turn up the source signals. Under-determined completeness matrix and equation n<m, the signals are not able to be recovered. The reason is that matrix H is not a square matrix, but a m×n matrix ; although H is a square matrix, determinant of H is equal to zero. If the matrix H^{-1} don't exist, $\hat{S} = H^{-1}x$ can't be built.

Therefore, $H^+=H^T(HH^T)^{-1}$ is assumed to be generalized inverse matrix of H, it is defined by Moore-Penrose inverse matrix, and it is satisfied with conditions of the generalized inverses of matrix uniqueness $HH^+H=H$, $H^+HH^+=H^+$, $(HH^+)^T=H^+H$.

Here E is identity matrix, and $(H^TH)^{-1}$ inverse matrix exists. From the generalized inverses of matrix $H^+=H^T(HH^T)^{-1}$, we can finish the solution of $\hat{S}$ estimation value. Under the situation n>m, the equation system number is smaller than the number of unknown numbers, the equation is called underdetermined. Supposing the number of receiver antennas is m; the rank of matrix HH^T is m; there are relations as $HH^T(HH^T)^{-1}$ =E_R , E_R is R order unit matrix.

Theorem 1: If X=HS solution exist (under-determined), $\hat{S} = H^+X$ is the solution of minimal norms in all equation solutions.

Theorem 2: If X=HS solution don't exist (over-determined), $\hat{S} = H^+X$ is the vector of minimal norm of the approximate solution in all of the methods of least squares.

In addition, it is the optimum estimation using generalized inverse operations instead of solving inverse under the least squares.

3.1 The Least Squares Estimation of Over-Determined Equation

The least squares estimation requires the error square norm $\|X-H\hat{S}\|^2$ of vector $\hat{S}$ to be minimum. The signal vector $H\hat{S}$ of least square estimation closes to the receiver signal vector X and MMSE is the smallest [3,4,5].

Find the vector $L \in R^n$ that minimizes the cost function

$$L = \| X - HS \|^2 \tag{6}$$

Where $e_i(s) = x_i - h_i^T s = x_i - \sum_{j=1}^{n} h_{ij} s_j$

The cost function approaches the global minimum when its gradient equals zero

$$\frac{\partial \| X - H\hat{S} \|}{\partial \hat{S}} = 0$$

$$\nabla L = H^T (X - HS) = 0$$

Since $\hat{S}^T H^T X = X^T H \hat{S}$,

$$\frac{\partial \| X - H\hat{S} \|^2}{\partial \hat{S}} = \frac{\partial \{ X^T X - \hat{S}^T H^T X - X^T H \hat{S} + \hat{S}^T H^T H \hat{S} \}}{\partial \hat{S}}$$

$$= \frac{\partial \{ X^T X - 2\hat{S}^T H^T X + \hat{S}^T H^T H \hat{S} \}}{\partial \hat{S}}$$

$$= -2H^T X + 2H^T H \hat{S}$$

Hence,

$$\hat{S} = (H^T H)^{-1} H^T X \tag{7}$$

Where $(H^T H)^{-1} H^T$ is the generalized inverse of matrix. Under over-determined, the inverse matrix exist $\hat{S} = H^{-1} X$.

3.2 The Solution of Underdetermined

When n>m, a least square approximate error is the vector of minimal norm. Under the Gaussian noise and channel interference, the generalized inverse matrix is instead of inverse matrix to solve the problem without concerning for the solution and solution uniqueness.

Let $\hat{S} = H^+ X$ on the basis of Gaussian noise, $\hat{S} = H^+ HS + H^+ n$. The source signal S_i and noise n can be separated from mixing signals by using SVD (singular value decomposition) and ICA (Independent component analysis). Channel matrix H is decomposed by the generalized inverse of matrix way as:

$$H = U \Lambda^{\frac{1}{2}} V^T = \sum_{i=1}^{R} \lambda_i^{\frac{1}{2}} u_i v_i^T \tag{8}$$

Where λ_i is eigenvalue of eigen vectors corresponding with difference transmitter wireless signal. Here u_i and v_i eigenvalue is equal. HH^T and H^TH eigen vectors are u_i and v_i respectively.

$$H^+ = V[\Lambda]^{-\frac{1}{2}} U^T = \sum_{i=1}^{R} \frac{1}{(\lambda_i)^{\frac{1}{2}}} v_i u_i^T \tag{9}$$

4 Minimizing Mutual Information and Gradient Algorithm

The blind source separation problem can be transferred into an optimization problem of multi-channel minimizing mutual information. Supposed that,

$$H(y;G) = I(y1,\ldots,yn;G) = -H(y1,y2,\ldots,yn\mid G) + H(y1,y2,\ldots,yn)$$
$$= H(G) - H(G\mid y1,y2,\ldots,yn)$$

$$H(y;G) = \sum H(y_i,G) - H(y;G) \tag{10}$$

Where $H(y_i;G) = -\int P_i(y_i;G)\ln P_i(y_i;G)dy_i$ and $H(y;G) = -\int P(y;G)\ln P(y;G)dy$ are the marginal PDF(probability distribution function) of y_i (i =0,1,2,…,m-1) and the joint probability density function of y respectively. In order to solve the temporarily independently and spatially mutual independent, we adapt the K-L divergence as well as mutual information to be a cost function

$$I(W) = I(y_1, y_2, \ldots, y_n; G) = \sum_{i=1}^{n} H(y_i, G) - H(y; G)$$

$$L(W) = I(W) = I(y_1, y_2, \ldots, y_n; G) = \sum_{i=1}^{n} H(y_i, G) - H(y; G) \tag{11}$$

Assuming that partitioned matrix V which front column n consist of sub matrix V_1, hind column (m-n) are formed by zero matrix V_2

$$Y = GX = U\Lambda V = U\Lambda V_1$$

According to the

$$H(y;G) = \ln|\det(U\Lambda)| + H(V^T_i x)$$
$$\det(\Lambda) = \sqrt{\det(W)}$$

$$L(W) = \sum_{i=1}^{n} \log P_i(y_i(k), W) - \frac{1}{2}|\det(W)|$$

When m=n, the equation system is completeness,

$$L(W) = \sum_{i=1}^{n} H(y_i; G) - \ln|\det(W)| \tag{12}$$

5 Simulation

Supposed that each signal of separating is a combination of sigmoid functions. The mixture model can be thought as

$X(t) = A \tanh(A_1 s(t))$, $X(t) = A\, (A_1 s(t))^{\frac{1}{3}}$, or $X(t) = A\, (A_1 s(t))^3$

Where the source vector is $s(t)$.

$$s(t) = [s1, s2, s3, s4, s5, s6, s7, s8, s9]^T$$

The algorithm performance can be measure by the performance index defined by

$$E = \sum_{j=1}^{m} [(\sum_{l=1}^{m} \frac{|a_{jl}|}{\max_k |a_{jk}|} - 1) + (\sum_{l=1}^{m} \frac{|a_{lj}|}{\max_k |a_{kj}|} - 1)] \quad (13)$$

Where $A = [a_{jl}]$ expresses the transmission matrix of system model, the properties of the system model are illustrated as shown in Fig1,2. The nine sub source signals shown have been mixed to be the mixing matrix. Uncorrelated Gaussian noise signals are added to every $X(k)$. Channel interference is Rayleigh distribution which elements

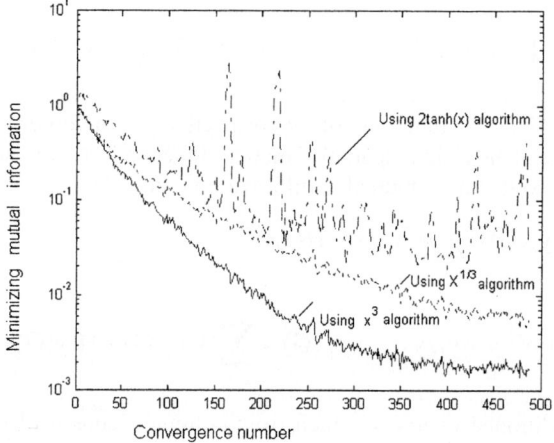

Fig. 2. The adaptive blind separating convergence speed

m_i is the even probability distribution $[0, +1]$, Rayleigh distribution sequence $s_i = \mu\sqrt{2 \ln m_i}$, where μ is the mean of Rayleigh distribution. With the associated learning rules and nonlinearity $x_i = f(As_i)$ and $v(y_i) = \tanh(10x_i)$, the first nine signals x_i are the mixed signal, and the second nine signals are the estimated source signals using the adaptive learning algorithm. The horizontal axis represents time in seconds. We have observations in which the order and amplitude of signals are indefinite.

The simulation observation indicates that, when the typical function $2\tanh(x)$, $x^{\frac{1}{3}}$ and x^3 are used in the nonlinear separating, the convergence rate is shown as Fig2 with adaptive algorithm. The ways of using $x^{\frac{1}{3}}$ and x^3 are faster in convergence and better in performance than the function 2tanh(x). The best way is the function x^3. The minimizing mutual information is the criterion of measuring the quality of source signal separating.

6 Conclusion

The paper discusses BSS problem of mixture signals based on adaptive minimizing mutual information gradient algorithm, SVD and ICA. The general adaptive natural gradient cost function method of completeness, under-determined and over-determined BSS evaluated separation quality. It separated source signals from observed data subspace and noise subspace successfully. The optimized minimizing mutual information gradient algorithm realizes minimizing cost function. The works aim at reducing signals interference and extracting noise signals. Above all, despite not having known the channel parameters and source signal information, the system is able to recover the transmitter source signals. The way of minimizing mutual information not only recovers mixing signals, but also attains better convergence and stability.

Acknowledgements

Supported by the National Natural Science Foundation of China under Grant 60372055, 30400101, and the Xian Jiao Tong University Natural Foundation xjj2004013.

References

1. zhang L., Amari S.: Estimating function approach to multi-channel blind deconvolution. Circuits and Systems IEEE APCCAS 2000, 12(4-6). (2000) 587-590
2. Amari S.: superefficiency in blind source separation. IEEE trans. on signal processing. 47(4).(1999) 936-944
3. Tsatsanis M.K., Giannakis G.B.: Blind estimation of direct sequence spread spectrum signals in multipath. IEEE Trans. Signal Processing. 45(5).(1997)1241-1252
4. Tugnait J.K.: Blind spatio-temporal equalization and impulse response estimation for MIMO channels using a Godard cost function. IEEE Trans. Signal Processing. 45(1). (1997) 268-271
5. Tugnait J.K.: Adaptive blind separation of convolutive mixtures of independent linear signals", EURASIP Journal Signal Processing .73(1-2).(1999)139-152
6. Cruces-Alvarez S.A., Cichocki A., Amari A.: From blind signal extraction to blind instantaneous signal separation: criteria, algorithms, and stability. IEEE Trans. on Neural Networks. 15(4).(2004) 859-873
7. Belouchrani A., Abed-Meraim K.: Blind separation of nonstationary sources. IEEE Signal Processing Letters. 11(7).(2004) 605-608

8. Ferreol A., Chevalier P.: Second-order blind separation of first- and second-order cyclostationary sources-application to AM, FSK, CPFSK, and deterministic sources. IEEE Trans. on Signal Processing. 52(4).(2004) 845-861
9. Asano F., Ikeda S., Ogawa M., Asoh H.: Combined approach of array processing and independent component analysis for blind separation of acoustic signals. IEEE Trans. Speech and Audio Processing. 11(3). (2003) 204- 210
10. Cardoso J.-F., Souloumiac A.: Blind beamforming for non Gaussian signals. IEE-Proceedings-F. 140(6). December. (1993) 362 –370
11. Jutten C., Herault J.: Separation of sources. Part i. Signal Processing. 24(1).July (1991) 1 –10
12. Bell A. J., Sejnowski T. J.: An information maximization approach to blind separation and blind deconvolution. Neural Computation. 7(6). (1995) 1129-1159
13. Comon P.: Independent component analysis, a new concept. Signal Processing. 36(3). April, (1994) 287 -314
14. Amari S., Cichocki A., Yang H. H.: A new learning algorithm for blind signal separation. Advances in Neural Information Processing Systems. Vol. 8. (1996) 757 –763

Training Conditional Random Fields with Unlabeled Data and Limited Number of Labeled Examples*

Tak-Lam Wong and Wai Lam

Department of Systems Engineering and Engineering Management,
The Chinese University of Hong Kong, Shatin, Hong Kong
{wongtl, wlam}@se.cuhk.edu.hk

Abstract. Conditional random fields is a probabilistic approach which has been applied to sequence labeling task achieving good performance. We attempt to extend the model so that human effort in preparing labeled training examples can be reduced by considering unlabeled data. Instead of maximizing the conditional likelihood, we aim at maximizing the likelihood of the observation of the sequences from both of the labeled and unlabeled data. We have conducted extensive experiments in two different data sets to evaluate the performance. The experimental results show that our model learned from both labeled and unlabeled data has a better performance over the model learned by only considering labeled training examples.

1 Introduction

Many research problems such as language processing and bioinformatics can be formulated as sequence labeling tasks [1,2]. For example, automatic part-of-speech (POS) tagging considers a sentence as a sequence of tokens. Its objective is to identify the part of speech of the tokens, based on the observation from the sentence. In essence, sequence labeling aims at assigning the class labels to the states of a sequence given the observation of the states. Various approaches applying machine learning techniques have been proposed to automatically train a sequence labeling system from a set of manually prepared training examples. For instance, Hidden Markov Models (HMM) has been applied in different kinds of text documents to extract information [3-5]. Linear classification models have also been studied to handle sequential data [6,7]. The trained system can then be applied to automatically label the sequence.

Recently, Lafferty et al. proposed to apply undirected graphical model known as *conditional random fields* to solve the sequence labeling problem [8]. Conditional random fields is a probabilistic framework employing the discriminative approach.

---

* The work described in this paper is substantially supported by grants from the Research Grant Council of the Hong Kong Special Administrative Region, China (Project Nos: CUHK 4179/03E and CUHK4193/04E), the Direct Grant of the Faculty of Engineering, CUHK (Project Code: 2050363), and CUHK Strategic Grant (No: 4410001). This work is also affiliated with the Microsoft-CUHK Joint Laboratory for Human-centric Computing and Interface Technologies.

There are several characteristics of conditional random fields. The first characteristic is that it can model the long range dependence between the state and the observation, as well as the inter-dependency between neighbouring states. The second characteristic is that unlike Naive Bayesian approach, it allows the use of dependent or overlapping features. The third characteristic is that iterative methods such as improved iterative scaling [9,10] and conjugate-gradient method [11] can be applied for parameter estimation. In general, conditional random fields achieves very good results in sequence labeling learning task.

Though the proposed learning algorithms including conditional random fields can automate the labeling process, one major problem exists is that quite a lot of human effort is required to manually prepare the labeled training examples in advance. Preparation of large number of labeled training examples can be expensive and time consuming. In normal circumstances, unlabeled data can be easily obtained with relatively less cost. Recently, many works in different research fields demonstrate that unlabeled training examples can be valuable for learning. For instance, Nigam et al. presented that both labeled and unlabeled training examples can be exploited in parameter estimation under the expectation-maximization (EM) framework and showed that their method gives substantial improvement in the text classification task [12]. Co-training is another method for using both labeled and unlabeled training examples [13]. Another example is in the parameter estimation of HMM. Unlabeled training examples can be easily incorporated by using the well developed Baum-Welch training algorithms. Previous literatures also reveal that generative models such as HMM can take the advantage of unlabeled training examples in the training process under the EM framework (Baum-Welch basically is an EM algorithm) by treating the class variables as the unobserved or hidden variables [14-16]. Essentially, unlabeled training examples can be incorporated in generative models because generative models consider the joint probability of all the observed and unobserved variables in the learning process.

Discriminative models are normally not obvious for incorporating unlabeled data since they consider the mapping from the observed variables to the unobserved variables based on the labeled training examples instead of gathering all the distribution information. In this paper, we are interested in tackling this problem by developing a technique which can train the conditional random fields using a small amount of labeled training examples and a set of unlabeled data. We develop a method which can improve the parameter estimation by making use of both labeled and unlabeled training examples. We conducted experiments in two different domains to demonstrate the effectiveness of our method.

2 Review of Conditional Random Fields

2.1 Basic Model and Inference

In sequence labeling, we consider the graph shown in Figure 1. Let X and Y be the entire sequence of observed and unobserved variables consisting of N states respectively. In the figure, x_i is the sequence of observed variables $\{x_i \in X : i=1,2,\ldots, N\}$ and

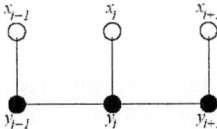 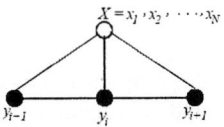

Fig. 1. An undirected chain graph representing the sequence of observed variables X and unobserved variables Y. x_i and y_i represent the observed variable and unobserved variable at the i-th state respectively, where $i=1,2,\ldots,N$.

Fig. 2. An undirected graph which is a generalization of the one shown in Figure 1

y_i is the sequence of unobserved variables $\{y_i \in Y : i=1,2,\ldots,N\}$ where i represents the i-th state. According to the Hammersley-Clifford Theorem, the joint probability of all the variables in an undirected graph is in the form of Gibbs distribution as follows:

$$P(W) = \frac{1}{Z} \exp\{ \sum_{\Omega_i \in \Omega} \Omega_i(W) \} \qquad (1)$$

where $W = X \cup Y$; Ω is the collection of all the cliques and $\Omega_i(W)$ is the clique potential function for the i-th clique. A clique is defined as the maximum complete sub-graph. Z is called the partition function which is defined as follows:

$$Z = \sum_W \exp\{ \sum_{\Omega_i \in \Omega} \Omega_i(W) \} \qquad (2)$$

so that the constraint $\sum_W P(W) = 1$ must be satisfied. Equation 1 can be rewritten as:

$$P(W) = \exp\{ \sum_{\Omega_i \in \Omega} \Omega_i(W) - \log Z \} \qquad (3)$$

Computing the log partition function is intractable for moderate number of variables in W. Therefore, some techniques such as Markov Chain Monte Carlo are proposed to approximate the log partition function.

To avoid the problem in the calculation of the log partition function, we can consider the following conditional probability:

$$P(Y|X = x) = \exp\{ \sum_{\Omega_i \in \Omega} \Omega_{i|X=x}(Y) - \log Z(x) \} \qquad (4)$$

where $\Omega_{i|X=x}(Y)$ is the i-th clique potential function given $X=x$ and $Z(x)$ is a function defined as:

$$Z(x) = \sum_Y \exp\{ \sum_{\Omega_i \in \Omega} \Omega_{i|X=x}(Y) \} \qquad (5)$$

Contrary to the partition function Z in Equation 2, $Z(x)$ can be computed efficiently using dynamic programming for the chain graph as shown in Figure 1. Consider the graph in Figure 1, Equation 4 can be rewritten as:

$$P(Y|X = x) = \exp\{ \sum_{i=1}^{N} \lambda_i f_i(x_i, y_i) + \sum_{i=2}^{N} \mu_i g_i(y_{i-1}, y_i) - \log Z(x) \} \qquad (6)$$

where λ_i and μ_i are the weights, f and g are binary feature functions. For example, $f(x_i, y_i) = 1$ if x_i="computer" and y_i="NNP" at the i-th token in the part-of-speech tagging task. Without losing generality, Equation 6 can be rewritten as:

$$P(Y|X=x) = \exp\{\sum_{i=2}^{N} \gamma_i h_i(x, y_{i-1}, y_i) - \log Z(x)\} \qquad (7)$$

where γ_i is the weights and $h_i(x, y_{i-1}, y_i)$ is the binary feature function which associates with x, y_{i-1}, and y_i. Equation 7 essentially refers to the graph shown in Figure 2 which is the generalization of the one shown in Figure 1. Figure 2 reveals that conditional random fields can model the long range dependence between the state and the observation because each state variable y_i is connected to all the observed variables $X = x_1, x_2, \ldots, x_N$.

Given the set of parameters γ and the observation x of a sequence, the optimal labeling y can be calculated using the Viterbi-like algorithm. In essence, the solution can be found by solving the following problem:

$$\hat{y} = \arg\max_{y} P(Y = y | X = x) \qquad (8)$$

2.2 Parameter Estimation

Suppose there are L labeled training examples and let Λ be the set of all labeled training examples. The conditional likelihood for the occurrence of this set of labeled training examples given the set of model parameters γ is:

$$P_\gamma(\Lambda) = \prod_{j=1}^{L} P(Y = y^{(j)} | X = x^{(j)}) \qquad (9)$$

The log likelihood function is:

$$L(\gamma|\Lambda) = \sum_{j=1}^{L} \{\sum_{i=2}^{N} \gamma_i h_i(x^{(j)}, y_{i-1}^{(j)}, y_i^{(j)}) - \log Z(x^{(j)})\} \qquad (10)$$

The parameter estimation is achieved by maximizing the log likelihood function. Equation 10 can be proved to be convex and the gradient is expressed as follows:

$$\frac{\partial L(\gamma|\Lambda)}{\partial \gamma_i} = \sum_{j=1}^{L} h_i(x^{(j)}, y_{i-1}^{(j)}, y_i^{(j)}) - \sum_{j=1}^{L} E_{P_\gamma(Y|X=x^{(j)})}[h_i(x^{(j)}, y_{i-1}, y_i)] \qquad (11)$$

where $E_{P(\cdot)}[h]$ is the expected value of h over the probability distribution $P(\cdot)$. Therefore, the maximum of Equation 10 is obtained if the following expression holds:

$$E_{\tilde{p}(X,Y)}[h_i(x, y_{i-1}, y_i)] = \frac{1}{|L|}\{\sum_{j=1}^{L} E_{P_\gamma(Y|X=x^{(j)})}[h_i(x^{(j)}, y_{i-1}, y_i)]\} \qquad (12)$$

where $\tilde{p}(\cdot)$ is the empirical distribution of the labeled training examples. However, we cannot obtain the analytical solution in closed form. Therefore, iterative methods such as improved iterative scaling and conjugate gradient methods can be employed to find the solution of γ.

3 Incorporate Unlabeled Data

The parameter estimation in conditional random fields is achieved by maximizing the conditional likelihood function stated in Equation 9. Owning to this, it is not easy to incorporate unlabeled data in the parameter estimation process. Let U be the number of unlabeled data and Λ' be the set of unlabeled data. Then the conditional likelihood of the occurrence of the data is expressed as

$$P_\gamma(\Lambda,\Lambda') = \prod_{j=1}^{L} P(y^{(j)}|x^{(j)}) \prod_{k=1}^{U} P(y^{(k)}|x^{(k)}).$$

Since the value of Y is unknown in unlabeled data, if we perform similar operation in EM replacing $P(y^{(k)}|x^{(k)})$ with $\Sigma_{y' \in Y} P(Y=y'|x^{(k)})$, $P_\gamma(\Lambda,\Lambda')$ becomes

$$\prod_{j=1}^{L} P(y^{(j)}|x^{(j)}) \prod_{k=1}^{U} \sum_{y' \in Y} P(Y = y'|x^{(k)})$$

which can be expressed as $\Pi_{j=1}^{L} P(y^{(j)}|x^{(j)})$. This shows that the unlabeled data has no effect in the conditional likelihood. Therefore, to incorporate unlabeled data, we modify the criteria in parameter estimation. Instead of maximizing the conditional likelihood function of the unobserved variable Y, our objective is to maximize the likelihood of the observed variable X, i.e., $P'_\gamma(\Lambda,\Lambda') = \Pi_{j=1}^{L} P(x^{(j)}) \Pi_{k=1}^{U} P(x^{(k)})$. Maximizing this likelihood function is equivalent to minimizing the following Kullback-Leibler (KL) divergence:

$$D(\tilde{P}(X)\|P_\gamma(X)) = \sum_{x \in X} \tilde{P}(x) \log \frac{\tilde{P}(x)}{P_\gamma(x)} \tag{13}$$

To minimize this KL divergence, we have:

$$\begin{aligned}
\min_\gamma & D(\tilde{P}(X)\|P_\gamma(X)) \\
= \min_\gamma & \sum_{x \in X} \tilde{P}(x) \log \frac{\tilde{P}(x)}{P_\gamma(x)} \\
= \min_\gamma & \sum_{x \in X} \tilde{P}(x) \log \frac{\tilde{P}(x)}{Z(x)/Z} \\
= \min_\gamma & \sum_{x \in X} \tilde{P}(x) \log \tilde{P}(x) - \sum_{x \in X} \tilde{P}(x) \log Z(x) \\
& + \sum_{x \in X} \tilde{P}(x) \log Z \\
= \min_\gamma & \sum_{x \in X} \tilde{P}(x) \log \tilde{P}(x) - \sum_{x \in X} \tilde{P}(x) \log Z(x) \\
& + \log Z \\
= \min_\gamma & - \sum_{x \in X} \tilde{P}(x) \log Z(x) + \log Z
\end{aligned}$$

Proposition 1. Equation 9 and Equation 13 achieve their maxima and minima respectively in the same condition if the expected value of any feature over the empirical distribution in the labeled training examples is the unbiased estimator for the expected value of the corresponding feature in the population.

Proof: Let $G(\gamma) = -\Sigma_{x \in X} \tilde{P}(x) \log Z(x) + \log Z$. Consider the gradient of $G(\gamma)$:

$$\frac{\partial G(\gamma)}{\partial \gamma_i} = - \sum_{x \in X} \tilde{P}(x) E_{P_\gamma(Y|X=x)}[h_i(x, y_{i-1}, y_i)] + E_{P_\gamma(X,Y)}[h_i(x, y_{i-1}, y_i)] \tag{14}$$

Setting the gradient to zero yields the following equation:

$$E_{P_\gamma(X,Y)}[h_i(x, y_{i-1}, y_i)] = \sum_{x \in X} \tilde{P}(x) E_{P_\gamma(Y|X=x)}[h_i(x, y_{i-1}, y_i)] \tag{15}$$

Suppose S is the set containing sufficiently large number of samples drawn from $P_\gamma(X,Y)$. Equation 15 can be written as follows:

$$E_{P_\gamma(X,Y)}[h_i(x, y_{i-1}, y_i)] = \frac{1}{|S|} \{ \sum_{j=1}^{|S|} E_{P_\gamma(Y|X=x^{(j)})}[h_i(x^{(j)}, y_{i-1}^{(j)}, y_i^{(j)})] \} \tag{16}$$

where $|S|$ denotes the size of S. In optimal condition, $P_\gamma(X,Y) = \tilde{P}(X,Y)$ and the expected value of any feature over the model distribution is equal to the expected value of the corresponding feature over the empirical distribution. Therefore,

```
# Conditional random fields learning algorithm using labeled and unlabeled data
Input:  A set of labeled training examples L; A set of unlabeled data U;
        An initial conditional random fields model γ₀
Output: A refined conditional random fields model γ*

Algorithm
1. Randomly partition U into two disjoint sets U_A and U_B
2. t ← 0
3. Until convergence
4.     Compute Ψ using Equation 18
5.     Compute Φ using Equation 19
6.     Compute the gradient of G(γ) using the formula: ∂G(γ)/∂γᵢ = Ψ − Φ
7.     Obtain the new model γ_{t+1} using the newly computed gradient
8.     t ← t + 1
9. γ* = γ_t
```

Fig. 3. The outline of the conditional random fields learning algorithm using labeled and unlabeled data

$$E_{\tilde{P}_\gamma(X,Y)}[h_i(x, y_{i-1}, y_i)] = \frac{1}{|S|}\{\sum_{j=1}^{|S|} E_{P_\gamma(Y|X=x^{(j)})}[h_i(x^{(j)}, y_{i-1}^{(j)}, y_i^{(j)})]\} \tag{17}$$

which is equivalent to Equation 12.

Suppose we have a set of labeled and unlabeled data, Proposition 1 reveals that if we can obtain the empirical expected value of the features for the entire set of data, the minima of Equation 13 can be achieved by updating the parameters γ such that Equation 17 is satisfied. Since the calculation of the right hand side (RHS) of Equation 17 does not require the true value of Y, it can be calculated using both of the labeled and unlabeled data. As the calculation of the empirical expected value of the features requires the information of X and Y of the data, we need to solve the problem of obtaining the empirical expected value of the features for the entire set of data which is composed of labeled and unlabeled data.

We develop an algorithm addressing the above issue. Figure 3 depicts the outline of our algorithm. The idea of our algorithm is to update the empirical expected value for the entire set of data by making use of a portion of unlabeled data and the current model. We first partition the unlabeled data U into two disjoint sets, namely, U_A and U_B. In each iteration of the learning process, we update the empirical expectation of the features by computing Ψ which is defined as follows:

$$\Psi = \frac{1}{|L|+|U_A|}\{\sum_j^{|L|} h_i(x^{(j)}, y_{i-1}^{(j)}, y_i^{(j)}) + \frac{|U_A|}{|U_B|}\sum_k^{|U_B|} E_{P_{\gamma_t}(Y|X=x^{(k)})}[h_i(x^{(k)}, Y_{i-1}, Y_i)]\} \tag{18}$$

Ψ is composed of two parts. The first part is to directly count the number of occurrence of the feature i in L. The second part is an estimation of the expected value of the feature i in U_B using the current model γ_t. As the model improves, Ψ converges to the empirical expected value according to Proposition 1. In Step 5, we compute Φ, which is basically the model expected value of the feature i in the sets L and U_A. Φ is defined as follows:

$$\Phi = \frac{1}{|L|+|U_A|}\{\sum_j^{|L|} E_{P_{\gamma_t}(Y|X=x^{(k)})}[h_i(x^{(j)}, Y_{i-1}, Y_i)] + \sum_k^{|U_A|} E_{P_{\gamma_t}(Y|X=x^{(k)})}[h_i(x^{(k)}, Y_{i-1}, Y_i)]\} \tag{19}$$

Next the gradient is the difference between Ψ and Φ. After the gradient is obtained, the new model γ_{t+1} can be computed using iterative procedures such as limited-memory quasi-Newton method (L-BFGS) [12].

Table 1. The 24 binary features used in the information extraction experiment

1.	Begin with number	13.	Contain question mark
2.	Begin with ordinal numbers or symbols	14.	Contain question word
3.	Begin with punctuation	15.	Terminate with question mark
4.	Begin with question word	16.	First alphabet is capitalized
5.	Begin with the string ``subject''	17.	Indented
6.	Blank line	18.	Indented from 1 to 4 spaces
7.	Contain alpha-numeric tokens	19.	Indented from 5 to 10 spaces
8.	Contain bracketed number	20.	More than one third of the line is space
9.	Contain the string ``http''	21.	Contain only punctuation
10.	Contain non-space string	22.	Previous line is a blank line
11.	Contain number	23.	Previous line begins with ordinal numbers or symbols
12.	Contain the string ``pipe''	24.	Less than 30 characters

4 Experiment Results

We have conducted extensive experiments in two different tasks to evaluate the performance of our approach. The first task is information extraction from the documents about the seven Usenet multi-part FAQs downloaded from the Internet [17]. In this task, each line of the documents is labeled with either *head*, *question*, *answer*, or *tail*. Our goal is to predict the label of each line based on the texts observed from the documents. The second task is noun phase (NP) chunking of the natural language texts investigated in the Conference on Computational Natural Language Learning (CoNLL) [18]. In each of the documents, the tokens are labeled with one of the three labels: beginning of a chunk (B), continuation of a chunk (C), and outside of a chunk (O). For example, in the text fragment "East Rock Partners Limited said it proposed to ...", the tokens and the corresponding labels are as follows:

East	Rock	Partners	Limited	said	it	Proposed	to
B	C	C	C	O	B	O	O

The objective of this task is to predict the label of each token found in a document.

Table 2. The experimental results in the information extraction task. P, R, and F refer to precision, recall, and F-measure respectively. CRF refers to conditional random fields.

	P(%)	R(%)	F(%)
HMM	41.3	52.9	46.4
MEMM	86.7	68.1	76.3
Ordinary CRF	79.6	76.1	76.9
CRF with unlabeled data	81.0	76.4	77.6

These two tasks are selected for evaluation because of two reasons. The first reason is that the characteristic of the documents in these two tasks are different. In the NP chunking task, the documents are natural language texts. They are largely grammatically correct. On the other hand, the documents used in the information extraction task may not be grammatical and they often have some special formatting structure. We commonly refer such documents as semi-structured documents. The second reason is the difference in the feature size. In the information extraction task, we follow the experimental setup in [17] and only 24 features are selected. In the NP chunking task, thousands of features are used. These characteristics of the tasks can demonstrate the robustness of our approach.

We adopt two evaluation metrics, namely, *precision* (P) and *recall* (R) for the evaluation. Precision is defined as the number of lines (or tokens) for which the system correctly labeled divided by the total number of lines (or tokens) it labeled. Recall is defined as the number of lines (or tokens) for which the system correctly labeled divided by the total number of actual lines (or tokens). We also adopt *F-measure* which combines precision and recall as a harmonic mean which is defined as $2PR/(P+R)$.

4.1 Evaluation on Information Extraction

The documents used in the information extraction task are collected from seven Usenet multi-part FAQs in the Internet. We follow the same experimental setup stated in [17]. In the experiment, we train the model for each of the categories, using one document as the labeled training example from the corresponding category. The remaining documents are regarded as unlabeled data and are used for testing purpose. The trained model is then applied to the testing documents in the same category for evaluation. Suppose there are n documents in the category, we conduct the experiment n times. In each run, a different document is selected as labeled training example to train the model and the remaining n-1 documents become the unlabeled data and are used for testing. The results are the average precision and recall for these n runs. We use the same set of 24 binary features as in [17] as depicted in Table 1. As stated in the algorithm shown in Figure 3, we need to divide U into U_A and U_B. We randomly select one unlabeled document in U to form the set U_A and the remaining documents become U_B.

We compare the performance of our approach with hidden Markov model (HMM), maximum entropy Markov model (MEMM), and ordinary conditional random fields (CRF). Table 2 depicts the results of different methods. The second, third, and fourth columns show the precision, recall, and F-measure respectively. The performance of HMM and MEMM are extracted from the paper stated in [17]. Ordinary conditional random fields shows a better performance over HMM and MEMM because of its discriminative power and the avoidance of label bias problem found in MEMM as stated in [8]. Our approach of incorporating unlabeled data in conditional random fields shows a better result over ordinary conditional random fields. The reason is that if we only learn the model parameters from the labeled training examples, we can just obtain a model which is the fittest to the set of labeled training examples. However, if we incorporate the unlabeled data in parameter estimation, the learned model can be more close to the actual model of the entire set of data composed of labeled and unlabeled data.

4.2 Evaluation on NP Chunking

The data used in the NP chunking experiment is the Wall Street Journal (WSJ) corpus of the Penn Treebank Project [19]. The corpus is divided into several sections. In the original chunking scheme used in CoNLL [18], sections 15-18, which consist of about nine thousand sequences, are used for training. Section 20, which consists of about two thousand sequences, is used for testing. Since our method aims at reducing the human effort in preparing labeled training examples, we used different number of labeled training examples from sections 15, and the remaining sequences in sections 15-18, and 20 as the unlabeled data to train the model. The learned model was then applied to the two thousand sequences in section 20 for testing.

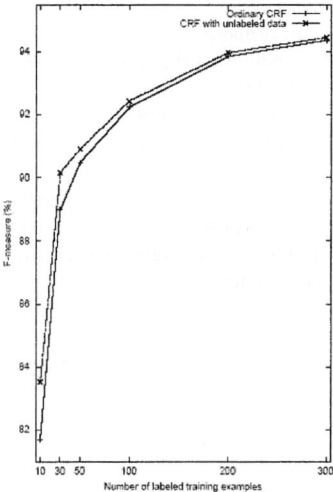

Fig. 4. The experimental results of ordinary conditional random fields and our approach using unlabeled data. The X-axis and Y-axis represent the number of labeled training examples used in the experiment and the F-measure respectively.

In our experiment, we use the same set of features as in [11]. The features of each token mainly consider the words, the part-of-speech tags, and the labels of the token and the tokens around within the window size of two. Figure 4 depicts the results of ordinary conditional random fields and our method for learning conditional random fields with unlabeled data using various number of labeled training examples. It shows that our approach can improve the learned model and achieves better performance. We have also conducted an experiment using all the sequences in section 15 as the labeled training examples. The F-measures for ordinary conditional random fields and conditional random fields with unlabeled data are 95.95 and 95.97 respectively. Another experiment which uses all the sequences from sections 15-18 as labeled training examples and section 20 for unlabeled data was also conducted. This setting is the same experimental setup as in [18]. The performance of ordinary conditional random fields and conditional random fields with unlabeled data are both 96.30. We can notice that if the number of labeled training examples increases, the impact of unlabeled data diminishes. The reason is that the number of labeled training examples is sufficient to reflect the statistics of the entire set of data. Adding more unlabeled data can no longer improve the learned model. However, if a limited amount of labeled training examples are available, unlabeled data can be very useful.

References

1. Brill, E.: Transformation-based error-driven learning and natural language processing: A case study in part-of-speech tagging. Computational Linguistics 21 (1995) 543–565
2. Ratnaparkhi, A.: A maximum entropy model for part-of-speech taggind. In: Proceedings of the Conference on Empirical Methods in Natural Language Processing (EMNLP). (1996) 133-142
3. Bikel, D.M., Schwartz, R., Weischedel, R.M.: An algorithm that learns what's in a name. Machine Learning 34 (1995) 211-231
4. Freitag, D., McCallum, A.: Information extraction with HMM structures learned by stochastic optimization. In: Proceedings of the Seventh National Conference on Artifical Intelligence (AAAI). (2000) 584-589
5. Wong, T.L., Lam, W.: Hot item mining and summarization from multiple auction web sites. In: Proceedings of the Fifth IEEE International Conference on Data Mining (ICDM) (2005) 797-800
6. Punyakanok, V., Roth, D.: The use of classifiers in sequential inference. In: Advances in Neural Information Processing Systems 13. (2000) 995–1001
7. Kudo, T., Matsumoto, Y.: Chunking with support vector machines. In: The Second Meeting of the North American Chapter of the Association for Computational Linguistics. (2001) 192-199
8. Lafferty, J., McCallum, A., Pereira, F.: Conditional random fields: Probabilistic models for segmenting and labeling sequence data. In: Proceedings of Eighteenth International Conference on Machine Learning (ICML). (2001) 282-289
9. McCallum, A.: Efficiently inducing features of conditional random fields. In: Proceedings of the Nineteenth Conference on Uncertainty in Articifical Intelligence (UAI). (2003) 403–410
10. Pietra, S.D., Pietra, V.D., Lafferty, J.: Inducing features of random fields. IEEE Transaction on Pattern Analysis and Machine Intelligence 19 (1985) 380-393
11. Sha, F., Pereira, F.: Shallow parsing with conditional random fields. In: Proceedings of the Human Language Technology Conference of the North American Chapter of the Association for Computational Linguistics (HLT-NAACL). (2003) 213-220
12. Nigam, K., Mccallum, A.K., Thrun, S.: Text classification from labeled and unlabeled documents using EM. Machine Learning 39 (2000) 103-134
13. Blum, A., Mitchell, T.: Combining labeled and unlabeled data with co-training. In: Proceedings of the Eleventh Annual Conference on Computational Learning Theory. (1998) 92-100
14. McLachlan, G.J., Krishnan, T.: The EM Algorithm and Extensions. John Wiley & Sons, Inc. (1997)
15. Wong, T.L., Lam,W.: A probabilistic approach for adapting information extraction wrappers and discovering new attributes. In: Proceedings of the 2004 IEEE International Conference on Data Mining (ICDM). (2004) 257-264
16. Wong, T.L., Lam, W.: Learning to refine ontology for a new web site using a Bayesian approach. In: Proceedings of the 2005 SIAM International Conference on Data Mining (SDM). (2005) 298-309
17. McCallum, A., Freitag, D., Pereira, F.: Maximum entropy markov models for information extraction and segmentation. In: Proceedings of Seventeenth International Conference on Machine Learning (ICML). (2000) 591-598
18. Sang, E.F.T.K., Buchholz, S.: Introduction to CoNLL-2000 shared task: Chunking. In: Proceedings of the Conference on Computational Natural Language Learning (CoNLL). (2000) 127-132
19. Marcus, M.P., Santorini, B., Marcinkiewicz, M.A.: Building a large annotated corpus of English: The penn treebank. Computational Linguistics 19 (1994) 313-330

An Effective and Efficient Two Stage Algorithm for Global Optimization

Yong-Jun Wang[1], Jiang-She Zhang[1], and Yu-Fen Zhang[2]

[1] Institute of Information and System Science, School of Science,
Xi'an Jiaotong University, Xi'an 710049, China
{wangyj, jszhang}@mail.xjtu.edu.cn
[2] Faculty of Mathematics and Computer Science,
Hebei University, Baoding 071002, China
Happy6002_cn@sina.com

Abstract. A two stage algorithm, consisting of gradient technique and particle swarm optimization (PSO) method for global optimization is proposed. The gradient method is used to find a local minimum of objective function efficiently, and PSO with potential parallel search is employed to help the minimization sequence to escape from the previously converged local minima to a better point which is then given to the gradient method as a starting point to start a new local search. The above search procedure is applied repeatedly until a global minimum of the objective function is found. In addition, a repulsion technique and partially initializing population method are also incorporated in the new algorithm to increase its global search ability. Global convergence is proven, and tests on benchmark problems show that the proposed method is more effective and reliable than the existing optimization methods.

1 Introduction

A global differential optimization problem (GOP) can be denoted by:

$$\min f(x) \quad subject\ to \quad x \in S. \tag{1}$$

where $f(x)$ is a differential real value function defined on $S \subseteq R^n$. A vector $x^* \in S$ satisfying $f(x^*) \leq f(x)$ for all $x \in S$ is called a global minimizer of $f(x)$ over S and the corresponding value f^* is called a global minimum. In this paper, we will focus on box constrained and differential global optimization problems.

Global optimization finds wide applications in an extremely broad spectrum of fields, e.g. bio-medical engineering, computer engineering and system engineering, to name only a few. However, the existence of multiple locally optimal solutions and non-convexity of objective functions or feasible regions make GOPs a great challenge. Therefore, finding the global optimal solution of an arbitrary function becomes an important challenge.

In the last four decades, many approaches have been proposed in literature in different fields to meet this challenge. Most methods realize global search by their capability of jumping from one local minimum to a better one until convergence. These methods can be classified into two main categories: namely i) deterministic methods and ii) stochastic methods. The first class relies on some deterministic information to solve GOPs and the better known deterministic methods include tunneling method [1], filled function method [2], etc. The main feature of these methods is to use gradient type methods coupled with certain auxiliary functions to jump successfully from one local minimum to another, better one. However, the latter class depends on probabilistic technique to escape from local minima and these methods include genetic algorithm (GA) [3], simulated annealing algorithm (SA) [4], and particle swarm optimization (PSO) [5], [6], [7]. Though the stochastic optimization approaches provide a relatively good methodology to move away from stationary points to a global one, they are generally computationally intensive to be applied and the final solution qualities are not high. In view of the above, a method designed for global optimization which can keep the rapid convergence and high accuracy of deterministic methods and the robustness of stochastic methods is an effective algorithm. Some reported papers have tried to hybridize different techniques to design such an algorithm [8-10].

Now, let's recall some referenced techniques propose our idea for this paper.

Gradient based algorithms are very effective deterministic methods in finding a stationary point near the initial one [11]. There are many existing efficient gradient descent methods for finding a local minimum of one function, e.g. steepest descent method, Newton method, various quasi Newton methods, trust region method and conjugate gradient method. In general, these methods converge more rapidly and can obtain solutions with higher precision than stochastic approaches in fulfilling the task of a local search. And they have been used extensively in a very broad class of problems, especially as a vital component of sophisticated algorithms [9-10]. However, these approaches often rely heavily on the initial point, the topology of the feasible region and the surface associated with the objective functions. A good starting point is vital for these methods to be executed successfully.

PSO method is a recently proposed stochastic optimization algorithm, which belongs to the category of swarm intelligence methods. This algorithm is inspired by the social behavior of flocking organisms, such as swarms of bees and schools of fish. It gradually probes promising regions of the search space by communicating swarm the information of each individual and the whole population. The core of PSO is the updating formula of the particle, which can be represented by (2) and (3).

Updating of the velocity (2) and updating of the location (3)

$$V_i(t+1) = wV_i(t) + c_1 r_1 \left(pBest_i - X_i(t) \right) + c_2 r_2 \left(gBest - X_i(t) \right). \tag{2}$$

$$X_i(t+1) = X_i(t) + V_i(t+1). \tag{3}$$

For the meaning of the symbols see [7]. Although the PSO algorithm is simple in concept, few in parameters, and easy in implementation, it has found applications in many areas due to its effectiveness in jumping out of a local minimum to convergence of a global one. However, it can often only detect the sub-optimal solutions and the improvement of the solution precision is time consuming for this algorithm.

Paper [8] proposes one hybrid method which incorporates gradient information into the velocity updating formula of each particle. The location updating formula is the same as (3). However, this method doesn't make good use of the high effective local search ability of existing traditional gradient based methods and the useful information that the individual has encountered (the best solution found so far), and the inertia weight w is set to constant 1. Moreover, it is a heuristic algorithm and has partly changed the core of the PSO algorithm. Getting a solution with high predefined precision implicates that the population and iteration number have to be very large, which means the function value computation will be extensive in return. This is truly illustrated by testing in Section 3.

Paper [9] combines the gradient method with the dynamic tuning method, resulting in an efficient approach. Inspired by it, we hybridize gradient based methods and the PSO approach in the present study. The new hybrid method uses gradient descent techniques to speed up the local search and improve solution precision, and uses the PSO approach to move away from the obtained minimizer to a better point from which the gradient method can restart a local search. The above stages are repeated until convergence. Thus, the new hybrid method may not only keep the rapid speed of gradient based methods but also retains the robustness of stochastic approaches. Furthermore, some techniques e.g. repulsion technique, which makes use of the obtained local minima information, and a method of initialing part of the population, which can increase the diversity of the population to prevent the swarm from premature convergence, are incorporated in the proposed algorithm to increase convergence probability. The effectiveness of the new proposed method is demonstrated on ten typical problems, including comparisons with some existing methods.

The motive of this paper, therefore, is to combine the existing gradient methods and PSO to construct an effective and efficient algorithm for complex GOPs. Thus, two major problems, namely having a good initial point for gradient techniques and an effective local search for PSO approach, can be dealt with.

The rest of the paper is organized as follows: Section 2 presents the new method and the global convergence is proven. The numerical results and comparisons between different methods are reported in Section 3. And finally, conclusions are drawn and further research is detailed in Section 4.

2 The New Algorithm

2.1 The New Algorithm

By examining gradient algorithms, we see that their main advantage is high efficiency and high accuracy in finding a local minimum near the initial point. However, the PSO method has good properties for escaping from the local minimum by relying on its effective potential parallel search and updating mechanism. Therefore, using the PSO method to obtain good starting points and then employing gradient based methods to fulfill the local searches effectively may make good use of their respective advantages to form an effective and efficient two stage strategy.

Phase 0. Generate $x^{(0)}$ randomly in feasible region S. Set $k = 0$.

Phase 1. *(local search)* Start from $x^{(k)}$ and use gradient descent method to search for a feasible local minimizer $x^{(k*)}$.

Phase 2. *(global search)* Use $x^{(k*)}$ as an initial point and execute N particle swarm optimization iterations until a point $x^{(k+1)}$ which at least is as good as $x^{(k*)}$ is obtained, such that $f\left(x^{(k+1)}\right) < f\left(x^{(k*)}\right)$. Set $k = k+1$ and turn to Phase 1.

Repeat Phase 1 and Phase 2 until convergence.

Fig. 1. A hybrid gradient and particle swarm optimization algorithm (GRPSO)

In Phase 2, the PSO algorithm can be implemented as in Figure 2.

Step 1. Initialize the particle population randomly in feasible region S. Find the best one *gBest* among the population. If $f(gBest) < f\left(x^{(k*)}\right)$, set $x^{(k+1)} = gBest$ and return. Else, set $gBest = x^{(k*)}$ and turn to Step 2.

Step 2. While (maximum iterations is not attained) do
 1. Update $pBest_i$ if the current fitness is better than $f(pBest_i)$ $(i = 1, 2 \cdots N)$, N is population scale.
 2. Update *gBest* if the best fitness of the population is better than $f(gBest)$.
 3. If $f(gBest) < f\left(x^{(k*)}\right)$, set $x^{(k+1)} = gBest$ and break while.
 4. Compute particle velocity according to 1.
 5. Compute particle location according to 2.
 6. Execute repulsion steps.*[12]*
    End while.

Step 3. If maximal iterations are attained in step 2 and $f(gBest) > f\left(x^{(k*)}\right)$, re-initialize part of the population, execute repulsion steps and turn to step 2. Otherwise, set $x^{(k+1)} = gBest$ and return.

Fig. 2. Steps of PSO algorithm in phase 2 of Fig. 1

In addition, because the new algorithm is an iterating population based algorithm, we can incorporate repulsion technique [12]. We can also incorporate the technique for reinitializing part of the population (its meaning is outlined below) in an algorithm as the best solution can't be improved any more in the PSO search stage. The repulsion technique here makes use of already obtained local minima information to repulse particles to fly from the already detected area to more promising regions and the partial reinitializing technique is used to keep population diversity and prevent the population from premature convergence. This new method is noted as GRPSO in the present study, whose main steps are in Fig.1.

In Step 3 of Figure 2, "Reinitialize part of the population" is implemented as follows:

Assume N is the population scale and M is a random generated number, and $M \in \{1, 2, \ldots N\}$. Individuals of the current population are sorted according to their objective function values. Select M worst individuals from current population and replace them by M randomly generated individuals (e.g. M independent samples from uniform distribution in feasible region) to form part of a new population.

Note that in Step 3 of Figure 2, we firstly reinitialize part of the population and then execute repulsion steps to assure the new M individuals move away from the obtained minimizers and distribute into more promising regions. We can also say that the diversity of the population is increased after Step 3.

2.2 The Global Convergence

Now, we prove the asymptotic convergence of the GRPSO method. Suppose that the local minimization sequence is strictly descent and can converge to a local minimizer. Let f_L^* be the least local minimum which is larger than the global minimum f^* and the *Lebesgue measure* of the set $m(S_L^*) > 0$, where $S_L^* = \{x \in S \mid f(x) < f_L^*\}$.

Definition 1: Let $y_k (k = 1, 2, \cdots)$ be the minimization sequence of the algorithm. Suppose f^* is a global minimum. If $p\{f^* \in \lim_{k \to +\infty} y_k\} = 1$, we say the algorithm converges with a probability of 1 to a global one.

Lemma 1: With an initial point $x' \in S_L^* = \{x \in S \mid f(x) < f_L^*\}$, the minimization sequence generated by minimizing $f(x)$ on S will converge to a global minimizer of $f(x)$ on S.

Proof: With an initial point $x' \in S_L^*$, the minimization sequence will converge to a local minimizer (denoted by x_1^*) of $f(x)$ on S. Since $f(x') < f_L^*$ and the minimization sequence is strictly descent, it follows that $f(x_1^*) < f_L^*$. By the assumption that f_L^* is the least local minimal value of problem (1) which is larger than f^* (f^* is a global minimum), we have $f(x_1^*) = f^*$, i.e. the minimization sequence converges to a global minimizer of $f(x)$ on S.

Let $x^{(k)}$ be the restart point in the kth iteration of the gradient algorithm, and y_k be the corresponding local minimum.

Theorem 1: let L be the maximum number of gradient local searches to be performed. If $L \to +\infty$, then y_L converges to the global minimum f^* of problem (1) on S with a probability of 1. Namely:

$$p\left\{\lim_{L \to +\infty} y_L = f^*\right\} = 1. \tag{4}$$

Proof: To prove Theorem 1 is equivalent to proving that:

$$p\left\{\bigcap_{k=1}^{\infty} \bigcup_{L=k}^{\infty} \left(|y_L - f^*| \geq \varepsilon\right)\right\} = 0, \forall \varepsilon > 0.$$

According to the descent property of the algorithm, it is obvious that $f^* \leq y_K \leq y_{K-1}$ i.e. $\{y_k\}_{k=0}^{\infty}$ is monotonically decreasing.

Let $q = 1 - \dfrac{m(s_L^*)}{m(X)}$. By Lemma 1 and the monotonic property of $\{y_k\}_{k=0}^{\infty}$, $\forall \varepsilon > 0$,

We have:

$$p\{y_L - f^* \geq \varepsilon\} = p\left\{\bigcap_{i=1}^{L}(y_i - f^*) \geq \varepsilon\right\} \leq p\left\{\bigcap_{i=1}^{L}(x \notin S_L^*)\right\}$$

$$= \prod_{i=1}^{L} p(x \notin S_L^*) = \prod_{i=1}^{L} p\left(1 - \frac{m(s_L^*)}{m(X)}\right) = q^L.$$

Thus:

$$p\left\{\bigcap_{k=1}^{\infty} \bigcup_{L=k}^{\infty}\left(|y_L - f^*| \geq \varepsilon\right)\right\} \leq \lim_{k \to +\infty} p\left\{\bigcup_{L=k}^{\infty}(y_L - f^*) \geq \varepsilon\right\}$$

$$\leq \lim_{k \to +\infty} \sum_{L=k}^{\infty} p(y_L - f^* \geq \varepsilon) \leq \lim_{k \to +\infty} \sum_{L=k}^{\infty} q^L = \lim_{k \to +\infty} \frac{q^k}{1-q}.$$

Since $m(S_L^*) > 0$, we have $0 < q < 1$ and $\dfrac{q^k}{1-q} \to 0$. If $k \to +\infty$,

$$p\left\{\bigcap_{k=1}^{\infty} \bigcup_{L=k}^{\infty}\left(|y_L - f^*| \geq \varepsilon\right)\right\} = 0, \forall \varepsilon > 0. \tag{5}$$

Formula (5) is obtained according to **Borel-Canteli Lamma**. Hence (4) holds.

3 Numerical Experiments

In this section, the proposed algorithm is examined against ten benchmark problems taken from literature [10]. The computational results are summarized in tables which indicate the comparisons of the new algorithm GRPSO with other methods, especially with HGPSO and GRDT. Since the solution quality (regardless of the initial system parameters), the convergence speed and the frequency of finding optimal solutions are the main requirements of a practical optimization technique, in order to make a fair comparison, we performed 20 independent runs on the 10 complex functions. The solution quality, average success rate or objective function evaluations are listed in Tables 1 to 3. And some typical cases are displayed in figures. Since the GRDT algorithm was executed against the ten test problems in [10], Tables 1 and 2 include all of the available results from [10]. The predefined precision is 1e-6 and the maximal number of function evaluations is 2,100. The algorithm terminates when the solution with the predefined accuracy is found. If one algorithm can't find the minimum with a predefined error within the maximal computation function values, we say that it fails.

The involved nomenclatures in Tables 1 to 3 are listed as follows:

PRS:	Pure random search [13]
MS:	Multi-start method [14]
SA1:	Simulated annealing based on stochastic differential equations [14]
SA2:	Basic simulated annealing [14]
TS:	Taboo search [15]
TA:	Tree annealing [16]
TT:	TRUST [17]
GRDT:	Hybridization of gradient descent algorithms with dynamic tunneling methods [10]
HGPSO:	Simulation of a new hybrid PSO algorithm [9]
GRPSO:	Proposed method in this paper

As can be seen from Table 1, the proposed method can locate the best global minima among the reported methods for the ten test functions, especially when compared with the similar hybrid method GRDT; SH and H3 are two typical cases. Furthermore, the success rate of finding the global minima is 100% for the new proposed method.

It is observed from Table 2 that the proposed technique displays better performance than many known algorithms in terms of the numbers of function evaluations, such as PRS, MS, SA1, SA2, TS, TA, TT, GRAD and HGPSO method. The cases of GP and H3 are two typical examples. It implicates that GRPSO method converges more rapidly than the existing methods. It can also be seen from Table 2 that the existing methods can't solve some of the test problems because of extensive computation, while GRPSO applies to all the test cases.

Table 1. The global minima found by GRDT, GRPSO and other reported method

	CA	GP	RA	SH	BR	H3	Sqrn5	Sqrn7	Swrn10	H6
Reported	-1.0316	3.	-2.	-186.7309	0.3979	-3.86	-10.14	-10.39	-10.53	-3.32
GRDT	-1.0316	3.	-2.	-186.7035	0.3979	-3.8406	-10.1532	-10.4029	-10.5364	-3.3224
GRPSO	-1.0316	3.	-2.	-186.7309	0.3939	-3.8621	-10.1532	-10.4029	-10.5364	-3.3224

Table 2. Average number of function evaluations for referenced methods

	CA	GP	RA	SH	BR	H3	Sqrn5	Squr7	Sqrn10	H6
PRS	-	5125	5964	6700	4850	5280	-	-	-	18090
MS	-	4400	-	-	1600	2500	-	-	-	6000
SA1	10822	5439	-	241215	2700	3416	-	-	-	3975
SA2	-	-	-	780	505	1459	-	-	-	4648
TS	-	486	540	727	492	508	-	-	-	2845
TA	-	6375	-	-	4172	1113	3700	2426	3463	17262
TT	31	103	59	72	55	58	-	-	-	-
GRDT	290	5175	822	502	466	2811	298	533	469	963
HGPSO	2100&	2100&	2100&	2100&	2100&	2100&	2100&	2100&	2100&	2100&
GRPSO	**53**	**134**	**309**	**308**	**32**	**88**	**303**	**554**	**450**	**47**

"&" indicates within the predefined maximal number of function evaluations 2,100, the success rate is at most 20% in 20 runs. Success rate is in Table 3.

Hyphen "-" indicates that the algorithms don't apply to the problems because of extensive computations.

Table 3. Success rate of HGPSO and GRPSO

	CA	GP	RA	SH	BR	H3	Sqrn5	Sqrn7	Sqrn10	H6
HGPSO	20%	20%	15%	10%	20%	20%	15%	10%	10%	20%
GRPSO	100%	100%	100%	100%	100%	100%	100%	100%	100%	100%

Though both GRPSO and HGPSO methods are hybrid methods which make use of gradient information and the PSO approach, we can say the GRPSO method runs more efficiently and effectively than the recently proposed HGPSO method in terms of average number of function evaluations and success rate, as can be clearly seen from Table 2 and Table 3. Meanwhile, this comparison implicates that the GRPSO method can reach a solution with higher precision than the HGPSO method provided the same computation of function values is employed.

It should be pointed out that the results of the proposed algorithm in Tables 1 to 3 are a mean of twenty runs. However, results of other algorithms except HGPSO are a mean of four runs [10]. That indicates the obtained number by the GRPSO method is more objective.

The monotonic convergence is also a very desirable property of the proposed method. For example, a typical convergence history for the algorithm in test SH is displayed in Figure 3, and typical trajectories of convergence in test GP are shown in Figure 4. Since the PSO method is mainly used for bypassing the previously converged local minimum and discovering the descent point, the decrease in function value after executing each PSO search might be small.

In addition, we point out that the traditional PSO method failed more than 18 times in 20 runs in finding the global minimum at the predefined computation and predefined solution error, namely maximal number of function evaluations 2,100 and solution precision 1e-6. Therefore, the comparisons between the proposed method and traditional PSO method aren't detailed here.

In conclusion, the GRPSO method proposed in this paper displays better performance in solving global optimization problems, especially in convergent speed, reliability and final solution quality than other existing algorithms.

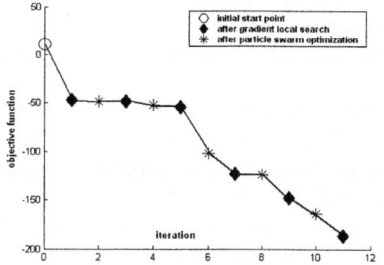

Fig. 3. A typical convergence history for the new algorithm (GRPSO) in SH function

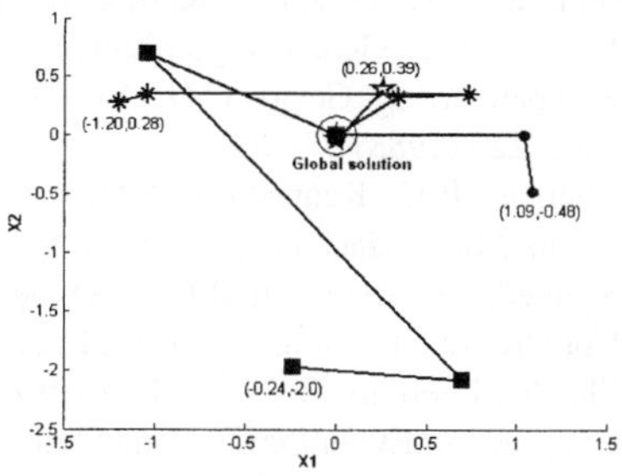

Fig. 4. Some typical trajectory convergence histories for the new algorithm (GRPSO) in RA function

4 Conclusions and Further Research

A new simple but effective and efficient two stage search method which combines the two well known search algorithms, namely gradient descent methods and PSO method, is proposed this present paper to solve global optimization problems. The gradient based method helps the hybrid algorithm execute the local search effectively, and the PSO technique plays the role of moving to a better descent point from which the local search restarts. In the new algorithm, a repulsion technique that uses already known information and a method of initializing part of the population to increase population diversity and prevent the swarm from premature convergence are used to improve its effectiveness. Different to the algorithm HGPSO, the effective classical gradient methods and a PSO with high jumping ability are combined reasonably well in the proposed algorithm. Numerical experiment results clearly underline that the monotonic method is computationally efficient and robust in most test cases, compared with some similar existing methods.

How the new algorithm will behave for large scale problems, e.g. molecular structure prediction requires further research, and as such we are conducting further research in these respects.

Acknowledgements

This work is supported by National Natural Science Foundation of China (NSFC) (# 60373106).

References

1. Ge, R.: A Filled Function Method for Finding a Gobal Minimizer of a Function of Several Variables. Mathematical Programming. 146 (1990) 191-204
2. Levy, A., Montalvo, A.: The Tunneling Algorithm for the Global Minimization of Functions. SIAM Journal of Scientific and Statistical Computing. 6 (1985) 15-29
3. Holland, J.H.: Genetic algorithms, Scientific American. 4 (1992) 44-50
4. Kirkpatrick, S., Gelatt, C.D., Vecchi, M.P.: Optimization by Simulated Annealing. Science. 220 (1983) 671-680
5. Eberhart, R.C., Kennedy, J: A New Optimizer Using Particle Swarm Theory, in Proc. 6 th Symp, Micro Machine and Human Science, Nagoya, Japan, (1995) 39-43
6. Kennedy, J., Eberhart, R.C.: Particle Swarm Optimization. Proc of IEEE International Conference on Neural Networks, Piscataway, NJ, (1995) 1942-1948
7. Shi, Y., Eberhart, R.C.: A Modified Particle Swarm Optimizer. Proceedings of the IEEE Congress on Evolutionary Computation (CEC 1998), Piscataway, NJ, (1998) 69-73
8. Noel, M.M., Jannett, T.C.: Simulation of a New Hybrid Particle Swarm Optimization Algorithm. System Symposium, Proceedings of the Thirty-Sixth Southeastern Symposium On. (2004) 150-153
9. RoyChowdhury, P., Singh, Y.P., Chansarkar, R. A.: Hybridization of Gradient Descent Algorithms with Dynamic Tunneling Methods for Global Optimization. IEEE Transactions on Systems, Man, and Cybernetics. 30 (2000) 384-390
10. Yiu, K.F.C., Liu, Y., Teo. K.L.: A hybrid Descent Method for Global Optimization. Journal of Global Optimization. 28 (2004) 229-238
11. Deb, K.: Optimization for Engineering Design, Algorithms and Examples. New Delhi, India: Prentice-Hall. (1995)
12. Parsopoulos, K.E., Vrahatis, M.N.: On the Computation of All Global Optimizers Through Particle Swarm Optimization. IEEE Transactions on Evolutionary Computation. 8 (2004) 211-223
13. Cvijovic, D., Klinowski, J.: Taboo search, An Approach to the Multiple Minima Problem. Science. 267 (1995) 664-666
14. Bilbro, G.L., Snyder, W.E.: Optimization of Functions With Many Minima. Transacton on Systems, Man, and Cybern. 21(7) (1991) 840-849
15. Anerssen, R.S., Jennings, L.S., Ryan D.M.: Optimization, St. Lucia, Australia: University of Queensland Press. (1972)
16. Dekkers, A., Aarts, E.: Global Optimization and Simulated Annealing. Mathematical Programming. 50 (1991) 367-393
17. Barhen, J., Protopopescu, V., Reister, D.: TRUST: A Deterministic Algorithm for Global Optimization. Science. 276 (1997) 1094-1097

Evolutionary Multi-objective Optimization Algorithm with Preference for Mechanical Design

Jianwei Wang[1,2], Jianming Zhang[2,3], and Xiaopeng Wei[2,3]

[1] School of Mechanical Engineering, Dalian University of Technology,
Dalian 116023, China
wangjw72@163.com
[2] Center for Advanced Design Technology, Dalian University,
Dalian 116622, China
{wangjw72, zjm_james}@163.com
[3] University Key Lab. of Information Science & Engineering, Dalian University,
Dalian 116622, China

Abstract. Although many techniques have been developed to deal with either multi-criteria or constrained aspect problems, few methods explicitly deal with both features. Therefore, a novel method of evolutionary multi-objective optimization algorithm with preference is proposed. It aims at solving multi-objective and multi-constraint problems, where the user incorporates his/her preferences about the objectives at the very start of the search process, by means of weights. It functions by considering the satisfaction of the constraints as a new objective, and using a multi-criteria decision aid method to rank the members of the EA population at each generation. In addition, the Analytic Hierarchy Process (AHP) is adopted to determine the weights of the sub-objective functions. Also, adaptivity of the weights is applied in order to converge more easily towards the feasible domain. Finally, an example is given to illustrate the validity of the evolutionary multi-objective optimization with preference.

1 Introduction

The Evolutionary Algorithms (EAs) were introduced by Schaffer[1] in 1984 to tackle the multi-objective optimization problem. Since 1990, the multi-objective optimization problem using EAs has attracted the attention of researchers. Though many optimization studies [2-4] deal with only one objective, this approach is often not realistic for industrial applications. More and more real-life cases need several objectives to be handled simultaneously; for instance, minimizing both the mass and cost of a mechanical structure, which can be a dilemma when, say, specially machined components are lighter but more expensive than other components, or heavier but with standard pieces. Another important aspect for the designer is to obtain a product which satisfies all the constraints, i.e. all the technical requirements. So far, there exists an overwhelming number of methods created to handle either multi-objective or constraints optimization with evolutionary algorithms (EAs). However, when the simultaneous tackling of both aspects is considered, very few specific methods are available.

In many cases, objectives are incommensurable, meaning they are not comparable with respect to magnitude and value, and conflicting, meaning that the different objectives cannot be arbitrarily improved without decreasing the value of another. The result is a trade-off between the objectives. Insight into such trade-offs is often of crucial importance for decision making. Due to the impossibility of achieving optimal values in all objectives simultaneously, multiple criteria decision making (MCDM) always involves a choice problem. The final solution represents a compromise between the different objectives depending on the preferences of the decision maker. There are four classes[5] determining when the decision maker's preferences enter the formal decision making process: no articulation of preference information, priori articulation of preference information, progressive articulation of preference information or posteriori articulation of preference information. Although the methods presented above are widespread in the EA community, and generally easy to implement in standard EAs, no systematic rule can be adopted to determine which one is the best.

Constraint handling methods used in classical optimization algorithms can be classified into two groups: (i) generic methods[6] that do not exploit the mathematical structure (whether linear or nonlinear) of the constraint, and (ii) specific methods[7] that are only applicable to a special type of constraint. Generic methods, such as the penalty function method, the Lagrange multiplier method, and the complex search method are popular, because each one of them can be easily applied to any problem without much change in the algorithm. But since these methods are generic, the performance of these methods in most cases is not satisfactory. However, specific methods, such as the cutting plane method, the reduced gradient method, and the gradient projection method, are applicable either to problems having convex feasible regions only or to problems having a few variables, because of increased computational burden with a large number of variables. Therefore, how to tackle constraints in EAs is a difficult issue for the users.

In this paper, a novel method of evolutionary multi-objective optimization algorithm with preference is proposed. It aims at solving multi-objective and multi-constraint problems, where the user incorporates his/her preferences about the objectives at the very start of the search process, by means of weights. It consists of considering the satisfaction of the constraints as a new objective, and using a multi-criteria decision aid method to rank the members of the EA population at each generation. Furthermore, adaptivity of the weights is applied in order to converge more easily towards the feasible domain.

In the remainder of the paper, we describe in detail the proposed evolutionary algorithm based on preference in Section 2. In Section 3, an application example is given to illustrate the presented algorithm as effective and practical. Finally, we outline the conclusions of this paper.

2 Evolutionary Algorithm Based on Preference

Many search and optimization problems in science and engineering involve a number of constraints which the optimal solution must satisfy. A constrained optimization problem is usually written as follows:

$$\text{Minimize } f(\vec{x})$$

$$\text{Subject to } g_j(\vec{x}) \geq 0, j=1,2,\ldots,p;$$
$$h_k(\vec{x}) = 0, k=1,2,\ldots,q; \quad (1)$$
$$x_i^l \leq x_i \leq x_i^u, i=1,2,\ldots,n;$$

In the above NLP problem, there are m objectives (that is, $f(x)^T=[f_1(x)\ f_2(x)\ \ldots\ f_m(x)]$), n variables (that is, $\vec{x}$ is a vector of size n), p greater-than-equal-to type inequality constraints, and q equality constraints. The function $f(\vec{x})$ is the objective function, $g_j(\vec{x})$ is the jth inequality constraints, and $h_k(\vec{x})$ is the kth equality constraints. The ith variable varies in the range [x_i^l, x_i^u].

2.1 Constraints Handling

The constraints are considered as a new objective, and then the $m+1^{th}$ objective can be formulated as follows:

$$f_{m+1}(\vec{x}) = \sum_{g_j<0} \frac{|g_j(\vec{x})|}{k_j} \quad (2)$$

where the equality constraints are transformed into inequalities as in Eq.(3). This increases the total number of inequality constraints to $p+q$ and the term p in Eq. (1) can then be replaced by $p+q$ to include all inequality and equality constraints. The factor k_j are scaling factors which can be estimated by Eq.(4):

$$\varepsilon_k - |h_k(\vec{x})| \geq 0, k=1,2,\cdots,q; \quad (3)$$

$$k_j = \frac{\sum_{n=1}^{N}|g_j^{(t)}(\vec{x})|}{N} \quad (4)$$

where ε_k is a small positive value. N is population size; $g_j^{(t)}(\vec{x})$ is the value of the jth constraint for $\vec{x}$ at generation t.

2.2 Choice of the Weights

The priori articulation of preference information is selected to tackle the multi-objective[8]. The method of evolutionary multi-objective optimization with preference seems like the weighted sum method. They the same in that the m objective functions are aggregated into one. The difference is that the weights of the former are variant, but that of the latter are stated throughout the entire process. As in any priori method, weights are initially chosen by the user for the m objectives in the following way:

The Analytic Hierarchy Process, developed by Saaty [9], addresses how to determine the relative importance of a set of alternatives in a multi-criteria decision problem. There are three steps in the AHP: the design of the hierarchy, the prioritization procedure, and the calculation of the results.

Once the hierarchy has been constructed, the decision maker begins the prioritization procedure to determine the relative importance of the elements of each level. The AHP can be used to make relative measurements through paired comparisons of criteria and of alternatives or to make rating measurements of the alternatives with respect to the criteria.

If there are m objectives to compare, the AHP performs the multi-objective decision making process as follows:

a) Develop the comparison matrix A:

$$A = (a_{ij}) = \begin{bmatrix} a_{11} & a_{12} & \cdots & a_{1m} \\ a_{21} & a_{22} & \cdots & a_{2m} \\ \cdots & \cdots & \cdots & \cdots \\ a_{m1} & a_{m1} & \cdots & a_{mm} \end{bmatrix} \quad (5)$$

Table 1. Assessment of a_{ij} values

Value of a_{ij}	Interpretation
0	Weak importance of i over j
1	Equal importance of i and j
2	Importance of i over j

where a_{ij} indicates how much more important the ith objective is than the jth objective, while making the suitable material handling equipment selection decision. For all i and j, it is necessary that $a_{ii}=1$. The possible assessment values of a_{ij} in the pairwise comparison matrix, along with their corresponding interpretations, are exhibited in Table 1.

b) Develop the judgment matrix based on the method of poles difference:

$$C = (c_{ij}) = \begin{bmatrix} c_{11} & c_{12} & \cdots & c_{1m} \\ c_{21} & c_{22} & \cdots & c_{2m} \\ \cdots & \cdots & \cdots & \cdots \\ c_{m1} & c_{m2} & \cdots & c_{mm} \end{bmatrix} \quad (6)$$

where $c_{ij} = f(r_i, r_j) = c_b^{(r_i - r_j)/R}$, $r_i = \sum_{j=1}^{m} a_{ij}$, c_b is a constant($c_b=5$), difference of poles $R = r_{max} - r_{min}$, $M_i = \prod_{j=1}^{m} c_{ij}$, $W_i = \sqrt[3]{M_i}$, $w_i = \dfrac{W_i}{\sum_{i=1}^{m} W_i}$, $\sum_{i=1}^{m} w_i = 1$.

c) Check the consistency of judgments:
$D = (d_i)_{n \times 1} = C \cdot w_i^T$, then the maximum eigenvalue of the comparison matrix:

$$\lambda_{max} = \sum_{i=1}^{m} \frac{d_i}{mw_i} \tag{7}$$

$$P_{C.I.} = \frac{\lambda_{max} - m}{m-1} \leq \varepsilon \tag{8}$$

where $\varepsilon = 0.001$.

The original weights of every objective can be obtained, but in order to take into account the objective relating to the satisfaction of the constraints, the actual weights are computed in the following way:

$$w_i^{(t)} = w_i \cdot R^{(t)} \quad \text{for } i=1,2,\ldots,m \tag{9}$$

$$w_{m+1}^{(t)} = 1 - R^{(t)} \tag{10}$$

where $R^{(t)}$ is the ratio of the population which satisfies all the constraints at the previous generation. At the first generation, $w_{m+1}^{(1)} = 1$ and $w_i^{(1)} = 0$ for $i=1,2,\ldots,m$. One can easily check that:

$$\sum_{i=1}^{m+1} w_i^{(t)} = 1 \tag{11}$$

The weights are a variance during the evolutionary process, when the number of feasible individuals is small; the relative importance given to the $m+1$th objective is high.

Then, if a growing part of the population tends to satisfy the constraints, a decrease of $w_{m+1}^{(t)}$ automatically occurs.

The flow-chart of the algorithm is illustrated in Fig.1.

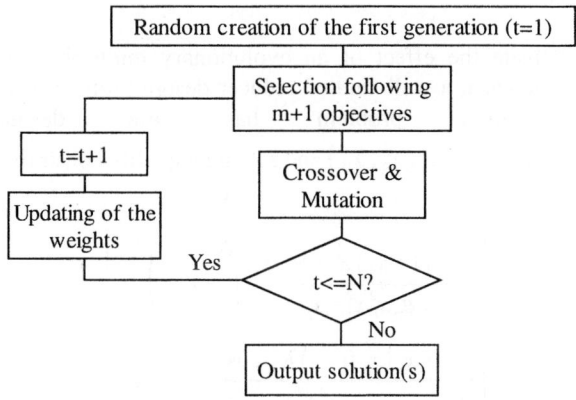

Fig. 1. The flow-chart of algorithm

2.3 Ranking the Individuals

For each objective f_i, a preference function $P_i(a,b)$ is created, which allows comparison of any couple (a,b) of individuals. $P_i(a,b)$ is calculated as follows:

$$P_i(a,b) = \begin{cases} -1 & f_i(a) > f_i(b) \\ 0 & f_i(a) = f_i(b) \\ 1 & f_i(a) < f_i(b) \end{cases} \quad (12)$$

Then, the preference index of a over b is defined by:

$$\pi(a,b) = \sum_{i=1}^{m+1} w_i \cdot P_i(a,b)$$

$$\sum_{i=1}^{m+1} w_i = 1 \quad (13)$$

The weights w_i reflect the relative importance assigned to each objective, and are chosen by the user.

Finally, to compare a solution a with the $N-1$ other solutions of a set E, the preference flow $\phi(a)$ is calculated as follows:

$$\phi(a) = \frac{1}{N-1} \cdot \sum_{\substack{b \in E \\ b \neq a}} \pi(a,b) \quad (14)$$

Consequently, the multi-objective problem is transformed into the maximization of the preference flow Φ, which acts like the fitness function of a single-objective problem. Finally, the optimal solution is obtained.

3 Case Studies

In order to investigate the effect of an evolutionary multi-objective optimization algorithm with preference, a well-studied reducer design problem is considered. The resulting optimization problem has nine design variables $\vec{x} = (x_1, x_2, x_3, x_4, x_5, x_6, x_7, x_8, x_9)$ and seven inequality constraints:

Minimize:

$$f_1(\vec{x}) = \left| \left(\frac{2T_1(1+x_5)K_1 \cos^2 x_4}{\varepsilon_a x_1^2 x_2^2 x_3 x_5} \right)^{1/2} \cdot Z_\mathrm{I} - \left(\frac{2T_1 x_5 (x_5/i - 1) K_\mathrm{II} \cos^2 x_9}{\varepsilon_a x_6^2 x_7^2 x_8} \right)^{1/2} \cdot Z_\mathrm{II} \right|$$

$$f_2(\vec{x}) = \left[x_1 x_2 (1+x_5)/\cos x_4 + x_6 x_7 (1+i/x_5)/\cos x_9 \right]/2$$

$$f_3(\vec{x}) = \Delta_1 \cdot x5/31.5 + \Delta_2$$

$$\Delta_1 = |1450/x_5 - 1450 x_2 /[x_2 x_5]|/(1450/x_5)$$

$$\Delta_2 = |1450/31.5 - 1450 x_2 x_7 /[31.5 x_2 x_7]|/(1450/31.5)$$

Subject to:

$$g_1(\vec{x}) = [\sigma]_{HI} - \left[2T_1(1+x_5) K_1 \cos^2 x_4 /(x_1^2 x_2^2 x_3 x_5) \right]^{1/2} \cdot Z_1 \geq 0$$

$$g_2(\vec{x}) = [\sigma]_{HII} - \left[2T_1 x_5 (x_5/i+1) K_{II} \cos^2 x_9 /(x_6^2 x_7^2 x_8) \right]^{1/2} \cdot Z_{II} \geq 0 \quad (15)$$

$$g_3(\vec{x}) = [\sigma]_{FI} - 2T_1 \cos x_4 /(x_1^3 x_2 x_3 \varepsilon_\alpha) K_1 Y_1 \geq 0$$

$$g_4(\vec{x}) = [\sigma]_{FII} - 2T_1 x_5 \cos x_9 /(x_6^3 x_7 x_8 \varepsilon_\alpha) K_{II} Y_{II} \geq 0$$

$$g_5(\vec{x}) = 31.5 \times x_6 x_7 \cos x_4 /(x_1 x_2 x_5^2 \cos x_9) - 1 \geq 0$$

$$g_6(\vec{x}) = 1.3 - 31.5 \times x_6 x_7 \cos x_4 /(x_1 x_2 x_5^2 \cos x_9) \geq 0$$

$$g_7(\vec{x}) = x_6 x_7 (1+i/x_5) \cos x_4 - x_1 x_2 x_5 \cos x_9$$
$$- 2\cos x_4 \cos x_9 (x_1 + 50) \geq 0$$

$$2 \leq x_1 \leq 5, 15 \leq x_2 \leq 50, \ 10 \leq x_3 \leq 50, \ 0.1396 \leq x_4 \leq 0.2618,$$
$$5.8 \leq x_5 \leq 7, 2 \leq x_6 \leq 10, 15 \leq x_7 \leq 50, 10 \leq x_8 \leq 50, 0.1396 \leq x_9 \leq 0.2618$$

where x_1 and x_6 are the module of gears, they are discrete-value variables, where x_2 and x_7 are the number of teeth in gears, so they are integer-value variables, others are real-value variables, so the coding of the variables adopts binary coding and real coding in evolutionary algorithms.

The Std-EA, albeit simple, is sufficiently general and efficient to be adapted to multi-objective and multi-constraint optimization problems. The genetic parameters of the Std-EA are collected in Tab. 2.

Table 2. EA parameters for test case

Parameter	Value
Environment	Std-EA Matlab
Coding of the variable	Binary and real coding
Size of the population	100
Number of generations	500
Type of selection	Tournament
Number of individuals participating to a tournament	2
Probability of crossover	0.90
Type of crossover	SBX
Probability of mutation	0.01
Type of mutation	Flip and PBM
Distribution index for crossover	1
Distribution index for mutation	100+t

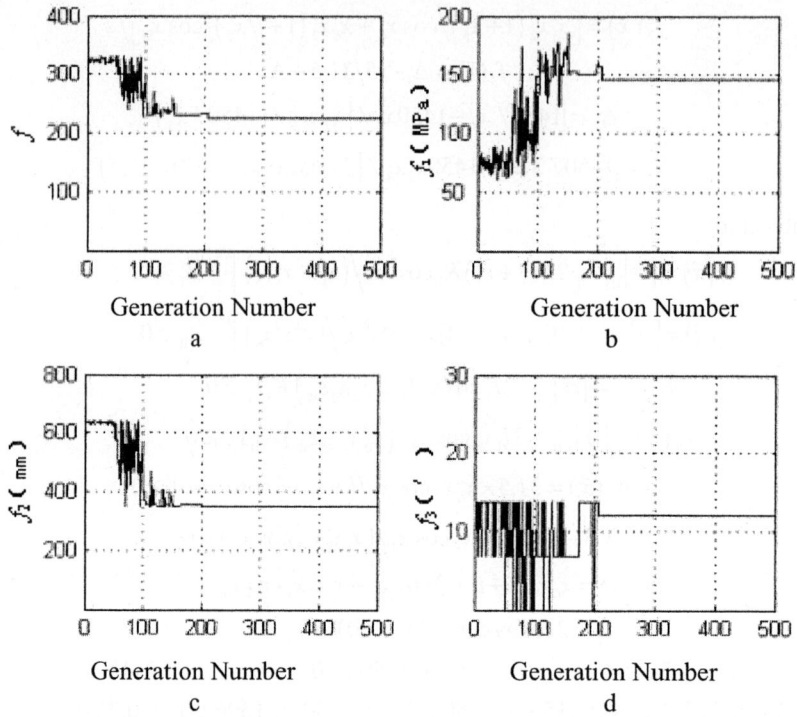

Fig. 2. Simulation solutions. a) Objective f, b) Sub-objective f_1, c) Sub-objective f_2, d) Sub-objective f_3.

Table 3. Comparison of results for test case

	Original design	Literature 8	This paper
x_1(mm)	2	2.75	2.75
x_2	19	18	16
x_3(mm)	15	11	24.8
x_4	15°	10°	13° 11′ 42″
x_5	6.7	6	5.92
x_6(mm)	3.5	4.5	3
x_7	19	15	20
x_8(mm)	27.6	15	29.5
x_9	15°	13°	8° 35′ 40″
f_1(MPa)	178.6615	176.9641	146.5037
f_2(mm)	347.7231	392.4080	348.1503
f_3(′)	28.8827	22.8330	11.9646
f	242.1044	261.1195	226.1444

The optimal solutions are illustrated in Fig. 2, which shows the convergence trend of objectives and the results of every objective. The best EA results obtained in this paper are summarized in Tab.2 and compared with the best reported results in earlier studies[10]. Tab.2 shows that the solution obtained here is better than this previously known best solution.

Numerical results show that the results of sub-objective f_1, f_2, f_3 are improved 18%, -0.12% and 58.6% respectively n that of the original design. The results of sub-objective f_1, f_2, and f_3 are improved 17.2%, 11.3% and 47.6% respectively on that in Ref. [10]. At the same time, the validity and practicability of the presented algorithm is proved.

4 Conclusion

In order to solve multi-objective and multi-constraint problems simultaneously, a novel method of evolutionary multi-objective optimization algorithm with preference was proposed. The constraints as a new objective are considered, a prior method including the user preferences is adopted, and a multi-criteria decision aid method to rank the members of the EA population at each generation is used. Also, the weights are tunable in order to converge quickly towards the feasible domain. The results on the test problems studied here are interesting and promising for a reliable and efficient multi-objective and multi-constraint optimization task through the presented algorithm.

Acknowledgement

The project is supported by the National Natural Science Foundation of China (grant Nos.50275013 and 50575026) and open funds of University Key Lab. of Information Science & Engineering, Dalian University.

References

1. Schaffer, J.D.: Some Experiments in Machine Learning Using Vector Evaluated Genetic Algorithms. Nashville TN:Vanderbilt University (1984)
2. Azid, I.A., Kwan, A.S.K.: A GA-based Technique for Layout Optimization of Truss with Stress and Displacement Constraints. International Journal for Numerical Methods in Engineering, 53 (2002) 1641-1674
3. Osyczka, A., Kundu, S.: A New Method to Solve Generalized Multicriteria Optimization Problems Using the Simple Genetic Algorithm. Structural Optimization, 10 (1995) 94-99
4. Zitzler,E., Thiele, L. et.al.: Performance Assessment of Multiobjective Optimizers: An Analysis and Review. IEEE Transactions on Evolutionary Computation, 7 (2003) 117-131
5. Hwang, C.L., Masud, A.S.M.: Multiple Objectives Decision Making—methods and Applications. Springer-Verlag, Berlin Heidelberg New York (1979)
6. Kundu, S.: A Note on Optimizality vs. Stability—A Genetic Algorithm Based Approach. In: Proceedings of 3rd World Congress on Structural and Multidisciplinary Optimization (WCSMO-3), Buffalo,New York (1999) 17-21
7. Brans, J.P., Mareschal, B.: How to Select and How to Rank Projects: The PROMETHEE Method for MCDM, European Journal of Operational Research, 24 (1986) 228-238

8. Coelho, R.F., Bouillard, Ph.: A Multicriteria Evolutionary Algorithm for Mechanical Design Optimization with Expert Rules. International Journal for Numerical Methods in Engineering, 62 (2005) 516-536
9. Saaty, T.L.: The Analytic Hierarchy Process.New York: McGraw-Hill (1980)
10. Yugen, G., Guobiao, W., et.al.: Optimization Design Based Genetic Algorithm for Helical Gear Reducer. Hoisting and Conveying Machinery, 6 (2003) 47-49

A New Adaptive Crossover Operator for the Preservation of Useful Schemata

Fan Li, Qi-He Liu, Fan Min, and Guo-Wei Yang

College of computer science and engineering,
University of Electronic Science and Technology of China,
Chengdu, Sichuan 610051, P.R. China
{lifan, qiheliu, minfan, guoweiyang}@uestc.edu.cn

Abstract. In genetic algorithms, commonly used crossover operators such as one-point, two-point and uniform crossover operator are likely to destroy the information obtained in the evolution because of their random choices of crossover points. To overcome this defect, a new adaptive crossover operator based on the Rough Set theory is proposed in this paper. By using this specialized crossover operator, useful schemata can be found and have a higher probability of surviving recombination regardless of their defining length. We compare the proposed crossover operator's performance with the two-point crossover operator on several typical function optimization problems. The experiment results show that the proposed crossover operator is more efficient.

1 Introduction

Genetic algorithms (GAs) have been validated by their outstanding performance in optimization and machine learning for poorly understood, irregular and complex spaces [1]. The basic idea of GAs is to simulate the mechanisms of natural evolution such as selection, recombination, and mutation. In canonical GAs [2], population is composed of individuals represented as fixed length binary vectors, and the population is generational. Recombination is implemented as a crossover operator, and mutation is an additional operator to provide diversity in a population. Recombination is one of the most salient features in GAs. Especially many researchers have more interest in the crossover operator than other operators, because it is the important element that performs the exchanging and recombining of genetic information from parents chosen through the selection mechanism [4]. In essence, through recombination, those distributed schemata are collected to form a better solution. The mechanism of this process can be explained by the schema theory [1]. Unfortunately, due to choosing crossover points randomly, commonly used crossover operators such as one-point, two-point and uniform crossover operator are likely to destroy useful schemata with a high defining length. This destruction does not have any significant effects on the performance of GAs, especially at the early state of the convergence process.

Furthermore, experiment results suggest that human DNA does not choose recombination loci randomly [3]. Therefore, as a bio-inspired methodology, GA should simulate this phenomenon. This means the crossover operator should be designed to enable both exchange of genes and preservation of information obtained in evolution. This kind of crossover operator is desired to make GAs converging to the optimal solution effectively.

For this purpose, several crossover operators have been developed. HRO [5] considers only restricted region which shows homology over a specified threshold value when it selects crossover points. In the Puzzle Algorithm [6], there are two coevolving populations: candidate solutions and candidate building blocks. The fitness of an individual in the building-blocks population depends on individuals from the solutions population. The choice of recombination loci in the solutions population is affected by individuals from the building-blocks population.

In this paper, a new adaptive crossover operator based on the Rough Set theory, RSO, is presented. The main idea is to place constrains on the choice of crossover points in recombination. First, candidates for useful schemata are found by using the attribute reduction, a basic notion in the Rough Set theory. Then, they are evaluated through recombination, and useful ones are preserved in this process. Thus, a useful schema has a higher probability of surviving recombination even if its defining lengthis very high.

The rest of this paper is organized as follows. In Section 2, basic notions of the Rough Set theory are briefly reviewed. In Section 3, the mechanism of the proposed crossover operator is discussed. In Section 4, the efficiency of the proposed crossover operator is tested by computation experiments. We conclude the paper with a summary in Section 5.

2 Preliminaries

In this Section, basic concepts of the Rough Set theory are briefly reviewed. More details can be found in [7][8][9].

Definition 1. *An Information system (IS) is a triplet $T = <U, AT, f>$, where U is a non-empty finite set of objects and AT is a non-empty finite set of attributes, $f_a : U \rightarrow V_a$ for any $a \in AT$, where V_a is called domain of an attribute a. Here, we assume that an object $x \in U$ possesses only one value for an attribute a, $a \in AT$. In an IS, if AT is composed of two disjoint subsets of attributes, called condition and decision attributes set respectively, then the IS is called a decision table, denoted by $DT = <U, C \cup D, f>$, where $C \cup D = AT, C \cap D = \emptyset$.*

Definition 2. *In an IS $T = <U, AT, f>$, each subset of attributes $A \subseteq AT$ determines a binary indiscernibility relation IND(A) of U:*

$$IND(A) = \{(x, y) \in U \times U | \forall a \in A, f_a(x) = f_a(y)\} . \quad (1)$$

The relation $IND(A)$ is an equivalence relation and constitutes a partition of U, denoted by $U/IND(A)$, in short U/A. Let $I_A(x)$ denote the set of objects $\{y \in U \mid (x,y) \in IND(A)\}$. $I_A(x)$ is the equivalence class that contains the object x, and objects from $I_A(x)$ are indiscernible with regard to their description in the IS.

Definition 3. Let $T = <U, AT, f>$ be an IS, $A \subseteq AT$ and $X \subseteq U$. The lower approximation and upper approximation of the set X with respect to A are defined as:

$$\underline{A}X = \{x \in U \mid I_A(x) \subseteq X\}. \quad (2)$$

$$\overline{A}X = \{x \in U \mid I_A(x) \cap X \neq \emptyset\}. \quad (3)$$

Definition 4. Let $DT = <U, C \cup D, f>$, the positive region of D with respect to C is denoted by:

$$POS_C D = \bigcup_{X \in U/D} \underline{C}X. \quad (4)$$

If $POS_C D = U$, then the decision table DT is consistent, otherwise it is inconsistent.

Definition 5. Let $DT = <U, C \cup D, f>$, a subset $A \subseteq AT$ is a relative reduct of DT iff:

$$POS_A D = POS_C D. \quad (5)$$

$$\forall a \in A, \; POS_{A \setminus \{a\}} D \neq POS_C D. \quad (6)$$

Definition 6. Let $RED_D C$ be the set containing all relative reducts of DT. The relative core is denoted by:

$$CORE_D C = \bigcap_{R \in RED_D C} R. \quad (7)$$

3 RSO - Crossover Operator Based on Rough Set Theory

In this section, the mechanism of RSO, a new adaptive crossover operator that helps to preserve schemata of promising performance, is discussed.

3.1 Inspiration from Nature

In canonical GAs, the schema theory suggests that those schemata with high defining length have lower probability to survive recombination, even if they have higher fitness [1]. Research results show that this destruction does not have any significant effects on the performance of GAs, especially at the early stage of the convergence process. This is due to the premise that the crossover operator chooses crossover points at random. But experiment results suggest that human DNA can be partitioned into long blocks, such that recombinants within each block are rare or altogether nonexistent [3]. We can consider that these blocks contain useful information obtained in evolution. Apparently, this means nature does not choose recombination loci randomly. To reflect this phenomenon, crossover points should be limited to those points that when they are used as crossover points in recombination, useful schemata do not be destroyed.

However, it is clear that we can hardly identify which schema is useful in the search space. Fortunately, using the concept of attribute reduction in the Rough Set theory, we can find key genes in the chromosome that can distinguish whether or not a schema has promising performance. Intuitively, we can choose schemata determined by those key genes as candidates and evaluate them. If the evaluation proves that they are useful, we can preserve them during recombination by placing constraints on the choice of crossover points, such that useful schemata have a higher probability of surviving recombination.

3.2. Implementation

Constructing chromosome decision table. In order to find schemata of promising performance, the chromosome decision table should be constructed first. The strategy we use in this paper is that each individual in population is treated as an object in DT and each bit of the corresponding chromosome string is treated as a condition attribute. The decision value of each object is determined by its fitness value. Formally, we can define a chromosome decision table as follows:

Definition 7. *Let population $\vec{X}(t) = \{X_1(t), X_2(t), \ldots, X_n(t)\}$, and m be the length of the chromosome string, the chromosome decision table is denoted by:* $DT_{chromosome} = <U, C \cup \{d\}, f>$, *where* $U = \vec{X}(t)$, $C = \{c_1, c_2, \ldots, c_m\}$ *and* $\forall c_i \in C$, $V_{c_i} = \{0, 1\}$. *Also,* $V_d = \{0, 1\}$, *each object of the decision table is assigned a decision value defined as*:

$$f_d(X_i(t)) = \begin{cases} 1 & J(X_i(t)) \geq J_{av}(\vec{X}(t)) \\ 0 & J(X_i(t)) < J_{av}(\vec{X}(t)) \end{cases}, \quad (8)$$

where:

$$J_{av}(\vec{X}(t)) = \frac{1}{n} \sum_{j=1}^{n} J(X_j(t)) \ . \quad (9)$$

means the average fitness of population $\vec{X}(t)$.

It is easy to prove that a chromosome decision table is a consistent decision table.

Here, we employ two examples to illustrate some concepts and computations involved in our proposed method. The aim of both examples is to maximize a function $f(x) = x^2, 0 \leq x \leq 31$.

Example 1: The initial population $\vec{X}(0) = \{20, 15, 2, 5, 8\}$.

Example 2: The initial population $\vec{X}(0) = \{18, 16, 9, 7\}$.

In both examples, the length of the chromosome is 5. The chromosome decision tables are constructed as follows:

Table 1. Chromosome decision table 1

	c_1	c_2	c_3	c_4	c_5	d
$X_1(0)$	0	0	1	0	1	1
$X_2(0)$	1	1	1	1	0	1
$X_3(0)$	0	1	0	0	0	0
$X_4(0)$	1	0	1	0	0	0
$X_5(0)$	0	0	0	1	0	0

Table 2. Chromosome decision table 2

	c_1	c_2	c_3	c_4	c_5	d
$X_1(0)$	0	0	0	0	1	1
$X_2(0)$	0	1	0	0	1	1
$X_3(0)$	1	0	0	1	0	0
$X_4(0)$	1	1	1	0	0	0

Finding candidate schemata. By the definition, a reduct of the chromosome decision table is a minimal subset of attributes in the sense of inclusion that enables us to classify objects with high fitness (decision values are 1) and those with low fitness (decision values are 0). Intuitively, we can choose schemata determined by a reduct to be candidate schemata with promising performance. It is clear that finding all reducts then choosing the most suitable one is the best scheme. But it has already proven to be an NP-hard problem [10]. Therefore, it is more feasible to use a heuristic algorithm to acquire the optimal or hypo-optimal result.

Definition 8. Let $DT = <U, C \cup \{d\}, f>$ be an decision table and $A \subseteq C$, then the significance for each attribute $a \in C \setminus A$ is defined as:

$$SGF(a, A) = \eta_{A \cup \{a\}} - \eta_A , \qquad (10)$$

where:

$$\eta_A = \frac{|POS_A D|}{|U|} . \qquad (11)$$

Based on the definition above, an attribute reduction algorithm is presented as follows:

Algorithm 1. Attribute Reduction Algorithm
Input: A chromosome decision table $DT_{chromosome} = <U, C \cup \{d\}, f>$.
Output: A reduct of $DT_{chromosome}$.
Step 1. Compute η_C for $DT_{chromosome}$.
Step 2. Compute $CORE_{\{d\}}C$. Let $RED = CORE_{\{d\}}C$, and compute η_{RED}.
Setp 2.1. Let $B = C \setminus RED$. For each attribute $a \in B$, compute $\eta_{RED \cup \{a\}}$.

Setp 2.2. Choose an attribute b such that $\eta_{RED \cup \{b\}}$ is maximal (thus $SGF(b, RED)$ is maximal), inserting it to the end of RED. Then, set $\eta_{RED} = \eta_{RED \cup \{b\}}$.

Setp 2.3. If $\eta_{RED} = \eta_C$ then go to Setp3. Otherwise, go to Setp2.1.

Setp 3. From the end to the head of RED, test whether an attribute e is redundant:

- If $\eta_{RED \setminus \{e\}} = \eta_C$ then e is redundant, deleting it from RED.
- If all the attributes in RED have been tested, the algorithm completes.

The time complexity of Alogorithm 1 is $O(|C|^2|U|\log|U|)$, if we use the algorithm in [12] to compute positive regions. In general, the size of the population is not very large, so the computational cost is acceptable. But the side effect is that only one reduction can be obtained.

Another choice is RAD [11], the scalable attribute reduction algorithm which can find all reducts of decision tables. In this case, we can choose the most suitable one to determine useful schemata, but the computational cost is rather high.

Next, we use the output of the attribute reduction algorithm to determine candidate schemata with promising performance. The set of all those schemata is denoted as S_{can}. The order of each schema in S_{can} is the cardinality of the reduct. Positions with fixed genes are determined by attributes in the reduct, and the values of those positions on the schema are those of the corresponding genes in the "good" chromosome. In example 1, supposing that we have $RED = \{c_1, c_4, c_5\}$, $S_{can} = \{(0, *, *, 0, 1), (1, *, *, 1, 0)\}$. In example 2, supposing that we have $RED = \{c_3, c_4\}$, $S_{can} = \{(*, *, 0, 0, *)\}$. But schemata in S_{can} are not always useful, so the recombination strategy is proposed as follows to evaluate them as well as exchanging genes on the chromosome.

Recombination strategy. In the method proposed in this paper, each recombination uses two parents, say $X_1(t)$ and $X_2(t)$, to create two children. During recombination two parents are selected through the selection mechanism and their fitness is checked by their decision values.

- If $f_d(X_1(t))=1 \wedge f_d(X_2(t))=1$ or $f_d(X_1(t))=0 \wedge f_d(X_2(t)) = 0$, crossover points are chosen randomly, and the recombination is executed like a standard GA.
- Otherwise, genes on the position determined by the corresponding candidate schema in S_{can} are exchanged, with probability p_c.

After recombination the two new children and two parents are evaluated and the replacement selection is employed.

The main idea of this strategy is as follows:

- If the fitness of either parent is greater than or less than $J_{av}(\vec{X}(t))$, then crossover points are chosen randomly. If a single child's fitness is less than the fitness of its parent, it is eliminated through the replacement selection. Otherwise, the parent is replaced by its child. This is done to reflect the genes' contribution to the fitness increase.
- If the fitness of one parent is greater than $J_{av}(\vec{X}(t))$ and the fitness of the other is less than $J_{av}(\vec{X}(t))$, say $f(X_1(t))=1$ and $f(X_2(t))=0$, we intend to preserve schemata in S_{can} through recombination. At the same time, they are checked by

this process. If the corresponding schema in S_{can} is useful, through the recombination, the fitness of the child of $X_2(t)$ is greater than its father, and the fitness of the child of $X_1(t)$ is less than its father. After the replacement selection, this schema exists in both survivors. Otherwise, the fitness of the child of $X_1(t)$ is greater than its father, and the fitness of the child of $X_2(t)$ is less than its father. Thus, if the corresponding schema in S_{can} is not useful, it does not exist in both survivors after the replacement selection.

Fig. 1 and Fig. 2 illustrate the mechanism for the above examples.

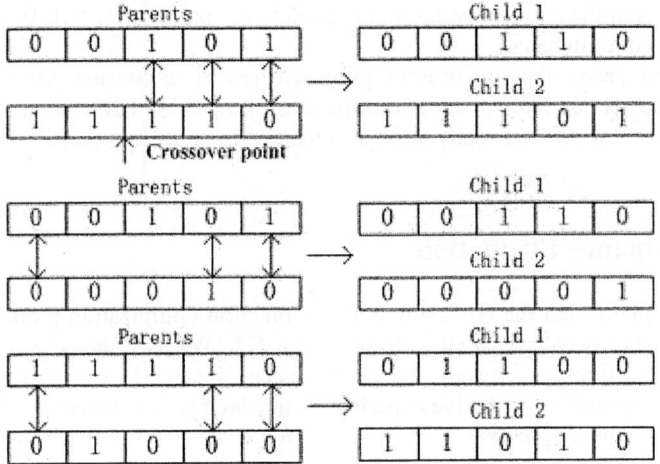

Fig. 1. Recombinations in example 1

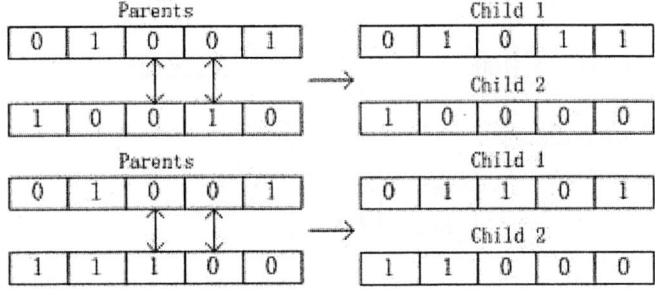

Fig. 2. Recombinations in example 2

In the first recombination of Fig. 1, the fitness of either parent is greater than $J_{av}(\vec{X}(t))$, so the crossover point is chosen randomly. Child 2 has an increase in fitness hence parent 1 and child 2 come into the next generation. In the second and the third recombination, children of "bad" parents (parents whose fitness is less than

$J_{av}(\vec{X}(t))$ have an increase in fitness after exchanging genes determined by schemata in S_{can}. Meanwhile, children of "good" parents (parents whose fitness is greater than $J_{av}(\vec{X}(t))$ have a decrease in fitness. Thus, (0, *, *, 0, 1) and(1, *, *, 1, 0) in S_{can} can be regarded as useful. After the replacement selection, schemata in S_{can} survive in spite of their high defining length.

But in either recombination of Fig. 2, after exchanging genes determined by schemata in S_{can}, children of "bad" parents have a decrease in fitness while children of "good" parents have an increase in fitness. That means (*, *, 0, 0, *) in S_{can} is not the schema with promising performance. After the replacement selection, it does not exist in survivors and the corresponding schemata in "bad" parents, (*, *, 1, 0, *) and (*, *, 0, 1, *), are not eliminated.

In a word, recombination strategy proposed here is responsible for not only exchanging and recombining genetic information from parents but evaluating schemata in S_{can} to decide if they are really those schemata with promising performance up until now.

4 Performance Evaluation

We have implemented the GA using RSO on function optimization problems and its performance has been compared with the simple GA. We used the "mean best" of all function evaluations to measure the performance (averaged over 10 runs). In this paper, we performed comparative experiments for three typical functions. They were:
(1) Schwefel's sphere function:

$$f_1(x) = \sum_{i=1}^{30} x_i^2 \quad -5.12 \leq x_i \leq 5.12 . \tag{12}$$

(2) DeJong's function:

$$f_2(x) = \sum_{i=1}^{29} (100(x_i^2 - x_{i+1})^2 + (x_i - 1)^2) \quad -5.12 \leq x_i \leq 5.12 . \tag{13}$$

(3) Griewangk's function:

$$f_3(x) = 1 + \sum_{i=1}^{20} \frac{x_i^2}{800} - \prod_{i=1}^{20} \cos \frac{x_i}{\sqrt{i}} \quad -512 \leq x_i \leq 512 . \tag{14}$$

Functions $f_1(x)$ and $f_2(x)$ are unimodal functions, and $f_3(x)$ is a multimodal function where the number of local minima increases exponentially with the dimension. In all experiments, the crossover rate is 0.85; the mutation rate is 0.001; the population size is 100; maximum number of generations is 10000. The simple GA uses two-point crossover operator. We use linear ranking selection with $\eta = 1.05$. During the whole optimization process we kept the best value found in all generations, beginning with the initial population. Experiment results show that for all test functions the GA using RSO performs better than the simple GA.

Table 3. Experiment results

Algorithm	simple GA	GA using RSO
f_1^{avg}	32.853	10.602
f_2^{avg}	13078.212	3642.138
f_3^{avg}	9.622	3.237

5 Conclusions and Discussions

In this paper, we have described a new adaptive crossover operator based on the Rough Set theory, called RSO, for GAs. Unlike conventional crossover operators such as one-point, two-point and uniform crossover operator, it allows exploitation of good schemata regardless of their defining length.

RSO uses the attribute reduction, a concept in the Rough Set theory, to find candidate schemata with promising performance. Then, a recombination strategy is used to evaluate whether these schemata are useful as well as to exchange genetic information from parents.

Experiment results indicate that GA using RSO performs better than traditional GA, which uses two-point crossover, on a set of test functions.

We conclude that the initial results of this study indicate that RSO may be a good candidate for a crossover operator in which practitioners can have more confidence to use as a starting point for an adaptive GA system. But there are still some issues which need to be discussed in future works.

- Currently, when assigning the decision values for each object in $DT_{chromosome}$, we just consider its fitness value. But maybe this is not an efficient way because the diversity of the population is not taken into account. For example, we can consider the fitness value and the Hamming distance to the best object at the same time.
- In this paper, we only focus on the crossover operator. But the mutation operator is another important factor that influences the performance of GAs. So if we reconstruct the mutation operator by the Rough Set theory, the performance of GAs is promising.
- Further experiments should be carried out to compare RSO with other adaptive crossover operators. We also intend to analyse the creation, propagation and disruption of a schema to determine exactly why and how GAs benefit from RSO and use these findings towards more reliable and adaptive crossover operators.
- In this paper, we only use reduct as defined by Pawlak [7][8]. This is easy to implement but may not be the most reasonable choice. For an example, dynamic reduct [13] shows better performance in reasoning with data. So it is necessary to incorporate different kinds of reducts to improve the result.

References

1. Holland, J.: Adaptation in Natural and Artificial Systems. Michigan University Press, Ann Arbor, MI (1975)
2. Goldberg, D. E.: Genetic Algorithms in search, optimization and machine learning. Addison-Wesley, (1989)
3. Gabriel, S. B., et al.: The structure of haplotype blocks in the human genome. Science, 296(5576)(2002) 2225-2229
4. Davis, L.: Handbook of Genetic Algorithms. Van Nostrand Reinhold, New York (1991)
5. Jong-man Park, Jeon-gue Park, et al.: Robust and Efficient Genetic Crossover Operator: Homologous Recombination. Proceedings of 1993 International Joint Conference on Neural Networks, Nagoya, October (1993) 2975-2978.
6. Assaf Zaritsky, Moshe Sipper: The Preservation of Favored Building Blocks in the Struggle for Fitness: The Puzzle Algorithm. IEEE Transactions on Evolutionary Computation, 39(5)(2004) 443-455
7. Pawlak, Z., Grzymala-Busse,J., Slowinski, R., Ziarko,W.: Rough sets. Communication of the ACM, 38(11)(1995) 89-95.
8. Pawlak Z.: Some issues on Rough Sets. Transactions on Rough Sets I, LNCS 3100 (2004) 1-58.
9. Wen-Xiu Zhang, Wei-Zhi Wu, Ji-Ye Liang, De-Yu Li: Rough Set Theory and Approach. Science Press, Beijng (2001).
10. Wong,S. K. M., Ziarko, W.: Optimal decision rules in decision . Bulletin of Polish Academy of Science, 33(11-12)(1985) 693-696
11. Kryszkiewicz, M., Cichon K.: Towards Scalable Algorithms for Discovering Rough Set Reducts. Transactions on Rough Sets I, LNCS 3100 (2004) 120-143.
12. Liu Shao-Hui, Sheng Qiu-Jian, Wu Bin, et al.: Research on Efficient Algorithms for Rough Set Methods. Chinese Journal of Computer, 26(5)(2003) 524-529.
13. Bazan,J.: Dynamic reducts and statistical inference. Proceedings of the Sixth International Conference, Information Processing and Management of uncertainty in Knowledge-Based Systems, Granada, Spain, July (1996) 1147-1152
14. Emmanouilidis,C., Hunter,A., MacIntyre,J.: A Multiobjective Evolutionary Setting for Feature Selection and a Commonality-Based Crossover Operator. Proceedings of the 2000 Congress on Evolutionary Computation, La Jolla (2000) 309-316
15. Peter, A. N., Bosman, Dirk Thierens: The Balance Between Proximity and Diversity in Multiobjective Evolutionary Algorithms. IEEE Transactions on Evolutionary Computation, 7(2)(2003) 443-455
16. Fan Li, Qihe Liu, Guowei Yang: A Heuristic Algorithm for Attribute Reduction in Incomplete Information Systems. Progress in Intelligence Computation and Applications, Wuhan, April (2005) 574-580

Refinement of Fuzzy Production Rules by Using a Fuzzy-Neural Approach

Dong-mei Huang[1], Ming-hu Ha[2], Ya-min Li[4], and Eric C.C. Tsang[3]

[1] College of Sciences, Agriculture University of Hebei, Baoding 071001, China
tinghb@sina.com
[2] Faculty of Mathematics and Computer Science, Hebei University,
Baoding 071002, China
mhha@mail.hbu.edu.cn
[3] Artificial Intelligence Research Center, Agriculture University of Hebei,
Baoding 071001, China
[4] Department of Computing, HongKong Polytechnic University,
Kowloon, Hong Kong

Abstract. In this paper we develop a fuzzy neural network (FNN) with a new BP learning algorithm using some smooth function, which is used to tune the local and global weights of fuzzy production rules (FPRs) so as to enhance the representation power of FPRs. The aim of including local and global weights in FPRs and the tuning of these weights is to improve the learning and testing accuracy without increasing the number of rules. By experimenting with some existing benchmark examples (Iris data, Wine data, Pima data and Glass data) the proposed method is found to have high accuracy in classifying unseen samples without increasing the number of the extracted FPRs, and furthermore, the time required to consult with domain experts for gaining a rule is reduced. The synergy between WFPRs and an FNN offers a new insight into the construction of better fuzzy intelligent systems in the future.

1 Introduction

Fuzzy production rules (FPRs) have long been the easiest and most popular way to capture and represent fuzzy, vague, imprecise and uncertain domain knowledge. They have been used in many fuzzy systems, such as fuzzy controllers or fuzzy expert systems. The heart of these fuzzy systems is their knowledge (the FPRs) that is captured or stored in the knowledge base. Fuzzy systems built on fuzzy rules have been successfully applied to various classification tasks [1]. Fuzzy systems either depend on linguistic rules that are provided by experts, or else the rules are extracted from a given training data set. Traditionally, these fuzzy production rules are provided by domain experts. It is very difficult and time-consuming to obtain accurate and reasonable FPRs.

In recent years there has been a lot of research on how to generate and produce FPRs from a set of data. Many learning techniques can be found in the literature [2-9], such as in [2], where an algorithm to generate fuzzy production rules from training data by using a fuzzy decision tree induction technique is given. While in [3], a way to process individual fuzzy attributes for fuzzy rule induction is given. A GA method to select fuzzy if-then rules for classification problems can be found in [4]. A method is proposed to generate FPRs from training data with noise for classification problems in [5]. In [8] D. Chakraborty uses a four-layered feed-forward network, which learns the important features and the classification rules for realizing a fuzzy rule-based classifier, and then proposes a neuro-fuzzy scheme for designing a classifier, and so on. Although we can use these learning techniques to generate a set of FPR, these extracted rules are found to be far from optimal and sometimes redundant. Tsang et al developed a fuzzy neural network to refine the local and global weights so as to enhance the representation power of the fuzzy production rules [9]. This paper develops a fuzzy neural network (FNN) with a new BP learning algorithm using some smooth function, which is used to refine or tune the local and global weights of fuzzy production rules. By testing our method with some existing benchmark examples, such as Iris data, Glass data, Pima data etc, the proposed method is found to have high accuracy in classifying unseen samples without increasing the number of the extracted FPRs and, furthermore, the time required to consult with domain experts for gaining a rule is greatly reduced.

In this paper, we begin our work with a set of rough, crude and raw FPRs extracted or generated by some learning techniques and the weights (local and/or global) of FPRs are not assigned. In order to enhance the representation power of FPRs, some knowledge representation parameters such as local and global weights are included in these FPRs. These local and global weights had been proposed by Yeung et al. [10, 11]. A fuzzy neural network (FNN) is proposed to tune the local and global weights of FPRs and a set of weighted FPRs (WFPRs) will be obtained. The obtained weighted fuzzy production rules will be more optimal and accurate in recognizing and classifying unseen examples. It is because those weights with values more or less equal to zero could be deleted so that smaller numbers of propositions in the antecedent of WFPRs (so-called simple WFPRs) are generated and the extracted WFPRs with local and global weights capturing more domain experts' knowledge will have higher accuracy in solving recognition and classification problems. Furthermore, we map WFPRs into an FNN and the connection weights of the FNN are the local and global weights respectively, and we use a back propagation (BP) learning algorithm to tune, refine and even acquire these parameters. Our FNN is used to represent WFPRs that could be refined or tuned so that optimal rules and higher testing accuracy can be obtained.

2 Weighted Fuzzy Production Rule and Similarity-Based Reasoning Algorithm

In general, a fuzzy production rule (FPR) takes the form of "IF A THEN B" where A, is called proposition of the antecedent and B is the consequent of the rule. The propositions and the consequent in an FPR can be linguistic terms such as "big", "high", etc, which are regarded as fuzzy subsets. Usually, all propositions of the antecedent are assumed to have an equal degree of importance and a number of rules leading to the same consequent are also regarded as having the same relative degree of importance. But in many fields, the weights of each proposition of the antecedent of a rule and the whole rule have different degrees of importance. For example, in a medical diagnosis system, there are many symptoms that are combined together to lead to a disease. For different diseases, the degree of importance of each symptom is different. So it is very useful to assign a weight to each symptom to show and capture the degree of importance.

2.1 Weighted Fuzzy Production Rule

To enhance the knowledge representation power of fuzzy production rules, a generic form of FPR is suggested in [10, 11] where a threshold value and a local weight are assigned to each proposition while a global weight is assigned to the entire rule. This paper only discusses a type of FPR in which two important knowledge parameters, the local and global weights, are emphasized. The local weight is introduced for the purpose of indicating the relative degree of importance of a proposition contributing to its consequent while the global weight concept is used to represent the relative degree of importance of each rule's contribution to reach a final goal.

For instance, a conjunctive Weighted Fuzzy Production Rule takes the form of:

R: If V_1 is A_1 [Lw_1] AND ... AND V_n is A_n [Lw_n] then U is B, [Gw]
Fact 1: V_1 is A_1^*, ... , Fact n: V_n is A_n^*
Conclusion: U is B^* ,

Where $V_1, \ldots, V_n$ and U are attributes and $A_1, \ldots, A_n$ and B are the values of these attributes, which are fuzzy. Lw_i $(1 \le i \le n)$ is the local weight of the proposition "V_i is A_i" and each Lw_i is non-negative. Gw denotes the global weight assigned to the entire rule R ($Gw \ge 0$).

2.2 A Similarity-Based Reasoning Algorithm

Now let us state our reasoning algorithm. We can regard the method as a kind of similarity-based reasoning algorithm. The similarity degree between the attribute values of an example and the antecedent of the rule is considered as the membership value that indicates to what degree the example belongs to the corresponding term. For instance, the similarity between attribute value "0.6/Hot + 0.4/Mild + 0.0/Cool" and the antecedent "Temperature = Hot" is 0.6.

Consider a set of fuzzy production rules $S = \{R_i, i = 1, 2, \cdots, m\}$ where R_i takes the form of:

R_i: If V_1 is $A_1^{(i)}$ [$Lw_1^{(i)}$] AND ... AND V_n is $A_n^{(i)}$ [$Lw_n^{(i)}$] then U is $B^{(i)}$, [Gw_i]
The observed object has attribute values in the following form:
Fact: V_1 is $C_1^{(i)}$, Fact 2: V_2 is $C_2^{(i)}$, ... , Fact n: V_n is $C_n^{(i)}$

For each rule $R_i \in S$, the similarity between the proposition $A_j^{(i)}$ and the observed attribute-value $C_j^{(i)}$, denoted by $SM_j^{(i)}$, is defined as the membership value that indicates to what degree the example belongs to the corresponding term. The overall similarity $SM^{(i)}$ is defined as:

$$SM^{(i)} = Min_{1 \leq j \leq n} \left(Lw_j^{(i)} \cdot SM_j^{(i)} \right) \tag{1}$$

Let there be K fuzzy sets of conclusions, the conclusions of the given m rules can be classified into K groups, denoted by $CLASS_1, \ldots, CLASS_K$. The inferred result is regarded as a vector $(x_1, x_2, \cdots, x_K)$. The x_k is determined by the following equation:

$$x_k = \sum_{B^{(i)} = CLASS_k} Gw_i \cdot SM^{(i)} \qquad (k=1,2,\ldots,K). \tag{2}$$

The normalized form of the inferred result is defined as $(d_1, d_2, \cdots, d_K)$ where d_k is the value which indicates to what degree the observed object belongs to $CLASS_k$ ($k = 1,2,\ldots, K$).

$$d_k = x_k \Big/ Max_{1 \leq j \leq K} x_j \qquad (k=1,2,\ldots,K). \tag{3}$$

When the crisp inferred result is needed, one can take the consequent $CLASS$ with maximum $d_k (1 \leq k \leq K)$.

Example 1. Consider the following three weighted fuzzy rules R1, R2, R3 and one observed case F:

R1: If T is Hot [1.0] AND O is Sunny [0.6] then U is Swimming, [1.0]
R2: If T is Hot [0.9] AND O is Cloudy [1.0] then U is Swimming, [0.8]
R3: If T is Mild [0.4] AND W is Not-windy [0.9] then U is Volleyball, [1.0]

Case: F = 1.0/Sunny + 0.2/Cloudy + 0.5/Hot + 0.5/Mild + 0.0/Windy + 1.0/Not-windy. (T: Temperature = {Hot, Cool, Mild}, O: Outlook = {Sunny, Cloudy, rain}, W: Wind = {Windy, Not-Windy}).

In terms of our reasoning algorithm, the normalized inferred vector of the case is (1/Swimming, 0.3/Volleyball). It is then easy for us to make a decision.

3 Mapping a Set of WFPR to an FNN and BP Algorithm

A set of WFPR and the proposed similarity-based reasoning algorithm can be mapped exactly into a three-layer FNN. The first layer is the input layer called

Term layer, the second layer is the Rule layer and the third layer is the output layer called Classification layer. We describe the structure of the mapped FNN as follows:

Term layer (layer 1): Each node in layer 1 represents an input linguistic term of an attribute. Since each linguistic term corresponds to an attribute value, the input of each node is regarded as the similarity degree between the observed attribute value and the corresponding term (proposition) of the antecedent in a WFPR. The similarity degree can also be the membership value that indicates to what degree the observed fact belongs to the corresponding linguistic term. Thus, the number of nodes in this layer is equal to the number of attribute values.

Rule layer (layer 2): This is the only hidden layer. Each node in this layer represents a given antecedent part of a weight fuzzy production rule. According to linguistic terms, when propositions appear in the antecedent part of a WFPR, the connections between the term layer (layer 1) and the rule layer (layer 2) are determined.

Classification layer (layer 3): This is the output layer. Each node in this layer represents a class. Since the inferred result of WFPRs generally has the form of a vector, which is a discrete fuzzy set defined on the space of cluster labels, the output of the network has more than one value. Thus, if there are c classes then there will be c nodes in layer 3. The meaning of each output value after normalization is the membership value that indicates to what degree the training object belongs to the class corresponding to the node.

Connection weights: The local weights (shown as Lw_{ij}) of a set of WFPR are regarded as the connection weights between the term layer (layer i) and the rule layer (layer j). The global weights (shown as Gw_{jk}) of the set of WFPR are regarded as the connection weights between the rule layer (layer j) and the classification layer (layer k).

4 An FNN Used to Tune the Local and Global Weights

4.1 Generic FNN

Now we consider a generic case of our proposed FNN used to tune the local and global weights as shown in Fig. 1 and formulate the back-propagation algorithm. Where there are L_0 Term nodes in layer 1, L_1 Rule nodes in layer 2 and L_2 Classification nodes in layer 3, for a given input vector, e.g. the n-th input vector, the feed forward propagation process is described as follows:

Layer 1 (The Term layer):

$$\{y_i^{(0)}[n] \mid i = 1, 2, \cdots, L_0\} \quad \text{(the given input vector);} \tag{4}$$

Layer 2 (The Rule layer):

$$y_j^{(1)}[n] = \wedge_{i=1}^{L_0}\left(Lw_{ij} \cdot y_i^{(0)}[n]\right) \quad j=1,2,\cdots,L_1 \tag{5}$$

Layer 3 (The Class layer):

$$y_k^{(2)}[n] = \sum_{j=1}^{L_1} Gw_{jk} \cdot y_j^{(1)}[n] \quad, k=1,2,\cdots,L_2 \tag{6}$$

Let there be N training sample data. Then, the total error function is usually defined as:

$$E = \frac{1}{2}\sum_{n=1}^{N}\sum_{k=1}^{L_2}(d_k[n] - y_k[n])^2 = \sum_{n=1}^{N}\left(\frac{1}{2}\sum_{k=1}^{L_2}(d_k[n] - y_k[n])^2\right) = \sum_{n=1}^{N} E_n \tag{7}$$

Where:

$$d_k[n] = \frac{y_k^{(2)}[n]}{\max_{1 \le k \le L_2}\{y_k^{(2)}[n]\}} \tag{8}$$

is a normalization value of the k-th actual output of the n-th training sample ($1 \le k \le L_2$). It is easy to see from (5), (6) and (7) that the error E is a function with respect to the local weight Lw_{ij} and the global weight Gw_{jk} ($i=1,\cdots,L_0; j=1,\cdots,L_1; k=1,\cdots,L_2$). The main objective of learning is to adjust these weights so that the error function reaches the minimum or is less than a given small value ε.

4.2 A Back-Propagation Algorithm for the FNN

A back-propagation is one of the most popular and powerful learning algorithms; it has been used for many years to learn multi-layer neural networks. In our proposed FNN, we establish a back-propagation algorithm by modifying the smooth derivative, which is briefly described as follows:

$$\frac{\partial(x \vee c)}{\partial x} = \begin{cases} 1 & \text{if } x \ge c \\ \dfrac{1}{1+|x-c|} & \text{if } x < c \end{cases}$$

$$\text{and} \quad \frac{\partial(x \wedge c)}{\partial x} = \begin{cases} 1 & \text{if } x \le c \\ \dfrac{1}{1+|x-c|} & \text{if } x > c \end{cases} \tag{9}$$

In terms of the principle of gradient descent, the back-propagation equations for the FNN as shown in Fig. 1 can be written as:

$$Lw_{ij} = Lw_{ij} - \alpha \frac{\partial E_n}{\partial Lw_{ij}} \quad \text{and} \quad Gw_{jk} = Gw_{jk} - \beta \frac{\partial E_n}{\partial Gw_{jk}} \qquad (10)$$

where α and β are the learning rate. Therefore, the problem of derivation is how to evaluate the two partial derivatives appearing in (10).
The results are presented as follows:

$$\frac{\partial E_n}{\partial Gw_{jk}} = \frac{\partial}{\partial Gw_{jk}} \left(\frac{1}{2} \sum_{k=1}^{L_2} (d_k[n] - y_k[n])^2 \right)$$

$$= (d_k - y_k) \cdot \frac{\partial (d_k - y_k)}{\partial Gw_{jk}}$$

$$= (d_k - y_k) \cdot y_j^{(1)} \cdot \frac{\partial (d_k - y_k)}{\partial y_k^{(2)}}$$

$$\begin{cases} (d_k - y_k) \cdot y_j^{(1)} \cdot \dfrac{\text{Max}\{y_k^{(2)}\} - y_k^{(2)}}{\left(\text{Max}\{y_k^{(2)}\}\right)^2} & \text{if } y_k^{(2)} \geq \vee_{p \neq k} y_p^{(2)} \\[2ex] (d_k - y_k) \cdot y_j^{(1)} \cdot \dfrac{\text{Max}\{y_k^{(2)}\} - y_k^{(2)} \cdot \left(\dfrac{1}{1 + \left|y_k^{(2)} - \vee_{p \neq k} y_p^{(2)}\right|}\right)}{\left(\text{Max}\{y_k^{(2)}\}\right)^2} & \text{if } y_k^{(2)} < \vee_{p \neq k} y_p^{(2)} \end{cases} \qquad (11)$$

$$\frac{\partial E_n}{\partial Lw_{ij}} = \frac{\partial}{\partial Lw_{ij}} \left(\frac{1}{2} \sum_{k=1}^{L_2} (d_k[n] - y_k[n])^2 \right)$$

$$= \frac{1}{2} \sum_{k=1}^{L_2} \left(\frac{\partial}{\partial Lw_{ij}} (d_k - y_k)^2 \right)$$

$$= \sum_{k=1}^{L_2} (d_k - y_k) \cdot \frac{\partial (d_k - y_k)}{\partial y_k^{(2)}} \cdot \frac{\partial y_k^{(2)}}{\partial Lw_{ij}} \qquad (12)$$

$$= \sum_{k=1}^{L_2} (d_k - y_k) \cdot \frac{\partial (d_k - y_k)}{\partial y_k^{(2)}} \cdot \frac{\partial y_k^{(2)}}{\partial y_j^{(1)}} \cdot \frac{\partial y_k^{(1)}}{\partial Lw_{ij}}$$

$$= \begin{cases} \sum_{k=1}^{L_2} [(d_k - y_k) \cdot y_i^{(0)} \cdot Gw_{jk}] \cdot \frac{Max\{y_k^{(2)}\} - y_k^{(2)}}{(Max\{y_k^{(2)}\})^2} \\ \qquad \text{if } y_k^{(2)} \geq \vee_{p \neq k} y_p^{(2)}, \quad Lw_{ij} \cdot y_i^{(0)} \leq \wedge_{p \neq i} (Lw_{pj} \cdot y_p^{(0)}) \\[6pt] \sum_{k=1}^{L_2} \left[(d_k - y_k) \cdot y_i^{(0)} \cdot Gw_{jk} \cdot \frac{Max\{y_k^{(2)}\} - y_k^{(2)}}{(Max\{y_k^{(2)}\})^2} \cdot (\frac{1}{1 + |Lw_{ij} \cdot y_i^{(0)} - \wedge_{p \neq i}(Lw_{pj} \cdot y_p^{(0)})|}) \right] \\ \qquad \text{if } y_k^{(2)} \geq \vee_{p \neq k} y_p^{(2)}, \quad Lw_{ij} \cdot y_i^{(0)} > \wedge_{p \neq i} (Lw_{pj} \cdot y_p^{(0)}) \\[6pt] \sum_{k=1}^{L_2} (d_k - y_k) \cdot y_i^{(0)} \cdot Gw_{jk} \cdot \frac{Max\{y_k^{(2)}\} - y_k^{(2)} \cdot (\frac{1}{1 + |y_k^{(2)} - \vee_{p \neq k} y_p^{(2)}|})}{(Max\{y_k^{(2)}\})^2} \\ \qquad \text{if } y_k^{(2)} < \vee_{p \neq k} y_p^{(2)}, \quad Lw_{ij} \cdot y_i^{(0)} \leq \wedge_{p \neq i} (Lw_{pj} \cdot y_p^{(0)}) \\[6pt] \sum_{k=1}^{L_2} \left[(d_k - y_k) \cdot y_i^{(0)} \cdot Gw_{jk} \cdot A \cdot (\frac{1}{1 + |Lw_{ij} \cdot y_i^{(0)} - \wedge_{p \neq i}(Lw_{pj} \cdot y_p^{(0)})|}) \right] \\ \qquad \text{if } y_k^{(2)} < \vee_{p \neq k} y_p^{(2)}, \quad Lw_{ij} \cdot y_i^{(0)} > \wedge_{p \neq i} (Lw_{pj} \cdot y_p^{(0)}) \end{cases} \qquad (13)$$

$$\text{where} \quad A = \frac{Max\{y_k^{(2)}\} - y_k^{(2)} \cdot (\frac{1}{1 + |y_k^{(2)} - \vee_{p \neq k} y_p^{(2)}|})}{(Max\{y_k^{(2)}\})^2} \qquad (14)$$

and the attached [n] has been omitted from each $y_h^{(t)}$ ($h = i, j, k$; $t = 0,1,2$) and all notations have the same meaning as that in (5) and (6).

5 Applications to Classification Problems

In the following experiments, we aimed to increase the testing accuracy by tuning the local and global weights but with no intention of reducing the number of the extracted rules.

We chose some well known and widely used machine learning classification problems such as Iris data, Wine data, Pima data and Glass data to verify our enhanced back-propagation learning algorithm found in Section 4 for tuning and refining the local and global weights in conjunctive with WFPRs.

5.1 Iris Data

The Iris data set comprises 150 examples with 4 numerical attributes which are Sepal Length(SL), Sepal Width(SW), Petal Length(PL) and Petal Width(PW). The entire data set is categorized into three classes: Setosa, Versicolor and Virginica. The main task of our study is to generate a set of WFPRs from the 100 training examples so that the number of fuzzy rules generated is as small as possible and the testing accuracy of these WFPRs with the remaining 50 examples is as high as possible. We set $\alpha = \beta = 0.1$.

To fuzzify the initial Iris data, we need to fuzzify numerical numbers into linguistic terms. Y. Yuan [7] describes a simple algorithm for generating certain types of membership functions.

For the Iris data, the number of linguistic terms for each of the four attributes can be assumed to be three. The abbreviations used are as follows: SM – Small; MED – Medium; LRG – Large.

Next is the issue of extracting the initial FPRs and mapping them to an FNN. According to the linguistic terms SM, MED and LRG, a set of FPRs can be generated by using one of the machine learning techniques. We expect the number of generated rules to be as small as possible and the generated fuzzy rules to have as high a predictive power as possible. For the Iris data, we quote three fuzzy rules extracted by fuzzy ID3 Algorithm. These three rules will be regarded as three initial FPRs and are shown in the following rules R1 to R3.

R1: IF PL is SM [Lw1] THEN Setosa [Gw1]
R2: IF PL is MED [Lw2] THEN Versicolor [Gw2]
R3: IF PL is LRG [Lw3] THEN Virginica [Gw3]

In rules R1 to R3, we assume that they are not assigned with any weights, i.e., local and global weights (Lwi=Gwj=1 for all i and j) are assumed to be equal to one. These rules are used to test 50 unseen examples of Iris data by means of the Similarity-Based Reasoning Algorithm presented in Section 2. The testing accuracy of the three generated rules is 86.0%.

We then have to train the FNN and obtain the WFPRs. We can train the FNN, obtained by mapping the FPRs R1 to R3, by using the back-propagation learning algorithm proposed in the previous section. After training the FNN with 100 examples, a set of connection weights is obtained. Three WFPRs are shown in the following rules, R1 to R3.

R1: IF PL is SM [32.06] THEN Setosa [5.4]
R2: IF PL is MED [0.49] THEN Versicolor [0.22]
R3: IF PL is LRG [0.92] THEN Virginica [0.98]

When we use the above WFPRs, R1 to R3, to test the 50 unseen examples of Iris data, the testing accuracy of the three WFPRs has increased to 92% from 86 %.

5.2 Testing Results

The results of Iris data, Wine data, Pima data and Glass data are summarized in Table 1.

Learning rate $\alpha=\beta= 0.1$, training examples are 67% of all examples. For this data, the number of linguistic terms for each attribute can be assumed to be three, and according to the linguistic terms SM, MED and LRG, a set of FPRs can be generated by using a fuzzy ID3 algorithm.

We know that the learning and testing accuracy and the number of generated rules depend on both the learning algorithm and the selected linguistic terms. When the learning and testing accuracy cannot satisfy user requirements, one may improve the learning and testing accuracy by increasing the number of linguistic terms. However, increasing the number of linguistic terms will result in increasing the number of generated rules, i.e., increasing the number of linguistic terms will affect the quality of the generated rules. In our study we propose one way of improving learning and testing accuracy by including local and global weights in FPRs while keeping the same number of rules. This concept has been demonstrated by using the benchmark examples in this section. The advantages of our proposed method are that we can obtain a high learning and testing accuracy while keeping the same number of rules.

Table 1. Testing Results

Data	Number of rules	Accuracy of testing $L_{wi}=G_{wj}=1$	Accuracy of testing after refinement
Iris	3	86.0%	92%
Pima	28	74.7%	77.8%
Glass	34	41.0%	71.1%
Wine	21	93%	96.7%

6 Conclusion and Future Work

This paper proposes a method to generate and obtain a set of WFPRs by training the local and global weights with an FNN. We know that the simpler the form of the extracted rules, the stronger the generalization capability of the extracted rules. As the computational complexity of finding an optimal set of fuzzy rules is generally NP-hard, the approach to find an optimal set of fuzzy rules becomes very important.

From the experimental results, one may notice that the representative power of WFPRs is significantly enhanced and better than that of FPRs without weights because the testing accuracy of WFPRs is higher than that of FPRs without weights. Moreover, owing to the learning capability of the proposed FNN, the time required to consult with domain experts to extract a set of WFPRs will greatly be reduced. The proposed back-propagation and the weight training algorithm have been applied to some benchmark problems – Iris, Glass, Wine and Pima classification problems and the results show that the accuracy of testing the extracted WFPRs after training increases. Furthermore, the synergy between WFPRs and an FNN offers a new insight into the future construction of better fuzzy intelligent systems.

Our future research work will be on determining the trade-off and attempting to strike a balance between the number of rules extracted and the testing accuracy of the extracted rules. We will look into the problems of how we could achieve an optimal number of rules by deleting those rules with small or zero global weights.

Acknowledgement

This work was supported by the Natural Science Foundation of Hebei Province (No. F2004000129 & 603137) and by the Foundation for applicational development of Agriculture University of Hebei.

References

1. K.Nozaki, H. Ishibuchi, and H. Tanaka: Adaptive Fuzzy Rule-Based Classification Systems. IEEE Trans. On Fuzzy Systems, vol. 4 (1996) 238-250
2. Dongmei Huang, J. Yang, X.Z Wang, M.H. Ha: Induction of Decision Ttree With Fuzzy Number-Valued Attribute .The Second International Conference on MLC, Vol.2 (2003) 1446-1452
3. T.P. Hong and J.B. Chen: Processing Iindividual Fuzzy Attributes for Fuzzy Rule Iinduction. Fuzzy Sets and System, vol. 112, no. 1 (2000) 127-140
4. H. Ishibuchi, K. Nozaki, N. Yamaoto and H.Tanaka: Selecting Fuzzy If-Then Rrules for Classification Problems Using Genetic Algorithms. IEEE Transactions on fuzzy Systems, vol. 3 (1995) 260-270
5. C.H. Kao and S.M. Chen: A New Method to Generate Fuzzy Rules From Trainig Data Containing Noise for Handling Classification Problems. Proceedings of the Fifth Conference on Artificial Intelligence and Applications, Taipei, Taiwan, Republic of China (2000) 323-331
6. V. Ravi, P.J. Reddy and H.-J. Zimmermann: Fuzzy Rule Base Generation for Classification and Its Minimization via Modified Threshold Accepting. Fuzzy Sets and Systems, vol. 120, no.2 (2001) 271-279
7. Y. Yuan and M. J. Shaw: Induction of Fuzzy Decision Trees. Fuzzy Sets and Systems, vol. 69 (1995) 125-139
8. D.Chakraborty and N. R. Pal: Neuro-Fuzzy Scheme for Simultaneous Feature Selection and Fuzzy Rule-Based Classification. IEEE Transactions on Neural Networks, vol.15, no. 1 (. 2004) 110-123
9. Eric Tsang, D. S. Yeung, J.W.T. Lee, D.M. Huang and X.Z Wang: Refinement of Generated Fuzzy Production Rules by Using a Fuzzy Neural Network. IEEE Transactions on Systems, Man, and Cybernetics---part B : cybernetics, vol.34, No.1 (2004) 409-418
10. D. S. Yeung and E. C. C. Tsang: Weighted Fuzzy Production Rules. Fuzzy Sets and Systems, vol. 88 (1997) 299-313
11. D. S. Yeung and E. C. C. Tsang: A Multilevel Weighted Fuzzy Reasoning Algorithm for Expert Systems. IEEE Transactions on Systems, Man and Cybernetics, vol.28, no. 2 (1998) 149-158

A Particle Swarm Optimization-Based Approach to Tackling Simulation Optimization of Stochastic, Large-Scale and Complex Systems

Ming Lu[1], Da-peng Wu[2], and Jian-ping Zhang[3]

[1] Assist. Professor, Dept. of Civil and Structural Engineering,
Hong Kong Polytechnic University, Hong Kong, China
cemlu@polyu.edu.hk
[2] Master's student, Dept. of Civil Engineering,
Tsinghua University, Beijing, China
wdp03@mails.tsinghua.edu.cn
[3] Professor, Dept. of Civil Engineering,
Tsinghua University, Beijing, China
zhangjp@tsinghua.edu.cn

Abstract. In this research, the methodology of particle swarm optimization (PSO) combined with discrete system simulation is described and employed for enhancing logistical and operational efficiencies of practical one-plant-multi-site concrete delivery systems. In a case study using data from a concrete plant in Hong Kong, PSO was compared with the genetic algorithms (GA) in assessing two mechanisms for optimizing stochastic simulation systems, namely, "steady, averaging" and "non-steady, stochastic". The results show our PSO-based approach could rapidly (5 minutes) converge at the minimum level for an output of the simulation model while GA failed to converge or required a long time (about 1.5 hours) in search of the minimum. In conclusion, the proposed optimization procedures hold the potential to provide a generic, efficient approach to tackling simulation optimization of stochastic, large-scale and complex systems.

1 Background and Introduction

Ready mixed concrete (RMC) accounts for an increasingly high proportion of concrete consumed in residential building, heavy and highway construction projects. Compared with on-site mixed concrete, RMC affords the advantages of stable quality, less pollution and less working space requirement, which are of significance to construction sites within urban areas. There are many central concrete plants in operation and more being established in order to meet the growing RMC demand in construction. A study benchmarking the performance of placing concrete in buildings found that metropolitan areas typically adopt the one-plant-multi-site RMC production and supply system [1]; site productivity is influenced not only by the placing method and other site factors but also by an inevitable imperfect concrete supply. Timely concrete delivery by truckmixers on site contributes to not only continuous, productive site operations on the side of contractors, but also the efficient utilization of limited truckmixer resources on the side of the plant. In order to become profitable and competitive, it is also crucial for a RMC business to be able to deploy less truckmixer resources and marshal more efficiently its truck-mixer fleet in running its daily operations.

HKCONSIM [1] was developed to facilitate building the one-plant-multi-site RMC production system simulation model. The HKCONSIM first collected information on the attributes for each pour and site and the plant and truckmixer resources available; then it generated a model in the SDESA simulation platform[2], including flow entity queue (holding site orders) and resource entity queue (holding all plant and site resources utilized in the system). Because of the probabilistic and stochastic nature of the real world operation, statistical distributions for traveling time and activity duration were fitted based on the Hong Kong's operations data as input models. By executing the HKCONSIM simulation model in SDESA, we can look into both the service level achieved on individual sites and the utilization level achieved for the resources involved.

The present research is, in general, concerned with how to devise a feasible, reliable, and cost efficient approach that integrates emerging evolutionary optimization techniques into stochastic operations simulation modeling. In the practical context of addressing a complex construction logistics problem using real world operations data, the research has placed emphasis on finding practical, efficient, cost-effective solutions to simulate and optimize stochastic, large-scale and complex systems. We apply the particle swarm optimization (PSO) technique to optimize a HKCONSIM simulation model, aimed at improving the overall operational efficiency by minimizing the nonproductive time incurred on multiple sites. A performance measure called total operations inefficiency (TOI), which adds up (1) the truckmixers' waiting time due to their early arrivals and (2) crews' idle time due to truckmixers' late arrivals, is evaluated through HKCONSIM simulation and minimized by PSO. The remainder of the paper first introduces PSO, followed with a comparison of PSO and GA and an overview of existing methodologies for optimization of stochastic simulation systems.

2. Particle Swarm Optimization

2.1 PSO Algorithms

Particle swarm optimization (PSO) is one of the evolutionary optimization techniques proposed by Kennedy and Eberhart in 1995[3]. The basic idea of PSO was inspired by natural flocking and swarm behavior of birds and insects. Analogous to GA, PSO is also a population-based optimization algorithm and starts with a population of randomly generated solutions called particles, which evolve over generations in approaching the optimum solution by the following rules:

Each particle is treated as a point in a D-dimension space, and the ith particle is represented as $x_i = (x_{i1}, x_{i2}, ..., x_{iD})$. Each particle has a *fitness* measure, which is the performance measure of the function or system being studied, and the velocity and position in the hyperspace of a particle are tracked. Each particle's best position that corresponds with the minimum fitness measure achieved so far in the search process is denoted as *pbest*. Likewise, the best position of all particles in the population achieved so far is denoted as *gbest*. Both *pbest* and *gbest* are constantly updated over iterations of seeking the optimum.

Once the *pbest* and *gbest* are identified in the current iteration, each particle updates its velocity and position by Equations (1) and (2) prior to entering the next iteration.

$$v_{id}^{k+1} = v_{id}^{k} + c_1 \times r_1 \times (p_{id}^{k} - x_{id}^{k}) + c_2 \times r_2 \times (p_{gd}^{k} - x_{id}^{k}) \tag{1}$$

$$x_{id}^{k+1} = x_{id}^{k} + v_{id}^{k+1} \tag{2}$$

Where v is the particle's velocity, x is its position; p_{id} and p_{gd} are respectively *pbest* and *gbest*; the superscript k denotes the kth iteration, c_1 and c_2 are the *cognitive* parameter and the *social* parameter respectively, both of which are generally set as 2; r_1 and r_2 are random numbers uniformly distributed on the range (0, 1). The pseudo code of the basic PSO algorithm is as follows:

```
For each particle {
Initialize particle;
}
Do{
   For each particle {
   Calculate fitness value;
   If (fitness value < pbest){
   Update pbest;
   If (pbest < gbest) Update gbest;
   }
   }
   For each particle {
   Calculate particle velocity v according to Eq. (1);
   If (v > Vmax) v = Vmax;
   Else if (v < -Vmax) v = -Vmax;
   Calculate particle position x according to Eq. (2);
   If (x > Xmax) x = Xmax
   Else if (x < -Xmax) x = -Xmax
   }
} While maximum iterations not attained;
```

What distinguishes the global version from the local version of PSO –both of which are commonly applied– lies in the *gbest* part of Eq. (1) [4]. In the global version, particles move toward the stochastic average of *pbest* and *gbest*; while in the local version, particles only have reference to information as of their own and their nearest neighbors' bests, thus, particles move toward the positions as guided by *pbest* and *lbest*. Note *lbest* represents the position of the particle with the best evaluation in the nearest neighborhood of the current particle. The following Eq. (3) describes the local version, where p_{ld} is *lbest*.

$$v_{id}^{k+1} = v_{id}^{k} + c_1 \cdot r_1 \cdot (p_{id}^{k} - x_{id}^{k}) + c_2 \cdot r_2 \cdot (p_{ld}^{k} - x_{id}^{k}) \tag{3}$$

A parameter called inertia weight w was introduced into PSO to balance the global and local search strategies in [5, 6]. It can be a positive constant or even a positive linear or nonlinear function of time. A large inertia weight facilitates global search, while a small inertia weight accelerates local search. The modified equation is as follows:

$$v_{id}^{k+1} = w \cdot v_{id}^k + c_1 \cdot r_1 \cdot (p_{id}^k - x_{id}^k) + c_2 \cdot r_2 \cdot (p_{gd}^k - x_{id}^k) \qquad (4)$$

Another parameter k called a constriction coefficient was introduced in [7], intended to guarantee PSO to converge.

$$v_{id}^{k+1} = k \cdot [v_{id}^k + c_1 \cdot r_1 \cdot (p_{id}^k - x_{id}^k) + c_2 \cdot r_2 \cdot (p_{gd}^k - x_{id}^k)] \qquad (5)$$

$$k = \frac{2}{\left| 2 - \varphi - \sqrt{\varphi^2 - 4\varphi} \right|}, \varphi = c_1 + c_2 \quad \varphi > 4 \qquad (6)$$

PSO has attracted attention of researchers around the world. Several investigations have been undertaken to improve the performance of PSO since 1995 [8-10]. In addition, PSO has been successfully applied to some computer science and engineering problems [11, 12].

2.2 Comparison of GA and PSO

PSO is observed to share many common traits with GA. Both algorithms start with randomly generated solutions (particles in PSO or chromosomes in GA); both rely on fitness measures to evaluate and evolve solutions over iterations or generations; and both contain stochastic elements and do not guarantee success in finding the global optimum. In GA, the chromosomes share information with one another, and the whole population moves collectively toward the optimum over generations of evolution through crossover and mutation. By contrast, PSO does not involve any genetic operators; instead, from one generation to the next, particles update themselves by adjusting their internal velocities and positions. And the fact that particles also keep memory of their previous best positions (*pbest*) is unique to the PSO algorithm and sets PSO apart from GA. As such, the best solution identified in global, collective terms (such as *gBest* or *lBest*) and the best solution identified for each individual particle combine to inform the adjustment of the current velocity and position of one particle. Compared with GA, PSO may provide a more effective and efficient solution to optimizing a stochastic system, which features high variability in system responses under a fixed set of input factors and hence the system state of which is regarded unsteady as opposed to a deterministic system.

Many previously proposed methods essentially transform a stochastic problem into a deterministic one in search of a combination of inputs to a stochastic simulation system that result in the optimum system state. For instance, in optimizing an output performance measure on a stochastic simulation model, given a certain input scenario, one Monte Carlo run of simulation randomly samples statistical distributions to derive an observed value of the system output, and a large number of the Monte Carlo simulation runs (n) give an average of the system output, which, as the fitness measure, is then fed back to the optimization engine. Given a large enough n, the averaged system output is generally steady, resembling a constant output from a deterministic system. Many commercial simulation software tools integrated with optimum-seeking packages [13] are implementation of the above quasi-deterministic optimization strategies on stochastic simulation models. The interactions between the optimization package and the simulation model are shown in Fig. 1. Note in addition to the quality of the optimum solution obtained, one important performance indicator of a practical simulation optimization methodology is the amount of execution time required to arrive at the solution on a commonly available PC (rather than a supercomputer), which is determined by (1) the number of system configurations (scenarios) that need to be evaluated, (2) the number of simulation runs needed to obtain the average output for every system configuration, and (3) the execution time per simulation run.

The remainder of the paper uses the optimization of the HKCONSIM concrete delivery simulation model as a case to compare the performances of PSO with GA in "steady, averaging" and "non-steady, stochastic" settings respectively.

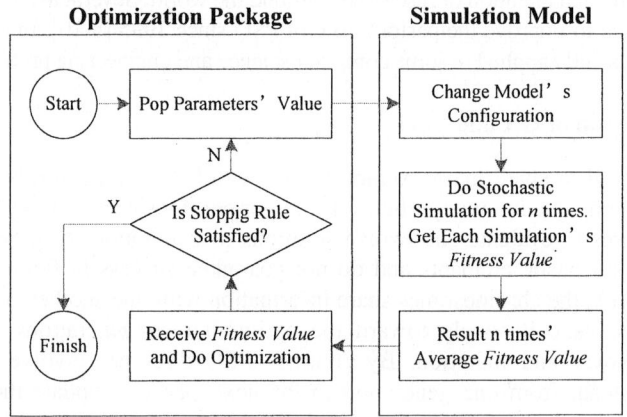

Fig. 1. Optimization method on Stochastic Simulation

3 Case Study

3.1 Optimization Model Formulation

We first describe the formulation of the PSO algorithm in the specific context of a HKCONSIM concrete delivery simulation model. Given n as the number of sites served by a central plant, we have a search space in $n+2$ dimensions and the

Table 1. Parameters limits

	MIN	MAX
Inter-arrival time	2	60
$5m^3$ Truckmixer	5	10
$7m^3$ Truckmixer	5	30

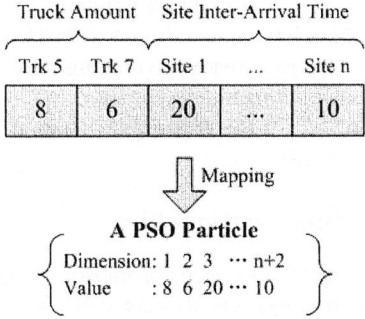

Fig. 2. PSO particle mapping

problem's parameters in a HKCONSIM simulation model are mapped to a PSO particle as in Fig. 2. Note the first two dimensions are the amounts of 5m³ and 7m³ truckmixers respectively, the remaining n dimensions are the inter-arrival time estimates (min) for each site. And Table 1 lists the practical lower and upper limits for all input parameters. Fig. 3 shows the overall PSO algorithm and how it interplays with the simulation model during optimization. We used the SDESA platform to run the HKCONSIM simulation model and obtain the simulation output of TOI as particles' fitness measure. Then we used Eq. (4) to update the particles' velocity and Eq. (2) to update the particles' position. At the end of optimization, we obtained the *gbest* position value as the final optimum result.

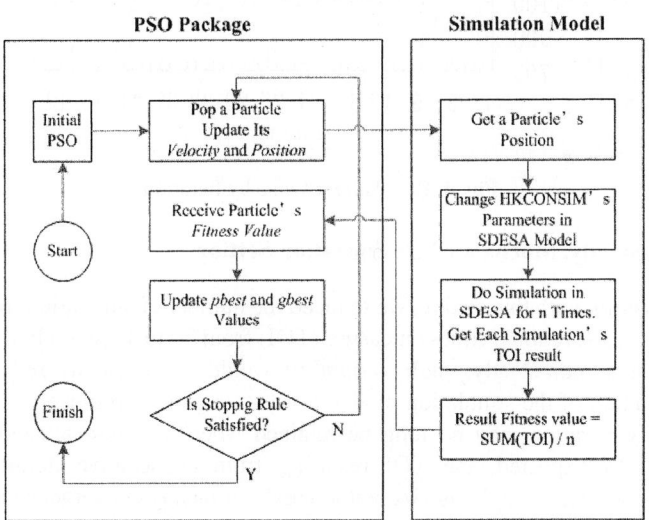

Fig. 3. PSO Package and Simulation Model

The proposed PSO algorithm was coded in C++ into an add-in package of the SDESA platform. The case study simulated the operations at a Hong Kong concrete plant on a particular day, serving 11 sites and supplying a total of 934 m³ concrete in its daily operations. Next, 50 iterations (generations) were executed so as to compare the performance of PSO and GA in "steady, averaging" and "non-steady, stochastic" settings respectively. Related optimization parameters used in the following case study are as: the population size of 30; the inertia weight w from initial 0.9 down to 0.4 in the end; and $c1$ and $c2$ both set as 2.0

3.2 "Steady, Averaging" Optimization Setting

In this setting, each PSO particle's (or each chromosome's as for GA) fitness measure in terms of the average TOI (min) was evaluated based on 30 simulation runs, i.e. $n = 30$. Fig. 4 contrasts the changes of the best fitness values over iterations for GA and PSO. We can see PSO and GA performed closely in bringing down the original TOI of around 2000 min to an level of 1100 min, both requiring about 1 hour and 30 minutes on a Pentium IV 2.0 GHz PC to run through 50 iterations.

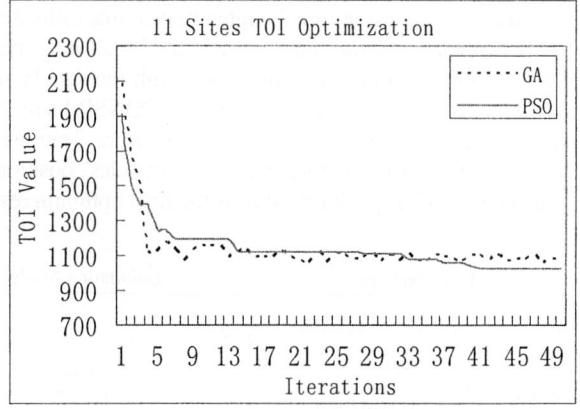

Fig. 4. Best *Fitness Value* by Iterations

3.3 "Non-steady, Stochastic" Optimization Setting

In experimenting with this setting, we reduced the number of simulation runs as needed for evaluating a solution's fitness measure (TOI) from 30 to 1. As such, the simulation system became non-steady: high variability would occur on its response due to stochastic nature of the simulation model. For GA, a good chromosome (solution) for the current generation may no long be retained when it is re-evaluated in the next generation. As expected, the TOI resulting from consecutive iterations broadly fluctuate in the case of applying GA, without exhibiting any convergence trend (Fig.5). Fig. 5 also shows results of independently repeating the 50-iteration GA optimization experiment for 20 times.

In contrast, under the same "Non-Steady, Stochastic" setting, the PSO required less than 4 minutes on a Pentium IV 2.0 GHz PC to complete 50 iterations and converged

TOI to a lower level around 1000 min. Note the PSO's superiority over GA in the "non-steady, stochastic" setting is in large part due to the PSO's special mechanism of memorizing the previous best position of each particle. As a result, PSO's optimization performance is exempt from being compromised by the non-steady response of the stochastic system under the "nonsteady, stochastic" setting. We further assessed the effects of the systemic randomness due to Monte Carlo sampling and PSO itself upon the PSO's optimization performance through independently repeating the 50-iteration optimization experiments. As shown in Fig. 6, PSO consistently converged at the TOI level of 1000 min for the simulation model over 20 independent experiments, with controllable variability of TOI observed (bounded between 900 and 1100 min). Fig. 7 sums up the performance of PSO and GA as given in Figs. 5 and 6 by showing the changes of TOI –averaged on 20 independent experiments– over 50 optimization iterations. In our case study, PSO was able to rapidly find the optimum on an output of a stochastic simulation model in the "non-steady, stochastic" setting, achieving

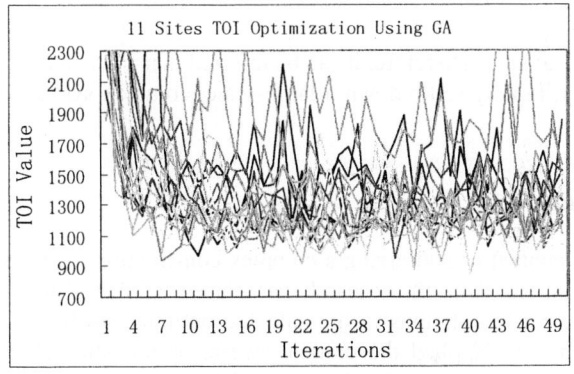

Fig. 5. Best *Fitness Value* Using GA

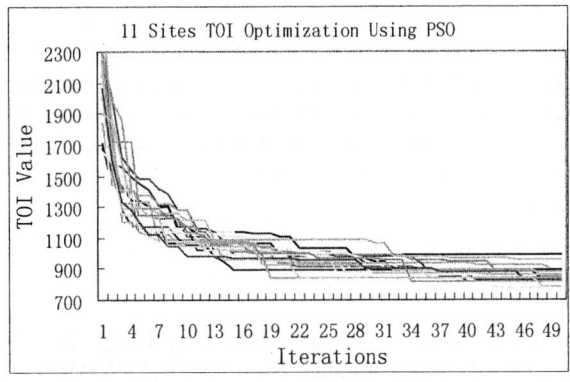

Fig. 6. Best *Fitness Value* Using PSO

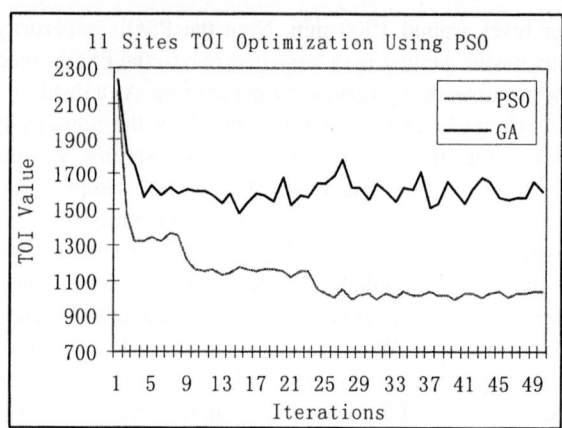

Fig. 7. PSO vs. GA in "nonsteady, stochastic" setting: TOI averaged over 20 independent experiments against 50 iterations

significant time savings. Therefore, it can be inferred that a few such PSO experiments can comfortably, rapidly settle down a large-scale, complex system simulation at its optimum state.

4 Conclusions

In the practical context of addressing a complex construction logistics problem using real world operations data, the research has placed emphasis on finding practical, efficient, cost-effective solutions to simulate and optimize stochastic, large-scale and complex systems. We applied the particle swarm optimization (PSO) technique to optimize a concrete delivery simulation model, aimed at improving the overall operational efficiency by minimizing the nonproductive time incurred on multiple sites. A performance measure called total operations inefficiency (TOI), which adds up (1) the truckmixers' waiting time due to their early arrivals and (2) crews' idle time due to truckmixers' late arrivals, is evaluated and minimized. The results show that on the same PC, PSO could converge at the minimum level for an output of the simulation model in 5 minutes while GA failed to converge or required a long time of about 1.5 hours in search of the minimum. In conclusion, the proposed optimization procedures are significant to practical system simulation research and application and hold the potential to provide a generic, efficient approach for optimizing stochastic, large-scale and complex systems.

Acknowledgement

The research presented in this paper was funded by Hong Kong Research Grants Council (Project A/C: B-Q686; Project No.: PolyU 5149/03E). The writers also acknowledge the Hong Kong Polytechnic Univ. – Tsinghua Univ. Research Center for Construction IT for facilitating the research.

References

1. Ming Lu, Michael Anson, S. L. Tang, Y. C. Ying.: HICONSIM: A Practical Simulation Solution to Planning Concrete Plant Operations in Hong Kong, ASCE Journal of construction engineering and management, vol. 129, (2003) 547-554
2. Ming Lu.: Simplified Discrete-Event Simulation Approach for Construction Simulation, ASCE Journal of Construction Engineering and Management, vol. 129, (2003) 537-546
3. James Kennedy, Russel Eberhart.: Particle Swarm Optimization, Proceeding of IEEE International Conference on Neural Networks, vol. 4, (1995) 1942-1948
4. Russel Eberhart, James Kennedy.: A New Optimizer Using Particle Swarm Theory, Proceeding of the sixth international symposium on micro machine and human science, (1995) 39-43
5. Yuhui Shi, Russel Eberhart.: A Modified Particle Swarm Optimizer, Proceedings of the IEEE International Conference on Evolutionary Computation, (1998) 69-73
6. Yuhui Shi, Russel Eberhart.: Parameter selection in particle swarm optimization, Proceedings of 7th Annual Conference on Evolution Computation, (1998) 591-601
7. Maurice Clerc.: The swarm and the queen: towards a deterministic and adaptive particle swarm optimization, Proceedings of the 1999 Congress of Evolutionary Computation, vol. 3, (1999) 1951-1957
8. Huiyuan Fan.: A modification to particle swarm optimization algorithm, Engineering Computations (Swansea, Wales□, vol. 19, (2002) 970□989
9. Peter J. Angeline.: Using Selection to Improve Particle Swarm Optimization, Proceedings of the IEEE Conference on Evolutionary Computation, ICEC, (1998) 84□89
10. Keiichiro Yasuda, Azuma Ide, Nobuhiro Iwasaki.: Adaptive particle swarm optimization, Proceedings of the IEEE International Conference on Systems, Man and Cybernetics, vol. 2, (2003) 1554□1559
11. Ayed Salman, Imtiaz Ahmad, Sabah Al-Madani.: Particle swarm optimization for task assignment problem, Microprocessors and Microsystems, vol. 26, (2002) 363□371
12. Hong Zhang, Xiaodong Li, Heng Li, Fulai Huang. : Particle swarm optimization-based schemes for resource-constrained project scheduling, Automation in Construction, vol. 14, (2005) 393-404
13. Ming Cao, Ming LU, Jian-ping Zhang.: Concrete plant operations optimization using combined simulation and genetic algorithms, Proceedings of the Third International Conference on Machine Learning and Cybernetics, vol. 7, (2004) 4204-4209

Combination of Multiple Nearest Neighbor Classifiers Based on Feature Subset Clustering Method

Li-Juan Wang[1,2], Qiang Hua[2], Xiao-Long Wang[1], and Qing-Cai Chen[1]

[1] Department of Computer Science and Technology, Harbin Institute
of Technology, Harbin 150001, China
{ljwang, wangxiaolong, qcchen}@insun.hit.edu.cn
[2] Machine Learning Center, Faculty of Mathematics and Computer Science,
Hebei University, Baoding 071002, China
huaq@mail.hbu.edu.cn

Abstract. This paper proposes a new method called FC-MNNC based on feature subset clustering for combining multiple NNCs to obtain better performance than that of using a single NNC. In FC-MNNC, the component NNCs based on the reasonably partitioned feature subsets are parallel and independently able to classify one pattern and the final decision is aggregated by the majority voting rule. Here, two methods are used to partition the feature set. In method I, GA is used for clustering features to form different feature subsets according to the accuracy of the combination classification. And method II is the transitive closure clustering method based on the pair-wise correlation between features. To demonstrate the performance of FC-MNNC, we select four UCI databases for our experiments. The experimental results show that: (i) in FC-MNNC, the performance of method II isn't better than that of method I; (ii) the accuracy of FC-MNNC based on method I is better than that of the standard NNC and feature selection using GA in individual classifier; (iii) the performance of FC-MNNC based on method I is not worse than that of feature subset selection using GA in multiple NNCs; and (iv) FC-MNNC is robust against irrelevant features.

1 Introduction

Classifier combination is a sub-branch of pattern recognition, which attempts to improve the accuracy of a single classifier. Although there is lack of theoretical study, much empirical study has been done. For example, papers [1,2] introduce how to combine multiple neural networks using a fuzzy integral for robust classification. In paper [3], K. Tumer and J. Ghosh apply the training data set alteration method in the combination system. And the combination system based on different feature sets is studied in paper [4].

By combining the diverse and accurate component classifiers, the accuracy of the whole may be improved. There are many methods available to design the combination system with the above properties; for example, the method of altering the training data set or feature set. By altering the training data set, the performance of neural networks, or the decision tree, is significantly improved [5]. Unfortunately, this method can't improve the accuracy of the nearest neighbor classifier (NNC) [5].

NNC is a simple, popular and nonparametric classifier, which assumes that the class label of an unknown pattern is the same as its nearest neighbor. In NNC, the training data is simply stored as opposed to abstracting general rules. So Bremain [6] demonstrates that NNC, unlike a decision tree, stores a large number of prototypes and is stable against the changes of the training data set. The alteration of a training data set could not improve the performance of NNC. Langley and Iba [7] find out that NNC is varied drastically with the addition of irrelevant features. Bay [5] combines multiple NNCs each using only a random subset of features (MFS). The experimental results show that the accuracy of MFS outperforms that of standard NNC. When the size of dimensionality is high, random selection could not find the optimal feature subsets for a combination of multiple NNCs. In [8], P. Visswanath et al apply a greedy algorithm to partition the feature set into different uncorrelated feature subsets and then form a PPC-tree data structure. By majority voting rule, the combination of multiple NNCs based on PPC not only improves the accuracy of standard NNC but also reduces the computation time. The greedy algorithm is a locally optimized algorithm, which is unable to find the best solution. In [9], L.I. Kunenva and L. C. Jain use GA to combine a multiple classifiers system. GA is used to select feature subsets for the multiple classifiers system, which consists of a three-classifier system and the basic types of individual classifier (the linear and quadratic discriminant classifier and logistic classifier). They find out that GA is appropriate for a combination multiple classifiers system because the encoding of the problem in terms of GA is easy and straightforward unlike other optimized algorithms.

This paper proposes a new method called FC-MNNC based on feature subset clustering for combining multiple NNCs to obtain a better performance than that of using a single NNC. Feature subset clustering partitions the feature set into disjoint feature subsets, which is an extension of feature selection. In feature selection, the feature set is partitioned into two sets; one is used to classify and the classification decision from the other set is omitted, whereas in feature subset clustering, the number of feature subsets is more than two, and the multiple decisions from different feature subsets may be consensus or conflict, which is aggregated by a combination technique.

In FC-MNNC, the component NNCs based on the reasonably partitioned feature subsets are parallel and independent to classify one pattern and the final decision is aggregated by majority voting rule. The key point of FC-MNNC is how to reasonably partition the feature set. There are two methods. In method I, GA is used for clustering features to form different feature subsets according to the accuracy of combination classification. In method II, the feature subset is partitioned by the transitive closure clustering method based on the pair-wise correlation between features. To demonstrate the performance of FC-MNNC, we select four UCI databases in our experiments. First, the FC-MNNC's classification accuracy of two feature subset clustering methods is compared. In method II, there is one phenomenon in that a feature subset only includes a single feature. Due to this phenomenon, the improvement of FC-MNNC based on method II has been greatly affected. So in the following, FC-MNNC based on feature subset clustering method I is compared with (i) standard NNC, (ii) feature selection using GA in individual NNC and (iii) feature subset selection using GA in multiple NNCs. The experimental results show that the accuracy of FC-MNNC based on method

I is better than that of the standard NNC and feature selection using GA in an individual classifier. The performance of FC-MNNC based on method I is no worse than that of feature subset selection using GA in multiple NNCs. It is also demonstrated that FC-MNNC is robust against irrelevant features.

The remainder of the paper is organized as follows: Section 2 introduces the basic terms and some concepts about NNC and the majority voting rule. Section 3 explains the developed FC-MNNC algorithm and two feature subset clustering methods. The experimental results are shown in Section 4. Finally, Section 5 presents the conclusion.

2 NNC and the Majority Voting Rule

Let $X = \{X_1, X_2, \cdots X_n\}$ be a set of patterns, where X_i represents the *ith* pattern; let $A = \{A_1, A_2, \cdots A_m\}$ be the feature set, where $A_m = \{C_1, C_2, \cdots C_c\}$ is the decision feature denoting the pattern's class label and the others $A_j (1 \leq j \leq m-1)$ are the conditional features describing the character of one pattern. For each item of the pattern X_i, A_j has a definite value $X_i(A_j)$. A classifier is a map:

$$X_i(A_j) \rightarrow X_i(A_m) \ (1 \leq i \leq n, 1 \leq j \leq m-1)$$

2.1 NNC

NNC is a simple classifier whose decision rule is that the unknown pattern's class label is the same as that of its nearest neighbor's. The nearest neighbor is defined by computing the standard Euclidean distance. The classification algorithm is described as follows:

i) **Training**: Store the pattern $X_i (1 \leq i \leq n)$ with class label in the training data set.
ii) **Classification**:
  Step 1 Give a query pattern X_q to be classified.
  Step 2 Compute the Euclidean distance d_{qi} between X_q and each pattern $X_i (1 \leq i \leq n)$ in the training data set, where d_{qi} is defined as:

$$d_{qi} = \sqrt{\sum_{j=1}^{m-1}(X_q(A_j) - X_i(A_j))^2} \qquad (1)$$

  Step 3 Select the nearest pattern $X_{nearest}$ as its nearest neighbor, where:

$$nearest = \{p | d_{qp} = \min d_{qi}, 1 \leq i \leq n\} \qquad (2)$$

  Step 4 $\qquad X_q(A_m) = X_{nearest}(A_m) \qquad (3)$

Usually the dataset is partitioned into two sets: a training data set and a testing data set. The training data set is stored in memory, while the testing data set is used to testify the classification accuracy. The performance of the classifier is determined according to the testing accuracy.

2.2 Majority Voting Rule

For an individual classifier, the final decision is $d = X_q(A_m)$. If there are l $(l \geq 1)$ classifiers, each classifier has one decision $d_j (1 \leq j \leq l)$. The multiple decisions maybe consensus or conflict. In a combination system, the final decision is aggregated by the combination technique as follows:

$$D = F(d_1, d_2, \cdots d_l) \tag{4}$$

where D is the combined decision and F is the combined technique. Let $N(d_j = C_k) 1 \leq j \leq l, 1 \leq k \leq c$ be the number of classifiers, which denote the unknown pattern belonging to class C_k.

Majority voting rule is a simple combination technique. Although it's a simple method, it is as effective as the other three complicated methods: Bayesian, logistic regression and neural network [10]. Majority voting rule can be described as follows:

$$D = F(d_1, d_2, \cdots d_l) = \begin{cases} C_k & N(d_j = C_k) >= \lfloor l/2 \rfloor + 1 \\ \Phi & \text{otherwise} \end{cases} \tag{5}$$

3 FC-MNNC and Two Features Subset Clustering Method

One method of generating a diverse combination of classifiers is to perturb some aspect of the training input for which the classifier is unstable [5]. Since NNC is sensitive to the change of feature sets, the combination of NNC based on different feature subsets may lead to a better performance. In this paper, FC-MNNC combination system is proposed and demonstrated in Figure 1. One pattern's feature

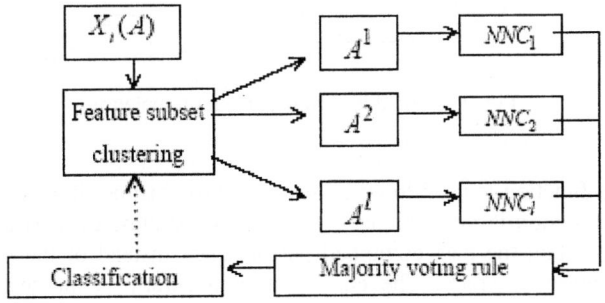

Fig. 1. FC-MNNC combination system

set, A, has been partitioned into l $(l \geq 1)$ feature subsets $A^j (1 \leq j \leq l)$ by a feature subset clustering method. The component classifiers (NNCs) are based on the corresponding feature subsets and are independent and parallel when classifying one pattern. The decisions from different NNCs may be consensus or conflict. Majority voting rule aggregates the multi-decisions. From the classification to the feature subset clustering method, there is a feedback loop, although not all of the combination system needs the loop, which depends on the method of feature subset clustering. For example, GA needs the feedback loop to dynamically adjust the partition of the feature subset, while in transitive closure clustering the partition of the feature subset is fixed. Therefore, it is unnecessary to utilize the feedback loop in the combination system based on transitive closure clustering. In the following, two feature subset clustering methods are introduced:

3.1 Method I (GA)

In GA, the encoding rule and fitness function should be specified first. Encoding rule transforms the problem to the chromosome S. Here one chromosome S represents the feature set, except for the decision feature. The *ith* gene in the chromosome corresponds to the *ith* feature. We use integer encoding representation where one integer includes $\lfloor \log l \rfloor +1$ bits of binary code. The value of the gene is set in the interval $[1,l]$, which represents l feature subsets corresponding to l NNCs. According to the value of the gene, the feature is divided into different subsets. For example, let $l = 3$ and the number of features is seven. A possible chromosome is shown in Figure 2. It can be seen that NNC_1 uses a two dimensional feature subset $[A^2, A^5]$, NNC_2 uses a three dimensional feature subset $[A^1, A^4, A^7]$ and NNC_3 uses a two dimensional feature subset $[A^3, A^6]$.

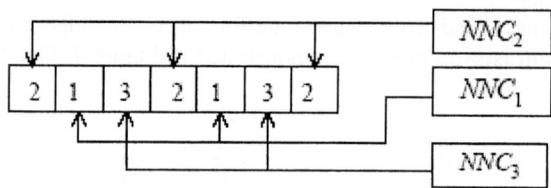

Fig. 2. A possible chromosome representation

The fitness function is used to evaluate each chromosome. In this case, the value of the fitness function is proportional to the combined classification accuracy. Here we attempt to obtain the best combined performance instead of the best individual NNC classification accuracy. The classification accuracy is the testing accuracy, which is the ratio of the number of correctly identified data N_c based on the majority voting rule over the whole number of testing data N, defined as follows:

$$fitness = \frac{N_c}{N} \qquad (6)$$

$$N_c = \begin{cases} N_c + 1 & if\ D = X_i(A_m) \\ N_c & otherwise \end{cases} \qquad (7)$$

where D is defined as Formula (5).

The operator of crossover, mutation and selection is the basic form of GA. The detail may be referred to in [11].

In FC-MNNC, GA dynamically adjusts the partition of feature subsets according to classification accuracy, which makes the partitions more appropriate.

3.2 Method II (Transitive Closure Clustering)

Transitive closure clustering is a popular way of clustering in which the similarity matrix needs to transform into its transitive closure.

First, the similarity measure ρ is defined as the pair-wise correlation between features. Then, by computing the similarity between each pair of features, a similarity matrix, S, is obtained. The similarity matrix S satisfies symmetry and reflectivity. In addition, the similarity matrix needs to satisfy the transitive condition. By searching for an integer, k, in which S^k is transitive, the transitive closure $T(S)$ is obtained. Finally, according to the transitive closure $T(S)$, the feature set is partitioned into several clusters.

Before classification, transitive closure clustering may find a fixed partition in that the average correlation between features within one cluster is high and that between features of different clusters is low [8].

4 Experiments

In order to testify as to FC-MNNC's performance, we select four UCI[12] databases, which are described in Table 1. The experiment results are shown in Table 2-6. When the number of feature subsets is equal to one in Table 2-6, it means the whole feature set is used. And the row or column of note in Table 2-6 specifies the partition of feature subsets.

Example 1. The classification accuracy of FC-MNNC based on two feature subset clustering methods is compared. For wine, the comparison result is shown in Table 2. Because the number of features in wine is thirteen, we only partition the feature set into three feature subsets and five feature subsets. From Table 2, it can be seen that after partition by method II, some feature subsets only include a single feature. The classification based on one feature is not satisfied. Due to this phenomenon, the classification accuracy of FC-MNNC based on method II isn't any better than that of FC-MNNC based on method I. Especially, when the number of feature subsets is three, the accuracy of FC-MNNC based on method II has been greatly affected.

In the following, the classification accuracy of FC-MNNC based on GA is compared with: (i) standard NNC; (ii) feature selection using GA in individual NNC; and, (iii) feature subset selection using GA in multiple NNCs. In addition, the robustness against irrelevant features is compared between FC-MNNC and standard NNC.

Table 1. The property of the four UCI databases

Data set	No. of training instances	No. of testing instances	No. of features	No. of Classes	Feature's property
Ionosphere	182	169	35	2	numerical
Thyroid	3772	3428	23	3	numerical
Sonar	139	39	62	2	numerical
Wine	110	68	15	3	numerical

Table 2. The classification accuracy of Standard NNC and FC-MNNC

		No. of feature subsets	Wine	
			accuracy	note
Standard NNC		1	0.808	
FC-MNNC	Method I	3	0.971	3,1,2,2,1,3,2,2,1,1,3,3,1
		5	0.985	5,2,1,3,4,2,5,1,4,1,5,3,4
FC-MNNC	Method II	3	0.779	1,1,1,2,1,1,1,1,1,1,1,1,3
		5	0.897	1,1,1,2,1,3,4,3,1,3,1,1,5

Example 2. Table 3 shows the classification accuracy of Standard NNC and FC-MNNC. It can be seen from Table 3 that the accuracy of FC-MNNC is better than that of standard NNC. The improvement of FC-MNNC varies with different databases. For the thyroid database, there is no obvious improvement, whereas for the wine database, the improvement is obvious - from 0.808 to 0.985. The optimal number of feature subsets also varies with different databases. For sonar database, the optimal number of feature subsets is seven. For thyroid database, the optimal number of feature subsets is three. The experimental results in Table 3 show that if the size of dimensionality is high, the optimal number of feature subsets may be high; and vice versa.

Table 3. The classification accuracy of Standard NNC and FC-MNNC

	No. of feature subsets	Ionosphere	Sonar	Thyroid	Wine
Standard NNC	1	0.817	0.391	0.919	0.808
FC-MNNC	3	0.911	0.565	0.943	0.971
	5	0.934	0.594	0.940	0.985
	7	0.952	0.623	0.936	-

Table 4. The classification accuracy of Ionosphere database by NNC based on GA feature selection and FC-MNNC

Ionosphere	No. of subsets	Accuracy	Note
Standard NNC	1	0.817	
GA feature selection for individual NNC	2	0.911	00101000011100011001111110111010100
FC-MNNC	3	0.911	3,3,3,1,2,3,3,2,3,1,2,1,1,3,2,2,1,1,3,1,3,3,1,3, 3,2,2,2,3,1,3,3,3,1
	5	0.935	2,5,1,5,4,4,2,1,2,3,1,3,2,3,2,4,2,1,5,5,3,3,5,1, 3, 5,2, 5,3,2,1,3,3,3
	7	0.952	1,7,4,1,3,7,6,2,2,1,5,6,5,5,7,3,1,1,6,6,3,4,1,2, 7,1,1,3,4,6,1,5,4,4

Example 3. GA can not only be used to select feature subsets for multiple classifiers, but is also fit for selection features for an individual classifier. Here the classification accuracy of an ionosphere database by NNC based on GA feature selection is compared with that by FC-MNNC. The results are shown in Table 4. It can be concluded from Table 4 that: (i) the accuracy of the standard NNC is 0.817; (ii) after feature selection by GA, the accuracy of NNC increases to 0.911; and, (iii) when the number of feature subsets is three, five or seven, the accuracy is not less than that of the GA feature selection for an individual classifier. Especially, when the number of feature subsets is seven, the accuracy raises to 0.952, which significantly improves the performance of standard NNC and feature selection using GA in an individual NNC.

Table 5. The classification accuracy of Ionosphere database by GA feature selection for multiple NNC and FC-MNNC

Ionosphere	No. of feature subsets	Accuracy	Note
FC-MNNC	3	0.911	1,2,3,1,3,1,3,2,3,3,3,2,2,3,3,3,2,3,2,1,3,3,3,3,2,1,3,3,3,1,2,1,3
	5	0.934	2,5,1,5,4,4,2,1,2,3,1,3,2,3,2,4,2,1,5,5,3,3,5,1,3,5,2,5,3,2,1,3,3,3
	7	0.952	1,7,4,1,3,7,6,2,2,1,5,6,5,5,7,3,1,1,6,6,3,4,1,2,7,1,1,3,4,6,1,5,4,4
GA feature selection for multiple NNC (disjoint)	3	0.946	1,2,1,3,2,2,3,0,2,3,1,3,2,0,0,3,3,2,1,3,1,2,1,1,3,3,2,3,2,0,3,3,0,1
	5	0.934	2,0,1,0,4,4,2,1,2,3,1,3,2,3,2,4,2,1,0,0,3,3,0,1,3,0,2,0,3,2,1,3,3,3
	7	0.952	6,5,1,1,2,0,4,1,3,7,5,6,4,1,2,6,4,4,1,1,6,6,1,1,3,7,0,1,6,3,7,4,5,2
GA feature selection for multiple NNC (joint)	3	0.923	2,1,2,5,3,2,0,2,0,4,0,6,7,3,1,0,4,2,0,1,6,1,6,7,0,6,6,5,1,0,0,1,2,0
	5	0.911	19,2,16,10,11,17,27,21,8,8,24,18,23,1,17,4,1,14,24,5,23,6,14,14, 13,12,30,0,31,24,0,10,17,30

Example 4. Paper [9] presents two versions of feature subset selection by GA in a multiple classifiers system. Version 1 is similar to our encoding rule which selects the

disjoint feature subsets but the value of one gene is in the range from 0 to l, where 0 represents that the ith feature is not used. In GA, the solution space of version 1 is $2^l *2$ while the solution space of a feature subset clustering is half of that. Because the consensus or conflict decisions are aggregated by the combination technique, it's unnecessary to discard features in the combination system. The experiment results in Table 5 show that the best accuracy of FC-MNNC is not worse than that of feature subset selection using GA in multiple NNCs. In paper [9] Version 2 selects not only the overlapping feature subsets but also the types of the individual classifiers. Here we only use NNC. Therefore it's unnecessary to select the type of classifier. The classification performance of Version 2 is better than that of Version 1. When the number of classifiers and the size of dimensionality are larger, the solution space of Version 2 is much larger than that of Version 1. Meanwhile Version 2's encoding rule is difficult to interpret. Under the same parameters of GA, the performance of Version 2 is limited. When the number of feature subsets is three or five, the accuracy of Version 2 is not better than Version 1 or FC-MNNC.

Table 6. The robustness against irrelevant features of NNC and FC-MNNC

Thyroid database	No. of feature subsets	The original feature set	The original feature set +3 irrelevant features
NNC	1	0.919	0.887
FC-MNNC	3	0.943	0.939
	Note	2,1,1,3,1,2,2,3,2,3,3,1,3,1,3,3,3,2, 3,2,1,1,	2,2,2,3,3,1,2,3,2,2,1,1,1,1,1,2,3 ,2,1,3,3,3,1,

Example 5. With the knowledge that NNC is sensitive to irrelevant features, this example looks at the robustness of FC-MNNC against irrelevant features. In Table 6, we compare the reduction of classification accuracy between NNC and FC-MNNC when some irrelevant features are added. For example, the thyroid database has 23 features. The accuracy of NNC is 91.9% and the accuracy of FC-MNNC raises this to 94.3%. When three irrelevant features with uniform distribution in the interval [0,1] are added, the accuracy of standard NNC reduces 3.2% while the accuracy of FC-MNNC reduces slightly by 0.4%. From the above discussion, it's concluded that FC-NNC is more robust against irrelevant features than standard NNC.

5 Conclusions

The classification accuracy of FC-MNNC based on GA outperforms standard NNC. Furthermore, FC-MNNC based on GA improves the robustness against irrelevant features of standard NNC. Similar to standard NNC, FC-MNNC dose not need the training phrase to obtain the global target function. Each NNC in the FC-MNNC combination system is parallel and independently able to classify one pattern based on the corresponding feature subsets. Since the number of features in one feature subset is fewer, the computing time of one NNC is greatly reduced. Notice that the time complexity of the combination system is not simply sum up each NNC; it is still a difficult problem to analyze the time complexity of the combination system. In addition, we should further study how to prevent the phenomenon that one feature subset only includes a single feature in feature subset clustering method II.

Acknowledgement

The investigation was supported by the National Natural Science Foundation of China (60435020).

References

1. Sung-Bae Cho and Jin H. Kim: Combining multiple neural networks by fuzzy integral for robust classification, IEEE trans. on SMC, Vol 25, (1995) 380-384.
2. Sung-Bae Cho and Jin H. Kim, Multiple network fusion using fuzzy logic. IEEE trans on NN, Vol 6, (1995) 497-501.
3. K. Tumer and J. Ghosh, Error correction and error reduction in ensemble classifiers. Connection science, vol 8, no 314, (1996) 385-404.,.
4. J. Kittler, A. Hojjatoleslami and T. windeatt, Strategies for combining classifiers employing shared and distinct representations. Pattern recognition letters, Vol 18, (1997) 1373-1377.,.
5. S. D. Bay, Nearest neighbor classifiers from multiple feature subsets, Intelligent data analysis, Vol 3, (1999) 191-209.,.
6. L. Breiman, Bagging predictors, Machine learning, Vol 24, (1996) 123-140,.
7. P. Langley, W. Iba, Average–case analysis of a nearest neighbor algorithm, Proc. of the thirteenth international joint conference on artificial intelligence, (1993) 889-894.
8. P. Vishwath, M. N. Murty, C. Bhatnagar, Fusion of multiple approximate nearest neighbor classifier for fast and efficient classification, Information fusion, Vol 5, (2004) 239-250.
9. L.I. Kuncheva, L.C. Jain, Designing classifier fusion systems by genetic algorithms, IEEE trans on evolutionary computation, Vol 4, (2000) 327-336.
10. L. Lam, C.Y. Suen, Application of majority voting to pattern recognition: An analysis of its behavior and performance. IEEE trans on SMC Vol 27, (1997) 553-568.
11. T. M. Mitchell, Machine learning, China machine press, Beijing, (2003).
12. UCI repository of machine learning databases and domain theories. FTP address: www.ics.uci.edu/~mlearn.

A Statistical Confidence-Based Adaptive Nearest Neighbor Algorithm for Pattern Classification

Jigang Wang, Predrag Neskovic, and Leon N. Cooper[*]

Institute for Brain and Neural Systems,
Department of Physics,
Brown University, Providence RI 02912, USA
jigang@brown.edu, pedja@brown.edu,
Leon_Cooper@brown.edu

Abstract. The k-nearest neighbor rule is one of the simplest and most attractive pattern classification algorithms. It can be interpreted as an empirical Bayes classifier based on the estimated *a posteriori* probabilities from the k nearest neighbors. The performance of the k-nearest neighbor rule relies on the locally constant *a posteriori* probability assumption. This assumption, however, becomes problematic in high dimensional spaces due to the curse of dimensionality. In this paper we introduce a locally adaptive nearest neighbor rule. Instead of using the Euclidean distance to locate the nearest neighbors, the proposed method takes into account the effective influence size of each training example and the statistical confidence with which the label of each training example can be trusted. We test the new method on real-world benchmark datasets and compare it with the standard k-nearest neighbor rule and the support vector machines. The experimental results confirm the effectiveness of the proposed method.

1 Introduction

One of the simplest and most attractive pattern classification algorithms, first proposed by Fix and Hodges in 1951, is the nearest neighbor rule [1]. Given a set of n labeled examples $D_n = \{(\boldsymbol{X}_1, Y_1), \ldots, (\boldsymbol{X}_n, Y_n)\}$, where $\boldsymbol{X}_i$ are the feature vectors in some input space and $Y_i \in \{\omega_1, \ldots, \omega_M\}$ are the corresponding class labels, the nearest neighbor rule classifies an unseen pattern $\boldsymbol{X}$ into the class of its nearest neighbor in the training data D_n.

It can be shown that, at any given point $\boldsymbol{X}$ in the input space, the probability that its nearest neighbor $\boldsymbol{X}'$ belongs to class ω_i converges to the corresponding *a posteriori* probability $P(\omega_i|\boldsymbol{X})$ as the size of training sample goes to infinity, namely, $P(\omega_i|\boldsymbol{X}) = \lim_{n\to\infty} P(\omega_i|\boldsymbol{X}')$. Furthermore, it was shown in [2,3] that under certain continuity conditions on the underlying distributions, the asymptotic probability of error L_{NN} of the nearest neighbor rule is bounded by

$$L^* \leq L_{\text{NN}} \leq L^*(2 - \frac{M}{M-1}L^*) \,, \tag{1}$$

---

[*] This work was partially supported by ARO under Grant W911NF-04-1-0357. Jigang Wang was supported by a dissertation fellowship from Brown University.

where L^* is the optimal Bayes probability of error. Therefore, the nearest neighbor rule, despite its extreme simplicity, is asymptotically optimal when the classes do not overlap, i.e., $L^* = 0$. However, when the classes do overlap, the nearest neighbor rule is suboptimal. In this case, the problem occurs at overlapping regions where $P(\omega_i|\boldsymbol{X}) > 0$ for more than one class ω_i. In those regions, the nearest neighbor rule deviates from the Bayes decision rule by classifying $\boldsymbol{X}$ into class ω_i with probability $P(\omega_i|\boldsymbol{X})$ instead of assigning $\boldsymbol{X}$ to the majority class with probability one.

Theoretically, this shortcoming of the nearest neighbor rule can be overcome by a natural extension, the k-nearest neighbor rule. As the name suggests, this rule classifies $\boldsymbol{X}$ to the class that appears most frequently among the k nearest neighbors. Indeed, as shown by Stone and Devroye respectively in [4,5], the k-nearest neighbor rule is universally consistent provided that the speed of k approaching n is properly controlled, i.e., $k \to \infty$ and $k/n \to 0$ as $n \to \infty$. However, in practical applications where there is only a finite amount of training data, choosing an optimal value for k is a non-trivial task, and people usually use methods such as cross-validation to pick the best value for k.

With only a finite number of training examples, the k-nearest neighbor rule can be viewed as an empirical Bayes classifier based on the estimated *a posteriori* probabilities from the k nearest neighbors. Its performance, therefore, relies heavily on the assumption that the *a posteriori* probability is approximately constant within the neighborhood determined by the k nearest neighbors. With the commonly used Euclidean distance measure, this method is subject to severe bias in a high dimensional input space due to the curse of dimensionality [7]. To overcome this problem, many methods have been proposed to locally adapt the metric so that a neighborhood of constant *a posteriori* probability can be produced. These methods include the flexible metric method by Friedman [7], the discriminant adaptive method proposed by Hastie and Tibshirani [8], and the adaptive metric method proposed by Domeniconi et al. [9]. Although differing in their approaches, the common idea underlying these methods is that they estimate feature relevance locally at each query point. The locally estimated feature relevance leads to a weighted metric for computing the distance between a query point and the training data. As a result, neighborhoods get constricted along the most relevant dimensions and elongated along the less important ones. These methods improve the original k-nearest neighbor rule because they are capable of producing local neighborhoods in which the *a posteriori* probabilities are approximately constant. However, the computational complexity of such improvements is high. Furthermore, these methods usually introduce more model parameters, which need to be optimized along with the value of k via cross-validation, therefore further increasing the computational load.

In this paper, we propose a simple adaptive nearest neighbor rule for pattern classification. Compared to the standard k-nearest neighbor rule, our proposed method has two appealing features. First, with our method, each training example defines an influence region that is centered on the training example itself and covers as many as training examples from the same class as possible. Therefore, the size of the influence region associated with each training example depends on its relative position to other training examples, especially training examples of other classes. In determining the nearest neighbors of a given query point, the distance from a query point to each training example is divided by the size of the corresponding influence region. As a result, training examples identified as nearest neighbors according to the scaled distance measure are more likely to have the same class label as the query point. The second feature of our proposed method is that it takes into account possible labeling errors in the training data by weighting each training example with the statistical confidence that can be associated with it. Our experimental results show that the proposed method significantly improves the generalization performance of the standard k-nearest neighbor rule.

This paper is organized as follows. In Section 2, we define the probability of error in decisions made by the majority rule based on a finite number of observations, and show that the probability of error is bounded by a decreasing function of the confidence measure. We then use the defined probability of error as a criterion for determining the influence region and the statistical confidence that can be associated with each training example. Finally, we present a new adaptive nearest neighbor rule based on the influence region and statistical confidence. In Section 3, we test the new algorithm on several real-world datasets and compare it to the original k-nearest neighbor rule. Concluding remarks are given in Section 4.

2 Adaptive Nearest Neighbor Rule for Classification

One of the main reasons for the success of the k-nearest neighbor rule is that for an arbitrary query point $\boldsymbol{X}$, the class labels Y' of its k nearest neighbors can be treated as approximately distributed from the desired *a posteriori* probability $P(Y|\boldsymbol{X})$. Therefore, the empirical frequency with which each class ω_i appears among the k-nearest neighbors provides an estimate of the *a posteriori* probability $P(\omega_i|\boldsymbol{X})$. The k-nearest neighbor rule can thus be viewed as an empirical Bayes decision rule based on the estimate of $P(Y|\boldsymbol{X})$ from the k nearest neighbors. Therefore, in practice, the performance of the k-nearest neighbor rule to a large extent depends on how well the constant *a posteriori* probability assumption is met. In addition, even if the constant *a posteriori* probability assumption holds, there is still a probability that the empirical majority class turns out to be different from the true majority class based on the underlying distribution. In this section, we will address these issues.

2.1 Probability of Error and Confidence Measure

For simplicity we consider a two-class classification problem. Let $R \in \Omega$ be an arbitrary region in the input space, and $p = P(Y = +1|\boldsymbol{X} \in R)$ be the *a posteriori* probability of the class being $+1$ given that $\boldsymbol{X} \in R$. Let $\boldsymbol{X}_1, \ldots, \boldsymbol{X}_n$ be n independently and identically distributed (i.i.d.) random feature vectors that fall in R. The n corresponding labels $Y_1, \ldots, Y_n$ can then be treated as i.i.d. according to the Bernoulli distribution $Bern(p)$. According to the binomial law, the probability that n_+ of them belong to class $+1$ (therefore $n_- = n - n_+$ belong to -1) is given by $\binom{n}{n_+} p^{n_+}(1-p)^{n_-}$.

Without loss of generality, let us assume that R contains n_- examples of class -1 and n_+ examples of class $+1$, with $n_- - n_+ = \delta > 0$, i.e., R contains δ more negative examples than positive examples. By the majority rule, R will be associated with the class -1. In practice, p is unknown; hence whether $p \in [0, 0.5)$ or $p \in (0.5, 1]$ is unknown. However, there are only two possibilities: if $p \in [0, 0.5)$, the class with the maximum a *posteriori* probability is also -1 and the classification of R to -1 is correct; however, if $p \in (0.5, 1]$, the class with the maximum a *posteriori* probability is $+1$ and the classification of R to -1 is a false negative error. Therefore, given $p \in (0, 5, 1]$, the expression

$$P_{err}(p; \delta; n) = \sum_{i=0}^{\lfloor (n-\delta)/2 \rfloor} \binom{n}{i} p^i (1-p)^{n-i} \qquad (2)$$

is the probability of false negatives. It is easy to show that, when R contains δ more positive examples than negative examples, the probability of false positives can be defined similarly.

To keep the probability of false negatives or false positives small, it is important to keep Eq. (2) under control. It is easy to check that $P_{err}(p; \delta; n)$ is a decreasing function of p, which means that it is bounded above by

$$P_{err}(\delta; n) = \sup_{p \in (0.5, 1]} P_{err}(p; \delta; n) = \frac{1}{2^n} \sum_{i=0}^{\lfloor (n-\delta)/2 \rfloor} \binom{n}{i} \approx \Phi\left(-\frac{\delta - 1}{\sqrt{n}}\right), \qquad (3)$$

where Φ is the cumulative distribution function (CDF) of a standard Gaussian random variable. The approximation of the upper bound is obtained by applying the normal approximation to the binomial distribution, which is in turn based on the central limit theorem. The probability of error $P_{err}(p; \delta; n)$ can also be bounded by applying other concentration of measure inequalities. For example, applying Hoeffding's inequality [10], one can obtain

$$P_{err}(\delta; n)_{max} = \frac{1}{2^n} \sum_{i=0}^{\lfloor (n-\delta)/2 \rfloor} \binom{n}{i} \approx e^{-\delta^2/2n}. \qquad (4)$$

In the following, we use the normal approximation of the upper bound (3) to illustrate the relationship between $P_{err}(\delta; n)_{max}$ and $(\delta - 1)/\sqrt{n}$. Obviously, $P_{err}(\delta; n)_{max}$ is decreasing in $(\delta - 1)/\sqrt{n}$ because as a cumulative distribution function, $\Phi(x)$ is an increasing function of x. Eq. (3) also tells us quantitatively how large $(\delta - 1)/\sqrt{n}$ should be in order to keep the probability of error under some preset value. For $n < 200$, we enumerate all possible values of δ and n and calculate $(\delta - 1)/\sqrt{n}$ and the corresponding value of $P_{err}(\delta; n)_{max}$. The results are shown in Fig. 1. As we can see, the upper bound of the probability of error is a rapid decreasing function of $(\delta - 1)/\sqrt{n}$.

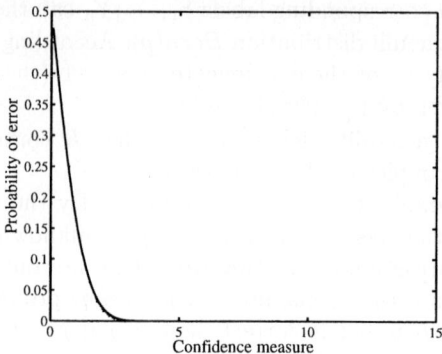

Fig. 1. Probability of error as a function of the confidence measure

Since $P_{err}(\bar{p}; \delta; n)$ is the probability that the observation is at odds with the true state of nature, $1 - P_{err}(\bar{p}; \delta; n)$ is the probability that the observation agrees with the true state of nature. We therefore define

$$\alpha(\bar{p}; \delta; n) \equiv 1 - P_{err}(\bar{p}; \delta; n) \tag{5}$$

to be the confidence level. From Eq. (3), it follows that the confidence level is bounded below by

$$\alpha(\delta; n) = 1 - P_{err}(\delta; n)_{max} \approx erf(\frac{\delta - 1}{\sqrt{n}}) , \tag{6}$$

and the larger $(\delta - 1)/\sqrt{n}$, the higher the confidence level. For this reason and for convenience, we will call $(\delta - 1)/\sqrt{n}$ the confidence measure.

An alternative way to define the probability of error for a decision that is made by the majority rule based on a finite number of observations is to use the Beta prior model for the binomial distribution. Based on the same argument, the probability of error can be defined as

$$P_{err}(\delta; n) = \frac{\int_{0.5}^{1} p^{\frac{n-\delta}{2}}(1-p)^{\frac{n+\delta}{2}} dp}{\int_{0}^{1} p^{\frac{n-\delta}{2}}(1-p)^{\frac{n+\delta}{2}} dp} , \tag{7}$$

which gives the probability that the actual majority class of the posterior probability distribution differs from the one that is concluded empirically from the majority rule based on n and δ. Likewise, the confidence level can be defined as

$$\alpha(\delta; n) = 1 - P_{err}(\delta; n) = \frac{\int_{0}^{0.5} p^{\frac{n-\delta}{2}}(1-p)^{\frac{n+\delta}{2}} dp}{\int_{0}^{1} p^{\frac{n-\delta}{2}}(1-p)^{\frac{n+\delta}{2}} dp} . \tag{8}$$

In Fig. 2, the probability of error based on the Beta prior model is plotted against the confidence measure. Numerically, the two different definitions give about the same results, which can be seen by comparing Figs. 1 and 2. More precisely,

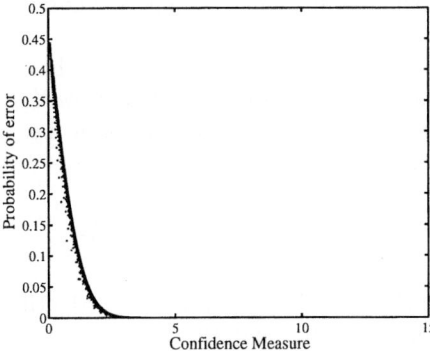

Fig. 2. Probability of error (based on the Beta prior model) against the confidence measure

the first definition of the probability of error can be better approximated as a function of the confidence measure, which is easily computable. In addition, for the same value of n and δ, the first definition gives a higher probability of error value than the second one since it is based on the worst case consideration.

2.2 Adaptive Nearest Neighbor Rule

Given a training data set $D_n = \{(\boldsymbol{X}_1, Y_1), \ldots, (\boldsymbol{X}_n, Y_n)\}$ and a query point $\boldsymbol{X}$, the k-nearest neighbor rule first finds the k-nearest neighbors of $\boldsymbol{X}$, denoted by $\boldsymbol{X}_{(1)}, \ldots, \boldsymbol{X}_{(k)}$, and then assigns $\boldsymbol{X}$ to the majority class among $Y_{(1)}, \ldots, Y_{(k)}$, where $Y_{(i)}$ are the corresponding class labels of $\boldsymbol{X}_{(i)}$. Commonly used distance measures $d(\boldsymbol{X}, \boldsymbol{X}_i)$ include the Euclidean distance and the L_1 distance. For a binary classification problem in which $Y \in \{-1, 1\}$, it amounts to the following decision rule:

$$f(\boldsymbol{X}) = \operatorname{sgn}(\sum_{i=1}^{k} Y_{(i)}) \ . \tag{9}$$

The adaptive nearest neighbor rule starts off by first constructing an influence region for each training example. For each training example $\boldsymbol{X}_i$, $i = 1, \ldots, n$, its influence region is constructed as follows. Centered on $\boldsymbol{X}_i$, we draw a sphere that is as large as possible without enclosing a training example of a different class. For simplicity, we call the influence region a sphere even if other metric such as L_1 metric is used to compute the distance. Denote the radius of the sphere as r_i. We then count the number of training examples that fall inside the sphere and compute the statistical confidence level α_i according to Eq. (8). Depending on the value of the computed confidence level, there are two possibilities. If the confidence level is above a preset threshold, e.g., 75%, we keep the influence region as it is. Otherwise, we would enlarge the sphere to include more training examples until its confidence level reaches the preset threshold. In the second case, the radius r_i is set to the radius of the sphere that achieves the desired confidence level, and so is the actual confidence level α_i. Therefore, we associate with each training example an influence sphere whose radius is r_i and whose confidence level is α_i.

Given a query point X, the adaptive nearest neighbor rule works as follows. It first finds the k-nearest neighbors of X, denoted by $X_{(1)}, \ldots, X_{(k)}$, according to the scaled distances $d(X, X_i)/r_i$ for $i = 1, \ldots, n$, i.e., the distance measure according to which the training examples are sorted is

$$d_{new}(X, X_i) = \frac{d(X, X_i)}{r_i} . \quad (10)$$

Once the k nearest neighbors $X_{(1)}, \ldots, X_{(k)}$ are identified, it classifies X according to the following weighted majority rule:

$$f(X) = \text{sgn}(\sum_{i=1}^{k} \alpha_{(i)} Y_{(i)}) , \quad (11)$$

where $\alpha_{(i)}$ is the confidence level associated with $X_{(i)}$, i.e., each neighbor is weighted by the confidence level associated with the corresponding influence sphere. Therefore, as one can easily imagine, a neighbor that happens to be close to decision boundary would have less weight because of the lower confidence level.

3 Results and Discussion

In this section, we present experimental results obtained on several real-world benchmark datasets from the UCI Machine Learning Repository [11]. Throughout our experiments, we used the 10-fold cross validation method to estimate the generalization error of our algorithm and the nearest neighbor rule. Table 1 shows the error rates and the corresponding standard deviations of the nearest neighbor (NN) rule and our adaptive nearest neighbor (A-NN) rule.

Table 1. Comparison of error rates

Dataset	NN	A-NN
Breast Cancer	4.85(0.91)	3.53(0.63)
Ionosphere	12.86(1.96)	7.14(1.15)
Pima	31.84(1.05)	29.74(1.38)
Liver	37.65(2.80)	37.94(1.93)
Sonar	17.00(2.26)	13.00(1.70)

As we can see from the results, the adaptive nearest neighbor rule outperforms the nearest neighbor rule on almost all 5 datasets being tested. On some datasets, such as the Ionosphere and Sonar datasets, the improvement of the adaptive nearest neighbor rule is statistically significant. These results show that the nearest neighbor identified according to the scaled distance measure is more likely to have the same class label as the query point.

Table 2 shows the corresponding results of the k-nearest neighbor (k-NN) rule and the adaptive k-nearest neighbor (A-k-NN) rule. On each dataset, we run the two algorithms at various values of k from 1 to 99. We report the lowest generalization errors obtained by these two algorithms together with the corresponding standard deviations. For comparison, we also obtained the best results obtained by the support vector machines (SVMs) equipped with Gaussian kernels. The kernel parameter and the regularization parameter for the support vector machines were determined via cross-validation.

Table 2. Comparison of results

Dataset	k-NN	SVMs	A-k-NN
Breast Cancer	2.79(0.67)	3.68(0.66)	2.65 (0.84)
Ionosphere	12.86(1.96)	4.86(1.05)	4.00 (0.87)
Pima	24.61(1.36)	27.50(1.68)	24.21(1.39)
Liver	30.88(3.32)	31.47(2.63)	30.59(2.33)
Sonar	17.00(2.26)	11.00(2.33)	13.00(1.70)

As we can see from Table 2, the adaptive k-nearest neighbor rule outperforms the k-nearest neighbor rule on all 5 datasets being tested. On the Ionosphere and Sonar datasets, the improvement of the adaptive k-nearest neighbor rule is significant. These results further confirm that, by modulating the distance with the size of the influence region associated with each training example, better neighbors are found by the adaptive nearest neighbor rule. Furthermore, the adaptive nearest neighbor also outperforms the support vector machines on all except the Sonar dataset.

In Table 3, we compare the numbers of nearest neighbors used by the two different nearest neighbor rule when the respective lowest generalization error is achieved. As we can see, on three out of the 5 datasets being tested, namely, the Breast Cancer, Pima, and Liver datasets, the adaptive k-nearest neighbor uses significantly less nearest neighbors for decision making. Combining the results in Tables 2 and 3, we can see that the adaptive k-nearest neighbor rule achieves better classification performance while using less nearest neighbors. On the Ionosphere dataset, although the adaptive k-nearest neighbor rule uses more nearest neighbors than the k-nearest neighbor rule, its performance is much better than the latter when using the same number of nearest neighbors. For example, as we can see from Table 1, using only a single nearest neighbor, the adaptive nearest neighbor rule is already performing much better than the simple nearest neighbor rule.

Using the data from the Wisconsin Breast Cancer dataset, Figure 3 shows how the generalization error of the two algorithms varies as the value of k changes. The solid line represents the error rate of the adaptive k-nearest neighbor rule at different values of k. The dashed line is the corresponding result of the

Table 3. Comparison of the number of nearest neighbors

Dataset	k-NN	A-k-NN
Breast Cancer	13	7
Ionosphere	1	15
Pima	31	7
Liver	55	29
Sonar	1	1

k-nearest neighbor rule. From Fig. 3, we can see that, when k is very small or very large, the generalization error of both algorithms is large due to the large variance or bias, respectively. This is a result of the so called bias/variance dilemma [6]. The best tradeoff between the bias error and the variance is achieved somewhere in the middle. Also clear from this figure is that the adaptive k-nearest neighbor rule performs almost always better than the k-nearest neighbor rule on this particular dataset. The flat shape of the adaptive k-nearest neighbor rule also suggests that it is less prone to the bias as k increases.

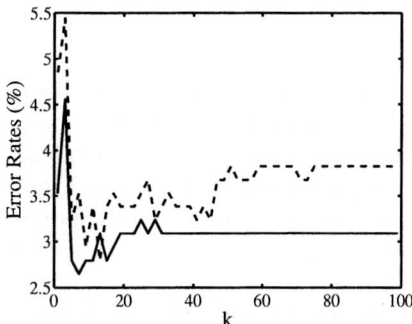

Fig. 3. Error rates at different values of k

4 Conclusion

In this paper, we presented an adaptive nearest neighbor rule for pattern classification. This new classifier overcomes the shortcomings of the k-nearest neighbor in two aspects. First, before a query point is presented to the classifier, it constructs an influence region for each training example. To determine the k nearest neighbors of the query point, it divides the standard distance from the query point to each training example by the size of the corresponding influence region. As a result, training examples with large influence regions have relatively large influence on determining the nearest neighbors, and the nearest neighbors identified according to the new distance measure are more likely to have the same class labels as the query point. Secondly, each training example is weighted according to the corresponding statistical confidence measure. This weighting mechanism leads to a lower influence of boundary points on the classification decision, therefore reducing the generalization error.

We tested the adaptive k-nearest neighbor rule on real-world benchmark datasets and compared it with the original k-nearest neighbor rule and the support vector machines. It outperforms both the k-nearest neighbor rule and the support vector machines on almost all datasets being tested and demonstrates better generalization performance.

References

1. E. Fix and J. Hodges, Discriminatory analysis, nonparametric discrimination: consistency properties. Tech. Report 4, USAF School of Aviation Medicine, Randolph Field, Texas, 1951.
2. T. M. Cover, and P. E. Hart, Nearest Neighbor Pattern Classification, IEEE Transactions on Information Theory, Vol. IT-13, No. 1, Jan. 1967, pp. 21-27.
3. L. Devroye, On the inequality of Cover and Hart. IEEE Transactions on Pattern Analysis and Machine Intelligence, Vol. 3, 1981, pp. 75-78.
4. C. J. Stone, Consistent nonparametric regression. Annals of Statistics, Vol. 5, 1977, pp. 595-645.
5. L. Devroye, L. Györfi, A. Krzyżak and G. Lugosi, On the strong universal consistency of nearest neighbor regression function estimates, Annals of Statistics, Vol. 22, 1994, pp. 1371-1385.
6. S. Geman, E. Bienenstock, and R. Doursat, Neural networks and the bias/variance dilemma, Neural Computation, Vol. 4. No. 1, 1992, pp. 1-58.
7. J. Friedman, Flexible metric nearest neighbor classification. Technical Report 113, Stanford University Statistics Department, 1994.
8. T. Hastie, R. Tibshirani, Discriminant adaptive nearest neighbor classification. IEEE Transactions on Pattern Analysis and Machine Intelligence, 18, 1996, pp. 607-615.
9. C. Domeniconi, J. Peng, and D. Gunopulos, Locally adaptive metric nearest-neighbor classification. IEEE Transactions on Pattern Analysis and Machine Intelligence, 24, 2002, pp. 1281-1285.
10. W. Hoeffding. Probability inequalities for sums of bounded random variables. *Journal of the American Statistical Association*, 58, 1963, pp. 13-30.
11. C. L. Blake, and C. J. Merz, UCI Repository of machine learning databases, Dept. of Information and Computer Sciences, University of California, Irvine, http://www.ics.uci.edu/~mlearn/MLRepository.html, 1998.

Automatic 3D Motion Synthesis with Time-Striding Hidden Markov Model

Yi Wang[1], Zhi-qiang Liu[2], and Li-zhu Zhou[1]

[1] Department of Computer Science and Technology,
Tsinghua University, Graduate School at Shenzhen, China
wangy01@mails.tsinghua.edu.cn
[2] School of Creative Media,
City University of Hong Kong, Hong Kong, China
ZQ.LIU@cityu.edu.hk

Abstract. In this paper we present a new method, time-striding hidden Markov model (TSHMM), to learn from long-term motion for atomic behaviors and the statistical dependencies among them. TSHMM is a 2-layer hidden Markov model, which approximates a variable-length *hidden* Markov model by first-order statistical dependencies. An EM algorithm is proposed to learn the TSHMM.

1 Introduction

Earlier 3D character motion editing relies heavily on skillful and intensive labor of art to create sequences of representative poses called *key-frames* manually. In recent years, a new trend appears to automate motion synthesis by making use of Bayesian learning techniques to extract underlying rules of human motion from 3D motion capture data. Given the learned statistical model, new motion sequences can be generated automatically following some high level directions provided by the artists. In order to cope with the highly complex dynamics of human motion, most related works based their learning approaches on variants of hidden Markov models (HMM), e.g., [1], [2], [3], and [4].

The initial motivation of our work comes from the fact that the first-order stochastic transitions modeled by HMM is restrictive to capture long-term statistical dependencies among the motion frames. The short context limits the prediction performance of the HMM and results in discontinuities, or gaps, to appear in the synthesized motion. A reasonable solution is to increase the order of HMM, but it also increases the complexity of learning exponentially faster. A better solution is the variable-length Markov model (VLMM), which is based on the fact that it is not necessary to increase the order for all contexts and learns only the shortest but necessary contexts with different lengths. However, VLMM is not *hidden*, so when it is used to model human motion, the training sequences over the high dimensional continuous pose space must be discretized and projected to one-dimensional before learning. And, learning VLMM captures only the transition probabilities embedded in the discretized training sequences, rather than fits the actual training motion. But extending VLMM to be hidden will face the same complexity problem as the fixed-high-order HMM.

To address the above problems, the time-striding hidden Markov model (TSHMM) is proposed and features two interesting properties: (1) TSHMM is a *hidden* model that fits the motion data itself instead of its discretized version. (2) As a first-order approximation to high-order HMM, TSHMM decreases the complexity of learning to a practical level.

TSHMM follows the dividing-and-recombining strategy similar with [3], where a long-term motion sequence is divided into segments as the basic motion elements, named *motion textons*, which can then be recombined to generate new motion sequences. While [3] models motion textons by linear dynamic systems (LDS), TSHMM does not constrain *linear dynamics* for textons. Instead, TSHMM learns the statistical properties from the training motion to ensure every motion textons are the shortest but long enough to carry complete statistical semantics. This property gives TSHMM the ability to discover atomic behaviors from long-term motion, e.g., leaping and rolling from ballet, or ducking and punching from boxing.

2 The Time-Striding Hidden Markov Model

TSHMM is a 2-layer hierarchical hidden Markov model. The top layer approximates the high-order statistical transitions, namely *time-stridings*, with first-order transition probabilities. The corresponding high-order states are modeled by a set of left-to-right hidden Markov models at the bottom layer. The learning algorithm of TSHMM contains two stages. The first stage initializes the model by approximately detecting the time-stridings from the training motion. The second stage estimates the parameters of the TSHMM by fine-tuning the detected time-stridings to maximize the likelihood of the model. This two-stage scheme ensures that when TSHMM is used for human motion modeling, each state of a learned TSHMM corresponds to an atomic behavior, i.e., a shortest motion segment that is long enough to predict the next pose.

2.1 Definition and Detection of Time-Striding

To explain how time-stridings are defined and learned, we need to start from the concepts of Markov chain. A Markov chain is a discrete and stationary stochastic process $\ldots, X_t, \ldots$, where $-\infty \leq t \leq \infty$ and all X_t share the same domain $\mathcal{X}$. The value of each X_t conditionally dependents only on finite number of previous values, denoted as,

$$P(X_t \mid X_{t-1}, \ldots, X_{-\infty}) = P(X_t \mid X_{t-1}, \ldots, X_{t-T}) . \quad (1)$$

If T is the same for all possible combinations of $X_{t-1}, \ldots, X_{t-T}$, namely the *contexts*, this Markov chain can be modeled with a Markov model with fixed order of T, which describes the transition probabilities given all the $|\mathcal{X}|^T$ contexts as a $|\mathcal{X}|^T \times (|\mathcal{X}| - 1)$ matrix. Otherwise, the lengths of conditional dependencies vary for different contexts, and are usually described by a context function $c(\cdot)$: $\mathcal{X}^T \to \bigcup_{l=1}^{T} \mathcal{X}^l$, which maps one or more contexts with length T to a shorter one. In [5], it is shown in detail that the range of this context function can be represented as a tree, namely the *context tree*.

For high-order (either fixed or with variable length) Markov models, the states are strings defined on the alphabet $\mathcal{X}$ and with length $1 \leq l \leq T$. A transition appends a letter to the string of the starting state and forms a new string, which is then shortened by the finite length of memory and becomes the string of the ending state of the transition. For example, suppose a Markov model with fixed order of 3 and alphabet $\mathcal{X} = \{a, \ldots, z\}$. Transition from state $\langle a, b, c \rangle$ to $\langle d, e, f \rangle$ requires at least three steps: $\langle a, b, c \rangle \to \langle b, c, d \rangle \to \langle c, d, e \rangle \to \langle d, e, f \rangle$.

The concept of time-striding is based on the observation that in some cases, the states $\langle b, c, d \rangle$ and $\langle c, d, e \rangle$ rarely appear in the training sequences but $\langle a, b, c, d, e, f \rangle$ appears one or more times. In such cases, it is reasonable to abbreviate the multiple steps of transitions into a single step that transits from $\langle a, b, c \rangle$ directly to $\langle d, e, f \rangle$. We name such abbreviations as *time-stridings*. Given the N_c substrings that are *frequently* appeared in the training sequences, their transition probabilities can be approximated by TSHMM with a $N_c \times N_c$ matrix.

As pointed out in [6], mining of frequently appeared substrings is an NP-hard problem, so an approximation algorithm is required for the job. In our work, we constrain that the maximum length of substrings is a given number T, and that the candidates of substrings are selected from the range of the context function $c(\cdot)$ of the VLMM learned from the training sequences. The approximation algorithm contains three steps:

1. Discretize the high-dimensional continuous training sequence by clustering similar elements of the sequences and substituting the elements with the indices to their clusters.
2. Learn a VLMM from the sequence of cluster indices,
3. Divide the training sequence into segments by parsing the context tree of the learned VLMM, so that each segment is a terminal[1] of the tree.

As terminals of a VLMM context tree learned from the training sequence, these divided segments are ensured to have appeared in the sequence frequently. Moreover, the statistical properties of VLMM ensures them as the atomic behaviors as explained below.

As discussed in [7], learning VLMM is to prune the context tree of a infinite order Markov process from one with infinite depth into a smaller one with variable and finite length of terminals, as the example shown in Fig. 1. Assume $q_{t-1}, \ldots, q_{t-T}$ ($q_i \in \mathcal{X}$) is a terminal of the context tree used as a memory to predict the next letter x according to an estimate $\hat{P}(x \mid q_{t-1}, \ldots, q_{t-T})$ of $P(x \mid q_{t-1}, \ldots, q_{t-T})$. The learning algorithm determines whether a shorter memory $q_{t-1}, \ldots, q_{t-T+1}$ is enough as a predictor to substitute $q_{t-1}, \ldots, q_{t-T}$ by measuring whether $\hat{P}(x \mid q_{t-1}, \ldots, q_{t-T})$ is significantly different from

---

[1] A terminal is a path starting from the root of a tree ending at a leaf node.

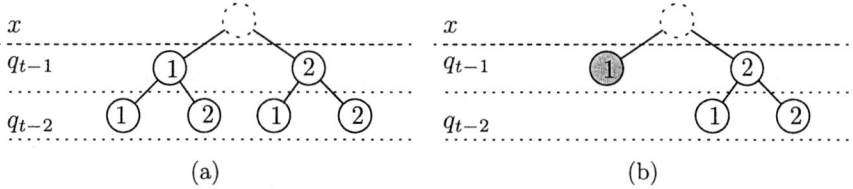

Fig. 1. (a) The context tree of a 2nd-order Markov model, which is pruned from the context tree with infinite depth. (b) The context tree is further pruned to be a VLMM, under the case that the prediction is accurate enough with memory length of 1 when $q_t = 1$.

$\hat{P}(x \mid q_{t-1}, \ldots, q_{t-T+1})$. Such a measurement can be chosen as a weighted Kullback-Leibler divergence:

$$\Delta H(wq_{t-T}, w) = \hat{P}(wq_{t-T}) \sum_{x \in \mathcal{X}} \left(\hat{P}(x \mid wq_{t-T}) \log \frac{\hat{P}(x \mid wq_{t-T})}{\hat{P}(x \mid w)} \right), \quad (2)$$

where w is an abbreviation of the string $q_{t-1}, \ldots, q_{t-T+1}$. If $\Delta H(\cdot)$ is larger than a given threshold ϵ, the longer memory is kept from pruning, otherwise, it is replaced by the shorter one.

Because the pruning process ensures that the terminals of the VLMM context tree are the shortest segments but long enough to predict the next pose with given accuracy, if any of them is further broken, the subdivision cannot be predictor with the same accuracy. Such property of unbreakable, or atomic, makes these terminals sensible as the basic building blocks to construct realistic long-term human motion. So, the segments divided by the above algorithm are named *atomic behaviors* in the sequel.

2.2 Learning TSHMM by Expectation-Maximization

The TSHMM, as illustrated in Fig. 2, is designed to model the first-order transitions among the set of atomic behaviors, which are represented by a set of left-to-right hidden Markov models named *behavior machines*, which in turn describe sequences of *prototypical poses* with the output densities. So the parameterization of TSHMM includes N_b behavior machines $\{\Lambda^{(i)}\}_{i=1}^{N_b}$ and the $N_b \times n_b$ transition matrix $\Gamma^{(0)}$. For each behavior machine $\Lambda^{(i)}$, the transition probabilities among its $N_p^{(i)}$ prototypical poses $\{\lambda_j^{(i)}\}_{j=1}^{N_p^{(i)}}$ is denoted as $\Gamma^{(i)}$.

Constraining the topology of behavior machines to be left-to-right helps preserving original form of the atomic behaviors. This constraint implies that the duration of a prototypical poses is encoded by its self-transition probability. For example, the duration of prototypical pose λ_j can be estimated as the expectation,

$$d(j) = \sum_{t=1}^{\infty} \left(t \cdot \left(\Gamma_{j,j}^{(i)} \right)^{t-1} \cdot \left(1 - \Gamma_{j,j}^{(i)} \right) \right) = \frac{1}{1 - \Gamma_{j,j}^{(i)}} \quad (3)$$

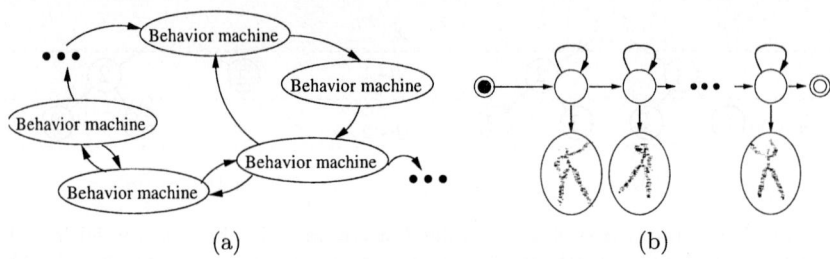

Fig. 2. (b) An example of TSHMM. The first-order transitions among behavior machines are the time-stridings. (b) An example of behavior machine.

Initialization of TSHMM. The initial set of behavior machines are estimated from the atomic behaviors detected by the algorithm discussed in Sect. 2.1. All segments corresponding to the same terminal of the context tree are used to estimate a behavior machine. So N_b equals to the number of terminals that appeared in the training motion. The initial transition matrix $\Gamma^{(0)}$ can be estimated by counting the times of transitions between two atomic behaviors. Such an initialized TSHMM can be considered as an optimal estimation that maximizes the likelihood to the discretized motion sequence, but it is not optimized with the maximum likelihood of the real motion data.

The EM Learning Algorithm. Given the initialized TSHMM, the boundaries of the detected motion segments need to be fine-tuned to maximize the likelihood of TSHMM given the training sequence of motion frames $\{f_t\}_{t=1}^T$:

$$\left\{\hat{\Gamma}^{(0)}, \{\hat{\Lambda}^{(i)}\}_{i=1}^{N_b}\right\} = \underset{\left\{\Gamma^{(0)}, \{\Lambda^{(i)}\}_{i=1}^{N_b}\right\}}{\operatorname{argmax}} P\left(\{f_t\}_{t=1}^T \mid \Gamma^{(0)}, \{\Lambda^{(i)}\}_{i=1}^{N_b}\right) . \quad (4)$$

In order to make the optimization computationally tractable, two sets of auxiliary variables are introduced as (1) the starting time of the atomic behaviors are marked as $\{h_i\}_{i=1}^{N_s}$, and (2) each atomic behavior is assigned a behavior label m_i to indicate which behavior machine the segment belongs to. Given $\{h_i\}_{i=1}^{N_s}$ and $\{m_i\}_{i=1}^{N_s}$, an EM algorithm can be derived by considering the auxiliary function $Q(\hat{\Gamma}^{(0)}, \{\hat{\Lambda}^{(i)}\}_{i=1}^{N_b} \mid \Gamma^{(0)}, \{\Lambda^{(i)}\}_{i=1}^{N_b})$, where $\Gamma^{(0)}, \{\Lambda^{(i)}\}_{i=1}^{N_b}$ are the current value of the parameters of the model and $\hat{\Gamma}^{(0)}, \{\hat{\Lambda}^{(i)}\}_{i=1}^{N_b}$ are the updated value of the parameters. Q is the expected value of the log likelihood of the observable and hidden data together given the observable and current parameter value $\Gamma^{(0)}, \{\Lambda^{(i)}\}_{i=1}^{N_b}$:

$$Q\left(\hat{\Gamma}^{(0)}, \{\hat{\Lambda}^{(i)}\}_{i=1}^{N_b} \mid \Gamma^{(0)}, \{\Lambda^{(i)}\}_{i=1}^{N_b}\right) = \log P\left(\{f_t\}_{t=1}^T \mid \Gamma^{(0)}, \{\Lambda^{(i)}\}_{i=1}^{N_b}\right)$$
$$= \sum_{\{h_i\}_{i=1}^{N_s}, \{m_i\}_{i=1}^{N_s}} \log P\left(\{f_t\}_{t=1}^T, \{h_i\}_{i=1}^{N_s}, \{m_i\}_{i=1}^{N_s} \mid \Gamma^{(0)}, \{\Lambda^{(i)}\}_{i=1}^{N_b}\right) . \quad (5)$$

By introducing the first-order Markovian property, the auxiliary function can be rewritten as,

$$Q\left(\hat{\Gamma}^{(0)}, \{\hat{\Lambda}^{(i)}\}_{i=1}^{N_b} \mid \Gamma^{(0)}, \{\Lambda^{(i)}\}_{i=1}^{N_b}\right)$$

$$= \sum_{\{h_i\}_{i=1}^{N_s}, \{m_i\}_{i=1}^{N_s}} \left\{ \log \prod_{s=1}^{N_s} \left[P\left(\{f_t\}_{t=h_s}^{h_{s+1}-1} \mid \Lambda^{(m_s)}\right) \Gamma^{(0)}_{h_s, h_{s+1}} \right] \right\} \quad (6)$$

$$= \sum_{\{h_i\}_{i=1}^{N_s}, \{m_i\}_{i=1}^{N_s}} \left\{ \sum_{s=1}^{N_s} \left[\log P\left(\{f_t\}_{t=h_s}^{h_{s+1}-1} \mid \Lambda^{(m_s)}\right) \Gamma^{(0)}_{h_s, h_{s+1}} \right] \right\},$$

Since the proof of the convergence of EM algorithm holds under fairly weak assumptions on the form of the distribution of hidden variables, an inference algorithm similar to [3] can be used to compute the most likely hidden variables $\{h_i\}_{i=1}^{N_s}$ and $\{m_i\}_{i=1}^{N_s}$ as the E-step:

Use $L_n(t)$ to represent the maximum likelihood derived from dividing the motion sequence ending at frame t into a concatenated sequence of n segments. $M_n(t)$ and $H_n(t)$ are used to represent the behavior label and beginning frame of the last segment of the sequence to achieve $L_n(t)$. We define S_{min} to be the least number of frames a behavior segment must have as a constraint on the range of boundaries adjustment. To allow maximum possible adjusting, S_{min} should be set to 1, or to restrict the learning result be close to the initialization by setting S_{min} to $\min_s\{h_{s+1} - h_s\}$.

1. Initialization:

$$L_1(t) = \max_{1 \leq i \leq N_b} P\left(\{f_t\}_{S_{min}}^T \mid \Lambda^{(i)}\right)$$

$$M_1(t) = \operatorname*{argmax}_{i} P\left(\{f_t\}_{S_{min}}^T \mid \Lambda^{(i)}\right)$$

$$H_1(t) = 1$$

2. Loop while $2 \leq n \leq \frac{T}{S_{min}}$, $n \cdot S_{min} \leq t \leq T$.

$$L_n(t) = \max_{\substack{1 \leq i \leq N_b \\ (n-1)S_{min} \leq b \leq (t-S_{min})}} \left[L_{n-1}(b-1) \cdot P\left(\{f_t\}_b^t \mid \Lambda^{(i)}\right) \cdot \Gamma^{(0)}_{l, m_i} \right]$$

$$M_n(t), H_n(t) = \operatorname*{argmax}_{i, b} \left[L_{n-1}(b-1) \cdot P\left(\{f_t\}_b^t \mid \Lambda^{(i)}\right) \cdot \Gamma^{(0)}_{l, m_i} \right]$$

where, $l = M_{n-1}(b-1)$.

3. The final solution is achieve by

$$L(T) = \max_{1 \leq n \leq \frac{T}{S_{min}}} L_n(T)$$

And $\{h_s\}_1^{N_s}$ and $\{m_s\}_1^{N_s}$ can be back traced from $M_n(t)$ and $H_n(t)$

The proof of the convergence of EM algorithm shows that if, during each EM iteration, the model parameters are updated to increase the value of Q, then the likelihood of the observed data increases as well. So, when the output densities of behavior machines are parametric models, such as Gaussian and mixture of Gaussian, the Baum-Welch algorithm can be used to update the behavior machines from the segments with corresponding behavior label. This forms the M-step of the TSHMM learning algorithm.

3 Synthesis of New Motion

The synthesis algorithm contains two levels. In the first level, a program is developed to allow users to select the starting and ending behaviors, and a paths connecting the two behavior machines is selected to maximize the sum of transition probabilities along the path. Some previous works like [3] applied the Dijkstra's algorithm on the Markov model with transition probability negated to find such a path. Unfortunately, the longest-path problem is not a dual to the shortest-path problem that is solved by the Dijkstra's algorithm. Indeed, it is NP-hard [6]. In our work, a modified Dijkstra's algorithm is used to find the smallest cycles (with least sum of transition probabilities) in the TSHMM as shown in Fig. 3(a). And then, the path of behavior machines can be constructed by concatenating such cycles under user interactions. Experiments show that such a semi-automatic approach is more suitable for the art work of motion synthesis.

In the second level, a B-spline curve $T(u)$ across the pose space is constructed as illustrated in Fig. 3(b) by taking the part of mean vector of each output density along the behavior path that representing the static prototypical poses (e.g., global positions and joint angles) as control points, and taking the part of mean vector representing the first derivatives of dynamics (e.g., global velocity and joint angular velocities) as local derivatives on the control points. Such a curve ensures that interpolating along the parameter u results in frames whose dynamics is consistent with the local derivatives of the curve, which is then consistent with the dynamics of training motion. This insurance is important to maintain the generated frames in correct temporal order.

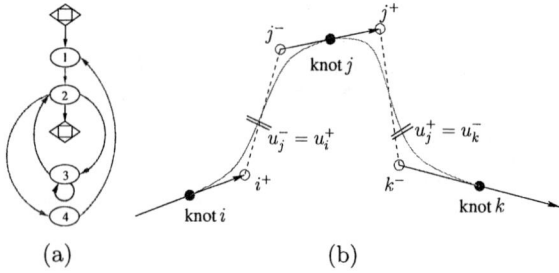

Fig. 3. (a) An example of cycles of behavior machines that can be detected by the Dijkstra algorithm. (b) Construction of the pose trace $T(u)$.

4 Experiments

Several human motion samples were gathered to test TSHMM as listed in Table 1.

As discussed in previous sections, an implicit parameter of learning TSHMM is the number of atomic behaviors found in the training motion N_s, which is determined by the threshold ϵ discussed in Sect. 2.1. A larger ϵ results in deeper context tree and longer atomic behaviors, and because the length of the training motion sequence is fixed, so less atomic behaviors are contained in the training motion, and less behavior machines are learned. As shown in Fig. 4(a) and 4(b), too long atomic behaviors been detected and too less behavior machines been learned make the TSHMM fail to discover cyclic patterns in sample w. The corresponding topology of learned TSHMM shown in Fig. 4(c) and 4(d).

Although shorter atomic behaviors results in more possible combinations of behavior machines during synthesis, too many and too short atomic behaviors also increase the possibility that several successive atomic behaviors been clus-

Table 1. Human motion samples gathered for experiments

name	style	length	complexity
w	walk	191	regular walk with 6 paces
c	chop tree	700	contains 6 repetitive patterns of chopping
bw	Ballet walk	146	walk in Ballet style with 6 paces
br	Ballet roll	169	a segment of Ballet containing 4 rolling patterns
d1	Disco	600	without visually salient cyclic patterns
d2	complexer Disco	612	dance while walk, no visually salient cyclic patterns

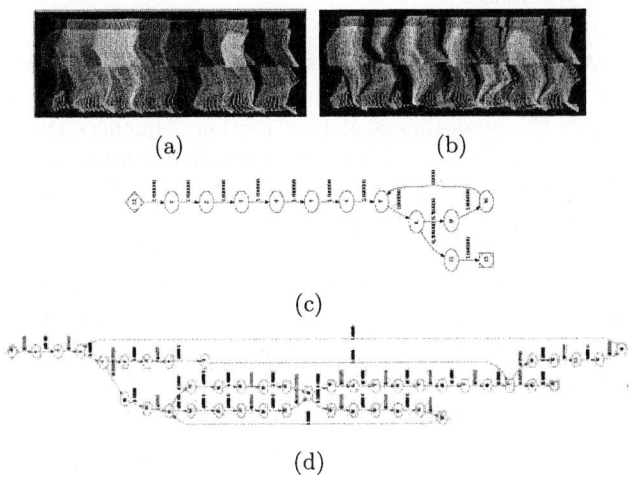

Fig. 4. Learning the sample w with too less (a)(b) and correct number (b)(d) of elementary behaviors

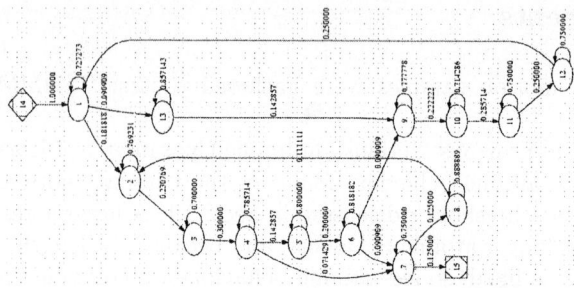

Fig. 5. Learning sample bw with too many elementary behaviors results many self-transitions on behavior machines

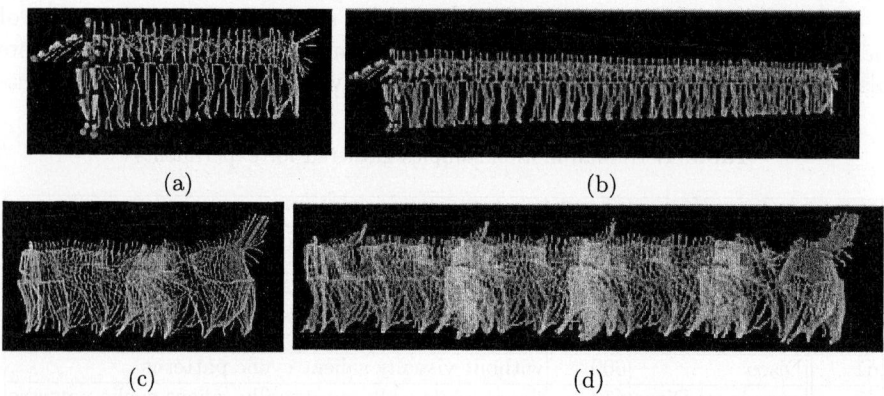

Fig. 6. From motion sample br (a) and d2 (c), and longer motion (b) and (d) with double length are synthesized

tered as the same behavior machine. This phenomena manifests as large number of self-cycles in the learned TSHMM topology, as the example shown in Fig. 5, which degenerates the smoothness of new motion sequences synthesized with the algorithm discussed in Sect. 3. In the experiment system, a probe strategy is proposed to gradually increase the length atomic behaviors until the number of self-transitions reduces to an acceptable level.

As shown in Fig. 6, by learning sample br (Fig. 6(a)), TSHMM detected the cycles of rolling, which are used to generated longer motion with 419 frames (Fig. 6(b)). The cycles in Disco sample d2 is not salient to human eyes (Fig. 6(c)), but still been found by TSHMM and used to generated longer motion with 1429 frames (Fig. 6(d)).

5 Conclusions

We present a new model TSHMM as a first-order approximation of high-order hidden Markov model. Compared with high-order HMM, the complexity of learning TSHMM is more tractable. Compared with other first-order models for motion learning, TSHMM has the ability to discover statistically atomic behaviors embedded within the training motion sequences. We also proposed an algorithm to synthesize new motion sequences from a learned TSHMM. The automatic motion synthesis based on machine learning is a prospective solution for alleviating the intensive manual work of artists in the entertainment and film industry.

Acknowledgments

This research has been supported in part by research grants from Natural Science Foundation of China (No. 60173008), Hong Kong RGC CityU 1062/02E and CityU 1247/03E.

References

1. Tanco, L.M., Hilton, A.: Realistic synthesis of novel human movements from a database of motion capture examples. IEEE Workshop on Human Motion (2000)
2. Brand, M., Hertzmann, A.: Style machines. In: Proc. ACM SIGGRAPH. (2000) 183–192
3. Li, Y., Wang, T., Shum, H.Y.: Motion texture: A two-level statistical model for character motion synthesis. Proc. ACM SIGGRAPH (2002) 465–472
4. Grochow, K., Martin, S.L., Hertzmann, A., Popović, Z.: Style-based inverse kinematics. In: Proc. ACM SIGGRAPH. (2004) 522 – 531
5. Mächler, M., Bühlmann, P.: Variable length markov chains: Methodology, computing and software. Journal of Computational and Graphical Statistics **13** (2004) 656–664
6. Cormen, T., Leiserson, C., Rivest, R.: An introduction to algorithms. MIT Press (1990)
7. Ron, D., Singer, Y., Tishby, N.: The power of amnesia: Learning probabilistic automata with variable memory length. Machine Learning **25** (1996) 117–149

Learning from an Incomplete Information System with Continuous-Valued Attributes by a Rough Set Technique

Eric C.C. Tsang[1], Suyun Zhao[2], Daniel S. Yeung[1], and John W.T. Lee[1]

[1] Department of Computing, Hong Kong Polytechnic University,
Hung Hom, Kowloon, Hong Kong
{csetsang, csdaniel, csljohn}@inet.polyu.edu.hk
[2] Department of Mathematics and Computer Science, Hebei University,
Baoding, Hebei, P.R. China
zhaosy@mail.hbu.edu.cn

Abstract. Many methods based on rough sets to deal with incomplete information system have been proposed in recent years. However, they are only suitable for the nominal datasets. So far only a few methods based on rough sets to deal with incomplete information system with continuous-valued attributes have been proposed. In this paper we propose one generalized model of rough sets to reduce continuous-valued attributes and learn some rules in an incomplete information system. The definition of a relative discernible measure is firstly proposed, which is the underlying concept to redefine the concepts of knowledge reduction such as the reduct and core. We extend a number of underlying concepts of knowledge reduction (such as the reduct and core), and finally propose a heuristic algorithm to generate fuzzy reduct from initial data. The main contribution of this paper is that the underlying relationship between the reduct and core of rough sets is proved to be still correct after our extension. The advantage of the proposed method is that instead of preprocessing continuous data by discretization or fuzzification, we can reduce an incomplete information system with continuous-valued attributes directly based on the generalized model of rough sets, Finally a numerical example is given to show the feasibility of our proposed method.

1 Introduction

The theory of rough sets proposed by Pawlak[1] provides a formal tool to deal with imprecise or insufficient information. It has successfully been applied to many areas including machine learning, pattern recognition, decision support, data mining and process control etc. In the Pawlak's rough set model, the values of attributes are nominal data, i.e., symbols. However, in many practical problems, the attribute-values are continuous. For example, the attribute "temperature" may take the values in the intervals of [0,100]. The Pawlak's rough set model needs to discretize or fuzzify those values to symbols. Some information included in the continuous-valued attributes is ignored in Pawlak's model. It implicitly means that the ability of rough sets to deal with these initial data is poor [13]. Furthermore, all those applications of rough set model are based on the same assumption that the information system is complete.

However, in the real world, the dataset we deal with are always incomplete. By the incompleteness of an information system, we mean that there exist unknown data (null data) in the system.

Though knowledge acquisition methodologies have been developed mainly for complete information system over years [2-7], some important results have recently been obtained for incomplete information systems [8-11]. Kryszkiewicz in [8,9] has proposed a method to obtain attributes reduction and decision rules in incomplete decision tables whose distinctive feature is that it can acquire rules in an incomplete information system without changing the size of the original information system. Leung and Li [10] have used the concept of maximal consistent block technique for knowledge acquisition in incomplete information systems which not only achieves in keeping the size of the original information system, but also puts forth a set of discernibility function simpler than that in [8,9] for finding all reducts. Leung and Wu [11] have constructed a new rough set model for an incomplete information system in which two new quantitative measures have been proposed to capture different characteristics of the rules. All the above research results have focused on information systems with nominal data i.e. symbols. The research based on rough set theory to deal with an incomplete information system with fuzzy data (as seen in table 1) is very few.

Table 1. Incomplete decision table with continuous-valued attributes

	Price	Mileage	Size	Max-speed	d
1	0.9	0.8	0.9	0.1	Good
2	0.2	*	0.8	0.2	Good
3	*	*	0.5	0.7	Poor
4	1	*	1	1	Good
5	*	*	0.7	0.7	Excel.
6	0.3	0.9	0.8	0.2	Good

In order to improve the performance of the Pawlark's rough set model when dealing with initial fuzzy or continuous data, many methodologies [13-17], which generalize rough sets to the fuzzy environments, are proposed in recent years. Roughly speaking, there are two types of fuzzy generalization models of rough sets. One is the concept approximation [15,17], which proposed different pairs of lower and upper approximations to approximate the subset of a universe. The other is the learning fuzzy rules from fuzzy examples based on the rough set techniques [13,14]. Most studies on generalization of rough sets have focused on the concept approximation. Compared with the study on concept approximations, less effort has been made on the study of learning rules from an information system with continuous-valued attributes based on rough set technique [13,14].

For an incomplete information system with continuous-valued attributes, there exists one way to deal with them using rough set technique, i.e., first discretizing the continuous data to crisp data, and then finding the attribute reduction using the methods proposed in [8-11]. It is well known that when preprocessing continuous data and null data, a lot of information is lost. In this paper we propose one method to deal with incomplete information systems without preprocessing continuous data. We introduce the relative discernible measure to measure the relative discernible ability of the attributes. Based on the relative discernible measure, we redefine the underlying concepts of the knowledge reduction such as the reduct and core. The advantage of the proposed method is that we can directly reduce attributes in an incomplete information system without preprocessing continuous data by fuzzification or discretization.

The present paper has the following organization: Section 2 outlines the information system and proposes the definition of the relative discernible measure. Sections 3 and 4 extend a number of underlying concepts of knowledge reduction such as the reduct and core. In section 5 an algorithm is provided to find all the attribute reductions from an incomplete information table with continuous-valued attributes. An illustrative example in section 5 shows the feasibility of the proposed approach. The last section concludes this paper.

2 Information System

2.1 Information System

Let a finite nonempty set of objects $U = \{x_1, x_2, \cdots, x_n\}$ be the universe of discourse, A be a set of attributes $A = b_1, b_2, \cdots, b_m$. The function $f_b : U \to V_b$ for any attribute b is called the information function, where V_b is called the domain of an attribute b. The ordered pair $IS = (U, A)$ is called an information system.

When $A = C \cup D$ is a set of attributes where $C = b_1, b_2, \cdots, b_m$ denotes the set of condition attributes and $D = b_{m+1}, b_{m+2}, \cdots, b_{m+k}$ denotes the set of decision attributes, the information system is called a decision system/table, denoted by $DS = (U, C \cup D)$.

In the real world, many information systems are incomplete. By the incomplete information system we mean that a system with unknown data (null data).

If V_b contains null values for at least one attribute b, then the information system $IS = (U, A)$ is called an incomplete information system[8], denoted by IIS. If a decision system/table is incomplete, we denote it by IDS. Furthermore, we will denote null value by $*$.

We need to assume in this paper that the attribute values of the considered IIS (or IDS) are symbolic or continuous. We also assume that the real value of the missing attribute could be found from the domain of an attribute, however, we do not assume which one it is.

2.2 Indiscernibility Relation and Relative Discernible Measure

Firstly we need to define the degree of indiscernibility of two objects on a certain attribute b in an IIS (or IDS):

$$ind_{i,j}^{b} = \begin{cases} 1 & b(x_i) = * \text{ or } b(x_j) = * \\ SIM(b(x_i), b(x_j)) & \text{others} \end{cases} \quad (1)$$

Where $SIM(b(x_i), b(x_j))$ is the similarity degree of two examples x_i, x_j on b, whose values belong to $[0,1]$. Then we call $ind_{i,j}^{b}$ the indiscernible degree on the attribute b of x_i, x_j. It is obviously that $ind_{i,j}^{b} \in [0,1]$.

Definition 1. Let $IIS = (U, A)$, Each subset of attributes $\forall B \subseteq A$ determines an indiscernibility relation IND^B on B :

$$IND^B = \left\{ \frac{ind_{i,j}^{B}}{(x_i, x_j)} \middle| (x_i, x_j) \in U \times U, \alpha_{i,j}^{B} = \inf_{b \in B} \alpha_{i,j}^{b} \right\} \quad (2)$$

We call $ind_{i,j}^{B}$ the indiscernibility degree on the attributes "B" of x_i, x_j. Notice that IND^B is reflexive and symmetric, but may not be transitive, thus the indiscernibility relation IND^B is a fuzzy similarity relation.

For an incomplete information system with continuous-valued attributes, the similarity measure or the distance measure is not enough to describe the discernible ability of the attributes. By considering the relative similarity or relative distance measure, we introduce a new definition: relative discernible measure. This definition will help us redefine the concepts of the knowledge reduction in an incomplete information system.

Let $IDS = (U, C \cup D)$ be an incomplete decision system. For any two objects i and j in U, the relative discernible degree of the attribute a with respect to the set of attributes $A \subseteq C$ is

$$IDM_{i,j}^{a,A/D} = \begin{cases} 0 & , ind_{i,j}^{D} = 1 \text{ or } ind_{i,j}^{A} = 1 \\ 1 - \dfrac{ind_{i,j}^{a} - ind_{i,j}^{A}}{1 - ind_{i,j}^{A}} & , \text{others} \end{cases} \quad (3)$$

When $ind_{i,j}^{A} = 1$, it means that the objects i and j are indiscernible on the attribute sets A.

3 The Concepts of knowledge Reduction

In an incomplete decision system $IDS = (U, C \cup D)$, let:

$$din_{C/D}^{a} = \max_{i,j=1,\cdots n} \left(IDM_{i,j}^{a,C/D} - \sup_{b \in C - \{a\}} IDM_{i,j}^{b,C/D} \right)$$

then the degree of indispensability of an attribute a in the set of the attributes C is $din_{C/D}^{a}$.

Definition 2. Let $IDS = (U, C \cup D)$ be an incomplete decision system, the subset of attributes $\forall B \subseteq C$ is the β–reduct, denoted by $Red_C^\beta(D)$, if and only if the following two formulas hold:

$$\max_{i,j=1,\cdots n} (\sup_{b \in C} IDM_{i,j}^{b,C/D} - \sup_{b \in B} IDM_{i,j}^{b,C/D}) \leq \beta \qquad (4)$$

$$\forall a \in B, \quad \max_{i,j=1,\cdots n} (\sup_{b \in C} IDM_{i,j}^{b,C/D} - \sup_{b \in B-\{a\}} IDM_{i,j}^{b,C/D}) \geq \beta \qquad (5)$$

Definition 3. The set which consists of attributes whose degree of indispensability is bigger than β is the β–core, denoted by $Core_C^\beta(D)$.

Theorem 1. The intersection of all the reducts is equal to the core, i.e. $\cap Red_C^\beta(D) = Core_C^\beta(D)$, where $Red_C^\beta(D)$ is the set of all the reducts of C with respect to D.

Proof. Firstly we prove that $\cap Red_C^\beta(D) \subset Core_C^\beta(D)$. We will prove it by contradiction.

Suppose that there exists $b_k \in \cap Red_C^\beta(D)$, but $b_k \notin Core_C^\beta(D)$. By definition 3, we get that $\max_{i,j=1,\cdots n} \left(IDM_{i,j}^{b_k,C/D} - \sup_{b \in C-\{b_k\}} IDM_{i,j}^{b,C/D} \right) \leq \beta$. Then there must exist the subset of fuzzy attributes set $B \subseteq C - \{b_k\}$, where B satisfies $\max_{i,j=1,\cdots n} (\sup_{b \in C} IDM_{i,j}^{b,C/D} - \sup_{b \in B} IDM_{i,j}^{b,C/D}) \leq \beta$; and $\forall a \in B$, the formula $\max_{i,j=1,\cdots n} (\sup_{b \in C} IDM_{i,j}^{b,C/D} - \sup_{b \in B-\{a\}} IDM_{i,j}^{b,C/D}) \geq \beta$ always holds. This shows that B is the reduct of C and $b_k \notin B$. That is to say $b_k \notin \cap Red_C^\beta(D)$. This contradicts our supposition. We prove that if $b_k \in \cap Red_C^\beta(D)$, then $b_k \in Core_C^\beta(D)$. i.e. $\cap Red_C^\beta(D) \subset Core_C^\beta(D)$.

Next, we prove $\cap Red_C^\beta(D) \supset Core_C^\beta(D)$, that is to say that we need to prove that if there exists $b_k \notin \cap Red_C^\beta(D)$, then $b_k \notin Core_C^\beta(D)$.

Suppose that B is a reduct of C. If $B = C$, then C has only one β–reduct. By the definition of reduct and core, we know that B is also the β–core of C. i.e. $\cap Red_C^\beta(D) = Core_C^\beta(D)$; if $B \subset C$, let $b_k \in C - B$, then we have $b_k \notin \cap Red^\beta(C)$. By the definition of indiscernibility relation, we know that if $B \subseteq C - \{b_k\}$ and $B \subseteq C$, then we have

$$\max_{i,j=1,\cdots n} (\sup_{b \in C} IDM_{i,j}^{b,C/D} - \sup_{b \in B-\{b_k\}} IDM_{i,j}^{b,C/D}) \leq \beta \qquad (6)$$

From the formula (6) and the definition of the core, we get $b_k \notin Core^\beta(C)$. This shows that $\cap Red_C^\beta(D) \supset Core_C^\beta(D)$. This completes the proof.

4 Fuzzy Reduct and Fuzzy Core of Rule

For an information system, it is not enough to just reduce attributes. It is necessary to reduce the superfluous attribute-values.

In a decision table, an example corresponds to an initial rule. Then, reducing every initial rule is equivalent to reducing the attribute-values.

In this section we introduce some concepts to reduce the initial rules in incomplete information system. First, let us define the concept of indispensability in an initial rule.

Definition 4. Let $IDS = (U, C \cup D)$ be an incomplete decision system, for the initial rule x_i and the attribute-value $a(x_i)$ on the attribute a of the initial rule x_i, let

$$\beta = \max_{j=1,\cdots,i-1,i+1,\cdots,n} \left(IDM_{i,j}^{a,C/D} - \sup_{b \in C-\{a\}} IDM_{i,j}^{b,C/D} \right)$$

then we will say that attribute-value $a(x_i)$ is β – indispensable in the initial rule x_i. We can also say that the indispensability degree of attribute-value $a(x_i)$ in the initial fuzzy rule x_i is β.

In the following definition, $\tilde{B}'$ is composed by several modified attributes which are formed by removing one or several attribute-values from condition attributes.

Definition 5. Let $IDS = (U, C \cup D)$ be an incomplete decision system, for the initial rule x_i and a certain threshold β, $\beta \in [0,1]$, if the following two formulae hold:

$$\max_{j=1,\cdots,i-1,i+1,\cdots,n} (\sup_{b \in C} IDM_{i,j}^{b,C/D} - \sup_{b \in B'} IDM_{i,j}^{b,C/D}) \leq \beta \quad (7)$$

$$\forall a \in B', \max_{j=1,\cdots,i-1,i+1,\cdots,n} (\sup_{b \in C} IDM_{i,j}^{b,C/D} - \sup_{b \in B'-\{a\}} IDM_{i,j}^{b,C/D}) \geq \beta \quad (8)$$

then $B'(x_i) \to D(x_i)$ is called β – reduct rule of the initial rule x_i, denoted by $Reduct_D^\beta(B')(x_i) \to D(x_i)$.

Notice that β – reduct rule of the initial rule x_i is not unique.

Definition 6. For the initial rule x_i and a certain threshold β, $\beta \in [0,1]$, the set P consists of the attribute value whose indispensability degree in the initial rule x_i is greater than $1-\beta$. Then $P \to D(x_i)$ is called the β – core rule of the initial rule x_i, denoted by $Core_D^\beta(B')(x_i) \to D(x_i)$.

Theorem 2. For an arbitrary threshold $\beta \in [0,1]$, $Reduct_D^\beta(B')(x_i) = Core_D^\beta(B')(x_i)$, $1 \le i \le n$.

The proof is similar to Theorem 1. We omit the proof details.

For the sake of reducing initial rules, we need to propose three new definitions: rule covering, covering rule number and the rank of rule.

Definition 7. For $i, j = 1, 2, \cdots, n$ and $j \ne i$, if the indiscernibility degree between the former of the initial rules x_i and x_j is greater than or equal to β, and the indiscernibility degree between the latter of the initial rules x_i and x_j is greater than or equal to β, then we will say that the rule x_i β – covers the rule x_j.

Definition 8. For the k th β – reduct rule of an initial rule x_i, find out all initial rules of this reduct rule β – covering and sum the number of these initial rules to N_{ik}, we will say that the sum N_{ik} is the β – covering rule number of the k th β – reduct rule of the initial rule x_i.

Definition 9. For any rule, if the attribute-values describing all condition attributes amount to γ, then we call that γ is the rank of this rule.

In this section we try to give the approach to reduce initial rules by ignoring the small perturbation. The small perturbations are visualized by the value 1-β. The smaller the threshold β, the less and simpler the decision rules. But this does not mean that the smaller threshold is the better. The choice of the threshold is dependent on the tolerance of the small perturbations of initial data. It shows that the approach of reducing the fuzzy information proposed in this paper is flexible and less sensitive to the small perturbation of initial data.

5 The Algorithm to Find the β – Reduct in an Incomplete Information System

In this subsection, we propose the following algorithm to find all reducts of an incomplete decision system with continuous-valued attributes.

    Input: Let $IDS = (U, C \cup D)$ be an incomplete decision system, where $C = b_1, b_2, \cdots, b_m$ denotes the set of condition attributes and $D = b_{m+1}, b_{m+2}, \cdots, b_{m+k}$ denotes the set of decision attributes and the given threshold β.

    Output: RED is the set of all β – reducts.

    Step1: Initialize $RED = \phi$, $CORE = \phi, i = 0$.

Step2: For each $b_k \in C$, calculate the indiscerinibility degree of the attribute b_k.

Step3: Choose the attribute b whose degree of indispensability is bigger than β, put these attributes to $CORE$. And let $C = C - CORE$.

Step4: Compute the power set P of C.

Step5: If there exists such set $N_i \in P$ which has only i element, goto **step7**; otherwise, goto **step6**.

Step6: Let $i = i + 1$, goto **step5**.

Step7: Select a set $M_i \in P$ which has i element. And let $H' = M_i \cup CORE$.

Step8: According to definition 2, determine whether H' is the reduct. If yes, then add it to the set RED, let $P = P - \{M \in P | M_i \subset M\}$ goto **step9**; Otherwise, let $P = P - \{M_i\}$, goto **step9**.

Step9: If $P \neq \phi$, goto **step5**; otherwise **stop**.

By using the above algorithm, we can compute all the β – reducts.

6 The Numerical Example

In this section we will show that the approach proposed in this paper is feasible and compare it with the method found in [8].

Example 5.1: Let us consider an incomplete decision table IDT with continuous-valued attributes as shown in table 1. {Price, Mileage, Size, Max-speed} is the set of condition attributes and d={acceleration} is the decision attribute.

Given the threshold $\beta = 0.4$, and by using the algorithm proposed in this paper to reduce attributes in the table 1, we have $Reduct_d^{0.4} = $ {Size, Max-speed}.

We firstly fuzzify the data of table 1 using the FCM algorithm [12] and then discrtize the fuzzification result. Then we obtain the table 2.

Table 2. Incomplete decision table with symbolic values

	Price	Mileage	Size	Max-speed	d
1	High	High	High	Low	Good
2	Low	*	High	Low	Good
3	*	*	Compact	High	Poor
4	High	*	High	High	Good
5	*	*	High	High	Excel.
6	Low	High	High	Low	Good

By using the approach in [8] to deal with table 2, we can obtain the attribute reduct as {Size, Max-speed}.

By comparing these two methods, one may find that the method in [8] needs to select one suitable algorithm to discretize the continuous data and the final result of attribute reduction is sensitive to the selected algorithm of discretization. Our proposed method does not need to go through the preprocessing of the continuous data.

7 Conclusion

In this paper we attempt to construct a new rough set model to deal with incomplete information system with continuous-valued attributes. The proposed rough set approach enables us to reduce the incomplete dataset directly without fuzzifying or discretizing the data. The concept of relative discernible measure is firstly proposed in this paper and is used to redefine the concepts of knowledge reduction, which saves us from having to preprocess the continuous data. We can find the informative attributes directly. The final numerical example illustrates that the proposal of this paper is feasible.

Acknowledgement

This work was also supported by the Hong Kong Research Grant Council under the Grants B-Q826 and B-Q943.

References

1. Pawlak Z.. Rough sets. International Journal of Computer and Information Sciences, 11(1982), 341-356
2. Pawlak Z., Rough Sets: Theoretical Aspects of Reasoning about Data [M]. Dordrecht: Kluwer Academic Publishers, 1991.
3. Quafafou M., a-RST: a Generalization of Rough Set Theory, Information Sciences 124 (2000) 301-316.
4. Yao Y. -Y., Lin T. -Y., Generalization of Rough Sets Using Modal Logic, Intelligent Automation and Soft Computing, an International Journal 2 (1996) 103-120.
5. Yao Y.Y., Generalized rough set model, in: L. Polkowski, A. Skowron (Eds.), Rough Sets in Knowledge Discovery 1. Methodology and Applications, Physica-Verlag, Heidelberg, 1998, pp. 286–318.
6. Yao Y.Y., Combination of Rough and Fuzzy Sets Based an a-Level Sets, in: T.Y. Lin, N. Cercone (Eds.), Rough Sets and Data Mining: Analysis for Imprecise Data, Kluwer Academic Publishers, Boston, 1997, 301-321.
7. Thiele H., Fuzzy Rough Sets Versus Rough Fuzzy Sets--an Interpretation and a Comparative Study Using Concepts of Modal Logics, University of Dortmund, Tech. Report No CI-30=98, 1998; also in Proc. EUFIT'1997, 159-167.
8. Kryszkiewicz M., Rough set approach to incomplete information systems, Information Sciences 112 (1998), 39-49.
9. Kryszkiewicz M., Rules in incomplete information systems, Information Sciences 113 (1999), 271-292.

10. Leung Y., Li D.Y., Maximal consistent block technique for rule acquisition in incomplete information systems. Information Sciences 153 (2003), 85-106.
11. Leung Y., Wu W.Z., Zhang W.X., European Journal of Operational Research 168(2006) 164-180.
12. Bezdek J.C., Pattern Recognition with Fuzzy Objective Function Algorithm. Plenum, New York. (1981).
13. Wang X. -Z., Hong J. -R.. Learning optimization in simplifying fuzzy rules. Fuzzy Sets and Systems, 106 (1999), 349-356
14. Slowinski R., Vanderpooten D., Similarity Relation as a Basis for Rough Approximations, in: P.P. Wang (Ed.), Advances in Machine Intelligence and Soft-Computing, Department of Electrical Engineering, Duke University, Durham, NC, USA, 1997, pp. 17–33.
15. Chakrabarty K., Biswas R., Nanda S., Fuzziness in Rough Sets, Fuzzy Sets and Systems 110(2000), 247-251.
16. Dubois D., Prade H., Rough Fuzzy Sets and Fuzzy Rough Sets, International Journal of General Systems 17 (1990) 191-208.
17. Dubois D., Prade H., Twofold Fuzzy Sets and Rough Sets--Some Issues in Knowledge Representation, Fuzzy Sets and Systems 23 (1987) 3-18.

Reduction of Attributes in Ordinal Decision Systems

John W.T. Lee[1], Xizhao Wang[2], and Jinfeng Wang[2]

[1] Department of computing, The Hong Kong Polytechnic University,
Hung Hom, Kowloon, Hong Kong
john.lee@polyu.edu.hk
[2] Machine Learning Center, Faculty of Mathematics and Computer Science,
Hebei University, Baoding 071002, China
wangxz@mail.hbu.edu.cn,
cmc_wangjf@cmc.hbu.edu.cn

Abstract. Rough set theory has proven to be a very useful tool in dealing with many decision situations where imprecise and inconsistent information are involved. Recently, there are attempts to extent the use of rough set theory to ordinal decision making in which decisions are made on ordering of objects through assigning them to ordinal categories. Attribute reduction is one of the problems that is studied under such ordinal decision situations. In this paper we examine some of the proposed approaches to find ordinal reducts and present a new perspective and approach to the problem based on ordinal consistency.

1 Introduction

We are often called upon to deal with data that are imprecise and inconsistent in decision situations. Many theories, such as fuzzy set theory and Dempster-Shafer theory of evidence, have been developed to handle these types of data in analysis and decision making. Rough set theory introduced by Pawlak in [7] is one of the more recent developments in this area. Since its introduction rough set theory has found to be useful in a broad spectrum of applications [3, 6]. Rough set theory acknowledges the fact that in real world situations, objects can only be identified by their known attributes and objects sharing the same attribute values become indiscernible. The indiscernible groups of objects resulting from the limited information we have about them are the basis upon which analysis and decisions must be made.

In the original rough set formulation, the attributes considered in an information system, including decision attributes, are assumed to take on nominal values. Objects sharing the same attribute values form equivalent groups which partition the object space. In such environment we may not be able to completely specify an arbitrary set of objects using the attributes available. We can approximate the set by a rough set consisting of a lower and an upper approximation, definable in the available attributes. One important area in data analysis is the selection of a suitable set of attributes among available attributes which may contain redundancy. Redundant attributes cause ineffectiveness in data analysis and induction of decision models. In rough set theory selection of attribute is studied under the topic of reducts which are minimal attribute sets with same descriptive power of the original attribute set.

Subsequent to its introduction, rough set theory has been extended in various ways, for example, by combining it with fuzzy set theory, or replacing the equivalence relation defining the indiscernibility groups with other weaker forms of relations. In this paper we consider the formulation in which the decision is based on a set of ordered labels. In such decision situation, an ordering is created in a set of objects by assigning them ordinal class labels as in the case of assigning students A, B, C, ... grades in a test. In the previous studies on application of rough set theory in ordinal decisions, the conditional attributes used to determine the decisions are also considered to be ordinal in nature [1, 2, 4, 8]. Greco et al studied the ordinal information system in the context of multicriteria decision making in [2]. They defined a reduct based on quality of approximation, using upper and lower set approximation similar to those in the classic rough set model. We will describe this system in greater details in Section 3 to contrast it with our approach. Bioch and Popova [1] studied reducts in monotone information systems by examining the monotone discernibility matrix, which corresponds to discernibility matrix in classic rough set, in finding monotone reducts. In [8], the authors examine the concept of reduct by considering the partitioning of binary relation space by ordering expressions in the set of attributes concerned. We have also studied this problem by focusing on the approximation of the implicit decision ordering using the available ordinal attributes in [4]. In this paper, we examine the situation where the ordinal decision is made based on condition attributes which take nominal values. Certainly nominal attributes are common, and in some situations like absence of monotonic relation, it may be more effective in decision analysis to treat ordinal attributes as nominal. We will examine reducts required for approximation of the decision ordering in this environment. We formulate a new type of discernibility matrix which we use to find ordinal reducts and illustrate this with an example.

In the following, we first present an overview of rough set in Section 2. We discuss ordinal information systems in Section 3. In Section 4 we examine the approximation of decision ordering and the associated concept of ordinal reducts. Section 5 introduces the new definition of ordinal separability and ordinal discernibility matrix and how it can be used to find ordinal reducts. The last section concludes with some of our ongoing investigation directions.

2 Rough Sets Overview

In this section we recap some of the basic formulation of rough set theory and related concepts we used in this paper. More details can be found in the tutorial paper [3]. An information system is a pair $S = (U, A)$ where U is the universe of discourse with a finite number of objects, and A is a set of attributes defined on U. Each attribute a of A is a function $a: U \to V_a$ which maps objects of U to the value set V_a. A decision system is a special information system $\Delta = (U, A \cup \{d\})$ in which there is a distinguished attribute d called the decision attribute with corresponding decision value set V_d. For any subset of attributes $B \subseteq A$, an indiscernibility relation $I_B = \{(x, y): a(x) = a(y) \forall a \in B\}$ is generated which partitions U into equivalence classes U/I_B of objects indistinguishable with respect to attributes in B. The equivalence class containing $x \in U$ can be defined by $[x]_B = \{y : a(x) = a(y) \forall a \in B\}$.

For any subset $X \subseteq U$ and $B \subseteq A$, X can be approximated by a rough set consisting of a lower and an upper approximation defined respectively as:

$$\underline{B}X := \{x : [x]_B \subseteq X\} \quad (1)$$

$$\overline{B}X := \{x : [x]_B \cap X \neq \emptyset\} \quad (2)$$

These rough set approximations form a pair of tight bounds over X based on B in the inequalities $\underline{B}X \subseteq X \subseteq \overline{B}X$. The boundary set $\tilde{B}X = \overline{B}X \setminus \underline{B}X$ [1] contains objects that we cannot say for certain to be inside or outside of X given their B attributes.

In a decision system, the family of equivalence classes generated by the decision attribute d is given by $D = U/I_{\{d\}}$. As for any set $X \subseteq U$, each equivalence class in D can be approximated by using a given attribute set B. The corresponding quality of approximation of the decision d by a set of attributes B can be measured by:

$\gamma_B(D) = \dfrac{\sum_{X \in D} |\underline{B}X|}{|U|}$. This measure constitutes the proportion of U which can be unambiguously classified using their attribute values in B. A reduct R of A with respect to D is a minimal subset of A that preserves this approximation quality. Thus R is a reduct if $\gamma_R(D) = \gamma_A(D)$ and $B \subset R \Rightarrow \gamma_B(D) < \gamma_A(D)$. The set of reducts with respect to d in A is denoted by $Red_d(A)$.

3 Ordinal Attributes and Ordinal Decision Systems

It is quite common for attributes and decisions to assume ordinal labels like alphabetic grading systems for student's performance or Likert scales used in opinion surveys. An ordinal decision system is one in which the decision attribute is ordinal. An ordinal attribute a has an attribute value set V_a which is a linearly ordered sets of labels. We represent the label set in the form of $V_a = \{l_1^a > l_2^a > ... > l_{\perp a}^a\}$. An ordinal attribute induces a corresponding weak order $\geq_a$ (a complete and transitive relation) in U thus $\geq_a = \{(x, y) : a(x) \geq a(y)\}$. In [5] we showed that any weak order $\geq_a$ corresponds uniquely to the nested sets in the family $U_a^\uparrow = \{[x]_a^\uparrow : x \in U\}$ where $[x]_a^\uparrow = \{y : y \geq_a x\}$. These nested sets correspond to the equivalence classes defined by nominal attribute values in the classic rough set theory. Thus in the case of an ordinal decision system, the induced decision order is $\geq_d$ and the corresponding nested sets is given by $U_d^\uparrow = \{[x]_d^\uparrow : x \in U\}$. We further define the following notations used in this paper.

---

[1] We use X\Y to represent difference of set X and Y.

$$[x]_a^\downarrow := \{y : x \geq_a y)\} \qquad (3)$$

$$[x]_B^\uparrow = \{y : y \geq_a x, \forall a \in B\} \qquad (4)$$

$$[x]_B^\downarrow = \{y : x \geq_a y, \forall a \in B\} \qquad (5)$$

$$a^{\uparrow i} := \{x : a(x) \geq l_i^a\} \qquad (6)$$

$$a^{\downarrow i} := \{x : l_i^a \geq a(x)\} \qquad (7)$$

In [2], the authors consider an ordinal decision system in which all attributes, both condition and decision attributes, are ordinal. They proposed to approximate an ordinal decision system in a similarly way to approximating sets. The sets in this context are now the nested sets $d^{\uparrow i}$ and $d^{\downarrow i}$ induced by the ordinal decision. Thus for any subset of attributes $B \subseteq A$, the lower and upper approximation of these sets are given by:

$$\underline{B}d^{\uparrow i} = \{x : [x]_B^\uparrow \subseteq d^{\uparrow i}\} \qquad (8)$$

$$\overline{B}d^{\uparrow i} = \{x : [x]_B^\uparrow \cap d^{\uparrow i} \neq \emptyset\} = \bigcup_{x \in d^{\uparrow i}} [x]_B^\uparrow \qquad (9)$$

$$\underline{B}d^{\downarrow i} = \{x : [x]_B^\downarrow \subseteq d^{\downarrow i}\} \qquad (10)$$

$$\overline{B}d^{\downarrow i} = \{x : [x]_B^\downarrow \cap d^{\downarrow i} \neq \emptyset\} = \bigcup_{x \in d^{\downarrow i}} [x]_B^\downarrow \qquad (11)$$

The corresponding boundary sets are similarly defined:

$$\tilde{B}d^{\uparrow i} = \overline{B}d^{\uparrow i} \setminus \underline{B}d^{\uparrow i} \qquad (12)$$

$$\tilde{B}d^{\downarrow i} = \overline{B}d^{\downarrow i} \setminus \underline{B}d^{\downarrow i} \qquad (13)$$

The quality of approximation of d using the set of attributes B is then defined as:

$$\gamma_B(d) = \frac{|U \setminus \left(\left(\bigcup_i \tilde{B}d^{\uparrow i}\right) \cup \left(\bigcup_i \tilde{B}d^{\downarrow i}\right)\right)|}{|U|} \qquad (14)$$

Reduct is then defined as any minimal subset that preserves this quality of approximation. Thus a subset $R \subseteq A$ is a reduct if and only if $\gamma_R(d) = \gamma_A(d)$ and $B \subset R \Rightarrow \gamma_B(d) < \gamma_A(d)$. In [4], we showed some problems associated with this definition of ordinal reduct and provide an alternative model to resolve these problems.

In this paper we focus on the case where in the decision system $\Delta = (U, A \cup \{d\})$, the decision attribute d is ordinal while the other attributes in A are nominal. Furthermore, similar to the approach in [4], our goal is the approximation, not of the ordinal classes, but of the underlying decision ordering $\geq_d$ generated by the ordinal decision labels in V_d. This is based on the assumption that in making an ordinal decision, the assignment of ordinal labels to objects is solely for the purpose of creating the underlying ordering $\geq_d$.

4 Approximating the Decision Ordering

Thus we regard the decision ordering as the meaning of the label assignment process and hence is more important than the actual labels assigned to the objects. To give a simple illustrate of this perspective: if we have a universe of two objects x and y, and ordinal labels 1>2>3, then the label assignments $\{x\rightarrow1, y\rightarrow2\}$, $\{x\rightarrow1, y\rightarrow3\}$, and $\{x\rightarrow2, y\rightarrow3\}$, will be equivalent from this perspective since they represent the same decision ordering of $x>y$. Our goal is therefore to provide a rough set approximation, in the sense of a tight upper and lower bound, for the decision ordering $>_d$ [2] base on information granules generated by the nominal attributes A. First of all, we observe that $U_d^\uparrow = \{[x]_d^\uparrow : x \in U\} = \{d^{\uparrow i}\}_i$ is the family of nested sets corresponding to the weak order $>_d$ and they are related by:

$$(>_d) = \bigcup_{X \in U_d^\uparrow} (X \times U \setminus X) = \bigcup_i \left(d^{\uparrow i} \times U \setminus d^{\uparrow i}\right) = \bigcup_i \left(d^{\uparrow i} \times d^{\downarrow(i+1)}\right) \quad (15)$$

This formulation provides us the means to create the upper and lower approximations for $>_d$. Since for all i and $B \subseteq A$, we have $\underline{B} d^{\uparrow i} \subseteq d^{\uparrow i} \subseteq \overline{B} d^{\uparrow i}$, thus

$$\left(\underline{B} d^{\uparrow i} \times \underline{B} d^{\downarrow(i+1)}\right) \subseteq \left(d^{\uparrow i} \times d^{\downarrow(i+1)}\right) \subseteq \left(\overline{B} d^{\uparrow i} \times \overline{B} d^{\downarrow(i+1)}\right) \quad (16)$$

provides an upper and a lower bound for the ordering generated by each level of the ordinal decision label l_i^d. Aggregating over all i's,

$$\bigcup_i \left(\underline{B} d^{\uparrow i} \times \underline{B} d^{\downarrow(i+1)}\right) \subseteq (>_d) = \bigcup_i \left(d^{\uparrow i} \times d^{\downarrow(i+1)}\right) \subseteq \bigcup_i \left(\overline{B} d^{\uparrow i} \times \overline{B} d^{\downarrow(i+1)}\right) \quad (17)$$

So the sets $\left(>_d^{\underline{B}}\right) = \bigcup_i \left(\underline{B} d^{\uparrow i} \times \underline{B} d^{\downarrow(i+1)}\right)$ and $\left(>_d^{\overline{B}}\right) = \bigcup_i \left(\overline{B} d^{\uparrow i} \times \overline{B} d^{\downarrow(i+1)}\right)$ provide respectively the lower and upper approximation to the decision ordering $>_d$. (Note: We use the same symbols for the upper and lower approximations as in [4], with the understanding that the attribute types are different and hence the approximations are also different. In the following, we will also continue to use the same symbols as in the paper for the corresponding concepts in our current formulation bearing in mind the definitions will depend on the attribute type concerned.) These are also tight bounds in as far as $\left(\underline{B} d^{\uparrow i}, \overline{B} d^{\uparrow i}\right)$ and $\left(\underline{B} d^{\downarrow i+1}, \overline{B} d^{\downarrow i+1}\right)$ are tight bounds for $d^{\uparrow i}$ and $d^{\downarrow i+1}$ respectively. The upper and lower bounds can also be written in the more familiar forms:

$$\left(x >_d^{\underline{B}} y\right) \Rightarrow \left(x >_d y\right) \quad (18)$$

$$\left(x >_d y\right) \Rightarrow \left(x >_d^{\overline{B}} y\right) \quad (19)$$

---

[2] We consider approximation of $>_d$, the asymmetric part of $\geq_d$, instead of $\geq_d$. The two order relations are related by a simple formula. $>_d$ is chosen because it offers more elegant conceptual formulations.

When all d^i's are definable in $B \subseteq A$, i.e. $\underline{B}d^{\uparrow i} = d^{\uparrow i} = \overline{B}d^{\uparrow i}$, the upper and lower boundaries for the order approximation also merge and we have $(>_d^B) = (>_d) = (>_d^{\overline{B}})$. The quality of ordinal approximation given $B \subseteq A$ can be measured in a similar manner as for set approximation as:

$$\gamma_B^o(d) = \frac{|>_d^B|}{|>_d|} = \frac{|\bigcup_i (\underline{B}^\uparrow d^{\uparrow i} \times \underline{B}^\downarrow d^{\downarrow i+1})|}{|>_d|} \quad (20)$$

This measure varies between 0 and 1. It is obvious that $\gamma_B^o(d)$ will become 1 if the d^i's (the decision classes when the decision labels are treated as nominal instead of ordinal) are definable in terms of B. However it can be shown this is not a necessary condition for $\gamma_B^o(d)$ be equal to 1. As in the classic rough set theory, this approximation measure helps to define the concept of ordinal d-reduct. Thus an ordinal d-reduct is defined as a minimal subset of A which preserves this approximating quality. Formally $R \subseteq A$ is an ordinal d-reduct of $\Delta = (U, A \cup \{d\})$ if and only if $\gamma_R^o(d) = \gamma_A^o(d)$ and $\gamma_R^o(d) > \gamma_B^o(d)$, $\forall B \subset R$. We represent the set of ordinal d-reducts in the context of A as $Red_d^o(A)$.

An alternative formulation of the ordinal d-reduct concept is through the concept of dispensability and independence. Under such consideration, the relation $(>_d^B)$ corresponds to the positive region in classic rough set theory. An attribute $a \in B$ is said to be ordinally d-dispensable if $(>_d^B) = (>_d^{B \setminus \{a\}})$, otherwise it is ordinally d-indispensable. A set of attributes $B \subseteq A$ is said to be ordinally d-independent if no attribute in B is ordinally d-dispenable. Then B is an ordinal d-reduct if it is ordinally d-independent and $(>_d^B) = (>_d^A)$.

5 Ordinal Separability and Ordinal Discernibility Matrix

In traditionally rough set theory, a discernibility matrix can be used to compute all the reducts within a decision system. In our ordinal decision context, we can develop a similar approach to compute ordinal d-reducts. To do so, we need to introduce the concept of ordinal separability. Any $x, y \in U$ are ordinally separable in B if $x >_d^B y$ or $y >_d^B x$. Alternatively, x and y separability can be expressed in terms of their equivalence classes as $[x]_B \subseteq d^{\uparrow i}$ and $[y]_B \subseteq d^{\downarrow(i+1)}$ for some i, or vice versa. So x, y separability in B means B is a set of attributes which is sufficient to discriminate x and y in the decision ordering. Furthermore, if x, y are separable in $B \setminus \{a\}$ for some $a \in B$, we will say a is ordinally dispensable for x, y in B. Otherwise a is ordinally indispensable. A subset $R \subseteq B$ is called an ordinal reduct for x, y in B if they are separable in R and every a in R is ordinally indispensable. Thus an ordinal reduct for x

and y is a minimal set of attributes that can discriminate them in the decision ordering. The set of ordinal d-reduct for x and y in B is denoted by $Red_d^{x,y}(B)$.

To compute the ordinal d-reduct for an ordinal decision system, we next define an ordinal discernibility matrix. For $x, y \in U$, the element c_{xy} in the ordinal discernibility matrix is defined by: $c_{xy} = Red_d^{x,y}(A)$ if x, y are ordinally separable in A, else $= \emptyset$. Thus each element of the matrix contains the minimal sets of attributes that are required to ordinally discriminate between the two object elements concerned.

From this we define an ordinal discernibility (Boolean) function:

$$f_d^o(A) = \prod_{(x,y) \in U^2} \left\{ \sum_{R \in c_{xy}} \pi(R) \right\} \text{ where } \pi(R) = \prod_{a \in R} a \tag{21}$$

Proposition

All constituents in the minimal disjunctive normal form of the function $f_d^o(A)$ are ordinal d-reducts of A.

While we will not provide our proof here, it can be observed that an ordinal d-reduct must be able to ordinally separate any pair of objects, and hence must contain at least one of the ordinal d-reduct in $Red_d^{x,y}(A)$ for any separable x, y. Therefore an ordinal d-reduct is a minimal set of attributes form from the union of selecting one member from each non-empty $Red_d^{x,y}(A)$.

We provide an example with the ordinal decision system showed as Table 1 to illustrate ordinal reducts and the use of ordinal discernibility matrix to compute them. In this example U consists of seven objects $\{x_1, x_2, x_3, x_4, x_5, x_6, x_7\}$. There are 4 condition attributes in $A = \{a_1, a_2, a_3, a_4\}$ which we assumed to be nominal, and an ordinal decision attribute d with ordinal labels $V_d = \{0 > 1 > 2\}$.

Table 1. An ordinal decision system

Attribute / Objects	a_1	a_2	a_3	a_4	d
x_1	1	0	2	1	1
x_2	1	0	2	0	1
x_3	1	2	0	0	2
x_4	1	2	2	1	0
x_5	2	1	0	0	2
x_6	2	1	1	0	2
x_7	2	1	2	1	1

To facilitate the computation of ordinal d-reducts for pairs of objects, we first compute the decision intervals, d-intervals, for equivalence classes of different attributes subsets. The d-interval of a set $X \subseteq U$ is the range of d values covered by the set, which will be represented by $int^d(X) = d^{max} : d^{min}$, where

$d^{max} = Max_{x \in X}\{d(x)\}$ and $d^{min} = Min_{x \in X}\{d(x)\}$. It can easily be shown that x, y are ordinally separable in B if and only if $int^d([x]_B)$ and $int^d([y]_B)$ do not intersect. Tables corresponding to each combination of attributes are created. Separability of any x, y can then be readily observed from these tables. In Table 2 we showed an example of d-interval table for $B = \{a_1, a_4\}$. It can be seen from this table that objects x_1 and x_4 are in the same equivalence class and the decision interval is 0:1. Objects x_1, x_2 are not separable in B since their corresponding decision intervals 0:1 and 1:2 overlap, and x_1, x_5 are separable as their intervals 0:1 and 2 do not intersect.

Table 2. d-interval table example

Equivalence Class / Attribute	a_1	a_4	d-interval
x_1, x_4	1	1	0:1
x_2, x_3	1	0	1:2
x_5, x_6	2	0	2
x_7	2	1	1

Table 3. The ordinal discernibility matrix

	x_1	x_2	x_3	x_4	x_5	x_6
x_2	$\varnothing$					
x_3	$\{a_3\}$ $\{a_2, a_4\}$	$\{a_3\}$ $\{a_2, a_4\}$				
x_4	$\{a_2, a_3\}$ $\{a_2, a_4\}$	$\{a_2, a_3\}$ $\{a_2, a_4\}$	$\{a_3\}$ $\{a_2, a_4\}$			
x_5	$\{a_3\}$ $\{a_1, a_4\}$ $\{a_2, a_4\}$	$\{a_3\}$ $\{a_1, a_4\}$ $\{a_2, a_4\}$	$\varnothing$	$\{a_3\}$ $\{a_1, a_4\}$ $\{a_2, a_4\}$		
x_6	$\{a_3\}$ $\{a_1, a_4\}$ $\{a_2, a_4\}$	$\{a_3\}$ $\{a_1, a_4\}$ $\{a_2, a_4\}$	$\varnothing$	$\{a_3\}$ $\{a_1, a_4\}$ $\{a_2, a_4\}$	$\varnothing$	
x_7	$\varnothing$	$\varnothing$	$\{a_3\}$ $\{a_2, a_4\}$	$\{a_2, a_3\}$ $\{a_2, a_4\}$	$\{a_3\}$ $\{a_1, a_4\}$ $\{a_2, a_4\}$	$\{a_3\}$ $\{a_1, a_4\}$ $\{a_2, a_4\}$

Using this method of judging separability, we can obtain the ordinal discernibility matrix shown as Table 3. The ordinal discernibility function for Table 3 is as follow:

$$\begin{aligned}f_d^o(B) &= (a_3 + a_2a_4)(a_3 + a_1a_4 + a_2a_4)(a_2a_3 + a_2a_4) \\ &= (a_3 + a_2a_4)(a_2a_3 + a_2a_4) \\ &= a_3a_2a_3 + a_2a_4 \\ &= a_2a_3 + a_2a_4\end{aligned} \qquad (22)$$

where *a+b* and *ab* denotes the Boolean sum and product of *a* and *b* respectively. It is obvious that after simplification we can obtain two ordinal *d*-reducts $\{a_2, a_3\}$ and $\{a_2, a_4\}$.

As in the classic rough set theory, we also have the concept of core attributes with respect to the ordinal decision *d*. The core attributes of *A* with respect to ordinal decision *d*, $CORE_d^o(A)$, are attributes which are ordinally *d*-indispensable in *A* and it can be shown that:

$$CORE_d^o(A) = \bigcap Red_d^o(A) \qquad (23)$$

In the example therefore, $CORE_d^o(A) = \{a_2\}$.

6 Conclusion and Future Works

In this paper we have examined the application of rough set approach in ordinal decision making in a context where the decision attribute consists of ordinal classes while the conditional attributes are nominal as in the classic rough set theory. Taking the perspective that the ordinal label assignments in the decision is to generate an ordering of the objectives concerned, we focus our goal on approximation of this underlying ordering instead of the classes generation by label equalities. Based on this consideration, we defined the quality of approximation to be the ability of the granules of information from a set of attributes to approximate this ordering. We defined a new concept of ordinal separability and ordinal reduct for a pair of elements in the universe of discourse. From this we introduced the ordinal discernibility matrix which we used to compute ordinal reducts for an ordinal decision system.

At the moment our computation of the discernibility matrix still requires exhaustive search for all ordinal reducts for pairs of elements which is quite computationally intensive. We are working on more efficient algorithm to achieve this process. On the other hand we are testing this concept of ordinal reducts in making ordinally classifications more effective with data sets from machine learning databases.

Acknowledgement

This project is supported by the Hong Kong Polytechnic University research grant G-T667.

References

1. Bioch, J., Popova, V.: Rough sets and ordinal classification. A.S.H. Arimura, S. Jain, editor, Algorithmic Learning Theory, Lecture Notes in Artificial Intelligence 1968 (2000) 291-305
2. Greco, S., Matarazzo, B., Slowinski, R.: Rough sets theory for multicriteria decision analysis. European Journal of Operational Research, Vol. 129 (2001) 1-47
3. Komorowski, J., Polkowski, L., Skowron, A.: Rough sets: a tutorial. S.K. Pal and A. Skowron, editors, Rough-Fuzzy Hybridization: A New Method for Decision Making, Springer-Verlag (1998)
4. Lee, J.W.T., Yeung, D.S., Tsang, E.C.C.: Rough Sets and Ordinal Reducts. Journal of Soft Computing - A Fusion of Foundations, Methodologies and Applications (to appear)
5. Lee, J.W.T., Yeung, D.S., Tsang, E.C.C.: Ordinal Fuzzy Sets. IEEE Transactions on Fuzzy Systems, Vol. 10, No. 6 (2002) 767-778
6. Pal, S.K., Skowron, A., eds.: Rough-Fuzzy Hybridization: A New Trend in Decision Making, Springer (1999)
7. Pawlak, Z.: Rough Sets. International Journal of Information & Computer Sciences, Vol. 11 (1982) 341-356
8. Sai, Y., Yao, Y. Y., Zhong, N.: Data analysis and mining in ordered information tables. Proc. of the IEEE Int'l Conf. on Data Mining (2001) 497-504

On the Local Reduction of Information System

Degang Chen[1] and Eric C.C. Tsang[2]

[1] Department of Mathematics and Physics, North China Electric Power University,
102206, Beijing, P.R. China
chengdegang@263.net
[2] Department of Computing, Hong Kong Polytechnic University,
Hung Hom, Kowloon, Hong Kong

Abstract. In this paper the definition of local reduction is proposed to describe the minimal description of a definable set by attributes of the given information system. The local reduction can present more optimal description for single decision class than the existing relative reductions. It is proven that the core of reduction or relative reduction can be expressed as the union of the cores of local reductions. The discernibility matrix of reduction and relative reduction can be obtained by composing discernibility matrixes of local reduction.

1 Introduction

The theory of rough sets, proposed by Pawlak[1], is an extension of set theory for the study of intelligent systems characterized by insufficient and incomplete information. With more than twenty years development, rough set theory has been found to have very successful applications in the fields of artificial intelligence. The theory of rough sets deals with the approximations of an arbitrary subset of a universe by two definable or observable subsets called lower and upper approximations. By using the concepts of lower and upper approximations in rough set theory, knowledge hidden in information systems may be unraveled and expressed in the form of decision rules. Another application of rough set theory is that of attribute reduction in databases. Given a dataset with discrete attribute values, it is possible to find a subset of the original attributes that are the most informative. Attributes reduction by rough sets can be viewed as a pure structural approach that only depend on data set and need not other knowledge. Many efforts have been concentrated on the characterization of the structure of reduction. [2] was a pioneering work to study the structures of reductions of rough sets in detail. The most valuable contribution in [2] is the development of approach of discernibility matrix to compute all the reductions. It not only presents algorithms of computing reductions, but also gives a deep insight of the structure of reductions. It is indicated in [2] that every element in the reduction is indispensable to distinguish certain pair of objects in the universe. But it has not told whether every element in the reduction is indispensable for certain decision class. In [3] the reductions of rough sets are described by belief and plausibility functions in evidence theory, while in [4] they are described by information entropy. In [5,6,7] the reduction of variable precision rough set model is studied and in [8,9] the reduction of incomplete information system is studied.

All of these reductions of rough sets can be viewed as global reductions since they are defined for the whole system and aim to keep some factors relative to the decision attribute invariant. For example, positive region, belief and plausibility functions and information entropy are global invariant factors in [2], [3] and [4] respectively. On the other hand, in many practical problems people always pay more attention on some special decision values than other decision values, and attributes support these special decision values always draw much attention. The global reductions need more features to evaluate all the decisions, which means high prediction cost. From the theoretical viewpoint, every attribute in the reduction may play different role for different decision class, thus more precise recognition to the properties of reductions can be presented by further study to the interior structure of the reductions. In this paper the definition of local reduction relative to several definable sets is proposed based on our initial idea of part reduction in [13]. It is proven that the core of reduction or relative reduction can be expressed as the union of the cores of local reductions. The discernibility matrix of reduction and relative reduction can be obtained by composing discernibility matrixes of local reduction. With results in reference [2] and this paper, the structure of reduction is totally clear.

The rest of this paper is structural as following. In Section 2 we recall some basic contents on rough set and its reductions. In Section 3 we define local reduction and study its properties.

2 Rough Sets and Its Reductions

An information system is a pair $A = (U, A)$, where $U = \{x_1, x_2, ..., x_n\}$ is a nonempty, finite set of objects called the universe and $A = \{a_1, ..., a_m\}$ is a nonempty, finite set of attributes. With every subset of attributes $B \subseteq A$ we associate a binary relation $IND(B)$, called $B-$ indiscernibility relation, and defined as

$$IND(B) = \{(x, y) \in U : a(x) = a(y), \forall a \in B\}.$$

Then $IND(B)$ is an equivalence relation and $IND(B) = \bigcap_{a \in B} IND(a)$. By $[x]_B$ we denote the equivalence class of $IND(B)$ including x. For $X \subseteq U$ the sets $\{x \in U : [x]_B \subseteq X\}$ and $\{x \in U : [x]_B \cap X \neq \phi\}$ are called $B-$ lower and $B-$ upper approximation of X in A, respectively, and they are denoted by $\underline{B}X$ and $\overline{B}X$, respectively.

By $M(A)$ we denote an $n \times n$ matrix (c_{ij}), called the discernibility matrix of A, such that $c_{ij} = \{a \in A : a(x_i) \neq a(x_j)\}$ for $i, j = 1, ..., n$.

A discernibility function f_A for an information system A is a Boolean function of m Boolean variables $\overline{a_1}, ..., \overline{a_m}$ corresponding to the attributes $a_1, ..., a_m$, respectively, and defined as follows:

$$f_A(\overline{a_1},...,\overline{a_m}) = \wedge\{\vee(c_{ij}): 1 \le j < i \le n, c_{ij} \ne \emptyset\}$$

where $\vee(c_{ij})$ is the disjunction of all variables $\overline{a}$ such that $a \in c_{ij}$.

An attribute $a \in B \subseteq A$ is dispensable in B if $IND(B) = IND(B - \{a\})$, otherwise a is indispensable in B. The set of all indispensable attributes in A is called the core of A, and is denoted by $CORE(A)$. We say that $B \subseteq A$ is independent in A if every attribute from B is indispensable in B. A set $B \subseteq A$ is called a reduction in A if B is independent in A and $IND(B) = IND(A)$. The set of all reductions in A is denoted by $RED(A)$. Let g be the reduced disjunctive form of f_A by applying the multiplication and absorption laws as many times as possible. Then there exist l and $X_i \subseteq A$ for $i = 1,...,l$ such that $g = (\wedge X_1) \vee ... \vee (\wedge X_l)$, we have $RED(A) = \{X_1,..., X_l\}$.

A decision system is a pair $A^* = (U, A \cup \{a^*\})$, a^* is called the decision attribute, attributes in A are called conditional attributes. We say $a \in B \subseteq A$ is relatively dispensable in B if $POS_B(a^*) = POS_{B-\{a\}}(a^*)$, otherwise a is said to be relatively indispensable in B, here $POS_B(a^*)$ is the union of B − lower approximations of all the equivalence classes of a^*. If every attribute from B is relatively indispensable in B, we say that B is relatively independent in A^*. A subset $B \subseteq A$ is called a relative reduction in A^* if B is relatively independent in A^* and $POS_B(a^*) = POS_A(a^*)$. The set of all relatively indispensable attributes in A is called the relative core of A, and is denoted by $CORE(A^*)$.

Suppose $M(A^*) = (c_{ij})$ We define a matrix $\mathbf{M}(A^*) = (\mathbf{c}_{ij})$ in the following way:

1) $\mathbf{c}_{ij} = c_{ij} - \{a^*\}$, if ($a^* \in c_{ij}$ and $x_i, x_j \in POS_A(a^*)$) or $pos(x_i) \ne pos(x_j)$;

2) $\mathbf{c}_{ij} = \emptyset$, otherwise

All the relative reductions can be computed in an analogous way as reductions of $M(A)$.

3 Local Reduction Relative to Several Definable Sets

Suppose $A = (U, A)$ is an information system. A subset $X \subseteq U$ is called A−definable if $\overline{A}X = \underline{A}X$, denote the collection of all the A− definable sets of

$A = (U, A)$ as $D(U, A)$. Suppose $\mathbf{X} = \{X_1, ..., X_N\} \subseteq D(U, A)$, $a \in A$, if $\mathbf{X} \subseteq D(U, A - \{a\})$, then a is called dispensable in A for $\mathbf{X}$, otherwise a is called indispensable in A for $\mathbf{X}$, the collection of all the indispensable elements in A is called the local core of A for $\mathbf{X}$ and denoted as $CORE_\mathbf{X}(A)$. We say that $B \subseteq A$ is independent in A for $\mathbf{X}$ if every attribute from B is indispensable in B for $\mathbf{X}$. A set $B \subseteq A$ is called a local reduction in A if B is independent in A for $\mathbf{X}$, i.e., B is the minimal subset of A keeping $\mathbf{X} \subseteq D(U, B)$ (not $\bigcup_{i=1}^{N} X_i \subseteq D(U, B)$). The set of all local reductions in A for $\mathbf{X}$ is denoted by $RED_\mathbf{X}(A)$, $CORE_\mathbf{X}(A) = \bigcap RED_\mathbf{X}(A)$.

The reduction of information system $A = (U, A)$ aims to keep $IND(A)$ invariant, it is just to keep $\{[x]_A : x \in U\}$ invariant. The relative reduction of decision system $A^* = (U, A \bigcup \{a^*\})$ aims to keep the positive region invariant, it is just to keep the lower approximation of every decision class invariant. These statements imply reduction of information system and relative reduction of decision system are all special cases of our proposed local reduction. Elements in $\mathbf{X} = \{X_1, ..., X_N\}$ may have nonempty overlaps, thus it can deal with the case that decision classes have nonempty overlap, this statement implies the local reduction is the generalization of part reduction in [13]. For example, the generalized decision classes for inconsistent information system in [10] may have nonempty overlaps. On the other hand, if the relative reduction of decision systems is defined to keep upper approximations of every decision class invariant such as approximation reduction in [11], then these upper approximations may have nonempty overlaps. The approximate reduction and μ-reduction for inconsistent decision system in [12] are also special cases of local reduction in this paper since they also aim to keep some elements in $D(U, A)$ invariant. Thus local reduction in this paper is a more general framework than the existing reductions of rough sets and different $\mathbf{X} = \{X_1, ..., X_N\}$ determines different kind of reduction. If elements in $\mathbf{X} = \{X_1, ..., X_N\}$ have nonempty overlaps, then there exists a $\mathbf{X}'$ satisfying elements in $\mathbf{X}'$ have empty overlaps and $RED_\mathbf{X}(A) = RED_{\mathbf{X}'}(A)$. We only prove this statement when $\mathbf{X} = \{X_1, X_2\}$.

Theorem 1. Suppose $\mathbf{X} = \{X_1, X_2\}$ and $X_1 \cap X_2 \neq \emptyset$, $\mathbf{X}' = \{X_1 \cap X_2, X_1 - X_2, X_2 - X_1\}$, then $RED_\mathbf{X}(A) = RED_{\mathbf{X}'}(A)$.

Proof. For any $B \subseteq A$, $\mathbf{X} \subset D(U, B) \Leftrightarrow \mathbf{X}' \subset D(U, B)$, thus we finish the proof. Following we always assume elements in $\mathbf{X} = \{X_1, ..., X_N\}$ have empty overlaps. We have the following theorem for the local core.

Theorem 2. Suppose $\mathbf{X} = \{X_1,...,X_N\}$ and $X_i \cap X_j = \phi$, then we have $CORE_\mathbf{X}(A) = \bigcup_{i=1}^{N} CORE_{\{X_i\}}(A)$.

Proof. For any $a \in A$, $a \in Core_\mathbf{X}(A) \Leftrightarrow$ there exists X_i satisfying $X_i \not\subseteq D(U, A-\{a\}) \Leftrightarrow a \in Core_{X_i}(A) \Leftrightarrow a \in \bigcup_{i=1}^{N} Core_{X_i}(A)$.

By Theorem 2 $CORE(A) = \bigcup_{x \in U} CORE_{\{[x]_A\}}(A)$ and $CORE(A^*) = \bigcup_{x \in U} CORE_{\{[x]_{a^*}\}}(A)$ hold, this implies elements in core of information system and relative core of decision system is indispensable for certain decision classes. If we pay more attention to special decision classes, then local reduction may offer less conditional attributes only being indispensable for these special decision classes. This is the objective of local reductions. Following we study the computing of local reductions.

Suppose $\mathbf{A} = (U, A)$ is an information system, $\mathbf{X} = \{X_1,...,X_N\}$, by $M_\mathbf{X}(A)$ we denote an $n \times n$ matrix (c_{ij}), called the discernibility matrix of $\mathbf{A}$, such that 1) $c_{ij} = \{a \in A : a(x_i) \neq a(x_j)\}$ if there exists $X_k \in \mathbf{X}$ such that $x_i \in X_k$ and $x_j \notin X_k$; 2) $c_{ij} = \phi$, otherwise for $i, j = 1,...,n$.

Clearly $M_\mathbf{X}(A)$ is symmetry. The proofs of following two theorems are straightforward.

Theorem 3. $CORE_\mathbf{X}(A) = \{a : c_{ij} = \{a\}\}$ for some i and j.

Theorem 4. $B \subseteq A$ is a local reduction in A for $\mathbf{X}$ if and only if $B \cap c_{ij} \neq \phi$ for $c_{ij} \neq \phi$.

A discernibility function $f_A(\mathbf{X})$ for an information system $\mathbf{A}$ is a Boolean function of m Boolean variables $\overline{a_1},...,\overline{a_m}$ corresponding to the attributes $a_1,...,a_m$, respectively, and defined as follows:

$$f_A(\mathbf{X})(\overline{a_1},...,\overline{a_m}) = \wedge\{\vee(c_{ij}) : 1 \leq j < i \leq n, c_{ij} \neq \phi\}$$

where $\vee(c_{ij})$ is the disjunction of all variables $\overline{a}$ such that $a \in c_{ij}$.

Let $g_A(\mathbf{X})$ be the reduced disjunctive form of $f_A(\mathbf{X})$ by applying the multiplication and absorption laws as many times as possible. Then there exist t and $A_i \subseteq A$ for $i = 1,...,t$ such that $g_A(\mathbf{X}) = (\wedge A_1) \vee ... \vee (\wedge A_t)$, we have the following theorem.

Theorem 5. $RED_\mathbf{X}(A) = \{A_1,...,A_t\}$.

Proof. For every $k = 1,\ldots,t$, we have $\wedge A_k \leq \vee c_{ij}$, so $A_k \cap c_{ij} \neq \phi$ if $c_{ij} \neq \phi$.
Let $A'_k = A_k - \{\mathbf{C}\}$, then $g_A(\mathbf{X}) \neq \bigvee_{r=1}^{k-1}(\wedge A_r) \vee (\wedge A'_k) \vee (\bigvee_{r=k+1}^{t} A_r)$ and
$g_A(\mathbf{X}) < \bigvee_{r=1}^{k-1}(\wedge A_r) \vee (\wedge A'_k) \vee (\bigvee_{r=k+1}^{t} A_r)$. If for every $c_{ij} \neq \phi$ we have
$A'_k \cap c_{ij} \neq \phi$, then $\wedge A'_k \leq \vee c_{ij}$ for every $c_{ij} \neq \phi$. This implies
$g_A(\mathbf{X}) \geq \bigvee_{r=1}^{k-1}(\wedge A_r) \vee (\wedge A'_k) \vee (\bigvee_{r=k+1}^{t} A_r)$ and
$g_A(\mathbf{X}) = \bigvee_{r=1}^{k-1}(\wedge A_r) \vee (\wedge A'_k) \vee (\bigvee_{r=k+1}^{t} A_r)$ which is a contradictinion. Hence there
exists $c_{i_0 j_0} \neq \phi$ such that $A'_k \cap c_{i_0 j_0} = \phi$ which implies A_k is a local reduction of
(U, A) for $\mathbf{X}$ For every $B \in RED(\Delta)$, we have $B \cap c_{ij} \neq \phi$ for every $c_{ij} \neq \phi$,
so we have $f_A(\mathbf{X}) \wedge (\wedge B) = \wedge(\vee c_{ij}) \wedge (\wedge B) = \wedge B$, this implies
$\wedge B \leq f_A(\mathbf{X}) = g_A(\mathbf{X})$. Suppose for every k we have $A_k - B \neq \phi$, then for
every k one can find $a_k \in A_k - B$. By rewriting $g_A(\mathbf{X}) = (\vee_{k=1}^{l} a_k) \wedge \Phi$, then
we have $\wedge B \leq \vee_{k=1}^{l} a_k$. So there is a_{k_0} such that $\wedge B \leq a_{k_0}$, this implies
$a_{k_0} \in B$ which is a contradiction. So $A_{k_0} \subseteq B$ for some k_0, since both B and
A_{k_0} are reductions, we have $B = A_{k_0}$. Hence $RED_\mathbf{X}(A) = \{A_1,\ldots,A_t\}$.

If $M_{\{X_k\}}(A) = (c_{ij}^k)$, then $c_{ij} = \bigcup_{k=1}^{N} c_{ij}^k$. Further more, if $x_i \in X_k$ and
$x_j \notin X_k$, then $c_{ij} = c_{ij}^k$, thus $M_\mathbf{X}(A)$ can be viewed as the composition of
$M_{\{X_k\}}(A)$, $k = 1,\ldots,N$.

Acknowledgement

This work was supported by the Hong Kong Research Grant Council under the Grants B-Q826 and B-Q943. The work of Dr. Chen was also supported by a grant of North China Electric Power University.

References

1. Z. Pawlak, Rough sets, International Journal of Computer and Information Sciences 11(1982)341-356
2. A. Skowron, C. Rauszer, The discernibility matrices and functions in information systems, Intelligent Decision support, Handbook of applications and advances of the rough sets theory, Ed.by R. Slowinski, 1992 Kluwer Academic Publishers

3. Wei-Zhi Wu, Mei Zhang, Huai-Zu Li and Ju-Sheng Mi, Knowledge reduction in random information systems via Dempster–Shafer theory of evidence, Information Sciences, In Press
4. Wang G. Y., Yu H. and Yang D.C., Decision table reduction based on conditional information entropy, Chinese J. Computers, 25(7)(2002)759-766
5. Malcolm Beynon, Reducts within the variable precision rough sets model: A further investigation, European Journal of Operational Research, 134(3)(2001) 592-605
6. Dominik lzak and Wojciech Ziarko, Attribute Reduction in the Bayesian Version of Variable Precision Rough Set Model, Electronic Notes in Theoretical Computer Science, 82(4)(2003)1-11
7. Ju-Sheng Mi, Wei-Zhi Wu and Wen-Xiu Zhang, Approaches to knowledge reduction based on variable precision rough set model, Information Sciences, 159(3-4)(2004)255-272
8. Marzena Kryszkiewicz, Rough set approach to incomplete information systems, Information Sciences, 112(1-4)(1998)39-49
9. Yee Leung and Deyu Li, Maximal consistent block technique for rule acquisition in incomplete information systems, Information Sciences, 153(2003)85-106
10. Roman W. Swiniarski and Andrzej Skowron, Rough set methods in feature selection and recognition, Pattern Recognition Letters, 24(6)(2003) 833-849
11. Zhang Wenxiu, Mi Jusheng and Wu Weizhi, Approaches to knowledge reductions in inconsistent systems, International Journal of Intelligent Systems, 18(2003)989-1000
12. Marzena Kryskiewicz, Comparative study of alternative types of knowledge reduction in inconsistent systems, International Journal of Intelligent Systems, 16(2001)105-120
13. Chen Degang, The part reduction in information systems, Rough Sets and Current Trends in Computing, LNAA3066, 477-482

Spectral Analysis of Protein Sequences

Tuan D. Pham

Bioinformatics Applications Research Centre
School of Information Technology,
James Cook University, Townsville,
QLD 4811, Australia
tuan.pham@jcu.edu.au

Abstract. Analysis of protein sequences can avoid many problems inherently existing in the study of nucleotide sequences given the knowledge that DNA sequences contain all the information for regulating protein expression. This paper presents a spectral approach for calculating the similarity of protein sequences, which can be useful for the inferences of protein functions. The proposed method is based on the mathematical concepts of linear predictive coding and cepstral distortion measure. We show that this spectral approach can reveal non-trivial results from an experimental study of a set of functionally related and functionally non-related protein sequences, and has advantages over some existing approaches.

1 Introduction

Genes have attracted significant attention from the community of computational biology and bioinformatics; however, it is the proteins which perform essential roles for controlling, effecting and modulating biochemical, cellular, and phenotypic functions. A novel protein function can be inferred from the known functions of homologous proteins and this type of prediction is based on the *similar sequence-similar structure-similar function* paradigm [1]. Protein sequence comparison is the most powerful tool for such inference and analysis [2]. Therefore, the development of effective methods for comparing protein sequences is one of the major tasks of biological research for gaining better understanding of the complexity of molecular machines.

It has been known that each conventional sequence comparsion method has its own advantage and disadvantage. For alignment-based similarity measures, the term *alignment* can be changed to *edit*, and similarly, *alignment score* be changed to *edit distance*. Moreover, some edits can change the original function of proteins. Hence, when there is an edit, some penalty should be given. The problem is that, in general, the lengths of biological sequences are quite different. For example, the length of human α hemoglobin and human basic FGF are 143 and 288 respectively. When the global pairwise alignment of these sequences are executed by using EMBOSS (http://www.ebi.ac.uk/emboss/align/), the gaps are about 70%. Therefore, it is clear that alignment-based similarity measures have some disadvantages. As a result, bioinformaticians have sought to find new methodologies for measuring similarity between protein sequences. One of promising methodologies for dealing with biological data is the signal-processing based approach [3, 4, 5, 6, 7]. It has been pointed out by Anastassiou [8] that if protein or DNA sequences can be mapped into one or more numerical sequences, then digital signal processing would be very useful for solving highly relevant problems in bioinformatics and computational biology.

Cosic [9] developed the resonant recognition model (RRM), which is based on the mapping of a protein sequence into a numerical sequence in which each amino acid can be assigned with a real constant called the electron-ion interaction potential (EIIP) value [10, 11] to analyze protein interaction using the discrete Fourier transform. Trad et al. [12] applied the wavelet transform for comparing protein sequences at different scales of the protein signals. This method transforms each protein sequence into a corresponding numerical sequence using the RRM. This numerical sequence is then normalized to have zero mean and unit deviation. Shorter sequences were zero-padded to have the same length of the longest sequence in order to enable the calculation of the cross-correlation coefficients. However, the zero-padding may cause error in defining peak frequencies, which leads to undesirable effect on the analysis of biological sequences [3]. Moreover, interpretation of similarities between two protein sequences in terms of multi-scales indicating contrasting results such as strong, weak, and no correlations which would be difficult for making decision.

In this paper, we first converted the character-based protein sequences into the corresponding numeral-based protein sequences using the EIIP values for twenty amino acids, and then applied the method of linear predictive coding and its cepstral distortion measure to identify the similarities between protein sequences. Experimental results of this study have shown that the LPC-based cepstral distortion measure could identify more related protein sequences than a wavelet-transform based method.

2 Linear Predictive Coding of EIIP-Based Protein

To proceed with the linear predictive coding (LPC) of protein sequences, we adopt the electron-ion interaction potential (EIIP) values for the twenty amino acids. The EIIP values [10, 11] for an amino acid can be determined by the general model of pseudopotentials [13]. Thus, each amino acid located at at any sequential position can be represented by a real EIIP constant, which is the

Table 1. EIIP values for 20 amino acids [12]

Amino Acid	Leu	Ile	Asn	Gly	Val	Glu	Pro	His	Lys	Ala
EIIP	0.0000	0.0000	0.0036	0.0050	0.0057	0.0058	0.0198	0.0242	0.0371	0.0373
Amino Acid	Tyr	Trp	Gln	Met	Ser	Cys	Thr	Phe	Arg	Asp
EIIP	0.0516	0.0548	0.0761	0.0823	0.0829	0.0829	0.0941	0.0946	0.0959	0.1263

average energy state of all valence electrons in a particular amino acid. Table 1 shows the EIIP values for 20 amino acids.

Let $s(n)$, $n = 1, 2, \ldots, N$ be a protein sequence of length N whose elements are represented by the EIIP values for the corresponding amino acids. The estimated EIIP value at position n, denoted by $\hat{s}(n)$, can be calculated as a linear combination of the past p EIIP-valued samples. This linear prediction can be expressed as

$$\hat{s}(n) = \sum_{k=1}^{p} a_k \, s(n-k) \tag{1}$$

where the terms $\{a_k\}$ are called the linear prediction coefficients.

The prediction error $e(n)$ between the observed EIIP-valued sample $s(n)$ and the predicted EIIP value $\hat{s}(n)$ can be defined as

$$e(n) = s(n) - \hat{s}(n) = s(n) - \sum_{k=1}^{p} a_k \, s(n-k) \tag{2}$$

The prediction coefficients $\{a_k\}$ can be optimally determined by minimizing the sum of squared errors

$$E = \sum_{n=1}^{N} e^2(n) = \sum_{n=1}^{N} \left[s(n) - \sum_{k=1}^{p} a_k \, s(n-k) \right]^2 \tag{3}$$

To solve (3) for the prediction coefficients, we differentiate E with respect to eack a_k and equate the result to zero:

$$\frac{\partial E}{\partial a_k} = 0, \; k = 1, \ldots, p \tag{4}$$

The result is a set of p linear equations

$$\sum_{k=1}^{p} a_k \, r(m-k) = r(m), \; m = 1, \ldots, p \tag{5}$$

where $r(m)$ is the autocorrelation of $s(n)$, that is

$$r(m) = \sum_{n=1}^{N} s(n) \, s(n+m) \tag{6}$$

Equation (5) can be expressed in matrix form as

$$\mathbf{R}\,\mathbf{a} = \mathbf{r} \tag{7}$$

where $\mathbf{R}$ is a $p \times p$ autocorrelation matrix, $\mathbf{r}$ is a $p \times 1$ autocorrelation vector, and $\mathbf{a}$ is a $p \times 1$ vector of prediction coefficients. Thus

$$\mathbf{a} = \mathbf{R}^{-1}\,\mathbf{r} \tag{8}$$

where $\mathbf{R}^{-1}$ is the inverse of $\mathbf{R}$.

3 LPC-Based Cepstral Distortion Measure

Methods for measuring similarity or dissimilarity between two vectors or sequences is one of the most important algorithms in the field of pattern comparison/recognition. The calculation of vector similarity is based on various developments of distance and distortion measures. Before proceeding to the mathematical description of a distortion measure, we wish to point out the difference between distance and distortion functions, where the latter is more restricted in mathematical sense.

Let **x**, **y**, and **z** be the vectors defined on a vector space V. A metric or distance d on V is defined as a real-valued function on the Cartesian product $V \times V$ if it has the following properties:

1. Positive definiteness: $0 \leq d(\mathbf{x}, \mathbf{y}) < \infty$, $\mathbf{x}, \mathbf{y} \in V$ and $d(\mathbf{x}, \mathbf{y}) = 0$ iff $\mathbf{x} = \mathbf{y}$;
2. Symmetry: $d(\mathbf{x}, \mathbf{y}) = d(\mathbf{y}, \mathbf{x})$ for $\mathbf{x}, \mathbf{y} \in V$;
3. Triangle inequality: $d(\mathbf{x}, \mathbf{z}) \leq d(\mathbf{x}, \mathbf{y}) + d(\mathbf{y}, \mathbf{z})$ for $\mathbf{x}, \mathbf{y}, \mathbf{z} \in V$.

If a measure of dissimilarity satisfies only the property of positive definiteness, it is referred to as a distortion measure which is considered very common for the vectorized representations of signal spectra [14] In this sense, what we will describe next is the mathematical measure of distortion which relaxes the properties of symmetry and triangle inequality. From now on, the term d will be used to denote a distortion measure. There are several measures of distortion developed for speech recognition [15] such as the Itakura-Saito distortion, the likelihood-ratio distortion, the log-likelihood-ratio distortion, and the LPC cepstral distortion measure. However, the LPC cepstral distortion is the most widely used distortion measure for speech recognition.

Let $S(\omega)$ be the power spectrum (magnitude-squared Fourier tranform) of a signal. The complex cepstrum of the signal is defined as the Fourier transform of the log of the signal spectrum:

$$\log S(\omega) = \sum_{n=-\infty}^{\infty} c_n e^{-jn\omega} \quad (9)$$

where $c_n = -c_n$ are real and referred to as the cepstral coefficients.

Consider $S(\omega)$ and $S'(\omega)$ to be the power spectra of the two (protein) signals and apply the Parseval's theorem [16], the L_2-norm cepstral distance between $S(\omega)$ and $S'(\omega)$ can be related to the root-mean-square log spectral distance as [14]

$$d_2^2 = \int_{-\pi}^{\pi} |\log S(\omega) - \log S'(\omega)|^2 \frac{d\omega}{2\pi}$$
$$= \sum_{n=-\infty}^{\infty} (c_n - c'_n)^2 \quad (10)$$

where c_n and c'_n are the cepstral coefficients of $S(\omega)$ and $S'(\omega)$ respectively.

Since the cepstrum is a decaying sequence, the infinite number of terms in (10) can be truncated to some finite number $L \geq p$, that is

$$d^2(L) = \sum_{m=1}^{L} (c_m - c'_m) \tag{11}$$

The cepstral coefficients can be directly derived from the LPC parameters using the following recursive procedure.

$$c_0 = \ln(G) \tag{12}$$

$$c_m = a_m + \sum_{k=1}^{m-1} \left(\frac{k}{m}\right) c_k a_{m-k}, \ 1 \leq m \leq p \tag{13}$$

$$c_m = \sum_{k=1}^{m-1} \left(\frac{k}{m}\right) c_k a_{m-k}, \ m > p \tag{14}$$

where G is the LPC gain, whose squared term is given as [17]

$$G^2 = r(0) - \sum_{k=1}^{p} a_k r(k) \tag{15}$$

4 Protein Sequences

We used the same data set that was studied by Trad et al. [12]. The data set consists of 8 closely-related, distantly-related, and unrelated sequences. These protein sequences are: human hemoglobin α-chain (HAHU), horse hemoglobin α-chain (HAHO), human hemoglobin β-chain growth factor (HBHU), pig cytochrome c (CCPG), lupine leghemoglobin (LEGH), rat lysozome (LZRT), sperm whale myoglobin (MWHP), and basic human FGF (FGFBH). Six functional groups of proteins involve in this analysis are described as follows.

Hemoglobin is the iron-containing oxygen-transport metalloprotein in the red cells of the blood in mammals and other animals. It transports oxygen to tissues. It is one of the most well-known globin proteins. From the structural point of view, hemoglobin is a tetrameric molecule whose quaternary structure is comprised of two α and two β peptide chains. The subunits are both similar in structure and size. Each subunit of hemoglobin contains one heme, therefore each hemoglobin can bind four oxygens. The name hemoglobin is the concatenation of heme and globin, because oxygen-binding proteins are called as a globin protein and each subunit of hemoglobin has one heme. Although the sequences of α hemoglobin and β hemoglobin are not completely identical, they have exactly the same biological function [18].

Myoglobin is a single-chain molecule, which contains a heme group. It is also an oxygen-carrying protein like hemoglobin. The main role of this molecule is to carry oxygen to muscle tissues. The myoglobin molecule is built up of eight helices, which compose a box-like structure with a hydrophobic pocket. The heme group being responsible for oxygen binding is fixed in this pocket only by weak bonding [12]. Myoglobin also belongs to globin family, and it has the highest oxygen affinity compared with other globin proteins, such as hemoglobin [19].

Leghemoglobin is an iron-containing, hemoglobin-like oxygen binding red pigment(s) produced in root nodules during the symbiotic association between bradyrhizobium or rhizobium and legumes. The pigment resembles but is not identical to mammalian hemoglobin. The red pigment has a molecular weight being approximately a quarter of hemoglobin and acts as an oxido-reduction catalyst in symbiotic nitrogen fixation.

Cytochrome c is another heme-containing protein, which is soluble protein. Unlike other cytochromes, it transfers electrons from the QH2-cytochrome c reductase complex to the cytochrome c oxidase complex [12]. It is capable of undergoing oxidation and reduction, but does not bind oxygen. Therefore it is considered to be different from globin family protein.

Lysozyme is an enzyme and referred to as the 'body's own antibiotic'. It is abundantly present in a number of secretions such as tears. This protein is present in cytoplasmic granules of the polymorphonuclear neutrophils and released to the mucosal secretions. Basically, this enzyme does not share any biological function with globin proteins.

Fibroblast growth factors (FGFs) are pleiotropic mitogenic activators. Acidic FGF and basic FGF bind negatively charged heparin-like molecules, as dose VEGF. FGFs play multiple roles as embryonic inducers, endothelial mitogens, and stimulators of protease activity. FGFs are not functionally related to the globin family [19].

HAHU, HAHO, HBHU, LEGH, and MWHP, which are of the globin-like superfamily, are referred to as heme containing protein. These globin proteins perform the oxygen binding function. It is also noted that cytochrome c has the heme group, however it does not hold oxygen. Thus it is the major biological difference between cytochrome c and globin-like proteins. It is known that lysozyme and hemoglobin do not share any biological function [12].

As for closely related sequences, HAHU and HAHO are referred to as orthologous sequences [20]. HAHU and HBHU are paralogous sequences, which have been known to be related through gene duplication events.

As for distantly related sequences, although MWHP and LEGH have only 15% identical residues, these sequences belong to the same family, and the same class as they share very similar biological function and have similar structure [21]. The sequence similarity of myoglobin and hemoglobin is in the twilight zone. Those sequences have about 24% of identical residues. Leghemoglobin and hemoglobin are also distantly related protein sequences which have 14 $\sim$ 20% sequence identity. Therefore, they are also difficult to detect using existing protein sequence comparison methods, even though they are in the same superfamily and family.

FGFBH and LZRT belong to different super families, and their biological functions are far from globin-like proteins. Thus, the similarity of those sequences should be low when being compared with the globin-like proteins.

5 Experiment 1

Because the lengths of the eight protein signals range from 104 to 288 amino acids, which are significantly shorter than speech signals, we chose $p=3$ and $L = 6$ for the LPC analysis and LPC-based cepstrum distortion measure respectively. To evaluate the performance of the present method, we used the criteria of *sensitivity* and *selectivity* where HAHU is the reference sequence. Sensitivity is expressed by the number of HAHU-related sequences found among the first closest 4 library sequences; whereas selectivity is expressed in terms of the number of HAHU-related sequences of which distances are closer to HAHU than others and are not truncated by the first HAHU-unrelated sequence. As a result, both sensitivity and selectivity criteria gave 3 out of 4 correct sequences (HAHO, HBHU, and MWHP) whereas the falsely accepted sequence is LZRT. However, LEGH is the fifth closest sequence to HAHU. Meanwhile, both *sensitivity* and *selectivity* given by an alignment-based method using EMBOSS (http://www.ebi.ac.uk/emboss/align/) resulted 2 out of 4 correct sequences (HAHO, and HBHU), where the falsely accepted sequences are LZRT, and CCPG.

Based on the fact that lysozyme and hemoglobin do not share any biological function, we therefore chose the lowest value, which is 0.005, of the distortion measures between LZRT and (HAHU, HAHO, HBHU, LEGH, MWHP) to establish the threshold for identifying similar sequences. Using this threshold, we could safely infer that (HAHO, HBHU, MWHP) are similar to HAHU; (HAHU, HBHU, MWHP) being similar to HAHO; (HAHU, HAHO, MWHP) being similar to HBHU; and (HAHU, HAHO, HBHU) being similar to MWHP. We could also confirm the unrelatedness between FGFBH and LZRT because the distortion measure (0.079) between these two sequences is relatively much larger than the threshold value. Moreover, LEGH was found to be closest to MWHP, whose distortion measure is 0.007 being slightly larger than the threshold value

Table 2. Similarity comparison using LPC-based distortion measure

	HAHU	HAHO	HBHU	CCPG	LEGH	LZRT	MWHP	FGFBH
HAHU	0.000	0.003	0.001	0.058	0.015	0.005	0.002	0.051
HAHO		0.000	0.004	0.075	0.017	0.010	0.004	0.055
HBHU			0.000	0.049	0.013	0.008	0.003	0.048
CCPG				0.000	0.037	0.086	0.056	0.038
LEGH					0.000	0.033	0.007	0.011
LZRT						0.000	0.010	0.079
MWHP							0.000	0.035
FGFBH								0.000

Table 3. Similarity comparison using sequence-scale cross-correlation [12]

	HAHU	HAHO	HBHU	CCPG	LEGH	LZRT	MWHP	FGFBH
HAHU	5S	5S	1S1W3N	1W4N	2W3N	5N	2W3N	5N
HAHO		5S	1S1W3N	1W4N	2W3N	5N	2W3N	5N
HBHU			5S	1W4N	2W3N	5N	2W3N	5N
CCPG				5S	1W4N	1W4N	5N	5N
LEGH					5S	1W4N	1W4N	2W3N
LZRT						5S	5N	1W4N
MWHP							5S	1W4N
FGFBH								5S

of 0.005. It has been mentioned earlier that the sequence similarity of LEGH and MWHP is far below the twilight zone (15% identity), but they both have similar secondary and tertiary structures and bind oxygen [21]. Table 2 shows the symmetrical distortion measures between the eight protein sequences.

Table 3 shows the symmetrical similarity comparisons between the same eight protein sequences studied by Trad *et al.* [12], in which the pairwise comparison was analyzed at five scales using the discrete wavelet transform. In Table 3, the numerals from 1 to 5 indicate the number of scales; whereas the symbols S, W, and N denote strong correlation, weak correlation, and no correlation respectively. This method could confirm only the similarity between HAHU and HAHO, while showing only the first out of five scales of similarity between (HAHU, HBHU) and (HAHO, HBHU).

6 Experiment 2

We used 41 protein sequences (HAHU: query sequence, 7 pre-experimented sequences, and 33 additional sequences) to further test the proposed spectral method with regard to *sensitivity* and *selectivity*. The structural classification of query sequence (HAHU) and other 40 is based on SCOP (Structural Classification of Proteins), available at http://scop.mrclmb.com.ac.uk/scop, which classifies proteins by class, fold, superfamily, and family.

The query sequence HAHU (α hemoglobin) belongs to all α proteins class, globin-like fold, globin-like superclass, and globins family. Among the 40 sequences, 14 sequences belong to the same class, fold, superfamily and family as the query sequence (HAHU). They all belong to the globins family. The remainders belong to 11 different protein families. Therefore, the criterion of this experiment was that the distances between query sequence (HAHU) and 14 globins family proteins should be closer than any other proteins of different groups.

Sensitivity is defined as the top 14 sequences being most similar to the query sequence. The local alignment-based methods detected 5 globin proteins among 14 globins proteins. On the other hand, our proposed method, LPC cepstrum based similarity measure, detected 10 globin proteins out of 14. Table 4 presents the sensitivity obtained by the alignment-based method and our pro-

Table 4. Sensitivity and selectivity by local alignment and cepstral-distortion

	Local alignment	Cepstral distortion
Sensitivity	5/14	10/14
Selectivity	3/14	4/14

posed method. The LPC cepstral based method shows better performance than the alignment method.

Selectivity is expressed in terms of the number of query-related sequences of which distances are closer to the query sequence (HAHU) than others and are not truncated by the first HAHU-unrelated sequence. The local alignment-based method obtained 3 out of 14 related sequences. For the local alignment method, the identity of protein sequence number 20 (1HFY), which belong to α and β proteins class, lysozyme-like fold and superfamily, and c-type lysozyme family, is 83.3%. However, this protein is from a totally different class, fold, superfamily and family. The LPC cepstral based method obtained 4 out of 14 related sequences. Our proposed method shows a slightly better performance than the local alignment method. Table 4 also shows the comparison in terms of the selectivity between the LPC cepstral distortion measure and the alignment-based method.

7 Concluding Remarks

We have introduced the LPC cepstral distortion measure for computing the similarity of protein sequences. The model is both physically reasonable and mathematically tractable. The experimental results have shown the effectiveness of the proposed approach.

Acknowledgement. Byung-Sub Shim carried out the computer implementation, training, and testing of the proposed method under the supervision of the author.

References

1. Nagl, S.B.: Function prediction from protein sequence, in *Bioinformatics: Genes, Proteins & Computers*, eds. C.A. Orengo, D.T. Jones, and J.M. Thornton. BIOS Scientific Publishers, Oxford, UK, 2003.
2. Bishop, M., and Rawlings, C.: *Nucleic Acid and Protein Sequence Analysis – A Practical Approach*. Oxford, IRL Press, 1987.
3. Veljkovic, V., Cosic, I., Dimitrijevic, B., and Lalovic, D.: Is it possible to analyze DNA and protein sequences by the methods of digital signal processing? *IEEE Trans. Biomed. Eng.*, **32** (1985) 337-341.
4. Anatassiou, D.: Frequency-domain analysis of biomolecular sequences, *Bioinformatics*, **16** (2000) 1073-1082.
5. Lio, P.: Wavelets in bioinformatics and computational biology: state of art and perspectives, *Bioinformatics*, **19** (2003) 2-9.

6. Li, L., Jin, R., Kok, P.L., and Wan, W.: Pseudo-periodic partitions of biological sequences, *Bioinformatics*, **20** (2004) 295-306.
7. del Carpio-Munoz, C.A., Carbajal, J.C.: Folding pattern recognition in proteins using spectral analysis methods, *Genome Informatics*, **13** (2001) 163-172.
8. Anatassiou, D.: Genomic signal processing, *IEEE Signal Processing Magazine*, **18** (2001) 8-20.
9. Cosic, I.: Macromolecular bioactivity: Is it resonant interaction between macromolecules? – theory and applications, *IEEE trans. Biomedical Engineering*, **41** (1994) 1101-1114.
10. Veljkovic, V., and Slavic, I.: General model of pseudopotentials, *Physical Review Lett.*, **29** (1972) 105-108.
11. Lazovic, J.: Selection of amino acid parameters for Fourier transform-based analysis of proteins, *CABIOS*, **12** (1996) 553-562.
12. de Trad, C.H., Fang, Q., and Cosic, I.: Protein sequence comparison based on the wavelet transform approach, *Protein Engineering*, **15** (2002) 193-203.
13. Pirogova, E., Simon, G.P., and Cosic, I.: Investigation of the applicability of dielectic relaxation properties of amino acid solutions within the resonant recognition model, *IEEE Trans. Nanobioscience*, **2** (2003) 63-69.
14. Rabiner, L., and Juang, B.H.: *Fundamentals of Speech Recognition*. New Jersey, Prentice Hall, 1993.
15. Nocerino, N., Soong, F.K., Rabiner, L.R., and Klatt, D.H.: Comparative study of several distortion measures for speech recognition, *IEEE Proc. Int. Conf. Acoustics, Speech, and Signal Processing*, **11.4.1** (1985) 387-390.
16. O'Shaughnessy, D.: *Speech Communication – Human and Machine*. Reading, Massachusetts, Addison-Wesley, 1987.
17. Ingle, V.K., and Proakis, J.G.: *Digital Signal Processing Using Matlab V.4*. Boston, PWS Publishing, 1997.
18. Lehninger, A.L., Nelson, D.L., and Cox, M.M.: Principles of Biochemistry, Worth Publishing, New York, 1993.
19. Epstein, R.J.: *Human Molecular Biology: An Introduction to the Molecular Basis of Health and Disease*. Cambridge, Cambridge University Press, 2003.
20. Mount, D.W.: *Bioinformatics - Sequence and Genome Analysis*. New York, Cold Spring Harbor Laboratory Press, 2nd edition, 2004.
21. Doolittle, R.: Similar amino acid sequences: Chance or common ancestry? *Science*, **214** (1981) 149-159.

Volatility Patterns of Industrial Stock Price Indices in the Chinese Stock Market

Lan-Jun Lao

Department of Finance, School of Management, Fudan University,
Shanghai, 200433, China
lao@fudan.edu.cn

Abstract. This paper will use real data from the Shenzhen Stock Exchange to investigate the ranking stability of short run volatilities of industrial stock price indices. Four well-constructed volatility measures are used to estimate the industrial short run volatilities, with total volatilities being decomposed into industry-unique and market-related components. The method of Kendall's coefficient of concordance is utilized to test whether the cross-sectional volatility ranking of industrial indices remains stable over time. Empirical results show that in the Chinese stock market, the ranking of total volatilities of industrial indices is consistent from period to period, and that the ranking of market-related volatilities is not stable while the ranking of industry-unique parts is highly and significantly consistent. Tests inside manufacturing show there is a significant volatility structure of sub-industries in manufacturing. This sort of inter-industry volatility pattern provides useful information for a deeper understanding of the Chinese stock market and for constructing investment strategies in the Chinese market.

1 Introduction

The analysis of financial market volatilities plays an important role in the field of financial engineering, supplying useful information for the construction of investment strategies and portfolio management. Some topics such as the influence of industry factors on variations of stock prices or returns, the dynamic characteristic of stock price indices' volatilities, and volatility patterns among different stocks or industries etc., are of lasting interest to both academic researchers and professional investment managers in the real financial market.

Numerous industry-related empirical studies (e.g., [1], [2], [3], [4] and [5]) suggest that, compared with other factors, e.g. factors of country and exchange rate, the industry factor has a more important influence on the volatilities of stocks' prices and returns, over both the long term and the short term. Schwartz and Altman [6] investigated whether or not an industry can be classified according to its stock price volatility, and if inter-industry volatility differentials remain constant over time. Their empirical results show that the stability of volatility ranking is of high significance by non-parametric statistical tests.

There are also many studies on the volatility characteristics of the Chinese stock market. For example, Song and Jiang [7] utilized three typical models to estimate the volatility in the Chinese stock market. They indicated that the total risk in China's stock market is similar to that in mature markets since 1998, but systematic risk is larger all along and relative stability is less in the Chinese stock market than in mature markets. They also discussed the inter-firm volatility patterns to some extent by calculating the Spearman correlation coefficients. According to the available literature, there are very few empirical research works on the inter-industry volatility patterns in the Chinese stock market. Therefore, this becomes the topic of this paper.

This paper will focus on the short run volatility patterns of industry stock price indices, which are of particular interest for the investors who have relatively short time horizons. We mainly investigate whether the industries' volatility ranking during different periods is significantly consistent in the statistical sense. A cross-sectional volatility ranking of different industrial stock price indices might remain stable over time even when for any individual industry, the volatility is not constant enough, and the pattern of volatility change is unstable.

In this paper, four well-defined short run volatility measures are employed to estimate the total, the industry-unique and the market-related volatilities of stock price indices of 13 industries and 9 sub-industries of manufacturing during different periods. Kendall's coefficients of concordance and Chi-square tests are adopted in the empirical study with real financial data from the Shenzhen Stock Exchange to examine the stability of inter-industry volatility ranking.

2 Volatility Measures

It is important to find suitable measures of short run volatility of prices. Four volatility measures developed by [6] will be used in this paper to estimate the volatility of the industrial price indices.

Suppose there are m different industry price indices in a stock market. They are labeled as P_{it}, $i = 1, \cdots, m$, $t = 1, \cdots, n$, where t stands for discrete time. t can be used to represent day, week, month etc., depending on the context. In this paper, daily closing data of industry price indices will be used. Thus P_{it} is the ith industry price index at the end of tth day.

2.1 Ratio of Variation Coefficients

The first volatility measure is based on the traditional risk measure of standard deviation. Making an adjustment for the level of an industry's price index, and for general market turbulence, we take the following volatile statistic:

$$V_{Ci} = \frac{\sigma_i / \overline{P_i}}{\sigma_I / \overline{P_I}} \tag{1}$$

as a short run volatility measure of an industrial price index, where σ_i and σ_I are, respectively, the standard deviations of the ith industry's price index and of the overall market index; $\overline{P_i}$ and $\overline{P_I}$ are average values for the industry and market indices, respectively. V_C is actually the ratio of the coefficient of variation computed for the industry to the associated coefficient of variation for the market.

2.2 Market Adjusted Volatility and Volatility Decomposition

To obtain the market adjusted volatility, we first regress an industry's price index on time using the equations:

$$\ln(P_{it}) = a_i + b_i t + u_{it} \qquad (2)$$

$$\ln(P_{It}) = a_I + b_I t + u_{It} \qquad (3)$$

where P_{it}, $i = 1, \cdots, m$, $t = 1, \cdots, n$, stands for the ith industry's index at the end of the tth day; P_{It} for the market index at the end of the tth day; u_{it} and u_{It} are error terms. The left terms in equations (2) and (3) are the natural logarithms of price indices, since the price indices are usually expected to be log-normally distributed. We then calculate the residuals from the above regressions:

$$R_{it} = \ln(\frac{P_{it}}{\hat{P}_{it}}) \qquad (4)$$

$$R_{It} = \ln(\frac{P_{It}}{\hat{P}_{It}}) \qquad (5)$$

where $\hat{P}$ denotes the estimated value of the corresponding index. The set of residuals, R_{it}, represents short run index movements which are not explained by long-term growth.

The residual variance of an industry index yields one trend-adjusted volatility measure, denoted by V_T as follows:

$$V_{Ti} = \sigma^2_{R_{it}} \qquad (6)$$

which reflects the total variability of the residuals, i.e. the short run volatility.

Now decompose the volatility V_T into industry unique and market-related components. Each set of residuals for the m industries is regressed on the set of residuals computed for the market index as follows:

$$R_{it} = \alpha_i + \beta_i R_{It} + \varepsilon_{it} \qquad (7)$$

where ε_{it} is the error term; t stands for time periods, i for industries, and I for the market index. Within each regression equation, t varies from the first to the last day in a given time span. Denote the sum of error squares by:

$$V_{Ui} = \sum_{t=1}^{n}(R_{it} - \hat{R}_{it})^2 \qquad (8)$$

which is not explained by change in the independent variable (R_{It}, the residual of the market index) and naturally taken as the industry-unique component of V_T. Thus the total residual volatility minus the market unrelated (industry unique) component, i.e.

$$V_{Mi} = V_{Ti} - V_{Ui} \qquad (9)$$

can be explained as the market-related volatility of an industry index. Further it can be shown that V_{Mi} is equal to the total residual volatility of the aggregate market index, V_{TI}, times the square of the slope parameter, β_i, of the regression equation (7), i.e.

$$V_{Mi} = \beta_i^2 V_{TI} \qquad (10)$$

To focus on the effect of general market volatility upon an industry price index, we examine the elasticity component of V_M. The market-related volatility measure is finally taken as the form of:

$$V_{\beta i} = \beta_i^2 \qquad (11)$$

In our empirical researches, the four above-defined volatility measures, $V_{Ci}, V_{Ti}, V_{Ui}, V_{Mi}$, $i = 1, \cdots, m$, will be used with daily data of industry price indices from the Shenzhen Stock Exchange.

3 Empirical Researches

In this section, we mainly test the ranking stability of short run volatilities of industrial stock price indices using real data from the Shenzhen Stock Exchange.

3.1 Industries and Data

This paper focuses on the volatility of prices, rather than on the volatility of return, using real data of 13 industrial stock price indices according to the classification in

Table 1. Industrial classification

Codes	Industries
A	Farming, foresting, herding and fishing
B	Fossicking
C	Manufacturing
D	Water, electricity, coal and gas
E	Construction
F	Transport and storage
G	Information technology
H	Wholesale and retail
I	Finance and insurance
J	Real estate
K	Social service
L	Spread and culture
M	Synthesis

Table 2. Sub-industries of manufacturing

Codes	Sub-industries
C0	Food, drink
C1	Weave, clothing
C2	Wood, furniture
C3	Paper making, print
C4	Oil, chemical and plastic
C5	Electronics
C6	Metal, nonmetal
C7	Machine, equipment
C8	Medicine, biology

the Shenzhen Stock Exchange. The 13 industries are listed in Table 1. The sub-industries of manufacturing will also be investigated separately since, in the Chinese stock market, more than half the listed companies belong to the manufacturing industry. Table 2 gives the 9 sub-industries of manufacturing industry. Daily closing observations are utilized for each industry stock price index. The whole time span is from July 2001 to December 2004, being divided into 14 periods of quarters.

3.2 Tests of the Stability of Volatility Ranking

The primary emphasis of this paper is on evaluating the stability of inter-industry volatility ranking. We separate the whole time span into K periods and rank the volatilities of the m industries' price indices every period. If we only wished to compare one period's ranking with another we would simply compute the Spearman's rank correlation coefficient as done by Song and Jiang [7]. However, in this paper we consider several rankings (K periods) of m objects (volatilities of m industries or sub-industries). The null hypothesis is that the K periodical rankings of m industries or sub-industries are unrelated to (independent of) each other. If we accept the null hypothesis, the volatility statistics are of no value for inter-industry comparisons. This also means that the rank of the industries' or sub-industries' price indices is not predictable in the sense of statistics.

To investigate the multiple rank correlations, we compute Kendall's coefficient of concordance (W); the significance of W is assessed by a chi-square test.

The method of Kendall's coefficient of concordance is used to test the divergence of actual rankings from perfect agreement. The statistic bears a linear relation to the average of all simple rank correlation coefficients. To compute Kendall's coefficient of concordance, we sum the K ranks for each industry:

$$S_i = \sum_{k=1}^{K} S_{ik}, \quad i=1,\cdots,m \tag{12}$$

where S_{ik} is the rank of the ith industry in the kth period. Kendall's coefficient of concordance is then defined by:

$$W = \frac{12S}{K^2(m^3 - m)} \tag{13}$$

where

$$S = \sum_{i=1}^{m}(S_i - \bar{S})^2 \tag{14}$$

$$\bar{S} = \frac{\sum_{i=1}^{m} S_i}{m} = \frac{K(m+1)}{2} \tag{15}$$

Empirically, we may test the significance of a W value when $m > 7$ by the following statistic:

$$\chi^2 = \frac{12S}{Km(m+1)} = K(m-1)W \tag{16}$$

which approximately follows the chi-squared distribution with $n-1$ degrees of freedom, $\chi^2(n-1)$, under the null hypothesis.

The resulting W, chi-square values and their P-values of four volatility measures, V_C, V_T, V_U and V_β, are listed in Table 3 and Table 4 for 13 industries and 9 sub-industries of manufacturing respectively.

Table 3. Tests of Kendall's coefficient of concordance for 13 industries

Volatility measures	V_C	V_T	V_U	V_β
W	0.2139	0.1921	0.5563	0.0691
$\chi^2(12)$	35.9435	32.2700	93.4662	11.6044
P-value of $\chi^2(12)$	0.0003	0.0013	<0.0001	0.4780

Table 4. Tests of Kendall's coefficient of concordance for 9 sub-industries

Volatility measures	V_C	V_T	V_U	V_β
W	0.4485	0.3917	0.4437	0.2187
$\chi^2(8)$	50.2286	43.8667	49.6952	24.4952
P-value of $\chi^2(8)$	<0.0001	<0.0001	<0.0001	0.0019

For the 13 main industries, the empirical results show that the W tests relating to V_C, V_T and V_U are highly statistically significant at the 0.0015 level. Therefore, the null hypothesis is rejected, which denotes that the rankings are not independent, but remain stable over time. This ranking stability implies that the industrial volatilities are predictable with respect to the measures V_C, V_T and V_U, and that the industry-unique volatilities dominate the whole inter-industry volatility patterns. This result coincides with the result of Schwartz and Altman [6], who used real weekly data from the New York Stock Exchange and divided the whole time span into semi-annual periods. However, being different to their work, the test on V_β in this paper shows an unstable ranking relation among industries over time, which can be explained as the Chinese stock market having less systematic stability than mature stock markets. At this point, the result of this paper is consistent with Song and Jiang's discovery to some extent although their research was done from other aspects using the historical data of individual stock prices.

For the 9 manufacturing sub-industries, it is shown that the rankings of all the four volatility measures are statistically stable over periods at the significant level of 0.002. Thereinto, the P-values of $\chi^2(8)$ of measures V_C, V_T and V_U are very small, less than 0.0001, which means that the ranking of these three measures are remarkably stable over time. This gives strong reason for predicting the rankings of total risks and unique risks of sub-industries of manufacturing based on the historical ranking relations, and means that there is a significant volatility pattern inside the manufacturing industry.

3.3 Volatility Classification

At the end of this paper's empirical research work, the classifications of industries and sub-industries of manufacturing based on the stability of volatility rankings are

Table 5. Volatility categories of 13 industries

Industries	V_C	V_T	V_U
A	LH	LH	LL
B	LH	LH	H
C	L	L	L
D	LL	LL	LL
E	H	H	LH
F	L	LL	L
G	LH	LH	LH
H	LL	LL	L
I	LH	LH	H
J	LH	LH	LH
K	LL	LL	LL
L	H	H	H
M	LL	LL	LL

given in Table 5 and Table 6 respectively for the reference of investment managers. To get the classifications, the ranks of individual industries and manufacturing sub-industries are examined and, for the 13 main industries, each industry is assigned to the High(H, $\bar{S}_i \leq 5$), Less High(LH, $5 < \bar{S}_i \leq 7$), Less Low(LL, $7 < \bar{S}_i \leq 9$) and Low(L, $\bar{S}_i > 9$) volatility categories; for the 9 sub-industries of manufacturing, High(H, $\bar{S}_i \leq 3$), Middle(M, $3 < \bar{S}_i \leq 5.5$) and Low(L, $\bar{S}_i > 5.5$), according to its average rank of all the 14 periods, $\bar{S}_i = \frac{1}{14}\sum_{k=1}^{14} S_{ik}, i = 1, \cdots, 13$. It is reasonable to classify all the industries or sub-industries in this way, since the above-mentioned results show the consistence of volatility rankings.

Table 6. Volatility categories of 9 sub-industries of manufacturing

Sub-indus.	C0	C1	C2	C3	C4	C5	C6	C7	C8
V_C	L	L	H	L	M	M	M	L	M
V_T	L	L	H	L	M	M	M	L	M
V_U	M	L	H	M	L	M	L	L	M
V_β	L	L	M	L	M	M	M	M	M

4 Conclusion

In this paper, the empirical research work using real data from the Shenzhen Stock Exchange shows that in the Chinese stock market, the rankings of total volatilities and the industry-unique volatilities of industrial stock price indices are consistent from period to period. The evidence that some industries or sub-industries of manufacturing are consistently more volatile than others suggests that grouping firms by industry or sub-industry would be useful for analytical purposes. Further, from the volatility decomposition, it is indicated that the ranking of market-related volatilities is not stable for the 13 main industries while the ranking of industry-unique parts is highly and significantly consistent, which implies the dominance of industry-unique risk across the industrial variations and less systematic stability in the Chinese stock market than in mature stock markets. The investigation of the manufacturing industry suggests there is a significant volatility structure of the 9 sub-industries. Hopefully, the discussion of inter-industry and inter-sub-industry volatility patterns in this paper could provide useful information for a better understanding of the Chinese stock market and for constructing sound investment strategies for managing portfolios in that market.

Acknowledgement

This paper is financially supported by National Natural Science Foundation of China (NSFC, No. 70371010).

References

1. Cavaglia S., Brightman, C., Aked M.: The increasing importance of industry factors. Financial Analysts Journal, Sep./Oct. (2000) 41–54
2. van Dijk, R., Keijzer, T.: Region, Sector and Style Selection in Global Equity Markets. Journal of Asset Management 5 (2004) 293–307
3. Heston, S. L., Rouwenhorst, K. G.: Does Industrial Structure Explain the Benefits of International Diversification? Journal of Financial Economics 36 (1994) 3–27
4. Moskowitz, T. J., Grinblatt, M.: Do industries explain momentum? Journal of Finance 4 (1999) 1249–1290
5. Roll, R.: Industrial Structure and the Comparative Behavior of International Stock Market Indices. Journal of Finance 47 (1992) 3–42
6. Schwartz, R. A., Altman, E. I.: Volatility Behavior of Industrial Stock Price Indices. Journal of Finance 4 (1973) 957–971
7. Song F. M., Jiang J.: Empirical study on volatility characteristic of Chinese stock market. Journal of Financial Research 4 (2003) 13-22

Data Migration in RAID Based on Stripe Unit Heat

Yan Liu, Chang-Sheng Xie, Huai-yang Li, and Zhen Zhao

Key laboratory of Data Storage System, School of Computer Science and Technology,
Huazhong University of Science and Technology, Wuhan 430074, China
to-liuyan@sohu.com, csxie@263.net, lhycly@263.com,
zhaozhen@163.net

Abstract. Traditional RAID has the characteristics that location of stripe unit in each disk is stochastic and static, and that the outer zone of the disk has higher data transfer rate as compared to the inner one. Facing this situation, to exploit RAID I/O performance fully, this paper proposes a new algorithm PMSH (Placement and Migration based on Stripe unit Heat) for RAID stripe unit data to be placed optically and migrated dynamically. Based on the heat of RAID stripe unit, PMSH keeps migrating the frequently accessed stripe unit to the disk zone with higher data transfer rate to optimize the location of data in RAID disks and make the data distribution adapt to the evolution of file access pattern dynamically as well. Simulation results demonstrate significant RAID I/O performance improvement using PMSH.

1 Introduction

The circumference increases with the radius of the track in a disk. If all tracks in a disk keep the peak linear storage density that disk drive can hold, then the longer track can store much data and the disk achieves the largest storage capacity. However, it requires more powerful electronics to manage the varied recording/accessing activity. To meet the demands for higher storage capacity and not too complicated controlling components, almost all modern disk drives employ a technology called *zoning*, e.g. *Zone Bit Recording (ZBR)* or *Zoned Constant Angular Velocity (ZCAV)* [1], [2]. Disk cylinders are grouped into zones according to their distance from the spindle of the disk. A zone is a contiguous collection of disk cylinders whose tracks have the same number of sectors. A sector is the minimum unit of data storage, typically holding 512 bytes of data. So the outer zones have more sectors per track than the inner zones located near the disk spindle, thus have larger storage capacity. The outer zones also have faster transfer rate because (1) data transfer rate is proportional to the rate of disk storage media rotating under the read/write head, (2) the track of the outer zone has larger storage capacity compared to the track of the inner zone, and (3) disk platters rotate at a constant angular velocity. Presently, a disk contains 3 to 20 zones, and the number tends to increase. The difference in data transfer rate between the fastest outermost zone and that of the slowest innermost zone can reach 120% or more [3]. So, the placement of date can significantly affect the I/O performance of storage system.

There are many researches about the effect of zoning technology on file system performance. Meter [2] analyzed theoretically that BSD Fast File System can not achieve the full disk transfer rate due to ZBR effect, and he measured about 25% performance degradation. Ghandeharizadeh, Ierardi [6], Meter et al. [2] proposed a placement scheme for file on multi-zone disk to maximize the bandwidth of storage system. They only studied the traditional file system with the restriction to read access. J. Wang and Y. Hu[7] extended their research to read and write access of Log File System (LFS). Chen and Thapar [8] described several data placement strategies to improve video I/O performance. Nerjes et al. [9] built an accurate performance analysis model of multimedia data on multi-zone disks.

But little has been published about the effect of zoning on RAID yet, So we propose a new RAID data placement strategy to improve the RAID I/O performance, making use of the characteristics that different disk zone has different transfer rate.

The rest of this paper is organized as follows. Section 2 describes the design of PMSH algorithm in detail, including how to calculate and trace the heat of RAID stripe units, and the steps by which stripe units migrate among different disk zones. Section 3 demonstrates our proposal through simulation results and analysis. The summarization and future research work are given in section 4.

2 The Design of PMSH Algorithm

2.1 The Reason for PMSH

To reduce the performance gap between CPU and memory, RAID [4] takes advantage of parallelism to boost I/O performance, through interleaving file data across multiple disks. Traditional RAID hasn't take the effects of zoning on performance into account, but the fact is that the layout of stripe units on disk zones can significantly affect the I/O performance of the RAID system, since a file is broken into several stripe units which interleaved across RAID disks, thus the access time of the file is determined by that of the slowest stripe unit [4]. The main idea of PMSH is to optimize the stripe unit layout in each RAID disks through reorganizing each stripe unit of each disk on appropriate zone with corresponding transfer rate according to its access rate, thus to improve the RAID I/O performance.

PMSH chooses stripe unit as the basic unit of data placement and migration, conforming to the data layout characteristics of RAID, and without incurring any change in data structure of stripe unit map. Obviously, such zone reorganization will incur extra overhead, which should be kept to minimal to avoid a negative performance impact. Fortunately, previous studies [5] have shown that file system activities are very gusty with long idle periods. So, our PMSH can perform stripe unit reorganization when the system is idle.

2.2 Stripe Unit Heat

PMSH improves RAID performance by putting frequently accessed stripe unit on high-transfer-rate zone of its located disk. Therefore an important issue is how to define and evaluate the access rate of stripe unit. Taking the *file heat* [7] as reference, we use *stripe unit heat* to identify the access rate of stripe unit. To calculate the heat of a stripe unit, first we calculate the heat of file, and then we get the heat of stripe unit from the average heat value of all resident files in this stripe unit.

The file access rate is designated as *file heat*. The file system gets the heat of files by gathering the statistics from issued requests. It is a heuristic learning process—file system maintains a time stamp queue and a heat value for every file. All the queues are initially empty and the heat values are uniformly set to 0. With the arrival of a request referencing file f_x, the current time is recorded in the stamp queue of file f_x. Whenever the timestamp queue of file f_x becomes full, the heat value of the file is updated according to the following formula.

$$heat_{new}(f_x) = (1-d) \times \frac{1}{\frac{1}{K} \times \sum_{i=1}^{K-1}(t_{i+1}-t_i)} + d \times heat_{old}(f_x); \quad (0 \le d \le 1) \quad (1)$$

Where $heat_{new}(f_x)$ and $heat_{old}(f_x)$ is the value of file heat after and before update respectively, K is the length of timestamp queue, d is a constant between 0 and 1, t_i is the ith timestamp. After the update is completed, the queue of f_x is flushed and new timestamp can be recorded. Since $\frac{1}{K} \times \sum_{i=1}^{K-1}(t_{i+1}-t_i)$ calculates the average interval of timestamps in queue, say the average interval of arriving requests, and since it takes into account the old value of file heat, formula (1) can smooth out short term fluctuations and maintains a longer trend of access pattern. Constant d and K can be set to different value according to different application—a small d favors recent access rate of file, then the evaluated heat value will be accurate at system startup time, however the margin of error increases with the number of requests. A smaller K means system updating file heat value more frequently, resulting in increased fluctuation of evaluated file heat value and system overhead.

The access rate of RAID stripe unit, called the *heat of stripe unit*, is calculated according to the heat of resident files as the following formula:

$$heat(S_y) = \frac{1}{P} \times \sum_{x=1}^{P} heat(fx). \quad (2)$$

Where $heat(S_y)$ is the heat value of stripe unit S_y, P is the number of resident file.

2.3 Disk Zone Tracing Table

System maintains a *disk zone tracing table* for each RAID disk to monitor the status of its zones. The structure of disk zone tracing table is shown in figure 1. Assume that

Z_0	Max. SU heat	Min. SU heat	1:1:0:0: 1:1:1:0:	Z_0 status bitmap
Z_1	Max. SU heat	Min. SU heat		Z_1 status bitmap
Z_m	Max. SU heat	Min. SU heat		Z_m status bitmap

Fig. 1. Disk Zone Tracing op Table (SU stands for stripe unit)

a RAID disk have m zones, designated as $Z_0, Z_1, \ldots Z_j, \ldots Z_m$ respectively, then each zone has a corresponding entry that traces the stripe units in it. Each entry contains the disk zone ID, the maximum stripe unit heat and the minimum stripe unit heat, and a bitmap of available information on *stripe unit blocks* in that zone. The maximum and minimum stripe unit heat help data reorganization progress to find target zone for migrating stripe unit quickly. Through setting the value of each bit which is assigned for different stripe unit blocks, bitmap records the available status of all stripe unit blocks in that zone—if the stripe unit blocks are occupied, then the corresponding bit is set to 1, and if a bit in bitmap is set to 0, then it means its corresponding stripe unit blocks is vacant and available. The bitmap helps data reorganization progress to find available stripe unit for migrating stripe unit swiftly. The size of disk zone tracing table is relatively small—assuming the storage capacity of a RAID disk is 10G, the stripe unit size is 4k, then the size of zone tracing table will be about 30KB, that is acceptable. Here, we need to explain two terms used in this paper: *stripe unit* and *stripe unit blocks* – stripe unit refers to the data interleaved from files to multiple RAID disks, while *stripe unit blocks* refer to the storage space of disks for locating the stripe unit.

The heat of each stripe unit in each disk is kept in *stripe unit heat table*, another data structure to which stripe unit data placement and migration should refer. We will not describe the content of stripe unit heat table in detail because it is rather similar to the file heat table [7].

2.4 PMSH Algorithm

To be consistent with the assumption in former subsection, we partition a RAID disk into m sequential zones, $Z_0, Z_1, \ldots, Z_j, \ldots Z_m$, in an order of descending transfer rate. We denote the transfer rate of the ith zone $tfr(Z_j)MB/s$, then $tfr(Z_i)>tfr(Z_i+1)$, where $i=0, 1,\ldots,m-1$.

To reduce the slowdown of access to a RAID-resident file caused by the slowest stripe unit, for each RAID disk, we should put the most frequently accessed stripe unit in the fastest zone according to Amdahl's Law. Under 2 assumptions that (1) $heat(S_y)$, the heat of stripe unit S_y, remains constant, where S_y represents one stripe unit in RAID, (2) files are not added to or deleted from RAID. We propose the *optimal*

Table 1. Zone parameters of disk hp_c3323a model

Zone	Cylinders in zone	Sectors per track	Data Xfer Rate (MB/s)
0	994	120	5.53
1	141	116	5.35
2	176	112	5.16
3	315	104	4.79
4	341	96	4.42
5	289	88	4.06
6	353	80	3.69
7	373	72	3.32

Table 2. Zone parameters of disk IBM_DNES-309170W

Zone	Cylinders in zone	Sectors per track	Data Xfer Rate (MB/s)
0	378	390	18.0
1	886	374	17.2
2	984	364	16.8
3	1219	351	16.2
4	1037	338	15.6
5	1023	325	15.0
6	1518	312	14.4
7	1717	286	13.2
8	1054	273	12.6
9	867	260	12.0
10	791	247	11.4

stripe unit layout in a RAID disk as follows: first, order the stripe units in that disk by their heat from maximum to minimum. Then layout the sequential stripe units contiguously, starting with zone Z_0 and proceeding progressively towards Z_m. A stripe unit can span multiple zones, but no stripe unit blocks are left unoccupied.

The optimal stripe unit layout in a RAID disk is static, however, we should expect file creation and deletion, and evolving file heat as well. (The location for newly created file differs with different algorithm. In this paper, to improve response time of the write access, the stripe unit of new file locates on the available stripe unit blocks with the fastest transfer rate. As for the deleted file, the corresponding bits in stripe unit status bitmap are set to 0; the stripe unit blocks are available then. Limited to the space of this paper, we will not discuss the cases of file creation and deletion in detail). So the system needs to update the stripe unit heat according to formula (2), and migrates the hotter stripe units to faster zones, in order to approximate the layout obtained by the optimal stripe unit layout. The stripe unit migration strategy of PMSH is swapping the locations of hotter stripe unit blocks and target stripe unit blocks, thus the key issue becomes how to choose the target stripe unit blocks for the migrating stripe unit.

Without loss of generality, we describe the processing steps of PMSH in RAID disk as follows:

(1) Sort all stripe units in disk by their heat in descending order. Then layout the sequential stripe units contiguously, starting with zone Z_0 and proceeding progressively towards Z_m, with no stripe unit blocks left unoccupied. This step complies with the *optimal stripe unit layout*. Since the stripe unit blocks of inner zones are occupied firstly, the stripe unit blocks of outer zones are reserved, so the write of new stripe unit can be completed fast.

(2) Once the heat of a stripe unit increases, it is regarded as the migrating stripe unit.

(3) System picks out all zones on which reside at least one stripe unit whose heat is greater than that of the migrating one according to the disk zones tracking table. If there is no such a zone, it means the migrating stripe unit has the greatest heat value

Table 3. Statistic characteristics of each trace (512byte/block)

Traces		hp_c2490a	hp_c2247a	Ibm_18es
Total NO. of request		11770	12402	12926
read/write ratio		0.58/0.42	0.41/0.59	0.51/0.49
request size(block)	Average	14.88	14.34	5.99
	Std. deviation	15.33	15.17	3.41
	Max.	138	134	44
Request size distribution (request size:NO. of request)	hp_c2490a	=1:814 =2:739 =3:714 =4:753 <7:1237 <9:1300 <13:1395 <17:1082 <21:808 21+:2928		
	hp_c2247a	=1:896 =2:852 =3:792 =4:743 <7:1316 <9:1592 <13:1420 <17:1122 <21:819 21+:2850		
	Ibm_18es	=1:0 =2:0 =3:0 =4:8533 <7:0 <9:3063 <13:865 <17:315 <21:102 21+:48		

in whole disk, then the migrating stripe unit will be put in the vacant stripe unit blocks of the fastest zone among which are not totally vacant, the migrating progress is completed; if there no stripe unit block is available in that zone, then move to another neighbor faster zone. If there are several qualified zones, then

(4) System chooses an intermediate transfer rate zone, for the sake of balancing the performance of write and read access—the fastest zone among qualified ones is reserved for new stripe unit to write in, the lowest zone is not chose considering the read response time.

(5) If the intermediate zone has available stripe unit blocks, then the migrating stripe unit plugs in and the migrating progress is completed. Otherwise, the zone is full, then System checks every stripe unit in that intermediate zone sequentially, until a stripe unit whose heat is greater than the migrating one is found and regarded as 'target stripe unit', then swap the migrating stripe unit and the target stripe unit.

(6) Now the target stripe unit is regarded as 'migrating stripe unit', turn to step (3).

3 Simulation and Results Analysis

3.1 Simulation

We used a trace driven simulation to investigate the effectiveness of the PMSH algorithm. The simulator is DiskSim [11], a widely-used, powerful storage system simulator.

We simulated two RAID models, designated as RAID_hp and RAID_IBM respectively. Their data layout is left symmetric, and both of them are level-5 RAID composed of eight 3.5inch disks. The disk model in RAID_hp is hp_c3323a whose rotation speed is 5400 RPM and formatted capacity is 1.0GB. The disk model in RAID_IBM is IBM_DNES-309170W whose rotation speed is 7200 RPM and formatted capacity is 9.0GB. Table 1 and table 2 list the zone parameters of hp_c3323a and IBM_DNES-309170W respectively.

Three traces validated by DiskSim have been used in our simulation, including hp_c2490a, hp_c2247a and Ibm_18es. The statistic characteristics of these three traces are described in detail in table 3.

Our objective is to compare the performance of traditional RAID and that of RAID applying PMSH. Overall storage system response time is the performance metric used in this paper. So in case of not applying PMSH and in case of applying PMSH, with stripe unit size ranging from 4 blocks (512bytes/block) to 12 blocks, the response time of RAID_hp under trace hp_2247 and hp_2490a respectively, and the response time of RAID_IBM under trace ibm_es are recorded. (We haven't put RAID_hp under trace ibm_es, because the trace size is greater than the storage capacity of RAID_hp. On the other hand, loading RAID_IBM with the other two trace will lead to the utilization of the RAID be too small to get effective simulation results.)

3.2 Simulation Results and Analysis

With stripe unit size ranging from 4 blocks to 12 blocks, figure 2 and figure 3 compare the performance of RAID_hp applying PMSH and that of RAID_hp without applying PMSH under trace hp_2490a and trace hp_c2247a, respectively. Figure 4 compares the performance of RAID_IBM with PMSH and that of RAID_IBM without PMSH under trace ibm_18es. Figure 2(a), figure 3(a) and figure 4(a) show the absolute performance (in term of overall storage system request response time), while figure 2(b), figure 3(b) and figure 4(b) show relative performance improvement of RAID with PMSH over traditional RAID.

With various stripe unit sizes we simulated, RAID achieves performance improvement via PMSH. Under trace hp_2490a, RAID_hp reduced request response time by 5.4%-16.7% through applying PMSH, and under trace hp_2247a, the same RAID reduced request response time by 5.4%-18.5% via PMSH, while under trace ibm_18es, RAID_IBM improved performance by 2.8%-10.5% through PMSH. But no obvious relationship between performance improvement ratio and the size of stripe unit size has been observed.

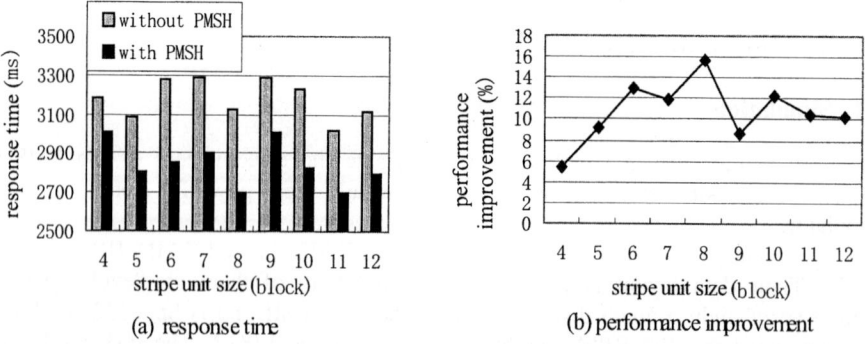

Fig. 2. Performance of RAID_hp, trace hp_c2490a (a) response time (b) performance improvement

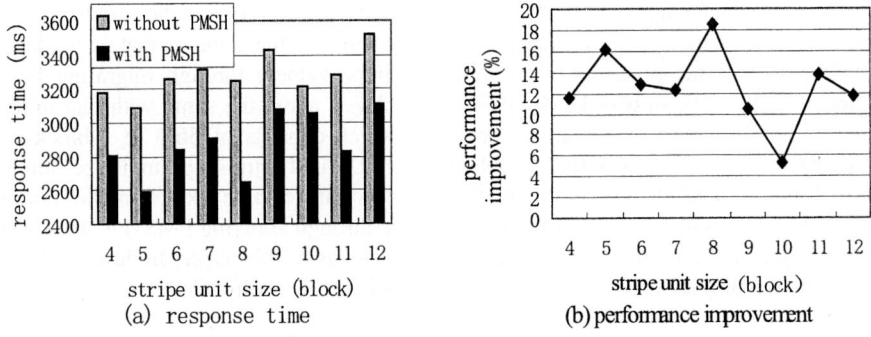

Fig. 3. Performance of RAID_hp, trace hp_c2247a (a) response time (b) performance improvement

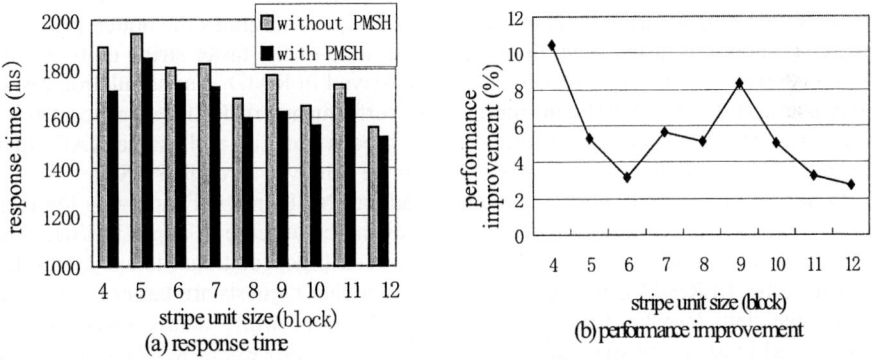

Fig. 4. Performance of RAID_IBM, trace ibm_18es (a) response time (b) performance improvement

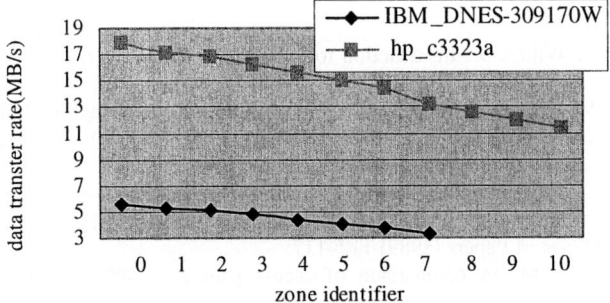

Fig. 5. Data transfer rate in each zone of disk hp_c3323a and disk IBM_DNES-309170W

We noticed that by applying PMSH, the performance improvement of RAID_IBM is relatively less than that of RAID_hp. The reason lies *not in* the disk zones, as we can see from figure 5 — the number of zones in disk IBM_DNES-309170W is more than that of disk RAID_c3323a. Moreover, the ascending rate of transfer rate from inner zones to outer zones of the former disk is approximately the same as that of the latter. Leading to that the potential of performance improvement through migrating hotter stripe to faster zone in disk IBM_DNES-309170W is about the same with that in disk hp_c3323a. However, in the trace ibm_18es which consists of 66% of 4-block-size requests that incur "small write" problem in RAID_IBM with stripe unit size ranging from 4 blocks to 12 blocks. As for small write, data transfer time takes a smaller portion of access time, thus the effect of I/O performance through applying PMSH is weakened. (The choice of stripe unit size in RAID is not the focus of this paper) In despite of that, the reduction of response time of RAID via PMSH is still worthwhile.

4 Conclusion and Future Work

We propose a new data reorganization scheme called PMSH. Using the information that different zones in multi-zone disk have different data transfer rates, this scheme monitors the heat of stripe units in each RAID disk, and migrates the hotter stripe unit to a corresponding faster zone, to minimize the time of the faster stripe units waiting for the slower ones when retrieving a file interleaved in RAID. Our simulation results demonstrate that (1) PMSH can improve the performance of RAID significantly. (2) The greater the transfer rate difference among each zone of multi-zone RAID disk, the greater the potential performance boost can be achieved through PMSH.

In our future research work, we intend to adopt PMSH in RAID applying log technology [11], [12]. Instinctively, we regard it as the better case to apply PMSH, since the access time of data consists of three parts: seek time, rotational latency, and data transfer time. In RAID with log technology, most data requests are larger request, for which the data transfer time takes a greater portion, while data transfer time is determined by data transfer rate. There is a 'cleaning' process in RAID applying log technology, so stripe unit migration can perform either during system idle period or during 'cleaning' process.

References

1. Rummer, C., Wildes, J.: Introduction to disk drive modeling. IEEE Computer 27(1993) 17–29.
2. Meter, R. V.: Observing the effects of multi-zone disks. Annual Technical Conference, Anaheim, CA (USENIX, ed.), (Berkeley, CA, USA), USENIX (1997) 19–30.
3. Seagate. Seagate Web Page. http://www.seagate.com. 2000.
4. Patterson, D. A., Chen, P., Gibson, G., Katz, R. H.: Introduction to Redundant Array of Independent Disk. 34th IEEE Computer Society International Conference, Intellectual Leverage, Digest of Papers (1989) 112–117.
5. Sivan - Zimet, M.: A comparison of access pattern (92-99). UCSC CS290S Project (2000).
6. Ghandeharizadeh, S., Ierardi, D., Kim, D., Zimmermann, R.: Placement of Data in Multi-Zone Disk Drives. Second International Baltic Workshop on DB and IS (1996).
7. Wang, J., Hu, Y.: PROFS-Performance-Oriented Data Reorganization for Log-Structured File System on Multi-Zone. Modeling Analysis and Simulation of Computer and Telecommunication Systems, Proceedings. Ninth International Symposium (2001) 285–292.

8. Chen, S.: Thapar. M.: Zone-bit-recording-enhanced video data layout strategies. Proceedings of the 4th int'l Workshop on Modeling, Analysis and Simulation of Computer and Telecommunication Systems (1996).
9. Nerjes, G., Muth, P., Weikum, G.: Stochastic service guarnantees for continuous data on multi-zone disks. Proceedings of the Sixteenth ACM SIGACT-SIGMOD-SIGART Symposim on Principles of Database Systems, Tucson, Arizona (1997) 154–160.
10. Ganger, G. R., Patt, Y. N.: Using system-level models to evaluate I/O subsystems designs. IEEE Transactions on Computers (1998) 667–678.
11. Gabber, E., Korth, H. F.: Data Logging: A Method for Efficient Data Updates in Constantly Active RAIDs. Data Engineering, Proceedings, 14th International Conference (1998) 144 –153.
12. Menon, J.: A Performance Comparison of RAID-5 and Log-structured Arrays. Proceedings of the 4th IEEE International Symposium (1995) 167–178.

Distribution Channel Coordination Through Penalty Schemes

Quansheng Lei[1] and Jian Chen[2]

[1] School of Automation, Beijing University of Posts and Telecommunications,
Beijing 100876, China
`Leiqshz@163.com`
[2] School of Economics and Management, Tsinghua University, Beijing 100084, China

Abstract. This paper studies a stochastic inventory problem from the viewpoint of minimizing distribution system costs. First, the order quantity of every period must be greater than some minimal level and less than some upper limit, and we apply penalties to the retailer when his/her purchase quantity exceeds these specified boundaries. Then the dynamic programming equation for the problem is established, and we prove the existence of an optimal policy and characterize the dynamic programming equation both in finite and infinite horizons. Finally, an example is provided, and computational results indicate that penalty schemes can lead to significant savings in total expected distribution system costs.

1 Introduction

This paper considers a distribution system which consists of one distribution center and one retailer. Customer demand arises at the retailer, and the retailer orders from the distribution center (DC). The phenomenon of the variance in demand faced by DC compared to the one faced by the retailer, is now widely known as the bullwhip effect. Lee et al. [1] offered four factors to explain the existence of the bullwhip effect (demand forecast updating, order batching, price fluctuation, and shortage gaming). One intuitive attempt to mitigate this variance propagation effect is via the penalty mechanism to the retailer. With more regulated demand patterns, the DC can plan for inventory and transportation easily and reduce costs for the distribution system.

To reduce lead-time and its variability, modern supply and transportation contracts often specify in advance the frequency and volume to be reserved by the carrier for a particular customer's future deliveries [2]. Once such a contract is signed, a given prepaid volume is available to the customer periodically at no incremental cost; the contract parameters' values (volume and frequency) need to be chosen simultaneously with the contingent inventory policy, taking into account the demand's randomness [2], [3]. Henig et al. [4] explore the joint optimization of contract parameters and inventory control policy in such environments. They derive the optimal periodic review inventory policy corresponding to a given supply contract, and there is a range of stock levels for which the quantity ordered equals the contract volume. Genues [5] generalizes that the model provided by Henig et al. [4], which applies a premium only to quantities exceeding a contracted value between supplier and customer, penalizes positive as well as negative deviations of actual order quantities from the mean. For a recent summary of work on inventory-routing models, see [6].

Our research is different from [4], [5] in the following ways: (i) This paper considers a supply contract in which the order quantity every period must be greater than some minimal level, and less than some upper limit, and we apply penalties to the retailer when his purchase quantity exceeds the specified bounds; (ii) This paper considers general discrete demand distribution.

The plan of the paper is as follows: the next section introduces some notions and the inventory model. The main results are listed in Section 3. We provide a numerical example and analysis in Section 4 and draw conclusions in Section 5.

2 The Inventory Model

This paper considers a single-item distribution system which consists of one distribution center (DC) and one retailer. We suppose that the retailer and the distribution center use a periodic-review order policy, and lead time of supply is assumed to be zero.

The demand D in a period is a nonnegative, discrete random variable. For the real application, we assume that demand D is bounded by some positive N.

Let $p(j) = \Pr(D = j)$, $j = 0, 1, \ldots$, where $\sum_{j=0}^{N} p(j) = 1$.

The notions in this paper are as follows:
n period index
x inventory level at the start of a period before an order is placed
y inventory level after an order arrives but before the demand is realized
c unit cost of ordered goods
b unit cost per period of back-ordered goods
h unit cost per period of holding inventory
β discount factor
U the upper limit on the purchase quantity each period
L the lower limit on the purchase quantity each period
p_1 penalty for each unit ordered exceeding the order quantity U
p_2 penalty for each unit ordered below the order quantity L
$L(y)$ expected single-period inventory cost

$$L(y) = \begin{cases} \sum_{j=0}^{y} h(y-j)p(j) + \sum_{j=y+1}^{N} b(j-y)p(j) & y \geq 0 \\ \sum_{j=0}^{N} b(j-y)p(j) & y < 0 \end{cases}$$

$f_n(x)$ is the expected discounted cost for an n-period horizon problem, if the beginning inventory level is x and optimal policies are followed over the n periods.
$G_n(y) = L(y) + cy + \beta E f_{n-1}(y - D)$.

2.1 Distribution Center Model

We consider DC with a singer retailer. After receiving the retailer's order, the DC fills the entire order at the beginning of the following period. If the DC's stock is insufficient to meet the retailer's demand, the DC receives an emergency shipment from the supplier at a per unit emergency shipment cost. The DC then transports the entire order to the retailer using its own transportation capacity. If the total order size exceeds the distribution center's in-house delivery capacity, the distribution center uses outside sources to handle any overage, plus that of a third party LTL carrier if necessary (see [5]).

The costs of the DC include the inventory cost and the transportation cost; the inventory costs involve unit purchasing c_{dc}, holding cost h_{dc} and emergency shipping cost b_{dc}. So the single period inventory cost equation for the DC with a starting inventory of x, is given by:

$$c_{dc}(y-x)+L_{dc}(y)$$

$$L_{dc}(y)=\begin{cases}\sum_{j=0}^{y}h_{dc}(y-j)p(j)+\sum_{j=y+1}^{N}b_{dc}(j-y)p(j) & y\geq 0\\ \sum_{j=0}^{N}b_{dc}(j-y)p(j) & y<0\end{cases}$$

The expected transportation cost per period is given by:

$$T(C)=(T_L+T_R)C-T_R\sum_{j=0}^{C}(C-j)p(j)+T_C\sum_{j=C+1}^{N}(j-C)p(j)$$

Where C denotes truck capacity, T_L is a scalar, T_R denotes per unit shipped via regular truck, T_C denotes per unit shipped via outside carrier.

2.2 Retailer Model

We consider a single retailer and one item. The retailer observes demand each week and attempts to satisfy demand with its stock on hand. If consumer demand exceeds the retailer's available stock, then the excess demand is backordered. After observing the week's demand, the retailer places an order to the DC based on its inventory position. The retailer's demand distribution uniquely determines the distribution of the DC's demand.

The expected single period holding and shortage cost is as follows:

$$c(y-x)+L(y)$$

$$L(y)=\begin{cases}\sum_{j=0}^{y}h_r(y-j)p(j)+\sum_{j=y+1}^{N}b_r(j-y)p(j) & y\geq 0\\ \sum_{j=0}^{N}b_r(j-y)p(j) & y<0\end{cases} \quad (1)$$

2.3 The Total Distribution System Costs Model

From the above analysis, the expected total distribution system costs is as follows:
Minimize E {[DC Inventory Costs + Transportation Costs] + [Retailer Inventory Costs]}

3 The Optimal Order Policy

The dynamic program formulation of the retailer's inventory problem is given by:

$$\begin{cases} f_n(x) = \min_{y \geq x} \{c(y-x) + p_1(y-x-U)^+ \\ \qquad\qquad + p_2(L-y+x)^+ + L(y) + \beta E f_{n-1}(y-D)\} \\ f_0(x) \equiv 0 \end{cases} \quad (2)$$

Lemma 1. In the finite horizon inventory model, $S_{1,n}, S_{2,n}$ minimize (3), (4) respectively, and S_n minimizes $G_n(y) = L(y) + cy + \beta E f_{n-1}(y-D)$

$$\min \quad p_1 y + G_n(y) \quad (3)$$
$$\min \quad -p_2 y + G_n(y) \quad (4)$$

then:
$$S_{1,n} \leq S_n \leq S_{2,n}$$

Proof. From $S_{1,n}, S_{2,n}$ respectively minimize (3) and (4), S_n minimizes $G_n(y)$

$$p_1 S_{1,n} + G_n(S_{1,n}) \leq p_1 S_n + G_n(S_n)$$
$$-p_2 S_{2,n} + G_n(S_{2,n}) \leq -p_2 S_n + G_n(S_n)$$

then:
$$p_1(S_n - S_{1,n}) \geq G_n(S_{1,n}) - G_n(S_n) \geq 0$$
$$p_2(S_{2,n} - S_n) \geq G_n(S_{2,n}) - G_n(S_n) \geq 0$$
$$S_{1,n} \leq S_n \leq S_{2,n} \qquad \square$$

Consider the policy $(S_{1,n}, S_n, S_{2,n}, L, U)$, which, depending on the initial inventory of the period, brings the inventory to the following levels:

$$y = \begin{cases} x & (\Rightarrow q = 0), & \text{if } S_{2,n} < x \\ S_{2,n} & (\Rightarrow q < L), & \text{if } S_{2,n} - L < x \leq S_{2,n} \\ x + L & (\Rightarrow q = L), & \text{if } S_n - L < x \leq S_{2,n} - L \\ S_n & (\Rightarrow L \leq q \leq U) & \text{if } S_n - U \leq x \leq S_n - L \\ x + U & (\Rightarrow q = U), & \text{if } S_{1,n} - U < x \leq S_n - U \\ S_{1,n} & (\Rightarrow q > U), & \text{if } x < S_{1,n} - U \end{cases}$$

Lemma 2. (Heyman, [7]) Let X be a nonempty set with A_x a nonempty set for each $x \in X$. Let $C = \{(x, y): y \in A_x, x \in X\}$, let J be a real-valued function on C, and define:

$$f(x) = \inf\{J(x, y): y \in A_x\}, \ x \in X$$

If C is a convex set and J is a convex function on C, then f is a convex function on any convex subset of $X^* = \{x: x \in X, f(x) > -\infty\}$.

Proposition 1. If $G_n(y)$ is a convex function, then policy $(S_{1,n}, S_n, S_{2,n}, L, U)$ is an optimal policy for minimizing $f_n(x)$.

Proof. Let $M(x) = p_2(L+x) - cx + \min_{x \leq y \leq x+L}\{-p_2 y + G_n(y)\}$

$$N(x) = -p_1(U+x) - cx + \min_{y \geq x+U}\{p_1 y + G_n(y)\}$$

$$F(x) = -cx + \min_{x+L \leq y \leq x+U} G_n(y)$$

Then $f_n(x) = \min\{M(x), N(x), F(x)\}$, and now we consider the following cases:

(i) $x > S_{2,n}$

Because $-p_2 y + G_n(y)$ is a continuous convex function, therefore, there exists a global minimizing point x of $-p_2 y + G_n(y)$, $M(x) = p_2 L - cx + G_n(x)$
$N(x) = -cx + G_n(x+U)$, $F(x) = -cx + G_n(x+L) = M(x+L)$
With $x > S_{2,n} \geq S_n$, and we have $G_n(x+L) \leq G_n(x+U)$, so $F(x) \leq N(x)$

From Lemma 2, $M(x)$ is a convex function, then $M(x) \leq M(x+L) = F(x)$, and an optimal solution is to order up to x, in this case, $q = 0$.

(ii) $S_{2,n} - L < x \leq S_{2,n}$

From $S_{2,n} - L < x \leq S_{2,n}$ we have $x + L > S_{2,n} \geq x$, and $M(x)$ achieves a global minimum at $S_{2,n}$, from $x + U \geq x + L > S_{2,n} \geq S_n$,

$$M(x) \leq M(x+L) = F(x) \leq F(x+U) = N(x)$$

and an optimal solution is to order up to $S_{2,n}$, in this case, $q = S_{2,n} - x$

(iii) $S_n - L < x \leq S_{2,n} - L$

From $S_n - L < x \leq S_{2,n} - L$ we have $S_n < x + L \leq S_{2,n}$, and $M(x)$ achieves a global minimum at $x + L$, $M(x) = -cx + G_n(x+L)$

Since $x+U \geq x+L > S_n \geq S_{1,n}$, then
$$F(x) = -cx + G_n(x+L), N(x) = -cx + G_n(x+U))$$
Since $x+U \geq x+L > S_n$, then $G(x+L) \leq G(x+U), F(x) \leq N(x)$
and an optimal solution is to order up to $L+x$, in this case, $q = L$;

(iv) $S_n - U \leq x \leq S_n - L$

From $S_n - U \leq x \leq S_n - L$, we have $x+U \geq S_n \geq x+L$,
$$x+U \geq S_n \geq S_{1,n} \Rightarrow N(x) = -cx + G_n(x+U)$$
$$x+U \geq S_n \geq x+L \Rightarrow F(x) = -cx + G_n(S_n)$$
$$S_{2,n} \geq S_n \geq x+L \Rightarrow M(x) = -cx + G_n(x+L)$$
and an optimal solution is to order up to S_n, in this case, $q = S_n - x$.

(v) $S_{1,n} - U \leq x < S_n - U$

From $S_{1,n} - U \leq x < S_n - U$ we have $S_{1,n} \leq x+U < S_n$,
$$x+L \leq x+U < S_n \Rightarrow M(x) = -cx + G_n(x+L)$$
$$x+L \leq x+U < S_n \Rightarrow F(x) = -cx + G_n(x+U)$$
Since $G_n(x+U) \leq G_n(x+L)$, then $F(x) = -cx + G_n(x+U) \leq M(x)$
$$S_{1,n} \leq x+U \Rightarrow N(x) = -cx + G_n(x+U)$$
and an optimal solution is to order up to $U+x$, in this case, $q = U$;

(vi) $x < S_{1,n} - U$

From $x < S_{1,n} - U$ we have $x+U < S_{1,n}$, and $N(x)$ achieves a global minimum at $S_{1,n}$, $N(x) = p_1(S_{1,n} - x - U) - cx + G_n(S_{1,n})$
$$N(x) \leq N(x+U) = -cx + G_n(x+U)$$
Since $x+L \leq x+U < S_{1,n} \leq S_n \leq S_{2,n}$, then
$$M(x) = -cx + G_n(x+L), F(x) = -cx + G_n(x+U)$$
Since $x+L \leq x+U < S_{1,n} \leq S_n$, then $G_n(x+U) \leq G_n(X+L)$,

So we have $N(x) \leq F(x) \leq M(x)$, and an optimal solution is to order up to $S_{1,n}$, $q = S_{1,n} - x$. □

Theorem 1. If $L(y)$ is convex, then the policy $(S_{1,n}, S_n, S_{2,n}, L, U)$ is optimal for problem $f_n(x)$ in period n.

Proof. From proposition 1, we need to prove that $G_n(y)$ is convex, so we shall show inductively that each of the functions $G_1(y), G_2(y)$....are convex.

Since $G_1(y)$ equals $cy + L(y)$, $G_1(y)$ is clearly convex. Let us assume $G_1(y), G_2(y),..., G_n(y)$ are convex, because:

$$G_{n+1}(y) = cy + L(y) + \beta E[f_n(y-D)]$$

For demonstrating the convex of $G_{n+1}(y)$, it is to show that $f_n(\cdot)$ is convex, where:

$$f_n(x) = \min_{y \geq x}\{-cx + p_1(y-(x+U))^+ + p_2(L-(y-x))^+ + G_n(y)\}$$

The convex of $G_n(y)$ implies that:

$$p_1(y-(x+U))^+ + p_2(L-(y-x))^+ - cx + G_n(y)$$

is convex, and $f_n(x)$ is convex from Lemma 2. □

Theorem 2. If $\beta < 1$, then $\lim_{n \to \infty} S_{1,n} = S_1$, $\lim_{n \to \infty} S_n = S$, $\lim_{n \to \infty} S_{2,n} = S_2$, $\lim_{n \to \infty} f_n(x) = f(x)$, where S_1, S, S_2 minimize $p_1 y + G(y)$, $G(y)$ and $-p_2 y + G(y)$ respectively, where:

$$G(y) = L(y) + cy + \beta E f_{n-1}(y - D_1)$$
$$f(x) = \min_{y \geq x}\{c(y-x) + p_1(y-x-U)^+ + p_2(L-y+x)^+ + G(y)\}$$

Proof. It is easy to verify that conditions (a)-(d) and (f) in Theorem 8-15 in [7] hold here (with inf instead of sup). □

Supposing that the item is sold in discrete units, we model the inventory positions as a discrete-time Markov chain. Let x_t denote the inventory position at the beginning of period t, and let $p_{ij} \equiv P(x_{t+1} = j | x_t = i)$ be the one-step transition probability of this Markov chain. Given the policy parameters S_1, S, S_2, L, U, we can represent the state transitions as follows (see [4]):

$$p_{ij} = \begin{cases} P(D_i = i - j) & \text{if } S_2 < i \\ P(D_i = S_2 - j) & \text{if } S_2 - L < i \leq S_2 \\ P(D_i = i + L - j) & \text{if } S - L < x \leq S_2 - L \\ P(D_i = S - j) & \text{if } S - U \leq x \leq S - L \\ P(D_i = i + U - j) & \text{if } S_1 - U < x \leq S - U \\ P(D_i = S_1 - j) & \text{if } x < S_1 - U \end{cases}$$

4 Numerical Examples

We conduct a numerical study to illustrate the impact of the penalty schemes to total distribution system costs, where we consider one retailer and one distribution center (DC) with a single product, as shown in Figure 1.

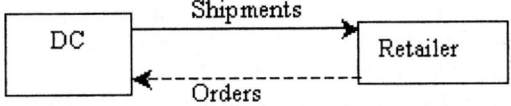

Fig. 1. The relation between DC and retailer

The demand distribution of the retailer is Poisson distribution with a mean of 10, and the following parameters are used for the retailer:

$$c = 200, \ h = 100, b = 900, \ \alpha = 0.9,$$
$$p_1 = p_2 = \{0,50,100,150,200,250,300,350,400,450,500\}$$

The follow parameters are used for the DC:

$$c = 150, b = 510, \ h = 90, \ \alpha = 0.9; \ T_L = 14.65, T_R = 2.71, T_C = 13.59.$$

We set the unit deviation premium values $p = p_1 = p_2$, the choice p will affect the amount of the retailer's order variability, i.e. the higher the premium, the lower the order variability. We wish to set p to some finite value to find the best level of order variability for the retailer and the DC. The method we will follow to set p begins by setting $p = 0$ and increasing p as long as the sum of the retailer's and the DC's costs decreases as p increases. This will allow us to at least find a local minimum for system costs for $p \geq 0$. The results are as follows:

Table 1. The total distribution system costs for given premium value of p

p	0	50	100	150	200	250
Cost	5277.6	5175.4	5091.2	4841.9	4809.2	4705.4
p	300	350	400	450	500	
Cost	4684.5	4685.8	4745.4	4746.5	4942.9	

Where cost denotes the long-run average cost per period for the distribution system.

In Table 1, we can see that as the value of p increases the distribution system costs decrease, and equal 5277.6 when $p = 0$; they then decrease to 4684.5 when $p = 300$, a decrease of 11.24%. However, when $p > 300$, we find that costs increase as p increases, and the long-run average cost per period for the distribution system costs attains a local minimum when $p = 300$.

The number results show that we can determine the long-run average cost per period for the distribution systems under the premium mechanism. For a given demand distribution and unit premium value p, we can determine the corresponding long-run average cost per period for the retailer. The corresponding retailer demand distribution determines the distribution of the retailer's order (DC demand), which we use to find the optimal DC stock level and truck capacity and the corresponding DC average cost per period. The sum of average retailer and DC costs per period gives the average system costs per period. We sequentially increase the value of p to determine the optimal distribution system costs.

5 Conclusions

This paper characterizes the structure of the retailer's optimal policy under the penalty schemes; the numerical results show that changing the value of p can allow us to find better levels of ordering variability from a system-wide view.

The model can be extended to consider lost sales. In this paper, we assume that the excess demand unfilled is backlogged. In fact, when a customer goes to one supermarket or a department store to choose a competitive brand, he/she will go to another store if his/her preferred brand is out of stock.

We can expand the model to consider the manufacturer; in addition, we can expand the model to include multiple retailers and multiple products.

Acknowledgement

The work is supported by the Chinese Postdoctoral Science Foundation (No.2004036266) and the National Natural Science Foundation of China (No.70401021).

References

1. Lee, H.L., V. Padmanabhan, and S. Whang.: Information Distortion in a Supply Chain: The Bullwhip effect, Management Science.43(1997)546-558
2. Yano, C.A., Gerchak, Y.: Transportation contracts and safety stocks for just-in-time deliveries. Journal of Manufacturing and Operations Management.2(1989) 314-330
3. Ernst, R., Pyke, D.F.: Optimal base stock policies and truck capacity in a two-echelon system. Naval Research Logistics. 40(1993) 879-904
4. Hening, M., Y. Gerchak, R.Ernsst, and D.F.Pyke.: An Inventory Model Embedded in Designing a Supply Contract, Management Science. 43 (1997) 184-189.
5. Geunes, J.: Models To Optimize Multi-Stage Linkages In Manufacturing And Distribution Operations, Ph.D. Thesis, Penn State University (1999)
6. Qu, W.W., Bookbinder, J.H., Iygun,P.: An integrated inventory-transportation system with modified periodic policy for multiple products. European Journal of Operational Research.115 (1999) 254-269
7. Heyman, D.P., and M.Sobel.: Stochastic models in operations research, vII, McGraw-Hill,New York (1984)

Automatic Keyphrases Extraction from Document Using Neural Network

Jiabing Wang, Hong Peng, and Jing-song Hu

School of Computer Science and Engineering, South China University of Technology,
Guangzhou 510641, China
{jbwang, mahpeng}@scut.edu.cn, hujingsong@yahoo.com

Abstract. Keyphrase extraction is a task with many applications in information retrieval, text mining, and natural language processing. In this paper, a keyphrase extraction approach based on neural network is proposed. To determine whether a phrase is a keyphrase, the following features of a phrase in a given document are adopted: its term frequency and inverted document frequency, whether to appear in the title or headings (subheadings) of the given document, and its frequency appearing in the paragraphs of the given document. The algorithm is evaluated by the standard information retrieval metrics of precision and recall, and human assessment.

1 Introduction

With the explosive growth of online information, it sometimes becomes simple to determine where to go to find information. At the same time, it makes us embarrassed: the size of query result sets returned by web search engines and academic databases is too large, commonly hundreds or thousands. It is infeasible for users to read each document of the result set to determine whether or not they might be useful. Therefore, document surrogates, such as title, abstract, etc., become very important for users to decide whether they would like to read a whole document or not.

Some types of document, especially in scientific and technical literature, contain a list of key words—keyphrases—specified by authors. Since the keyphrases are assigned by authors, they actually offer a brief and precise description of a document's contents. Users can approximately know a document's content and find whether the document is useful through the keyphrases. However, not all documents contain keyphrases: even in collections of scientific papers those with keyphrases are in the minority [14, 20], say nothing of web pages. For documents with no keyphrases, it is necessary to assign keyphrases with each of those documents, either manually or automatically. Manual keyphrase assignment is tedious and time-consuming. So automatic methods benefit both the developers and the users of large document collections. Consequently, many automatic keyphrase extraction algorithms have been proposed based on different techniques [3-4, 6-9, 11-20], especially on machine learning.

Azcarraga et al [1] proposed a keyword extraction method for the SOM-based (Self-Organizing Map) archives. The algorithm was based on the distribution of weights in the weight vectors of the trained map and a manipulation of the random projection matrix used for input compression.

Barker and Cornacchia [3] proposed an algorithm to choose noun phrases from a document as keyphrases. A noun phrase is chosen based on its length, its frequency and the frequency of its head noun. Noun phrases are extracted from a text using a base noun phrase skimmer and an off-the-shelf online dictionary.

Chien [4] developed a PAT-tree-based keyphrases extraction system. Based on the definitions of LCD (Left Context Dependency) and RCD (Right Context Dependency), the system can efficiently extract domain-specific keyphrases patterns CLP (Complete Lexical Patterns) and SLP (Significant Lexical Patterns), from a text collection or an on-line textual database, written particularly in Chinese and other oriental languages.

Gayo-Avello et al [7] proposed a keyphrase extraction algorithm inspired by the protein biosynthesis process. A document is considered as an individual from a population, a document corpus, and documents are composed of passages, divided into sentences built upon words. Following this analogy, they hypothesized that two documents written in the same language or semantically related would show similar "document genomes". The document genomes are extracted and then translated into "significance proteins" (i.e., keywords, keyphrases and summaries).

HaCohen-Kerner et al [8-9] proposed a model for keyphrase extraction based on supervised machine learning and combinations of the baseline methods. Experiments show that a combination of a relatively high number of baseline methods is very successful for academic papers.

Hulth et al [12] proposed a keyphrase extraction algorithm in which the domain knowledge, i.e., the hierarchically organized thesaurus, and the frequency analysis were integrated. The combination of evidence from frequency analysis and thesaurus was done by inductive logic programming.

Kea [14, 20] is a keyphrase extraction algorithm based on naïve Bayes classifier. Three attributes of each remaining phrase are calculated: whether or not it is an exemplar keyphrase of the document, the distance into a document that it first occurs, and its TF × IDF value. The distance value is real and in the range 0 to 1, indicating the proportion of the document occurring before a phrase's first appearance. TF × IDF is a standard information retrieval metric that estimates how specific a phrase is to a document [2]. TF (term frequency) is a measure of how frequently a phrase occurs in a particular document, and DF (document frequency) is a measure of how many other documents contain the phrase. The candidate phrases from each document are combined and used to construct a Naïve Bayes classifier that predicts whether or not a given phrase is a keyphrase based on its distance and TF × IDF attributes.

The AKE (one part of the OmniPaper project) [15] is a keword extraction system that is used to extract keywords from news article. AKE uses statistical approaches and integrated linguistic techniques.

Matsuo et al [16] used a graph model to extract keyphrases from a document. A document is represented as a network: the nodes represent terms, and the edges represent the co-occurrence of terms. They find that the network has the characteristics of a small world, i.e., nodes are highly clustered yet the path length between them is small. Whether a term is a keyword is determined by measuring its contribution to the graph being small.

Turney [19] proposed a keyphrase extraction algorithm based on supervised learning. A document is treated as a set of phrases, which must be classified as either positive or negative examples of keyphrases based on examination of their features. Nine features are observed in the training data, including the number of words in a phrase, the location of the first occurrence of a phrase in a document, the frequency with which a phrase occurs within a document, whether the phrase is a proper noun and whether a phrase matches a human-generated keyphrase. It is shown that specialized procedural domain knowledge is valuable for learning to extract keyphrases from text.

In this paper we propose a keyphrase extraction approach based on multilayer feed-forward neural network. In order to determine whether or not a phrase is a keyphrase, the following features (attributes) of a phrase in a given document is considered: the term frequency TF, the inverted document frequency IDF, whether or not the phrase appears in the title or headings (subheadings) of the given document, and its distribution in the paragraphs of the given document. These features of a phrase are input to a neural network, and with which keyphrases are selected using backpropagation algorithm. The experiment results show that this approach is competitive with known methods.

The rest of the paper is organized as follows. We define the neural network model for keyphrase extraction in section 2. In section 3, we apply the neural network model to keyphrase extraction and give experiment results. We give some discussion about the experiment results in section 4. This paper concludes with some comments.

2 The Neural Network Model for Keyphrase Extraction

The backpropagation algorithm performs learning on a multilayer feed-forward neural network [5]. An example of such a network is shown in Figure 1. The inputs correspond to the attributes measured for each training sample. The inputs are fed simultaneously into a layer of units making up the input layer. The weighted outputs of these units are, in turn, fed simultaneously to a second layer of "neuronlike" units, known as a hidden layer. The hidden layer's weighted outputs can be input to another hidden layer, and so on. The number of hidden layers is arbitrary, although in practice, usually only one is used. The weighted outputs of the last hidden layer are input to units making up to the output layer, which emits the network's prediction for given samples.

Backpropagation learns by iteratively processing a set of training samples, comparing the network's prediction for each sample with the actual known class label. For each training sample, the weights are modified so as to minimize the mean squared error between the network's prediction and the actual class. These modifications are made in the "backwards" direction, that is, from the output layer, through each hidden layer down to the first hidden layer. Although it is not guaranteed, in general the weights will eventually converge, and the learning process stops.

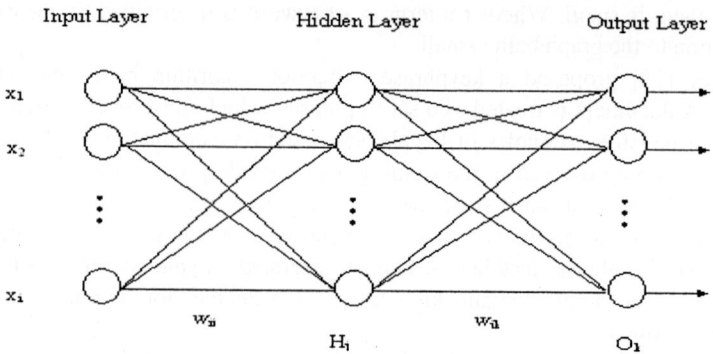

Fig. 1. A multilayer feed-forward neural network: A training sample, $X = (x_1, x_2, ..., x_i)$, is fed to the input layer. Weighted connections exist between each layer, where w_{ij} denotes the weight from a unit j in one layer to a unit i in the previous layer.

Before applying the neural network to keyphrase extraction, features (or attributes) of a phrase for judging whether it is a keyphrase should be defined. We have the following consideration and hypothesis when deciding to adopt what features to determine a keyphrase:

1. TF (Term Frequency) provides one measure of how well the term describes the document contents.
2. The motivation for usage of IDF (Inverted Document Frequency) is that tems which appear in many documents are not very useful for distinguashing a relevent document from a non-relevent one [2].
3. Title and headings (and subheadings) are the most common summaries in documents and usually describe the main issue discussed in the document.
4. If a phrase recurs in different paragraphs of a document, then the phrase may be an important concept to the document.

Based on the above discussion, we use the following four features to determine whether a phrase is a keyphrase: the normalized term frequency TF, the inverted document frequency IDF, whether or not a phrase appears in the title or heading (subheading) THS, and the normalized paragraph distribution frequency PDF.

TF: the normalized frequency of the phrase in the given document. For a phrase i and a document d, let n_i be the number of times the phrase i is mentioned in the document d, then the TF of i is computed by the formula (1).

$$\text{TF} = n_i / \max_{l \in d} n_l \,. \tag{1}$$

IDF: the inverted document frequency. For a phrase i and a document set (sample documents) with size Q, let q_i be the number of documents in which the phrase i appears, then the IDF of i is computed by the formula (2).

$$\text{IDF} = \log(Q/q_i) \,. \tag{2}$$

PDF: PDF is a structural measure feature. For a phrase i and a document d, let m_i be the number of paragraphs (of the document d) in which the phrase i appears, then the PDF of i is computed by the formula (3).

$$PDF = m_i / \max\nolimits_{l \in d} m_l . \qquad (3)$$

THS: existence of the phrase in the title or headings (subheadings) of a given document. If the phrase appears in the title or headings (subheadings) of a given document, THS is equal to one, otherwise zero.

Therefore, we have the neural network model for keyphrase extraction as shown in Figure 2. In the input layer, there are four neurons corresponding to a phrase's four features in a given document. In the output layer, there is only one neuron corresponding to whether or not a phrase is a keyphrase: in the training stage, if a phrase is a keyphrase, then O_1 is equal to 1, otherwise 0; in the keyphrase extraction stage, if the output O_1 for a feature vector input of a phrase i is more than 0.5, then i is extracted as a keyphrase, otherwise i is not a keyphrase.

The algorithm is implemented in MATLAB neural network toolbox. In our neural network implementation, there are ten neurons in the hidden layer and the network is trained for up to 500 epochs to the mean squared error goal of 0.00001.

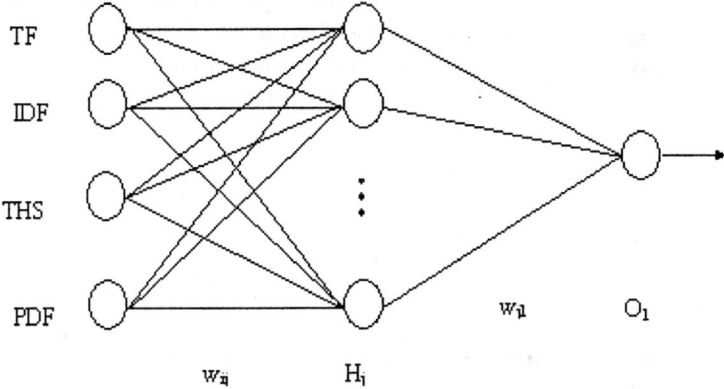

Fig. 2. The neural network model for keyphrase extraction

3 Experiment Results

Before computing the feature values of a phrase, it is necessary to get a collection of sample documents. The sample collection of documents is required to set the value of IDF of each phrase contained in a particular document. We use the web search engines *google* (www.google.com) and *Baidu* (www.baidu.com, a popular search engine in China) to search and download web documents (including *word*, *pdf*, and *ps* file formats). 300 documents are selected as the sample documents, including 250 documents written in English and 50 documents written in Chinese. The subjects of those documents are various, including mathematics, physics, chemistry, engineering science, information science, biology, manage science, and economics.

Among those 300 sample documents, 237 documents have been assigned keyphrases by authors, and 63 documents have not been assigned. The number of the author's keyphrases ranges from three to seven, and the length of keyphrases ranges from two to six.

In order to obtain the feature matrix of each document, we use a text segmentation tool to break up the document into phrases (for Chinese document) and then manually extract a set of candidate phrases for each document. For each document, every sequence of one to four (for English document) or two to six (for Chinese document) words is identified. Stems that are equivalent are merged into a single canonical form. Many phrases are discarded at this stage, including those that begin or end with a stopword, those which consist only of a proper noun, etc. This work is very tedious, but we can get more credible candidate phrases of each document.

There are two basic methods for evaluating automatically generated keyphrases. The first adopts the standard information retrieval metrics of precision and recall to reflect how well generated phrases match a set of "relevant" phrases. The second gathers subjective assessments from human readers.

The first approach requires a set of "relevant" phrases against which extracted phrases can be compared. The keyphrases provided by authors are usually used as gold standard set of keyphrases for a document. Performance is measured using precision and recall. Let N_e be the number of extracted phrases, N_a the number of keyphrases assigned by authors, and $N_{e \cap a}$ the number of extracted phrases that are also keyphrases assigned by authors, then precision and recall is computed by formula (4) and (5) respectively:

$$\text{Precision} = N_{e \cap a} / N_e . \tag{4}$$

$$\text{Recall} = N_{e \cap a} / N_a . \tag{5}$$

This approach is simple, but there are several problems with using author's keyphrases [3]:

1. Author's keyphrases are not always taken from the text. So, if a phrase is not contained in a given document, it is never extracted as a keyphrase of the given document by the automatic keyphrase extraction algorithm.
2. Author's keyphrases are often restricted to a very small number of phrases (two or three, for example) because of the journal (and proceedings) publication policy and other consideration.
3. Author's keyphrases are often chosen for a specific purpose (for classification according to an existing set of keyphrases, to steer review of a document, to distinguish a document from others in one specific collection of documents, etc.)
4. Author's keyphrases are usually only available for the very few kinds of documents for which authors supply keyphrases.

The second approach, human assessment, has been used in several previous studies. Human evaluation also suffers some disadvantages: it can be time-consuming and expensive; assessors may not make consistent judgements, etc. However, the evaluation may be closer to the nature of decisions that users will make in the course of their interactions with systems exploiting keyphrases [14].

We evaluate our keyphrase extraction algorithm using the above two approaches. For the documents that the keyphrases have been assigned by authors, we use the precision and recall to evaluate the algorithm and the experiment result is shown in table 1; for the documents that the keyphrases are unavailable, we use human assessment approach. The judges in our experiments are graduate students, and the experiment result is shown in table 2.

In table 3, the number of phrases is the sum of 237 (or 63) documents' number of phrases, where each document is seen as a list of different phrases manually extracted from the original document. We run the algorithm on a PC with Pentium 1.7Hz CPU and 256M memory and the value in the last column of table 3 is the CPU time for neural network with Levenberg-Marquardt training algorithm [10].

Table 1. The Experiment Result—Precision and Recall

The number of extracted keyphrases	The number of author's keyphrases	Precision (%)	Recall (%)
1208	1019	31.6	37.5

Table 2. The Experiment Result—Human Assessment

The number of extracted keyphrases	The proportion of good keyphrases (%)	The proportion of fair keyphrases (%)	The proportion of poor keyphrases (%)
327	64.7	15.8	19.5

Table 3. The Experiment Result—CPU time

	The number of phrases	CPU Time for classification of phrases (seconds)
237 documents	9762	15.368
63 documents	2501	3.796

4 Discussion

From table 1 we can see that the approach presented in this paper seems to be dissatisfactory in terms of the precision and recall. In fact, the experiment results show that the approach presented in this paper is competitive with other known algorithms [3, 9, 14] in terms of not only precision and recall but also human assessment.

The reasons that the precision and recall are low have been mentioned in section 3. Author's keyphrases are not always taken from the text and often restricted to a very small number of phrases. Therefore, if a phrase is not contained in a given document, it has no chance to be extracted as a keyphrase of the given document. In this case, it is impossible for recall to reach 100 percent.

For example, the paper *"A Chinese web page classifier based on support vector machine and unsupervised clustering"*, appearing in the *Chinese Journal of computer*, have three author's keyphrases: *"support vector machine"*, *"clustering"*, and *"web page classification*". The keyphrase extraction algorithm extracts the following five keyphrases from the paper: *"support vector machine"*, *"unsupervised clustering"*, *"web page classification"*, *"Recognition"*, and *"Web page representation"*. So, the recall for this paper is 3/3 = 100%, while the precision is only 3/5 = 60%. Actually, the phrase *"web page representation"* could be selected as one keyphrase of the paper considering the fact that one section of the paper discusses how to represent web pages.

From table 2, we can see that over 80 percent of the keyphrases extracted by backpropagation is acceptable. At the same time, the algorithm is also fast: the CPU time of training and classification for 9762 phrases is only 15.368 seconds and the CPU time of classification for 2501 phrases is only 3.796 seconds.

5 Conclusions

In this paper we propose a keyphrase extraction approach based on neural network and use the backpropagation as the training algorithm. To determine whether a phrase is a keyphrase or not, we use the frequency analysis, i.e., term frequency and inverted document frequency, and the phrase structural features, i.e., the distribution of a phrase in a given document. The approach is evaluated by the standard information retrieval metrics of precision and recall, and human assessment. Experiment results show that this approach is competitive with other known methods and practical, especially in the situation where the keyphrases are unavailable.

In order to increase further the precision and recall, we think that the term association rule mining and ensemble neural networks learning may be useful approaches, on which we are investigating.

Acknowledgement

This work was supported partially by Natural Science Foundation of China under Grant 30230350 and 60574078, and Natural Science Foundation of Guangdong Province under Grant 031454.

References

1. Azcarraga A. P., Yap Jr.T., Chua T. S.: Comparing Keyword Extraction Techniques for WEBSOM Text Archives. International Journal on Artificial Intelligence Tools, 11(2) (2002) 219 – 232.
2. Baeza-Yates R., Ribeiro-Neto B.: Modern Information Retrieval. Reading, Addison-Wesley Publishing Company, MA (1999).
3. Barker K., Cornacchia N.: Using Noun Phrase Heads to Extract Document Keyphrases. In: H. Hamilton, Q. Yang (eds.): Canadian AI 2000. Lecture Notes in Artificial Intelligence, Vol. 1822, Springer-Verlag, Berlin Heidelberg (2000) 40 – 52.
4. Chien L. F.: PAT-tree-based Adaptive Keyphrase Extraction for Intelligent Chinese Information Retrieval. Information Processing and Management, 35 (1999) 501 – 521.

5. Freeman J. A., Skapura D.M.: Neural Networks: Algorithms, Applications, and Programming Techniques. Addison-Wesley Publishing Company, MA, 1992.
6. Freitag D.: Machine Learning for Information Extraction in Informal Domains. Machine Learning, 39 (2000) 169 – 202.
7. Gayo-Avello D., Álvarez-Gutiérrez D, Gayo-Avello J.: Naïve Algorithms for Keyphrase Extraction and Text Summarization from a Single Document Inspired by the Protein Biosynthesis Process. In: A. J. Ijspeert et al (eds.): BioADIT 2004. Lecture Notes in Computer Science, Vol. 3141, Springer-Verlag, Berlin Heidelberg (2004) 440 – 455.
8. HaCohen-Kerner Y.: Automatic Extraction of Keywords from Abstracts. In: V. Palade, R. J. Howlett, L. C. Jain (eds.): KES 2003. Lecture Notes in Artificial Intelligence, Vol. 2773, Springer-Verlag, Berlin Heidelberg (2003) 843 – 849.
9. HaCohen-Kerner Y., Gross Z, Masa A.: Automatic Extraction and Learning of Keyphrases from Scientific Articles. In: A. Gelbukh (ed.): CICLing 2005. Lecture Notes in Computer Science, Vol. 3406, Springer-Verlag, Berlin Heidelberg (2005) 657 – 669.
10. Hagan M. T., Menhaj M.: Training Feed-forward Networks with the Marquardt Algorithm. IEEE Transactions on Neural Networks, 5(6) (1994) 989 – 993.
11. He J., Tan A-H., Tan C-L.: On Machine Learning Methods for Chinese Document Keyphrases Categorization. Applied Intelligence, 18 (2003) 311 – 322.
12. Hulth A., Karlgren J., Jonsson A., Boström H.: Automatic Keyword Extraction Using Domain Knowledge. In: A. Gelbukh (ed.): CICLing 2001. Lecture Notes in Computer Science, Vol. 2004, Springer-Verlag, Berlin Heidelberg (2001) 472 – 482.
13. Ikeda D., Hirokawa S.: Extracting Positive and Negative Keywords for Web Communities. In: S. Arikawa, S. Morishita (eds.): DS 2000. Lecture Notes in Artificial Intelligence, Vol. 1967, Springer-Verlag, Berlin Heidelberg (2000) 299 – 303.
14. Jones S., Paynter G. W.: Automatic Extraction of Document Keyphrases for Use in Digital Libraries: Evaluation and Applications. Journal of the American Society for Information Science and Technology, 53(8) (2002) 653 – 677.
15. Martínez-Fernández J. L., Gacía-Serrano A., Martínez P., Villena J.: Automatic Keyword Extraction for News Finder. In: A. Nürnberger, M. Detyniecki (eds.): AMR 2003. Lecture Notes in Computer Science, Vol. 3094, Springer-Verlag, Berlin Heidelberg (2004) 99 – 119.
16. Matsuo Y., Ohsawa Y., Ishizuka M.: KeyWorld: Extracting Keywords from a Document as a Small World. In: K. P. Jantke, A. shinohara (eds.): DS 2001. Lecture Notes in Computer Science, Vol. 2226, Springer-Verlag, Berlin Heidelberg (2001) 271– 281.
17. Rydberg-Cox J. A.: Keyword Extraction from Ancient Greek Literacy Texts. Literary and Linguistic Computing, 17(2) (2002) 231 – 244.
18. Soderland S.: Learning Information Extraction Rules for Semi-structured and Free Text. Machine Learning, 34 (1999) 233 – 272.
19. Turney P.D.: Learning Algorithms for Keyphrase Extraction. Information Retrieval, 2(4) (2000) 303-336.
20. Witten I.H., Paynter G.W., Frank E., et al: KEA: Practical Automatic Keyphrase Extraction. In: E. A. Fox, N. Rowe (eds.): Proceedings of Digital Libraries'99: The Fourth ACM Conference on Digital Libraries. ACM Press, Berkeley, CA (1999) 254 – 255.

A Novel Fuzzy Anomaly Detection Method Based on Clonal Selection Clustering Algorithm

Fenghua Lang, Jian Li, and Yixian Yang

Information Security Center,
State Key Laboratory of Networking and Switching,
Beijing University of Posts and Telecommunications,
Beijing 100876, P.R. China
lang_feng_hua@yahoo.com.cn

Abstract. This paper presents a novel unsupervised fuzzy clustering method based on clonal selection algorithm for anomaly intrusion detection in order to solve the problem of fuzzy k-means algorithm which is particularly sensitive to initialization and fall easily into local optimization. This method can quickly obtain the global optimal clustering with a clonal operator which combines evolutionary search, global search, stochastic search and local search, then detect abnormal network behavioral patterns with a fuzzy detection algorithm. Simulation results on the data set KDD CUP99 show that this method can efficiently detect unknown intrusions with lower false positive rate and higher detection rate.

1 Introduction

With the development of network technology and the improvement of information science, network and information security has already become a globally unavoidable problem. To protect the core information in systems and networks, many methods for intrusion detection have been presented and much attention has been paid to it.

In general, an Intrusion Detection Systems(IDS) is categorized into two general approaches: misuse detection and anomaly detection. Misuse detection, which is based on attack signatures, is efficient and accurate in detecting known intrusions, but is unable to detect new intrusions. Anomaly detection, which is based on statistical knowledge about the normal activity of the computer system, can detect novel and unknown attacks, but its false positive rate is high. Therefore, many anomaly detection methods are applied to intrusion detection for reducing the false positive rate and improving the detection efficiency.

Many different approaches and techniques, such as genetic algorithm[1], hide Markov model[2] , support vector machine[3] etc, have been applied to anomaly intrusion detection. However, many above mentioned methods totally depend on the training data sets, which should not only be "clean" data sets but also involve most of the normal behavioral patterns of the detected object. But, in fact, it is very difficult and costly to meet both these requirements.

In order to solve the above mentioned problems, this paper proposes a novel unsupervised Fuzzy K-Means(FKM) clustering anomaly detection method based on Clonal Selection Algorithm(CSA). This method can quickly obtain the global optimal clustering with a clonal operator which combines evolutionary search, global search, stochastic search and local search, and then detect abnormal network behavioral patterns with a fuzzy detection algorithm. The advantage of this method is that it does not need to collect and classify the training data sets with artificial or other methods. Simulation results on the data set KDD CUP99 show that this method can efficiently detect unknown intrusion with a lower false positive rate and a higher detection rate.

The subsequent sections are organized as follows: Section 2 briefly describes the fuzzy clustering theory used in this paper. Section 3 details an unsupervised k-means fuzzy clustering method based on clonal selection algorithm for intrusion detection. Simulation and results analysis are presented in Section 4 followed by the conclusion remarks and future directions for this work in Section 5.

2 Fuzzy Clustering Theory

Let data set $X = \{x_1, x_2, \cdots, x_n\} \subset R^s$ be a feature vector set of s-dimensional mode or pattern space. Sample set X is divided into fuzzy subsets $X_1, X_2, \cdots X_k$, where k is an integer in $[2, n)$, and the fuzzy classified space M_f is denoted as follows:

$$M_f = \left\{ \mu_{il} \mid \mu_{il} \in [0,1]; \sum_{i=1}^{k} \mu_{il} = 1, \forall l;\ n \geq \sum_{l=1}^{n} \mu_{il} \geq 0, \forall i \right\} \quad (1)$$

where μ_{il} is the membership degree of x_l belonging to the i-th cluster.

For any given dataset X, fuzzy clustering analysis can easily obtain its fuzzy k-partition: $U = [\mu_{il}]_{k \times n}$, where U is a fuzzy partition matrix. To obtain an optimal cluster, we firstly define an appropriate partition principle operator $D(\cdot)$, and assume set p_i as the clustering prototype of each fuzzy subset, the nearness degree between the sample x_l and the fuzzy data set X_i can be measured by distortion $d_{il} = D(x_l, p_i)$ between the sample x_l and the clustering prototype p_i, where $D(\cdot)$ is generally defined as a different measurement of some kinds of distance such that Euclidean distance or Mahalanobis distance.

To ensure the clustering result can make things of one kind, researchers generally establish the objective function of a fuzzy cluster by minimizing the distortion between each sample and its modes, thus obtaining optimal fuzzy k-partition $U^* = [\mu_{il}]_{k \times n}$ where U^* is the clustering prototype set and optimal clustering prototype $P^* = \{p_i \mid 1 \leq i \leq k\}$ of each cluster by optimizing its objective function. The general objective function of a fuzzy cluster is represented as follows:

$$C(U, P) = \sum_{i=1}^{K} \sum_{l=1}^{N} (\mu_{il})^m [D(x_l, p_i)]^2, \ \mu_{il} \in [0,1] \quad (2)$$

where parameter m is the fuzzy control factor. Fuzzy k-means algorithm obtains its final clustering result by iteratively optimizing and minimizing the objective function. Fuzzy k-means algorithm is simple and has a high convergence rate, so it is widely used in intrusion detection fields. However, fuzzy k-means algorithm is very sensitive to initialization and falls easily into local optimization, unless excellent initialization is obtained. A few years ago researchers presented another clustering algorithm which is base on genetic algorithm. This kind of clustering algorithm can converge at the global optimal point with high probability, but its disadvantage is that the convergence rate is low and the prematurity is easily occurred.

3 Fuzzy Detection Algorithm Based on CSA

To overcome the drawbacks of the conventional fuzzy k-means algorithm which is particularly sensitive to initialization and falls easily into local optimization, we optimize the objective function of unsupervised fuzzy k-means clustering based on clonal selection algorithm and then introduce this improved algorithm into anomaly detection. This novel clustering algorithm can not only performs cluster analysis with multi-type prototypes but also automatically determines the proper cluster number and cluster structures.

3.1 Clonal Selection Algorithm

Jeme proposed the immune network theory[4] in 1974, and in 2002, De Castro and Von Zuben[5] presented the clonal selection algorithm. The clonal selection algorithm is a novel artificial immune algorithm, which has the clonal operators to be applied to artificial intelligence according to the antibody clonal selection mechanism of biology immune system. Since the clonal selection algorithm has a colony search mechanism in nature, which helps to prevent it from falling into the trap of local optimization, it can converge to global optimization with a higher probability and higher speed. Therefore, compared with the clustering algorithms based on genetic algorithm, the novel fuzzy clustering algorithm based on clonal selection algorithm will have higher efficiency, and be more suitable for clustering analysis of large data sets. The advantage of the fuzzy clustering algorithm proposed in this paper is that it is extremely appropriate for the need of large data sets and high real-time characteristics in IDS.

Clonal selection algorithm[6] is represented as follows:

Step 1: $n=0$; initialize the population of antibody $A(0)$, and set parameters of algorithm, then calculate the affinity of initial population;

Step 2: Conduct clonal operator operation, and obtain the following generation population $A(n+1)$ based on affinity and scale of antibody clones in Step 1;

Step 3: $n++$; repeat Step 2 until the proposed iterations are completed;

Step 4: Stop.

3.2 Fuzzy Clustering Algorithm Based on CSA

To obtain optimal fuzzy clustering based on clonal selection algorithm, it is most important that we firstly encode the solution of clustering problem to antibody, then construct the affinity functions of antibody and antigen, and then finally select the most appropriate clonal operator. The detailed encoding scheme can be referred to can be found in reference [6]. The clonal operator plays a very important role in the process of the clustering algorithm, which mainly involves clonal operation T_c^c, clonal gene operation T_g^c which consist of clonal recombination and clonal mutation, clonal selection operator T_s^c and clonal death operation T_d^c, and its flow is described as follows:

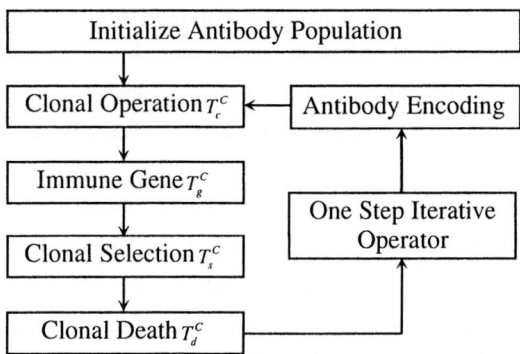

Fig. 1. The flow of a fuzzy clustering algorithm based on clonal selection algorithm

3.3 Fuzzy Detection Method Based on Clonal Selection Clustering Algorithm

The unsupervised fuzzy k-means algorithm based on clonal selection algorithm for anomaly detection is based on two assumptions. First, the number of normal samples should far exceed the number of attacks. Second, the attacks themselves should be significantly different to the normal samples. This algorithm is guided by the knowledge that since the intrusions are correspondingly rare in number and are different to the normal samples, they show the special features in the data which can be detected.

The algorithm proposed in this paper basically includes three parts: the data pre-processing, the unsupervised fuzzy clustering algorithm based on the clonal selection algorithm, and the detection algorithm based on the unsupervised fuzzy k-means clustering algorithm.

The first step of the data pre-processing process is encoding, which is essentially to establish a mapping between the solution space of problem and the searching space of algorithm. Because the aim of clustering is to get a fuzzy dividing matrix U and a clustering prototype P of data set X, where U and P are not irrelevant. We assume the clustering prototype P as an antibody, and encode its quantization as an antibody by connecting all the k features in the prototype based on each range of the value. The second step is the cluster process. The detail of the pre-processing process is represented as follows:

Step 1: Create initial population, then generate randomly initial antibody $A(0) = [A_1(0), A_2(0), \cdots A_K(0)]$ and each antibody represents a combined features with binary digital coding;

Step 2: $k = 0$; calculate affinity and decode each antibody into a corresponding combination feature to get a new training samples set, then calculate corresponding affinity $\{J(A(0))\}$ with the following formula

$$f(A) = \frac{1}{1+C(U,P)} \tag{3}$$

Step 3: If the iterative termination conditions have been satisfied (the conditions such as the affinity threshold or the iterative times), then we consider the optimal individual of current populations as the global optimal solution, else continue;

Step 4: Perform the clonal operation T_c^c to obtain $A'(k)$;

Step 5: Perform the immune gene operation T_g^c to obtain $A^*(k)$;

Step 6: Perform the clonal selection operation T_s^c to obtain a new antibody population $A(k+1)$;

Step 7: Perform the clonal death T_d^c: if $A(k+1)$ involves $A_i(k+1)$ and $A_j(k+1)$ which satisfies the condition of $f(A_i(k+1)) = f(A_j(k+1)) = \max\{f(A(k+1))\}, i \neq j$, then randomly generate a new antibody, and randomly die $A_i(k+1)$ or $A_j(k+1)$;

Step 8: Calculate the affinity: obtain a new feature subset based on individual code in population, and then calculate affinity $\{J(A(k+1))\}$ of $A(k+1)$ with formula (3) in Step 2;

Step 9: $k++$; return Step 3;

Step 10: Stop.

After creating fuzzy k-means clusters with the above algorithm, we should label the clusters. According to the first and second assumptions we can deduce that the number of clusters containing normal data will be larger than that of clusters

---

Algorithm: Labeling algorithm
    Input: Cluster C_i, threshold r and number of cluster $cluster\_num$
    Output: Type of Cluster C_i corresponding to r
    Process:
        Begin
            $j=1$;
            $k = r \times cluster\_num$;
            While ($j \leq cluster\_num$)
                Selection
                If ($j < k$)
                    $C_j \in \{\text{Normal Cluster}\}$;
                Else
                    $C_j \in \{\text{Abnormal Cluster}\}$;
                Mutation
                    $j++$;
        End

Fig. 2. Pseudo-code of labeling algorithm

containing abnormal data. So we can set a detection threshold r, then clusters with a larger number corresponding to r are labelled as "normal" classes and the rest of the clusters are labelled as "abnormal" classes.

Assume $C_i, i=1,2,\cdots,cluster\_num$ as the created original clusters, and r as the detection threshold. The labeling algorithm is described in Figure 2.

This labeling algorithm[7] is simple and easily implemented. However, its validity depends on the sub-type number of normal samples. To reduce the false positive rate, we should ensure that the percentage of the normal samples in the training set is large enough to assure that each type of the normal samples used will have adequate representation compared to each sub-type of intrusion.

The detection algorithm proceeds as below:
Assume x as the network data packet to be detected.

Step 1: Get $x \in C_i, 1 \le i \le cluster\_num$ with data pre-processing algorithm;
Step 2: Get the attribute of C_i with labeling algorithm;
Step 3: If $C_i \in \{$Normal Clusters$\}$, then $x \in \{$Normal data$\}$;
Step 4: Else $x \in \{$Abnormal data$\}$;
Step 5: Stop.

4 Simulation and Analysis

In this section, we experiment with the unsupervised fuzzy k-means clustering detection algorithm based on clonal selection algorithm by using the data set of KDD CUP99[8] which is one of the authoritative testing data set in current intrusion detection fields.

KDD CUP99 data set is a version of the 1998 DARPA intrusion detection evaluation data set prepared and managed by MIT Lincoln Labs, which contained a wide variety of intrusions simulated in a military network environment. It consists of 4,898,431 records, of which 3,925,650 are attacks, and contains 22 different types of attacks that can be classified into four main categories: denial of service(DoS), unauthorized access from a remote machine(R2L), unauthorized access to local superuser(root) privileges (U2R) and surveillance and other probing (Probing).

The whole KDD CUP99 data set is too large, so we must filter the raw training data sets in order to satisfy the two assumptions above. About 1.73 percent(84,582) of instances which include 930(less than 1.1 percent of total training sets) attack

Table 1. Numbers and types of attacks of training data set

Classes	Name and number of sub-classes
DoS(400)	neptune(196) smurf(204)
R2L(210)	imap(4) xsnoop(12) xlock(15) phf(5) ftp_write(12) named(17) sendmail(19) guess_passwd(45) warezmaster(41) multihop(40)
R2L(210)	loadmodle(2) buffer_overflow(30) xterm(35) rootkit(20) ps(27) perl(4)
Probing(202)	ipsweep(80) nmap(38) satan(84)

instances as a training set is used to evaluate the performance of the system. Table 1 shows the number and types of attacks in the training data set.

Before using the detection algorithm for anomaly detection, we should firstly normalize the attributes of the data, because the original data set includes numeric and symbolic characteristic variables and different characteristic variables have different measuring standards. If we don't pre-process the data sets there will be an abrupt deviation. The pre-treatment is described as follows:

(1) Convert symbolic characteristic variables into numeric characteristic variables.
(2) Normalize every field of every data to the closed interval [0,1].

In order to evaluate the performance of the clustering method presented in this paper, we choose 4 groups of data sets, and every group includes 42,791 records. Group 1 and group 2 are selected from training sets while the other two group data sets are selected from KDD CUP99 data set which does not include training sets so that we can evaluate the efficiency of unknown attack by using the algorithm proposed in this paper.

To evaluate the performance of the algorithm proposed in this paper, we use two elements to define the accuracy of an anomaly detection approach: Detection Rate(DR) and False Positive Rate (FPR). DR equals the number of intrusions divided by the total number of intrusions in the data sets. And FPR equals the number of normal instances divided by the number of normal instances in the data sets. The value of DR is expected to be as large as possible, while the value of FPR is expected to be as small as possible.

DR and FPR are the most important indicators in the anomaly detection system, and always correlate tightly with the performance of the anomaly detection. DR, which is the percentage of abnormal samples correctly classified(considered abnormal), can be enhanced at the cost of increased FPR, which is the percentage of the normal samples incorrectly classified(considered abnormal), so we must choose an approximate detection rate and false positive rate in order to get a higher detection performance.

Table 2. Detection results of group 1 and group 2 with different threshold r

r (%)	Group 1		Group 2	
	DR(%)	FPR(%)	DR(%)	FPR(%)
14	90.04	9.04	95.26	4.71
16	88.49	3.85	92.12	2.63
18	87.14	2.18	84.75	1.30
20	84.10	1.29	82.54	1.12
22	83.25	1.24	73.58	0.88
24	80.15	1.54	77.78	1.56
26	76.25	1.82	71.25	1.37
28	70.24	3.34	70.45	1.64
30	69.57	2.90	68.52	2.14
32	69.47	6.95	40.25	1.75
34	62.14	10.36	39.45	3.95

Table 3. Detection results of group 3 and group 4 with different threshold r

r (%)	Group 3		Group 4	
	DR (%)	FPR(%)	DR (%)	FPR(%)
14	82.24	9.14	87.54	4.86
16	81.58	5.44	76.25	4.77
18	76.58	2.39	76.06	1.85
20	76.25	1.27	75.65	1.45
22	74.21	1.28	74.12	1.09
24	70.58	1.96	73.25	1.13
26	69.65	1.66	62.15	1.05
28	64.54	1.90	54.25	2.71
30	62.12	1.73	48.54	3.73
32	60.25	3.35	40.15	3.35
34	54.25	9.04	40.02	4.00

Table 2 and Table 3 show the results of DR and FPR when different thresholds r are chosen. To determine the most appropriate value of threshold r, we use a trial-and-error method to carry out the experiment. Initially, we assume the value of r as 14, and then change the value of r to obtain different DR and FPR. From Table 2 we can conclude that DR and FPR of every group reduce with our estimation. The smaller the value of r, the greater the number of the instances labelled as "anomaly"; and the larger the detection rate, larger the false positive rate.

Figure 3 shows the relationship between the detection threshold r and the ratio DR/FPR. From Figure 3 we obtain the most appropriate value of the detection rate r when r is equal 22 percent, so we adopt this value for the next experiment.

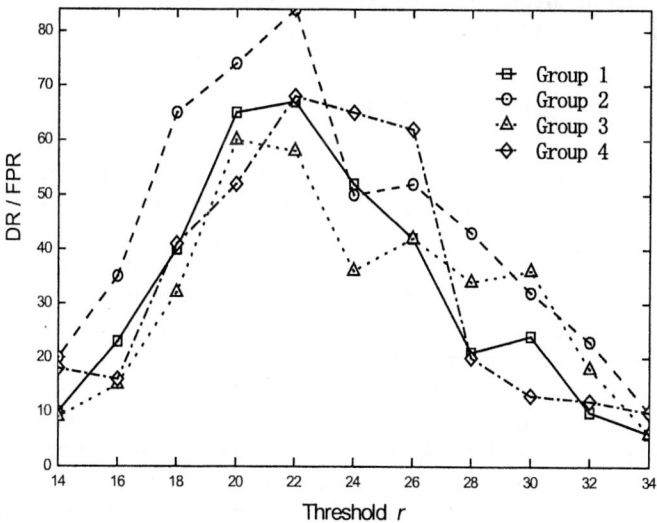

Fig. 3. Detection results with different threshold r

When r is equal to 22 percent, we conduct the experiment with group 3 and group 4. The experiment results are shown in Table 4. The known attacks(KA) are defined as attacks including both training sets and the test sets, such as intrusions listed in Table 1. The unknown attacks(UA), however, are intrusions which include test sets but do not include training sets, such as udpstorm intrusion in DoS and portsweep intrusion in Probing.

Table 4. Detection rate to known and unknown attack when r is equal to 22 percent

Classes	Group 3		Group 4	
	KA (%)	UA (%)	KA (%)	UA (%)
DoS	64.84	48.45	67.54	52.23
R2L	48.53	28.42	44.40	10.10
U2R	80.04	68.85	89.87	58.75
Probing	78.49	76.45	82.41	80.85
Average	67.98	55.54	71.06	50.48

From Table 4, we can see that the algorithm proposed in this paper obtains high detection rates in U2R and R2L, this result also coincides with our estimation too. Because many R2U attackers pretend to be legal users to use the network or use it in a seemingly legitimate way, their features are similar to the normal samples. Therefore, the algorithm may cluster these instances together and the attacks will be undetected. In addition, just because there are so many instances of the intrusion that it occurs in a similar number to normal samples, the algorithm has difficulty in the detection of DoS attacks, and may also label these samples as normal samples. The over 50 percent average detection rate of unknown attacks in group 3 and group 4 shows that the fuzzy clustering algorithm based on clonal selection algorithm proposed in this paper can efficiently detect unknown intrusions.

5 Conclusion and Future Work

The aim of this paper is to increase the detection rate and reduce the false positive rate of anomaly detection systems by using the unsupervised fuzzy k-means clustering algorithm based on clonal selection algorithm, it overcomes two disadvantages of conventional k-means algorithm, which is sensitive to initialization and fall easily into local optimization. Simulation results on data set KDD CUP99 show that the method proposed in this paper can not only detect unknown intrusion but also have lower false positive rate and higher detection rate.

However, we must clearly realize that there is still a lack of efficient methods for choosing threshold r which is a standard of normal clusters and abnormal clusters, and we can only determine the value of threshold r by experiment. One direction that we are pursuing after this study is to applied swarm intelligence technology, such as Ant Colony Optimization(ACO), Particle Swarm Optimization(PSO) or Marriage in Honey Bees Optimization(MBO) to the research on anomaly intrusion detection for further lower false positive rate and higher detection rate.

Acknowledgement

The authors gratefully acknowledge the help from Institute of Intelligent Information Processing, Xidian University. We wish to thank anonymous reviewers for their suggestions and comments. This work was supported by the National High-Tech Research and Development Program of China under the Grant No. 2005AA143040.

References

1. Dasgupta, D., and Gonzalez, F.: An Immunity-Based Technique to Characterize Intrusions in Computer Networks. IEEE Trans. Evol. Comput., Vol. 6, (2002) 281-291
2. Sugbae C., and Sangjun H.: Two Sophisticated Techniques to Improved HMM-Based Intrusion Detection Systems. Proceeding of RAID, Pittsburgh, Sept. (2003) 207-219
3. He, D., and Leung, H.: CFAR Intrusion Detection Method Based on Support Vector Machine Prediction. Proceeding of CIMSA2004, Boston, Jul. (2004) 10-15
4. Jeme N.K.: Towards a Network Theory of the Immune System. Ann. Immunol., Jan. (1974) 373-389
5. Castro L. N., and Von Zuben F. J.: Learning and Optimization Using the Clone Selection Principal. IEEE Trans. Evol. Comput., Vol. 6, No. 3, (2002) 239-251
6. Jie L., Xinbo G., and Licheng J.: A Novel Clustering Method with Network Structure Based on Clonal Algorithm. Canada, Proceeding of ICASSP2004, Canada, May (2004) 793-796
7. Portnoy L., Eskin E., and Stolfo S.: Intrusion Detection with Unlabeled Data Using Clustering. Proceedings of DMSA2001, Philadelphia Nov. (2001) 5-8
8. KDD CUP99 Data Set. http://kdd.ics.uci.edu/databases/kddcup99/kddcup99.html, 1999.

An Anti-worm with Balanced Tree Based Spreading Strategy

Yi-xuan Liu[1], Xiao-chun Yun[1], Bai-ling Wang[1], and Hai-bin Sun[2]

[1] Harbin Institute of Technology
{liuyixuan, yxc, wbl}@hit.edu.cn
[2] The Chinese University of Hong Kong
hbsun@cse.cuhk.edu.hk

Abstract. The traditional prevention methods of anti-virus software cannot provide a safe network against malicious worms. In this paper, we research an anti-worm mechanism that actively distributes the anti-worm code to the authorized hosts. We propose a Balanced Tree based Propagation strategy(BTP) for an anti-worm strategy with a mathematic model. By varying the model parameters, the impacts can be studied. Some simulation results show us that the new strategy is effective and feasible.

1 Introduction

Recent virus and worm outbreak have demonstrated that network computers continue to be vulnerable to new attacks. Security flaws still exist. First, the software itself is often written in an insecure manner. Also, when vulnerabilities are announced with corresponding software patches, many people are slow to apply patches to their computers for various practical reasons [1]. Weakly protected computers can be compromised, putting the entire community at risk, including secured computers that can still be impacted by the traffic effects of a worm outbreak. Besides, the non real-time characteristics of current defense approaches such as antivirus software render it highly ineffective against zero-day worms [2] (such as Witty, which appeared one day after the exploited vulnerability was announced).

Slammer provided the first real-world demonstration of a high-speed worm's capabilities [3], quickly reaching far beyond the speed of human's reaction. It is reasonable to predict that in the near future attackers will continue to implement a variety of strategies to increase their worms' spreading speed and overcome our defenses in spite of new countermeasures.

To recover from a worm quickly, defense measures such as the patch code or worm killing signals should be distributed as quickly as possible. However, once hundreds and thousands of nodes have an urgent demand for the same code, the network and patch management system will collapse. However, as soon as one transporting patch code finishes, the network then has two 'servers', with which it can then serve other nodes. As this process evolves it is easy to see that the number of served nodes in the network will grow exponentially. This behavior will act as the worm itself: choose the victim node; transfer itself to that node and the newly received nodes began to serve others.

In this paper we consider a fast self-spreading method to distribute worm defense codes. We propose the BTP (Balance Tree-based Propagation) algorithm for anti-worm propagation and study its performance characteristics. We model the propagation based on age limited branching processes. We also model the malicious worm and anti-worm, two of its cross-propagation 'competitors'. In addition to our mathematical model, packet based experiments are also carried out to prove its efficiency. Our analytical results and experiments suggest how quickly and smoothly our worm defense code can spread to fight malicious worm disease.

The paper is organized as follows. Section 2 introduces related work on this topic. Section 3 gives a definition for anti worm. Section 4 presents the balance tree based propagation strategy. Simulation results are shown in section 5. We conclude with section 6.

2 Background

To date, most existing so-called anti-worm strategies have proven to be poor examples. But there are some good examples of beneficial self-replicating codes, usually in the form of automatic update programs or antivirus software. However, these approaches are insufficient when a malicious worm breaks out and thousands of hosts are under threat.

Early work by [4] in studies on transforming a malicious worm into an anti-worm and an anti-worm generation architecture is given. A Few researchers have used analytical models to study several worms' propagation. For example, [5] constructed a propagation model of worms together with anti-worms and gave an action-based taxonomy of Internet worms which differentiate the malicious worm from the friendly worm. The author in [6] also proposed a worm-anti-worm model based on the two factor model [7]. Some related research topics without further studies are suggested in this paper. These are the foundations for future work. The proposed anti-worm in its current form still has some practical issues, such as ethical and trust problems, although private companies or schools can use anti-worm in local networks where they have full legal access authority.

This paper focuses on a worm propagation strategy with controllability and cost efficiency. How to exploit a vulnerability, how to kill the malicious worm and how to patch systems are not part of our discussion.

3 What is an Anti Worm

In this section, we will give a general description of anti-worm to differentiate the anti-worm from the malicious worm. Some characteristics are provided to limit its capabilities.

3.1 Definition

Anti-worm is a self-replicating program to fight against the malicious worm. As an example, host A knows that a host B is vulnerable to the particular exploit that the worm uses to propagate, unless the worm itself removes that vulnerability. By using the authorized interface, host A can automatically transfer its defense code to host B and try to cure it from infection and even patch it. So, the anti-worm can be also regarded as a worm-to-worm agent, an agent with more autonomy, more reactivity, and more social ability.

Definition 1. Anti-worm is an active defense mechanism with mobile code to remove the vulnerabilities on the authorized network host which have or will have been used by attackers.

Anti worm will not take charge of all internet security. Instead, its aim is to spread over the authorized hosts to protect those hosts from being threatened. Therefore, the attacking components are not necessary for anti-worm and we could use more legality methods such as a real time client to receive the anti-worm. Below, vulnerable hosts will refer to the authorized hosts with security flaws.

3.2 Spreading Process

A worm may consist of several parts and here we talk only about how the spreading process works. The spreading process can be separated into four stages: selection, probing, attacking and self-propagating (See Figure 1). These issues may greatly impact on the efficiency of anti-worm propagation.

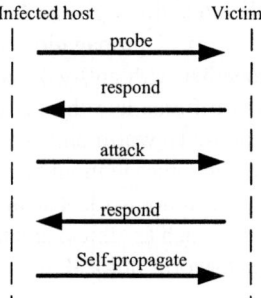

Fig. 1. Spreading Process

4 The Study of Anti-worm Spreading Strategy

The greedy spreading strategy of the malicious worm represents a persistent threat to the Internet. The strategy of the anti-worm is to avoid from such rapid unlimited scanning, as well as some useless re-scanning and frequency scanning from one local network to the other.

4.1 The Balanced Tree Based Propagation

Our aim is to have each vulnerable hosts receive only one copy of the anti-worm via the shortest route path. We denoted the whole network as an undirected graph

$G = G(V, E)$, while $V = \{v_1, \ldots, v_n\}$ is the set of vulnerable hosts in the network and $E = \{e_{ij}\}, e_{ij} \in E$ if there is an edge connecting two nodes v_i and v_j. Then, $G_1 \subset G$ is a directed graph denoting the anti-worm path in the network, while $V_1 \subseteq V$ represent the infected hosts in the network and $E_1 \subseteq E$ is the worm's spreading path, $e_{ij} \in E_1$ if host v_i sends a worm copy to host v_j. So G_1 is growing with time and in each time unit there will not be an added edge such as e_{ij} if e_{kj} or e_{ji} is already exist. This means there will not be a repeated edge and the indegree of each node is only one. We also hope the outdegree of each node in G_1 is almost equal.

Balanced Tree based Propagation (BTP): the full histlist we obtained is the set V, which is composed with nodes marked with $v_1, \ldots, v_n$. Anti worm spreads from one node (v_1 for example), infects the node and then sends the copy to the next nodes (v_2, v_3, ... for example). The worm will spread forward through the descendant's node and usually every non-leaf node has fixed descendant nodes. Usually, G_1, the worm spreading path graph, is a balanced tree at a time step (Figure 2 with degree 2). Noted that all the vulnerable host addresses are given in advance from the information collected in steps, some of which may already be down, and some of which may not vulnerable. We consider all the nodes in the list and organize them to be a balanced tree.

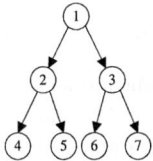

Fig. 2. Worm Spreading Path of BTP

Below, we present the pseudo-code of BTP.

BTP algorithm
$v_i(i = 1, \cdots, n)$ is the ith hosts with vulnerability.
Λ_i is the subtree list of nodes, and v_i is the root node of the subtree.
$|\Lambda_i|$ is the number of nodes in the subtree list.

1. **foreach** (infected host v_i)
2. {
3.   send the ok signals to his father;
    kill the malicious worm; patch the host;
4.   **while** ($|\Lambda_i| - 1 > 0$) {
5.   **foreach** ($v_j \in$ {immediate subsequence of v_i}) {
6. $tmp\_v = v_j$;
7.   **while** (Send_probe(tmp_v) == Fail || Is _infected(tmp_v) == True) {
8. $\Lambda_{tmp\_v} = \Lambda_{tmp\_v} - tmp\_v$;
9. tmp_v = GenerateTree (Λ_{tmp_v}) // tmp_v is the root of subtree Λ_{tmp_v}
10.   }
11.   Send_worm(tmp_v);

```
12.     Send_list($\Lambda_{tmp\_v}$);
13.     if (Waiting_response()== Null) {
14.         $\Lambda_{tmp\_v} = \Lambda_{tmp\_v} - tmp\_v$;
15.         tmp_v = GenerateTree ($\Lambda_{tmp\_v}$) // tmp_v is the root of subtree $\Lambda_{tmp\_v}$
16.     }
17.     else
18.         $\Lambda_i - = \Lambda_{tmp\_v}$;
19.     write the log file;
20.     }
21. }
22. add an infected identifier to $v_i$; kill itself;
23. }
```

Anti-worm on each node will kill itself after it sends copies to its sons. The number of sons is limited, so the time consumption for each node is constant. If there is N vulnerable hosts, the BTP strategy will spread over the hosts in $O(logN)$.

4.2 Epidemic Model Introduction

First, we briefly introduce the epidemic model [8,9] to give a general evaluation for random scan strategy, which is widely used by malicious worms. The traditional epidemic model assumes that each host owns one of two states: susceptible and infected. The model also assumes that once a host is infected by a worm, it remains in the infected state forever. Suppose $I(t)$ is the number of infected hosts at time t, N is the number of all vulnerable hosts in the network, then $N - I(t)$ is the number of susceptible hosts at time t. k is the infection rate of the worm. Some of the scans will hit invulnerable hosts in the network, so that k should be retouched as the effective infection rate which is the number of infected hosts hit by a host per unit time. And Δt is the small time interval. Thus the number of newly infected hosts during $(t, t+\Delta t)$ equals the number of hosts which receive the worm scanning. That is: $I(t+\Delta t) - I(t) = kI(t)[N - I(t)]/N$.

If $\Delta t \rightarrow 0$, we derive the traditional epidemic model:

$$\frac{dI}{dt} = kI(1 - \frac{I}{N}) \tag{1}$$

Equation(1) gives the increasing rate of infected nodes varying with time. It shows us the random scan worm will infect all N vulnerable hosts in $O(logN)$ time.

The epidemic model provides the basic intuition for the worm spreading. However, the model is somewhat idealized. We have assumed that there is no congestion and that there are no patching factors in the system.

4.3 Modeling the Anti-worm

Next we consider about the BTP model for anti-worm spreading. Assume that each host owns one of three states: susceptible, infected and quarantined. A host infected by a BTP worm recovers from the infected state and stays in the quarantined state after it sends d copies forward. Suppose $S'(t)$ is the number of susceptible host at time t. $I'(t)$ is the number of active infected hosts which are sending scans at time t. $Q'(t)$ is the number of quarantined hosts at time t, N is the number of all vulnerable hosts in the network, and $N = S'(t) + I'(t) + Q'(t)$. k' is the infection rate of the worm. Thus, it will spend the worm d/k' unit time long to send d scans. In other words, each infected host will send scans at d speed, branch its hitlist to its descendants and die after d/k' unit time.

Using the assumptions listed above, the BTP model can be written as:

$$\begin{cases} \dfrac{dI'(t)}{dt} = k'I'(t) - \dfrac{dQ'(t)}{dt} & \text{if } t > 0 \\ \dfrac{dI'(t)}{dt} = 0 & \text{if } t \leq 0 \\ \dfrac{dQ'(t)}{dt} = \dfrac{dI'(t - d/k')}{dt} & \end{cases} \quad (2)$$

Simulating with Matlab Simulink, we obtain the numerical solutions of BTP model (Equation 2) and plot them in Figure 3(a) for parameters $N = 6 \times 10^6$, $I'(0) = 1$, $Q'(0) = 0$, $k' = 2$, $d = 2$ in BTP model equation 2 and $I(0) = 1$, $k = 1$ in epidemic model Equation 1. Y axis for BTP model in Figure 3(a) indicates both active infected and quarantined hosts by the BTP worm. Figure 3(a) shows that the time T taken by the BTP worm to spread around the network is shortened compared to the random scan worm since the effective infection rate k' is increased.

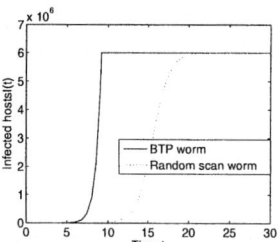

(a) BTP worm model vs Random scan model

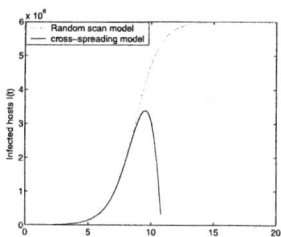

(b) Cross-spreading model vs Random scan model

Fig. 3. Worm Model Results

We reconsidered about Equation 2. If $d \to \infty$, than $dI(t)/dt \to k'I(t)$. That is to say if the degree of worm tree is unlimited, the BTP worm turns out to be the perfect worm [10]. That is once a node gets infected, it sends the scans at its top speed, and every one of its scans can reach the target and infect a new host. We limit the degree of the worm tree, or its living age, for an infected host because scanning every infected host at top speed will keep the computing resources occupied and bandwidth exhausted.

4.4 Modeling Two Worms

The goal of an anti-worm is to restrain the propagation of a malicious worm. We give the cross-spreading model of two worms.

We release the BTP worm at $t = t_0$, when the number of susceptible hosts is $S(t)$ and the number of hosts infected by a random scan worm is $I(t)$. The average effective number of scan sent by the random scan worm is $kI(t)S(t)/N$ per time unit.

BTP worm will remove both the susceptible and random-scan-infected hosts. The number of hosts removed from susceptible state hosts at time t is called as $R(t)$, and the number of hosts removed from random-scan-infected state hosts at time t is called $Q(t)$.

Considering Equations (1) and (2), the cross-spreading model can be derived.

We can also plot the numerical solutions of the cross-spreading model and plot them in Figure 3(b), compared with the random scan worm propagation (Equation 1). Parameters are $N = 6 \times 10^6$, $I(0) = 1000$, $k = 1$, $Q(0) = I'(0) = 1$, $R(0) = 0$, $Q'(0) = 0$, $k' = 1.7$, $d = 2$. Y label in Figure 3(b) indicates the number of hosts infected by the random scan worm.

The curve of the cross-spreading model rises into its peak value, which is much lower than the original random scan model, and falls down rapidly because the number of recovered hosts by the anti-worm in a time unit is greater than the number of newly generated vulnerable hosts at the same time.

We can also find other characteristic of the anti-worm's spreading. As the infection rate of anti worm k' grows, the maximized value of infected hosts is greatly decreased. As the $I(0)$ decreases, it takes less time to kill the malicious worm. That is to say, the earlier we release the anti-worm, the better the result we will obtain. This complies with our intuition. The effect of the degree on worms' propagation, is that the increase will slow this down. However, it has its limits. When the degree value gets much bigger, the slowing down space gets much smaller.

5 Experiments

In this section, we present a set of packet based simulation results that demonstrate the feasibility of BTP model.

5.1 Simulation Methods

The traditional epidemic model gives us some significant abstraction from worm behavior. That is, considering all individuals to be units of a population with certain states and the detailed transmission mechanics are translated into a probability to get the node infected. These simplifications provide fundamental assumptions about worm models which are also limitations for the models. Then, a more reliable simulation method should be taken to study the characteristics of anti-worm spreading.

The propagation procedures are concluded as: identify a vulnerable host, compromise the target host, transfer the worm and activate it. For some cases all of these steps can be combined into a single packet. Still, vulnerability details are negligible.

We carry out experiments using PDNS (Parallel Distributed Network Simulator) [14]. Our network is composed of 100 interconnected campus network (CN). Each CN has 12 subnets. And each subnet has one Class B IP network spaces, where the vulnerable hosts are uniformly distributed.

Table 1 provides an overview of all worm and network parameters implemented by our simulator.

Table 1. Simulation Parameters

Parameters	Unit	Value
Hosts in the Network	Hosts	307,200
Vulnerable Hosts	Hosts	50,400
Start Population	Hosts	307,200
Scanning Rate	Hosts /second	1
Bad Worm Length	Bytes	404
Anti worm Length	Bytes	700
Protocol (TCP/UDP)	–	UDP
Degree of BTP worm	–	2

5.2 Results

We have conducted simulation for both single worm spreading and two worms' cross spreading. Due to space restrictions, we will only present the results of the cross spreading simulation. For detailed information, please refer to our technical report.

Experiment 1 (Single Worm Spreading). The first experiment is about single worm spreading, including both the random scan worm and the BTP worm. The main goal of the proposed anti-worm is to stop the spreading of the bad worm. Therefore the anti-worm itself needs to spread faster than the original worm.

Figure 4(a) shows our simulation results with a single infected host. With the parameters listed in Table 1, the effective scan rate can be computed as $1 \times (50400/307200) \approx 0.16$ hosts per second. It takes the random scan worm more than 100s to infect 50,400 hosts. Compared with Figure 3(a) in the mathematical model, the worm's spread slowed down in the PDNS platform. That is because some factors such as bandwidth and transport delays are ignored in the mathematical model.

Experiment 2 (Two Worms Cross-spreading). The second experiment is about two worms cross-spreading. The hosts infected by BTP worm will be immune to the random scan worm attacks. We take our experiments with different relatively released time $t = 0s$ and $t = 120s$. We also plot the random scan worm spreading curve for reference. Parameters are the same as the first experiment.

We can see from Figure 4(b) that in spite of limited bandwidth and increased latency, BTP worm spreading can still decrease the number of vulnerable hosts rapidly. Besides, owing to packet loss and latency in simulation, the curve experiences a slight deviation compared with the one in Figure 3(b). Its survivability is proved to be acceptable and its effect is remarkable during any stage of malicious worm spreading.

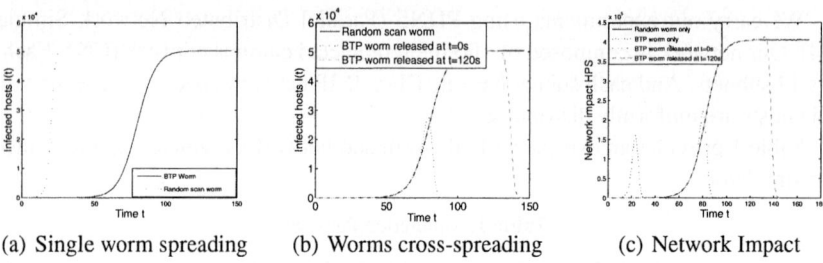

(a) Single worm spreading (b) Worms cross-spreading (c) Network Impact

Fig. 4. Simulation Results

Experiment 3 (Network Impact). We give the notion HPT (hops per time unit, the whole hops that worm packets have ever passed during spreading) to depict the network impact of the worm. In this case, HPT taken by the anti worm is as destructive as that taken by the bad worm. We hope that introducing the anti-worm won't make things even worse.

We keep the trace files of experiments listed above and compute their HPT values. Figure 4(c) shows the network impact curves. We can see clearly from the random worm and BTP worm curves that the network impact taken by BTP worm is much lower than the random scan worm. And the maximal value in the curve of BTP worm is earlier than that of random scan worm because the former spreads with more efficiency. Besides, the curve of BTP worm rises to the maximal value and falls down to zero quickly because the BTP worm in each host has a fixed age time and then kills itself. The other two curves are about the HPT curves in Experiment 2, two worms cross-spreading with different relative release times. No matter when it is released, the anti-worm can spread over the network quickly to kill the malicious worm and quarantine the system. Its spreading won't aggravate the disease as the HPT of two worms spreading is lower than the HPT of a random scan spreading at any time. And when the relative release time is earlier, the network impact is lower, which fits our intuition.

5.3 Discussions

We considered two parameters above in different scenarios to show the efficiency of our model. One is the host infected by the malicious worm, and the other is the packet hops of the worm as it spreads. We know from the falling curve of the first parameter that the BTP worm can spread rapidly and has the ability to fight against the random scan worm. The curve of the second parameter tells us that anti-worm spreading will help to ease the traffic burden taken by the random scan worm.

However, we also noted that a series of standards should be made for anti-worm spreading. For instance, the maximum speed of the anti-worm, the maximum impact value we can withstand, etc. We leave these problems to further research.

6 Conclusions

In this paper, we have proposed the BTP algorithm for anti-worm spreading. We give the mathematical model and also discuss the BTP worm spreading together with the random scan worm. The result shows that the BTP worm is rapid in spreading over the network in O(logN) time. After releasing the anti-worm, the epidemic situation will be slowed, and the anti-worm will not bring greatly increase the traffic load on the network. Besides, the controllability and traceability of BTP are shown to be acceptable. The experiments taken on the PDNS platform shows us its feasibility.

References

1. Thomas M. Chen, Trends in Viruses and Worms. The Internet Protocol Journal. Volume 6, No. 3, September 2003.
2. Levy, E. Approaching Zero, In IEEE Security & Privacy Magazine, Volume 2, Issue 4, pages 65-66. 2004.
3. Moore, D., Paxson, V., Shannon, C. Inside the Slammer Worm. In: IEEE Security and Privacy, 2003.
4. Frank Castaneda, Emre Can Sezer, Jun Xu. WORM vs. WORM: Preliminary Study of an Active Counter-Attack Mechanism. In Proceedings of ACM Workshop on Rapid Malcode (WORM'04), Oct 2004.
5. Wang Bai-ling, Fang Bin-xing, Yun Xiao-chun. The Propagation Model and Analysis of Worms Together with Anti-Worms. WSEAS Transactions on Information Science and Applications. Issue 4, Volume 1, October 2004.
6. Wen Wei-Ping, Qin Si-Han, et. al. Research and Development of Internet Worms. Journal of Software. Vol15, No.8, 2004.
7. Zou CC, Gong W, Towsley D. Code Red worm propagation modeling and analysis. In: Proc. of the 9th ACM Symp. on Computer and Communication Security. Washington, 2002.
8. J.O.Kephart and S.R.White. Measuring and Modeling Computer Virus Prevalence. Proceedings of the IEEE Symposimum on Security and Privacy, 1993.
9. J. O. Kephart, D.M. Chess, and S. R. White. Computers and Epidemiology. IEEE Spectrum, 1993.
10. Cliff Changchun Zou, Don Towsley, Weibo Gong. On the Performance of Internet Worm Scanning Strategies. Technical Report: TR-03-CSE-07.
11. S. Staniford, et al. The Top Speed of Flash Worms. in ACM Workshop on Rapid Malcode (WORM 2004), George Mason University, Fairfax, Virginia, USA, 2004.
12. Ivan Arce, Elias Levy. An Analysis of the Slapper Worm. IEEE Security & Privacy, 2003.
13. Jiang Wu, Sarma Vangala, Lixin Gao. An Effective Architecture and Algorithm for Detecting Worms with Various Scan Techniques. Network and Distributed System Security Symposium, 2004.
14. PDNS - Parallel/Distributed NS. http://www.cc.gatech.edu/computing/compass/PDNS/.

EFIS: Evolvable-Neural-Based Fuzzy Inference System and Its Application for Adaptive Network Anomaly Detection

Muhammad Fermi Pasha[1], Rahmat Budiarto[1], Mohammad Syukur[2], and Masashi Yamada[3]

[1] School of Computer Sciences, University of Sains Malaysia,
11800 Minden, Pulau Pinang, Malaysia
{fermi, rahmat}@cs.usm.my
[2] Faculty of Mathematics and Natural Sciences,
University of Sumatera Utara, 20155 Medan, Sumut, Indonesia
mhdsyukur@usu.ac.id
[3] School of Computer and Cognitive Sciences, Chukyo
University, 101 Tokodachi, Kaizu-cho, Toyota, 470-0383, Japan
myamada@sccs.chukyo-u.ac.jp

Abstract. This paper presents an application of a new type of fuzzy inference system, denoted as evolvable-neural-based fuzzy inference system (EFIS), for adaptive network anomaly detection in the presence of a concept drift problem. This problem cannot be avoided to happen in every network. It is a problem of modeling the behavior of normal traffic while it keeps changing over time in continuous manner. EFIS can solve the concept drift problem by having dynamic network traffic profile creation and adaptation. The profile is then being further used to detect anomaly. An enhanced evolving clustering method (ECMm), which is employed by EFIS for online network traffic clustering, is also presented. It is demonstrated, through experiments, that EFIS can evolve in a growing network and also successfully detect network traffic anomalies.

1 Introduction

The complexity and dynamic feature of network monitoring and traffic measurement task require sophisticated methods and tools for building online and adaptive intelligent systems. Such systems should be able to grow as they operate, to update their knowledge and refine its structure through interaction with the network. Numerous research works have been devoted to propose new methods and techniques in profiling network traffic. The approaches are taken ranging from using statistical method with K-Means clustering and approximate distance clustering [1]. The previous work included of using data mining techniques to mine the network traffic and generate the profiles in terms of rules [2], and using three different approaches to specifically profile network application behavior by rough sets, fuzzy C-Means clustering and Self Organizing Maps [4], etc.

Thus far, most of the works were done in offline mode which requires data collection, data analysis, and profile creation phase to be completed first. The drawback of this offline approach is its static nature. Static here means if changes happened to the network traffic behaviors, all the phases need to be repeated again in order to adapt to the new network characteristics. This problem is known as the concept drift problem. The concept drift problem may happen if, in the future, there are changes in the system and network activities as well as user behavior due to hardware upgrades, type of software that being used in the network, topology changes, more nodes added into the network, etc.

Apart from that, there are some works, which use online mode, proposed to detect network anomaly. They include using inductively generated sequential pattern to detect anomaly [6], using nearest neighbor classifiers based online learning scheme to examine the issues of incremental updating of system parameters and instance selection [7], using reinforcement learning method that uses feedback from the protected system to detect network attack [8], and using fuzzy association rule mining architecture to adaptively detect anomaly [9]. But unfortunately, all these works require prior knowledge of the underlying network traffic data distribution in advance, in order to train the system first. Most of it will only adapt its previously trained structure instead of growing from the scratch. The main issue is that none of these works can learn and adapt automatically without the presence of an expertise (network administrator) at the beginning of each adaptation cycle.

In this paper, we propose a model called evolvable-neural-based fuzzy inference system (EFIS) for online and adaptive network traffic profiling and anomaly detection in the presence of a concept drift problem. A clustering method, which is used by EFIS for online network traffic clustering, called an enhanced evolving clustering method (ECMm) is also proposed.

The rest of the paper is organized as follows. Section 2 gives a description of an enhanced evolving clustering method (ECMm) which is used in the EFIS model for partitioning the input space. In Section 3, the design and structure of EFIS are presented. Section 4 presents the results from the first experiment which focuses on demonstrating the ability of ECMm to profile network traffic input streams and EFIS ability to evolve the profile. In Section 5, the results from experiments with the 1999 DARPA intrusion detection evaluation benchmark corpus are presented. Finally we summarize our conclusions and future work in Section 6.

2 ECMm: An Enhanced Evolving Clustering Method

As an online clustering method, the original Evolving Clustering Method (ECM) algorithm performs well on one-pass partitioning of an input space. Together with its extension for offline optimization ECMc, it is a powerful method to partition scarce inputs. ECM is one of the ECOS branches for online unsupervised online clustering. It is a fast one-pass algorithm for dynamic clustering of an input stream of data, where there is no predefined number of clusters. It is a distance-based clustering method where the cluster centers are presented by evolved nodes in an online mode [5].

Here we introduce ECMm, an enhanced evolving clustering method for the purpose of clustering network traffic data streams. ECMm is used by EFIS to obtain network traffic profile from the results of the clustering process. The ECMm algorithm itself is basically a combination of ECM algorithm and its extension ECMc so that it can use the number of cluster created in previous process and optimize its cluster center in online mode. By having a continuous process of online clustering, the system can adapt accordingly in the presence of concept drift. Below is the algorithm of ECMm:

Step 1. If it is not the first time, initialise the cluster centre C_{Cj}, $j = 1,2,3,...,n$, that already produced before. Else, go straight to Step 6 to start creating new clusters.

Step 2. Determine the membership matrix U in which each of its element u_{ij} derived from:

$$\text{IF } \|x_i - C_{Cj}\| \leq \|x_i - C_{Ck}\|, \text{ for } k = 1,2,3,..., n, j \neq k, \\ \text{THEN } u_{ij} = 1, \text{ else } u_{ij} = 0 \tag{1}$$

Step 3. Employ the constrained minimisation method to modify the cluster centres. The constraint can be expressed as,

$$\|x_k - C_{Cj}\| \leq Dthr \tag{2}$$

Step 4. Calculate the objective function J defined by the following equation:

$$J = \sum_{j=1}^{n} J_j \tag{3}$$

where $J_j = \Sigma_{k, xk \ast Cj} \|x_k - C_{Cj}\|$ is the objective function within cluster center C_j for each $j = 1,2,3,..., n$.

Step 5. Go to Step 7, if the result is below a certain tolerance value, or the result when compared with the previous iteration is below a certain threshold, or the iteration number is the optimizing operation is over a certain value. Else, go back to Step 2.

Step 6. Create the new cluster C_1 (if the first time) by simply taking the position of the first example from the input data stream as the first cluster centre C_{C1}, and setting a value 0 for its cluster radius R_{U1}.

Step 7. If all examples from the data stream have been processed, the clustering processes finished. Else, the current input example, x_i, is taken and the normalized Euclidean distance D_{ij}, between this example and all n already created cluster centres C_{Cj},

$$D_{ij} = \|x_i - C_{Cj}\|, j = 1,2,3,...,n \tag{4}$$

is calculated.

Step 8. If there is a cluster C_m with a centre C_{Cm}, a cluster radius R_{Um} and distance value C_{C1} such that:

$$D_{im} = \|x_i - C_{Cm}\| = min \{D_{ij}\} = min \{ \|x_i - C_{Cj}\| \}, \text{ for } j = 1,2,3,...,n; \tag{5}$$

and

$$D_{im} < R_{Um} \tag{6}$$

when the current x_i belong to this cluster, then go back to Step 7.

Step 9. Find a cluster C_a with a centre C_{Ca} a cluster radius R_{Ua}, and a distance value D_{ia} which has a minimum value S_{ia}:

$$S_{ia} = D_{ia} + R_{Ua} = min\{S_{ij}\}, j = 1,2,3,..., n \tag{7}$$

Step 10. If S_{ia} is greater than 2 x *Dthr*, the example x_i does not belong to any existing cluster. Then repeat the process from Step 6 to create a new cluster.
Step 11. If S_{ia} is not greater than 2 x *Dthr*, the cluster C_a is updated by moving its centre, C_{Ca}, and increasing its radius value R_{Ua}. The updated radius R_{Ua}^{new} is set to be equal to $S_{ia}/2$ and the new centre C_{Ca}^{new} is located on the line connecting input vector x_i and the old cluster centre C_{Ca}, so that the distance from the new centre C_{Ca}^{new} to the point x_i is equal to R_{Ua}^{new}. Back to Step 7.

There are two types of traffic data model to be clustered. The first one is overall data (without filtering) and the second one is application based (currently we only focus on http, icmp and NetBIOS packet) data. The clustering process will then be performed on each model by using captured time, total packet and its size information.

3 EFIS: An Evolvable-Neural-Based Fuzzy Inference System

Here we propose EFIS, an evolvable-neural-based fuzzy inference system for profile creation and network traffic anomaly detection in online mode. EFIS utilizes the evolving connectionist systems framework which makes it able to evolve in open space to dealt with concept drift problem and continuously monitor the network traffic to detect anomaly in online and lifelong mode. The general idea of EFIS comes from a combination of the features and structures of HyFIS [10] and DENFIS [5] model so that it is more suitable for network traffic data.

The connectionist structure of EFIS closely follows the HyFIS model but the input partitioning method, rule extraction and creation method, and membership function type closely follow the one in DENFIS model. The choice of adopting the feature of DENFIS in partitioning the input space into EFIS is inline with our work in proposing ECMm (see Sect. 2) since DENFIS uses ECM as the clustering method and ECMm is based on ECM.

Just like HyFIS and DENFIS, one of EFIS main feature is that it is adaptable; the membership functions of the fuzzy predicates and the fuzzy rules can be adapted if necessary. EFIS uses triangular type of membership functions following the DENFIS structure. While the fuzzy rules that EFIS uses in its neuro-fuzzy model structure (will be explained shortly) is the type of rule with certainty degree or known as Certainty Factors (CF) similar to the one on HyFIS model and the format is given below:
```
IF (T is A₁) AND (P is A₂) AND (B is A₃) THEN status is C
```
where T, P, and B represent time, total packet, and total byte respectively, while A_n and C are fuzzy values.

There are two main parts of EFIS structure, the first one is the Profile Creation and Management (PCM) module which creates and extracts rules from ECMm results, and the second one is the Neuro-Fuzzy Model (NFM) module which is a 5 layer neural network-based fuzzy system. The PCM module connects EFIS model with ECMm in order to partition the input space. Fig. 1 shows the proposed general EFIS architecture.

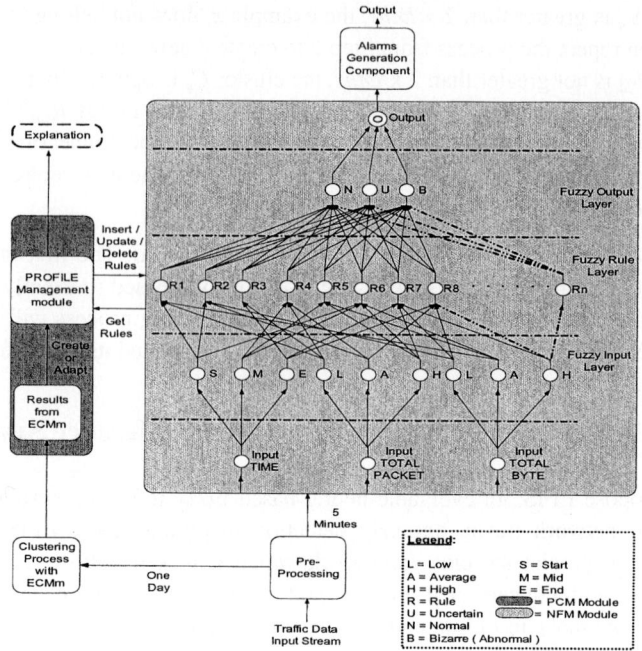

Fig. 1. EFIS model general schematic block architecture

The results from ECMm are passed to the first module and it then extracts the rules using information of each created cluster (following DENFIS model), thus each rule is representing each cluster. Basically all the resulted rules are showing the normal condition, hence to detect anomalies simply match any deviation from this rules. That is, clusters resulted as outliers are not extracted as rule. Clusters are considered as outliers using the following scheme:

$$\text{IF } R_{Ua} \leq Dthr/3 \text{ OR total instances in } C_a \leq 6 \qquad (8)$$
$$\text{THEN } C_a \text{ considered as } outlier$$

For membership functions of total packet and total byte, the number of total packet and total byte are doubled for the upper fuzzy intervals boundary value while the lower value is zero. One thing to note is that the three membership functions of total packet are similar to membership functions of total byte as total packet and total byte are strongly correlated.

Based on those rules, the module then creates and adapts the profile of that particular day. The presence of these profiles can be manually evaluated by network administrator since EFIS provides explanation module which can be used to view all the rules in a particular profile. This would avoid black box symptoms like most connectionist systems do (especially neural network based systems) and network administrator can derive why such alarms was raised. Then these profiles are later being passed to the second module to be inserted into the neuro-fuzzy structure. The adaptation of the rule is following the evolving procedures given below:

1. Compare the newly resulted profile with the last week profile, and mark all the changes.
2. Check for generated alarms and recorded actions by the administrator and match every event with the previously marked profile changes.
3. If an action is taken by the administrator, keep the old rules unchanged. Else, evolve the rules by:

$$A_{Vn}^{new} = A_{Vn}^{old} \pm \left\| \frac{(A_{Vn}^{resulted} - A_{Vn}^{old})}{2} \right\| \tag{9}$$

where n = sets of profile changes event without action taken by network administrator, and each is calculated such that A_V are the antecedent of total packet for $v=1$ and antecedent of total byte for $v=2$. Meanwhile the adaptation of the time interval is done by shifting the beginning and ending time accordingly.

Each rule extracted from ECMm results has several fuzzy rules with CF in this neuro-fuzzy structure. These fuzzy rules are basically all the possible connections that can be made between nodes in fuzzy input layer and nodes in fuzzy rule layer where each connection represents one rule. In choosing which connection to be inserted, the initial CF is randomize for each node according to its membership degree, and then calculated as the product of CF in one particular connection. Nine connections that involve pair connection of total packet and total byte (e.g. *S-L-L, S-H-H, M-L-L*) are inserted by default regardless the CFs value. The rest connections will be inserted only if the final CF is above 0.06 for connection that involves *S*, connections that involve *M* must have final CF above 0.18, and connections that involve *E* must have final CF above 0.25.

We also propose a new strategy and procedure as an add-in to the NFM module to generate alarms. Instead of directly raise an alarm when EFIS detect anomaly, we further apply the proposed strategy and procedure to carefully raise the alarms. The proposed strategy and procedure is implemented as alarms generation component (see Fig. 1) and it is designed to reduce the number of false alarms rate to as minimum as possible. Our general assumption in applying this strategy is that no one is using the network at late night, no heavy workload on holiday, and working day is Monday to Friday only.

Our strategy is to divide the time of day into three periods of peak-time, off-peak-time, and midnight-time. Furthermore, the lengths of these periods are different on each day. There are three types of alarms generated by this strategy, Warning Alarms (WA), Attention Alarms (AA) and Critical Alarms (CA). While AA is raised if a sequence of WA exists, the procedures in generating WA and CA are different in the three given periods. In general, the procedure involves manipulating the outputs from EFIS as the degree of mismatch between normal and anomalous. If the output degree from EFIS is in normal range of [0.4:0.6], no alarms will be generated as this range is considered normal. That is, only output degree outside this normal range will be process to generate alarms. Basically we can state that the process in generating alarms is the process of defuzzification from EFIS fuzzy output value into alarms.

The standard mechanism procedure in raising an alarm (both WA and CA) is expressed by $\forall$ traffic, $\exists$ x, where x is a set of traffic which violates the threshold degree. Basically by default, WA is raised if the threshold degree from EFIS output is below 0.7 otherwise CA is raised. While AA is raised if WA is raised 4 times in a row or AA is raised at once with CA if WA is raised 8 times in a row.

4 Network Traffic Profiling with ECMm

The system was experimented at the School of Computer Sciences USM network for the duration of two months. The Monitoring Agent was installed on different network segments in our school's switched network. The primary objective of this experiment is to see how the system evolves in real network where no clean and attack-free training data are available.

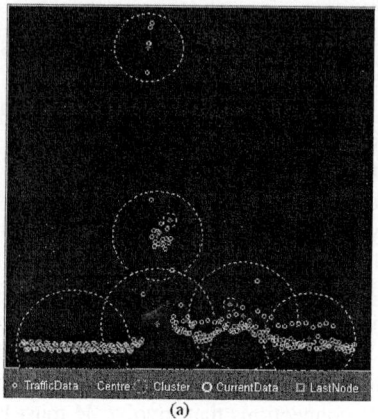 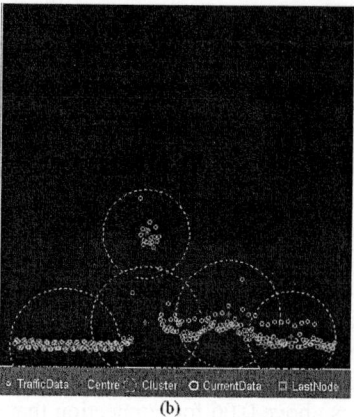

Fig. 2. ECMm's results on Friday, January 21, 2005 profile. (a) Initial results. (b) Results after ignoring the outlier cluster.

Fig. 2 visualizes the process of ECMm in detecting outliers in a noisy network traffic data stream on Friday, January 21, 2005. In Fig. 2 (a), we show that ECMm successfully finds three outlier clusters and two of them are located inside the normal clusters and another one differs significantly from other clusters but only contain four instances. In general system workflow, these outliers are triggered with WA alarms as they are different from normal instances and therefore EFIS is not considering these clusters in creating or adapting the profiles. Especially for the last outlier cluster, AA is generated since four WA are triggered in a row.

The final clusters shown in Fig. 2 (b) are the one used by EFIS in adapting the profiles. As we can see all the outlier clusters are ignored and are not considered as normal. In this way, the system is able to learn from scratch and grow in online mode on noisy network traffics under assumption that at first time running, the network condition is considerably normal in a sense that the number of normal instances vastly outnumbers the anomalous instances.

Fig. 3 shows the simple statistic record on how many rules created in each day profile and the total counts on how many rules are evolved in each day profile. It can be seen that week days profile (Monday-Friday) has more rules compare to week-end profile (Saturday and Sunday) since the network has more traffics at those days. This statistic was made based on a counter that we put on the system to record all the necessary events on the system. As such, no weekly statistic, which can show the number of times each rules evolved after the initial rules, are recorded.

In this experiment, EFIS detects some device failures (especially our switches) happened in some network segments. A simple DoS attack that we simulate was also successfully detected by EFIS. As a whole, EFIS performance on this experiment was satisfactory.

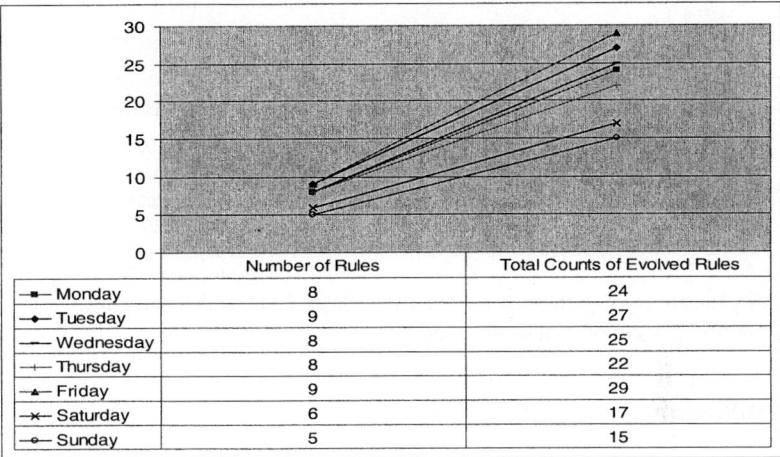

Fig. 3. The statistic of EFIS' results in terms of the number of rules created and counts on how many times the rules are evolve

5 Network Traffic Anomaly Detection with EFIS

In this Section, we applied the EFIS model to detect anomalous behavior in the 1999 DARPA intrusion detection evaluation corpus data. These data has been used as a benchmark in the areas of intrusion detection and anomaly detection system. The 1999 DARPA intrusion detection evaluation corpus have four different types of attacks which, in total, consist of more than 200 attacks. In this experiment, we only consider two types of attack, DoS and probes attacks, since the rest are typically a host-based attack and will not be considered. Therefore, the total number of attacks (that our system focuses to detect) is only 52.

Fig. 4 shows the overall system performance obtained by one of participants that has published their results [11]. As a comparison, we add our system performance into the previous published result. It is obvious that our system has the best performance compared to other systems. In addition, in terms of false alarms generation per day, in average our system has a lower number of false alarms during its process. It is typically about 5 false alarms per day while the other systems could have 10 false alarms per day.

However, we do not claim that our system is better than other systems as seen in Fig. 4 since our system and others have a different total number of attacks focus. In general, most of the system is specifically designed as an intrusion detection system and they perform a detail analysis of all the given information such as the audit data, file listing and the sniffed raw traffic data. In this analysis we only consider the sniffed raw traffic data and try to model its normal condition.

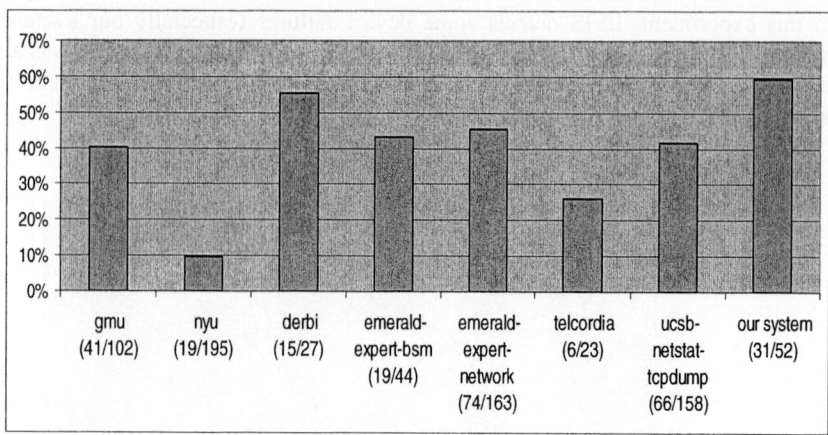

Fig. 4. A comparison of performance from all available systems that participate in the 1999 DARPA intrusion detection evaluation program

6 Conclusion

This paper presents the principles of a fuzzy inference system, EFIS, for adaptive network anomaly detection in the presence of a concept drift problem. In both experiment conducted, we show that EFIS is able to evolve its structure to accommodate new traffic behavior. The obtained results also show that ECMm is successfully partitioning the network traffic data streams.

There are several ways to improve our system. Firstly, the structure of our connectionist model can still be improved to detect more types of network intrusion. This can be achieved by further analyzing each packet's information or, perhaps, performing an analysis on the information on network packet's layer 2.

Secondly, implementing a signature based intrusion detection engine should also be taken into consideration to improve the detection engine's performance. Finally, we need to add an intelligent module in order to produce a pilot automation response system to prevent a network outage. This pilot system can significantly reduce an involvement of a network administrator in all critical time.

References

1. Marchette, D.: A Statistical Method for Profiling Network Traffic. Workshop on Intrusion Detection and Network Monitor (1999) 119–128
2. Pasha, M.F., Budiarto, R., Sumari, P., Osman, A.: Data Mining and Rule Generation in Network Traffic using Fuzzy Clustering Techniques. MMU International Symposium on Information and Communications Technologies (2004) TS4B-5: 17–20
3. Budiarto, R., Pasha, M.F.: Developing Online Adaptive Engine for Profiling Network Traffic using Evolving Connectionist Systems. Conference on Neuro-Computing and Evolving Intelligence (2004) 69–70

4. Lampinen, T., Koivisto, H., Honkanen, T.: Profiling Network Application with Fuzzy C-Means Clustering and Self Organizing Map. First International Conference on Fuzzy System and Knowledge Discovery: Computational Intelligence for the E-Age (2002) 300–304
5. Kasabov, N.: Evolving Connectionist System: Methods and Applications in Bioinformatics, Brain Study and Intelligent Machines. Springer-Verlag, London Berlin Heidelberg (2002)
6. Teng, H.S., Chen, K., Lu, S.C.: Adaptive real-time anomaly detection using inductively generated sequential patterns. IEEE Symposium on Security and Privacy (1980) 278–284
7. Lane, T., Brodley, C.: Approaches to online learning and conceptual drift for user identification in computer security. ECE and the COAST Laboratory Tech. Rep. (Coast TR 98-12), Purdue University (1998)
8. Cannady, J.: Next generation intrusion detection: Autonomous reinforcement learning of network attacks. 23rd National Information Systems Security Conference (2000) 1–12
9. Hossain, M., Bridges, S.M.: A framework for an adaptive intrusion detection system with data mining. 13th Annual Canadian Information Technology Security Symposium (2001)
10. Kim, J., Kasabov, N.: HyFIS: Adaptive Neuro-Fuzzy System and Their Application to Non-Linear Dynamical Systems. Neural Network. Elsevier (1999) 12(9): 1301–1319
11. Barbara, D., Couto, J., Jajodia, S., Popyack, L., Wu, N.: ADAM: Detecting intrusions by data mining. IEEE Workshop on Information Assurance and Security (2001) 11–16

Fast Detection of Worm Infection for Large-Scale Networks

Hui He, Mingzeng Hu, Weizhe Zhang, and Hongli Zhang

Department of Computer Science and Engineering,
Harbin Institute of Technology, Harbin 150001, China
{hehui, mzhu}@hit.edu.cn, {zwz, zhl}@pact518.hit.edu.cn

Abstract. Internet worms constitute a major threat to the security of today's networks. They work by exploiting vulnerabilities in operating systems and application software that run on end systems. In this paper, an effective algorithm for fast detection of worms is proposed. It integrates the worms' behavior attributes with their traffic distribution and detects abnormal behavior by their similarity distribution and changes in some of their attributes. The process of fast detection based on similarity is discussed in detail including threshold selection, similarity detection algorithm and fine analysis. Simulation experiments show that the detection algorithm can locate the worm infection prior to it spreading over the large-scale network.

1 Introduction

Internet worms constitute a major threat to the security of today's large-scale networks. They work by exploiting vulnerabilities in operating systems and application software that run on end systems. Worms such as CodeRed I [1] [2] and CodeRed II [3] have caused tremendous financial losses in our society. CodeRed I worm attack was widespread across the world and wasted more than 20 billion dollars and the Code Red II worm cost more than 12 billion dollars.

As the Internet grows, future attacks will be considerably faster through simple optimizations and alternate strategies, allowing all vulnerable machines to be infected in far less than an hour, faster than humans can react. Hence, the sooner we detect a worm, the less damage it does. A fast detection system is essential in fighting against Internet disasters, and a just-in-time warning can be invaluable in saving money and limiting damages. Using Internet traffic measurements to detect worms, David Moore [4] proposed "network explore" to detect the abnormal event and Cliff Zou [5] conducted research in a similar way on early worm detection. Zou et al. [6], explored the possibility of monitoring Internet traffic with small sized address spaces and proposed a Kalman filter-based detection algorithm. Weaver et al. [7] and Jung [8] put forward worm containment based on the observation that scanning worms caused high failed connection ratios. Recently, Vincent Berk [9] introduced the idea of monitoring the number of ICMP destination unreachable packets generated by routers to its detection system, as Internet worms probe many vacant IP addresses. In [10], Guofei Gu employed a fast detection algorithm based on local victim information, and

Xuan Chen [11] proposed framework DEWP, which detects worm probing traffic by matching destination port numbers.

Previous researchers have mostly focused on single character matching such as ICMP unreachable packets, TCP SYN packets or TCP RST packets and destination ports. They failed to consider that single character matching may identify some legitimate traffic as potential worm traffic. With respect to other studies, they depend on the attacking traffic to be large enough or have attempted to perform detection on a local network but not on the large-scale network. Thus, in order to detect worms more effectively, two factors are introduced in this paper. First, in the time aspect, we consider that the faster we find the attack behavior, the better our detection method. Second, in the attacking intensity degree, the less attack intensity compared to the background traffic, the better our detection method. In this paper, our studies preliminarily emphasize the latter. However, to some degree, worm probing traffic is always too small to sense and the probing behavior is just at the very early stage of the worm's attack. So if we solve the latter problem efficiently, we also contribute to solving the former one to some extent. In our paper, we propose a multi-similarity fast detection method, which integrates a novel technique that detects the concerted scan activity of an ongoing worm attack earlier, especially when the probing traffic is covered by the background. Further studies on the effectiveness of the similarity algorithm will be summarized in our next study.

This paper is organized as follows: Section 2 introduces definitions of similarity. Section 3 describes the detection process of the fast detection algorithm based on similarity, and how to apply the multi-similarity detection method to the worm's detection is discussed in detail including threshold selection, similarity detection algorithm and fine analysis. Section 4 describes the simulation environment and shows the experiment results of the fast detection algorithm. Section 5 concludes the paper.

2 Related Definitions

Definition 1. (similarity coefficient). The similarity coefficient is denoted as:

$$\psi(X,Y) = Cov(X, Y)/\sqrt{DX}\sqrt{DY},$$

where $X: \{x_1, x_2 .... x_n | x_i \in R\}$ and $Y :\{ y_1, y_2 .... y_n | y_i \in R\}$ are two stochastic variable sequences, $Cov(X, Y)$ is the covariance between X and Y, and DX and DY are the variances of the stochastic variable sequence X and Y respectively.

Definition 2. (traffic attributes space). Let $TAS = \{A_1, A_2....A_n\}$ be the set of traffic attributes such as port number, packet size, protocol, IP address etc, which characterize the traffic flow. Concerning different attribute factor A_i, its value space may be different. For example, $A_{port\ number} = \{a_i | a_i \in N\}$, while $A_{packet\ size} = \{a_i | a_i \in R\}$.

Definition 3. (attribute distribution sequence). Given an attribute factor $A \in TAS$, there is $\{a_1, a_2 ... a_n\} \in \{A\}$ at time τ. The attributed distribution sequence of A at time τ can be denoted as $(\tau_1, \tau_2, \tau_3.... \tau_n)$ where τ_i denotes the ratio of a_i to the overall traffic.

Definition 4. (s-similarity). Given an attribute factor $A \in TAS$ and two different attribute distribution sequences at time τ and τ', then $S_{\tau,\tau'}^{A} = \psi(\tau,\tau')$ is defined as s-similarity of τ' according to τ.

Definition 5. (m-similarity). For all the $A_i \in TAS$, $S_{\tau,\tau'}^{TAS} = \sum_{i=1}^{n} \varepsilon^{A_i} \delta^{A_i} S_{\tau,\tau'}^{A_i}$ is defined as m-similarity of τ' according to τ. $\varepsilon^{A_i} = \left|\Delta S_{\tau,\tau'}^{A_i}\right| / \sum_{i=1}^{n}\left|\Delta S_{\tau,\tau'}^{A_i}\right|$ is defined as the contributor factor, which reflects the changing magnitude of s-similarity of A_i. δ^{A_i} is defined as the selector factor, where $\delta^{A_i} \in \{0,1\}$, if the changing scope is above a threshold ξ during a span of time, then $\delta^{A_i} = 1$, inversely $\delta^{A_i} = 0$. (ξ is a parameter described in Section 3.2).

3 The Fast Detection Algorithm

3.1 The Detection Process Based on Similarity Algorithm

The process shown in Figure 1 is composed of several steps. First, its data collection module gathers the original datagram at the network interface. We then calculate the N-top statistical value of attributes. Next, we compute the s-similarity and multi-similarity values. According to the condition judgment of abnormal, we track the abnormal attribute and apply it to the fine analysis module for further exact conclusion. It effectively decreases the false positive rate. Next, a record is taken into the RRD database and an alarm is produced as a result of the above. "Condition judgment of abnormal" and "fine analysis" are the key stages along the whole detection process.

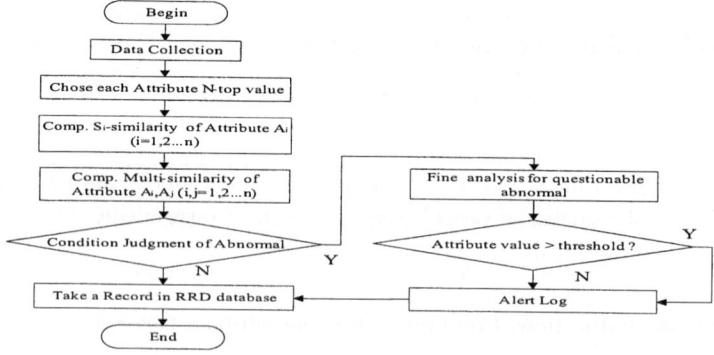

Fig. 1. Flow chart of abnormal detection based on similarity

Given time sequence denoted as $T_1, T_i, ... T_n$ ($n<m$), the similarity value is defined as $R_1,...R_i,...R_n$. The condition judgment of abnormal is as following:

1. $R_i-R_{i+1} > \theta$ indicates the decline scope of similarity when an attack starts, where θ is the decrease threshold.
2. $R_{i+2}-R_{i+1} > \beta\theta$, if $0<\beta<1$, then it shows the increased scope of similarity when the attack is underway.
3. $|R_{j+1}-R_j| < \varepsilon$, if $i+2<j<n$, then it indicates the stable similarity when the attack is underway in a period, that ε is stable threshold as the attack is going on.

If it settles for the three conditions above at T_n, then we conclude that it is abnormal at T_n.

In order to obtain the proper value of threshold θ, an auto-adaptive method is introduced into this paper. ΔR_i is denoted as a variation of similarity measured and ΔE_i represents the variation of similarity evaluated, as shown in formulas (1) (2) and (3).

$$\Delta R_i > \Delta E_i \tag{1}$$

$$\frac{1}{n-k+1}\sum_{j=k}^{n} r_j - r_1 > \beta \Delta R_i, \quad 0 < \beta < 1 \tag{2}$$

$$\left|\Delta R_j\right| < \gamma \Delta E_i, \quad k < j < n \tag{3}$$

In order to decrease the false positive rate, we employ fine analysis to the abnormal results from the module of condition judgment. This part is discussed in section 3.2.3.

3.2 Worm Detection Based on Multi-similarity

The multi-similarity detection algorithm is the key component of the detection module, which consists of three parts: threshold selection, similarity detection and fine analysis.

3.2.1 Threshold Selection

Adaptive threshold T is needed to determine whether traffic is abnormal or not. And it is important to judge when a similarity surge is large enough. If the similarity downwards scope is larger than the threshold, then we consider it to be abnormal; in reverse, we look it as a normal jitter of the network. To select an appropriate threshold, we usually employ the following two methods: one is static threshold and the other is dynamic threshold. As we know, the internet is a huge and complex system; none can predict its traffic status at any given time. So, according to the above analysis, the dynamic threshold is subjected to being selected, and is expressed in Formula (4):

$$T_{new} = (1.0-\beta) * T_{old} + \beta * \text{decline of similarity} \tag{4}$$

Adaptive threshold is not effective until the program has been running for a short period of time, so we consider the value of the initial threshold as 1. β is denoted as a weighted coefficient, which is specified as old threshold ratio to new ones. In the experiment, the ratio of old threshold to new ones is 0.5. This means that the old threshold is equal to the same scope of similarity decline as the gain of the new threshold.

For an example, given an initial threshold=1, $\beta=0.5$. When the decline scope of similarity is 2, then $T_{new} = (1-0.5)*1+0.5*2=1.5$. In the same way, when the decline scope of similarity is 0.6, then $T_{new} = (1-0.5)*1.5+0.5*0.6=1.05$. So, it is simply the advantage of the adaptive threshold compared to the static one that judges the decline scope by its historical time.

3.2.2 Multi-similarity Detection Algorithm

After analyzing the aggregation result of the real-world data, we can see that the distribution of traffic employed to similarity is relatively stable. The similarity curve has leveled off, although with a small jitter. That is, we can't detect a sharp download movement without worm traffic. When the worm traffic is injected, the similarity curve changes also. First, when worms start to probe, there will be a great move downwards in the curve of similarity and the range is larger than the threshold. It is the first step we can use to judge for abnormalities. Second, after the attack has gone on for a few seconds, the traffic with malice flow is stable again, and at this moment, we have two other changes in the similarity curve. One is that there is a visibly upwards movement to previous values. And the other is that the curve comes into stabilization again. The judgement algorithm is shown in Figure 2.

```
BEGIN
    Alert=0
    IF (the difference of similarity at previous time and at next time >threshold)
    Alert=1;
        IF (have no great upwards during attack persistence )
            Alert=0;
        ENDIF
        IF (have great upwards during attack persistence )
            Alert=0;
        ENDIF
    ENDIF
    IF (ALERT=1)
        Find out attribute k;   // Abnormal
        Write attribute k into log;
        Start the Fine analysis module ;
    ENDIF
END
```

Fig. 2. The abnormal judgement algorithm of worm detection

3.2.3 Fine Analysis

After detecting the abnormal behaviour based on multi-similarity, we need to filter some of the normal behaviour that brought about the change of similarity. As a server provides services to a great many hosts in the same moment, it will also destroy the balance of certain port traffic distribution and result in a change of similarity. Likewise, as with the communication between two computers with high bandwidth, it can also bring about a change of similarity. So it is necessary to introduce the fine analysis module to filter these normal events and decrease the rate of false alarm.

Then we take the port abnormal event for example to indicate how to filter out the normal behaviour. After the coarse analysis of abnormal detection is processed, it is used to trace these suspicious port behaviours in the next period of time. If a server provided services to many clients, the destination ports of their connection request packets are certain, such as 80, 25 and 21 etc. but the source ports of the request packets are random. Likewise, the destination ports of their reply packets are random which is different from worm scan packets with certain ports. Hence, it will be filtered out in the fine analysis step. Otherwise, if two high bandwidth computers are sending data to each other at the same time, and we find out the destination and source port of their transfer packets are all certain, and it doesn't also accord with the worm's behaviour, then it will be filtered out by the step of fine analysis.

4 Experiments

In this section, we evaluate our worm detection and early warning methods based on the traffic characteristic similarity. We study the following problems:

- Is the worm detection method based on s-similarity suitable for fast early warnings?
- What is the effectiveness of the worm detection method based on m-similarity compared with detection based on s-similarity?

We use network simulation experiments to answer these questions.

4.1 Environmental Setup

In order to assure that the experimental environment is controllable and results can be replayed, we set up a local network platform as shown in Figure 3. The configuration of the test bed is: (1) Three 800 MHZ dual xeon CPU Dawning workstations, equipped with 2 GB memory, 24 GB disks and 100M Ethernet Card. (2) One CISCO Router 3524. All three workstations are connected by the router and are running Red Hat Linux 8.0 as their operating system. The detection program runs on one of the workstations. The background traffic is replayed and the simulated worm traffic is assigned to the other two machines. Meanwhile, the router plays an important role in which it synthesizes and mirrors all the background traffic and the simulated worm traffic to the detection engine.

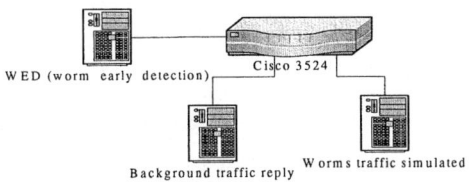

Fig. 3. Local network simulation test bed

Based on the theory analysis in Section 3, we conclude that it is crucial to detect worm activity in its earlier stage. Therefore, we have conducted two experiments, summarized in Table 1, where the worm traffic simulates the first and second phase behavior of worm spread.

Table 1. Summary of experiment configuration

	Experiment 1	Experiment 2
Background resource	Data of CERNET, Sep.,2004	Data of CERNET, Sep.,2004
Begin time-End time (attack)	9.35 am - 10:00 am	18:27pm - 18:32 pm
Total traffic (before attack)	35MBps~45MBps	35MBps~45MBps
Attack intensity	5 thread	10 thread
Rule of attack	Port, Packet Size	Packet Size, Protocol
Total traffic (attack on going)	300Mbps-350Mbps	320Mbps-400Mbps
Percent of victim port traffic	3% - 4%	0%
Percent of victim protocol traffic	0%	10%-12%
Percent of victim packet size traffic	0.5%-1%	1.5%-2%

4.2 Single-Similarity Experiment Results

The effect of port, packet size and protocol s-similarity are shown in Figure 4 after the worm has injected scanning packets into the background traffic in the scenario of Experiment 1. In detail, Figure 4(a) presents the trend of port similarity values, as can been seen from the diagram, and great changes have taken place at about 9:35. That is the moment that the worm begins to scan the network and it destroys the balance of port traffic distribution and results in the great changes to the similarity values on the curve. And from Figure 4(b) and Figure 4(c), we see that the similarity value of packet size and protocol remain to be approximately one line. It shows that its similarity distribution is still stable. Because the worm's attack focuses on port scanning, the port single-similarity is effective in this scenario.

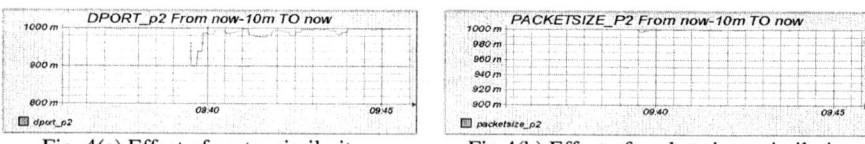

Fig. 4(a) Effect of port s-similarity   Fig.4(b) Effect of packet size s-similarity

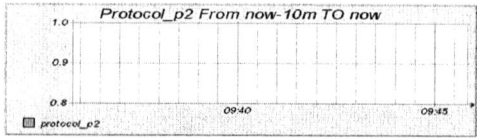

Fig.4(c) Effect of protocol s-similarity

Fig. 4. Effect of s-similarity in Experiment 1

4.3 Multi-similarity Experiment Results

Comparing the above graphs of single attribute similarity in Figure 4 and Figure 5, we can find that no single similarity can detect a worm's attack effectively and independently without the other ones. So, we introduce two kinds of multiple similarity methods in our experiments. One is the static weighted average similarity; the other is the dynamic weighted average similarity, which is called multi-similarity in our paper. As for the static weighted average similarity, we designate that the weight value of each is a constant 1/3. Namely, the port similarity, packet size similarity and the protocol similarity are equally weighted. Although it considers all of these effective factors, it is not feasible to use it for complete detection.

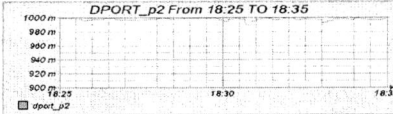
Fig.5(a) Effect of port s-similarity

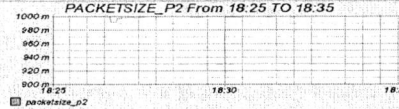
Fig.5(b) Effect of packet size s-similarity

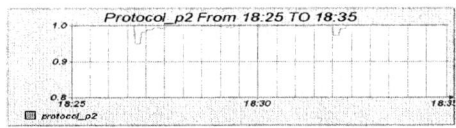
Fig.5(c) Effect of protocol s-similarity

Fig. 5. Effect of s-similarity in Experiment 2

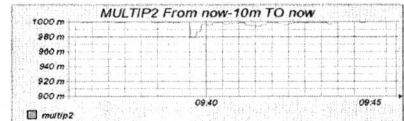
Fig.6(a) Effect of static weighted average s-similarity

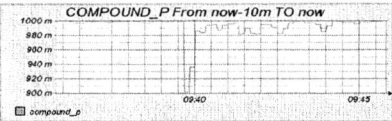
Fig.6(b) Effect of dynamic weighted m-similarity

Fig. 6. Effect of m-similarity in Experiment 1

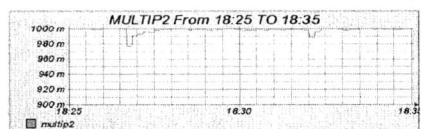
Fig.7(a) Effect of static weighted average s-similarity

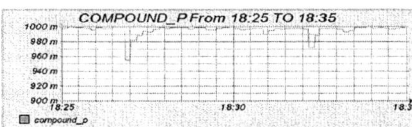
Fig. 7(b) Effect of dynamic weighted m-similarity

Fig. 7. Effect of m-similarity in Experiment 2

Multi-similarity approach aims to avoid the problems mentioned above. We also take all necessary attributes into account for our detection. But, multi-similarity integrates the characteristic according to its contribution by computing parameter ξ, which we can see in Figure 6 and Figure 7, by comparing the result of static weighted similarity and multi-similarity. When we use static weighted similarity, we have a lower downwards movement in Figure 6 (a) than in Figure 4 (a) in Experiment 1, and that is the same for Experiment 2. It is because the static similarity method weakens the change of abnormal and decreases the precision of detection. But on the contrary, as can be seen from Figure 6(b), the downward movement is even larger than the single port similarity without use of static weighted similarity. It can be further proved to be effective in Experiment 2. Hence, we can make a conclusion that multi-similarity is better than s-similarity on unknown characteristic worm detection. It can capture the abnormal exactly and effectively enlarge it. So we can sense the abnormal change more quickly and with a lower percentage of the traffic. That's why we can effectively detect a worm scanning earlier against the large scale network traffic.

5 Conclusions

This paper proposes an early worm detection method based on multi-similarity. On the basis of analyzing characteristics of normal network traffic distribution, this paper makes three contributions:

1. that the proposed detection algorithm based on multi-similarity is a different approach combining traffic distribution and similarity. It effectively detects the worm at its early probing stage.
2. the method we proposed can effectively detect the worm's attack when the attacking traffic is too little to be aware under background. Especially, it can be adapted to early detection for large-scale networks.
3. this approach does not require knowledge of worm packet contents; it can automatically detect worms due to their unusual distribution of traffic.

From the above experiment result, we prove that this method can obtain an effective rate of detection on an on-going worm attack before it is propagated across the Internet; in fact, proving that worms can be detected in their early-burstout stage by this method.

Acknowledgements

This research was supported by the National Natural Science Foundation of China funding made available through grant no.60403033.

References

1. David Moore, Colleen Shannon, Jeffery Brown, "Code-Red: a case study on the spread and victims of an Internet worm", In Proceedings of the ACM SIGCOMM Internet Measurement Workshop, Marseille, France, pp.273-284, November 2002.
2. D. Moore, and C. Shannon, The spread of the code-red worm (CRv2), Technical report, CAIDA, the Cooperative Association for Internet Data Analysis, USA, 2002.
3. R. Russell, and A. Mackie, Code red II worm, Incident analysis report, Security Focus, USA, August 2001.

4. D. Moore, "Network Telescopes: Observing Small or Distant Security Events", Proceedings of the 11th USENIX Security Symposium, CA, USA, pp.167-174 Aug. 2002.
5. Cliff Changchun Zou, Lixin Gao, Weibo Gong, and Don Towsley, "Monitoring and early warning for internet worms", Proceedings of the 10th ACM conference on Computer and communication security, Washington D.C., pp.190-199, USA, 2003.
6. C. C. Zou, L. Gao, W. Gong, and D. Towsley, "Monitoring and early warning for internet worms", In Proceedings of the ACM conference on Computer and Communication Security, Washington D.C., USA, pp.190-199, October 2003.
7. Nicholas Weaver, Stuart Staniford, and Vern Paxson, "Very Fast Containment of Scanning Worms", In Proceedings of the 13th USENIX Security Symposium, USA, pp.29-44, August 2004.
8. JUNG J., Paxson V., Berger A. W. and Balakrishnan, H., "Fast Portscan Detection Using sequential Hypothesis Testing", In proceeding of the IEEE Symposium on Security and Privacy, USA, pp.211-225, May 2004.
9. V.Berk, G.Bakos., and R. Morris, "Designing a Framework for Active Worm Detection on Global Networks", In Proceedings of the IEEE International Workshop on Information Assurance, Darmstadt, Germany, pp. 13-23, March 2003.
10. Guofei Gu, Monirul Sharif, Xinzhou Qin, and David Dagon, "Worm Detection, Early Warning and Response Based on Local Victim Information", 20th Annual Computer Security Applications Conference, Arizona, pp. 1063-9527, December 2004.
11. Xuan Chen, and John Heidemann, "Detecting Early Worm Propagation through Packet Matching", Technical Report ISI-TR-2004-585, USC/Information Sciences Institute, February 2004.

Empirical Study on Fusion Methods Using Ensemble of RBFNN for Network Intrusion Detection

Aki P.F. Chan, Daniel S. Yeung, Eric C.C. Tsang, and Wing W.Y. Ng

Hong Kong Polytechnic University,
Department of Computing, Hong Kong, China
{csaki, csdaniel, csetsang, cswyng}@comp.polyu.edu.hk
http://www.comp.polyu.edu.hk/~cike/

Abstract. The network security problem has become a critical issue and many approaches have been proposed to tackle the information security problems, especially the Denial of Service (DoS) attacks. Multiple Classifier System (MCS) is one of the approaches that have been adopted in the detection of DoS attacks recently. Fusion strategy is crucial and has great impact on the classification performance of an MCS. However the selection of the fusion strategy for an MCS in DoS problem varies widely. In this paper, we focus on the comparative study on adopting different fusion strategies for an MCS in DoS problem.

1 Introduction

Although a secure computer system provides guarantees regarding the confidentiality, integrity and availability of its objects, the system generally contains design and implementation flaws which result in security vulnerabilities. According to the CSI/FBI survey in 2004, the Denial of Service (DoS) attack, which is a class of attacks initiated by individual or group of individuals exploiting security vulnerabilities to prevent legitimate users or victims from accessing the compromised system and information, is reported as the most costly in computer crime because of its use for computer extortion [18]. The DoS attack is perhaps the most detrimental attack because they have been proven capable of shutting an organization off from the Internet or dramatically slowing down network links [4]. This causes a great impact on those e-commerce systems or critical systems, which results in incalculable losses, trust and loyalty reduction for the e-commerce companies. Misuse and anomaly detection are the two approaches to intrusion detection. Both of them possess different merits and limitations and the details can be found in [6, 8]. The DoS problem involves large sample size and detecting novel attacks may need to be included in the future.

An MCS is a young and active research area which gives better performance than a single classifier [5, 17]. Many researchers found that just selecting a single classifier that performs well may not be the optimal choice. Alternatively, one may divide the problem into several small problems and deal with each of them using simpler classifiers. Thus an MCS approach is suggested as a solution which merges several simpler classifiers together to solve a given problem.

Design successful classifier fusion system consists of two important issues: the selection of the base classifiers [7, 15], and design classifier fusion mechanism [13].

The fusion of different base classifiers within an MCS plays the key role of successful MCS training.

Neural network is widely adopted as base classifiers for an MCS in different application areas [17]. Every base classifier within an MCS is unique and they may be different in training data, initialization or architecture. After training, their results will be combined by one of the fusion methods introduced in Section 2. Multi-Layer Perceptron Neural Networks (MLPNN), Radial Basis Function Neural Networks (RBFNN) and Support Vector Machine (SVM) are the common base classifiers for an MCS [8, 16]. An MLPNN consists of a set of sensory units that merge together to implement the complex mapping function. It is capable of performing multiclass classifications. However it is not able to handle problem involving a large number of samples. An SVM is a learning machine which transforms the data into a high-dimensional feature space and solves the classification problem by solving a quadratic optimization problem. It does not depend on the number of input features. An SVM is capable of solving problem having a large number of features, however it can only perform two-class classification and is very slow in solving large sample sizes problem. On the other hand, an RBFNN performs classification by the distances between the sample and the centers of the RBFNN's hidden neurons. It has 3 layers, the input layer, the hidden layer with the RBFNN non-linearity and a linear output layer. The RBFNN does not employ time-consuming back-propagation algorithm and solve a linear equation to find the connection weights between the hidden neurons and output neurons. It is much faster and more suitable for problem with large sample size, e.g. the DoS problems.

Fusion strategy is one of the critical issues in an MCS that yields a big impact on the performance of an MCS [14]. The major research problem in an MCS is to find the most appropriate fusion strategy to combine the results from the base classifiers while maintaining the classification accuracy for unseen samples. In DoS detection problem, the goal is to maximize the classification accuracy and minimize the false alarm rate simultaneously. There are two major types of fusion strategy: winner-take-all and weighted sum. The winner-take-all category decides the final decision based on the highest measurement value only while the weighted sum type combines the decisions from all of the base classifiers. In this work, we provide a comparative study of using different fusion methods in an MCS to solve a DoS problem. A brief survey on the fusion approaches is given in Section 2. Section 3 presents the experimental results and empirical comparisons are discussed. Finally, Section 4 gives the conclusion of this work.

2 Fusion Approaches of MCS

Fusion method adopted in an MCS will greatly affect the decision of the final output of the MCS. A choice of an appropriate fusion method can improve further on the performance of the MCS. Traditionally the fusion method is categorized according to the output of the base classifiers which are the crisp outputs and the soft outputs while we provide an alternative categorization of the fusion method based on their algorithms. The fusion method is grouped into winner-take-all and weighted sum by considering how they combine the decisions from base classifiers.

2.1 Winner-Take-All Type

Majority vote, Weighted Majority vote, Behavior Knowledge Space, Naïve-Bayes combination and Dempster-Shafer combination are categorized as winner-take-all type since they all have a measurement for each base classifier and the final decision of an MCS is the one with the highest measurement value.

2.1.1 Majority Vote

Majority vote [3] can be applied to an MCS by assuming that each classifier gives a single class label as the output and the final output is assigned to the class where most of the base classifiers give this as class outputs. Let the output of the classifiers from the decision vector d be defined as $d = [d_{i,1},......,d_{i,c}]^T \in \{0,1\}^c, i = 1,....L$, where L is the number of classifier and $d_{i,j} = 1$ if D_i assigns x in ω_j, and 0 otherwise. The majority vote results in the final decision for class ω_k if

$$\sum_{i=1}^{L} d_{i,k} = \max_{j=1}^{c} \sum_{i=1}^{L} d_{i,j} \qquad (1)$$

The main advantage of this rule is its simplicity and no training is required. However this rule ignores the diversity of the base classifiers.

2.1.2 Weighted Majority Vote

This fusion rule assigns a weight to each base classifier which indicates the degree of importance of the classifier's output with respect to the final decision. The weights vary according to the ability of the base classifiers in classifying the samples.

$$\sum_{i=1}^{L} b_i d_{i,k}(x) = \max_{j=1}^{c} \sum_{i=1}^{L} b_i d_{i,j}(x) \qquad (2)$$

The final decision of an MCS is based on the base classifiers' output $d_{i,j}(x)$ and pre-selected weights b_i.

This method assigns more weight to the accurate base classifiers but ignore the other inaccurate base classifiers. The weights for the base classifiers need to be chosen apriori and are difficult to obtain and adjust. Thus, it is difficult to adopt novel network attacks.

2.1.3 Naïve-Bayes Combination

The Naïve Bayes (NB) combination [17] approach makes the assumption that the decisions of the individual classifiers are independent. The decision of each base classifier is weighted according to the confusion matrix on the training set. Using L base classifiers where each picks a particular class s, the NB decision rule is

$$\mu_D^i(x) = \prod_{j=1}^{L} P(i \mid D_j(x) = s) \quad (3)$$

$$P(k \mid D_j(x) = s) = \frac{cm_{k,s}^j}{cm_{\cdot,s}^j} \quad (4)$$

where $cm_{k,s}^j$, which is an entry of the confusion matrix, is the number of element of the dataset whose true class label was k, and were assigned by classifier D_j to class s and $cm_{\cdot,s}^j$ is the total number of elements labeled by D_j to class s. For two-class problem with two classifiers, we will have cm^1 and cm^2, which are 2x2 confusion matrix.

The independent assumption of Naïve-Bayes combination approach is too strict and is always violated in real world problems.

2.1.4 Dempster-Shafer Combination

The Dempster-Shafer (DS) combination [12] adopts the decision templates as its measures. It calculates the proximity between decision templates and the output of classifiers, belief degrees and the support for each class.

The proximity between DT_j^i, which is the ith row of the decision template for class j, and $D_i(x)$, which is the ith row of the decision profile $DP(x)$, for every class $j = 1,....,c$ and for every classifier $i = 1,....,L$ is calculated as

$$\Phi_{j,i}(x) = \frac{(1 + \|DT_j^i - D_i(x)\|^2)^{-1}}{\sum_{k=1}^{c}(1 + \|DT_k^i - D_i(x)\|^2)^{-1}} \quad (5)$$

The belief degrees for each class and each classifier can then be calculated as

$$b_j(D_i(x)) = \frac{\Phi_{j,i}(x)\prod_{k \neq j}(1 - \Phi_{k,i}(x))}{1 - \Phi_{j,i}(x)[1 - \prod_{k \neq j}(1 - \Phi_{k,i}(x))]} \quad (6)$$

The final degrees of support are

$$\mu_j(x) = K\prod_{i=1}^{L} b_j(D_i(x)) \quad (7)$$

where $j = 1,....,c$ and K is a normalizing constant.

Although this method does not make any assumption on the base classifiers, its computational complexity and memory requirement are very high. These limit the use of this method to DoS detection problem.

2.2 Weighted Sum

Each base classifier is given a weight which depends on the ability of individual base classifier. All of them compute a weight for each base classifier using different methods and then sum up their outputs with the weights to give a final decision.

2.2.1 Average

This fusion method is the one that frequently used. The sum of each output of the base classifiers is averaged to give the final decision [3].

$$\mu_o(x) = \frac{1}{L}\sum_{i=1}^{L} d_{i,j}(x) \qquad (8)$$

where μ_o is the final output, L is the number of classifiers and $d_{i,j}$ is the output of the base classifier D_i for class ω_j.

This method lacks the ability to handle the imbalance of base classifiers' accuracy where each base classifier contributes the same amount to the final output.

2.2.2 Neural Network

A neural network is employed to combine the results from the base classifiers by using the base classifiers' outputs as its inputs.

$$\mu_o(x) = f(\sum_{i=1}^{L} \omega_i d_i) \qquad (9)$$

where μ_o is the final output, the ω_i is the weight associated with the input line i, d_i is the output of the base classifier D_i and $f()$ is the activation function.

The advantage of a neural network is its ability to automatically adjust the connection weights without any domain-specific knowledge while other approaches use preselected weights to combine the outputs. The main disadvantage of this approach is the lack of standard and effective criteria on how to create, select and combine the results from base classifiers. For examples, one may use multilayer perceptron or radial basis function to find the fusion weights and their architecture may also be different.

2.3 Fusion Approaches for DoS Problem

The DoS detection problem is formulated as a pattern classification problem of classifying a sample to be a DoS attack or a normal sample. The sample in the DoS detection problem comprises the current network information and the packet passing through the DoS detection system which has been installed in the network system. Multiple classifier systems (MCS) [2, 9] have been applied in the DoS detection due to its ability to realize arbitrary continuous mappings between the inputs and outputs. A choice of an appropriate fusion method can improve further on the performance of an MCS. Since the classification of DoS problem involves a large number of samples and the class distribution is unbalanced, the selection of fusion approaches for an

MCS in DoS problem depends on their characteristics. However the choice of the fusion method for an MCS in DoS problem varies widely. In [9], majority vote is adopted to combine the results from the base classifiers of an MCS for detecting network intrusions while Naïve-Bayes combination is applied in [2]. There is a lack of standard on choosing the fusion method for an MCS.

In this paper, the fusion approaches are grouped into winner-take-all and weighted sum based on how they combine the decisions from the base classifiers and also the appropriate fusion method for detecting DoS problem is investigated. The fusion methods in winner-take-all category except the majority vote and the weighted majority vote require high computational resources due to the calculation of measurement that involves pair-wise comparison. This computational requirement is unacceptable for the problem having large number of samples. Majority vote is a simple fusion method which does not require any training or complex calculation. However it ignores the diversity of the base classifiers which is one of the motivations of building an MCS. The weighted majority vote assigns weights to the base classifiers according to their performance. However the weights have to be manually set prior.

The fusion methods in weighted sum category assign a weight to each of the base classifier and combine their outputs to give the final decision. The average method combines the base classifiers' output where each classifier contributes the same amount to the final decision. Neural network solves this problem which determines and adjusts the weights automatically. Although there are no standard and effective criteria to select and combine the outputs from base classifiers, it gives the final decision without a prior knowledge and is efficient if suitable neural network is chosen. Thus neural network is a suitable fusion method and the RBFNN is the one that could handle a large number of samples efficiently and is suitable for DoS problem.

3 Experimental Results

In this section, an experiment is conducted on KDDCUP 1999 dataset which is prepared from the 1998 DARPA intrusion detection evaluation program to evaluate the performance of adopting different fusion approaches. In the dataset, there are substantial amount of network connections and each connection is represented by 41 features. Among the five classes of network connections, normal traffic and Denial of Service (DoS) attacks are selected for the experiment. For the DoS attack in the dataset, only 6 kinds of them will be used for experiments which are Smurf, Neptune, Back, Land, Teardrop and Ping of Death. Thus an MCS for DoS detection by adopting different fusion methods are experimented.

In the experiment of an MCS with different fusion methods, the number of base classifiers is chosen as the number of attack classes in the dataset, 6 in this case and each base classifier is designated to detect one attack type. The architecture of an MCS is shown in Figure 1. This architecture design aids the addition of novel attack types in the future by including one more classifier designated for detecting the novel attack [1]. All features were used to train each of the base classifier.

In each experiment, the dataset is randomly split into two half: training dataset and testing dataset. The testing dataset serves as future unseen samples to evaluate the final result of the different methods and the training of an MCS use only the training dataset in all the methods. All the input values are normalized to [0,1] and different fusion methods were adopted for combining the results of base classifiers. 10-fold cross-validation was adopted for the experiment and the result was averaged.

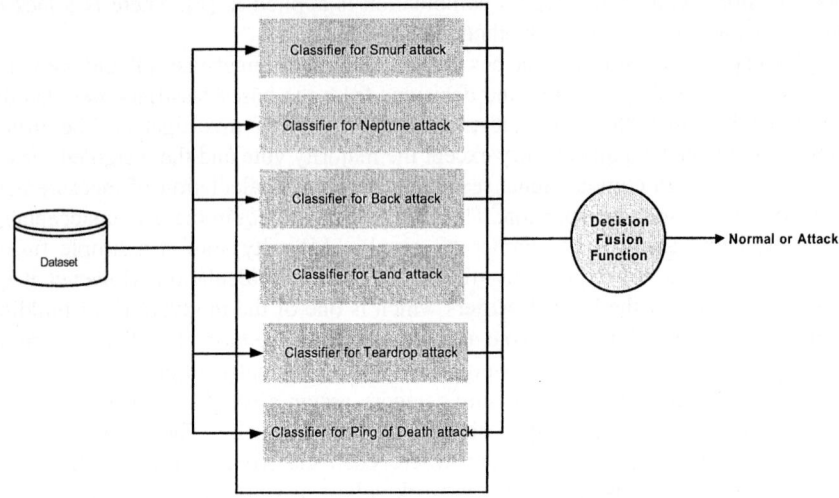

Fig. 1. The architecture of an MCS for DoS detection

The performance of an MCS with different fusion methods for detecting DoS attacks is shown in Tables 1 and 2.

Table 1. Average testing accuracy for an MCS using different fusion methods on KDDCUP'99 Dataset

Fusion Methods	Average Testing Accuracy
Neural Network	**99.59%**
Dempster-Shaffer	99.08%
Weighted Majority Vote	80.66%
Majority Vote	80.09%
Average	80.01%
Navie-Bayes	79.86%

Table 2. Average false alarm rate for an MCS using different fusion methods on KDDCUP'99 Dataset

Fusion Methods	Average False Alarm Rate
Neural Network	**0.63%**
Dempster-Shaffer	0.71%
Weighted Majority Vote	1.91%
Majority Vote	2.27%
Average	2.29%
Navie-Bayes	4.99%

An MCS built using the Naïve-Bayes combination method attains unsatisfactory testing accuracy and has relatively high false alarm rate. This indicates that this method is not suitable for detecting DoS attacks and this may be due to the violation in the independent assumption of Naïve-Bayes combination and a relationship exists between base classifiers. On the other hand, the performances of an MCS built using the average, majority vote and weighted majority vote fusion methods are comparable, however these methods have nearly 20% lower testing accuracy and 2% higher false alarm rate than the neural network and Dempster-Shaffer combination approaches. The majority vote fusion method yielding lower accuracy may be due to most of the base classifiers not recognizing the attacks belonging to their own type. This occurs even if each classifier is not designated to one attack type. It also ignores the diversity of the base classifiers while the average fusion method ignores the different ability of the base classifiers and weights the same amount for each base classifier. The weighted majority vote fusion method magnifies the ability of the accurate classifier by assigning more weight to it but less to the less accurate classifiers. But the weights are set manually and are difficult to adjust which cannot truly represent the importance of the accurate classifiers. The neural network and Dempster-Shaffer combination approaches attain 99% and 98% testing accuracy respectively and the false alarm rate is only 1% to 2% for the two fusion methods. These methods provide the best performance which yields high accuracy and low false alarm rate among the considered fusion rules. However the Dempster-Shaffer combination approach has the deficiency that novel attacks may be undetected due to the use of decision template.

Neural network posses the ability to adjust the weights of the base classifiers and reveal the importance of the base classifiers. Therefore, an MCS using neural network as the fusion method is shown to have better performance than the other fusion methods experimentally in detecting DoS attacks. The neural network fusion in the experiment employs the RBFNN to compute the weights. This is efficient for large sample size while the Dempster-Shaffer method is not.

4 Conclusion and Future Works

Different fusion methods of an MCS for DoS problem are compared. It shows that fusion method is an important issue in an MCS that yields a big impact on the performance of an MCS. The fusion methods are categorized into winner-take-all and weighted sum and a brief survey of different fusion methods is also provided. The DoS detection problem is discussed and different fusion methods of an MCS are applied to detect the DoS attacks so as to evaluate their performance. In DoS detection problem, the major characteristic is the large sample size and the experimental results shown that the neural network (RBFNN) fusion approach performs better than the other fusion methods due to its ability to adjust weights automatically without prior assumption.

Acknowledgements

This paper is jointly supported by the Hong Kong Research Grant Council Projects Number B-Q571 and Number B-Q676.

References

1. A. P. F. Chan, W. W. Y. Ng, D. S. Yeung and E. C. C. Tsang, "Multiple Classifier System with Feature Grouping for Intrusion Detection: Mutual Information Approach", Knowledge-Based Intelligent Information and Engineering Systems: 9th International Conference, KES 2005, LNAI 3683, pp.141-148.
2. G. Giorgio, R. Fabio & D. Luca, "Fusion of multiple classifiers for intrusion detection in computer networks", Pattern Recognition Letters, Vol.24, pp. 1795-1803, 2003.
3. L. Hanson and P. Salamon, "Neural Network Ensembles", IEEE Trans. on Pattern Analysis and Machine Intelligence, Vol.12, pp.993-1001, 1990.
4. A. Householder, A. Manion, L. Pesante, G. Weaver, and R. Thomas, "Managing the Threat of Denial-of-Service Attacks," Carnegie Mellon CERT Coordination Center, Pittsburgh, PA, Oct. 2001.
5. J. Kittler, M. Hatef, R. P. W. Duin and J. Matas, "On Combining Classifiers", IEEE Trans. on Pattern Analysis and Machine Intelligence, Vol.20, pp. 226-239, 1998.
6. S. Kumar and E. H. Spafford, "A pattern matching model for misuse intrusion detection", Proceedings of the 17th National Computer Security Conference, pp.11-21, 1994b.
7. L. I. Kuncheva, "Switching between selection and fusion in combining classifiers: An experiment", IEEE Trans. on Systems, Man and Cybernetics, Part B, Vol.32, pp.146-156, 2002.
8. W. Lee and S. J. Stolfo, "Data mining approaches for intrusion detection", Proceedings of the 7th USENIX Security Symposium, 1998.
9. S. Mukkamala, A. H. Sung, A. Abraham, "Intrusion Detection Using Ensemble of Soft Computing and Hard Computing Paradigms", Journal of Network and Computer Applications, Vol.28, pp. 167-182, 2005.
10. W. W. Y. Ng, A. P. F. Chan, D. S. Yeung and E. C. C. Tsang, "Quantitative Study on the Generalization Error of Multiple Classifier Systems", To appear in IEEE Proc. of International Conference on Systems, Man and Cybernetics, Hawaii, USA, October 2005.
11. W. W. Y. Ng, R. K. C. Chang and D. S. Yeung, "Dimensionality Reduction for Denial of Service Detection Problems Using RBFNN Output Sensitivity", IEEE Proceedings of the International Conference on Machine Learning and Cybernetics, Vol.2, pp.1293 – 1298, 2003.
12. G. Rogova, "Combining the results of several neural network classifiers", Neural Networks, Vol.7, pp.777-781, 1994.
13. F. Roli, G. Giacinto and G. Vernazza, "Methods for Designing Multiple Classifier Systems", MCS, LNCS 2096, pp.78-87, 2001.
14. K. Tumer, J. Ghosh, "Classifier combining: analytical results and implications", National Conference on Artificial Intelligence, 1996.
15. K. Tumer and J. Ghosh, "Error correlation and error reduction in ensemble classifiers", Connection Science, Vol.8, pp.385-404, 1996.
16. T. Verwoerd, R. Hunt, "Intrusion detection techniques and approaches", Computer communications, Vo.25, pp. 1356-1365, 2002.
17. L. Xu, A. Krzyzak and C. Y. Suen, "Methods for combining multiple classifiers and their applications to handwriting recognition", IEEE Trans. on SMC, Vol.22, pp. 418-435, 1992.
18. http://www.businessweek.com/magazine/content/04_32/b3895106_mz063.htm

A Covariance Matrix Based Approach to Internet Anomaly Detection

Shuyuan Jin[1], Daniel So Yeung[1], Xizhao Wang[2], and Eric C.C. Tsang[1]

[1] Department of Computing, HongKong Polytechnic University, HongKong
{cssyjin, csdaniel, csetsang}@comp.polyu.edu.hk
[2] School of Mathematics and Computer Science, Hebei University, Baoding, China
wangxz@mail.hbu.edu.cn

Abstract. Detecting multiple network attacks is essential to intrusion detection, network security defense and network traffic management. This paper presents a covariance matrix based detection approach to detecting multiple known and unknown network anomalies. It utilizes the difference of covariance matrices among observed samples in the detection. A threshold matrix is employed in the detection where each entry of the matrix evaluates the covariance changes of the corresponding features. As case studies, extensive experiments are conducted to detect multiple DoS attacks – the prevalent Internet anomalies. The experimental results indicate that the proposed approach achieves high detection rates in detecting multiple known and unknown anomalies.

1 Introduction

Detecting multiple network attacks is essential to intrusion detection, network security defense and network traffic management. For example, effective detection of multiple attacks can guarantee the good performance of an intrusion detection system (IDS). All of the on-line intrusion-prevention systems (IPS), such as Internet Security Systems (ISS) Proventia G Series, NetScreen Technologies' NetScreen-IDP 100 and TippingPoint, have some level of attack detection mechanisms to identify malicious traffic [7]. Detecting multiple attacks also helps the Internet Service Providers (ISP) to effectively manage the traffic and improve the Quality of Service(QoS) to end-users.

Generally speaking, two kinds of strategies exist in the field of intrusion detection: misuse and anomaly. Misuse detection utilizes signature-matching techniques to indicate the presence of an attack. It is only effective and practical to detect already-known attacks. Anomaly detection utilizes the significant deviation from the normal profile to identify suspicious behaviors. Compared with misuse detection, anomaly detection approaches offer an advantage of identifying unknown attacks.

In the context of Internet anomaly detection, statistical detection approaches are widely employed. Normally these statistical methods utilize the first-order statistical inferences of network features provided by the monitoring devices [1] [2] [3]. In this paper, we present a second-order statistical method to detect the cumulative changes exhibited by the network packet sequences of equal and fix length. The detection approach utilizes the covariance matrix to model the observed network packets. Totally different from traditional anomaly detection techniques, where covariance matrix structure is estimated to analyze the noise [4] [5] [6], the covariance matrix based detection approach presented in this paper utilizes the difference among covariance matrices directly in the detection. Under the effect of different thresholds for different classes obtained by training, the significant changes among covariance matrices are revealed in detecting different types of attacks.

Our design makes use of the following basic facts. First, the covariances among different first-order network features have specific meanings in the network engineering. For example, the covariance changes among first-order features (such as SYN and FIN) will indicate the ongoing phenomenon, i.e., a SYN flooding attack [10]. Second, as a statistical variable, covariance or covariance matrix should be calculated from a collection of data. Facing the large volume of network traffic, it is more reasonable to consider the traffic within a determined time interval or a fixed sequence length.

The rest of this paper is organized as follows. Section 2 describes the anomaly detection approach in details. Section 3 validates the performance of our approach by experiments. Section 4 gives some discussions and draws a conclusion.

2 Approach

2.1 Detection Algorithm

We regard the problem of detecting multiple attacks as a multi-class classification problem. The classifier should be able to not only distinguish multiple known classes, but also identify the unknown classes.

Suppose that we have samples from R already known classes: $\omega_1, \omega_2, \ldots, \omega_R$. For each class ω_r ($1 \leq r \leq R$), its training set ω_r consists of all the corresponding covariance matrices calculated on the sample sequences of equal, fixed length. For example, when selecting the sequence length as n, M_r^1 is obtained by calculating all the samples $x_1^1, x_2^1, \ldots, x_n^1$ in the temporal sequence T_1; and M_r^l is obtained from the samples $x_1^l, x_2^l, \ldots, x_n^l$ in the temporal sequence T_l. A covariance matrix M_r^l based on all the samples $x_1^l, x_2^l, \ldots, x_n^l$ in the temporal sequence T_l is defined as:

$$M_l = \begin{pmatrix} \sigma_{f_1^l, f_1^l} & \sigma_{f_1^l, f_2^l} & \cdots & \sigma_{f_1^l, f_p^l} \\ \sigma_{f_2^l, f_1^l} & \sigma_{f_2^l, f_2^l} & \cdots & \sigma_{f_2^l, f_p^l} \\ \vdots & \vdots & \ddots & \vdots \\ \sigma_{f_p^l, f_1^l} & \sigma_{f_p^l, f_2^l} & \cdots & \sigma_{f_p^l, f_p^l} \end{pmatrix} \quad (1)$$

$$\sigma_{f_u^l, f_v^l} = \frac{1}{n} \sum_{k=1}^{n} \left(f_u^{l,k} - \mu_{f_u^l} \right)\left(f_v^{l,k} - \mu_{f_v^l} \right) \quad (2)$$

where

f_u and f_v is the first-order features of the observed network packet
$\mu_{f_u^l}$ ($1 \leq u \leq p$) is the expectation of f_u

$f_u^{l,k}$ is the value of f_u in the k-th observation during the l-th time interval
u is the number of features $(1 \le u \le p)$
k is the number of observations during T_l $(1 \le k \le n)$
l is the number of time intervals, such as $T_1, T_2, \ldots, T_l, \ldots$ $1 \le l \le \infty$

Assume that we can get a total of l covariance matrices for class $\omega_r : \{M_r^1, M_r^2 \ldots, M_r^l\}$ according to the above described procedure. The classifier will assign a class label to a presented M^{obs} in the detection according to the following discrimination function:

$$\begin{cases} \text{if } Dist(M^{obs}, E(\omega_r); \delta_r) = [0]_{p \times p}, & M^{obs} \in \omega_r \\ \text{if } \forall r, Dist(M^{obs}, E(\omega_r); \delta_r) \ne [0]_{p \times p}, & M^{obs} \in \text{unkown class} \end{cases} \quad (3)$$

where $E(\omega_r)$ is the mean of class ω_r and δ_r is the settled threshold matrix of class ω_r, $1 \le r \le R$. The dissimilarity function $Dist(M^{obs}, E(\omega_r); \delta_r) = [0]_{p \times p}$ is defined as

$$\forall m_{ij}^{obs} \in M^{obs}, \forall \overline{m}_{ij}^r \in E(\omega_r), \forall \delta_{ij}^r \in \delta_r, \forall d_{ij} \in Dist(M^{obs}, E(\omega_r); \delta_r)$$

$$\begin{cases} d_{ij} = 0 & \text{if } |m_{ij}^{obs} - \overline{m}_{ij}^r| \le \delta_{ij}^r \\ d_{ij} = 1 & \text{if } |m_{ij}^{obs} - \overline{m}_{ij}^r| > \delta_{ij}^r \end{cases} \quad (4)$$

Equations (3) and (4) mean that for an observed covariance matrix M^{obs}, the classifier will classify it to the same label as the average of any one of known classes ω_r, if and only if $Dist(M^{obs}, E(\omega_r); \delta_r) = [0]_{p \times p}$. For example, M^{obs} will be considered as normal when M^{obs} is δ_N-matrix nearest to the center of the normal class ω_N in all $p(p+1)/2$ different positions in the difference matrix of M^{obs} and ω_N. If we could not find any one of known classes to M^{obs} to be δ_r-matrix nearest, M^{obs} will be determined as the novelty.

2.2 Threshold Determination

The determination of multiple thresholds for multiple known classes is a complex optimization problem. Especially, that the threshold is a matrix as proposed in Equations (3) and (4) makes its determination more difficult. Here we propose a relatively simple but practical threshold determination algorithm. The algorithm attempts to set every entry of the threshold matrix as a value which covers all the variances of the corresponding covariance changes. Especially, the maximum statistic of the covariance changes is utilized as the initial value of each element in the threshold matrix. The aim of the threshold matrix determination algorithm is to achieve the minimal misclassification rate for each training class. We increase or decrease the threshold matrix by multiplying the threshold matrix with different multipliers. Correspondingly, the classification precision rate and misclassification rate will change with different product threshold matrices. Generally, we can obtain a set of product threshold matrices which can make the misclassification rate achieve the minimum. We select the minimal multiplier from the product set as the preferred threshold matrix multiplier. The preferred threshold matrix is the product of the preferred threshold matrix and the initial threshold matrix. In order to illustrate the threshold matrix determination process, a realization of threshold matrix determination for normal class is provided in Fig. 1. The threshold matrix determination of other attack classes will have the similar process. Because a misclassification of any normal sample will signal a false alarm, the false alarm rate is used in Fig. 1 instead of misclassification rate.

Notations

ω_r : Traing Data Set, $1 \le r \le R$

ϖ_r : Testing Data Set, $1 \le r \le S, \ S > R$

N: Normal Class Label, $N \in [1, R]$

ω_N : Traing Data Set of Normal Class

ϖ_N : Testing Data Set of Normal Class

δ_N : Threshold Matrix of Normal Class

Assume ω_N has a total of l covariance matrix training samples

---

$\forall \delta_{ij}^N \in \delta_N, \ \forall m_{ij}^N \in \omega_N, \ \forall \delta_{ij}^N \in \delta_N,$

init $\delta_{ij}^N = \max\limits_{k=1}^{l} \left| m_{ij}^N - \bar{m}_{ij}^N \right|$, *multiplier*=0.2;

do {

$\quad \delta_N = \delta_N * multiplier$

$\quad$ for each $M \in \varpi_N$

$\quad\quad$ if $Dist(M, E(\omega_N); \delta_N) \ne [0]_{p \times p}$ count=count+1;

$\quad$ endfor

$\quad FAR$(False Alarm Rate) = count/$\|\varpi_N\|$

$\quad$ *multiplier*=*multiplier*+0.01;

} until (*FAR* is converged or minimum)

Fig. 1. A realization of threshold determination algorithm for normal class

2.3 Detection Rules

As an on-line detection system, our detection approach employs a rule-like sequential detection procedure. Assume there are R classes in the training stage and we have obtained R threshold matrices according to the above threshold determination algorithm.

We label the training classes as follows. The normal class is labeled as class ω_1 and the attack classes are labeled based on the sample numbers they have. The more samples the attack class has, the smaller its label is. Therefore, a labeled training class sequence will be obtained as $\omega_1, \omega_2, \omega_3, ..., \omega_R$. The detection process is demonstrated in Fig. 2.

$\forall M^{obs}$
if $Dist(M^{obs}, E(\omega_1); \delta_1) = [0]_{p \times p}$, then $M^{obs} \in \omega_N$
elseif $Dist(M^{obs}, E(\omega_2); \delta_2) = [0]_{p \times p}$, then $M^{obs} \in \omega_2$
elseif $Dist(M^{obs}, E(\omega_3); \delta_3) = [0]_{p \times p}$, then $M^{obs} \in \omega_3$
... ...
else $M^{obs} \in$ unknown attack

Fig. 2. A rule-like realization of on-line detection

3 Experiments

3.1 Data and Feature Used

The dataset we use is KDD CUP 99 Dataset at http://kdd.ics.uci.edu/databases/kddcup99/kddcup99.html. It is constructed based on the raw data of TCP dump data from 1998 DARPA evaluations [11] for the purpose of network intrusion detector competition. The datasets contain a total of 24 training attack types, with an additional 14 types in the test data only. In our experiments, only the DoS attack classes which contain records greater than 200 are considered. The main reason is that it is not always possible to formulate a classification model to learn the anomaly detector with "insufficient" training data [12]. There are totally 6 types of DoS attacks in our experiments which include 3 known DoS attack types and 3 unknown DoS attack types. We use 3/5 samples as training set and 2/5 samples as testing set for each selected class. The detailed dataset description in our experiments is presented in Table 1.

We employ all the 9 time-based traffic features in our experiments. They are the features named *count, serror_rate, rerror_rate, same_srv_rate, diff_srv_rate, srv_count, srv_serror_rate, srv_rerror_rate* and *srv_diff_host_rate*. A detailed description of the 9 time-based traffic features is provided in [13].

Table 1. Data set description

Type	Training samples	Testing Samples
Normal	94722	63148
Smurf	266929	177952
Back	1981	1320
Neptune	99122	66080
apache2	0	794
mailBomb	0	5000
processtable	0	759

3.2 Results

In our experiment, the sequence length parameter n is set to 200 with a sliding window of 50, while the preferred threshold δ_r for each known classes is obtained in the training procedure described in Section 2.2.

As we know, different threshold matrix corresponds to different classification precision rate in detecting different class. Here we take the detection of the normal class as an example. Fig. 3 illustrates the performance of different threshold matrix used in detecting the normal class, in terms of different pairs of detection rate and false alarm rate.

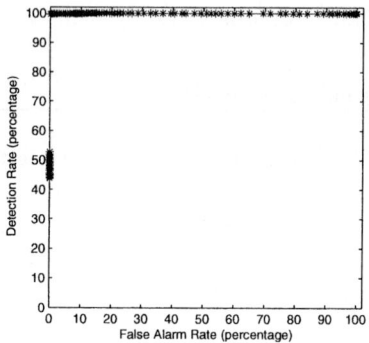

Fig. 3. ROC curve of the covariance matrix based detection approach

Remarks: Fig. 3 shows that the covariance matrix based detection approach achieves very high detection rates with very low corresponding false alarm rates. Two reasons contribute to this high detection results. One is the dataset itself. As we know that many flaws exist in the KDD CUP dataset [14], the normal traffic provided in the dataset is somewhat too simple. The other reason is that the threshold utilizes a matrix rather than a scalar to evaluate the covariance changes. Each entry in the threshold matrix evaluates the changes of the covariance of two corresponding features. Therefore, if the observed covariance matrix (e.g. the samples of the attack class) should not be labeled as the provided class profile (e.g. the profile of normal class), it is very easy to happen that the changes of some elements in the observed covariance matrix exceed the corresponding element in the threshold matrix, which will result in the failure of labeling the observed samples as the label of the provided profile. However, we will also notice that each entry of the initial threshold matrix is settled as the maximum statistic of the covariance changes, which increase the opportunity of labeling the observed sample of covariance matrix as its corrected class label. Therefore, the false alarm rate of the normal class or the misclassifications rates of the attack classes will be very low while the classification precision rate will be very high in the covariance matrix based detection approach.

Table 2 shows some pairs of false alarm rate and detection rate in details when different multipliers of the initial threshold matrix for normal class are used (refer to Fig. 1 for detailed threshold determination algorithm for the normal class).

Table 2. Different pairs of false alarm rate and detection rate under different threshold matrices of the normal class

Threshold Multiplier	False Alarm Rate	Detection Rate
1.15	0	99.60%
1.05	0.32%	99.66%
0.95	2.78%	99.70%
0.85	7.94%	99.84%
0.75	10.88%	99.86%
0.65	16.68%	100.00%

In order to show the performance difference of using different threshold matrices in detecting normal class, we list the classification precision rates in detecting testing samples of the normal class, under different threshold matrix with different multipliers of 1.15 and 0.65 (refer to Table 2), respectively. The classification precision results are shown in Table 4, where *New* represents the unknown attack class. Each entry in Table 3 shows the classification rate of detecting the testing samples of normal class as different known classes. For example, the entry of (2,2) in Table 3 means that the classification rate of detecting the testing samples of the normal class as the normal class is 100% under the threshold matrix with multiplier 1.15.

Table 3. Classification precision rates of detecting the testing samples of the normal class as known classes and unknown attack

Threshold Multiplier	normal	smurf	back	neptune	New
1.15	100.00%	0	0	0	0
0.65	83.32%	0	0	0	16.68%

In order to show the overall performance of the covariance based detection approach in detecting multiple known and unknown attacks, we list the classification results in Table 4. Because the threshold matrix determination algorithm proposed in Section 2.2 is only a practical solution, we only use 1.15 as the threshold multiplier for the normal class and simply use the initial threshold matrix as the preferred threshold matrix for each known attack class.

Table 4. Classification results of distinguishing multiple known and unknown classes using the preferred threshold in the threshold determination algorithm

	normal	smurf	back	neptune	New
normal	100.00%	0	0	0	0
smurf	0	100.00%	0	0	0
back	86.96%	0	4.35%	0	8.70%
neptune	0	0	0	98.86%	1.14%
apache2	0	0	0	0	100.00%
mailBomb	0	0	0	0	100.00%
processtable	0	0	0	0	100.00%

Table 5 summarizes the total classification precision rates of the results listed in Table 4, for the different whole dataset of 4 training classes (refer to column *Training*), 7 testing classes (refer to column *Testing*), 3 known attacks (refer to column *Known*) and 3 unknown attacks (refer to column *Unknown*), respectively. The row of *number of samples* presents the sample count of the dataset represented by the column in terms of the covariance matrix, where the covariance matrix samples are obtained under the fixed and equal sequence length 200 with a sliding window 50. The total precision rate is calculated as the number of correctly classified samples divided by the total samples.

Table 5. Total classification results of distinguish multiple known and unknown classes

	Training	Testing	Known	Unknown
Number of Samples	9241	6277	4897	121
Total Precision Rate	99.62%	99.41%	99.24%	100.00%

4 Discussions

The experimental results in Section 3 show that the covariance matrix based detection approach can achieve a high detection rate, high classification precision rate for the normal class, known attack and unknown attack classes. These experimental results in this extended paper are much better than that presented in our original paper [15]. In the original paper, the threshold is realized based on a scalar value, which evaluates the Euclidean distance of the difference matrix between an observed covariance matrix and the profile covariance matrix; while the threshold in this extended paper is based on a matrix where each entry is realized based on the maximum statistics of the covariance changes of two corresponding features. Therefore, the detection performance has improved a lot. It is true that the dataset employed in this paper has some bias on the detection results, because the flaws exist and the data is somewhat a little simple [14]. However, the detection results verify the effectiveness of employing the covariance matrix in the DoS attack detection; particularly, employing a matrix rather than a scalar to evaluate each entry of the observed matrix sample will greatly increase the effectiveness of the detection.

As the detection approach proposed in this paper utilizes statistical covariance matrix directly, another more relevant detection approach we want to mention is the Mahalanobis-distance based detection approach (M-detector). Both methods take into account variance and covariance of the variables measured, but our proposed method is very different from Mahalanobis Distance base detector in the following aspects:

- Similarity measurement: M-detector evaluates the M distance between the observed sample and the different means of different classes, while our method evaluates the difference of matrices between the covariance matrix of samples and the covariance matrix of different classes.
- Feature space: the feature space of M-detector consists of the samples of signals, while the feature space of our proposed method consists of the covariance matrix of a group of sampled data.

Compared with other outlier detection methods, our proposed method takes advantage of the following desirable characteristics:

- The employment of the *covariance* statistics makes the dissimilarity prominent among the normal and different types of attacks.
- The covariance matrix used in our detection approach has specific meaning, which characterizes each attack in terms of dispersion of its own corresponding *first-order* feature pairs.
- The detection approach overcomes the drawback [7] of the dependency of data specific distribution in traditional IDES/NIDES based anomaly detection techinques.

More research needs to be done. For example, we need to know how to evaluate the effect of physical features on the covariance feature space. We also need to conduct more experiments on different datasets. But these future works do not undermine the discussion of anomaly detection in this paper. The proposed covariance based second order statistical detection approach can be served as a new tool in detecting multiple anomalies.

Acknowledgements

This research work is supported by the Hong Kong RGC Project Research Grant B-Q571 and the Hong Kong Polytechnic University Research Grant GT-891.

References

1. Feinstein, L., Schnackenberg, D.: Statistical Approaches to DDoS Attack Detection and Response. Proceedings of the DARPA Information Survivability Confe-rence and Expostion(DISCEX'03), April 2003.
2. Manikopoulos, C., Papavassiliou, S.: Network Intrusion and Fault Detection: A Statistical Anomaly Approach. IEEE Communications Magazine, October 2002.
3. Blazek, R. B., Kim, H., Rozovskii, B., Tartakovsky, A.: A Novel Approach to Detection of Denial-of-Service Attacks Via Adaptive Sequential and Batch-Sequential Change-Point Detection Methods. Workshop on Statistical and Machine Learning Techniques in Computer Intrusion Detection, June 2002.
4. Conte, E., Maio, A.De., Ricci, G.: Covariance matrix estimation for adaptive CFAR detection in compound-Gaussian clutter. IEEE Transactions on Aerospace and Electronic Systems, Volume: 38, Issue: 2, April 2002.
5. Yang, Z., Wang, X.: Blind turbo multiuser detection for long-code multipath CDMA. IEEE Transactions on Communications, Volume: 50, Issue: 1, Jan. 2002.
6. Conte, E., Maio, A.De., Ricci, G.: Recursive estimation of the covariance matrix of a compound-Gaussian process and its application to adaptive CFAR detection. IEEE Transactions on Signal Processing, Volume: 50, Issue: 8, Aug. 2002
7. Ye, N., Emran, S,M., Chen, Q., Vilbert, S.: Multivariate Statistical Analysis of Audit Trails for Host-Based Intrusion Detection. IEEE Transaction on COMPUTERS, vol.51, No. 7, 2002.
8. G. Cormode, S. Muthukrishnan. What's New: Finding Significant Differences in Network Data Streams. IEEE INFOCOM 2004. March, 2004.

9. Estan, C., Varghese, G.: Data streaming in computer networks. In proceedings of workshop on Management and processing of Data Streams. http://www.research.att.com/conf/mpds2003/schedule/estanV.ps, 2003.
10. Jin, S., Yeung, D.: A Covariance Analysis Model for DDoS Attack Detection. Proceedings of IEEE ICC'2004. Paris, France, June 2004.
11. Lincoln Laboratories: 1999 DARPA Intrusion Detection Evaluation. http://www.ll.mit.edu/IST/ideval/index.html.
12. Lee, W. : A Data Mining Framework for Constructing Features and Models for Intrusion Detection Systems. Ph.D. dissertation, Columbia University,1999.
13. Lee, W., Stolfo, S.: A Framework for Constructing Features and Models for Intrusion Detection Systems. ACM Trans. Information and System Security, vol. 3, no. 4, pp. 227-261, Nov. 2000.
14. Mahoney M.V., Chan, P. K.: An Analysis of the 1999 DARPA/Lincoln Laboratory Evaluation Data for Network Anomaly Detection. RAID, pp. 220–237, 2003.
15. Jin S., Yeung, D., Wang, X., Tsang, E. C.C.: A Second-order Statistical Detection Approach with Application to Internet Anomaly Detection. IEEE International Conference on Machine Learning and Cybernetics, August, 2005.

Use of Linguistic Features in Context-Sensitive Text Classification

Alex K.S. Wong, John W.T. Lee, and Daniel S. Yeung

Department of Computing, The Hong Kong Polytechnic University,
Hung Hom, Kowloon, Hong Kong
{cskswong, csjlee, csdaniel}@comp.polyu.edu.hk
http://www.comp.polyu.edu.hk

Abstract. Many popular Text Classification (TC) models use simple occurrence of words in a document as features to base their classifications. They commonly assume word occurrences to be statistically independent in their design. Although such assumption does not hold in general, these TC models are robust and efficient in their task. Some recent studies have shown context-sensitive TC approaches were able to perform better in general. On the other hand, although complex linguistic or semantic features may intuitively be more relevant in TC, studies on their effectiveness have produced mixed and inconclusive results. In this paper, we present our investigation on the use of some complex linguistic features with two context-sensitive TC methods. Our experimental results show potential advantages of such approach.

1 Introduction

Automatic Text Classification is an important task in the management and use of textual data resources. Such task involves applying machine learning techniques to classify documents based on selected features. Typically, a set of training text documents is preprocessed, say, with stop word removal and stemming, followed by the extraction of feature vectors representing the documents for training a classifier. The simplest way to represent a document is the "bags-of-words" representation which treats each word in the document as an independent feature. This has been proven to be a robust, efficient model though with some limitation in its performance. Well-known approaches like Rocchio's algorithm [9] are based on this model.

In many TC approaches, the use of word occurrences as feature set is combined with the assumption of features independence to improve efficiency and simplify design. However, it is obvious that words are correlated and some words are significant pattern only when they co-occurred with other words. Context-sensitive classification methods identify and make use of words association information to improve the classification effectiveness. There are some good existing methods like IREP [4] and its extension RIPPER [2], [3], which can learn feature co-occurrences with fast heuristics for the classification task.

Another direction to improve the performance of TC is to use different or additional features other than words as basis for the classification task. The features may carry different level of syntactic and semantic properties, e.g. phrases [11], complex nominals [8] and hyponym by word sense disambiguation [1]. Unfortunately, no significant improvement has been observed by using these features. A possible explanation is the lack of good text processing techniques for extracting these features reliably.

In this research, we investigate the use of complex linguistic features in context-sensitive text classification. The features we investigated include lemma, part-of-speech (POS), and syntactic dependency among words. These features have closer association with semantics than plain words. On the other hand, word sense disambiguation studies have shown context plays an important role in determining word semantics. Thus the combination of these complex linguistic features and context-sensitive techniques may form an effective surrogate for semantics for text classification. This is the rationale of our investigation.

The rest of our paper is layout as follows. In the next section, we will review the general issues associated with common TC approaches, the context-sensitive TC techniques studied by Cohen in [3], and the use of complex linguistic features in TC. In Section 3 we describe our experimental setup and the associated results. In the final Section we draw our conclusion and discuss the direction of our future works.

2 Background and Related Works

2.1 Limitations of Common Approaches to TC

As mentioned above, there are two main characteristics in common approaches to TC that warrant more investigation, viz. the use of word occurrences as document features and the statistical independence assumption in these approaches.

A linear classifier using words as features is simple and efficient to implement, but it is against our normal understanding that words do have associations with one another when they are used. As demonstrated in [3], the presence of a word may influence the importance of other words. A context-sensitive representation can address this issue and will be discussed in the following section.

On the other hand the effectiveness in using words as features may also be questioned. Words are the fundamental components of a text document. It is the simplest features which is directly machine recognizable without aid of external knowledge. As a basic symbol in a textual document, words are very efficient and easy to use as indexing features for document search and retrieval, and their effectiveness has been demonstrated in search engine applications. However, for human readers, words convey meaning and meaning is often the basis on which people search and classify documents. It is a commonly known fact that words and concepts do not have unique and unambiguous relationships. The existence of *synonyms* not only increases the feature space in bags-of-words approaches, but also tends to reduce the recall rate in text retrieval and accuracy in classification tasks. Text document may be misclassified because of the use of some rare synonym in a document for a concept. An opposite situation is the existence of *polysemous words*. It is common for words to have multiple meanings. This phenomenon reduces the precision in word-based search and classification techniques.

2.2 Context-Sensitive Text Classification

Text classification approaches like Naïve Bayes and Rocchio's algorithms make use of the linear combination of words' weight. Since each word is considered as independent, the contextual effect among words is ignored. Such effect is addressed by context-sensitive learning methods such as the two approaches discussed in [3].

The first approach RIPPER discussed in the paper [2] is similar to association rule learning in data mining. RIPPER is a non-linear rule-based algorithm. It attempts to learn to classify using features described in a disjunctive normal form (DNF), consisting of the disjunction of a rule set, with each rule specifying a conjunction of features. The heuristic method to generate rules originated from the Incremental Reduced Error Pruning technique (IREP) [4] and its modified version IREP*. The main idea is to greedily add words (features) to the rule based on information gain evaluated on a grow data set, and subsequently simplify the rules by pruning words from the rules based on evaluation on a prune data set. Finally the rule set is further optimized as a whole by alternative rules replacement.

The second approach discussed in [3] is the "sleeping-experts", a technique based on ensemble classifiers. The technique itself does not basically cater to word contexts. It works by treating each feature as "expert" and classify document by weighted ensemble of multiple "experts". In [3], it handles the context effect through a preprocessing of feature set into "sparse phrase", each of them consisting of word sequences separated by "holes". For example, a learned phrase "X?Y" means there could be any other words between words X and Y. The information of X, Y co-occurrence and the position that X is in front of Y constitutes the identifying feature.

The experimental results in [3] showed that context-sensitive algorithms have generally better performance, pointing to the usefulness of context information in TC.

2.3 Use of Linguistic and Semantic Features in TC

Generally speaking, when people use a word with multiple meanings, some 60% of the time they use it in the most frequent sense. However, for some special domains or field of studies, an alternative meaning may be more prevalent. Furthermore, some specific concepts can only be recognized by consecutive combinations of multiple words. These *phrases* and *named entities* may refer to concepts which can be expressed in a variety of ways.

To use semantics in classification, we must first of all identify the meaning of words as they are used in their particular contexts. By looking up machine-readable dictionaries such as WordNet [6], we can identify multi-words phrases, word meanings and different semantic relations like hyponyms/hypernyms.

As mentioned in the previous section, some words may have several meanings. Word sense disambiguation (WSD) is one of the natural language processing tasks to identify the meanings of words as they are used in particular contexts. Unfortunately, it is not easy for machine to achieve this task accurately, as this may require common sense knowledge and specific knowledge in different domains. The current state of art WSD algorithm can achieve 90% precision at the expense of decreased coverage to 10%, but to balance the performance of precision and recall, most system hit a wall at 65%-70% [12]. Indeed, even if we do nothing but just take the most frequent sense of a word, we would be correct some 60% of the time [7]. The common approach in the WSD task is to use "contextual information", including POS and other syntactic features, together with co-occurrence of surrounding words to guide the selection of the word sense.

There are several studies that apply word sense and other semantic features in text classification. In [11] Scott attempted to enrich the feature space by including phrases and hyponyms. Hyponyms are obtained by looking up WordNet. The combined use of words and phrases has slightly improved the performance, while the inclusion of hyponyms has not. Bloehdorn [1] compared the effect of combining terms with senses identified by different word sense disambiguation techniques. They tried the combination of all senses from WordNet, first sense from WordNet, and senses identified by context-based sense disambiguation. Although there are no significant differences among the approaches, their results are comparable to term-based features. This may be caused by applying boosting technique to improve the performance of weak semantic features set.

A study in information retrieval shows the need for high precision disambiguation in order to improve performance [10]. Various studies in text classification have similar conclusion [11]. It is generally not efficient, nor effective, to use high-level or deep semantics in text processing task. Moschitti [8] submitted that the use of word token has generally better performance than adding complex nominal and POS information in Rocchio and SVM TC.

Thus from the above analysis of the various studies in text classification, we see that context-sensitive techniques have been able to perform well with words as features, but no investigation has been done with complex linguistic features with this type of techniques. As word senses are closely associated with their context, it is possible that the combination of complex linguistic features with their context may provide an effective environment for the text classification task. This motivated our research.

3 The Experiment

We have conducted experiments on the application of complex linguistic features using two different context-sensitive TC algorithms. A subset of documents from Reuters-21578 is selected for the evaluation. The documents are parsed to extract linguistic features. Two context-sensitive TC algorithms similar to those used in [3] were implemented and applied to different sets of linguistic features. Three-fold cross validations were performed for different combinations of linguistic features.

3.1 Test Collection

The test data we used in this research is the Reuters-21578 test collection. It is a well-known and popular corpus for evaluation of text classification techniques. The data set contains 21578 news stories which are classified into 135 topics. Each article consists of some metadata like date, author, title and body. The whole collection is annotated in SGML format and size of categories varies from nearly 4000 articles to 1 article. It provides a broad range of characteristics to test classifiers in different aspects.

For this research we selected classes of different sizes, and included both specialized and general topics in order to investigate our approaches in a more comprehensive context. Based on the information supplied by the data set, we have selected documents in which "Topic" tag has value of "YES" and "Topic List" is not empty. Also, we have filtered out documents which do not belong to our selected classes. As a result, a total of 7888 documents are selected for our experiment. The details of the selected categories are listed in Table 1 below.

Table 1. Selected classes from Reuters-21578 and their number of documents

	earn	acq	trade	interest	sugar	nat-gas	jobs	yen
Doc#	3986	2448	552	511	184	130	76	69

3.2 Feature Extraction

The linguistic features we investigated in our experiment including lemma, POS and words dependency. The extraction process involves the following steps:

1. Separating word tokens and punctuations by looking up the token combinations in machine-readable dictionary. We use *WordNet* [6] as the dictionary with *JWNL* [5] as the program interface.
2. Splitting paragraphs into sentences using simple punctuation rules.
3. Parsing each sentence to get POS and word dependency using the linguistic parser *Stanford Parser* [13].

After the above processes, we are able to obtain words tagged by their lemmas, POS and list of modifiers. The implementation of feature extraction process is based on the Java platform and directly adopting linguistic processing tool described above.

3.3 Learning Algorithms

In this study, two context-sensitive TC models were implemented and used in the experiments; they were both implemented as binary classifiers:

IREP [4]: It is a greedy heuristic algorithm which learns a rule set for classification. To learn a single rule, the training data is split into a grow set and a prune set. The rule generation process includes two phases: growing and pruning.

Using the grow set, the algorithm greedily selects the features which can best improve the relative information gain compare to previously selected features, to add to a rule. The rule growing process stops when no more features can be added to improve the information gain. By using the prune data set and an objective function, each rule feature is checked to see if the rule's performance can be improved based on the objective function by removing a feature.

The rule is then evaluated using the whole set of training data. If it can pass a threshold, it will be added to the rule set. The documents which are covered by the new rule are then removed from the set of training data. The rule generation process is repeated with the remaining documents to generate another rule. The process stops either when there is no more positive example left in the training data, or when a newly generated rule cannot reach some threshold of performance.

Sleeping-Experts [3]: It is a feature oriented algorithm based on weight update and can support ongoing learning when a new document is presented. We prohibit the learning in the testing phase in order to get a more stable and comparable experiment results.

In fact, Sleeping-Experts is not basically a context-sensitive algorithm unless context-sensitive features are included in the pool of "experts". In [3], sparse phrases are included as context-sensitive feature. In our implementation, we use simple co-occurrences of basic features as context information.

An "expert" is actually a feature appearing in a document. It carries a positive and a negative weight corresponding to the confidence of prediction by the expert of whether the document belongs to the target class or not. For each incoming document, features are extracted from the document and matched against the existing set of experts. For each new feature which could not match any expert in the existing pool, a new expert is generated and given an initial weight. For features that find a match with experts in the pool, their weights are retrieved. The weights for these active experts and the new experts are combined to produce a score which is used to determine the classification outcome. If the score passed a threshold, the document is classified as belonging to the target class, otherwise it is not. During training when the actual classification of the document is known, the weights of the active experts which made a wrong prediction will be penalized by multiplying them with a "weight update factor" less than 1. The weights of the active experts are then re-normalized. The testing process is similar except the creation of new experts and weight update process are not performed.

3.4 Experiment Design

Using the set of selected documents, we performed three-fold cross validations to evaluate the effectiveness of using complex linguistic feature in context-sensitive classification techniques.

The experiments are repeated for the eight selected classes and eight feature combinations listed in Table 4. The composition of feature set is prepared by merging the multiple feature sets concerned.

Table 2. Test combinations of linguistic features

Combination	Symbol
Word	W
Lemma	L
Lemma|POS	P
Lemma|Modifier	M
Lemma|POS + Lemma|Modifier	L+P
Lemma + Lemma|POS	L+M
Lemma + Lemma|Modifier	P+M
Lemma + Lemma|POS + Lemma|Modifier	L+P+M

In each experiment, one class is selected as classification target for the classifier. The positive and negative documents are randomly divided into three sets and three runs are performed each time with one group withheld as test set and the others as training set. The result is evaluated by averaging these three-fold cross validation results.

3.5 Results and Discussion

Results of experiments with IREP are summarized in Tables 3 and 4 at the end of this paper. Table 3 gives the Precision-Recall figures and Table 4 presents the overall performance by evaluating the f-measure, which is the harmonic mean of precision and recall. Similarly, results for Sleeping Experts are summarized in Table 5, 6. "W", "L", "P" and "M" denote testing with "word", "lemma", "lemma with POS" and "lemma with modifier word" respectively. The results from using "word" features only serve as a baseline for comparison with the use of other more complex linguistic features. Bolded value indicates that the test result is better than the corresponding baseline figure in the "word" feature test.

The overall performances of IREP showed some symptoms of over-fitting. Most of the recall rates are relatively high while the precision rates are comparatively low. This symptom is particularly significant in classes "acq" and "interest". There is no clear dominance of performance in the use of complex linguistic features over words or vice versa, although in many cases linguistic features do appear to help.

Table 3. Precision/Recall by IREP, bolded value means it outperforms the baseline of "W"

	earn		acq		trade		interest	
	P	R	P	R	P	R	P	R
W	81.7	93.8	75.5	85.5	71.7	93.3	57.1	77.7
L	90.0	95.8	79.4	81.7	83.0	81.7	59.7	83.8
P	87.9	90.4	65.2	82.1	73.5	80.2	54.1	81.0
M	91.2	73.9	74.5	70.3	69.4	51.0	70.7	60.7
L+P	81.6	94.9	64.7	84.2	76.7	87.3	58.7	82.0
L+M	76.6	93.2	78.4	89.2	80.1	79.5	58.0	84.7
P+M	83.7	92.1	68.6	83.7	54.3	79.5	66.1	58.3
L+P+M	80.9	94.9	54.0	88.2	70.1	85.5	57.2	83.4

	sugar		nat-gas		jobs		yen	
	P	R	P	R	P	R	P	R
W	88.6	96.7	75.1	60.0	89.7	90.9	45.7	58.0
L	88.2	96.7	48.2	67.8	91.7	88.3	42.3	69.6
P	93.7	89.6	48.4	70.7	86.3	81.7	71.6	65.2
M	91.8	48.6	81.0	31.6	81.0	43.0	38.1	23.9
L+P	87.5	97.8	68.9	70.0	88.1	87.0	25.4	81.2
L+M	88.6	96.7	66.5	73.1	96.2	81.7	33.9	15.2
P+M	93.8	90.7	62.7	67.7	65.4	88.1	49.1	65.2
L+P+M	88.7	97.8	61.6	74.6	92.7	84.4	54.5	75.4

On the other hand, the result from Sleeping Experts is much more conclusive. They generally give better results than the baseline using "word". Most results from the experiments using complex linguistic features demonstrate better performance except for the classes "sugar" and "job". Both precision and recall are improved by applying linguistic features.

However, the composition of multiple linguistic feature sets has not demonstrated absolute superiority over other more simple sets, although it accounts for the best results in many cases. This is probably the consequence of the fact that the underlying information contents of these features are similar and predominantly overlapping so that their union produces little added information for the classification task.

Table 4. F-measure on precision and recall by IREP, bolded value means it outperforms the baseline of "W"

	earn	acq	trade	interest	sugar	nat-gas	jobs	yen
W	86.8	80.1	81.1	58.0	92.5	66.7	90.1	48.4
L	92.8	80.4	82.2	63.5	92.2	55.6	89.9	48.9
P	88.7	71.4	75.0	61.5	91.6	52.8	83.4	68.2
M	81.6	72.1	56.1	65.2	60.7	45.1	54.1	27.4
L+P	87.5	72.8	81.1	63.4	92.3	69.3	87.2	31.0
L+M	83.0	83.4	79.7	63.5	92.5	69.1	87.8	14.8
P+M	87.5	74.5	61.1	59.0	92.2	64.8	64.7	55.7
L+P+M	87.2	66.9	76.7	63.1	93.0	67.1	88.3	54.5

Table 5. Precision/Recall by Sleeping-Experts, bolded value means it outperforms the baseline of "W"

	earn		acq		trade		interest	
	P	R	P	R	P	R	P	R
W	97.5	97.3	89.6	98.7	85.6	92.6	82.3	96.7
L	96.7	96.5	88.0	98.5	84.4	92.0	86.3	95.5
P	97.5	98.3	91.4	98.5	83.6	95.8	82.9	97.7
M	95.6	97.0	85.3	98.1	75.9	95.6	81.4	93.9
L+P	98.0	97.9	91.4	98.6	84.7	94.4	84.8	97.5
L+M	97.4	97.4	88.5	98.5	86.3	92.6	87.3	97.8
P+M	97.7	98.4	91.0	98.7	84.3	95.3	83.5	98.0
L+P+M	98.2	98.0	91.4	98.7	85.0	94.4	85.9	97.5

	sugar		nat-gas		jobs		yen	
	P	R	P	R	P	R	P	R
W	93.2	96.7	64.7	81.6	83.4	97.4	72.7	56.5
L	93.4	96.7	70.8	80.1	82.7	96.1	64.9	53.6
P	92.1	94.6	65.6	83.8	83.6	88.1	86.0	71.0
M	72.5	83.1	54.6	77.0	65.1	77.6	65.1	59.4
L+P	92.8	95.7	68.6	88.4	83.5	97.4	80.4	71.0
L+M	93.9	95.7	67.9	80.0	83.9	96.1	74.3	63.8
P+M	93.1	94.0	64.7	83.8	82.8	88.1	85.0	73.9
L+P+M	92.8	95.7	67.1	88.4	83.2	96.1	85.4	72.5

Table 6. F-measure on precision and recall by Sleeping-Experts, bolded value means it outperforms the baseline of "W"

	earn	acq	trade	interest	sugar	nat-gas	jobs	yen
W	97.4	93.9	88.9	88.9	94.9	72.1	89.5	63.2
L	96.6	93.0	88.0	**90.6**	**95.0**	**75.1**	88.5	58.7
P	**97.9**	**94.8**	**89.3**	**89.6**	93.3	**73.5**	85.7	**77.8**
M	96.3	91.3	84.7	87.2	77.1	63.8	69.9	61.7
L+P	**98.0**	**94.8**	**89.3**	**90.6**	94.1	**77.2**	**89.6**	**75.3**
L+M	97.4	93.3	**89.3**	**92.3**	94.7	**73.4**	89.1	**68.6**
P+M	**98.1**	**94.7**	**89.4**	**90.1**	93.5	**73.0**	85.2	**79.1**
L+P+M	**98.1**	**94.9**	**89.4**	**91.3**	94.1	**76.2**	88.9	**78.0**

4 Conclusion and Future Works

In this paper, we have presented an experiment to investigate the use of complex linguistic features in context-sensitive TC techniques. While the results of the IREP approach have not been conclusive, the results of Sleeping Experts have shown the effectiveness and potential for more complex linguistic features to improve performance of context-sensitive TC techniques. We are continuing our investigations in several directions:

1. Repeat the test to include more classes and other document collections.
2. Consider the use of other complex synthetic and linguistic features such as phrases, complex nominals, word senses and case frames.
3. Use the complex features with other context-sensitive TC approaches.
4. Investigate an effective way to combine different linguistic features under different classification problem contexts.

Acknowledgement

This project is supported by the Hong Kong Polytechnic University research grant G-T885.

References

1. Bloehdorn, S., and Hotho, A.: Boosting for Text Classification with Semantic Features. Proceedings of the MSW workshop at the 10th ACM SIGKDD Conference on Knowledge Discovery and Data Mining (2004) 70-87
2. Cohen, W. W.: Fast Effective Rule Induction. Proceedings of the 12th International Conference on Machine Learning, Lake Tahoe, CA (1995)
3. Cohen, W. W., Singer, Y.: Context-sensitive Learning Methods for Text Categorization. ACM Transactions on Information Systems Vol 13, No. 1 (1999) 100-111
4. Furnkranz, J., Widmer G.: Incremental Reduced Error Pruning. Proceedings of the 11th Annual Conference on Machine Learning, New Brunswick, NJ, Morgan Kaufmann Publishers Inc., San Francisco, CA (1994)

5. JWNL, http://jwordnet.sourceforge.net/
6. Miller, G. A.: WordNet: An On-line Lexical Database. International Journal of Lexicography, Vol 3, No. 4 (1990)
7. Miller, G. A., Chodorow, M., Landes, S., Leacock, C., Thomas, R.: Using a Semantic Concordance for Sense Identification. Proceedings of the Human Language Technology Workshop (1994)
8. Moschitti, A., Basili, R.: Complex Linguistic Features for Text Classification: A Comprehensive Study. ECIR (2004) 181-196
9. Rocchio, J.: Relevance Feedback Information Retrieval. The Smart Retrieval System – Experiments in Automatic Document Processing, G. Salton, Ed. Prentice-Hall, Englewood Cliffs, NJ (1971) 313-323
10. Sanderson, M.: Word Sense Disambiguation and Information Retrieval. Proceedings of the 17th Annual International ACM SIGIR Conference on Research and Development in Information Retrieval (1994) 142-151
11. Scott, S., Matwin, S.: Feature Engineering for Text Classification. Proceedings of ICML (1999) 379-388
12. SENSEVAL, http://www.itri.brighton.ac.uk/events/senseval/
13. Stanford Parser, http://nlp.stanford.edu/downloads/lex-parser.shtml

Using Term Relationships in a Structured Document Retrieval Model Based on Influence Diagrams

Jian-min Xu[1,2], Shuang Zhao[1], Zhen-peng Liu[1], and Bian-fang Chai[1]

[1] College of Mathematics and Computer Science, Hebei University, Baoding 071002, China
[2] Institute of Systems Engineering, Tianjin University, Tianjin 300072, China
yy.csi@mail.hbu.edu.cn

Abstract. The performance of an information retrieval system usually increases when it uses the relationships among the terms contained in a given document collection. This paper presents a new Influence Diagrams-based structured document retrieval model which contains two term-layers to represent the term relationships, gives the model's topology and inference process, and puts forward an efficient learning method based on co-occurrence analysis to capture the relationships among the terms.

1 Introduction

As more and more structured documents such as textbooks and scientific articles, whose contents are organized around a well-defined structure, become available on the Internet, it is becoming more important to design structured document retrieval models and systems. Some models have been presented for structured document retrieval during the last decade, such as SID, CID [1], BNR-SD[2], but these are less than perfect as the particular dependence relationships between terms are ignored. This paper presents a structured document retrieval model that takes into account the term relationships in an attempt to reduce these problems, and presents an efficient learning method based on the co-occurrence analysis to capture the relationships between terms.

The remainder of the paper is organized as follows: Section 2 introduces Influence Diagrams and the representation of the structured document. Section 3 presents related work on the structured document retrieval. Section 4 introduces a new retrieval model based on Influence Diagrams in detail. Section 5 shows the inference process and a way of applying the results to structured document retrieval. Section 6 puts forward the conclusions drawn from this work and some proposals for future research.

2 Preliminaries

(1) Influence Diagrams (ID)[3]: ID is a generalization of Bayesian network that provides a visual representation of a decision problem; it is a structure built by qualitative and quantitative information.

The qualitative part constitutes by a directed acyclic graph, which contains three kinds of node and two types of arc.

The three kinds of node are chance, decision, and utility. Chance nodes represent random variables or uncertain quantities drawn as circles. A decision node drawn as a rectangle stands for the collection of actions available at a particular time in the decision making process. The decision-maker must choose one action from this collection at that time. The last type is the utility node that represents the utility function associated with the decision problem and is drawn as a diamond [4].

Of the two types of arc, one is the arc pointing to a chance node or a utility node representing probability and function dependences (as occur in Bayesian networks), respectively; the other type, called an informative arc, points to a decision node, representing the variable that should be known when making the decision.

The quantitative part of the Influence Diagrams contains a number of conditional probability distributions that must be associated with the chance nodes, and a set of utility values for each utility node.

(2) Representation of the structured document: Each structured document is represented as a tree structure (see Figure 1), similar to those used in [1, 2].

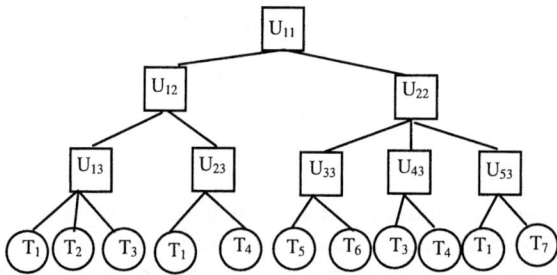

Fig. 1. Structured representation of a document

Each document is composed of a hierarchical structure of l abstraction levels $L_1, L_2, ..., L_l$, the document itself is noted as level 1, and the level l is specific because the units in this level join directly with some term nodes (term node noted as T_k). In order to simplify the notation, it is assumed that the number of levels is the same for all the documents in the collection. Each structural unit at level j is noted as U_{ij}, where i is the identifier of this unit. The number of structural units contained in level j is represented by $|L_j|$. Therefore, $L_j = \{U_{1j}, ..., U_{|L_j|j}\}$. The units are organized according to the actual structure of the document: every unit U_{ij} at level j, except the unit at level 1 (representing the document itself), is contained in only one unit $U_{z(i,j),j-1}$ of the lower level $j-1$, $U_{ij} \subseteq U_{z(i,j),j-1}$, where $z(i,j)$ is a function returning the index of the unit in level $j-1$ to which the unit U_{ij} belongs[1].

3 Related Work on Structured Document Retrieval

Two main models for structured document retrieval are discussed in this section, while other Bayesian network-based approaches can be found in [5~8].

The first model is the BNR-SD Model [2], which extends the Two-Layered Bayesian network retrieval model to a Multi-Layered Bayesian network for structured document retrieval. The representation of each structured document is the same as the one described in section 2. This model contains two different types of node: the structural unit node U_{ij}, and the term node T_j; and one type of arc leading from a given term node or structural unit node to the particular structural unit node which contains it. The topology of this model is depicted in Figure 2. The posterior probabilities of relevance of all the structural units can be computed in the inference process when a query is given. The relevant units are then sorted according to their corresponding probabilities and delivered to the user.

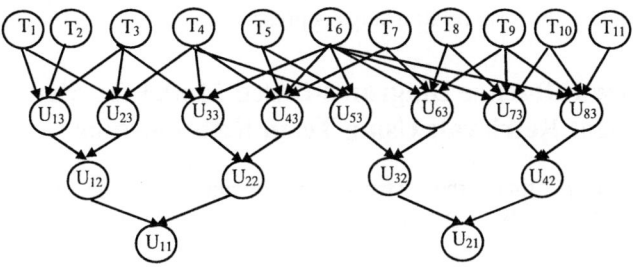

Fig. 2. The BNR-SD model

The second model is the Simple Influence Diagram (SID) [1], which regards the structured document retrieval as a decision-making problem. The representation of each structured document in this model is the same as the one in the BNR-SD. This model contains three different types of node and two different types of arc.

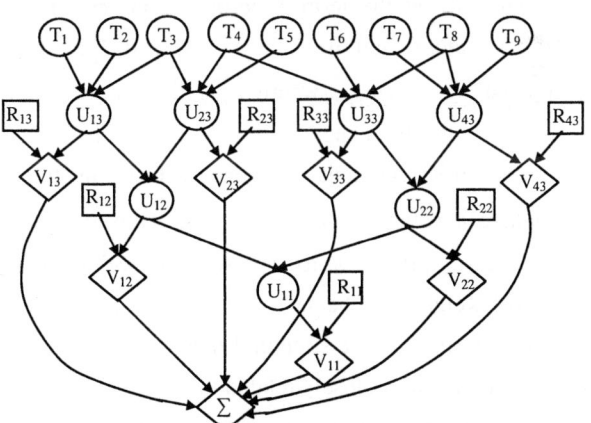

Fig. 3. Influence diagrams for the SID model

The chance nodes are comprised of two kinds: the structural unit node U_{ij} and the term node T_j. The decision node, R_{ij}, represents the decision variable related to whether or not to show U_{ij} to the user and the utility node, V_{ij}, measures the utility value of the corresponding decision. The arcs go from a given chance node (either a term or a structural unit) to the particular structural unit node which contains it; and the arcs go from a decision node and a structural unit node to the corresponding utility node.

The topology for the SID is shown in Figure 3. When a user submits a query, the expected utility of each decision given the query is computed. The retrieval system then presents the relevant units to the user in decreasing order of the utility.

Neither of the models above takes into account the particular dependence relationships between terms that can be mined from the structured document collection. However, the retrieval performance of an information retrieval system usually increases when it uses these relationships. In the following section, a new model containing the term relationships is presented.

4 The New Influence Diagrams-Based Model for Structured Document Retrieval: Using Term Relationships

It is assumed that the structured document collection D comprises s documents, $D = \{D_1, D_2, ..., D_s\}$, and the collection is indexed by k terms constituting the term set T, $T = \{T_1, T_2, ..., T_k\}$.

4.1 Learning Term Relationships

This paper adopts the method based on co-occurrence analysis [9] to measure the relationships between terms.

Before showing this approach, some additional notations should be introduced. Let N be the number of the structural units in the whole collection. Let $tf_{ij,kh}$ be the frequency of the term T_i and the term T_j co-occurs in the structural unit U_{kh}, and idf_{ij} be the inverse structural unit frequency of T_i and T_j in the whole collection. idf_{ij} can be computed by $\lg(N/n_{ij})$, where n_{ij} is the number of the units indexed by T_i and T_j. Let $tf_{j,kh}$ be the frequency of the term T_j in the structural unit U_{kh}, and idf_j be the inverse structural unit frequency of T_j in the whole collection ($idf_j = \lg(N/n_j)$, where n_j is the number of the units indexed by the term T_j). We use the weighting scheme $d_{j,kh} = tf_{j,kh} \times idf_j$ to represent the weight of the term T_j in the structural unit U_{kh}, the weighting scheme $d_{ij,kh} = tf_{ij,kh} \times idf_{ij}$ to represent the joint weight of the term T_i and the term T_j in the structural unit U_{kh}, and use the notation $Rn(T_j)$ to represent the set of n terms most closely related to T_j.

When all weights described above are obtained, the strength of two terms co-occurrence relationship can be computed, from the perspective of term T_j:

$$strength(T_j, T_i) = \frac{\sum_{kh} d_{ij,kh}}{\sum_{kh} d_{j,kh}} \times Weightfactor(T_i) \tag{1}$$

Some terms, which appeared in many places, are called general terms. These general terms should be penalized to some extent in the co-occurrence analysis. So a method similar to inverse document frequency is adopted to deal with this problem. We define:

$$Weightfactor(T_i) = idf_i / \lg N \qquad (2)$$

Therefore, to learn term relationships implies the need to determine the set $Rn(T_j)$. Thus, for each T_j, the measure $strength(T_j\ T_i)$ is computed.

4.2 The Qualitative Component of the Model

The different types of node are:

(1) Chance nodes. The model contains three types of chance nodes: structural unit node U_{ij}, term node T_j, and term node T_j' (we duplicate each term node T_j in T to obtain another term node T_j', forming a new term layer T', $T' = \{T_1',...,T_k'\}$). Each node represents a binary random variable: U_{ij} takes its values in the set $\{u_{ij}^+, u_{ij}^-\}$, representing whether the unit is relevant or not relevant, respectively; T_j (T_j') takes its values in the set $\{t_j^+, t_j^-\}$ ($\{t_j'^+, t_j'^-\}$), representing whether the term T_j (T_j') is relevant or not relevant, respectively.

(2) Decision nodes. For each structural unit U_{ij}, there is one decision node R_{ij}, which represents the decision about whether or not to retrieve the corresponding unit. R_{ij} takes its values in the set $\{r_{ij}^+, r_{ij}^-\}$, meaning 'retrieve U_{ij}' and 'do not retrieve U_{ij}', respectively.

(3) Utility nodes. There is also one utility node for each unit in the new model, denoted by V_{ij}, which measures the value of utility of the corresponding decision. It is assumed that all the values belong to the interval [0, 1], because the result of evaluating an Influence Diagram is invariable with respect to change in the scale of the utilities [1].

The different types of arc are:

(1) Arcs between the chance nodes. There are arcs going from the term node T_i' to the term node T_j, $T_i' \in Rn(T_j)$ (the arc from T_j' to T_j always exists), from the term node T_j to the structural unit node U_{il} (U_{il} is indexed by T_j), and from the structural unit node to the particular structural unit node which contains it.

(2) Arcs pointing to the utility nodes. There are arcs from the decision node R_{ij} and the chance node U_{ij} to the utility node V_{ij}.

In addition, the utility function is also influenced by the query. Since this is a query independent model (i.e., the query node is not a part of the IR system), the arcs from the query node to the utility node do not show in the model.

Figure 4 shows an example of the new model.

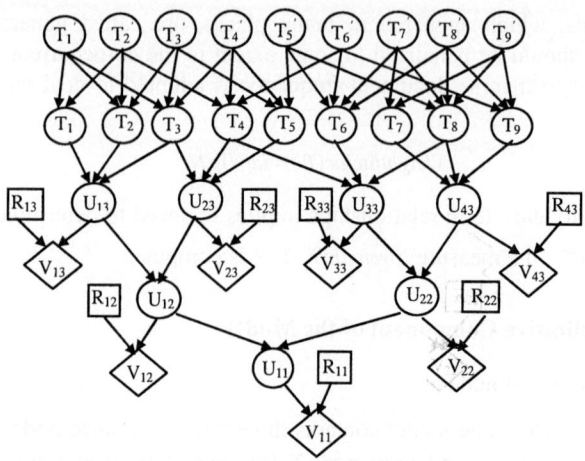

Fig. 4. The new structured document retrieval model

4.3 The Quantitative Component of the Model

4.3.1 Probabilities in Chance Node

For each chance node X in the graph, a set of conditional probability distributions $p(x | pa(X))$, one for each configuration $pa(X)$ of the parent set of X, $Pa(X)$, should be defined.

Term nodes T_i', i.e., the term nodes in the first layer ($T_i' \in T'$), do not have parents, $Pa(T_i') = \emptyset$, hence $p(t_i'^+ | pa(T_i'))$ equals $p(t_i'^+)$. We use the following estimator:

$$p(t_i'^+) = 1/k \tag{3}$$

where k is the number of the terms.

Term nodes in the second layer ($T_j \in T$) must store the conditional probabilities $p(t_j^+ | pa(T_j))$. We use a probability function defined in [10] to estimate them:

$$p(t_j^+ | pa(T_j)) = \sum_{T_i' \in Pa(T_j), t_i'^+ \in pa(T_j)} W_{ij} \tag{4}$$

where the weight W_{ij} measures the influence of each term $T_i'(T_i' \in Pa(T_j))$ on the term T_j, with $W_{ij} \geq 0$. It is then defined in the following:

$$W_{ij} = \begin{cases} \alpha & T_i' \in Pa(T_j), i = j \\ (1-\alpha) strength(T_j, T_i') / \sum_{T_i' \in Pa(T_j), i \neq j} strength(T_j, T_i') & \forall T_i' \in Pa(T_j), i \neq j \end{cases} \tag{5}$$

where α is a parameter, $0 < \alpha < 1$, and it is used to control the importance of the contribution of the term relationships being considered for a term T_j to its final degree of relevance.

For the structural unit nodes U_{ij}, the conditional probabilities $p(u_{il}^+ \mid pa(U_{il}))$ and $p(u_{ij}^+ \mid pa(U_{ij}))$, $j \neq l$, must be assessed using the probability function [10].

First, the conditional probabilities of relevance of U_{il}:

$$p(u_{il}^+ \mid pa(U_{il})) = \sum_{T_j \in Pa(U_{il}), t_j^* \in pa(U_{il})} W(T_j, U_{il}) \qquad (6)$$

where the weight $W(T_j, U_{il})$ is associated with each term T_j indexing the unit U_{il}, with $W(T_j, U_{il}) \geq 0$. We define:

$$W(T_j, U_{il}) = tf_{j,il} \times idf_j \Big/ \sum_{T_h \in Pa(U_{il})} tf_{h,il} \times idf_h \qquad (7)$$

Second, the conditional probabilities of relevance of U_{ij} ($j \neq l$):

$$p(u_{ij}^+ \mid pa(U_{ij})) = \sum_{U_{h,j+1} \in Pa(U_{ij}), u_{h,j+1}^* \in pa(U_{ij})} W(U_{h,j+1}, U_{ij}) \qquad (8)$$

where $W(U_{h,j+1}, U_{ij})$ is a weight measuring the importance of the unit $U_{h,j+1}$ within U_{ij}, with $W(U_{h,j+1}, U_{ij}) \geq 0$.

Before defining the weight $W(U_{h,j+1}, U_{ij})$, a new notation should be introduced: for any unit U_{ij}, let $A(U_{ij}) = \{ T_k \in T \mid T_k \text{ is an ancestor of } U_{ij} \}$, i.e., $A(U_{ij})$ is the set of terms that are included in the unit U_{ij} [1]. This also means a unit U_{ij} in level $j \neq l$ containing all the terms indexing structural units in level l that are included in U_{ij}. Then the weight is defined:

$$W(U_{h,j+1}, U_{ij}) = \sum_{T_k \in A(U_{h,j+1})} tf_{k,(h,j+1)} \times idf_k \Big/ \sum_{T_k \in A(U_{ij})} tf_{k,ij} \times idf_k \qquad (9)$$

4.3.2 Values in Utility Nodes

In our case, for each node V_{ij}, two values influencing the final utility value should be determined: one is the numeric value that represents the utility for the corresponding combination of the decision node R_{ij} and the structural unit node U_{ij}; the other is the value influenced by the query Q.

(1) Four values should be defined in case one: $v(r_{ij}^+ \mid u_{ij}^+)$, $v(r_{ij}^- \mid u_{ij}^+)$, $v(r_{ij}^- \mid u_{ij}^-)$ and $v(r_{ij}^+ \mid u_{ij}^-)$. The ordering of the four values is shown below (this is the guideline used to assign these values) [1]:

$$1 = v(r_{ij}^+ \mid u_{ij}^+) \geq (r_{ij}^- \mid u_{ij}^-) \geq (r_{ij}^+ \mid u_{ij}^-) \geq (r_{ij}^- \mid u_{ij}^+) = 0 \qquad (10)$$

(2) The value influenced by query Q can be computed by Equation (11):

$$Mfactor(U_{ij}) = \sum_{T_k \in A(U_{ij}) \cap Q'} tf_{k,ij} \Big/ \sum_{T_k \in Q'} tf_{k,*} \qquad (11)$$

where Q' represents a set of terms in T whose parents in T' belong to the query Q, and $tf_{k,*}$ means the frequency of the term T_k in the whole document collection. It is easy to understand that the unit will be more useful to the user when it is indexed by more terms belonging to a given query.

(3) The final value of each utility node is defined as following:

$$v'(r_{ij} \mid u_{ij}) = v(r_{ij} \mid u_{ij}) \times Mfactor(U_{ij}) \tag{12}$$

5 Evaluation of the Model

In order to make a decision about whether or not to retrieve a structural unit, the expected utility of each decision should be computed.

5.1 Inference with the Model

The expected utility for each structural unit U_{ij} in the model can be computed by means of:

$$EU(r_{ij}^+ \mid Q) = \sum_{u_{ij} \in \{u_{ij}^+, u_{ij}^-\}} v'(r_{ij}^+ \mid u_{ij}) \, p(u_{ij} \mid Q) \tag{13}$$

$$EU(r_{ij}^- \mid Q) = \sum_{u_{ij} \in \{u_{ij}^+, u_{ij}^-\}} v'(r_{ij}^- \mid u_{ij}) \, p(u_{ij} \mid Q) \tag{14}$$

Before computing the expected utility above, the probabilities $p(u_{ij} \mid Q)$ must first be determined. There are different algorithms that efficiently perform the propagation progress used to compute these probabilities. Since the field of structured document retrieval contains a large number of variables, it is time consuming to perform the general purposed inference algorithms. In this model, we use a specific inference process designed for a non-structured document Bayesian network retrieval model (see [11]), which is also used in structured document retrieval (see [1, 2]).

The first step is evaluating the posterior probability of relevance of the term nodes T_j belonging to T, $p(t_j^+ \mid Q)$, by the following expression:

$$p(t_j^+ \mid Q) = \sum_{T_i \in Pa(T_j)} W_{ij} \, p(t_i^{'+} \mid Q) \tag{15}$$

where $p(t_i^{'+} \mid Q) = 1$ if $T_i' \in Q$, otherwise $p(t_i^{'+} \mid Q) = \frac{1}{k}$, hence Equation (15) becomes:

$$p(t_j^+ \mid Q) = \sum_{T_i \in Pa(T_j) \cap Q} W_{ij} + \frac{1}{k} \sum_{T_i \in Pa(T_j) \setminus Q} W_{ij} \tag{16}$$

The second step is computing the structural units in level l by using the information obtained in the previous step, in the following way:

$$p(u_{il}^+ \mid Q) = \sum_{T_j \in Pa(U_{il})} W(T_j, U_{il}) \, p(t_j^+ \mid Q) \tag{17}$$

Finally, the posterior probability of the structural units in level j, $j \neq l$, can be computed by means of:

$$p(u_{ij}^+ \mid Q) = \sum_{U_{h,j+1} \in Pa(U_{ij})} W(U_{h,j+1}, U_{ij}) \, p(u_{h,j+1}^+ \mid Q) \tag{18}$$

The probabilities $p(u_{ij}^-|Q)$ will be obtained by duality ($p(u_{ij}^-|Q)=1-p(u_{ij}^+|Q)$). Therefore all the required probabilities can be computed starting from level l and going down to level 1.

5.2 Decision-Making

In a typical decision-making problem, the decision with the greatest utility will be chosen, while in the field of information retrieval making the decision about whether or not to retrieve a unit (retrieving the structural unit U_{ij} if $EU(r_{ij}^+|Q) \geq EU(r_{ij}^-|Q)$ and not retrieving it otherwise) is not enough. The retrieval system must present the relevant units in a decreasing order according to their relevance to the user. So this paper adopts the method used in [1], which is ranking the relevant units according to the corresponding expected utility, $EU(r_{ij}^+|Q)$.

6 Conclusions and Further Work

This paper presents a model considering the relationships between terms based on Influence Diagrams for structured document retrieval. Although some work has been done in the research of structured document retrieval, the retrieval model containing the direct relationships between terms is rare, although these relationships are already introduced in many non-structured document retrieval models (see [10] [11]).

Our model can be improved in several ways; for instance, the terms should directly connect to any structural units, but not be limited to the structural units in level l; other factors influencing the utility value should be considered as well, such as the user's preference. In addition, we can introduce the semantic similarity into our model in order to represent the term relationships more accurately.

Acknowledgement

This work was supported by National Natural Science Foundation of China Grant No.70471049.

References

1. L.M. de Campos, J.M. Fern´andez-Luna, and J.F. Huete, "Using context information in structured document retrieval: an approach based on influence diagrams", Information Processing and Management, Vol 40, pp. 829~847, 2004.
2. F. Crestani, L.M. de Campos, J.M. Fern´andez-Luna, and J.F. Huete, "A Multi-Layered Bayesian Network Model for Structured Document Retrieval", Lacture Notes in Artificial Intelligence, Vol 2711, pp. 74~86, 2004.
3. Shachter,R, "Probabilistic inference and influence diagrams", Operations Research, Vol 36, pp. 527~550, May 1988.
4. A. Sharif Heger, Janis E. White, "Using influence diagrams for data worth analysis", Reliability Engineering and system safety, Vol 55, pp. 195~202, 1997.

5. A. Graves and M. Lalmas, "Video retrieval using an MPEG-7 based inference network", Proceedings of the 25th ACM–SIGIR Conference, pp. 339~346, 2002.
6. S.H. Myaeng, D.H. Jang, M.S. Kim, and Z.C. Zhoo, "A flexible model for retrieval of SGML documents", Proceedings of the 21th ACM-SIGIR Conference, pp. 138~145, 1998.
7. B. Piwowarski, G.E. Faure, and P. Gallinari, "Bayesian networks and INEX", Proceedings of the INEX Workshop, pp. 7~12, 2002.
8. F. Crestani, L.M. de Campos, J.M. Fern´andez-Luna, and J.F. Huete, "Ranking structured documents using utility theory in the Bayesian network retrieval model", Lecture Notes in Computer Science, Vol.2857, pp.168~182, 2003.
9. Zheng Yi, Wu Bin, Shi Zhong-zhi, "A Concept Space Based Text Retrieval System", Computer Engineering and Applications, pp. 67~69, December 2002.
10. L.M. de Campos, J.M. Fern´andez-Luna, and J.F. Huete, "Clustering terms in the Bayesian network retrieval model: a new approach with two term-layers", Applied Soft Computing, pp. 149~158, April 2004.
11. L.M. de Campos, J.M. Fern´andez-Luna, and J.F. Huete, "The BNR model: foundations and performance of a Bayesian network-based retrieval model", International Journal of Approximate Reasoning, Vol 34, pp. 265~285, 2003.

Kernel-Based Metric Adaptation with Pairwise Constraints

Hong Chang and Dit-Yan Yeung

Department of Computer Science,
Hong Kong University of Science and Technology,
Clear Water Bay, Kowloon, Hong Kong
{hongch, dyyeung}@cs.ust.hk

Abstract. Many supervised and unsupervised learning algorithms depend on the choice of an appropriate distance metric. While metric learning for supervised learning tasks has a long history, extending it to learning tasks with weaker supervisory information has only been studied very recently. In particular, several methods have been proposed for semi-supervised metric learning based on pairwise (dis)similarity information. In this paper, we propose a kernel-based approach for nonlinear metric learning, which performs locally linear translation in the kernel-induced feature space. We formulate the metric learning problem as a kernel learning problem and solve it efficiently by kernel matrix adaptation. Experimental results based on synthetic and real-world data sets show that our approach is promising for semi-supervised metric learning.

1 Introduction

Many machine learning and pattern recognition methods, such as nearest neighbor classifiers, radial basis function networks, support vector machines for classification and the k-means algorithm for clustering involve the use of a distance metric. The performance of these methods often depends very much on the metric of choice. Instead of determining a metric manually, a promising approach is to learn an appropriate metric from data.

For supervised learning applications such as classification and regression tasks, one can easily formulate the distance function learning problem as a well-defined optimization problem based on the supervisory information available in the training data. This approach can be dated back to early work on optimizing the metric for k-nearest neighbor density estimation [1]. More recent research continued to develop locally adaptive metrics for nearest neighbor classifiers [2,3,4,5]. Besides, there are other methods that also perform metric learning based on nearest neighbors, e.g., radial basis function networks and variants [6].

While class label information is available for metric learning in classification (or supervised learning) tasks, such information is not available in standard clustering (or unsupervised learning) tasks. Under the unsupervised learning setting, the distance function learning problem is ill-posed with no well-defined optimization criteria. In order to adapt the metric to improve the clustering results, some additional background knowledge or supervisory information is required. The supervisory information may be in the form of labeled data, which are typically limited in quantity. For such problems, the classification accuracy can usually be improved with the aid of additional unlabeled data. Some methods that adopt this approach include [7,8,9].

Another type of supervisory information is in the form of pairwise similarity or dissimilarity constraints. This type of supervisory information is weaker than the first type, in that pairwise constraints can be derived from labeled data but not vice versa. Wagstaff and Cardie [10] and Wagstaff et al. [11] first used such pairwise constraints to improve clustering results. Extensions have also been made to model-based clustering based on the expectation-maximization (EM) algorithm for Gaussian mixture models [12,13]. However, these methods do not incorporate metric learning into the clustering algorithms. Recently, some methods have been proposed for learning global Mahalanobis metrics and related distance functions from pairwise information [14,15,16,17]. However, the distance functions learned are either nonmetric or globally linear metrics. Chang and Yeung [18] generalized the globally linear metrics to a new metric that is linear locally but nonlinear globally. However, the criterion function of the optimization problem defined in that paper has local optima, and the algorithm is not efficient enough.

In this paper, we propose a new kernel-based metric learning method along the same direction we pursued before [18]. Instead of applying metric adaptation in the input space, we define locally linear translation in the kernel-induced feature space, where data points have higher separability. Instead of formulate the metric learning problem as an optimization problem, we formulate it as a kernel learning problem, and solve it by iterative kernel matrix adaptation. As a nonparametric approach, the new method has higher computational efficiency than that proposed in [18].

The rest of this paper is organized as follows. In Section 2, we present our metric learning method, where we perform metric learning in kernel-induced feature space and formulate the metric learning problem as a kernel learning problem. Experimental results on both synthetic and real data are presented in Section 3, comparing our method with some previous metric learning methods. Finally, some concluding remarks are given in the last section.

2 Kernel-Based Metric Adaption

2.1 Basic Ideas

Let us denote a set of n data points in a d-dimensional input space by $\mathcal{X} = \{\mathbf{x}_1, \mathbf{x}_2, \ldots, \mathbf{x}_n\}$, the set of similar pairs by $\mathcal{S}$, and the set of dissimilar pairs by $\mathcal{D}$. $\mathcal{S}$ and $\mathcal{D}$ are both represented as sets of point pairs, where each pair $(\mathbf{x}_i, \mathbf{x}_j)$ indicates that $\mathbf{x}_i$ and $\mathbf{x}_j$ are similar or dissimilar to each other, respectively. Intuitively, we want to adjust the locations of the data points, such that similar pairs tend to get closer while dissimilar pairs tend to move away from each other. (1) For computational efficiency, we resort to locally linear translation. (2) Instead of applying locally linear translation in the input space, we define the translation in the kernel-induced feature space, where data points have higher separability. (3) To preserve the topological relationships between data points, we move not only the points involved in the similar and dissimilar pairs but also other points in their neighborhoods. Locally linear translation is equivalent to changing the metric of the feature space implicitly. In this section, we will propose a nonparametric metric learning algorithm in kernel space and establish the relationship between metric learning with kernel matrix adaptation.

2.2 Centering in the Feature Space

Suppose we use a kernel function $\hat{k}$ which induces a nonlinear mapping $\hat{\phi}$ from $\mathcal{X}$ to some feature space $\mathcal{F}$.[1] The images of the n points in $\mathcal{F}$ are $\hat{\phi}(\mathbf{x}_i)$ ($i = 1, \ldots, n$), which in general are not centered (i.e., their sample mean is not zero). The corresponding kernel matrix $\hat{\mathbf{K}} = [\hat{k}(\mathbf{x}_i, \mathbf{x}_j)]_{n \times n} = [\langle \hat{\phi}(\mathbf{x}_i), \hat{\phi}(\mathbf{x}_j) \rangle]_{n \times n}$.

We want to transform (simply by translating) the coordinate system of $\mathcal{F}$ such that the new origin is at the sample mean of the n points. As a result, we also convert the kernel matrix $\hat{\mathbf{K}}$ to $\mathbf{K} = [k(\mathbf{x}_i, \mathbf{x}_j)]_{n \times n} = [\langle \phi(\mathbf{x}_i), \phi(\mathbf{x}_j) \rangle]_{n \times n}$.

Let $\boldsymbol{\Phi} = [\phi(\mathbf{x}_1), \ldots, \phi(\mathbf{x}_n)]^T$, $\hat{\boldsymbol{\Phi}} = [\hat{\phi}(\mathbf{x}_1), \ldots, \hat{\phi}(\mathbf{x}_n)]^T$ and $\mathbf{H} = \mathbf{I} - \frac{1}{n}\mathbf{1}\mathbf{1}^T$, where $\mathbf{1}$ is a column vector of ones. We can express $\boldsymbol{\Phi} = \mathbf{H}\hat{\boldsymbol{\Phi}}$. Hence,

$$\mathbf{K} = \boldsymbol{\Phi}\boldsymbol{\Phi}^T = \mathbf{H}\hat{\boldsymbol{\Phi}}\hat{\boldsymbol{\Phi}}^T\mathbf{H} = \mathbf{H}\hat{\mathbf{K}}\mathbf{H}. \tag{1}$$

2.3 Locally Linear Translation in the Feature Space

For each similar pair $(\mathbf{x}_k, \mathbf{x}_l) \in \mathcal{S}$, we define a translation vector

$$\mathbf{a}_k = [\phi(\mathbf{x}_l) - \phi(\mathbf{x}_k)]/2,$$

pointing from $\phi(\mathbf{x}_k)$ to the midpoint of $\phi(\mathbf{x}_k)$ and $\phi(\mathbf{x}_l)$. $\phi(\mathbf{x}_k)$ and $\phi(\mathbf{x}_l)$ are translated towards their midpoint, indicated by vector $\mathbf{a}_k$ and $-\mathbf{a}_k$, respectively. For each dissimilar pair $(\mathbf{x}_u, \mathbf{x}_v) \in \mathcal{D}$, we define a translation vector

$$\mathbf{b}_u = [\phi(\mathbf{x}_u) - \phi(\mathbf{x}_v)]/2,$$

pointing from the midpoint of $\phi(\mathbf{x}_u)$ and $\phi(\mathbf{x}_v)$ to $\phi(\mathbf{x}_u)$. $\phi(\mathbf{x}_u)$ and $\phi(\mathbf{x}_v)$ are moved away from their midpoint, indicated by vector $\mathbf{b}_k$ and $-\mathbf{b}_k$, respectively. If a data point is involved in more than one point pair, we consider the linear translation for each pair separately.

To preserve the topological relationships between data points, we apply the above linear translations to other data points in the neighborhood sets of the

---

[1] We use RBF kernel in this paper.

similar or dissimilar pairs. Therefore, the new location $\psi(\mathbf{x}_i)$ of $\phi(\mathbf{x}_i)$ in the feature space is the overall translation effected by possibly all similar and dissimilar point pairs (and hence neighborhood sets):

$$\psi(\mathbf{x}_i) = \phi(\mathbf{x}_i) + \alpha \sum_{(\mathbf{x}_k, \mathbf{x}_l) \in \mathcal{S}} \pi_{ki} \mathbf{a}_k + \beta \sum_{(\mathbf{x}_u, \mathbf{x}_v) \in \mathcal{D}} \tau_{ui} \mathbf{b}_u, \qquad (2)$$

where π_{ki} and τ_{ui} are Gaussian functions. If $\phi(\mathbf{x}_i)$ is closer to $\phi(\mathbf{x}_k)$ than $\phi(\mathbf{x}_l)$,

$$\pi_{ki} = \exp\left[-\frac{1}{2}(\phi(\mathbf{x}_k) - \phi(\mathbf{x}_i))^T \Sigma_k^{-1} (\phi(\mathbf{x}_k) - \phi(\mathbf{x}_i))\right],$$

otherwise

$$\pi_{ki} = -\exp\left[-\frac{1}{2}(\phi(\mathbf{x}_k) - \phi(\mathbf{x}_i))^T \Sigma_k^{-1} (\phi(\mathbf{x}_k) - \phi(\mathbf{x}_i))\right],$$

with Σ_k being the covariance matrix. For simplicity, we use a hyperspherical Gaussian function, meaning that the covariance matrix is diagonal with all diagonal entries being σ^2. Thus π_{ki} can be rewritten as

$$\pi_{ki} = \exp[-\|\phi(\mathbf{x}_k) - \phi(\mathbf{x}_i)\|^2/(2\sigma^2)],$$

if $\phi(\mathbf{x}_i)$ is closer to $\phi(\mathbf{x}_k)$ than $\phi(\mathbf{x}_l)$, and

$$\pi_{ki} = -\exp[-\|\phi(\mathbf{x}_k) - \phi(\mathbf{x}_i)\|^2/(2\sigma^2)],$$

otherwise. For dissimilar constraints, τ_{ui} is defined in the same way.

Let $\boldsymbol{\Psi} = [\psi(\mathbf{x}_1), \ldots, \psi(\mathbf{x}_n)]^T$, $\boldsymbol{\Pi}^S = [\pi_{ki}], k = 1, \ldots, |\mathcal{S}|$ and $\boldsymbol{\Pi}^D = [\tau_{ui}], u = 1, \ldots, |\mathcal{D}|, i = 1, \ldots, n$. Let $|\mathcal{S}|$ and $|\mathcal{D}|$ denote the number of similar or dissimilar pairs in $\mathcal{S}$ and $\mathcal{D}$, respectively. Let $\mathbf{A}$ and $\mathbf{B}$ denote the translation matrices decided by similar or dissimilar constraints, with each of the $|\mathcal{S}|$ or $|\mathcal{D}|$ columns representing a different translation vector. From 2, the adaptation of data set $\boldsymbol{\Phi}$ can be expressed as

$$\boldsymbol{\Psi} = \boldsymbol{\Phi} + \alpha \mathbf{A} \boldsymbol{\Pi}^S + \beta \mathbf{B} \boldsymbol{\Pi}^D. \qquad (3)$$

2.4 Iterative Kernel Matrix Adaptation

We first apply the centering transform as described in Section 2.2 to give the kernel matrix $\mathbf{K}$. Then, we compute the new kernel matrix $\tilde{\mathbf{K}}$ after performing the locally linear translation defined in Section 2.3. It is worthy to note that we can use kernel trick to avoid explicit embedding of data points in the feature space. Metric learning with pairwise constraints is actually formulated as a kernel learning problem. Let us omit the derivation details due to page limit. The kernel matrix will be adapted as follows:

$$\begin{aligned}
\tilde{\mathbf{K}} &= \boldsymbol{\Psi}^T \boldsymbol{\Psi} \\
&= \mathbf{K} \\
&+ \alpha[(\mathbf{K}^{\Phi S_2} - \mathbf{K}^{\Phi S_1})\boldsymbol{\Pi}^S + \boldsymbol{\Pi}^{S^T}(\mathbf{K}^{S_2\Phi} - \mathbf{K}^{S_1\Phi})]/2 \\
&+ \beta[(\mathbf{K}^{\Phi D_1} - \mathbf{K}^{\Phi D_2})\boldsymbol{\Pi}^D + \boldsymbol{\Pi}^{D^T}(\mathbf{K}^{D_1\Phi} - \mathbf{K}^{D_2\Phi})]/2 \\
&+ \alpha^2 \boldsymbol{\Pi}^{S^T}(\mathbf{K}^{S_2 S_2} - 2\mathbf{K}^{S_2 S_1} + \mathbf{K}^{S_1 S_1})\boldsymbol{\Pi}^S/4 \\
&+ \beta^2 \boldsymbol{\Pi}^{D^T}(\mathbf{K}^{D_1 D_1} - 2\mathbf{K}^{D_1 D_2} + \mathbf{K}^{D_2 D_2})\boldsymbol{\Pi}^D/4 \\
&+ \alpha\beta \boldsymbol{\Pi}^{S^T}(\mathbf{K}^{S_2 D_1} - \mathbf{K}^{S_2 D_2} - \mathbf{K}^{S_1 D_1} + \mathbf{K}^{S_1 D_2})\boldsymbol{\Pi}^D/4 \\
&+ \alpha\beta \boldsymbol{\Pi}^{D^T}(\mathbf{K}^{D_1 S_2} - \mathbf{K}^{D_2 S_2} - \mathbf{K}^{D_1 S_2} + \mathbf{K}^{D_2 S_1})\boldsymbol{\Pi}^S/4.
\end{aligned} \qquad (4)$$

We define $\mathbf{K}^{PQ}$ as a submatrix of $\mathbf{K}$, with P and Q specifying the indices of data points, corresponding to the rows and columns extracted from $\mathbf{K}$. Φ represents the indices of all data points in $\mathcal{X}$. $S_1 = \{k | (\mathbf{x}_k, \mathbf{x}_l) \in \mathcal{S}\}$, and $S_2 = \{l | (\mathbf{x}_k, \mathbf{x}_l) \in \mathcal{S}\}$. D_1 and D_2 are defined in the similar way.

As for the Gaussian window parameter, we make σ^2 depend on the average of squared Euclidean distance between all point pairs in the feature space:

$$\sigma^2 = \frac{\theta}{n^2} \sum_{i,j=1}^n \|\phi_i - \phi_j\|^2 = \frac{2\theta}{n}\left[\text{Tr}(\mathbf{K}) - n\bar{\mathbf{K}}\right],$$

where $\bar{\mathbf{K}}$ represents the mean value of the elements in matrix $\mathbf{K}$. The parameter θ is set to be the same ($= 0.5$) for all data sets in our experiments. Note that $\|\phi(\mathbf{x}_k) - \phi(\mathbf{x}_i)\|^2 = k(\mathbf{x}_k, \mathbf{x}_k) - 2\,k(\mathbf{x}_k, \mathbf{x}_i) + k(\mathbf{x}_i, \mathbf{x}_i)$, so the Gaussian functions defined in our method can be computed directly using kernel matrix $\mathbf{K}$. The parameter α and β in Equation (2) and (3) decide the learning rate as well as the relative effects of between similarity and dissimilarity constraints. We set them to be $1/|\mathcal{S}|$ and $1/|\mathcal{D}|$, respectively.

The locations of the data points in the feature space are translated iteratively, with the kernel matrix being adapted accordingly. As in [18], the Gaussian window parameter and learning rate should be decreased over time to increase the local specificity gradually. The iterative adaptation procedure will stop when either there is no much changes in the kernel matrix or the maximum number of iterations (T) is reached. We summarize the metric learning algorithm below:

3 Experiments

To assess the efficacy of our kernel-based metric learning method, we perform extensive experiments on toy data as well as real data from the UCI Machine Learning Repository.[2]

---

[2] http://www.ics.uci.edu/~mlearn/MLRepository.html

Input: $\mathcal{X} = \{\mathbf{x}_1, \mathbf{x}_2, \ldots, \mathbf{x}_n\}$, $\mathcal{S}$, $\mathcal{D}$
Begin
    $t = 0$
    Centering transform to get initial kernel $\mathbf{K}^0$ (Equation (1))
    Repeat {
       Update kernel matrix $\mathbf{K}^t$ to $\mathbf{K}^{t+1}$ (Equation (4))
       Decrease parameters σ^2, α, β
       $t = t + 1$
       $\lambda = \|\mathbf{K}^{t+1} - \mathbf{K}^t\|$
    } Until ($\lambda <$ threshold or $t = T$)
End

Fig. 1. Iterative metric learning by kernel matrix adaptation

3.1 Experimental Setting

We compare the our proposed method described in Section 2 with two previous methods. The first method is relevant component analysis (RCA) [14]. As a metric learning method, RCA changes the input space by a global linear transformation which assigns large weights to relevant dimensions and low weights to irrelevant dimensions. Another method is locally linear metric adaptation (LLMA) [18], which is more general in that it is linear locally but nonlinear globally. We also use the Euclidean distance without metric learning for baseline comparison. Since both RCA and LLMA make use of pairwise similarity constraints only, we also use such supervisory information only for our method. In summary, the following four distance measures for the k-means clustering algorithm are included in our comparative study (the short forms inside brackets will be used subsequently for convenience):

1. k-means without metric learning (Euclidean)
2. k-means with RCA for metric learning (RCA)
3. k-means with LLMA for metric learning (LLMA)
4. k-means with our kernel-based method for metric learning (Kernel-based)

There exist many performance measures for clustering tasks. As in [18,17,14], we use the Rand index [19] to quantify the agreement of the clustering result with the ground truth. For each data set, we randomly generate 20 different $\mathcal{S}$ sets to provide pairwise similarity constraints to the clustering task. In addition, for each $\mathcal{S}$ set, we perform 20 runs of k-means with different random initializations and report the average Rand index over the 20 runs.

3.2 Experiments on Synthetic Data

Figure 2 demonstrates the power of our proposed metric learning method on two synthetic data sets. One is exclusive four data set, the other is 2-moon data set which is commonly used in some recent semi-supervised learning work. However, the difference is that we do not exploit the underlying manifold structure here. Instead, only some limited pairwise similarity constraints are provided. The two

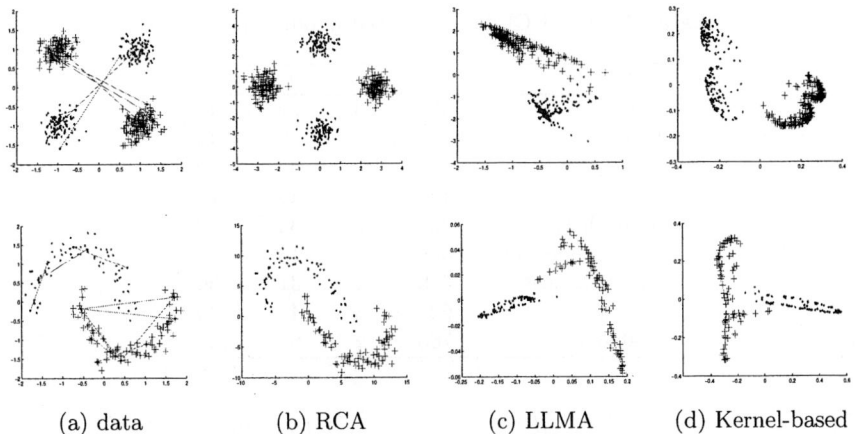

Fig. 2. Comparison of different metric learning methods on two synthetic data sets. (a) origianl synthetic data sets; and the data sets after applying (b) RCA; (c) LLMA; (d) our kernel-based method.

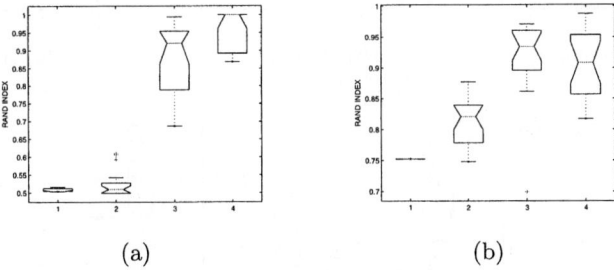

Fig. 3. Clustering results for (a) XOR data set and (b) 2-moon data set

data sets are shown in the first column of Figure 2. Data points with the same mark and color belong to the same cluster. Similar pairs are connected by solid lines. The second, third and fourth columns show the data sets after applying RCA, LLMA and our kernel-based method. Obviously, RCA, which performs globally linear metric learning, cannot give satisfactory results. The performance of LLMA is significantly better, although some points from the two classes are quite close to each other. On the other hand, our kernel-based approach can group the data points well according to their class.

We further perform some semi-supervised clustering experiments on the XOR and 2-moon data sets. The results are shown in Figure 3. For each trial, 10 point pairs are randomly selected to form $\mathcal{S}$.

3.3 Experiments on UCI Data

To access the efficacy of our metric learning methods for real-world data sets, we further perform experiments for semi-supervised clustering tasks on some

Table 1. Nine UCI data sets used in our experiments

Data set	n	c	d	$|\mathcal{S}|$
Soybean	47	4	35	10
Protein	116	6	20	15
Iris	150	3	4	20
Wine	178	3	13	20
Ionosphere	351	2	34	30
Boston housing	506	3	13	40
Breast cancer	569	2	31	50
Balance	625	3	4	40
Diabetes	768	2	8	50

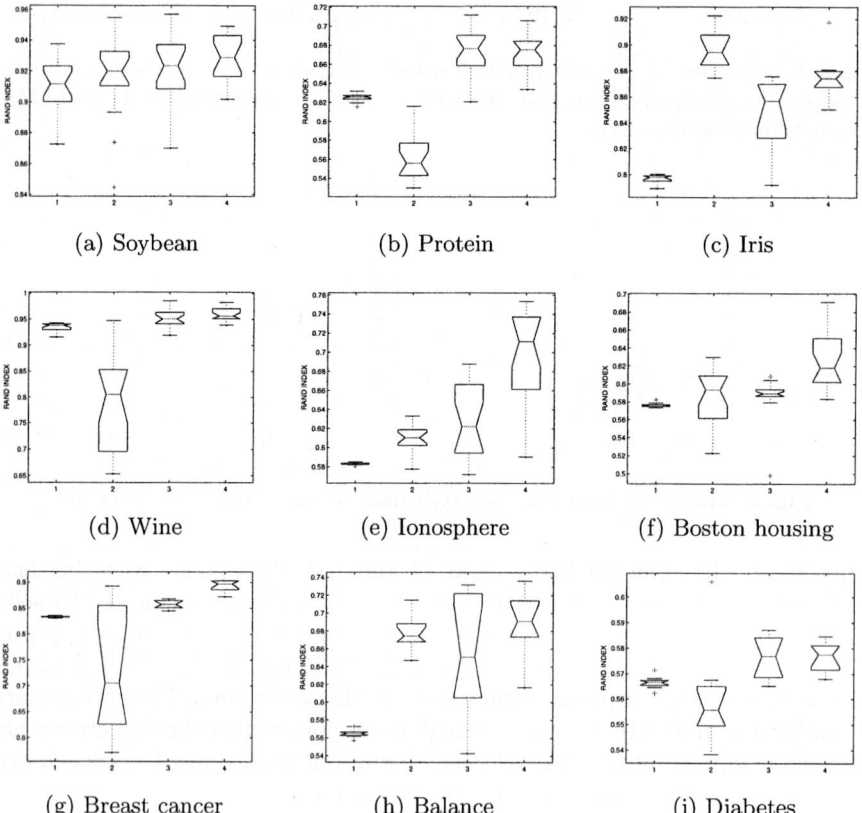

Fig. 4. Clustering results for nine UCI data sets

data sets from the UCI Machine Learning Repository. Table 1 summarizes the characteristics of nine UCI data sets used in our experiments. The number of data points n, the number of clusters c, the number of features d, and the number of randomly selected similar pairs $\mathcal{S}$ are shown in each line of Table 1.

The clustering results using different clustering algorithms numbered as in Section 3.1 are shown in Figure 4. From the clustering results, we can see that our kernel-based method outperforms RCA and is comparable or even better than LLMA.

4 Concluding Remarks

In this paper, we have proposed a new metric learning method based on semi-supervised learning. Unlike previous methods which perform metric learning in input space, our method performs metric learning in kernel-induced feature space by iterative kernel matrix adaptation. We neither have to formulate the metric learning as an optimization problem nor need to compute the explicit embedding of data points in the feature space. These characteristics make our method more powerful for solving some difficult clustering tasks as demonstrated through the synthetic and UCI data sets.

Although our kernel-based metric learning method is simple and still quite effective, there is still much space for it to be improved. We have only considered translation in the feature space, which is a restrictive form of locally linear transformation. One possible extension is to generalized it to more general linear transformation. Another limitation is that our method cannot preserve the topology structure during the metric learning procedure.

Except the illustrative examples shown in Figure 2, we access the performance of our proposed metric learning method by semi-supervised clustering. There may exist other machine learning tasks that can be used to evaluate different metric learning methods. One possible task is content-based image retrieval (CBIR), whose performance depends critically on the distance measure between images. We will pursue this direction and explore other applications as well in our future research.

Acknowledgments

The research described in this paper has been supported by two grants, CA03/04.EG01 (which is part of HKBU2/03/C) and HKUST6174/04E, from the Research Grants Council of the Hong Kong Special Administrative Region, China.

References

1. K. Fukunaga and L. Hostetler. Optimization of k-nearest neighbor density estimates. *IEEE Transactions on Information Theory*, 19(3):320–326, 1973.
2. J.H. Friedman. Flexible metric nearest neighbor classification. Technical report, Department of Statistics, Stanford University, Stanford, CA, USA, November 1994.
3. T. Hastie and R. Tibshirani. Discriminant adaptive nearest neighbor classification. *IEEE Transactions on Pattern Analysis and Machine Intelligence*, 18(6):607–616, 1996.

4. D.G. Lowe. Similarity metric learning for a variable-kernel classifier. *Neural Computation*, 7(1):72–85, 1995.
5. J. Peng, D.R. Heisterkamp, and H.K. Dai. Adaptive kernel metric nearest neighbor classification. In *Proceedings of the Sixteenth International Conference on Pattern Recognition*, volume 3, pages 33–36, Québec City, Québec, Canada, 11–15 August 2002.
6. T. Poggio and F. Girosi. Networks for approximation and learning. *Proceedings of the IEEE*, 78(9):1481–1497, 1990.
7. S. Basu, A. Banerjee, and R. Mooney. Semi-supervised clustering by seeding. In *Proceedings of the Nineteenth International Conference on Machine Learning*, pages 19–26, Sydney, Australia, 8–12 July 2002.
8. J. Sinkkonen and S. Kaski. Clustering based on conditional distributions in an auxiliary space. *Neural Computation*, 14(1):217–239, 2002.
9. Z. Zhang, J.T. Kwok, and D.Y. Yeung. Parametric distance metric learning with label information. In *Proceedings of the Eighteenth International Joint Conference on Artificial Intelligence*, pages 1450–1452, Acapulco, Mexico, 9–15 August 2003.
10. K. Wagstaff and C. Cardie. Clustering with instance-level constraints. In *Proceedings of the Seventeenth International Conference on Machine Learning*, pages 1103–1110, Standord, CA, USA, 2000.
11. K. Wagstaff, C. Cardie, S. Rogers, and S. Schroedl. Constrained k-means clustering with background knowledge. In *Proceedings of the Eighteenth International Conference on Machine Learning*, pages 577–584, Williamstown, MA, USA, 2001.
12. Z. Lu and T. Leen. Penalized probabilistic clustering. In L. Saul, Y. Weiss, and L. Bottou, editors, *Advances in Neural Information Processing Systems 17*. MIT Press, Cambridge, MA, USA, 2005.
13. N. Shental, A. Bar-Hillel, T. Hertz, and D. Weinshall. Computing Gaussian mixture models with EM using equivalence constraints. In *Advances in Neural Information Processing Systems 16*. MIT Press, Cambridge, MA, USA, 2004.
14. A. Bar-Hillel, T. Hertz, N. Shental, and D. Weinshall. Learning distance functions using equivalence relations. In *Proceedings of the Twentieh International Conference on Machine Learning*, pages 11–18, Washington, DC, USA, 21–24 August 2003.
15. T. Hertz, A. Bar-Hillel, and D. Weinshall. Boosting margin based distance functions for clustering. In *Proceedings of the Twenty-First International Conference on Machine Learning*, pages 393–400, Banff, Alberta, Canada, 4–8 August 2004.
16. M. Schultz and T. Joachims. Learning a distance metric from relative comparisons. In *Advances in Neural Information Processing Systems 16*. MIT Press, Cambridge, MA, USA, 2004.
17. E.P. Xing, A.Y. Ng, M.I. Jordan, and S. Russell. Distance metric learning, with application to clustering with side-information. In S. Becker, S. Thrun, and K. Obermayer, editors, *Advances in Neural Information Processing Systems 15*, pages 505–512. MIT Press, Cambridge, MA, USA, 2003.
18. H. Chang and D.Y. Yeung. Locally linear metric adaptation for semi-supervised clustering. In *Proceedings of the Twenty-First International Conference on Machine Learning*, pages 153–160, Banff, Alberta, Canada, 4–8 August 2004.
19. W.M. Rand. Objective criteria for the evaluation of clustering methods. *Journal of the American Statistical Association*, 66:846–850, 1971.

Generating Personalized Answers by Constructing a Question Situation

Yanwen Wu, Zhenghong Wu, Yan Li, and Jinling Li

Department of Information & Technology,
Central China Normal University, 430079, Wuhan, China
wzh_hongzheng@hotmail.com

Abstract. This paper proposes a methodology to generate the personalized answer based on a question situation. To construct the question situation, personal learning characteristics should be obtained by principal component analysis and question type vector is used in the process of semantic analysis. After these analyses, the question situation is constructed based on a harmony network. The answer parameters, including answer depth and answer presentation pattern, are calculated by harmony function. According to these parameters, the personalized answer is matched by the adaptive neuro-fuzzy inference (ANFI). The system architecture of personalized answer generation is proposed in this paper and takes a learner's question to demonstrate.

1 Introduction

Intelligent question answering has been discussed for a long time. Most experts and scholars have researched some aspects of intelligent question answering, e.g., natural language understanding, question identification, problem model analysis, answer matching, system structure[1][2][3]. After considering how to identify and execute a question, the personalized answer is an interesting topic for discussion. This paper focuses on personal learning characteristics and their relationships in the question situation to provide a personalized answer.

Learner analysis is one of the critical tasks in helping learners to study. The difficulty lies in that people learn in different ways because of their learning characteristics, e.g., personalities, innate abilities, educational backgrounds, prior experiences and knowledge, learning and cognitive styles, and psychosocial or physical traits[4][5][6]. Also, original cognitive structure, enthusiasm, initiative, and learning mind-set all affect a learner's study[7]. So, despite the same question, different learners demand different answer depths and answer presentation patterns because of their inherent or external differences. The answer has to be available assimilation for learners which also allows them to acquire information, practice activities, and construct their knowledge.

Section 2 describes the learning characteristics of the learner and principal component analysis for analyzing personal learning characteristics. After considering the learning characteristics, the construction process of the question situation and the matching method of a personalized answer are discussed in Section 3. A personalized answer generating system which is given as an example for showing the process is built in Section 4 and a brief conclusion is described in Section 5.

2 Personal Learning Characteristics

Personal learning characteristics give information on effective learning methods for a learner. Information on personal learning characteristics is an important factor for a personalized answer. Different learners have different personal characteristics, such as cognitive structure, learning motivation, and so on. These differences cause the need for different answer depths and answer presentation patterns. However, it's not an easy task for an intelligent question answering system. In order to help an online intelligent question answering system analyze learners and determine personalized answers, the principal component analysis is used to gather personal learning characteristics. It provides the key help for matching the most available answer materials, especially in inter-correlated characteristics.

Table 1. Learning Characteristics

Learning Characteristics	
C1: Cognitive Structure	C7: IQ
C2: Study Style	C8: Personality
C3: Preliminary Knowledge	C9: Learning Speed
C4: Learning Motivation	C10: Score
C5: Cognitive Style	C11: Aptitude
C6: Psychology Development Level	C12: Others

Table 2. Examples of Some Learning Sub-Characteristics

C1: Cognitive Structure Utilizing degree Distinguishing degree Consolidating degree	C4: Learning Motivation Surface state Deep state Achievement state
C2: Study Style Perceptual orientation Motivation and value Best learning time Physic environment partiality Social environment partiality	C5: Cognitive Style Field dependence/ Field independence Impulsiveness/Introspecting Gathering thinking/Dispersing thinking Introversion/Extroversion
C3: Preliminary Knowledge Zero degree Low degree	C6: Psychology Development Level Low Middle High

2.1 Learning Characteristics

In Table 1, the learning characteristics are detailed. Each characteristic has its own sub-characteristics. Table 2 lists some examples of these learning characteristics' sub-characteristics. All sub-characteristics are inter-correlated for a learner. These innate relationships are useful for providing the personalized answer.

2.2 Personal Learning Characteristics Analysis

In all learning characteristics, only some learning characteristics, *personal learning characteristics*, are a leading action for a learner. The principal component analysis is used to draw the personal learning characteristics. Assume the number of learner samples is n. m is the number of all learning characteristics. p is the new number of synthesized learning characteristics. To a learner sample $\mathbf{X}$, it is a p-dimension vector, which is expressed by $X = \{X_1, X_2, ..., X_p\}$. Expression 1 shows the linear relations between m and p. The average is u, and variance is not equal to zero.

$$\begin{cases} y_1 = b_{11}x_1 + b_{12}x_2 + ... + b_{1p}x_p \\ y_2 = b_{21}x_1 + b_{22}x_2 + ... + b_{2p}x_p \\ ...... \\ y_m = b_{m1}x_1 + b_{m2}x_2 + ... + b_{mp}x_p \end{cases} \quad (1)$$

and

$$b_{k1}^2 + b_{k2}^2 + ... + b_{kp}^2 = 1 \quad k=1\sim m . \quad (2)$$

$$X_i = \{X_{i1}, X_{i2}, ..., X_{ip}\} \quad i=1\sim n . \quad (3)$$

X_i stands as a sample. First, standardize the sample data. Then calculate the relevant matrix R. According to character equation $|R-\lambda I|=0$, it can obtain character values λ_i. Corresponding to λ_i, Q_i is the character vector of a character value. Then we have:

$$Q_i = (b_{i1}, b_{i2}, ..., b_{ip}), \quad i=1\sim m . \quad (4)$$

and $\lambda_1 > \lambda_2 > \lambda_3 > ... > \lambda_p > 0$.

Based on Q_i, the synthesized learning characteristics can be expressed by expression 5:

$$\begin{cases} y_1 = b_{11}x'_1 + b_{12}x'_2 + ... + b_{1p}x'_p \\ y_2 = b_{21}x'_1 + b_{22}x'_2 + ... + b_{2p}x'_p \\ ...... \\ y_m = b_{m1}x'_1 + b_{m2}x'_2 + ... + b_{mp}x'_p \end{cases} \quad (5)$$

and:

$$x'_i = \frac{x_i - \frac{1}{n}\sum_{j=1}^{n} x_{ij}}{\sqrt{\frac{1}{n-1}\sum_{j=1}^{n}(x_{ij} - \overline{x_i})^2}} \quad (i=1, 2, \ldots, p). \tag{6}$$

The variance of every synthesized learning characteristic decreases gradually. The accumulated contribution ratio determines the personalized learning characteristics. Expression 7 gives the calculation method:

$$r = \sum_{i=1}^{q} \lambda_i \Big/ \sum_{i=1}^{m} \lambda_i . \tag{7}$$

r is the accumulated contribution ratio. q could stand for the number of personalized learning characteristics when $r \geq 0.85$. Through the prediction and revision in practice, it is possible to obtain the personalized learning characteristics of learners to realize personalized intelligent question answering. In our experiment, we input a lot of learners' data. For example, for LiMing (a learner sample), his personalized learning characteristics is q. It can be described as $LM = \{c_1, c_2, \ldots, c_q\}$.

3 Question Situations and Matching Method

A question exists when someone has a goal and tries to find a way to reach the target. That means when someone has a goal and the goal is blocked for lack of resources or information, there's a question[8]. There are many instruments available for educators to design an intelligent question answering system. Two metaphors, problem graph and problem matrix, can be represented for solving a problem[3]. To construct a standard information-processing framework, a question is constructed by some states: one end state, which is the goal of a question; one starting state, which is the initial description of the question; and several intermediate states, which describe the possible solution paths of the question[9].

To a learner, his question has his own special features, e.g., cognitive structure, feeling orientation, learning motivation, and so on. These features compose the question situation. This same question in a different question situation will need a different answer depth and answer presentation pattern to solve it.

3.1 Constructing Question Situation

In this paper, construct a standard question network structure to form a question situation. In Figure 1, the question situation is constructed by a knowledge-atom, expression character and knowledge vector.

Knowledge-atom, which is the knowledge needed for solving the question, is presented by m. Knowledge-atom has its own active variable presented by m_m. If the active variable is activity, its value is one. Otherwise, its value is zero. The set of active variables $\{m_m\}$ is active vector m.

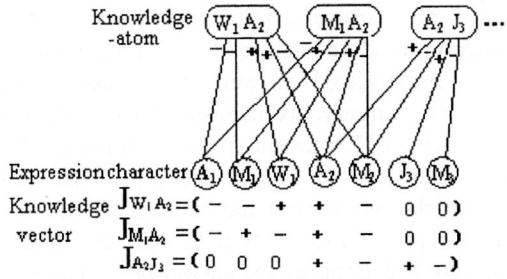

Fig. 1. Network Structure of Question Model

Expression character, which is the description of personal learning characteristics, is presented by c. For LiMing, the expression character is $c = \{c_1, c_2, ..., c_q\}$. Each expression character has three expression variable values: positive one, negative one and uncertain (zero).

Knowledge vector, which is the connection from active variable to expression variable, is presented by J_m. The value of J_m may be positive one, negative one, or zero.

There are many knowledge vectors. The harmony function (Expression 8) is used to calculate the question situation and get the personalized answer parameters.

$$H_J = (c, m) = \sum_m \theta_m m_m h_J(c, J_m) \quad (8)$$

and

$$h_J(c, J_m) = (c \cdot J_m)/|J_m| - j \quad (9)$$

$$c \cdot J_m = \sum_i c_i (J_m)_i \quad (10)$$

$$|J_m| = \sum_i |(J_m)_i| \quad (11)$$

$$\pi(c) \propto e^{u(c)} \quad (12)$$

$$u(c) = \sum_{m \in 0} \lambda_m \chi_m(c) \quad (13)$$

$h_J(c, J_m)$ is the contribution of active knowledge-atom in any expression character. The value of j is from negative one to positive one. π is the biggest entropy under a learner's individualized environment. x_m (c) is the form of factor in a question situation. According to the value of $|J_m|$, the number of personal learning characteristics n can be known. When the value of j exceeds the value of b, and $b = 1 - 2/n$, the personal learning characteristics and knowledge-atom needing consideration in question are basically matched. Therefore, the question situation is dynamically constructed by a series of knowledge-atoms offering personalized answers.

The parameters of adaptive answer depth and presentation pattern are decided by the probability distribution of all knowledge-atoms. If a certain knowledge-atom has more influence for a personalized answer, its intensity force adds $\Delta\theta$, then $\Delta\lambda=\Delta\theta$ $(1-j)$. On the contrary, its intensity force reduces $\Delta\theta$. According to Expression 8, Expression 9 and Expression 10, we can make a harmony calculation for a personal learning characteristic. Finally, every personal learning characteristic has an ended value, which can confirm the suitable parameter of a personalized answer. For example, for presentation pattern E, there are three kinds of situation: hearing, vision and mixed. E determines the answer presentation pattern on the basis of the intensity value of the three factors. When the value of λ makes the expression 13 tenable, λ is the answer presentation pattern parameter.

3.2 Matching Personalized Answer

Make answer parameters as the input, which is the premise parameter of ANFI (Figure. 2). According to general rule sets:

Rule 1: if x is D_1 and y is E_1, then $f_1 = p_1 x + q_1 y + r_1$
Rule 2: if x is D_2 and y is E_1, then $f_2 = p_2 x + q_2 y + r_2$
Rule 3: if x is D_3 and y is E_1, then $f_3 = p_3 x + q_3 y + r_3$
Rule 4: if x is D_1 and y is E_2, then $f_4 = p_4 x + q_4 y + r_4$
Rule 5: if x is D_2 and y is E_2, then $f_5 = p_5 x + q_5 y + r_5$
Rule 6: if x is D_3 and y is E_2, then $f_6 = p_6 x + q_6 y + r_6$
Rule 7: if x is D_1 and y is E_3, then $f_7 = p_7 x + q_7 y + r_7$
Rule 8: if x is D_2 and y is E_3, then $f_8 = p_8 x + q_8 y + r_8$
Rule 9: if x is D_3 and y is E_3, then $f_9 = p_9 x + q_9 y + r_9$

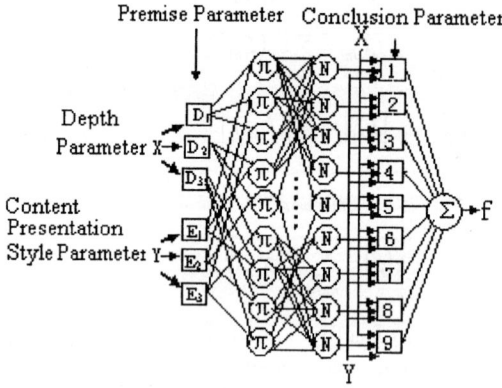

Fig. 2. Personalized Answering Reasoning Network

The concrete answer that is most appropriate for the learner's personality can be matched in the knowledge base by ANFI function (Expression 14, Expression 15). In this function, w_i is the encouragement intensity of the rule i at the node of i. And f_i is the value of rule i at the node of i.

$$f = \frac{\sum_i \overline{w_i} f_i}{\sum_i w_i} . \qquad (14)$$

$$\overline{w_i} = \frac{w_i}{w_1 + w_2 + \ldots + w_9} . \qquad (15)$$

4 Personalized Answer Generating System

In previous research, the personalized intelligent question answering algorithm is used in an intelligent question answering system. Figure 2 shows the generating system architecture of personalized answer. To guarantee efficiency, the system needs semantic analysis. And this system introduces a question type of vector for judging the question's type by semantic analysis. In the process of semantic analysis, the main goal is to identify the question core and its vector type. After the research on the question core has been conducted, we discover that the answer to each question involves one or more knowledge points. Attributes of knowledge points, such as concept, essence and time, etc., form an answer. Question manner is diversification, including reason, relation, instance, and so on. So, each question can be classified to some vector type according to the relationship between its involved knowledge points and its manner. Question type vector is helpful for locating questions to improve answer precision and shorten matching time.

The knowledge base includes a question base and an answer base. The question base stores the question type vector and other data. It is organized by knowledge points based on ontology. The answer base is organized by content levels (low, middle and high) and content styles (text, picture, and multimedia).

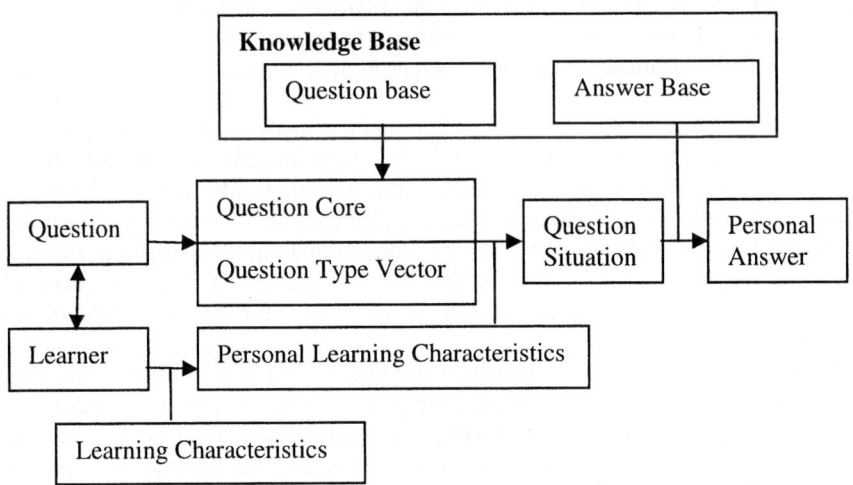

Fig. 3. Personalized Answer Generating System

Take LiMing's question as example: what is cuttlefish? Using semantic analysis, the system obtains his question core. Then, it classifies the question type vector on the basis of question base. At the same time, his personal learning characteristics are calculated by principal component analysis. Subsequently, his question situation is constructed using the harmony network. We get several vectors to explain the network structure of a question situation. In Figure 1, his expression character can be described as follows: A_1 (words statement); M_1 (vision partiality); W_1 (psychological development level); A_2 (object presentation); M_2 (hearing partiality); M_3 (blending pattern/vision and hearing); J_3 (knowledge background). J_{W1A2} is decided by W_1 and A_2 because the value of W_1 and A_2 are one. By analogy, the question integrated with personal learning characteristics can dynamically construct a question situation suitable to his personality. To LiMing, his psychological development, knowledge background and vision partiality can influence the assimilation of the answer. The answer parameters are calculated by harmony function. These parameters show that the premise depth parameter is easy and the premise content presentation pattern parameter is vision presentation. Then, the conclusion parameters X and Y are calculated by the application of ANFIS. Also, it obtains concrete factors for the learner's personality. According to these, the personalized answer is obtained from the knowledge base. Namely, the output f, a personalized answer, is presented to the learner.

5 Conclusions

This paper has described a methodology for generating a personalized answer. According to our questionnaire, we have compared judgments by others and our system. As a result, we have seen that our method is useful if the question situation is decided by learning characteristics. At the same time, according to the feedback information of learners, the system has added harmony functions. Learners feel that the personalized answer pays more attention to their personalized learning. And they can more easily assimilate the answer content in their cognitive structure to solve the question.

In this paper, we applied the principal component analysis to analyze personalized learning characteristics according to the associational factors of learning characteristics. After semantic analysis, the question situation is dynamically constructed based on personalized learning characteristics. Answer parameters are ascertained by the application of harmony function in a question situation. According to answer parameters, the system matches the personalized answer to the learner by using ANFI. The personalized answer is efficiency for an intelligent question answering system.

Some measures which solve questions are enumerated as a result of some studies However, in order to realize the adaptive personalized answer, it is necessary to consider the personal learning characteristics automatically assumed by computers. Therefore, we have defined the question situation along the personalized answering process and proposed the mechanism of personalized answer calculation in this paper. The next target of our research is to realize a function to locate a question type vector in a knowledge base by semantic analysis.

References

1. Shuang, Li., Li Chen: The Comparison of Domestic and International Online Intelligent Question Answering System. China Educational Technology, No.1 (2003) 80-83
2. Fumito, MASUI., Masayuki, MIYAGUCHI: MAIMAI: A Question Answering System at NTCIR3 QAC-1. National Institute of Informatics.(2003)
3. Rita, Kuo., Wei-Peng, Lien., Maiga, Chang., Jia-Sheng, He.: Analyzing Problem's Difficulty based on Neural Networks and Knowledge Map. Educational Technology & Society, Vol. 7, No.2. (2004) 42-50
4. Jonassen, D. J., & Grabowski, B. L.: Handbook of Individual Differences, Learning and Instruction, Lawrence Erlbaum Associates. Inc. (1993)
5. John,Wiley., Sons Inc., Rothwell, W.J., Kazanas, H.S. (3rd ed): Mastering the Instructional Design: a Systematic Approach Process,., Pfeiffer: San Francisco, CA. (2004)
6. Kramarski, B., Feldman, Y.: Internet in the Classroom: Effects on Reading, Comprehension, Motivation and Metacognitive Awareness. Education Media International,Vol. 37, No.3, (2000)149-155
7. Ruizhen, Shao. (1st ed): Educational Psychology. Educational Press of Shanghai, Shanghai, (1997)
8. Kahney, H. (2nd ed.): Problem Solving: Current Issue, Milton Keynes. UK: Open University Press,(1993)
9. E. D. Gagné., Carol Walker Yekovich.,Frank R. Yekovich: The Cognitive Psychology of Scholl Learning. New York : HarperCollins College Publishers, (1993)
10. Weihua, Li: The Design of Intelligent Answering Expert System in Web Teaching System. Journal of Beijing Union University(Natural Sciences), Vol. 18,No. 3, (2004) 42-45
11. Yajun, Liu., Yi, Xu., Lisha, Gao (Nat Sci Ed): Research and Implementation of Quick Location Algorithm for Intelligent Question Answering System. Journal of Southeast University, Vol. 30, No. 4, (2003) 410-413
12. Peng, Han., Ruimin, Shen., Fan, Yang: Application of Case Based Reasoning on Q&A System. Journal of Shanghai Jiao Tong University, Vol. 37, No. 3, (2003)393-396
13. Sadler-Smith, E., Allinson, C. W., Hayes, J.: Learning Preferences and Cognitive Style: Some Implications for Continuing Professional Development. Management Learning, Vol. 31, No.2, (2000)239-256
14. Qun, Su., Ruimin, Shen., Wu, Wang: Generalization and Association Pattern Mining Intelligent Answering Model Based on Knowledge Tree. Computer Engineering, Vol. 29, No. 17, (2003)124-125
15. Joo, Y-J., Bong, M., Choi, H-J.: Self-efficacy for Self-regulated Learning, Academic Aelf-efficacy, and Internet Self-efficacy in Web-based Instruction. Educational Technology Research and Development, Vol. 48, No. 2, (2000) 5-17

A Multi-stage Chinese Collocation Extraction System

Ruifeng Xu and Qin Lu

Dept. of Computing, The Hong Kong Polytechnic University,
Hung Hom, Kowloon, Hong Kong
{csrfxu, csluqin}@comp.polyu.edu.hk

Abstract. Most of the existing collocation extraction systems are based on globally significant statistical behaviors without mechanisms to handle different types of collocations. By taking compositionality, substitutability, modifiability and internal associations into consideration, collocations are categorized into four different types in this work. Based on the analysis for each type of collocation, a multi-stage extraction system is designed using different combinations of discriminative features so as to identify different types of collocations in different stages. Perceptron training is employed to optimize the consolidation of discriminative features from different sources. Experiment results show that the achieved performance is much better than most reported work.

1 Introduction

Collocation is a lexical phenomenon in which two or more words are habitually used in text as a conventional saying. It is essential to many natural language processing tasks such as machine translation, information retrieval, and word sense disambiguation [1]. Even though collocations are commonly used by human beings, they are still difficult to describe [1-2] since collocations are mostly habitual use in a language. In this study, *collocation* is defined as *a recurrent and conventional expression consisting of at least two content words that hold syntactic and semantic relations*. More specifically, content words in Chinese include noun, verb, adjective, adverb, determiner, and directional word.

In the past decade, there have been a number of studies on collocation extraction for both English and Chinese [2-5]. They can be categorized into window-based and syntax-based approaches, respectively [2-4]. The window-based approach utilizes lexical statistics between a chosen word, called the *headword*, and its context words within a fixed window to estimate the association between these words. The common lexical statistics are based on co-occurrence frequencies and co-occurrence distribution. Different criteria including frequency, mutual information [3], mean and variance [2], *t*-test or *chi*-square for hypothesis test [1], and log-likehood ratio test [1] are employed. The syntax-based approach applies the syntax dependency parsing results to refine the candidate search space before the association estimations are done using lexical statistics [5]. The use of semantic information such as synonym substitution testing [6] and translation testing [1] are also tried as a way to strengthen existing collocation extraction techniques and have proven to be useful, although they are not used alone.

The main issues affecting the performance of current collocation extraction systems are the elimination of *pseudo collocations* (the word combinations extracted with high lexical statistics but which are not true collocations) and the extraction of true collocations with low occurrences. Furthermore, most of the existing systems identify collocations by using a single set of criteria and a single set of threshold values. However, collocations fall between, at one extreme, idiom, and at the other extreme, free word combinations, and thus have very different behaviors varying from lexical statistics, syntax and semantics. This work categorizes collocations into four types according to their compositionality, substitutability, modifiability, and internal associations. A multi-stage collocation extraction system, referred to as *CXtract*3 (the third version of a Chinese collocation extraction system), is implemented according to different features of different types. Perceptron training is employed to optimize the weighting of features from different sources. Some heuristic rules based on dependency grammar are also used to reduce pseudo collocations. The largest up-to-date experiment results on Chinese collocation extraction have shown the performance is much better than all the existing systems. The rest of the paper is organized as follows: Section 2 presents the categorization scheme and Section 3 presents the characteristics observation of the different types of collocations. The design and implementation of the multi-stage extraction system are presented in Section 4. Section 5 gives experiment results and evaluations analysis. Section 6 concludes this paper.

2 Categorization of Chinese Collocations

Collocations have different characteristics. Based on the linguistic characteristics observation and the co-occurrence statistics of typical collocations, Chinese collocations are characterized into four types. They are:

Type 0: Idiomatic Collocation
Type 0 collocations have fixed forms. Components cannot be shifted around. Also, their components are non-substitutable allowing no syntactic transformation or internal lexical variation. Type 0 collocations are *non-compositional* meaning that they cannot be predicted from the meanings of their component parts such as in 缘 木 求 鱼 (to climb a tree to catch a fish, meaning a fruitless effort) whose underlying meaning cannot be derived directly from the meanings of the individual characters. Since most Type 0 collocations are already listed as idioms in idiom dictionaries and are treated as known words, there little need to extract them.

Type 1: Fixed Collocation
Type 1 collocations are non-substitutable and non-modifiable, meaning that their components cannot be substituted, reordered or modified. Components of Type 1 collocations cannot be substituted by synonyms. For example, the collocation 外 交/n 豁 免 权/n (diplomatic immunity), is compositional. However, none of these two component words can be substituted by other words to carry the same meaning. Since compositionality is a linguistic characteristic and it is difficult to test by computational methods using monolingual resources, the non-substitutability and non- modifier-insertion characteristics become the main discriminative features for Type 1 collocations.

Type 2: Strong Collocation

Type 2 collocations allow limited modifier insertion while the order of components must be kept unchanged. Strong collocations have very limited-substitutability where the components can be substituted by a very few synonyms in only certain limited combinations, and the newly generated word combinations have nearly the same meaning. For example, 缔结/v 同盟/n and 缔结/v 联盟/n (form alliance). This means that for Type 2 collocation, a synonym substitution ratio can be an important discriminative feature. Meanwhile, Type 2 collocations are limited modifiable and thus, their co-occurrences normally have one or two peak distributions.

Type 3: Loose Collocation

Type 3 collocations allow modifier insertion and component order alteration. Their components may be substituted by some of the synonyms and the newly generated word combinations usually have the same meaning. This means that more substitutions of their components are allowed; yet the replacement is not arbitrary. Here are some examples of Type 3 collocations including 合法/v 收入/n (lawful income), 正当/v 收入/n (legitimate income), and 合法/v 收益 (lawful income).

The varying types of collocations are quite different in terms of their compositionality, substitutability, modifiability, and internal strength. These differences warrant different target features on the extraction for different types of collocations.

3 Feature Analysis Based on Collocation Types

CXtract3 is developed based on the data-driven principle. That is, extraction is based on the observations of the characteristics of different types of collocations in real data. A set of typical collocations based on linguistics knowledge is firstly prepared. A so called *typical collocation set*, labeled as *TCS*, which contains 35,742 typical collocations corresponding to a set of 3,643 headwords, labeled *THS,* are taken from the linguistic resource "The Dictionary of Modern Chinese Collocation" [7]. Two linguists manually categorized these collocations into Type 1 to Type 3 collocations according to the definitions with reference to co-occurrence statistics in the training corpus. Since n-gram collocation extraction for a window-based approach is straightforward and existing systems have already achieved 92% in precision and 88% in recall which is sufficiently accurate [4], this work focuses only on bi-gram collocation extraction. The numbers of Type 1- Type 3 bi-gram collocations in *TCS* are 224, 13,461, and 220,577 respectively. The observations based on the extracted statistics corresponding to different types of collocations are summarized below.

1. The co-occurrence peaks of word bi-grams have shown a good discriminative capability, especially for identifying Type 1 and Type 2 collocations. As for Type 3 collocations, the distribution statistics are flatter, although many of them still have quite a number of low peaks.
2. The distributions of word combinations as collocations with different Part-of-Speech (POS) tags are quite different. For example, a noun often collocates with a noun, verb, or adjective, yet it seldom collocates with an adverb.
3. The distributions of certain fixed POS combinations are similar for different collocations, yet the distributions of different POS combinations are quite different.

Such co-occurrence distributions have shown strong inner-class cohesion and inter-class differentia. Naturally, this can be used as a discriminative feature.
4. Synonym substitution testing has proven to be an effective feature in reported works to identify true collocations [6], especially for Type 1 and Type 2 collocations, and thus it should be applied in identifying Type 1 and Type 2 collocations.

4 The Design of a Multi-stage Collocation Extraction System

The framework of CXtract3 is summarized as follows. For a given headword, the bi-gram words co-occurring in its context windows with significant lexical statistics are identified as bi-gram collocation candidate in the 1st stage. In the 2nd stage, the continuous multiple bi-gram combinations are extracted as n-gram collocations. In the 3rd stage, Type 1 and Type 2 bi-gram collocations are identified. In the 4th stage, a set of heuristic rules based on Dependency Grammar [8] is employed to eliminate pseudo collocations based on the identified Type 1 and Type 2 bi-gram collocations. Finally, in the 5th stage, Type 3 collocations are extracted.

Stage 1. Co-occurrence Concordance and Extraction

This stage includes concordance production, statistical data preprocessing and bi-gram collocation extraction based on the bi-directional bi-gram statistics, where a word co-occurrence table *WT* is compiled for headword w_{head} to record all co-occurred words w_{co-i} ($i=1$, to k) within the context window of w_{head}. The word pairs having bi-directional strength (*bi-strength*) and bi-directional spread (*bi-spread*) above a certain threshold are extracted as bi-gram collocation candidates. The details of this part are given in [4].

Stage 2. N-gram Collocation Extraction

The n-gram collocation extraction algorithm developed in [2] is used directly. For each co-word of w_{head}, only those occurring in certain positions with a frequency over a given threshold *T*, are kept. Only if all bi-grams in a continuous series have an occurrence frequency are they considered n-gram collocations. When the n-gram collocations are identified, their corresponding word bi-gram co-occurrences in *WT* are removed to produce WT_1 for future processing.

Stage 3. Type 1 and Type 2 Bi-gram Collocation Extraction

Since Type 1 and Type 2 bi-gram collocations have nearly fixed co-occurrence positions and they tend to be semantically collocated rather than syntactically collocated, the peak distribution and synonyms substitution ratios are used as important discriminative features to identify them. For a bi-gram collocation candidate pair (w_{head}, w_{co-i}), if the co-occurrence frequency at position *m* fulfils the following condition:

$$f(w_{head}, w_{co-i}, m) \geq \overline{f(w_{head}, w_{co-i})} + \sqrt{\frac{1}{10} \cdot \sum_{j=-5}^{5}(f(w_{head}, w_{co-i}, j) - \overline{f(w_{head}, w_{co-i})})^2} \quad (1)$$

then (w_{head}, w_{co-i}) is considered to have a peak co-occurrence at position *m*.

Synonym substitution ratio is a feature for estimating the semantic restrictions within a bi-gram pair. For each bi-gram pair (w_{head}, w_{co-i}), suppose there are two corresponding synonym sets, denoted by $S_{sym}(w_{head})$ and $S_{sym}(w_{co-i})$. For each w_{sh} in $S_{sym}(w_{head})$, if the bi-gram pair (w_{sh}, w_{co-i}) is also found in WT_1 with a frequency larger than a threshold, we say w_{head} can be substituted by w_{sh} when w_{head} is collocated with w_{co-i}. The synonym substitution ratio of w_{head} collocated with w_{co-i}, is calculated by:

$$substitution\ ratio(w_{head}) = \frac{number\ of\ w_{head}\ can\ be\ substituted\ by\ w_{sh}}{total\ number\ of\ synonyms\ of\ w_{head}} \cdot 100\% \qquad (2)$$

The value of the synonym substitution ratio ranges from 0 to 1, and a small value means that this word combination is less substitutable and more likely to be semantically collocated. The synonym substitution ratio of w_{co-i} can be obtained in the same way. To summarize, Type 1 collocations are identified using the following criteria:

1. The value of *bi-strength*(w_{head}, w_{co-i}) is larger than a threshold S_1;
2. The value of *bi-spread*(w_{head}, w_{co-i}) is larger than a threshold D_1;
3. Bi-gram $w_{head}w_{co-i}$ has one and only one peak co-occurrence position m, and $f(w_{head}, w_{co-i}, m)$ is larger than a threshold $FP_1\%$ of $f(w_{head}, w_{co-i})$.
4. Synonym substitution ratio for any one of the two words is lower than SR_1.

Then, Type 2 collocations are identified by using a set of looser criteria as follows:

1. The value of *bi-Strength*(w_{head}, w_{co-i}) is larger than a threshold S_2;
2. The value of *bi-Spread*(w_{head}, w_{co-i}) is larger than a threshold D_2;
3. Bi-gram pair $w_{head}w_{co-i}$ has one or two peak co-occurrences, and the summary of co-occurrence at its peak positions is larger than a $FP_2\%$ of $f(w_{head}, w_{co-i})$.
4. Synonym substitution ratio for any one of the two words is lower than SR_2.

The above thresholds, $(S_1>S_2, D_1>D_2, FP_1>FP_2, SR_1<SR_2)$, are obtained experimentally. After Type1 and Type 2 bi-gram collocations are identified, their corresponding bi-gram co-occurrences are eliminated from WT_1, and a revised WT_2 is then obtained.

Stage 4. Pseudo Collocation Filtering
Theoretically speaking, collocated words must be directly related or dependent. If collocation candidates have no direct dependency relationships, they are naturally regarded as pseudo collocations. Based on the identified Type 1/2 bi-gram collocations, a set of heuristic rules, which are manually compiled based on the dependency grammar and observation of real text, are employed to filter out pseudo collocations around the identified collocations. Below is an example:

> Example Rule 1: For an adverb headword, if an adverb-verb collocation is identified, the headword should not collocate with any verb in the opposite direction and thus the verb on the other side should be eliminated.
> E.g. 公开/ad 审理/v (*public hearing*) is an identified collocation for headword 公开/ad, then the underlined verb doesn't collocate with 公开/ad in the following examples, 反对/v 公开/ad 审理/v (*opposed to public hearing*)

By means of the pseudo collocation filtering in this stage, WT_3 is obtained.

Stage 5. Type 3 Collocation Extraction
The identification of Type 3 bi-gram collocations is difficult because there are no obvious semantic discriminative criteria. Since most Type 3 collocations are

grammatically collocated, two new discriminative features are introduced. The first one is the expected probability of two POS tags which may be collocated. This can be estimated by using lexical statistics extracted from *TCS*. Suppose t_1 and t_2 are two POS tags, the probability of t_1 collocating with t_2 is calculated as:

$$cp(t_1,t_2) = 2 \cdot c(t_1,t_2) / (c(t_1) + c(t_2)) \qquad (3)$$

where, $c(t_1)$ and $c(t_2)$ are the occurrences of tags t_1 and t_2, in all bi-gram collocations of *TCS*, respectively. $c(t_1, t_2)$ is the co-occurrences of bi-gram collocations consisting of two words with POS tags t_1 and t_2. The value of $cp(t_1, t_2)$ ranges from 0 to 1. A larger value means a higher probability that t_1 and t_2 are collocated. Another discriminative feature is the distribution similarity between the candidate and the statistically expected distribution. For bi-gram collocation with POS pattern $(t_1 t_2)$, the occurrences of all the bi-gram collocations in *TCS* are $c(t_1, t_2)$, and for each position m from -5 to 5, the co-occurrence frequencies are $c(t1,t2,m)$. A normalized vector $sam(t_1,t_2)$ is used to characterize the distribution as follows:

$$sam(t_1,t_2) = (sam_{-5},...,sam_5) = (c(t_1,t_2,-5)/c(t_1,t_2),...,c(t_1,t_2,+5)/c(t_1,t_2)) \qquad (4)$$

Once an observed bi-gram candidate (w_{head}, w_{co}) has POS tags of t_1 and t_2, its distribution can be characterized by the vector $can(t_1, t_2)$:

$$can(w_{head}, w_{co}) = (can_{-5},...,can_5) = (f(w_{head}, w_{co},-5)/f(w_{head}, w_{co}),...,f(w_{head}, w_{co},+5)/f(w_{head}, w_{co})) \qquad (5)$$

The distribution similarity between the bi-gram candidate and the training data is then calculated by the production of the two vectors $sam(t_1,t_2)$ and $can(t_1,t_2)$:

$$sim(w_{head} w_{co}, t_1, t_2) = \sum_{m=-5}^{5}(sam_m \times can_m) \qquad (6)$$

The value of the distribution similarity ranges from 0 to 1. A larger value means the distribution of the observing bi-gram candidate is similar to the expected distribution.

Six features are incorporated to measure the observing bi-gram (w_{head}, w_{co}) with POS tags of t_1 and t_2. Assuming that these features are independent, the probability of w_{head} collocated with w_{co}, notated as $P_{col}(w_{head}, w_{co})$, can be estimated by:

$$P_{col}(w_{head}, w_{co}) = \lambda_1 \cdot bi\text{-}strengh(w_{head}, w_{co}) + \lambda_2 \cdot bi\text{-}spread(w_{head}, w_{co}) \qquad (7)$$
$$+ \lambda_3 \cdot cp(t_1,t_2) + \lambda_4 \cdot (1 - substitutionratio(w_{head}))$$
$$+ \lambda_5 \cdot (1 - substitutionratio(w_{co})) + \lambda_6 \cdot sim(w_{head}, w_{co}, t_1, t_2)$$

where, λ_1 to λ_6 are the weight parameters which are trained by employing the perceptron learning rule on the examples of the true collocation with the value of the above features. If a bi-gram candidate has the $Pcol(w_{head}, w_{co})$ value larger than a threshold, which is experimentally obtained, it is identified as a Type 3 collocation..

Parameter Optimization Based on Perceptron Training Rule
Perceptron training rule [9] is used to optimize the weight parameters in Equation 7. A perceptron is a linear unit that (1) takes a vector of real-value inputs, (2) calculates a weighted linear combination of these inputs, and then (3) outputs 1 if the result is greater than a threshold θ and -1 otherwise. When applying perceptron training to collocation extraction, if the output value of the perceptron is 1, the word bi-grams are

regarded as collocated, otherwise, they are non-collocated. Using the true collocations in *TCS* and their values of each attribute in Equation 7 as positive learning examples, and using other co-occurred bi-grams as negative learning examples, the perceptron training algorithm is described as follows:

Perceptron Training for Parameter Optimization
Input: Each training example is a pair of $\{x_1, \ldots, x_n, d\}$, where $x_1, \ldots, x_n$ is the vector of the attribute values. In this task, n equals 6, and $x_1, \ldots, x_6$ correspond to *bi-strength*(w_{head}, w_{co}), *bi-spread*(w_{head}, w_{co-j}), $cp(t_1, t_2)$, *substitutionratio* (w_{head}), *substitutionratio*(w_{co}), and $sim(w_{head}w_{co}, t_1t_2)$, respectively. If the input training example corresponds to a true collocation, the value of the target output value, d, is 1, otherwise -1. η is the learning rate which is used to moderate the degree to which weights are changed at each step (η is a small value, say 0.05 or 0.1) and θ is a pre-defined threshold for determining the perceptron output.

    Initialize each $w_i(0)$, to a randomly generated small value. Here, $w_i(t)$, $1 \leq i \leq 6$ denotes the weight for the *i-th* attribute at time t.
$t=0;$
Until the termination condition is met, Do
    Initialize each Δw_i to zero;
    For each training example, $\{x_1, \ldots, x_6, d\}$, Do
        Compute the linear perceptron $O(x_1, \ldots, x_6)$ using Equation 7;
        If the value of Equation 7 with current weight, $w_i(t)$ is greater than θ, the perceptron output is 1, otherwise it is -1;
        For each weight vector w_i, $1 \leq i \leq 6$ Do
            If the perceptron output is the same as the target given in the training example, the weight parameters are not changed, otherwise,
$$\Delta w_i(t) \leftarrow \eta \cdot (d - O(x_1, \ldots, x_6)) \cdot x_i$$
$$w_i(t+1) \leftarrow w_i(t) + \Delta w_i(t)$$
$t=t+1$

For input training examples, the perceptron is applied iteratively and its weight parameters are modified whenever it misclassifies an example. Such a learning process is repeated until the termination condition is met. The theoretical termination condition is that all training examples are correctly classified if they are linearly separable. Due to the fact that not all true collocations and pseudo collocations are linearly separable, the algorithm may not converge within a finite number of training steps to achieve 100% correct classification. Thus, the termination condition should be reasonably set. A small value of η is helpful to ensure the learning process converges. However, it decreases the training speed. On the other hand, a large value of η increases the training speed, yet it sometimes leads the algorithm to convergence failure. Thus a reasonable η is also important.

5 Experiment Results and Evaluations

Experiment Data Preparation
A Chinese Corpus is constructed with 97 million segmented and POS tagged words. Tong Yi Ci Lin [10], a Chinese synonyms dictionary, is employed as a manually

prepared synonyms resource. The processed Tong Yi Ci Lin records 43,987 entries that are categorized into 4,321 synonym sets to be used in Equation 2.

To fairly evaluate the performance of CXtract3, two sets of collocation answers are prepared. The first is a manually prepared complete collocation list, labeled as *CCS*, containing 4,668 collocations of 134 randomly selected headwords (labeled as *CHS*) with diverse frequency and POS properties. The second is *TCS*, the typical collocations corresponding to the headword set *THS* mentioned in Section 3. The prepared training corpus and the two collocation answer sets are the largest up-to-date resources for Chinese collocation extraction research. By using *CCS*, both precision and recall of the collocation extraction on 134 headwords can be measured. And by using *TCS*, the precision and coverage ratio, an indicator of recall, of the collocation extraction on 3,643 headwords can be evaluated.

Experiment on Weighting Parameter Optimization

The first experiment evaluates the contributions of parameter optimization based on perceptron training to CXtract3. Figure 1 gives the precisions corresponding to five sets of weight parameters are given in Figure 1. These weight parameters are the obtained after 100, 200, 300 and 390 training cycles is done, respectively when the learning rate is set to 0.05. It is observed that the optimized value of weights leads to a better precision over that of equal weights. Also, updated weight parameters after more training cycles leads to better precision of collocation extraction, which means the weight parameters are optimized during the whole process of training, especially after 200 training cycles.

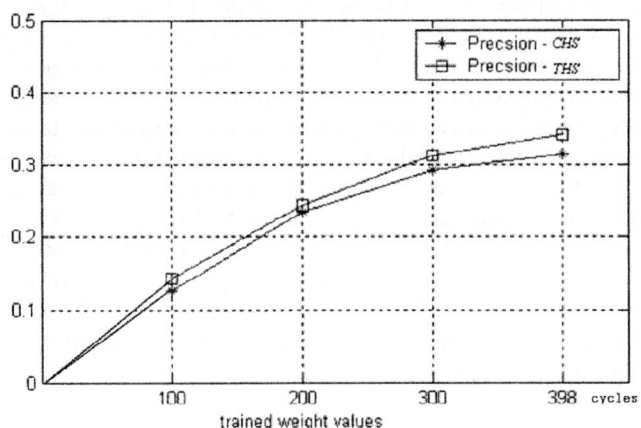

Fig. 1. The precisions of collocation extraction with different weights

Experiment on Multi-stage Collocation Extraction

In this experiment, the effectiveness of the multi-stage extraction strategy and pseudo collocation elimination is evaluated. The precision, recall and F1 performance achieved by Stage 1, by using Formula 7 in single stage, by multi-stage extraction, and the whole CXtract3 incorporating pseudo collocation elimination are charted in Figure 2. Also, some existing statistical-based extraction systems based on mutual

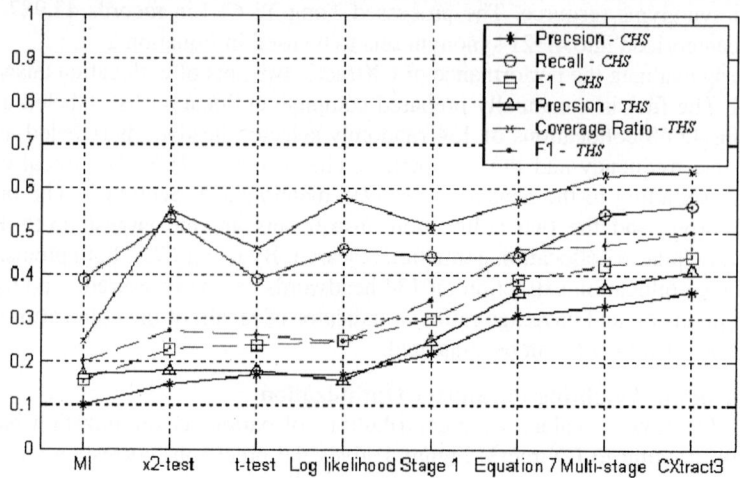

Fig. 2. The performance improvements by different collocation extraction techniques

information (MI), χ^2 test, t-test, log-likelihood, are evaluated and compared by using the same training corpus and answer set. The performances achieved are also shown.

Since the discriminative features and weight parameters are obtained from the statistics of the typical collocations in *TCS*, the experiment on *THS* is regarded as a close test, while the experiment on *CHS* is regarded as an open test. That is why all of the performances on *THS* are better. From the results, it is found that by incorporating synonyms and syntax information, the F1 performance is obviously improved from the pure statistics-based Stage 1. Then, the multi-stage collocation extraction strategy leads to a better result compared to the single-stage strategy, since the discriminative features for identifying Type 3 collocations are not optimal for Type 1/2 collocations. Finally, by appending a pseudo collocation elimination stage, CXtract3 achieves 45.6% and 47.0% F1 performance improvement on *CHS* and *THS* respectively, by comparison with the pure statistics-based Stage 1. Such an improvement has shown the effectiveness of the multi-stage extraction strategy. It is also shown that CXtract3 achieves a much higher F1 performance with any statistical-based system. This result has shown that our research approach is correct, and the collocation extraction performance is significantly improved.

5 Conclusions

In this paper, a multi-stage Chinese collocation extraction system is presented. By categorizing Chinese collocations into four types, a multi-stage collocation extraction system is established in which appropriate features from different sources are consolidated to identify different types of collocations in separate stages. The F1 performance achieved by CXtract3 improves our previous system [4] by about 45%, and it is about 75%-100% higher than the existing statistics-based systems. In the undergoing research, the chunking information is trying to incorporate in CXtract3, and a further improvement is expected.

Acknowledgements

This research is supported by Hong Kong Polytechnic University (Project Code A-P203) and a CERG Grant (Project code 5087/01E).

References

1. Manning C. D. and Schutze H.: Foundations of Statistical Natural Language Processing. The MIT Press, Cambridge, Massachusetts, (1999)
2. Smadja, F.: Retrieving Collocations from Text: Xtract. Computational Linguistics, 19, 1, (1993) 143-177
3. Church K. and Hanks P.: Word Association Norms, Mutual Information, and Lexicography. Computational Linguistics, 16, 1, (1990) 22-29
4. Xu R.F., Lu Q., and Li Y.: An Automatic Chinese Collocation Extraction Algorithm Based on Lexical Statistics, Proc. IEEE Int. Conf. NLPKE (2003)
5. Lin, D. K.: Extracting Collocations from Text Corpora. First Workshop on Computational Terminology, (1998)
6. Li, W.Y., Lu, Q., Xu, R.F.: Similarity based Chinese Synonyms Collocation Extraction, Int. J. Computational Linguistics and Chinese Language Processing, 10, 1, (2005) 123-144
7. Mei, J.J.: Dictionary of Modern Chinese Collocations, Hanyu Dictionary Press (1999)
8. Robinson, J.J.: Dependency Structures and Transformation Rules. Language, 46, (1970)
9. Mitchell T. M.: Machine Learning, The McGraw-Hill Press (1997)
10. Mei, J. J. and Zhu, Y. M.: Tong_Yi_Ci_Lin, Shanghai Dictionary Press, (1996)

Monitoring Glaucomatous Progression: Classification of Visual Field Measurements Using Stable Reference Data

Shuanghui Meng[1], Mihai Lazarescu[1], Jim Ivins[1], and Andrew Turpin[2]

[1] Department of Computing, Curtin University of Technology,
GPO Box U1987, Perth 6845, Western Australia
{sharonm, lazarescu, jim}@cs.curtin.edu.au
[2] School of Computing Science & Information Technology, RMIT,
GPO Box 2476V, Melbourne, Victoria 3001, Australia
aht@cs.rmit.edu.au

Abstract. Glaucoma is a common disease of the eye that often results in partial blindness. The main symptom of glaucoma is the progressive deterioration of the visual field. Glaucoma management involves monitoring the progress of the disease using regular visual field tests but currently there is no standard method for classifying changes in visual field measurements. Sequence matching techniques typically rely on similarity measures. However, visual field measurements are very noisy, particularly in people with glaucoma. It is therefore difficult to establish a reference data set including both stable and progressive visual fields. We describe method that uses a *baseline* computed from a query sequence, to match stable sequences in a database collected from volunteers. The results suggest that the new method is more accurate than other techniques for identifying progressive sequences, though there is a small penalty for stable sequences.

1 Introduction

Glaucoma is a common eye disease that affects the optic nerve. Its prevalence in Australia is about 3% of the population [1], [2]. Most people with glaucoma have no symptoms until some blindness occurs. A common feature in all patients is that the optic nerve fibers are damaged irreversibly [3], though with treatment the damage process can be slowed. Early detection of the disease is therefore crucial. If a patient continues to lose visual function after treatment, the glaucoma is said to be *progressing*, otherwise it is said to be *stable*.

Accurate evaluation of visual function is an important aspect of glaucoma management. It requires a series of visual field tests as described in the next section. However, it is difficult to separate true visual field loss from fluctuations that arise from learning effects, fatigue, and the inherent variation in the tests [4]. The high level of "noise" makes the correct diagnosis of glaucoma and the detection of progression difficult. A number of mathematical, statistical, and data mining methods have been proposed to determine visual field progression [5], [6], [7], [8], [9], [10]. At present, however, there is no universally accepted standard against which to validate them [11]. Different clinical trials use different definitions of "progressing". Nevertheless, all agree that visual field measurement is an essential tool for detecting progression.

Sequence matching techniques have been widely used in applications such as DNA analysis, signal processing, and anomaly detection for computer security [12[, [13]. This study investigates sequence-matching techniques applied to glaucomatous visual fields. This problem is complex becauseS of the noise in the data, and the lack of a universally accepted standard for detecting progression. Hence we propose a method using *baselines* (Section 4) to match a database of stable sequences. The aims of this work are as follows: (1) for a given query sequence, to find the closest matches in a set of reference sequences and then classify the query sequence using the matches; (2) to compare the performance of the new method with the Glaucoma Change Probability (GCP) method that is widely used by clinicians to identify visual field loss.

The rest of this paper is organized as follows. Section 2 briefly describes the standard technique for measuring visual fields. The data sets used in this paper are described in Section 3. Section 4 describes the methods. The results are presented in Section 5, and conclusions are presented in Section 6.

2 Visual Field Measurement

Regular eye tests are essential to detect glaucoma early and prevent significant loss of sight. The Standard Automated Periphery (SAP) test currently employed in glaucoma management requires subjects to place their chins on an immobile stand and fixate on a central spot. Subjects are then asked to press a button whenever they see a flash of light. Lights of varying intensity are shown in each of 76 locations in the visual field. The marginally visible light intensity is recorded as the *threshold sensitivity value*. Each of the 76 locations has a threshold value reported in decibels (dB), printed on a map of the visual field [14]. The threshold values range from 0 to 40 dB. 0 dB indicates that the brightest light could not be seen - in other words, that the location is

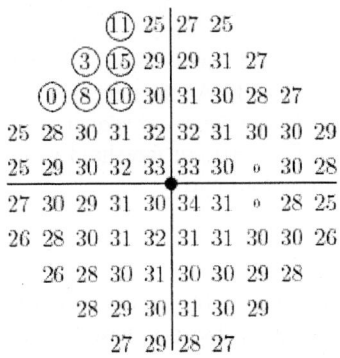

Fig. 1. A map of the 76 locationsin a SAP visual field showing loss in the top left quadrant

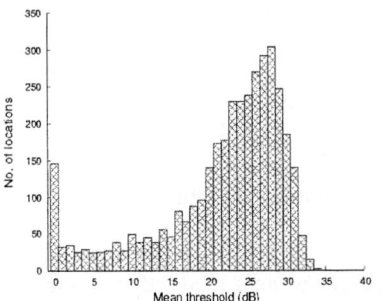

Fig. 2. Distribution of the means of five visual field measurements, at all 74 SAP for 50 subjects. There are relatively few measurements outside the range16–31dB.

blind. Threshold values of 35-40 dB indicate exceptional vision. Figure 1 shows a visual field with localized loss in the top left corner. There are two physiological blind spots, indicated by small zeros. By convention, visual fields of the left eye are reflected into the right eye format.

When visual field measurements are repeated over time, the key task for an ophthalmologist is to determine whether change has occurred. This is a classification problem: each location must be classified as either *non-progressing* (which includes *stable* and *improving*) or *progressing*. Several techniques exist to aid the clinician in this task. The most widely used of these is the Glaucoma Change Probability method described in Section 4.

3 Data

The sequence matching method proposed in this paper is based on a reference database consisting only of stable sequences. To test the method, we used both synthetic and real data. The synthetic data consisted of two artificial datasets to simulate glaucomatous progression and stable glaucoma and are described in the remainder of this section.

3.1 Reference Database

The SAP data in the reference set were taken from 15 subjects with normal eyes and 35 subjects with stable glaucoma. The subjects ranged from 34 to 82 years of age (average, 60.9 years). The first five follow-up visual fields for each subject were used, even in cases where subjects had more than five SAP tests. Hence a total of 250 visual fields were analyzed. The time between tests for patients with stable glaucoma was typically about one week. The test interval for subjects with normal eyes was six months.

Together, these subjects provide $50 \times 74 = 3700$ sequences measured at locations which are known to be stable. For a stable sequence, because of noise in the data the best overall estimate of the threshold value is the mean of the five measurements for that sequence. The distribution of the 3700 means is shown in Figure 2. The data cover the entire range of stable visual field values (0–34dB). All sequences were used to form a reference data set. Let $R = \{S_1, S_2, ..., S_n\}$ denote the set of sequences where $n=3700$, and $S_i = \{y_{i1}, y_{i2}, ..., y_{i5}\}$ ($i =1, 2, ..., 3700$) is a series of threshold values for one location of either a normal eye or a stable glaucomatous eye.

3.2 Simulated Data Sets

Spry *et al* [15], [16] describe an approach to generate stable and progressive sequences using a model that includes short-term fluctuation (location-based noise) and long-term fluctuation (age-based noise). To test the effectiveness of the sequence matching method, we created a synthetic dataset using a simulation similar to that of Spry et al. This provided sequences from individual locations in the visual field, with stable, linear, bilinear, and convex exponential degradation over time.

3.2.1 Progressive Visual Field Data

To simulate progressive visual field data, the first visual fields of 15 normal subjects were randomly distributed into three groups of five. All 15 visual fields were used as the initial values in the simulation. The visual field values in the three groups were then duplicated, but with 12dB, 18dB, or 24dB subtracted from all locations. These new fields were used as the final values. If the final value at any point was less than 0dB then this value was changed to zero. The standard deviation of long-term fluctuation (with normal distribution) was 1dB. The standard deviation of short-term fluctuation was varied as $|x_n - N| \times 0.4/5$ as described by Spry et al [15]. Finally, five new visual fields were interpolated between the initial and the final fields, with average decreases of 2dB, 3dB or 4dB between consecutive fields for the 3 groups respectively. The linear, bilinear and convex exponential procedures were applied to each of the 15 visual fields, providing a total of 45 progressive visual fields.

3.2.2 Stable Visual Field Data

To simulate stable visual field data, the first visual field from each of the 50 real subjects was used as both the first and last values. To generate the middle five visual fields, short-term and long-term fluctuations were used as described above. Thus, 50 virtual eyes with stable glaucoma were generated.

To avoid repetition, the initial and final values were removed from the simulated data. The number of sequences simulated in each group is shown in Table 1.

Table 1. Number of simulated sequences per group (5 patients × 74 locations = 370 sequences)

	Linear	Bilinear	Convex	Total
Progressing 12dB	370	370	370	1110
Progressing 18dB	370	370	370	1110
Progressing 24dB	370	370	370	1110
Stable	3700	0	0	3700
Sum	4810	1110	1110	7030

4 Methods

The 7030 simulated sequences (95 visual fields) were evaluated using the Glaucoma Change Probability (GCP) method described in subsection 4.1, and using the new baseline matching method described in subsection 4.2.

4.1 GCP Method

Given a sequence of n threshold measurements: $X = \{x_1, x_2, ..., x_n\}$, the *baseline* is defined as $(x_1 + x_2)/2$ where x_1 and x_2 were taken in a short period so that no natural decline or glaucomatous progression occurred.

The GCP method calculates the difference between a threshold measurement and a baseline on a point-by-point basis, and then determines whether the difference falls inside or outside the 95% confidence interval established from a set of stable glaucomatous visual fields [17]. If the difference for one location is less than the lower limit of the confidence interval, the location is said to be progressing. If the difference falls inside the confidence interval, the location is said to be stable. Otherwise, it is said to improving.

We present two methods of building a confidence interval by using the reference set R. One method is similar to that used by Spry et al [11], and is as follows.

(1) The mean of all five values in a sequence: $\{x_1 + x_2 + x_3 + x_4 + x_5\}/5$ is calculated, and then rounded to the nearest integer. These integers are used to divide the sequences into groups.
(2) The difference between test and retest values is calculated for each sequence in each group. That is, $x_i - x_{i+1}$, $i = 1, 2, 3, 4$.
(3) The differences in each group are sorted from the smallest to the largest, and then the 2.5% and 97.5% percentiles are computed to form a 95% confidence interval for that group. This method for building a confidence interval is called SA in this paper.

Because there is no consensus as to how the underlying confidence interval should be derived, we modified the second step by taking $(x_1 + x_2)/2 - x_i$, $(i = 3, 4, 5)$ instead of $x_i - x_{i+1}$. This method for building a confidence interval is called SB in this paper.

4.2 Baseline Matching Stable Sequences

Let query $Q = \{x_1, x_2, ..., x_m\}$ be a sequence of values for one location, where x_i is the ith value, and m is the number of measurements. We are unlikely to find a sequence in R to match Q exactly due to noise, and because all reference sequences in R are stable, whereas the query sequence may be progressing. We therefore used a similarity measure D which is calculated as follows:

$$D = |\overline{baseline} - \overline{S_i}| \le cutoff \qquad (1)$$

Where $\overline{S_i}$ is the average of five visual field measurements from a stable sequence, and the baseline is from Q. This function is used to choose the best matching reference sequences in R for the query sequence Q.

The rationale behind this method is that the baseline value for each query sequence Q is an observation of the initial condition, and is subsequently used for comparison with follow-up examinations [14]. For a stable sequence $S_i = \{y_{i1}, y_{i2}, ..., y_{i5}\}$, $\overline{S_i}$ is an unbiased estimate of the population mean at the corresponding location. By using the similarity measure for a given query Q, we select stable sequences that are closest to the baseline of Q. The degree of similarity depends on the cutoff.

For a given cutoff and query Q, we collected all measurements from matched sequences and sorted them from the smallest to the largest. The 2.5% and 97.5% percentiles in this range were calculated to form a 95% interval. If the mth value x_m in Q fell into the 95% interval, the query sequence was said to be stable. If x_m was less than the lower limit of the interval, the query sequence was said to be progressing. Otherwise, the sequence was improving. Improving and stable sequences were classified together as non-progressing. This method is called MH in this paper.

4.3 Experiments

In the experiments, the first interpolated field was taken as the baseline for each query. That is, for a query sequence $Q = \{x_1, x_2, ..., x_m\}$, x_1 was the baseline value.

This study was restricted to baseline values from 16 to 31dB because the stable dataset included only small numbers of sequences outside this range (see Figure 2). The evaluation of an interval requires an adequate sample size, otherwise the classification method may not be reliable [18]. The formula for calculating the required sample size n is:

$$n = Z^2 \times \sigma^2 / E^2 \qquad (2)$$

where E is the maximum allowable error (the difference between the population mean and the sample mean). Z is obtained by using the given confidence interval coefficient, and σ is the population standard deviation. For this study, $E = 1$, $Z = 1.96$ (computed by using $\alpha = 0.95$), and σ is computed using Henson's [19] standard deviation:

$$log_e(\sigma) = -0.081 dB + 3.27 \qquad (3)$$

In equation (1), we used values between 0.1 and 1.0 as the cutoff to select matches in R. The results are examined in Section 5.

5 Results

5.1 Simulated Dataset

Figures 3 and 4 show the results obtained using the new method on the simulated datasets for classifying the *3rd, 4th* and *5th* visual field measurements at different cutoffs. As the cutoff increases, the accuracy of classification also increases for stable sequences, while it decreases for progressing sequences. This is because when the cutoff is less than 0.4, some query sequences cannot get enough points as required by equation (2). For these sequences, the result of classification is not reliable. On the other hand, when the cutoff is greater than 0.6, query sequences may obtain enough points from the matched stable sequences. However, the means of some matched stable sequences are closer to the integer "baseline + 1" or "baseline − 1"[1]. That is, the interval formed by taking all points from matched stable sequences is too wide. When the cutoff is 0.4, the minimum number of points necessary to satisfy equation (2) is 120. Figures 3 and 4 show that when the cutoff is 0.4, 0.5, or 0.6, the results are very similar for the *3rd, 4th* and *5th* visual field measurements.

We used a cutoff of 0.5 to compare the GCP methods. We also used the GCP criteria: (1) for a given location, if progression at this location was identified in two of three consecutive fields (denoted by 2of3), this location was said to be progressing; or (2) in three of three consecutive fields (denoted by 3of3) [21]. The results are shown in Table 2 using five visual field measurements.

---

[1] |baseline − mean| ≤ cutoff ⇒ baseline - cutoff ≤ mean ≤ baseline + cutoff.

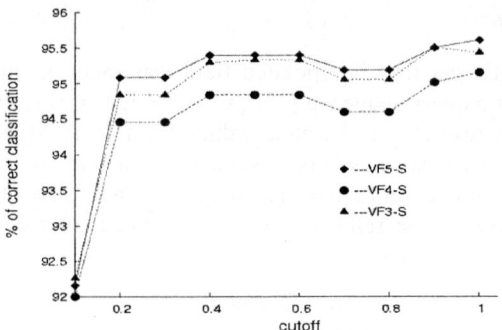

Fig. 3. Percentage correct classification for stable sequences (S) with baseline values from 16 to 31dB at different cutoffs, using the *3rd, 4th* and *5th* visual field measurements

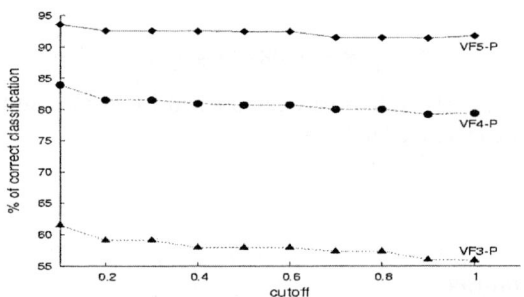

Fig. 4. Percentage correct classification for progressing sequences (P) with baseline values from 16 to 31dB at different cutoffs, using the *3rd, 4th* and *5th* visual field measurements

Table 2. Percentage correct classification for baselines between 16 and 31dB. SA and SB are the GCP methods described in Section 4.1. MH is the method proposed in Section 4.2.

Criterion	SA		SB		MH	
	P	S	P	S	P	S
2of3	68.35	99.06	74.10	98.95	82.72	97.11
3of3	36.24	99.83	41.52	99.79	52.99	99.30

Tables 2 and 3 show that the GCP method using confidence interval SB is statistically significantly more accurate compared with GCP using SA when classifying progressive sequences. The accuracy of GCP with SB in classifying stable sequences decreases slightly, but the loss is not statistically significant. The new method MH is the best for correctly classifying progressing sequences. It increases accuracy by between 8% and 14% compared with GCP using confidence interval SB and SA respectively. It decreases accuracy by less than 2% for detecting stable sequences when GCP criterion (1) was used. When GCP criterion (2) was used, the method offers about 11% and 16% increase respectively for progressing sequences, with about 0.5% decrease for stable sequences.

Table 3. Percentage difference (of correct classification) between methods. Statistically significant differences are underlined ($\alpha<0.05$).

Criterion	Group	SB-SA	MH-SA	MH-SB
2of3	12dB	+<u>7.8</u>	+<u>21.7</u>	+<u>13.9</u>
	18dB	+<u>4.9</u>	+<u>12.1</u>	+<u>7.2</u>
	24dB	+<u>3.8</u>	+<u>7.4</u>	+<u>3.6</u>
	Stable	-0.1	-<u>1.5</u>	-<u>1.4</u>
3of3	12dB	+<u>3.8</u>	+<u>45.4</u>	+<u>41.6</u>
	18dB	+<u>5.9</u>	+<u>48.4</u>	+<u>42.6</u>
	24dB	+<u>5.4</u>	+<u>39.3</u>	+<u>33.9</u>
	Stable	0.0	-<u>2.1</u>	-<u>2.1</u>

5.2 Real Dataset

The proposed method MH and the GCP method using confidence intervals SA and SB described in this paper were also evaluated using a real dataset which differs from the reference dataset R. The difference is that the sequences in the real dataset contained 8 values instead of the 5 used for the simulated dataset. The real dataset consists of 60 progressive and 62 stable patients with 8 visual fields. We used the same GCP criteria for the real dataset: (1) for a given patient, if progression at four or more locations were identified in two of three consecutive fields (denoted by (4, 2of3)), this patient was said to be progressing; or (2) in three of three consecutive fields (denoted by (4, 3of3)) [21]. The results are shown in Table 4 using the first five visual field measurements.

Table 4. Percentage correct classification. SA and SB are confidence intervals described in Section 4.1. MH is the method proposed in Section 4.2.

Criterion	SA		SB		MH	
	P	S	P	S	P	S
(4, 2of3)	45.00	83.87	53.33	79.03	68.33	70.97
(4, 3of3)	11.67	98.39	20.00	96.77	26.67	95.16

Tables 4 shows that the GCP method using confidence interval SA is the most specific and MH is the most sensitive. When using the criterion (4, 2of3), MH offers a 23% increasing for identifying progressive visual fields, decreases 13% for identifying stable visual fields compared with the GCP method using SA. When criterion (4, 3of3) was used, MH offers about 15% increasing for progressing visual fields, with 3% decrease for stable visual fields. When compared with the results obtained from the simulated dataset, the real dataset results show a decrease in accuracy for both the stable and the progressive sequences. This, we believe is due to the significantly larger variability visual field sequences extracted from the real data, and the difference between classification methods based on whole visual field and a location.

6 Conclusion

This paper has described an application of sequence matching to the problem of classifying change in visual field measurements. It is difficult to establish a set of reference sequences that includes progressing sequences because different techniques can give different results for a patient with progressing glaucoma. We have therefore focused on the use of the baseline for a given query sequence. In this way, the set of reference sequences can be constructed only from stable sequences. The sequence matching methods were tested with both synthetic and real datasets. The results indicate that using the new method can significantly improve the accuracy of identifying progressing sequences, though there is a small penalty for stable sequences.

Acknowledgement

This research was supported by the Australian Research Council. The stable visual field data set used for constructing the reference sequences was provided by Prof. Bal Chauhan at Dalhousie University, Canada.

References

1. Mitchell P., Smith W., Attebo K., Healey P.R. Prevalence of Open-Angle Glaucoma in Australia. The Blue Mountains Eye Study. Ophthalmology (1996) 103: 1661-1669
2. Rochtchina E., Mitchell P. Projected Number of Australians with Glaucoma in 2000 and 2030. Clin Experiment Ophthalmol (2000) 28: 146-148
3. Johnson C. A., Sample P. A., Zangwill L. M., et al. Structure and Function Evaluation (SAFE): 2. Comparison of Optic Disk and Visual Field Characteristics. American Journal of Ophthalmology (2003) 135: 148-154
4. Flammer J., Drance S. M., Zulauf M., Differential Light Threshold. Vol. Arch Ophthalmol (1984) 102: 704-706
5. Heijl A., Lindgren G., Olsson J., Asman P. Visual Field Interpretation with Empiric Probability Maps. Arch Ophthalmol (1989) 107: 204-208
6. Katz J., Congdon N., Friedman D. S. Methodological Variations in Estimating Apparent Progressive Visual Field Loss in Clinical Trials of Glaucoma Treatment. Arch Ophthalmol (1999) 117: 1137-1142
7. Lazarescu M., Turpin A. Classifying Glaucomatous Progression using Decision Trees. Proceedings of IASTED International Symposia on Applied Informatics. Innsbruck, Austria (2003) 205-210
8. Lin A., Hoffman D., Gaasterland D. E., Caprioli J. Neural Networks to Identify Glaucomatous Visual Field Progression. Vol. 135. American Journal of Ophthalmology (2003) 49-54
9. Morgan R. K., Feuer W. J., Anderson D. R. Statpac 2 Glaucoma Change Probability. Arch Ophthalmol (1991) 109: 1690-1692
10. Turpin A., Frank E., Hall M., Witten I. H., Johnson C. A. Detecting Progression in Glaucoma using Data Mining Techniques. Proceedings of the 5th Pacific Asia Conference on Knowledge Discovery and Data Mining (2001) 136-147

11. Spry P. G., Johnson C. A., Chauhan B. C. Identification of Progressive Glaucomatous Visual Field Loss. Survey of Ophthalmology (2002) 47: 158-173
12. Lane T., Brodley C. E. Sequence Matching and Learning in Anomaly Detection for Computer Security. AI Approaches to Fraud Detection and Risk Management (Fawcett, Haimowitz, Provost, Stolfo. Eds.) AAAI Press (1997) 43-49
13. Navarro G.. A Guided Tour to Approximate String Matching. ACM Computing Surveys (2001) 33: 31-38
14. Anderson D. R., Patella. V.M. Automated Static Perimetry. Second ed., Mosby (1999)
15. Spry P.G., Bates A.B., Johnson C.A., Chauhan B.C. Simulation of Longitudinal Threshold Visual Field Data. Investigative Ophthalmology and Visual Science. (2000) 41:2192-2200
16. Vesti E., Spry P.G., Chauhan B.C., Johnson C.A. Sensitivity Differences between Real Patient and Computer Stimulated Visual Fields. Journal of Glaucoma (2002) 11:35-45
17. Heijl A., Lindgren A., Lindgren G. Test-Retest Variability in Glaucomatous Visual Fields. American Journal of Ophthalmology (1989) 108:130-135
18. Hughes A., Grawoig D. Statistics: A Foundation for Analysis. Addison-Wesley (1971)
19. Henson D.B., Chaudry S., Artes P.H., Faragher E.B., Ansons A. Response Variability in the Visual Field: Comparison of Optic Neuritis, Glaucoma, Ocular Hypertension, and Normal Eyes. Investigative Ophthalmology and Visual Science (2000) 41:417-421
20. Sheskin D.J. Handbook of Parametric and Nonparametric Statistical Procedures. Second ed., Chapman & Hall/CRC (2000)
21. Vesti E, Johnson C.A., Chauhan B.C. Comparison of Different Methods for Detecting Glaucomatous Visual Field Progression. Investigative Ophthalmology and Visual Science (2003) 44: 38733879

A New Intelligent Diagnostic Method for Machine Maintenance

Qianjin Guo[1,2], Haibin Yu[1], and Aidong Xu[1]

[1] Shenyang Inst. of Automation, Chinese Academy of Sciences,
Shenyang, Liaoning, 110006, China
[2] Graduate School of the Chinese Academy of Sciences,
Beijing 100039, China
guoqianjin@sia.cn

Abstract. Fuzzy neural networks display good capacity for self-adaptation and self-learning, and wavelet transformation or analysis reveals time frequency location characteristics and a multi-scale ability. Inspired by these advantages, a new intelligent diagnostic method for machine maintenance, wavelet fuzzy neural network (WFNN), is proposed in this paper. This new intelligent diagnostic method uses wavelet basis function as a membership function whose shape can be adjusted on line so that the networks have better learning and adaptive ability. An on-line learning algorithm is applied to automatically construct the wavelet fuzzy neural network. There are no rules initially in the wavelet fuzzy neural network, they are created and adapted as on-line learning proceeds via simultaneous structure and parameter learning. The advantages of this learning algorithm are that it converges quickly and the obtained fuzzy rules are more precise. The results of simulation show that this new intelligent diagnostic method has the advantages of a faster learning rate and higher diagnostic precision.

1 Introduction

Recently, artificial intelligence techniques such as expert system, neural network, fuzzy logic and genetic algorithm, have been employed to assist the diagnostic task of correctly interpreting fault data. Motivated by the results in each of these areas and the potential for mutual progress in computational modeling, an integration of these concepts is very important [1]. ANNs and the fuzzy model have been used in many application areas [2-4], and each pairing has its own advantages and disadvantages. Therefore, the main focus of this research is on how to successfully integrate these two approaches, ANNs and fuzzy modeling, for use in machine diagnostic systems.

Generally, the traditional fuzzy system is based on experts' knowledge. However, it is not very objective and it is also very difficult to acquire robust knowledge and find available human experts [6]. Recently, ANN's learning algorithm has been applied to improve the performance of a fuzzy system and has shown itself to be a new and promising approach. Takagi and Hayashi [5] introduced a feedforward ANN into fuzzy inference. Jang [6] proposed a method that transforms the fuzzy inference system into a functional equivalent adaptive network, and then employs the EBP-type algorithm to update the premise parameters and least square method to identify the consequence parameters. Meanwhile, Wang and Mendel [7], Shibata et al. [8], and Fukuda and Shibata [9] also presented similar methods. Nakayama et al. [10] proposed a so-called FNN (fuzzy neural network) that has a special structure for realizing a fuzzy inference system.

In recent years, the wavelet theory [11][12] has received wide attention in the analysis of transient disturbances and signal compression [13][14]. The wavelets transform, with characteristics similar to those of band-filters, decomposing a signal into scales of signals at various resolution levels. Coupled with the timing information, each scale of the signal denotes the distinct frequency contents of the original signal.

The combination of soft computing and wavelet theory has lead to a number of new techniques such as wavelet networks[15], wavelets[16] and fuzzy-wavelet[17]. In this paper, a self-constructing wavelet based fuzzy neural network approach (SWFNN) is introduced as a new research direction of intelligent monitoring and fault detection for Condition Based Maintenance. The structure and the parameter learning phases are created concurrently and on-line in the SWFNN. The advantages of this learning algorithm are that it converges quickly and the obtained fuzzy rules are more precise.

2 Architecture of the Neural Network

The basic configuration of the SWFNN system includes a fuzzy rule base, which consists of a collection of fuzzy IF-THEN rules in the following form:

$$R^l : \text{IF } x_1 \text{ is } F_1^l \text{ and ... and } x_n \text{ is } F_n^l \text{ THEN } y_1 \text{ is } G_1^l \text{ and ... and } y_m \text{ is } G_m^l \quad (1)$$

where R^l is the lth rule ($1 \leq l \leq M$), $\{x_i\}_{i=1,...,n}$ are input variables, and $\{y_j\}_{j=1,...,m}$ are the output variables of the SWFNN system, respectively, F_i^l are the labels of the fuzzy sets characterized by the membership functions(MF) $\mu_{F_i^l}(x_i)$, and G_l^l are the labels of the fuzzy sets in the output space. The semantic meaning and function of the neurons in the proposed fuzzy neural network are as follows.

Layer 1 (input layer): For every node i in this layer, the net input and the net output are related by:

$$I_i^{(1)} = x_i \quad (2)$$

$$O_i^{(1)} = I_i^{(1)} \quad i = 1, 2, ..., m, \quad (3)$$

where $I_i^{(1)}$ and $O_i^{(1)}$ denote, respectively, the input and output of ith neuron in layer 1.

Layer 2 (membership layer): In this layer, each neuron represents the membership function of a linguistic variable. The most commonly used membership functions are in shape of a triangle, trapezoid and bell, etc. In this paper, the wavelet basis function is adopted as the membership function, and five fuzzy sets (very small, small, medium, large, and very large) are used for the above-mentioned fuzzy diagnostic rules. For the jth term neuron associated with $O_i^{(1)}$:

$$\mu(x_i) = \psi_{a_{ij},b_{ij}}(x_i) = \psi\left(\frac{x_i - b_{ij}}{a_{ij}}\right) = \cos(0.25 \cdot \frac{x_i - b_{ij}}{a_{ij}}) \cdot \exp\left[-\frac{(x_i - b_{ij})^2}{2a_{ij}^2}\right] \quad (4)$$

where $i=1,2,\ldots,m$; $j=1,2,\ldots,p$, p ($p=5$) represents the number of linguistic values for each input, a_{ij} and b_{ij} are a dilation parameter and translation parameter accordingly.

In this layer the relation between the input and output is represented as:

Net input: $I_{ij}^{(2)} = O_i^{(1)}$ (5)

Net output: $O_{ij}^{(2)} = \mu_{ij}(I_{ij}^{(2)}) = \cos(0.25 \cdot \frac{O_i^{(1)} - b_{ij}}{a_{ij}}) \cdot \exp\left[-\frac{(O_i^{(1)} - b_{ij})^2}{2a_{ij}^2}\right]$ (6)

where $i=1,2,\ldots,m$; $j=1,2,\ldots,p$.

Layer 3 (rule layer): The input and output of the nodes in this layer are both numerical. The links in this layer perform precondition matching of fuzzy logic rules. Hence, the rule nodes should perform the fuzzy AND operation. The most commonly used fuzzy AND operations are intersection and algebraic product [3,4]. If intersection is used, we have:

$$O_i^{(3)} = \min(O_1^{(2)}, O_2^{(2)}, \ldots, O_i^{(2)}) \quad (7)$$

On the other hand, if algebraic product is used, we have:

$$O_i^{(3)} = O_1^{(2)} O_2^{(2)} \ldots O_i^{(2)} \quad (8)$$

Each node in this layer is denoted by Π, which multiplies the incoming signal and outputs the result of the product, and the relation between the input and output is represented as:

Net input: $I_i^{(3)} = O_{1i_2}^{(2)} * O_{2i_2}^{(2)} * \ldots * O_{mi_m}^{(2)} = \min\{O_{1i_2}^{(2)}, O_{2i_2}^{(2)}, \ldots, O_{mi_m}^{(2)}\}$ (9)

Net output: $O_i^{(3)} = I_i^{(3)}$, (10)

where $i=1,2,\ldots,s$, $s = \prod_{i=1}^{m} p^m = \prod_{i=1}^{m} 5^m$

Layer 4 (defuzzifier layer) is the output layer of the consequent network. Nodes in this layer represent the output variables of the system. Each node acts as a defuzzifier and computes the output value.

Net input: $I_{i,k}^{(4)} = \sum_{j=1}^{s} W_{ij} O_j^{(3)}$ (11)

Net output: $Y_i = O_i^{(4)} = I_i^{(4)}$ $i=1,2,\ldots,n$ (12)

where W_{ij} are the connection weights, Y_i represents the ith output to the node of layer 4.

3 Training Algorithms for the Neural Network

Two phases of learning, structure learning and parameter learning, are used for constructing the neurofuzzy network. In the first phase the structure learning algorithm is used to find proper fuzzy partitions in the input space and create fuzzy logic rules. In the second phase all parameters are tuned using a supervised learning scheme. The backpropagation algorithm to minimize a given cost function adjusts the weights in the consequent part and the parameters of membership functions. There are no rules (i.e., no nodes in the network except the input–output nodes) in the SWFNN initially. They are created dynamically and automatically as learning proceeds upon receiving on-line incoming training data by performing the structure and parameter learning processes. The procedure of the structure/parameter learning algorithm is through inputting the training pattern to learn successively. Then, we can gain proper rules.

3.1 The Structure Learning Algorithm

The proposition of the structure learning algorithm is to decide proper fuzzy partitions by the input patterns. The procedure of our structure learning algorithm is to find the proper fuzzy logic rules. However, the structure learning algorithm determines whether or not to add a new node in layer 2 via the input pattern data, and decides whether or not to add the associated fuzzy logic rule in layer 3.

After the input pattern is entered in layer 2, the firing strength of the wavelet based membership function will be obtained from Equation (4), and is used as the degree measure $\mu_{F_i^j}$. For computational efficiency, we can use the firing strength obtained from $\prod \mu_{F_i^j}$ directly as the precondition part's degree measure.

$$P = \prod_{j=1}^{R(t)} \mu_{F_i^j} \quad (13)$$

where i is input dimension, $i = 1,\ldots,m; j$ is rule number, $j=1,\ldots,R(t), R(t)$ is the number of existing rules at time t.

Using this degree measure, we can obtain the following criterion for the generation of a new fuzzy rule of new incoming data. The method is described as follows:

Preset a positive threshold $P_{min} \in (0,1)$ that decays during the learning process. Find the maximum degree P_{max}

$$P_{max} = \max_{1 \leq j \leq R(t)} P_j \quad (14)$$

where $R_{(t)}$ is the number of existing rules at time t.

If $P_{max} \leq P_{min}$, the structure learning needs to add a new node in the SWFNN, and a new rule is generated. Once a new rule is generated, the next step is to assign initial mean and variance of the new membership function. Since our goal is to minimize an objective function, the mean and variance are all adjustable later in the parameter learning phase. Hence the mean and variance deviation of the new membership function are set as follows:

$$a_{ij}^{(R_{(t+1)})} = x_i \quad (15)$$

$$\sigma_{ij}^{(R_{(t+1)})} = \sigma_{init} \quad (16)$$

where x_i is the new input pattern; σ_{init} is preset constant; i is input dimension; j is rule number. To avoid the newly generated membership function being too similar to the existing one, the similarities between the new membership function and existing ones must be checked. If the new fuzzy rule is different to the existing fuzzy rule, we confirm the new fuzzy rule would be added in the SWFNN. It can improve the performance of the neural fuzzy inference system. Therefore, we use the similarity measure of membership functions to estimate the rule's similarity degree. Suppose the fuzzy sets to be measured are fuzzy sets A and B with membership function $\mu_A(x) = \psi((x-m_1)/\sigma_1)$ and $\mu_B(x) = \psi((x-m_2)/\sigma_2)$, respectively. Assume $m2 \geq m1$ as in [11], we can compute $|A \cap B|$ by:

$$|A \cap B| = \frac{1}{2} \cdot \frac{h^2(m_2 - m_1 + (\sigma_2 + \sigma_1)\sqrt{\pi})}{(\sigma_2 + \sigma_1)\sqrt{\pi}} + \frac{1}{2} \cdot \frac{h^2(m_2 - m_1 + (\sigma_1 - \sigma_2)\sqrt{\pi})}{(\sigma_2 - \sigma_1)\sqrt{\pi}} + \frac{1}{2} \cdot \frac{h^2(m_2 - m_1 + (\sigma_2 - \sigma_1)\sqrt{\pi})}{(\sigma_1 - \sigma_2)\sqrt{\pi}} \quad (17)$$

where $h(x) = max\{0, x\}$. So the approximate similarity measure of fuzzy sets is:

$$E(A,B) = \frac{|A \cap B|}{|A \cup B|} = \frac{|A \cap B|}{\frac{1}{2}(\sigma_1 + \sigma_2)\sqrt{\pi} - |A \cap B|} \quad (18)$$

where we use the fact that $|A| + |B| = |A \cap B| + |A \cup B|$.

The similarity measure E between the new membership function and all existing ones is calculated and the maximum one E_{max} is found as follows:

$$E_{max} = \max_{1 \leq j \leq M(t)} E(\mu(a_{new}, \sigma_{new}), \mu(a_j, \sigma_j)) \quad (19)$$

If $E_{max} \leq E_{min}$, where $E_{min} \in (0,1)$ is a prespecified value, then the new fuzzy logic rule is adopted and the rule number is incremented:

$$M = M + 1 \quad (20)$$

Therefore, the new mean, deviation and link weight are generated randomly.

3.2 The Parameter Learning Algorithm

In general, an efficient learning algorithm must have fast learning as well as good computational capacity and generalization capacity. Here, the backpropagation learning algorithm with adaptive learning rate is introduced. The adaptive learning rate guarantees the convergence and speeds up the learning. The task of the learning algorithm for this architecture is to tune all the modifiable parameters, namely wavelet node parameters, a, b and SWFNN weights, w_{jk}, to make the SWFNN output match the training data. The cost function can be written as:

$$E = \frac{1}{2}(D - Y)^T(D - Y) \quad (21)$$

where D is the desired output acquired from specialists, and Y is the SWFNN's current output. For the multi-output case, $Y = [y_1, y_2,..., y_n]$.

According to the gradient descent method, the weights in the output layer are updated by the following equation:

$$\Delta W_{ij} = -\frac{\partial E}{\partial W_{ij}} = -\frac{\partial E}{\partial O_i^{(4)}} \cdot \frac{\partial O_i^{(4)}}{\partial I_i^{(4)}} \cdot \frac{\partial I_i^{(4)}}{\partial W_{ij}} = (D_i - Y_i) \cdot O_j^{(3)} \qquad (22)$$

where $i=1,2,\ldots,n;\ j=1,2,\ldots,s$.

The weights of the output layer are updated according to the following equation:

$$W_{ij}(t+1) = W_{ij}(t) + \eta \cdot \Delta W_{ij} = W_{ij} + \eta \cdot (D_i - Y_i) \cdot O_j^{(3)} \qquad (23)$$

where η is the learning-rate parameter.

The selection of the mother wavelet is very important and depends on the particular application. There are a number of well-defined mother wavelets such as Morlet, Harr, Mexican Hat, and Meyer. Groups of them are called families, such as Daubechies, Biorthogonals, Coiflets, and Symmlets [18]. For this wavelet fuzzy neural network, Morlet wavelet has been chosen to serve as an adoption basis function to the network's hidden layer, which has been the preferred choice in most work dealing with WNN, due to its simple explicit expression.

$$\psi_{a,b}(t) = \cos(0.25\, t_z) e^{-\frac{t_z^2}{2}} \qquad (24)$$

where $t_z = \left(\dfrac{t-b}{a}\right)$

$$\psi_{a,b}'(t) = -\left(0.25\sin(0.25 t_z)\exp(-\frac{t_z^2}{2}) + \cos(0.25 t_z)\exp(-\frac{t_z^2}{2}) t_z\right) \qquad (25)$$

such that

$$\Delta a_{ij} = -\frac{\partial E}{\partial a_{ij}} = -\frac{\partial E}{\partial O_i^{(4)}} \cdot \frac{\partial O_i^{(4)}}{\partial I_i^{(4)}} \cdot \frac{\partial I_i^{(4)}}{\partial O_k^{(3)}} \cdot \frac{\partial O_k^{(3)}}{\partial I_k^{(3)}} \cdot \frac{\partial I_k^{(3)}}{\partial O_{ij}^{(2)}} \cdot \frac{\partial O_{ij}^{(2)}}{\partial I_{ij}^{(2)}} \cdot \frac{\partial I_{ij}^{(2)}}{\partial a_{ij}}$$

$$= 2\sum_l\left[(D_l - Y_l) \cdot \sum_{k,k_1,k_2,\ldots,k_n}(Q_{l_k} * \ldots * Q_{l-1k_{l-1}} * Q_{l+1k_{l+1}} * \ldots * Q_{mk_m}) \cdot W_{lk}\right] \cdot \exp\left[-\frac{(Q^{(1)}-b_{ij})^2}{2 q_{ij}^2}\right] \cdot \frac{Q^{(1)}-b_{ij}}{q_{ij}^2} \cdot \left[0.25\sin(0.25 \cdot \frac{Q^{(1)}-b_{ij}}{q_{ij}}) + \cos(0.25 \cdot \frac{Q^{(1)}-b_{ij}}{q_{ij}})\right] \cdot \frac{Q^{(1)}-b_{ij}}{q_{ij}} \qquad (26)$$

$$\Delta b_{ij} = -\frac{\partial E}{\partial b_{ij}} = -\frac{\partial E}{\partial O_i^{(4)}} \cdot \frac{\partial O_i^{(4)}}{\partial I_i^{(4)}} \cdot \frac{\partial I_i^{(4)}}{\partial O_k^{(3)}} \cdot \frac{\partial O_k^{(3)}}{\partial I_k^{(3)}} \cdot \frac{\partial I_k^{(3)}}{\partial O_{ij}^{(2)}} \cdot \frac{\partial O_{ij}^{(2)}}{\partial I_{ij}^{(2)}} \cdot \frac{\partial I_{ij}^{(2)}}{\partial b_{ij}}$$

$$= 2\sum_l\left[(D_l - Y_l) \cdot \sum_{k,k_1,k_2,\ldots,k_n}(Q_{l_k} * \ldots * Q_{l-1k_{l-1}} * Q_{l+1k_{l+1}} * \ldots * Q_{mk_m}) \cdot W_{lk}\right] \cdot \exp\left[-\frac{(Q^{(1)}-b_{ij})^2}{2 q_{ij}^2}\right] \cdot \frac{1}{q_{ij}} \cdot \left[0.25\sin(0.25 \cdot \frac{Q^{(1)}-b_{ij}}{q_{ij}}) + \cos(0.25 \cdot \frac{Q^{(1)}-b_{ij}}{q_{ij}})\right] \cdot \frac{Q^{(1)}-b_{ij}}{q_{ij}} \qquad (27)$$

The wavelet node parameters are then updated as follows:

$$a_{ij}(t+1) = a_{ij}(t) + \eta \Delta a_{ij} \qquad (28)$$

$$b_{ij}(t+1) = b_{ij}(t) + \eta \Delta b_{ij} \qquad (29)$$

where η is the learning rate. We let the learning rate η vary to improve the speed of convergence, as well as the learning performance (accuracy).

4 Experiments for Machine Maintenance

Experiments were performed on a machinery fault simulator, which can simulate the most common faults, such as misalignment, unbalance, resonance, radial rubbing, oil whirling and so on. The schematic of the test apparatus mainly consists of a motor, a coupling, bearings, discs and a shaft etc.

In this system, the rotor is driven by an electromotor, and the bearing is the journal bearing. The fault samples are obtained by simulating a corresponding fault on the experiment rotating system. For example, adjusting the simulator plane highness and degree simulates the misalignment faults; adding an unbalance weight on the disc at the normal condition creates an unbalance. A radial acceleration was picked up from an accelerometer located at the top of the right bearing housing. The shaft speed was obtained by one laser speedometer. The measurements of acceleration, velocity, or displacement data from rotating equipment are acquired by the NI digital signal acquisition module, and then are collected into an embedded controller. A total of six conditions were tested: resonance, stable condition after resonance, bearing housing looseness, misalignment, oil whirling, and unbalance. Each condition was measured with a given times continuously. The frequency of used signal is 5000Hz and the number of sampled data is 1024.

4.1 Feature Extraction

The features of vibration signals are extracted with wavelet packet analysis and FFT, the time-frequency spectrum of data is computed and fed into the training stage, in which six faults and seven frequency bounds are selected to form a feature vector. These feature vectors are used as input and output of the wavelet based fuzzy neural network.

4.2 Fault Diagnosis and Analysis

4.2.1 Experimental Data Sets

The network architecture used for fault diagnosis consists of seven inputs corresponding to the seven different ranges of the frequency spectrum of a fault signal and six outputs corresponding to six respective faults, such as unbalance, misalignment, oil whirling, oil oscillating, radial rubbing and twin looseness.

In the experiment, 200 groups of feature data are acquired on a machinery fault simulator; 50 groups of feature data are used as the training set and the remaining 150 groups are used as the diagnostic set samples. Feature vectors are used as the input and output of neural networks.

After all possible normal operating modes of the fault are learned, the system enters the fault diagnosis stage, in which the machinery vibration data are obtained and are subjected to the pre-processing and feature extraction methods described in the signal processing and feature extraction stage.

4.2.2 Fuzzy Sets and Fuzzy Control Rules

Described in Section 2, five fuzzy sets are used for fuzzy diagnostic rules, corresponding to very small, small, medium, large and very large (labeled as VS, S, M, L and VL respectively). Morlet wavelet function is chosen as the membership function for these five fuzzy sets. Here, the five fuzzy sets for the input and output linguistic variables of the SWFNN diagnostic system have both been designed in the same range of [0,1] (shown in Fig. 1). Once the shape of the fuzzy sets is given (shown in Fig. 1), the relationship between input and output variables of the SWFNN based diagnostic system is defined by a set of linguistic statements that are called fuzzy rules. The corresponding fault diagnosis rules are listed in table 1.

Table 1. The learned fuzzy logic rules for fault diagnosis

Rules	$<0.40\omega_0$	$0.4\sim0.5\omega_0$	$0.51\sim0.99\omega_0$	$1\omega_0$	$2\omega_0$	$3\sim5\omega_0$	$>5\omega_0$	Conclusions
If	VS	VS	VS	VL	VS	VS	VS	Unbalance
If	VS	VS	VS	L	VL	VS	VS	Misalignment
If	VS	L	VS	VL	VS	VS	VS	Oil whirling
If	VS	VL	VS	VL	VL	VS	VS	Oil oscillating
If	S	S	S	VL	S	S	S	Radial rubbing
If	VS	VS	VS	S	S	M	S	Twin looseness

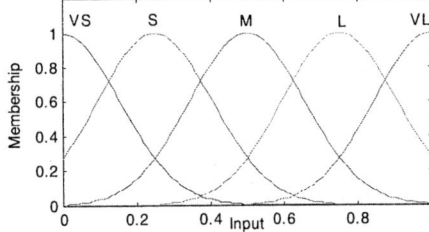 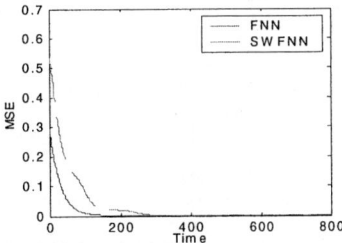

Fig. 1. The membership functions of the input linguistic value "very small"(X1), "small"(X2), "large"(X3) in Example.

Fig. 2. Convergence curves for SWFNN and FNN

4.2.3 Performance of the Fuzzy Network-Based Diagnostic System (Network Training and Determination)

To demonstrate the performance of the SWFNN-based approach on fault classification, comparisons are made with other types of artificial neural networks, namely fuzzy neural networks, wavelet neural networks and BP networks. Both the WNN networks and BP networks have three layers with seven inputs corresponding to the seven sources of information, and six outputs corresponding to the six faults considered, the number of hidden neurons was fixed at ten, and the MSE function is the same as Equation (21). Expecting output error threshold is 0.001, and training processes terminate in given fitness evaluation times. In all experiments, each experiment was run 50 times for given iterations, and the results were averaged to account for stochastic difference.

Fig.2, Fig.3 and Fig.4 demonstrate the training history and the performance of the SWFNN, FNN, WNN and BP networks by using the GD algorithm respectively. By looking at the shapes of the curves in Figure 2, it is easy to see the SWFNN trained with GD algorithm (with average 720 epochs) converges more quickly than the FNN trained with GD (with average 800 epochs). By looking at the shapes of the curves in Figure 3, it is easy to see the SWFNN trained with GD algorithm converges more quickly than the WNN trained with GD (with average 1550 epochs). As seen in Figure 4, it is clear that the simulation time obtained by the SWFNN trained with GD algorithm is comparatively less compared to the BP networks trained with GD algorithm (with average 2490 epochs).

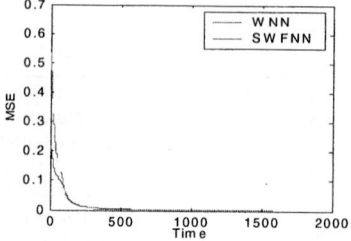
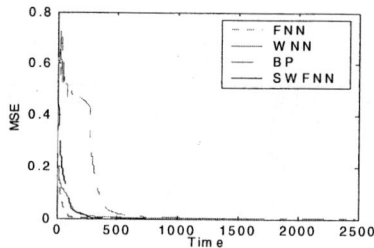

Fig. 3. Convergence curves for SWFNN and WNN

Fig. 4. Convergence curves for SWFNN, FNN, WNN and BP

Table 2. Comparisons of WFNN, WNN and BP method

Method	Diagnosis accuracy (%)	Sum error	Epochs
BP	90.67	0.001	2490
WNN	95.33	0.001	1550
FNN	96.67	0.001	800
SWFNN	98.67	0.001	720

Table 2 shows the comparison results of SWFNN, FNN, WNN and BP methods on the fault diagnosis. The second column in this table lists the diagnostic accuracy on the 150 actual sample data. The third column in this table lists the average number of error function evaluations used during training, until running terminated with the network converged or the epochs exceeding the maximum epochs. Compared with the BP method, the SWFNN method has 8.0% improvement in diagnostic accuracy; compared with the WNN method, the SWFNN method has 3.34% improvement on the diagnostic accuracy, and compared with the FNN method, the SWFNN method has 2.00% improvement on the diagnostic accuracy. The test results confirm that, in all compared cases, the proposed SWFNN method has a better capability for generalization than the other methods.

From the comparison of various methods, it can be seen that the SWFNN method outperformed all the other architectures. The SWFNN architecture is decidedly superior, yielding errors that are smaller than the FNN, WNN and BP architecture. Another benefit of the SWFNN approach is the reduced training time.

5 Conclusions

A novel online self-constructing wavelet based fuzzy network for fault diagnosis has been proposed. The SWFNN network synergistically integrates the standard fuzzy inference system and a one-pass supervised learning concept of neural networks. Morlet wavelet functions are used as the membership functions in the antecedent parts of the fuzzy inference system. The network has been validated using the fault diagnosis data sets. The results have shown that an SWFNN based diagnostic system has better trainsing performance, a faster convergence rate, and a better diagnostic ability than the other modules selected.

References

1. Kosko, B.: Neural Networks and Fuzzy Systems Ð A Dynamical Systems Approach to Machine Intelligence. Prentice-Hall, Englewood Cli.s. NJ.992.
2. Lee, C.C.:Fuzzy logic in control systems: fuzzy logic controller: part I, IEEE Transactions on Systems, Man, and Cybernetics.20 (1990)404- 418.
3. Lee, C.C.: Fuzzy logic in control systems: fuzzy logic controller: part II, IEEE Transactions on Systems, Man, and Cybernetics.20 (1990)419- 435.
4. Liu, P.: Universal approximations of continuous fuzzy-valued functions by multilayer regular fuzzy neural networks. Fuzzy Sets and Systems. 119 (2001)313-320.
5. Takagi,T.,Hayashi,I.: NN-driven fuzzy reasoning.Internat.J. Approx. Reasoning.5 (1991) 191-212.
6. Jang ,J.-S.R.:Fuzzy controller design without domain expert, IEEE Inter. Conf. on Fuzzy Systems. (1992)289-296.
7. Wang,L.-X., Mendel,J.M.: Back-propagation fuzzy system as nonlinear dynamic system identifiers. IEEE Internat. Conf. on Fuzzy Systems, (1992)1409-1418.
8. Shibata,T., Fukuda,T., K. Kosuge, F. Arai: Skill based control by using fuzzy neural network for hierarchical intelligent control. Proc. IJCNN. (1992) 81-86.
9. Fukuda,T., Shibata,T.:Hierarchical intelligent control for robotic motion by using fuzzy. artificial intelligence, and neural network, Proc. IJCNN'92.(1992)269-274.
10. Nakayama,S., Horikawa, Furuhashi,S., T., Uchikawa,Y.: Knowledge acquisition of strategy and tactics using fuzzy neural networks, Proc. IJCNN'92, (1992) 751-756.
11. Daubechies,I.: The wavelet transform, time–frequency localization, and signal analysis. IEEE Trans. Inform. Theoryl. 36(1990) 961–1005.
12. Mallat,S.:A theory for multi-resolution signal decomposition: The wavelet representation. IEEE Trans. Pattern Anal. Machine Intell. 11(1989) 674–693.
13. Pillay,P., Bhattachariee,A.:Application of wavelets to model short-term power system disturbances. IEEE Trans. Power Syst.. 11(1996)2031–2037.
14. Santoso,S., Powers ,E. J., Grady, W. M.:Power quality disturbance data compression usingwavelet transform methods. IEEE Trans. Power Delivery. 12(1997)1250–1257.
15. Zhang,Q., Benveniste,A.:Wavelet networks. IEEE Trans. On Neural Networks.3 (1992)889-898.
16. Thuillard, M.:Applications of wavelets and wavenets in soft computing illustrated with the example of fire detectors. SPIE Wavelet Applications VII, April 24-28 2000 (Orlando), in press (2000b).
17. Ho,D.W.C., Zhang,P.-A., Xu,J.: Fuzzy Wavelet Networks for Function Learning. IEEE Transactions on Fuzzy Systems.9(2001) 200-211.
18. Misiti, M., Misiti Y et al: Wavelet Toolbox User's Guide, The Math Works Inc, 1996.

Prediction of Human Behaviour Using Artificial Neural Networks

Zhicheng Zhang[1], Frédéric Vanderhaegen[2], and Patrick Millot[2]

[1] Division of I&C and Electrical Systems, Framatome ANP,
Tour Areva, 92084 Paris La Defense Cedex, France
zhicheng.zhang@framatome-anp.com
[2] CNRS UMR 8530, Laboratoire d'Automatique,
de Mécanique et d'Informatique industrielles et Humaines, University of Valenciennes,
Le Mont Houy, 59313 Valenciennes Cedex 9, France
{vanderhaegen, millot}@univ-valenciennes.fr

Abstract. This paper contributes to the analysis and prediction of deviate intentional behaviour of human operators in Human-Machine Systems using Artificial Neural Networks that take uncertainty into account. Such deviate intentional behaviour is a particular violation, called Barrier Removal. The objective of the paper is to propose a predictive Benefit-Cost-Deficit model that allows a multi-reference, multi-factor and multi-criterion evaluation. Human operator evaluations can be uncertain. The uncertainty of their subjective judgements is therefore integrated into the prediction of the Barrier Removal. The proposed approach is validated on a railway application, and the prediction convergence of the uncertainty-integrating model is demonstrated.

1 Introduction

The study of human factors plays an increasingly important role in the design of new complex Human-Machine Systems (HMS) or in the updating of older systems. Behaviours that deviate from a given prescription are interpreted as errors when the behaviors or their consequences are not intentional, and as violations when they are intentional [1]. Though human error has received close attention for about a century, the study of intentional violations is still in its early stages [2]. The awareness of the importance of taking safety violations into account in the risk analysis process increased after the Chernobyl accident. According to J. Reason, five of the seven human actions that led directly to the accident were deliberate deviations from written rules and instructions, rather than slips, lapses or mistakes. As a matter of fact, though violations have been mentioned in a number of contexts, research on violations is still insignificant compared to research about slips, lapses, and rule & knowledge-based mistakes.

This paper takes a connectionist approach that allows uncertainty to be taken into account when analyzing and predicting the deviate intentional behavior (violations) of the human operators in an HMS. The following section of the paper presents our predictive Benefit-Cost-Deficit (BCD) model. The third section proposes an uncertainty-based prediction approach to Barrier Removal (BR) using Artificial Neural Networks.

In the fourth section, the validation of this approach on a railway simulator experiment is described and the convergence of the uncertainty-based predictions is discussed. The final section presents our conclusions and offers perspectives for future research.

2 A Three-Dimentional BCD Model

In an HMS, human operator actions are initially delimited by such boundaries as cost acceptability, available resources and acceptable safety practices (Figure 1).

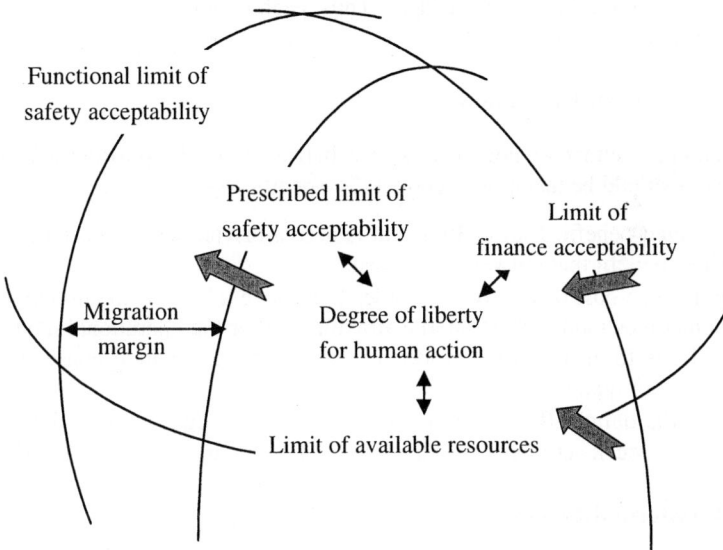

Fig. 1. Human behavioural boundaries

How much these boundaries can migrate depends on the maximum functional limits that users of a given system can accept in all safety. Human operators continually manage a compromise between three joint and sometimes contradictory objectives: performance objectives imposed by the organization or by the operators themselves, safety objectives for the system and for the operator, and objectives related to the cognitive and physiological costs of operator activities (e.g., workload, stress). These objectives limit and bound the field of human actions. An action that crosses the set boundaries can lead to loss of control, an incident, or even an accident. In this paper, any action that crosses a boundary is called a Barrier Removal (BR). BR are specific violations, made without any intention of subjectively damaging the HMS, and may indicate that system designers and system users accept divergent degrees of risk. The analysis of system user's activities is three-dimensional: the reference-based, the BCD factor-based and the criteria-based dimensions to identify and analyze the benefits, costs and potential deficit generated by BR within a BCD framework.

2.1 Multi-reference BR Evaluation

There are often differences between the task prescribed by the designer and the actual activity in its operational context, due to a variety of individual, technical and/or environmental factors. For HMS designers, risk analysis is usually limited to assessing safety risks, which is a mono-criterion process. Once the machine is operating on-site, the validation process stops evolving and remains quite stable since the process was the result of a common decision. However, this type of designer-based risk evaluation is done independently of the users and is limited to the technical failures. Users, on the other hand, control the risks associated with operational situations by evaluating them after they are detected and by intervening in the piloted process to avoid their occurrence or to limit their consequences. Thus, each operational BR is motivated by several factors.

2.2 Multi-factor BR Evaluation

When deciding whether or not to remove a barrier, both the positive and negative consequences should be taken into account [3], specifically:

- The expected benefit: Barrier Removal is a goal-driven behavior seen to offer an immediate benefit that outweighs the cost.
- The immediate cost of removal: In order to remove a barrier, the human operator must sometimes modify the material structure and/or the operational mode, which usually leads to an increased workload and can have negative consequences on productivity or quality.
- The potential deficit: Because removing a barrier introduces a potentially dangerous situation, such actions creates a potential deficit, due to the related risk.

2.3 Multi-criteria BR Evaluation

Evaluating operational BR is more or less a multi-criteria risk control process that takes into account not only system safety criteria, but also economic criteria (e.g., production and quality) or social criteria (e.g., motivation or workload). Since it depends on the variability of the operational situations to be controlled, as well as on inter- and intra-individual differences, this risk control process is dynamic and variable. Moreover, it can be used to evaluate a variety of elements, such as technical failures, human and organisational errors, and violations, to name only a few.

During BR analysis, all three factors mentioned above (Benefit, Cost, potential Deficit) are evaluated for each barrier class in terms of several performance criteria, making it complicated to identify the removal status of a barrier directly and/or to easily group similar BRs together. Clearly, determining the complex nonlinear relationships that exist between the different criteria is not easy, nor is identifying the similaries/proximities of all BRs. In fact, BR analysis is a two-phase process. First, all BRs must be classified in terms of the various performance criteria, and if possible, the contributive BR criteria for a given HMS must be identified by looking for and memorizing the similarities/proximities of all BRs. Second, the likelihood of the new/changed barriers being removed must be predicted, according to the identified criteria and the memorized similarities/proximities.

Artificial Neural Networks have the potential to accomplish the above tasks. A series of approaches for predicting Barrier Removal using ANN have already been developed to anticipate or predict the removal of a given barrier in a given system using the retained criteria by either considering a network according to one performance criterion (mono-performance) or by considering a network according to several performance criteria (multi-performance) [4]. Based on these connectionist models and methods (i.e. mono-performance ANN and multi-performance ANN), the uncertainty of subjective human operator evaluations can be analyzed and processed, allowing it to be integrated in the overall prediction methodology.

3 A Connectionist BCD Model and Prediction with Uncertainty

As stated above, BR is a safety-related violation. Its impact can be analyzed in terms of benefits, costs, and potential deficits. In order to allow designers to integrate BR into the risk analysis during the design phase or during re-design work, we have already proposed three Self-Organizing Map (SOM) predictive algorithms [5] used to model the activation or the removal of barriers by the human operators. Designers conceive their systems according to the pertinent regulations, standards and technical guidelines, paying particular attentions to safety concerns. They equip their systems with barriers in order to reduce human errors, limit failure propagation and/or protect human operators from technical failures.

However, particular operational contexts require the definition of a series of connectionist models and BR methods using ANN that allow the different contexts to be dealt with and still obtain optimal results. Like an artificial neural network, the Self-Organizing Map was originally designed for multidimensional data reduction with topology-preserving properties [6]. The proposed connectionist methods were thus validated through experimental manipulation designed to analyse and/or predict the removal of a given barrier in a given system by integrating both the subjectivity and the uncertainty of operator BCD evaluations and by considering both mono-performance and multi-performance approaches.

Each evaluation of a BR factor incorporates a certain degree of uncertainty. Factor evaluations with different uncertainty levels may have different numbers of subsets, and thus weights should be allocated to each subset element, respectively. Different weight allocations can be defined, for example:

- The lower the uncertainty level, the more representative the given value, making the associated weight high.
- The lower the uncertainty level, the less numerous the values in the corresponding subset.
- The closer a value is to the one evaluated by the human operator, the less its weight differs from the evaluated one.
- The sum of the attributed weights is equal to 1.

Once the weight allocations have been defined, the subsets of all the factor evaluations can be combined. Table 1 illustrates the final format of BR data for which uncertainty has been factored in.

Table 1. The final format of BR data with uncertainty

		Barrier Removal Factors					
		Benefit		Cost		Potential Deficit	
		Evaluation	Uncertainty	Evaluation	Uncertainty	Evaluation	Uncertainty
	Criterion 1	Variable 1	Variable 2	Variable 3	Variable 4	Variable 5	Variable 6
	Criterion 2	Variable 7	Variable 8	Variable 9	Variable 10	Variable 11	Variable 12
Performance criteria	Criterion 3	Variable 13	Variable 14	Variable 15	Variable 16	Variable 17	Variable 18
	Criterion 4	Variable 19	Variable 20	Variable 21	Variable 22	Variable 23	Variable 24
	……	……	……	……	……	……	……

As mentioned above, the human operators' evaluation of the BR factors incorporates a degree of uncertainty, and thus the uncertainty data must be pre-processed in order to create cases or scenarios for which all the BCD values and their associated uncertainties appear linearly for each criterion. For each case or scenario, an additional data element is required: the boolean value of the BR, which indicates whether or not the corresponding barrier was removed. Figure 2 shows the basic uncertainty-based BR prediction process.

Each predictive network has two phases: a learning phase and a prediction phase. During the first phase, the learning needed for BR classification requires all the data for a given case, and is accomplished via USOM, SSOM, and/or HSOM:

- In Unsupervised Self-Organizing Map (USOM) learning, the input data are the subjective evaluations of benefit, cost and potential deficit in terms of the different performance criteria;
- In Supervised Self-Organizing Map (SSOM) learning, the input data are the same as those in Unsupervised SOM, but include a removal label for the corresponding barrier;
- In Hierarchical Self-Organizing Map (HSOM) learning, the input data are the same as those in Supervised SOM, except that network is formed by classifying the data into parallel subsets, according to the personalities of the human operators. For example, experimental BR data can be grouped into several subsets related to the controllers' cultural background (e.g., ethnic characteristics).

During the second phase, barrier removal predictions are made, based on the identified criteria and the similarity/proximity data that was memorized during the learning process. For a known target value, the SSOM algorithms are used to classify the data & to predict barrier removal: the input data are all the variables for a given case, except the BR boolean value that has to be predicted. In addition, because different people have different characteristics, the HSOM algorithms are used to group BR data into subsets based on personality. Finally, for an unknown target value, the USOM algorithms are used in order to classify the input data and identify two groups (i.e. the group of removed barriers and the group of unremoved barriers), as is the case in data mining, for example.

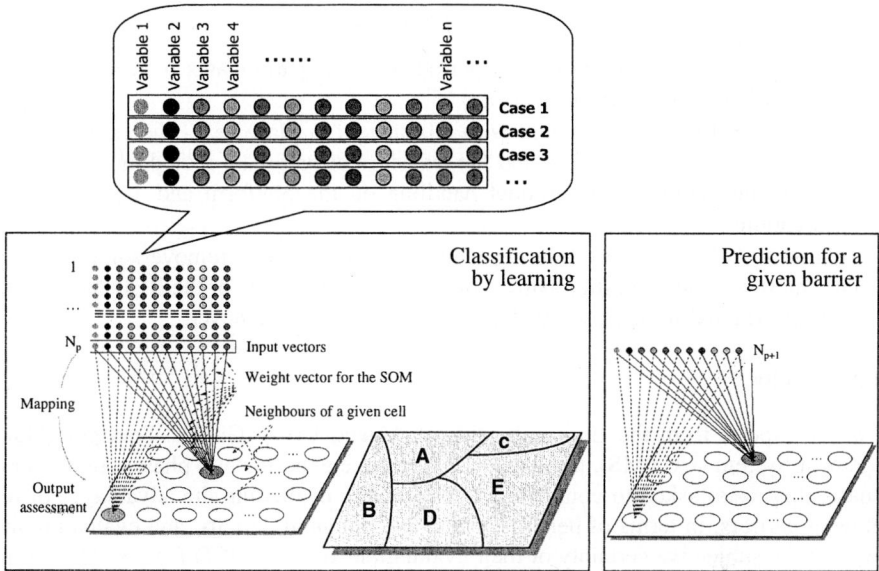

Fig. 2. The basic uncertainty-based BR prediction process

4 Case Study Using a Railway Simulator

This case study was performed on an experimental platform called TRANSPAL.

4.1 Platform Configuration

The TRANSPAL platform simulates train movements from depot to depot, via several transformation stations at which human operators load/unload the products located on a train stopped at the station platform. [7]. A human operator controls the train traffic flow.

Several risks have been identified for this controlled process:

- Train derailment: if the corresponding switching device is not operated correctly when a train is authorised to move, the train may derail.
- Shunting error: a train may be directed toward the wrong route.
- Train collision: trains may crash head-on or during an overtaking maneuver.
- Operator injury: an injury may occur because the human operators are not aware that a train is entering or leaving a transformation area.
- Planning delay: the products on the trains may not be loaded/unloaded on time or may be only partially loaded/unloaded.

In order to limit the risks due to control errors, several barriers exist in order to organize the traffic flow and the train routes, to prevent collisions or derailments, and to keep operators in the transformation areas informed.

The proposed experiment was run in 3 phases:

- Phase 1: A 5-min familiarization period to allow participants to understand the TRANSPAL process and interface;
- Phase 2: A 15-min experiment with all barriers in place (e.g., the signals at the depots, the switching device and the transformation areas) including a presentation of the planning, the product handling on the platform and a performance evaluation;
- Phase 3: A 10-min period during which participants may remove some barriers, but must complete questionnaires assessing the importance of the BCD factors and the uncertainty of their own evaluation for each barrier removed.

4.2 Results

Twenty experts from the European railway project, Urban Guided Transport Management System (UGTMS), participated in the three experimental phases. In the third phase, they were asked to complete a questionnaire evaluating the advantages of removing barriers, in terms of benefits, costs, and potential deficits, and evaluating the level of the subjective certainty of their evalutations of these BCD factors. They were asked to take four performance criteria into account:

- The quality of the planning.
- The production, based on the percentage of the product loaded/unloaded at the stations.
- The traffic safety, based on possible collisions, derailments and injuries due to incorrectly synchronized announcements of train movement at the transformation stations.
- The human workload, based on the occupational rate (i.e. number of actions on the interface).

The results focus on the perceived impact of the BR and were grouped into five barrier families:

- The signals for trains entering the depots.
- The signals for trains exiting the depots.
- The signals for trains approaching a shunting device.
- The signals for trains entering and leaving the transformation stations.
- The signals for trains stopping at transformation areas.

Prior to predicting human actions based on their perceptions about barrier removal, a learning step was required in order to determine the data distribution. The tested algorithm exploits the SSOM approach, meaning that the input vectors of the neural network were the barrier removal factors (i.e. the benefit, cost and potential deficit associated with barrier removal for each performance criterion, the decision to respect or remove the corresponding barrier, as well as the associated uncertainty level).

An example comparing prediction with uncertainty and prediction without uncertainty. After constructing the vectors for sample data without uncertainty and reconstructing the vectors for sample data with uncertainty, predictions with uncertainty and without uncertainty were compared. Table 2 summarizes the comparative

Table 2. Comparison of prediction with and without uncertainty

	10: learning ; 10: prediction			Prediction rate
	Prediction	Observation	Variations	
Without uncertainty	9 Not removed 21 Removed	12 Not removed 18 Removed	9 cases out of 30	70%
With uncertainty	81 Not removed 108 Removed	69 Not removed 120 Removed	33 cases out of 189	83%

results for the depot entrance signals in the mono-performance mode, based on data for the productivity criterion.

As this table shows, the sample data for the first 10 subjects were used for the learning phase, and the sample data for the last 10 subjects were used to identify the variations between prediction and observation. The result of comparing the prediction with uncertainty and the prediction without uncertainty (column "Prediction rate" in the table) shows that the prediction rate taking the uncertainty of the human operator's evaluation into account is higher than the one not taking uncertainty into account. Input data with uncertainty increased the number of studied cases because extrapolations were made regarding the uncertainty values on the BCD factors. This paper does not develop this extrapolation.

Convergence of prediction integrating uncertainty. In order to verify the accuracy of predictions integrating the uncertainty of barrier removal factor evaluations,

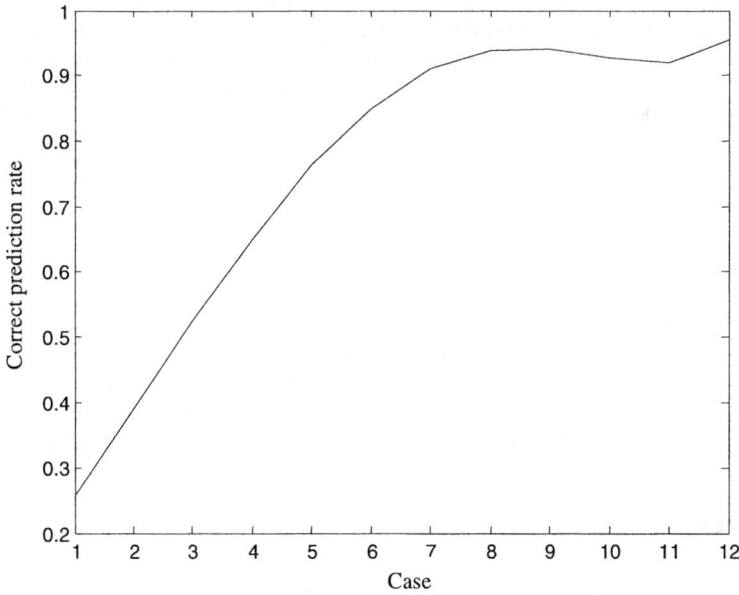

Fig. 3. Convergence of prediction with uncertainty data

prediction convergence was studied. Figure 3 provides an example showing the impact of the quantity of learning phase input vectors on the prediction rate. In this figure, several cases are defined: case 1 corresponds to a learning phase that integrates the input vectors of 5 human experts and the prediction phase concerns the 15 other experts; case 12 considers the input vectors of 16 human experts, and makes predictions for the last 4 human experts. The prediction rate is determined by comparing the prediction produced by the SSOM algorithm and the real behaviour of the human experts.

The results show that the number of input vectors used for the learning phase has an impact on the convergence of the prediction rate. The accurate prediction rate converges toward 95% when the uncertainty evaluation is taken into account.

4 Conclusions

This paper has presented a method using Artificial Neural Networks to analyze and predict BR based on evaluations of the uncertainty and subjectivity of the data. Representing BR results within a BCD framework as a constraint network can provide designers/users with tools that will allow them to predict the likelihood that new/changed barriers will be removed.

Human operator evaluations incorporate a degree of uncertainty. Analyzing and processing the uncertainty and subjectivity of human operator evaluations allows these two elements to be integrated into the prediction. Given enough learning cases and enough sample data, competitive neural networks can be configured, and the SOM maps obtained from a learning set can be used to predict barrier removal for any given barrier.

The experiment with 20 specialists from a European transportation project shows that the prediction rate based on BR data that integrate uncertainty is higher than the rate based on data that doesn't integrate uncertainty. The result with the uncertainty-based BR data converges toward 95% of accurate predictions.

It should be noted that the results presented here constitute only a preliminary analysis of uncertainty in BR prediction. Our approach is able to deal with not only subjective data but also objective data if available. In the mean time, it can be used as a statistical data mining method to aide in the identification of the most contributive BR criteria.

Acknowledgements

The research presented in this paper was supported by the European framework project, Urban Guided Transport Management System. The authors would like to thank the 20 experts from the project consortium for their contributions to this project.

References

1. Reason, J.: Human error, Cambridge University Press, Cambridge, 1990.
2. Reason, J.: A system approach to organizational error. Ergonomics, 38, 8, 1708–1721, 1995.

3. Vanderhaegen, F.: Analyse et contrôle de l'erreur humaine. Hermes science, Paris, France, 2003.
4. Zhang, Z., Polet, P., Vanderhaegen, F., and Millot, P.: Artificial Neural Network for Violation Analysis. Reliability Engineering and System Safety, 84, 1, 3–18, 2004.
5. Zhang, Z., and Vanderhaegen, F.: A method integrating Self-Organizing Maps to predict the probability of Barrier Removal. Chapter 30 in H. Bozdogan (ed.), Statistical Data Mining and Knowledge Discovery, CRC Press, New York, July 2003.
6. Kohonen, T.: Self-Organizing Maps. Springer-Verlag, Third edition, Berlin, Heidelberg, Germany, 2001.
7. Zhang, Z. : Fiabilité humaine: prédiction des violations par réseaux de neurones et application aux systèmes de transport. PhD Thesis, Universite de Valenciennes, France, March 2004.

Iterative Learning Controller for Trajectory Tracking Tasks Based on Experience Database

Xuesong Wang, Yuhu Cheng, and Wei Sun

School of Information and Electrical Engineering,
China University of Mining and Technology, Xuzhou, Jiangsu, 221008, China
{wangxuesongcumt, chengyuhu, sw3883204}@163.com

Abstract. An iterative learning controller based on experience database is proposed for a class of robotic trajectory tracking tasks. It is very general for supporting all types of iterative learning control schemes. The experience database consists of previously tracked trajectories and their corresponding control inputs. The initial control input of an iterative learning controller can be selected properly using a dynamic RBF neural network by properly considering the past experience of tracking various trajectories. Moreover, the RBF network can be created dynamically to ensure the network size is economical. Simulation results of trajectory tracking of a planar two-link manipulator indicate that the convergence speed of the iterative learning controller can be improved by using this method.

1 Introduction

Trajectory tracking problem is one of the main topics in the robot control research field. There are various types of trajectory tracking control methods such as optimal control [1], inverse dynamics control [2] and robust control [3]. These all depend on an exact dynamic model of the robot. It's known that a robot is a very complex, strong coupling and nonlinear dynamics system; moreover, there always exist imprecise measurements and modeling, the load changes, and the influence of outer disturbances. Therefore, we cannot obtain an exact dynamic model of a robot. A human being has the abilities of strong learning and adaptability to the environment; in comparison, learning control technique within adaptive control theory was summarized by Fu in 1970 [4]. When the parameters of the system change, adaptive control can achieve a certain performance index by identification, learning and tuning control law in time. But as it requires huge computational labor to identify parameters on-line, its structure is very complex. In addition, adaptive control cannot guarantee the stability when non-parameterized uncertainties exist.

As another important branch of learning control method, iterative learning control (ILC) can track any desired trajectory with arbitrary precision within a given time span for an unknown controlled system. Iterative learning control considers the systems which perform the required task repetitively, thus utilizing the repetition of the task as an experience to improve the control quality. The beauty of the iterative learning control lies in its structural simplicity and it does not require identification of the system. Therefore it is found to be effective for repetitive control tasks such as manipulators tracking control [5, 6]. However, its low learning speed limits the actual application of iterative learning control. Aiming at the above low learning speed problem, Gu and Loh [7] proposed an iterative learning algorithm combining multi-step error, and simulation results indicated that the convergence speed is improved. But they did not detail the selection method of learning gains in their paper, thus the iterative learning algorithm could not be used for the common plant. Togai and Yamano [8] et al. gave a kind of D-type ILC to solve the optimal problem of discrete systems, and the optimal methods are gradient method, Newton-Raphson method and Gauss method. But the optimal control variable could not be achieved except that the mathematical model is exact. Lee and Bien [9] pointed out that the dynamic process could be improved greatly using sup-norm rather than λ-norm. Based on the analysis of Lee and Bien, all the research until now has concentrated on the selection of the optimal norm and H_∞ norm for linear systems. However, how to select these norms for nonlinear systems has not been detailed in iterative learning literature. Arif, Ishihara and Inooka [10] researched a prediction-based ILC and analyzed the convergence. But the proposed ILC is only applicable for slowly varying desired trajectories.

In order to obtain quick convergence speed, we now put forward in this paper an iterative learning controller based on experience database (ILCED) by using the experience of the previously tracked various trajectories to properly select the initial control input. During the iterative learning controller design phase, a new desired trajectory can be at first decomposed into many query points, and then a dynamic RBF network is applied to predict the control variable for each query point that can be set as the initial control input for the new trajectory. The structure of the RBF network can be created dynamically to ensure the network size is economical.

The paper is organized as follows. An ordinary ILC for manipulator is given in Section 2. In Section 3, the configuration and the detailed design steps of the ILCED system along with the structure learning method of the RBF network are proposed. In order to verify the validity of the proposed ILCED method, simulation results are presented and analyzed in Section 4. Finally, conclusions are drawn in Section 5.

2 Iterative Learning Controller

The dynamic model of an n-link rigid manipulator can be described as:

$$M(q)\ddot{q} + C(q,\dot{q})\dot{q} + G(q) + F(\dot{q}) = u. \quad (1)$$

where, q, $\dot{q}$ and $\ddot{q}$ denote joint position, velocity and acceleration vectors respectively, $M(q) \in R^{n \times n}$ is the symmetrical inertia matrix, $C(q,\dot{q}) \in R^n$ is the Coriolis or centrifugal force vector, $G(q) \in R^n$ is the gravity vector, $F(\dot{q}) \in R^n$ is the friction vector, and $u \in R^n$ is the external control force or torque vector. The dynamics of Eq. (1) can be represented in the form as follows:

$$f(x) = f(q,\dot{q},\ddot{q}) = u. \quad (2)$$

Supposing that the control task of the manipulators is of a repetitive nature, and it's required that the system output $q(t)$ track the desired trajectory $q_d(t)$ exactly within the time range $t \in [0,T]$ where T is the total time for one iteration. The concept of iteration learning control is as follows: in the ith iteration, a control input $u_i(t)$ is applied to the system for $t \in [0,T]$, and the response of the system $q_i(t)$ is recorded in computer memory. After the end of the ith iteration, the iterative learning control algorithm modifies the control input $u_i(t)$ by adding a modification term $g(e_i(t), \dot{e}_i(t))$ to $u_i(t)$ and stores it as a new control input $u_{i+1}(t)$ to be used in the next, i.e., $(i+1)$th iteration. Hence, the iterative learning control algorithm of the $(i+1)$th iteration takes the following form [11]:

$$u_{i+1}(t) = u_i(t) + g(e_i(t), \dot{e}_i(t)), \forall t \in [0,T]. \tag{3}$$

where, $e_i(t) = q_d(t) - q_i(t)$, $\dot{e}_i(t) = \dot{q}_d(t) - \dot{q}_i(t)$, $u_i(t)$ is the control input of the ith iteration, and g is a linear or nonlinear operator. The modification term $g(e_i(t), \dot{e}_i(t))$ is constructed by using the information about error $e_i(t)$ or error rate $\dot{e}_i(t)$ or both $e_i(t)$ and $\dot{e}_i(t)$ of the ith iteration. We can obtain different iterative learning control schemes according to different forms of $g(e_i(t), \dot{e}_i(t))$, in which the main iterative learning control schemes are P-type ILC, D-type ILC, and PID-type ILC. Presently, some new iterative learning control schemes are proposed by combing these conventional learning schemes with the other control methods such as the optimal ILC and model referenced ILC.

3 Iterative Learning Controller Based on Experience Database

The iterative learning control algorithm (3) for manipulators can be described in the following form:

$$u_{i+1}(t) = u_i(t) + g(e_i(t), \dot{e}_i(t)) = u_0(t) + \sum_{l=0}^{i} g(e_l(t), \dot{e}_l(t)). \tag{4}$$

Arimoto, Kawamura, and Miyazaki [11] gave the convergence criterion of the system under consideration when iterative learning controller takes the form as Eq. (4).

$$\|e_{i+1}\|_\lambda \leq \rho \|e_i\|_\lambda, \; \rho < 1. \tag{5}$$

where, $\|\cdot\|_\lambda$ denotes λ-norm that is defined as:

$$\|e(t)\|_\lambda = \sup_{0 \leq t \leq T} e^{-\lambda t} \|e(t)\|_\infty. \tag{6}$$

If Eq. (5) is described in progression form, we can obtain:

$$\|e_{i+1}\|_\lambda \leq \rho^i \|e_0\|_\lambda, \; \rho < 1 \tag{7}$$

It can be seen from Eq. (7) that the error of the ith iteration depends not only on parameter ρ, but also on the initial error $e_0(t)$. Therefore, we can take advantage of the knowledge of the previously tracked various trajectories to construct the new initial control input $u_0(t)$ of the iterative learning controller properly to decrease $e_0(t)$, and so increase convergence speed.

The structure of the iterative learning control system for manipulators based on experience database is shown in Fig. 1. Compared to an ordinary ILC system, the proposed ILCED system has an extra part that is emphasized by the dashed line.

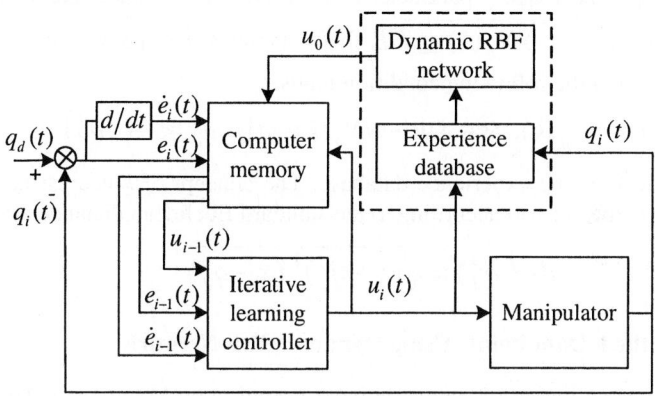

Fig. 1. Iterative learning control system based on experience database

The inverse dynamic model of an n-link rigid manipulator shown in Eq.(1) can be defined as:

$$u(t) = \psi(q(t), \dot{q}(t), \ddot{q}(t)). \qquad (8)$$

where ψ is a nonlinear function that can be approximated by a neural network.

The trajectory tracking task of the manipulator is that the system output $q(t)$ tracks the desired trajectory $q_d(t)$ exactly within the time range $t \in [0, T]$. The inverse model then can be represented by the experience database which stores the past experience of various tracked trajectories $Z_K = [q_K, \dot{q}_K, \ddot{q}_K]$ and their corresponding control inputs u_K. $[Z_K, u_K]$ is called a data point within the experience database.

The selection of the initial control input of iterative learning control is based on the premise that the classification of a new case is similar to that of its neighbor cases. Based on the above analysis, during the phase of designing an iterative learning controller for manipulators, we can decompose the desired trajectory q_d into m query points q_d^j, $j = 1, 2, \cdots, m$, and then compare each query point with data points within the database, and at last use an RBF network to approximate the k nearest cases for each query point so as to predict the control variable corresponding to each query point. In this way, the predicted control variable can then be used as an initial control input by the iterative learning controller for the new desired trajectory. The steps of the proposed method of constructing initial control input in this paper are described as follows.

3.1 Selecting the Nearest k Data Points Near Every Query Point

We select the nearest k cases by using the k-nearest neighbor search method. Given a query point q_d^j and a query parameter k, the k-nearest neighbor search method will return the smallest set $NN_q(k) \subseteq DB$ that contains k data points from the database of experience, and the following condition holds:

$$\forall p \in NN_q(k), \forall s \in DB - NN_q(k):\ d(p, q_d^j) < d(s, q_d^j). \tag{9}$$

where, DB denotes the experience database. The concept of k-nearest neighbor of a query point can be defined according to the standard Euclidean distance as:

$$d(x, q_d^j) = \sqrt{(x - q_d^j)^T (x - q_d^j)}. \tag{10}$$

3.2 Fitting the k Data Points Using Dynamic RBF Network

RBF network is an important neural network proposed by Moody and Darken [12]. It is a three-layer feedforward network with a single hidden layer. Because an RBF network imitates the network structure of a human with local tuning and overlapping receptive regional properties, it is a locally approximative network. It has been proven that an RBF network can approximate any nonlinear function with arbitrary precision and without a local minimum problem.

The output of the hth hidden unit of the RBF network is:

$$v_h = \Phi(\|x - c_h\|). \tag{11}$$

where, $x \in R^I$ is the input vector, $c_h \in R^I$ is the center of the hth hidden unit, $h = 1, 2, \cdots, H$ where H is the number of the hidden units, $\|\cdot\|$ is the Euclidean norm, and $\Phi(\cdot)$ denotes the RBF basis function. The basis function $\Phi(\cdot)$ has a local receptive property, which embodies that the RBF network has nonlinear mapping ability. $\Phi(\cdot)$ is defined as a Gauss function as follows:

$$\Phi(\|x - c_h\|) = \exp(-\|x - c_h\|^2 / 2\sigma_h^2). \tag{12}$$

where σ_h is the width of the hth basis function.

The output of the rth unit in the output layer is the linear combination of the outputs of all the hidden units described as:

$$u_r = f(x) = \sum_h w_{rh} v_h - \theta_r. \tag{13}$$

where, w_{rh} is the connect weight between v_h and u_r, and θ_r is the threshold of the rth output unit.

The learning functions of an RBF network includes the network structure learning and the parameters learning. Generally speaking, the parameters learning function of an RBF network can be divided into two phases. The first phase is to determine the parameters of basis function such as c_h and σ_h, and the second phase is to update the weight between the hidden layer and the output layer. The commonly used learning methods of an RBF network are k-means clustering method, least squares method, and local training method.

Structure learning means that the number of hidden units of the RBF network can be added or deleted according to the dynamic changes to ensure that the network size remains economical [13]. There are two criteria for adding a new unit to the hidden layer as follows:

$$\|x_K - c_{nearest}\| > \xi = \frac{D_{max}}{\sqrt{2H}}. \tag{14}$$

$$|\varepsilon| = |u_d - u| > \varepsilon_{max}. \tag{15}$$

where, $\|x_K - c_{nearest}\|$ is the Euclidean distance between the Kth input vector x_K and its nearest center $c_{nearest}$, and ξ is a critical value that can be understood as the precision of the model and is defined as $\frac{D_{max}}{\sqrt{2H}}$, where D_{max} is the largest distance of all the centers and H corresponds to the number of hidden units. u_d and u are the desired and the actual output of the RBF network respectively.

At the initial learning phase, there are no units in the hidden layer, and the first input observation data is viewed as the first unit. As for the following input, we can judge whether to add a unit or not according to the above two criteria. If a new input variable meets the above two criteria, we will add a hidden unit to the RBF network. The corresponding center vector of the added unit is equal to the current input vector, while the width is:

$$\sigma_{new} = \tau \|x_K - c_{nearest}\|. \tag{16}$$

where τ is an overlapping coefficient of input space.

We know that the greater the number of basis functions, the better the function fitting effects the RBF network has. But it is at the expense of a long learning time. The structure will be enlarged continuously with the process of learning, thus a scheme of combining basis functions is put forward. However, some hidden units are active and have larger contributions to the overall network outputs initially, but the contributions will attenuate gradually with the changing system and this will produce some useless 'dead' units. Therefore, we get the following determining rule: if there are M successive input samples all satisfying Eq. (17), then we should delete the useless unit.

$$\Phi(\|x_\kappa - c_h\|) < th, \quad \kappa = 1, 2, \cdots M . \tag{17}$$

where th is an active threshold.

The training samples of the RBF network are the nearest k data points produced by the k-nearest neighbor search method. The input of the RBF network is the state variables vector of manipulators $x = [q, \dot{q}, \ddot{q}]$, and the outputs of network are control variables u corresponding to the desired trajectory.

The detailed structure learning algorithm of the RBF network can be summarized as follows, based on the above analysis:

Step 1. Set the first input observation data as the first hidden unit;

Step 2. Feed a new input data x_κ to the network and judge whether to add a unit or not according to the adding criteria Eqs. (14) and (15); add a new unit if the criteria are satisfied;

Step 3. Else, tune network parameters;

Step 4. Delete useless unit according to the deleting criterion Eq. (17);

Step 5. $\kappa = \kappa + 1$, go to Step 2.

3.3 Predicting the Control Input of Query Point

When the RBF network can approximate the nonlinear function $f(x)$ with a definite precision after a period of off-line learning of inverse dynamics of manipulators, the RBF network then can be used to predict the control input corresponding to the given query point q_d^j. Thus the predicted value (the output of the RBF network) is the initial control input $u_0(t)$ of the iterative learning controller.

4 Simulation Research

In order to verify the proposed iterative learning controller, trajectory tracking control of a planar two-link manipulator is simulated. The dynamic model of the manipulator is described in Eq. (1), and friction force is neglected for simplification.

The inertia matrix $M(q)$ is:

$$M(q) = \begin{bmatrix} M_{11} & M_{12} \\ M_{21} & M_{22} \end{bmatrix} \tag{18}$$

$$= \begin{bmatrix} m_1 l_1^2 + m_2(l_1^2 + l_2^2 + 2l_1 l_2 \cos(q_2)) & m_2(l_2^2 + l_1 l_2 \cos(q_2)) \\ m_2(l_2^2 + l_1 l_2 \cos(q_2)) & m_2 l_2^2 \end{bmatrix}$$

The Coriolis or centrifugal force vector is:

$$C(q,\dot{q}) = m_2 l_1 r_2 \sin(q_2) \begin{bmatrix} -\dot{q}_2 & -(\dot{q}_1 + \dot{q}_2) \\ \dot{q}_1 & 0 \end{bmatrix} \quad (19)$$

The gravity vector is:

$$G(q) = \begin{bmatrix} m_2 l_2 g \cos(q_1 + q_2) + (m_1 + m_2) l_1 g \cos(q_1) \\ m_2 l_2 g \cos(q_1 + q_2) \end{bmatrix} \quad (20)$$

Let $m_1 = 1.09kg$, $m_2 = 1.12kg$, $l_1 = 1.0m$, $l_2 = 1.3m$ and $g = 9.81 m/s^2$.

Given the desired trajectory of the manipulator as $q_{d1} = \sin(0.5t)$ and $q_{d2} = \sin(t + 0.2)$, the control task is moving two links from the initial position [0, 0.2] to the goal position [0.5, 1]. During the simulation, the sampling period is $t_s = 0.01s$, D-type iterative learning scheme based on an experience database is applied to control the manipulator, and the learning gains of D-type ILC are [0.01, 0.01]. The input of the RBF network is $x = [q_1, \dot{q}_1, \ddot{q}_1, q_2, \dot{q}_2, \ddot{q}_2]$, and the output of the network is $u = [u_1, u_2]$. The parameter learning algorithms of the RBF network are selected as k-means clustering and least squares methods.

Performance index J is defined as follows to evaluate the performance:

$$J = \sqrt{\frac{1}{T} \int_0^T e^2(t) dt} = \sqrt{\frac{1}{N} \sum_{j=0}^{N} e_j^2} \quad (21)$$

where, T is the total time for one iteration, and N is the number of iterations, $N = T/t_s$. An ordinary D-type ILC and the proposed D-type iterative learning

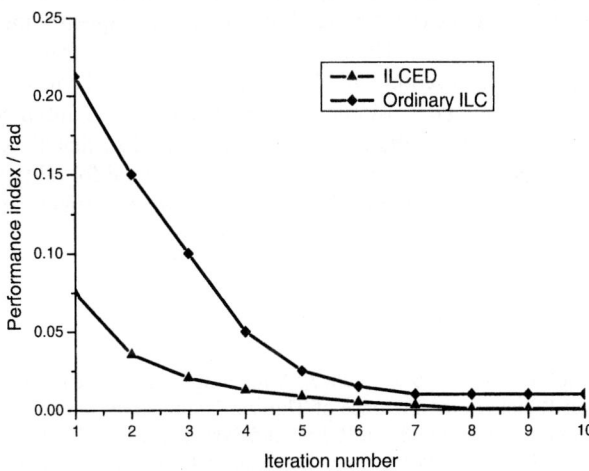

Fig. 2. Tracking performance index of joint 1

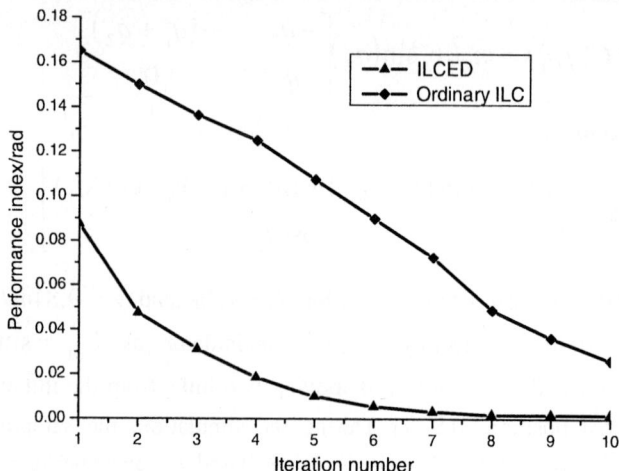

Fig. 3. Tracking performance index of joint 2

scheme based on the experience database are applied to control the manipulator respectively, and simulation results are shown in Fig. 2 and Fig. 3.

5 Conclusions

It can be clearly seen from the above simulation results that the proposed iterative learning controller can converge to the desired value more quickly than that of an ordinary D-type ILC. The reason is that the proper selection of the initial control input using previous experience stored in the database can decrease the number of iterations. A new desired trajectory can be decomposed into many query points at first, and then an RBF network is applied to construct inverse dynamics of the manipulator by fitting the k data points near every query point and subsequently these are used to predict the initial control input. Hence, with a lower initial error bound, the error bound in each succeeding iteration will also reduce for a certain convergence speed as determined by the learning gains. Moreover, the selection of the initial control input is independent of the structure of the controller despite the fact that D-type ILC is exemplified in this paper. Therefore, this method is very general for all types of iterative learning control schemes. Simulation results have shown the effectiveness of trajectory tracking of manipulators.

References

1. Hanai, A., Choi, H.T., Choi, S.K., Yuh, J.: Minimum Energy Based Fine Motion Control of Underwater Robots in the Presence of Thruster Nonlinearity. Proceedings of IEEE International Conference on Intelligent Robots and Systems, (2003) 559-564
2. Lee, S.H., Song, J.B., Choi, W.C., Hong, D.: Position Control of a Stewart Platform Using Inverse Dynamics Control with Approximate Dynamics. Mechatronics. 13(6) (2003) 605-619

3. Yagiz, N.: Robust Control of a Spatial Robot Using Sliding Modes. Mathematical & Computational Applications. 7(3) (2002) 219-228
4. Fu, K.S.: Learning Control System-Review and Outlook. IEEE Transactions on Automatic Control. 15 (1970) 210-221
5. An, G., Zhang, L., Liu, J.T.: A Sort of Iterative Learning Algorithm for Tracking Control of Robot Trajectory. Robot. 23(1) (2001) 36-39
6. Norrlof, M., Gunnarsson, S.: Experimental Comparison of Some Classical Iterative Learning Control Algorithms. IEEE Transactions on Robotics and Automation. 18(4) (2002) 636-641
7. Gu, Y.L., Loh, N.K.: Learning Control in Robotic Systems. Proceedings of IEEE International Symposium on Intelligent Control, (1987) 360-364
8. Togai, M., Yamano, O.: Analysis and Design of an Optimal Learning Control Scheme for Industrial Robots: A Discrete System Approach. Proceedings of the 24th IEEE Conferences on Decision and Control, Ft. Lauderdale. Florida (1985) 1399-1404
9. Lee, H.S., Bien, Z.: A Note on Convergence Property of Iterative Learning Controller with Respect to Sup Norm. Automatica. 33(8) (1997) 525-528
10. Arif, M., Ishihara, T., Inooka, H.: Prediction-based Iterative Learning Control (PILC) for Uncertain Dynamic Nonlinear Systems Using System Identification Technique. Journal of Intelligent and Robotic Systems. 27 (2000) 291-304
11. Arimoto, S., Kawamura, S., Miyazaki, F.: Bettering Operation of Robots by Learning. Journal of Robotic Systems. 1(2) (1984) 123-140
12. Moody, J., Darken, C.: Fast Learning in Networks of Locally-Tuned Processing Units. Neural Computation. (1) (1989) 281-294
13. Cheng, Y.H., Yi, J.Q., Zhao, D.B.: Application of Actor-Critic Learning to Adaptive State Space Construction. Proceedings of The Third International Conference on Machine Learning and Cybernetics, (2004) 26-29

MGPC Based on Hopfield Network and Its Application in a Thermal Power Unit Load System

Peng Guo and Taihua Chang

Department of Automation, North China Electric Power University,
102206 Beijing, China
huadiangp@163.com

Abstract. Multivariable General Predictive Control (MGPC) is an effective application in the control of plant with inertia and delay. But it has some defects such as requiring a large amount of computation online and poor treatment of constraints. This paper introduces Hopfield neural network into MGPC. Firstly, the MGPC was decomposed into several multi-input and single-output systems, then they were converted into several quadratic constrained optimizing problems. Several Hopfield networks were used to solve each quadratic constrained optimizing problem respectively. The Hopfield network has the merits of simple arithmetic and rapid computation. The combination of the two methods can overcome the defects of MGPC. Then the new method was applied to the control of a unit load system in a thermal power plant that is a 2×2 multivariable plant with coupling and constraints. Simulation proved that the new method has effective control performance.

1 Introduction

Multivariable General Predictive Control (MGPC) has the characteristics of predictive model, rolling optimization and feedback correction, and shows good control performance and robustness. But MGPC also has some defects such as requiring a large amount of computation online and poor treatment of constraints. Neural network is effective at dealing with parallel computation and nonlinear problems. The Hopfield network especially is an effective application in solving quadratic constrained optimizing problems. The Hopfield network has a simple structure and can be implemented with a circuit network. The optimizing computation can be finished within milliseconds. This paper introduces multiple Hopfield networks to MGPC, and applies the new method into the control of a unit load system in a thermal power plant that is a 2×2 multivariable plant with coupling and constraints. Simulation showed that the new method has a satisfactory performance.

2 Decoupling of MGPC

Considering the following MIMO plant:

$$A(z^{-1})y(t) = B(z^{-1})u(t-1) + \xi(t)/\Delta, \tag{1}$$

$\{u(t)\} \in R^m$, $\{y(t)\} \in R^m$, $\xi(t) \in R^m$. The mean value of $\xi(t)$ is zero and its variance is σ^2. $A(z^{-1})$ is assumed as a diagonal matrix. Consider the following two inputs and two outputs system:

$$\begin{bmatrix} A_{11}(z^{-1}) & 0 \\ 0 & A_{22}(z^{-1}) \end{bmatrix} \begin{bmatrix} y_1(t) \\ y_2(t) \end{bmatrix} = \begin{bmatrix} B_{11}(z^{-1}) & B_{12}(z^{-1}) \\ B_{21}(z^{-1}) & B_{22}(z^{-1}) \end{bmatrix} \begin{bmatrix} u_1(t-1) \\ u_2(t-1) \end{bmatrix} + \begin{bmatrix} \xi_1(t) \\ \xi_2(t) \end{bmatrix} / \Delta . \quad (2)$$

Change Equation 2 into the following two-input and one-output equations[1]:

$$A_{11}(z^{-1})\Delta y_1(t) = B_{11}(z^{-1})\Delta u_1(t-1) + B_{12}(z^{-1})\Delta u_2(t-1) + \xi_1(t), \quad (3a)$$

$$A_{22}(z^{-1})\Delta y_2(t) = B_{21}(z^{-1})\Delta u_1(t-1) + B_{22}(z^{-1})\Delta u_2(t-1) + \xi_2(t). \quad (3b)$$

As to Equation 3(a), use Diophantine equation, then Equation 3(a) can be rewritten as follows:

$$\begin{aligned} y_1(t+j) &= G_j^{11}(z^{-1})\Delta u_1(t+j-1) + F_j^{11}(z^{-1})y_1(t) + H_j^{11}(z^{-1})\Delta u_1(t-1) + \\ &\quad G_j^{12}(z^{-1})\Delta u_2(t+j-1) + H_j^{12}(z^{-1})\Delta u_2(t-1) + E_j^{11}(z^{-1})\xi_1(t+j) \end{aligned} \quad (4)$$

Rewrite Equation 4 into vector format:

$$Y_1(t+1) = G_{11}U_1(t) + F_{11}y_1(t) + H_{11}\Delta u_1(t-1) + G_{12}U_2(t) + H_{12}\Delta u_2(t-1) + E_{11}. \quad (5)$$

In Equation 5,

$$Y_1(t+1) = [y_1(t+1), y_1(t+2), \cdots, y_1(t+N_1)]^T,$$

$$U_1(t) = [\Delta u_1(t), \Delta u_1(t+1), \cdots, \Delta u_1(t+N_u-1)]^T,$$

$$F_{11} = [F_1^{11}, F_2^{11}, \cdots, F_{N_1}^{11}]^T, \quad H_{11} = [H_1^{11}, H_2^{11}, \cdots, H_{N_1}^{11}]^T,$$

$$H_{12} = [H_1^{12}, H_2^{12}, \cdots, H_{N_1}^{12}]^T,$$

$$G_{11} = \begin{bmatrix} g_0^{11} & 0 & \cdots & 0 \\ g_1^{11} & g_0^{11} & \cdots & 0 \\ \vdots & & & \\ g_{N_u-1}^{11} & g_{N_u-2}^{11} & \cdots & g_0^{11} \\ \vdots & & & \\ g_{N_1-1}^{11} & g_{N_1-2}^{11} & \cdots & g_{N_1-N_u}^{11} \end{bmatrix}, \quad G_{12} = \begin{bmatrix} g_0^{12} & 0 & \cdots & 0 \\ g_1^{12} & g_0^{12} & \cdots & 0 \\ \vdots & & & \\ g_{N_u-1}^{12} & g_{N_u-2}^{12} & \cdots & g_0^{12} \\ \vdots & & & \\ g_{N_1-1}^{12} & g_{N_1-2}^{12} & \cdots & g_{N_1-N_u}^{12} \end{bmatrix}.$$

Use Diophantine equation to 3(b), following which Equation 6 can be obtained:

$$Y_2(t+1) = G_{22}U_2(t) + F_{22}y_2(t) + H_{22}\Delta u_2(t-1) + G_{21}U_1(t) + H_{21}\Delta u_1(t-1) + E_{22}. \quad (6)$$

The known components of Equations 5 and 6 are:

$$Y_{P01}(t) = F_{11}y_1(t) + H_{11}\Delta u_1(t-1) + H_{12}\Delta u_2(t-1) + E_{11},$$

$$Y_{P02}(t) = F_{22}y_2(t) + H_{22}\Delta u_2(t-1) + H_{21}\Delta u_1(t-1) + E_{22}. \quad (7)$$

Then Equations 5 and 6 become:

$$Y_1(t+1) = G_{11}U_1(t) + G_{12}U_2(t) + Y_{P01}(t), \quad (8)$$

$$Y_2(t+1) = G_{22}U_2(t) + G_{21}U_1(t) + Y_{P02}(t). \tag{9}$$

The cost functions of control loop 1 and control loop 2 are:

$$\begin{aligned} J_{P1} &= [Y_1(t+1) - Y_{r1}(t+1)]^T Q_1 [Y_1(t+1) - Y_{r1}(t+1)] + U_1^T \lambda_1 U_1 \\ &= [G_{11}U_1(t) + G_{12}U_2(t) + Y_{P01}(t) - Y_{r1}(t+1)]^T Q_1 \\ & [G_{11}U_1(t) + G_{12}U_2(t) + Y_{P01}(t) - Y_{r1}(t+1)] + U_1^T(t)\lambda_1 U_1(t) \end{aligned} \tag{10a}$$

$$\begin{aligned} J_{P2} &= [Y_2(t+1) - Y_{r2}(t+1)]^T Q_2 [Y_2(t+1) - Y_{r2}(t+1)] + U_2^T \lambda_2 U_2 \\ &= [G_{22}U_2(t) + G_{21}U_1(t) + Y_{P02}(t) - Y_{r2}(t+1)]^T Q_2 \\ & [G_{22}U_2(t) + G_{21}U_1(t) + Y_{P02}(t) - Y_{r2}(t+1)] + U_2^T(t)\lambda_2 U_2(t) \end{aligned} \tag{10b}$$

Y_{r1}, Y_{r2} are respectively the reference track of y_1, y_2.

By removing the known components, the new cost function ϕ_1, ϕ_2 can be obtained.

$$\begin{aligned} \phi_1 &= U_1^T(t) G_{11}^T Q_1 G_{11} U_1(t) + 2U_2^T(t) G_{12}^T Q_1 G_{11} U_1(t) + \\ & U_2^T(t) G_{12}^T Q_1 G_{12} U_2(t) + 2(Y_{P01}^T - Y_{r1}^T) Q_1 [G_{11}U_1(t) + \\ & G_{12}U_2(t)] + U_1^T(t)\lambda_1 U_1(t) \end{aligned} \tag{11a}$$

$$\begin{aligned} \phi_2 &= U_2^T(t) G_{22}^T Q_2 G_{22} U_2(t) + 2U_1^T(t) G_{21}^T Q_2 G_{22} U_2(t) \\ & + U_1^T(t) G_{21}^T Q_2 G_{21} U_1(t) + 2(Y_{P02}^T - Y_{r2}^T) Q_2 [G_{22}U_2(t) \\ & + G_{21}U_1(t)] + U_2^T(t)\lambda_2 U_2(t) \end{aligned} \tag{11b}$$

In Equation 11(a), $U_2(t)$ can be approximately replaced by $U_2(t-1)$. Many simulations prove that the error is very small when the sample time is small. Then $U_2(t)$ can be treated as a known part and removed from 11(a). Equation 11(a) can be further simplified as:

$$\begin{aligned} \phi_1' &= U_1^T(t) G_{11}^T Q_1 G_{11} U_1(t) + 2U_2^T(t-1) G_{12}^T Q_1 G_{11} U_1(t) \\ & + 2(Y_{P01}^T - Y_{r1}^T) Q_1 G_{11} U_1(t) + U_1^T(t)\lambda_1 U_1(t) \end{aligned} \tag{12a}$$

$$\begin{aligned} \phi_2' &= U_2^T(t) G_{22}^T Q_2 G_{22} U_2(t) + 2U_1^T(t-1) G_{21}^T Q_2 G_{22} U_2(t) \\ & + 2(Y_{P02}^T - Y_{r2}^T) Q_2 G_{22} U_2(t) + U_2^T(t)\lambda_2 U_2(t) \end{aligned} \tag{12b}$$

The constraints of the multivariable MGPC are as follows:
Amplitude constraints:

$$u_{\min 1} \leq u_1(t) \leq u_{\max 1}, \quad u_{\min 2} \leq u_2(t) \leq u_{\max 2}.$$

Velocity constraints:

$$|\Delta u_1(t)| \leq \Delta_1, \quad |\Delta u_2(t)| \leq \Delta_2.$$

The MGPC problem is converted into two independent quadratic constrained optimizing problems. Optimizing the cost functions ϕ_1' and ϕ_2' provides the predictive control sequences $U_1(t)$ and $U_2(t)$.

3 Using the Hopfield Network to Solve MGPC with Constraints

The Hopfield network is an effective application in solving quadratic constrained optimizing problems. By introducing the Hopfield network into MGPC, complex computation can be avoided while producing the predictive control sequences $U_1(t)$ and $U_2(t)$.

The Hopfield network used to solve the quadratic optimizing problem is:

$$\begin{cases} \min \varphi(x) = \dfrac{1}{2}x^T G x + I^T x \\ \text{s.t.} A_j^T x \geq J_j, j = 1,2,\cdots m \end{cases} \tag{13}$$

where $x \in R^n$ is optimizing vector, $G \in R^n$ is positive definite matrix; I, $A_j \in R^n$ are constant vectors. Define $A^T = [A_1 \ A_2 \ \cdots \ A_m]_{n \times m}$ as constraint equation coefficient matrix, J_j is scalar of constraint equations.

Add constraints to the first item of predictive control sequences $U_1(t)$ and $U_2(t)$.

$$u_{\min 1} \leq \Delta u_1(t) + u_1(t-1) \leq u_{\max 1},\ -\Delta_1 \leq \Delta u_1(t) \leq \Delta_1. \tag{14a}$$

$$u_{\min 2} \leq \Delta u_2(t) + u_2(t-1) \leq u_{\max 2},\ -\Delta_2 \leq \Delta u_2(t) \leq \Delta_2. \tag{14b}$$

Two Hopfield networks were used to obtain $U_1(t)$ and $U_2(t)$ respectively.

Compare Equations 12(a) and 14(a) with a standard quadratic optimizing problem (13), and Equation 15(a) can be obtained:

$$G_1 = 2(G_{11}^T Q_1 G_{11} + \lambda_1),\ I_1 = 2(U_2^T(t-1)G_{12}^T Q_1 G_{11} + (Y_{p01}^T - Y_{r_1}^T)Q_1 G_{11})^T,$$

$$A_1 = \begin{bmatrix} 1 & 0 & \cdots & 0 \\ -1 & 0 & \cdots & 0 \\ 1 & 0 & \cdots & 0 \\ -1 & 0 & \cdots & 0 \end{bmatrix}_{4 \times M_1},$$

$$J_1 = [u_{\min 1} - u_1(t-1) \ -(u_{\max 1} - u_1(t-1)) \ -\Delta_1 \ -\Delta_1]^T. \tag{15a}$$

Compare Equations 12(b) and 14(b) with Equation 13, and Equation 15(b) can be obtained:

$$G_2 = 2(G_{22}^T Q_2 G_{22} + \lambda_2),\ I_2 = 2(U_1^T(t-1)G_{21}^T Q_2 G_{22} + (Y_{p02}^T - Y_{r_2}^T)Q_2 G_{22})^T,$$

$$A_2 = \begin{bmatrix} 1 & 0 & \cdots & 0 \\ -1 & 0 & \cdots & 0 \\ 1 & 0 & \cdots & 0 \\ -1 & 0 & \cdots & 0 \end{bmatrix}_{4 \times M_2},$$

$$J_2 = [u_{\min 2} - u_2(t-1) \ -(u_{\max 2} - u_2(t-1)) \ -\Delta_2 \ -\Delta_2]^T. \tag{15b}$$

M_1 and M_2 are the control horizons of loop 1 and loop 2 respectively.

4 Construct Two Hopfield Networks

The structure of a Hopfield network is shown in Figure 1.

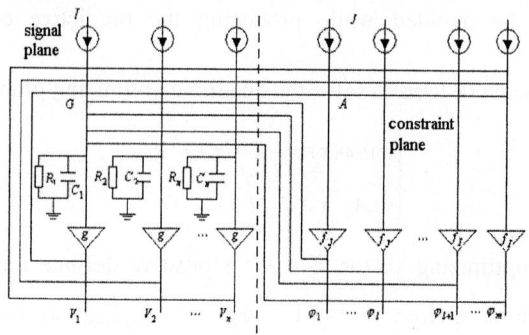

Fig. 1. Structure of Hopfield network

Construct two Hopfield networks with Equation 15 in order to obtain $U_1(t)$ and $U_2(t)$.

(1) Control predictive series $U_1(t) \in R^{M_1}$, $U_2(t) \in R^{M_2}$ as outputs V_1, V_2 of the two signal planes.
(2) I_1, I_2 as input vectors of two signal planes;
(3) J_1, J_2 as input vectors of two constraint planes;
(4) G_1, G_2 as self-conductive matrix of two networks;
(5) A_1, A_2 as correlated conductive matrix of two networks;
(6) $\varphi_1, \varphi_2 \in R^4$ as output vectors of two constraint planes.

The dynamic equation of Hopfield network one is:

$$C_i \frac{du_i}{dt} = -I_i - \frac{u_i}{R_i} - \sum_{j=1}^{M_1} g_{ij} V_j - \sum_{j=1}^{4} a_{ji} \varphi_j, \ i=1,2,\cdots,M_1, V_i = g(u_i) = \rho u_i. \quad (16)$$

$$\varphi_i = f_I(-J_i + \sum_{j=1}^{M_1} a_{ij} V_j), \ f_I(x) = \alpha x \cdot 1(-x). \quad (17)$$

$1(x)$ is a step function. Network two is the same as network one.

5 Simulation

The thermal power unit load system is a 2×2 system:

$$\begin{bmatrix} N_e \\ P_t \end{bmatrix} = \begin{bmatrix} W_{NT}(s) & W_{NB}(s) \\ W_{PT}(s) & W_{PB}(s) \end{bmatrix} \begin{bmatrix} u_t \\ u_b \end{bmatrix}. \quad (18)$$

Where, N_e, P_t are actual power and main steam pressure, their counterparts are y_1, y_2.

u_t and u_b are respectively turbine valve instruction and burning rate instruction, and their counterparts are u_1, u_2.

$$W_{NT}(s) = \frac{68.81s}{(1+12s)(1+82s)}, \quad W_{NB}(s) = \frac{1}{(1+82s)^2},$$

$$W_{PT}(s) = -2.194(\frac{0.064}{1+3s} + \frac{0.936}{1+124s}), \quad W_{PB}(s) = \frac{2.194}{(1+80s)^2}.$$

Sample time is 3 seconds, predictive horizon $P=12$, control horizon $M_1 = M_2 = 6$. The constraints are: $\Delta_1 = 0.05$, $\Delta_2 = 0.05$, $u_{\min 1} = -0.15$, $u_{\max 1} = 0.15$, $u_{\min 2} = -0.15$, $u_{\max 2} = 0.15$.

Figure 2 and Figure 3 are simulation results when N_e has a step disturbance.

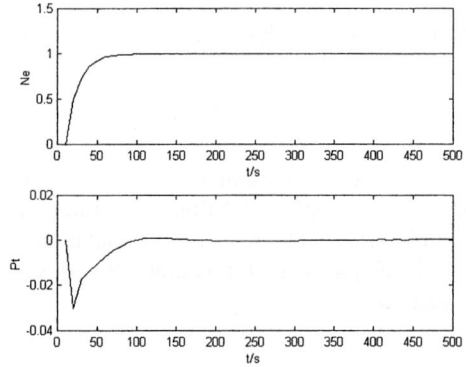

Fig. 2. Simulation result of N_e with step disturbance

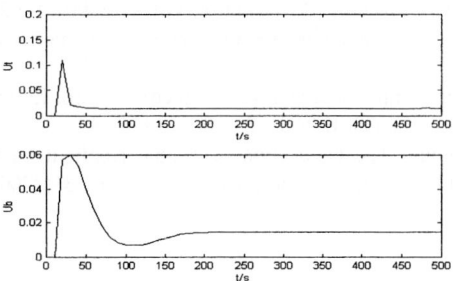

Fig. 3. Simulation result of control output

The robustness of the new method is also very satisfactory. Figure 4 is the simulation result when plant changes.

$$W'_{NT}(s) = \frac{68.81s}{(1+20s)(1+100s)}, \quad W'_{NB}(s) = \frac{1}{(1+90s)^2},$$

$$W'_{PT}(s) = -2.194(\frac{0.064}{1+3s} + \frac{0.936}{1+150s}), \quad W'_{PB}(s) = \frac{2.194}{(1+65s)^2}.$$

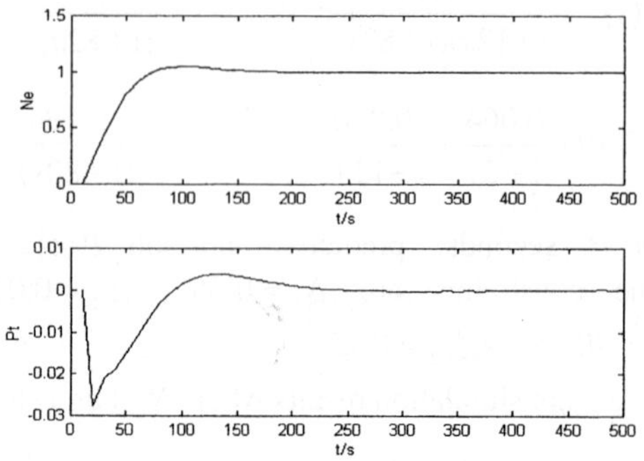

Fig. 4. Simulation result when plant has some changes

6 Conclusion

Unit load system is a plant with multivariable coupling and control constraints. The existing GPC method is very complex and time consuming. This paper proposes a new GPC with multiple Hopfield networks. Simulations prove its effective performance. With the development of the neural network chip, the method has a promising future in industry.

References

1. Wang Dongfeng: Decoupling design of generalized predictive control for multivariable control system. Electric Machines And Control, Vol. 4. (2000) 243-245
2. Wang Wei: The theorem and application of generalized predictive control. Science Press, Beijing (1998)
3. Ju Gang, Wei Hongqi: Multivariable model predictive control for thermal power unit load system. Proceedings of the CSEE, Vol. 22. (2002) 144-148
4. Guo Peng, Guo Junjun: The application of double Hopfield network in unit dispatch. Proceedings of North China Electric Power University, Vol. 31. (2004) 48-50

Solving the Minimum Crossing Number Problem Using an Improved Artificial Neural Network

Rong Long Wang and Kozo Okazaki

Faculty of Engineering,
Fukui University, Fukui-shi, 910-8507, Japan
wang@fuee.fukui-u.ac.jp

Abstract. The minimum crossing number problem has important applications in printed circuit board layout, VLSI circuit routing, and automated graph drawing. In this paper, we propose an improved Hopfield neural network algorithm for efficiently solving the minimum crossing number problem. To evaluate the proposed algorithm, a large number of instances have been simulated. The simulation results show that the proposed algorithm is much better than previous works for solving the minimum crossing number problem in terms of the computation time and the solution quality.

1 Introduction

The objective of the minimum crossing number problem is to embed the edges of a graph so that the total number of crossings is minimized. Recently, several linear graph layout problems have been the subject of study. Given a set of vertices, the problem involves placing the vertices along a horizontal "node line" in the plane and then adding edges as specified by the interconnection pattern. The crossing number problem [1] is related to the more general planar crossing number problem. The objective of this problem is to embed the edges so that the total number of crossings is minimized. This problem has important applications in printed circuit board layout, VLSI circuit routing, and automated graph drawing [2]. The crossing number problem is NP-hard [1]; hence research has focused on finding efficient heuristics or on methods for special families of graphs. In 1996 Shahrokhi et al. [3] proposed a one-page heuristic. For solving such problems, the Hopfield neural network [4] constitutes an important avenue. Using the neural network technique, Cimikowski et al. [5] proposed a parallel algorithm for the linear crossing number problem. Unfortunately, due to its inherent local minimum problem, the probability of obtaining the minimum number of crossings using Hopfield network is very low.

In this paper, we present an improved neural network algorithm to efficiently solve the crossing number problem. In the proposed neural network algorithm, the internal dynamics is modified to permit temporary increases in the energy function in order to help the network escape from local minima and increase the exchange of information between neurons. The proposed algorithm is tested on a larger number of graphs and compared with some existing algorithms. The experimental results indicate that the proposed algorithm could yield optimal or near-optimal solutions and outperform the other compared algorithms.

2   The Minimum Crossing Number Problem

We use standard graph-theoretic terminology. In the linear crossing number problem, the crossing number, $\nu(G)$, of a graph $G(V, E)$, is the minimum number of edge crossings required in any drawing of G in the plane. In the 2-page drawing representation used here, each edge is embedded in either the upper page or the lower page. Then any pair of edges ij and kl cross in a drawing $iff\ i < k < j < l$ and both lie in the same page. We use neuron y_{ij} to express the edge between vertices i and j. The state $y_{ij} = 1$ indicates that the edge ij is embedded in the upper page, and the state $y_{ij} = 0$ indicates that the edge ij is embedded in the lower page. The number of edges in a given graph determines the number of neurons required.

Thus, the linear crossing number problem can be mathematically stated as finding the minimum of the following objective function:

$$\frac{1}{2}\sum_{ij}\sum_{kl}(g_{ij}g_{kl}d_{ijkl}y_{ij}y_{kl}) + \frac{1}{2}\sum_{ij}\sum_{kl}(g_{ij}g_{kl}d_{ijkl}(1-y_{ij})(1-y_{kl})) \quad (1)$$

where d_{ijkl} is crossing condition and can be described as:

$$d_{ijkl} = \begin{cases} 1 & if\ i < k < j < l\ or\ k < i < l < j \\ 0 & otherwise \end{cases} \quad (2)$$

g_{ij} indicates whether the edge ij exist.

$$g_{ij} = \begin{cases} 1 & if\ edge\ ij\ exists \\ 0 & otherwise \end{cases} \quad (3)$$

Then, the energy function for the linear crossing number problem is given by:

$$E = A\sum_{ij}\sum_{kl}(g_{ij}g_{kl}d_{ijkl}y_{ij}y_{kl}) + B\sum_{ij}\sum_{kl}(g_{ij}g_{kl}d_{ijkl}(1-y_{ij})(1-y_{kl})) \quad (4)$$

The Hopfield network can find the solution of the linear crossing number problem by seeking the local minimum of the energy function E using the motion equations of neurons. Unfortunately, the quality of the solution by the neural network is not very good; since the Hopfield network will attempt to take the best path to the nearest minimum, whether global or local. If a local minimum is reached, the network will fail to update. It is usually difficult for the Hopfield network to find the global minimum that corresponds to the minimum number of crossings.

3 The Improvement of the Internal Dynamics of Hopfield Network

Without loss of the generality, we consider a general Hopfield neural network. The motion equation is composed of the partial derivation term of the energy function as the gradient descent method.

$$dx_i/dt = \sum_{i,j}^{N} w_{ij} y_j + h_i \qquad (5)$$

where w_{ij} is the weight from #i neuron to #j neuron, h_i is the threshold and y_i is the output of #i neuron. The internal potential x_i of neuron is updated according the following equation [6]:

$$x_i(t+1) = x_i(t) + \frac{dx_i(t)}{dt} \Delta t \qquad (6)$$

The state y_i of neuron #i is updated from x_i using a non-linear function called neuron model. The following sigmoid function is always used as neuron model for optimization problems:

$$y_i = 1/(1 + e^{(-x_i/T)}) \qquad (7)$$

In order to efficiently solve the minimum crossing number problem, we now propose an improved neural network algorithm. The proposed method modifies the updating mode of the internal potential. The modified updating equation of the internal potential is given by:

$$x_i(t+1) = \alpha_i(y_i, t) \cdot x_i(t) + \frac{dx_i(t)}{dt} \Delta t \qquad (8)$$

where $0 \leq \alpha_i(y_i, t) \leq 1$. The modified internal dynamic behavior means that the change of the internal potential in neuron #i is now controlled by a new parameter $\alpha_i(y_i, t)$ which represents the stabilization of neuron #i. When the state of neuron is far from 0 and 1 or the network is in the initial stage of updating (far from the stable state), the stabilization of neuron is very low ($\alpha_i(y_i, t)$ is near 0). Thus, the internal potential of neuron ($x_i(t+1)$) is mainly determined by the weight state of other neuron (the second term of Eq.(8)). As time proceeds and the state of neuron approaches to 0 or 1, the stabilization of neuron will increase. Finally the stabilization of neuron ($\alpha_i(y_i, t)$) will get near to 1, and the internal dynamic behavior of neuron will tend toward original updating mode. This guarantees that the network can always converge to a stable state. We define the parameter $\alpha_i(y_i, t)$ as following:

$$\alpha_i(y_i, t) = 1 - e^{-\frac{(0.5 - y_i(t))^2}{\epsilon} \cdot \frac{t}{\lambda}} \qquad (9)$$

where y_i is the state of neuron #i, t is the updating iteration, ϵ and λ are positive constant which decide the increase speed of $\alpha_i(y_i, t)$.

Now we show that if sigmoid function (Eq.(7)) is used as input/output function of neuron, the proposed method allows increases in energy initially, with such increases becoming less as updating proceeds, until finally the network tends toward a steepest descent algorithm.

In general, energy function of a Hopfield network can be written as following equation.

$$E = -\frac{1}{2}\sum_i\sum_j w_{ij} y_i(t) y_j(t) - \sum_i h_i y_i(t) \tag{10}$$

The change of energy caused by the change in the states of neurons is:

$$\Delta E = -\frac{1}{2}\sum_i\sum_j w_{ij}(y_i(t+1)y_j(t+1) - y_i(t)y_j(t))$$
$$- \sum_i h_i(y_i(t+1) - y_i(t)) \tag{11}$$

Adding and subtracting $y_i(t+1)y_j(t)$, and simplifying, we get:

$$\Delta E = -\frac{1}{2}\sum_i\sum_j w_{ij} y_i(t+1)\Delta y_j(t+1)$$
$$-\frac{1}{2}\sum_i\sum_j w_{ij} \Delta y_i(t+1) y_j(t)$$
$$-\sum_i h_i \Delta y_i(t+1) \tag{12}$$

In the asynchronous parallel mode, we can suppose that at time t, the state of neuron #k is changed. The change in the state of neuron #i is:

$$\Delta y_i(t+1) = y_i(t+1) - y_i(t) \tag{13}$$

We have $\Delta y_k(t+1) \neq 0$ and $\Delta y_i(t+1) = 0$ for $i \neq k$. Thus, Eq.(12) can be reduced to:

$$\Delta E = -\frac{1}{2}\sum_{i\neq k} w_{ik} y_i(t+1)\Delta y_k(t+1)$$
$$-\frac{1}{2}\sum_{i\neq k} w_{ki} \Delta y_k(t+1) y_i(t)$$
$$-h_k \Delta y_k(t+1) \tag{14}$$

Because of the facts that $\Delta y_i(t+1) = 0$, i.e., $y_i(t+1) = y_i(t)$ for $i \neq k$ and $w_{ik} = w_{ki}$, Eq.(14) can be rewritten to:

$$\Delta E = -\Delta y_k(t+1)(\sum_{i\neq k} w_{ki} y_i(t) + h_i) \tag{15}$$

Using $\Delta t = 1$, Eq.(5) and Eq.(8), Eq.(15) can be rewritten as follow:

$$\Delta E = -\Delta y_k(t+1)(x_k(t+1) - \alpha_k(y_k,t) \cdot x_k(t)) \tag{16}$$

Consider the case of $x_k(t) > x_k(t+1)$, according to the characteristic of sigmoid function, we can know that:

$$\Delta y_k(t+1) < 0 \tag{17}$$

Moreover, even $x_k(t) > x_k(t+1)$, if $\alpha_k(y_k,T)$ is sufficiently small, it is possible for:

$$x_k(t+1) > \alpha_k(y_k,t) \cdot x_k(t) \tag{18}$$

Using Eqs.(17) and (18), we can know from Eq.(16) that when $\alpha_k(y_k,t)$ is small, $\Delta E > 0$ is possible in the case of $x_k(t) > x_k(t+1)$. The possibility of the increase in energy becomes less as $\alpha_k(y_k,t)$ increases until finally the network tends toward a steepest descent algorithm. Thus we can say that the proposed method which uses Eq.(8) and Eq.(9) provides a mechanism for escaping from local minima and converging to a good stable state by introducing a stabilization parameter $\alpha_k(y_k,t)$ for neurons.

4 Algorithm

The algorithm procedure of solving the minimum crossing number problem using the proposed improved Hopfield neural network can be described as follow:

(1) Set constant A, B, T, ϵ and λ and set iteration step $t = 1$.
(2) Randomly initialize the internal potential x_{ij} for $i, j = 1, \cdots, N$.
(3) Update the state y_{ij} of neuron $\#ij$ for $i, j = 1, \cdots, N$ using sigmoid function.
(4) set $loop\_time = 1$.
(5) Loop until $loop\_time \geq 2*M$, where M is the number of edges. (a) Randomly select a neuron $\#ij$.
   (b) Use Eq.14 and Eq.15 to update the internal potential x_{ij} of neuron $\#ij$.
   (c) Use Eq.13 to update the state y_{ij} of neuron $\#ij$.
   (d) Increment the $loop\_time$ by 1.
(6) Increment the t by 1. If the network reaches an equilibrium state go to step 8, else go to step 4.
(7) Compute the crossing number using the stable state of the network.

5 Simulation Results

The proposed algorithm was experimented on PC station to some complete graph K_n. We simply set $A = B = 1.0$. ϵ and λ were selected to 0.1 and 135 respectively, the temperature parameter T in sigmoid function was set to 2.5. To evaluate our results, one-page heuristic [3] and Cimikowski et al.'s parallel

Table 1. Computational results

Graph	Edges	Optimal	One-page [3]	Cimikowski et al.'s algorithm [5]	This work
K5	10	1	1	1	1
K6	15	3	3	3	3
K7	21	9	9	9	9
K8	28	18	19	18	18
K9	36	36	36	36	36
K10	45	60	62	60	60
K11	55	100	100	100	100
K12	66	150	154	150	150
K13	78	–	265	225	225

algorithm [5] were also executed for comparison. The reason of selecting these methods for comparison is that these methods are typical one for solving the linear crossing number problem. The solutions found by different algorithms were shown in Table 1. From this table, we can see that one-page heuristic had the worst performance on these complete graphs. Both Cimikowski et al.'s algorithm and the proposed method found optimal solutions or near-optimal solutions. Besides, our simulations found that the rate to find good solutions by Cimikowski et al.'s algorithm was very low, while the proposed algorithm could find one hundred percent good solutions. Table 2 shows the detail simulation results by Cimikowski et al.'s algorithm and the proposed algorithm in 100 runs with different initial values of neuron, where the the average solution, the best solution, the rates of best solution were summarized. From this table, we can see that the proposed algorithm works better than Cimikowski et al.'s algorithm.

Table 2. Simulation results on complete graph in 100 runs with different initial value

Graph	Cimikowski et al.'s Algorithm			This work		
	Average	Best	Rate	Average	Best	Rate
K5	1.0	1	100%	1	1	100%
K6	3.6	3	42%	3	3	100%
K7	10.0	9	37%	9	9	100%
K8	19.8	18	19%	18	18	100%
K9	38.9	36	44%	36	36	100%
K10	63.6	60	12%	60	60	100%
K11	108.0	100	29%	100	100	100%
K12	166.0	150	13%	150	150	100%
K13	239.0	225	18%	225	225	100%

6 Conclusions

We have proposed an improved neural network algorithm for the linear crossing number problem and shown its effectiveness by simulation experiments. The proposed algorithm is based on an improved Hopfield neural network in which the internal dynamics is modified to permit temporary increases in the energy function in order to help the network escape from local minima. To verify the proposed algorithm, we tested it on some complete graphs. The experimental results indicated that the proposed algorithm could yield optimal or near-optimal solutions.

References

1. M. R. Garey and D. S. Johnson, "Crossing number is NP-complete," SIAM J. Alg. Disc. Meth. **4** (1983) 312–316
2. F. T. Leighton, "New lower bound techniques for VLSI," Math. Sys. Theory, **17** (1984) 47–70.
3. F. Shahrokhi, L. A. Szekely, O. Sykora and I. Vrto, "The book crossing number of a graph," J. Graph Theory, **21** (1996) 413–424
4. J.J. Hopfield and D.W.Tank, "Computing with neural circuits: A model." Science, **233** (1986) 625–633
5. R. Cimikowski and P. Shope, "A neural network algorithm for a graph layout problem," IEEE Trans on Neural Network, **7** (1996) 341–345
6. Y. Takefuji and K. C. Lee, "Artificial neural networks for four-coloring map problems and K-colorability problems," IEEE Trans. Circuits Syst., **38** (1991) 326–333

The Design of a Fuzzy-Neural Network for Ship Collision Avoidance

Yu-Hong Liu[1], Xuan-Min Du[2], and Shen-Hua Yang[1]

[1] Merchant Marine College of Shanghai Maritime University,
200135 Shanghai, China
yhliu@cen.shmtu.edu.cn
[2] Shanghai Marine Electronic Equipment Research Institute,
200025 Shanghai, China

Abstract. A fuzzy-neural network for ship collision avoidance where ships are in sight of one another is proposed in this article. There are three subsets: the subset of classifying ship encounter situations and collision avoidance actions, the subset of calculating the membership functions of speed ratio, and the subset of inferring alteration magnitude and action time. The weight values of the former two subsets are obtained by self-learning from a number of samples, while those of the last subset are obtained from experience. The test results show that by the use of this network, some valuable decisions can be made.

1 Introduction

An intelligent decision making system is an effective solution for ship collision avoidance by integrating some quantitative and qualitative methods. Fuzzy technology proposes a useful way of knowledge description and processing, which can also change qualitative reasoning into quantitative computation. But during the working process of the intelligent system created and based on fuzzy technologies, some membership functions and fuzzy rules are difficult to change or adjust. Neural networks have a strong capability for learning and imitating any nonlinear function. But the knowledge stored inside a neural network is unreadable and it is difficult to interpret how it is used. So, we make use of the advantages of fuzzy technology and a neural network, and combine them together to construct a fuzzy-neural inference network model for ship collision avoidance. The model not only has certain intelligibility to make some valuable decisions, but can also be conveniently modified.

2 Structure of the Fuzzy-Neural Inference Network

A simple ship collision avoidance process includes following several steps:

1. Collect and analyze data to obtain some important information about target ships, such as the course, speed, orientation and distance, etc.
2. Estimate the encounter situation and collision danger degree between own ship and each target ship.

3. Give some collision avoidance decisions, such as action's type, time and magnitude, according to the navigation regulations and above judgments.

There are many usable experiences, data and rules accumulated during navigation, and these can be used to construct the fuzzy-neural inference network in line with the above process. However, it is quite difficult and unpractical to carry out the above three steps with a single fuzzy-network. So, we divide the single network into several subsets, and each subset has a specific function, respective structure and learning algorithm. After being constructed and properly trained, these subsets are integrated into a compound fuzzy-neural inference network. The compound network is easy to develop, and to interpret and modify.

In reference [1] "the primary factors affecting collision avoidance action in sight of each other" and reference [2] "the turning range of give way ship in different speed and encounter angle", some important data and rules on encounter situations and collision avoidance action are given. Thereby, the basic structure of a fuzzy-neural inference network for ship collision avoidance is shown in Figure.1.

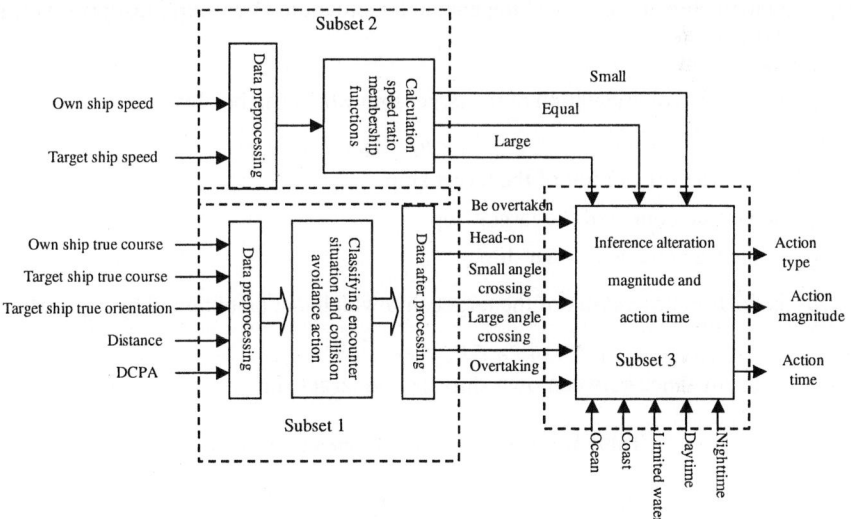

Fig. 1. The structure of a fuzzy-neural inference network for ship collision avoidance

Three subsets are involved in the above model. There is the subset of classifying encounter situation and collision avoidance action (Subset 1), the subset of calculating speed ratio membership functions (Subset 2) and the subset of inference alteration magnitude and action time (Subset 3). The inputs of Subset 1 and Subset 2 are the data coming from the user and other equipment by respective interface to describe the current ship encounter situation, while the outputs (after being processed) are taken as inputs of Subset 3. These final outputs of Subset 3 are the decisions for collision avoidance at the time.

The structures of each subset are independent, and their learning algorithms are also different, which will be discussed in the following sections.

3 Classifying Encounter Situation and Collision Avoidance Action

Ship encounter situation is an important factor for collision avoidance in sight of one another. Three kinds of encounter situation are presented in International Regulations for Preventing Collisions at Sea, 1972. There are overtaking (or being overtaken), head-on and crossing (with large angle and small angle). According to these regulations, different responsibilities, rules and actions should be obeyed, depending on the encounter situation.

There are 14 rules to be used to classify the encounter situations and collision avoidance actions. Eight of these rules are about non-overtaking situations and the other six rules are about overtaking situations. Each rule has the form as follows:

If $000° \leq \theta_T \leq 005°$, $\left|180° - |\varphi_T - \varphi_O|\right| \leq 5°$ and $R_T \leq 6$ n mile, then own ship and the target ship are in head-on encounter situation. Own ship must give way and should turn starboard. (Non-overtaking)

If $112.5° \leq \theta_O \leq 180°$, $|\varphi_T - \varphi_O| \leq 67.5°$, $R_T \leq 3$ n mile and $DCPA < 0$, then own ship and target ship are in overtaking encounter situation. Own ship must give way and should turn port. (Overtaking)

Where:

θ_T is the relative orientation of the target ship which can be obtained by a_T and φ_O.

$$\theta_T = a_T - \varphi_O$$

a_T is the true orientation of the target ship.

φ_T is the true course of the target ship.

φ_O is the true course of own ship.

θ_O is the true orientation of the target ship which can be obtained by a_T and φ_T.

$$\theta_O = a_T - \varphi_T + 180°$$

R_T is the distance between own ship and the target ship.

Table 1. Encoded rules of overtaking situations

Premise	θ_O	112.5° ~180°	00
		180° ~210°	01
		210° ~247.5°	10
		Others	11
	DCPA	<0	0
		>=0	1
Conclusion	Collision avoidance action	Turn starboard	00
		Turn port	01
		Stand-on	10
		No meaning	11

These rules can be encoded as a sample set and then stored in Subset 1 by self-learning and use of the rules can be carried out by forward reasoning in Subset 1.

All of these can make use of advantages of the network, such as parallel reasoning, data error tolerance and self-learning, etc.

For non-overtaking and overtaking situations, the premises and conclusions of all rules are encoded respectively in Table 1 and Table 2.

Table 2. Encoded rules of non-overtaking situations

Premise	θ_T	0° ~ 5°	000
		5° ~ 67.5°	001
		67.5° ~ 112.5°	010
		112.5° ~ 247.5°	011
		247.5° ~ 355°	100
		355° ~ 360°	101
	$|\varphi_T - \varphi_O|$	<=5°	0
		>5°	1
	R_T	0~3 n mile	0
		3~6 n mile	1
Conclusion	Encounter situation	Head-on	00
		Crossing	01
		Be overtaken	10
		No meaning	11
	Collision avoidance action	Turn starboard	00
		Turn port	01
		Stand-on	10
		No meaning	11

Two independent networks are built up respectively to process these non-overtaking and overtaking situation rules. Take the former as an example. The structure of the BP network contains three layers, five input neurons, four output neurons and five hidden neurons. 24 samples are used to train the network and the final connection values between the three layers and the thresholds of the hidden neurons are shown in Figure.2.

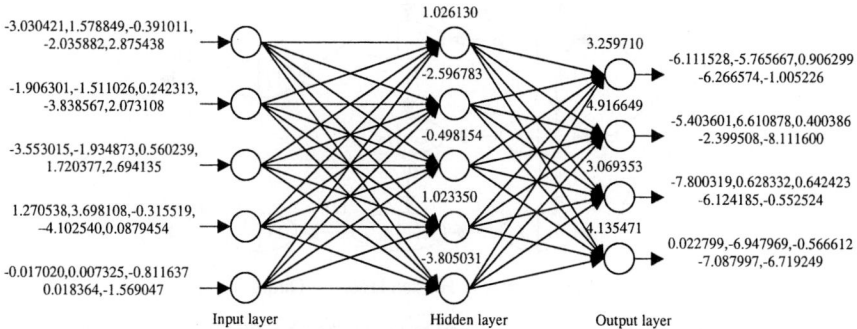

Fig. 2. The connection values and thresholds of a non-overtaking situation network

4 Calculation Speed Ratio Membership Functions

In order to make a problem simpler, the fuzzy words used to describe the speed ratio of own ship and target ship are "small", "equal" and "large". The range of the speed ratio is restricted form 0 to 2.0. These three membership functions are shown in Figure.3.

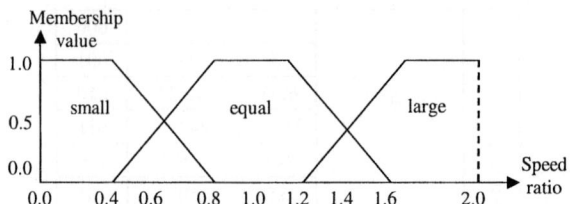

Fig. 3. Membership function of speed ratio

Theorem 1. (Kolmogorov theorem) For any given continuous function, $\Phi: E^m \to R^m$, $\Phi(X) = Y$. Here E is a close section [0,1], so Φ can be achieved accurately by a three layer neural network.

According to the theorem, each continuous membership function corresponding to the fuzzy word can be described and performed with a neural network. Generally, the monotone functions (such as the fuzzy words "small" and "large") can be achieved by a network with only one hidden neuron, while the non-monotone function (such as the fuzzy word "equal") can be achieved by a network with at least two hidden neurons. The network of calculation speed ratio membership functions with their connection values and thresholds is shown in Figure.4.

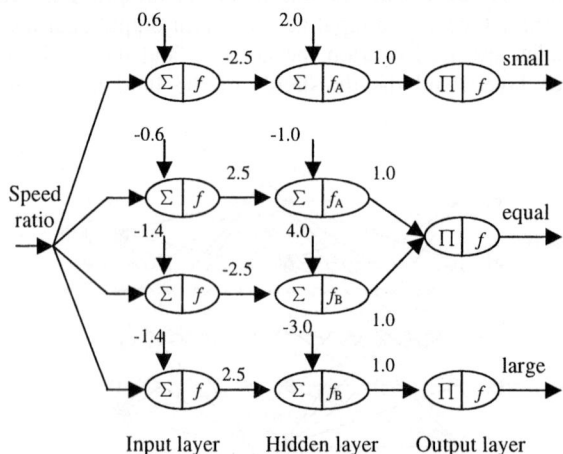

Fig. 4. The network of speed ratio membership functions

The value above each neuron is its threshold. The transfer functions of input and output layer neurons are linear functions, while the hidden layer neurons have two types of piecewise-linear function, namely f_A and f_B:

$$f_A(x) = \begin{cases} 0.4 & x \leq -0.2 \\ x + 0.6 & -0.2 < x < 0.2 \\ 0.8 & x \geq 0.2 \end{cases} \quad (1)$$

$$f_B(x) = \begin{cases} 1.2 & x \leq -0.2 \\ x + 1.4 & -0.2 < x < 0.2 \\ 1.6 & x \geq 0.2 \end{cases} \quad (2)$$

5 Inference Alteration Magnitude and Action Time

From the performance of Subset 3, the turning angle magnitude and action time can be obtained. Some connected values come from other subsets, such as part values between Layer 2 and Layer 3 which come from Subset 1, while some connected values come from navigation experiences, and can be revised conveniently, such as the values between Layer 1 and Layer 2. The transfer functions of neurons in Subset 3 are all linear functions. The basic structure of Subset 3 is shown in Figure.5.

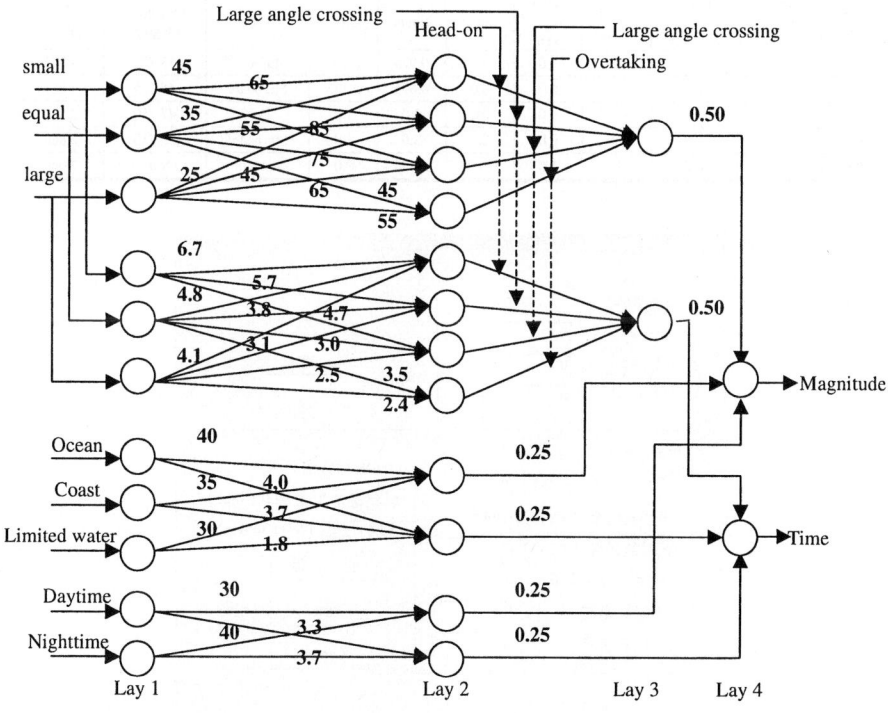

Fig. 5. The subset structure of inference alternation magnitude and action time

6 Conclusions

From the calculation of the fuzzy-neural inference network in some given ship encounter situation examples, the corresponding collision avoidance decisions (action type, turning magnitude and action time) are obtained and some of these are shown in Table 3.

Table 3. Encounter instances and performing results of the fuzzy-neural inference network

Input data

Own ship true course (degree)	Target ship true course (degree)	Target ship true orientation (degree)	Distance between two ships (nmile)	DCPA	Own ship speed (kts)	Target ship speed (kts)	Water area			Weather	
							Sea	Coast	Limit water	Day time	Night time
0	184	3	5	none	10	13	0.8	0.2	0.0	1.0	0.0
18	200	25	4.5	none	12	9	1.0	0.0	0.0	0.3	0.7
330	270	70	4	none	16	8	0.0	0.0	1.0	0.9	0.1
30	0	10	3	>0	11	6	0.0	0.6	0.4	0.0	1.0
270	230	190	3	none	7	14	1.0	0.0	0.0	1.0	0.0

Output data

Classifying encounter situation and collision avoidance action					Calculation speed ratio membership function			Inference alteration magnitude and action time		
Head-on	Small angle crossing	Large angle crossing	Overtaking	Been overtaken	Small	Equal	Large	Type	Magnitude (degree)	Time (nmile)
1.0	0.0	0.0	0.0	0.0	0.075	0.925	0.0	Starboard	35.125	4.281
0.0	1.0	0.0	0.0	0.0	0.0	0.675	0.325	Starboard	45.125	3.681
0.0	0.0	1.0	0.0	0.0	0.0	0.0	1.0	Port	47.750	2.535
0.0	0.0	0.0	1.0	0.0	0.0	0.0	1.0	Starboard	35.750	2.860
0.0	0.0	0.0	0.0	1.0	0.750	0.250	0.0	Stand on	None	None

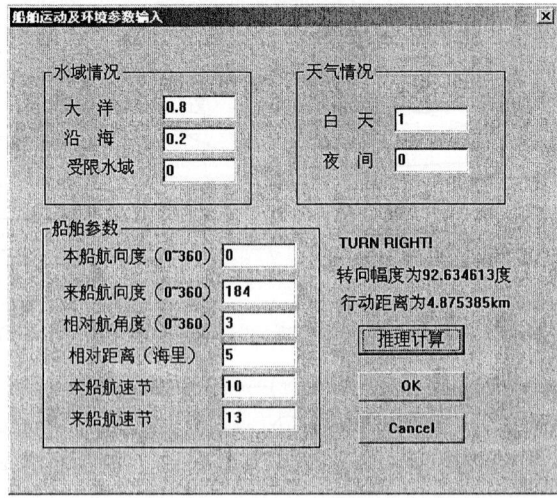

Fig. 6. Parameter input interface

It is clear from these instances that, by use of the fuzzy-neural inference network, some valid collision avoidance plans can be deduced from given facts. The network is simple and convenient. The whole of the reasoning process can be carried out by means of neuron connection and the calculations upon them. Figure 6 is the interface to input initial parameters. By depressing the button "inference and calculate", the output of the network can be obtained.

The network is also flexible. The great mass of connection values in Figure.5 can be revised easily according to real application or actual circumstance (see Figure 7), so that the network can have more practical worthiness.

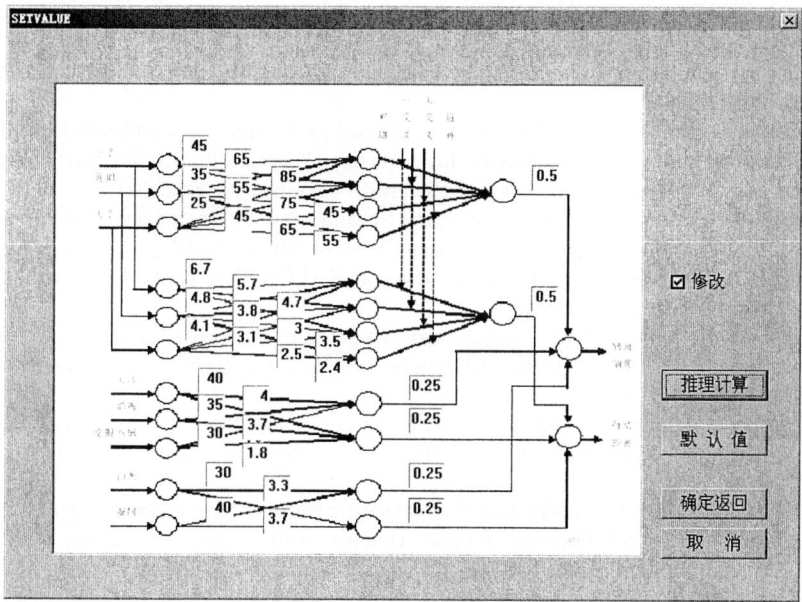

Fig. 7. Connect value update

Acknowledgement

This paper is supported by Doctor Subject Special Scientific Research Foundation for University from Ministry of Education Science and Technology Development Center under grant No. 20050254001 and also supported by Shanghai Leading Academic Discipline Project, Project Number T0603.

References

1. Jinsong Zhao, Fengchen Wang. The Principles of Collision Prevention at Sea. Publishing Company of Dalian Maritime University, 1999.
2. Zhongyi Zheng, Zhaolin Wu. Decision-making of Vessel Collision Avoidance. Publishing Company of Dalian Maritime University, 2000.

3. Xiedong Cao. Fuzzy Information Processing and Application. Science Publishing Company, 2003.
4. Bart Kosko. Fuzzy Engineering. Prentice Hall, 1999.
5. Licheng Jiao. Theory of Neural Network System. Publishing Company of Sian Electronic Technology University, 1995.
6. Alexander I. Galushkin. The Theory of Neural Network. Publishing Company of Tsinghua, 1999.
7. Martin T.Hagan, Howard B.Demuth, Mark H.Beale. Neural Network Design. PWS Publishing Company, 2003.
8. Luoya Zeng. The Application and Study of Fuzzy Neural Network. Guangxi Normal University, Master paper, 2000.
9. Jian Zhang. The Study and Application of Fuzzy Neural Network Model and Algorithm. Daqing Oil College, Master paper, 2002.
10. Jun Gao. Introduction of Intelligent Information Processing Methods. China Machine Press, 2004(6) 33-39.
11. Martha Grabowski, Stephen D.Sanbornc. Human performance and embedded intelligent technology in safety-critical systems. Int. J. Human-Computer Studies 58 (2003) 637–670.
12. Vassilios Petridis, Vassilis George Kaburasos. Fuzzy Lattic Neural Network: A Hybrid Model for Learning. IEEE Trans. on Neural Networks, Vol.9. No. 5, September 1998.
13. Sinan Altug, H.Joel Trussell, and Mo-yuen Chow. A "Mutual Update" Training Algorithm for Fuzzy Adaptive Logic/Decision Network (FALCOMN). IEEE Trans. on Neural Networks, Vol.10. No.1, January 1999.
14. Byoung-Jun Park, Witold Pedrycz and Sung-Kwan Oh. Fuzzy Polynomial Neural Networks: Hybrid Architectures of Fuzzy Model. IEEE Trans. On Fuzzy System, Vol.10, No.6, June 2002.
15. Jean-Shing Wang, C.S.George Lee. Self-adaptive Neuro-Fuzzy Inference Systems for Classification Applications. IEEE Trans. on Fuzzy System, Vol.10, No. 6, June 2002: 790-802.
16. Ludmil Mikhailov, Madan G.Singh. Fuzzy Analytic Network Process and its Application to the Development of Decision Support Systems. IEEE Trans. on System, Man and Cybernetics-Part C: Applications and Reviews, 2003, 33(1).
17. Nauck, Kruse. A Neuro-Fuzzy Approach to Obtain Interpretable Fuzzy Systems for Function Approximation. IEEE International Conference on Fuzzy Systems 1998 (FUZZ-IEEE'98), Anchorage, AK, May 4-9, 1998, pp. 1106-1111.
18. Nauck. Neuro-Fuzzy Systems: Review and Prospects. Fifth European Congress on Intelligent Techniques and Soft Computing (EUFIT'97), Aachen, Sep. 8-11, 1997, pp. 1044-1053.
19. Nauck/Kruse. Neuro-Fuzzy Systems for Function Approximation. International Workshop Fuzzy-Neuro Systems 1997 in Soest.
20. He Qiang, Hua Qiang, Wang Xizhao. Learning Weights of Fuzzy Production Rules by a MAX-MIN Neural Network. Fuzzy Systems and Mathematics, 2002(16), P388-392

A Genetic Algorithm-Based Neural Network Approach for Fault Diagnosis in Hydraulic Servo-Valves

Hao Huang, Kuisheng Chen, and Liangcai Zeng

College of Machinery & Automation, Wuhan University of Science and Technology,
Wuhan 430081, China
yellowrat@sohu.com, kschen@mail.wust.edu.cn

Abstract. The hydraulic servo-valve is the key component of the electro-hydraulic system. But it is difficult to diagnose faults in a hydraulic servo-valve. In this paper, a Genetic Algorithm-based Artificial Neural Network model for fault diagnosis in hydraulic servo–valves is proposed. We use a known set of servo-valve faults as the outputs to the valve-behavior model. Adoption of this approach brings about the advantages of reducing training time and increasing accuracy when compared with the traditional Back Propagation Neural Network.

1 Introduction

The hydraulic servo-valve is the key component of the electro-hydraulic system, and it is also the component with the highest fault rate in the system [1]. Unwanted faults in a hydraulic servo-valve lead to reduce controlling accuracy and endanger the stability of the system. Therefore, it is vital to diagnose the faults in a hydraulic servo-valve correctly and quickly [2].

A servo-valve fault is often characterized by the complex coupling of mechanical, electrical and hydraulic faults. Only an expert can diagnose the fault correctly and quickly. It is difficult to solve complicated faults in a servo-valve due to the nonlinear relationship between the fault phenomenon and the fault reason of the servo-valve. As a widely used and mature method, the neural networks (NN) model can be adopted in fault identification of a servo-valve. But in practical application, there are two problems that the traditional NN finds difficult to solve: one is the low speed of training, the other is the difficulty gaining access to the local minimum. Presently, there are many methods to improve the training speed of the network, such as improving the error function, adjusting the study rate dynamically and so on. But we must choose other optimization methods in order to overcome the difficulties of accessing the local minimum [3].

Genetic algorithm (GA) is an intelligent searching algorithm which can obtain the best result compared to other algorithms when its searching space is complex. It can search the global extremum easily, but GA is not suitable for result trimming and has difficulty determining the precise position of the result. In this paper, we establish an NN where the link weights between the nodes of the NN are calculated with the genetic learning algorithm. Based on this algorithm, the faults in a hydraulic servo-valve can be more easily identified and diagnosed [3].

2 Configuration of Experimental Hydraulic System

The performance of the servo-valve is the static characteristic of the servo-valve, which mainly includes pressure characteristic and flow characteristic. In the Computer Aided Test experiment table, we can obtain the performance curve of a servo-valve. The signal data of the fault is processed by the GA-BPNN.

The experimental hydraulic circuit for the servo-valve is shown in Fig. 1[4]. The pump (3) is driven by an electrical motor, and fluid is sucked into the pump (3) from the reservoir (1) through the filter (2). Oil driven by the pump flows through the fine filter (4) to the relief valve (7) and the tested servo-valve (8). The relief valve is used to adjust the circuit pressure and the pump flow goes to the reservoir (1) via the relief valve (7) except the flow goes to the tested servo-valve (8). If a positive current is input to the servo-valve (8), the valve will be shifted to the right mode. The valve will be shifted to the left mode with a negative current. If no current is input, the valve will at neutral position. The flow through the valve and the pressure at A and B will be different if the value of the current is changed. The flow and pressure of the servo-valve can be achieved with the pressure transducer and speed measuring motor. The different values of pressure and flow will be used as the sample data for the NN.

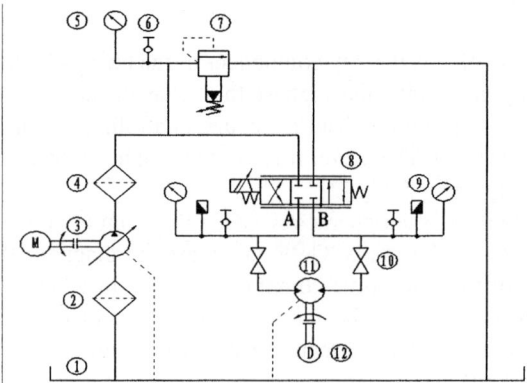

Fig. 1. Experimental hydraulic circuit for servo-valve. 1-reservoir, 2-filter, 3-electrical motor and pump, 4-filter, 5-manometer, 6-pressure tapping, 7-relief valve, 8-servo valve, 9-pressure transducer, 10-cut-off valve, 11-oil motor, 12-speed measuring motor.

3 Neural Network Based on Genetic Algorithm

3.1 The Steps of GA-BPNN

In this study, GA is inducted into the training process of the BPNN. First, optimize the initial weights of BPNN by using GA. Second, seek the best chromosome in the optimized initial weights. Third, utilize the BP algorithm to find the best individual. Finally, repeat the step until the precision requirement is met. GA-BP algorithm combines the advantages of BP and GA, while dispensing with their disadvantages. Thereby, its efficiency and effective training is better than that of BP algorithm [4]. The block diagram of the GA-BPNN system is shown in Fig. 2 [5].

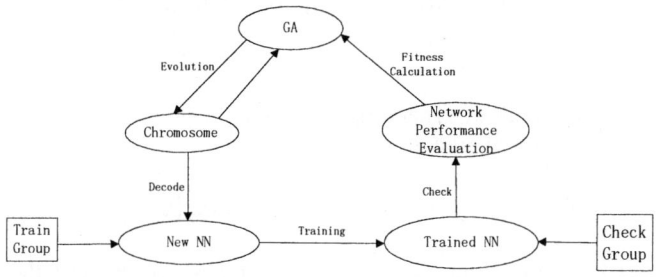

Fig. 2. The block diagram of GA – BPNN system

3.2 The Detailed Process of GA-BPNN

The chromosome and the evaluation function of GA are the weight and the error function of BPNN. The final result of GA is the weight vector of BPNN when optimizing the initial weights of BPNN with GA.

In the process of GA, a coding scheme of real numbers is applied. Each link weight is directly represented by a real number. An array of real numbers represents the weight distribution of BPNN, and assigns the weights corresponding to the real numbers. This method is very simple and possesses high precision.

An important characteristic of BPNN is that if the sum of a square error between the output value and the expected output value is smaller, the performance of the network is better. Consequently, we define the fitness function as $f=1/E$, and E is the sum of the square error.

The initial population is generated randomly. Selection operation affects the dimensions of the group greatly. The numbers of individuals of the group range between tens and hundreds.

The roulette selection method is employed in this study. The selection probability of each individual is proportional to individual fitness value. If the best individual in the parents group is better than the new group, the best individual in the parents group will reproduce to the next new group directly.

The genotype in coding scheme uses real numbers, so the intercross mode differs from the binary code mode. In general, arithmetic intercross mode is adopted. Its detailed operation process shows as follows [6][7].

Incoherent mutation operator is applied in this study. It combines the mutation operator with the evolution algorithms. The mutation range is comparatively larger in the initial stages of evolution and subsequently becomes less and less. It can be described as follows:

$x = (x_1, x_2, \cdots, x_k, \cdots, x_m)$ is the parents' result vector.

$x_k \in [a_k, b_k](1 \leq k \leq m)$ is selected to mutate.

The child is $x' = (x_1, x_2, \cdots, x_k', \cdots, x_m)$ after mutation.

$$x_k' = \begin{cases} x_k + \Delta(t, b_k - x_k), & if \quad rnd(2) = 0 \\ x_k - \Delta(t, b_k - x_k), & if \quad rnd(2) = 1 \end{cases} \quad (1)$$

where, rnd(2) is the result of generating a positive integral number 2 at random, and t is the current generation of evolution,

$$\Delta(t, y) = y(1 - r^{(1-t/T)^\lambda}), \Delta(t, y) \in [0, y] \quad (2)$$

where $r \in (0,1)$ is a random number, T is the highest epoch, λ is the parameter of incoherence degree, and $\lambda \in [2, 5]$.

A difficulty of using GA is how to decide the intercross probability and mutation probability. Intercross probability controls the rate of intercross operation. If the intercross probability is too great, then the best result is probably destroyed quickly; and if its value is too small, then searching is stagnated. Mutation probability is a factor that increases the diversity of the group, but if its value is too great, then the better mode is probably destroyed, the result is far from the best result and GA turns to random searching; and if its value is too small, then it isn't easy to generate new genes and it is unable to get rid of the result that gets into the local extremum.

In order to speed up the searching of the GA and to avoid getting into the local extremum, the self-adaptation adjusting method to intercross probability and mutation probability is shown as follows:

$$P_c = \begin{cases} k_1(f_{max} - f_c')/(f_{max} - \bar{f}) & f_c' \geq \bar{f} \\ k_3 & f_c' \prec \bar{f} \end{cases} \quad (3)$$

$$P_m = \begin{cases} k_2(f_{max} - f)/(f_{max} - \bar{f}) & f_c' \geq \bar{f} \\ k_4 & f_c' \prec \bar{f} \end{cases} \quad (4)$$

where, f_c' is the better individual's fitness in the parents before intercross, f is the individual's fitness that must be mutated, and $\bar{f}$ is the average individual's fitness. $k_1 = k_3 = 1, k_2 = k_4 = 0.5$.

In order to shorten the learning time, the self-adaptation learning rate of BP is shown as follows:[7]

$$w(k+1) = w(k) + \alpha(k)D(k) \quad (5)$$

$$\alpha(k) = 2^{\lambda}\alpha(k-1) \quad (6)$$

$$\lambda = sign[D(K)D(K-1)] \quad (7)$$

where $\alpha(k)$ is the learning rate and $D(k)$ is the gradient.

4 Diagnosis of the Experiment Data

We set the five experimental states of the hydraulic servo-valve as:

- the normal state,
- with the seal in one control chamber being damaged 8.33%,
- with the seal in one control chamber being damaged 50%,
- with the seal in one control chamber being damaged 100%, and
- with the fixed orifice of the pilot valve in one side being blocked.

These states are represented by the outputs of the GA-BPNN. In these states, the pressure characteristics of the servo-valve are measured. In the pressure characteristics, near the zero position of the servo-valve, pressure differences at the same current are the inputs GA-BPNN uses to form training samples (Table 1 details one of the samples). The learning method possesses tutor information, the sample's target output "1 0 0 0 0" shows that the corresponding fault occurred. Network training and the identification of mode are accomplished by the GA-BP diagnosis software. The BPNN requires 74 cells in the input layer, five cells in the output layer, one hidden layer, and the nodes of the hidden layer can be changed. In the previous five states of the servo-valve, 30 training samples can be acquired at the pressure of 2Mpa, 2.5Mpa, 3Mpa, 4Mpa, 4.5Mpa and 5Mpa to train the network. The dimensionless data that was acquired at 3.5Mpa testing-pressure of the five states is sent to the trained network to confirm the network and check whether the output values are within the error scope. It is the process of the artificial NN fault mode identification. The GA-BPNN structure of fault diagnosis is shown in Fig. 3.

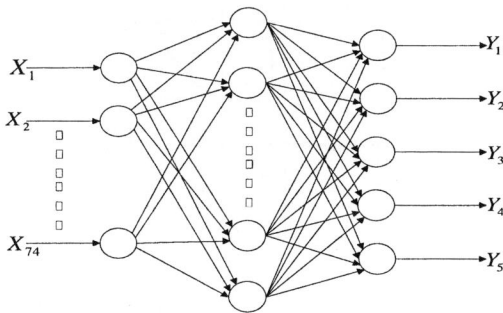

Fig. 3. GA-BPNN structure

Table 1. Testing-pressure is 2MPa and the hydraulic servo-valve is in normal state

I	-40	-37.8	-35.6	-33.3	-31.1	-28.9	-26.7	-24.5	-22.2	-
P	-0.96	-0.95	-0.93	-0.92	-0.89	-0.84	-0.76	-0.64	-0.53	-
P'	-0.99	-0.98	-0.98	-0.98	-0.98	-0.98	-0.98	-0.98	-0.98	-
I	-20	-17.8	-15.6	-13.3	-11.1	-8.9	-6.7	-4.5	-2.2	0
P	-0.44	-0.36	-0.29	-0.24	-0.18	-0.09	0.38	0.80	0.89	0.94
P'	-0.98	-0.98	-0.98	-0.98	-0.98	-0.98	-0.98	-0.97	-0.97	-0.95
I	2.2	4.5.	6.7	8.9	11.2	13.4	15.6	17.8	20	22.2
P	0.96	0.98	0.99	0.99	0.99	0.99	0.99	1.0	1.0	1.0
P'	-0.92	-0.88	-0.84	-0.78	-0.61	0.24	0.31	0.39	0.44	0.55
I	24.5	26.7	28.9	31.1	33.3	35.6	37.8	40	-	-
P	1.0	1.0	1.0	1.0	1.0	1.0	1.0	1.0	-	-
P'	0.66	0.78	0.89	0.93	0.96	0.98	0.98	0.99	-	-

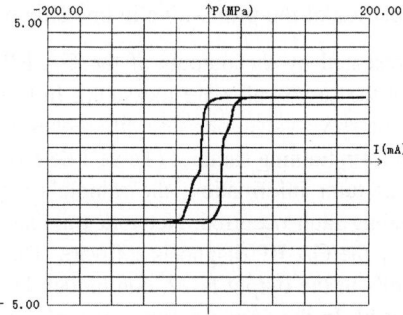

Fig. 4. Normal condition at 2.0Mpa

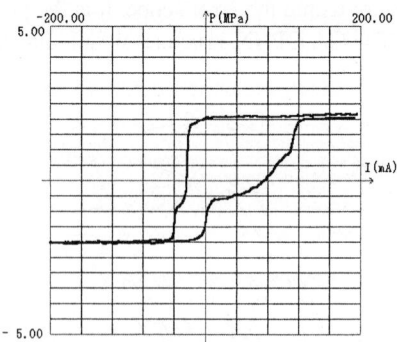

Fig. 5. One side of fixed throttle hole of the pilot valve being blocked at 2.0Mpa

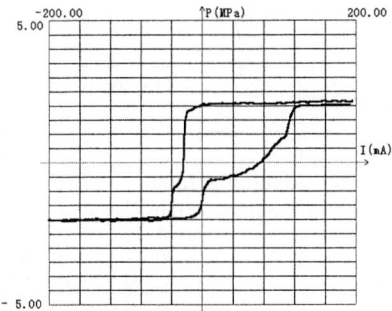

Fig. 6. The seal in one control chamber being 100% damaged at 2.0Mpa

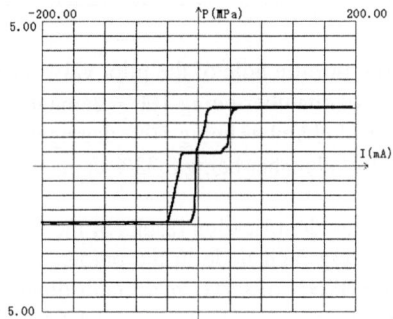

Fig. 7. The seal in one control chamber being 50% damaged at 2.0Mpa

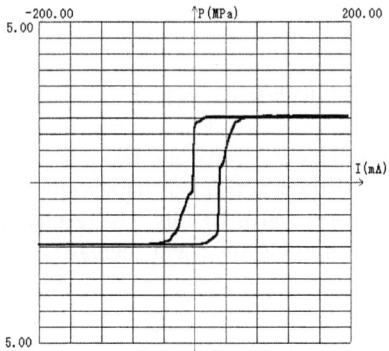

Fig. 8. The seal in one control chamber being 8.33% damaged at 2.0Mpa

The pressure characteristics of the servo-valve when the testing pressure is at 2.0Mpa, are shown in Fig.4 ~ Fig.8.

Table 2. The Result Of GA-BPNN Training And Mode Identification

Network training record				The result of Fault mode identification record					
Permissible error	The hidden layer node	GA's parameters	Training cycle	Input state	Network output				
					Y1	Y2	Y3	Y4	Y5
0.1	28	Group size M=80 P_c=0.4 P_m=0.05	242	A	0.9514	0.0105	0.0060	0.0236	0.0264
				B	0.0151	0.9743	0.0245	0.0167	0.0045
				C	0.0149	0.0186	0.9666	0.0132	0.0120
				D	0.0270	0.0151	0.0056	0.9695	0.0126
				E	0.0291	0.0007	0.0206	0.0053	0.9746

A - normal condition.
B - one side of the fixed throttle hole of the pilot valve being blocked.
C - the seal in one control chamber being 100% damaged.
D - the seal in one control chamber being 50% damaged.
E - the seal in one control chamber being 8.33% damaged.

Table 2 is a group of mode identification results of the GA-BPNN. From Table 2, it is clear that the corresponding fault node in the output mode is close to 1, and else where it is close to 0. In a BPNN of servo-valve fault diagnosis, the training cycle is 2858, and the permissible error is 0.3 [1]. In a GA-BPNN, the training cycle reduces to 242, and the permissible error is 0.1. It is clear that the method presented in this paper can be used to diagnose the servo-valve faults quickly and accurately, and the network can memorize the studied knowledge.

5 Conclusion

It is clear that when the GA-BPNN is applied to fault diagnosis of the hydraulic servo-valve, it can memorize the studied knowledge quickly and accurately. In this paper, five states of hydraulic servo-valve are taken as the network output and the processed pressure characteristic data taken as input values. The method presented in this study can simulate the servo-valve's faults. The results prove that GA-BPNN has the advantages of reducing training time and increasing accuracy when compared with the BPNN.

Acknowledgement

This work is supported by the Hydraulic Laboratory of Wuhan University of Science and Technology. Their help is highly appreciated. We are also grateful for the help of Dr. Qi Luo and Mr. Xinyuan Chen, who have given the authors a lot of incentive to write this paper.

References

1. LiangCai Zeng, GuoZheng Sun: Fault Diagnosis for Electro-hydraulic Servo-valve Based on Neural Network. Application of science and technology, Vol 29, No. 4, pp. 4-6, Apr. 2002.
2. YiMin Xu: Study of the fault mode identification for Electro-hydraulic Servo-valve based on BP Neural Network. Journal of Wuhan University of Science and Technology, Vol 22, No. 2, pp. 164-166, June 1999.
3. Shengwei Wang, Zhiming Jiang: Valve fault detection and diagnosis based on CMAC neural networks. Journal of Energy and Buildings, Vol 36, No. 3, pp.599-610, June 2004.
4. T. Knohl, H. Unbehauen: Adaptive position control of electrohydraulic servo systems using ANN. Mechatronics, Vol 10, pp.127-143,2000.
5. Jinn-Moon Yang, Jorng-Tzong Horng and Cheng-Yan Kao: A Genetic algorithm with adaptive mutations and family competition for training neural networks. International Journal of Neural Systems, Vol. 10, No. 5, pp. 333-352, 2000.
6. FengQin Wang, Yin Gao, Jun Zhao: Optimization of neural network based on genetic algorithm. Journal of Yanshan University, Vol. 25, No. 3, pp. 234-238, July 2001.
7. Baoshu Wang: The application of ANN and GA in Data. XiDian University Press, XiAn,2001.
8. Lewen Fan, Haiping Fang, Zhifang Lin: Efficiency of modified genetic algorithms on two-dimensional system. International Journal of Modern Physics C, Vol. 11, No. 3, pp.593-605, 2000.

Sensitivity Analysis of Madalines to Weight Perturbation

Yingfeng Wang[1], Xiaoqin Zeng[1], and Daniel S. Yeung[2]

[1] Department of Computer Science and Engineering, Hohai University,
Nanjing 210098, China
{wangyf, xzeng}@hhu.edu.cn
[2] Department of computing, The Hong Kong Polytechnic University,
Hung Hom, Kowloon, Hong Kong
csdaniel@comp.polyu.edu.hk

Abstract. This paper aims at exploring the behavior of the sensitivity for an ensemble of Madalines. An algorithm is first given to compute the Madalines' sensitivity, and its efficiency is verified by computer simulations. Then, based on the algorithm, the sensitivity analysis is conducted, which shows that the dimension of input has little effect on the sensitivity as long as the dimension is sufficient large, and the increases in the number of Adalines in a layer and the number of layers will lead the sensitivity to increase under an upper bound. The analysis results will be useful for designing robust Madalines.

1 Introduction

Generally, an artificial neural network is aimed at realizing a mapping between its input and output by establishing its connection weight during training. Therefore, the sensitivity of a neural network's output to the weight perturbations is a fundamental issue with both theoretical and practical values in neural network researches. It is hopefully expected that the analysis of the sensitivity can be helpful for designing robust networks. This paper focuses on exploring the behavior of the sensitivity for ensemble Madalines.

In the past two decades, many researchers paid attention to the sensitivity of neural networks [1~8], including the Madaline networks. Stevenson et al. [1] first systematically investigated the sensitivity of Madalines to weight errors by using a hypersphere model. They theoretically analyzed the sensitivity of Madalines under the assumption that the input and weight perturbations are small and the number of Adalines per layer is sufficiently large. Recently, we made use of a hypercube model instead of the hypersphere model to consider the sensitivity of Madalines [8]. However, the two approaches are only suitable for an individual Madaline with fixed weigh.

With a goal to explore the behavior of the sensitivity for an ensemble of Madalines, we employ a new approach to consider the sensitivity of Madalines without fixed weight. In the approach, a probability model is set up, then a formula is derived for calculation of the sensitivity of Adalines, and finally an algorithm is designed to compute the sensitivity of Madalines. Using the formula and the algorithm, we analyze the effects of some network parameters on the sensitivity. The analysis results show that the dimension of input has little effect on the sensitivity as long as the dimension is sufficient large, while increasing the number of Adalines in a layer and the number of layers will lead the sensitivity to increase under an upper bound.

The rest of this paper is arranged as follows. The model of Madalines is briefly described in Section 2. The sensitivity of Adalines is discussed in Section 3, and that of Madalines is in Section 4. In Section 5, the effects of some network parameters on the sensitivity of Madalines are analyzed separately. Finally, Section 6 concludes the paper.

2 The Madaline Model

A Madaline in general can have L layers, and each layer l ($1 \leq l \leq L$) has n^l ($n^l \geq 1$) Adalines. The form $n^0 - n^1 - ... - n^L$ is used to represent a Madaline with certain structural configuration, in which each n^l ($0 \leq l \leq L$) not only indicates the number of Adalines (n^0 is an exception which indicates the dimension of input), but also stands for a layer from left to right. n^0 stands for the input layer and n^L for the output layer. The number of Adalines in layer $l-1$ is equal to the output dimension of that layer, which is also equal to the input dimension of layer l, thus the input dimension of layer l is n^{l-1}. For Adaline i ($1 \leq i \leq n^l$) in layer l, its input vector is $X^l = (x_1^l, ..., x_{n^{l-1}}^l)^T$, its weight vector is $W_i^l = (w_{i1}^l, ..., w_{in^{l-1}}^l)^T$, and its output is $y_i^l = f(X^l W_i^l)$, where $f()$ is the following commonly used hard-limit function:

$$f(x) = \begin{cases} 1 & x \geq 0 \\ -1 & x < 0 \end{cases} \tag{1}$$

For each layer l, all Adalines in it have the same input vector X^l. Its weight set is $W^l = \{W_1^l, ..., W_{n^l}^l\}$. For an entire Madaline its input is the vector X^1, its weight is $W = W^1 \cup ... \cup W^L$. Let $\Delta W_i^l = (\Delta w_{i1}^l, ..., \Delta w_{in^{l-1}}^l)^T$ be the perturbation of weight vector, and $X'^l = (x_1'^l, ..., x_{n^{l-1}}'^l)^T$ and $W_i'^l = (w_{i1}'^l, ..., w_{in^{l-1}}'^l)^T$ be the corresponding perturbed input and weight vectors, respectively.

3 The Sensitivity of Adalines

A perturbation in the direction of the input vector can alter the output of an Adaline and a perturbation in the weight vector can also alter the Adaline's input-output mapping. In this section, the effect of those perturbations on the output of the Adaline is studied. Because the network is studied before training, it is assumed that all inputs of n-dimension are uniformly distributed and all weight elements are independently uniformly distributed in the interval $[-a, a]$, where a is a given positive real number. Simultaneously, all elements of the weight perturbation vector satisfy $|\Delta w_i| < a$.

Definition: The sensitivity of Adaline i in layer l is defined as the mathematical expectation of half of deviated output of the Aadaline due to its input and weight perturbations with respect to all input patterns and all possible weights in the range of $[-a,a]$, which is expressed as

$$s_i^l = E(\frac{1}{2}|f(X^l W_i^l) - f(X'^l W_i'^l)|) \qquad (2)$$

Since the perturbation of an Adaline's input element can only result in either $x_j' = x_j$ or $x_j' = -x_j$, it is obvious that an affected product in $X'W$ can be expressed as $x_j' w_j = (-x_j)w_j = x_j(-w_j)$, this means that the effective perturbation of x_j is equivalent to the change of the sign of w_j. In this way, the input perturbation can easily be converted to the weight perturbation. Without the loss of generality, only weight perturbation is considered in the following discussions of the sensitivity computation. Besides, for the sake of expression simplicity, the superscript and the subscript that mark an Adaline's layer and its order in the layer are omitted since the Adaline's position in the network has no interest to us in this section.

According to (1), it is obvious that whether there is an output deviation due to weight perturbation at input $X^q (1 \leq q \leq 2^n)$ is totally dependent on the signs of $X^q W$ and $X^q W'$, namely, the output deviation occurs if and only if $X^q W$ and $X^q W'$ have opposite signs ($X^q W$ and $X^q W'$ or $X^q W$ and $X^q W'$). This inspires us to consider the sensitivity as the probability of XW and $X^q W'$ having different signs for all input patterns, and give the following notations and expressions.

$$s = P(f(XW) \neq f(XW')) = 1 - P(f(XW) = f(XW'))$$
$$= 1 - (P((XW \geq 0) \cap (XW' \geq 0)) + P((XW < 0) \cap (XW' < 0))) \qquad (3)$$

In order to derive a computable expression for the sensitivity, we will follow such a clue that is first to derive the distributions of XW and $X^q W'$ separately, then the joint distribution of them, and finally the probability obtained by using the joint distribution.

Let $\xi_i = x_i w_i$, then $\xi_1, \xi_2, ..., \xi_n$ are independent each other. Since x_i and w_i are independent, the expectation is $E(\xi_i) = E(x_i)E(w_i) = 0$ and the variance is $D(\xi_i) = E(x_i^2 w_i^2) - [E(x_i w_i)]^2 = E(w_i^2) = a^2/3$.

Because $\xi_1, \xi_2, ... \xi_n$ are independent identical distribution, according to the center limited theorem XW converges in distribution to a random variable with normal distribution $N(0, na^2/3)$.

Let $\xi_i' = x_i w_i'$, then $\xi_1', \xi_2', ..., \xi_n'$ are independent each other. Since x_i and w_i' are independent, the expectation is $E(\xi_i') = E(x_i)E(w_i') = 0$ and the variance is

$$D(\xi_i') = E(x_i^2 w_i'^2) - [E(x_i w_i')]^2 = \frac{a^2}{3} + \Delta w_i^2 \qquad (4)$$

For each ξ'_j, we have

$$F_j(x) = P\{\xi'_j \leq x\} = \begin{cases} 1 & x \geq a+|\Delta w_i| \\ \dfrac{x+3a-|\Delta w_i|}{4a} & a-|\Delta w_i| \leq x < a+|\Delta w_i| \\ \dfrac{x+a}{2a} & -a+|\Delta w_i| \leq x < a-|\Delta w_i| \\ \dfrac{x+a+|\Delta w_i|}{4a} & -a-|\Delta w_i| \leq x < -a+|\Delta w_i| \\ 0 & x < -a-|\Delta w_i| \end{cases} \quad (5)$$

Then, due to the *Lindeberg condition*

$$\forall \tau > 0, \quad \lim_{n \to \infty} \frac{1}{B_n^2} \sum_{j=1}^n \int_{|x-u_j| \geq \tau B_n} (x-u_j)^2 dF_j(x) = 0 \quad (6)$$

where $B_n^2 = \sum_{i=1}^n D(\xi_i)^2$ and $u_j = E(\xi_j)$. The following equation can be derived,

$$\frac{1}{B_n^2} \sum_{j=1}^n \int_{|x-u_j| \geq \tau B_n} (x-u_j)^2 dF_j(x) = \frac{1}{B_n^2} \sum_{j=1}^n \int_{|x| \geq \tau B_n, |x| \leq a+|\Delta w_j|} x^2 dx \quad (7)$$

Then, we have

$$0 \leq \frac{1}{B_n^2} \sum_{j=1}^n \int_{|x| \geq \tau B_n, |x| \leq a+|\Delta w_j|} x^2 dx \leq \frac{1}{B_n^2} \sum_{j=1}^n \int_{|x| \leq a+|\Delta w_j|} x^2 dx = \frac{1}{B_n^2} \sum_{j=1}^n \left.\frac{x^3}{3}\right|_{-a-|\Delta w_j|}^{a+|\Delta w_j|} = \frac{2\sum_{i=1}^n (a+|\Delta w_i|)^2}{3(n\frac{a^2}{3} + \sum_{j=1}^n \Delta w_j^2)} \quad (8)$$

We have $\displaystyle\lim_{n \to \infty} \frac{1}{B_n^2} \sum_{j=1}^n \int_{|x| \geq \tau B_n, |x| \leq a+|\Delta w_j|} x^2 dx = 0$, because $\displaystyle\lim_{n \to \infty} \frac{2\sum_{i=1}^n (a+|\Delta w_i|)^2}{3(n\frac{a^2}{3} + \sum_{j=1}^n \Delta w_j^2)} = 0$.

So, the *Lindeberg condition* is satisfied by $\xi'_1, \xi'_2, \ldots, \xi'_n$. Then XW' converges in distribution to a random variable with normal distribution $N(0, \dfrac{na^2}{3} + \sum_{i=1}^n \Delta w_i^2)$.

With the aim at deriving the joint probability density function of XW and XW', it is required to obtain the covariance and the correlation coefficient of them. The covariance can be derived as follows,

$$Cov(XW, XW') = E\{[\sum_{i=1}^{n} x_i w_i - E(\sum_{i=1}^{n} x_i w_i)][\sum_{i=1}^{n} x_i w'_i - E(\sum_{i=1}^{n} x_i w'_i)]\}$$

$$= E(\sum_{\substack{i=1 \\ j=1}}^{n} x_i x_j w_i w'_j) = \sum_{\substack{i=1 \\ j=1}}^{n} E(x_i x_j) E(w_i w'_j) \quad (9)$$

while $i = j$, we have $E(x_i x_j) = 1$. As to $i \neq j$, because the probabilities of x_i and x_j being 1 or -1 are the same, the probability of $x_i x_j$ must also be so, and we have $E(x_i x_j) = 0$. Then,

$$\sum_{\substack{i=1 \\ j=1}}^{n} E(x_i x_j) E(w_i w'_j) = \sum_{i=1}^{n} E(w_i w'_i) = \sum_{i=1}^{n} E[w_i (w_i + \Delta w_i)] = na^2/3$$

Therefore we obtain

$$Cov(\sum_{i=1}^{n} x_i w_i, \sum_{i=1}^{n} x_i w'_i) = na^2/3 \quad (10)$$

With (10) the correlation coefficient of XW and XW', which is denoted as ρ, can be written as

$$\rho = \frac{Cov(\sum_{i=1}^{n} x_i w_i, \sum_{i=1}^{n} x_i w'_i)}{\sqrt{D(\sum_{i=1}^{n} x_i w_i)} \sqrt{D(\sum_{i=1}^{n} x_i w'_i)}} = \frac{\frac{na^2}{3}}{\sqrt{\frac{na^2}{3}} \sqrt{\frac{na^2}{3} + \sum_{i=1}^{n} \Delta w_i^2}} = \frac{na}{\sqrt{n^2 a^2 + 3n \sum_{i=1}^{n} \Delta w_i^2}} \quad (11)$$

So, the joint probability function of XW and XW' can be approximately expressed as the following bivariate normal integral:

$$F(x, y) = P\{\sum_{i=1}^{n} x_i w_i \leq x, \sum_{i=1}^{n} x_i w'_i \leq y\}$$

$$\approx \int_{-\infty}^{x} \int_{-\infty}^{y} \frac{1}{2\pi B_n B'_n \sqrt{1-\rho^2}} \exp(\frac{-1}{2(1-\rho^2)}(\frac{x^2}{B_n^2} - 2\rho \frac{xy}{B_n B'_n} + \frac{y^2}{B_n'^2})) dx dy \quad (12)$$

where $B_n = \sqrt{D(\sum_{i=1}^{n} x_i w_i)}$ and $B'_n = \sqrt{D(\sum_{i=1}^{n} x_i w'_i)}$,

and the corresponding joint probability density function is:

$$f(x, y) \approx \frac{1}{2\pi B_n B'_n \sqrt{1-\rho^2}} \exp(\frac{-1}{2(1-\rho^2)}(\frac{x^2}{B_n^2} - 2\rho \frac{xy}{B_n B'_n} + \frac{y^2}{B_n'^2})) \quad (13)$$

Now, based on the above discussion, it is possible to calculate the probability. However, the following transformation needs to be introduced in advance, which solution can be found in [9].

$$\Psi(-\beta_1,-\beta_2,\rho) = \int_{-\infty}^{-\beta_1}\int_{-\infty}^{-\beta_2} \frac{1}{2\pi\sqrt{1-\rho^2}} \exp(-\frac{1}{2} \cdot \frac{x_1^2+x_2^2-2\rho x_1 x_2}{1-\rho^2})dx_1 dx_2$$

$$= \Phi(-\beta_1)\Phi(-\beta_2) + \int_0^\rho \frac{1}{2\pi\sqrt{1-t^2}} \exp(-\frac{1}{2} \cdot \frac{\beta_1^2+\beta_2^2-2\beta_1\beta_2 t}{1-t^2})dt \quad (14)$$

where $\Phi(x) = \int_{-\infty}^x \frac{1}{\sqrt{2\pi}} \exp(-\frac{1}{2}x^2)dx$.

By means of (13), (14) and the symmetry property: $\int_0^{+\infty}\int_0^{+\infty} f(x,y)dxdy = \int_{-\infty}^0\int_{-\infty}^0 f(x,y)dxdy$, the probability, i.e. the sensitivity, can finally be derived as

$$s = 1-(P((XW \geq 0)\cap(XW' \geq 0)) + P((XW < 0)\cap(XW' < 0)))$$

$$\approx 1-(\int_0^{+\infty}\int_0^{+\infty} f(x,y)dxdy + \int_{-\infty}^0\int_{-\infty}^0 f(x,y)dxdy) = 1-2\int_{-\infty}^0\int_{-\infty}^0 f(x,y)dxdy$$

$$= 1-2\Psi(0,0,\rho) = 1-2(\frac{1}{2}\cdot\frac{1}{2} + \frac{1}{2\pi}\int_0^\rho \frac{1}{\sqrt{1-t^2}}dt) = \frac{\arccos\rho}{\pi}. \quad (15)$$

To verify the efficiency of the formula, the sensitivity results for three Adalines with input dimensions of being 3, 4 and 5 were separately computed by (15) with $a = 1$ and the elements of weight perturbations being identical and ranging from 0 to 0.1 with an increment of 0.01. Meanwhile, computer simulations were run to compute the actual probability of the output deviations for the three Adalines with the same parameters as in the sensitivity computation. The results are shown in Fig. 1-1. Form Fig. 1-1 it can be concluded that our theoretical results have the same tendencies with the simulation results.

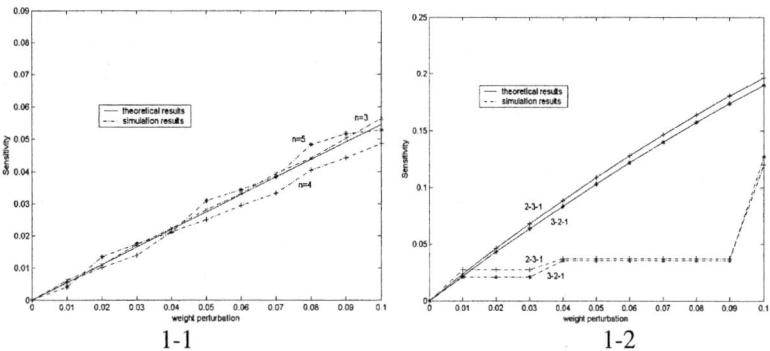

1-1   1-2

Fig. 1. Sensitivity of Adalines and Madalines to weight perturbation

4 The Sensitivity of Madalines

Our final goal is to determine the sensitivity of Madalines to input and weight perturbations. Based on the structural characteristics of Madalines and the sensitivity of Adalines discussed in last section, we define the sensitivity of Madalines as follows.

Definition: *The sensitivity of a Madaline is a vector in which each element corresponds to one Adaline on the output layer and is the sensitivity of the corresponding Adaline due to input and weight perturbations, which is expressed as*

$$S = S^L = (s_1^L, s_2^L, \ldots, s_{n^L}^L)^T . \tag{16}$$

There are two sources of perturbations for a Madaline. One is the weight perturbation of all layers; the other is the input perturbation from input layer denoted as $S^0 = (s_1^0, s_2^0, \ldots, s_{n^0}^0)^T$ that indicates the probability of each input element's perturbation. In a Madaline network, the output of layer l is the input of its immediately succeeding layer. For Adaline i ($1 \leq i \leq n^l$) in layer l, its sensitivity is the probability of the ith element of the input vector being perturbed in layer $l+1$. To each layer, it is obvious that there are many kinds of the different combinations while some elements of the input vector are perturbed. For layer l, the mean value of s_i^{l-1} is expressed as

$$\overline{s^{l-1}} = \frac{1}{n^{l-1}} \sum_{i=1}^{n^{l-1}} s_i^{l-1} . \tag{17}$$

In the following derivations, $s_1^l, s_2^l, \ldots, s_{n^{l-1}}^l$ are approximately replaced by $\overline{s^{l-1}}$, which is the mathematical expectation of s_i^{l-1}.

Thus, the probability of k elements being perturbed in the input of layer l can be approximately expressed as

$$p_k^l \approx C_{n^{l-1}}^k (1 - \overline{s^{l-1}})^{n^{l-1}-k} (\overline{s^{l-1}})^k . \tag{18}$$

In order to compute the corresponding correlation coefficient for an Adaline with both input and weight perturbations, (15) needs to be modified to merge the input perturbation into the weight perturbation. Let ρ_{ik}^l denote the correlation coefficient of the ith Adaline in layer l with k input elements perturbed and $W_i''^l = (w_{i1}''^l, \ldots, w_{in^{l-1}}''^l)^T$ represent the perturbed weight after the merge, (14) can be modified as follows by noticing that we have either $w_{ij}''^l = w_{ij}'^l$, i.e. $w_{ij}''^l = w_{ij}^l + \Delta w_{ij}^l$, when jth input element is not perturbed or $w_{ij}''^l = -w_{ij}'^l$, i.e. $w_{ij}''^l = -w_{ij}^l - \Delta w_{ij}^l$, when jth input element is perturbed. Then we have

$$E(x_i^l w_{ij}''^l) = E(x_i^l w_{ij}''^l) = E(x_i^l) E(w_{ij}''^l) = 0 \tag{19}$$

According to (4), it can be derived that,

$$D(x_i'^l w_{ij}''^l) = D(x_i^l w_{ij}''^l) = \frac{a^2}{3} + \Delta w_i^2 \tag{20}$$

Because $E(w_{ij}^l w_{ij}''') = a^2/3$, while $w_{ij}''^l = w_{ij}'^l$ and $E(w_{ij}^l w_{ij}'') = -a^2/3$, while $w_{ij}'''^l = -w_{ij}'^l$, so by (9) and (10), it follows that

$$\rho_{ik}^l = \frac{\sum_{i=1}^{n^{l-1}} \frac{a^2}{3} - 2\sum^k \frac{a^2}{3}}{\sqrt{\frac{n^{l-1}a^2}{3}}\sqrt{\frac{n^{l-1}a^2}{3} + \sum_{i=1}^{n^{l-1}} \Delta w_i^2}} = \frac{(n^{l-1} - 2k)a}{\sqrt{(n^{l-1})^2 a^2 + 3n^{l-1}\sum_{i=1}^{n^{l-1}} \Delta w_i^2}} \quad (21)$$

With (18) and (21), the sensitivity s_i^l can be expressed as

$$s_i^l \approx \sum_{k=0}^{n^{l-1}} p_k^l \left(\frac{\arccos \rho_{ik}^l}{\pi}\right) \quad (22)$$

In summary, an algorithm for the computation of the sensitivity of a Madaline can be given as follows.

MADALINE_SENS $(W, \Delta W, S^0, ...)$
For layer l from 1 to L do:
    For Adaline i from 1 to n^l do:
        Calculated s_i^l with (17), (18), (21) and (22);
$(s_1^L, s_2^L, ..., s_{n^L}^L)^T$ is the sensitivity of the Madaline.

To verify the effectiveness of our algorithm, two Madalines, 2-3-1 and 3-2-1, were implemented with $a = 1$ and the elements of weight perturbations being identical and ranging from 0 to 0.1 with an increment of 0.01. Meanwhile, computer simulations were run to compute the actual probability of the output deviations for the three Adalines with the same parameters as in the sensitivity computation. The results are shown in Fig. 1-2. Form Fig. 1-2 it can be concluded that our theoretical results have the same tendencies with the simulation results.

5 Analysis of the Sensitivity

Using the results obtained above, we can reveal some behavior of Madalines in this section.

According to (15), while the absolute values of elements of weight perturbation, say, $|\Delta w_i|$, are identical, we have

$$\rho = \frac{na}{\sqrt{n^2 a^2 + 3n\sum_{i=1}^{n} \Delta w_i^2}} = \frac{a}{\sqrt{a^2 + 3\Delta w^2}}, \quad (23)$$

where $\Delta w = |\Delta w_1| = ... = |\Delta w_n|$. It seems that sensitivity almost has no change while increasing the dimension of input if the dimension of input is sufficient large.

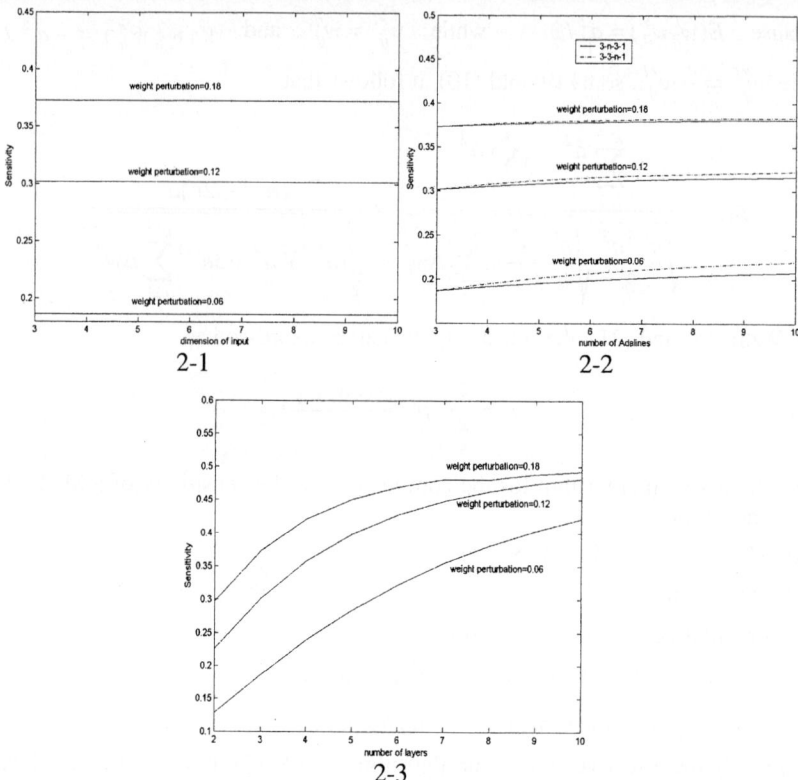

Fig. 2. Sensitivity of Madalines to the dimension of input, the number of Adalines in a layer and the number of layers

To verify the valid of the analysis result, a set of Madalines, $\{n-3-3-1 | 3 \leq n \leq 10\}$, was constructed. MADALINE_SENS $(W, \Delta W, S^0, ...)$ is used to compute the sensitivities shown in Fig. 2-1. It is clear that the experimental results coincide with the analysis result.

Since the number of Adalines in different layers may have different effects, two sets of Madalines $\{3-n-3-1 | 3 \leq n \leq 10\}$ and $\{3-3-n-1 | 3 \leq n \leq 10\}$, were constructed to study the effect of the number of Adalines in different layers. The sensitivities computed by MADALINE_SENS $(W, \Delta W, S^0, ...)$ are shown in Fig. 2-2. By Fig. 2-2, it is clear that, for the same weight perturbation, the sensitivity slightly increases with the number of Adalines in a layer, but the increase has an upper bound. The nearer a layer to the output layer is, the more effect the number of Adalines in the layer has. This, from another angle, shows us that the number of layers in the Madaline has an effect on the sensitivity.

In order to study the effects on the number of layers, nine Madalines are implemented. They are 3-3-1, 3-3-3-1, ..., 3-3-3-3-3-3-3-3-3-3-1. From the second to the last, we each time add a layer with 3 Adalines and keep the output layer with only one

Adaline. The Sensitivities computed by MADALINE_SENS $(W, \Delta W, S^0, ...)$ for these Madalines are shown in Fig. 2-3. It is found that the sensitivity increases with the number of layers and the increase has an upper bound.

6 Conclusion

After deriving an analytical expression and giving an algorithm to compute the sensitivity of Adalines and Madalines to weight perturbation, this paper analyzes the effects of some network parameters on the Madalines' sensitivity. The analysis results show that the dimension of input has little effect on the sensitivity as long as the dimension is sufficient large, and the increases in the number of Adalines in a layer and the number of layers will lead the sensitivity to increase with an upper bound. These analysis results, which have been verified by experiments, can provide useful rules for designing robust Madalines with appropriate architecture.

Acknowledgements

This work was supported by the Provincial Natural Science Foundation of Jiangsu, China under Grant BK2004114 and the National Natural Science Foundation of China under Grant 60571048.

References

1. M. Stevenson, R. Winter, and B. Widrow, "Sensitivity of Feedforward Neural Networks to Weight Errors," IEEE Trans. on Neural Networks, vol. 1, no. 1, pp. 71-80, 1990.
2. J. Y. Choi and C. H. Choi, "Sensitivity Analysis of Multilayer Perceptron with Differentiable Activation Functions," IEEE Trans. on Neural Networks, vol. 3, no. 1, pp. 101-107, 1992.
3. L. Fu and T. Chen, "Sensitivity Analysis for Input Vector in Multilayer Feedforward Neural Networks," Proc. of IEEE Int. Conf. on Neural Networks, vol. 1, pp. 215-218, San Francisco, CA, 1993.
4. S. W. Piché, "The Selection of Weight Accuracies for Madalines," IEEE Trans. on Neural Networks, vol. 6, no. 2, pp. 432-445, Mar. 1995.
5. S. H. Oh and Y. Lee, "Sensitivity Analysis of a Single Hidden-Layer Neural Networks with Threshold Function," IEEE Trans. on Neural Networks, vol. 6, no. 4, pp. 1005-1007, 1995.
6. X. Zeng and D. S. Yeung, "Sensitivity Analysis of Multilayer Perceptron to Input and Weight Perturbations," IEEE Trans. on Neural Networks, vol. 12, no. 6, pp. 1358-1366, 2001.
7. X. Zeng and D. S. Yeung, "A Quantified Sensitivity Measure for Multilayer Perceptron to Input Perturbation," Neural Computation, vol.15, no.1, pp.183-212, 2003.
8. Yingfeng Wang, Xiaoqin Zeng and Lixin Han, "Sensitivity of Madalines to Input and Weight Perturbations," Proceedings of IEEE International Conference on Machine Learning and Cybernetics, pp.1349-1354, Nov. 2003
9. Jinxin Gong and Guofang Zhao "An approximate algorithm for bivariate normal integral," Computational Structural Mechanics and Applications, vol. 13, no. 4, pp.494-497, 1996.

Fault Diagnosis for the Feedwater Heater System of a 300MW Coal-Fired Power Generating Unit Based on RBF Neural Network

Liangyu Ma, Yongguang Ma, and Jin Ma

School of Control Science and Engineering,
North China Electric Power University, Baoding 071003, China
mlydw@163.com

Abstract. In this paper, a new style radial basis function (RBF) neural network is used for fault diagnosis of the high-pressure feed-water heater system of a coal-fired power generating unit. The structure of the RBF network and its training algorithm are given. Another important factor to realize neural network based fault diagnosis, fault symptom fuzzy calculating methods for two different fault symptoms and their integrated calculation, are discussed in detail. The high-pressure feed-water heater system of a 300MW coal-fired power generating unit is taken as a fault diagnosis example. The fault knowledge library of the system is summarized. The fault diagnosis is further realized based on the above RBF neural network. It is shown that good diagnostic results can be acquired with RBF neural network method by using the fault fuzzy knowledge library of the high-pressure heater system.

1 Introduction

Artificial neural networks (ANN) have been widely used in parameter prediction and fault diagnosis for various technical processes due to their good inner adaptability for such things. Among which BP network is most widely applied in fault diagnosis field. But as we know, BP network is with many limits, such as possible local optimum, slow learning speed and low convergence efficiency, etc.

Radial basis function (RBF) neural network is a new-style network with good fitting and sorting ability and with fast learning speed. So in this paper RBF network will be used to realize thermodynamic system fault diagnosis. The structure of RBF network and its training method will be discussed.

Besides these, another important factor to realize fault diagnosis with neural network is the fault symptom calculation. The fault feature parameters such as temperature, pressure etc in the thermal system of a power unit, must be pre-treated into scattered fault symptoms among range of set [-1,1] from actual continuous parameter values. The calculating methods for different fault symptoms are then discussed in detail.

At last, the high-pressure feed-water heater system of a 300MW thermal power generating unit is taken as an example of fault diagnosis. The fault knowledge library of the system is summarized with the fault symptom calculation method, and the fault diagnosis is further realized based on the above RBF neural network.

2 RBF Network Structure and Its Training Algorithm

2.1 Structure of RBF Network and Its Characters

Suppose that x、$x_0 \in R_n$, then the function series{ $k(x)=O \parallel x\text{-}x_0 \parallel$ }, whose center is x_0 and radius is the distance between x and x_0, is called radial basis function(RBF). Radial basis function neural network is a kind of forward network. RBF network often uses Gauss kernel as its hidden-layer transfer function.

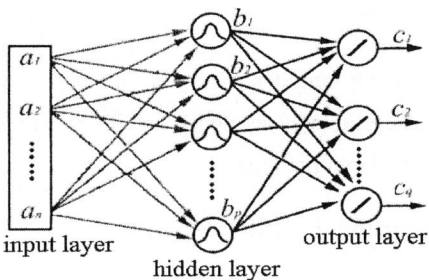

Fig. 1. Structure of RBF neural network

The RBF network shown in Fig.1 is a three-layer network made up of input layer, hidden layer and output layer. Nerve cells for each layer separately are n, p, q. For above network, the hidden-layer output vector is $\vec{B}_k = (b_1, b_2, ..., b_p)$, the output layer vector is $\vec{C}_k = (c_1, c_2, ..., c_q)$, and the input pattern vector is $\vec{A}_k = (a_1^k, a_2^k, ..., a_n^k)$. Suppose expected output vector is $\vec{Y}_k = (y_1^k, y_2^k, ..., y_q^k)$, where $k=1, 2, ..., m$. There are m pattern pairs used for network train.

Here we take Gauss kernel function centered by $\vec{S}_j$ as the hidden-layer transfer function of the RBF network. For the kth input sample $\vec{A}_k = (a_1^k, a_2^k, ..., a_n^k)$, the corresponding output for the jth hidden unit is:

$$b_j^k = \Phi(\|\vec{A}_k - \vec{S}_j\|) = \exp\left[-\sum_{i=1}^{n} \frac{(a_i^k - s_{ji})^2}{2\sigma_j^2}\right]$$

$$i=1,2,...,n;\ j=1,2,...,p;\ k=1,2,...,m. \tag{1}$$

where, $\vec{S}_j$ is the center transfer vector for the jth hidden unit; σ_j is the shape control parameter for the jth hidden unit center vector, which is used for weighting in how wide range the input sample and the typical sample could be considered as similar. The output value of the radial basis function increases with the distance decrease between the input vector and the center transfer vector. So the function of the hidden layer is equivalent to a process to transform the fewer-dimension input pattern data into a higher-dimension space, which can be considered as feature extraction of the input data.

The output value of each output-layer unit is the liner weighted sum of the hidden layer outputs. The value of the tth output layer unit can be written as:

$$c_t^k = \sum_{j=1}^{p} w_{t,j} b_j^k + \theta_t = \sum_{j=0}^{p} w_{t,j} b_j^k , \ t=1,2,\ldots,q. \qquad (2)$$

where : q is number of the output nodes; p is number of the hidden-layer nodes, $w_{t,0} = \theta_j$, $b_0^k = 1$. The output layer nodes are linear calculation units with good classification ability to the input patterns.

2.2 OLS Training Algorithm for RBF Network

Orthogonal Least Square (OLS) method is the common used training method for RBF network with the advantages of simple and fast and with no local optimum problem. OLS method is used here to modify the network weight values. Its training process is as follows.

In a given group of training samples, The learning object is to make following error evaluation function to minimum value:

$$E = \sum_{k=1}^{m}\sum_{t=1}^{q}(c_t^k - y_t^k)^2 / 2 \qquad (3)$$

Here: c_t^k, y_t^k are the actual output and expected output of the tth node corresponding to the kth input pattern, separately. Suppose W_{gh} is the connection weight from the hth node of hidden layer to the gth node of output layer, the weight value to make E reach minimum should satisfy:

$$\frac{\partial E}{\partial W_{gh}} = \sum_{k=1}^{m}\{[(\sum_{j=0}^{p}W_{tj}b_j^k - y_t^k)\cdot b_h^k]\} = 0 \qquad (4)$$

If

$$M_{jh} = \sum_{k=1}^{m} b_j^k b_h^k \qquad (5)$$

the formula (4) can be rewritten as:

$$\sum_{j=0}^{p} w_{tj} M_{jh} = \sum_{k=1}^{m} y_t^k b_h^k \quad (6)$$

Supposing matrix M is composed of Mjh and M is nonsingular, from (6) we can get:

$$W_{tj} = \sum_{j=0}^{p} (M^{-1})_{jh} (\sum_{k=1}^{m} y_t^k b_h^k). \quad (7)$$

From above deduction, it can be seen that the train process of RBF network is a problem of solving linear equation. The calculation quantity needed is far less than BP neural network. So the learning speed is very fast.

For fault diagnosis problem, the diagnostic knowledge can be expressed in form of network weight matrix and threshold matrix by training the network with typical fault samples. The fault diagnosis process is in fact a forward reasoning process to acquire a output pattern(fault vector) from a input pattern(symptom vector) by calling the fault knowledge library (network train data).

Supposed the nerve cells for a 3-layer RBF network are n、p、q, The reasoning process of RBF network includes:

(1) To call fault knowledge library, which is the weight matrix and the threshold matrix; (2) To input a group of fault symptom values $[x_1^i, x_2^i, ..., x_n^i]$, $i=1,2,...k$, which is the input vector to be recognized; (3) To calculate the output value of each hidden-layer node by formula (1); (4) To calculate the output value of each output-layer node by formula (2).

3 Calculations for Different Fault Symptoms

3.1 Semantic Symptom Calculation

It is supposed that the change of the feature parameter y is bi-directional under different faults and its maximum amplitude is (y_0-a, y_0+b). If we choose a square root function for fault symptom calculation and let the symptom take value 0, 1, -1 separately corresponding to normal value y_0, maximum value y_0+b, minimum value y_0-a, the fuzzy expression of the semantic fault symptom $\mu(y)$ can be written as:

$$\mu(y) = \begin{cases} 1 & y \geq y_0 + b \\ \sqrt{\frac{y-y_0}{b}} & y_0 < y < y_0+b \\ 0 & y = y_0 \\ -\sqrt{\frac{y_0-y}{a}} & y_0 - a < y < y_0 \\ -1 & y \leq y_0 - a \end{cases} \quad (8)$$

Where: y_0 is the expected value of parameter y under normal condition; a is maximum width for parameter decrease; b is maximum width for parameter increase. The relation between fault symptom value calculated by formula (6) and the feature parameter value y is shown in fig. 2.

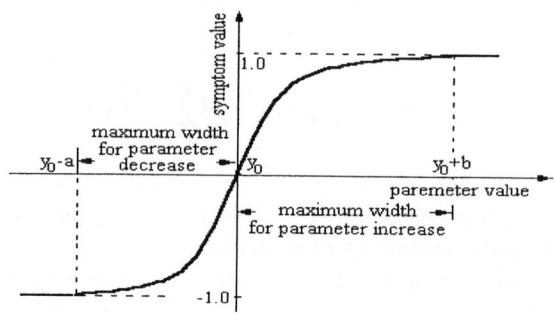

Fig. 2. Relation between the fault symptom value and the feature parameter

3.2 Trend Symptom Calculation

Representation of the trend symptom is similar to the semantic symptom. It is supposed that the change of the feature parameter y is bidirectional under different faults and the maximum amplitude of the changing rate y' for parameter y is (-c, d). If we also choose a square root function for trend symptom calculation, and have trend symptom take value 0 , 1, -1 separately corresponding to normal steady condition (rate of change y' equals 0), maximum positive rate value d, maximum negative rate value -c, the fuzzy expression form of the trend symptom $\mu(y')$ is similar to the semantic symptom expression (6).

3.3 Synthetic Calculation of Above Two Symptoms

Both of the semantic symptom and the trend symptom have their merit and demerits. It is better to use them synthetically in order to acquire good diagnostic result. Therefore, it is necessary to discuss their synthetic calculation method. Following two cases exist:

1) The value of semantic symptom $\mu(y)$ and the value of trend symptom $\mu(y')$ for parameter y take same sign, both greater than zero or both less than zero, which is shown in fig. 3(a). The expression of their synthetic symptom $\mu(+)$ is given as:

    IF $\mu(y)>0$ and $\mu(y')>0$ THEN $\mu(+)=max[\mu(y), \mu(y')]$
    IF $\mu(y)<0$ and $\mu(y')<0$ THEN $\mu(+)=min[\mu(y), \mu(y')]$

2) The value of semantic symptom $\mu(y)$ and the value of trend symptom $\mu(y')$ for parameter y take different sign, which is shown as the section e-f in fig. 3(b). Under this condition, the semantic symptom value can better reflect the transient relation between the feature parameter and the fault than the trend symptom value, So the synthetic symptom takes the value of the semantic symptom. That is:

    IF $\mu(y)>0$ and $\mu(y')<0$ OR IF $\mu(y)<0$ and $\mu(y')>0$ THEN $\mu(+)=\mu(y)$

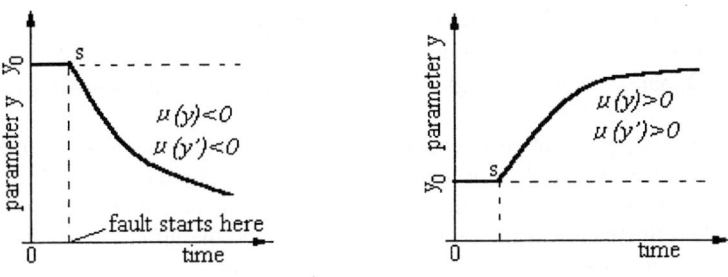

(a) Trend symptom value and semantic symptom value take same sign

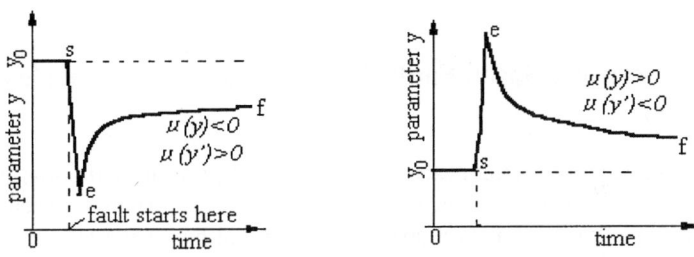

(b) Trend symptom value and semantic symptom value take different sign

Fig. 3. Relation of the two kings of fault symptoms

3.4 Conversion from Continuous-Value Symptom to Discrete-Value Symptom

The symptom values got by above-mentioned fuzzy expression method are continuous values between −1 and +1. It is necessary to convert them from continuous values to discrete values in order to acquire normative typical fault sample knowledge library and to use them conveniently for fault diagnosis. The fault symptom can either be

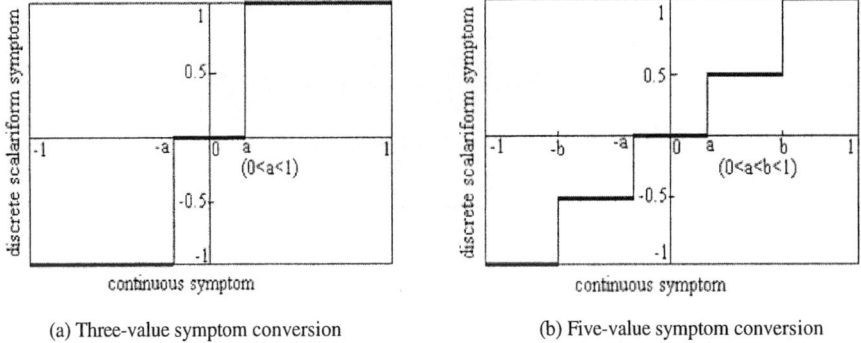

(a) Three-value symptom conversion   (b) Five-value symptom conversion

Fig. 4. Conversion from continuous-value symptom to discrete-value symptom

three–value symptom set {-1, 0, +1}, which represents parameter decrease, fixedness and increase, or be five-value symptom set {-1, -0.5, 0, 0.5, 1} corresponding to parameter apparent decrease, slight decrease, fixedness, slight increase and apparent increase.

The sticking point of this process is to determine reasonably each transforming threshold value, which often needs try of many times. The threshold value should be more propitious to fault separation. At same time it should filtrate the disturbance of the random fluctuation of the measured parameter and the influence of the instrument measure error. Moreover, it should reserve the slight symptom signal for inchoate fault and mild fault. Fig 4 (a) and (b) are the sketch map for symptom transforming from continuous symptom to three-value and five–value discrete symptom, in which a and b are threshold values.

4 RBF Network Based Fault Diagnosis for Feedwater Heater System

The high-pressure feed-water heater system of a 300MW coal-fired power unit (shown in Fig.5) is taken as an example. The three high–pressure heaters between feed-water pumps and the drum water-level control valve are all horizontal U-pipe double-flow heaters manufactured by Shanghai Power Station Auxiliary Equipment Factory. They are separately called No.1, No.2 and NO.3 HP heaters according to their extraction steam pressure high-to-low sequence and their models are JG810-1, JG1100-1, JG830-1 in turn. All of them include three heat transfer phases: overheat steam phase, steam condensation phase and drain water sub-cooling phase.

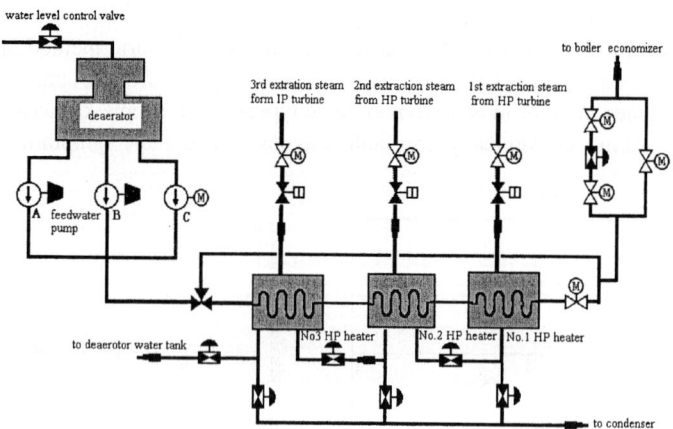

Fig. 5. Structure of the high-pressure feed-water heater system

4.1 Fault Fuzzy Knowledge Library of the High-Pressure Heater System

By regarding the three HP heaters in Fig. 5 as a whole system and considering the structure and performance of the heaters and the onsite system configuration, 19

Table 1. Typical faults set of the HP heater system

u_1	No. 1 heater feedwater pipe leakage	u_{11}	No. 2 heater feedwater pipe foul or dirty
u_2	No. 2 heater feedwater pipe leakage	u_{12}	No. 3 heater feedwater pipe foul or dirty
u_3	No. 3 heater feedwater pipe leakage	u_{13}	No. 1 heater shell side air accumulation
u_4	No. 1 heater inlet/outlet water room short	u_{14}	No. 2 heater shell side air accumulation
u_5	No. 2 heater inlet/outlet water room short	u_{15}	No. 3 heater shell side air accumulation
u_6	No. 3 heater inlet/outlet water room short	u_{16}	No. 1 heater extraction valve choke or not
u_7	No. 1 heater feedwater pipe jammed partially	u_{17}	No. 2 heater extraction valve choke or not
u_8	No. 2 heater feedwater pipe jammed partially	u_{18}	No. 3 heater extraction valve choke or not
u_9	No. 3 heater feedwater pipe jammed partially	u_{19}	Inlet bypass valve not full closed and feedwater partially bypassed
u_{10}	No. 1 heater feedwater pipe foul or dirty		

Table 2. Feature parameters used for fault symptom calculation

x_1	No.1 heater terminal temperature difference	x_{11}	No.3 heater terminal temperature difference
x_2	No.1 heater drain sub-cooler approach	x_{12}	No.3 heater drain sub-cooler approach
x_3	No.1 heater feedwater temperature rise	x_{13}	No.3 heater feedwater temperature rise
x_4	Total opening of No.1 heater's drain valves (or water level)	x_{14}	Total opening of No.3 heater's drain valves (or water level)
x_5	No.1 heater entrance steam pressure	x_{15}	No.3 heater entrance steam pressure
x_6	No.2 heater terminal temperature difference	x_{16}	Feedwater pump exit pipe water pressure
x_7	No.2 heater drain sub-cooler approach	x_{17}	Pressure drop from pump exit pipe to
x_8	No.2 heater feedwater temperature rise	x_{18}	Average speed of the feedwater pumps
x_9	Total opening of No.2 heater's drain valves (or water level)	x_{19}	Water level of the deaerator
x_{10}	No.2 heater entrance steam pressure		

Table 3. Fault fuzzy knowledge library of the high-pressure feedqater heater system

	x_1	x_2	x_3	x_4	x_5	x_6	x_7	x_8	x_9	x_{10}	x_{11}	x_{12}	x_{13}	x_{14}	x_{15}	x_{16}	x_{17}	x_{18}	x_{19}
u_1	0.5	-0.5	-0.5	1	-0.5	-0.5	1	0	1	-0.5	-0.5	0.5	0	1	0	0.5	0.5	1	-1
u_2	0	0.5	0	-0.5	0.5	0.5	-0.5	1	-0.5	-0.5	0.5	-0.5	1	-0.5	0.5	0.5	1	-1
u_3	0	0	0	0	-0.5	0	0	0.5	0	-0.5	0.5	-0.5	-0.5	1	-0.5	0.5	0.5	1	-1
u_4	1	0.5	-1	-0.5	1	0.5	-0.5	0	-0.5	0.5	0.5	-0.5	0	-0.5	0.5	-0.5	-0.5	-0.5	0
u_5	-0.5	0.5	1	0.5	-1	1	1	-1	0	0.5	0	0	0.5	0	0.5	0	0	0	0
u_6	0	0.5	0.5	0	-0.5	-0.5	0.5	1	0.5	-0.5	1	1	-1	0	0.5	0	0	0.5	0
u_7	1	-1	-1	-0.5	1	0.5	-0.5	0	-0.5	0.5	0.5	-0.5	-0.5	0.5	1	1	1	1	-0.5
u_8	-0.5	0.5	1	0.5	-1	1	-1	-1	-0.5	0.5	0	-0.5	-0.5	0	0	1	1	1	-0.5
u_9	0	0.5	0.5	0	-0.5	-0.5	0.5	0.5	0.5	-0.5	1	-1	-1	-0.5	0.5	1	1	1	0
u_{10}	0.5	1	-0.5	0	0.5	0	0	0	0	0	0	0	0	0	0.5	0.5	0.5	0
u_{11}	-0.5	0.5	0.5	0.5	-0.5	0.5	1	-0.5	0	0.5	0	0	0.5	0	0.5	0.5	0.5	0.5	0
u_{12}	0	0	0.5	0	-0.5	-0.5	0.5	0.5	0.5	-0.5	1	1	-0.5	0	0.5	0.5	0.5	0.5	0
u_{13}	1	-1	-1	-0.5	1	0.5	-0.5	0	-0.5	0.5	0.5	-0.5	0	-0.5	0.5	-0.5	-0.5	-0.5	0
u_{14}	-0.5	1	1	0.5	-1	1	-1	-1	-0.5	0.5	0	-0.5	0	-0.5	0	-0.5	-0.5	-0.5	-0.5
u_{15}	0	0.5	0.5	0.5	-1	-0.5	1	1	0.5	-1	1	-1	-1	-0.5	1	-0.5	0	-0.5	-0.5
u_{16}	0.5	-1	-1	-0.5	1	0.5	-0.5	0.5	0.5	-0.5	-0.5	0.5	-0.5	-0.5	-0.5	-1	0
u_{17}	-0.5	1	1	0.5	-1	0.5	-1	-1	0.5	-1	0	-0.5	0	-0.5	0.5	0	0	0	0
u_{18}	0	0.5	0.5	0.5	-0.5	1	0.5	-1	0.5	-1	-1	0.5	-1	0.5	0.5	0.5	0
u_{19}	-0.5	0.5	-0.5	-0.5	1	-1	0.5	0	-1	1	1	1	-1	1	-1	-1	-1	0

typical faults are generalized as listed in table 1: u_1, u_2, ..., u_{19}. At the same time, 19 feature parameters are chosen for fault diagnosis as shown in table 2: x_1, x_2, ..., x_{19}, which are either directly taken from onsite DAS parameters or got through simple calculation with these DAS parameters.

In order to summarize the fuzzy knowledge library of the faults in table 1, the dynamic simulation model for the high-pressure heater system is built and is integrated to the model of the full-scope power station simulator to make detailed fault simulation tests. The {-1, -0.5, 0, 0.5, 1} five–value type fault fuzzy knowledge library are summarized as listed in table 3.

4.2 Fault Diagnosis Examples of the High-Pressure Feedwater Heater System

Various faults of the high-pressure heater system are diagnosed with RBF neural network method by simulating the faults with a full-scope power station simulator. The diagnostic results of the fault "No.1 heater inlet and outlet water room short circuit"(u_4) 10% and 30% after the system has stepped into another steady state are given in table 4. The shape control parameter for the network kernel function is 1.1 times of 0.8325. The weight matrix of the hidden-layer is a 19*19 matrix corresponding to the fault fuzzy knowledge library of the high-pressure feedwater heater system. The input layer and the output layer of the RBF network both include 19 neuron nodes corresponding with 19 input feature parameters and 19 typical system faults.

From table 4 we can see RBF neural network diagnosis method is with higher fault separation degree, which is similar to BP network.While the accurately designed RBF network needs far less training calculation than BP network. What we need do is to determine the shape control parameter of the network kernel function properly by several tests.

Table 4. Diagnostic results of "No. 1 heater water room short circuit "fault of different degree with RBF network

Fault degree	u_1	u_2	u_3	U_4	u_5	u_6	u_7	u_8	u_9	u_{10}
10%	0.000	-0.000	-0.003	**0.738**	0.000	0.003	0.000	-0.001	-0.001	0.138
30%	-0.000	0.000	0.001	**0.843**	-0.000	-0.001	-0.003	0.000	0.000	-0.036

Fault degree	u_{11}	u_{12}	u_{13}	u_{14}	u_5	u_{16}	u_{17}	u_{18}	u_{19}	Right ?
10%	-0.0013	0.001	0.119	0.000	0.000	0.005	-0.000	0.0001	0.0004	Yes
30%	0.001	0.001	0.203	0.000	0.000	-0.010	0.000	0.000	-0.000	Yes

5 Conclusions

(1) A new style RBF neural network method for fault diagnosis of the thermodynamic system is introduced and its training method is discussed. Compared with BP network, the RBF network needs less training calculation and is with good fault recognition ability. So the RBF network is with favorable application prospect in function approximation and fault recognition field.

(2) The high-pressure feedwater heater system of a 300 MW coal-fired power generating unit is taken as a fault diagnostic example. The fault fuzzy knowledge library of it is summarized..
(3) Fuzzy representation method for two kinds of fault symptoms and their integrated calculation are discussed thoroughly for the first time. By using these two symptoms synthetically, it is propitious to diagnose the fault accurately and timely.
(4) It is shown by examples that good diagnostic results can be acquired with RBF neural network method by using the fault fuzzy knowledge library of the high-pressure heater system built in this paper.

Acknowledgements

This paper is supported by the scientific and technical project of the State Power Company (SPKJ016-22) and the doctoral degree teacher research fund (20041209) of North China Electric Power University.

References

1. James A, Leonard, Mark A. Kramer. "Radial basis function networks for classifying process fault", IEEE control systems, April, (1991) 31-37
2. K.G. Narendra, V.K. Sood, K. Khorasani, R. Patel. "Application of a radial basis function(RBF) neural network for fault diagnosis in a HVDC system", IEEE Trans. on power systems. Vol 13, No. 1, Feb. (1998) 177-183
3. Chen S. Cowan C F N,Grant P M. "Orthogonal least squares learning algorithm for radial basis function network", IEEE trans. on neural networks. Vol 2, No. 2, (1991) 302-309
4. Ma Liangyu, Gao Jianqiang, Ma Yongguang. "Fault intelligent diagnosis for high-pressure feed-water heater system of a 300MW coal-fired power unit based on improved BP neural network", 2002 IEEE/PES international conference on power system technology proceedings, Kunming, Vol.3, (2002) 1535-1539
5. Ma Liangyu,Wang Bingshu,Gao Jianqiang. " A new intelligent approach to diagnose the slight and incipient fault during the production process",Proceedings of the CSEE,Vol 22, No.6, Jun. (2002) 115-118

The Application of Modified Hierarchy Genetic Algorithm Based on Adaptive Niches

Wei-Min Qi[1], Qiao-ling Ji[2], and Wei-You Cai[2]

[1] College of Physics and Information engineering,
Jianghan University, Wuhan, 430056, China
{Wei-Min, qwmin}@126.com
[2] College of Power and Mechanical engineering,
Wuhan University, Wuhan, 430072, China
{Qiao-ling, Wei-you, jql7605}@126.com

Abstract. Traditional genetic algorithms have the defects of pre-maturity and stagnation when applied in optimizing problems. In order to avoid the shortcomings, an adaptive niche hierarchy genetic algorithm (ANHGA) is proposed. The algorithm is based on the adaptive mutation operator and crossover operator to adjust the crossover rate and probability of mutation of each individual, whose mutation values are decided using individual gradient. This approach is applied in Percy and Shubert function optimization. Comparisons of niche genetic algorithm (NGA), hierarchy genetic algorithm (HGA) and ANHGA have been done by establishing a simulation model and the results of mathematical model and actual industrial model show that ANHGA is feasible and efficient in the design of multi-extremum.

1 Introduction

Since Genetic Algorithms (GAs) were firstly put forward by J.H.Holland in 1970s [1], it has been widely used in optimizing complex functions, identifying parameters, optimizing neural networks and so on. GAs are stochastic optimization methods based on the mechanics of natural evolution and natural genetics [2,3]. They have been successfully applied to finding a global optimum of a single objective problem [4]. In the optimization of multimodal functions, however, the standard GA converges to only one peak since it cannot maintain controlled competition among the competing operation corresponding to different peaks.

In recent years much work has been done with the aim of extending genetic algorithms to make it possible to find more than one local optimum of a function. One of the techniques developed for this purpose is known as a niching method [5]. In natural ecosystems, a niche can be viewed as an organism's task, which permits species to survive in their environment.

Though niche GA has strong searching ability and is easy to find many global optimums, its local searching ability should be improved. In this paper, a modified niche GA is proposed in order to improve its performance.

In Section 2, the niche genetic algorithm (NGA) is reviewed. In order to improve the local searching ability of NGA, we combined niche with hierarchy technology and introduced adaptive mutation probability in Section 3, then the adaptive niche hierarchy genetic algorithm (ANHGA) is proposed. In Section 4, the simulation result shows that the ANHGA has strong searching ability and is easy to find many global optimums. An industrial model is used to test the reliability of ANHGA in Section 5. Finally, we give some comments in Section 6.

2 Niche Genetic Algorithm

Niching methods have been developed to minimize the effect of genetic drift resulting from the selection operator in the traditional GA in order to allow the parallel investigation of many solutions in the population. The niche technology mainly adjusts the fitness of individuals and replacement strategy when generating the new generation. This makes the individuals evolve in special environment, ensures diversity of evolution population and gets many global optimums at the same time [6]. Representative niche methods are preselecting, crowding and sharing technology. Table.1 describes the procedure of NGA in simple programs.

Table 1. Genetic algorithm with niching method

Generate initial population: parents		
Iterate		
Choose: =random-value		
Case choose		
generation	mutation	crossover
Find smallest HD (child, parents)		
of those find parent with worst fitness		
If better fitness: exchange (child, parent)		
Show best designs		

As the niche technology is an effective measure to maintain diversity when GAs are applied to optimize functions with many apices or tasks with many targets, it is mainly used to improve GA operators and doesn't change encoding structure. The research found the niche technology and hierarchy GA are mutual complementary in mechanism. The advantages of their combination will be better than those of single method. Based on this thought, we put forward adaptive niche hierarchy genetic algorithm (ANHGA). ANHGA changes in the following aspects: hierarchy structure is used in encoding method, niche technology is used in individuals operation and mutation probability is changed adaptively.

3 The Modified Niche Hierarchy Genetic Algorithm

Using niche technology, ANHGA adopts speedup strategies during the process of encoding, selection and replacement to maintain reasonable population diversity and make GA not only converge but also discover many apices. ANHGA uses hierarchy structure to encode. Before selection, it adjusts individual fitness based on sharing strategy to increase selecting probability of small-scale species. During replacement, it selects individuals as the new generation ones based on density and fitness [7,8].

3.1 Hierarchy Encoding Structure

In hierarchy encoding method, each chromosome is composed of two parts: control gene and constitution gene. Control gene determines whether constitution genes are active. Chromosome includes dominant genes and recessive genes. The active constitution genes are dominant and effective. The inactive constitution genes are recessive and ineffective. The two kinds of genes are inherited to the next generation at the same time. The corresponding control genes determine whether they are transformed [9].

The control genes in hierarchy encoding are often binary encoding. The constitution genes are float encoding or binary encoding in allusion to practical problems. The number of constitution genes controlled by each control gene is variable with specific problems. The structure of hierarchy encoding is shown as Fig.1.

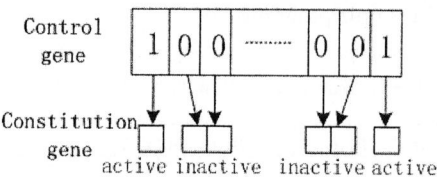

Fig. 1. Structure of hierarchy encoding

In Fig.1, the upper-layer is control genes. The below-layer is constitution genes. In control genes layer, "1" indicates the active and dominant corresponding constitution genes and "0" expresses that the corresponding constitution genes are inactive and recessive. Decoding the dominant genes gets the solutions of the given problems. The recessive genes are inherited to the next generation with the dominant genes and may be activated during the process of evolution. The effective gene segments are adjusted continually until getting the satisfied solutions.

3.2 Individual Density

Similarity of individual gene codes embodies close degree among individuals. We define sharing function to express the density of individuals. So we introduce the concepts of sharing function and individual density.

In order to describe the problem conveniently, some definition should be made as follows:

$\vec{X}(t)$: Population of t th generation;

$X_i(t)$: Constitution genes of i th individual;

N : The size of population;

$d(i, j)$: The distance between i th individual and j th individual.

Then sharing function is defined in Eq.(1):

$$sh(d(i,j)) = \begin{cases} 1 - \left(\dfrac{d(i,j)}{\Delta(t)}\right)^{\alpha} & d(i,j) \leq \Delta(t) \\ 0 & else \end{cases} \quad (1)$$

Where $\Delta(t)$ is a variable, which describes the close degree between $i\,th$ and $j\,th$ constitution genes. Its value is determined according to practical problems. α is a parameter that controls the shape of sharing function. Usually α is set to be 1.

It can be seen from Eq.(1) that when individuals are similar, the value of sharing function is bigger. Whereas when individuals are different, the value of sharing function is small.

Equation 2 set $sh(d(i,j))$ as sharing function of $i\,th$ individual and $j\,th$ individual. The density of $i\,th$ individual is defined as:

$$C_i(t) = \frac{1}{N}\sum_{j=1}^{N} sh(d(i,j)) \ . \quad (2)$$

Obviously individual density can be used to appraise population diversity. The larger $C_i(t)$ is, the more number of individuals whose constitution genes are similar to those of $i\,th$ individual is. In such case, the population may concentrate and lose diversity.

3.3 Fitness Sharing

In fact, for individuals in certain range $\Delta(t)$ can be regarded as a species [10,11]. Large individual density means the corresponding species are large too. Whereas, if some species' density are too large, the fitness of all individuals in this species should be reduced and their selecting probabilities be decreased to maintain the population diversity, create niche evolution environments and encourage small number species to multiply. As for population of t generation, the fitness of $X_i(t)$ after sharing can be defined as:

$$f_i^{'}(t) = f_i(t) / C_i(t) \ . \quad (3)$$

Where, $f_i(t)$ is individual fitness of $X_i(t)$ before sharing. GA carries out selection according to the Eq.(3).

Supposing that the fitness of all individuals in $i\,th$ species is f_i, the number of individuals in this species is N_i, k is the number of species. Then the stable state of fitness sharing can be expressed as

$$f_i / N_i = f_j / N_j \ . \quad (4)$$

where $i \neq j$ and $\sum_{i=1}^{k} N_i = N$.

3.4 Adaptive Mutation

In fact, for individuals in certain range $\Delta(t)$ can be regarded as a species. Large individual density means the corresponding species are large too. Whereas, if some species' density are too large, the fitness of all individuals in these species should be reduced and their selecting probabilities be decreased to maintain the population diversity, create niche evolution environments and encourage small number species to multiply. As for population of t generation, the fitness of $X_i(t)$ after sharing can be defined as: when individual density $C_i(t)$ is bigger, larger probability should be applied to mutation operation. Considering both the evolution time and individual density as well as ensuring algorithm to converge, the mutation probability should be limited to (0,0.5). Based on these considerations, we put forward the following adaptive mutation probability.

$$P_m(t) = 1 - \frac{1}{1+\exp(-t/C_i(t))} \tag{5}$$

3.5 Individual Replacement Based on Crowding Strategy

If we define parent population as $\vec{X}(t)$ and the population after mutation as $\vec{X}'(t)$, then mix population $\vec{X}(t)$ and $\vec{X}'(t)$, adjust individual fitness according to the following equation:

$$fit'_j(t) = \beta \frac{f_j(t)}{\sum_{k=1}^{N} f_k(t)} + (1-\beta) \frac{\frac{1}{C_j(t)}}{\sum_{k=1}^{N} \frac{1}{C_j(t)}}, \quad j=1,2,\ldots,2N. \tag{6}$$

Where β is a weight coefficient. The adjustment of fitness balances between individual fitness and density. Rank $fit'_j(t)$ in descent order and select the first N individuals of parent generation to compose the next generation. It is obvious that the individual replacement strategy based on crowding method can make uniform distribution and maintain population diversity preferably.

4 Simulations

In order to compare and test the searching ability of two function optimization problems named as Percy and Shubert function, the simulations of GA, NGA, HGA and ANHGA are performed respectively.

Percy function is defined as:

$$\max f_1(x_x, x_2) = \frac{x_1^2 + x_2^2}{2} + \cos(20\pi x_1)\cos(20\pi x_2) + 2 \quad, -10 \le x_1, x_2 \le 10 \ . \tag{7}$$

The figure of Percy function is shown in Fig.2. It includes 4 global optimal solutions and the Apex's height is 103.0.

Shubert function is defined as:

$$\min f_2(x_1, x_2) = \left\{\sum_{i=1}^{5} i \times \cos[(i+1)x_1 + i]\right\} \times \left\{\sum_{i=1}^{5} i \times \cos[(i+1)x_2 + i]\right\}, \tag{8}$$
$$-10 \le x_1, x_2 \le 10$$

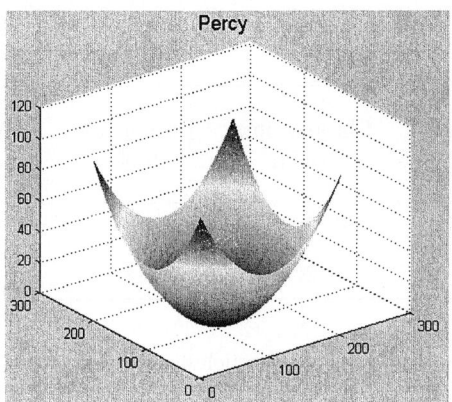

Fig. 2. Percy function

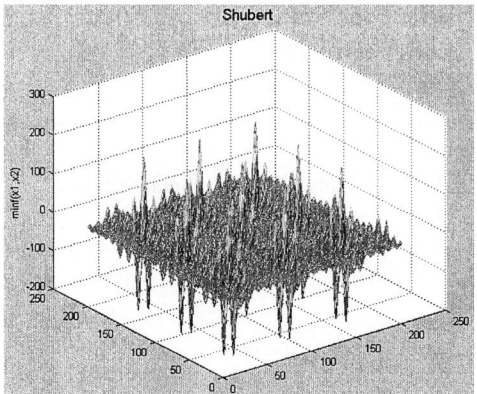

Fig. 3. Shubert function

As shown in the Fig.3, it's known that Shubert function has 760 local optimal solutions. Among which there are 18 optimums and the value is -186.7310. The objective function is converted to fitness value using the following equation:

$$F(x_1, x_2) = \begin{cases} 1 - 0.05 f_2(x_1, x_2), & \text{if} \quad f_2(x_1, x_2) < 0 \\ 1, & \text{if} \quad f_2(x_1, x_2) \geq 0 \end{cases}. \qquad (9)$$

Simple hierarchy genetic algorithm (HGA) can improve the diversity of population by hierarchy encoding [12], but the simple genetic operators adopted causes limitations on premature convergence avoidance and efficiency improvement. In following simulations, all four genetic algorithms (GA, NGA, HGA, ANHGA) utilize the same control parameters listed in Table 2. All four algorithms adopt proportional selection, single point crossover, $P_c = 0.8$. Each algorithm began with the same initial population and was simulated 20 cycles for each optimized function respectively. The simulation results are listed in Table 3 and 4.

Table 2. Control parameters

	Population size	Chromosome length	Termination time	Weight Coefficient	$\Delta(t)$
Percy	30	20	200	0.75	0.5/t
Shubert	50	20	300	0.75	0.5

Table 3. Percy function simulation results

	GA	NGA	HGA	ANHGA
Number of average global optimums	1.2	3.8	2.3	3.94
Number of global optimum individual	3	29	10	31
Average evolutional generations of global optimums		57	30	42

Table 4. Shubert function simulation results

	GA	NGA	HGA	ANHGA
Average numbers of global optimums	2.1	5.5	3.9	12
Average individual numbers of global optimums	3	18	11	30

Comparing the tables above, it can be seen from simulation results that the space searching ability of GA and simple HGA is unsatisfactory and its optimizing efficiency is inferior to NGA and ANHGA apparently. Under the same condition the solution quality of NGA and ANHGA performs better, which demonstrates that the fitness sharing and the crowding strategy are effective in optimizing functions with many apices. Shubert function is a complicated optimization problem. It is very difficult to find 18 global optimums at the same time. Although GA is easy to carry out, there lie some problems such as premature and convergence speed. HGA can found 2~5 global optimums and the number of global optimum individual is 11. However ANHGA can find a dozen of optimums and sometimes even get 18 global optimums, which proved that hierarchy encoding with niche methods can maintain population diversity effectively and converge rapidly.

5 Example of Application

A reliability optimum design theory and method of a jaw clutch has been introduced [13]. The design goal is to seek a set of design parameters (outside diameter of clutch: D; number of gear: Z; structure coefficient K_1; structure coefficient K_2) under the condition of probability restriction. The relation of S_b and design parameters are defined as:

$$S_b = \frac{15.6T_n}{\left(\frac{Z}{2}+0.5\right)\left[\frac{\pi D(1-K_2)}{4Z}\right]^2 (1+K_1)D} \quad (10)$$

In Eq.(10), T_n is a constant. Obviously, S_b is the nonlinear function of the design parameters. The paper presents the values of (S_b, D, Z, K_1, K_2) using the restraint random directional methods. Under the completely same design condition, we employ ANHGA and NGA and HGA to genetic optimization calculation. After 400 iterative cycle the calculation is shown in Table 5.

Table 5. Optimization result of a jaw clutch

	Z	K_1	K_2	D(mm)	S_b (MPa)
NGA	25	0.74	0.34	45	2099.264
HGA	25	0.74	0.341	42	2203.24
ANHGA	25	0.7442	0.3348	64.777	692.934

From Table 5, it is obvious that ANHGA is more efficient than NGA and SHGA in optimum design of jaw clutch.

6 Conclusion

In this paper, niche technology and hierarchy genetic algorithm were combined and adaptive niche hierarchy GA based on sharing and crowding was put forward. The adaptive niche hierarchy genetic algorithm improves GA from not only encoding but also operators. These measures also increase searching ability of the GA effectively, ensuring population diversity and finding many solutions of complicated problems. The application of the modified genetic algorithm shows it is great effective to the multimodal optimization and appropriate for the design of multi-extremum complex system.

References

1. Holland J.H.: Adaptation in nature and artificial systems. Ann Arber, MI, University of Michigan Press (1975)
2. B. Sareni, L. Krahenbuhl, and A. Nicolas.: Niching genetic algorithms for optimization in electromagnetics, in Proc. 11th COMPUMAG'97, Rio de Janeiro (1997) 563-564
3. D. E. Goldberg.: Genetic Algorithms in Search, Optimization and Machine Learning. Reading, MA, Addison Wesely (1989)
4. Rudolph G.: Convergence analysis of canonical genetic algorithms, IEEE Trans. Neural networks, special issue on evolution computing, Vol.5, (1994) 96-101
5. S.W. Mahfoud.: Niching methods for genetic algorithms, Ph.D. dissertation, Univ. Illinois at Urbana-Champaign, Illinois genetic Algorithm Lab., Urbana, IL (1995)
6. C. G. Lee, D. H. Cho, and H. K. Jung.: Niching genetic algorithm with restricted competition selection for multimodal function optimization, IEEE Trans. Magn., Vol.34, No.1, (1999) 1722-1755
7. Beiyue Zhou, Bin Deng, Guanqi Guo.: Research of a class of improved genetic algorithm based on niches[J]. Journal of Mechanical Strength, Vol.24, No.1, (2002) 13-16
8. Shouyi Yu, Guanqi Guo.: A class of niche used in genetic algorithms for improving efficiency of searching global optimum. Information and Control, Vol.30, No.6, (2001) 326-331
9. Dunwei Gong, Fengping Pan, Shifan Xu.: Adaptive niche hierarchy genetic algorithms. Proc. Of the 2002 IEEE Region 10 Conf. On computers, communicatona, Control and Power Engineering, Beijing: Posts & Telecom Press (2002) 39-42
10. Xin-jie Yu, Zan-ji Wang.: Fitness sharing crowding genetic algorithm, Control and decision, Vol.16, No.6, (2001) 926-929
11. Zhiyong Liu, Mandan Liu, Feng Qian.: The application of one improved niche genetic algorithm for Elman recurrent neural networks. Proceedings of the 5th World congress on Intelligent control and Automation, Hangzhou, (2004)1978-1981
12. Dunwei Gong, Xiaoyan Sun, Xijin Guo, yong Zhou.: Adaptive hierarchy genetic algorithm. Proceedings of IEEE TENCON'02, Vol.1, (2002)81-84
13. Liu Weishan.: Optimization of reliability design of machine components. Beijing: China Science and Technology Press (1993)

Construction of High Precision RBFNN with Low False Alarm for Detecting Flooding Based Denial of Service Attacks Using Stochastic Sensitivity Measure

Wing W.Y. Ng, Aki P.F. Chan, Daniel S. Yeung, and Eric C.C. Tsang

Hong Kong Polytechnic University, Department of Computing,
Hong Kong, China
{cswyng, csaki, csdaniel, csetsang}@comp.polyu.edu.hk
http://www.comp.polyu.edu.hk/~cike/

Abstract. High precision and low false alarm rate are the two most important characteristics of a good Intrusion Detection System (IDS). In this work, we propose to construct a host-based IDS for detecting flooding-based Denial of Service (DoS) attacks by minimizing the generalization error bound of the IDS to reduce its false alarm rate and increase its precision. Radial basis function neural network (RBFNN) will be applied in the IDS. The generalization error bound is formulated based on the stochastic sensitivity measure of RBFNN. Experimental results using artificial datasets support our claims.

1 Introduction

Nowadays a computer system generally contains design and implementation flaws which result in security vulnerabilities. Malicious users may exploit these vulnerabilities and cause significant disruptions to the system. The Denial of Service (DoS) attack, which is a class of attacks initiated by an individual or a group of individuals exploiting aspects of the Internet to prevent legitimate users or the victims from accessing the compromised system and information, is reported as the most expensive computer crime in CSI/FBI survey in 2004 because of its use for computer extortion 1. The DoS attack has been proven capable of shutting an organization off from the Internet or dramatically slowing down network links 6 and may consider as the most detrimental attack. Misuse and anomaly detection represent two main approaches to detect intrusions. They have different merits and limitations and details can be found in 9, 10.

Rule-based systems are most widely deployed in network intrusion detection products. They are easy to understand and use, but require human domain experts to find the rules and their generalization power depends on the expertise knowledge in the attacks. Research works on applying statistical approaches to detect DoS attacks could be found in 4, 11. However, they depend on the assumption of the distribution of the normal and attack packets. Machine learning and data mining techniques are possible solutions to these drawbacks 2.

A serious drawback of machine learning or pattern recognition based techniques is high false alarm rate 5. The major reason is that a classifier learns from training samples by minimizing the training error only, which does not necessarily lead to a good generalization capability of the classifier. Hence the classifier may not be able to distinguish attack-like legitimate traffics. For example, the signature of flooding-based DoS attacks is extremely high bit-rate. However, one may notice that legitimate high bit-rate may also occur in rush hours, such as on mid-night.

Furthermore, machine learning techniques depend so much on the training dataset such that, for instance, an unbalanced ratio of the normal and attack packets in a training data set may most likely cause difficulty for a classifier to learn the attack signatures.

Jin et al. studied the covariance between the features describing the DoS problems 7, 8. The covariance matrix between features for samples fetched from the network within a given period is used as a sample and the decision of attack or normal is made by comparing this covariance matrix with the templates of various attack types. In 7, 8 it was shown that the covariance between input features could be used to indicate the occurrence of network intrusion. Chan et al. 3 makes use of the mutual information to capture the nonlinear relationship between features and also between features and target output of the training samples. They have also shown that, by making use of these nonlinear correlations for feature selection, one could improve the classification accuracy and reduce false alarm rate.

It could be stated that the major objective of solving a flooding-based DoS problem is to achieve a 100% detection of the attacks with the lowest false alarm rate, given that the number of normal (legitimate) packets greatly outnumbers the attack packets. One way to solve all these problems ultimately is to train a classifier with the best generalization capability, instead of best training error only. In 12 Ng et al. derived a localized generalization error model (R_{SM}) using the stochastic sensitivity measure. In this paper, we focus on the flooding-based DoS problems and study the effectiveness of applying R_{SM} in the construction of IDS for flooding-based DoS problems. In particular, the Radial Basis Function Neural Network (RBFNN) is used in this paper because of its fast training and responses to large datasets. One may notice that the proposed method is a host-based detection system which operates in a host, such as a router or web server. The works in this paper could be applied directly to detect Distributed Denial of Service (DDoS) attacks because there is no difference between detecting DDoS and DoS attack using a host-based system.

Section 2 describes the localized generalization error model. The corresponding model selection method for constructing the IDS is introduced in Section 3. Section 4 provides experimental results and its analysis. Section 5 concludes the paper.

2 Localized Generalization Error Model (R_{SM})

In this section, we introduce the localized generalization error model (R_{SM}) proposed in 12. The Q-neighborhood ($S_Q^{(b)}$) of a training sample $\vec{X}^{(b)}$ is defined as $S_Q^{(b)}$ = { $\vec{X} = \vec{X}^{(b)} + \Delta\vec{X}$ } $\forall \Delta\vec{X}$ that satisfy $0 < |\Delta x_i| \leq Q \ \forall i = 1, \cdots, N$, where N denotes the number of features of the training sample, Q is a selected real number and $\Delta\vec{X} = (\Delta x_1, \cdots, \Delta x_N)$. The Q-union (S_Q) is defined to be the union of all $S_Q^{(b)}$.

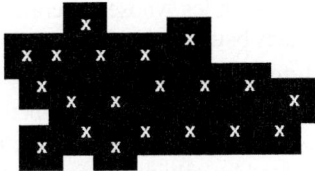

Fig. 1. An Illustration of Q-Union (S_Q) with 20 training samples. The X is the training samples and any point in the shaded area except X is an unseen sample.

We define the R_{SM} to be the generalization error for the unseen samples located within the Q-union, i.e. the shaded region in Figure 1. With a probability of $1-\eta$, we have 12

$$R_{SM}(Q) = \int_{S_Q} (f_\theta(\vec{x}) - F(\vec{x}))^2 p(\vec{x}) d\vec{x}$$

$$\leq \left(\sqrt{E_s((\Delta y)^2)} + \sqrt{R_{emp}} + \sqrt{A} \right)^2 + \varepsilon = R_{SM}^*(Q) \quad (1)$$

The ST-SM ($E_s((\Delta y)^2)$) for RBFNN is defined as:

$$E_s((\Delta y)^2) = \frac{1}{l} \sum_{b=1}^{l} \int_{Q}^{(b)} (f_\theta(\vec{x}) - f_\theta(\vec{x}^{(b)}))^2 \frac{1}{(2Q)^2} d\vec{x}$$

$$\approx \frac{1}{3} Q^2 \sum_{j=1}^{M} v_j + \frac{0.2}{9} Q^4 N \sum_{j=1}^{M} \zeta_j \quad (2)$$

Specifically for any RBFNN, with a probability of $1-\eta$, we have 12

$$R_{SM}^*(Q) \approx \left(\sqrt{\frac{1}{3} Q^2 \sum_{j=1}^{M} v_j + \frac{0.2}{9} Q^4 N \sum_{j=1}^{M} \zeta_j} + \sqrt{R_{emp}} + \sqrt{A} \right)^2 + \varepsilon \quad (3)$$

where $v_j = \varphi_j \left(\sum_{i=1}^{N} (\sigma_{x_i}^2 + (\mu_{x_i} - u_{ji})^2) / v_j^4 \right)$, $\zeta_j = \varphi_j / v_j^4$, $E(s_j) = \sum_{i=1}^{N} (\sigma_{x_i}^2 + (\mu_{x_i} - u_{ji})^2)$,

$\varphi_j = (w_j)^2 \exp((Var(s_j)/2v_j^4) - (E(s_j)/v_j^2))$, $s_j = \|\vec{x} - \vec{U}_j\|^2$, $R_{emp} = (1/l) \sum_{b=1}^{l} (err)^2$,

$err^{(b)} = f_\theta(\vec{x}^{(b)}) - F(\vec{x}^{(b)})$, $A = (\max(F(\vec{x})) - \min(F(\vec{x})))$, $B = \max((f_\theta(\vec{x}) - F(\vec{x}))^2)$,

$Var(s_j) = \sum_{i=1}^{N} (E_D[(x_i - \mu_{x_i})^4] - (\sigma_{x_i}^2)^2 + 4E_D[(x_i - \mu_{x_i})^3](\mu_{x_i} - u_{ji}) + 4\sigma_{x_i}^2 (\mu_{x_i} - u_{ji})^2)$,

$\Delta y = f_\theta(\vec{x}) - f_\theta(\vec{x}^{(b)})$, $\varepsilon = B\sqrt{\ln \eta (-2l)}$ and l, F and f_θ denote the number of training samples, the unknown true input-output mapping of the given problem, and the RBFNN output with the parameter set θ selected from its domain Λ respectively.

For every trained classifier, one could compute the maximum Q value in which the R_{SM} bound is less than or equal to a threshold a. For example, if $F(\vec{x}) \in \{1, 2, \cdots, K\}$ for a K-class problem, the threshold a could be selected to be 0.25 which is the threshold of the squared error between the classifier output and the target output of a sample being classified correctly. So, intuitively the Q value provides an indication on how big the area of coverage of the unseen samples whose generalization errors in MSE are less than a. Thus, a larger Q indicates better generalization of a classifier in the probability sense 12. On the other hand, for two classifiers yielding the same R^*_{SM} with different Q values, the one that yields a larger Q value has better generalization capability. Moreover, this unique Q could also be used to compute the R_{SM} for feature selection purpose. The Q value is computed by solving the following quadratic equation:

$$Q^4 \frac{0.2}{3} N \sum_{j=1}^{M} \zeta_j + Q^2 \sum_{j=1}^{M} v_j - 3\left(\sqrt{a-\varepsilon} - \sqrt{R_{emp}} - \sqrt{A}\right)^2 = 0 \qquad (4)$$

There are a maximum of four solutions for Equation (4) and the smallest real-valued solution will be used as the final result. If no real solution exists, zero will be used as the final result.

3 Model Selection Method Using R^*_{SM} (MC²SG) for Intrusion Detection

The generalization error for a parameter set of a classifier could be estimated empirically using a popular technique, the leave-one-out cross-validation. It trains a total of l classifiers, with the pth classifier leaving out the pth sample as a validation sample. The average of the validation errors for the l classifiers is used as the unbiased estimation of the generalization error for the given model parameter set. However, it is difficult, if not impossible, to apply this technique to an intrusion detection problem due to the huge number of samples involved. For example, a training dataset with 500,000 training samples requires 500,000 classifiers being trained for the leave-one-out cross-validation method. Hence it appears that the provision of an analytical estimation of the generalization error using the R^*_{SM} with time complexity independent of the number of training samples is appropriate for intrusion detection problems.

The Maximal Coverage Classifier with Selected Generalization (MC²SG) was proposed in 12. For any given threshold, the R_{SM} model allows us to find the best classifier by maximizing Q, assuming that the MSE of all samples within the Q-Union is smaller than the given threshold value. One can formulate the model selection problem as a Maximal Coverage Classification problem with Selected Generalization Error (MC²SG), i.e.,

$$\max_{\theta \in \Lambda} Q \quad s.t. \ \left(R^*_{SM}(Q)\right) \le a \qquad (5)$$

In RBFNN training, once the number of hidden neurons is fixed, the center positions and widths could be determined by an automatic clustering algorithm such as k-means clustering, self-organizing map or hierarchical clustering. So we only need to concentrate on the problem of determining the number of hidden neurons. This means that $\theta = M$ and $\Lambda=\{1,2,\ldots,l\}$ because it is not reasonable to have the number of hidden neurons more than the number of training samples.

Problem (5) is a two-dimensional optimization problem. The first dimension is the number of hidden neurons (θ) and the second dimension is the Q for a fixed θ. For every fixed θ and Q, we can determine a $R^*_{SM}(Q)$. Problem (5) has two adjustable parameters, θ and Q, and these two parameters are independent of each other. Furthermore, by substituting Equation (2) into the constraint in Equation (1), with probability $(1-\eta)$ we have,

$$R_{SM}^*(Q) \approx \left(\sqrt{\frac{1}{3}Q^2\sum_{j=1}^{M}v_j + \frac{0.2}{9}Q^4 N\sum_{j=1}^{M}\zeta_j} + \sqrt{R_{emp}} + \sqrt{A}\right)^2 + \varepsilon \qquad (6)$$

Let $R_{SM}^*(Q) = a$. For every θ, let the Q that satisfies $R^*_{SM}(Q) = a$ to be Q^*, where a is a constant real number. $R^*_{SM}(Q) = a$ exists because the second order derivative of Equation (6) is positive. We could solve Equation (6) as follow,

$$Q^4 \frac{0.2}{3} N\sum_{j=1}^{M}\zeta_j + Q^2\sum_{j=1}^{M}v_j - 3\left(\sqrt{a-\varepsilon} - \sqrt{R_{emp}} - \sqrt{A}\right)^2 = 0 \qquad (7)$$

There will be at most 4 solutions of Q and let Q^* be the solution which is the smallest real number among the four. Q is the width of the Q-neighborhood and as such it must be a real number. If there exists no real solution, let $Q^* = 0$.

$$h(M,Q^*) = \begin{cases} 0 & R_{emp} \geq a \\ Q^* & else \end{cases} \qquad (8)$$

So, for RBFNN model selection, Problem (5) becomes:

$$\max_{M\in\Lambda} h(M,Q^*) \qquad (9)$$

The determination of the constant a is made according to the classifier's output schemes for classification. For instance, if class outputs are different by one, then a may be selected as 0.25 because a sample is misclassified if the square of its deviation from the target output is larger than 0.25. Same as the other methods, $h(M,Q^*)$ is generally not differentiable with respect to M (not a smooth function). One must try out all possible M values in order to find the optimal solution. Our experimental results show that $h(M,Q^*)$ drops to zero when the classifier becomes too complex, i.e. M is too large, and heuristically early stop could be applied to reduce the number of classifier trainings when Q approaches zero. In the experiments presented in the next section, we stop the search when the Q values drop below a threshold. In fact, Q does not increase significantly after it drops below 10% of the maximum value of Q being found and thus it is used as the threshold to speed up the MC²SG.

4 Experimental Results and Discussion

In this section, we generate three artificial datasets to simulate the bit rates of I/O to the Internet during weekdays. The first dataset, Artificial Dataset 1, consists of first 5 weekdays as training dataset and the 5 weekdays of the incoming week are used as testing dataset. The second dataset, Artificial Dataset 2, is similar to the first one, but having 10 weekdays in both training and testing datasets. The two features in the datasets are the average bit rate within 2 minutes and the current time. We simulate the real operating environment when more than 90% of the time is free from attack, and attacks occur only in a very small portion of time. The flooding-based attacks use up all the bandwidths and thus the server is disabled from serving legitimate users. Figures 2 and 3 (4 and 5) are the bit rate of the server connection to the Internet and the corresponding occurrences of DoS attack for the training dataset of the Artificial Dataset 1 (Artificial Dataset 2). One may find that only few DoS attacks occur randomly during all the 3 weeks of simulation and this should be very difficult for neural network to learn the attacks from the training dataset.

For each of the artificial datasets, one RBFNN is trained and the corresponding number of hidden neurons is selected by the MC^2SG method. The numerical results are shown in Table 1. The bit rate plot of the testing dataset of Artificial Dataset 1 (Artificial Dataset 2) could be found in Figure 6 (7). Figures 8 and 9 (10 and 11) show the RBFNN network outputs and the DoS attack occurrences for Artificial Dataset 1 (Artificial Dataset 2), respectively.

Both RBFNNs consist of 4 hidden neurons. The selection of the RBFNN architecture using the MC^2SG guarantees a low generalization error for unseen samples, in a probability sense. Thus, one may notice that the false alarm rates for both experiments are zero and the precision of DoS attack detection is very high. Those DoS attacks which are missed by the RBFNN occur at the beginning of the attacks and the RBFNN does not have enough confidence to flag for attacks. This problem may be solved by adding more input features to the RBFNN.

The Artificial Dataset 3 is specially designed to demonstrate the adaptability of the machine learning approach we applied in this work. The training dataset follows the pattern we described for the Artificial Dataset 2 while the testing dataset has a 12 hours time shift in the peak periods. This is to simulate the servers serving overseas

Table 1. Numerical Results for the Experiments on two Artificial Datasets

	Artificial Dataset 1	Artificial Dataset 2
# Hidden Neurons in the RBFNN	4	4
Precision	99.94%	99.96%
False Alarm	0.00%	0.00%
DoS Detection Rate	96.97%	98.29%

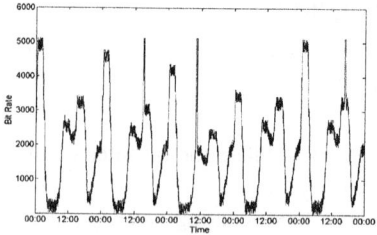

Fig. 2. Bit Rate vs Time forTraining Dataset of Artificial Dataset 1

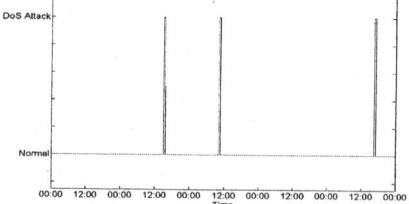

Fig. 3. Occurrence of the DoS Attacks for Training Dataset of Artificial Dataset 1

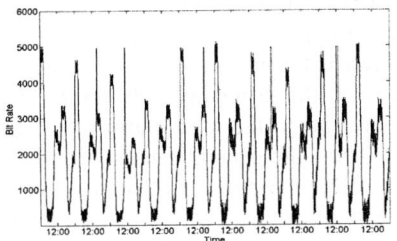

Fig. 4. Bit Rate vs Time For Training Dataset of Artificial Dataset 2

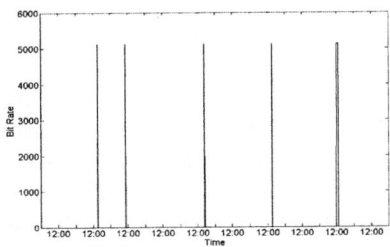

Fig. 5. Occurrence of the DoS Attacks for Training Dataset of Artificial Dataset 2

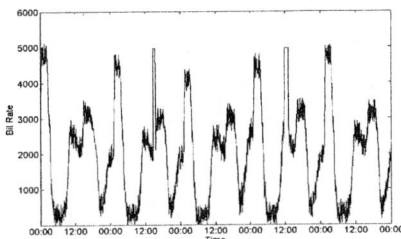

Fig. 6. Bit Rate vs Time for Testing Dataset of Artificial Dataset 1

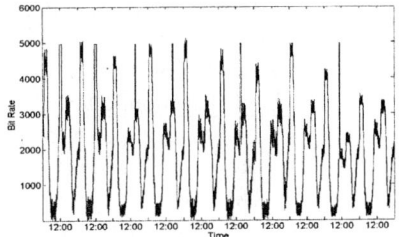

Fig. 7. Bit Rate vs Time for Testing Dataset of Artificial Dataset 2

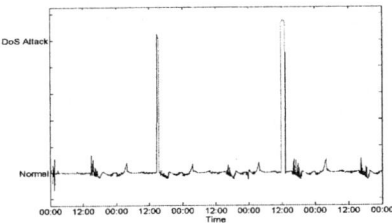

Fig. 8. RBFNN Outputs for the Testing Dataset of Artificial Dataset 1

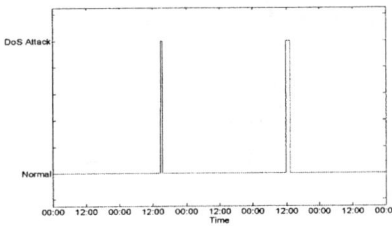

Fig. 9. Occurrence of the DoS Attacks for Testing Dataset of Artificial Dataset 1

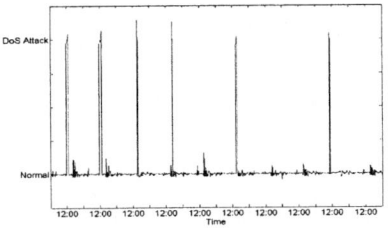

Fig. 10. RBFNN Outputs for the Testing Dataset of Artificial Dataset 2

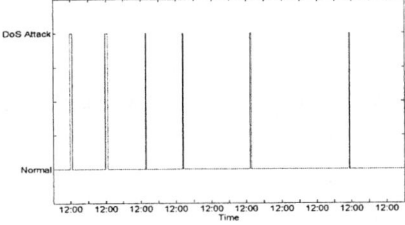

Fig. 11. Occurrence of the DoS Attacks for Testing Dataset of Artificial Dataset 2

clients. The numerical results are shown in Table 2. One may notice that the DoS detection rate is little bit worse than the one for Artificial Dataset 2. Moreover, Figure 15 shows that the confident of the RBFNN is lower than those in the previous experiments of the two datasets. These are due to the difference between the peak periods in the training and testing datasets. Fortunately, the false alarm rate is zero and the precision of the RBFNN is very high. Thus, the generalization capability of the trained RBFNN is very good because we select the number of hidden neurons based on its generalization error bound. This experiment also shows that the adaptability of RBFNN and machine learning techniques in the time shifting and they are not affected by the change of peak periods of traffics.

Table 2. Numerical Results for the Experiments on Artificial Dataset 3

# Hidden Neurons in the RBFNN	4
Precision	99.94%
False Alarm	0.00%
DoS Detection Rate	98.18%

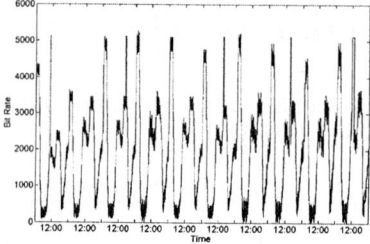

Fig. 12. Bit Rate vs Time For Training Dataset of Artificial Dataset 3

Fig. 13. Bit Rate vs Time For Testing Dataset of Artificial Dataset 3

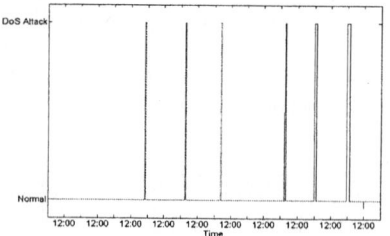 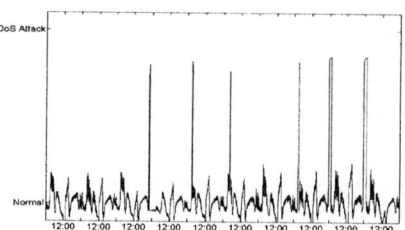

Fig. 14. Occurrence of the DoS Attacks for Testing Dataset of Artificial Dataset 3

Fig. 15. RBFNN Outputs for the Testing Dataset of Artificial Dataset 3

The performances of machine learning techniques and neural networks depend on the training datasets. If the training datasets are not similar to the future unseen samples and testing datasets, one could not expect the trained classifiers to have good performances on them. This is the philosophy that guided us to develop the localized generalization error bound (R^*_{SM}) and is applicable to general machine learning problems. In the experiment using the Artificial Dataset 3, we demonstrated that the machine learning techniques are able to adapt to unseen patterns which differ from the training datasets. However, the performance of the classifiers in such case will be weakened.

5 Conclusion and Future Works

The applications of machine learning techniques in intrusion detection problems encounter two major problems: high false alarm rate and the difficulty in learning from samples having a very small portion of attack packets. We demonstrated to the possibility of solving a flooding-based DoS detection by building a RBFNN with minimization of its generalization error bound. The generalization error bound is constructed using the stochastic sensitivity measure of RBFNN. The experimental results show that the proposed system tackles the two mentioned problems very well.

The time complexity of the proposed method is very low and independent of the number of training samples. This is particularly important to intrusion detection problems because the training dataset size is usually very large. In contrast to other machine learning techniques which minimize the training error only, our approach directly minimizes the estimated generalization error bound using stochastic sensitivity measure.

This work serves as a pilot study of applying the generalization error bound based on stochastic sensitivity measure for intrusion detection problems. Further investigation using real world dataset is needed. Moreover, this will be an interesting research topic to explore the intrusion detection system which recognizes multiple types of intrusions using our proposed method.

Acknowledgements

This work was supported by the Germany/Hong Kong Joint Research Scheme R.G.C. grant #G_HK029/02.

References

1. S. Baker and B. Grow, "Gambling Sites, This Is A Holdup", http://-www.businessweek.com/magazine/content/04_32/b3895106_mz063.htm, Business Week, 2004.
2. D. Barbará and S. Jajodia, "Applications of Data Mining in Computer Security", Kluwer Academic Publishers, 2002.
3. A. P. F. Chan, W. W. Y. Ng, D. S. Yeung and E. C. C. Tsang, "Multiple Classifier System with Feature Grouping for Intrusion Detection: Mutual Information Approach", Lecture Notes in Computer Science, vol. 3683, pp. 141 - 148, 2005.
4. L. Feinstein, D. Schnackenberg and R. Balupari and D. Kindred, "Statistical Approaches to DDoS Attack Detection and Response", Proc of the DARPA Information Survivability Conference and Expostion, pp. 303 - 314, 2003.
5. G. Giorgio, R. Fabio and D. Luca, "Fusion of multiple classifiers for intrusion detection in computer networks", Pattern Recognition Letters, pp. 1795-1803, 2003.

6. A. Householder, A. Manion, L. Pesante, G. Weaver, and R. Thomas, "Managing the Threat of Denial-of-Service Attacks," Carnegie Mellon CERT Coordination Ceter,Pittsburgh,PA, [Online]Available:http://www.cert.org/archive/pdf/Managing_DoS.pdf, Oct. 2001.
7. S. Jin and D. S. Yeung, "DDoS detection based on feature space modeling", Proc. of International Conference on Machine Learning and Cybernetics, pp.4210-4215, 2004.
8. S. Jin and D. S. Yeung, "A Covariance Analysis Model for DDoS Attack Detection", IEEE Proc. of International Conference on Communications, pp. 1882 - 1886, 2004.
9. S. Kumar, EH. Spafford, "A pattern matching model for misuse intrusion detection", Proceedings of the 17th National Computer Security Conference, 1994.
10. W. Lee, S. J. Stolfo, "Data mining approaches for intrusion detection", Proceedings of the seventh USENIX Security Symposium, 1998.
11. C. Manikopoulos and S. Papavassiliou, "Network Intrusion and Fault Detection: A Statistical Anomaly Approach", IEEE Communications Magazine, 2002.
12. W. W. Y. Ng, D. S. Yeung, D. Wang, E. C. C. Tsang and X-Z. Wang, "Localized Generalization Error and Its Application to RBFNN Training", Proc. of International Conference on Machine Learning and Cybernetics, pp. 4667 - 4673, 2005.

Context-Sensitive Kernel Functions: A Distance Function Viewpoint

Bram Vanschoenwinkel*, Feng Liu**, and Bernard Manderick

Vrije Universiteit Brussel,
Computational Modeling Lab,
Pleinlaan 2, 1050 Brussel, Belgium
{bvschoen, fengliu, bmanderi}@vub.ac.be
http://como.vub.ac.be/

Abstract. This paper extends the idea of weighted distance functions to kernels and support vector machines. Here, we focus on applications that rely on sliding a window over a sequence of string data. For this type of problems it is argued that a symbolic, context-based representation of the data should be preferred over a continuous, real format as this is a much more intuitive setting for working with (weighted) distance functions. It is shown how a weighted string distance can be decomposed and subsequently used in different kernel functions and how these kernel functions correspond to real kernels between the continuous, real representations of the symbolic, context-based representations of the vectors.

1 Introduction

In support vector machine (SVM) learning the data is mapped non-linearly from the original input space X to a high-dimensional feature space F and subsequently separated by a maximum-margin hyperplane in that space F. By making use of the kernel trick, the mapping to F can stay implicit, and we can avoid working in the high-dimensional space. Moreover, because the mapping to F is non-linear, the decision boundary which is linear in F, corresponds to a non-linear decision boundary in X. One of the most important design decisions in SVM learning is the choice of kernel function K because the hyperplane is defined completely by inner products between vectors in F and calculated through the kernel function K. Moreover, K takes vectors from the input space X and directly calculates inner products in F without having to represent or even know the exact form of these vectors, hence the implicit mapping and computational benefit [1]. In the light of the above it is not hard to see that the way in which K is calculated is crucial for the success of the classification process.

Notice that an inner product is in fact one of the most simple similarity measures between vectors as it gives much information about the position of these vectors in relation to each other. In that sense the learning process can benefit a lot from the use of special purpose similarity or dissimilarity measures in the calculation of K [2, 3, 4].

---

* Author funded by a doctoral grant of the institute for advancement of scientific technological research in Flanders (IWT).
** Author funded by a doctoral grant of the Vrije Universiteit Brussel.

However, incorporating such knowledge in a kernel function is not trivial as a kernel function has to satisfy a number of properties that result directly from the definition of the inner product.

This paper concentrates on the use of SVMs on string data. Applying SVMs on such data involves a number of issues that need to be addressed, i.e. SVMs are defined on real vectors and not on string data. In general two approaches exist : i) the transformation approach, i.e. transform the discrete data to real vectors and ii) the direct approach, i.e. define kernel functions that work on string data but calculate real inner products in F. The transformation approach has been successfully applied to the classification of large texts and is in that context generally known as the *bag-of-words* approach [5]. For other applications, where classification is done more at the word level, and where a word that has to be classified (the focus word) is represented by a context of p words in front and q words after the focus word, the data is transformed to a real format in a order preserving way. We will refer to this approach as the *orthonormal vector* approach [4, 6].

This paper focuses on classification problems at the word level as described above, but in contrast to what is commonly done we will not be making use of the transformation approach and orthonormal vectors but we will be making use of the direct approach. It will be argued that it is better to work directly on the contexts in stead of working on a transformed high-dimensional sparse format because, in this way it is much easier to incorporate special purpose (dis)similarity measures into the kernel function as such measures are defined on the string data itself and not on a high-dimensional representation of that data. This approach will be referred to as the *context-based* approach.

2 Sliding Windows and Contexts

Consider a collection S of sequences $\mathbf{s}$. Every sequence $\mathbf{s}$ consists of an ordered succession of symbols, i.e. $\mathbf{s} = \left(s_{k_0} \ldots s_{k_{|\mathbf{s}|-1}}\right)$ with $|\mathbf{s}|$ the length of the sequence and with $s_{k_i} \in D$ a set (henceforth called a dictionary) of symbols indexed according to $k_i \in \{0, \ldots, n\}$ with $|D| = n$ the cardinality of the dictionary D and $i = 0, \ldots, |\mathbf{s}| - 1$. Contexts are now formed by sliding a window over the sequences $\mathbf{s} \in S$, i.e. for every sequence $\mathbf{s}$ a set of instances $I(\mathbf{s})$ containing $|\mathbf{s}|$ contexts with a window size $r = (p+q+1)$ is constructed as follows $I(\mathbf{s}) = \{\mathbf{s}\,[(i-p) : (i+q)] \mid 0 \le i \le |\mathbf{s}| - 1\}$ with p the size of the left context, q the size of the right context and with $\mathbf{s}\,[i : j] = \left(s_{k_i} \ldots s_{k_j}\right)$ the subsequence of symbols from index i to j in the sequence $\mathbf{s}$. The total set of contexts is now formed by taking the union of all the $I(\mathbf{s})$, i.e. $I(S) = \bigcup_s I(\mathbf{s})$. Notice that for subsequences with indexes $i < 0$ and $j > |\mathbf{s}| - 1$ corresponding positions are filled with the special symbol ' − ' which can be considered as the empty symbol. Also note that this symbol is assigned the index 0 in the dictionary D.

2.1 Representing Contexts by Orthonormal Vectors

A well-known approach to representing contexts as suitable vectors to do SVM learning is by encoding them with *orthonormal* vectors. An orthonormal vector is a vector of length n representing a symbol from D. An orthonormal vector has all zero components except for the component corresponding to the index in D of the symbol it represents, in total there are n orthonormal vectors, i.e. one for each symbol in D. Usually the only non-zero component takes the value of 1 (although other values are also possible as we will see in Section (3.2)), complete vectors are now formed by concatenating all orthonormal vectors corresponding to the symbols in the sequence, the dimensionality of such a complete vector is $n*r$ with only r non-zero components. Consider the following example.

Example 1. Gene finding systems have the purpose to identify regions that encode proteins in a raw DNA sequence. One subtask in this process is known as *splice site prediction*. Note that a DNA sequence is essentially a sequence of nucleotides represented by a four letter alphabet (or dictionary) $D = \{A, C, G, T\}$. Without going into detail splice site prediction instances can be represented by considering adjacent nucleotides at fixed positions relative to the candidate splice site, i.e. a context of p positions upstream and q adjacent positions downstream the candidate. Assuming that the symbols in the dictionary are indexed alphabetically we get the following four orthonormal vectors: A $= (v_1, 0, 0, 0)$, C $= (0, v_2, 0, 0)$, G $= (0, 0, v_3, 0)$ and T $= (0, 0, 0, v_4)$. In its most basic form $\mathbf{v} = \mathbf{1}$ although other values are possible as it will be shown in Section 3. For now assume that $\mathbf{v} = \mathbf{1}$. Next, complete instances are formed by concatenating above vectors according to the occurrence of the symbols in the sequence, i.e. the sequence (A, T, G, C, A) becomes (1, 0, 0, 0, 0, 0, 0, 1, 0, 0, 1, 0, 0, 1, 0, 0, 1, 0, 0, 0).

Reasoning about such vectors, e.g. reasoning about the similarity between orthonormal vectors is not easy because it is not directly observable what context they represent. Moreover, similarity measures one would like to use in the kernel function are defined on contexts and not on orthonormal representations of such contexts.

2.2 Representing Contexts by Their Index in the Dictionary

For the reasons mentioned above, we believe that it is better to reason about contexts at the level of the symbols themselves. However, calculating with such context vectors is not efficient at all because the different symbols of the context will have to be checked for equality and the complexity of comparing 2 strings is proportional to the length of the longest string in the comparison. Note that one of the most important requirements for a kernel is for it to be computationally efficient as it has to be calculated for all pairs of vectors in the training set. For these reasons we will represent the symbols by their index k_i in the dictionary D. In this way we only have to compare integers and not strings.

3 Context Kernels from a Distance Function Viewpoint

Notice that from now on we will be reasoning about vectors $\mathbf{x}, \mathbf{x}' \in X$ with $X \subseteq \mathbb{S}^l$ the input space of the SVM with $\mathbb{S}^l$ the space of all contexts with r the window size as before and l the total length of the contexts with components $x_i, x_i' \in D$. When doing calculations and talking about implementation, for reasons of efficiency, the contexts will be represented by the index of the symbols in D as discussed in the previous section. Next, orthonormal vectors will be denoted by $\tilde{\mathbf{x}}, \tilde{\mathbf{x}}' \in \tilde{X}$ with $\tilde{X} \subseteq \mathbb{R}^{l*n}$ with n the cardinality of D as before.

Before we start however, we need to define what it means for a kernel to be valid. It was already mentioned in the introduction that kernels need to satisfy a number of conditions that follow directly from the fact that they define inner products in a *Reproducing Kernel Hilbert Space* (RKHS) associated with the kernel.

3.1 Positive Semi-definite and Conditionally Positive Definite Kernels

Let's start with a general definition of a kernel function and subsequently refine it to two more specific types of kernels known as *positive semi-definite* (PSD) and *conditionally positive definite* (CPD) kernels.

Definition 1. *A kernel is a symmetric function* $K : X \times X \to \mathbb{R}$ *so that for all* $\mathbf{x}_i$ *and* $\mathbf{x}_j$ *in* X, $K(\mathbf{x}_i, \mathbf{x}_j) = \langle \phi(\mathbf{x}_i), \phi(\mathbf{x}_j) \rangle$ *where* ϕ *is a (non-linear) mapping from the input space* X *into the Hilbert space* F *provided with the inner product* $\langle ., . \rangle$.

But not all symmetric functions over $X \times X$ are kernels that can be used in a SVM. Since a kernel K is related to an inner product, cfr. the definition above, it has to satisfy some conditions that arise naturally from the definition of an inner product and are given by Mercer's theorem: the kernel function has to be positive semi-definite (PSD).

Definition 2. *A symmetric function* $K : X \times X \to \mathbb{R}$ *which for all* $m \in \mathbb{N}$, $\mathbf{x}_i, \mathbf{x}_j \in X$ *gives rise to a positive semi-definite (PSD) kernel matrix, i.e. for which for all* $c_i \in \mathbb{R}$ *we have:*

$$\sum_{i,j=1}^{m} c_i c_j \mathbf{K}_{ij} \geq 0, \text{ where } \mathbf{K}_{ij} = K(\mathbf{x}_i, \mathbf{x}_j) \qquad (1)$$

is called a positive semi-definite (PSD) kernel.

In practice, the requirement of a kernel to be PSD turns out to be a very strict assumption. Many special purpose or sophisticated similarity and dissimilarity measures that one would like to incorporate in the learning process do not satisfy the requirement of being PSD.

One particular class of non-PSD kernels is the class of *conditionally positive definite* (CPD) kernels. For this type of kernel functions it has been shown that they can be used as generalized distances in the feature space [7, 2].

Definition 3. *A symmetric function* $K : X \times X \to \mathbb{R}$ *which satisfies (1) for all* $m \in \mathbb{N}$, $\mathbf{x}_i \in X$ *and for all* $c_i \in \mathbb{R}$ *with the extra condition:*

$$\sum_{i=1}^{m} c_i = 0, \qquad (2)$$

is called a conditionally positive definite (CPD) kernel.

3.2 A Weighted Distance Between Contexts

Consider the following weighted distance function that works on contexts $\mathbf{x}$ and $\mathbf{x}' \in X \subseteq \mathbb{S}^l$ with $\mathbf{x}, \mathbf{x}'$ and D with $|D| = n$ as before:

$$d_w : X \times X \to \mathbb{R}^+ : d_w(\mathbf{x}, \mathbf{x}') = \sum_{i=0}^{l-1} w_i d(x_i, x_i') \qquad (3)$$

with $d(x_i, x'_i) = 0$ if $x_i = x'_i \neq$ '$-$', else 1. Notice that in order for d_w to be always positive and make sense, all the w_i should be greater than 0. Next, when doing calculations, we will present the contexts by their index in D as discussed before. Therefore, consider the following alternative expression to calculate the RHS of Equation (3):

$$w_i d(x_i, x'_i) = w_i - \delta(k_i, l_i) \qquad (4)$$

with $k_i, l_i \in \{0 \ldots n\}$ the indexes of x_i and x'_i in D and with $\delta : \{0 \ldots n\} \times \{0 \ldots n\} \to \{w_i, 0\}$:

$$\delta(k_i, l_i) = w_i \text{ if } k_i = l_i \neq 0, \text{ else } 0 \qquad (5)$$

Notice that by making use of Equations (4) and (5) we avoid doing any string comparisons and moreover isolating the w_i in (4) and (5) will allow us to calculate our weighted inner product by at most l integer comparisons and floating point sums. This will be shown in the next section.

3.3 A Weighted Inner Product Between Contexts

We start by defining an inner product based on the distance from Equation (3) and making use of the alternative formulation in (4) and (5) gives rise to the following definition:

$$\langle . | . \rangle : X \times X \to \mathbb{R} : \langle \mathbf{x} | \mathbf{x}' \rangle = \sum_{i=0}^{l-1} \delta(k_i, l_i) \qquad (6)$$

Next, it will be argued that above inner product is equivalent to the standard inner product between the corresponding orthonormal vectors. This is stated in the following proposition.

Proposition 1. *Let $X \subseteq \mathbb{S}^l$ be a discrete space with contexts $\mathbf{x}$ and $\mathbf{x}'$ with l the length of the contexts, with components x_i and $x'_i \in D$ and with $|D| = n$ as before. Let $\tilde{X} \subseteq \mathbb{R}^{n*l}$ be the space of $n * l$-dimensional vectors $\tilde{\mathbf{x}}$ and $\tilde{\mathbf{x}}'$ the corresponding orthonormal vector representation of the vectors $\mathbf{x}$ and $\mathbf{x}'$ as follows: $\tilde{\mathbf{x}} = ([\tilde{\mathbf{x}}]_0, \ldots, [\tilde{\mathbf{x}}]_{l-1})$, $\tilde{\mathbf{x}}' = ([\tilde{\mathbf{x}}']_0, \ldots, [\tilde{\mathbf{x}}']_{l-1})$, with $[\tilde{\mathbf{x}}]_i$ and $[\tilde{\mathbf{x}}']_i$ the orthonormal vectors as defined in Example 1 and corresponding to the symbols x_i and x'_i respectively and with $\mathbf{v} = \left(\sqrt{w_0}, \ldots, \sqrt{w_n}\right)$. Then, the function $\langle . | . \rangle$ as defined in Equation (6) is positive semi-definite (PSD) and $\langle \mathbf{x} | \mathbf{x}' \rangle = \langle \tilde{\mathbf{x}}, \tilde{\mathbf{x}}' \rangle$.*

Proof. We will prove that $\langle \mathbf{x} | \mathbf{x}' \rangle = \langle \tilde{\mathbf{x}}, \tilde{\mathbf{x}}' \rangle$, the positive definiteness of the function $\langle . | . \rangle$ will follow automatically. We start by noting that the vectors $\tilde{\mathbf{x}}$ and $\tilde{\mathbf{x}}'$ are composed out of l orthonormal vectors and every $[\tilde{\mathbf{x}}]_i$ corresponds with the symbol x_i from the vector $\mathbf{x}$. For $l = 1$ and $\forall \mathbf{x}, \mathbf{x}' \in X \subseteq \mathbb{S}^1$ we have the following:

$$\langle \mathbf{x} | \mathbf{x}' \rangle = \delta(k_0, l_0) = \begin{cases} w_0 & \text{if } x_0 = x'_0 \\ 0 & \text{if } x_0 \neq x'_0 \end{cases}$$

For the discrete case this follows directly from the definition of the kernel function and the distance function it is based on, see Equations (4),(5) and (6). For the orthonormal case it is sufficient to note that for the inner products between all orthonormal vectors $[\tilde{x}]_i$, $[\tilde{x}']_i$ it holds that:

$$\langle [\tilde{x}]_i, [\tilde{x}']_i \rangle = \begin{cases} w_i & \text{if } [\tilde{x}]_i = [\tilde{x}']_i \\ 0 & \text{if } [\tilde{x}]_i \neq [\tilde{x}']_i \end{cases} \quad (7)$$

Next, because $l = 1$ we need only one orthonormal vector to construct complete instances, i.e. $\tilde{x} = [\tilde{x}]_0$ and $\tilde{x}' = [\tilde{x}']_0$ and thus:

$$\langle \tilde{x}, \tilde{x}' \rangle = \sum_{i=0}^{l-1} \langle [\tilde{x}]_i, [\tilde{x}']_i \rangle \quad (8)$$
$$= \langle [\tilde{x}]_0, [\tilde{x}']_0 \rangle$$
$$= \delta(k_0, l_0)$$

Where the last step is justified by Equation (7) and by the assumption that $[\tilde{x}]_i$ is the orthonormal vector corresponding to the symbol x_i. Next, assume that the proposition holds for $l = m$. Subsequently, we will prove that the proposition holds for $l = m + 1$ and by induction we will be able to conclude that it holds for all l. We start by showing that the calculation of the kernel values for $l = m + 1$ can be decomposed in terms of $l = m$:

$$\langle \mathbf{x}|\mathbf{x}' \rangle = \sum_{i=0}^{m-1} \delta(k_i, l_i) + \begin{cases} w_m & \text{if } x_m = x'_m \\ 0 & \text{if } x_m \neq x'_m \end{cases} \quad (9)$$

Now it can be readily seen that the the proposition holds for $l = m+1$ because we know by assumption that for the left part of the RHS of Equation (9) it holds that $\sum_{i=0}^{m-1} \delta(k_i, l_i) = \sum_{i=0}^{m-1} \langle [\tilde{x}]_i, [\tilde{x}']_i \rangle$ and for the right part of the RHS making use of Equations (7) and (8) $x_m = x'_m$ and $x_m \neq x'_m$ implies $\langle [\tilde{x}]_m, [\tilde{x}']_m \rangle = w_m$ and 0 respectively. □

Next, it will be shown how the above inner product can be used in more complex kernel functions that are suited to do SVM learning for problems with more complicated non-linear decision boundaries.

3.4 Context-Sensitive Kernel Functions

Two kernels will be described in this section, both based on standard kernel functions, i.e. the polynomial kernel and the radial basis kernel [1]. For $\mathbf{w} = \mathbf{1}$ the kernels are actually equal to these kernels, however for $\mathbf{w} \neq \mathbf{1}$ they are not the same and in that case we call them context-sensitive as they take into account the amount of information that is present at every position i in the contexts through the weights w_i. We start with the polynomial based kernel, consider the following proposition:

Proposition 2. *Let $X \subseteq \mathbb{S}^l$ be a discrete space with contexts $\mathbf{x}$ and $\mathbf{x}'$ with l the length of the contexts, with components x_i and $x'_i \in D$ with indexes k_i and l_i respectively and with $|D| = n$ as before. Let $\tilde{X} \subseteq \mathbb{R}^{n*l}$ be the space of $n * l$-dimensional vectors $\tilde{\mathbf{x}}$ and*

$\tilde{\mathbf{x}}'$ the corresponding orthonormal vector representation of the vectors $\mathbf{x}$ and $\mathbf{x}'$ as in Proposition 1, then the kernel function $K : X \times X \to \mathbb{R}$:

$$K(\mathbf{x}, \mathbf{x}') = \left(\sum_{i=0}^{l-1} \delta(k_i, l_i) + c \right)^d \tag{10}$$

is positive semi-definite. For $\mathbf{w} = \mathbf{1}$ we call the kernel K_{SOK} (Simple Overlap Kernel) and for $\mathbf{w} \neq \mathbf{1}$ we call the kernel K_{WOK} (Weighted Overlap Kernel).

Proof. The proof is very simple and follows directly by application of Proposition 1, i.e. $\sum_{i=0}^{l-1} \delta(k_i, l_i) = \langle \mathbf{x} | \mathbf{x}' \rangle = \langle \tilde{\mathbf{x}}, \tilde{\mathbf{x}}' \rangle$ and the closure properties of kernels [1]. □

Notice that in practice K will often be normalized, i.e. scaled between 0 and 1.

Next, we describe the radial basis function based kernel, but first we need a result by Christian Berg dating back to 1984 [7].

Theorem 1. *Let X be the input space as before and let $K : X \times X \to \mathbb{R}$ be a kernel then K is CPD if and only if $\exp(\gamma K)$ is PSD for all $\gamma > 0$.*

Note that the following kernel has already been introduced in previous work [8, 4] however here we give a proof of its validity and in addition we link it back to the distance d_w the inner product from Equation 6 is based on.

Proposition 3. *Let $X \subseteq \mathbb{S}^l$ be a discrete space with contexts $\mathbf{x}$ and $\mathbf{x}'$ with l the length of the contexts, with components x_i and $x'_i \in D$ with $|D| = n$ as before. Let $\tilde{X} \subseteq \mathbb{R}^{n*l}$ be the space of $n*l$-dimensional vectors $\tilde{\mathbf{x}}$ and $\tilde{\mathbf{x}}'$ the corresponding orthonormal vector representation of the vectors $\mathbf{x}$ and $\mathbf{x}'$ as in Proposition 1, then the kernel function $K : X \times X \to \mathbb{R}$:*

$$K(\mathbf{x}, \mathbf{x}') = \exp(-2\gamma d_w(\mathbf{x}, \mathbf{x}')) \tag{11}$$

is positive semi-definite. For $\mathbf{w} = \mathbf{1}$ we call the kernel K_{ORBF} (Overlap Radial Basis Function) and for $\mathbf{w} \neq \mathbf{1}$ we call the kernel K_{WRBF} (Weighted Radial Basis Function).

Proof. First of all it is noticed that for real vectors the negative squared Euclidean distance $-\|.-.\|^2$ is CPD, for more details the reader is referred to [7, 2]. Next, by making use of Equations 6 and 4 and by application of Proposition 1 it can be readily seen that:

$$\begin{aligned}
-2d_w(\mathbf{x}, \mathbf{x}') &= -2 \sum_{i=0}^{l-1} (w_i - \delta(k_i, l_i)) \\
&= -\left(\sum_{i=0}^{l-1} w_i - 2 \sum_{i=0}^{l-1} \delta(k_i, l_i) + \sum_{i=0}^{l-1} w_i \right) \\
&= -(\langle \mathbf{x} | \mathbf{x} \rangle - 2 \langle \mathbf{x} | \mathbf{x}' \rangle + \langle \mathbf{x}' | \mathbf{x}' \rangle) \\
&= -\|\tilde{\mathbf{x}} - \tilde{\mathbf{x}}'\|^2
\end{aligned} \tag{12}$$

with $\tilde{\mathbf{x}}, \tilde{\mathbf{x}}' \in \mathbb{R}^{n*l}$ the orthonormal vectors corresponding to the symbolic vectors $\mathbf{x}, \mathbf{x}' \in \mathbb{S}^l$ and thus we can conclude that (12) is CPD which makes Equation 10 PSD by application of Theorem 1. □

As a final remark note that the factor 2 in Equation 11 can actually be dropped as γ can be used to scale d_w in any way we want.

4 Experiments

We will be describing experiments on two different tasks where instances can be represented by sliding a window over a sequence of strings as described in Section 2. Note that it is not our purpose here to improve the state of the art results for each task, but that we are interested in comparing the weighted kernels with the unweighted kernels. The experiments have been done with LIBSVM, a C/C++ and Java library for SVMs [9]. As a weighting scheme we used a quantity called *information gain ratio* which calculates for every feature the amount of information it contains with respect to the determination of the class label, for more details we refer to [8].

4.1 Part-of-Speech Tagging

Part-of-speech (POS) tagging is the process of marking up the words in a text with their corresponding parts of speech, i.e. the syntactic categories that words belong to, for more information the reader is referred to [10]. For the experiments we used a dataset that has been extracted from the WSJ corpus, it consists of a training set of 497522 instances and a test set of 46512 instances. Every instance consists out of one single symbol, i.e. the word in the sentence, in total we consider 37 syntactical categories and we use a window size 10. Finally, for multi-class classification a *one-against-one* method is used [9] and for the evaluation of the results we use a python script which calculates for every class the precision, recall and $F_{\beta=1}$ rate. Additionally it also calculates the *overall* precision, recall and $F_{\beta=1}$ rate. The $F_{\beta=1}$ rate serves to assess the global performance, it is calculated by a combination of precision and recall, i.e. $F_{\beta=1} = \frac{(\beta^2+1)*precision*recall}{\beta^2*precision+recall}$.

Next we give the results for POS tagging with the polynomial based kernel from Equation 10. Notice that for a classification problem with 37 classes 666 classifiers have to be trained. For this reason we did not do a complete parameter optimization, but we give the results for 3 different values of the SVM cost parameter C. The other parameters are fixed as $c = 0$ and $d = 2$ because previous work has shown that this is actually the best choice. To start note that the indicated significance intervals for the F rates have been obtained with bootstrap resampling [11]. F rates outside of these intervals are assumed to be significantly different from the related F rate ($p < 0.05$). In the left side of Table 1 it can be seen that the WOK outperforms the SOK for all values of C although the differences are rather small, for $C = 1$ and $C = 25$ the differences are not significant, for $C = 5$ the results are considered to be significantly different although

Table 1. Results for POS tagging. The F rates and the number of support vectors for the simple overlap kernel (SOK) and the weighted overlap kernel (WOK) with information gain ratio.

	$F_{\beta=1}$		#SVs	
C/kernel	$SOK(d=2, c=0)$	$WOK(gr)(d=2, c=0)$	SOK	WOK(gr)
1	77.80 ± 1.11	78.80 ± 1.02	237231	206256
5	79.98 ± 1.03	81.11 ± 1.06	240211	208635
25	79.90 ± 1.17	80.85 ± 1.08	242787	208629

only with a small margin. Nevertheless, there is another positive side effect in the use of gain ratio weights : both the model complexity and the time needed for the SVM to converge drop significantly, for the model complexity this can be seen in the right side of Table 1.

Note that in previous work [6] we performed more in-depth experiments on a natural language task called named entity recognition. In these experiments the same tendencies can be observed. In addition as a motivation for the use of gain ratio as weights the reader is referred to [8].

4.2 Splice Site Prediction

In Example 1 it was already explained that splice site prediction is a subtask in the gene finding process where it is the purpose to identify regions that encode proteins in a raw DNA sequence. In general a gene is not a continuous sequence in the DNA but usually consists of a set of coding fragments known as exons that are separated by non-coding fragments known as introns. Most of such introns start with the GT *consensus dinucleotide* called a *donor* site and end with the AG *consensus dinucleotide* called an *acceptor* site. In splice site prediction it is the purpose to automatically predict which GT, AG dinucleotides are donor or acceptor sites. In this paper we will only be predicting donor sites making use of a data set of human genes called *HumGS* making use of a context of 10 nucleotides both before and after the candidate splice site, for more details the reader is referred to [12].

To optimize the parameters we perform 2–fold cross-validation and a fine-grained grid search on a subset of 17278 candidate donor sites (4778 actual and 12500 pseudo donor sites). Notice that accuracy here is given as a measure known as $FP95\%$ which measures the number of false positive classifications at a sensitivity rate of 95% with sensitivity calculated as the number of true positive predictions over the sum of false negative and true positive predictions, for more details see [12]. Testing is done on a test set with 955 actual and 2500 pseudo donor sites. From Table 2 it can be seen that the WRBF with gain ratio weights performs best. Furthermore, in the same way as for POS tagging all weighted kernels perform better than their unweighted counterparts both in terms of $FP95\%$ and model complexity.

Table 2. Results for splice site prediction. False positive rate at a sensitivity level of 95% (top) and model complexity (bottom). Note that lower $FP95\%$ rates are better than higher ones.

	SOK	$WOK(gr)$	$ORBF$	$WRBF(gr)$
$FP95\%$	7.28%	7.12%	7.36%	6.76%
#SVs	3677	2947	3419	2971
parameters	$(C=0.5, d=2, c=0)$	$(C=2, d=2, c=0)$	$(C=2, \gamma=0.03)$	$(C=8.0, \gamma=0.5)$

5 Conclusion

This paper described the use of SVMs on applications characterized by sliding a window over a sequence of symbols. For this type of applications we described a different viewpoint completely based on distance functions defined on contexts. The advantage of this approach is a much more intuitive setting to design and reflect about this type of kernel functions. The latter was illustrated by extending the idea of a weighted distance function to kernel functions and SVMs. In general the approach is also usable on continuous data and with different distance functions. Finally, the experimental results showed that the weighted kernel functions making use of information gain ratio weights outperform their unweighted counterparts not only in terms of accuracy but also in terms of model complexity.

References

1. Cristianini, N., Shawe-Taylor, J.: An Introduction to Support Vector Machines and other Kernel-based Learning Methods. Cambridge University Press (2000)
2. Schölkopf, B.: The kernel trick for distances. Technical report, Microsoft Research (2000)
3. Vanschoenwinkel, B.: Substitution matrix based kernel functions for protein secondary structure prediction. In: Proceedings of ICMLA-04 (International Conference on Machine Learning and Applications). (2004)
4. Vanschoenwinkel, B., Manderick, B.: Appropriate kernel functions for support vector machine learning with sequences of symbolic data. Deterministic and Statistical Methods in Machine Learning, Lecture Notes in Artificial Intelligence **3635** (2005)
5. Joachims, T.: Learning to Classify Text Using Support Vector Machines. Kluwer Academic Publishers (2002)
6. Vanschoenwinkel, B., Liu, F., Manderick, B.: Weighted kernel functions for svm learning in string domains: A distance function viewpoint. In: International Conference on Machine Learning and Cybernetics (ICMLC), Guangzhou, China, Vrije Universiteit Brussel, Belgium, Brussels (2005)
7. Berg, C., Christensen, J.P.R., Ressel, P.: Harmonic Analysis on Semigroups. Springer-Verlag, New York, Berlinj Heidelberg, Tokyo (1984)
8. Vanschoenwinkel, B., Manderick, B.: Context-sensitive kernel functions : A comparison between different context weights. In: Belgisch Nederlandse Artifcial Intelligence Conference (BNAIC) 2005 , Brussels, Belgium, Vrije Universiteit Brussel, Belgium, Brussels (2005)
9. Chih-Chung, C., Chi-Jen, L.: LIBSVM : A Library for Support Vector Machines. (2004)
10. Daelemans, W., Zavrel, J., Berck, S.: Mbt: A memorybased part of speech tagger-generator (1996)
11. Noreen, E.W.: Computer-Intensive Methods for Testing Hypotheses. John Wiley & Sons (1989)
12. Degroeve, S.: Design and Evaluation of a Linear Classification Strategy for Gene Structural Element Recognition. PhD thesis, Universiteit Gent, Faculty of Sciences, Gent, Belgium (2004)

A Parallel Genetic Algorithm for Solving the Inverse Problem of Support Vector Machines

Qiang He, Xizhao Wang, Junfen Chen, and Leifan Yan

Faculty of Mathematics and Computer Science,
Hebei University, Baoding 071002, Hebei, China
{heq, wangxz}@mail.hbu.edu.cn

Abstract. Support Vector Machines (SVMs) are learning machines that can perform binary classification (pattern recognition) and real valued function approximation (regression estimation) tasks. An inverse problem of SVMs is how to split a given dataset into two clusters such that the maximum margin between the two clusters is attained. Here the margin is defined according to the separating hyper-plane generated by support vectors. This paper investigates the inverse problem of SVMs by designing a parallel genetic algorithm. Experiments show that this algorithm can greatly decrease time complexity by the use of parallel processing. This study on the inverse problem of SVMs is motivated by designing a heuristic algorithm for generating decision trees with high generalization capability.

1 Introduction

Support vector machines (SVMs) are a classification technique of machine learning based on statistical learning theory [1, 2]. Considering a classification problem with two classes, SVMs are used to construct an optimal hyper-plane that maximizes the margin between two classes. According to Vapnik statistical learning theory [1, 3], the maximum of margin implies an extraordinary generalization capability and good performances of SVM classifiers [4, 5]. So far, SVMs have already been successfully applied to many real fields. This paper aims to make preparation for SVM's application to decision tree generation.

Given a training set, a general procedure for generating a decision tree can be briefly described as follows:

The entire training set is first considered as the root node of the tree. Then the root node is split into two sub-nodes based on appropriate heuristic information. If the instances in a sub-node belong to one class, then the sub-node is regarded as a leaf node, else we continue to split the sub-node based on the heuristic information. This process repeats itself until all leaf nodes are generated. The most popular heuristic information used in the decision tree generation is the minimum entropy. This heuristic information has many advantages such as small leaf numbers and less computational effort. However, it has a serious disadvantage – the poor generalization capability.

The investigation into the inverse problem of SVMs is motivated by designing a new decision tree generation procedure to improve the generalization capability of existing decision tree programs based on minimum entropy heuristic. Due to the relationship between the margin of SVMs and the generalization capability, the split with maximum margin may be considered as the new heuristic information for generating decision trees.

This paper has the following organization; Section 2 briefly reviews the basic concept of support vector machines. Section 3 proposes the inverse problem of SVMs and designs a parallel genetic algorithm to solve this problem. Section 4 gives some experiment results to demonstrate the feasibility and effectiveness of the parallel genetic algorithm, especially in the way of time complexity. And the last section briefly concludes this paper.

2 Support Vector Machines

2.1 The Basic Problem of SVMs

Let $S = \{(x_1, y_1), (x_2, y_2), \cdots, (x_N, y_N)\}$ be a training set, where $x_i \in R^n$ and $y_i \in \{-1, 1\}$ for $i = 1, 2, \cdots, N$. The optimal hyper-plane of S is defined as $f(x) = 0$, where

$$f(x) = (w_0 \cdot x) + b_0 \tag{1}$$

$$w_0 = \sum_{j=1}^{N} y_j \alpha_j^0 x_j \tag{2}$$

$(w_0 \cdot x) = \sum_{i=1}^{n} w_0^i \cdot x^i$ is the inner product of the two vectors, where $w_0 = (w_0^1, w_0^2, \cdots, w_0^n)$ and $x = (x^1, x^2, \cdots, x^n)$. The vector w_0 can be determined according to the following quadratic programming [1]

$$\begin{cases} \text{Maximum } W(\alpha) = \sum_{i=1}^{N} \alpha_i - \frac{1}{2} \sum_{i,j=1}^{N} y_i y_j \alpha_i \alpha_j (x_i \cdot x_j) \\ \text{Subject to } \sum_{j=1}^{N} y_j \alpha_j = 0; C \geq \alpha_i \geq 0, \ i = 1, 2, \cdots, N \end{cases} \tag{3}$$

where C is a positive constant. The constant b_0 is given by

$$b_0 = y_i - \left(x_i \cdot \sum_{j=1}^{N} y_j \alpha_j^0 x_j \right) \tag{4}$$

Substituting (2) for w_0 in (1), we have

$$f(x) = \sum_{i=1}^{N} y_i \alpha_i^0 (x_i \cdot x) + b_0 \tag{5}$$

We can identify separability of two subsets by checking whether the following inequalities

$$y_i(w_0 \cdot x_i + b) \geq 1; \quad i = 1, 2, \cdots, N \tag{6}$$

hold well[1].

A procedure to compute a maximum margin for two subsets is described below.

Procedure 1. The constant C in equation (3) is selected to be large at first.

Step 1. Solve the quadratic programming (3).
Step 2. Determine the separating hyper-plane (5) according to (4).
Step 3. Check the separability between two subsets according to inequalities (6).
Step 4. Let the margin be 0 if the two subsets are not separable.
Step 5. Compute the maximum margin according to $1/(w_0 \cdot w_0)$ for the separable case where the vector w is determined by (2).

2.2 Generalization in Feature Space

In practice, the performance of SVMs based on the previous section may not be very suitable for the nonlinear-separable cases in the original space. To improve the performance and to reduce the computational load for the nonlinear separable datasets, Vapnik [1] extended the SVMs from the original space to the feature space. The key concept of the extension is that a SVM first maps the original input space into a high-dimensional feature space through some nonlinear mapping, and then constructs an optimal separating hyper-plane in the feature space. Without any knowledge of the mapping, the SVM can find the optimal hyper-plane by using the dot product function in the feature space. The dot function is usually called a kernel function. According to the Hilbert-Schmidt theorem [1], there exists a relationship between the original space and its feature space for the dot product of two points. That is

$$(z_1 \cdot z_2) = K(x_1, x_2) \tag{7}$$

where it is assumed that a mapping Φ from the original space to the feature space exists, such that $\Phi(x_1) = z_1$ and $\Phi(x_2) = z_2$, and $K(x_1, x_2)$ is conventionally called a kernel function satisfying the Mercer theorem [1]. Usually the following three types of kernel functions can be used: polynomial with degree p, radial basis function and sigmoid function [1]. Replacing the inner product $(x_1 \cdot x_2)$ in (5) with the kernel function $K(x_1, x_2)$, the optimal separating hyper-plane becomes the following form:

$$f(x) = \sum_{i=1}^{N} y_i \alpha_i^0 K(x_i, x) + b_0 \tag{8}$$

It is worth noting that the conclusion of section 2.1 is still valid in the feature space if we substitute $K(x_1, x_2)$ for the inner product $(x_1 \cdot x_2)$.

3 An Inverse Problem of SVMs and Its Solution Based on Genetic Algorithms

For a given dataset for which no class labels are assigned to instances, we can randomly split the dataset into two subsets. Suppose that one is the positive instance subset and the other is the negative instance subset, we can calculate the maximum margin between the two subsets according to Procedure 1 where the margin is equal to 0 for the non-separable case. Obviously, the calculated margin depends on the random split of the dataset. Our problem is how to split the dataset such that the margin calculated according to Procedure 1 attains the maximum.

It is an optimization problem. We mathematically formulate it as follows:

Let $S = \{x_1, x_2, \cdots, x_N\}$ be a dataset and $x_i \in R^n$ for $i = 1, 2, \cdots, N$, $\Omega = \{f \mid f \text{ is a function from } S \text{ to } \{1, -1\}\}$. Given a function $f \in \Omega$, the dataset can be split into two subsets and the margin can then be calculated by Procedure 1. We denote the calculated margin (the functional) by $\text{Margin}(f)$. Then the inverse problem is formulated as

$$\text{Maximum}_{f \in \Omega} (\text{Margin}(f)) \tag{9}$$

Due to the exponentially increased complexity, it is not feasible to enumerate all possible functions in Ω for calculating their margins according to Procedure 1. It is difficult to give an exact algorithm for solving the optimization problem (9). Here we can design a genetic algorithm to solve (9).

First, we briefly review the main steps of a general simple genetic algorithm [9].

Procedure 2. A general procedure of genetic algorithms for solving an optimization problem with several variables:

Step 1. Determine the encoding mechanism for representing the optimization problem's variables.

Step 2. Initialize the population, which contains a number of encoded samples (called chromosomes) based on the encoding mechanism.

Step 3. Specify the fitness function, which normally takes the values in [0, 1] and is defined in the set of all chromosomes.

Step 4. Select parents (chromosomes) from the current population according to their fitness values.

Step 5. Produce their offspring via the crossover operation, which usually means to partially exchange genes of two parent chromosomes.

Step 6. Conduct mutation operation, i.e., genes of the offspring chromosome change with a certain probability.

Step 7. Consider all offspring as the new population and check whether a termination criterion is reached. If yes, go to step 8, else, go to step 4.

Step 8. Stop.

Then, we can design a genetic algorithm to solve the proposed inverse problem of SVMs according to the above Procedure 2.

Procedure 3. A general procedure of genetic algorithms for solving the proposed inverse problem of SVMs:

Step 1. Each function $f \in \Omega$ corresponds to a binary partition of the dataset S. Therefore each f can be viewed as a N-dimensional vector such as 100011101$\cdots$01 with N bits. Each bit taking value 0 or 1 is regarded as a gene corresponding to an instance in S. Thus, each chromosome (a bit string such as 100011101$\cdots$01) consisting of N genes represents a function in Ω where, if a bit is 1, it means that the corresponding instance is positive; and a value 0 represents that the corresponding instance is negative. The fixed length of each chromosome's coding is N, the number of instances of the initial dataset.

Step 2. Given an integer M denoting the size of the population, uniformly generate N random numbers (0 or 1), which constitute a chromosome. Repeat M times and hence generate M chromosomes.

Step 3. Noting that each chromosome can determine a training set given in Section 2, we define the fitness value for each chromosome as the margin value computed by Procedure 1. Here the fitness value is 0 if the chromosome corresponds to a non-separable training set, and is the real margin of the SVM if the chromosome corresponds to a separable training set.

Step 4. Reproduction. This is a process in which individual strings are copied in terms of their fitness values. In traditional textbook manner, the reproduction is conducted by a technique of roulette-wheel parent selection, which indicates that the probability with which an individual is selected is proportional to its fitness value. This technique can be implemented algorithmically as follows [7]:

(1) Let the population be $\{1, 2, \cdots, M\}$ and $f(j)$ denotes the fitness value of the j-th individual. Compute $s_i = \sum_{j=1}^{i} f(j)$ $(i = 1, 2, \cdots, M)$.

(2) Generate a random number α uniformly distributed in the interval $[0, s_M]$.

(3) Return the first individual whose fitness value plus the values of fitness of the previous individuals are greater than or equal to α. That is, this step returns the k-th individual with the property $s_{k-1} < \alpha \leq s_k$.

The reproduction is used to generate M parent candidates. We suppose that the M parent candidates contain the individual with the highest fitness. (If not, we can specify the individual with the highest fitness as a candidate).

Step 5. Crossover. Reproduction results in a mating pool consisting of M parent candidates. Then $M/2$ pairs of parents are randomly selected from the pool. The crossover site (a bit position) is also selected randomly. The crossover happens with probability p_c for each selected pair. This crossover operator leads to $M/2$ pairs of offspring, i.e., M new chromosomes.

Step 6. Mutation. It means that a bit of an offspring chromosome is replaced with a randomly chosen bit. The mutation is performed with probability p_m for each chromosome.

Step 7. Calculate the M parents' fitness values and place them with their M children to form a set of 2M chromosomes. Sort the 2M chromosomes based on their fitness values from big to small, and then choose the first M chromosomes with the highest fitness values as the population of the next generation.

Step 8. The predefined maximum number of generations, T, is chosen as the termination criterion. If the generation number is less T then go to Step 4; else go to Step 9.

Step 9. Output the first chromosomes and its fitness value. According to this chromosome, in which value 1 corresponds to a positive instance and value 0 corresponds to a negative instance, the final partition (split) of the initial dataset is obtained. And the outputted fitness value is the maximum margin. Stop.

The decision function f obtained through the above algorithm denotes the optimal or approximately optimal solution of problem (9) when the parameters in GA are selected properly. In addition, it is worth mentioning that genetic algorithms cannot be guaranteed to obtain the optimal solution every time, so it is expected they will have a big probability for obtaining the optimal or approximately optimal solution. To raise the probability of obtaining the optimal solution, one needs to increase the population size or the maximum number of generations, which obviously is at the price of increased running time.

One main reason that the proposed genetic algorithm has large time complexity is the process of solving quadratic programs; that is, calculating each chromosome's fitness value. How to reduce the time complexity of the algorithm (for large databases especially) is a very important issue to be investigated. Here we use the method of parallel processing on Linux Clusters to solve this problem.

Procedure 4. A parallel procedure of genetic algorithms for solving the proposed inverse problem of SVMs:

Step 1. Choose the same encoding mechanism as Procedure 3. Specify the penalty factor C, the maximum number of generations MaxG, the population size M, the crossover probability p_c, the mutation probability p_m and the fixed length of each chromosome's coding N, which is the number of instances of the initial dataset.

Step 2. Let the master process generate M chromosomes as the first population on the master node of Linux Clusters.

Step 3. Calculate each chromosome's fitness value on slave nodes by parallel method, that is, the margin value computed by Procedure 1. We describe it in detail by pseudo codes as follows:

for $i = 1$ to *numtask* par-do
    calculate each chromosome's fitness value;
end for

This is a parallel statement, where *numtask* is the number of chromosomes processed by every slave process on the corresponding slave node, and i is the number of slave processes (slave node). It is important that a synchronization mechanism is used in order to avoid any problems when parallel computation is completed.

Step 4. Reproduction. This is the same as Procedure 3; however, it is only done on the master node. The reproduction will generate another set of M parent candidates, which are put into the buffer called a mating pool.

Step 5. Crossover. This operation is just for the M candidates from the mating pool, and is done on the master node.

Step 6. Mutation. It is also for the M candidates and is done on the master node.

Step 7. Calculate the M candidates' fitness values as in Step 3. In succession, sort the 2M chromosomes based on their fitness values from big to small, and then choose the first M chromosomes with the highest fitness values as the population of the next generation.

Step 8. If the generation number is less MaxG then go to Step 4; else go to Step 9.

Step 9. Output the final result, the first chromosome and its fitness value, i.e., the best chromosome and the maximum margin. Stop.

Here our parallel algorithm is a global single-population master-slave genetic algorithm [8]. In a master-slave genetic algorithm there is a single population (just as in a simple genetic algorithm), but the process to get each chromosome's fitness value, which consumes more time, is distributed among slave nodes and done by means of parallel processing. Since in this type of parallel genetic algorithm, selection and crossover consider the entire population, it is also known as a global parallel genetic algorithm.

4 Experimental Results

Experimental environment refers to Table 1(a) & (b).

To verify the effectiveness of the parallel genetic algorithm, we construct a small dataset with 20 2-dimensional points (Table 2). The parameters specified in the parallel algorithm are shown in Table 3. Table 4 is the experimental results of the above dataset on the original space for the parallel genetic algorithm, which shows the relationship between the running time and the number of computing nodes. From Table 4 one can see that the running time of the parallel genetic algorithm is significantly reduced with the number of computing nodes increased.

A well-known dataset called Iris [9] is selected to verify the advantage of the parallel algorithm. We used 50 samples of the dataset (25 from the second class and another 25 from the third class) for the verification. Table 5 shows the running time change with the increase of computing nodes. From Table 5 we observe that the running time rapidly decreases with the computing nodes. The decrease is significant, because the process to get each chromosome's fitness value, which has larger time complexity, is done by means of parallel processing.

Table 1(a). Node devices configuration

CPU	Intel Pentium 4 Xeon 3.06GHz ×2
Memory	512MB DDR
Bus	PCI-X
Disk	80G IDE

Table 1(b). Cluster configuration

No. of computing nodes	16
No. of management nodes	2
Network	100M-Ethernet, 2G-Myrinet
Operating system	Redhat 9.0
Programming environment	MPICH

Table 2. A small dataset

Case	Feature1	Feature2	Case	Feature1	Feature2
1	0.116	0.710	11	0.422	0.306
2	0.248	0.860	12	0.574	0.396
3	0.362	0.798	13	0.748	0.308
4	0.254	0.642	14	0.560	0.194
5	0.116	0.532	15	0.598	0.308
6	0.150	0.852	16	0.656	0.512
7	0.188	0.760	17	0.626	0.562
8	0.282	0.750	18	0.766	0.436
9	0.168	0.640	19	0.780	0.562
10	0.358	0.640	20	0.666	0.398

Table 3. Parameters in genetic algorithm

POPSIZE=90	Size of population
PC=0.7	Probability of crossover
PM=0.6	Probability of mutation
NB=0.3	Gen mutation proportion
MAXGENERATION=20	Maximum generation
C=100	Penalty factor

Table 4. Experimental results on the original space of the dataset (Table 2)

No. of computing nodes	Time (minutes)	The best margin
3	9.567	0.421
6	5.825	0.421
15	4.507	0.421

Table 5. Running time with an increase of computing nodes in the Iris dataset

No. of computing nodes	3	6	9	10	15
Time (minutes)	69.971	35.185	28.956	27.125	22.048

5 Concluding Remarks

Motivated by design of a new heuristic procedure of generating decision trees with higher generalization capability, a genetic algorithm can be used to solve an inverse problem of SVMs, but its time complexity is larger. To overcome this disadvantage, this paper proposes an improved version, the parallel genetic algorithm, which can reduce time complexity significantly.

Acknowledgement

This paper is supported by the National Natural Science Foundation of China(Project No. 60473045) and the Young Research Fund of Hebei University.

References

1. V. N. Vapnik, Statistical learning theory, New York, Wiley, 1998, ISBN: 0-471-03003-1
2. V. N. Vapnik, The Nature of Statistical Learning Theory, Springer-Verlag, New York, 2000, ISBN: 0-387-98780-0
3. V. N. Vapnik, An Overview of Statistical Learning Theory, IEEE Transactions on Neural Networks, Vol. 10, No.5, Pages 88 - 999, 1999.
4. B. E. Boser, I. M. Guyon, and V. N. Vapnik, "A training algorithm for optimal margin classifiers," in Proc. Fifth Annual Workshop on Computational Learning Theory. ACM Press, Pittsburgh. Guyon, D. Haussler, Ed., 1992, pp. 144-152.
5. R. Schapire, Y. Freund, P. Bartlett, and W. Sun Lee, "Boosting the margin: A new explanation for the effectiveness of voting methods," Ann. Statist., vol. 26, no. 5, pp. 1651–1686, 1998
6. J. Shawe-Taylor, P. L. Bartlett, R. C. Williamson, and M. Anthony, "Structural risk minimization over data-dependent hierarchies," IEEE Trans. Inform. Theory, vol. 44, pp. 1926–1940, Sept. 1998
7. Chin-Teng Lin and C.S. George Lee, Neural Fuzzy Systems: A Neuro-Fuzzy Synergism to Intelligent Systems, Prentice Hall PTR, 1996, 797 pages ,ISBN 0-13-235169-2.
8. Erick Cantú-Paz, "A survey of parallel genetic algorithms," Tech. Rep., The University of Illinois, 1997, IlliGAL Report No. 97003, FTP address: ftp://ftpilligal.ge.uiuc.edu/pub/papers/IlliGALs/97003.ps.Z.
9. UCI Repository of machine learning databases and domain theories. FTP address: ftp://ftp.ics.uci.edu/pub/machine-learning-databases.

Short Term Load Forecasting Model Based on Support Vector Machine

Dong-Xiao Niu, Qiang Wang, and Jin-Chao Li

School of Business Administration, North China Electric Power University,
Baoding, 071003, P.R. China
ndx@ncepu.edu.cn

Abstract. An artificial neural network was used for sample preprocessing in this paper. Firstly, the data points were classified into three types as follows: the high load type, the medium load type and the low load type. Then, the artificial neural network was adopted to forecast the load type of the predict point. Finally, a support vector machine forecasting model was created on the basis of data points whose load type is the same as the predict point. Comparisons were made between different methods. The results show that the model established in this paper is better than other methods in forecasting accuracy and computing speed.

1 Introduction

Load is the foundation of a power system operation and planning. Short-term power load forecasting is very important to the electric network's economic and stable running. With the development of the electric power market in China, a much higher forecasting precision is required than previously. According to research in Britain, an increase in forecasting errors of just 1% will result in an additional annual running cost of 17 million US dollars [1].

The traditional models for short-term power load forecasting such as the time series model and the regression analysis model [2], [3] are too simple to simulate the complex and fast changes of the short–term power load.

With the development of artificial intelligence technique, the artificial neural network, radial based function network [4] and fuzzy logic method [5] are all now widely used in short-term load forecasting. As they can deal with the non-liner relation between the influencing factors and the load output, the forecasting precision is raised. Since all the artificial intelligence models are developed on the basis of the training sample, their forecasting speed and precision are, to a great extent, determined by the sample preprocessing.

In this paper, the artificial neural network is adopted to forecast the load type of the predict point. Data points of the same load type will be selected as the training sample set for the support vector machine. After training, the support vector machine will be used to forecast the load of the predict point. It is the first time that the artificial neural network (ANN) will be combined with the support vector machine (SVM) in short-term load forecasting. This model is named as ANN-SVM model in this paper. The practical examples show that the ANN-SVM model outperforms other methods in forecasting accuracy and computing speed.

2 The Principle of Support Vector Machine

In recent years, support vector machine (SVM) has been introduced by Vapnik [6] to solve machine learning tasks such as regression, pattern recognition and density estimation.

This approach is developed on the basis of statistical learning theory. Unlike most traditional neural network models which implement the empirical risk minimization principle, the SVM implements the structural risk minimization principle which seeks to minimize the training error and a confidence interval term. This eventually results in a satisfactory performance of generalization. Due to its superior properties such as automatic selection on models (parameters and locations of basis functions), being trained with quadratic programming (global optimal solution exists) and good learning ability for small samples, the SVM has been receiving greater attention in recent years [7,8].

2.1 The Regression Function of SVM

Let $\{(\widetilde{X}_i, y_i)\}_{i=1}^{N}$ be a given set of data points where $\widetilde{X}_i$ is the i th input vector and y_i the corresponding desired output. The output of the neural network is:

$$y = f(\widetilde{X}) = \langle \widetilde{W}, \varphi(\widetilde{X}) \rangle + b \tag{1}$$

where $\widetilde{W}$, is the weight vector, b the bias and $\varphi(\widetilde{X})$ the nonlinear mapping from the input space to the high dimensional feature space. $\langle \cdot, \cdot \rangle$ represents the inner product.

According to the statistical learning theory, Function (2) is minimized to train $\widetilde{W}$ and b.

$$R_{SVM} = c \frac{1}{N} \sum_{i=1}^{N} L_\varepsilon \left(y_i, f(\widetilde{X}_i) \right) + \frac{1}{2} \|\widetilde{W}\|^2 \tag{2}$$

where c is the regularized constant determining the trade-off between the empirical error and the regularization term, L_ε is the commonly used ε-insensitive loss function introduced by Vapnik.

The ε-insensitive loss function is shown as the following:

$$L_\varepsilon = \begin{cases} 0 & \left| y_i - f(\widetilde{X}_i) \right| \leq \varepsilon \\ \left| y_i - f(\widetilde{X}_i) \right| - \varepsilon & \text{elsewhere} \end{cases} \tag{3}$$

After the introduction of positive slack variables and Lagrange multipliers, Function (2) is equivalent to the following standard quadratic programming problem:

$$\min_{\alpha,\alpha^*} \frac{1}{2}\sum_{i=1}^{N}\sum_{j=1}^{N} Q_{ij}(\alpha_i - \alpha_i^*)(\alpha_j - \alpha_j^*) +$$

$$\varepsilon \sum_{i=1}^{N}(\alpha_i + \alpha_i^*) - \sum_{i=1}^{N} y_i(\alpha_i - \alpha_i^*) \quad (4)$$

$$s.t. \begin{cases} 0 \le \alpha_i, \alpha_i^* \le C \\ \sum_{i=1}^{N}(\alpha_i - \alpha_i^*) = 0 \end{cases}, i = 1, 2 \cdots N$$

where $Q_{ij} = K(\widetilde{X}_i, \widetilde{X}_j)$ is a kernel function, and α_i and α_i^* are two kinds of Lagrange multipliers.

Finally, Function (1) can be rewritten as the following:

$$f(\widetilde{X}) = \sum_{i=1}^{N}(\alpha_i - \alpha_i^*) K(\widetilde{X}_i, \widetilde{X}_j) + b \quad (5)$$

According to the scarcity feature of SVM, the values of α_i and α_i^* are not always equivalent to zero. Those vectors whose α_i and α_i^* values are not equivalent to zero are the support vectors and they can determine the regression function $f(\widetilde{X})$ [9].

2.2 The Training of SVM

The training of SVM is the process used to solve Equation (4), which is also a quadratic programming problem. Usually the ISMO method is used in this process.

The idea of the ISMO is to turn the problem of quadratic programming to a series of sub programming problems which only include two parameters. Neither additional matrix storage nor value iteration program in quadratic programming is necessary in ISMO because each sub-programming problem has an exact solution. This characteristic results in a high convergence rate [9].

The ISMO consists of three parts as follows: analytic expression of bivariate programming, heuristic rule used in the selection of optimum variables and the computing method for b.

The minimum necessary condition for the optimized solution to Equation (4) is that a group of a_i, a_i^* satisfies the Karush-Kuhn-Tucker (KKT) condition. Those variables that do not satisfy the KKT condition are selected directly as the optimum variables in ISMO. Shevade discovered that the information in a_i and a_i^* can be used to judge the sample's position in relation to the curved surface as expressed by Equation (5). For example, if b_u is the smallest possible value of the samples above the curved surface, and b_l is the largest possible value of the samples below the curved surface, then the minimum necessary condition for KKT is as follows:

$$b_l \leq b_u \tag{6}$$

The ISMO method selects the optimum variables according to the condition mentioned above, which increases the computing efficiency. In order to guarantee the stability, the following condition is used to test the optimality of the solution:

$$b_l \leq b_u + 2\tau \tag{7}$$

where τ is the machine error [10].

3 ANN-SVM Model

The short-term load forecasting system is a problem of multi-variables, which can be regarded as a process of function regression. The actual load is regarded as the output value of the function, while the corresponding influencing factors such as the history load, the meteorological information and the date type will be used as input variables. The training sample set is confirmed by ANN, which is used to deal with the historical data. The final purpose is to find a mapping of good generalization performance from the influencing factors to the actuarial load.

3.1 Create the Sample Set

According to the collected history data, the sample set is created as $\{(\widetilde{X}_i, y_i)\}_{i=1}^{N}$. $\widetilde{X}_i$ is the influencing factor set and y_i is the actual load value on the i th point. The total number of the data points is N.

The influencing factor set is shown as the following:

$$\widetilde{X}_i = \{L_i^{i-1}, L_i^{i-2}, T_i, M_i, W_i, H_i\} \tag{8}$$

Where L_i^{i-1} is the actual load at the $(i-1)$ th point, L_i^{i-2} the actual load at the $(i-2)$ th point, T_i the temperature, M_i the humidity, W_i the week type and H_i the holiday type on the i th point.

The value of the week type is calculated, using:

$$W_i = w/7 \tag{9}$$

Where $w = 1, 2, 3, 4, 5, 6, 7$ is the week value for the i th point.

The value of the holiday type is calculated, using:

$$H_i = \begin{cases} 1 & holiday \\ 0 & others \end{cases} \tag{10}$$

Treat all the data of the sample with normalization and smoothing processing so that computing overflow will be avoided.

3.2 Load Type Classification

According to the actual load value, the data points are classified into three types as follows: the high load type, the medium load type and the low load type. Correspondingly, the given set of data points $\{(\widetilde{X}_i, y_i)\}_{i=1}^{N}$ is divided into three sub-sets, which are high load sub-set H, medium load sub-set M and low load sub-set S:

$$\begin{cases} H = \{(\widetilde{X}_i, y_i)\}_{i=1}^{m} & y_i \in \left[y^{\max} - y^*, y^{\max}\right] \\ M = \{(\widetilde{X}_i, y_i)\}_{i=1}^{n} & y_i \in \left[y^{\min} + y^*, y^{\max} - y^*\right] \\ S = \{(\widetilde{X}_i, y_i)\}_{i=1}^{l} & y_i \in \left[y^{\min}, y^{\min} + y^*\right] \end{cases} \quad (11)$$

$$s.t. \begin{cases} m+n+l = N \\ y^* = \frac{1}{3}\left(y^{\max} - y^{\min}\right) \end{cases}$$

where m, n, l is the quantity of the data points for each sub-set, $y^{\max}$ is the largest load value in the given data point set and $y^{\min}$ the lowest load.

Each load type is given a value as the output of the artificial neural network. The value for high load type is 0, the medium load type is 1/3 and the low load type is 1.0.

3.3 Sample Preprocessing by ANN

3.3.1 The Main Idea of ANN

ANN is a network system containing a large number of simple processing elements, which are fully interconnected. In order to make the actual output close to any complex nonlinear mapping, its information processing procedure includes back propagation, forward propagation and weight adjustment.

Since the multiplayer feed forward neural network based on BP algorithms has good capabilities in analogue classification, it is used here to simulate the mutual relations between the influencing factors and the load type of the data points. It has been proven that a single intermediate layer neural network can be close to any continuous function. Thereby the single intermediate layer neural network model is used in this paper.

3.3.2 The Learning Algorithms of ANN

ANN of BP algorithms is developed and its architecture is three layers comprised of the input layer, the intermediate layer and the output layer.

In this paper the input equates to the influencing factors and the output is the load type. The learning algorithm of the BP Network is as follows:

The first step: Set the initial parameter ω and θ (ω is the initial weight, θ is the critical value; randomly let both of them be a fairly small number).

The second step: Input the known sample to the Network and calculate the output value y_j, using:

$$y_j = \left[1 + e^{-(\sum_i \omega_{ij} x_i - \theta_j)}\right]^{-1} \tag{12}$$

where x_i is the input of that junction $(i = 1, \cdots, m)$, ω_{ij} is the connection weight from i to j $(i = 1, \cdots, m, j = 1, \cdots, n)$, and let the initial weight be a fairly small number within [0,1]. θ_j is the critical value and y_j is the calculated value.

The third step: Adjust the weight coefficient ω on the basis of the difference $(d_j - y_j)$ between the known output value and the calculated one.

The adjustment is calculated using:

$$\Delta \omega_{ij} = \eta \delta_j x_j \tag{13}$$

where η is the ration coefficient (learning rate), x_j the input, d_j the actual output of the sample, and δ_j the output deviation.

Regarding η, it is a small number within the range [0,1]. Under the presupposition that oscillation is not stirred and a fairly high precision is guaranteed, the value of η can be increased step by step until a satisfactory training speed is reached.

Regarding x_j, it is the network input to the junctions in the intermediate layer, but to junctions in the output layer, it is the intermediate junctions' output $(j = 1, \cdots, n)$.

Regarding δ_j, it is a value related to the output deviation. To the junctions in the output layer, it is calculated using:

$$\delta_j = \eta_j (1 - y_i)(d_j - y_j) \tag{14}$$

To the junctions in the intermediate layer whose output are hard to compare, its value can be acquired by counter calculation using:

$$\delta_j = x_j (1 - x_j) \sum \delta_k \omega_{jk} \tag{15}$$

where k means all the junctions in the output layer that should be taken into account, the deviation δ_j is obtained by reverse calculation from the output.

After being adjusted, the weight of the neuron in each layer is as follows:

$$\omega_{ij}(t) = \omega_{ij}(t-1) + \Delta \omega_{ij} \tag{16}$$

where t is the learning time.

This algorithm is an interaction process in which all the values of ω are adjusted in each round. Such interaction is repeated until the output deviation is less than an acceptable value, and then a good network is successfully trained. It is the essence of the BP algorithms to turn the first grade sample input question into a nonlinear optimized question. The gradient decreasing method used in the BP algorithms is one of the most common methods in optimization technology, while calculation of the weight value by interactive computation is equal to the learning memory question.

3.3.3 Data Preprocessing

The ANN model of load type classification is a three-layer BP network, which contains the input layer including six nodes, the intermediate layer including ten nodes and the output layer including one node.

According to the classification mentioned above, train the BP network. The influencing factor set is used as the input of the BP neural network, while the load type value is the output. Both the input data and the output data will be normalized before the training.

Sigmoid Function is selected as the activated Function F_1 in the intermediate layer, that is:

$$F_1(x) = 1/(1+e-x) \qquad (17)$$

The activated Function F_2 in output layer is Pureline Function, which is:

$$F_2(x) = ax \qquad (18)$$

where a is a linear coefficient.

As the sample data has been normalized, the variables of Sigmoid Function are within [-1, 1] and a real nonlinear transference is successfully made. Using the ANN tool box of MATLAB5.3, selecting the gradient decreasing method to train the trained function, letting the convergence precision be 2e-7, setting the dynamic parameter as 0.05 and the largest training number as 2000, we can acquire the demanded precision within 1000 interactions.

After being trained, the BP network is used to forecast the load type of the predict point. The sub-set (the high load sub-set H, the medium load sub-set M or the low load sub-set S) of the same load type will be selected as the training sample set for the SVM in the next step.

3.4 Load Forecasting by SVM

The selected training sample set above is used to train the support vector machine and the ISMO algorithm is adopted.

The influencing factor set is used as the input of the SVM, with the load value as the output. Both the input data and the output data will be normalized before the training.

The input layer has six nodes and the output layer has only one node. The Gauss function is selected as the kernel function.

$$K\left(\widetilde{X}_i, \widetilde{X}_j\right) = \exp\left(-\frac{\left\|\widetilde{X}_i - \widetilde{X}_j\right\|^2}{\sigma}\right) \qquad (19)$$

where the σ is the width parameter of the Gauss kernel.

According to experience, the value of parameters is selected as follows:
$c = 10, \varepsilon = 0.01, \sigma = 1, \tau = 10^{-5}$

First, the training samples will be used to set up Function (4); then the ISMO algorithm will solve the function whose result is the value of α_i and α_i^*. Finally, with the value of α_i and α_i^*, we will obtain Function (5) which can be used in short term forecasting.

Input the influencing factors of the predict point into the trained SVM, and the output is the forecasted value.

The whole process is realized on a computer with the following configuration: EMS is 256MB, hard disk is 80GB.

4 Example Application and Analysis

This model is applied in the 24-point daily load forecasting. Data points between 01/01/2005 to 01/30/2005 of Baoding Hebei Province are collected and the total number of data points is 720. The data points between 01/01/2005 to 01/25/2005 are used to train the ANN-SVM model and the rest are used to test the model.

Besides the ANN-SVM model in this paper, the traditional ANN model and SVM model are used to forecast the test points.

The average relative error of each day is used to indicate the precision performance of the model. Comparisons are made among the three models above. The result is shown in Table 1.

Table 1. Precision Comparison for Different Models

Date(points)	ANN MRE (%)	SVM MRE (%)	ANN-SVM MRE (%)
01/26/2005 (24)	2.636	2.541	2.312
01/27/2005 (24)	2.664	2.762	2.513
01/28/2005 (24)	2.804	2.753	2.600
01/29/2005 (24)	3.021	2.923	2.714
01/30/2005 (24)	3.243	3.177	2.901

It can be learned from Table 1 that the ANN-SVM model created in this paper is better than the either the ANN model or the SVM model alone.

5 Conclusions

An ANN-SVM model for short term load forecasting is created in this paper. The data points are classified according to the load type. The load type is forecast first by the ANN, which not only deletes the unnecessary points, but also narrows the load variation. Finally the data points of the same type are collected as the training samples for SVM. After training, the SVM can be used to forecast the load of the predict point.

The comparison and examination of actual forecasting results of a few models show that the proposed method is obviously superior to the traditional SVM model and ANN model in the respect of prediction precision.

Acknowledgements

This paper was supported by Doctor Funding of NCEPU(20040079008),Natural Science Funding of Hebei Province (G2005000584) and Great Pre-research Project Funding of NCEPU.

References

1. Liu K.: Comparison of very short-term load forecasting technique [J]. IEEE Trans. Power System, 1996,11(2):877-882
2. Niu Dongxiao, Cao Shuhua, Zhao lei, et al: Power Load Forecasting Technology and Its Application. Beijing: China Electric Power Press, 2001
3. T.Masters: Neural Novel & Hybrid Algorithms for Time Series Prediction[M]. John Wiley & Sons. Inc, 1995.
4. A.D.Papalexopoulos, T.C.Hesterberg: A regression based approach to short term system load forecasting[C]. Proceedings of 1989 PICA Conference, 1989 : 414-423.
5. A.M.Lanchlan: An improved novelty criterion for resource allocating networks[C]. IEE, Artificial Neural Networks, Conference Publication, 1997: 48-52.
6. V.N.Vapnik: The Nature of Statistical Learning Theory . New York : Springer -Verlag,1995
7. Flake.G.W.et al: Efficient SVM regression training with SMO . Machine Learning,2002,46 : 271. .
8. V.N.Vapnik: The nature of statistical learning theory[M]. New York: Springer, 1999.
9. J.S.Ma, J.Theiler and S.Perkins: Accurate Online Support Vector Regression [R]. Tech. Rep. Los Alamos National Laboratory, 2002.
10. Li Yuan-cheng, Fang Ting-jian,Yu Er-keng: Study of Support Vector Machine for Short-term Load ForecastingProceedings of the CSEE 2003,23(6) : 55-58.

Evaluation of an Efficient Parallel Object Oriented Platform (EPOOP) for Control Intensive Intelligent Applications

Chun Che Fung[1], Jia-Bin Li[1], and Douglas G. Myers[2]

[1] Centre for Enterprise Collaboration in Innovative Systems,
School of Information Technology, Murdoch University,
Murdoch, 6150, Western Australia
{L.Fung, J.Li}@murdoch.edu.au
[2] Department of Electrical and Computer Engineering, Curtin University of Technology,
Bentley, 6102, Western Australia
myersd@bauhaus.ece.curtin.edu.au

Abstract. A small scale distributed computing system that is able to meet the needs of parallel intelligent techniques for engineering and science applications is reported. The system is a cluster of powerful yet low cost general-purpose PCs interconnected in a network. While, most applications written for cluster systems are programmed in MPI-C, results from the proposed system have shown that it is advantageous to use Java due to its simplicity, distribution enabling, and mobility. These results suggest there are advantages in considering a Java-enhanced cluster platform for many engineering and science applications.

1 Introduction

Data intensive applications such as bioinformatics, climate prediction, biological analysis, chemical reaction analysis and power grid analysis generally require a high performance computer system to obtain results within a reasonable time. Traditionally, these tasks were computed on a super computer costing millions of dollars to purchase and substantial sums to maintain. Further, these "big-box" machines were hard to program and were offered with limited software support. More recently, there has been a dramatic shift in such computation towards cluster computing. Clusters offer low purchase costs, low maintenance costs and support for software development is becoming increasingly sophisticated.

While this is a welcome trend, not all large scale computing problems of interest are necessarily data intensive. In addition, there are control intensive tasks such as those based on computation intelligent techniques such as neural networks and genetic algorithms. A question of importance is whether clusters can support these computations, and if not, is there any simple modification of hardware or software or both that allows them to be usefully employed.

A cluster is simply a computing system constructed from a set of commodity computers interconnected with some form of standard or special networks. The guiding principle in forming a cluster is covered by the acronym COTS; common off-the-shelf technology, meaning both hardware and software building a cluster means focusing on the five abstract levels listed in Fig. 1. The current industry standard for the distributed programming model is message-passing interface (MPI) [11].

Although MPI is an efficient programming model, it is generally not convenient to program and maintain. Java is an object oriented programming language and it has become more and more popular due to its simplicity and modularity. Furthermore, it provides support for distributed programming and object mobility. However, Java does not support transparent distributed programming. Thus, it is necessary to design a Java-based distributed programming model that provides location transparency, dynamic object distribution and runtime load balancing.

In this paper, we will focus on issues of design of a distributed programming model, referred to as EPOOP, for cluster computing systems based on object-oriented technologies. In particular, scalability is one of the most important questions in such design. Hence, A benchmarking test had been conducted to examine the scalability of our model. Test results and analysis are given in Section 4.

This paper is structured as follows: Section 2 discusses the architecture of the Efficient Parallel Object Oriented Platform (EPOOP), which consists of a set of Java-based distributed programming models and computational agents for task scheduling and resource management. Section 3 gives an overview of our cluster computing system. Section 4 benchmarks the performance of EPOOP using a simple control intensive program that calculates the value of π.

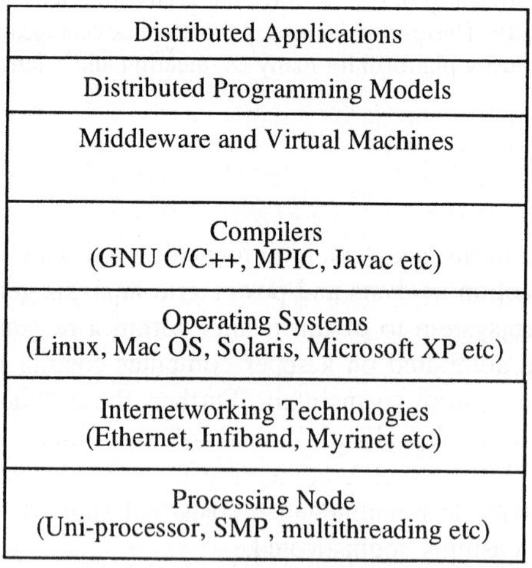

Distributed Applications
Distributed Programming Models
Middleware and Virtual Machines
Compilers (GNU C/C++, MPIC, Javac etc)
Operating Systems (Linux, Mac OS, Solaris, Microsoft XP etc)
Internetworking Technologies (Ethernet, Infiband, Myrinet etc)
Processing Node (Uni-processor, SMP, multithreading etc)

Fig. 1. A hierarchical structure of a cluster computing system. The five essential components include Internetworking, Processing Node, Operating System, Distributed Programming Library and Middleware and Virtual Machine.

2 Efficient Parallel Object-Oriented Platform (EPOOP)

Fig. 2 gives an overview of our project. Using the perCluster system (for personal cluster system) as an operating environment, a number of distributed applications have been developed and assessed. These have been primarily of two classes.

- Computational Intelligent (CI) applications include Generic Algorithms (GA), Artificial Neural Networks (ANN) and Fuzzy Logic (FL); and
- Image processing applications, e.g. a content-based retrieval system.

These applications were developed based on a set of programming libraries that implement various parallel and distributed programming models. They have been used to benchmark the performance of the distributed programming libraries and the underlying hardware structures. Then in an ongoing process, we are seeking to optimize both the programming libraries and the hardware structures to improve the performance of those applications.

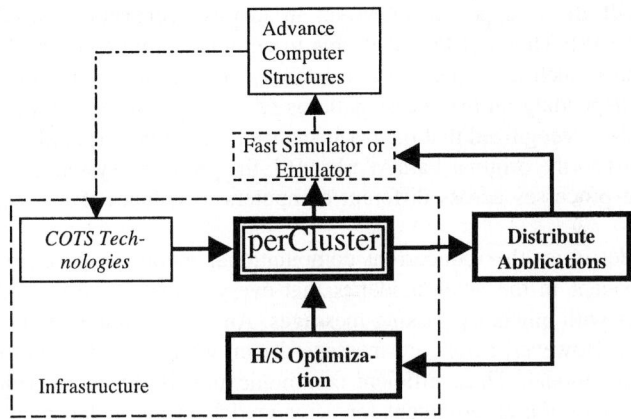

Fig. 2. An overview of the perCluster project. The key goal of the system is to efficiently execute computational intelligence techniques and image processing algorithms.

Most of our interest has focused on one programming environment that we currently refer to as EPOOP. The goal of EPOOP is to develop an object-based distributed execution environment, focusing on transparent distributed programming, fine-grained mobility, autonomous scheduling and dynamic load balancing. However, the most important issue is how to design a distributed programming model support for transparency, efficiency and scalability.

2.1 Architecture of EPOOP

Many different distributed programming models had been proposed and have been discussed [7]. We have developed our own model termed Efficient Parallel Object-Oriented Platform (EPOOP). While similar to MPI in terms of overall objectives, EPOOP is Java based. However, EPOOP also includes features that offer support for other types of computational models such as distributed shared memory (DSM) model and the Actor model [1]. EPOOP has been implemented like MPI as a distributed programming software package based on libraries.

In broad terms, there are two main forms of parallel computation; shared memory and message passing. Clusters follow the former. Traditionally, shared memory struc tures have been seen as easier to program, but as a physical system, they are extremely difficult to construct. Distributed shared memory is a concept whereby the virtual machine appears to be shared memory, but the physical system is based on message passing. While relatively easy to support, a problem with DSM is maintaining apparent memory consistency.

Consistency has been a topic of some interest in recent years in engineering circles as processor speeds begin to become very high indeed while memory speeds remain largely fixed. A number of consistency policies have been proposed and many implemented on current high performance units. Examples of such developments are Sequential Consistency [10], Lazy Release Consistency [2] and Entry Consistency [3].

EPOOP will allow support of DSM via an adaptive consistency model similar to Para Worker 2 [8]. That is, EPOOP is able to automatically choose between the different protocols, such as sequential consistency, lazy release consistency and entry consistency, depending on the access patterns of the application and the workload in the network. It is recognized that the performance of a protocol is application dependent. In contrast to the original Para Worker [6], the proposed system allows dynamically allocate processes across different computers to balance the workload on the system.

Actor model is another concurrent computational model proposed by Agha [1]. The basic concept in the actor model is that every object is active and the object communicates with others by passing messages. An actor is quite similar to a thread object in Java. However, actors are message-driven while threads tend to focus on a shared memory model. Thus, efficient communication is the most critical issue in design of an execution environment for actor model. In particular, naming problem [9] has to be addressed to cope with the dynamic nature of objects.

EPOOP is an extension to previous developed programming models, Para Worker and Para Worker 2, to support message passing programming models such as actor model. Hence, a programmer is allowed to choose the most appropriate model for developing distributed applications. In this paper, we will concentrate on the scalability issue in design of EPOOP as given in Section 4.

2.2 Computational Intelligent (CI)

In this section and the next section, we will briefly discuss two distributed applications: computational intelligent and image processing applications, which are being developed using EPOOP.

The first and the most important application of EPOOP is to develop distributed computational intelligent techniques. Computational Intelligent (CI) techniques primarily concern three major disciplines: Artificial Neural Network (ANN), Fuzzy Logic (FL) and Evolutionary Computation (EC). Such techniques are frequently used to solve many complex problems in system engineering. In particular, problems with a non-linear or nondeterministic nature as these are often not easily solved via traditional methods.

Many problems in electrical power system engineering requiring massive computational effort are of this type. Examples are the Economic Dispatch (ED) model to resolve the economic loading of electric generators so that the load demand can be met where the loading must be within the feasible operating region of the generators [13]. Solving such a problem requires finding a global maximum point to satisfy the model. Fung et al [6] applied the evolutionary computation technique to this task including implementation of a Genetic Algorithm (GA), Simulated Annealing (SA), and Tabu Search (TS). Two implementations, namely, cluster structure and parallel structure, on a cluster system had been reported [6]. Fung shows that the distributed implementations could improve the overall computational time to complete the problem. These models are available in the form of a CI toolbox.

2.3 Image Processing (IP) Applications

The second application of EPOOP is to apply distributed programming to improve performance of feature analysis in image processing systems. In particular, the system of interest is a content-based image retrieval system.

Although it is possible to retrieve images from database using a unique identification defined by a human operator as an index to images, it is more convenient and natural to search images based on their contents. The principle of Content-Based Image Retrieval (CBIR) system is to retrieve images based on the content of the images. One of the important components in CBIR system is to extract the visual features of the images for performing more abstract analysis. However, deriving these features is computationally expensive. To solve this issue, a more flexible architecture is desired to improve the extraction time for the system. Consequently, a parallel framework based on the perCluster system has also been proposed aims at improving the feature analysis process [4-5].

3 The perCluster System

Two cluster computing systems were used in our test. One was constructed from nodes representative of current commodity systems and the other of the previous generation. Table 1 shows the configurations of the two systems. The use of different configurations enables the performance scalability of cluster systems and our distributed programming libraries to be assessed. That in turn enables us to assess what software and hardware enhancements could be usefully employed to improve clusters, particularly for control-intensive tasks.

Table 1. Configurations of two cluster computing systems. The faster machine consists of six Pentium 4 nodes with 1GB memory while the slow machine consists of ten Pentium 3 nodes.

	Node #	CPU Type	CPU Speed	RAM	HD	LAN	OS
1	10	Pentium III	800MHz (H) 433MHz (S)	256MB (H) 130MB (S)	6GB (H) 2GB (S)	100Mb/s	Redhat Linux 8.0
2	6	Pentium 4	3GHz	1GB	40GB	100Mb/s	Microsoft XP Pro

4 Performance Evaluation

The performance of EPOOP was evaluated with a benchmark program called CPI. CPI is an example program included in the MPICH software – a portable implementation of MPI [12]. CPI simply computes the value of π by using integral approximation (see Eq. 1). Basically, the larger number of N will provide a more accurate value of π. That is, it produces a higher resolution result. With a large value of N, it is obvious that the program will run a great deal of loops to compute the π value.

$$\pi = \int_{a=1}^{N} \frac{4}{1+(\frac{a-0.5}{N})^2} \quad (1)$$

A Java-based CPI was implemented for testing based on Eq 1. The implementation is based on a server-client model. A server is responsible to distribute the initial parameters and to collect results from the clients. A client, also known as worker, computes only a subset of the workload, which it is the sub-range of the loops in such case, and it submits its result to the server after completion. There is no collaboration needed for clients. Hence each runs independently during execution.

4.1 Evaluation of EPOOP

During testing, we ran two versions of CPI: distributed and sequential on our two cluster computing systems. The distributed implementation is based on the server-client model while the sequential one is optimized for running on a single process machine.

Fig. 3 shows the execution time of two implementations with various computing loops on a Pentium 4 cluster. Furthermore, the distributed implementation was executed using different sets of processing nodes. The execution time is obtained by taking the average value over three executions.

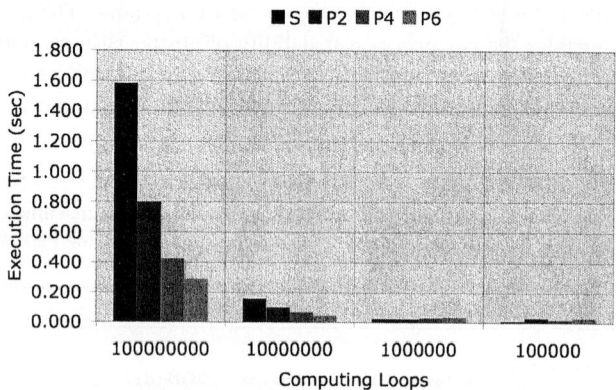

Fig. 3. Testing of two implementations on the Pentium 4 cluster. The parallel implementation executing on six nodes delivered the best performance while the sequential execution is superior on the low resolution. S – sequential implementation; P2 – two nodes cluster; P4 – four nodes cluster; P6 – six nodes cluster.

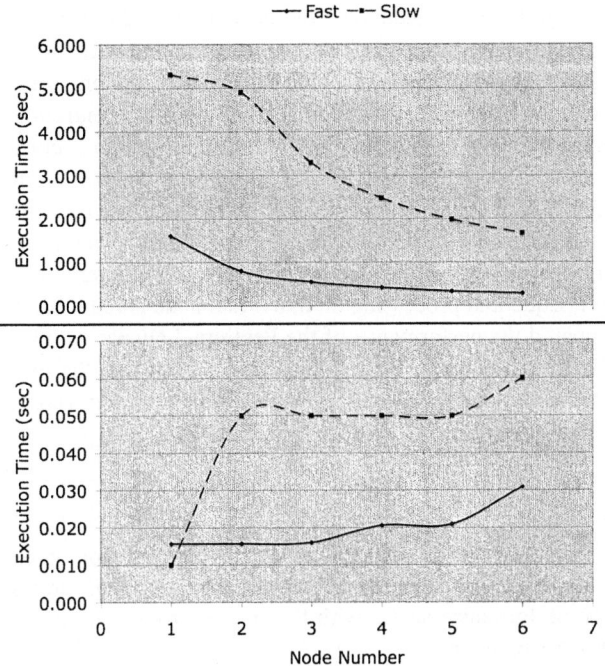

Fig. 4. Comparison of two cluster computing systems. The figure above shows the performance of two systems computing 1.E+8 loops using 1 to 6 nodes. The figure below shows the performance of two system computing 1.E+4 loops using 1 to 6 nodes. Fast – Pentium 4 cluster; Slow – Pentium 3 cluster.

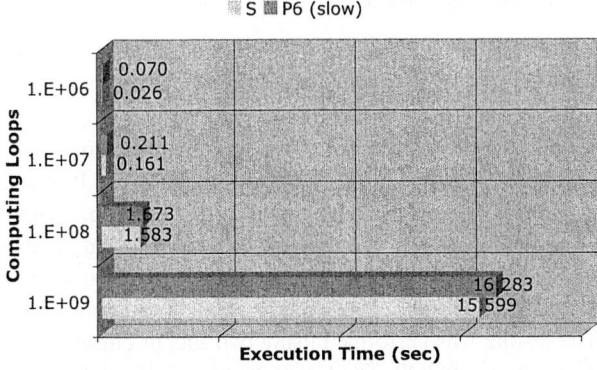

Fig. 5. Comparison of sequential and parallel implementations. The sequential implementation was performed on the single Pentium 4 system while the parallel one was performed on the Pentium 3 cluster system.

As mentioned before, the number of computing loops affects the accuracy of the computation value of π. For high resolution, the sequential computation spent the longest execution time. The execution time decreases as the number of processing nodes increases. The performance of two implementations was roughly equal when calculating 10E+6 loops. The single machine became efficient on 10E+3 loops.

Similar results had been observed when executing on the Pentium 3 cluster. However, the Pentium 4 cluster performed faster than the Pentium 3 cluster crossing all sets of nodes (see Fig. 4). However, the execution time on the Pentium 3 system is falling dramatically as more nodes were used in computation. Particularly, when using six nodes, the difference in performance became small. When the same workload is shared by more processing nodes, the performance of the internetworking becomes significant as the sequential processing on individual node is reduced.

We also compared the performance of the Pentium 3 cluster with a single Pentium 4 processor system as shown in Fig. 5. The result shows that the execution time of two systems are very close even though the Pentium 4 system runs at much faster clock rate than that of each node in the Pentium 3 cluster.

4.2 Remarks

Remark 1. The testing results indicate the parallel implementation based on EPOOP is superior to the sequential implementation when calculating high precision of results. Furthermore, the performance scales with the size of processing node and the power of individual processing node.

Remark 2. The performance of networks becomes significant when a large number of processing nodes in use. Thus, message passing between objects must be carefully analyzed and optimized to reduce communication overheads.

Remark 3. Design of efficient scheduling mechanisms for distributed computation is still an open question. Particularly, the mismatch between processor and network in speed and latency causes more trouble in such design.

5 Conclusions

This paper gives an overview of the perCluster project. The core of the project is to develop an object based distributed platform, termed EPOOP. It is a Java-based distributed framework that utilizes cluster computing for the implementation of intelligent techniques for computation of complex engineering and science applications such as image processing. Performance of the system is illustrated by running a basic function that computes the value of π. Both sequential and parallel implementations were created. The testing was performed using two sets of cluster computing systems to study the scalability of EPOOP. The test results have shown the good scalability in EPOOP. That is, the execution speed can be improved by adding more nodes. However, with a large size of nodes, the performance of networks becomes bottleneck in execution. Hence, it is important to design an efficient communication scheme for message passing. Furthermore, hardware and software optimization techniques are required to improve execution efficiency and load balancing.

Acknowledgements

This paper is supported by the Murdoch University Research Excellence Grant Scheme and Mr. J.B. Li is supported by an International Postgraduate Research Scholarship.

References

1. Agha G. A., *"Actors: A Model of Concurrent Computation in Distributed Systems"*, Cambridge, Mass. MIT Press, (1986).
2. Amza C., Cox A. L., Dwarkadas S., Jin L.-J., Rajamani K., and Zwaenepoel W., "Adaptive protocols for software distributed shared memory" *Proceedings of the IEEE, Special Issue on Distributed Shared Memory*, vol. 87, no. 3, (1999) 467-75.
3. Bershad, B. N., Zekauskas, M. J. & Sawdon, W. A., 1993, "The Midway Distributed Shared Memory System", *Proceeding of IEEE COMPCON* (1993) 528 - 537.
4. Chung K.P., Li J.B., Fung C.C. and Wong K.W., "A parallel architecture for feature extraction in content-based image retrieval system", To be appeared in *Proceedings of the 2004 IEEE International Conference on Cybernetics and Intelligent Systems (CIS 2004)*, Dec. (2004) 468-473.
5. Chung K.P., Fung C.C., and Wong K.W., "A Feature Selection Framework for Small Sampling Data in Content-based Image Retrieval System," *5th International Conference on Information, Communications and Signal Processing*, December 6-9 (2005).
6. Fung, C. C., Chow, S. Y. and Wong, K. P., "A Low-Cost Parallel Computing Platform for Power Engineering Applications", (APSCOM'00), *Proceedings of Advances in Power System Control, Operation and Management*, (2000) 354-358.
7. Fung C.C., Li J.B. and Wong K.W., "Development of a Java-based distributed platform for the implementation of computational intelligence techniques", *Proceedings of the Third International Conference on Machine Learning and Cybernetics (ICMLC)*, Vol. 7, (2004) 4156-4161.
8. Fung C. C., Li J. B., Wong K. W., and Wong K. P., "A java-based parallel platform for the implementation of evolutionary computation for engineering applications," *The International Journal of Systems Science*, Vol. 35, (2004) 13-14.
9. Li J. B., Fung C. C., and Myers D. G., "Naming models in object-based distributed systems," *The 2004 Postgraduate Electrical Engineering and Computing Symposium (PEECS04)*, (2004).
10. Li K. and Hudak P., "Memory Coherence in Shared Virtual Memory Systems," *ACM Transactions on Computer Systems*, vol. 7, no. 4, (1989) 321-59.
11. Message Passing Interface (MPI) standard, [URL] http://www-unix.mcs.anl.gov/mpi/ Accessed on 10/04/2005
12. MPICH – a portable implementation of MPI, [URL] http://www-unix.mcs.anl.gov/mpi/mpich/Accessed on 10/04/2005
13. Wong K.P and Wong Y.W, "Genetic and genetic/simulated-annealing approaches to economic dispatch"; *IEEE Proceedings of Genetic Transmission Distribution* Vol. 141, No.5, September (1994) 507-513.

Location of Tropical Cyclone Center with Intelligent Image Processing Technique

Q.P. Zhang[1], L.L. Lai[1], and W.C. Sun[2]

[1] Energy Systems Group, City University,
London EC1V 0HB, United Kingdom
abbn397@city.ac.uk, l.l.lai@city.ac.uk
[2] Dept. of Computer Science and Engineering, Fudan University,
Shanghai 200433, China
wcsun@fudan.edu.cn

Abstract. Digital imaging techniques have been applied to locate tropical cyclone centers. In order to improve the precision of location, a novel intelligent automatic system framework will be proposed, to locate the tropical cyclone center intelligently and automatically, based on satellite photographs. After pre-processing, several center location technologies will be considered, based on combining movement of whirl and translation. According to the tropical cyclone's symmetry shape and its spiral movement feature, logarithmic helix is used to fit the edge or skeleton of the cyclone feature cloud, which can be used to estimate the center of the cyclone. According to its movement feature, a rotation matching methodology will be proposed to catch the track through imaging sequence. As an example, the computing methodology produced was applied in cyclone forecasting by the Shanghai Meteorology Center. The proposed solution was confirmed to have a potential for successful application to tropical cyclone center tracking.

1 Introduction

Tropical cyclones (TC) are low pressure systems that form in the tropics which, in the southern hemisphere, have well defined clockwise wind circulations with average surface winds exceeding gale force. Short period wind gusts are often 40 per cent or more higher than the average wind speed. Severe tropical cyclones have surface winds greater than hurricane force. The circular eye of a tropical cyclone is an area characterized by light winds and often by clear skies. The eye is typically 20 nautical miles (nm) or so across but the eye of a cyclone can range from under 5 to over 50nm wide. The eye is surrounded by a dense ring of cloud known as the eye wall which is the area of heaviest winds and seas. Following the passage of the eye the winds shift to the opposite direction with equal force.

Tropical cyclones vary in both size and intensity. Small cyclones such as Chloe (April 1995) may be only 60nm across whereas large storms, such as Orson (April 1989) and Joan (December 1975), may be up to 300nm across. Both large and small cyclones can have equally devastating wind speeds near the centre. Radar and satellite images often show that the eye wall clouds are the innermost coil of a series of spiral rain-band clouds. These bands may extend up to 300nm from the eye wall and are often associated with thunderstorms and very strong wind.

A tropical cyclone is characterized by a non-frontal synoptic scale low-pressure weather system over tropical or sub-tropical waters with organized convection and definite cyclonic surface wind circulation [1]. Tropical cyclones are one of many atmospheric circulation systems, surveyed by geostationary meteorological satellites. Additionally, they often cause significant damage and loss of lives in affected areas. To reduce the loss, warning centers should issue warnings early based on a forecast of the TC track, which requires the accurate location of the circulation center, or the eye, of the tropical cyclone. This is normally done by the analysis of remote sensing data from weather radars or satellites.

A typhoon cyclone's inner movement is very complex and tropical hurricane theorists still argue on the cause and movement mechanism. The life cycle of a typhoon can be divided into approximately three phases: gestate from the offing, grow up to maturity and weaken to death. Since the original force is dictated during gestation, which comes from the effect of Corioli's force brought by the Earth's rotation, tropical hurricanes usually appear in latitude between -5 and +5 degrees. Later northwest Pacific tropical cyclones move towards the northwest. If a cyclone doesn't meet too much impeding force, it will keep this direction and disembark on the east coast of China. Typhoons begin to weaken about six hours before disembarkation. Thus locating the typhoon center in the mature phase while it's still in the offing is very important in central power estimation and later moving path forecast.

One of the most widely accepted techniques is the Dvorak technique [2], which assigns a wind intensity value (called the TC number) based on the size, shape, and vorticity of the dense cloud shield adjacent to the center of the storm. Owing to the high variation of cloud patterns and lack of efficient scene analysis techniques for the isolation and extraction of cloud systems from satellite pictures, the TC pattern matching jobs in Dvorak analysis are so far all done by subjective human justification [3]. Reference [4] introduces genetic algorithm into the template matching method which is proposed to solve a subclass of TC eye problems and higher the accuracy in latitude/longitude; however, processing performance is lowered. The methodology proposed in this paper is mainly based on image processing theories and mathematic morphology, to increase the performance and precision. At the same time, more characteristics of a typhoon's movement have also been considered, based on which, feature based matching and some neural networks could be used to perform the location of a tropical cyclone center automatically and intelligently [5].

This paper is organized as follows: Section 2 introduces several pre-processing methodologies for filtering, smoothing, and segmentation on satellite images. In Section 3, some helix matching based procedures and models will be proposed to detect the center of a tropical cyclone according to its natural shape, e.g. edge feature detection operator and skeleton feature detection operator. Subsequently, based on its spiral movement feature, a rotation matching methodology will be put forward in Section 4. Finally, a brief conclusion and discussion on the findings and future targets of our work are provided.

2 Noise Reduction and Image Segmentation

Image segmentation is one of the most frequently addressed problems in computer vision. The complexity of such a problem varies on the application, where, in the most general case, one would like to partition an image in regions with consistent properties. Such properties can be either visual or geometric. Knowledge based approaches consider a problem of lower complexity where some prior knowledge on the object to be recovered is available. Visual appearance of the object as well as its geometric form can be considered to encode prior knowledge on the segmentation.

Image segmentation is used to distinguish objects from their background. For intensity images (that is, those represented by point-wise intensity levels), four popular approaches are: threshold techniques, edge-based methods, region-based techniques, and connectivity-preserving relaxation methods.

Threshold techniques make decisions based on local pixel information, and are effective when the intensity levels of the objects fall outside the range of levels in the background. Because spatial information is ignored, however, blurred region boundaries can create problems.

Edge-based methods center around contour detection. The weakness is in connecting together broken contour lines, which makes them prone to failure in the presence of blurring.

In the region-based method, the image is partitioned into connected regions by grouping neighboring pixels of similar intensity levels. Adjacent regions are then merged under some criterion involving perhaps sharpness of region boundaries.

A connectivity-preserving relaxation-based segmentation method was recently proposed. The main idea is to start with some initial boundary shape represented in the form of spline curves, and iteratively modified by applying various shrink/expansion operations according to some energy function. Although the energy-minimizing model is not new, coupling it with the maintenance of an "elastic" contour model gives it an interesting new twist. As is usual with such methods, getting trapped into a local minimum is a risk against which one must guard; this is no easy task.

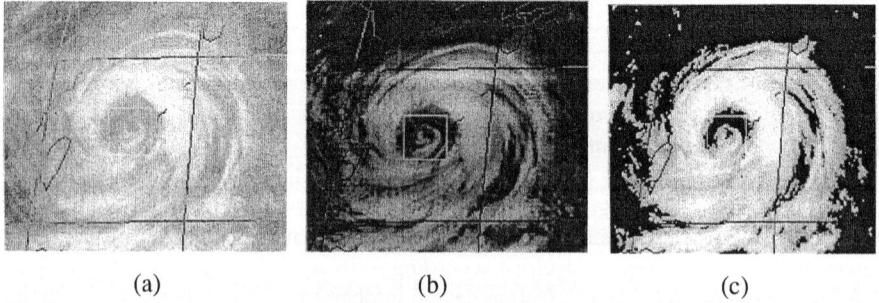

Fig. 1. Original image and images after delamination.(a) Original image with 256 gray-scale. (b)Image with 128 gray-scale, which will be used for further processing. (c) Image with lower scale, which sharpens the differences.

In general, cloud movement information is collected by meteorological satellites and represented through multiple modalities of images. An example of an original image is shown in Figure.1 (a). Satellite cloud image is a 256-gray-scale digital image, with 1Pic/Hour sampling frequency. In this meteorological project, the data resources include 16 hours continuous sequence images, color-temperature relation table, path file (central positions for previous pre-determined hours) to locate the tropical cyclone center in real time. Satellite images are easily deformed and polluted by ambient interferences. There is a relative range for the tropical cyclone gas temperature, which is demonstrated by pixel gray-level value. Various temperature ranges can be utilized to locate the sensitive cloud that represents the typhoon center. In order to separate the relevant information from lots of mess, it is necessary to down sample the images from 256 color scale to 128, while the highest part of the gray-level value ought to be cleared to zero, as shown in Figure. 1 (b).

Traditionally, the delaminating of a nephogram can be implemented through the down sampling method. In order to lower the grade of satellite images, accumulated frequency curves based on the statistical gray scale of the nephogram are taken into consideration; through experiments, some thresholds can be specified. All gray-scale that is smaller than such a threshold should be adjusted to zero. Figure.1 (c) shows an example image after delamination to lower the gray-scales. The procedure can also be termed the bucketing process.

3 Helix Matching Model

The helix matching model proposed in this paper can be divided into these phases: feature cloud extraction, feature cloud smoothing, skeleton extraction of feature cloud, and the simulation based on the least square algorithm.

3.1 Feature Cloud Extraction

Feature extraction is a set of techniques in scientific visualization aiming at algorithmic, automated extraction of relevant features from data sets. This leads to a small set of numbers (the attributes) describing the properties of the features. Hence,

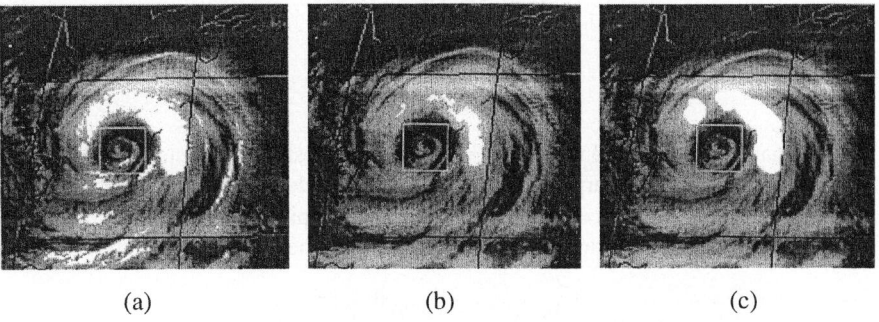

Fig. 2. Feature cloud extraction and smoothing. (a) Image with feature cloud extraction. (b) Image after morphological eroding processing. (c) Image after morphological dilating processing.

feature extraction lifts the data to a higher abstraction level, and comes down to a major data reduction. Since an "interesting feature" is different for each application, many application-specific feature extraction techniques exist, such as vortex extraction [7].

Based on the mentioned method of delamination in Section 2, a fairly reasonable threshold can be chosen to separate the feature cloud in some temperature ranges. Figure. 2 (a) shows the enhanced effect of the feature cloud with gray-level value delaminated in [205, 225] (corresponding temperature range is [-72.13, -52.01]). A helix cloud strip near the typhoon center can easily be marked up according to the demonstration of the figure.

3.2 Feature Cloud Smoothing

As shown in Figure. 2 (a), the extracted feature cloud strip is disturbed by the noise and other tiny burs, which can be reduced by a Minkowski structural operator [8]; the operation definition of Minkowski is briefly introduced as follows:

Suppose A is a point set on a plane, $\overline{A}$ is the complement of A. Choose a point set B with a simple set shape, which includes the origin O, and set the origin as the symmetric center. B is named Minkowski element. If the structural elements shift, e.g. shift original point to z, which can be described as Bz.

Minkowski subtraction can also be referred to as eroding or shrinking, and the definition is:

$$A\ominus B=\{z:B_z\in A\} \tag{1}$$

Minkowski addition is also referred to as dilating or expanding, and the definition is:

$$A\oplus B=\{z:B_z\cap A\neq\phi\} \tag{2}$$

Where ϕ indicates a void set, $\ominus$ means the eroding operation, and $\oplus$ the delegating dilating operation, and, according to the joint operation between Minkowski subtraction and addition, hybrid Minkowski is defined as:

Open operation:

$$A_B=(A\ominus B)\oplus B \tag{3}$$

Close operation:

$$A^B=(A\oplus B)\ominus B \tag{4}$$

For binary gray scale images, open operation can restrain the details of an image and identify clearly the sharp and shrink parts, while close operation can be used to fill up cavities and clearances. In the processing of tropical cyclone satellite images, ground filtering algorithm can also be used to increase the processing quality:

$$\overline{A} = \begin{cases} A_B, & \text{if } (A - A_B \geq A^B - A) \\ A^B, & \text{if } (A - A_B < A^B - A) \end{cases} \tag{5}$$

Figure. 2 (b) and (c) are the results after mathematical morphological eroding and dilating processing. The experiment result shows that after such mathematical morphological operating sequences, non-useful disturbing cloud is successfully filtrated and the remainder is the feature cloud with a smooth border.

3.3 Skeleton Extraction of Feature Cloud

Skeleton is a lower dimensional shape description of an object. The requirements of a skeleton differ with applications. For example, object recognition requires skeletons with primitive shape features to make similarity comparisons. On the other hand, surface reconstruction needs skeletons that contain detailed geometry information to reduce the approximation error in the reconstruction process. Whereas many previous works are concerned about skeleton extraction, most of these methods are sensitive to noise, or are time consuming or restricted to specific models.

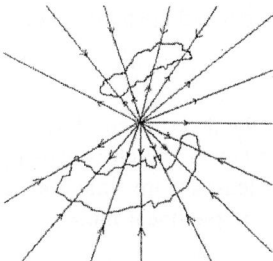

Fig. 3. Sketching map for radiating scan

Although border and skeleton are important features for image processing, it is not the focus and the main task is to focus on the extraction of enough information to simulate the logarithmic helix. Due to the spiral structure feature of tropical cyclones, central outward radiating scan arithmetic is adopted here, based on which only one time scanning can extract inner & outer borders, and skeleton information. The detection and reduction of false skeletons is achieved by weighting the detected skeleton points based on their local height (intensity). Then, binary thresholding is applied, followed by small connected component detection and elimination, morphological reconstruction by dilation, and thinning [9,10].

Based on the extrapolating method [11], the typhoon center traces can be forecast in one hour, two hours or three hours according to the cloud images' history path list. Such calculated point is used as the central position in the radiating scan algorithm, which is of course only a reference value and may not be the actual center. The only requirement is that it must be in the central area of the helix feature cloud strip, which provides safety when using the predicted extrapolating point as the radiating scan center. Figure. 3 shows the principle of this algorithm, which includes drawing the feature cloud binary strip.

3.4 Simulation with the Least Square Algorithm

Given the skeleton information of the feature cloud, the next task is to find a standard logarithmic helix to simulate this feature cloud strip. Points on inner border, outer border or the skeleton curve can be used to simulate the helix, and the data set is:

$$T_i=\{(x_i,y_i)\}_{i=1}^{n} \tag{6}$$

which represents the points used to carry out the simulation. Subsequently, the least square algorithm can be used to find a logarithmic helix:

$$\rho=e^{\alpha\theta} \tag{7}$$

which will match the spire cloud strip's inner, outer, and skeleton curve perfectly. And the helix center is the tropical cyclone center reference point.

Since the extracted helix feature cloud strip may have a different initial rotary angle, a parameter θ' is introduced, and the helix is represented as follows:

$$\rho=e^{\alpha(\theta+\theta')} \tag{8}$$

in which α, θ' is the constant to be determined (θ' stands for helix's initial rotary angle and α stands for obliquity parameter), which is actually a non-linear model for α, θ'. Since the method of non-linear least square simulation is complex, firstly equation (8) is Minkowski transformed to a simple linear mode.

$$\lg\rho = \alpha\theta\lg e + \alpha\theta'\lg e \tag{9}$$

By setting $u = \lg\rho$, $A = \alpha\lg e$, and $B = \alpha\theta'\lg e$, a linear model is obtained as follows:

$$u=A\theta+B \tag{10}$$

The relative normal equation group is:

$$\begin{bmatrix} \sum_{i=1}^{n} 1 & \sum_{i=1}^{n} \theta_i \\ \sum_{i=1}^{n} \theta_i & \sum_{i=1}^{n} \theta_i^2 \end{bmatrix} \begin{bmatrix} B \\ A \end{bmatrix} = \begin{bmatrix} \sum_{i=1}^{n} u_i \\ \sum_{i=1}^{n} \theta_i u_i \end{bmatrix} \tag{11}$$

By solving this equation, the values of A, B can be obtained. Thus the parameter α, θ' can be calculated. Since this is only a simple quadratic equation, it won't have an ill-conditioned coefficient matrix.

The procedure of feature cloud extraction, smoothing, and skeleton is organized mainly in consideration of how to implement the location with minimal manual assistance. The simulation computation can also be carried out, based on which many means of performance tuning and improvement can be introduced to make the proposed intelligent methodology practical.

4 Rotation Center Method

The movement characteristic of the typhoon is the combination of rotating and translating. Although a typhoon is a non-rigid object, its center area, with high pressure and moving speed, has less distortion and as such can be treated as a rigid object. Thus, from the theoretical view, the typhoon center point has the feature that its rotation vector is zero.

If a point could be found in the central area of the typhoon, it is the typhoon center point. The method is only suitable for the typhoon in mature status and has small distortion. While in the small central area, the rotation can be treated as circumferential movement. As such after counteracting the translating effect, certain points in different time can be treated as circling around the center point. If two points and their position are found in two hours, the center point can be determined. It is known that by any given four points, it is easy to find the center of a circle. The intersection point of the two perpendicular bisectors is the center of the circle. The arithmetic is demonstrated in Figure. 4

In calculating the typhoon center, the feedback method is used to improve the precision. Given the two continuous pictures Pk-1(xi, yj, tk-1) and Pk(xi, yj, tk) at temporal points tk-1, tk respectively, and the center position at tk-1 is Ck-1. The current center at tk is calculated by using the extrapolating method. The center position Ck, is treated as the initial value.

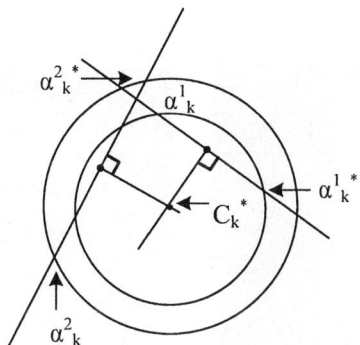

Fig. 4. Scheme of rotating center method

The translating vector is assumed to be $u = \overrightarrow{C_{k-1}C_k}$. Set the two feature points at tk-1 and the time in the picture Pk-1(xi, yj, tk-1) as α_{k-1}^1 and α_{k-1}^2. And the matching points in tk time are α_k^1 and α_k^2. Using the translating vector u, the corresponding points of α_{k-1}^1, α_{k-1}^2, in picture Pk-1(xi, yj, tk) are α_k^{1*}, α_k^{2*}, thus in picture Pk(xi, yj, tk), α_k^{1*} is corresponding to α_k^1 and α_k^{2*} is corresponding to α_k^2. The displacement is created by rotating an angle. In generally, feature point α_k^{1*} and α_k^1

are in the same circle with the typhoon center as the circle center, which means that the same argument can be applied to α_k^{2*} and α_k^2. The typhoon center point C_k^* can then be calculated. The error is $e = \left|C_k^* - C_k\right|$. Feedback the error e to the input value, which means modifying the initial C_k by e. Repeat the same steps until the error e is less than the given error threshold ξ or the repeat time is larger than given time N. The calculated center C_k^* is the typhoon center point. As discussed above, the feedback based correction scheme is approximated with the Neural Network technology, which introduces both automatic and intelligent features to the approach.

5 Results

These methods are usually combined together to fulfill the practical requirement, and the geometric center of several calculated values is used as the real center of the tropical cyclone. Figure. 5 (a) and Figure. 5 (b) give the result of a single helix simulating experiment result. Figure. 5 (a) is the satellite cloud image for No. 11 typhoon at 21 o'clock on 8/17/1997. Using image analysis, we choose the cloud in the temperature range [-72.13, -52.01] as the feature cloud. The darkened dot on Figure. 5 (a) is the typhoon center. The result is accurate enough to predict the center confidently. For the cloud image that may not be intuitionist, according to Figure. 5(b), the result is also satisfactory.

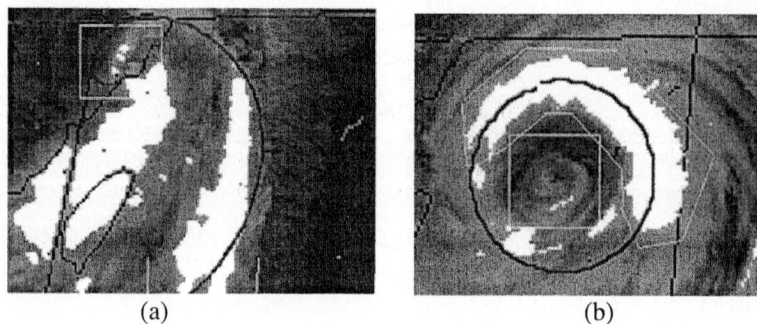

(a)   (b)

Fig. 5. Result of simulation. (a) Single helix simulating location. (b) Another instance of simulation.

6 Conclusions

Tropical hurricane is a kind of ether action, which is affected by atmospheric movement, earth rotation deflection force and offing temperature. Usually, those with central wind power larger than 8 degrees are called typhoons. Determined by the cause of formation, there are two main typhoon centers; one is in the west Pacific Ocean, the other one is in the Atlantic Ocean. China belongs to the west Pacific area and the number of typhoon occurrences is the highest in the world. 36% of total typhoon occurrences happen in China [12].

It is both complex and meaningful to use computer technology and image processing techniques to aid tropical cyclone center location. In this helix simulation method, there are a few points which could be improved. The proposed methodology focuses on the extracted skeleton information to simulate the best matching helix. If the whole feature cloud is taken into account, and a best matching helix is found for the whole strip, the result could be better.

Acknowledgements

This research project is sponsored by National 973 Plan of China [Ref code: 2001CB309401]. The project is co-operated between City University London, Fudan University, and Shanghai Meteorology Center.

References

1. Poon, C.H., Chau, C.P., Ghadiali, M.I.: Using Fuzzy Mathematical Morphology for Locating Tropical Cyclones in Satellite Imagery. IEEE International Symposium on Circuits and Systems. (1997) 1353-1356
2. Dvorak, V.F.: A technique for the Analysis and Forecasting of Tropical Cyclone Intensities from Satellite Pictures. U.S. Dept. Commerce, Washington, D.C., NOAA Tech. Memo. NESS 45, (1973)
3. Lee, S.T., Liu, N.K.: An Elastic Contour Matching Model for Tropical Cyclone Pattern Recognition. IEEE Transactions on Systems, Man, and Cybernetics. (2001) 413-417
4. Chi Lap Yip, Ka Yan Wong: Efficient and Effective Tropical Cyclone Eye Fix Using Genetic Algorithms. Springer-Verlag Berlin Heidelberg. (2004) 654-660
5. Lai L.L., Braun, H., Zhang, Q.P., Wu, Q., Ma, Y., Sun, W.C., Yang, L.: Intelligent Weather Forecast. Proceedings of the Third International Conference on Machine Learning and Cybernetics. IEEE. Shanghai China. (2004) (Invited paper)
6. Zhang, Q.P., Lai, L.L., Sun, W.C.: Intelligent Location of Tropical Cyclone Center. Proceedings of the Fourth International Conference on Machine Learning and Cybernetics. IEEE. Guangzhou China. (2004) (Invited paper)
7. Banks, D.C., Singer, B.A.: A Predictor-corrector Technique for Visualizing Unsteady Flow. IEEE Transactions on Visualization and Computer Graphics, Vol. 1. No. 2., (1995) 151-163
8. Serra, J.: Image Analysis and Mathematical Morphology, Academic Press. (1982)
9. Wang, L., Pavlidis, T.: Direct Gray-Scale Extraction of Features for Character Recognition. IEEE Transactions on Pattern Analysis and Machine Intelligence. Vol. 15. No. 10. (1993) 1053–1067
10. Vincent, L.: Morphological Grayscale Reconstruction in Image Analysis: Applications and Efficient Algorithms. IEEE Transactions on Image Processing, Vol. 2. No.2. (1993) 176–201
11. Neumann, C.J.: Global Overview - Chapter 1, Global Guide to Tropical Cyclone Forecasting, WMO/TC-No, 560, Report No. TCP-31, World Meteorological Organization, Geneva. (1993)
12. Atmosphere and Physical Research Institute of China Academy, China Metrological Center: Satellite Nephogram Manual., Agriculture Publication. Beijing. (1975)

A Hybrid Genetic Algorithm/Particle Swarm Approach for Evaluation of Power Flow in Electric Network

T.O. Ting, K.P. Wong, and C.Y. Chung

Computational Intelligence Applications Research Laboratory,
Department of Electrical Engineering, The Hong Kong Polytechnic University, Hung Hom,
Kowloon, Hong Kong
{chan.xiuyan, eekpwong, eecychun}@polyu.edu.hk

Abstract. This paper presents an investigation of possible hybrid genetic algorithm / particle swarm optimization approaches to evaluate the flow of electric power in power transmission network. The possible schemes are presented and their performances are illustrated by applying them to the power flow problem of the Klos Kerner 11-busbar system. The performance of the hybrid algorithm in terms of reliability is further improved by applying the optimal values for both inertia weight and mutation probability which are found through parameter sensitivity analyses.

1 Introduction

The Newton-Raphson Power flow (NRPF) method has been widely applied in solving the power flow problem [1] in power system planning and operation. It is well known that when the load in a power system is heavy, the system becomes stressed and it will be difficult for the NRPF to converge [2]. This is also true for other conventional approaches such as the Gauss-Seidel method and fast decouple power flow method.

Generally, the power flow equation set has multiple solutions [2, 3]. In the multiple solutions, there only exits one normal solution while others are abnormal solutions. However, if the system is operating at its steady-state ceiling point there is only one solution. A limiting condition of the system is indicated when the existence of near solutions is found. The estimation of the steady-state operating limit is important since any extra loading imposed on the system beyond the limit can lead to voltage collapse. To achieve this, a power flow algorithm which can determine multiple solutions is required. Although an optimal multiplier method [2] has been developed and incorporated in the NRPF method to find a pair of near solutions, it is not general enough to find all the multiple solutions. Moreover, since this method is based on NRPF, it will not be able to determine the solution at the steady-state point of the system.

Recently, the advent of power electronic devices provides new ways of improving and expanding the performance and capacity of power transmission systems. Transmission systems which adopt power electronic devices for the control of power transmission have been referred to as flexible AC transmission system (FACTS). The load flow equations of a power system containing FACTS will be much more nonlinear and the equation set may be nonconvex, which is not solvable with any conventional

tional methods. A great deal of interest in modeling nonlinear loads and in investigating the effects of these loads on the stability of power systems using chaos and bifurcation theory [4, 5] has been done. Before the stability can be determined, the steady-state operating point of the system is obtained by solving the load-flow equations. However, the inclusion of nonlinear load models in the load-flow equations can cause gradient based method such as the NRPF to fail.

In [6, 7], a constrained genetic algorithm for power flow (CGAPF) has been developed and found to be effective. This algorithm has incorporated the concept of virtual population in which the qualities of the candidate solutions are improved using the numerical and gradient accelerators [7]. The algorithm has been shown to be able to find both the normal and abnormal power flow solutions of a number of IEEE test systems.

With the advent of Particle Swarm Optimization (PSO), which can be viewed as a general form of numerical accelerator in the context of virtual population, the numerical accelerator in [7] can be replaced using PSO. Like the other solution accelerators, PSO here can be regarded as a pseudo mutation operator. As the effect of normal uniform mutation can be small in the presence of PSO, then PSO can be used as the mutation operator in CGAPF. The combination of GA and PSO in the above manner provides a hybrid approach to solving the power flow problem. This paper reports the preliminary investigation made on the performance of such a hybrid approach. The hybrid method is applied to solve the power flow problems of the Klos-Kerner 11-node system [8] under heavy-load conditions.

The paper further investigates and reports the finding of the optimal values of the inertia weight and mutation probability for use in executing the proposed hybrid method for the power flow problem.

2 Power Flow Problem Formulation

In an interconnected n node power system, there are N_{PQ} load nodes, N_{PV} voltage-controlled nodes and one slack bus. In rectangular coordinates, there are $2(n-1)$ unknowns to find. The load flow problem in this paper is formulated as nonlinear optimization problem, i.e. the objective function results from the summation of squares of the power mismatch and voltage mismatch whose minimum coincides with the load flow solution. At any node i the nodal active power, P_i and reactive power, Q_i are given as follows:

$$P_i = E_i \sum_{j=1}^{n}(G_{ij}E_j - B_{ij}F_j) + F_i \sum_{j=1}^{n}(G_{ij}F_j + B_{ij}E_j) \tag{1}$$

$$Q_i = F_i \sum_{j=1}^{n}(G_{ij}E_j - B_{ij}F_j) - E_i \sum_{j=1}^{n}(G_{ij}F_j + B_{ij}E_j) \tag{2}$$

where G_{ij} and B_{ij} are the $(i, j)th$ element of the admittance matrix. E_i and F_i are real and imaginary parts of the voltage at node i. If node i is a PQ-node where the load demand is specified, then the mismatches in active and reactive powers, ΔP_i and ΔQ_i respectively, are given by:

$$\Delta P_i = \left| P_i^{sp} - P_i \right| \tag{3}$$

$$\Delta Q_i = \left| Q_i^{sp} - Q_i \right| \tag{4}$$

in which P_i^{sp} and Q_i^{sp} are the specified active and reactive powers at node i. When node i is a PV-node, the magnitude of the voltage, V_i^{sp} and the active power generation at i are specified. The mismatch in voltage magnitude at node i can be defined as:

$$\Delta V_i = \left| V_i^{sp} - V_i \right| \tag{5}$$

In eqn. (5), V_i is the calculated nodal voltage at PV-node i and is given by:

$$V_i = \sqrt{E_i^2 + F_i^2} \tag{6}$$

The unknown variables in this problem are:

(i) The voltages at the PQ-nodes and
(ii) The real and imaginary parts of the voltages at the PV-nodes and the reactive powers of the generators connected to the PV-nodes.

It is required to determine the values of the variables in (i) and (ii) such that the mismatches in eqns. (3)-(5) are zero. Apart from solving the load-flow problem by the conventional methods, the problem can be viewed as an optimization problem, in which an objective function H is to be minimized:

$$H = \sum_{i \in N_{pq} + N_{pv}} \Delta P_i^2 + \sum_{i \in N_{pq}} \Delta Q_i^2 + \sum_{i \in N_{pv}} \Delta V_i^2 \tag{7}$$

where N_{pq} and N_{pv} are the total numbers of PQ-nodes and PV-nodes respectively. When the power flow problem is solvable, the value of H is zero or in the vicinity of zero at the end of the optimization process. If the problem is unsolvable, the value of H will be greater then zero. The square root of H can be regarded as the minimum distance between the solution point in the unsolvable region and the boundary of the solvable region. In the previous constrained genetic algorithm for the power flow problem [7], to minimize the objective function in eqn (7), the following fitness function has been suggested:

$$F = \frac{M}{10^{-5} + H + (H - H_{av})} \tag{8}$$

where M is a constant for amplifying the fitness, with the value given in section 6. The value of F will increase when H approaches zero towards convergence. This fitness function is also used in the present work.

3 Constrained Genetic Algorithm Power Flow (CGAPF)

The details of the CGAPF algorithm can be found in [6, 7]. The chromosomes are encoded in real value number. The algorithm can be described as:

1. Initialize the chromosomes (real and imaginary parts of the voltage) in the population
2. Fitness evaluation
3. Generate new population of candidate solutions using roulette-wheel selection, 2-point crossover and uniform mutation.
4. Accelerate candidate solutions using numerical acceleration [7].
5. Constraint satisfaction (PV and PQ) [6].
6. Gradient technique to accelerate the candidate solutions [7].
7. Elitism - Update the best candidate solution or chromosome.
8. Go to step 3 until termination criterion met.

There are two criteria for termination criterion in step 7 above. The algorithm will terminate when all the PV and PQ nodes are within the tolerance given. If the first criterion is not met, the algorithm will proceed until it reaches maximum generation.

4 Particle Swarm Optimization (PSO)

Kennedy and Eberhart first introduced the Particle Swarm Optimization (PSO) method in the year 1995 [10]. It is one of the optimization method categorized in the family of evolutionary computation. The method has been found to be promising in solving real-world problems featuring non-differentiability, high dimension, multiple optima and non-linearity. The PSO concept consists of, at each time step, changing the velocity of each particle toward its *pbest* and *gbest* solutions. The movement is weighted by a random term, with separate random numbers being generated toward *pbest* and *gbest* values. For example, the ith particle consisting d dimensions is represented as $X_i = (X_{i,1}, X_{i,2}, X_{i,3}, ..., X_{i,d})$. The same notation applied to the velocity, $V_i = (V_{i,1}, V_{i,2}, V_{i,3}, ..., V_{i,d})$. The best previous position of the ith particle is recorded and represented as $pbest_i = (pbest_{i,1}, pbest_{i,2}, pbest_{i,3}, ... pbest_{i,d})$. In the case of minimization, the value of *pbest$_i$* with lowest fitness is known as *gbest*. The modification of velocity and position can be calculated using the current velocity and the distance from *pbest$_i$* to *gbest* as shown in the following formulas:

$$V_{i,j}^t = w \times V_i^{t-1} + 2r_1(gbest_j - X_{i,j}^{t-1}) + 2r_2(pbest_{i,j} - X_{i,j}^{t-1}) \qquad (9)$$

$$X_{i,j}^t = X_{i,j}^{t-1} + V_{i,j}^t \qquad (10)$$

where $i \in 1...N, j \in 1...d, t \in 1...T$ with N is the number of population size, d is the number of dimension and T is the number of maximum generation. The position, X of each particle is updated for every dimension for all particles in each iteration. This is done by adding the velocity vector to the position vector, as described in eqn. (10) above. In eqn. (9), w is known as the inertia weight. This parameter was introduced by Shi and Eberhart to accelerate the convergence of PSO [11]. Suitable selection of w provides a balance between global and local explorations, thus requiring less iteration on average to find sufficiently optimal solution. Low values result in particles moving in the region far from the optimum value before being tugged back. On the other hand, high values result in abrupt movement toward target regions. The parameters r_1 and r_2 are two random values, uniformly distributed in [0, 1]. In the above equations, the parameter V is limited in $V_{min} \leq V \leq V_{max}$. These boundaries determine the resolution, with which regions be searched between the present position and target position. If the range of V is too high, particles may search a large area, lacking the ability to converge.

5 A Proposed Hybrid GA/PSO Algorithm

The proposed hybrid GA/PSO power flow algorithm is to use the PSO as the mutation operator and solution accelerator in the CGAPF algorithm in section 3. In the procedure of section 3, the mutation action in step 3 and the solution acceleration in Step 4 are now replaced by PSO. Hereby, PSO acts as a mutation strategy with the mutation probability found in section 6 below.

6 Application Studies

The proposed hybrid GA/PSO method is applied to the Klos-Kerner 11-node system under the heavy load conditions. The settings of the parameters of the algorithm and the power flow tolerances are given in Table 1 below:

Table 1. Setting for the relevant parameters in Hybrid GA/PSO

Parameter	Setting
PV tolerance	0.001 p.u. on a 100MVA base
PQ tolerance	0.001 p.u. on a 100MVA base
M	100
Maximum Generation, T	100
Population size, N	100
Range for initialization	Voltage: 0.7 p.u. to 1.2 p.u., θ: -30° to 0°
Selection in GA	Roulette wheel selection
Crossover	2-point crossover with probability 0.9
Mutation	Uniform mutation with probability = 0.01
Inertia weight, w	0.7
r_1 and r_2	Random numbers uniformly distributed in [0,1].

The details on the network data of Klos-Kerner 11-node system are available in [6], together with the specified generation for heavy load case.

7 Results

Results of the schemes as depicted in Table 2 are shown in Tables 3. For simplicity, the notation CGA in Table 2 refers to CGAPF as mentioned in section 3. In these tables, the meanings of the attributes are given below.

Ave Time: Average time taken to complete a trial
S.R. : A trial is considered successful if all nodes value is within the tolerance before maximum generation, T is reached. Success rate can be obtained from the number of successful trials within 50 trials.
Std Dev : A small standard deviation of H denotes that the algorithm is stable.
Best : The best results obtained within 50 trials.
Average : Average of H for all 50 trials.
Worst : The worst result among 50 trials.

For the heavy load case in Table 3, the four schemes have significant differences when reliability is taken into account. From Table 3, CGA (Scheme A), records a success rate of 76% whereas CPSO (Scheme B) records a success rate of 60%. CPSO fails to obtain a competent results and the time recorded is doubled compared to the one obtained by CGA. It can be observed in Scheme C that the reliability of CGA can be increased by incorporating the numerical accelerator suggested in [6]. At the same time, the average time recorded is decreasing from 0.74 second to 0.52 second. With PSO as mutation operator with mutation probability of 0.01, the proposed hybrid GA/PSO method (Scheme D) has a success rate of 96% and the time recorded is competent to the time recorded by CGA in Scheme A. This shows that the strategy of incorporating PSO as mutation operator while having GA as the backbone is an efficient approach in solving power flow problem.

Table 2. List of Schemes

Scheme	Description
A	CGA.
B	CPSO.
C	CGA with numerical accelerator.
D	Hybrid GA/PSO.

Table 3. Heavy Load of KK11 system with 0.04% load reduction (50 trials)

Scheme	Ave Time[ms]	S.R. (%)	Std Dev	H Best	H Average	H Worst
A	740	76	6.39E-7	6.0E-6	7.4E-6	9.0E-6
B	1690	60	5.80E-7	6.0E-6	6.7E-6	8.0E-6
C	520	92	5.36E-7	6.0E-6	7.28E-6	8.0E-6
D	730	96	5.73E-7	6.0E-6	7.28E-6	9.0E-6

8 Further Investigation on Hybrid GA/PSO

In this section, the performance of Hybrid GA/PSO is further enhanced by improving the reliability of the hybrid algorithm and by reducing the computational cost. The high reliability can be achieved by choosing the optimal value for the inertia weight, w, and the mutation probability, mp, applied in the hybrid algorithm. This is done through parameter sensitivity analysis for both w and mp. In achieving the reduction in computational cost, it is best to reduce the number of population to the lowest size possible while maintaining the solution success rate close to 100%. The population size applied in the previous simulation has been 100. Empirical study shows that the population size could possibly be reduced to increase the speed of the algorithm while maintaining a high reliability. Therefore, for the following parameter sensitivity analyses in section 8.1 and 8.2, the population size is fixed at a size of 8 individuals. All the other settings as given in section 6 remains intact. The convergence characteristic of the hybrid algorithm is described in section 8.3. The technical information of the best result is also included in the same section.

8.1 Determining Optimal Inertia Weight, *w* Value

In the previous studies, the inertia weight, w has been set to 0.7. Recent work shows that a lower inertia weight value might help to improve the convergence of PSO algorithm. Therefore, a series of inertia weight starting from 0.7 to 0.1 with a decrement of 0.1 are chosen for analysis. Meanwhile, the mutation probability of 0.01 as given in section 6 remains unchanged as the main focus here is to analyze the influence of w in the hybrid algorithm. Results for this analysis are recorded in Table 4. From the results, the best reliability achieved is obtained by setting $w=0.1$, with a success rate of 53%. The best result is highlighted in the same table.

Table 4. Parameter sensitivity analysis of inertia weight (w) for KK11-node system with 0.04% load reduction. (100 trials)

w	Ave Iter	Ave Time[ms]	S.R. (%)	Std Dev	H Best	H Average	H Worst
0.7	32.51	48.0	37	5.60E-07	7E-06	7.73E-06	9E-06
0.6	32.62	48.0	43	6.71E-07	7E-06	7.81E-06	9E-06
0.5	33.47	49.0	49	7.55E-07	7E-06	7.82E-06	1E-05
0.4	35.18	53.0	50	7.07E-07	7E-06	7.70E-06	9E-06
0.3	31.6	47.0	48	6.17E-07	7E-06	7.71E-06	9E-06
0.2	34.92	49.0	50	7.08E-07	7E-06	7.78E-06	9E-06
0.1	**45.36**	**66.0**	**53**	**7.23E-07**	**6E-06**	**7.70E-06**	**1E-05**

8.2 Determining Optimal Mutation Probability, *mp* Value

Having the optimal value of w from the sensitivity analysis in the previous section, further analysis to obtain the optimal mutation probability, mp is carried out. This is done through parameter sensitivity analysis and results for this analysis are recorded in Table 5. At this point, the inertia weight, w is fixed at 0.1 as this is best value found in the previous parameter sensitivity analysis. From the table, the performance of the hybrid algorithm varies with different setting of the mp values, which is varied from 0.00 to 0.10 with the increment of 0.01. Results are tabulated accordingly in Table 5 with Fig. 1 showing the average iteration, average time in millisecond and success rate in percentage. From the graph, the optimal mutation probability, mp is clearly no other than 0.04 as highlighted in the table. With this mp value, the hybrid GA/PSO algorithm is able to achieve the best success rate of 95% with low computational time. The algorithm takes 81ms when it is executed on a Pentium IV computer with 3.0 GHz processor and the average number of iterations needed is 53.97 iterations. This is a significant improvement as the algorithm with optimal w and mp settings is much faster than when it is without, in which case as shown in Table 3, the average computational time is 730ms.

Table 5. Parameter sensitivity analysis of mutation probability (*mp*) for KK11-node system with 0.04% load reduction. (100 trials)

mp	Ave Iter	Ave Time[ms]	S.R. (%)	Std Dev	H Best	H Average	H Worst
0.00	26.38	35.0	34	7.16E-07	7E-06	7.82E-06	9E-06
0.01	33.47	49.0	49	7.55E-07	7E-06	7.82E-06	1E-05
0.02	56.14	79.0	81	6.29E-07	6E-06	7.61E-06	9E-06
0.03	55.5	84.0	88	6.03E-07	7E-06	7.57E-06	9E-06
0.04	**53.97**	**81.0**	**95**	**5.62E-07**	**7E-06**	**7.47E-06**	**9E-06**
0.05	56.4	89.0	89	5.43E-07	7E-06	7.44E-06	9E-06
0.06	59.01	113.0	86	6.47E-07	7E-06	7.53E-06	9E-06
0.07	59.16	108.0	81	6.06E-07	6E-06	7.4E-06	9E-06
0.08	60.62	106.0	74	5.23E-07	7E-06	7.41E-06	9E-06
0.09	69.4	107.0	62	5.88E-07	6E-06	7.4E-06	9E-06
0.10	62.31	98.0	59	5.69E-07	7E-06	7.47E-06	9E-06

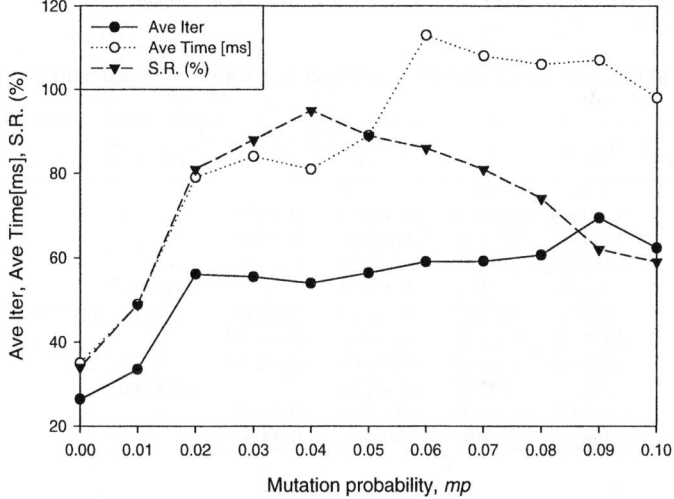

Fig. 1. Parameter sensitivity analysis for mutation probability, *mp*

8.3 Convergence Characteristic

Fig. 2 shows the convergence characteristic of the hybrid GA/PSO for the case of heavy load with 0.04% load reduction. With the optimal parameter settings of w=0.1 and mp=0.04, the hybrid algorithm converges very quickly in less than 10 iterations and only a slight improvement is observed after 10 iterations until the maximum iteration. The best power flow solution is tabulated in Table 6. As mentioned in section 3, the algorithm will stop when all the PV and PQ nodes are within the tolerance of 0.001. From Table 6, all the deviations for P, Q and V are within this tolerance with a total squared mismatched, H as 6.54×10^{-6}. Hence, this verifies that the solution obtained is a valid solution.

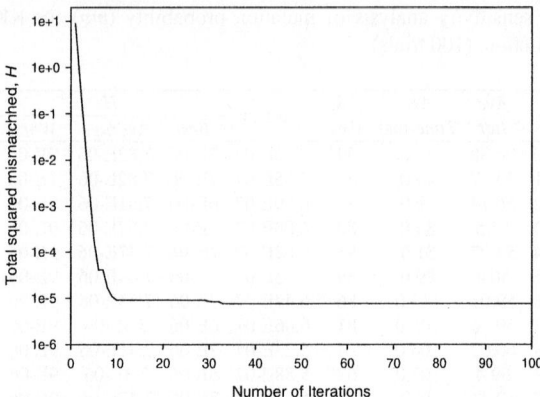

Fig. 2. Convergence characteristics of Hybrid GA/PSO in finding the solution for the heavy-load case with 0.04% load reduction with optimal settings of w and mp

Table 6. Best solution for the heavy-load case with 0.04% load reduction

Node no.	V_i(p.u)	$\theta°$	Mismatches (p.u) $P_i^{sp} - P_i$	$Q_i^{sp} - Q_i$	$V_i^{sp} - V_i$	H
1	1.05	0	-	-	-	
2	0.724899	-36.6266	-0.000559	-0.000557	-	
3	0.714302	-57.7219	-0.000982	-0.000856	-	
4	0.817615	-56.145	-0.000622	-0.000538	-	
5	1.05	-40.1	-0.000500	-	0.000000	
6	0.817783	-54.1989	-0.000714	-0.000573	-	0.00000654
7	0.905145	-45.2183	-0.000487	-0.000564	-	
8	0.920989	-34.3729	-0.000361	-0.000603	-	
9	1.0375	-15.396	-0.000504	-	0.000000	
10	0.965471	-20.5319	-0.000434	-0.000522	-	
11	0.888985	-38.9962	0.000568	-0.000606	-	

9 Conclusion

This paper has described a hybrid GA/PSO algorithm for solving the power flow problem. The proposed algorithm has been applied to the Klos Kerner 11 node system. It has been found to be very promising and PSO may be used as the mutation operator and to replace the numerical accelerator in Reference [7]. The parameter sensitivity analysis has been carried out to find the optimal settings for the inertia weight, w, and the mutation probability, mp, in the hybrid algorithm. With these optimal settings, the proposed algorithm has a high solution success rate and requires a small population size consisting of 8 candidates solutions. Thus, the hybrid GA/PSO has been much faster with the optimal settings. Further work is being undertaken to investigate the robustness of the proposed hybrid algorithm in analyzing larger power systems.

Acknowledgements

This work was supported by Research Grants Council of Hong Kong (PolyU 5225/04E) and the Department of Electrical Engineering of The Hong Kong Polytechnic University. Mr. T.O. Ting is grateful to The Hong Kong Polytechnic University for an International Postgraduate Scholarship.

References

1. Hadi Saadat: *Power system analysis*, McGraw-Hill, 2004.
2. Iba, K., Suzuki, H., Egawa, M., and Watanabe. T.: A method for finding pair of multiple load flow solutions in bulk power systems, IEEE Trans. Power Syst., 1990, vol 5, (2), pp. 582-591.
3. Grainger, J.J., and Stevenson, W.D. Jr.: *Power system analysis*, McGraw-Hill, 1994.
4. Chiang, H., Hiu, C., Varaiya, P., WU, F., and Lauby, M.: Chaos in simple power system, IEEE Trans. Power Syst., 1993, 4, (4), pp. 1407 – 1417.
5. Ajjarapn, V., and Lee, B.: Bifurcation theory and its application to nonlinear dynamical phenomena in an electrical power system, IEEE Trans. Power Syst., 1992, 7, (1), pp. 424-431.
6. K.P. Wong, A. Li and M.Y. Law: Development of constrained-genetic-algorithm load-flow method, IEE Proc. Gener. Transm. Distrib., Vol. 144, No. 2, March 1997.
7. K.P. Wong, A. Li and T.M.Y. Law: Advanced constrained genetic algorithm load flow method, IEE Proc. Gener. Transm. Distrib., Vol. 146, No. 6, November 1999.
8. Klos, A., and Kerner, A.: The non-uniqueness of load-flow solutions, Proceedings of 5th Power system computation conference (PSCC), Cambridge, UK, July 1975, (V.3.1/8).
9. J. H. Holland: *Adaptation in Natural and Artificial Systems,* Ann Arbor, MI: Univ. Michigan Press, 1975.
10. Kennedy J and Eberhart R.C (1995): Particle swarm optimization, Proceedings of the 1995 IEEE International Conference on Neural Networks, vol. 4, pp. 1942, IEEE Press.
11. Shi Y and Eberhart R.C (1998): A modified particle swarm optimizer, Proceedings of the IEEE International Conference on Evolutionary Computation, Anchorage, Alaska, May 4-9, 1998.

A Method to Construct the Mapping to the Feature Space for the Dot Product Kernels

Degang Chen[1], Qiang He[2], Chunru Dong[2], and Xizhao Wang[2]

[1] Department of Mathematics and Physics, North China Electric Power University,
102206, Beijing, P.R. China
chengdegang@263.net
[2] Department of Mathematics and Computer Science, Hebei University,
Baoding, Hebei, 071002, P.R. China

Abstract. Dot product kernels are a class of important kernel in the theory of support vector machine. This paper develops a method to construct the mapping that map the original data set into the high dimensional feature space, on which the inner product is defined by a dot product kernel. Our method can also be applied to the Gaussian kernels. Via this mapping, the structure of features in the feature space is easy to be observed, and the linear separability of data sets in the feature space is studied. We obtain that any two finite sets of data with empty overlap in the original space will become linearly separable in an infinite dimensional feature space, and a sufficient and necessary condition is also developed for two infinite sets of data in the original data space being linearly separable in the feature space, this condition can be applied to examine the existences and uniqueness of the hyperplane which can separate all the possible inputs correctly.

1 Introduction

Support vector machine(SVM) is a new learning theory presented by Vapnik[1,2]. From the pattern recognition viewpoint, it can briefly be stated as follows. When a given sample set K is linearly separable, the separating hyperplane with the maximal margin, the optimal separating hyperplane, is constructed in the original space. When the sample set is linearly non-separating, the input vectors are mapped into the high-dimensional feature space through some kernel functions. Then in this high-dimensional feature space an optimal separating hyperplane is constructed. The inner product in the high-dimensional feature space is just the employed kernel, so the complex computing of inner product in the high-dimensional feature space is avoided. This is one of the advantages of SVM. SVM has been shown to provide higher performance than traditional learning machines[3] and has been introduced as powerful tools for solving classification problems, at mean time the research on its theory and applications has drawn more and more attention in recent years.

However, if we only consider the computing of the inner product in the feature space, the kernel is enough, it is unnecessary to consider the mapping from the original data set to the feature space. But if we want to know more about the SVM, for example, analysis of the shape of mapped data in the feature space, consideration of the construction of features, and selection of optimal kernels with better generalization properties, the mapping from the original data set to the feature space can not be ignored. In the existing statistical learning theory[6], there are mainly two approaches to obtain the mapping from the original data set to the feature space. One is to employed the well known Mercer Theorem, by this way the mapping is constructed as a vector whose entries are N_H eigenfunctions of an integral operator, and the kernel corresponds a dot product in $l_2^{N_H}$. Another approach is to consider the Reproducing Kernel Hilbert Space, by this way each pattern is turned to a function on the domain. In this sense, a pattern is now represented by its similarity to all other points in the input domain.

However, for the first approach, sometimes it is very difficult to compute the eigenvalues and eigenfunctions of an integral operator defined by a kernel even they really exist. For the second approach, the structures of features are difficult to observe since the image of every input pattern is a function and not a vector. All of these two approaches are mainly designed from the mathematical viewpoint to ensure the existence of such mapping, they are too abstract to be applied to analysis practical problems. Thus an intuitive and general method to construct the mapping from the original data set to the feature space with legible feature structure is clearly necessary from both of the theoretical and practical viewpoints.

As well known, dot product kernels are an important class of kernels in common use. The well known dot product kernels in the theory of SVM are homogeneous polynomial kernels, inhomogeneous polynomial kernels. Both the homogeneous polynomial kernels and inhomogeneous polynomial kernels map the original data set into a finite dimensional polynomial space(feature space) and the structures of features are clear(there is a whole field of pattern recognition research studying polynomial classifiers[4]). By using of the power series expansion of a dot product kernel, we can develop a mapping from the original dataset into a polynomial space(may not be finite dimensional) for every dot product kernel. Via this mapping, the structures of features are clear. This method can also be applied to the Gaussian kernels. Furthermore, the linear separability of data set is also investigated. It can be proven the images of any finite data set are linear independent in the feature space relative to certain dot product kernels, this implies any two finite subclasses of the original data set are linear separable in the feature space. We also develop a sufficient and necessary condition for two infinite subclasses of the original data set being linear separable in the feature space, this condition offer a theoretical characterization to examine the existences and uniqueness of the hyperplane which can separate all the possible inputs correctly.

This paper is organized as follows. In section 2 we mainly review some basic content of kernels in SVM. In section 3 the method of constructing mapping for dot product kernels is developed. In section 4 we mainly discuss the separability of infinite sets in the feature space via our proposed mapping.

2 Kernels for SVM

In this paper we only consider the binary classification problem. Let $\{(x_1, y_1),...,(x_l, y_l)\} \subset R^n \times \{+1,-1\}$ be a training set, A is the sample set with label $+1$ and B is the sample set with label -1. A and B are called linear separable in R^n if there is a hyperplane $<w, x> + b = 0$ and $\delta > 0$ such that $<w, x> + b > \delta$ for

$x \in A$ and $<w,x>+b<-\delta$ for $x \in B$ (this definition is also suitable when A and B are infinite set), clearly $d(A,B)>0$ holds when A and B are linear separable, and the separating hyperplane with the maximal margin, the optimal separating hyperplane, could be constructed in R^n. If A and B are not linear separable in R^n, the SVM learning approach projects input patterns x_i with a nonlinear function $\Phi: x \to \Phi(x)$ into a higher dimension space Z and, then, it separates the data in Z with a maximal margin hyperplane. Therefore, the classifier is given by $f(x) = sign(w^T \Phi(x) + b)$ and parameters w and b are obtained through the minimization of functional $\tau(w) = \frac{1}{2}\|w\|^2$ subject to $y_i(<w,x_i>+b) \geq 1$ for all $i=1,...,l$. Since the solution of the linear classifier in Z only involves inner products of vectors $\Phi(x_i)$, we can always use the kernel trick[6], which consists on expressing the inner product in Z as an evaluation of a kernel function in the input space $<\Phi(x),\Phi(y)> = k(x,y)$. By this way, we do not need to explicitly know $\Phi(\cdot)$ but just its associated kernel $k(x,y)$. When expressed in terms of kernels, the classifier results $f(x) = sign(\sum_{i=1}^{l} y_i \alpha_i k(x_i,x) + b)$, where coefficients $\{\alpha_i\}$ are obtained after a QP optimization of functional $L(w,b,\alpha) = \frac{1}{2}\|w\|^2 - \sum_{i=1}^{l} \alpha_i \{[<x_i,w>-b]y_i - 1\}$ which can be solved by the KKT complementarity conditions of optimization theory[3].

However, if we not only consider the computing of inner product in the feature space, but also aim to present deep insight to SVM such as analysis of the shape of mapped data in the feature space, consideration of the construction of features, and selection of optimal kernels with better generalization properties, we must deal with the mapping from original dataset into the feature space. As pointed in [6], there are mainly two approaches to develop the mapping. One is the utilization of the well known Mercer theorem. Suppose X is a nonempty set and $k \in L_\infty(X^2)$ is a kernel, then the integral operator $T_k: L_2(X) \to L_2(X)$ defined as $(T_k f)(x) = \int_X k(x,x') f(x') d\mu(x')$ is positive definite. Let $\psi_j \in L_2(X)$ be N_H normalized orthogonal eigenfunctions of T_k associated with the eigenvalues $\lambda_j > 0$, then $k(x,x')$ corresponds to a dot product in $l_2^{N_H}$ with $\Phi: X \to l_2^{N_H}$ defined as $\Phi(x) = (\sqrt{\lambda_j} \psi_j(x))_{j=1,...,N_H}$. For this method, sometimes it is very difficult to compute the eigenvalues and eigenfunctions of T_k even they really exist.

Another approach is utilizing the Reproducing Kernel Hilbert Space. We can define a map from X into the space of functions mapping X into R, denoted as $R^X = \{f: X \to R\}$, via $\Phi(x) = k(x',x)$, $x' \in X$, the feature space is spanned by k and is a Reproducing Kernel Hilbert Space. Clearly $\Phi(x) = k(x',x)$ is a function and not a vector, and the structures of features are hardly to be observed.

Two kinds of kernels are always applied in SVM. They are translation invariant kernels and dot product kernels. The translation invariant kernels are independent of the absolute position of input x and only depend on the difference between two inputs x and x', so it can be denoted as $k(x,x') = k(x-x')$. The well known translation invariant kernel is the Gaussian radial basis function kernel $k(x,x') = \exp(-\frac{\|x-x'\|^2}{2\sigma^2})$, other translation invariant kernels include B_n − splines kernels[7], Dirichlet kernels[6] and Periodic kernels[6]. A second important family of kernels can be efficiently described in term of dot product, i.e., $k(x,x') = k(<x,x'>)$. The well known dot product kernels are Homogeneous Polynomial Kernels $k(x,x') = <x,x'>^p$, inhomogeneous Polynomial Kernels $k(x,x') = (<x,x'> + c)^p$ with $c \geq 0$. Both Homogeneous Polynomial Kernels and inhomogeneous Polynomial Kernels map the input set into a finite dimensional Polynomial space. In [11] we have also considered a class of infinite Polynomial kernels on a compact subset U_n of the open unit ball $\{x \in R^n : \|x\| < 1\}$, defined as $k_c(x,x') = \frac{1 - <x,x'>^p}{(1 - <x,x'>)^p}$, for every $x,x' \in U_n$, $p \in N - \{1\}$, via an infinite Polynomial kernel, the input dataset is projected into an infinite dimensional Polynomial space.

3 The Mapping for Dot Product Kernels

In this section we will focus on developing a general method to construct the mapping from the original dataset into the feature space for the dot product kernels. This method is also suitable to deal with the Gaussian kernels. We can prove if the feature space is an infinite dimensional Polynomial space, then any two finite sets of data in the original space will become linearly separable in the feature space.

For the dot product kernels, the following theorem is always useful.

Theorem 1.[8] A function $k(x,x') = k(<x,x'>)$ defined on an infinite dimensional Hilbert space, with a power series expansion $k(t) = \sum_{n=0}^{\infty} a_n t^n$ is a positive definite kernel if and only if for all n, we have $a_n \geq 0$.

This theorem implies many kinds of dot product kernels can be considered in SVM. Suppose $k(x,x') = k(<x,x'>)$ is a dot product kernel on $X \subset R^n$ with the power series expansion $k(<x,x'>) = \sum_{n=0}^{\infty} a_n <x,x'>^n$. For every $x \in X$, define C_n to map $x \in X$ to the vector $C_n(x)$ whose entries are all possible nth degree ordered products of the entries of x, and define Φ_k by compensating for the multiple occurrence of certain monomials in C_n by scaling the respective entries of Φ_n with the square roots of their numbers of occurrence. Then, by the construction of C_n and

Φ_n, we have $<C_n(x), C_n(x')> = <\Phi_n(x), \Phi_n(x')> = <x, x'>^n$. This fact can be found in [6] and is well known for the Homogeneous Polynomial Kernels $k(x, x') = <x, x'>^p$.

Define $\Phi(x) = (a_0, \sqrt{a_1}\Phi_1(x), ..., \sqrt{a_n}\Phi_n(x), ...)$, then we have $<\Phi(x), \Phi(x')> = k(x, x')$. Clearly $\Phi_1(x) = x$ holds, this implies if $a_1 \neq 0$, then $\Phi(x)$ is the extension of x by adding features and keeps all the original entries of x, thus $\Phi(x)$ keeps the original information of x. This statement is a goodness of our proposed Φ. The entries of $\Phi(x)$ is constructed by the entries of x, thus the structure of the appending features are clear and easy to be analyzed since these appending features are constructed by the original features. The feature space with respect to $k(x, x')$ can be selected as the Hilbert space spanned by $\Phi(X)$.

First we consider the properties of the above proposed Φ when the feature space is finite dimensional. If there is $n_0 \in N$ such that $a_n = 0$ when $n > n_0$, then we have $k(x, x') = \sum_{n=0}^{n_0} a_n <x, x'>^n$, thus $k(x, x')$ is just the weighted sum of some Homogeneous Polynomial Kernels, and the feature space is a finite dimensional Homogeneous Polynomial Kernels. However, for $k(x, x') = <x, x'>^n$, it is possible that Φ is not a one to one mapping, i.e., different inputs may have the same image, which is clearly unreasonable. This statement can be illustrated by the following example.

Example 2. If $n = 2$, and $x = (x_1, x_2)$, then $\Phi(x) = \Phi_2(x) = (x_1^2, x_2^2, \sqrt{2}x_1x_2)$. For two different inputs $x = (1, -1)$, $y = (-1, 1)$, clearly $x \neq y$, but $\Phi(x) = \Phi(y)$. If x and y belong to different classes, then every separating hyperplane in the feature space relative to the kernel $k(x, x') = <x, x'>^2$ can not distinguish x and y. Similar cases will appear frequently when n is an even. If we select a weighted sum form kernel predigest satisfying $a_1 \neq 0$, then the entries of x is a part of $\Phi(x)$, thus we can avoid this case.

By using of our proposed Φ, we have the following useful theorem.

Theorem 3. Suppose $\{x_1, ..., x_m\} \subset X$ satisfying $x_i \neq 0$, $x_i \neq x_j$ if $i \neq j$, then there is a dot product kernel $k(x, x') = \sum_{n=0}^{n_0} a_n <x, x'>^n$ such that $\Phi(x_1), ..., \Phi(x_n)$ are linear independent.

Proof. Suppose $x_i = (a_{i1}, a_{i2}, ..., a_{in})$, $k(x, x') = \sum_{n=0}^{m-1} <x, x'>^n$, then $k(x, x')$ is a dot product with expression $k(x, x') = \dfrac{1 - <x, x'>^m}{1 - <x, x'>}$.

Let $f_i(x) = a_{i1} + a_{i2}x + ... + a_{in}x^{n-1}$, $i = 1,...,m$. If $i \neq j$, then $x_i \neq x_j$, we have $f_i(x)$ and $f_j(x)$ are two different equations. By the algebraic basic theorem we know every $f_i(x) - f_j(x) = 0$ has finite roots. Thus there exists $n_0 \in N$ such that any two of $\{f_i(n_0) : i = 1,...,m\}$ are different. Let $\beta_i = \{1, f_i(n_0),..., f_i^{m-1}(n_0)\}$, $i = 1,...,m$, then we have $\beta_1, \beta_2,..., \beta_m$ are linear independent.

Suppose $\alpha_1 \Phi(x_1) + \alpha_2 \Phi(x_2) + ... + \alpha_m \Phi(x_m) = 0$, then $\sum_{i=1}^{m} \alpha_i a_{i1}^{l_1} a_{i2}^{l_2} ... a_{in}^{l_n} = 0$, $l_1 + l_2 + ... + l_n \leq m - 1$, $l_1, l_2,..., l_n \in N \cup \{0\}$, we have $\sum_{i=1}^{m} \alpha_i f_i^n(n_0) = 0$, this implies $\alpha_1 \beta_1 + ... + \alpha_m \beta_m = 0$, thus every $\alpha_i = 0$ and $\Phi(x_1),..., \Phi(x_n)$ are linear independent.

In the proof of Theorem 3 we choice the kernel as $k(x, x') = \dfrac{1 - <x, x'>^m}{1 - <x, x'>}$ in order to predigest the proof. However, every kernel $k(x, x') = \sum_{n=0}^{n_0} a_n <x, x'>^n$ satisfying $n_0 \geq m - 1$ and $a_n > 0$ for $n \leq m - 1$ satisfies the condition in Theorem 3.

Suppose Φ is a mapping relative to a kernel $k(x, x')$ such that $\Phi(x_1),..., \Phi(x_n)$ are linear independent, A and B are two nonempty subsets of X and $A \cap B = \phi$, then we have $\Phi(X) = \Phi(A) \cup \Phi(B)$ and $\Phi(A) \cap \Phi(B) = \phi$. $\Phi(x_1),..., \Phi(x_n)$ are linear independent implies any element in the convex hull of one class cannot be the convex combination of the elements of another class, this implies the two convex hulls of A and B have empty overlap, notice these two convex hulls are compact, so $\{\Phi(x_1),..., \Phi(x_l)\}$ and $\{\Phi(x_{l+1}),..., \Phi(x_m)\}$ are linear separable in the feature space. Thus we can derive the following fact.

Theorem 4. Suppose $\{(x_1, y_1),...,(x_l, y_l)\} \subset X \times \{+1\}$, $\{(x_{l+1}, y_{l+1}),...,(x_m, y_m)\} \subset X \times \{-1\}$, then there is a mapping relative to a dot product kernel which map X into a finite dimensional Polynomial space such that these two classes are linear separable in the feature space.

Suppose $k(<x, x'>) = \sum_{n=0}^{\infty} a_n <x, x'>^n$ satisfies for every $n_0 \in N$ there exists $n > n_0$ such that $a_n > 0$, without losing universality, we assume every $a_n > 0$, i.e., every coefficient in its power series is positive, for example, Vovk's infinite polynomial kernel $k(x, x') = (1 - (<x, x'>))^{-1}$ [6]and our proposed infinite polynomial kernel $k_c(x, x') = \dfrac{1 - <x, x'>^p}{(1 - <x, x'>)^p}$ [11]. The following theorem implies the feature space relative to such kernels is infinite dimensional.

Theorem 5. Suppose $\{x_1,...,x_m\} \subset X$ satisfies $x_i \neq 0$ for $i = 1,2,...,m$, $x_i \neq x_j$ if $i \neq j$, Φ is the mapping relative to $k(<x,x'>) = \sum_{n=0}^{\infty} a_n <x,x'>^n$ such that every $a_n > 0$, then $\Phi(x_1),...,\Phi(x_n)$ are linear independent.

Proof. Suppose $x_i = (a_{i1}, a_{i2},...,a_{in})$ and $\Phi(x_1),...,\Phi(x_m)$ are linear dependent, then there exists $\alpha_1, \alpha_2,...,\alpha_m$ satisfying at least one of them is not equal to zero and $\alpha_1 \Phi(x_1) + \alpha_2 \Phi(x_2) + ... + \alpha_m \Phi(x_m) = 0$ holds. Thus we have $\sum_{i=1}^{m} \alpha_i a_{i1}^{l_1} a_{i2}^{l_2}...a_{in}^{l_n} = 0$ where $l_1, l_2,...,l_n \in N \cup \{0\}$.

Let $f_i(x) = a_{i1} + a_{i2}x + ... + a_{in}x^{n-1}$, $i = 1,...,m$. Then there exists $n_0 \in N$ such that any two of $\{f_i(n_0) : i = 1,...,m\}$ are different. Let $\beta_i = \{1, f_i(n_0),..., f_i^{m-1}(n_0)\}$, $i = 1,...,m$, then we have $\beta_1, \beta_2,..., \beta_m$ are linear independent. But by $\sum_{i=1}^{m} \alpha_i a_{i1}^{l_1} a_{i2}^{l_2}...a_{in}^{l_n} = 0$ we have $\alpha_1 \beta_1 + ... + \alpha_m \beta_m = 0$, this is a contradiction. Thus we have $\Phi(x_1),...,\Phi(x_n)$ are linear independent.

For $\{x_1,...,x_m\} \subset X$, Theorem 3 implies there exists a finite dimensional feature space such that the images of $\{x_1,...,x_m\}$ are linear independent in this feature space, while Theorem 5 implies the images of $\{x_1,...,x_m\}$ are linear independent in the feature space relative to a kernel satisfying every coefficient in its power series is positive, so these two theorems are different. For the kernel satisfying every coefficient in its power series is positive, similar to Theorem 4 we have the following result.

Theorem 6. Suppose $\{(x_1,y_1),...,(x_l,y_l)\} \subset X \times \{+1\}$, $\{(x_{l+1},y_{l+1}),...,(x_m,y_m)\} \subset X \times \{-1\}$, then they are linear separable in every feature space relative to a kernel satisfying every coefficient in its power series is positive.

However, as pointed in section 2, for a fixed kernel $k(x,x')$, the feature space is not uniqueness. The following theorem implies the selection of feature space does not influence the linear independence of a finite class of data in the feature space.

Theorem 7. Suppose $\{x_1,...,x_m\} \subset X$ satisfies $x_i \neq 0$ for $i = 1,2,...,m$, $x_i \neq x_j$ if $i \neq j$, then the Gram matrix $M = (k(x_i, x_j))$ has full rank for a dot product kernel $k(x,x')$ satisfying every coefficient in its power series is positive.

Proof. If $M = (k(x_i, x_j)) = (<\Phi(x_i), \Phi(x_j)>)$ has not full rank, then there exists $\alpha_1, \alpha_2,...,\alpha_m$ satisfying at least one of them is not equal to zero such that $\sum_{l=1}^{m} \alpha_l <\Phi(x_l), \Phi(x_i)> = 0$, $i = 1,...,m$. So we have

$$< \alpha_i\Phi(x_i), \sum_{l=1}^{m}\alpha_l\Phi(x_l) >= 0 \quad , \quad i=1,\ldots,m \quad \text{which} \quad \text{implies}$$

$$< \sum_{i=1}^{m}\alpha_i\Phi(x_i), \sum_{l=1}^{m}\alpha_l\Phi(x_l) >= 0 \quad , \quad \text{thus} \quad \sum_{i=1}^{m}\alpha_i\Phi(x_i) = 0 \quad \text{and}$$

$\Phi(x_1),\ldots,\Phi(x_n)$ are linear dependent. Hence $M = (k< x_i, x_j >) = <\Phi(x_i), \Phi(x_j)>$ has full rank.

If Φ' is another mapping that project X into a different feature space, then it is easy to prove $\Phi'(x_1), \Phi'(x_2),\ldots,\Phi'(x_m)$ are linear independent by $M = (k(x_i, x_j))$ has full rank.

For two dot product kernels k_1 and k_2, suppose Φ_1 and Φ_2 are mappings relative to k_1 and k_2 respectively, we have the following straightforward but useful theorem.

Theorem 8. If Φ_2 is the extension of Φ_1, then $\Phi_1(x_1),\ldots,\Phi_1(x_n)$ are linear independent implies $\Phi_2(x_1),\ldots,\Phi_2(x_n)$ are linear independent.

Our proposed method to construct mapping for dot product kernels can be applied to the Gaussian kernels on the surface of the unit ball. Suppose every $x \in X$ is an unit vector, i.e., $\|x\|=1$, then $\|x-x'\|^2 = <x-x', x-x'>= 2-2<x, x'>$, thus the Gaussian kernels $k(x, x') = \exp(-\frac{\|x-x'\|^2}{2\sigma^2})$ have an equivalence expression as dot product kernels as $k(x, x') = \exp(\frac{<x,x'>-1}{\sigma^2})$, and we can construct the mapping for the Gaussian kernels by its power series by our proposed method. In [6] it has been pointed the Gaussian Gram Matrices are full rank, i.e., if Φ_G is the mapping relative to a Gaussian kernel, then $\Phi_G(x_1),\ldots,\Phi_G(x_m)$ are linear dependent for $\{x_1,\ldots,x_m\} \subset X$, this statement is very important for analysis of the properties of Gaussian kernels. By Theorem 5 we can also get this conclusion and we propose a new straight proof for this result, our proof is different with the original one in [13].

For a finite data set $\{x_1,\ldots,x_m\} \subset X$, $\Phi(x_1),\ldots,\Phi(x_n)$ are linear independent implies any binary partition of $\{x_1,\ldots,x_m\}$ are linear separable in the feature space. So $\Phi(x_1),\ldots,\Phi(x_n)$ being linear independent is a sufficient condition of $\{x_1,\ldots,x_m\}$ being linear separable in the feature space and clearly not a necessary condition. This sufficient condition illustrates the rationale of the kernel trick in SVM. However, it seems this sufficient condition is too strong since we always just need to separate two subsets of $\{x_1,\ldots,x_m\}$ in stead of separating all its possible binary partitions. The equivalence description of linear separability of a binary classifications problem by using of kernel is a meaningful problem.

4 On the Linear Separability of Infinite Data Sets in Feature Space

In this section we mainly discuss the linear separability of infinite data sets in feature space. At first glance, it is unnecessary to consider infinite data sets since the data sets we deal with in practical problems are all finite. This opinion is from the viewpoint of designing algorithm for practical applications. If we consider the classification problem from the theoretical viewpoint, the following three arguments indicate it is meaningful to investigate the linear separability of infinite data sets.

First, separating two finite sets linearly is equivalence to separating their convex hulls linearly, and their convex hulls are infinite sets, so we have implicitly considered the linear separability of special infinite data set when separating finite sets linearly. Second, most feature values are real valued, this implies the possible data may be infinite even the samples are infinite, for instance, if we take stature as a feature with value range 0.5 to 2.5 meter, then every number between 0.5 and 2.5 is possible to be the stature of somebody. So after we construct a learning machine based on finite independent and identically distributed samples, the possible data we deal with by this machine is always drown from an infinite set and we can not exactly forecast its detail structure, i.e., exact values of the possible data taking for every feature, this also need to take account of all possible cases drown according to a probability distribution. At last, for a practical binary problem, certainly we desire to know the existence and uniqueness of optimal hyperplane that can separate all the possible data without misclassification, this also inspires us to consider all the possible data.

Thus it is necessary to investigate the linear separability of infinite data sets at least from the theoretical viewpoint, and such investigation can offer guidance to improve algorithm for practical problems.

For any two finite data sets, by our discussion in Section 3 there must exists a feature space relative to a dot product kernel such that they are linear separable in feature space, and the optimal hyperplane in the feature space is always available. For the infinite data set this statement may not hold, we have the following sufficient and necessary condition to characterize the linear separability of two infinite data sets.

Theorem 9. Suppose $X \subset R^n$ is compact and $X = A \cup B$, $A \cap B = \phi$. Then there exists a feature space relative to a dot product such that $\Phi(A)$ and $\Phi(B)$ are linear separable in feature space if and only if the crowed point sets of A and B have empty overlap, i.e., the boundary points set of A and B is empty.

Proof. Without losing universality, we assume X is a subset of the open unit ball. We select Vovk's infinite polynomial kernel $k(x, x') = (1 - (<x, x'>))^{-1}$ in the following proof, Φ is the mapping relative to $k(x, x') = (1 - (<x, x'>))^{-1}$.

$\Rightarrow$ Since X is compact, we know the crowed points of X are still in X, thus the crowed points of $\Phi(X)$ are still in $\Phi(X)$ by $\Phi(X)$ is compact. If the crowed point sets of A and B have nonempty overlap, then the crowed point sets of $\Phi(A)$ and

$\Phi(B)$ also have nonempty overlap by Φ is continuous, this implies $d(\Phi(A), \Phi(B)) = 0$, so $\Phi(A)$ and $\Phi(B)$ can not be linear separable in feature space.

$\Leftarrow$ Suppose the crowed point sets of A and B have empty overlap. Clearly A and B are compact, this implies $\Phi(A)$ and $\Phi(B)$ are compact in the feature space in case of Φ being continuous. By Theorem 5 the overlap of convex hulls of $\Phi(A)$ and $\Phi(B)$ are empty, thus they are linear separable in the feature space and $\Phi(A)$ and $\Phi(B)$ are linear separable in the feature space.

Other kernels $k(<x, x'>) = \sum_{n=0}^{\infty} a_n <x, x'>^n$ satisfies for every $n_0 \in N$ there exists $n > n_0$ such that $a_n > 0$ can also be employed to prove this theorem.

For a binary pattern recognition problem, if there is a hyperplane which can not only separate the training simple but also can classify every possible data properly, i.e., it can separate all the possible data of two classes without misclassification, we call this binary pattern recognition problem can be totally solved. Theorem 9 develops a sufficient and necessary condition under which a binary pattern recognition problem is possible to be solved totally, i.e., for every sample of one class, there exists a sufficient small neighborhood of this sample satisfying none sample of another class is in this neighborhood. Thus we can conclude that for a binary pattern recognition problem, if it can be solved totally, then generally the selection of optimal separating hyperplane is not unique, if it can not be solved totally, then the optimal separating hyperplane does not exist. The following figure illustrates our idea of Theorem 5.

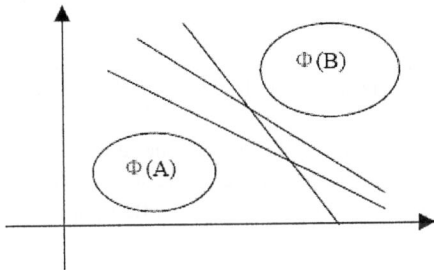

Fig. 1. If X is compact and $X = A \cup B$, $A \cap B = \phi$, all the possible data are in X. If the crowed point sets of A and B have empty overlap, then $\Phi(A)$ and $\Phi(B)$ are linear separable in the feature space as shown in above figure. Since every separating hyperplane can classify all the possible input data without misclassification as the three lines in the figure, each of them can be selected as an optimal separating hyperplane.

As pointed out in [12], since one has to make assumptions about the structure of the data(otherwise no generalization is possible), it is natural to assume that two points that are close are likely to belong to the same class, informally, we want similar inputs to lead to similar output[6]. Most classical classification algorithms rely, implicitly or explicitly, on such an assumption(e.g. nearest-neighbors classifiers, and the simplest possible justification for large margins in SVM in [6]). Applying this assumption to the binary pattern recognition problems, it just implies the crowed points of the two classes have an empty overlap, thus the optimal separating hyperplane in the feature space always exists and is not unique.

If the binary pattern recognition problems do not satisfy this assumption, i.e., the two classes have conjunct crowed points, then the optimal separating hyperplane that can separate all the data without misclassification is not available. By this way, in an infinite dimensional feature space relative to a dot product kernel, two classes of data distribute along the different sides of the crowed points, and the best separating hyperplane should pass through the crowed points. We employ the following simple example to illustrate our idea.

Example 3. Suppose we have two tangent ellipses as two classes, thus the tangent point is the conjunct crowed point. If we want to separate them by a line, then clearly the tangent is the best selection. The following figure can explain this example straightforward.

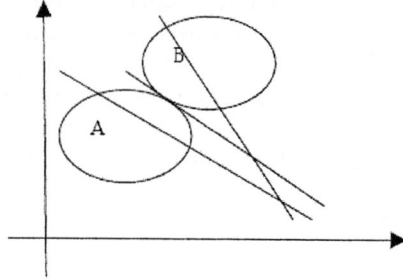

Fig. 2. To separate two tangent ellipses by a line, clearly the tangent is the best selection

Clearly the conjunct points may not be unique, and the number of conjunct points will influence the selection of separating hyperplane. We omit detail discussion on this topic here and will focus on it in detail in another paper.

Acknowledgements

This paper is supported by a Foundation of North China Electric Power University, the National Natural Science Foundation of china(NSFC60473045) and the Natural Science Foundation of Hebei Province (603137)

References

1. Vapnik V. N.: The Nature of Statistical Learning Theory. New York: Springer- Verlag(1995)
2. Vapnik V. N.: Statistical Learning Theory. New York: Wiley(1998)

3. Burges C.: A Tutorial on Support Vector Machines for Pattern Recognition, Data Mining and Knowledge Discovery, 2(2)(1998)121-167
4. Schurmann J.: Pattern Classification: A Unified View of Statistical and Neural Approaches. Wiley, New York(1996)
5. Micchelli C. A.: Algebraic Aspects of Interpolation, Proceedings of Symposia in Applied Mathematics, 36(1986) 81-102
6. Scholkopf B., Smola A. J.: Learning with Kernels, MIT Press, Cambridge, MA(2002)
7. Smola A. J.: Regression Estimation with Support Vector Learning Machines, Diplomarbeit, Technische Universitat Munchen(1996)
8. Schoenberg I. J.: Positive Definite Functions on Spheres, Duke Mathematical Journal, 9(1942) 96-108
9. Steinwart I.: On the Influence of the Kernel on the Consistency of Support Vector Machines, Journal of Machine Learning Research 2(2001)67-93
10. Saunders C., Stitson M. O., Weston J., Bottou L., Scholkopf B., and Smola A. J.: Support Vector Machine Reference Manual. Technical Report CSD-TR-98-03, Department of Computer Science, Royal Holloway, University of London, Egham, UK(1998)
11. Chen Degang, He Qiang, Wang Xizhao.: The infinite polynomial kernel for support vector machine, Lecture Notes in Artificial Intelligence 3584(2005): 267-275
12. Matthias Hein, Olivier Bousquet, Bernhard Scholkopf.: Maximal margin classification for metric spaces, Journal of Computer and System Sciences 71(2005)333-359
13. C. A. Micchelli.: Algebraic aspects of interpolation. Proceedings of Symposia in Applied Mathematics 36(1986)81-102

An Edge Detection Method by Combining Fuzzy Logic and Neural Network

Rong Wang, Li-qun Gao, Shu Yang, and Yu-hua Chai

Institute of Information Science & Engineering, Northeastern University, Shen Yang
110004, China
dbdxwangrong@163.com

Abstract. An edge detection method by combining fuzzy logic and neural network is proposed in this paper. First, the distance measures between the feature vector in 4 directions and the six edge prototype vectors for each pixel are taken as input pattern and fed into input layer of the self-organizing competitive neural network. Classifying the type of edge through this network, the thick edge image is obtained. After classification, we utilize the competitive rule to thin the thick edge image in order to get the fine edge image. Finally, the speckle edges are discarded from the edge image, thus the final optimal edge image is got. We compared the edge images obtained from our method with that from Canny's one and Sobel's one in our experiments. The experimental results show that the effect of our method is superior to other two methods and the robusticity of our method is better.

1 Introduction

Because the edges include the most important information in the image, such as the edges which are used for labeling the abrupt points and the points with a significant variation in gray level, and can provide the information of the object's position, so the edge detection plays an important role in applying of image analysis. Edge detection is an important link in computer vision and other image processing, widely used in contour extraction, feature detection and texture analysis. Most previous edge detection techniques used first-order derivative operators [1], such as the Sobel edge operator, the Prewitt edge operator and the Robert edge operator. The Laplacian operator is a second-order derivative operator for functions of two-dimension operators and is used to detect edges at the locations of the zero crossing. However, these points of zero crossing aren't certainly the edge points and can only be determined to be edge points by further detection. Another gradient operator is the Canny operator that is used to determine a class of optimal filters for different types of edges [2], e.g., step edges or ridge edges. A major problem in Canny's work is that a trade-off is emerged between detection and localization: as the scale parameter increases, the detection accuracy increases but the localization accuracy decreases. In order to set the appropriate value for the scale parameter, the noise energy must be known. However, it is not an easy task to locally measure the noise energy because both noise and signal affect the local measure. Many researchers have proposed the statistical or stochastic methods of boundary detection, but these methods don't always perform well since they lack powerful two-dimensional structure knowledge and employ only a single formula to treat different edge patterns [3]. Due to the effects of noise and other factors, all the edge detection methods above may lead a result not satisfied, such as false edge or missing edges, for many complicated actual images.

In recent years, an increasing number of researchers have been involved in research of the subjects of fuzzy logic and neural network in the hope of combining the superiority of fuzzy logic and neural network to achieve a more useful tool for fuzzy information processing [4], [5], [6], [7], [8]. In this paper, a new edge detection method of combining fuzzy logic and neural network is presented. To verify the method proposed in this paper, we compare it with Canny method and Sobel method in the term of images which have no noise and noise respectively. The experimental results show that the effect of our method is superior to that of Canny method and Sobel method.

2 Pixel Edge Classification and Neural Network

Fig.1 shows the 3×3 neighborhood of pixels about the center pixel p_5 as well as the four edge directions which may appear. The bi-directional grey level summed magnitude of differences between p_5 and its neighbors are designated respectively by d_1, d_2, d_3 and d_4 for directions 1, 2, 3 and 4, are shown in Fig.1 and are calculated by,

$$\begin{aligned} d_1 &= |p_1 - p_5| + |p_9 - p_5| \\ d_2 &= |p_2 - p_5| + |p_8 - p_5| \\ d_3 &= |p_3 - p_5| + |p_7 - p_5| \\ d_4 &= |p_4 - p_5| + |p_6 - p_5| \end{aligned} \quad (1)$$

For each pixel in an input image that is not on the outer boundary of the image, we define its four-dimensional feature vector in four directions on its 3×3 neighborhood as $x = (d_1, d_2, d_3, d_4)$.

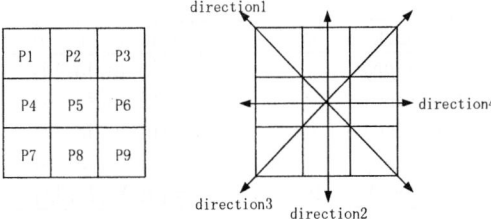

Fig. 1. Pixels and directions in 3×3 neighborhood

Each edge class has a single feature vector of four directional grey level summed magnitudes of differences as far as the low and high values are concerned. According to the feature vector of pixel, we classify pixels into 6 classes (four edge classes, a background class and a speckle edge class). Four typical neighborhood situations are shown in Fig.2. Among them the grey level summed magnitudes of differences of class 1 are 'lo' in direction 1 and 'hi' in directions 2, 3, 4. The summed magnitudes of differences of class 2 are 'lo' in direction 2 and 'hi' in directions 1, 3, 4; the grey level summed magnitudes of differences of class 3 are 'lo' in direction 3 and 'hi' in directions 1, 2, 4; the grey level summed magnitudes of differences of class 4 are 'lo' in direction 4 and 'hi' in directions 1, 2, 3; the background class is for the pixel whose neighborhood has low grey level summed magnitude of differences in the four directions; the speckle edge class is used for pixels on whose neighborhood the change magnitudes in all directions are high.

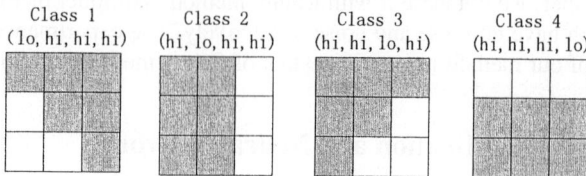

Fig. 2. Situation for typical edge classes

Given a pixel, any neighborhood has a situation that determines a feature vector such as $x = (3, 35, 26, 4)$, of magnitudes of differences in each of the four directions shown in Fig.1. We construct 6 prototype vectors $C_0, \ldots, C_5$ to be the respective centers of the 6 classes (four edge classes, one background class and one speckle edge class). These centers or prototypes for the respective classes have component values 'lo' and 'hi' that represent low and high grey level summed magnitude of differences in the directions indicated. The construction of these class centers are listed in Table 1. The parameters lo and hi are set by the user depending on the image region contrasts and the noise sensitivity desired. For example, lo could be set to a gray level difference of 5 and hi set to a value from 30 to 40. These low and high values decide the prototype vectors $C_0, \ldots, C_5$.

Table 1. The edge classification and their prototype vectors

Class 0 (background)	$C_0 = $ (lo, lo, lo, lo)
Class 1 (edge)	$C_1 = $ (lo, hi, hi, hi)
Class 2 (edge)	$C_2 = $ (hi, lo, hi, hi)
Class 3 (edge)	$C_3 = $ (hi, hi, lo, hi)
Class 4 (edge)	$C_4 = $ (hi, hi, hi, lo)
Class 5 (speckle edge)	$C_5 = $ (hi, hi, hi, hi)

2.1 The Self-organization Competitive Neural Network

Self-organization competitive neural network is a neural network which conducts the network training by no teacher's guiding and has the function of self-organization. Through training itself the network classifies the input pattern automatically. The simple working process of self-organization competitive neural network is that after inputting the pattern vector, the network lets the neurons of output layer start competition according to a rule, and when a neuron winned network lets the connective weights structure to be updated along the direction which can make the winning neuron more sensitive to this pattern. When the network inputs again this pattern or similar pattern, this neuron wins easier. At the same time, the other neurons are restrained and aren't sensitive to this pattern, thus difficult to win. When there are other pattern inputtings, these neurons take part in the hopeful competition again. These characteristics of self-organization competitive neural network make it have high application value in pattern classification.

The neural network proposed in this paper is a self-organization competitive neural network (shown as Fig.3), consisted of two layers of neuron(input layer and competitive layer) and a set of connective weight. There are six neurons in input layer, indicating respectively the distance measures between the feature vector of pixel and the six edge prototype vectors. (u_0 indicates the distance measure from feature vector to background, $u1$ to class 1 edge, $u2$ to class 2 edge, $u3$ to class 3 edge, $u4$ to class 4 edge, $u5$ to speckle edge.) There are six neurons in the competitive layer which correspond respectively to the six edge classes. (C_0 indicates background, C_1 class 1 edge, C_2 class 2 edge, C_3 class 3 edge, C_4 class 4 edge, C_5 speckle edge.)

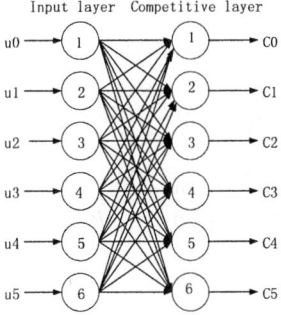

Fig. 3. The competitive neural network

Due to the Euler distance between the feature vector of the pixel and the edge prototype vectors in different images is differ in thousands ways and the near distance in a image may be the far distance in another image, so only upon providing more training samples can we make the network recognize the edge pixels in different type images. In fact, the 'far' or 'near' distance is a fuzzy concept in the given patterns. For this, we propose a 'measure' concept, and the Euler distance between the feature vector of pixel and the edge prototype vector is fuzzified. If the measure approaches 1, it indicates the near distance; if the measure approaches 0, it indicates the far distance.

$$u_i = 1 - \|x - c_i\|/\omega \quad . \tag{2}$$

where, ω is the biggest Euler distance obtained from computing in the image, and the quality of edge detection depends mainly on the parameters lo, hi and ω.

Feeding the preprocessed distance measures into the above self-organization competitive neural network, the network will recognize automatically which edge type the pixel belongs to.

Suppose that the connectional weights of the network are $\{W_{i,j}\}$, $i = 1,2,...,6$, $j = 1,2,...,6$, and the restrictive condition is,

$$\sum_{i=1}^{6} W_{ij} = 1 \qquad (3)$$

and suppose $P_k = (p_1^k, p_2^k, ..., P_6^k)$ is one of the studying patterns, then the input value of the neurons of the competitive layer is,

$$S_j = \sum_{i=1}^{6} W_{ij} p_i^k, \quad i = 1,2,...,6, \quad j = 1,2,...,6 \qquad (4)$$

According to the rule of 'the winner is the king', the neuron corresponding to the maximum value in S_j ($j = 1, 2, ..., 6$) is considered as the 'winner' and its output status is set as 1, while the output status of all the other neurons are set as 0, then the connectional weights connected with the winning neuron are updated by the following equation and the other connectional weights keep unchangeable.

$$\begin{aligned} W_{ij} &= W_{ij} + \Delta W_{ij} \\ \Delta W_{ij} &= \eta * (\frac{p_i^k}{m} - W_{ij}) \end{aligned} \qquad (5)$$

where, η is the studying coefficient, and $0 < \eta < 1$, m is the number of elements with value '1' in the study pattern $P_k = (p_1^k, p_2^k, ..., P_6^k)$.

2.2 The Competitive Rules

After recognizing the edge type of each pixel by the network, a competitive selection is conducted for each edge pixel according to its assigned class. Only the edge pixels that are first classified as edge pixels and then wined in the edge competition, or speckle edge pixels, are mapped as the edge pixels in the new output map, and all other pixels are mapped as background.

Once a pixel is classified as an edge class, it will compare with the two adjacent edge pixels along the edge direction. For these three pixels, only the one with the largest grey level summed magnitude of difference is saved as a white edge, the others are saved as black background, thus the thick edge image got from the self-organization competitive neural network is thinned. These competitive rules are as follows:

If x is class 0 (background), then change pixel to black.
If x is class 1 (edge), then compare this pixel with d_3 value of neighborhood pixels in direction 3.
If it wins, then change it to white (edge), else change to black.

If x is class 2 (edge), then compare this pixel with d_4 value of neighborhood pixels in direction 4.
    If it wins, then change it to white (edge), else change to black.
If x is class 3 (edge), then compare this pixel with d_1 value of neighborhood pixels in direction 1.
    If it wins, then change it to white (edge), else change to black.
If x is class 4 (edge), then compare this pixel with d_2 value of neighborhood pixels in direction 2.
    If it wins, then change it to white (edge), else change to black.
If x is class 5 (speck edge), then change pixel to white (edge).

3 The Realization of the Algorithm of Edge Detection

Because the speckle edge mapped as a white edge pixel is not always an edge, we implement a despeckler that removes isolated single and double edge pixels from the edges after the edge competition have been done. Before the edge detection is done we pretreated image by a smoothing opertator. There are three steps in the edge detection algorithm. First, the feature vector $x = (d_1, d_2, d_3, d_4)$ of each pixel and the distance measures between it and the six prototype vectors (C_0, C_1, C_2, C_3, C_4, C_5) are computed, and the distance measures are fed into the self-organization competitive neural network for edge classification, and the thick edge image is got. Afterwars the edge image obtained is thinned with competitive rules and at last the speckles are removed to get the final edge image.

3.1 Fuzzy Classification

I: set parameters lo and hi.
II: for each pixel in the image,
    compute and save the bi-directional gray level summed magnitudes of differences,
    construct the feature vector x and compute the distance measures between it and the six prototype vectors and feed the distance measures into the neural network,
    the type of the edge of pixel is recognized by the network automatically and the thick edge image is obtained.

3.2 Competition of Edge Strengthening

I: for each pixel in the image,
    if it is edge class, then apply appropriate competition rule and record pixel value,
    if it is background class, then change the pixel as black,
    if it is speckle edge class, then change the pixel as black.

3.3 Despeckling

I: for each pixel in the image,
    If it is isolated single or double speckle, then change the pixel as black.

4 The Experimental Results

The source image used for simulating experiment is shown in Fig.4 (a). All of our experimental results were obtained by detecting every pixel in the image using a 3×3 neighborhood. The appropriate parameters lo and hi must be provided to achieve good results. From the experimental results, we think that the detective result is the best when lo = 5 and hi = 40. The smaller is the hi value, the more sensitive edges and the more noise are produced; whereas the larger is the lo value, the more false edges are produced. We also use Canny method to detect the edges in the source image. In Canny method, we found that a smaller threshold T gives more details and noises, and a smaller σ also gives more details but no noise. So T is the most sensitive. Through experiments, we found that the effect of Canny edge detection method is best when T = 0.04 and σ = 0.6.

Fig. 4. Source image without noise and its simulating results

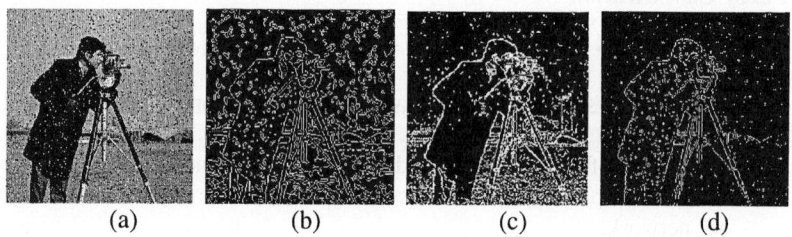

Fig. 5. Source image with noise and its simulating results

Fig.4 (b), Fig.4 (c) and Fig.4 (d) show respectively the best results obtained with Canny edge detection method, our fuzzy neural network edge detection method and Sobel edge detection method. It is can be seen from these figures that the edge image obtained with our method detected many details which are not detected by Canny method and Sobel method, thus having the best effect. The edge image obtained with Sobel method lacks lots of details and its effect is the worst. The effect of Canny method is between our method and Sobel method. Fig.5 (a) shows the image obtained after corruption of the source image by noise (salt & pepper). Fig.5 (b), Fig.5 (c) and Fig.5 (d) show respectively the best results we obtained with Canny method, our method and Sobel method. It is can be seen from these figures, under noisy condition, our method can still get the best edge image, although existed the noise in the edge image. But it has little effect on recognizing the image contour and many details. There are many false edges in the edge image obtained with Canny method which are brought by the noise, making some details can not be recognized. The effect of Sobel method is the worst.It can only detect the edges in the area which has higher contrast, and has many weak edges affecting the recognition effect.

5 Conclusions

We define the gray level summed magnitude of differences in four directions on 3×3 neighborhood of each pixel as a feature vector, construct six edge prototype vectors and take the distance measures between the feature vector and the prototype vectors as inputs and feed them into the self-organization competitive neural network to recognize whether the pixel is the edge, speckle or background to get the thick edge image . The thin edge image is obtained by using the competitive rule in the thick edge image. From the experimental results, it can be seen that the edge detection method proposed in this paper is superior to Canny method and Sobel method, this advantage is more prominent under the noisy condition and the robusticity is better.

References

1. Lily Rui, Liang, Carl G., Looney.: Competitive Fuzzy Edge Detection. Applied Soft Computing, 3 (2003) 123-137.
2. J. Canny.: A Computational Approach to Edge Detection. IEEE Trans, Pattern Anal. Mach. Intell. 8 (6) (1986) 679-687.
3. W. Deng, S.S. Iyengar.: A New Probabilistic Relaxation Scheme and Its Application to Edge Detection. IEEE Trans, Pattern Anal. Mach. Intell. 18 (4) (1996) 432-437.
4. H.S. Wong, L. Guan.: A Neural Learning Approach for Adaptive Image Restoration Using a Fuzzy Model-based Network Architecture. IEEE Trans, Neural Network 12 (3) (2001) 516-531.
5. C.G. Looney.: Nonlinear Rule-based Convolution for Refocusing. Real Time Imaging, 6 (2000) 29-37.
6. H. Maturino-Lozoya, D. Munoz-Rodriguez, F. Jaimes-Romero, H. Tawfik.: Handoff Algorithms Based on Fuzzy Classifiers. IEEE Trans, Vehicular Technol, 49 (6) (2000) 2286-2294.
7. R. Joe. Stanley, Randy Hays Moss.: A Fuzzy-based Histogram Analysis Technique for Skin Lesion Discrimination in Dermatology Clinical Images. Computerized Medical Imaging and Graphics. 27 (2003) 387-396.
8. Lionel Valet, Gilles Mauris.: A Fuzzy Rule-based Interactive Fusion System for Seismic Data Analysis. Information Fusion. 4 (2003) 123-133.

Fast Face Detection Integrating Motion Energy into a Cascade-Structured Classifier

Yafeng Deng, Guangda Su, Jun Zhou, and Bo Fu

Department of Electronic Engineering, Tsinghua University, Beijing, 100084, China
Dyf02@mails.tsinghua.edu.cn

Abstract. In this paper, we propose a fast and robust face detection method. We train a cascade-structured classifier with boosted haar-like features which uses intensity information only. To speed up the process, we integrate motion energy into the cascade-structured classifier. Motion energy can represent moving the extent of the candidate regions, which is used to reject most of the candidate windows and thus accelerates the evaluation procedure. According to the face presence situation, we divide the system state into three modes, and process input images with an intensity detector, or motion integrated dynamic detector, or else keep the pre-results. Since motion energy can be computed efficiently, processing speed is greatly accelerated. Furthermore, without depending on any supposed motion model, the system is very robust in real situations without the limitation of moving patterns including speed and direction.

1 Introduction

Given any static image or an image in a video, face detection is used to determine whether there are faces in the image and, if so, return the number of faces, location and extent of each face [4]. As the necessary first-step of a face recognition system, face detection can also be implemented in video coding, video conferencing, crowd surveillance, and intelligent human computer interfaces [5]. Recently, with the application of face detection in the above-mentioned fields, face detection in video is attracting more attention than ever before. Compared to static face detection, face detection in video must be fast with less computational complexity, not only because the whole system must run in real-time but also because other tasks which are more complex must be able to run while face detection is used.

Many works have been proposed to detect face in video. Viola et al. [1] proposed a framework for rapid object detection, which can process 15 frames per second. Their work realized the first robust real-time face detection system in the world. But their approach detects faces for every frame without using the temporal information, and thus they cost much more in computational resources than is necessary.

Some works including [6], [11] have made use of temporal information to predict the detection parameters to narrow the searching areas and scales and thus accelerate the algorithm. But there are still some problems. First, all works based on prediction will suppose a temporal model of motion pattern, and if the real face movements do not fit the model, the algorithm will not work well. Second, most of the approaches can not deal with situations such as new faces appearing, faces intersecting, sudden face motion etc. Camera translation is another situation most of the previous methods can not process.

In this paper, we concentrate on a new approach to detect face in video, which is not only fast with low computational complexity, but also robust without limitation by the moving patterns of faces.

If a face appears or moves, evident change will occur at the new position of the face. Without introducing limitation to the moving patterns of the face, we use variable named motion energy to represent the moving extent of the candidate regions. We integrate a motion energy classifier into a cascade-structured classifier proposed in [1] to evaluate the candidate windows. (In this paper, the cascade-structured classifier integrated with motion energy is curtailed as CSCIME classifier for convenience.) The motion energy classifier can be computed efficiently with an integral image of a motion image, and can reject most of the candidate windows. Thus the computational complexity of the system is greatly reduced.

Considering such situations as a static background or still faces presenting, and in order to avoid the error of a departing face being kept in the following frames, we divide the state of the system into three. The three states are decided by pre-detection results, and switch between each other internally. According to the different states of the system, we use different processing methods to deal with the input images.

The approach does not depend on any supposed model, and thus is out of the limitation of moving patterns including speed, direction, and new faces appearing. The algorithm is very suitable for the real situation, and the implemented system has achieved an acceptable performance in a dynamic face recognition system and also in a verification system used to check on work attendance.

The remainder of the paper is organized as follows: Section 2 introduces the framework of the whole system. The intensity detector is presented in Section 3. The detail of the dynamic detector is described in Section 4. Section 5 provides the experimental results and conclusions are given in Section 6.

2 System Framework

The state of the system is divided into three: face presenting state, background state, and temporary state, which is the transitory state between the first two. The three states are decided by pre-detection results, and the system can switch among the three

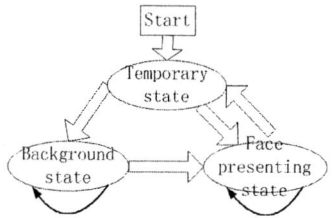

Fig. 1. Switching flowchart of system state

states internally. Figure 1 shows the switching procedure of the system states. First, we set the state of the system as a temporary state, and detect the whole image. If there is any face appearing, the state will transform to the face presenting state, and if no face appears, we set the new state as a background state. With the face presenting state, if any face is detected, the state is kept, and if no face is detected, the state will change to the temporary state. With the background state, if any face is detected, the state will transform to the face presenting state, otherwise, the background state is kept.

As shown in Figure 2, we use different processing methods to deal with different states. There are three processing modes: detecting with intensity detector, detecting with dynamic detector, and keeping pre-frame results. If the current state is the temporary state, we detect the whole image with the intensity detector which uses intensity information only. The intensity detector is constructed based on Viola et al.'s work, and searches the whole image thoroughly to evaluate all potential positions of the face. It is very sensitive to appearing faces but costs much in time. If the current state is the face presenting state, we detect the image with the dynamic detector, which uses motion information to reject that part of the potential regions which do not change evidently. The approach is very effective, and most of the potential rectangles are rejected with simple operations which thus greatly accelerate the speed of the whole system. Considering that with the background state, there is the situation that the background is static for a long time and no evident change occurs in the whole image, we process the background state in two different modes. If evident change occurs, we detect the image with the dynamic detector like processing the face presenting state and if no evident change occurs, we keep the frame results as pre-frame.

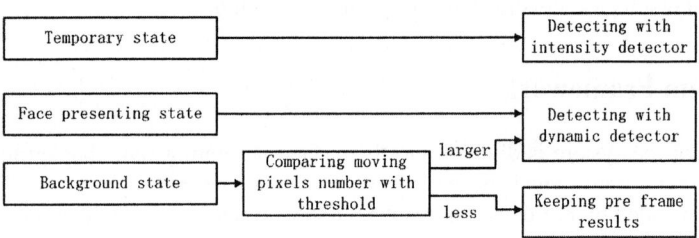

Fig. 2. Three processing modes

The system can switch among the three states internally, and process each state in the appropriate mode.

3 Intensity Detector

The intensity detector used in this paper is based on the method developed by Viola et al. [1]. Viola et al. [1] proposed a framework for robust and rapid object detection which achieved an equivalent accuracy of the state-of-the-art results [2] while being distinguished from others in its ability to detect faces extremely rapidly.

3.1 Cascade-Structured Classifier

Like Viola et al. [1], we trained a cascade-structured classifier as Figure 3 shows.

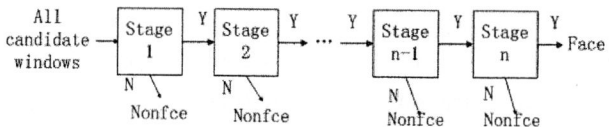

Fig. 3. Cascade-structured classifier

3.2 Candidate Weak Classifiers and Training Methods

We use the Real AdaBoost algorithm[8] to train every stage classifier. Domain-partitioning weak hypotheses are used to build weak classifiers. To minimize the upper limit on training errors, each weak classifier candidate is computed from the weighted histograms of face and non-face on several disjoint blocks, and to avoid the value in the histograms that might be very small or even zero, the weak classifiers prediction is smoothed as [8]:

$$h(x) = \frac{1}{2}\ln(\frac{W_{+1}^j + \varepsilon}{W_{-1}^j + \varepsilon}), \qquad (1)$$

where ε is a small positive constant, and W_{+1}^j, W_{-1}^j are the weighted histograms of features of face and non-face examples in block j.

To save training time, we use weight trimming method to select examples with larger weight to train while neglecting the samples with smaller weight [7].

3.3 Fast Feature Computation

Like Viola et al. [1], we use four types of haar-like feature to build the feature pool. The feature can be computed efficiently with an integral image. The haar-like features can be rescaled easily by avoiding calculating a pyramid of images and thus greatly accelerating the detector. For each scale level, we rescale the features and record the relative coordinate of the rescaled features to the top-left of the integral image in the look-up-table (LUT). After looking up the value of the rescaled rectangle's coordinate, we calculate features with a relative coordinate. Like Viola, we use image variance to correct lighting, which can be obtained using integral images of both the original image and the image squared. Rescaling needs to round rescaled coordinates to the nearest integer, which would degrade the performance of Viola's features [3]. Like R. Lienhart [3], we normalize the features by acreage, and thus reduce the rounding error.

4 Dynamic Detector

4.1 Motion Image

Considered to be of computational complexity, we use frame differencing of two images to model motion information. But a change of background can be introduced not only by the sudden and gradual change in illumination but also by image changes due to small camera displacements and motion in parts of the background [10]. To avoid such noise, we model the background image in a Gaussian model and use a threshold to acquire the motion image. At time t, there is a recording image $I_r(t)$ to record the pre-situation. Suppose that the intensity of pixel (x, y) in image $I_r(t)$ is $I_r(x, y, t)$. Note that the recording image is not always the pre-frame of the current processing image, and the rules of refreshing the recording image are described at Section 4.4. Set that the current input image at the time t is I(t), and the intensity of pixel (x, y) in image I(t) is I(x, y, t). Let D(t) be a binary image sequence indicating regions of motion which are called motion images. The value of pixel (x, y) in motion image at time t is defined as:

$$D(x,y,t) = \begin{cases} 1 & if \, |I(x,y,t) - I_r(x,y,T)| \geq \gamma, \\ 0 & others \end{cases} \quad (2)$$

where γ is the threshold to avoid background noise mentioned above. Figure 4 shows an example of the input image, the difference image, and the motion image. Difference image is the intensity difference between the input image and the recording image.

Fig. 4. An example of input image, difference image, and motion image

4.2 Motion Energy of Candidate Region

Motion image indicates the pixels which have shifted out of the change range of noise, but what we are concerned with is which candidate rectangle region has shifted up to the extent of the moving face. Suppose an image rectangle is specified by r(l, t, w, h), where l/t is the left/top and w/h is the width/height of the rectangle. We use the number of the moving pixels in the candidate rectangle region to represent the moving extent of the region which is called motion energy. To make the motion energy invariant to the region acreage, we normalize it with region acreage. Finally motion energy of candidate region r(l,t,r,b) is defined as:

$$E(l,t,r,b,t) = \frac{\sum_{y=t}^{b}\sum_{x=l}^{r} D(x,y,t)}{(r-l+1)*(b-t+1)}, \quad (3)$$

which can be computed efficiently with the integral image of the motion image.

4.3 Cascade-Structured Classifier Integrated with Motion Energy (CSCIME Classifier)

Motion energy indicates the moving extent of each candidate rectangle, which can be used to evaluate the moving state of the region. We set the motion energy classifier as:

$$H_m(x) = \begin{cases} 1 & if \quad E(x) > \theta \\ 0 & otherwise \end{cases}, \quad (4)$$

where $E(x)$ is the motion energy of candidate rectangle image x, and θ is the threshold. Because only part of the candidate windows can pass the motion energy classifier, we integrate it into a cascade-structured classifier to build a cascade-structured classifier integrated with motion energy (CSCIME classifier). Since a motion energy classifier can remove many candidate windows with one simple operation, it is reasonable to place it at the first stage. Figure 5 shows the structure of the CSCIME classifier. The cascade-structured intensity classifier is constructed as Figure 3 showed previously.

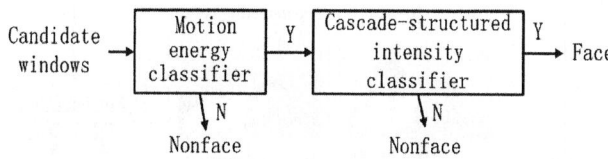

Fig. 5. Cascade-structured classifier integrated with motion energy

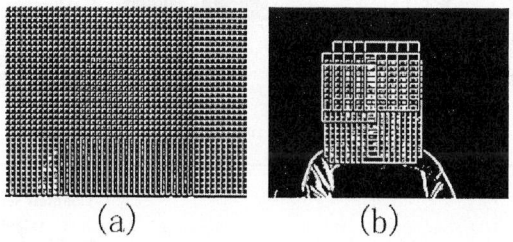

Fig. 6. Comparing candidate windows sent to motion energy classifier and that passing motion energy classifier

In most situations, the motion energy classifier at the first stage of the CSCIME classifier can reject most parts of the candidate window. Figure 6 (a) shows the evaluated windows being sent to the motion energy classifier, and Figure 6 (b) shows the windows passing the motion energy classifier which will be evaluated by the following cascade-structured intensity classifier. Obviously, the motion energy classifier accelerates the evaluation procedure by rejecting most of the candidate windows.

4.4 Dynamic Detector

If the current state is the face presenting state, or evident change occurs in the background state, we will detect the image with the dynamic detector. First, we obtain the motion image by image difference and threshold. As shown in Figure 7, if the current state is the face presenting state, we divide faces presented in pre-image into still faces and moving faces according to their motion energy in current motion image. The still faces are kept and merged in the final results. For moving faces, according to their motion energy, we divide the whole image into a thoroughly searching region and a coarsely searching region. For each moving face, we get its thoroughly searching region with the same center by enlarging it with the ratio:

$$R_e = 1 + \sqrt{E(r)} * \beta, \qquad (5)$$

where $E(r)$ is the motion energy of the face and β is the controlling parameter.

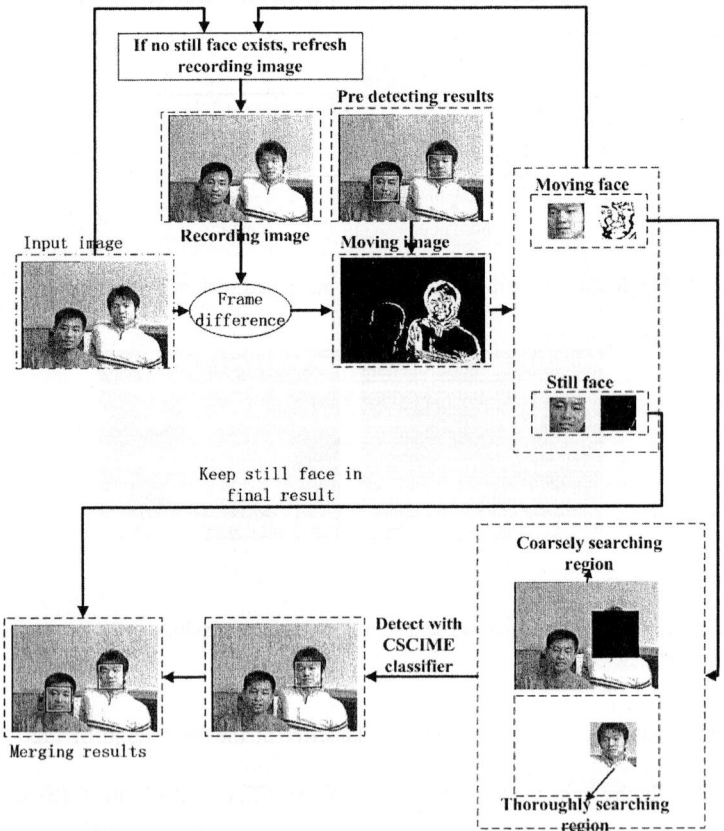

Fig. 7. Procedure of processing the face presenting state by dynamic detector

All the thoroughly searching regions are merged to build a final thoroughly searching region and the other part of the image is set to a coarsely searching region. The thoroughly searching region is searched in a refined step (step = 1.2 in the experiments) and the coarsely searching region is searched in a coarse step (step = 1.5 in the experiments). All candidate windows of both regions are evaluated by the CSCIME classifier.

If the current state is the background state, we will get the motion image and judge if the ratio of moving pixels in the whole image is larger than the threshold η. If the moving ratio is less than η, we regard it that no evident change occurs to the current image and return without further operation. Only if the moving ratio of the whole image is larger than η do we process the image using the dynamic detector with coarsely searching step as we process the coarsely searching region in the face presenting state.

Notice that the recording image is not always the pre-frame image. Due to the face presenting state with still faces, and the background state without evident change, we keep the recording image without change. This simple insight can avoid such situations where continuous small shifts occurring in continuous frames will accumulate to a large difference, and if the detector refreshes the recording image at every frame, it will not be sensitive to the small shifts and so will keep the detection results of the pre-frame only. But after several frames, an error will occur because a large difference has occurred to the image by the accumulating small ones.

In the dynamic detector, three integral images are used. The integral image of the input image and the squared input image are used to accelerate the cascade-structured intensity classifier, and the integral image of the motion image is used to compute the motion energy and evaluate the windows using the motion energy classifier. Using the integral image, the motion energy can be computed efficiently, and thus the performance of the whole system is very efficient at computational complexity.

5 Experiment Results

We use 8,466 original frontal faces to create 20,000 face patterns with random rotating, shifting, and mirroring, while 10,000 non-face samples which passed all prior stages are used to train the current stage which is called bootstrap. All the samples are resized to 24×24. With the training algorithm for building a cascade detector [1], we obtain a cascade-structured classifier with 15 stages. Due to each stage in training, the hit rate is no less than 0.9995, and the false alarm rate is no more than 0.2.

After reference to a large number of experiments, parameters of the dynamic detector are set as follows: γ in Equation (2) is set to 14, θ in Equation (4) is set to 0.35, β in Equation (5) is set to 1.2 and threshold η deciding if evident change occurs to the image is set to 0.037. All the following experiments are based on the above parameters.

The proposed algorithm has been implemented on a P4 2.53 GHz PC, and the inputs are 360×270 pixel images. In order to get the detection ratio and speed of the system, we test it in a real situation. The system is tested on ten persons in 16 videos which include various motion styles and degrees of movement. There are in all 4,516 images with

6,478 faces. The poses of the faces are limited to the following range: out-of-plane rotations in [-20, 20], up-down rotations in [-20, 20], and the in-plane rotations in [-10, 10]. The detection ratio is about 99% at false alarm 1.34E-7. Using the motion energy classifier, 60%~95% of the whole candidate windows are rejected by the dynamic detector. The speed of the system is about 6~22ms, which is about 2.6~7 times the speed of the system using the intensity detector to process all the frames. If there is only background in the input, the speed will be about 2ms. The speed of the system depends on the size of the face and the change extent of the motion image.

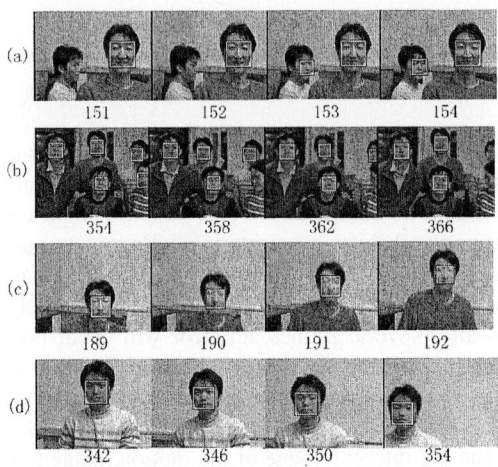

Fig. 8. Examples of detected faces in special situation

The approach is not limited by the motion patterns of the faces. Shown as Figure 8 (a), when a face newly appears in the image, the dynamic detector notices the change of the new face region, and finds the new face. Multi-face detection results are shown in Figure 8 (b). Shown as Figure 8 (c), if the face moves suddenly, which might be lost by the tracker in others' work, our detector can detect the face exactly. When the camera is moving, it can also work, but the speed descends, because most of the candidate regions are processed. Figure 8 (d) shows an example. The numbers under each image are the order of the image in the video.

The system is very robust in real situations, and we have implemented the approach to construct a three-route face detection system which is used in a dynamic face recognition system and a verification system used to check on work attendance. Running on a P4 2.53 GHz PC, with the face presenting state, the three-route system speed is about 40~80 ms, costing 50~80% of the CPU computational resource.

6 Conclusions

In this paper, we have suggested a fast and robust face detection algorithm in video. With motion image and a cascade-structured classifier integrated with motion energy, most of the candidate windows are rejected and computational complexity is greatly reduced. Furthermore, the algorithm does not suppose the model of moving patterns, so no matter how the faces move, it can work well. Experimental results show that newly appearing faces, multi-faces, suddenly moving faces and faces in a moving camera can all be detected.

The method is implemented on a PC, and the performance implies that it is very suitable for actual applications.

References

1. P. Viola and M. Jones, "Robust real time object detection", IEEE ICCV Workshop on Statistical and Computational Theories of Vision, Vancouver, Canada. July 13, 2001.
2. H. Rowley, S. Baluja, and T. Kanade, "Neural network-based face detection", IEEE Patt. Anal. Mach. Intell, volume 20, pp. 22-38, 1998.
3. R. Lienhart, A. Kuranov and V. Pisarevsky, "Empirical analysis of detection cascades of boosted classifiers for rapid object detection", DAGM'03, 25th Pattern Recognition Symposium, pp. 297-304, 2003.
4. Ming-Hsuan Yang, David Kriegman, and Narendra Ahuja, "Detecting Faces in Images: A Survey", IEEE Transactions on Pattern Analysis and Machine Intelligence (PAMI), vol. 24, no. 1, pp. 34-58, 2002.
5. E. Hjelm and B.K. Low, "Face Detection: A Survey", Computer Vision and Image Understanding, vol. 83, no. 3, pp. 236-274, Sept. 2001.
6. K. Mikolajczyk, R. Choudhury, and C.Schmid, "Face detection in a video sequence - a temporal approach", Computer Vision and Pattern Recognition, December 2001.
7. J. Friedman, T. Hastie and R. Tibshirani, "Additive logistic regression : a statistical view of boosting", Technical Report, Stanford University, 1998.
8. E. Schapire and Y. Singer, "Improved boosting algorithms using confidence-rated predictions", Proceedings of the Eleventh Annual Conference on Computational Learning Theory, pp. 80-91, 1998.
9. S.Z. Li, Z.Q. Zhang, H. Shum, and H.J. Zhang, "FloatBoost learning for classification", NIPS 15, December 2002.
10. Elgammal, R. Duraiswami, D. Harwood and L. S. Davis, "Background and Foreground Modeling using Non-parametric Kernel Density Estimation for Visual Surveillance", Vol 90, No. 7, Proceedings of the IEEE, July 2002.
11. S. McKenna, S. Gong, and J. Collins, "Face tracking and pose representation", British Machine Vision Conference, Edinburgh, 1996.

Adaptive Online Multi-stroke Sketch Recognition Based on Hidden Markov Model

Zhengxing Sun, Wei Jiang, and Jianyong Sun

State Key Lab for Novel Software Technology, Nanjing University, 210093, Nanjing
szx@nju.edu.cn

Abstract. This paper presents a novel approach for adaptive online multi-stroke sketch recognition based on Hidden Markov Model (HMM). The method views the drawing sketch as the result of a stochastic process that is governed by a hidden stochastic model and identified according to its probability of generating the output. To capture a user's drawing habits, a composite feature combining both geometric and dynamic characteristics of sketching is defined for sketch representation. To implement the stochastic process of online multi-stroke sketch recognition, multi-stroke sketching is modeled as an HMM chain while the strokes are mapped as different HMM states. To fit the requirement of adaptive online sketch recognition, a variable state-number determining method for HMM is also proposed. The experiments prove both the effectiveness and efficiency of the proposed method.

1 Introduction

Sketching is a natural input mode to help us convey ideas and guide our thinking process both by aiding short-term memory and by helping to make abstract problems more concrete [1]. Numerous researchers have been working on the subject of sketch recognition for many years either as a natural input modality [2][3][4] or to recognize composite sketches [5][6][7]. They can be mainly classified into two categories: feature-based and graph-based. Feature-based methods make use of some local or global features of sketchy shapes for sketch recognition. For example, Rubine [3] defined a gesture characterized by a set of eleven geometric attributes and two dynamic attributes. Fonseca et al [5] proposed a method of symbol recognition using fuzzy logic based on a number of rotation invariant global features. As one of the most prominent approaches to object representation and matching, graph-based methods have been recently applied to hand-drawn pattern recognition problems, such as in [6][7], where sketch recognition is formulated as a graph isomorphism problem. However, the poor efficiency of these recognition engines is always frustrating, especially for the newly added users and the multi-stroke sketchers. The difficulty comes from the fact that sketching is usually informal, inconsistent and ambiguous both in intra-person and inter-person settings in a given situation. To capture a user's sketching habit, adaptive sketch recognition is required [8], where the recognition engine should be trainable and adaptable to a particular user's drawing styles, especially for the multi-stroke sketchy shapes.

Obviously, one solution for adaptive sketch recognition is to construct appropriate classifiers based on machine learning. In our previous researches, we have developed an adaptive sketch recognition method based on incremental SVM learning [9]. It can actively analyze the users' incremental data, and can largely reduce the workload of artificial labeling and the classifier's training time. While it has been proven to be both effective and efficient in our experiments, it can still deal with only single-stroke sketches since the dimension of feature vectors of SVM must be fixed for all shapes.

Hidden Markov Model (HMM) is one of the most successful stochastic modeling tools that have been used in the analysis of non-stationary time series [10]. It has been used with great success in the stochastic modeling of speech [10][11] for years. In recent years, it has also been widely used in handwriting recognition [12][13][14]. In this paper, we will present our experiments in adaptive online multi-stroke sketch recognition in terms of HMM, where we view the drawing pattern as the result of a stochastic process that is governed by a hidden stochastic model and identified according to its probability of generating the output, inspired by its success in speech recognition and handwriting recognition.

The rest of the paper is organized as follows: in Section 2, the principle of our method of adaptive online multi-stroke sketch recognition based on HMM is introduced in detail, including feature representation for multi-stroke sketchy shape, modeling multi-stroke sketching with HMM and determination of HMM state-number for adaptive sketch recognition. Some experiment results are evaluated in Section 3 and conclusions are given in the final section.

2 Adaptive Sketch Recognition Based on Hidden Markov Model

2.1 Feature Representation for Multi-stroke Sketching

There have been many features used for representing the characteristics of a sketchy shape, including "Rubine features" [3], "turning function" [8], "curvature" and "pen speed" [6], "normalized curvature" [12], "centroidal radius" [5], "intersection type" and "number of strokes" [7], and so on. Some of them are prominent in describing the local characteristics of graphical symbols, such as "intersection type" and "number of strokes"; some are outstanding in outlining the global structure of symbols, such as "curvature"; and some may be only adaptable to simple-structural graphics or one-stroke drawn symbols, such as "Rubine features" and "turning function".

During our research experiments [1][7][8][9], we have realized that the sketchy shape in multi-stroke sketch recognition is closely related to both the symbol structures and peoples' drawing habits. That is to say, features used to represent sketches must include both the geometrical features of symbols and the dynamic features of a user's drawing. Accordingly, we consider the features selected for online multi-stroke sketch recognition must satisfy the following three criteria:

1. the features must contain both geometric (spatial) and dynamic (temporal) characteristics of a sketchy shape,
2. the features must be able to represent the spatial relationships between strokes, and

3. the features do not need to depict too much detailed local information of the symbols.

To satisfy these criteria, we define a composite feature in a seven-dimension vector, as shown in Table 1, which combines a few geometrical and dynamic features often used in graphics recognition, such as "centroidal radius", "curvature", "speed" and their means and standard variances. Each of them is briefly described as follows: "Centroidal radius" is the cumulated distances between every point in each of the strokes and the centroid of the graphical symbol. It can describe the characters of an engineering sketch. In our experiments, we choose only 20 points that are uniformly distributed on each of the strokes. "Pen speed" represents the ratio of distance between the current point and the previous point to the time spent during drawing the two points. "Curvature" indicates the cosine of the corner angle at the current point between two lines connected respectively to the previous point and the next point. In addition, we define a "pen-direction" with the slope of a virtual line, which connects the end-point of the previous stroke to the start-point of the current stroke, as a one-dimension vector to reflect the tendency of pen-movement between two continuous strokes.

Table 1. Component of our Composite Feature

Feature	Feature Description	Feature Characteristics	
f_1	Mean of centroid-radius	Global	Geometric
f_2	Standard deviation of centroid-radius	Global	Geometric
f_3	Mean of all pen speeds	Global	Dynamic
f_4	Standard deviation of all pen speeds	Global	Dynamic
f_5	Mean of all curvatures	Global	Geometric
f_6	Standard deviation of all curvatures	Global	Geometric
f_7	Pen-direction between two continuous stokes	Local	Dynamic

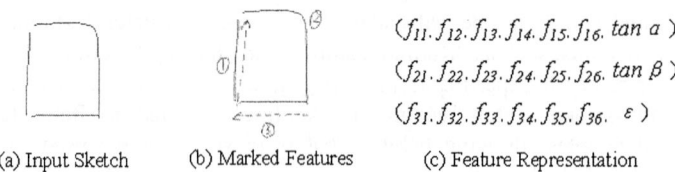

(a) Input Sketch   (b) Marked Features   (c) Feature Representation

$(f_{11}, f_{12}, f_{13}, f_{14}, f_{15}, f_{16}, \tan \alpha)$
$(f_{21}, f_{22}, f_{23}, f_{24}, f_{25}, f_{26}, \tan \beta)$
$(f_{31}, f_{32}, f_{33}, f_{34}, f_{35}, f_{36}, \varepsilon)$

Fig. 1. An example of the definition of our composite feature

During the training and recognition stage, we extract combined features from each of the strokes. The seventh feature is a variable vector according to the stroke type. If the stroke is not the last stroke of the sketch, the seventh feature is the "pen-direction". On the contrary, the seventh feature is the perimeter ratio of the sketch to its closure. Fig. 1 illustrates the definition of our composite feature. Fig. 1(a) shows a sketch drawn by a user. Fig. 1(b) indicates that a sketch is composed of three strokes, where the left dashed arrow represents the "pen direction" between the first stroke and the second, the bottom dashed arrow represents the "pen direction" between the second stroke and the third, and their elevations are α and β respectively. The perimeter ratio of the sketch to its closure is defined as ε. The vector representation of the sketch by combined feature is shown in Fig. 1(c).

2.2 Modeling Multi-stroke Drawing with a Hidden Markov Model

In Hidden Markov Models, the observed pattern is viewed as the result of a stochastic process that is governed by a hidden stochastic model. Each stochastic model represents a different class pattern capable of producing the observed output. The goal is to identify the model that has the highest probability of generating the output. One aspect that distinguishes Hidden Markov Models is their strong temporal organization; processes are considered to be the result of time-sequenced state transitions in the hidden model and the expectation of a particular observation is dictated by the current state in the model and (usually) the previous state.

In online sketch recognition, drawing sketches, especially drawing multi-stroke sketches, can be regarded as a time-sequenced process. Different users have different drawing styles. The input sketches for the same shape are quite different from user to user (e.g., when drawing a multi-stroke sketch, some users like to draw it in one sequence while others like to draw it in another), and even from time to time. Therefore, Hidden Markov Models can be used to model different sketches and they can easily represent the user's drawing styles.

The Hidden Markov Model topology used in pattern recognition can be divided into two categories: the chain topology and the network topology. HMM chain is a simple structure. It is easy to implement and is widely used in recognizing simple symbols, e.g. gesture recognition. An HMM network is constructed by grouping and interconnecting HMM chains and is largely used in recognizing handwritten characters [14]. To date, there has been no serious study or guidance in the use of HMM in sketch recognition, and it is the first time that we have used HMM in multi-stroke sketch recognition. In this paper, we have selected the simple HMM chain topology, as shown in Fig. 2, because it has been shown to be successful in speech and handwriting recognition.

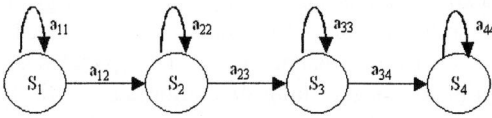

Fig. 2. Adaptive Hidden Markov Model Topology

According to the characteristics of the drawing sketch, the position and structure of the current stroke is usually dependent on the previous stroke, and the position and structure of the next stroke is dependent on the current stroke. We assume that the stroke of one sketch drawn by a user is only correlated with the previous stroke and the next stroke. Therefore, in our approach, we use a first-order left-to-right HMM chain, as shown in Fig. 2, to model each sketch. It is strictly causal: the current state depends only upon previous states. The experiments in handwriting recognition showed that this topology leads to high recognition accuracy.

In the training stage, we extract all composite features from each of the strokes and use the method mentioned in the previous section to determine the HMM state-number and some other parameters. Models are trained using the well-known iterative segmental training method based on Viterbi decoding. The transition probabilities indicate the relationships between strokes. The HMM chain can represent the user's drawing habit very well.

In the recognition stage, the recognizer calculates the probabilities using the trained HMM and returns the recognition results in the sequence of probabilities from high to low to the user.

2.3 HMM State-Number Determination for Adaptive Sketch Recognition

HMM needs enough free parameters to accommodate complexity of target patterns and to represent properties of the patterns. However, in practice, available training samples are usually limited, so it is often difficult to obtain enough free parameters. In our approach, we focus on one design parameter: the number of states in the HMM.

The number of HMM states is an important design parameter. For instance, a state could correspond to a certain phonetic event in a sketch recognition system. Thus, in modeling complex patterns, the number of states should be increased accordingly. When there are insufficient numbers of states, the discrimination power of the HMM is reduced, since more than one signal should be modeled on one state. On the other hand, the excessive number of states can generate the over-fitting problem when the number of training samples is insufficient compared to that of the model parameters.

There are two approaches to determining the HMM state-number used in handwriting recognition. The first is using a fixed state-number, which means using the same HMM state-number while training each category of samples. The second is using a variable state-number, which means the handwritten characters are divided into sub-components according to some given criterion (usually they are divided by strokes). Each subcomponent is modeled by one single HMM state.

Neither of the two methods mentioned above is fit for online multi-stroke sketch recognition because sketch has its own characteristics compared with handwritten character. First, the spatial relationships between strokes of a given sketch are more complex than that of the handwritten character. If we use a fixed state-number, we need to segment the sketch into subcomponents. The spatial relationships between strokes, which contain important sketching style information, will be broken, and the recognizer cannot capture enough information to represent the user's sketching habits. Obviously, the recognition accuracy will have high sensitivity to the segmentation process. Second, a number of standard character databases are present. In addition, in the handwritten characters are some fixed, predefined and well-known graphic objects among writers and readers, which have strict definition for strokes and stroke-sequence, so we can analyze all characters in the standard character databases and obtain the number of subcomponents, which are often used in different characters. In sketch recognition, there is no such standard database, so we cannot analyze all of the sketches and enumerate all of the constitutive subcomponents of sketches, and we cannot determine the state's number according to the number of subcomponents.

As mentioned above, we must find a new approach to determine the number of HMM states in multi-stroke sketch recognition. Although the sketches drawn by different users are very different from each other, they are all drawn stroke by stroke, which are then joined one by one. The stroke-number of one given sketch is different from every other among different sketching styles. Even if the numbers of strokes are the same, the structure of each stroke will be different from every other. Stroke is a natural representative of a user's sketching styles. The recognition performance will be upgraded if we make better use of the information contained in these strokes. In this paper, we proposed an adaptive HMM based on a variable state-number number for the purpose of generating a description of a multi-stroke sketch. In this approach, the number of HMM states is determined by the structural decomposition of the target pattern. Sketch is structurally simplified as a sequence of strokes.

The main idea behind the proposed approach is to use a single HMM state to model each stroke. While collecting samples, the recognition system will automatically store the stroke-number of each sample (which is defined to be *Snumber*). Before we train the HMM, we analyze the stored numbers and find out the maximum emergent number (which is defined to be *Tnumber*) for each category of sketches. We consider *TNumber* to be the state-number of HMM, because the samples corresponding to *TNumber* are frequently drawn by the user and they can represent the user's drawing habit. Then we train the HMM as follows:

i). If *Tnumber* > *SNumber*, we segment the last stroke of the sketch into *TNumber-SNumber+1* segments on average, and then model the remaining strokes and these segments to *TNumber* HMM states.

ii). If *Tnumber* < *SNumber*, we group the last *SNumber-TNumber+1* strokes to one virtual stroke, and then model the remaining strokes and the virtual stroke to *TNumber* HMM states.

Using this proposed approach to determine the HMM state-number, the inner structure of the HMMs is easily altered according to different users. Moreover, the approach does not need too much intervention by the user. After the user has become familiar with the input environment and the structure of sketches they usually draw, the user will draw one given sketch almost in the same style, and the stroke-number will become equal to *TNumber*. The recognizer will then seldom segment the sketch drawn by the user. Compared with other approaches, our approach is fit for online multi-stroke sketch recognition.

3 Experiment Results and Evaluation

The purpose of our experiments is to evaluate the effectiveness and efficiency of the recognition approach we have proposed above. In order to evaluate our proposed state-number determination approach, we carry out experiments for comparing the performance of variable state-number with that of fixed state-number. We also perform experiments to evaluate the performance of an adaptive online sketch recognition method based on our designed HMM. Our experiment environment is Pentium 4 1.6G CPU, 256MB memory, Windows 2000, Visual C++ 6.0.

By analyzing users' input strokes and some familiar graphics-based design software, we have set 9 classes of sketch, including straight line, arc, ellipse, poly-line 1, poly-line 2, poly-line 3, triangle, quadrangle and pentagon, as shown in Fig. 3. These are the most commonly used classes of sketch in the sketching process.

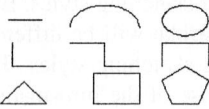

Fig. 3. All Nine Classes of Sketches

For the data collection, we collected two users' samples of these sketches. When using some present sketch recognition systems, the users are forced to draw only one stroke for simple shapes. However, a successful system should not restrict the user's drawing styles. For comparison, we asked the first user to draw these sketches in one-stroke and the second user to draw these sketches freely. The numbers of each class of sample are listed in Table 2.

Table 2. Number of samples collected from User 1 and User 2

Types	Straight Line	Arc	Poly-line 1	Poly-line 2	Poly-line 3
User 1	801	800	800	800	800
User 2	811	820	798	851	802
Types	Triangle	Quadrangle	Pentagon	Ellipse	Total
User 1	800	800	800	801	7,203
User 2	848	846	817	815	7,408

3.1 Comparison Between the Fixed and Variable State-Number HMM

In the previous section, we considered that variable state-number HMM is better than fixed state-number HMM in sketch recognition. The experiment in this section will confirm the conclusion. Because sketches, which have a greater number of strokes can easily lead to a multi-drawing-style, we choose polygon samples drawn by User 2 for the experiment. From the samples drawn by the second user, we obtain their drawing habits in the form of stroke-sequences, as shown in Fig. 4.

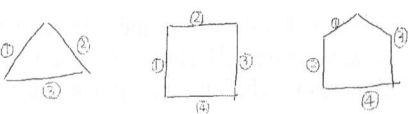

Fig. 4. Polygon Drawn by User 2

In the fixed state-number experiment, given the state-number to be 1, 2, 3 and 4, we obtain four different recognition precisions. In the variable state-number experiment, we use the state-number determining approach mentioned above to determine the state-number (in this experiment, the numbers of states are 2, 3 and 4) for each class.

Fig. 5. shows the result of our experiments. As we can see, the red pentagram corresponds to the precision of triangle recognition (using variable state-number), while the green one is for quadrangle and the blue one is for pentagon. The other points represent results for the fixed state-number experiment.

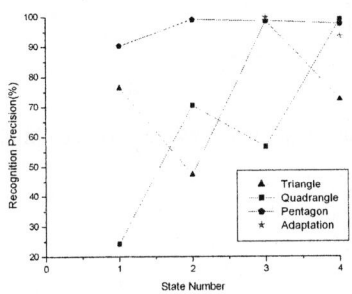

Fig. 5. Comparison of precisions of the fixed and variable state-number HMM

From Fig. 5., we can see that the recognition precision of different classes depends on state-number when a fixed state-number approach has been used. For one given fixed state-number, the recognition precisions of different classes of sketch are fluctuant and lower at the same time. Comparatively, when using a variable state-number approach, the recognition precisions of each class are nearly stable. Accordingly, we make a conclusion that a variable state-number approach can adapt different drawing styles, and it is better than a fixed state-number approach in on-line multi-stroke sketch recognition.

3.2 Performance of Adaptive HMM-Based Sketch Recognition

In this experiment, 60% of the first user's samples are used for training, while 75% of the second user's are used for training, and the remaining samples are used for testing. We divide the samples into 30 training sets for each user. The first five training sets contain 1%, 1%, 2%, 3% and 3% of the total samples of each user. Each of the remaining 25 training sets contains 3.6% of the total samples of each user. The experiment results are shown in Fig. 6.

From Fig. 6., we can see that our proposed method obtains a high performance; in multi-stroke sketching (for sketches drawn by the second user), the recognition precision reaches 95% after the second training, while in one-stroke sketching (sketches drawn by the first user), the recognition precision reaches 95% after the seventh training. The results show that our proposed adaptive online sketch recognition method based on HMM has a good performance in adaptation to user's drawing habits, especially under multi-stroke sketch and small training sets.

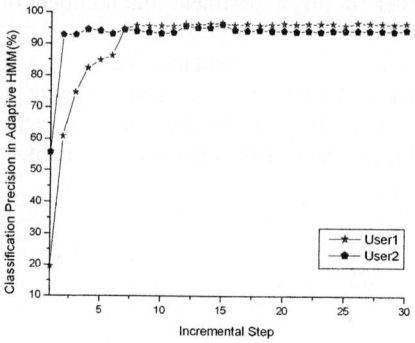

(a) Recognition precision of adaptive Hidden Markov Model

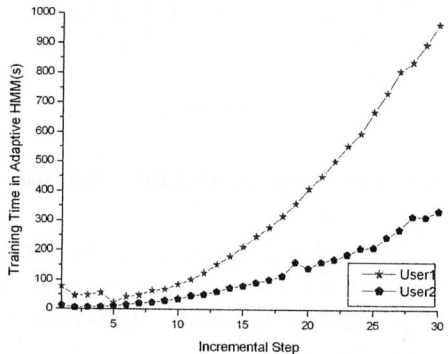

(b) Training time of adaptive Hidden Markov Model

Fig. 6. Experiment results of our proposed method

4 Conclusion

In this paper, we develop an HMM-based method for multi-stroke sketch recognition, where the drawing sketch is viewed as the result of a stochastic process that is governed by a hidden stochastic model and identified according to its probability of generating the output. To capture a users' drawing habit, a composite feature representation of each stroke is defined. To implement the stochastic process of online multi-stroke sketch recognition, multi-stroke sketching is modeled as an HMM chain while the strokes are mapped as different HMM states. To cater for the requirement of adaptive online sketch recognition, a variable state-number determining method for adaptive HMM is proposed. The experiments prove both the effectiveness and efficiency of the proposed method.

Acknowledgement

The work described in this paper is supported by the grants from the National Natural Science Foundation of China [Project No. 69903006 and 60373065] and the Program for New Century Excellent Talents in University of China (2004).

References

1. Zhengxing Sun and Jing Liu: Informal user interfaces for graphical computing, Lecture Notes in Computer Science, Vol. 3784, 2005, page 675-682.
2. Landay J. A. and Myers B. A.: Sketching Interfaces: toward more human interface design. IEEE Computer, Vol. 34, No. 3, 2001, page 56-64.
3. Rubine D, Specifying gestures by example, Computer Graphics, Vol. 25, 1991, page 329-337.
4. Newman M. W., James L., Hong J. I., et al: DENIM: An informal web site design tool inspired by observations of practice, HCI, Vol. 18, 2003, page 259-324.
5. Fonseca M. J., Pimentel C. and Jorge J. A.: CALI - an online scribble recognizer for calligraphic interfaces, In: AAAI Spring Symposium on Sketch Understanding, AAAI Press, 2002, page 51-58.
6. Chris Calhoun, Thomas F. Stahovich, Tolga Kurtoglu, et al: Recognizing multi-stroke symbols, AAAI Spring Symposium on Sketch Understanding, AAAI Press, 2002, page 15-23.
7. Xiaogang Xu, Zhengxing Sun, Binbin Peng, et al: An online composite graphics recognition approach based on matching of spatial relation graphs, International Journal of Document Analysis and Recognition, Vol. 7, No.1, 2004, page 44-55.
8. Zhengxing Sun, Wenyin Liu, Binbin Peng, et al: User adaptation for online sketchy shape recognition, Lecture Notes in Computer Science, Vol. 3088, 2004, page 303-314.
9. Zhengxing Sun, Lisha Zhang and Enyi Tang: An incremental learning algorithm based on SVM for online sketchy shape recognition, Lecture Notes in Computer Science, Vol. 3610, 2005, page 655-659.
10. Rabiner L. R.: A Tutorial on Hidden Markov Models and selected applications in speech recognition. Proceedings of the IEEE, Vol.77, No.2, 1989, page 257-286.
11. Jen-Tzung Chien: On-line unsupervised learning of hidden Markov models for adaptive speech recognition, Proceedings of Vision, Image and Signal Processing, Vol. 148, No. 5, 2001, page 315-324.
12. Hu Jianying: Michael K Brown and William Turin, HMM-based online handwriting recognition, IEEE Transactions on PAMI, Vol. 18, No. 10, 1996, page 1039-1045.
13. Mitsuru Nakai, Naoto Akira, Hiroshi Shimodaira, et al: Sub-stroke approach to HMM-based On-line Kanji Handwriting Recognition, International Conference on Document Analysis and Recognition, 2001, page 491-495.
14. Jay J.Lee, Jah Wan Kim and Jin H. Kim: Data-driven design of HMM Topology for on-line handwriting recognition. In: Hidden Markov models: applications in computer vision, World Scientific Series, 2001, page 107-121.

To Diagnose a Slight and Incipient Fault in a Power Plant Thermal System Based on Symptom Zoom Technology and Fuzzy Pattern Recognition Method

Liangyu Ma, Jin Ma, Yongguang Ma, and Bingshu Wang

School of Control Science and Engineering, North China Electric Power University,
Baoding 071003, China
maliangyu@ncepu.edu.cn

Abstract. To diagnose a slight and incipient fault in a power plant thermal system correctly and timely, a new fault recognition approach is put forward by using fault symptom zoom technology(SZT) and fuzzy pattern recognition method. By studying the rules of the faults pertinent to energy and mass balance in a power plant thermal system , a new fault symptom preprocessing method, which is called "fault symptom zoom technology", is put forward to preprocess the fault characteristic parameters. The complexity of the thermal system fault knowledge library can be effectively reduced and the slight fault recognition ability can be greatly enhanced with SZT. The fault fuzzy pattern recognition method is introduced. A new general-purpose fuzzy recognition function is given, which can fit for various kinds of fault symptoms and is with favorable fault classifying ability. Some examples for incipient and slight fault diagnosis for a power plant thermal system are given to verify the effectiveness of the method.

1 Introduction

Faults in the thermal system of a power unit or in other similar complex industrial process system often experience a gradual change from birth to growth, from slight to severe, especially the faults related to energy and mass balance, such as working medium leakage, pipe choke or device performance degradation, et al. During this process, the relative fault characteristic parameters will also experience a process from initial inconspicuous and incomplete ones to final conspicuous and complete ones.

It is more meaningful than regular severe fault diagnosis if a fault can be recognized accurately when it hasn't grown from slight one into severe one yet, which can be called slight fault recognition. Similarly, the operators can strive for more time to deal with the fault if it can be timely recognized when a fault just arises and the system state is not very far away from its normal state yet (thus the fault symptoms are incomplete), which is called incipient fault diagnosis.

Due to the importance of above incipient and slight fault diagnosis problem, by taking the power plant thermal system as an example, this paper proposes a new fault fuzzy recognition approach to diagnose a slight and incipient fault by joint application of fault symptom zoom technology (SZT) and fuzzy pattern recognition. This method can also be used for fault diagnosis of other complex industrial process system.

2 Flowchart of Incipient and Slight Fault Diagnosis

The flowchart of the fuzzy recognition approach for an incipient and slight fault is shown as Figure 1. It includes following steps: (1) To select the fault characteristic parameters from vast operating parameters coming from the DCS system or onsite instruments and to preprocess them, which mainly refers to the elimination of the signal disturbance and noise with digital filtering method. (2) To set a certain zoom factor for these characteristic parameters and calculate the fault symptoms with fuzzy knowledge expression method. (3) To recognize the fault with fuzzy pattern recognition model by using the real-time symptom values and the fault knowledge library. (4) To set a different zoom factor and repeat step 2 and step 3 until the optimum diagnostic result is achieved.

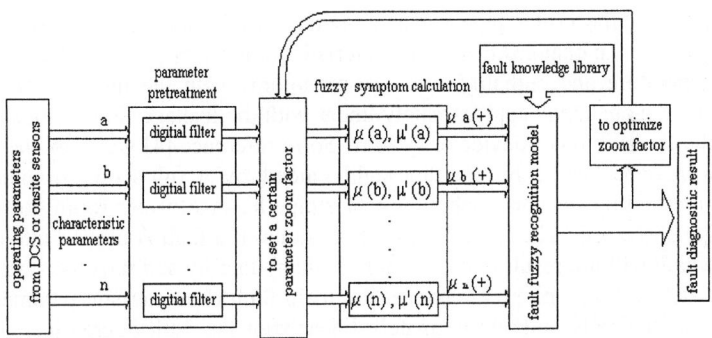

Fig. 1. Flowchart of slight and incipient fault diagnosis with fuzzy recognition method

3 Symptom Zoom Technology

3.1 Necessity of Symptom Zoom Technology and Its Basic Principle

As we know, the fault itself is very complex and the degree of a same fault may be slight, medium or severe. The fault diagnosis methods that we usually use, including a fuzzy recognition method or a neural network method, are substantively a process to match the abnormal work condition with the typical fault patterns, which brings difficulty in choosing the standard fault samples in the fault knowledge library. If a severe fault is selected as a standard sample the recognition ability for slight fault will decrease when the fault knowledge library is used for fault diagnosis. Similarly, if a slight fault is select as a standard sample the same problem exists when the actual fault is severe.

The ordinary disposing method is to classify a same fault into several levels and treat them as different faults. For example, a fault A can be classified into slight fault A, medium fault A and severe fault A, etc. Thus we need at least three samples for a fault. For a complex system when many types of faults exist the negative action of above measure is apparent. The fault knowledge library becomes so voluminous and complex and the accuracy of the fault diagnostic results may decrease. The diagnosis process becomes complex too no matter what fault diagnosis method you use.

To solve this problem, a new approach called "symptom zoom technology" (SZT) is put forward. With this technology only one typical sample is included in the fault knowledge library for a fault. If the actual fault degree is either slighter or severer than this typical sample, we can find out an optimum match with the typical fault sample by changing different zoom factors for the actual fault characteristic parameters. Thus the complexity of the knowledge library induced by the variety of the fault degree can be solved. The problem is transformed into a simple process to select the zoom factor of the characteristic parameters and to search for the optimum zoom value during the fault diagnosis process.

3.2 Theoretical Foundation of SZT and Its Key Point

In reference [3] the boiler pipe leakage fault is deeply studied and analyzed. It is pointed out that the changes of the characteristic parameters, such as the exhaust gas glow, temperature and enthalpy, etc., are monotonic with the increase of the fault degree, and the change is approximately linear with the leakage flow. Is this rule also true for the faults in other device or system? So In reference [4] we study the faults of the high-pressure heater system thoroughly aided by a full-scope simulator of a 300MW thermal power unit, including heater pipe leakage, water room short circuit, heater pipe choke, etc. The result is almost the same. If a fault is limited into a certain degree, which will not result in trip or isolate of any facility and thus the system topological structure keeps no great change, the main fault characteristic parameters will change monotonically and approximately linear with the fault degree increase. This research result is the theoretical foundation of the symptom zoom technology.

The sticking point of the SZT is how to choose the zoom factor properly. This is a parameter optimization problem. The optimal value should be found by taking the fault recognition model and the fault diagnostic result into consideration. The primary rule is that the zoom factor should make the diagnostic result have best fault separation effect.

4 Fuzzy Calculation for Different Fault Symptoms

Three types of fault symptoms are often used in thermodynamic system fault diagnosis, which include: (1) Parameter increase or decrease; (2) Parameter A greater than B; (3) Parameter fluctuation. The first type of symptom can reflects the change scope, change rate and change direction of the parameters. It can be further divided into semantic symptom and trend symptom. The semantic symptom value expresses the changing amplitude and direction of a characteristic parameter, while the trend symptom expresses the changing rate and direction of a characteristic parameter under a certain fault.

The fuzzy expression of the semantic symptom and the trend symptom and their synthesizing calculation are thoroughly discussed in reference [4]. The symptom transformation from continuous value [-1,+1] to discrete three–value symptom {-1, 0, +1} or five-value symptom {-1, -0.5, 0, 0.5, 1} are also discussed.

To improve the incipient fault recognition ability and to ensure the stability of the fault diagnostic result, above symptom calculation methods are jointly used with fuzzy pattern recognition method for slight and incipient fault diagnosis.

5 Fuzzy Pattern Recognition for Thermal System Fault Diagnosis

Fuzzy pattern recognition method can be divided into direct method and indirect method. During the fault diagnosis of the thermal system facilities, because the object to be recognized is usually clear, the direct method with the threshold value rule and maximum membership function rule are often used to recognize the fault. Firstly, the membership grade values of the symptoms to be recognized upon all typical fault patterns are calculated with the predetermined membership function. Then the membership grade values are compared with the given threshold to judge whether current symptom set is healthy. If it is healthy then the maximum membership function rule can be used to determine which typical fault is most possible.

The Fault recognition effect of above direct method heavily depends on the membership function form. Some rules must be followed to set up the membership function. (1) The function should have favorable fault separating effect. (2) The function should be sensitive to the fault time and the slight fault. (3) The function should avoid giving mistaken diagnosis result for normal operating condition when none fault happens.

Reference [5] adopts following membership function to diagnose the condenser fault:

$$\mu_{u_i}(u_0) = 1 - \frac{d_i(u_0, u_i)}{D} \tag{1}$$

$$d_i(u_0, u_i) = \sqrt{\sum_{j=1}^{S_{max}} (x_j - x_{ij})^2} \tag{2}$$

$$D = \max[d_i(u_0, u_i)] \tag{3}$$

where: $d_i(u_0, u_i)$ is a kind of distance between the object to be recognized $u_0=(x_1, x_2, \ldots, x_{S_{max}})$ and the typical fault pattern u_i. D is the maximum distance among them. x_{ij} is the symptom indices of typical fault pattern u_i, and here: $i=1,2,\ldots F_{max}$, $j=1,2,\ldots S_{max}$. F_{max}, S_{max} are separately the number of typical fault patterns and the number of characteristic parameters.

To diagnose the faults of the double-channel condenser with (1) shows its fault separation degree is distinct. But this function has one shortage. When the system is operating normally with none fault happening and all feature indices taking value 0, the membership grade values calculated with (1) are not all 0. So it may give mistaken diagnosis result for normal operating condition.

In order to overcome this shortage and to make the membership function fit for different symptom expression forms, such as {-1, 0, 1} three-value symptom set or {-1, -0.5, 0, 0.5, 1} five-value symptom set, etc, a new form of fuzzy membership function is put forward here, that is:

$$\mu_{u_i}(u_0) = \left[1 - \frac{d_i(u_0, u_i)}{D}\right]^2 \qquad (4)$$

$$d_i(u_0, u_i) = \frac{\sum_{j=1}^{S_{max}} |x_j - x_{ij}|}{\sum_{j=1}^{S_{max}} |x_{ij}|} \qquad (5)$$

$$D = \max[d_i(u_0, u_i)] \qquad (6)$$

It can be seen that all values of $d_i(u_0, u_i)$ got from (5) are 1.0 and thus all fault membership grade values got from (4) are zero when the system is working normally and the fault symptoms x_j are all taking value zero. So the new fuzzy membership function (4) overcomes the shortage of (1) and avoids giving a mistaken diagnostic result for normal work condition. The new function (4) also has favorable fault separation ability and can fit for different symptom expression forms.

A slight or incipient fault in the thermodynamic system can be diagnosed timely and correctly by integrating above fuzzy pattern recognition method with symptom fuzzy calculation and symptom zoom technology.

6 Slight and Incipient Fault Recognition Examples

The five-value fault fuzzy knowledge library of the high-pressure feedwater heater system for a 300MW thermal power unit is summarized in reference [4], in which 19 typical faults are included and 23 fault characteristic parameters are selected. By simulating faults with a 300MW full scope simulator, the fuzzy recognition approach for slight and incipient fault diagnosis is verified.

For the fault of "No.1 high-pressure heater water room short circuit" (u_4), of which the fault degree of the sample included in the knowledge library is 20% water flow leakage, we simulate the slight water room short circuit fault of 2% water leakage with the simulator. When the operating state of the system is stable again after several minutes, we select different parameter zoom factors (from 1 to 20) to diagnose the fault with fuzzy pattern recognition method. The results are shown as figure 2.

From figure 2 we can see, when the zoom factor changes from 1 to 20, the fuzzy pattern recognition model can recognize the possible fault u_4 correctly. When the zoom factor reaches 10, the u_4 gets maximum membership grade value 1.0. From 10 to 17 the membership grade value of u_4 keeps no change. If the zoom factor is greater than 17 the membership degree value begins to decrease. So 10 is the optimum zoom factor.

Because the fault degree of the typical fault sample is 10 times the actual fault, we can judge the fault degree difference between them approximately from the optimum zoom factor value 10.

To test the incipient fault diagnosis ability of the method, we simulate the fault of " No.1 heater tube water leakage 1%, of which the typical sample in the knowledge library is 9% water leakage. When the zoom factor takes value 1 and 10 separately, the fault diagnostic results with fuzzy pattern recognition method are listed in table 1.

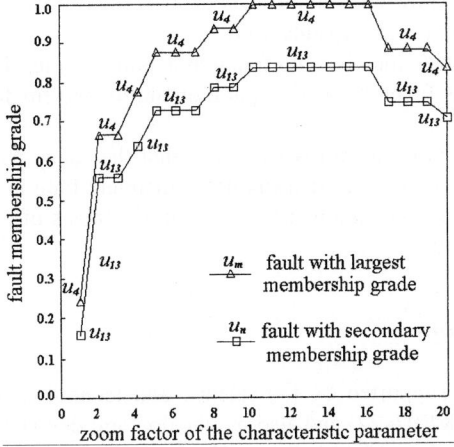

Fig. 2. Diagnostic results for "No.1 heater water-room short circuit 2%"(u_4)

Table 1. Diagnostic results for "No.1 heater water tubes leakage 1%" (u1)

zoom factor	fault lasting time		Fault diagnosis results (the greatest and secondary membership grade values
zoom factor taking value 1.0 (no zoom)	first time to give correct result	10s	u_1=0.455 u_9=0.146
	time to get stable fault diagnosis result	55s	u_1=0.571 u_2=0.376
zoom factor taking value 10	first time to give correct result	15s	u_1=0.825 u_7=0.251
	time to get stable fault diagnosis result	55s	u_1=0.623 u_2=0.529

From table 1 we can see, when the zoom factor takes value 1, the first time of the model to correctly recognize the fault is 10s after the fault arises when the trend symptom plays main roll. It needs 55s to get a stable and correct result when the semantic symptom begins to play main roll. The thermodynamic system needs about 4 to 5 minutes to run into another stable condition after the fault have arisen, so the model has favorable ability to recognize the incipient fault timely. By comparing the two diagnostic results with different zoom times, we can find that the zoom factor has less influence upon the timeliness to recognize the fault correctly and its main function lies in the slight fault diagnosis.

7 Conclusions

(1) A new fuzzy pattern recognition approach to diagnose a slight and incipient fault in power plant thermal system is put forward in this paper. By preprocessing the fault characteristic parameters with symptom zoom technology, the complexity of the

thermal system fault knowledge library can be effectively reduced and the slight fault recognition ability can be greatly enhanced.

(2) An improved fuzzy membership function is built for fault fuzzy pattern recognition. The function has favorable fault separation ability and fits for different symptom expression forms.

(3) It is proved by fault diagnosis examples that the fuzzy pattern recognition approach is very effective to diagnose a slight and incipient fault in thermal system. This method is versatile and can also be used for fault diagnosis of other similar complex industrial process system.

Acknowledgements

This paper is partly supported by the science and technology project of the State Power Company (SPKJ016-22) and also by the doctoral degree teacher research fund (20041209) of North China Electric Power University.

References

1. Ding Yanjun, Wang Peihong, Lu Zhenzhong. "A novel method of early fault detection and diagnosis for technical process", Proceedings of the CSEE, Vol 20, No. 3, Mar. (2001) 61-65
2. Hak-Yeong Chung, Zeungnam Bien, Joo-hyun Park, Poong-hyun Seong. "Incipient multiple fault diagnosis in real time with application to large-scale systems", IEEE trans. on nuclear science, Vol 41, No.4, Aug.(1994) 1692-1703
3. Yang Weijuan, Zhou Junhu, Cao Xinyu. "Analyse on heat calculation of boiler tubes leakage", Proceedings of the CSEE, Vol 20, No.8, Sep. (2000) 85-88
4. Ma Liangyu, Wang Bingshu, Gao Jianqiang. "Fault intelligent diagnosis for high-pressure feed-water heater system of a 300MW coal-fired power unit based on improved BP neural network", 2002 IEEE/PES international conference on power system technology proceedings, Kunming, Vol.3, (2002) 1535-1539
5. Wang Peihong, Zhu Yuna, Jia Junying. "Application of fuzzy pattern recognition to fault diagnosis of the condenser", Proceedings of the CSEE, Vol 19, No. 10, Nov. (1999) 46-49
6. Ma Liangyu, Wang Bingshu, Tong Zhensheng. "Fuzzy pattern recognition and artificial neural network used for fault diagnosis of the double-channel condenser", Proceedings of the CSEE, Vol. 21, No. 6, Jun. (2001) 68-73

Mandarin Voice Conversion Using Tone Codebook Mapping

Guoyu Zuo[1,3], Yao Chen[2], Xiaogang Ruan[1], and Wenju Liu[3]

[1] Institute of Artificial Intelligence and Robotics, Beijing University of Technology,
Beijing 100022, China
{zuoguoyu, adrxg}@bjut.edu.cn
[2] School of Computer Sciences, Beijing University of Technology,
Beijing 100022, China
yaochen@bjut.edu.cn
[3] Institute of Automation, Chinese Academy of Sciences, Beijing 100080, China
lwj@nlpr.ia.ac.cn

Abstract. A tone codebook mapping method is proposed to obtain a better performance in voice conversion of Mandarin speech than the conventional conversion method which deals mainly with short-time spectral envelopes. The pitch contour of the whole Mandarin syllable is used as a unit type for pitch conversion. The syllable pitch contours are first extracted from the source and target utterances. Time normalization and moving average filtering are then performed on them. These preprocessed pitch contours are classified to generate the source and target tone codebooks, and by associating them, a Mandarin tone mapping codebook is finally obtained in terms of speech alignment. Experiment results show that the proposed method for voice conversion can deliver a satisfactory performance in Mandarin speech.

1 Introduction

Voice conversion (speaker conversion) technique makes the speech of one speaker sound as if it were uttered by another speaker [1]. This technique has a variety of applications including customization of text-to-speech system, voice dubbing in movie and radio broadcasts, very low bandwidth speech transmission and preprocessing in speech recognition.

Much work has been directed at this speech technique and many conversion methods have been proposed, including VQ-based codebook mapping [2], mixture Gaussian mapping [3] etc. To a great degree, however, these algorithms focused on the acoustical features such as short-time spectral envelope represented as LPC, LSF, MFCC etc; they had few or even no concerns with the super-segmental characteristics such as the variations of F0 and duration, which play an important role in determining speaker identities. Some of these approaches only assumed a linear mapping method that F0 obeys uni-Gaussian distribution and estimated the mean and variance of it and performed linear transformation on F0 values between two speakers [4]. Therefore, these methods would not describe effectively the locally corresponding relations of pitch contours between two speakers.

Mandarin Chinese is a tonal language. The phonetics of Mandarin Chinese is characterized by clearly demarcated syllables with tonal phonemes [5]. Some results from a large number of experiments and investigations suggest that the tones behave differently between speech with isolated syllables and continuous speech respectively [6]. For the former, the syllables' pitch contours show a relatively steady state. In the continuous context, the tones of the neighboring syllables have an influence on each other, which shows the dynamic characteristics of tones. These include continuous tonal changes in a continuous speech stream, the changes in pitch contour and tonal range. The Chinese tones should be described using both the comparative relations between syllables and the up-down of pitches within syllables.

In terms of the phonetics characteristics of Mandarin Chinese, the pitch contour (F0 contour) of the whole Mandarin syllable can be used as a unit type for F0 conversion instead of an isolated F0 value of a frame-length speech, which is expected to find a better association in F0s between two speakers' speech. The F0 contours of associated syllables in the speech of two speakers are extracted after speech alignment for moving average filtering and length normalization. A clustering method is used to build the Mandarin tone codebooks for two speakers respectively, by which a tone mapping codebook is trained. When the source speech is converted into the target one, the converted speech will obtain the expected pitch contour by performing easy modification on the tone mode in the tone mapping codebook.

2 Pitch Processing

The auto-segmentation and pitch marking are conducted on the utterances in speech data before learning the tone codebooks of different speakers, which are processed by a speech analysis tool. To obtain a high pitch marking precision, the segmentation and pitch marking results are manually modified and the original pitch sequence of all the syllables in each utterance is obtained. In this preprocessing step, a preprocessing method similar to [7] is used to perform length normalization and moving average filtering on the original pitch before generating the syllable tone mode codebooks and tone mean codebooks of two speakers.

2.1 Time Normalization

The length of original pitch sequences varies across a wide range. To meet the clustering requirements, the pitch sequences of different lengths are warped to those of a normalized length. Assuming the pitch contour can be described as a function $p = f(t)$, stretch the time (length) coordinate by a variable scaling factor k which makes all the normalized pitch sequences to be the same length, and the original graph is mapped to $p' = f(kt)$. The jth pitch value in the normalized sequence can be calculated by interpolating several values of the corresponding i^{th} value in the original one, if the ith point is not exactly the original point. Repeat the step for all the pitch sequences.

2.2 Moving Average Filtering

A moving average filter is used to eliminate the influence of large fluctuant data in a short time, by which the changing trend of pitch contour can be obtained. The z-Transform of a moving average filter using FIR filter structure can be represented as follows:

$$H(z) = \frac{1}{N}\sum_{n=0}^{N-1} z^{-n} \qquad (1)$$

in which N is the integral length for moving average. N should be a proper number; the dynamic influence of data cannot be removed if it is too small, while there will be a heavy influence of the filter if it is too big. Given x, the output of a moving average filter can be shown as:

$$y_i = y_{i-1} + \frac{x_i - x_{i-N}}{N} \qquad (2)$$

After time-normalization and moving average filtering, the mean value of every pitch sequence is calculated, and subtracted. All the preprocessed pitch sequences are used for training the syllable tone codebook.

3 Learning Mandarin Tone Mapping Codebook

3.1 Clustering the Source and Target Tone Patterns

After being preprocessed, the original pitch sequence samples are converted into the new samples with the same length suitable for the training process. There are many clustering methods which can be used to perform the clustering behaviors, such as K-means, ISODATA, Max Tree, and SOM etc. We adopt here the LBG algorithm for its effectiveness to perform the clustering analysis on the pitch vectors and learn the tone codebooks. The similarity measure as follows was given to measure the distance between the two pitch sequences denoted by $p_i = \{p_{ik}\}$ and $p_j = \{p_{jk}\}$:

$$D(i,j) = \sqrt{\beta\sum_{k=1}^{L}(p_{ik} - p_{jk})^2 + (1-\beta)\sum_{k=1}^{L-1}(\Delta p_{ik} - \Delta p_{jk})^2} \qquad (3)$$

where p_{ik} is the kth dimension of the pitch vector p_i, L is the dimensional number of pitch vectors, and $\beta > 0$. Δp_{ik} is the first-order difference of p_{ik}, which reasonably explains the differences between pitch contours and makes each clustering center approximate the real pitch contour's shape. With the clustering process conducted on the source pitch sequence and the target one respectively, a source tone mode codebook P_s and a target codebook P_t are obtained (the word tone here is slightly different to its conventional four-tone meaning in Chinese phonetics). These tone words show the Mandarin tones' dynamic characteristics in different speech contexts.

3.2 Learning the Tone Mapping Codebook

In voice conversion, the codebook mapping method was first used in spectral mapping [2] and this method was also used in segmental F0 conversion [4]. In this section, the codebook mapping idea is adopted for performing Mandarin voice conversion. The mapping relation between the source tone space and the target one can first be captured from the source and target tone codebooks obtained as previously noted. The mapping algorithm under discussion assumes that both source and target speakers utter the same sentences. The Mandarin tone mapping codebook is introduced as follows:

step1: For each utterance in the training speech set, the phonetic alignment is performed using the marking labels of phones.

step2: Extract the source and target pitch sequences in each syllable pair using syllable alignment results. Perform time warping moving average filtering and zero-mean normalization on the two pitch contour series.

step3: After being preprocessed, the pitch sequences are vector-quantified using the two tone codebooks. For each syllable pair, the source pitch contour is quantified to be the ith source codeword p_s^i with the corresponding target pitch contour quantified to be the jth target word p_t^j.

step4: Accumulate the histogram h_{ij} of the two words p_s^i and p_t^j.

step5: Repeat for all the pitch contours in one utterance.

step6: Repeat for all the utterances and obtain an original mapping matrix $H_{m \times n}$, where m and n denote the sizes of the source and target codebook respectively.

step7: For each word p_s^i in the source book, calculate each w_{ij} corresponding to h_{ij}.

$$w_{ij} = \frac{\exp\left(\alpha \cdot h_{ij} / \sum_j h_{ij}\right)}{\sum_j \exp\left(\alpha \cdot h_{ij} / \sum_j h_{ij}\right)} \qquad (4)$$

where $\alpha > 0$ is the weighting factor.

step8: Corresponding to each p_s^i in the source book, each word in the mapping book for the target speaker can be represented as the linear combination of all the codes in the target book using the obtained weights, which is as follows:

$$p_c^i = \sum_{j=1}^{n} w_{ij} p_t^j \qquad (5)$$

A mapping codebook P_m of the same size as that of the source book can be derived from the source and target codebooks using the training set. When the weighting factor α is a small number, the synthesized pitch contour will contain a few more words in the mapping book; when α is set to be a large number, the code in the mapping book is determined by the target word which has the maximum in the histogram, i.e., if $\alpha \to \infty$, Equ. (5) becomes the following equation:

$$p_m^i = p_t^k, \; k = \arg\max_j h_{ij} \qquad (6)$$

3.3 Pitch Conversion

In the conversion stage, each syllable of the source input speech is preprocessed as noted above, and quantified to gets its tone codeword from the source book P_s. The target tone is found in the mapping book P_m and inversely warped to the suitable length of the synthesized syllable tone using the same time warping method. Thus, the final synthesized syllable pitch contour can be generated. The average value of the expected pitch contour is expected to have a linear relation to that of syllables in the source speech, which is shown as the following equation:

$$\overline{p}_m = (\overline{p}_s - \mu_s) \cdot \sigma_t / \sigma_s + \mu_t \qquad (7)$$

where μ and σ are the mean and variance of the average values of syllable pitch sequences, and s, t and m denote the source, target and converted utterances respectively. The converted pitch is obtained by adding $\overline{p}_m$ to the converted mapping code and the expected pitch contour to be used in synthesis is derived by time warping to the output length.

Fig.1 shows a conversion example of a Mandarin syllable 'gong1' from a four-word phrase 'gong1 gong4 an1 quan2'. It can be seen that the converted pitch contour (dotted line) in the bottom plot fits well with that of the target one in pitch developmental trend and pitch values. However, it is also seen that the converted pitch contours have some trouble in fully showing the pitch jitter phenomena.

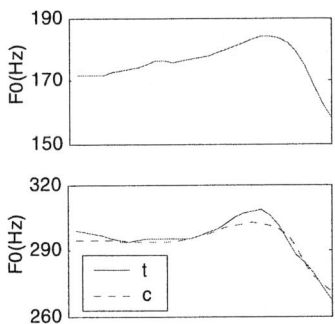

Fig. 1. Pitch contours for mandarin syllable 'gong1' in a four-word phrase for the source (top), target and converted utterances (bottom)

4 Voice Conversion

In general, voice conversion is performed in two steps. At the training stage, acoustical features of speech signals of both speakers are computed and the mapping relations between two acoustical spaces are obtained. In the conversion stage, the target features are converted using the mapping rules. The features to be converted include short-time spectral envelope and super-segmental features such as pitch contour. Since the spectral features contribute much to the conversion performance and are most often used in the conversational voice conversion methods, we summarize the spectral conversion algorithm adopted here, and then schematically describe the implementation of voice conversion including F0 conversion.

4.1 Spectral Conversion

The barked line spectral frequency (LSF) is used as the representation of the spectral feature for its efficient interpolating performance. LPC residuals can be obtained by the inverse filtering of each frame of speech using the associated LP coefficients.

In the mixture Gaussian mapping (MGM) method, the joint density approach [8] is applied to the density $p(x, y)$ and predicts the target y from the source x by finding $E[y \mid x]$, the expected value of y given x. In this method, a Gaussian mixture model is fit to determine the probability distribution of acoustic features, which is given by:

$$p(x) = \sum_{i=1}^{m} \alpha_i N(x; \mu_i, \Sigma_i), \quad \sum_{i=1}^{m} \alpha_i = 1, \quad \alpha_i \geq 0 \qquad (8)$$

where $N(x; \mu, \Sigma)$ denotes a p-dimensional normal distribution with mean vector μ and the covariance matrix Σ, m denotes the total number of Gaussian mixtures, and a_i denotes the weight of class i.

The features of the source speaker are converted into those of the target speaker using the mapping function as follows:

$$\hat{y} = \sum_{i=1}^{m} h_i(x)[\mu_i^y + \Sigma_i^{yx}(\Sigma_i^{xx})^{-1}(x - \mu_i^x)]$$

$$h_i(x) = \frac{\alpha_i N(x; \mu_i^x, \Sigma_i^{xx})}{\sum_{j=1}^{m} \alpha_j N(x; \mu_j^x, \Sigma_j^{xx})} \qquad (9)$$

where:

$$\mu_i^z = \begin{bmatrix} \mu_i^x \\ \mu_i^y \end{bmatrix}, \quad \Sigma_i^z = \begin{bmatrix} \Sigma_i^{xx} & \Sigma_i^{xy} \\ \Sigma_i^{yx} & \Sigma_i^{yy} \end{bmatrix} \qquad (10)$$

are the mean vector and covariance matrix of class i. These parameters are trained from the joint vectors $z = [x^T, y^T]^T$, which are composed of the time-aligned source vectors x and target vectors y and probabilistically described by a GMM whose parameters are trained by joint density distribution. μ_i^x and μ_i^y denote the mean vectors of class i for the source and target speakers. Σ_i^{xx} denotes the covariance matrix of class i for the source speaker, and Σ_i^{yx} is the cross covariance matrix of class i for the source and target speakers.

4.2 Implementation of Voice Conversion

In the training stage, the syllable tone mapping codebook and spectral conversion function are trained from the speech data set. In the conversion stage, the source speech is divided into overlapped blocks frame by frame in the pitch-synchronous way. Each frame speech is analyzed into both LSF spectral features and LPC residual signals. The input LSF vectors are mapped into the target vectors through the spectral conversion function described by Equation (9) and the output spectra are combined with residual signals. By extracting the pitch contour of each syllable, performing time normalization, moving average filtering on it, and finding the target tone curve in the mapping book, the overlapped frames are added into converted speech and TD-PSOLA is performed on the residual signals using the converted pitch and the expected duration. The residuals are then filtered by the converted spectral parameters to generate the converted speech.

5 Experiments and Results

5.1 Experiment Data

The speech of 4-word phrases in the 863DB synthesis corpus was used as the experiment data for training tone mapping codebooks. Considering the sandhi phenomena in Mandarin speech and the modest scale for experiment, the 1, 2 and 3-word phrase speech and the whole-sentence speech in the database have not been applied to these experiments. The speech of two males (M1 and M2) and two females (F1 and F2) were selected for training. All speech of the four speakers contains the same text content. 153 utterances from each speaker were used for training spectral mapping functions. The test speech came from the close-set data.

5.2 Experiment Schemes

The frame-based pitch conversion (FPC) and the tone codeword-based mapping method (TCB) were adopted to perform pitch modification. With different amounts of training data, the differences of mean pitches between the converted utterances respectively by FPC and TCB and those of the target ones were calculated. The male-to-male conversion (M1-M2) and the male-to-female conversion (M1-F1) were performed.

To evaluate the converted speech's degree of preference for the target speaker's identity, the ABX test was used as the subjective evaluation method, in which excitation X represents the converted speech while A and B denote one of the source and target speeches respectively and the speech most similar to X is chosen. ABX was performed by 10 listeners, each with 13 utterances. In the experiments, the converted speech was respectively generated in the following ways.

- FPC: frame-based pitch conversion
- TCB: pitch conversion by Mandarin tone codebook mapping
- MGM: spectral conversion by mixture Gaussian mapping.
- VQ: spectral conversion by VQ

- MGM/TCB: both spectral conversion by MGM and pitch conversion by TCB
- VQ/FPC: both spectral conversion by VQ and pitch conversion by FPC

5.3 Algorithm Evaluations

To compare VQ with MGM, the maximal 150 utterances were selected for spectral mapping and thus for pitch conversion. The comparative results of FPC and TCB were listed in Table 1 with different amounts of training data. We can see that before pitch conversion, the mean pitch difference between the converted and target pitches for M1-M2 conversion is 38.71Hz with 111.23Hz for M1-F1. In comparison, there are great decreases in the mean pitch differences by both methods for both conversions. However, the mean pitch differences by TCB are less than those by FPC at all levels of training data, which shows that TCB can better describe the dynamic characteristics of the target tone at the whole utterance level, and thus reduce the inherent discrete properties of FPC based on frame speech. It is also found that the mean differences have not shown a totally mono relation to the amount of data [2].

Table 1. Mean pitch differences with different amount of training data

		Number of Utterances (n)					
		$n = 0$	$n = 30$	$n = 60$	$n = 90$	$n = 120$	$n = 150$
M1-M2	FPC	38.71	14.68	13.42	14.14	13.53	13.75
	TCB	38.71	10.42	9.54	8.47	7.83	8.23
M1-F1	FPC	111.23	18.43	17.42	16.74	17.22	16.79
	TCB	111.23	11.92	10.54	11.60	9.43	10.64

According to the experiment schemes, the subjective evaluation results when using the converted speech generated by different methods are shown in Fig.2. When only pitch conversions are performed, TCB has a better performance than FPC for both the male-to-male and female-to-female conversions. We can see that when the pitch conversions are combined with spectral mapping, MGM/TCB behaves a little better than VQ/FPC, while nearly the same conversion results for the spectral mapping respectively by VQ and MGM only. Although pitch by itself contributes only about an average 45% to the listener's correct response in voice conversion of the same gender's speech, when it is converted with the spectral mapping, it brings improvements in the target speaker information in the converted speech. Generally, MGM/TCB can achieve the best performance of all the methods

Fig.2 shows that spectral conversions by both VQ and MGM contribute about 70% to the speaker information in the converted speech for the target speakers, which explains why the short-time spectral features are dominant factors in current voice conversion technology. However, the spectral features can not yet give enough reasons to explain the preferences for the target speakers. To obtain the maximal speaker recognition rates, it is evident that both spectral and prosodic information need to be processed in voice conversion.

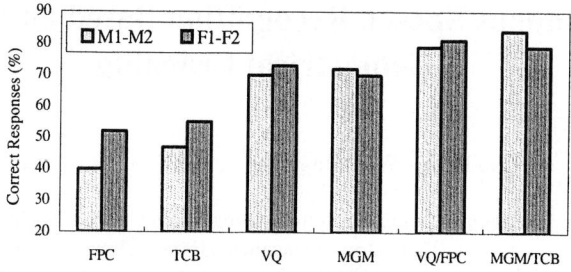

Fig. 2. Subjective evaluation on the preference performance of the converted speech using different ways

6 Conclusions

In addition to the short-time spectral envelope, pitch is an indispensable factor in identifying a speaker's individuality. In this paper, the pitch contour of the whole Mandarin syllable was selected as a unit type for pitch conversion instead of isolated fundamental frequency value of a frame-based speech in voice conversion of Mandarin speech. The experiment results showed that a better association can be found in fundamental frequencies between two speakers' speech using the proposed tone codebook mapping algorithm which improves the voice conversion performance for Mandarin speech.

Acknowledgements

This study was partially supported by National Natural Science Foundation of China (No. 60375017) and Beijing Natural Science Foundation (No. 40402025).

References

1. Moulines, E., Sagisaka, Y.: Voice conversion: state of the art and perspectives. Special Issue of Speech Communication, Vol. 16, No.2, Feb. (1995) 125-126
2. Abe, M., Nakamura, S., Shikano, K., Kuwabara, H.: Voice Conversion through Vector Quantization. In Proceedings of IEEE International Conference on Acoustics, Speech and Signal Processing, NY, USA (1988) 655-658
3. Stylianou, Y., Cappe, O., Moulines, E.: Continuous Probabilistic Transform for Voice Conversion. IEEE Transaction on Speech and Audio Processing, Vol.6, No.2, March (1998) 131-142
4. Türk, O.: New Methods for Voice Conversion [MS thesis]. Boğaziçi University, Turkey (2003)
5. Zhou, T.: Modern Chinese Phonetics. Beijing Normal University Press, Beijing (1990)
6. Chu, M.: Research on Chinese TTS system with high intelligibility and naturalness [Doctoral thesis]. Institute of Acoustic, Chinese Academy of Sciences, Beijing (1995)
7. Zhu, T., Gao, W.: Data Mining for Learning Mandarin Prosodic Models. Chinese Journal of Computer, Vol.23, No.11 (2000) 1179-1183
8. Kain, A., Macon, M.: Spectral Voice Conversion for Text-to-Speech Synthesis. In Proceedings of IEEE International Conference on Acoustics, Speech and Signal Processing, Seattle, USA, May (1998) 285-288

Continuous Speech Recognition Based on ICA and Geometrical Learning

Hao Feng[3], Wenming Cao[1,2], and Shoujue Wang[2]

[1] Institute of Intelligent Information System, Information College, Zhejiang University of Technology, Hangzhou 310032, China
[2] Institute of Semiconductors, Chinese Academy of Science, Beijing 100083, China
[3] Jiaxing University, 320000, China
zjhzfh@mail.zjxu.edu.cn

Abstract. We investigate the use of independent component analysis (ICA) for speech feature extraction in digits speech recognition systems. We observe that this may be true for recognition tasks based on Geometrical Learning with little training data. In contrast to image processing, phase information is not essential for digits speech recognition. We therefore propose a new scheme that shows how the phase sensitivity can be removed by using an analytical description of the ICA-adapted basis functions. Furthermore, since the basis functions are not shift invariant, we extend the method to include a frequency-based ICA stage that removes redundant time shift information. The digits speech recognition results show promising accuracy. Experiments show that the method based on ICA and Geometrical Learning outperforms HMM in a different number of training samples.

1 Introduction

Finding an efficient data representation has been a key focus for pattern recognition tasks. Popular methods for capturing the structure of data have been principal component analysis (PCA), which yields a compact representation, and more recently independent component analysis (ICA). In ICA, the data are linearly transformed such that the resulting coefficients are statistically as independent as possible. In a graphical model framework, the ICA can be regarded as a data generative model in which independent source signals activate basis functions that describe the observation. The adaptation of these basis functions using ICA has received attention since this adaptation leads to a highly efficient representation of the data. Efficiency is measured in terms of its coding lengths (bits) per unit. Fewer bits correspond to lower entropy of the transformed data. Examples in representing natural scenes include [4 and 5]. For audio signals, Bell and Sejnowski [3] proposed ICA to learn features for certain audio signals. Speech basis functions were also learned for speech recognition tasks [6]. Feature extraction for speech recognition aims at an efficient representation of spectral and temporal information of non-stationary speech signals. Conventionally, speech signals were transformed to the frequency domain by using the Fourier transform and then the spectral coefficients are transformed by the discrete cosine transform (DCT) to the cepstral domain to remove the correlation between adjacent coefficients. The DCT reduces the feature dimension and produces nearly uncorrelated coefficients, which is desirable when back-end speech recognizers are based on continuous hidden Markov models (HMMs) using Gaussian mixture observation densities with diagonal covariance matrices. The resulting mel frequency cepstral coefficients (MFCCs) are one of the most common base features to represent spectral characteristics of speech signals. Prior research on using ICA features for speech recognition resulted in significant improvements [7] but experiments were conducted under constraint settings (small training data). Our goal was to investigate this approach without any constraint setting and provide new analysis and options to cope with the main problems of the standard ICA features, namely in providing features that are phase insensitive and time-shift invariant.

In this paper, we apply ICA to speech signals in order to analyze its intrinsic characteristics and to obtain a new set of features for automatic digits speech recognition tasks. We would like to obtain features in a completely unsupervised manner since the ICA is a data-driven method. Eventually, digits speech recognition based on Geometrical Learning [8][9][10][11][12][14][15][16] is used. Compared with the conventional HMM-based method, the ICA and Geometrical Learning-based method (ICA-GL) mentioned in this paper has a noticeable advantage when the number of training samples is very few. The trend of recognition results shows that the difference in recognition rates between these two methods decreases as the amount of training increases but the recognition rate of the ICA-GL-based method is always higher than that of HMM-based. And both of these recognition rates will reach 100% if there are enough training samples. The recognition accuracy of the HMM-based method is lower than that of the HDSCT-based method. This is because ICA-GL-based method can describe the morphological distribution of the speeches in HDS. However, the HMM-based method can only calculate the probability distribution of them.

2 Feature Extraction Based on ICA

2.1 The Collection and Establishment of the Speech Database

There are two speech databases. One is spontaneous speech in daily life. It has no special preparation in terms of speech pattern. It is always slack, and goes with random events (filled pauses etc.). Other is the reading speech database. Its speech pattern and speech context should be prepared beforehand and accord with the grammar as well.

The continuous speech database we adopted in this paper lies between the reading and the spontaneous speech databases. The context of our database is telephone numbers. The read pattern is similar to the spontaneous speech that has some background noise (e.g. the hum of cars on the road).

We segment the continuous speech into syllables by hand and then select the better result as "the learning database". We must point out that these syllable samples are different to the isolated samples. They have characteristics of continuous speech. Finally, we classify these samples into 11 classes according to their pronunciation in Chinese and phoneticize them as shown in Table 1.

Table 1. The digits classification of pronunciation in Simplex Chinese

Digit	0	1	2	3	4	5	6	7	8	9
Pronunciation in Simplex Chinese	ling	Yi	yao	er	san	si	Wu	liu	Qi	ba	Jiu

These database items are collected in 8000Hz (the Sample Frequency) and 16bits (the Bit Depth).

2.2 Proposed Method

Phase sensitivity and time variance seemed to be the most profound factors prohibiting the use of the ICA-adapted basis functions for speech recognition tasks. We took a log of the obtained coefficients. The coefficients show large correlation because ICA was not learned to optimize the independence of the magnitude coefficients. Therefore, we apply an additional ICA transformation for the log of the spectral coefficients to obtain coefficients that are as independent as possible. The mel filter and log operation used in the conventional feature extraction were applied to the ICA coefficients in order to reflect the human speech perception characteristics. Figure 1 compares feature extraction methods using MFCC and ICA. The ICA in the time domain (ICA1) in the proposed method replaces the FFT of the MFCC-based method.

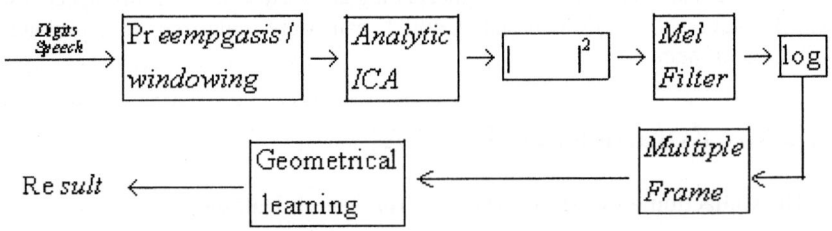

Fig. 1. In ICA-based feature method, speech signals are filtered by analytic ICA filters, the coefficients are logged as squared magnitude and split into mel frequency bands, and then multiple frames are concatenated

2.2.1 Pre-emphasis and Windowing

Speech signals are pre-emphasized by using a first-order FIR filter as pre-emphasis plays a role in weakening the correlation of speech signals. A stream of speech signals is segmented into a series of frames with N samples and each frame is windowed by a Hamming window. These two steps are the standard procedure in feature extraction for speech recognition. In the following sections, we omit the frame index t unless confused, assuming that all processing is done in the frame base.

2.2.2 Analytic ICA in the Time Domain (ICA1)

We used the Infomax algorithm with the natural gradient extension [1 and 2] to obtain the basis functions and the corresponding coefficients. To accelerate the convergence, we reduced the dimension of the windowed signals **x** and obtained a sphered signal **z** by multiplying the sphering matrix $\mathbf{V}_1$ obtained by eigenvector decomposition of the covariance matrix [13]:

$$z = V_1 x \tag{1}$$

where $\mathbf{V}_1$ is an $M \times N$ matrix and M is the reduced dimension of the input signals. The updated unmixing matrix $\mathbf{W}_1$ was constrained to an orthonormal matrix [13]. To reduce the phase sensitivity, we used the analytic version of the unmixing matrix, which was obtained via the Hilbert transform:

$$\mathbf{B} = B + j\hat{B} \tag{2}$$

where $\mathbf{B}_i$ is the Hilbert transform of **B** in the row direction and $j = \sqrt{-1}$. By using the analytic version of the unmixing matrix, we can obtain a smoother estimate of the ith coefficient magnitude $m(i)$, the energy of the windowed signal **x**:

$$m(i) = \| \mathbf{B}_i x \|^2 \tag{3}$$

where $\mathbf{B}_i$ is the ith row vector of the analytic unmixing matrix.

The difference from using the conventional FFT is that the ICA here uses the filters learned from speech signals which have non-uniform center frequencies and non-uniform filter weights but the FFT does not consider the fact that input signals are speech. Phase sensitivity is a common problem when localized basis functions are used to transform speech signals; energy components were used instead of time samples of filter outputs when the DWT was used for feature extraction.

2.2.3 Mel Filter

Mel band energies were obtained by weighting the magnitude coefficients considering the center frequency of the mel bands [6] and the center frequency of the ICA filters. This procedure can be formulated as follows:

$$fb(i) = F(i)m, i = 1...K, \tag{4}$$

where $\mathbf{F}(i)$ is the ith row vector denoting a mel filter whose center frequency is spaced in the mel scale and whose coefficients are weighted according to a triangular shape [6], and K is the number of the mel bands. Because the center frequencies of the ICA filters are different to those of the mel filters, we set the weight for the jth magnitude of the ith filter to:

$$F(i,j) = \begin{cases} \varepsilon & \text{otherwise} \\ \dfrac{|f_{ica}(j) - f_{mel}(i)|}{f_{mel}(i+1) - f_{mel}(i-1)}, & f_{mel}(i+1) \le f_{ica}(j) \le f_{mel}(i-1) \end{cases} \tag{5}$$

where $f_{ica}(j)$ is the center frequency of the jth ICA filters, $f_{mel}(i)$ is the center frequency of the ith mel band, and ε is a small constant to prevent underflow in taking the logarithm to the next step. The $f_{mel}(0)$ and $f_{mel}(M+1)$ are assumed to be 0 and half of the sampling frequency respectively. The center frequency of the ICA filters was determined by weighted frequency. The weight was proportional to the energy of each frequency component excluding the DC components. The weight of the DC component was set to zero. Therefore, we obtain a center frequency even if the basis functions have two lobes.

The logarithm of the resulting coefficients was taken from the fact that the human auditory system is sensitive to speech loudness in the logarithmic scale:

$$g = \log fb \qquad (6)$$

The output vector **g** is used as a base for the following feature transformation stage to remove temporal dependencies between frames and obtain components that are as independent as possible by using another ICA step. As will be shown later, **g** has a strong conditional dependency between components and thus needs further processing.

2.2.4 Concatenating Multiple Frames

We concatenate $2\Delta+1$ consecutive frames to form a new vector at time t, $\mathbf{h}(t)$,

$$h(t) = \begin{bmatrix} g(t-\Delta) \\ \vdots \\ g(t) \\ \vdots \\ g(t+\Delta) \end{bmatrix} \qquad (7)$$

Because the DC component of **h** does not have a sparse distribution, we subtracted the local mean of **h** [13]. If Δ is equal to 0, no temporal filtering is done and only spectral transformation takes place as the DCT in the MFCC computation.

2.2.5 Geometrical Learning

Now, the task of geometrical learning is to cover a given sample set by a chain of hyper sausage units with a minimum sum of volumes via determining the end points of each line segment and the radius of each hyper-sphere. BBBAs introduced in section 2.2 the main idea is similar to finding the center and radius of the outer hyper-sphere via successive projection from a higher dimensional space to a lower dimensional space in the hope of acquiring descriptive high dimensional geometry.

To simplify implementation, the HSN shape[9] is approximated by the shape (in the solid line) that can be computed by the following characteristic function:

$$f_{HSN}(X) = \text{sgn}\left[2^{\frac{d^2(X.\overline{X_1X_2})}{r^2}} - 0.5\right] \qquad (8)$$

which contains a radius parameter r and the distance between X and the line segment $\overline{X_1 X_2}$ as follows:

$$d^2(X, \overline{X_1 X_2}) = \begin{cases} \|X - X_1\|^2, & q(X, X_1, X_2) < 0 \\ \|X - X_1\|^2, & q(X, X_1, X_2) > \|X_1 - X_2\| \\ \|X - X_1\|^2 - q^2(X, X_1, X_2), & otherwise \end{cases} \quad (9)$$

here $q(X, X_1, X_2) = <(X - X_1), \dfrac{(X_1 - X_2)}{\|X_1 - X_2\|}>$. iven an ordered set of samples $P = \{x_i\}_{i=j}^{n}$. The set is sampled in a certain order, which obeys the rule that the mid sample is more like the anterior sample than the latter one. This assures that the set of the samples is a continuously mutative chain. We select a parameter, D, the distance between the two contiguous selected samples in S. This parameter determines the total of the HSN neurons. From P we choose a set $S\{s_i \mid d(s_{i+1}, s_i) \approx D, 1 \le i < m\}$ of n_j sample support points as the sausage parameters $\{X_{j1}, X_{j2}\}_{j=i}^{n}$ defined by (3) such that all the HSN units become overlapped, in aid of the algorithm that follows.

Let S denote the filtered set that contains the samples which determine the network and X denote the original set that contains all the samples sampled in order.

```
Begin:
Put the first sample into the result set S and let it be
the fiducial sample s_b, and the distance between the
others and it will be compared. Set S ={ s_b }. S_max = s_b and
d_max = 0
If no sample in the original set X, stop filtering.
Otherwise, check the next sample in X, then compute its
distance to s_b, i.e., d = ||s - s_b||.
If d > d_max, goto step 6. Otherwise continue to step 4.
If d < ε, set S_max = s, d_max = d, goto step 2. Otherwise
continue to step 5.
Put  s  into  the  result  set:  S = S∪{s}, and let
S_b = s, S_max = s, and d_max = d. Then go to step 2.
If |d_max - d| > ε_2, go to step 2. Otherwise put s_max into the
result set: S = S∪{s_max}, and let s_b = s_max, d_max = ||s - s_max||
go to step2.
```

3 Analysis of ICA Basis Functions

Fig.2 shows the basis functions sorted by the L2 norm and the corresponding frequency responses when the frame size is 128 ms and the number of sources is 67. The basis functions show an ICA waveform. To obtain these basis functions, we updated the ICA filter matrices every 1,000 frames, with the convergence factor, ε, linearly decreasing from 0.0001 to 0.000033.

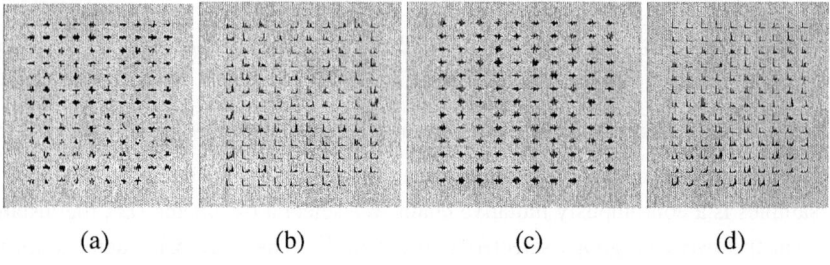

(a)   (b)   (c)   (d)

Fig. 2. Basis functions (a) and their frequency response (without sort order) (b) of ICA in the time domain (without sort order) (c) and their frequency response (d) of ICA in the time domain

4 Experiment and Analysis

This library includes 2,640 MFCC samples of single digital syllables from 24 people. They are divided into 5 groups (Table 1) according to different sample figures.

Table 2. The modeling samples of different figures

Sample distribution	1	2	3	4	5	6
Each person's sample figure of each class	1	2	4	5	7	10
The figure of each class's sample point	24	48	96	120	168	240

In Chinese continuous digital speech recognition, we need to consider enough of the influence of cooperating pronunciation among figures. The influence of a figure's preceding figure is crucial. And the following figure's influence to the subject figure is much lighter. When choosing every class's digital samples of each group, we review the position of every single digital syllable's modeling sample in 8 bit continuous numeric strand and the situation of its former figure. Let every chosen class's digital sample of each group include the situation that every figure connects with its former one. For example, the sample of number 0 in the first group chooses 11 classes' numbers that are those 0s that appeared before the 0, and the situation appears that the 11 classes' numbers influence the 0 equally. This sample set includes a bigger range and more situations.

Table 3. The HMM state figures and hybrid figures in the gauss probability density function

	The sample points' quantity of each class	10	20	40
HMM	State figures	4	4	5
	Hybrid figures in the gauss probability density function	2	4	3

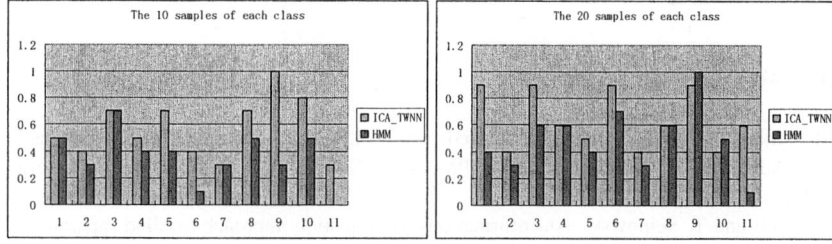

Fig. 3. (Left) Result compared with ICA-GL and HMM in the 10 samples of each class. (Right) Result compare with ICA-GL and HMM in the 20 samples of each class.

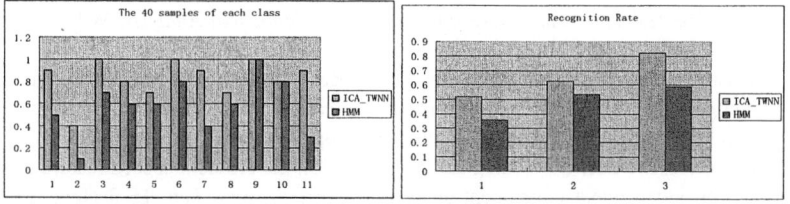

Fig. 4. (Left) Result compare with ICA-GL and HMM in the 40 samples of each class. (Right) Recognition Rate compared with ICA-GL and HMM.

There are 29 persons' totaling 7,308 single digital syllable samples used to test the correctness of the model. Construct each group's single digital syllable samples' HMM model. Use the HMM model that is from left to right without jumping. How many of the hybrid figures in the gauss probability density function have huge influence on the recognition? Adjust the state figures and hybrid figures in the gauss probability density function to let the test set obtain the highest recognition rate possible. Through repeated testing, each groups' states and hybrid figures in the gauss probability density function are displayed in Table 2 and each groups' results of recognition are displayed in Table 3.

Use the same samples to construct digital ICA-GL for 11 classes. Compared with the conventional HMM-based method, the trend of recognition results shows that the difference in recognition rates between these two methods decreases as the number of training samples increases.

5 Conclusion

Dividing continuous speech is difficult, and it also directly influences the digits speech recognition rate. This paper changes the traditional speech recognition's pattern that says to syncopate first then recognize. Instead, it uses the algorithm with ICA-GL and achieves the continuous speech recognition without syncopating. The paper derives from the complicated two weights geometrical structure and gives a new algorithm in speech with an ICA-GL learning algorithm. We hope it can be used in continuous speech recognition of a large vocabulary.

References

1. S. Amari, Neural learning in structured parameter spaces—natural Riemannian gradient, in: Advances in Neural Information Processing System, Vol. 9, MIT Press, Cambridge, MA, 1997, pp. 127–133.
2. A. Bell and T. Sejnowski, An information-maximization approach to blind separation and blind deconvolution. *Neural Comput.* **7** (1995), pp. 1129–1159.
3. A.J. Bell and T.J. Sejnowski, Learning the higher-order structure of a natural sound. *Network Comput. Neural Syst.* **7** (1996), pp. 261–266.
4. A.J. Bell and T.J. Sejnowski, The 'independent components' of natural scenes are edge filters. *Vision Res.* **37** 23 (1997), pp. 3327–3338.
5. G.E.P. Box and G.C. Tiao. *Bayesian Inference in Statistical Analysis*, Wiley, New York (1992).
6. J.H. Lee, H.Y. Jung, T.W. Lee, S.Y. Lee, Speech feature extraction using independent component analysis, in: Proceedings of the International Conference Acoustics, Speech, Signal Processing, Istanbul, Turkey, June 2000, pp. 1631–1634.
7. J.-H. Lee, T.-W. Lee, H.-Y. Jung and S.-Y. Lee, On the efficient speech feature extraction based on independent component analysis. *Neural Process. Lett.* **15** 3 (June 2002), pp. 235–245.
8. Wang ShouJue, A new development on ANN in China - Biomimetic pattern recognition and multi weight vector neurons, LECTURE NOTES IN ARTIFICIAL INTELLIGENCE 2639: 35-43 2003
9. Wang Shoujue,etc. Multi Camera Human Face Personal Identification System Based on Biomimetic pattern recognition ,Acta Electronica Sinica 2003,31(1): 1-3
10. Wang Shoujue,etc. Discussion on the basic mathematical models of Neurons in General purpose Neurocomputer, Acta Electronica Sinica 2001, 29(5): 577-580

11. Xiangdong Wang, Shoujue Wang: The Application of Feedforward Neural Networks in VLSI Fabrication Process Optimization. International Journal of Computational Intelligence and Applications 1(1): 83-90 (2001)
12. Wenming Cao, Feng Hao, Shoujue Wang: The application of DBF neural networks for object recognition. Inf. Sci. 160(1-4): 153-160 (2004)
13. A. Hyvärinen, J. Karhunen and E. Oja. Independent Component Analysis, Wiley, New York (2001).
14. W.M. Cao, Similarity index for clustering DNA microarray data based on multi-weighted neuron, LECTURE NOTES IN ARTIFICIAL INTELLIGENCE 3642: 402-408 2005
15. W.M. Cao, J.H. Hu, G. Xiao, et al. Application of multi-weighted neuron for iris recognition, LECTURE NOTES IN COMPUTER SCIENCE 3497: 87-92 2005
16. W.M. Cao, The application of Direction basis function neural networks to the prediction of chaotic time series, Chinese Journal of Electronics 13 (3): 395-398 (2004)

Underwater Target Recognition with Sonar Fingerprint

Jian Yuan and Guo-Hui Li

Department of System Engineering, School of Information System & Management,
National University of Defense Technology, 410073, Changsha, Hunan, China
`yuanjian@vip.163.com, guohli@nudt.edu.cn`

Abstract. To recognize an underwater target precisely is always a more difficult task for the navy compared to the air force due to the complicated watery environment which is very different from the aerial circumstance. Part of the reason is that there is much more interference under the sea. Sonar is the most efficient way to detect items in the underwater world at the present time. In this paper, a genetic-based classifier system is designed which recognizes targets by sonar fingerprints. This method will, to a certain degree, relieve the sonar man of some of his work. Experiments show that the system gains acceptable speed and accuracy in the classifying operation. The proposed underwater target classifier system is highly automatic, with quite finite hardware requirements for operation.

1 Introduction

Surface ships are the core power of a navy; their greatest dangers come from the air and the submarine. Detecting the aerial target depends on the radar system, and it works based on the electromagnetic wave. Electromagnetic waves spread in the air, and as there is less interference than in the underwater world, abundant methods in the area of radar target recognition have been put forward. For example, from the Monterey University in California, US, in the period 1983 to 1990, more than 40 papers on recognizing aerial targets were embodied into the AD Report [9], [11]. But the underwater world needs different methods despite the two looking apparently similar. Radar operates over high frequency electromagnetic waves, while sonar operates over sound waves. Sonar is in a much lower band, about $5kHz$—$30kHz$, and even the latest information shows that to detect the most advanced submarine requires infrasound wave [8], [13]. The Signal-to-Noise of a radar's echo is normally very high, and the dynamic range is small. However, the dynamic range of sonar is large, often between several micro volts to tens of volts, and *SNR* can range from minus decibel to tens of decibel [8].

The lack of an advanced method to efficiently recognize marine targets is a ridiculous situation; presently, target recognition still relies on the experienced sonarman's monitoring and listening. How can we trust this man's reliability? The weapon manufacturing technique has gone through its evolution; no country can collect all samples in the water. Under this finite condition, the sonar system must obtain the ability to classify.

Sonar fingerprint technique is designed to map sonar echo into fingerprint segments, which can then identify the original echo uniquely. It's composed with very limited data. It greatly decreases the difficulty of, and time consumed by, signal processing. Furthermore, the fingerprint has a thick skin so it can be stored in different formats i.e. no matter how the sound clips are stored, perceptual similarity always leads to an approximate fingerprint [6].

This paper describes a valid underwater target recognition system's architecture and working procedure. After focusing on the system's working precondition, sonar fingerprint's extracting guiding principle and the algorithm in Section 2 and the whole system's architecture in Section 3, we elaborate on the proposed special improvements to the system in Section 4. Experiments, discussion and future work are described in the last two sections.

2 Fingerprint Extraction Algorithm

Sonar fingerprint intends to capture the relevant perceptual features of echo, quickly and easily, and preferably with a small granularity to allow usage in some extreme applications (such as the warfare circumstance).

First, the echo signal is segmented into overlapping frames. For every frame a set of features is computed. Preferably the features are chosen such that they are invariant to signal degradations. Features that have been proposed are well known audio features such as Fourier coefficients [4], Mel Frequency Cepstral Coefficients (MFCC) [7], spectral flatness, sharpness, Linear Predictive Coding (LPC) coefficients and others [1]. Also items such as derivatives, means and variances of audio features are used. Generally, the extracted features are mapped into a more compact representation by using classification algorithms, such as quantization [5]. The compact representation of a single frame will be referred to as a sub-fingerprint. The global fingerprint procedure converts a stream of echo into a stream of sub-fingerprints. One sub-fingerprint usually does not contain sufficient data to identify an echo clip. The basic unit that possesses the ability to identify will be referred to as a fingerprint-block.

The overlapping frames have a length of 0.37 seconds and are weighted by a Hamming window with an overlap factor of 31/32. The extraction scheme extracts 32-bit sub-fingerprints for every interval of 11.6 milliseconds. A fingerprint block consists of 256 subsequent sub-fingerprints, corresponding to a granularity of only about 3 seconds. In the worst-case scenario the frame boundaries used during identification are 5.8 milliseconds. The large overlap assures that even in this worst-case scenario the sub-fingerprints of the echo clip to be identified are still very similar to the sub-fingerprints of the same clip in the database. Due to the large overlap subsequent sub-fingerprints have a large similarity and vary slowly in time.

The most important perceptual features live in the frequency domain. Therefore a spectral representation is computed by performing a Fourier transformation on every frame.

In order to extract a 32-bit sub-fingerprint value for every frame, 33 non-overlapping frequency bands are selected. These bands lie in the range from $300Hz$ to $2000Hz$ (most echo sound's energy lives in this range and it is the most relevant spectral range for the *HAS*) but not the whole band. They also have a logarithmic spacing, in accordance with the *HAS*'s operating principle. Experimentally, it was verified that the sign of energy differences (simultaneously along the time and frequency axes) is a property that is very robust to many kinds of processing.

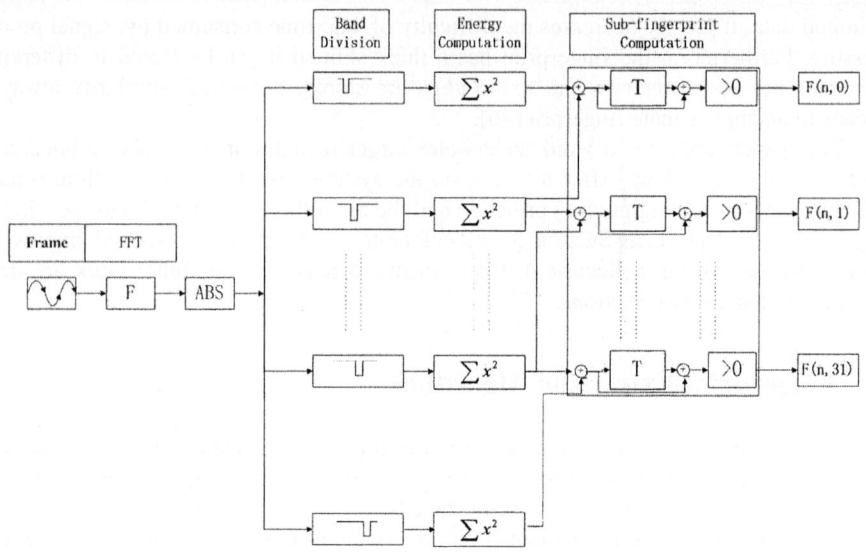

Fig. 1. Overview of fingerprint extraction scheme

If we denote the energy of band m of frame n by $E(n,m)$ and the m-th bit of the sub-fingerprint of frame n by $F(n, m)$, the bits of the sub-fingerprint are formally defined as:

$$F(n,m) = \begin{cases} 1 & if \quad E(n,m) - E(n,m+1) - (E(n-1,m) - E(n-1,m+1)) > 0 \\ 0 & if \quad E(n,m) - E(n,m+1) - (E(n-1,m) - E(n-1,m+1)) \leq 0 \end{cases} \quad (1)$$

The computing resources needed for the proposed algorithm are limited. Since the algorithm only takes into account frequencies below 2 *kHz* the echo is first down sampled to a mono stream with a sampling rate of 5 *kHz*. The sub-fingerprints are designed to be innately robust against signal degradations, therefore very simple down sample filters can be used. In the experiments, a 16-tap FIR filter is used to realize the operation mentioned above. The most computationally demanding operation is the pretreatment of the sound, i.e. the overlapped frame generating operation and Fourier transformation of every frame. In the down sampled signal a frame has a fixed length of 2,048 samples.

Figure 2 shows an example of 256 subsequent 32-bit sub-fingerprints (i.e. a fingerprint block), extracted with the above scheme from an echo of a submarine. A '1' bit corresponds to a white pixel and a '0' bit to a black pixel. Figure 2a and Figure 2b show a fingerprint block from an original echo sound and the compressed version of the same excerpt, respectively. The usage of a compressed version is to symbolize the degradation of the echo caused by the watery environment. Ideally these two figures should be identical, but due to the compression (corresponding to the attenuation in the water) some of the bits are retrieved incorrectly. These bit errors, which are used as the similarity measure for our fingerprint scheme, are shown in black in Figure 2c.

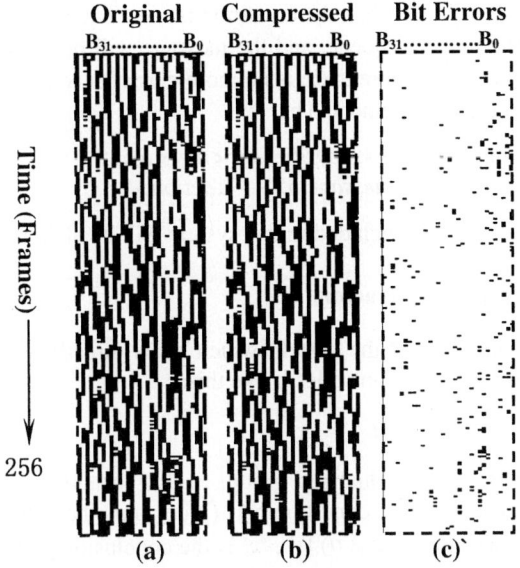

Fig. 2. (a) Fingerprint block of original echo clip, (b) fingerprint block of a compressed version, (c) the difference between (a) and (b) showing the bit errors in black (BER=0.034)

3 The Classifier System Architecture

In order to identify the correct class of a target, a well-designed classifier is necessary. The classifier receives the fingerprint information and can tell which class the current target belongs to by comparison with the well-trained fingerprint-rule set.

In this application, a well-defined system has the modules shown below in Figure 3:

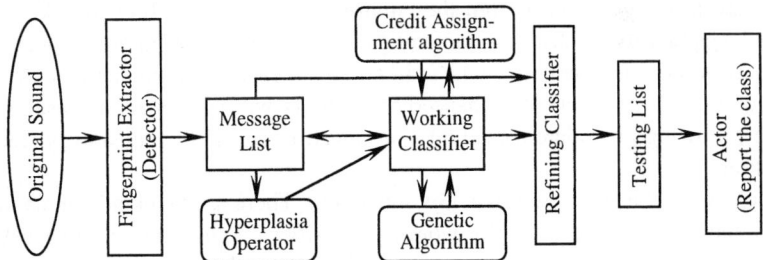

Fig. 3. Classifier System Architecture

Firstly, the detector distils the sonar fingerprint according to the CS's requirements, and once the information is sent to the CS, it becomes encoded environmental information, i.e. a piece of message is delivered to the message queue, and maybe it will trigger the rule (it is the so-called classifier). A rule's form is shown here [2]:

$$\text{IF } <condition> \text{ THEN } <action> \tag{2}$$

This means the rule will act when the condition is met. The triggered classifier will send a message to the message queue, and the message will probably trigger another classifier or bring an action (where there is no more classifier to be triggered). Finally the action will act on the environment. That is:

$$<environment\ information> \rightarrow <classifier1>:<message1> \rightarrow ... \rightarrow <classifier\ n>:<message\ n> \rightarrow <action> \quad (3)$$

Now five main components included in this system will be elaborated.

3.1 Detector (Fingerprint Extractor)

The detector is the interface of the system which deals directly with the echoes. It extracts the sonar fingerprint and encodes it like this:

$$M^i = [x^i, y^i] \quad (4)$$

Every piece of message is a dualistic group. In this formula, 'i' is the sequence number of the message, 'x' is the condition part (it contains the codes which embody all the classifying information), $x^i \in \{0,1\}^n$, 'y' is the conclusion part, and $y^i \in \{0,1\}^m$ (the class of the object), is added manually for training after encoding. For example, [(10001011), (1011)] is a piece of message which is composed by an 8-bit condition and a 4-bit conclusion.

3.2 Message List

The message list is the system's repository as it contains all the messages. It offers the raw materials that are needed in the following operation.

3.3 Classifier System

Rules are different in form from the environment messages. They should have enhanced adaptability, so that they can cover more information. Consequently the condition part of the rule contains a wildcard '#'. This means that a bit can be either '0' or '1', but it cannot be decided. Enhanced adaptability will lead to an increased rule set. In the following procedure a method is designed to avoid the redundancy caused by this strategy.

The classifier is generated by a GA subsystem. There are two kinds of classifier in the system, one of which is the working classifier. When the learning begins, it chooses a scheduled number of messages and mutates them to a certain degree. The following learning and evolution operation carry and achieve this. The other classifier is the refinement classifier. All the useful rules in the working classifier and the collision rules obtained from the message list form the refinement classifier. Some material handling takes place in it; this can merge the redundant rules.

Relative to traditional rule, the newly proposed rule is a triplet; its form is as follows:

$$C^i = [U^i, V^i, fitness^i] \quad (5)$$

U^i is the condition part, $U^i \in \{0,1,\#\}^n$, # is the wildcard, V^i is the conclusion part, $V^i \in \{0,1\}^m$, $fitness^i$ is a rule's fitness; it's two-tuples itself, and it intakes the form:

$$fitness^i = [\, fit1, fit2 \,] \qquad (6)$$

fit1 and *fit2* are positive integers; they separately mean the quantity that a piece of message matches in the rule's conclusion or not within the rule's coverage area. For example, [(1##0#0#1), (1011), (20, 4)] means the rule's condition part (1##0#0#1) covered 24 samples and among these, there are 20 samples holding the same conclusion with the rule, and four at variance.

3.4 Testing List

All the testing examples make up the testing list. A testing example T^i is like a piece of message, and one difference exists in its conclusion part, $y^i \in \{*\}^m$, * meaning it is not confirmed yet. After testing by the CS, it will obtain the same form as the message and the example itself will turn into a new message. Its conclusion can both act on the environment and feedback the new message through the environment, so that the system may continue its learning and can better adapt to the environment.

3.5 Actor

Actor turns the classifying result to the true output value, and then acts on the environment. It's the reverse process of detector; in fact, it's a decode course. In our application, we can learn from the actor which class an underwater target belongs to after the whole training and classifying procedure.

4 Improvements on Classifier System

Considering the application the system is likely to be used for, speed and accuracy are paramount. Here, the Comparing and Matching Algorithm (*CMA*), Hyperplasia Operator (*HO*), Refining Classifier (*RC*) and alterable mutation probability (P_m) are designed to meet these requirements.

4.1 Comparing and Matching Algorithm

Compared with the commonly used Bucket Brigade Algorithm (*BBA*), *CMA* is more convenient for users to acquire the fitness; it invests the fitness value with more explicit statistical meaning, and this allows users to explain the rule with background knowledge. Furthermore, the fitness which is elicited by the *CMA* can decide if the rule should be merged in the *RC*.

The designing idea of the *CMA* is to match the rules and the messages in the *ML* one by one, which modifies the rule's fitness based on the success or failure of the match. The fitness has been described in Formula 8. The ultimate purpose is to ensure the survival of the best rules and the elimination of the worst rules.

Here is the approach:

1. Initialize the rule's fitness, i.e. fit1← 0,fit2← 0;
2. Select a piece of message from ML; match the rules in the working classifier one by one.
    IF both the condition and the conclusion are matched,
        THEN   fit1 ← fit1 + 1;
    IF the condition matches while the conclusion not,
        THEN   fit2 ← fit2 + 1;
    IF the condition doesn't match,
        THEN   fitness ←fitness
Return to Step 2, do the match until the ML is out.

4.2 Hyperplasia Operator

The Hyperplasia Operator is designed for the avoidance of the situation where no rule matches the current message. Therefore, it gives the system a persistent learning ability.

Suppose that when the message matches the rule, it is found that there is no rule that can distinguish the message; what can be done? Here the *HO* will generate a new rule which can match the message.

The approach is to mutate the message's condition part in every bit with a fixed probability. While mutating, the 1 or 0 on this bit will be changed into "#". Make the result the condition part of a new rule, and then give a specific class artificially.

4.3 Refining Classifier

The purpose of *RC* (also called Merge Operator) is to reduce the quantity of the redundant rules. The smaller the scale of the rule set, the faster the classification is achieved.

1. For every rule in the original population, if its corresponding $fit1 \neq 0$ and $fit2=0$, the *RC* will reserve it, otherwise the *RC* will eliminate it.
2. Match the reserved rules to each other. Suppose R_1 and R_2 are two rules that survived.
    IF $R_1 \supseteq R_2$ and $fit1\ (R_1) = fit1\ (R_2)$,
    THEN keep R_2, eliminate R_1;
    IF $R_1 \supseteq R_2$ and $fit1\ (R_1) > fit1\ (R_2)$,
    THEN keep R_1, eliminate R_2.

4.4 Alterable Mutation Probability

In normal *GA*, the value of the parameter P_m is invariable. The classifier mutates according to the fixed probability from beginning to end. Experiments show that to set an alterable mutation probability correctly may increase the speed and the accuracy of classification.

In the prophase of the evolution, all the rules' fitness are relatively low; high mutation probability would probably destroy some potential rules. Lower mutation probability should be used in order to keep the stability of the evolution, and this can speed up the evolution. In the anaphase the fitness has already become steady; amplified mutation probability will enlarge the variety.

Furthermore, the training and the testing go hand in hand in the system, known from the normal classifier system. In general, the training samples cannot cover all the situations in reality, and the proportion of positive and negative samples is difficult to predict. However, the policy of simultaneous processing makes the system acquire persistent learning ability. Therefore, the samples decide the acquisition procedure, and consequently the rules correspond better with reality.

5 Experiment and Discussion

The class is specified compulsively when an echo is being used as a training example. If the system is well-trained, the recognition time will be swift. In practice, the main time consumed is in the processing of the echoes. If the Fourier transformation is implemented as a fixed point real-valued FFT, then the fingerprinting algorithm will run more efficiently.

In order to validate the performance, we took eight different kinds of targets for identification:

- submarines or surface ships
- wood ships
- buoyages
- fish torpedoes
- trail streams
- submerged rocks or rocky benthal
- shoals and benthal reverberations or
- fake echoes.

Each kind of target contained 50 echoes; we chose 40 randomly as training examples, the rest were test examples. The classification result is shown in Table 1.

Table 1. Result of the classification

Training set	Nr	TR	Testing set	C	Er	Er%	TE
320(40×8)	86	100%	80(10×8)	74	6	7.5%	92.5%

Nr is the rule quantity after training, C is the number of correctly recognized testing targets, TR is the recognition success rate of the training set, TE is the recognition success rate of the testing set, Er is the wrongly recognized target, and Er% is the error rate. In our opinion, the classification is successful only until TR>95% and TE>70%.

The difference between the improvements supplied and absent is shown in Table 2. Without the hyperplasia operation, it is necessary to collect a large number of training examples covering all kinds of classes. The hyperplasia operation can generate them gradually; therefore the system possesses persistent learning ability.

Table 2. Improvements can affect the system greatly

	With RC	Without RC	Alterable P_m	Invariable P_m
Number of Rules	86	231	—	—
Average Fitness	—	—	34.3	28.7
Training Time(Minute)	6	65	6	9

6 Conclusion and Future Work

Despite these achievements, there are still some issues requiring future work:

- Parallel identification. Sonar feedback has particular meaning; it's the decision support information, and the synthetic information will help to increase accuracy.
- Concise sonar fingerprint extracting algorithm. In order to reduce unnecessary processes and extracting complexity, further study into echo should be carried out.
- Extend the system's function. It's a promising idea to store the well-trained rules and the correlative equipment information in the database. Associated information can be shown after a class is recognized. The commander would then be able to use the system's support in making a more scientific decision on how to deal with a target.

References

1. Timothy J Murphy: Natural Resonance Extraction and Annihilation Filtering Methods for Radar Targets Identification. Master's thesis, Naval Postgraduate School, Monterey California, September 1990
2. T J Murphy: Natural Resonance extraction and annihilation filtering. AD-A241 038,September 1990
3. RunZhong Zhang, ZongYu Tang: Oceanic Acoustics Computation. No.715 Institute of China Shipbuliding Industry Corporation, 2000
4. XiaoPing Wang, LiMing Cao: Application of Genetic Algorithm and Software Realization. Xi'an, Xi'an Jiao Tong University Press, 2002
5. ChengMin Ding, ChuanSheng Zhang: Genetic Algorithm and Its Improvement. Information and control, 1997
6. Jaap Haitsma, Ton Kalker: A Highly Robust Audio Fingerprinting System. International Symposium on Music Information Retrieval (ISMIR) 2002
7. Cheng Y.: Music Database Retrieval Based on Spectral Similarity. International Symposium on Music Information Retrieval (ISMIR) 2001, Bloomington, USA, October 2001
8. Fragoulis D, Rousopoulos G., Panagopoulos T, Alexiou C and Papaodysseus C: On the Automated Recognition of Seriously Distorted Musical Recordings. IEEE Transactions on Signal Processing, vol.49, no.4, p.898-908, April 2001

9. Logan B.: Mel Frequency Cepstral Coefficients for Music Modeling. Proceeding of the International Symposium on Music Information Retrieval (ISMIR) 2000, Plymouth, USA, October 2000
10. Allamanche E, Herre J, Hellmuth O, Bernhard Fröbach B and Cremer M: AudioID: Towards Content-Based Identification of Audio Material. 100th AES Convention, Amsterdam, the Netherlands, May 2001
11. Haitsma J., Kalker T. and Oostveen J.: Robust Audio Hashing for Content Identification. Content Based Multimedia Indexing 2001, Brescia, Italy, Sep 2001
12. RunZhong Zhang, ZongYu Tang: Oceanic Acoustics Computation. No.715 Institute of China Shipbuliding Industry Corporation, 200
13. Technical Handbook of Model SJD-7 Sonar System. Jiangning Machine Factory, China State Shipbuilding Corporation, 2002
14. Jian Yuan, GuoHui Li: Recognition of the Underwater Target with an Improvement Genetic-Based Classifier System. Proceeding of ICMLC2003 Conference, Xi'an, pp. 3056-3061, November 2003

Multi-stream Articulator Model with Adaptive Reliability Measure for Audio Visual Speech Recognition

Lei Xie and Zhi-Qiang Liu

Center for Media Technology, School of Creative Media,
City University of Hong Kong, Kowloon, Hong Kong
{xielei, zq.liu}@cityu.edu.hk

Abstract. We propose a multi-stream articulator model (MSAM) for audio visual speech recognition (AVSR). This model extends the articulator modelling technique recently used in audio-only speech recognition to audio-visual domain. A multiple-stream structure with a shared articulator layer is used in the model to mimic the speech production process. We also present an adaptive reliability measure (ARM) based on two local dispersion indicators, integrating audio and visual streams with local, temporal reliability. Experiments on the AVCONDIG database shows that our model can achieve comparable recognition performance with the multi-stream hidden Markov model (MSHMM) under various noisy conditions. With the help of the ARM, our model even performs the best at some testing SNRs.

1 Introduction

Inspired by lipreading, audio visual speech recognition (AVSR) has recently received much interest in improving the speech recognition robustness under noisy conditions. Various audio visual fusion approaches have been proposed, among which the multi-stream hidden Markov model (MSHMM) [1] has shown superior performance. Derived from the conventional phoneme-based speech recognition, this model incorporates two streams of observations each of which represents one modality of speech (audio and video). The two streams share the same phoneme state sequence and the observation emission probabilities are integrated by a pair of stream reliability.

Recent nonlinear phonology has indicated that speech may be better described as the output of multiple streams of linguistic features, more specifically articulators. From the point view of speech production, each sound is originated from a group of articulators, such as glottis, vocal folds, velum, teeth, lips and tongue. These facts have motivated many researchers to work on articulator modelling for speech. Richardson et al [2] proposed a hidden-articulator Markov model (HAMM), which was actually a factorial HMM directly integrating the articulator information into speech recognition. Very recently, dynamic Bayesian networks (DBNs) have been used in articulator modelling due to their great expressive power. Bilmes et al [3] proposed a prototype of DBN-based articulator model which directly mimics the speech production process for audio speech. Saenko et al [4] extended their DBN-based articulatory feature model to visual modality for visual speech recognition; and their experiments have shown that a recognizer that models the inherent articulatory asynchrony outperforms one that does not.

In this paper, we propose a novel articulatory approach to integrate both audio and visual speech. Considering that audio visual speech may be better modelled in the same articulation process, we present a multi-stream articulator model (MSAM) for AVSR. This model takes on a DBN structure with two streams and a shared articulator layer. We also use stream reliability variables to reflect the confidences of both streams, where an adaptive reliability measure is proposed to estimate the reliability variables in a local, temporal level.

2 Multi-stream Articulator Model

2.1 Model Structure

Fig. 1 shows the repeating structure of the proposed MSAM which is composed of 5 layers of variables. Similar to that in [3], there is a set of articulator variables $\Psi_t = \{\psi_t^1, \psi_t^2, \cdots, \psi_t^D\}$ in each time frame t, each of which depends on the current state variable q_t and its own value in the previous frame $t-1$. The time dependency is to model the continuity constraints on articulator values, since they cannot change from one value to another very different one without going through some inter-values.

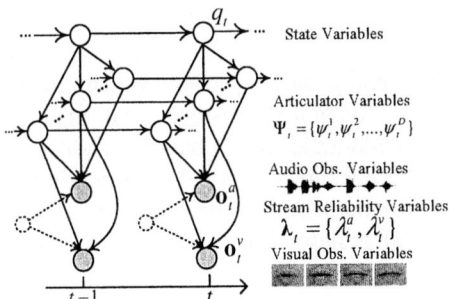

Fig. 1. Multi-Stream Articulator Model

Different from [3], our model includes two observation streams ($\mathbf{o}_t^a$ and $\mathbf{o}_t^v$) each of which describes one modality of speech–audio and video. Since the audio and visual observations are originated from the same articulator source, only a unique articulator layer is incorporated. However, as visual speech is the reflection of *visible* articulators, such as tongue, lips, teeth, visual observation variables are only up-linked to those visible articulator variables. This structure not only is intended to mimic the true human speech production process in some extent but also encapsulates the synchronization between the audio and video.

To achieve the best recognition performance, we use a pair of auxiliary stream reliability variables $\lambda_t^s, s \in \{a, v\}$ to reflect the confidence of each stream, where an adaptive reliability measure is adopted (see Section 3).

2.2 Model Parameters

A DBN specifies a set of variables and a factorization of the joint probability distribution using conditional probability distributions (CPDs) between variables. The CPDs are the parameters to be described. In our model, the CPDs associated with variables for each frame are

- $P(q_t|q_{t-1})$: state transition probability,
- $P(\psi_t^i|\psi_{t-1}^i, q_t), i = 1, 2, \cdots, D$: articulator generation probability, and
- $P(\mathbf{o}_t^s|\Psi_t^s, \lambda_t^s), s \in \{a, v\}$: audio (visual) observation emission probability.

Since q_t and ψ_t^i are discrete variables, the probabilities $P(q_t|q_{t-1})$ and $P(\psi_t^i|\psi_{t-1}^i, q_t)$ are described in a tabular way, known as conditional probability tables (CPTs). $P(\mathbf{o}_t^s|\Psi_t^s, \lambda_t^s)$ is defined as the following exponential Gaussian mixture:

$$P(\mathbf{o}_t^s|\Psi_t^s, \lambda_t^s) = [P(\mathbf{o}_t^s|\Psi_t^s)]^{\lambda_t^s} = \left[\sum_{k=1}^{K} \omega_{\Psi_t^s k} \mathcal{N}(\mathbf{o}_t^s; \mu_{\Psi_t^s k}, \Sigma_{\Psi_t^s k})\right]^{\lambda_t^s} \quad s \in \{a, v\}, \quad (1)$$

where $\mathcal{N}(\mathbf{o}_t^s; \mu_{\Psi_t^s k}, \Sigma_{\Psi_t^s k})$ is a multivariate Gaussian with mean vector $\mu_{\Psi_t^s k}$ and covariance matrix $\Sigma_{\Psi_t^s k}$, and $\omega_{\Psi_t^s k}$ denotes the mixture weight of the kth Gaussian. Stream reliability variables hold that $\lambda_t^a + \lambda_t^v = 1$. Each allowed combination of articulator values is implemented via a Gaussian mixture.

2.3 Articulator Variables

Speech production is a complicated process which involves various articulators. Prior to modelling, we must consider what articulatory configurations can be encapsulated. Pseudo-articulatory based variables are widely used in the speech processing literature where statistical classifications are applied to acoustic speech, resulting in abstract classes representing typical articulator configurations. We construct our articulator feature set (with discrete values) as follows[1]:

- **voicing**: on, off;
- **velum**: open, closed;
- **manner**: closure, sonorant, fricative, burst;
- **tongueBodyLH**: low, mid, mid-high, high;
- **tongueBodyBF**: back, mid, slightly front, front;
- **lipRounding**: rounded, slightly rounded, mid, wide;
- **lipSeparation**: closed, apart, wide apart;
- **tongueShow**: touching top teeth, near alveolar ridge, touching alveolar, others;
- **teethShow**: show, hide.

---

[1] The lipRounding, lipSeparation, tongueShow and teethShow are visible articulator variables.

2.4 Model Training

Since the articulator level transcriptions are not available, we use a two-step parameter training process. Firstly, we train the articulator generation probabilities $P(\psi_t^i|\psi_{t-1}^i, q_t)$ using probability factoring and HMM-based articulator value recognizers; secondly, we train the state transition probabilities $P(q_t|q_{t-1})$ and observation emission probabilities $P(\mathbf{o}_t^s|\Psi_t^s)$ using the EM algorithm with pre-trained articulator generation probabilities.

In order to constrain the articulator variables to their intended meanings, we use a probability factoring scheme. We factor $P(\psi_t^i|\psi_{t-1}^i, q_t)$ into the following form:

$$P(\psi_t^i|\psi_{t-1}^i, q_t) = \frac{P(\psi_t^i|q_t)P(\psi_t^i|\psi_{t-1}^i)}{N(\psi_t^i)}. \qquad (2)$$

Thus we build two separate CPTs:

- $P(\psi_t^i|q_t)$: state-to-articulator mapping probability (Abbr. mapping probability) and
- $P(\psi_t^i|\psi_{t-1}^i)$: articulator transition probability.

The final CPT of $P(\psi_t^i|\psi_{t-1}^i, q_t)$ is constructed by multiplying the appropriate items in the above two CPTs and normalized by a constant $N(\psi_t^i)$.

Since we use English phonemes as the linguistic units, we manually examine each phoneme state's articulatory characteristics to determine the best mapping to the articulator values and create a phoneme-state-to-articulators mapping table [1]. We use an HMM-based method to get reasonable state-to-articulator

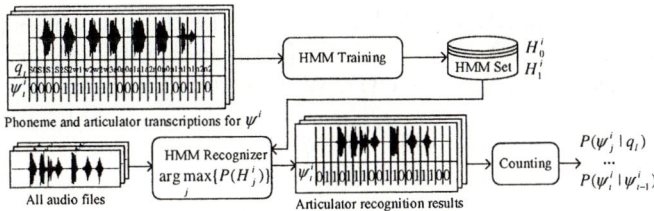

Fig. 2. The HMM-based method to get mapping probabilities and transition probabilities. For clarity, we suppose the articulator ψ^i has only two values (0 and 1).

mapping probabilities and articulator transition probabilities (see Fig. 2). We train an HMM for each possible value of each articulator ψ_j^i using the best mapping as the transcriptions, which is denoted as H_j^i. Here j denotes a possible value of articulator ψ^i. Then each audio snippet of an utterance can be classified into one of the values of each articulator by an HMM-based recognizer. Finally the mapping probabilities and articulator transition probabilities can be determined by counting the resultant recognition results.

2.5 Parameter Reduction

In our model, the observation emission probabilities $P(\mathbf{o}_t^s|\Psi_t^s)$ are described by Gaussian mixtures, and each allowed combination of articulator variable values Ψ^s is implemented by a Gaussian mixture. This induces a very large number of parameters. Specifically in our case, we have to train 24576 and 96 Gaussian mixtures for audio and video respectively according to the articulator variables defined in Section 2.3. To avoid the data sparseness and achieve robust parameter training, we use two parameter reduction schemes.

Physical Constraints. Restricted by the inherent physical constraints of human articulation system, some combinations of articulator variable values can never be realized. We use the following rules to reduce the combinations:

- if *lipSeperation* = *closed*, then *lipRounding* $\neq$ *rounded* or *wide*;
- if *lipSeperation* = *wide apart*, then *lipRounding* $\neq$ *rounded* or *wide*;
- if *tongueShow* = *touching alv. ridge*, then *tongueBodyLH* = *high* and *tongueBodyBF* $\neq$ *back*;
- if *velum* = *open*, then *voicing* $\neq$ *on*;
- if *velum* = *open*, then *tongueBodyBF* $\neq$ *front*.

Considering the above constraints, the number of audio and visual Gaussian mixtures to be estimated will be dramatically reduced to 5120 and 64.

Probability Factorization. To further reduce the audio Gaussian mixtures, we classify the articulator variables into some reasonable subsets and factorize the probability $P(\mathbf{o}_t^a|\Psi_t^a)$ into terms. Thus the number of mixtures to be trained is given by the sum of the subset cardinalities, rather than the product of cardinalities of all articulator variables.

Suppose we can classify $\Psi = \{\psi^1, \psi^2, \cdots, \psi^D\}$ (with cardinalities $\{c^1, c^2, \cdots, c^D\}$) into subsets $\mathbf{\Gamma} = \{\mathbf{U}^1, \mathbf{U}^2, \cdots, \mathbf{U}^M\}$ (with cardinalities $\{g^1, g^2, \cdots, g^M\}$), where $M < D$, $\mathbf{U}^k \subset \mathbf{\Gamma}$, and $\mathbf{\Gamma} = \cup \mathbf{U}^k$. We substitute $P(\mathbf{o}_t^a|\Psi_t^a)$ with

$$\frac{\prod_{k=1}^M P(\mathbf{o}_t^a|\mathbf{u}^k)}{N(\mathbf{o}_t^a)}, \qquad (3)$$

where $\mathbf{u}^k$ is a value vector of subset $\mathbf{U}^k$, and $N(\mathbf{o}_t^a)$ is a normalization constant. Therefore, the number of mixtures to be estimated will be reduced from $\prod_d c^d$ to $\sum_m g^m$, and $\sum_m g^m \ll \prod_d c^d$. According to the speech organs that the articulator variables involved, we define the subsets as follows [1]:

- $\mathbf{U}^1$ = *voicing*;
- $\mathbf{U}^2$ = *velum*;
- $\mathbf{U}^3$ = *manner*;
- $\mathbf{U}^4$ = [*tongueBodyLH, tongueBodyBF, tongueShow*];
- $\mathbf{U}^5$ = [*lipRounding, lipSeparation*];
- $\mathbf{U}^6$ = *teethShow*.

Therefore, the audio Gaussian mixtures to be estimated will be rapidly reduced from 24576 to 86. Finally considering the above two parameter reduction schemes together, we need to estimate only 82 Gaussian mixtures for audio stream.

3 Adaptive Reliability Measure

We calculate the values of stream reliability variables λ_t^s using a separate frame level classification process prior to the recognition process. Since the discriminative powers of audio and visual signals can vary temporally and real-world noise may burst dramatically, we propose an adaptive stream reliability measure technique based on two local dispersion measurements. To the best of our knowledge, Adjoudani el al [5] first proposed the concept of dispersion for AVSR. Normally, the *dispersion* is defined as the variance of the classifier output, as in

$$\mathcal{D}^2 = \frac{1}{N-1} \sum_{n=1}^{N} (R_n - \mu)^2, \quad (4)$$

where R_n is the nth output of the classifier, and μ is the mean of all outputs. Dispersion is a good indicator of stream confidence, where large difference in classifier outputs indicates a greater confidence [5]. Lucey et al [6] have theoretically proven that dispersion approximately reflects the cepstral shrinkage effect induced by additive noise. We propose two *local* dispersion measures to reflect the temporal reliability of the audio and visual streams. They are presented as follows.

3.1 Frame Dispersion

Frame dispersion is defined as

$$\mathcal{F}_t^s = \mathcal{D}(P(\mathbf{o}_t^s | q_t^s)), \quad (5)$$

where $\mathcal{D}(\cdot)$ denotes the dispersion function shown in Eq. 4, and $P(\mathbf{o}_t^s | q_t^s)$ is the observation emission probability where an HMM-based recognizer is adopted.

We introduce the frame dispersion to describe the temporal discriminative power of each stream (audio and video). We know that audio speech and visual speech have quite different discriminative powers on different speech classes (e.g. phonemes). For example, phoneme [m] is acoustically very close to [n], resulting in a lower discriminative power on audio recognizer. However, [m] can be easily distinguished visually from [n] since they are observed as quite different mouth shapes; phoneme [m] is normally perceived a closed mouth, while [n] induces an opened mouth. Phoneme pair [p] and [m] has a different story. They both take on a closed mouth which makes them visually confusable. But they are quite distinguishable acoustically because they present different acoustic spectra. Therefore, a reasonable confidence measure is to depict each recognizer (stream) in short time intervals (such as frames). A higher frame dispersion indicates a higher frame reliability, while a lower one means a lower confidence. Fig. 3(a) shows an example of frame dispersion measure, in which a 6-best calculation is implemented to a fragment of an utterance audio (SNR=30dB, free of acoustic noise) from the AVCONDIG database [1]. From Fig. 3(a) we can clearly see that the frame dispersion is changing over time, which demonstrates that the audio recognizer has different discriminating power in different time depending on the N-best classification results.

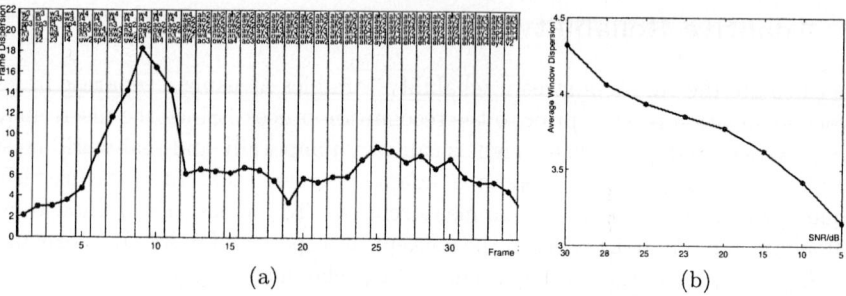

Fig. 3. Local Dispersion Measures. (a) Frame dispersions of a fragment of an utterance audio from the AVCONDIG database, where 6-best output hypotheses are given on the top. (b) Average window dispersions calculated on all the utterance audio from the AVCONDIG database at 8 different SNRs.

3.2 Window Dispersion

Window dispersion is defined as the local envelope of frame dispersions,

$$\mathcal{W}_t^s = \frac{1}{k} \sum_{r=t-k}^{t+k} \mathcal{F}_r^s, \tag{6}$$

where the window length is $2k+1$.

It is evident from the discussion earlier that in clean speech, the frame dispersion should be low for acoustically confusable sounds and high for relatively easily distinguishable sounds. In corrupted speech, however, due to noise the frame dispersions will vary. Consequently it is hard to judge whether the dispersion changes come from the varying discriminative powers of the recognizer or from the ambient noise presented in the audio channel. Hence, the frame-level dispersion measure is inadequate to decide the stream reliability. Therefore, we propose window dispersion to determine the noise level locally. Fig. 3(b) clearly illustrates the monotone relationship between the window dispersion and the noise level (SNR), where average window dispersions are calculated on all the utterance audio from the AVCONDIG database at 8 different SNRs.

3.3 Mapping to Stream Reliability Via MCE

Since we use two local measurements, frame dispersion and window dispersion, to determine the reliability of both audio and visual streams, that is,

$$\mathbf{C}_t^s = [\mathcal{F}_t^s, \mathcal{W}_t^s], \tag{7}$$

a mapping from $\mathbf{C}_t^s$ to stream reliability λ_t^s needs to be established. A simple and reasonable mapping is the following weight function:

$$\lambda_t^s = \mathbf{w}^s \mathbf{C}_t^s, \tag{8}$$

where $\mathbf{w}^s$ is called mapping weights. We are interested in finding a set of experiential values of $\mathbf{w}^s$ which leads to an optimal incorporation of the two local dispersion measures under some criterion. Since constrains $0 \leq \lambda_t^s \leq 1$ and $\sum_s \lambda_t^s = 1$ must be satisfied, we use the following normalized form:

$$\lambda_t^s = \frac{\mathbf{w}^s \mathbf{C}_t^s}{\sum_{s'} \mathbf{w}^{s'} \mathbf{C}_t^{s'}}. \tag{9}$$

We use minimum classification error (MCE) as the optimal criterion to train the mapping weights [7]. The goal of MCE is to choose an optimal weighting vector $\hat{\mathbf{w}}^s$ that maximizes the frame level classification performance on a training set $\mathcal{T}$. Suppose that L training sentences (audio and video) $\mathcal{O} = [\mathbf{O}^{(1)}, \cdots, \mathbf{O}^{(L)}]$ of duration $T_l (l = 1, \cdots, L)$ are available in $\mathcal{T}$. Given a state sequence x, the average conditional log-likelihood per frame is given by

$$\mathcal{L}_x^{(l)} = \frac{1}{T_l} \sum_{s=a,v} \sum_{t=1}^{T_l} \lambda_t^s \log P(\mathbf{o}_{st}^{(l)} | q_t^s). \tag{10}$$

Then the *misclassification measure* for utterance l is defined by

$$d^{(l)} = -\mathcal{L}_F^{(l)} + \log \left[\frac{1}{N_l} \sum_{n=1}^N \delta_{F,l}^{R_n} \exp(\mathcal{L}_{R_n}^{(l)}) \right], \tag{11}$$

where F denotes the state alignment of the correct word sequence W_l, and R_n denotes the state alignment of nth best hypothesis of the recognizer's output $W_l^{R_n}$. $N_l = \sum_{n=1}^N \delta_{F,l}^{R_n}$ is a normalization term. If $W_l^{R_n} \neq W_l$, $\delta_{F,l}^{R_n} = 1$; otherwise $\delta_{F,l}^{R_n} = 0$.

The *error function* is defined by

$$\epsilon^{(l)} = \frac{1}{1 + \exp[-\alpha(d^{(l)} + \beta)]}, \tag{12}$$

where α and β are constants and $\alpha > 0$. We estimate the mapping weights $\mathbf{w}^s$ using the following probabilistic gradient descent algorithm:

$$\mathbf{w}^{s,(k+1)} = \mathbf{w}^{s,(k)} - e_k \frac{\partial \epsilon^{(l)}}{\partial \mathbf{w}^{s,(k)}}. \tag{13}$$

The steps $e_k > 0$ and slowly decrease to 0.

4 Experiments

We have conducted experiments to investigate the performance of the proposed MSAM and the ARM. We have compared the MSAM with the MSHMM [1]. We have also made comparisons between the grid search (GS) [1] method and the proposed ARM method. The GS method searches in [0,1] for an optimal reliability pair which minimizes the word error rates (WERs). Once chosen, the reliability pair is fixed for all the utterances at the same SNR. Totally we built 4 AVSR systems, namely MSHMM-GS, MSHMM-ARM, MSAM-GS, and MSAM-ARM. For the 11-word digit vocabulary (one, two, $\cdots$, zero, oh), we trained state synchronized MSHMMs for the 22 phonemes with 3 states for each stream. For all the testing systems, a mixture of five continuous Gaussians was used for each MSHMM state or each allowed articulator value combination. An audio-only system (AO) with conventional left-to-right, three-state, five-continuous-Gaussian-mixture, phoneme HMMs was also built to benchmark the experiments. For the systems using ARM, we used two separate HMM-based recognizers for the audio and visual streams to collect the local dispersion measures before the recognition process.

The AVCONDIG database [1] was used for for all the experiments, which consisted of 100 audio visual recordings of a subject uttering strings of connected English digits. We separated the database into a training set (80 utterances) and a testing set (20 utterances). A set of 39 MFCCs with their velocity and acceleration derivatives was used as audio features, and 32 *Eigenlip* features were used for the visual stream. To evaluate the systems under various acoustic noise conditions, we artificially added babble noise into the testing audio at 6 SNRs from 28dB to 10dB. Table 1 shows the experimental results in terms of WER.

Table 1. Recognition results in terms of WER at 7 SNRs(Clean speech: SNR=30dB)

System	30dB	28dB	25dB	23dB	20dB	15dB	10dB
AO	1.8	19.7	22.7	34.8	48.5	57.6	84.9
MSHMM-GS	1.5	4.6	6.3	6.7	8.7	10.3	12.4
MSHMM-ARM	1.3	3.4	5.2	6.0	6.8	8.5	10.6
MSAM-GS	1.6	4.4	6.3	6.9	8.4	10.0	12.1
MSAM-ARM	1.3	3.0	5.1	6.1	6.8	9.6	11.9

Table 1 shows that the AO system is heavily affected by acoustic noise; and a 2dB small SNR degradation (30dB to 28dB) can result in a 17.9% absolute WER increase. Detailed analysis unveils that lots of insertion errors occur when speech is contaminated by the babble noise since the babble noise is also composed of speech. Not surprisingly, all the testing AVSR systems are able to dramatically decrease the WERs at noisy conditions. The MSAM-GS system achieve comparable results with the MSHMM-GS system. Moreover, at several testing SNRs such as 28dB, 20dB, 15dB, and 10dB, the MSAM-GS system even can achieve lower WERs than the MSHMM-GS system. With the help of the proposed ARM method, the MSHMM-ARM and MSAM-ARM systems can further decrease the WERs compared to those systems using the GS method. Also, the MSAM-ARM system achieve better results than the MSHMM-ARM system when SNR=28dB and SNR=25dB.

Fig. 4 clearly plots the frame dispersions of both audio and visual streams varying over time, where calculations are made on an utterance (SNR=30dB, free of noise) from the testing set. From Fig. 4 we can observe that frame dispersions change dramatically over time. In most occasions, frame dispersions of the visual stream are much lower than that of the audio stream, which indicates that audio speech conveys more information for classification than visual speech. Surprisingly in most non-speech area, frame dispersions of visual speech are higher than that of audio speech, especially at the long silence areas of the

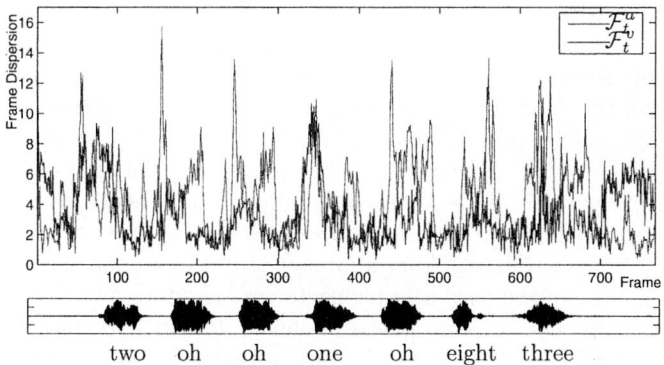

Fig. 4. Frame dispersions of both audio and visual streams for a testing utterance, whose waveform is shown on the bottom (SNR=30dB)

utterance start and end. This is probably because a fully closed mouth can be easily distinguished from other mouth shapes, thus providing higher confidence in making decisions.

Fig. 5 illustrates the window dispersions (SNR=30dB, 25dB and 10dB) of the same testing utterance. In the speech area, these dispersion curves obviously reflect the cepstral shrinkage effect. Interestingly in the speech intervals (non-speech areas), window dispersion curves *dilate* with the decrease of SNR. It unveils that the discriminative distance between classification units (sub-phonemes) expands with the addition of noise. It might be explained as follows. Under noise-free conditions, the HMM states of phonemes [sil] and [sp] have greater probabilities to get their entries into the 6-Best hypothesis list. But the observation emission probabilities of these states are very close as they are all non-speech snippets, inducing a lower dispersion. With the addition of babble noise (actually speech), non-silence phoneme states achieve greater opportunities to get into the 6-Best list, thus enlarging the distances between the observation probabilities.

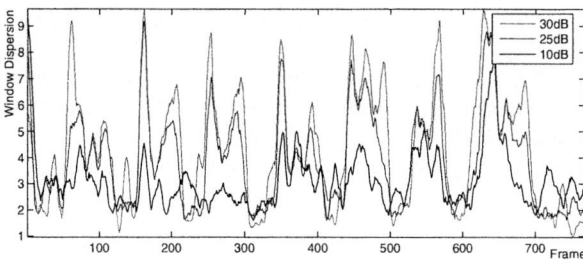

Fig. 5. Window dispersions of the audio stream for the same testing utterance when SNR=30dB, 25dB and 10dB

5 Conclusions

We have proposed a multi-stream articulator model for AVSR. Experiments have demonstrated that our model can achieve comparable recognition performance with the conventional phoneme-based MSHMM under various audio SNRs. We have also presented an adaptive reliability measure to integrate the audio and visual streams with local, temporal reliability. Experiments have shown that adaptive stream reliability outperforms the fixed one that maximizes the WER of the data set. Since our articulatory approach still uses a phoneme-to-articulator mapping scheme, we are currently trying to realize direct articulator modelling that totally eliminates the contiguous phoneme line-up structure. Moreover, as our stream reliability modelling technique is realized in a separate estimation process which adopts phoneme state emission probability, we are interested in modelling articulator-related stream reliability explicitly in the recognition process.

Acknowledgement

This paper is supported in part by a Hong Kong RGC grant (CityU 1062/02E).

References

1. Xie L.: Research on Key Issues of Audio Visual Speech Recognition. Ph.D Thesis of Northwestern Polytechnical University (2004)
2. Richardson, J., Bilmes, J., Diorio, C.: Hidden-Articulator Models for Speech Recognition. Speech Communication. **41** (2003) 511–529
3. Bilmes, J.A., Zweig, G. et al: Discrimiatively Structured Graphical Models for Speech Recognition. Technical Report of JHU 2001 Summer Workshop (2001)
4. Saenko, K., Livescu, K., Glass, J., Darrell T.: Production Domain Modeling of Pronunciation for Visual Speech Recognition. Proc. ICASSP 2005, Philadelphia (2005)
5. Adjoudani A., Benoit C.: On the Integration of Auditory and Visual Parameters on an HMM-based ASR. In: Stork, D.G., Hennecke, M.E. (eds.): Speechreading by Humans and Machines. Springer, Berlin, Germany (1996) 461–471
6. Lucey S.: Audio-Visual Speech Processing. Ph.D Thesis of Queensland University of Technology (2002)
7. Xie, L., Zhao, R.C., Liu, Z.Q.: Adaptive Stream Reliability Modelling based on Local Dispersion Measures for Audio Visual Speech Recognitin. Proc. ICMLC 2005, Guangzhou, China (2005)

Optical Font Recognition of Chinese Characters Based on Texture Features

Ming-hu Ha and Xue-dong Tian

College of Physics Science and Technology,
Hebei University, 071002 Baoding, Hebei, China
{mhha, xdtian}@mail.hbu.edu.cn

Abstract. Font recognition is a fundamental issue in the identification, analysis and reconstruction of documents. In this paper, a new method of optical font recognition is proposed which could recognize the font of every Chinese character. It employs a statistical method based on global texture analysis to recognize a predominant font, and uses a traditional recognizer of a single font to identify the font of a single character by the guidance of an obtained predominant font. It consists of three steps. First, the guiding fonts are acquired based on Gabor features. Then a font recognizer is run to identify the font of the characters one by one. Finally, a post-processing is fulfilled according to the layout knowledge to correct the errors of font recognition. Experiments are carried out and the results show that this method is of immense practical and theoretical value.

1 Introduction

In addition to the content of characters itself, there is also much layout information in a printed document such as the font and size of characters. However, neither keying by hand nor using OCR (Optical Character Recognition) system for data entry can extract the layout information, which is fatal when the original layout is restructured. So, font recognition is a fundamental issue in the identification and analysis of documents.

So far, most of the papers detailing research on font recognition have assumed that the documents are printed in a single predominant font. Khoubyari and Hulf[1] proposed an approach to identify the predominant font printed in a text. Their method has an advantage in the fact that most machine-printed documents are printed in a single predominant font. Repeated words, such as function words, can provide cues for font recognition, and can also be utilized to tackle the problem of noise corruption. Kuhnke et al. [2] proposed an approach for distinguishing machine-printed and hand-written characters. In their approach, two kinds of features, namely, the line isolation and the inner loop isolation, are obtained in the phase of feature extraction. Fan and Wang [3] presented a method to classify machine-printed and hand-written text automatically. In their proposed method, a run length histogram is constructed to extract the directional feature and long stroke ratio, which are both useful in identifying the type of a text block image. Their assumption is that machine-printed characters may have more long straight strokes than those of hand-written characters, thus the long stroke ratio of the machine-printed characters is larger. However, an erroneous result will be obtained if the printed fonts fail in satisfying the above assumption. Such is the case with the fonts of Fang-Song and Xing, etc. Zhu et al. [4] and Carlos et al. [5] takes the document as an image containing some specific textures and regards font recognition as texture identification. They extract digital statistical features through Gabor filters from the texture or window analysis, then match them with the template features in one single dictionary by calculating the weighted Euclidean distance.

All of the methods above are based on the hypothesis that most layouts are printed in a uniform font. So they can only identify the predominant font of a text paragraph. This results in the fatal loss of the font of single characters which is unfortunate because the character font has plenty of meaning in many cases. Although some methods of single character font recognition are also provided, they can not be applied in practice because of their low accuracy [6], [7], [8].

In our study, an approach of font recognition of single Chinese characters is developed which makes use of the predominant font as the guiding font to reduce the complexity of the recognizing algorithm. It consists of the following steps:

- Predominant font identification by Gabor texture analysis.
- Font recognition of individual character based on the guiding font.
- Post-processing based on the typesetting knowledge of the font.

This paper is arranged as follows: in Section 2 the identification method of predominant font based on Gabor texture analysis is described. The algorithms of font recognition of individual character are discussed and the post-processing rules of font recognition are shown in Section 3 and Section 4 respectively. The last two sections contain the experiment results and the conclusion for the entire paper.

2 Predominant Font Identification Based on Gabor Texture Analysis

Because font characteristics are often related to some local region, it is very difficult to draw the font features for every single Chinese character. However, according to the study conducted by Chang and Chen [9], more than 20% of Chinese characters in a document are predominated by the MFU (most frequently used) font. If the MFU font is detected before the OCR technology is employed, an approximate 20% saving in computation time can be expected. In our method, the Chinese characters are put together to form a kind of texture that appears as the font feature and a Gabor filter is used for analyzing this font texture because it can simulate the optical mechanism of a human being, and so perfectly obtain local characteristics in spatial and frequency domain at the same time. Gabor filters transform the input texture image with a fixed scale window, and the statistical value of the result is the texture feature.

2.1 Parameters Optimization of Gabor Filters

2D Gabor filters have the following general forms:

$$\begin{cases} h_e(x,y) = e^{-\frac{(x^2+y^2)}{2\sigma^2}} \cos(2\pi\omega_0(x\cos\theta_0 + y\sin\theta_0)) \\ h_o(x,y) = e^{-\frac{(x^2+y^2)}{2\sigma^2}} \sin(2\pi\omega_0(x\cos\theta_0 + y\sin\theta_0)), \end{cases} \quad (1)$$

where ω_0 is the central frequency, θ_0 is the angle of orientation and σ is the space constant of the Gabor envelope.

Since different combinations of those free parameter values define different Gabor filters, the design of the filters, whose purpose is to extract classing features with as few filters as possible, is in essence to select proper parameter values. Dimension of the texture feature is related to the number of the filters included in one filter group and usually the higher the dimension, the lower the recognition speed, but too few filters will result in the loss of this effective feature. So the angle parameter selection of the Gabor filter is very important when texture features are to be extracted with the Gabor filter.

Although the mentioned methods are different in frequency selection, the orientation values are all 0°, 45°, 90°, 135° [10], [11], [12], [13]. However, there is a great difference between the font texture and the natural texture. The texture features of a font may be only affected by the stroke orientation, density distribution and the stroke profile in some special degrees, therefore the orientation values should be selected strictly. In our method, classical GA (Genetic Algorithm)[14], [15] is employed to optimize the orientation set with the known frequency and spatial constant [16], [17].

Since the Gabor filters are symmetric and the orientation space covers from 0° to 180°, the orientation spans are taken as 15° and 5° respectively, thus 12 or 36 bits, which represent the corresponding orientation values, is either used or not in each orientation set, to form the chromosome in the GA. There are some font textures used as classifiers and other textures used as tuningsamples for calculating the font recognition rate. The GA searches for an orientation set that minimizes the number of orientations while maximizing classification accuracy from all possible orientation sets. So, the fitness function is designed as follows:

$$Fitness = a \times \frac{N_R}{N_{TS}} + \frac{b}{N_A} , \qquad (2)$$

where N_R is the number of correctly recognized samples, N_{TS} is the total count of samples, N_A is the orientation number of an angles set and a and b are constants whose value can be drawn by experience.

When the image on a newspaper is pretreated, text blocks on a natural background are arranged in a texture picture of 256x256 pixels as Fig. 1 shows.

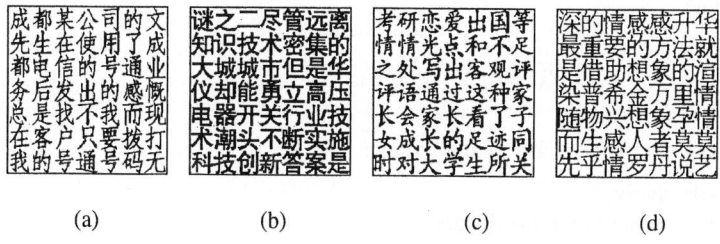

(a)   (b)   (c)   (d)

Fig. 1. Font Texture samples

Details of the genetic algorithm can be found in the related paper[17]. Here, we do not intend to repeat what has already been done.

The experiments show that a high accuracy of classification can be obtained by using 25°, 55°, and 75°, and the optimized filters can be expressed as:

$$\begin{cases} h_{ie}(x,y) = e^{-\frac{(x^2+y^2)}{2\sigma_i^2}} \cos(\omega_i(x\cos\theta_i + y\sin\theta_i)) \\ h_{io}(x,y) = e^{-\frac{(x^2+y^2)}{2\sigma_i^2}} \sin(\omega_i(x\cos\theta_i + y\sin\theta_i)) \end{cases} \quad (3)$$

2.2 Font Classification Based on Gabor Filters

The extraction of features is carried out in a channel that is formed with a pair of Gabor filters as shown in Formula 3. The image $p_i(x,y)$ is obtained from the font texture image $I(x, y)$ which is transformed by the channel i ($i =1, 2, \cdots, m$) of the Gabor filter.

$$p_i(x,y) = \sqrt{q_{ie}^2(x,y) + q_{io}^2(x,y)}, \quad (4)$$

$$\begin{cases} q_{ie}(x,y) = h_{ie}(x,y) \otimes I(x,y) \\ q_{io}(x,y) = h_{io}(x,y) \otimes I(x,y), \end{cases} \quad (5)$$

where $\otimes$ is the symbol of convolution.

Texture features of the same font, even drawn from the same document, are different in gray level, the distribution of stroke density and orientation being caused by different printing quality and randomly used characters in a document. Thus, one single dictionary cannot denote all the textures accurately. To solve this problem, several dictionaries are employed to obtain a robust classifier. Although the more dictionaries the better the fitness, only 4 feature vector templates $F_j^k (j=1\cdots 4)$ for font $k(k=1..K)$, which are saved in dictionary Dic_j respectively, are set to balance the space-time complexity and the performance [9]. Also, the dictionaries are initialized with the GA classifier features.

The Euclidean distance classifier is used to identify the font. Features of an unknown testing font are compared with the dictionaries' features. The distance can be calculated as:

$$D(F_S, F_j^k) = \sqrt{\sum_{i=1}^{2*l}(F_{Si} - F_{ji}^k)^2}, \quad (6)$$

where F_S is the unknown font feature vector, and F_{Si}, F_{ji}^k denote the ith feature of the vectors respectively.

Classifying is based on this distance:

$$D_{\min} = \min(D(F_S, F_j^k)) \, j=1\cdots 4, k=1\cdots K. \quad (7)$$

The font can be decided by the template corresponding to $D_{\min}$.

3 Font Recognition of Individual Characters Based on the Guidance of the Predominant Font

As a single-font recognizer adopts the feature dictionary of a certain font, it is ideal for recognizing the corresponding font, but totally inadequate for use with other kinds of font. This characteristic can be used for discerning fonts. By analyzing the different results among these single-font recognizers in identifying the same character, the font information can be drawn [19]. The recognition diagram is shown in Fig. 2.

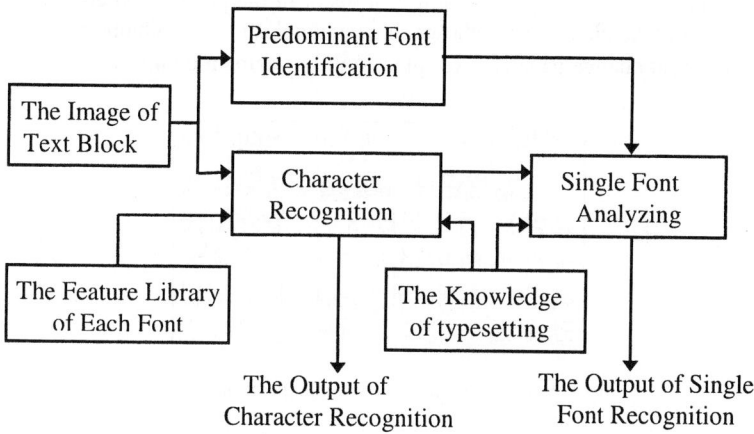

Fig. 2. The diagram of single font recognition

Let the feature vector of the unknown character be X $(x_1\ x_2\ \ldots\ x_T)$. The first character of a text block is recognized by the guidance of the predominant font of the block. The matching result is obtained according to the following rules:

Rule 1. R_i ($1 \leq i \leq K$) is the corresponding recognizer of the guidance font, and $D_i(X)$ is the matching result of R_i. If $D_i(X) < T_{min0}$, where T_{min0} is a threshold value obtained from the experiment, the font of the character is F_i. Otherwise, a new guidance font is chosen to recognize the unknown character again with the help of typesetting knowledge.

Rule 2. $D_i(X)$ ($1 \leq i \leq K$) is the match result of R_i. If $D_i(X) \geq T_{min0}$, the recognizing result of an unknown character is $D_j(X) = \min(D_1(X), D_2(X) \ldots, D_k(X))$. If $D_j(X) \leq T_{min1}$, where T_{min1} is a parameter measured by experiment, the font of the unknown character is the corresponding font with $D_j(X)$, otherwise it is the predominant font.

Rule 3. If the font of the unknown character is F_i (($1 \leq i \leq K$), then F_i is the guidance font of the next character.

Rule 4. Assume that the unknown character is an element of the sort L, which has N_1 standard character templates whose feature vectors are M_i (m_{i1}, m_{i2}, …, m_{iT}) ($1 \leq i \leq N_l$), the result of the feature match of X is:

$$D(X) = \min(D(X, M_1), D(X, M_2), \cdots, D(X, M_l)) . \qquad (8)$$

4 Post-processing of Font Recognition

Inevitably, there exist some errors in the results of font recognition. These errors are very harmful and distinct in the reconstructed document. To solve these problems, a post-processing section is proposed in this paper to correct the errors with the help of typesetting laws as follows:

- Most documents are printed in a single font.
- The font change rarely occurs on a single character.
- Generally, there is punctuation or a blank in the position where the changes of font take place. Fig. 3 shows some examples of these changes.
- The font change usually takes place within a semantic unit.

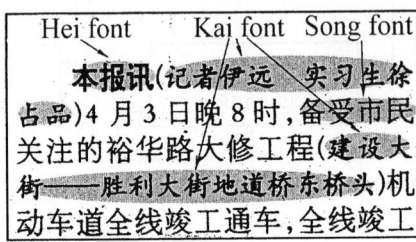

Fig. 3. The examples of font changes in layouts

Rule 5. Let $S_i(1 \leq i \leq K)$ be the character set between punctuations (including blanks). Assume that N_{ij} is the character number of the *j*th font in S_i. Then the local predominant font $LPF_i(1 \leq LPF_i \leq K)$ of S_i is finally identified as:

$$LPF_i = j \Big| N_{ij} = \max_{k=1,2,\ldots,K}(N_{ik}) \,. \tag{9}$$

Rule 6. Let C_{ij} be a character within S_i, and $F(C_{ij})$ be the font of C_{ij}. If $F(C_{ij}) \neq LPF_i$, then $F(C_{ij}) = LPF_i$.

5 Experiment Results

The fitness of the font recognizer rises remarkably with the decline in the number of angles when the Gabor angles are optimized by GA. The highest accuracy can be reached by using 45, 90, and 135 degrees with a span of 15 degrees, which reduces the dimension of the feature vector and improves the discerning speed. When 80 (20 pieces of each font) training samples of low quality are selected from recognized samples, two angles of 25 and 55 degrees are obtained by GA with a small range (such as 60) and a span of 5 degrees, and the accuracy rises to 93%.

By selecting samples of each kind of font (Song, Kai, Fang Song and Bold font) from a newspaper, 10,176 texture images of different fonts are formed. The accuracy of recognition using texture feature extracted by the optimized Gabor filter is as per

Table 1. It is remarkable that the texture feature drawn by using 25 and 55 degrees is more effective and the discernment rate is remarkably improved.

In the experiment of individual font recognition, four kinds of font are tested. Each kind has ten sets of samples, and each set of samples has 4,135 Chinese characters. This means that in a test of 40 sets of samples, 165,400 Chinese characters have been used. The result is shown in Table 2. In this table, the row represents the sample's actual font, and the column represents the result of the font recognition.

Table 1. The result of predominant font recognition

Font	Number	The result from traditional methods		The result from the optimized method	
		Correct number	Recognition Rate(%)	Correct number	Recognition Rate(%)
Song	3,257	2,644	81.18	3,029	92.99
Kai	3,102	1,955	63.02	3,050	98.32
Fang Song	2,733	1,967	71.97	2,301	84.19
Hei	1,084	1,051	96.96	1,078	99.45
Total	10,176	7,617	74.85	9,458	92.94

Table 2. The result of single font recognition

Font	Song	Kai	Fang song	Hei
Song	97.87%	0.10%	0.72%	1.31%
Kai	0.22%	98.37%	1.29%	0.12%
Fang song	0.75%	1.37%	97.45%	0.43%
Hei	1.86%	0.13%	0.58%	97.43%

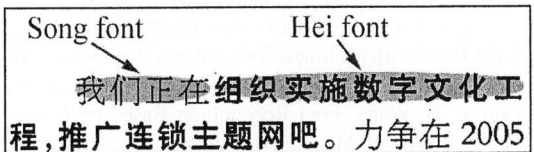

Fig. 4. The exceptional example of font changing

After the post-processing of font recognition, the average rate of font recognition achieves 99.28%, which indicates the validity of this method.

There exists an exceptional example shown in Fig.4 in which the font distribution is not according to the typesetting laws concluded in Section 4, and which will result in an error result of post-processing. In this case, more knowledge, such as the last typesetting law in Section 4, should be used to avoid the occurrence of these errors.

6 Conclusion

In this paper, an improved font recognition approach of individual character is put forward. There are three remarkable characteristics in this method. The first is that the single-font recognizer is started by a guidance font, which reduces the random selection of the recognizer. The second is that the GA algorithm is used to optimize the Gabor filters to obtain the predominant font. Finally, a post-processing step is employed which uses a set of rules about typesetting knowledge to improve the accuracy of font recognition. The results show that the method is of immense practical and theoretical value.

Our future research is to explore a method for correcting the errors in single font recognition as shown in Fig. 4. The semantic information is to be used in this work. A sentence will be segmented into words by the technique of Chinese word segmentation if different fonts of characters exist in it. Then the error correction rules discussed in the previous section will be applied to the individual word units.

Acknowledgements

This work is supported by National Natural Science Foundation of China (60573069), the National Natural Science Foundation of China (NSFC 60473045), the Natural Science Foundation of Hebei Province (603137), and Natural Science Foundation of Hebei Province (F2004000129; F2004000132).

References

1. S. Khoubyari, J. J. Hull. Font and Function Word Identification in Document Recognition. Computer Vision and Image Understanding. 1 (1996) 66-74
2. K. Kuhnke, L. Simoncini, Z. M. Kovacs-V. A System for Machine-written and Handwritten Character Distinction. Proceedings of the International Conference on Document Analysis and Recognition, 2, Montreal Canada (1995) 811-814
3. K. C. Fan, L. S. Wang. A Run Length Histogram Based Approach to the Identification of Machine-Printed and Handwritten Chinese Text Images. Proceedings of International Conference on Computer Vision, Graphics and Image Processing. Taiwan (1996) 416-420
4. Y. Zhu, T. N. Tan, Y. H. Wang. Font Recognition Based on Global Texture Analysis. IEEE Trans. Pattern Analysis and Machine Intelligence, 10(2001) 1192-1200
5. A. C. Carlos, R. K. Risto, R. A. Mario. High-order Statistical Texture Analysis–Font Recognition Applied. Pattern Recognition Letters. 26 (2005) 135–145
6. L. Chen, X. Q. Ding. Font Recognition of Single Chinese Character. In Huai, J. P. (Eds): Progress of Intelligence Computer Research, Tsinghua Press, Beijing China. (2001) 338-342

7. R. Zramdini. Optical Font Recognition Using Typographical Features, IEEE Transactions on Pattern Analysis and Machine Intelligence, 8 (1998) 877-882, 1998
8. M. C. Jung, Y. C. Shin, S. N. Srihari. Multifont Classification Using Typographical Attributes. Proc. of International Conference on Document Analysis and Recognition, Bangalore India (1999) 353-356
9. C. H. Chang, C. D Chen. A Study on Corpus based Classification of Chinese Words. Proceedings of the Int. Conf. on Chinese Computing, Singapore (1994) 310-316
10. C. F. Lin, Y. F. Fang, Y. T. Juang. Chinese Text Distinction and Font Identification by Recognizing Most Frequently Used Characters. Image and Vision Computing. 19 (2001) 329-338
11. A. C. Bovik, M. Clark, W. S. Geisler. Multichannel Texture Analysis Using Localized Spatial Filters. IEEE transactions on Pattern Analysis and Machine Intelligence. 1 (1990) 55-73
12. A. K. Jain, F. Farrokhnia. Unsupervised Texture Segmentation Using Gabor Filters. Pattern Recognition. 12(1991) 1167-1186
13. D. Patel, T. J. Stonham. Accurate Set-up of Gabor Filters for Texture Classification. Proceeding of SPIE, Visual Communications and Image Processing, 2501 (1995) 894-903,
14. M. Zhou, S. D. Sun. Genetic Algorithm: Theory and Applications. National defence industry press, Beijing, China (1999)
15. M. L. Raymer, W. F. Punch. Dimensionality Reduction Using Genetic Algorithm. IEEE transactions on Evolutionary Computation. 2 (2000) 164-171
16. X. D. Tian, B. L. Guo. Chinese Character Font Recognition Based on Texture Features. Computer Engineering, 6 (2002) 156-157
17. F. Yang, X. D. Tian. An Improved Font Recognition Method Based on Texture Analysis, Proceedings of the First International Conference on Machine Learning and Cybernetics, Beijing China (2002) 1726-1729
18. T. N. Tan. Texture Feature Extraction via Cortical Channel Modeling. Proc. 11th International Conference on Pattern Recognition, Assoc. for Pattern Recognition, Hague Netherlands (1992) 607-610
19. X. F. Miao, X. D. Tian. Individual Character Font Recognition Based on Guidance Font, Proceedings of the First International Conference on Machine Learning and Cybernetics, Beijing China (2002) 1715-1717

Some Characteristics of Fuzzy Integrals as a Multiple Classifiers Fusion Method

Huimin Feng[1], Xuefei Li[2], Tiegang Fan[1], and Yanju Chen[1]

[1] Department of Mathematics and Computer Science, Hebei University,
Baoding, Hebei, P.R. China
hmfeng@mail.hbu.edu.cn, yhmalyhmal@sina.com
[2] College of Science, Hebei Agriculture University, Baoding, Hebei, P.R. China
ddgbb@sin.com

Abstract. Fuzzy integrals have attracted the attention of many researchers as a solution for expressing the interactions between classifiers in multiple-classifier fusion. In a classifier fusion system based on fuzzy integrals, the fuzzy measures will have a major impact on a system's performance. Much work has been carried out by numerous authors on how to determine the fuzzy measures to improve results. Our paper presents some new characteristics of multiple-classifier fusion based on fuzzy integrals. This paper discusses the conditions under which the fusion system must give the incorrect classification and that the fusion system can give the correct classification even if all classifiers have given an incorrect classification. It will be helpful for improving classifier fusion systems and designing classifiers in application.

1 Introduction

In many classification problems, it is extremely difficult for a single classifier or a single algorithm to achieve highly reliable classification due to a number of reasons. For example, the common weakness of neural networks is the trap of the local optimal in the learning process and the decision tree's weakness is that the one-step-ahead node splitting without backtracking may not be able to generate the best tree. It is logical to combine multiple classifiers to achieve higher reliability. A variety of schemes have been proposed for combining multiple classifiers. The soft computing approaches used most often include the majority vote [1], averaging [2], weighted averaging [3], the fuzzy integral [4 - 7], the fuzzy templates [8], the Dempster-Shafer theory [9] etc. Among those methods, the value of the fuzzy integral in classifier fusion has been well established. The fusion of multiple classifiers is valuable in overcoming the inherent ambiguities present in a single classifier and in resolving conflicting information from separate classifiers. However, generating the importance of each subset of the classifiers in determining a crisp class label is a difficult and important task. In the past, many authors have performed much research work in determining the importance of each subset of classifiers group [4 –7, 10, 11].

A large advantage of using fuzzy integrals within classification is due to the unique behavioral property of the fuzzy integral. The fusion based on fuzzy integrals can deal with the information from multiple classifiers that may agree or conflict with each other. It can combine the objective evidence for a hypothesis with the system's expectation of the importance of that evidence to the hypothesis. And many experiences have proved that the fuzzy integral performs well in multiple classifier fusion[6,12]. To our knowledge, no paper has reported on the performance of fuzzy integral as a method of multiple classifier fusion in theory. This paper will attempt to analyze the performance of the fusion from a view other than experience.

Section 2 reviews the concepts and mathematical properties of fuzzy measure and fuzzy integrals. Section 3 contains the formalization of multiple classifier fusion based on fuzzy integrals. Section 4 describes our analyses of the performance of fusion based on fuzzy integrals and Section 5 presents our conclusion.

2 Background on Fuzzy Measure and Fuzzy Integral

In this section we briefly describe the basic concepts of the fuzzy measure and the fuzzy integral. Fuzzy measures and fuzzy integrals were first introduced by Sugeno [13]. In multi-classifier fusion, measure corresponds to the importance of the subset of a classifier group. Fuzzy integral is a nonlinear approach to combining multiple sources of uncertain information. In application, the integral is evaluated over the set of outputs of classifiers. The function being integrated supplies a confidence value for a particular hypothesis from which class the instance to be classified comes.

2.1 Fuzzy Measures

Fuzzy measures are the natural generalizations of classical measures. Let X be an arbitrary nonempty set and Ω a sigma-algebra of subsets of X. When X is finite, Ω is the power set of X. In information fusion (including fusion of classifiers) fuzzy measures are usually regular fuzzy measures. A set function $\mu : \Omega \to [0, 1]$ defined on Ω which has the following properties is called a *regular fuzzy measure*.

(1) $\mu(\emptyset) = 0$, $\mu(X) = 1$;
(2) If $A, B \in \Omega$ and $A \subset B$, then $\mu(A) \leq \mu(B)$ (Monotonicity);
(3) If $E_n \in \Omega$, for $1 \leq n < \infty$, and the sequence $\{E_n\}$ is monotone (in the sense of inclusion), then:
$$\lim_{n \to \infty} \mu(E_n) = \mu(\lim_{n \to \infty} E_n) \text{ (Continuity)}.$$

Since X is always finite in the fusion of multiple classifiers where X represents the set of classifiers, the continuity requirement (the third condition (3)) for μ is insignificant. Then μ satisfying the first two conditions is a fuzzy measure. Fuzzy measure μ is nonadditive in general (i.e. usually $\mu(A \cup B) \neq \mu(A) + \mu(B)$, $A \cap B = \emptyset$). The nonadditivity of μ means that, for the comprehensive numerical evaluation of the target, the combined contribution of classifiers in a set may be more or less than the sum of the contributions of each classifier in the set. In general, the measure of the union of two disjoint subsets cannot be directly computed by the components' measures.

If a fuzzy measure μ is called $\lambda-fuzzy\ measure$ when there exits $\lambda > -1$ (for regular fuzzy measure) such that:

$$\mu(A \cup B) = \mu(A) + \mu(B) + \lambda\mu(A)\mu(B), \quad A \subset X, B \subset X, A \cap B = \emptyset.$$

λ can be obtained uniquely through the following equation:

$$1 + \lambda = \prod_{i=1}^{n}(1 + \mu(\{x_i\}))$$

where $\mu(\{x_i\})$ is the fuzzy measure value on the single point of X. The fuzzy measure values on the single point are called fuzzy density. The $\lambda-$fuzzy measure value on the subset of X can be calculated as:

$$\mu(A) = \frac{1}{\lambda}\prod_{x \in A}(1 + \mu(\{x\})), \quad \lambda \neq 0$$

$$\mu(A) = \sum_{x \in A}\mu(\{x\}), \quad \lambda = 0$$

If we know the fuzzy density, we can know the $\lambda-$fuzzy measure value on each subset of X. So we often use the $\lambda-$fuzzy measure in classifier fusion instead.

2.2 Fuzzy Integrals

Let X={$x_1, x_2, x_3, ..., x_n$} be a finite set and μ is a fuzzy measure defined on the power set of X. f is a nonnegative function defined on X, $f : X \to [0, 1]$.

The Sugeno fuzzy integral of the function f with respect to the fuzzy measure μ on X is defined, in symbol $(s)\int f\ d\mu$, as:

$$(s)\int f\ d\mu = \max_{E \subset X}[\min(\min_{x \in E} f(x), \mu(E))] \\
= \max_{\alpha \in [0,1]}[\min(\alpha, \mu(f_\alpha))] \quad (1)$$

where f_α is the level set of f:

$$f_\alpha = \{x \mid f(x) \geq \alpha, x \in X\} \quad (2)$$

The Choquet fuzzy integral of the function f with respect to the fuzzy measure μ on X is defined, in symbol $(c)\int f\ d\mu$, as:

$$(c)\int f\ d\mu = \int_0^{+\infty} \mu(F_\alpha)d\alpha \quad (3)$$

where f_α is defined as in formula (2).

Let $f(x_i) = f_i$, and $f_1 \geq f_2 \geq \cdots \geq f_n$ (if not, f_i can be rearranged so that this relation holds). Then the Sugeno integral of f over X with respect to μ can be computed as follows:

$$(s)\int f \, d\mu = \max_{1 \leq i \leq n}[\min(f(x_i), \mu(A_i))] \tag{4}$$

where $A_i = \{x_1, x_2, \cdots, x_i\}$.

Let $f(x_i) = f_i$, and $f_1 \geq f_2 \geq \cdots \geq f_n$ (if not, f_i can be rearranged so that this relation holds). Then the Choquet integral of f over X with respect to μ can be computed as follows:

$$(c)\int f \, d\mu = \sum_{i=1}^{n}[f(x_i) - f(x_{i-1})]\mu(\{x_i, x_{i+1}, \cdots, x_n\}) \tag{5}$$

where $f(x_0) = 0$.

The following properties of the two types of fuzzy integral can be easily proven [14]. We denote the two types of fuzzy integral as $\int f \, d\mu$. We have:

1. If $f_1(x) \leq f_2(x)$, for all $x \in X$, then:

$$\int f_1 \, d\mu \leq \int f_2 \, d\mu \tag{6}$$

2. For any measure μ, it holds:

$$\min_{x \in X} f(x) \leq \int f \, d\mu \leq \max_{x \in X} f(x) \tag{7}$$

3 The Model of Multiple Classifiers Fusion

3.1 Classifier Fusion System

Let $D=\{O_1, O_2, \ldots\}$ be a set of instances which come from different classes $C_1, C_2, \ldots, C_q$. Given an instance, each class C_k will represent a hypothesis that the instance comes from class C_k. Let X=$\{x_1, x_2, \ldots, x_n\}$ be a finite set which represents a set of n classifiers and μ_k be the measure on the power set of X and corresponding class C_k. We denote the output of the ith classifier as $[h_{i,1}, h_{i,2}, \cdots, h_{i,q}]$, where $h_{i,j}$ is interpreted as the degree of "support" given by classifier x_i to the hypothesis that an instance comes from class C_j.

The classifier outputs can be organized in a *decision profile* (DP) as per the following matrix [8].

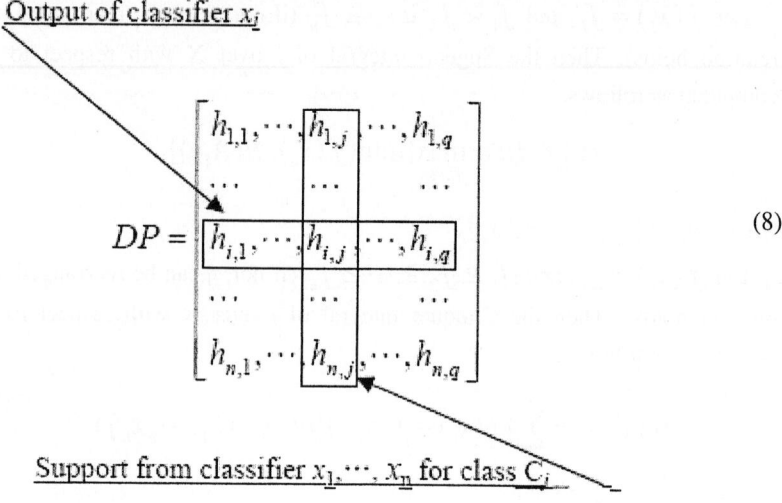

$$DP = \begin{bmatrix} h_{1,1}, \cdots, h_{1,j}, \cdots, h_{1,q} \\ \cdots \\ h_{i,1}, \cdots, h_{i,j}, \cdots, h_{i,q} \\ \cdots \\ h_{n,1}, \cdots, h_{n,j}, \cdots, h_{n,q} \end{bmatrix} \qquad (8)$$

We denote $[h_{1,j}, h_{2,j}, \cdots, h_{n,j}]^T$ (superscript T denotes transpose) as h_j which can been interpreted as a function $h_j : X \to [0,1]$, $h_j(x_i) = h_{i,j}$, $1 \leq i \leq n$. Given an instance O_k, we can obtain the h_j for the class C_j from the outputs of the n classifiers. We can then obtain the overall support from all classifiers through calculating the fuzzy integral of h_j with respect to the fuzzy measure μ_j defined in advance. In this process the objective evidence (i.e. h_j) supplied by each classifier and the expected importance (i.e. the measure μ_j on the power set of X) of each subset of classifiers are considered at the same time. Finally, the class C_t with the largest integral value is chosen as the output class.

$$C_t = \arg(\max_{1 \leq i \leq q} \int h_i \, d\mu_i) \qquad (9)$$

where fuzzy integral $\int h_i \, d\mu_i$ can be Choquet integral or Sugeno integral. And we denote both Choquet integral and Sugeno integral as $\int h_i \, d\mu_i$ in the following discussions.

Fig. 1 is the general frame of a classifier fusion system based on fuzzy integrals. In a classifier fusion system based on fuzzy integrals, the outputs of a classifier are between 0 and 1. Their sum can be equal to 1, or not. Here, the discussions are limited to the fusion process. Other processes of the fusion system are not so relevant to this discussion.

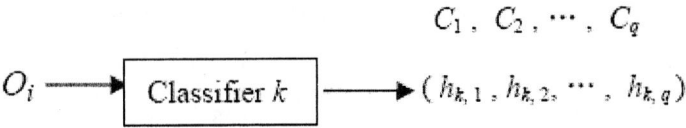

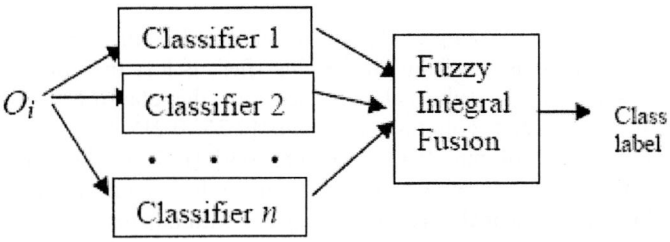

Fig. 1. A A single classifier in classifier fusion; **B** Architecture of classifier fusion system

4 Some New Opinions About the Performance of Fuzzy Integral as a Fusion Method

Definition 1. Given the classification task of q classes with n classifiers $x_1, x_2, \ldots, x_n$, an instance O is called *negative fixed point* with respect to classifiers $x_1, x_2, \ldots, x_n$, if there exists j, such that:

$$\max_{1 \le i \le n} h_{i,k} < \min_{1 \le i \le n} h_{i,j}, \quad j \ne k, \ 1 \le j \le q,$$

where k is the true class label of instance O, and h_j is the jth column of the decision profile of instance O.

We can see that for a negative fixed point all classifiers give incorrect classification. Now we analyze the performance of a fuzzy integral in classifier fusion primarily under the circumstances that for a given instance all classifiers give incorrect class labels. The aim of combining multiple classifiers is to overcome the conflicts among classifiers and obtain the synthetic evaluation about the true class label. Briefly, the ideal result is to obtain correct classification if partial classifiers give correct classification. How about the case that all classifiers give incorrect classification? In this case, the classifiers can perhaps still give us some useful information about the true class label of an instance. It will be better if we can obtain the correct class label under the above circumstance. In other words, can we classify correctly an instance if all classifications from classifiers are incorrect? This is the very question which we will discuss below.

Example 1. Let instance O_1 be from class C_2, for a classification task of 3 classes. And x_1, x_2 are two classifiers. Table 1 is the decision profile of instance O_1.

Table 1. The decision profile of instance O_1

Class→	C_1	C_2	C_3
Classifier x_1	0.83	0.25	0.1
Classifier x_2	0.9	0.2	0.12

Here instance O_1 is an example of a negative fixed point. The maximum of supports for the true class C_2 from all the classifiers is less than the minimum of supports for some of the other classes from all the classifiers. That is, the maximum of the second column ($0.25=max([0.25\ 0.2]^T$)) is less than the minimum of the first column ($0.83=min([0.83\ 0.9]^T)$). Then there are no fuzzy measures such that the classification after fusion based on fuzzy integrals is correct. And this is a reasonable result as it agrees with our reasoning logic. When all agrees with one opinion, then the opinion is chosen for the decision. This is the first result as follows.

Proposition 1. For a negative fixed point, there exist no fuzzy measures that make the classification after fusion based fuzzy integral, correct.
Prof. Let k be the true crisp label of instance O and:

$$\max_{1 \le i \le n} h_{i,k} < \min_{1 \le i \le n} h_{i,j}, \ j \ne k, \ 1 \le j \le q.$$

We have:

$$\int h_k\, d\mu_k \le \max_{1 \le i \le n} h_{i,k} < \min_{1 \le i \le n} h_{i,j} \le \int h_j\, d\mu_j,$$

where μ_k and μ_j present any fuzzy measure for class C_k and class C_j respectively. In other words, the class label cannot be k when we determine the instance O through the maximum. The classification of the fusion system will always be incorrect.

From another point of view, the error rate of a fusion system will greater or equal to the probability of the negative fixed point. It is the best we can obtain when the error rate is equal to the probability of the negative fixed point. In experiments, we can consider the fusion system effective if the error rate is equal to the probability of the negative fixed point. In this condition, we must improve the single classifier to obtain a better classification result.

On the other hand, the fuzzy integral is still able to obtain the correct classification by combining the useful information from each classifier when all classifiers have misclassified an instance. This an be seen from the following example.

Example 2. There is another instance O_2 from class C_2 in the same classification task of Example 1. The decision profile of instance O_2 is shown in Table 2.

Table 2. The decision profile of instance O_2

Class→	C_1	C_2	C_3
Classifier x_1	0.65	0.25	0.1
Classifier x_2	0.9	0.7	0.2

Let the fuzzy measure μ_1 for class be:

$$\mu_1(\{x_1\}) = \mu_1(\{x_2\}) = 0.1, \mu_1(\{x_1, x_2\}) = 1;$$

the fuzzy measure μ_2 for class C_2:

$$\mu_2(\{x_1\}) = 0.3, \mu_2(\{x_2\}) = 0.95, \mu_2(\{x_1, x_2\}) = 1;$$

the fuzzy measure μ_3 for class C_3:

$$\mu_3(\{x_1\}) = 0.2, \mu_3(\{x_2\}) = 0.4, \mu_3(\{x_1, x_2\}) = 1.$$

Thus, the following Table 3 shows us the fusion results by the two types of fuzzy integral based on the above fuzzy measures. The values for class C_2 are greater than the values for all other classes. Fusion system gives the right class label C_2, even though all classifiers x_1 and x_2 assign the instance into the wrong class C_1.

Table 3. The values of fuzzy integral with respect to the above fuzzy measures

Class→	C_1	C_2	C_3
Sugeno integral	0.6	0.7	0.2
Choquet integral	0.63	0.6775	0.14

Proposition 2. Given the classification task of q classes with n classifiers $x_1, x_2, \ldots, x_n$ and an instance O. If:

$$\max_{1 \leq i \leq n} h_{i,k} > \min_{1 \leq i \leq n} h_{i,j}, \quad j \neq k, 1 \leq j \leq q,$$

where k is the true crisp label of instance O, h_j is the jth column of the decision profile of instance O, at least there exists a fuzzy measure such that the classification of the fusion system is correct.

Prof. We denote $M_k = \max_{1 \leq i \leq n} h_{i,k}$, $m_k = \min_{1 \leq i \leq n} h_{i,k}$, $M_j = \max_{1 \leq i \leq n} h_{i,j}$, $m_j = \min_{1 \leq i \leq n} h_{i,j}$. μ_k is the fuzzy measure for class C_k, and μ_j is the fuzzy measure for class C_j.

If the fuzzy measure μ_k for class C_k satisfies:

$$\mu_k(\{x \mid h_k(x) = M_k, x \in X\}) = M_k$$

and the fuzzy measure μ_j for class C_j at the same time satisfies:

$$\mu_j(\{x' \mid h_j(x) > m_j, x \in X\}) = m_j$$

then we have:

$$(s)\int h_k d\mu_k \geq M_k > m_j \geq (s)\int h_j d\mu_j .$$

Thus the value of Sugeno integral for class C_k is greater than the value of Sugeno integral for class C_j.

For Choquet integral, it will be more complicated. Let $\delta \in (0,1)$ such that:

$$\delta M_k > m_j, \text{ and } \mu_k(\{x' \mid h_k(x) = M_k, x \in X\}) = \delta.$$

When $m_j = M_j$, we have:

$$(c)\int h_k d\mu_k \geq m_k + (M_k - m_k)\delta > m_j = (c)\int h_j d\mu_j$$

for any fuzzy measure μ_j. When $m_j \neq M_j$, the fuzzy measure μ_j satisfying:

$$\mu_j(\{x \mid h_j(x) > m_j, x \in X\})$$
$$< \min(\frac{M_k + m_k(1-\delta) - m_j}{M_j - m_j}, 1)$$

will lead to:

$$(c)\int h_k d\mu_k$$
$$\geq m_k + (M_k - m_k)\delta$$
$$> m_j + (M_j - m_j)\mu_j(\{x \mid h_j(x) > m_j, x \in X\})$$
$$\geq (c)\int h_j d\mu_j$$

In summary, there exist fuzzy measures such that the classification of the fusion system is correct for an instance satisfying the conditions of Proposition 2.

Proposition 2 can be extended to λ–fuzzy measure as per the following.

Proposition 3. Given the classification task of q classes with n classifiers $x_1, x_2, ..., x_n$ and an instance O. If:

$$\max_{1 \leq i \leq n} h_{i,k} > \min_{1 \leq i \leq n} h_{i,j}, \quad j \neq k, \ 1 \leq j \leq q,$$

where k is the true crisp label of instance O, h_j is the jth column of the decision profile of instance O, at least there exists a $\lambda-$ fuzzy measure such that the classification of the fusion system is correct.

5 Conclusions

In this paper, we analyze the performance of a multi-classifier fusion system based on fuzzy integrals. It shows us the limit of error rates of a fusion system that the error rate is greater than or equal to the probability of a negative fixed point. This can be used to estimate the methods determining fuzzy measures in a fusion system. It is the best fusion result through fuzzy integrals that we can obtain when the error rate is equal to the probability of the negative fixed point. In experiments, we can consider the fusion system efficient if the error rate is equal to the probability of the negative fixed point. In this condition, if we want to obtain a better classification rate we must improve the single classifier rather than improve the fusion process. On the other hand, our analysis indicates the potential of fuzzy integrals in classifier fusion. Under some conditions, the classifier fusion system based on fuzzy integral can give a correct classification even if all the classifiers misclassify an instance. If the classifiers are more diverse, we can obtain even higher correct classification rates through fusion. Therefore, it will be helpful in determining fuzzy measures, designing classifiers and other applications.

Acknowledgements

This research is supported by the National Natural Science Foundation of China (NSFC 60473045); the Natural Science Foundation of Hebei Province (603137).

References

1. L. Lam and C.Y. Suen, "Optimal combination of pattern classifiers," Pattern Recognition Letters, 1995, vol. 16, pp. 945-954
2. K. Tumer and J. Ghosh, "Analysis of decision boundaries in linearly combined neural classifiers," Pattern Recognition, 1996, vol. 29, no. 2, pp.341-348.
3. S. Hashem, "Optimal linear combinations of neural networks," Neural networks, 1997, vol.10, no.4, pp.599-614
4. Sung-Bae cho and Jin H. Kim, "Multiple Network Fusion Using Fuzzy Logic," IEEE Transaction on Nueral Networks, 1995, vol. 6, no. 2, pp. 497-501.
5. Jia Wang and Zhenyuan Wang, "Using Neural Networks to Determine Sugeno Measures by Statistics," Neural Networks, 1997, vol. 10, no. 1, pp.183-195.
6. Antanas Verikas and Arunas Lipnickas, "Fusing Neural Networks Through Space Partitioning and Fuzzy Integration," Neural Processing Letters, 2002, vol. 16, pp.53-65
7. James M. Keller and Jeffrey Osborn, "Training the Fuzzy Integral," International Journal of Approximate Reasoning, 1996, vol. 15, pp. 1-24.
8. Ludmila I. Kuncheva, James C. Bezdek, Robert P.W. Duin, "Decision templates for multiple classifier fusion: an experimental comparison," Pattern Recognition, 2001, vol. 34, pp. 299-314.

9. Isabelle Bloch, "Some aspects of Dempster-Shafer evidence theory for classification of multi-modality medical images taking partial volume effect into account," Pattern Recognition Letters, 1996, vol.17, pp. 905-919.
10. Zhenyuan Wang, Kwong-sak Leung, Jia Wang, "A genetic algorithm for determining nonadditive set functions in information fusion," Fuzzy Sets and Systems, 1999, vol. 102, pp. 463-469.
11. L. Mikenina, H.-J. Zimmermann, "Improved feature selection and classification by the 2-additive fuzzy measure," Fuzzy Sets and Systems, 1999, vol. 107, pp. 197-218.
12. Antanas Verikas, Arunas Lipnickas, Kerstin Malmqvist, "Soft combination of neural classifiers: A comparative study," Pattern Recognition Letters, 1999, vol. 20, pp. 429-444.
13. M. Sugeno, "Fuzzy measures and fuzzy integrals —A survey", Fuzzy Automata and Decision Processes, M.M. Gupta, G.N Saridis and B.R. Gaines, Eds. Amsterdam: North-Holland, 1977, pp: 89-102.
14. H. Tahani and J. M. Keller, "Information fusion in computer vision using the fuzzy integral", IEEE Trans. Syst. Man. Cybern. , 1990, Vol. 20, pp: 733-741.

Error Concealment Based on Adaptive MRF-MAP Framework*

Zhi-heng Zhou and Sheng-li Xie

College of Electronic & Information Engineering,
South China University of Technology,
510640 Guangzhou, China
crenna@21cn.com, adshlxie@scut.edu.cn

Abstract. Error concealment is a post-processing tool at the decoder side to recover the lost information of video sequences after transmitting over the noisy communication channels. An adaptive error concealment algorithm based on Markov Random Field (MRF) - Maximum a Posteriori (MAP) framework is proposed. Firstly, Discrimination Analysis is used to detect edges. So, edge threshold T for the Huber function of MRF is adaptively obtained, according to the edge or non-edge area that current pixel belongs to. Then, in order to eliminate the blocking artifacts, a slope k is also introduced to the linear part of the Huber function. Simulation results show that the proposed algorithm can recover images with the higher quality, comparing to the existing algorithms.

1 Introduction

Recently, there is a great demand on real time video transmission, because of the enough bandwidth of communication network and the development of efficient video compression techniques. Many video compression standards such as MPEG-2 and H.263 use the block-based DCT and motion compensation to eliminate the spatial and temporal redundancy. Although these compression techniques reduce the bit rate efficiently, the variable length coding is sensitive to the interference in the channel, especially the error prone wireless channel. A single bit error can destroy all blocks in the slice, and motion compensation method can make the error propagate temporally and spatially in the whole video sequence.

Error concealment by post-processing at the decoder is an efficient method to resist the interference in the channel [1]. It takes advantage of the fact that the values of temporally and spatially adjacent pixels vary smoothly. Recently an error concealment technique based on MRF-MAP is proposed. But usually in MRF-MAP method [2][3], iterations will cause edge blurring and inaccurate initial solution will cause blocking artifacts.

---

* This work is supported by the National Natural Science Foundation of China (Grant 60274006), the National Science Foundation of China for Excellent Youth (Grant 60325310), the Natural Science Key Fund of Guangdong Province, PR China (Grant 020826), and the Trans-Century Training Programme Foundation for Talents by the State Education Ministry.

In this paper, we want to construct a new adaptive Huber function of MRF model, which can make up the disadvantage of MRF-MAP method. In the second part of this paper, traditional error concealment algorithm based on MRF-MAP is presented. The third part proposes a new adaptive edge-preserving error concealment algorithm. The simulation results and conclusions are given respectively in the fourth and fifth part.

2 Traditional Error Concealment Algorithm Based on MRF-MAP

Assume that matrix X and Y represent original image and received damaged image of the current frame respectively. They both are modeled by discrete random fields, with x and y as the realizations of them. Given a prior distribution for x and the received damaged image y, a MAP estimation $\hat{x}$ of x is expressed by

$$\hat{x} = \arg\max_{x}(P(X = x | Y = y)) \tag{1}$$

Note that the received image Y is the same as the original image X except the damaged parts. And all of the damaged parts are regarded as to be lost, we have

$$P(Y = y | X = x) = \begin{cases} 1 & Y = X \\ 0 & Y \neq X \end{cases} \tag{2}$$

Assume that the size of the lost block is $M \times N$. Using equation (1), (2), the Bayesian rule and some knowledge of Markov Random Field, we have the following problem

$$\hat{x} = \arg\min_{x}(\sum_{i=1}^{M}\sum_{j=1}^{N}\sum_{k=i-1}^{i+1}\sum_{l=j-1}^{j+1}\rho(x_{ij} - x_{kl})) \tag{3}$$

where $\rho(\cdot)$ is the cost function and people usually appeal to the Huber function first introduced in robust statistics.

Iterated Conditional Modes (ICM) [4] is one of the most famous methods to solve this kind of problem. ICM is an iterative method, and it needs initial solution. The initial solution can be obtained following temporal error concealment methods [1], such as BMA [5].

3 New Adaptive Edge-Preserving Error Concealment Algorithm

In the existing error concealment algorithms [2][3] based on MRF-MAP, the main limitation is that the edge threshold T of Huber function is fixed. If T is too large, the strong edges will be blurred. If T is too small, new artifacts will appear. Another limitation is that inaccurate initial solution will cause blocking artifacts.

We want to construct a new adaptive Huber function, which can make up the disadvantage of MRF-MAP method.

3.1 Pixel's Membership

Pixel's membership is defined as the degree measuring the pixel belonging to edge or non-edge area. In fact, it implies the edge detection. In the video sequences, we can only use the traditional edge detection operators to process I frames and obtain the statistical characteristic of real edges. For the B and P frames, we take advantage of the characteristic to detect edges. On one hand, it will save lots of computations. On the other hand, it can avoid blocking artifacts influencing on edge detection. So, we use Discrimination Analysis to introduce the definition of pixel's membership.

Discrimination Analysis is a statistical method for judging which type the individual belongs to. It is also often used in Pattern Recognition. The edge area and smooth area in the image are two distinct parts. So, the edge detection can be achieved by dividing all pixels into two types, with one coming from edge population π_1 and the other coming from non-edge population π_2. This is a discrimination problem of two populations and Fisher's rule [6] will be used to solve it.

3.1.1 Edge Detection Based on Discrimination Analysis

Given an arbitrary pixel X_{ij} ($1 \le i \le M, 1 \le j \le N$) in the image, we use two factors to decide whether this pixel is an edge point. The two factors are the mean and standard deviation of X_{ij} and its neighboring pixels. Define an arithmetic operator

$$A: X_{ij} \to W \text{ or } AX_{ij} = W, \tag{4}$$

where W is a two dimensional vector and identifies pixel X_{ij},

$$W = \begin{pmatrix} W_\mu & W_\sigma \end{pmatrix}^T, \tag{5}$$

and

$$W_\mu = \frac{1}{9} \sum_{k=i-1}^{i+1} \sum_{l=j-1}^{j+1} X_{kl}$$

$$W_\sigma = \sqrt{\frac{1}{8} \sum_{k=i-1}^{i+1} \sum_{l=j-1}^{j+1} (X_{kl} - W_\mu)^2} \tag{6}$$

Firstly, we apply the traditional edge detection operators in I frames. Then the results of the edge detection will be used to estimate the parameters of the population. Denote the numbers of samples belonging to edge population π_1 and non-edge population π_2 by n_1 and n_2. The corresponding data matrixes are

$$\begin{aligned} w_1 &= (w_{11}, w_{12}, \cdots, w_{1n_1}), \\ w_2 &= (w_{21}, w_{22}, \cdots, w_{2n_2}) \end{aligned} \tag{7}$$

Then we have the mean vectors and covariance matrices of the samples

$$\overline{w}_i = \frac{1}{n_i} \sum_{k=1}^{n_i} w_{ik} \tag{8}$$

$$s_i = \frac{1}{n_i - 1} \sum_{k=1}^{n_i} (w_{ik} - \overline{w}_i)(w_{ik} - \overline{w}_i)^T, \quad i = 1, 2. \tag{9}$$

Supposing the two populations have the same covariance matrix Σ, we can combine s_1 with s_2 to obtain an unbiased estimation s_p of Σ

$$\begin{aligned} s_p &= \left[\frac{(n_1 - 1)}{(n_1 - 1) + (n_2 - 1)} \right] s_1 + \left[\frac{n_2 - 1}{(n_1 - 1) + (n_2 - 1)} \right] s_2 \\ &= \frac{(n_1 - 1)s_1 + (n_2 - 1)s_2}{(n_1 + n_2 - 2)} \end{aligned} \tag{10}$$

We have the Fisher sample discriminative function

$$z = l^T w = (\overline{w}_1 - \overline{w}_2)^T s_p^{-1} w, \tag{11}$$

and the estimation of the midpoint m of the means of two populations

$$m = \frac{1}{2}(\overline{z}_1 + \overline{z}_2) = \frac{1}{2}(\overline{w}_1 - \overline{w}_2)^T s_p^{-1} (\overline{w}_1 + \overline{w}_2). \tag{12}$$

According to Fisher's rule [6], we have the following discriminative formulas:

If $z - m < 0$, the pixel x_{ij} will be classified into the edge population π_1.

If $z - m \geq 0$, the pixel x_{ij} will be classified into the non-edge population π_2. (13)

3.1.2 Parameters Updating

Assume that adding a new sample into the edge population π_1 and it is the $n_1 + 1$ th sample of π_1. So $\overline{w}_1$ and s_1 are updated by $\overline{w}_1'$ and s_1' respectively,

$$\overline{w}_1' = \frac{1}{n_1 + 1}(n_1 \overline{w}_1 + w_{1, n_1 + 1}), \tag{14}$$

$$s_1' = \frac{1}{n_1} \sum_{k=1}^{n_1 + 1} (w_{1k} - \overline{w}_1')(w_{1k} - \overline{w}_1')^T = \frac{1}{n_1} \left(\sum_{k=1}^{n_1+1} w_k w_k^T - (n_1 + 1)\overline{w}_1'(\overline{w}_1')^T \right). \tag{15}$$

Substitute equation (14) into (15), we have

$$\begin{aligned} s_1' &= \frac{1}{n_1} \left[\sum_{k=1}^{n_1} w_k w_k^T + w_{1, n_1+1} w_{1, n_1+1}^T - \frac{1}{n_1 + 1} (n_1 \overline{w}_1 + w_{1, n_1+1})(n_1 \overline{w}_1 + w_{1, n_1+1})^T \right] \\ &= \frac{1}{n_1} \left[\sum_{k=1}^{n_1} w_k w_k^T + \frac{n_1}{n_1 + 1} (w_{1, n_1+1} w_{1, n_1+1}^T - n_1 \overline{w}_1 \overline{w}_1^T - \overline{w}_1 w_{1, n_1+1}^T - w_{1, n_1+1} \overline{w}_1^T) \right] \end{aligned} \tag{16}$$

If n_1 is big enough, $\dfrac{n_1-1}{n_1} \approx \dfrac{n_1}{n_1+1} \approx 1$. Then, equation (14) and (16) can be simplified by

$$\overline{w}_1' \approx \overline{w}_1 + \dfrac{1}{n_1+1} w_{1,n_1+1}, \qquad (17)$$

$$\begin{aligned} s_1' &\approx \dfrac{1}{n_1}\left(\sum_{k=1}^{n_1} w_k w_k^T - n_1 \overline{w}_1 \overline{w}_1^T + w_{1,n_1+1} w_{1,n_1+1}^T - \overline{w}_1 w_{1,n_1+1}^T - w_{1,n_1+1} \overline{w}_1^T \right) \\ &= s_1 + \dfrac{1}{n_1}\left(w_{1,n_1+1} w_{1,n_1+1}^T - \overline{w}_1 w_{1,n_1+1}^T - w_{1,n_1+1} \overline{w}_1^T \right) \end{aligned} \qquad (18)$$

We will have similar formulas when adding a new sample into the non-edge population π_2.

3.1.3 Pixel's Membership Function

We can find that the values of sample discriminative function distribute on both sides of m. The farther from m, the more specific population the pixels belong to. For the current pixel x_{ij}, we define pixel's membership D_{PM}

$$D_{PM} = \dfrac{z-m}{m} \times 100\% \qquad (19)$$

Combining with equation (4), (11) and (19), we have the pixel's membership function

$$D_{PM}(x_{ij}) = \dfrac{l^T A x_{ij} - m}{m} \times 100\% \qquad (20)$$

The D_{PM} represents the relationship between the pixel and edge population or non-edge population. It's easy to find that $D_{PM} \in (-\infty, \infty)$.

3.2 Adaptive Edge Threshold T

Now, we can take advantage of the D_{PM} to construct an adaptive function for edge threshold T. Note that the value of T is a positive integer and there is an upper limit T^* for it, with the relationship $T \leq T^*$. For the current pixel x_{ij}, define a function

$$T = \begin{cases} T^* & D_{PM}(x_{ij}) \geq 100\% \\ \left[\dfrac{D_{PM}(x_{ij}) \cdot T^*}{2}\right] + \left[\dfrac{T^*}{2}\right] & -100\% < D_{PM}(x_{ij}) < 100\% \\ 1 & D_{PM}(x_{ij}) \leq -100\% \end{cases} \qquad (21)$$

where $\lceil x \rceil$ rounds x to the nearest integers larger than x, $\lfloor x \rfloor$ rounds x to the nearest integers, and $D_{PM}(x_{ij})$ is the pixel's membership. In equation (20) and (21), we can find that if the pixel x_{ij} belongs to the edge area, $D_{PM}(x_{ij})$ will become smaller and the edge threshold T will become smaller; if the pixel x_{ij} belongs to the non-edge area, $D_{PM}(x_{ij})$ will become larger and the edge threshold T will become larger.

3.3 Adaptive Slope k

Further more, we consider the blocking artifacts problem. To reduce the computations, BMA [5] and other algorithms are often used to obtain the initial solution of ICM method. But these algorithms have limited ability to estimate the motion vectors, leading to the appearance of the blocking artifacts. If we take their result as the initial solution of ICM, the blocking artifacts will be preserved as edges.

In order to reduce the blocking artifacts, we introduce a slope parameter k for the Huber function

$$k = \left| \frac{1}{1-\sigma/m} \right| \qquad (22)$$

where σ and m are the standard deviation and mean of the pixels over one-pixel wide boundary ring of the lost block, respectively.

Using the adaptive threshold T and slope k, we can construct a new Huber function,

$$\rho(u) = \begin{cases} u^2 & |u| \leq T \\ T^2 + 2kT(|u|-T) & |u| > T \end{cases} \qquad (23)$$

as shown in Fig.1.

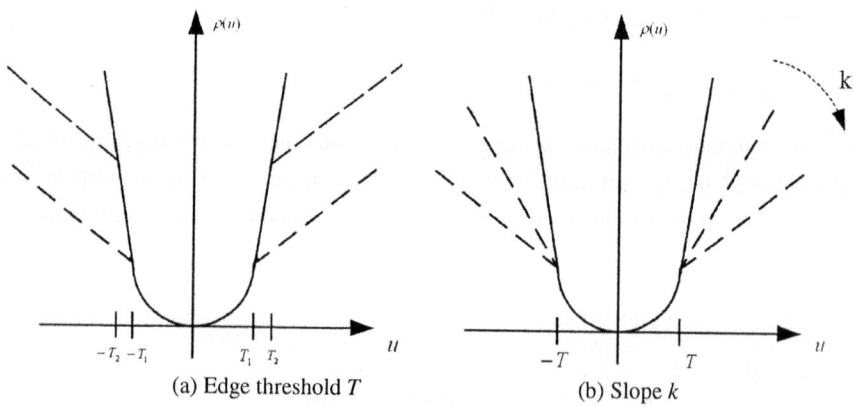

Fig. 1. Adaptive Huber function $\rho(u)$

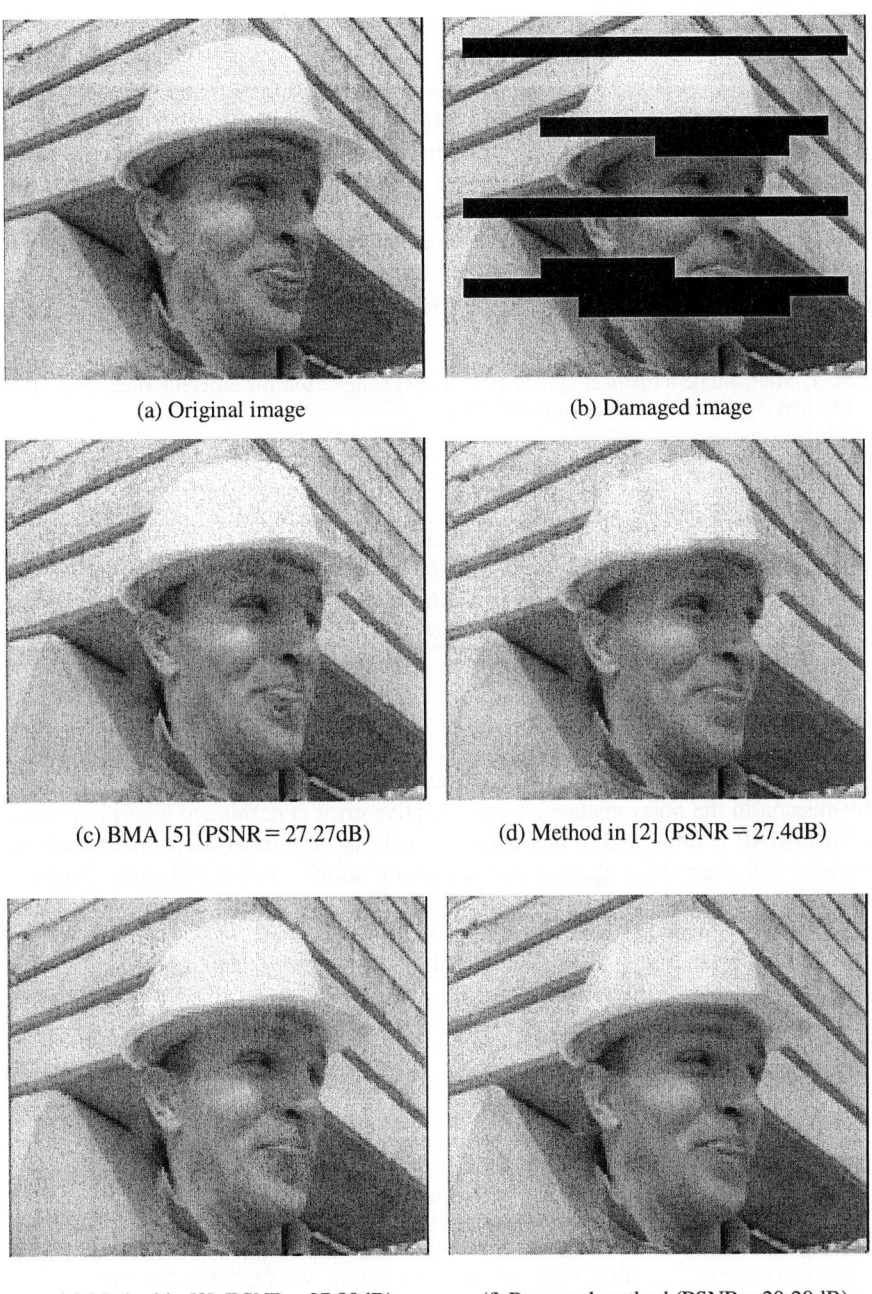

(a) Original image   (b) Damaged image

(c) BMA [5] (PSNR = 27.27dB)   (d) Method in [2] (PSNR = 27.4dB)

(e) Method in [3] (PSNR = 27.89dB)   (f) Proposed method (PSNR = 29.29dB)

Fig. 2. Visual quality comparison by different error concealment algorithms with block lost rate 25.3%

4 Simulation Results

We use the YUV (144×176) grayscale video sequences with the block size 8×8 to do the simulations. The recovered images of different error concealment algorithms for the 91st frame in "Foreman" video sequence are shown in Fig.2. Fig.2 (a) is the original undamaged image, (b) is simulated damaged image with block lost rate 25.3%, and (c)-(f) are the results of BMA [5], non-adaptive MRF-MAP method [2], Zhang's adaptive MRF-MAP method [3], and our proposed method, respectively. Table 1 shows the numerical results of different error concealment methods for 20 frames of different kinds of video sequences with block lost rate 20.2%. The value of T^* is set to 8 in our simulations.

Table 1. Multi-frame numerical quality (PSNR dB) comparison for different video sequences by different algorithms with block lost rate 20.2%

Video sequences	BMA [5]	Method in [2]	Method in [3]	Proposed method
Foreman	27.17	28.8	28.91	29.34
Coastguard	21.69	27.6	28.18	28.0
Claire	30.86	35.6	36.07	36.38
Carphone	27.02	28.9	29.0	30.28

5 Conclusions

Considering that encoded digital video sequences often lose image information after transmission in the noisy channel, a new adaptive error concealment algorithm based on MRF-MAP is presented in this paper. Usually in the former MRF-MAP method, iterations will cause edge blurring and inaccurate initial solution will cause blocking artifacts. We construct a new adaptive Huber function in MRF model, which can make up the disadvantage of MRF-MAP method.

Simulation results show that the proposed method in this paper outperforms the existing error concealment methods.

References

1. Wang Y. and Zhu Q.F.: Error control and concealment for video communication: a review. Proceeding IEEE, Vol.86, (1998) 974-997.
2. Salama P., Shroff N. B., Delp E. J.: Error concealment in MPEG video streams over ATM networks. IEEE J. Select. Areas Commun., vol. 18, (2000) 1129-1144.
3. Zhang Y., Ma K.K.: Error concealment for video transmission with dual multiscale Markov random field modeling. IEEE Trans. on Image Processing, Vol.12, (2003) 236-242.
4. Besag J.: On the statistical analysis of dirty pictures. J. R. Statist. Soc. B, vol. 48, (1986) 259-302.
5. Lam W.M., Reilbman A. R., Liu B.: Recovery of lost or erroneously received motion vectors. Proc. ICASSP, vol. 5, (1993) V417-V420.
6. Fisher R.A.: The use of multiple measurements in Taxonomie problems. Annals of Eqgencis, vol.7, (1936) 179-188.

Spatial Video Watermarking Based on Stability of DC Coefficients

Tianhang Chen[1], Shaohui Liu[1], Hongxun Yao[1], and Wen Gao[2]

[1] School of Computer Science and Technology, Harbin Institute of Technology,
Harbin 150001, P.R. China
{thchen, shaohl, yhx}@vilab.hit.edu.cn
[2] Institute of computing, Chinese Academy of Science, Beijing 100080, P.R. China
wgao@ict.ac.cn

Abstract. Watermarking technology plays an important role in digital rights management. Many high performance watermark algorithms have been developed. However, most of them focused on image media. This paper presents a novel blind video watermarking algorithm based on the stability of the direct current (DC) coefficient values in blocks. This algorithm first selects some frames by a key, and then embeds watermark into its luminance component of each selected frame. The luminance component to be watermarked first is divided into sub-blocks with size 8 by 8, and then discrete cosine transform (DCT) is used to process each sub-block to get the DC coefficients. Rearranging these DC coefficients into sub-sequences with equal length, and each such sub-sequence is transformed by DCT and get the highest frequency coefficient. Finally, the watermark is embedded in the high frequency coefficient array. The correlation metric is used in the detection process. The experimental results indicate that the correlation curve peaks emerge at the watermarked I frames and P frames which suffered from MPEG-4 and H.264 compression. The proposed watermarking method has strong robustness against some attacks such as frame deleting, frame inserting, frame shifting, frame statistical average and collusion attack.

1 Introduction

Digital technology has brought digital media products into our daily life, for example, MP3, CD (Compact Disc), VCD (Video Compact Disc), DVD (Digital Versatile Disc) and so on. In addition, personal computer and audio/video processing software are common used in current environment. Hence, high quality audio/video resources can be easily reproduced and distributed. Due to underlying huge profit, the problem of illegal copying and distribution of digital contents has become an urgent problem in the last decades, which has seriously affected the development of digital content industry. Hence, DRM (digital rights management) acts as a rights enforcement measure to prevent illegal copying and distribution, and it has attracted many researchers' interests. But it should note that the most important goal of DRM is to help legal people to enjoy legal digital contents in more efficient way, for example watching movies, listening songs and so on. Watermarking technology is an important part of DRM system. In fact, many commercial products use watermarking technology to protect copyright of high value digital contents. Of course, the functions of watermark not only include copyright protection but also include other many roles, such as providing added-value to content. Nowadays, watermark technology can be classified into image watermarking, video watermarking, audio watermarking and 3D model watermarking and so on according the type of host signal. Although current works are mainly image watermarking, video watermarking researches has made a great progress in recent years.

Video watermarking can be classified into two classes according the domain of embedding watermark, namely embedding watermark in the compressed domain [1-4] and in the uncompressed domain [5-8]. The typical method [1] of the first class embedded the watermark in VLC, which adjusted the VLC pairs to embed watermark bits. Some other methods embed the watermark in residual of motion vectors [2, 3], and Lagendijk [4] proposed XDEW algorithm to embed watermark both in I-frame and P-frame. XDEW algorithm grouped every two blocks into a unit, and it embedded a watermark bit into each unit by compared with energy of each block in a unit. For example, there exists a unit, and this unit includes block A and B. If the energy of block A is larger than one of block B, then algorithm will embed a watermark bit 1, otherwise it will embed a watermark 0. If the current watermark bit is 1, but the energy of block A is less than one of block B, then it will adjust the energies of these two block by cutting some coefficients until the energy of block A is larger than one of block B. These methods in compressed domain can gain low computational complexity, but they are not robust against some common attacks such as frame deleting, and re-compression with a different GOP (Group of Picture) structure. In order to improve the robustness of watermarking, the video watermarking methods in the uncompressed domain using 3D-DFT [5], 3-D DWT [6] and 3-D DCT [7] are proposed. These methods take temporal redundancy into account, but they require too high computational complexity to meet the real-time requirement. In addition, most methods embed watermark in spatial domain or transformed domain, and then the detecting watermark procedure will be performed in the same domain. And this will lead to increase the complexity of extracting watermark. For example, an algorithm embedded a watermark into video sequence in spatial domain, but the watermarked sequence has been compressed into compressed bitstream. How to detect the watermark correctly? What should we do? First, the compressed bitstream is decompressed into raw sequence, and then the watermark may be detected.

Considering these problems, a new method of watermarking is proposed to embed watermark into those frames chosen randomly from a raw video in this paper. The watermark will be embedded in the spatial domain, and it can be detected correctly from the compressed domain. The detecting procedure only needs some additional memory to store the DC coefficients. The main reason is that the embedding will consider the compatibility with video compression standard. Most video compression standards are based on block DCT transform, especially the common size of each block is 8 by 8. Hence in order to be compatible with video compression standard, the watermark is embedded in the DCT domain of luminance. These frames to be watermarked are first divided into 8 by 8 blocks, and then each block is transformed by DCT. We embed the watermark in the high frequency coefficient of some consecutive DC coefficients which have been transformed by DCT, because of the stability and the robustness of DC coefficients. Watermark detection is based on the correlation value between the high frequency coefficients and watermark without original video sequence. Compared with the 3-D DCT, the proposed method maintains the robustness against some attacks such as frame deleting, frame inserting, frame shifting, frame statistical average and collusion attack while alleviating the computational complexities.

The rest of this paper is organized as follows: the proposed embedding algorithm is presented in section 2. In section 3, the corresponding blind detecting watermark procedure is described in detail, and some experimental results for various attacks are shown in section 4. Finally, conclusions are obtained in section 5.

2 Embedding Watermark

2.1 Generating Watermark

Suppose watermark be a binary sequence W with size L. Nowadays, security of watermark algorithm is an important research topic [9]. In order to improve the safeness and robustness [9], the watermark is encrypted by modulating and intensified by mapping. Moreover, the logistic chaos map is used to produce modulating sequence by key K_1.

The description of logistic chaos map is:

$$x_{k+1} = \rho x_k (1 - x_k) \tag{1}$$

When $\rho = 4$ and $x_k \in (0,1)$, it can produce chaos phenomenon. It should note that the initial value of x_k can not choose the map's motionlessness points (0.25, 0.5, 0.75).

We use the key $K_1 \in (0,1)$ as the initial value to produce a chaos sequence X_k ($k = 1,2,3,\ldots,L$) by equation (1), then make it to binary sequence M_k by equation (2). The largest advantage of using logistic chaos map is the chaos sequence is very sensitive to the initial value.

$$M_k = \lfloor 10^n \times X_k \rfloor \bmod 2 \quad (n = 1,2,3,\ldots) \tag{2}$$

Then the encrypted watermark W' can be obtained by XOR operation between W and M:

$$W' = W \oplus M \tag{3}$$

In order to improve the intensity of embedding watermark in this paper, we use a simple map to intensify watermark.

$$\begin{cases} W''(i) = H & \text{if } W'(i) = 1 \\ W''(i) = -H & \text{if } W'(i) = 0 \end{cases}, \quad i = 1,2,\ldots,L \tag{4}$$

The encrypted and intensified watermark is denoted by W'', and its length is L.

2.2 Embedding Watermark

In order to be compatible with video compression algorithm, the watermark is embedded in DCT domain. In this paper, we embed the watermark in the high frequency coefficient of some consecutive DC coefficients which have been transformed by DCT, because the DC coefficients in DCT domain have strong stability and robustness. Let the video frames with size of $M \times N$, and then the luminance component of a frame is divided into 8×8 blocks and then each block is transformed by 2-D DCT. The DC coefficients are scanned from left to right and from top to bottom and form a 1-D sequence S. Then n consecutive DC coefficients are selected from S and transformed by 1-D DCT, We get a 1-D DCT coefficients sequence B_j. In order to improve the imperceptibility of watermark, the highest frequency DCT coefficients are choosen from B_j to embed watermark. Therefore the embedded capacity of a frame is L' bits.

$$L' = M \times N / 8 \times 8 \times n \tag{5}$$

The procedure of embedding watermark described as follows:

Step 1: We use nonnegative integer sequence produced by key K_2 as the distance between the selected frames to embedded watermark.

Step 2: The luminance component of each selected frame is partitioned into 8×8 blocks, and then every block is transformed by 2-D DCT. The DC coefficients are scanned from left to right and from top to bottom, and then a 1-D sequence S is created. The sequence S is scrambled by key K_3, and then a new sequence S' is created.

Step 3: We choose n consecutive DC coefficients from S' as a sub array and take DCT to every sub array, hence, we get L' sub arrays $B_j^i \left(1 \le i \le n, 1 \le j \le L' \right)$.

The highest frequency coefficient of every sub array is selected to embed watermark, describe as:

$$B_j^{"n} = B_j^n + \alpha W_j^{"} \tag{6}$$

Where B_j^n denotes n^{th} frequency coefficient of jth sub array, $j = 1, 2, ..., L'$. $W_j^{"}$ represents the jth bit of the intensified watermark, α denotes the strength of embedding.

Step 4: We make inverse DCT to every sub array and restore the scrambled sequence. Blocks are transformed by inverse DCT, getting the watermarked frame.

Step 5: We repeat steps 2 to 4 to embed watermark in the next selected frame.

3 Detecting Watermark

First, it should note that watermark detection and watermark extraction are different. Watermark detection is to determine whether the digital content has been embedded watermark, the detection result is a binary answer yes or no. But the watermark extraction is different, it not only needs to detect watermark, but also needs to extract every bit of the watermark. The detecting process is similar to embedding process. All of the highest frequency coefficient of every sub array are reshaped into a sequence, then the correlation value between the sequence and the intensified watermark is computed to judge whether the frame embed watermark.

The procedure of detecting watermark is described as follows:

Step 1. The luminance of a frame is divided into 8×8 blocks, and transformed by DCT. Then all the DC coefficients are formed into a 1-D sequence S. We scramble the sequence S by key K_3, and get the sequence S'.

Step 2. Divide sequence S' into L' sub arrays. We select the nth frequency coefficient of every sub array to form a new sequence S_H.

Step3. The correlation between the sequence S_H and the intensified watermark W'', denoted by S_{im}, is computed by equation (7), and compared with the threshold value T. If S_{im} is larger than the threshold value T, we can infer that the frame has been embedded watermark, otherwise, the frame is not embedded watermark. The value of T can be determined by multiple experimentation.

$$S_{im} = \frac{S_H \cdot W''}{W'' \cdot W''} \qquad (7)$$

4 Experimental Results

The "CITY" sequence is used to evaluate the performance of proposed algorithm, this sequence includes 35 frames with size 704×576 pixels per frame, as shown in Fig.1. At the same time, the watermark is generated with 792 bits ($704\times 576/8\times 8\times 8$) according the procedure described in section 2.1. In experiments, we select the 1st, 5th, 11th, 16th, 20th, 26th and 31st video frame to embed watermark. After the selected frames have been watermarked, all the video frames are compressed in MPEG-4 format. For example, Fig.2 shows the same frame as the frame shown in Fig.1 of watermarked sequence. The MPEG-4 compressing is performed under conditions which frame rate is 30, I frame interval is 15, and structure of the group pictures is that first frame is I frame and other frames are P frames. The watermarked frames consist of two types such as I and P frame. 1st, 16th and 31st are I frames, 5th, 11th, 20th and 26th are P frames. In this paper, we will afford the detection results of capability resisting video compression and

Fig. 1. A frame of original City sequence

Fig. 2. The same frame of watermarked City sequence as the one in Fig. 1

frame operations, for example deleting a frame, shift a frame and so on. Due to the limited space, extracting results will discuss in another paper.

In resisting H.264 compression experiments, we select the 1st, 5th, 10th, 16th, 25th, 29th and 31st video frame to embed watermark. All the video frames which have been embedded watermark are compressed in H.264 format. The H.264 compressed format is given that frame rate is 30, I frame interval is 15, and structure of the group pictures is IBBPBBPBBPBBPBB, consisting of 15 frames. Then there are three types of watermarked frame such as I, P and B frames. 1st, 16th and 31st are I frames, 10th and 25th are P frames, 5th and 29th are B frames.

Fig.3 shows correlation value curves between the watermark and the video frames which suffered from MPEG-4 compression-decompression with variable bit rate, which average bit rate is 4.4 M. It is clear that the correlation values between the watermark and the original frames approximate zero, whereas those between the watermark and the watermarked frames are much larger than zero. We can see from Fig.3 (b), whether the watermark is embedded in I or P frame, the peak values emerge at all the watermarked frames. And the correlation value S_{im} of the watermarked I-frame is obviously larger than the correlation value S_{im} of the watermarked P-frame.

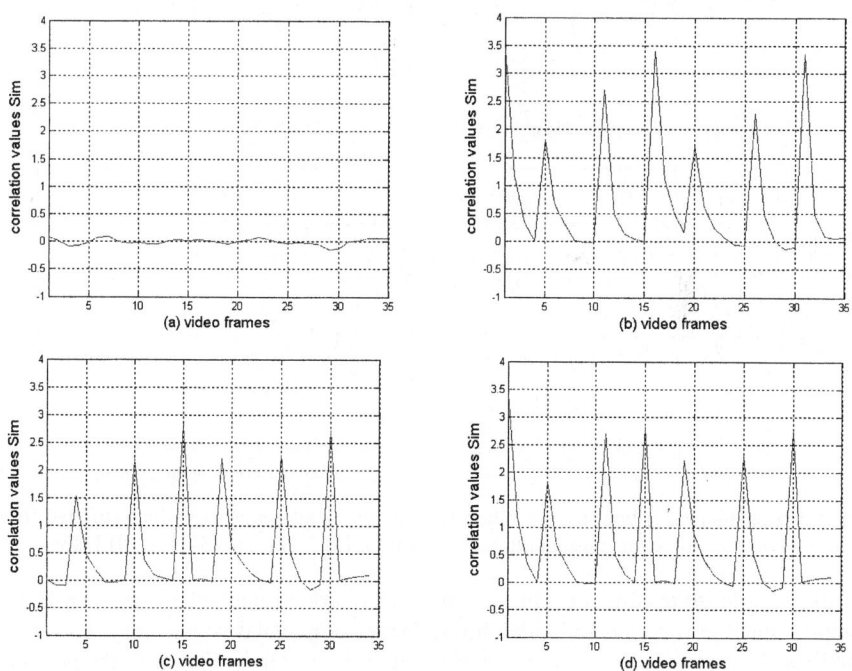

Fig. 3. Correlation curves between the watermark and the video sequence which suffered from MPEG-4 compression-decompression with variable bit rate: (a) the original video sequence case; (b) the watermarked video sequence case; (c) deleting the 1st frame of the watermarked sequence case; (d) deleting the 15th frame of the watermarked video sequence case.

The curves shown in Fig.3(c) and Fig.3(d) respectively describe the correlation values between the watermark and the watermarked video frames that attacked by deleting 1st frame (I frame) and 15th frame (P frame). We can see from Fig.3(c) that the peaks of correlation values curve emerge at the other watermarked frames when 1st frame was deleted. We can see from Fig.3 (d) that the correlation value between watermark and the frame before 11th are not changed, but the peaks behind 15th move forward.

In order to validate the robustness of the watermarking method against MPEG-4 compression in different bit rate, the watermarked video frames are compressed respectively with the constant bit rate of 7Mbps, 5Mbps, 3Mbps and 1Mbps, and then decompressed. The correlation values between watermark and decompressed frames are shown in Fig.4. It is clear that the watermarked frames can be detected clearly.

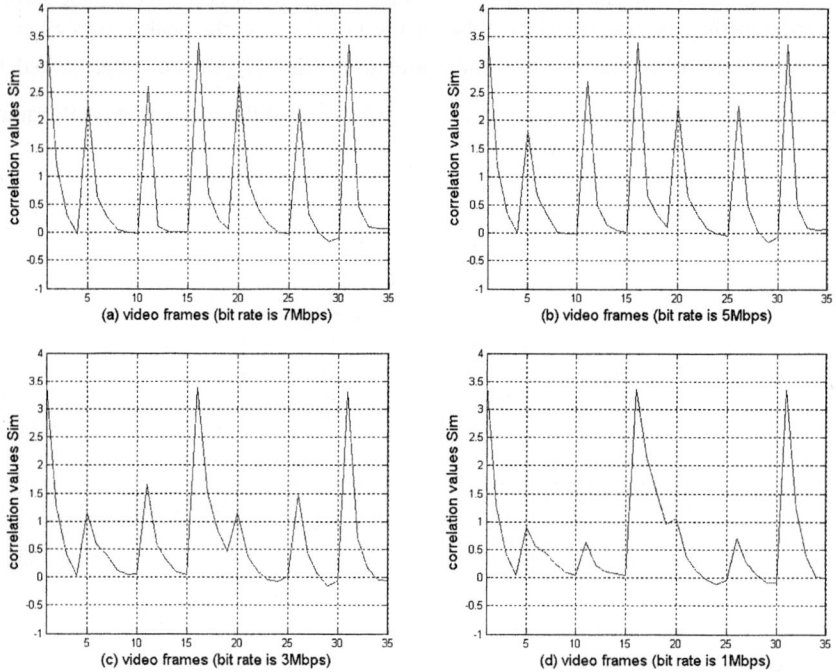

Fig. 4. Correlation cures between the watermark and the video sequences which suffered from MPEG-4 compression with constant bit rate: (a) 7Mbps; (b) 5Mbps; (c) 3Mbps; (d) 1Mbps

And in order to test the robustness of the watermarking method also against H.264 compression, the watermarked video frames were compressed with average bit rate of 2.0Mbps. The test results are shown in Fig.5. We can see from Fig. 5(b), the peaks of correlation values are larger than threshold at the watermarked frames which are I frame or P frame. The result shown in Fig.5(c) describes the correlation values between the watermark and the watermarked videos that suffered the attack of deleting 2nd frame. We can see from Fig.5(c) that the peaks of correlation values larger than threshold 1 emerge at the other watermarked frames which is I or P frame when 2nd frame was deleted. The curve shown in Fig.5 (d) describe the correlation values between the watermark and the watermarked videos that suffered the attack of shifting 5th frame (B frame) to 7th frame (P frame) and shifting 30th frame (B frame) to 31st frame (I frame). We can see from Fig.5 (d) that the peaks value is larger than threshold 1 at these watermarked frames which is I or P frame when suffered shifting attack.

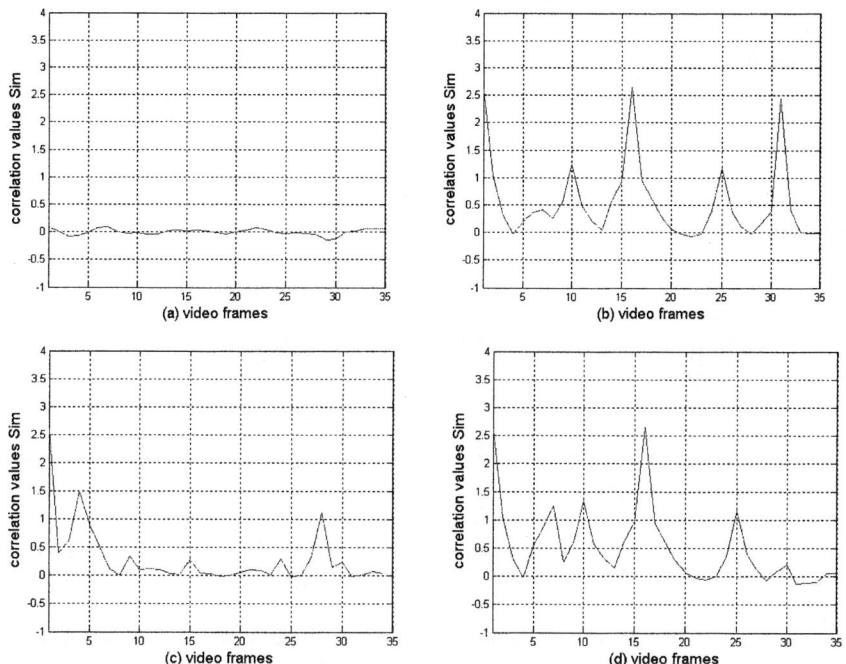

Fig. 5. Correlation curves between the watermark and the video sequence which suffered from H.264 compression-decompression with variable bit rate: (a) the original video sequence case; (b) the watermarked video sequence case; (c) deleting the 2nd frame of the watermarked video sequence case; (d) shifting the 5th frame and 30th frame of the watermarked video sequence to 7th frame and 31st frame respectively

When the watermarked video sequence suffered from deleting, inserting or shifting attack, the watermark can be detected as long as not all the watermarked frames are deleted or shifted to B frame position. As for those frames selected by randomly to embed watermark, the watermark method also can resist the static average attack.

5 Conclusions

The proposed algorithm takes advantage of the stability of DC coefficient and imperceptibility of high frequency coefficient to embed watermark in the spatial domain. For the compatibility with most of video compression standards, the algorithm considers only those blocks with size 8 by 8, which are common used in video standard based on DCT. Hence, the embedded watermark can be detected directly from compressed bit stream with a little improvement. The video frames such as I, P and B frame are selected randomly to embed watermark. When the video frames have been detected hiding watermark, we can extract watermark by using the source video. The experimental results demonstrate that the watermarking scheme is robust against multiple attacks, especially video compression and frame operations. The future works will increase the capability resisting trans-coding operations and resisting collusion attacks.

Acknowledgement

This work is supported by Natural Science Foundation of China (Grant No. 60472043).

References

1. Cross D., Mobasseri B. G.: Watermarking for Self-authentication of Compressed Video. IEEE ICIP, vol.2 (2002)913-916.
2. Zhao Z., Yu N. H., Li X. L.: A Novel Video Watermarking Scheme in Compressed Domain Based on Fast Motion Estimation. IEEE ICCT, (2003) 1878-1882
3. Dai Y. J., Zhang L. H., Yang Y. X.: A New Method of MPEG Video Watermarking Technology. IEEE ICCT, (2003)1845-1847
4. Setyawan I., Lagendijk R. L.: Low Bit Rate Video Watermarking Using Temporally Extended Differential Energy Watermarking (DEW) Algorithm. Proc. Security and Watermarking of Multimedia Contents III, vol. 4314(2001) 73-44
5. Deguillaume F., Csurka G., Ruanaidh J. O. and Pun T.: Robust 3D DFT Video Watermarking. Proceedings of Security and Watermarking of Multimedia Contents, SPIE, San Jose, Vol.3657(1999)113-124
6. Swanson M. D., Zhu B. *et al*: Multiresolution Scene-based Video Watermarking Using Perceptual Models. IEEE Journal on Selected Areas in Communications, vol. 16(4)(1998)540-550
7. Lim J. H., Kim D. J., Kim H. T., Won C. S.: Digital Video Watermarking Using 3D-DCT and Intra-Cubic Correlation. In: Ping Wah Wong, Edward J. Delp (eds): Security and Watermarking of Multimedia Contents III, Proceedings of SPIE Vol. 4314(2001)
8. Barni M., Bartolini F., Checcacci N.: Watermarking of MPEG-4 Video Objects. IEEE Transactions on Multimedia, Vol.7(1)(2005) 23-32
9. Su K., Kundur D., Hatzinakos D.: Statistical Invisibility for Collusion-Resistant Digital Video Watermarking. IEEE Transactions on Multimedia. Vol.7(1)(2005) 43-51

A Learning-Based Spatial Processing Method for the Detection of Point Targets

Zhijun Liu, Xubang Shen, and Hongshi Sang

Institute for Pattern Recognition and Artificial Intelligence,
Huazhong University of Science and Technology, Wuhan 430074, China
zjlieu@126.com

Abstract. In this paper, we present an efficient learning-based method for the detection of point targets in images. In the scheme, the probabilistic visual learning (PVL) technique is used for modeling the appearance of point targets and constructing a saliency measure function. Based on this function and the feature vector extracted at each pixel position and a target saliency map is formed by lexicographically scanning the input image. We treat such saliency map as a spatially filtered result of input image. Experimental results show that the proposed algorithm outperforms other filter-based methods.

1 Introduction

Detecting point targets in image data is fundamental to many image processing applications including point target detection in airborne infrared (IR) images, medical image processing, automatic inspection, and astronomy. In these relevant application cases, the searched targets appear as small spots in general with little internal structure information in an inhomogeneous background. A number of techniques for spatial detection of point targets have been developed in the past decades. The techniques developed aim at achieving a high true detection rate and at the same time a low false detection rate. Most of existing spatial domain detection methods are filter-based approaches. They include: 2-D least mean square (TDLMS) adaptive filter [1-2], 2-D normalized LMS (TDNLMS) adaptive filter [3], median subtraction (MS) filter [4], morphological filters [4], max-mean filter [5], max-median filter [5], and multilevel filter [6]. A standard technique for detecting a specified point target in an input image is to derive a matched filter for such object signal. But when background or the size, intensity and orientation of point targets are of variety, such method will be inefficient. Learning-based detection algorithms can tolerate the variance of such four characteristics because the detection is carried out by using the models learned from a set of training images, which capture the representative variability of object appearance. Recently, the learning-based methods using neural network filter [7] and/or support vector machine [8] are proposed for detecting point targets. These two methods all require two patterns of training samples: point target training samples and non-object training samples. Despite their success, the following two problems remain to be resolved: (1) construction of a proper non-object training set, and (2) detection of multiple neighboring point targets. Because the space of non-object samples is much larger than the space of point target images, it is very difficult to collect a "representative" set of non-object. The second problem is caused by interference from neighboring point targets when obtaining the subimage using a sliding window.

In this paper, we describe a learning-based scheme for the detection of point targets in image data, which requires only one training set of point target images and also solves the second problem well through adopting multiple sliding windows. In the scheme, the probabilistic visual learning (PVL) technique is used for modeling the appearance of point targets and constructing a saliency measure function. Based on this function and the feature vector extracted at each pixel position, a point target saliency map is formed by lexicographically scanning the input image. The saliency map can suppress clutter greatly and enhance the detectability of point targets at the same time.

The remainder of the paper is organized as follows. Section 2 briefly reviews the PVL technique. Section 3 presents the detail of proposed detection method. Finally, experimental results conducted on real-world optical and IR image data and conclusions are given in Section 4 and Section 5, respectively.

2 Probabilistic Visual Learning

Appearance-based models have received a remarkable attention from the computer vision community, due to their ability to encode shape, pose and illumination in a single, compact representation. PVL, a learning method proposed by Moghaddam and Pentland [9], is an efficient probabilistic approach to representing object appearance on low dimensional eigenspaces. In a PVL stage, a set of training samples is collected in such a manner that these images encompass the appearance of a pattern Ω under different orientation, different object intensity, and different size. PVL is based on density estimation. Given a training set of feature vectors $\{x_t\}_{t=1}^{N_T}$ from pattern model Ω where $x \in R^N$. In order to construct a probabilistic model of such pattern, the low-order statistics of the training set of vectors are used, namely, the mean vector $\overline{x}$ and covariance matrix Σ. For computational convenience, multivariate normal pdfs $N(\overline{x}, \Sigma)$ or mixtures of normal densities are considered, to represent the training set of feature vectors. In our case, the likelihood of an input vector x, corresponding to the pattern model Ω is expressed as:

$$P(x|\Omega) = \frac{\exp[-\frac{1}{2}(x-\overline{x})^T \Sigma^{-1}(x-\overline{x})]}{(2\pi)^{N/2}|\Sigma|^{1/2}} \quad (1)$$

Instead of applying estimation techniques directly to the original high dimensional space of the input feature vectors, Principal Component Analysis (PCA) [10], also known as the Karhunen-Loeve Transform (KLT), is used to yield a computationally feasible estimate. The KLT computation involves finding the eigenvectors of training samples covariance matrix Σ :

$$\Lambda = \Phi^T \Sigma \Phi \quad (2)$$

where Φ is the eigenvector matrix of Σ and Λ is the corresponding diagonal matrix of eigenvalues.

In PCA, the principal transformation is defined as:

$$y = \Phi^T (x - \bar{x}) \quad (3)$$

The partial KLT is defined as:

$$y_M = \Phi_M^T (x - \bar{x}) \quad (4)$$

where Φ_M is a submatrix of Φ containing the principal eigenvectors, which correspond to the $M (M \ll N)$ largest eigenvalues of Σ. The likelihood $P(x|\Omega)$ is approximated using the first M principal components:

$$\hat{P}(x|\Omega) = \left[\frac{\exp\left(-\sum_{i=1}^{M} \frac{y_i^2}{2\lambda_i}\right)}{(2\pi)^{M/2} \prod_{i=1}^{M} \lambda_i^{1/2}} \right] \left[\frac{\exp\left(-\sum_{i=M+1}^{N} \frac{y_i^2}{2\rho}\right)}{(2\pi\rho)^{(N-M)/2}} \right] \quad (5)$$

where y_i are the components of principal transformation vector y, the λ_i are the diagonal elements of matrix Λ, and the residual reconstruction error $\sum_{i=M+1}^{N} y_i^2$ here is calculated as:

$$\sum_{i=M+1}^{N} y_i^2 = (x - \bar{x})^T (x - \bar{x}) - \sum_{i=1}^{M} y_i^2 \quad (6)$$

The first term corresponds to the true marginal density in the principal subspace $F = \{\Phi_i\}_{i=1}^{M}$, whereas the second term is the estimated marginal density in the orthogonal complement subspace $\bar{F} = \{\Phi_i\}_{i=M+1}^{N}$. The optimal value of parameter ρ is the average of eigenvalues in the subspace $\bar{F}$:

$$\rho = \sum_{i=M+1}^{N} \lambda_i / (N - M) \quad (7)$$

3 PVL-Based Point Targets Detection

3.1 Model-Based Training Set

For learning the parameters of PVL and extracting feature vectors, a training set of point target images should be constructed. In our study, we use the Gaussian point target model [11] to generate the training images. The reasons for using model-based image data rather than actual image data are: 1) It is more difficult to construct training set with the latter, 2) the actual image data are far from ideal, due to the high amount of image clutter [7]. The training images encompass the appearance of point target under different orientation, intensity, size, and background illumination. There is only one point target at the center of each training image.

3.2 Extraction of Feature Vector

Before forming training vectors $\{x_t\}_{t=1}^{N_T}$ from training images for learning PVL parameters and forming test vectors x from a subimage in the detection stage, a normalization operation is carried out on such training images and subimages. The main purpose of normalization is to limit the illumination variance. Suppose g denotes a training image or subimage with size of $W \times W$, the normalization operation is implemented according to the following equation,

$$g_n(k,l) = [g(k,l) - \mu]/(\beta\sigma + \alpha)$$
$$k,l = 1,2,...,W$$
(8)

where g_n is the normalized image, μ is the mean brightness of g, σ is the standard deviation, β is a positive constant, and α a tiny positive constant to avoid dividing by zero. In our case, $\beta = 2.0$.

For a normalized training image g_n, the training vector x_t or test vector x is formed by lexicographic ordering of the pixel values in g_n. Once the training vectors are gathered, the PVL parameters, i.e., the mean vector $\overline{x}$, eigenvalue λ_i, eigenvectors, and the parameter ρ can be determined. In our case, we set $M=5$. The first 5 largest eigenvalues account for above 95% of total eigenvalues. Fig. 1 shows the plot of eigenvalues spectrum of covariance matrix Σ calculated from the training images with size of 11×11. From the figure and the ratio, it is can be seen that $M=5$ is reasonable.

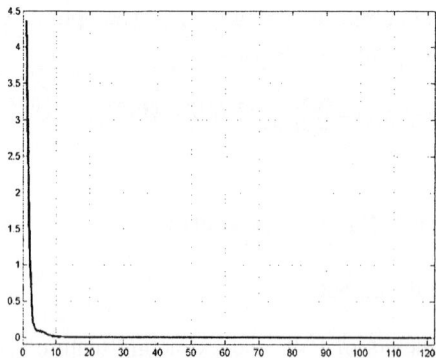

Fig. 1. Plot of eigenvalues spectrum

3.3 Formation of Saliency Map

The density estimate $\hat{P}(x|\Omega)$ in (5) is used to compute a local measure of point target saliency at each spatial position (i, j) in an input image based on the feature vector x extracted from the subimage centered at (i, j). For computational efficiency, instead of directly using $\hat{P}(x|\Omega)$ as saliency map, we define saliency map $S(i, j; W)$ using $W \times W$ sliding window as follows:

$$S(i, j; W) = \rho \bigg/ (1.0 + \rho \sum_{i=1}^{M} \frac{y_i^2}{\lambda_i} + \sum_{i=M+1}^{N} y_i^2) \qquad (9)$$

If there are no neighboring point targets in an input image, a single sliding window will work well. However, if there are multiple neighboring objects, the saliency value at targets may be very small due to the interference from neighboring point targets when capturing subimage. For solving such problem, we adopt three kinds of sliding windows to obtain subimage, the size of these sliding windows are 5x5, 9x9, and 13x13, respectively. In accordance, we constructed three independent training sets and thus obtained three PVL parameter sets. In our implementation, the saliency measure function $S(i,j)$, which is used for generating saliency map, is defined as follows,

$$S(i,j) = \sum_{k=1}^{3} S(i,j; W_k) \qquad (10)$$

After getting saliency map, the extraction of small targets can be carried out by thresholding such map with a threshold.

4 Experimental Results

Proposed detection scheme were tested on lots of real-world optical images and IR images. Fig. 2 (a)~(c) show three IR images with size of 240x320, which are intercepted from real-world IR video sequences. Fig. 3 shows a real-world optical image embedded with 15 point targets.

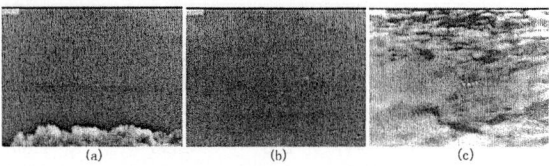

Fig. 2. Three real-world IR images. (a) with one dim object, (b) with two dim objects, (c) with four neighbouring objects in the clutter background.

To compare proposed method with other filter-based methods for the same test set, two techniques are employed to evaluate their detection performances. The first technique use the LSBR metric [1-2]. The LSBR here is defined as follows:

$$\text{LSBR} = 10\log_{10}\left(\frac{1}{H^2\sigma_b^2}\sum_{k=-(H-1)/2}^{(H-1)/2}\sum_{j=-(H-1)/2}^{(H-1)/2}[I(s-k,r-j)-m_b]^2\right)(dB) \quad (11)$$

where I is the input image, σ_b^2 is the variance and m_b is the mean of the background in the window described by the width and height H around the pixel of interest (s,r).

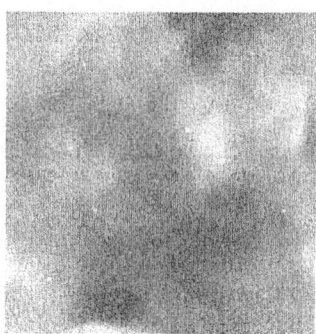

Fig. 3. A real-world optical image embedded with 15 point targets

Table 1 and table 2 show the LSBRs using different algorithms for Fig. 2 computing at each point target position.

From the tables, we can see that proposed scheme could get better LSBR Gain. Although LSBR does provide an indication of how well the filter has performed, it does not tell the whole story. Receiver Operating Characteristics (ROC) is another standard technique to evaluate their detection performances, which give us a true picture of the performance characteristics of each detection scheme and serve as an

Table 1. Comparison of LSBRs of point targets using different methods for Fig. 2 (a)~(b)

Methods/images		Fig.(a)	Fig.(b)	
		Obj.1	Obj.1	Obj.2
Unprocessed image		3.86	3.08	4.77
Max-mean	N=2	4.21	3.99	4.08
Filter	N=4	2.67	2.97	1.87
Max-median	N=2	4.23	4.40	5.35
filter	N=4	3.59	4.48	3.14
Median	5x5	4.51	4.50	5.63
subtraction	3x3	3.99	3.57	4.32
TDLMS filter	5x5	1.92	0.63	1.31
$\mu=5\times10^{-7}$	7x7	1.15	0.54	1.10
Saliency map		10.18	9.09	9.06

Table 2. Comparison of LSBRs of point targets using different methods for Fig. 2 (c)

Methods/images		Fig. (c)			
		Obj.1	Obj.2	Obj.3	Obj.4
Unprocessed image		0.56	0.55	0.22	0.77
Max-mean filter	N=2	1.72	0.95	1.25	1.25
	N=4	1.22	0.46	0.76	0.76
Max-median filter	N=2	1.82	1.21	1.42	1.42
	N=4	1.47	0.88	1.11	1.11
Median subtraction	5x5	1.25	1.34	1.51	1.43
	3x3	1.17	0.96	1.20	1.02
TDLMS filter $\mu=5\times10^{-7}$	5x5	0.69	1.01	2.01	1.99
	7x7	0.58	0.99	1.81	1.52
Saliency map		2.96	3.20	0.95	2.10

effective metric to compare them [7]. The ROC curves using different methods for Fig. 3 are shown in Fig. 4. For these four images, it is impossible to detect point targets by directly thresholding the original images. Also, the median subtraction, max-mean, and max-median filters fail to detect point targets in Fig. 3.

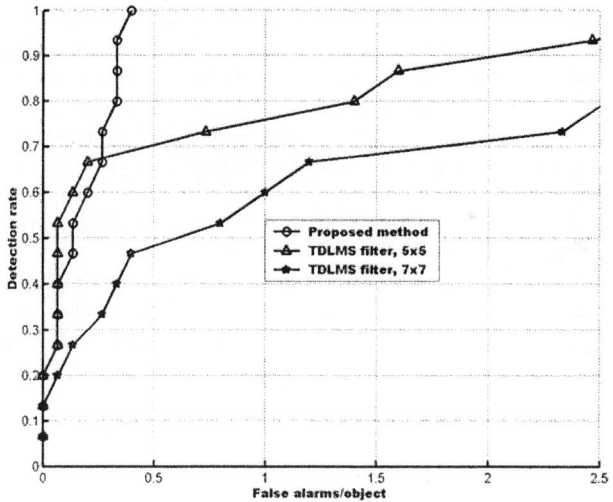

Fig. 4. The ROC curves using different methods for Fig. 3

From the tables and curves, we can see that the overall performance of proposed scheme is superior to the three filter-based methods.

5 Conclusions

In this paper we propose an efficient learning-based method for the detection of point targets in image data. Such method avoids the problem of constructing proper non-object training set and also successfully solves the problem of detecting multiple neighboring point targets taking place in other learning-based detection algorithms. Our experiments show that the proposed detection method outperforms several spatial filter-based methods for both bright objects and dim objects.

References

1. Soni, T., Zeidler, J.R., Ku, W.H.: Performance evaluation of 2-D adaptive prediction filters for detection of point targets in image data. IEEE Trans. Image Process. 2 (1993) 327-340
2. Ffrench, P.A., Zeidler, J.R., Ku, W.H.: Enhanced detectability of point targets in correlated clutter using an improved 2-D adaptive lattice algorithm. IEEE Trans. Image Process. 6 (1997) 383 – 397
3. Sang, H.S., Shen, X.B., Chen, C.Y.: Architecture of a configurable 2-D adaptive filter used for small object detection and digital image processing. Opt. Eng. 42 (2003) 2182-2189
4. Barnett, J.T., Billard, B. D., Lee, C.: Nonlinear morphological processors for point-target detection versus an adaptive linear spatial filter: a performance comparison. Proc. SPIE Int. Soc. Opt. Eng. 1954 (1993) 12-24
5. Deshpande, S.D., Er, M.H., Ronda, V., Chan, P.: Max-Mean and Max-Median filters for detection of small-targets. Signal and Data Processing of Small Targets SPIE, 3809 (1999) 74-83
6. Moon, Y.S., Zhang, T.X., Zuo, Z.R., Zuo, Z.: Detection of Sea Surface Small Targets in Infrared Images Based on Multilevel Filter and Minimum Risk Bayes Test. Int. J. Patt. Recogn. Artif. Intell. 14 (2000) 907 – 918
7. Shirvaikar, M.V., Trivedi, M.M.: A neural network filter to detect small targets in high clutter backgrounds. IEEE Trans. Neural Networks, 6 (1995) 252-257
8. El-Naqa, I., Yongyi, Y., Wernick, M.N., Galatsanos, N.P., Nishikawa, R.M.: A support vector machine approach for detection of microcalcifications. IEEE Trans. Medical Imaging 21 (2002) 1552-1563
9. Moghaddam, B., Pentland, A.: Probabilistic visual learning for object representation. IEEE Trans. Pattern Anal. Mach. Intell. 19 (1997) 696-710
10. Jolliffe, I.T.: Principal Component Analysis, Springer-Verlag, New York (1986)
11. Anderson, K.L., Iltis, R.A.: A tracking algorithm for infrared images based on reduced sufficient statistics. IEEE Trans. Aerospace and Electronic System 33 (1997) 464-472

CTFDP: An Affine Invariant Method for Matching Contours

Hui-Xuan Tang and Hui Wei

Lab of Algorithm for Cognitive Model, Department of Computer Science and Engineering,
Fudan University, Shanghai 200433, P.R. China
{hxtang, weihui}@fudan.ac.cn

Abstract. In this paper a new method for matching contours called CTFDP is presented. It is invariant to affine transform and can provide robust and accurate estimation of point correspondence between closed curves. This has all been achieved by exploiting the dynamic programming techniques in a coarse-to-fine framework. By normalizing the shape into a standard point distribution, the new method can compare different shapes despite the shearing and scaling effect of affine transform. Using the coarse-to-fine dynamic programming technique, the shapes are aligned to each other by iteratively seeking correspondences and estimating relative transform so as to prune the start points in the dynamic programming stage in turn. Experiments on artificial and real images have validated the robustness and accuracy of the presented method.

1 Introduction

Curve matching has been recognized as one of the most important issues in the literature of computer vision, and is useful across various applications, e.g. shape retrieval[8], object recognition[2], video tracking[3], etc.

Recent progress in curve matching[1,4,6,9,10,11,12] is roughly classified into local and global methods. The local methods are more efficient, but are not as stable as global methods. Global methods are more resistant to noise, but suffer from at least one of the following problems:

- Non-invariance to geometrical transformations. Many curve matching methods, if not all, only work well under RST transformations. While matching 3D planar curves, invariance to affine transformations is often desired.
- Resolution degradation. Since curves may be sheared or scaled, the points sampled along the curve can produce very different representations of the same shape.
- Expensive computational costs. A different starting point hypothesis may result in different matches; exhaustive matching processes have to be completed in matching two contours. This is obviously very expensive.

In this paper, an affine invariant curve matching method called CTFDP is proposed to solve the above problems. The first two problems are solved by using the shape normalization method. Assuming that the inputs of our algorithm are two contours related by an unknown affine transformation and some limited level of noise, we have derived a method to remove the effect of shear and scale in this transformation. Our method is somewhat similar to the affine invariant shape descriptor proposed by Zuliani et al. [12], yet in our formulation the translation is left for further estimations and some analysis on the shape normalization technique has been done to provide some intuitive insight on this skill.

Observing that starting point pruning has become a performance bottleneck in matching contours, we have developed a multi-scale method to resolve this problem by running the curve matching process through dynamic programming (DP) at different levels. Unlike most multi-scale matching techniques, if not all, the presented method fuses the matching processes into a coarse-to-fine (CTF) framework rather than fixing the matching process at a single scale. It not only benefits from great reduction of computational costs but also achieves satisfactory robustness and accuracy.

The remainder of this paper is organized as follows. Section 2 introduces the shape normalization technique, and some interesting properties of this skill are investigated. In Section 3, the dynamic programming algorithm is described, followed by discussion of the starting point pruning techniques. Section 4 illustrates some experiment results on both artificial and real images to prove the accuracy and robustness of the CTFDP method. Section 5 concludes the paper.

2 Shape Normalization

It was proposed by Kendall [7] that shape is what is left of the configuration after removing the effect of RST transforms. Before proceeding, we firstly introduce the definition of normalization of an arbitrary Jordan curve, which factors out affine transformations from the original curve:

Definition 1. Let Γ be a curve, the shape normalization transform is defined as:

$$T(\Gamma) = \Sigma^{-\frac{1}{2}} \Gamma \tag{1}$$

Where Σ is the covariance matrix of Γ.

This definition is equivalent to the definition of 'shape' proposed by Zuliani et al. [13], which factors out shear, scale and translation from the affine transformation. The only difference is that translation is left unknown in the normalization stage in our algorithm, and it will be estimated in the starting point pruning step in the curve matching stage.

Theorem 1. Let Γ_1 and Γ_2 be curves related by an affine transformation, $T(\Gamma_1)$ and $T(\Gamma_2)$ are related by a rotation and translation transform.

Proof: Given that Γ_1 and Γ_2 be curves related by an affine transformation, it has been proven by [13] that there exists a rotation, so that:

$$\Sigma_1^{-\frac{1}{2}}(\Gamma_1 - E\Gamma_1) = R\Sigma_2^{-\frac{1}{2}}(\Gamma_2 - E\Gamma_2) \qquad (2)$$

It is straightforward to derive that:

$$\Sigma_1^{-\frac{1}{2}}\Gamma_1 = R\left[\Sigma_2^{-\frac{1}{2}}\Gamma_2 - \left(\Sigma_2^{-\frac{1}{2}}E\Gamma_2 - R^{-1}\Sigma_1^{-\frac{1}{2}}E\Gamma_1\right)\right] \qquad (3)$$

Let:

$$t = \Sigma_2^{-\frac{1}{2}}E\Gamma_2 - R^{-1}\Sigma_1^{-\frac{1}{2}}E\Gamma_1 \qquad (4)$$

and we have:

$$T(\Gamma_1) = R[T(\Gamma_1) - t] \qquad (5)$$

Theorem 1 shows that the effect of shear and scale has been factored out from the original shape. The following properties provide a more intuitive explanation:

Theorem 2. The covariance of $T(\Gamma)$ equals a unit matrix for all curves Γ.

Proof: From the definition of $T(\Gamma)$, we have:

$$ET(\Gamma) = E\Sigma^{-\frac{1}{2}}\Gamma = \Sigma^{-\frac{1}{2}}E\Gamma \qquad (6)$$

Therefore:

$$\Sigma[T(\Gamma)] = \Sigma^{-\frac{1}{2}}\left(\Gamma^T\Gamma - (E\Gamma)^T(E\Gamma)\right)\left(\Sigma^{-\frac{1}{2}}\right)^T = I \qquad (7)$$

Therefore, the normalization method can be explained by saying that the point distribution of a shape varies with the affiliated geometric transforms. Consequently, the effect of shear and scaling can be removed by shaping the inputting contours into a standard point distribution.

3 Coarse-to-Fine Curve Matching Through Dynamic Programming

In the second stage, the algorithm commences by detecting local maximums in curvature as feature points, which are connected to generate a polygon to sketch the normalized shape at a given scale. At the coarsest scale, all pairs of features are hypothesized to be the start point of both curves and are matched through dynamic programming. After that, an estimation of the image transform is made and is used to prune the starting point at the finer levels.

3.1 Matching Features at the Coarsest Scale

Most dynamic programming methods first interpret the curves into syntactic descriptions and seek the minimum editing distance between them. Gdalyahu and Weinshall proposed a more flexible method [5] that combines syntactic and metric methods to match closed curves. The proposed dynamic programming algorithm is a variation of their work.

In the coarsest level, all the hypotheses of the start points are checked. During each matching process, the curves are first aligned to the line segment connecting the centroid and the start point of both curves. Subsequently, the curve sketches (polygons) are matched through filling a similarity scoring table, each entry $S(i,j)$ of which represents the minimum editing of cost matching the first i+1th and j+1th edges of the polygons. Initially, the first row and the first column of the table are filled by zeros:

$$\begin{cases} S(0,j) = 0 & 0 \leq j \leq N \\ S(i,0) = 0 & 0 \leq i \leq M \end{cases} \qquad (8)$$

Observing that the feature detection process does not guarantee stable extraction of feature points, it is necessary to merge continuous short edges into a longer one. Therefore, $S(i,j)$ is determined by taking all possible merging operations into account:

$$S(i,j) = \max_{0 \leq k < i, 0 \leq l < j} \{S(k,l) + similarity(V_{ik}, V_{jl})\} \qquad (9)$$

where V_{ik} (V_{jl}) are respectively the vector connecting the i+1th and k+1th (j+1th and l+1th) vertex. The function $Similarity(V_1, V_2)$ is defined to compare two vectors $V_1 = (l_1, \theta_1)$ and $V_2 = (l_2, \theta_2)$:

$$similarity(V_1, V_2) = \min(\frac{l_1}{l_2}, \frac{l_2}{l_1}) + \cos(\theta_1 - \theta_2) \qquad (10)$$

When the table has been completed, the maximum similarity gain for matching both contours is given by the last entry of the table. It is natural to establish correspondences with a backward tracing process. By the end of the first iteration, the set of correspondences with the maximum similarity is chosen.

3.2 Matching Features at a Finer Scale

At a finer level, the rotation and translation transformation is firstly estimated through a maximum likelihood method. The curves are then aligned according to the transformation and matched using the dynamic programming method introduced in the last section.

Theorem 3. Given a set of correspondences (Γ_i^1, Γ_i^2) where:

$$\Gamma_i^1 = (X_1, Y_1) \qquad (11)$$

and:
$$\Gamma_i^2 = (X_2, Y_2) \quad (12)$$

The maximum likelihood estimation of rotation and translation is:

$$\hat{R} = \begin{bmatrix} \dfrac{U}{\sqrt{U^2+V^2}} & -\dfrac{V}{\sqrt{U^2+V^2}} \\ \dfrac{V}{\sqrt{U^2+V^2}} & \dfrac{U}{\sqrt{U^2+V^2}} \end{bmatrix}$$

$$\hat{t} = [EX_1 \quad EY_1] - \hat{R}^{-1}[EX_2 \quad EY_2] \quad (13)$$

where:
$$U = \operatorname{cov}(X_1, X_2) + \operatorname{cov}(Y_1, Y_2)$$
$$V = \operatorname{cov}(X_2, Y_1) - \operatorname{cov}(X_1, Y_2)$$

Here "cov" is the covariance operator.

Proof: As mentioned in earlier sections, the normalization of curves is related by a rotation and a transformation:

$$\Gamma_2 = R(\Gamma_1 - t) + \varepsilon \quad (14)$$

where ε is assumed to be a zero-cross Gaussian noise:

$$g(\varepsilon) = \frac{1}{\sqrt{2\pi}\sigma} \exp\left\{-\frac{\varepsilon^2}{2\sigma^2}\right\} \quad (15)$$

Therefore, given a set of correspondences (Γ_i^1, Γ_i^2), the likelihood function is:

$$L(\Gamma_1, \Gamma_2; R, t) = \prod_i \frac{1}{\sqrt{2\pi}\sigma} \exp\left\{-\frac{\|\Gamma_{1i} - R(\Gamma_{2i} - t)\|^2}{2\sigma^2}\right\} \quad (16)$$

where:
$$R = \begin{bmatrix} \cos\gamma & -\sin\gamma \\ \sin\gamma & \cos\gamma \end{bmatrix}, \quad t = [t_x \; -t_y] \quad (17)$$

Since $\theta = (\gamma, t_x, t_y)$ is an open set and L is derivable with respect to γ, t_x and t_y, the parameters that maximize the likelihood function satisfy:

$$\left.\frac{\partial \log L(\Gamma_1, \Gamma_2; R, t)}{\partial \gamma}\right|_{\gamma = \hat{\gamma}} = 0$$

$$\left.\frac{\partial \log L(\Gamma_1, \Gamma_2; R, t)}{\partial t_x}\right|_{t_x = \hat{t}_x} = 0 \quad (18)$$

$$\left.\frac{\partial \log L(\Gamma_1, \Gamma_2; R, t)}{\partial t_y}\right|_{t_y = \hat{t}_y} = 0$$

Solving equation (18), we have:

$$\hat{R} = \begin{bmatrix} \dfrac{U}{\sqrt{U^2+V^2}} & -\dfrac{V}{\sqrt{U^2+V^2}} \\ \dfrac{V}{\sqrt{U^2+V^2}} & \dfrac{U}{\sqrt{U^2+V^2}} \end{bmatrix}$$

$$\hat{t} = [EX_1 \quad EY_1] - \hat{R}^{-1}[EX_2 \quad EY_2] \tag{19}$$

where:

$$U = \mathrm{cov}(X_1, X_2) + \mathrm{cov}(Y_1, Y_2)$$
$$V = \mathrm{cov}(X_2, Y_1) - \mathrm{cov}(X_1, Y_2)$$

After determining the rotation and translation, the second curve is aligned to the first curve and features are detected at a finer scale. The starting point is assumed to be the pair of correspondences that best matches the estimated rotation and translation, and more correspondences are established by running the dynamic programming algorithm described in Section 3.1.

4 Experiments

In this section we present experiment evaluations of the CTFDP method. Due to space limitation, scale and translation transformations are not shown in the figures.

In the first experiment, the method is tested on a set of artificial images simply related by an affine transform. The input shapes are shown in Figure 1. Figure 2 shows the results of aligned shapes. From these results, the CTFDP algorithm proves to be very accurate after matching normalized shapes at different scales.

To illustrate how the coarse-to-fine strategy works, Figure 3 depicts details in matching the curves shown in Figure 1(b) in the presence of a small level of noise. It is observed that, with the scale decreasing and the number of matched features

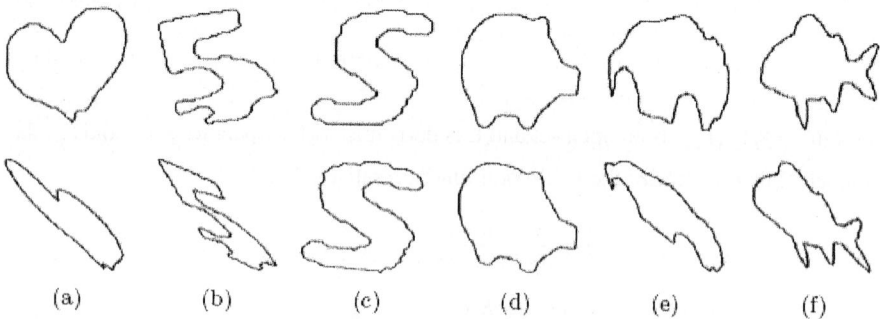

Fig. 1. Contours used in the curve matching experiment. The shapes are related by an affine transformation.

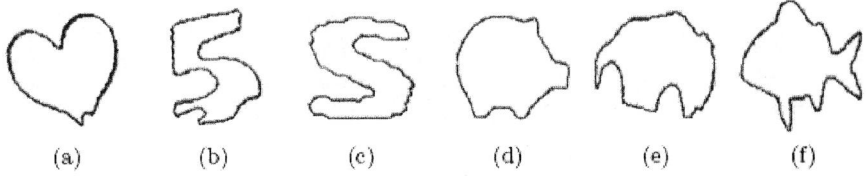

Fig. 2. Experiment results aligning shapes in Fig. 1. Blue contour: normalized shape in the first image. Red contour: aligned shape in the second image.

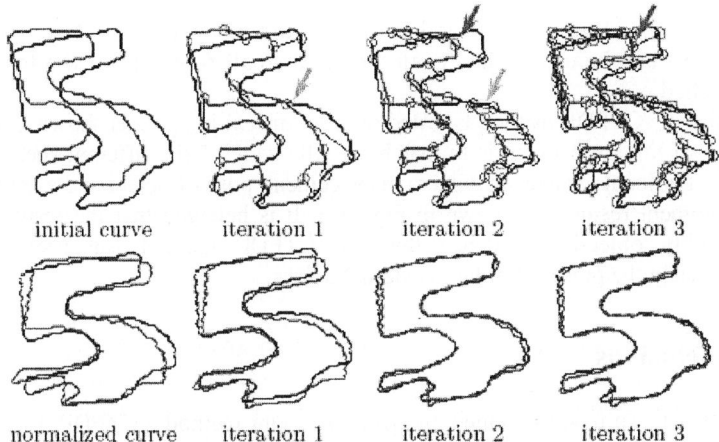

Fig. 3. The process of matching two contours related by an affine transformation. Each column refers to an iterative step in the matching process. The upper line shows registration of input contours and the bottom the alignment results. The selected scales are respectively 0.05, 0.25, 0.15 of the total length of the contours.

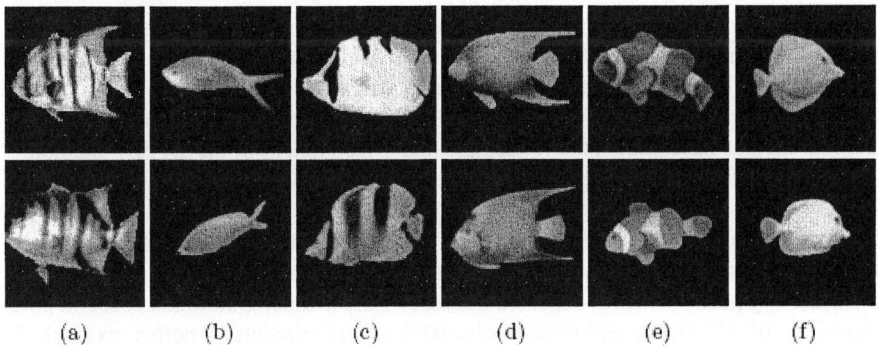

Fig. 4. Species of fish used in the object recognition experiments; the upper and bottom images are related by a variety of transforms

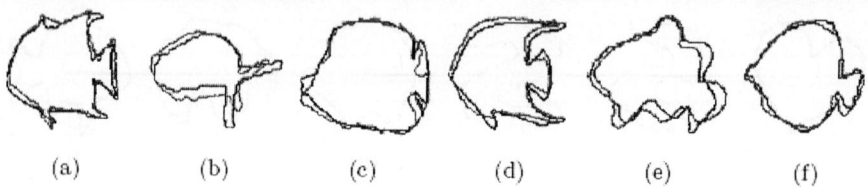

(a) (b) (c) (d) (e) (f)

Fig. 5. Results of matching contours in Fig. 5. The shapes are preliminarily normalized. Note that, though the shapes are related by perspective distortion, non-rigid motion and external noises, the CTFDP method manages to produce very satisfactory results.

increasing, the alignment estimation is more and more accurate. Note that robust estimations can be established even though a small fragment of the features are mismatched.

Finally the CTFDP method is tested on a set of real images, as shown in Figure 4. The task of this experiment is to match the silhouette of six different species of fish despite significant changes in camera displacement, pose of object and external noise. The alignment results are shown in Figure 5. It is believed that the results provide considerably objective evidence that the CTFDP method can provide robust estimations in the presence of large external noises.

5 Conclusions

In this paper, we have presented an affine invariant method - CTFDP, for matching contours. We approach this as a two stage process:

- Normalizing the two inputing shapes to factor out effects of shear and scale. This is achieved by shaping the curves into a standard point distribution.
- Running curve matching processes at different scales through dynamic programming in a coarse-to-fine framework so as to resist noise, translation and rotation.

The kernel of the presented method is the invention of a coarse-to-fine(CTF) matching framework through dynamic programming(DP). Both a dynamic programming based matching algorithm and a maximum likelihood based starting point pruning method are developed to realize this idea. Experiment results in artificial and real images have shown the robustness and effectiveness of the CTFDP method.

There is much opportunity for future research. A possible direction is to use the CTFDP method in shape retrieval and object recognition systems. By inventing a method for selecting optimal parameters, the curve matching algorithm is totally automatic, thus what is left for contour based recognition is just equation shuffling, and a satisfactory performance is expected because of the low computational cost and good capability of alignment estimations observed in experiments. Another example is revising the shape normalization method so that the CTFDP method can be reinvented to provide resistance to more complex transformations, e.g. perspective distortion, non-rigid motions. We will continue to work in these directions.

Acknowledgement

This work was supported by the NSFC under grant no. 60303007 and China Basic Research Project (973) under contract no. 2002CB309401.

References

1. Asada H., Brady M.: The Curvature Primal Sketch. IEEE Trans. on Pattern Analysis and Machine Intelligence. 8(1986) 2–14
2. Ayache N., Faugeras O. D.: HYPER: A New Approach for the Recognition and Positioning of Two-dimensional Objects. IEEE Trans. on Pattern Analysis and Machine Intelligence. 8 (1986) 44–54
3. Cohen F. S., Ayache N., Sulger P.: Tracking Points on Deformable Objects Using Curvature Information. Proc. European Conf. Computer Vision. (1992) 458–466
4. Cohen F. S., Huang Z., Yang Z.: Invariant Matching and Identification of Curves Using B-Spline Curve Representation. IEEE Trans. on Image Processing. 4(1995) 1–10
5. Gdalyahu Y., Weinshall D.: Flexible Syntactic Matching of Curves and Its Application to Automatic Hierarchical Classification of Sihouettes. IEEE Trans. on Pattern Analysis and Machine Intelligence. 21(1999) 1312–1328
6. Han M. H., Jang D.: The Use of Maxium Curvature Points for the Recognition of Partially Occluded Objects. Pattern Recognition. 23(1990) 21–33
7. Kendall D. G.: Shape Manifolds, Procrustean Metrics and Complex Projective Spaces. Bulletin of the London Mathematical Society. 16(1984) 81–121
8. Milios E., Petrakis E. G. M.: Shape Retrieval Based on Dynamic Programming. IEEE Trans. Image Processing. 9(2000) 141–146
9. Mokhtarian F., Bober M.: Curvature Scale Space Representation: Theory, Applications and MPEG-7 Standardization. Kluwer Academic Publishers (2003)
10. Orrite C., Blecua S., Herrero J. E.: Shape Matching of Partially Occluded Curves Invariant under Projective Transformation. Computer Vision and Image Understanding. 93 (2004) 34–64
11. Pajdla T. and Van Gool L.: Matching of 3-D Curves Using Semi-differential Invariants. International Conference on Computer Vision. (1995) 390–395
12. Tsai W. H. and Yu S. S.: Attributed String Matching with Merging for Shape Recognition. IEEE Trans. on Pattern Analysis and Machine Intelligence. 7 (1985) 453–462
13. Zuliani M., Bhagavathy S., Manjunath B. S., Kenney C. S.: Affine Invariant Curve Matching. Proc. International Conf. Image Processing. (2004) 3041–3044

A De-noising Algorithm of Infrared Image Contrast Enhancement

Changjiang Zhang, Xiaodong Wang, and Haoran Zhang

College of Information Science and Engineering,
Zhejiang Normal University, Postcode 321004 Jinhua, China
{zcj74922, wxd, hylt}@zjnu.cn

Abstract. An infrared image contrast enhancement algorithm based on discrete stationary wavelet transform (DSWT) and non-linear operator is proposed. Having implemented DSWT to an infrared image, de-noising is done by the method proposed in the high frequency sub-bands which are in the better resolution levels, and enhancement is implemented by combining a de-noising method with a non-linear gain method in the high frequency sub-bands which are in the worse resolution levels. Experiment results show that the new algorithm can effectively reduce the correlative noise (1/f noise), additive gauss white noise (AGWN) and multiplicative noise (MN) in the infrared image while also enhancing the contrast of the infrared image. In visual quality, the algorithm is better than the traditional unshaped mask method (USM), histogram equalization method (HIS), GWP method and WYQ method.

1 Introduction

Today, infrared images are used widely in many domains, however, the inherent character of infrared detectors and the effect of atmosphere cause bad contrast and high noise in the infrared images. It is very important to enhance the contrast of the infrared images, which will improve the quality of segmentation and target recognition. Algorithms, which are widely used to enhance the contrast in images, are histogram equalization, histogram matching, gray level transform and un-sharp mask algorithm. The common disadvantage of the above algorithms is that the noise in the image is magnified while the contrast is enhanced. Although many enhancing algorithms have been proposed[1-9], either noise in the image is not considered[12,4], high image quality is demanded[6], or the statistical properties are employed to approximate the de-noising threshold and the noise in the image is mostly considered to be gauss white noise[3]. However, the hypothesis cannot be achieved because, in general, accurate statistical properties for noise in the image cannot be obtained in practice. Not only white noise, but also correlated noise (1/f noise) corrupts the infrared image. It is very useful to reduce the correlated noise in the infrared image which contains faint targets[10-13]. The correlated noise can be considered to be additive noise[13]. The correlated noise (1/f noise) will not be discussed in detail here. Detailed information for the correlated noise in the infrared image can be found in Ref. [10-13].

An effective algorithm for enhancing the contrast of an infrared image, which is based on DSWT and a non-linear gain operator, is proposed. Because of the shift-invariance of the DSWT, and the fact that the number of wavelet coefficients at all the scales are equal to the number of the pixels in the original image, the asymptotic optimal threshold for de-noising will be assured while excellent visual quality for the reconstructed image can be obtained. The infrared image is decomposed by employing the DSWT[14]. Noise is reduced directly at the better resolution levels by employing the proposed de-noising algorithm. Contrast enhancement is implemented by combing the de-noising algorithm and the non-linear gain operator at the worse resolution levels. Experiment results show that the new algorithm can efficiently enhance the global contrast and the local contrast for the infrared image while the 1/f noise, gauss white noise and multiplication noise in the image can be noticeably reduced. Visual quality of the enhanced image employing the new algorithm is better than the traditional histogram equalization, un-sharpening mask algorithm, GWP algorithm and WYQ algorithm[3,5].

2   De-noising Principle Based on DSWT

DSWT has different names due to different applications, such as shift-invariant wavelet transform, or redundant wavelet transform[14]. Compared with discrete orthogonal wavelet transform, the main characters of DSWT are redundancy and shift-invariance and its ability to give a more approximate estimation to continuous wavelet transform.

Mallat and *Meyer* defined a series of sub-space V_j of $L^2(R)$ space in the $L^2(R)$ space, they are called multi-resolution analyses[15]. The operators T, R and D show translation, reproduction and scale operator respectively[14]. In general, we have:

$$\overline{D_i R_1 \psi} \supset \overline{D_j R_1 T_{\frac{k}{2^{j-i}}} \psi}, \quad i<j, k=0,\cdots,2^{j-i}-1 \qquad (1)$$

Two different styles can be adopted to segment the space:

$$\overline{D_{j-1} R_1 \psi} = \overline{D_j R_1 \psi} \oplus \overline{D_j R_1 \psi} = \overline{D_j R_1 T_{\frac{1}{2}} \psi} \oplus \overline{D_j R_1 T_{\frac{1}{2}} \psi} \qquad (2)$$

The above procedure is repeated and the space is divided into a series of redundant sub-spaces. When comparing DSWT with discrete orthogonal wavelet transform, their difference is in that the transformed matrix is not a square matrix and transform results are no longer orthogonal. A left inverse exists for the transformed matrix and its computation complexity is $O(N \log N)$. Traditional discrete orthogonal wavelet transform is a kind of non-redundant wavelet transform. It is suited to deal with non-correlated problems. DSWT is a kind of redundant wavelet transform and is compatible to correlated problems. It is more compatible to use DSWT to enhance the contrast for the infrared image because correlation between gray levels occurs in the infrared image.

3   De-noising Principle Based on DSWT

Wavelet transform of the correlated noise is non-stationary. The de-noising effect is worse if employing traditional "global threshold" to reduce noise in the image.

Fortunately, *I. M. Johnstone* has proven that wavelet transform of the correlated noise is still stationary at all scales of every resolution level[9]. Thus de-noising thresholds at all scales of every resolution level are calculated respectively so as to reduce noise in the image effectively.

We consider a discrete image model as follows:

$$g[i,j] = f[i,j] + \varepsilon[i,j] \tag{3}$$

The above equation can be written as a matrix as follows:

$$\mathbf{g} = \mathbf{f} + \mathbf{\varepsilon} \tag{4}$$

Where, $\mathbf{g} = \{g[i,j]\}_{i,j}$ is an observation signal, $\mathbf{f} = \{f[i,j]\}_{i,j}$ indicates an uncorrupted original image, $\mathbf{\varepsilon} = \{\varepsilon[i,j]\}_{i,j}$, $i = 1,\cdots,M; j = 1,\ldots,N$ is a stationary signal. DSWT is applied to Equation (4):

$$\mathbf{X} = \mathbf{Sf} \tag{5}$$

$$\mathbf{V} = \mathbf{S\varepsilon} \tag{6}$$

$$\mathbf{Y} = \mathbf{Sg} \tag{7}$$

$$\mathbf{Y} = \mathbf{X} + \mathbf{V} \tag{8}$$

where $\mathbf{S}$ shows two-dimensional stationary wavelet transform operator. "Soft-threshold" function, which was proposed by *Donoho*, is employed to reduce the noise in the image:

$$\mathbf{Y}_\delta = \mathbf{T}_\delta \circ \mathbf{Y} \tag{9}$$

$$\mathbf{T}_\delta = diag\{t[m,m]\}$$

$$t[m,m] = \begin{cases} 0, & |Y[i,j]| < \delta \\ 1 - \frac{\delta}{|Y[i,j]|}, & |Y[i,j]| \geq \delta \end{cases}$$

where, $i = 1,\cdots,M$, $j = 1,\cdots,N$, $m = 1,\cdots,MN$. Similarly, we have:

$$\mathbf{X}_\delta = \mathbf{T}_\delta \circ \mathbf{X} \tag{10}$$

According to Equations (7) and (9), inverse transformation for input signal is written as:

$$\mathbf{g}_\delta = \mathbf{S}^{-1} \circ \mathbf{Y}_\delta \tag{11}$$

The total operator can be expressed as:

$$\mathbf{g}_\delta = \mathbf{Z}_\delta \circ \mathbf{g} \tag{12}$$

$$\mathbf{Z}_\delta = \mathbf{S}^{-1} \circ \mathbf{T}_\delta \circ \mathbf{S} \tag{13}$$

where $\mathbf{T}_\delta$ is correlated to threshold δ and input signal $\mathbf{g}$. If the statistic properties of the noise are employed to approximate the optimal threshold δ, standard variance σ will be used[8-9]. This will be almost impossible in practice according to the above discussion. Generalized cross validation principle is employed to solve the problem[16].

4 De-noising Threshold Employing Generalized Cross Validation

Let the original signal $f[i,j]$ be expressed by employing the linear combination of its neighbor elements. Consider $\tilde{g}[i,j]$ as a linear combination of $g[k,l]$, thus special noise can be reduced. Because they can be replaced by weighted average values of their neighbor elements, and the noise in the image will be smoothed in the procedure, a cleaner signal can be obtained.

Revised signal $\tilde{\mathbf{g}}$ is employed to calculate the de-nosing threshold. $g[i,j]$, which is the $[i,j]$ element of $\mathbf{g}$, is replaced by $\tilde{g}[i,j]$:

$$\tilde{\mathbf{g}} = \mathbf{Z} \cdot (g[1,1],\ldots,\tilde{g}[i,j],\ldots,g[M,N])^T \tag{14}$$

We consider the ability of $\tilde{g}_\delta[i,j]$ to "predict" $g[i,j]$ as the standard to determine the optimal threshold. If the threshold δ is too small, the main component of $g[i,j] - \tilde{g}_\delta[i,j]$ is noise. If the threshold δ is too big, a useful signal will be reduced. The same processing is repeated to all the components and proper thresholds can be obtained by employing the following equation:

$$OCV(\delta) = \frac{1}{MN}\sum_{i=1}^{M}\sum_{j=1}^{N}(g[i,j] - \tilde{g}_\delta[i,j])^2 \tag{15}$$

The forms of $\tilde{g}[i,j]$ are many, here let $\tilde{g}_\delta[i,j] = \tilde{g}[i,j]$, and we have:

$$g[i,j] - \tilde{g}_\delta[i,j] = \frac{g[i,j] - g_\delta[i,j]}{1 - \tilde{z}[i,j]} \tag{16}$$

where, $\tilde{z}[i,j] = \dfrac{g_\delta[i,j] - \tilde{g}_\delta[i,j]}{g[i,j] - \tilde{g}_\delta[i,j]} \approx z'[m,n] = \dfrac{\partial g_\delta[i,j]}{\partial g[k,l]}$,

where, $m,n = 1,\cdots,MN$; $i,k = 1,\cdots,M$; $j,l = 1,\cdots,N$. However, in Equation (16), $z'[m,m]$ is either zero or 1. This will result in Equation (16) not being able to be calculated in practice. Thus a "generalized cross validation" formula in the wavelet domain will be given as follows:

$$SGCV(\delta) = \frac{\frac{1}{MN} \cdot \|\mathbf{Y} - \mathbf{Y}_\delta\|^2}{\left[\frac{trace(\mathbf{I} - \mathbf{Z}'_\delta)}{MN}\right]^2} \quad (17)$$

where $trace$ shows the trace of a matrix, $\|\cdot\|$ indicates Euclidean norm based on inner product, $\mathbf{I}$ shows unit matrix $M \times N$, and the meaning of other signs is the same as stated previously. Let $\delta^* = \arg\min MSE(\delta)$, and $\tilde{\delta} = \arg\min GCV(\delta)$, M. Jansen has proven that $\tilde{\delta}$, which is obtained by "generalized cross validation", is an asymptotic optimal solution[17].

5 Non-linear Enhancing Operator

Next, based on DSWT, a non-linear enhancement operator, which was proposed by A. Laine in 1994, is employed to enhance the local contrast for image[18]. For convenience, let us define the following transform function to enhance the high frequency of sub-band images in each decomposition level respectively:

$$g[i, j] = MAG\{f[i, j]\} \quad (18)$$

where $g[i, j]$ is the sub-band image enhanced, $f[i, j]$ is the original sub-band image to be enhanced, MAG is the non-linear enhancement operator, and M, N are the width and height of the image respectively.

Let $f_s^r[i, j]$ represent the gray values of pixels in the **r**th sub-band in the **s**th decomposition level, where $s = 1, 2, \cdots, L$; $r = 1, 2, 3$. $maxf_s^r$ is the maximum of the gray value of all the pixels in $f_s^r[i, j]$. $f_s^r[i, j]$ can be mapped from $[-maxf_s^r, maxf_s^r]$ to $[-1, 1]$. Thus the dynamic range of a, b, c can be set respectively. The contrast enhancement approach can be described by:

$$g_s^r[i, j] = \begin{cases} f_s^r[i, j], & |f_s^r[i, j]| < T_s^r \\ a \cdot \max f_s^r \{sigm[c(y_s^r[i, j] - b)] - \\ sigm[-c(y_s^r[i, j] + b)]\}, & |f_s^r[i, j]| \geq T_s^r \end{cases} \quad (19)$$

$$y_s^r[i, j] = f_s^r[i, j] / maxf_s^r \quad (20)$$

6 Total Cost Criterion for Enhanced Image Quality

A new criterion for evaluating the quality of an enhanced image is proposed to solve the above problem. The quality of an enhanced image is evaluated by employing the measure function, which was proposed in Ref. [19]:

$$C_{contrast} = \frac{1}{MN}\sum_{x=1}^{M}\sum_{y=1}^{N} f'^2(x,y) - \left| \frac{1}{MN}\sum_{x=1}^{M}\sum_{y=1}^{N} f'(x,y) \right|^2 \qquad (21)$$

where M and N show the width and height of the original image, and $f'(x, y)$ is the enhanced image. The higher the value of Equation (4), the better the image contrast is. Combining the ratio of signal-to-noise, a total evaluation criterion is proposed as follows:

$$C_{total} = \frac{C_{contrast} * C_{snr}}{\beta} \qquad (22)$$

where C_{snr} shows the ratio of signal-to-noise for the enhanced image, and β is a constant. It is obvious that the higher the value of Equation (22), the better the total visual quality is.

7 Experimental Results

The new algorithm is used to enhance three infrared images. In experiments, the three infrared images are added additive correlated noise (1/f noise), additive gauss white noise and multiplication noise. In order to simplify expression, HIS is employed to show histogram equalization, USH shows un-sharpening mask, SWT indicates discrete stationary wavelet transform, GWP shows the algorithm in Ref.[3] and WYQ indicates the algorithm in Ref.[5], RN shows correlated noise (1/f noise), GWN indicates additive gauss white noise, and MN shows multiplication noise.

It is very significant that RN (1/f noise) is reduced for detecting the faint targets in the infrared image. Thus for enhancing an infrared image, which is corrupted by RN, we select an infrared image, which contains a faint air target, to conduct the experiment. For enhancing the images, which are corrupted by GWN and MN, two infrared images, which contain face targets, are selected for the experiment by the new algorithm. In order to prove the efficiency of the new algorithm, we will compare the performance between HE, USH, GWP and WYQ. Figure1 shows a non-linear enhancing curve, where b=0.15, c=30. Figures 2- (a)-(g) indicate a faint air target image, image corrupted by RN (σ =6.36), enhanced image by USH, enhanced image by HIS, enhanced image by the new algorithm, enhanced image by GWP algorithm and enhanced image by WYQ algorithm respectively. Figure 3 (a) is an infrared tank image, Figure 3-(b) is an infrared tank image corrupted by GWN (σ =14.09), and Figures 3-(c)-(g) show enhanced images by USM, HIS, the new algorithm, GWP and WYQ respectively. Figure 4-(a) is an infrared hand image, Figure 4-(b) is an infrared hand image corrupted by MN (σ=0.032), and Figures 4-(c)-(g) show enhanced images by USM, HIS, the new algorithm, GWP and WYQ respectively.

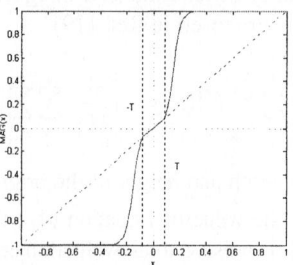

Fig. 1. Nonlinear function

(a) Small infrared target   (b) Image added with RN 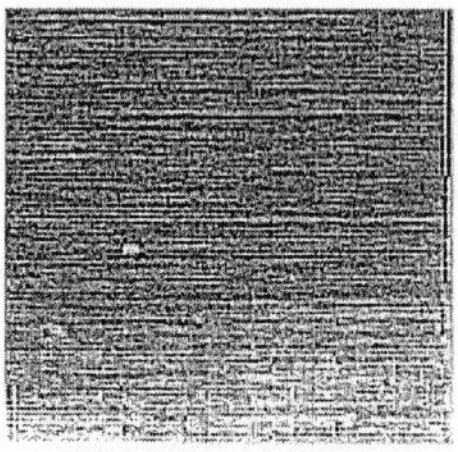   (c) Enhancement by USH

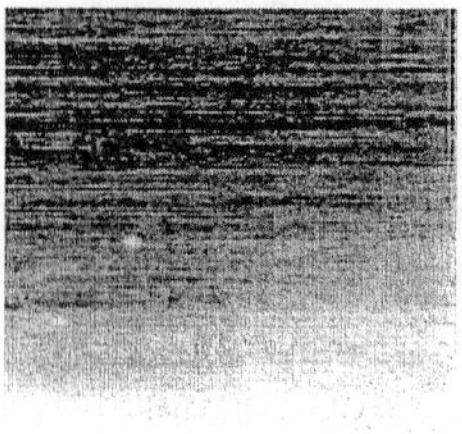

(d) Enhancement by HIS   (e) Enhancement by SWT 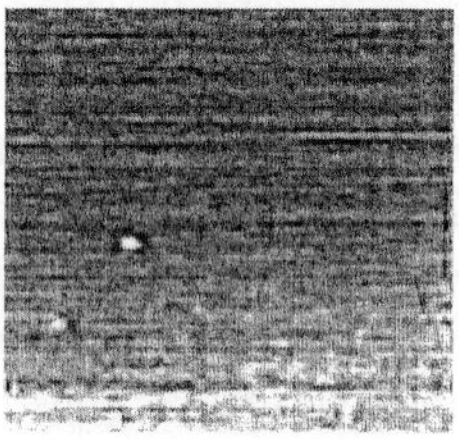   (f) Enhancement by GWP

(g) Enhancement by WYQ   (a) Infrared car    (b) Image added with GWN

Fig. 2. Enhanced image added with 1/f noise

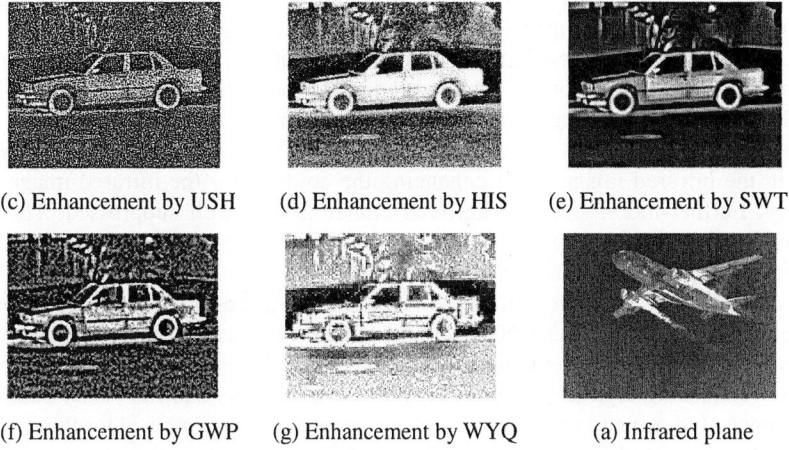

(c) Enhancement by USH (d) Enhancement by HIS (e) Enhancement by SWT

(f) Enhancement by GWP (g) Enhancement by WYQ (a) Infrared plane

Fig. 3. Enhancement results of image added with GWN

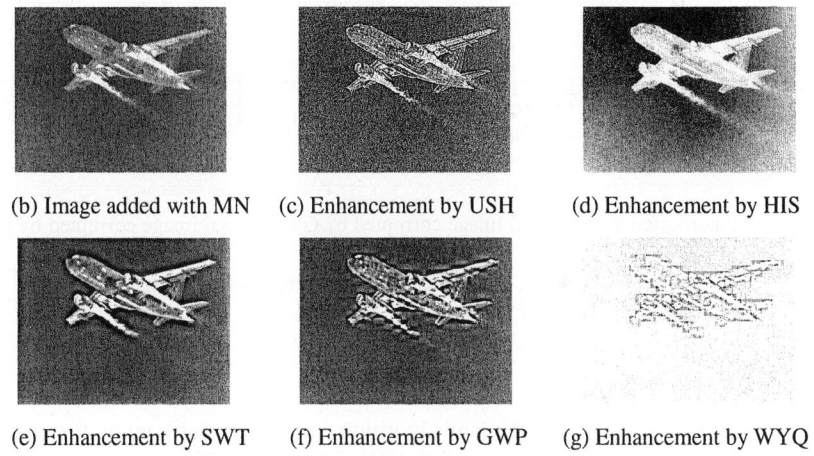

(b) Image added with MN (c) Enhancement by USH (d) Enhancement by HIS

(e) Enhancement by SWT (f) Enhancement by GWP (g) Enhancement by WYQ

Fig. 4. Enhancement results of image added with MN

From the experiment results above, the noise in the infrared image is enhanced greatly when USM and HIS are used to enhance the image, which is clear in Figures 2-(c)-(d), Figures 3-(c)-(d) and Figures 4-(c)-(d). Noise reduction is also considered in Ref.[3] and Ref.[5]. The total contrast is better when employing the GWP algorithm, however, it is not efficient at reducing the noise in the infrared image. From Figure 2-(f), Figure 3-(f) and Figure 4-(f), it is clear that the noise in the infrared image is enhanced greatly and the background clutter is also enlarged. Especially, for the faint air target in Figure 1, the background clutter has submerged the faint target in the infrared image, which will be of no benefit to detect a faint target in the infrared image. Although the WYQ algorithm can reduce the noise in the infrared image effectively, the whole brightness of the image is too high to prove some detail in the image from being lost. Especially, in Figure 2-(g), the faint target in the infrared image almost disappears completely so as not to be able to detect the faint target. Lots of burr is produced around the targets in Figure 3-(g) and Figure 4-(g), particularly at the edges of the car and the plane. Compared with the above four algorithms, the new algorithm can efficiently reduce RN, GWN and MN in the infrared image while enhancing the contrast for the infrared image efficiently. Further-more, some background clutter is also well suppressed. The new algorithm can keep the detail clear in the infrared image. For example, the faint target in Figure 2 (e) is extruded clearly.

In order to prove the effect of the new algorithm, Figures 5-(a)-(c) draw three cost curves when RN, GWN and MN corrupt the image respectively. Where the horizontal axis shows the standard averaging variance, the vertical axis indicates the total cost of the five enhancing algorithms. From Figure 5, it is obvious that the visual quality of the enhanced image and robustness to the noise employing the new algorithm is more excellent than with the other four algorithms. Thus we can draw the same conclusion as from Figures 2, 3 and 4.

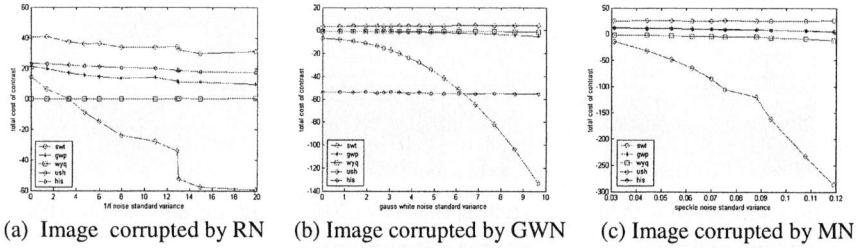

(a) Image corrupted by RN (b) Image corrupted by GWN (c) Image corrupted by MN

Fig. 5. Total cost of image added with three kinds of noise

8 Conclusion

Experimental results show that the new algorithm can enhance efficiently the contrast for the infrared image while reduce well the RN, GWN and MN in the infrared image. Employing the new algorithm, the detail in the infrared image can be kept. The visual quality of the new algorithm is much better than that obtained when using USM, HIS, GWP and WYQ.

References

1. Dekui Yin, Baomin Zhang, Lianfa Bai: 2D gray level transformation enhancement for infrared images. Infrared technology, **21** (1999) 25-29
2. Jun Xu, Changhong Liang, Jianqi Zhang: A new approach to IR image enhancement. Chinese Journal of XIDIAN University, **27** (2000) 546-549
3. Wupeng Gong, Yongzhong Wang: Contrast enhancement of infrared image via wavelet transform. Chinese Journal of National University of Defense Technology, **22** (2000) 117-119

4. Biwu Yang, Xiaosong Guo, Kejun Wang, Wanning Wei: New algorithm of infrared image enhancement based on nonlinear extension. Chinese J. Infrared and Laser Engineering, **32** (2003) 1-4
5. Yingqian Wu, Pengfei Shi: Approach on image contrast enhancement based on wavelet transform. Chinese J. Infrared and Laser Engineering, **32** (2003) 4-7
6. Honggui Li, Xingguo Li, Guozhen Li, Zhengfa Luo: A method for infrared image enhancement based on genitic algorithm. Chinese J. Systems Engineering and Electronics, **21** (1999) 44-46
7. Ming Tang, Songde Ma, Jing Xiao: Ehancing far infrared image sequences with model-based adaptive filtering. Chinese J. Computers, **23** (2000) 894-897
8. S.Grace Chang, Yu Bin, Martin Vetterli: Spatially adaptive wavelet thresholding with context modeling for image denoising. IEEE Trans on Image Processing, **9** (2000) 1522-1531
9. I.M.Johnstone, B.W.Silverman: Wavelet threshold estimators for data with correlated noise. Journal of the Royal Statistical Society, Series B, **59** (1997) 319-351
10. Qishun Su: Comparison between parallel-scan and serial-scan mechanisms of optomechanical scan infrared image systems. Chinese J. Infrared and Laser Engineering, **25** (1996) 27-35
11. Ying Zhang: The noise of thermoimaging system. Chinese J. Infrared Technology, **25** (2003) 33-36
12. Feng Yang, Hong Zhu, ZHAO Gong Yi: Prediction and compensation of 1/f noise in infrared imaging sensors. Chinese J. Infrared Millim. Waves, **22** (2003) 86-90
13. Mengyu Zhu, Baojun Zhao, Yueqiu Han: A method of removing 1/f noise based on wavelet transform. Chinese J. Journal of Beijing Institute of Technology, **21** (2001) 641-644
14. M.Lang,H.Guo,J.E. odegend, C.S. Burrus, R.O.Wells, Jr.: Nonlinear processing of a shift-invariant DWT for noise reduction. In SPIE Conference on wavelet applications, **2491** (1995) 76-82
15. S.G. Mallat: A theory for multiresolution signal decomposition: The wavelet representation. IEEE Transactions on Pattern Analysis and Machine Intellegence. **11** (1989) 674-693
16. P. Hall, I. Koch: On the feasibility of cross-validation in image analysis. SIAM J.Appl. Math, **52** (1992) 292-313
17. Maarten Jansen, Geert Uytterhoeven, Adhemar Bultheel: Image de-nosing by integer wavelet transforms and generalized cross validation. Technical Report TW264, Department of Computer Science, Katholieke Universiteit, Leuven, Belguim, August 1997
18. A. Laine, S. Schuler: Hexagonal wavelet processing of digital mammography. In Medical Imaging 1993, Part of SPIE's Thematic Applied Science and Engineering Series, 1993: 1345-1348
19. Azriel Rosenfield, Avinash C K.: Digital Picture Processing. New York: Academic Press, (1982)

Speckle Suppressing Based on Fuzzy Generalized Morphological Filter

Lihui Jiang and Yanying Guo

Tianjin Key Lab for Advanced Signal Processing,
Civil Aviation University of China, 300300, Tianjin, P.R. China
lhjiang@cauc.edu.cn

Abstract. A new filtering scheme using fuzzy generalized morphological operators is proposed for suppressing speckle noise in images. The algorithm employs generalized morphological close-open and open-close operations with a directional structuring element, and acquires the several filtered versions with different directional structure elements respectively, then computes the fuzzy membership of the versions' every pixel according to the designed fuzzy rule. The final filtered image is composed of all the pixels with corresponding maximal membership. Experiment result shows that performance of the proposed scheme is superior to that of lee's filter, F.safa's algorithm and weighted morphological filter.

1 Introduction

Radar images, SAR images and ultrasonic images are used very widely in remote sensing and nondestructive evaluation applications. Such images are often contaminated with speckle noise. Speckle noise usually falls into two types, based on the method of image formation. The first type involves the random phase variation of the wave-front originating from each source point. This occurs when imaging through a turbulent medium. The shear beam imaging technique greatly reduces the formation of this type of speckle, therefore it was not considered here. The second case involves the random interference of the various phasors when they are scattered by the microstructure fluctuations on the target's surface. This type of speckle is predominantly present in the current set of images, and usually causes high density spot-like fluctuations in the images, and degrades the quality of the image. Hence it has badly affected image interpretation and unscrambling, reduces the ability of human observer to discriminate fine details and decreases the accuracy of automated image classification and makes it difficult to identify features of interest.

For these reasons, many techniques for reducing speckle noise have been proposed in signal and image processing. The most notable include the Lee[1], Kuan[2], and Frost[3] filters applicable to SAR data. Meanwhile other filters not derived from speckle models, such as the mean filter, median filter[4], geometric filter[5], wavelet transform filter[6], and morphological filter[7][8] have also been applied for SAR speckle reduction. Evaluations of various filters can also be found elsewhere [9]. In recent years, morphological filter have attracted a lot of attention, and several morphological filters for reducing speckle noise have been developed, such as the F.Safa algorithm, and weighted morphological filter, etc [7][8]. In this paper, we construct a speckle noise suppression scheme based on fuzzy generalized directional morphological filter . First, a series of directional structuring elements are taken to implement a noise removal algorithm in the processing of speckle noise corrupted images. Next, generalized directional morphological filter is described. Then, membership function is designed and a combined filter structure is introduced. Finally, comparison is made in speckle noise suppression ability among our filter scheme and lee's filter, the F.Safa algorithm, weighted morphological filter, and concluding remarks are given.

2 Filter Scheme

2.1 Structuring Elements Selection

The morphological filters are combinations of two-dimensional morphological openings and closings or closings and openings, are not well adapted to the speckle case. This is due to the high variability of the speckle and to the tow-dimensional character of the structuring element. Even a 3×3 structuring element may contain one or several very sharp maxima or minima, so that an opening or a closing with respect to this element modifies the local value noticeably. To some degree, these drawbacks can be avoided by using linear structuring elements. Thus, In considerations of speckle noise removal and detail preserving abilities, our filter scheme is to use the structuring elements p(five pixels) of a size in four directions u_1, u_2, u_3, u_4 (Figure.1) and q(seven pixels) of a size in four directions u_1, u_2, u_3, u_4 (Figure.1) in generalized morphological opening and closing.

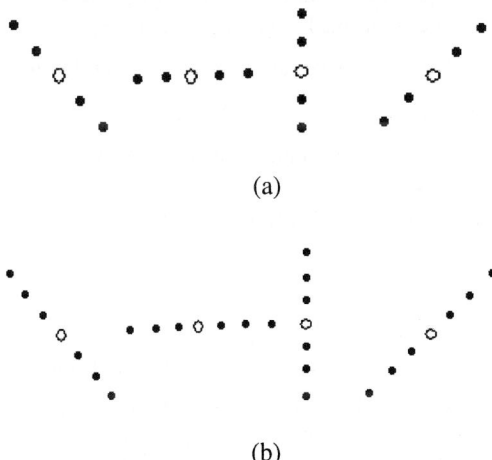

Fig. 1. (a) 5 points 4 directional linear structuring elements. (b) 7 points 4 directional linear structuring elements.

2.2 Generalized Directional Morphological Filter

Let $X(n)$ denotes input image, $Y(n)$ denotes output image. Generalized directional morphological filter[10] is defined as

$$Y(n) = (X(n) \circ B^{pu_i}) \bullet B^{qu_i} \quad Y(n) = (X(n) \bullet B^{pu_i}) \circ B^{qu_i} \quad (1)$$

Where $\circ$ denotes morphological opening operation, $\bullet$ does morphological closing operation, B^{pu_i} does structuring element with length p and direction u_i, B^{qu_i} does structuring element with length q and direction u_i, $B^{pu_i} \subset B^{qu_i}$, $n \subset Z^2$. Here, $X(n)$ is employed generalized morphological opening-closing operations and closing-opening operations with respect to 5 points 4 directional and 7 points 4 directional linear structuring elements, and acquire the eight filtered versions as

$$Y_i(n) = (X(n) \circ B^{pu_i}) \bullet B^{qu_i}$$
$$Y_j(n) = (X(n) \bullet B^{pu_i}) \circ B^{qu_i} \quad p=5, q=7, i=1,2,3,4, j=i+4 \quad (2)$$

The more directions taken, the more details of images will be preserved, but at the expense of a degradation of speckle noise removal ability. In consideration of speckle noise removal and detail preserving abilities, fuzzy logic will be applied for more effectively suppressing speckle noise.

2.3 Design of Fuzzy System

One of the key features of fuzzy logic is its ability to deal with the typical uncertainty, which characterizes any physical system. In fact, fuzziness really affects many aspects of an image process: input signal can be noisy and incomplete. In this section, a new inference mechanism using speckle noise removal will be presented.

Let the directional morphological filtered results $Y_i(n)$ be a digitized input signal. Let $X_n = X(n)$ be the noisy signal at position n, and let $W(n) = \{X_i\}$ be the set of neighboring samples, which belong to a window centered on X_n. Let $m(n) = Mean(W(n))$ be the mean of all elements of window $W(n)$.

The input variables of the fuzzy system are defined as the amplitude and *mean* differences given by the following relationship:

$$S(n) = Y(n) - m(n) \quad (3)$$

Because speckle-imaging model follows $Y(n) = X(n) + v(n)X(n)$ ($X(n), Y(n)$ are output and input signal, respectively, $v(n)$ is a random variable with mean 0 and variance σ_v^2), the smaller the absolute difference between amplitude of the pixel and *mean* of the filtering window, the higher the membership of the pixel. Thus the fuzzy set can be based on the following rules:

IF the absolute difference between amplitude of the pixel and its *mean* of all pixel amplitude in the filtering window is very large (e.g. larger than σ which is the standard variance of the amplitude in window $W(n)$), *THEN* the membership of the pixel is very low.

IF the absolute difference between amplitude of the pixel and *mean* of all pixel amplitude in the filtering window is very small (e.g. smaller than σ), *THEN* the membership of the pixel is very high.

Therefore, we use triangular-shaped fuzzy set by one parameter u for the purpose of reducing speckle noise: here u represents the width of the fuzzy set, and u can be associated with the standard variance σ. In particular, we adopt three fuzzy sets labeled small (SM), medium (ME), and *large (LA)* (Fig.2) for the purpose of reducing speckle noise and image enhancement. There, $|v| \geq |u|$. While the *mean* is small, fuzzy set labeled *SM* in Fig.2 is adopted, which the negative difference ($S(n)$) has higher membership than the corresponding positive difference. While the *mean* is large, fuzzy set labeled *LA* in Fig.2 is adopted, which the positive difference ($S(n)$) has higher membership than the corresponding negative difference.

According to these fuzzy sets, we can estimate the membership $C_{Y_i}(n)$ of $Y_i(n)$ ($i = 1, 2, \cdots, 8$) with respect to the filtering window $W(n)$. The fuzzy membership of every pixel is computed in the eight filtered visions. Then in the directional morphological filter, the output is modified as

$$\tilde{Z}(n) = Y_I(n) \text{ with } Max(C_{Y_i}(n)) \quad i = 1, 2, \cdots, 8 \qquad (4)$$

In some circumstances, $\tilde{Z}(n)$ may coincide with all $Y_i(n)$ ($i = 1, 2, \cdots, 8$). However, in the presence of speckle noise, the probability of coincidence will be very low. The output $\tilde{Z}(n)$ can therefore be expected to remove the speckle noise more effectively while edges are preserved.

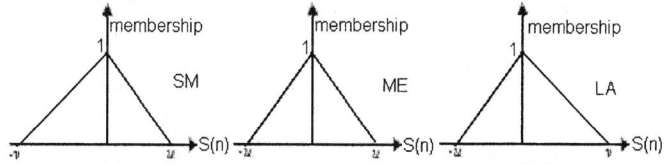

Fig. 2. Definition of triangular-shaped fuzzy set

3 Experimental Results

In this section, the performance of the proposed filter scheme is compared with that of Lee filter, F.Safa algorithm and weighted morphological filter. The original image of size 271×404(8 bits per pixel) is showed in Fig.3(a). The image Fig.3(b) are corrupted by speckle noise. The image Fig.4(a) is MSTAR(Moving and Stationary

Target Acquisition Recognition) data from USA. The images restored by the notable Lee filter, F.Safa algorithm, and the weighted morphological filter are showed in Fig.3(c), (d), (e) and Fig.4(b), (c), (d), respectively. A 5×5 square window is chosen for both Lee filter and the weighted morphological filter. The images restored by the proposed filter scheme is showed in Fig.3 (f) and Fig.4(e). Then, performance of various filters including Lee's filter, F.Safa's algorithm, weighted morphological filter and the proposed filter scheme is examined through speckle-index[11] and normalized mean square error (NMSE)[12]. The measured results are showed Table.1. The restored images show that Lee's filter and weighted morphological filter can not preserve the geometrical features of images, and the measured results support the fact that the speckle noise suppressing performance of the proposed scheme is superior to that of F.Safa's algorithm, weighted morphological filter, and nearly the same as that of Lee's filter.

Fig. 3(a). The original image

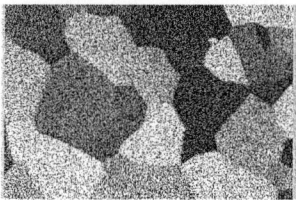

Fig. 3(b). Noisy image

Fig. 3(c). The image filtered by Lee's filter

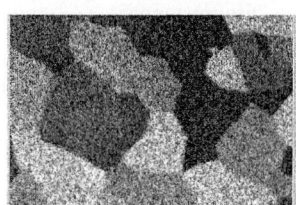

Fig. 3(d). The image filtered by F.Safa's algorithm

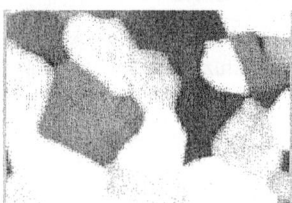

Fig. 3(e). The image filtered by weighted morphological

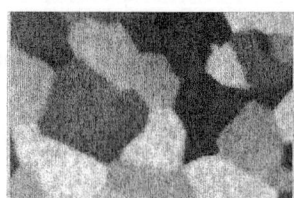

Fig. 3 (f). The image filtered by the proposed filter scheme

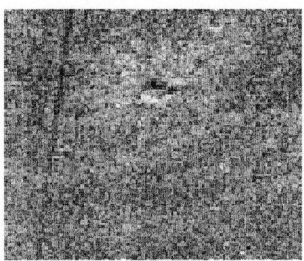
Fig. 4(a). noisy image

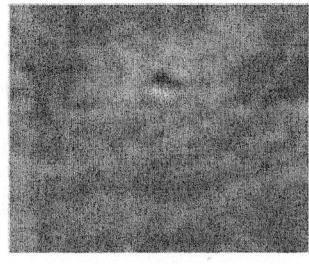
Fig. 4(b). The image filtered by Lee's filter

Fig. 4(c). The image filtered by F.Safa's algorithm

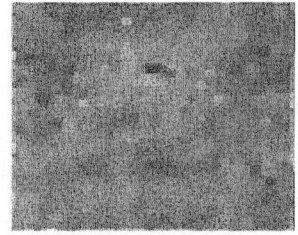
Fig. 4(d). The image filtered by weighted morphological filter

Fig. 4(e). The image filtered by the proposed filter scheme

Table 1. Speckle-index and NMSE of noisy image and processed image

Noisy image and algorithm	Speckle-index	NMSE	Speckle-index/MSTAR
Noisy image	0.3032	0.0795	0.1625
The proposed filter scheme	0.0382	0.0043	0.0364
Lee's filter	0.0417	0.0056	0.0358
F.safa's algorithm	0.2159	0.0617	0.0961
Weighted morphological filter	0.0688	0.1534	0.0438

4 Conclusions

We have presented a new filter scheme based on fuzzy morphological filter for reducing speckle noise in image. Experimental results show the filter scheme not only can suppress speckle noise more effectively but also can preserve the geometrical features of images. A comparison shows that the filter scheme is superior to lee's filter, F.safa's algorithm, weighted morphological filter although slightly more computation is required.

Acknowledgements

This paper is supported by the National Science Fund of China (60373034).

References

1. J. S. Lee. Speckle suppression and analysis for synthetic aperture radar. Opt. Eng.,Vol.25, No.5,pp.636-643,1986.
2. D. T. Kuan, A. A. Sawchuk, T. C. Strand, and P. Chavel. Adaptive restoration of images with speckle. IEEE Trans. Acoust. Speech Signal Processing, Vol. ASSP-35, No.2,pp.373-383,1987
3. V. S. Frost, J. A. Stiles, K. S. Shanmugan, and J. C. Holtzman. A model for radar images and its application to adaptive digital filtering of multiplicative noise. IEEE Trans. Pattern Anal. Machine Intell., Vol. PAMI-4,No.1,pp. 157-165,1982.
4. J. W. Tukey. Exploratory data analysis. MA: Addison-wesley, pp.18-68,1997.
5. T. R. Grimmins. Geometric filter for reducing speckle. Opt. Eng., Vol.25, No.4, pp.652-654,1986.
6. Y. Dong, B. C. Forster, A. K. Milne, and G. A. Morgan. Speckle suppression using recursive wavelet transform. Int. J. Remote Sensing, vol.19, no.2, pp.317-310, 1998.
7. F.Safa, G. Fiouzar. Speckle removal based on mathematical morphology. Signal Processing, Vol.16,No.4,pp.320-333,1989.
8. M. H. Sedaaghi, Q. H. Wu. Weighted morphological filter. Electronics Letters, Vol.34, No.16, pp.1566-1567,1998
9. J. S. Lee, I. Jurkevich, P. Dewalle, P. Wambacq, and A. Oosterlink. Speckle filtering of synthetic aperture radar images: A review. Remote Sensing Rev.,Vol.8, No.4,pp.313-340,1994.
10. Zhao ChunHui, Sun ShengHe and Qiao JingLu. A generalized morphological filter based on adaptive weighted average. Chinese Journal of Electronics. Vol.6, No.3,pp.76-81,1997.
11. XiaHua Yang, Peng Seng Toh. Adaptive fuzzy multilevel median filter. IEEE Trans. On Image Processing, Vol.4, No.5,pp. 680-682,1995
12. Dewaele P., Wambacq P, Oosterlinck A, et al. Comparison of some speckle reduction techniques for SAR Images.IGRASS'90,Maryland,USA:the University of Maryland college Park, 2417~2422

Research of Vehicle License Plate Location Algorithm Based on Color Features and Plate Processions

Yao-Quan Yang, Jie Bai, Rui-Li Tian, and Na Liu

Faculty of Control Science and Engineering, North China Electric Power University,
Baoding 071003, China
yyq2201@163.com

Abstract. Locating the region of a license plate is the key component of the vehicle plate recognition system. A novel method is adopted in this paper to replace the traditional method which is based on gray image. The method that sufficiently utilizes the color characteristics of the colored image is based on the color collocation of the plate's background and characters combined with the plate's structure and texture to locate the vehicle license plate. The plate's region would then be emended and binarized. The location rate reaches 98% in experiments.

1 Introduction

Intelligent traffic system is the main direction in the development of traffic management, and the technique of automatic vehicle license plate recognition is the key component of this system. It plays an important role in the management of city streets, ports, airports, highways and parking lots. In the vehicle license plate recognition system, the plate location system is the most important part. In the past, limited by the speed and memory capacity of the CPU, plate recognition was mainly based on the gray image in order to recognize the vehicle plate in real time. But the defect of the gray image processing technique is its high error rate when the contrast is low or the luminance is unequal, or some other region's structure and texture are similar to the plate's region. In recent years, computer performance has improved significantly, and it is now possible to process a great deal of color information quickly and efficiently. Nowadays, more and more scholars locate the plate region by the colored image processing technique. These methods are mainly as follows:

1. First, segmenting the colors in the image by use of a neural network. Second, the horizontal and vertical projections of the plate's background color are calculated. Then, the plate's region is located using the ratio of the plate's height and width [1].
2. Based on gray image, template matching is used to find the corner points of the plate. If four possible corner points are found, the content of the quadrangle is checked on its spatial frequencies. Certain spatial frequencies are expected due to the characters in a plate. Only in the case where this frequency content confirms its presence, are the four corner points accepted as being the corner points of a license plate [2].

3. Processing the image's edge with the distance of color space and similarity, and then segmenting the gray image from the candidates of plate region by texture to locate the plate [3].

The effect of the plate's location is improved by these methods, but when the luminance varied or the plate was oblique in the image, the locating error rates were very high. If increased reliability is wanted, then full use should be made of the color information provided by the colored image. There is an important attribute of Chinese vehicle plates: there are only four plate background colors namely, blue, black, white and yellow. And there are only three colors used for the characters on the plate: black, red and white. Their collocations are fixed. With this attribute, we can quickly and efficiently locate the plate region.

This paper is organized as follows. In the next section the methods overview is presented. The algorithm and other processes are discussed in detail in Section 3. The results of experiments are presented in Section 4 and Section 5 is the conclusion.

2 Methods Overview

All vehicle plates have the same important attributes such as structure and texture etc. These attributes are used to locate the plate's region where the methods used are based on gray images. But there is another important attribute of the vehicle plate, which is the color collocation of the plate's background and the characters. The image is made up of pixels. In a colored image, when the color model is RGB, every pixel is described by three vectors. They are R (red), G (green) and B (blue). We can find the plate's region in the colored image with the several given colors of the plate's background. But the color of the vehicle plate's background in different provinces is not completely the same. Otherwise, the color of the plate would fade when the plate has been used for a long time. The same color's R, G and B vectors will not be the same in luminance, either. To solve this problem, the color model should be transformed from RGB to HSV, because each color bolt is continuous in the HSV model. But when there are other objects in the image which have the same color as the plate's background, it becomes difficult to locate the plate's region. So we can utilize the color of the plate's background combined with the characters' color to detect the color edge. There are only five collocations of the plate's background and characters in China:

1. blue background with white characters on low-power cars;
2. yellow background with black characters on high-power buses and lorries;
3. black background with white characters on foreign organizations' vehicles;
4. white background with black characters or red characters on military or police vehicles.

When the program is used to detect the color edge, every pixel in the image is firstly scanned. If a pixel's color is found to be the same as a kind of plate's background color or characters' color, the program will look for the pixel with corresponding color around it. If the corresponding color appears on the pixel's left or right, it will be considered to be a horizontal edge point. If the corresponding color is under the pixel or above the pixel, it will be considered to be a vertical edge point.

The edge points detected by this method are much less than that detected by common methods. This will make the location of the plate easier.

3 Plate Locating Algorithm

Before detecting the edge, the digital image should be preprocessed to eliminate disturbances such as mud or dirt and make the follow steps easier.

3.1 Transformation of the Color Model

There are many color models to describe color information such as RGB, HSV, Lab and so on. Generally, the image is described by the RGB model, which includes the three vectors R, G and B. They represent red, green and blue. The defect of this model is that the three vectors would obviously change when the luminance or contrast varied slightly. But in the HSV model, color is presented by Hue (H), Saturation (S) and Value (V). The kind of color is decided by vector H, vector S decides the brightness of the color and vector V decides the color's contrast. Color in different brightness and contrast can be obtained by adjusting vectors S and V. The formula to transform the RGB model to the HSV model is as follows[4]:

$$Hl = \cos^{-1}\left\{0.5[(R-G)+(R-B)]/\sqrt{(R-G)^2+(R-B)(G-B)}\right\}. \qquad (1)$$

$$H = \begin{cases} Hl & \text{if } B \leq G \\ 360° - Hl & \text{if } B > G \end{cases}. \qquad (2)$$

$$S = (Max(R,G,B) - Min(R,G,B))/Max(R,G,B). \qquad (3)$$

$$V = Max(R,G,B)/255. \qquad (4)$$

3.2 Color Edge Detection Based on the Fixed Color Collocation

We can assume the color pixel that is waiting to be detected as S0 (x, y) = (H (x, y), S (x, y), V (x, y)). The H (x, y), S (x, y), V (x, y) in the equation are the hue, saturate and value vectors in the HSV color model. Getting pixels from S0's left, right, up and down establishes a 5×5 matrix as figure1 shows (we call the matrix a detection matrix).

Taking plates with a blue background and white characters for example, in order to decide whether the point that is waiting for detection is a horizontal edge point, vertical edge point or an oblique one; we clip the matrix into two parts in four different ways. The cutting lines in this method are the 3rd row, the 3rd column and the 45°, 135° diagonal of the matrix. Then setting up 16 variables, they are Left_Blue, Left_White, Right_Blue, Right_White, Up_Blue, Up_White, Down_Blue, Down_White, LeftUp_Blue, LeftUp_White, LeftDown_Blue, LeftDown_White, RightUp_Blue, RightUp_White, RightDown_Blue, and RightDown_White. Let them represent the number of the blue pixels and white pixels in the left part, right part, up part, down part, left up part, left down part, right up part and right down part. Among them, left and right, up and down, left down and right up, left up and right down make up position pairs in order to detect the horizontal edge, vertical edge and 45°, 135° oblique edges. When the points that are waiting for detection aren't blue or white, pass it. A corresponding detection matrix will be established if the pixel is blue (or white), and then every element in the matrix is scanned. Its position in the matrix should be found if an element is white (or blue), and then the corresponding variable adds one. For example, S2 is in the matrix's left part, right part, left up part and right up part simultaneously in figure1. If it is blue, the variables Left_Blue, Up_Blue, LeftUp_Blue and RightUp_Blue will be added 1. After all the elements in the matrix are detected, the difference value between the four position pairs' blue elements and white elements will be calculated. The equations are as follows:

Vertical=|Left_Blue − Right_Blue| + |Left_White − Right_White|
Horizon=|Up_Blue − Down_Blue| + |Up_White − Down_White|
Slope45=|RightUp_Blue − LeftDown_Blue| + |RightUp_White − LeftDown_White|
Slope135=|LeftUp_Blue − RightDown_Blue| + |LeftUp_White − RightDown_White|

S1	S2	S3	S4	S5
S6	S7	S8	S9	S10
S11	S12	S0	S13	S14
S15	S16	S17	S18	S19
S20	S21	S22	S23	S24

Fig. 1. 25 pixels around S0 make up of the detection matrix

Because there are absolute value signs in the equations, whether the edge is blue-white or is white-blue doesn't have any effect on the difference value. Assuming a threshold value, if the difference value of a position pair is bigger than the threshold value, S0 is considered to be an edge point.

3.3 Locating the Plate's Region by the Plate's Texture

The edge points detected by the methods in Section 3.2 are much less than that detected by the method of the color space's distance among the red, green and blue vectors. But when the color of the vehicle's body is the same as the color in the several collocations, there will still be many disturbances after edge detection. In order to locate the plate's region correctly, the plate's structure and texture should be utilized.

Because the number of characters on the plate usually ranges from 7 to 10 (including Chinese characters, Arab numerals and English letters), the edge points on the horizontal direction are regulated and concentrated and the variance ratio of the edge points is steady. A threshold value can be assumed so that a region with more edge points than the threshold value can be considered as a candidate plate. Then the plate can be correctly located from the candidate plates by its variance ratio on the horizontal direction. Through experiments, this method has proven to locate the vehicle plate from the colored image very well. It will fail only when there are some posters or advertisements that have the same color collocation with the plates in the image. But in practical situations, these cases are very few.

3.4 Line Detection and Plate Emendation

Restricted by the photo conditions, the image may be slightly oblique, which will make the following steps difficult. So, the plate's region should be emended before the recognizing process.

Because the oblique angle can't be known beforehand, it is necessary to detect the borders of the plate to obtain the oblique angle. Therefore, line detection is important for plates' emendation. Instead of the classic Hough transformations[5], this paper applies Random Algorithm to line detection[6]. This method's advantages are that the amount of calculation and storage it needs are much less than when using the Hough transformation. The steps of this algorithm are as follows:

- Detecting the image's edge and setting up an edge-point-space V(x, y) with all the edge points. X and Y are the coordinate of points in edge-point-space.
- Three points, which are $p_1(x_1, y_1)$, $p_2(x_2, y_2)$ and $p_3(x_3, y_3)$, are chosen at random from the edge-point-space then producing a line, L, by two of them. The equation of the line is as Equation (5).

$$y = ax + b. \quad (5)$$

Parameters in Equation (5) can be obtained from two points:

$$a = (y_j - y_i)/(x_j - x_i). \quad (6)$$

$$b = (y_i x_j - y_j x_i)/(x_j - x_i). \quad (7)$$

The distance between the third point and the line made by the other two points can be obtained by Equation (8). If d is smaller than a certain threshold T_d, the three points are considered to be on the same line L.

$$d = |y_k - ax_k - b|/\sqrt{a^2 + 1}. \quad (8)$$

A variable Num is set up to represent the number of edge points, which are on the line L. Then the edge-point-space is scanned point by point. If the distance between an edge point and the line L were smaller than threshold T_d, variable Num would add one. After scanning the space V, variable Num and another threshold T_s are compared. If Num is bigger than T_s, line L is the plate's border. All the points on line L will be deleted from space V, then go on to detect another border of the plate. If Num is smaller than T_s, obtain three other points at random from space V and repeat steps above.

The oblique cases of the image can be classified into horizontal oblique, vertical oblique and horizontal-vertical oblique[7] as figure. 2 shows.

Based on the slope K_i of the line, which is detected in the steps before, the plate's region can be horizontally emended at first. As figure 3(a) shows, the coordinates of point p0 change from (x0, y0) to (x1, y1), but the distance between point and origin doesn't change.

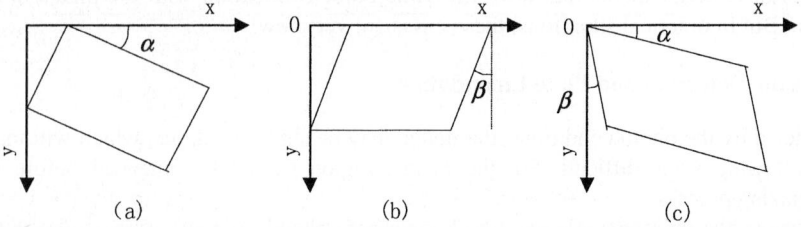

Fig. 2. Three oblique cases: horizontal oblique, vertical oblique and horizontal-vertical oblique

Based on the slope K_i of the line, which is detected in the steps before, the plate's region can be horizontally emended at first. As figure 3(a) shows, the coordinates of point p0 change from (x0, y0) to (x1, y1), but the distance between point and origin doesn't change.

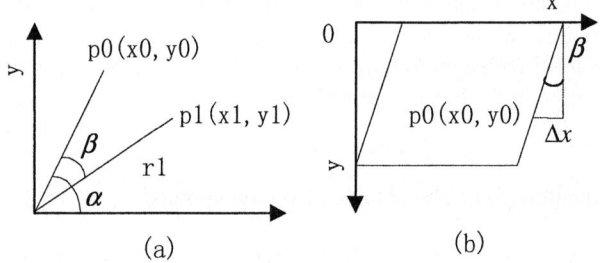

Fig. 3. This figure shows how to emendate the image horizontally and vertically

The horizontal-oblique-angle α in figure 3(a) can be obtained by Equation (9). The relation between (x0, y0) and (x1, y1) is as per Equation (10).

$$\alpha = \pi/4 - \arctan(k_i) \cdot \quad (9)$$

$$\begin{cases} x0 = r\cos(\alpha) \\ y0 = r\sin(\alpha) \end{cases} \cdot \quad (10)$$

$$\begin{cases} x1 = x0\cos(\beta) + y0\sin(\beta) \\ y1 = -x0\sin(\beta) + y0\cos(\beta) \end{cases} \cdot \quad (11)$$

The vertical-oblique-angle β also can be obtained by Equation (9). The point's ordinate needn't be changed; its abscissa variance can be obtained by Equation (12).

$$\Delta x = y_0 \tan(\beta) \cdot \quad (12)$$

3.5 Vehicle License Plate Binarization

To recognize the characters on the plate quickly and easily, binarization is necessary. This step of the process means the image can have only two colors. They are black and white. One of the difficulties with plate binarization is the plates' diversification. Because there are four types of plates with different colors of background and characters, there will be two types of binary image after binarization. For example, a plate with a blue background and white characters will be a black background with white characters after binarization. But a plate with a yellow background and black characters will become a white background with black characters. So they must be standardized to one form (black background with white characters) in order to make the subsequent steps easy.

Another difficulty is the selection of the threshold value. The iteration method is adopted in this paper to compute the most appropriate threshold value. The basic principle of this method is as follows:

$$T_{i+1} = K[(\sum_{l=0}^{Ti} h_l * l / \sum_{l=0}^{Ti} h_l) + (\sum_{l=Ti+1}^{L-1} h_l * l / \sum_{l=Ti+1}^{L-1} h_l)] \cdot \qquad (13)$$

First, the image should be made into gray. Second, the image's gray histogram is calculated. Third, select the median of the gray value's scope as the initial threshold value (assume that there are L gray levels in all), and then iterate the threshold value as Equation (13).

In Equation (13), h_l is the number of the gray level l. The iteration will be over when $T_{i+1}=T_i$. Making the final T_i is the threshold value T. The initial value of parameter K in Equation (13) is 0.6. Then iterate it by Equation (14).

$$S = \sum_{l=0}^{T_i} h / \sum_{l=T_i+1}^{L-1} h \cdot \qquad (14)$$

The principle is: the ratio between the total number of background pixels and the characters' pixels is fixed (about 2.0). In Equation (14), parameter S represents the ratio. Although S will vary a little along with the variation of the characters' complication in the plate (the scope is between 1.8 to 2.5 from experiments), the value of S can reflect approximately the correctness of the threshold value. So the parameter K should be adjusted on the basis of S every time it iterates as follows:

$$K = \begin{cases} S > 2.5 & \text{reduce K} \\ S < 1.8 & \text{increase K} \\ \text{others} & \text{no change} \end{cases} \cdot \qquad (15)$$

With this method, adjusting the iteration parameter automatically achieves an accurate threshold value. Its self-adapting ability is very strong, and the threshold value obtained by it is very accurate.

4 The Result and Analysis of Experiment

Figure 4 (a) is a blue mini bus with a plate of blue and white collocation. Though the vehicle's body is blue, there are not many blue-white boundaries around the region in the image. Therefore, edge points detected by the method of fixed color collocation (shown in figure 5 (b)) are much less than that detected by common methods (shown in figure 5 (a)). As figure 5 (b) shows, the plate's structure and texture are very apparent. The vehicle plate can be located easily and quickly as figure 5 (e).

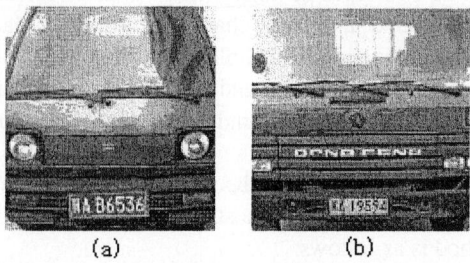

(a)　　　　(b)

Fig. 4. In this figure are colored vehicle images. The left vehicle in the figure is a mini-bus with a plate of blue and white collocation, and the right one is a lorry with a plate of yellow and black collocation.

Figure 4 (b) is a lorry with a plate of yellow and black collocation. The edge points detected by the method of fixed color collocation are shown in figure 5 (c). Figure 5 (d) shows the edge points detected by common methods. The plate's region is located as figure 5 (f) shows.

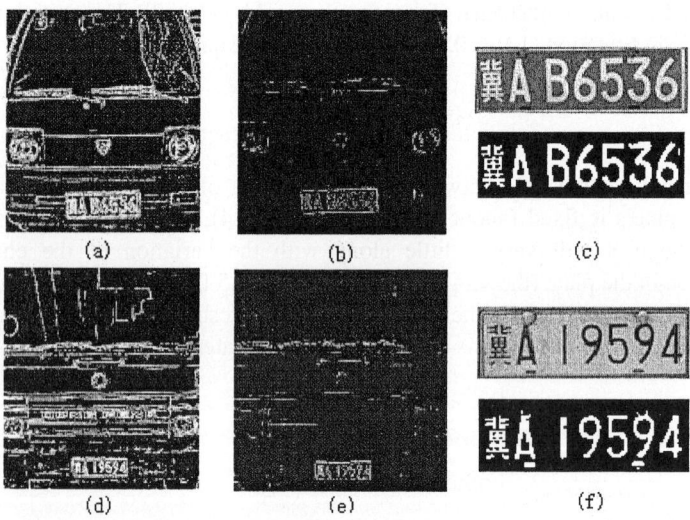

Fig. 5. This figure shows the comparisons between the result of edge detection used of traditional method and fixed color collocation. The plate's region that is located by the plate's texture is shown in this figure too.

The method is tested by locating 500 images of each kind of vehicle that were taken by digital camera in varying weather, illumination, vehicle speed, perspective and geometrical conditions. Each image contains the head of the vehicle, plate and natural scenery. In experiments, the program, which is written with Visual C++ 6.0 and launched on a computer with P4 2.4G CPU and 512M memory, takes 1 to 2 seconds. This proves that the program based on this method can fulfill the request of real-time. The number of plates located correctly is 491, so the correctly locating rate is 98.2%. The images that failed to be located can be categorized as follows:

1. The faded condition of the plate was so serious that the colors of the plate's background and characters couldn't be properly distinguished.
2. The camera was too far from the vehicle, so that the plate in the image was too small.
3. The characters on the plate merged into the plate's background. In the two cases where this occurred, the colors of the characters and background were almost the same; corresponding color collocation is not be well detected under this circumstance.

Therefore, the algorithm needs improving to cater for these conditions.

5 Conclusions

In this paper, a novel method based on fixed color collocation is put forward to locate vehicle plates. This method's characteristic is to locate the plate quickly and efficiently by the color collocation of the plates' background and characters combined with the plates' structure and texture. In this method, the color information from the colored image is reasonably utilized to greatly decrease the edge points. With this method, it also eliminates the disturbances of the fake plate's region whose structure and texture are similar to the vehicle plate but don't match the plate's fixed color collocation. Experiments prove that this method is efficient in locating vehicle plates in colored images.

Instead of the classic Hough transformation, an improved random algorithm for line detection is used in vehicle plate emendation to obtain the gradient angle of the image. Then the plate's region is emended and binarized. Experiments prove that the efforts are worthwhile.

References

1. Wei. W, X. Huang, M. Wang: An Automatic System of Vehicle Number-plate Recognition Based on Neural Networks. In: Journal of Systems Engineering and Electronics, Vol. 12. (2001) 63-72
2. Hans A. Hegt, Ron J. De la Haye, Nadeem A. Khan: A High Performance License Plate Recognition System. In: Proceedings of IEEE International Conference on Systems, Man, and Cybernetics, San Diego, Vol. 5. (1998) 4357-4362
3. Wen-Ju. Li, De-Qun. Liang, Qi. Zhang: A Novel Approach for Vehicle License Plate Location Based on Edge-Color Pair. In: China Journal of Computers, Vol.27. (2004) 204-208
4. Eun Ryung Lee, Pyeoung Kee Kim, Hang Joon Kim: Automatic Recognition of a Car License Plate Using Color Image Processing. In: Proceedings of IEEE International Conference on Image Processing, Austin, Texas (1994): 301-305
5. Xu L, Oja E, Kultanan P: Randomized Hough transform (RHT) [j]. In: Pattern Recognition Letters (1990): 331-338
6. Gang-Feng. Xu, Biao. Li, Zhen-Kang. Shen: An Efficient Random Algorithm for Lines Detection. In: Journal of Image and Graphics, Vol.8. (2003) 1418-1421
7. Wen-Ju. Li, De-Qun. Liang, Lian-Yan. Cui: Novel License Plate Image Preprocessing Approach for Character Segmentation. In: Application Research of Computers, Vol.21. (2004) 258-260

Fast Measuring Particle Size by Using the Information of Particle Boundary and Shape

Weixing Wang

Department of Computer Science & Technology,
Chongqing University of Posts & Telecommunications,
Post code: 400065, China
wangwx@cqupt.edu.cn, znn525d@yahoo.com

Abstract. To quickly and accurately estimate average size of densely packed particles on a fast moving conveyor belt, a new image processing method is designed and studied. The method consists of two major algorithms, one is a one-pass boundary detection algorithm that is specially designed for the images of densely packed particles (the word "particle" is used in a wide sense), and the other is average size estimation based on image edge density. The algorithms are cooperative. The method has been tested experimentally for different kinds of closely packed particle images which are difficult to detect by ordinary image segmentation algorithms. The new method avoids delineating and measuring every particle on an image, therefore, is suitable for real-time imaging. It is particularly applicable for a densely packed and complicated particle image sequence.

1 Introduction

In a quarry, the average size of aggregate particles is not only a quantity to be used for evaluating the quality of aggregates, but also important information for adjusting the crushers, e.g., their apertures. A main indicator of a normal crusher operation is average size. In control systems for automatic crushing, a feedback loop involving average aggregate particle size from real-time processing could mean substantial improvement of the crusher stage of the production flow. In this kind of applications, a CCD camera should be mounted looking down on a bed of crushed aggregates being transported on a conveyor belt from a crusher. Such work was reported in [1-6].

The aim of aggregate particle delineation is to measure the different parameters of an individual particle. From literature review, there are a large number of publications dealing with aggregate (or rock fragmentation) image segmentation and processing [1-6]. Since it is difficult to obtain the same type of aggregate images in different working environments, the image segmentation algorithms [1-6] should be different. In our case, the application properties are: (1) the complexity of images: where particles are wet and glue together, and the particles on belt surface are looking like clay sometimes, an ordinary segmentation algorithm is hard to be used for particle delineation; (2) image acquisition: ordinary cameras are difficult to close to belt to acquire high accuracy images, so, the number of pixels is limited for a particle, which causes image segmentation difficult too, and (3) speed of image processing: the industry manufacture needs an online processing, so, the time consuming and complex image processing and segmentation algorithms should not be used. One image example is shown in Fig.1, where, the belt moving speed is about 2.5 m per second, the particle size is between 0.1 and 3.0 mm, the particles are wet, and the average particle size is needed to be estimated online.

In this paper, we will illustrate a new method for quick estimation of densely packed aggregate particles on a fast moving conveyor belt. The method mainly consists of the two algorithms: (1) the algorithm of one-pixel-wide edge detection in one-pass (directly thresholded), and (2) the algorithm for directly converting image edge density to the average size of the aggregate particles.

To meet the engineering requirements of online inspection or monitoring, currently, real time image feature detection is a hot topic [7-8]. To estimate particle size based on edges, the similar work was done [1]. To overcome the problems in the previous work, new edge detection algorithm was studied. The new algorithm does not need any threshold algorithm for image binarisation, and particle size estimation can be done directly. The processing speed is suitable for online video image sequence.

Edge density is the percentage of particle boundary area to image area (particle inter area and void space area), and it may reflect average size. The underlying question is not whether or not edge density is used for estimating average aggregate size, but rather, more generally: is there a reliable short-cut method by which the standard procedure of first segmenting the image into aggregate particles and background is by-passed, so as to obtain direct estimates of average size?

A direct approach for estimating edge density may be based on, e.g., an edge detector. By size of aggregate particles, we mean the diameters or approximate diameters of aggregate particles, in what follows. Under the assumption of closely packed aggregates of roughly elliptical-like shape, we show that there is a relation between on one hand average size and on the other edge density, an average shape factor, and variance of size. If the variation of size is not too large, the edge density and an average shape factor are sufficient for estimating average size, and the estimation is within an accuracy of 5 to 10 percent. The estimation of average size involves average shape factor calculations as an intermediate step. We believe that average shape estimation could be done in cleverer ways in the future. The approach taken in this paper is just good enough to illustrate the usefulness of the edge density-base average size estimation, or, almost equivalently, automatic approximate counting of number of particles in an image, from edge density.

One image example is shown in Fig. 1a, where, belt moving speed is about 2.5 m per second, the particle size varies from 0.1 to 1.5 mm, the particles are wet, and the average particle size needs to be estimated online. It is impossible to use a traditional image segmentation algorithm to delineate an individual particle on this kind of images (Fig. 1b). To estimate the average size of a mass of aggregate particles, there are many ways, such as using the relationship between image grey level and particle average size. There is a large grey level variation on a belt even the average size being the same in a sequence of image frames, but the edges of particles may give stable information for estimation of the average size of particles. Therefore, the new methods of edge detection and average size estimation are presented in the following sections.

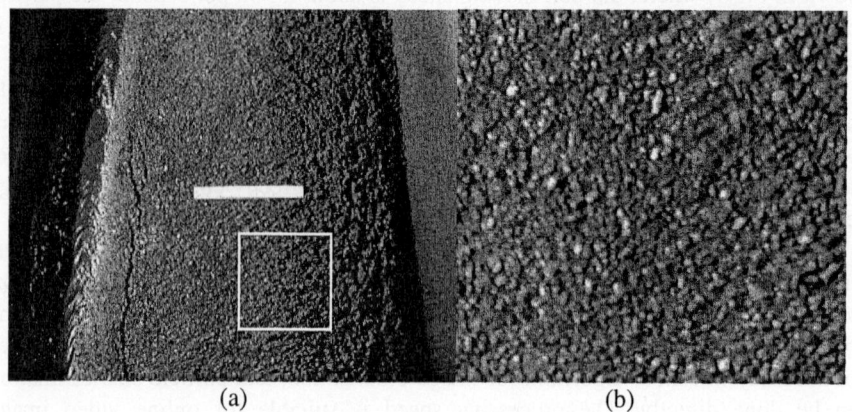

Fig. 1. (a) Particles on a moving belt. (b) A part of the image from the square in (a).

2 Edge Detection Algorithm

Edge (or ridge) detection is a fundamental operation in image processing and computer vision, because it is useful for object delineation and recognition. There are a huge number of papers dealing with this topic. Marr and Hildreth [9] described a method for determining the edges using the zero-crossings of the Laplacian of Guassian of an image. Haralick [10] determined edges by fitting polynomial functions to local image intensities and finding the zero-crossings of the second directional derivative of the functions. Canny [11] determined edges by an optimization process and proposed an approximation to the optimal detector as the maxima of gradient magnitude of a Gaussian-smoothed image. Clark [12] found a method to filter out false edges obtained by the Laplacian of Gaussian operator. Bergholm [13] introduced the concept of edge focusing and tracked edges from coarse to fine to mask weak and noisy edges. Elder and Zucker [14] determined edges at multitudes of scales. For a survey and comparison of the edge detectors, the reader can refer to [15]. Among the edge detection methods so far, the Canny edge detector is the most rigorously defined operator and is widely used. Canny also implemented a ridge detector. However, it is difficult to design a general edge detection algorithm which performs well in many contexts and captures the requirements of subsequent processing stages. Conceptually, the most commonly proposed schemes for edge detection include three operations: differentiation, smoothing and labeling.

The goal of edge detection in our case is to quickly and clearly detect the boundaries of particles, it is not necessary to close every particle's boundary (it is too hard), but it should produce less gaps on boundaries and less noise edges on the particles. To reach this goal, we tested several widely used edge detection algorithms for a typical particle image; in Fig. 2, (a) original image (150x240x8 bits), (b) Sobel edge detection result that includes too much white noise, (c) Robert edge detection result that is mass, (d) Laplacian edge detection result that miss boundaries much, (e) Prewitt edge detection result that is similar to (a), (f) and (g) Canny edge detection results which are thresholding value dependent, and (h) the result from our developed one-pass boundary detection algorithm (presented in this paper). By comparing results from the seven tests, the new algorithm gives the best edge (boundary) detection result. Our algorithm is actually a kind of ridge detector (or line detector).

To overcome the disadvantages of the above first six edge detection algorithms, we studied a new boundary detection algorithm (Fig. 2 (h)) based on ridge (or valley) information. We use the word valley as an abbreviation of negative ridge. The algorithm is briefly described as follows:

A simple edge detector uses differences in two directions: $\Delta_x = f(x+1, y) - f(x, y)$ and $\Delta_y = f(x, y+1) - f(x, y)$, where $f(x, y)$ is a grey scale image. In our valley detector, we use four directions. Obviously, in many situations, the horizontal and vertical grey value differences do not characterize a point, such as P (in Fig. 3), well.

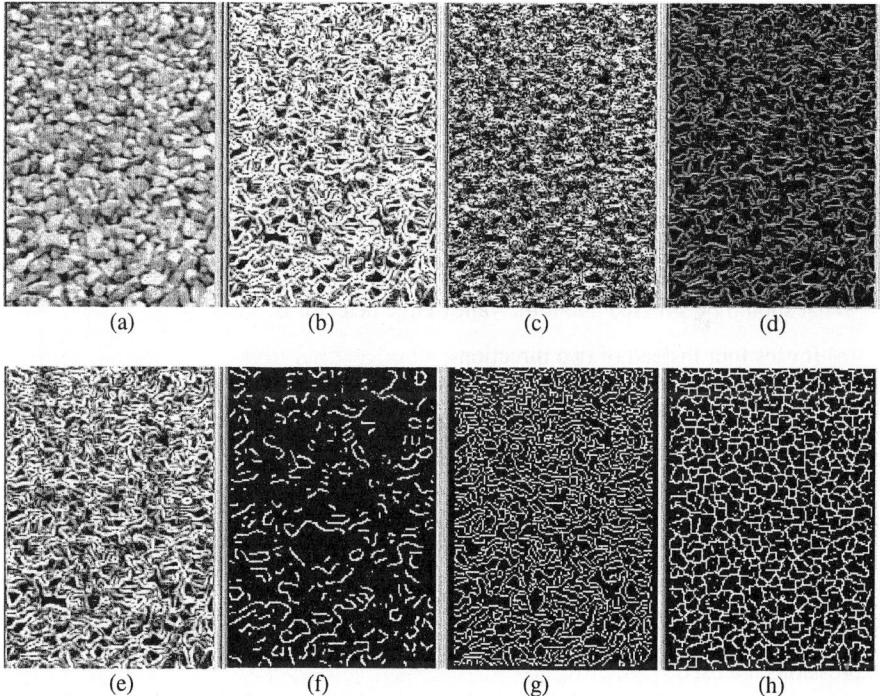

Fig. 2. Testing of edge detection algorithms. (a) Original image; (b) Sobel detection; (c) Robert detection; (d) Laplacian detection; (e) Prewitt detection; (f) Canny detection with a high threshold; (g) Canny detection with a low threshold; and (h) Boundary detection result by the new algorithm.

In Fig. 3, we see that P is surrounded by strong negative and positive differences in the diagonal directions:

$\nabla_{45} < 0$, and $\Delta_{45} > 0$, $\nabla_{135} < 0$, and $\Delta_{135} > 0$, whereas, $\nabla_0 \approx 0$, and $\Delta_0 \geq 0$, $\nabla_{90} \approx 0$, and $\Delta_{90} \approx 0$, where Δ are forward differences: $\Delta_{45} = f(i+1, j+1) - f(i, j)$, and ∇ are backward differences: $\nabla_{45} = f(i, j) - f(i-1, j-1)$ etc. for other directions. We use $\max(\Delta_\alpha - \nabla_\alpha)$ as a measure of the strength of an edge point. It should be noted that we use sampled grid coordinates, which are much more sparse than the pixel grid $0 \leq x \leq n$, $0 \leq y \leq m$. f is the original grey value image after slight smoothing.

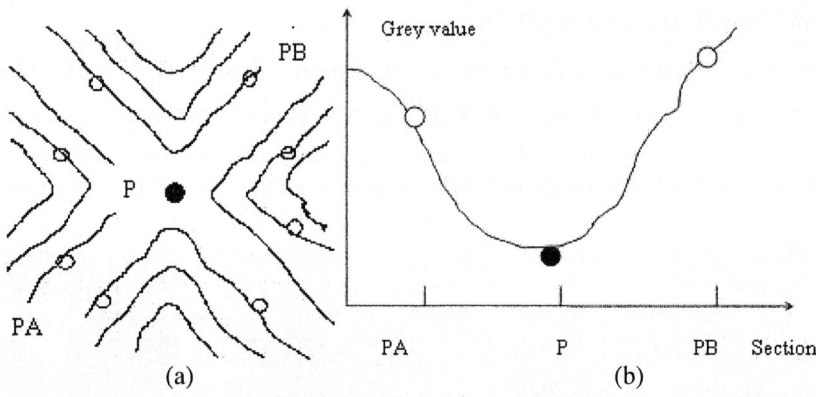

Fig. 3. Examine the point P, determining if it is a valley pixel, or not. Circles in the sparse (i, j)-grid. It moves for each P ∈ (x, y)-grid. (a) A grey value landscape over layered with a sample point grid. (b) PA-PB section.

What should be stressed about the valley edge detector is:

(a) It uses four instead of two directions;

(b) It studies value differences of well separated points: the sparse $i \pm 1$ corresponds to $x \pm L$ and $j \pm 1$ corresponds to $y \pm L$, where $L \gg 1$, in our case, $3 \leq L \leq 7$. In applications, if there are closely packed particles of area > 400 pixels, images should be shrunk to be suitable for this choice of L. Section 3 deals with average size estimation, which can guide choice of L;

(c) It is nonlinear: only the most valley-like directional response $(\Delta_\alpha - \nabla_\alpha)$ is used. By valley-like, we mean $(\Delta_\alpha - \nabla_\alpha)$ value. To manage valley detection in cases of broader valleys, there is a slight modification whereby weighted averages of $(\Delta_\alpha - \nabla_\alpha)$-expressions are used.

$w_1 \Delta_\alpha(P_B) + w_2 \Delta_\alpha(P_A) - w_2 \nabla_\alpha(P_B) - w_1 \nabla_\alpha(P_A)$, where, P_A and P_B are shown in Fig. 3. For example, $w_1 = 2$ and $w_2 = 3$ are in our experiments.

(d) It is one-pass edge detection algorithm; the detected image is a binary image, no need for further thresholding.

(e) Since each edge point is detected through four different directions, hence in the local part, edge width is one pixel wide (if average particle area is greater than 200 pixels, a thinning operation follows boundary detection operation);

(f) It is not sensitive to illumination variations, as shown in Fig. 4, an egg sequence image. On the image, illumination (or egg color) varies from place to place, for which, some traditional edge detectors (Sobel and Canny etc.) are sensitive, but the new edge detector can give a stable and clear edge detection result comparable to manual drawing result.

The new algorithm includes only some kind of differentiation - one of the three operations (differentiation, smoothing and labeling) by comparing to ordinary edge detectors. It is a kind of line detection algorithm, but detecting lines in four directions.

After boundary detection, the edge density will be counted and converted to particle size; the next section presents our particle size estimation algorithm.

3 Size Estimation Based on Edge Density

Consider the case of an image of closely packed aggregate particles, which can be approximated by ellipses in the image plane. The approximation is not done for the purpose of describing the shape of individual aggregate particle, but for setting up a model for relating edge density to average size. The concept size is defined below.

The ellipses are indexed $i = 1, 2, \cdots, n$. Let minor and major axes be W_i and L_i, with $W_i < L_i$ and $r_i = W_i/L_i$. Below, we use L_i as a measure of size, and call it length. Denote area and perimeter by A_i and P_i, respectively. Assume that there are no boundaries in the interior of the ellipses. Define the following edge density concept δ_*:

$$\delta_* = \frac{P_1 + P_2 + \cdots + P_n}{A_1 + A_2 + \cdots + A_n} \tag{1}$$

and related to size L_i:

$$\frac{\sum_i P_i}{\sum_i A_i} = \frac{\sum_i 2L_i E(\sqrt{1-r_i^2})}{\sum_i \pi r_i L_i^2 / 4} \approx \frac{4}{\sqrt{2}} \frac{\pi \sum_i \sqrt{1+r_i^2} L_i}{\pi \sum_i r_i L_i^2} = \frac{\frac{4}{\sqrt{2}}\sqrt{1+(r(\xi_1))^2}}{r(\xi_2)} \cdot \frac{\sum_i L_i}{\sum_i L_i^2} \tag{2}$$

where, E is the complete elliptic integral.

The last equality is due to the mean value theorem of integrals: $\int G(x)H(x)dx = G(\xi)\int H(x)dx$, which also applies to sums if we replace discrete functions by continuous step functions $\xi_1, \xi_2 \in [1, n]$. The more precisely:

$$\sum_{i=1}^n nr_i \cdot L_i^2 = \int_1^n r(x)(L(x))^2 dx = r(\xi_1)\int_1^n (l(x))^2 dx = r(\xi_1) \cdot \sum_{i=1}^n nL_i^2 \tag{3}$$

$$L(x) = L_i, r(x) = R_i, i/lex < i+1 \tag{4}$$

Where ξ_1 is a value between 1 and n for which equality holds?

The value $r(\xi_2)$ is by definition a weighted average of $r_1, r_2, \cdots, r_n$ with $L_i^2 / \sum L_i^2, i = 1, 2, \cdots, n$ as weights, and $\sqrt{1 + (r(\xi 1))^2}$ is another weighted average, but with $L_i / \sum L_i, i = 1, 2, \cdots, n$ as weights. Note that $r(\xi_1) \neq r(\xi_2)$, in general.

$$\frac{\sum L_i}{\sum L_i^2} = \frac{\frac{1}{n}\sum L_i}{\frac{1}{n}\sum L_i^2} = \frac{\overline{L}}{\overline{L}^2 + \sigma_L^2} = \frac{1}{\overline{L} + \sigma_L^2 / \overline{L}} \tag{5}$$

Where $\overline{L}$ is average length ($\overline{L} = n^{-1} \sum L$), and σ_L^2 the sample variance of L defined as $\sigma_L^2 = n^{-1} \sum (L_i - \overline{L})^2$. We call $si = (4/\sqrt{2})\sqrt{1 + r_i^2} / r_i$ the shape factor and call

$$\overline{s} = \frac{\frac{4}{\sqrt{2}}\sqrt{1 + (r(\xi_1))^2}}{r(\xi_2)}, \quad \overline{s}_{exact} = \frac{\frac{8}{\pi} E(\sqrt{1 - (r(\xi_1))^2})}{r(\xi_2)} \tag{6}$$

The "average shape factor".(When all ellipses are of the same form $r_i = r$, $\forall i$, it is easily seen that $s_i = \overline{s}$.) One may note that the shape factor is closely related to compactness P^2/A. The approximation $E(\sqrt{1-r^2}) \approx 0.5\pi\sqrt{(1+x^2)/2}$ comes from Spiegel 1992, and is fairly well known.

With known average shape factor $= \overline{s}$, average size $\overline{L}$ in a single frame can be solved from Eq.2, using Eqs.5-6:

$$\overline{L} + \frac{\sigma_L^2}{\overline{L}} = \frac{\overline{s}}{\sum P / \sum A} = \frac{\overline{s}}{\hat{\delta}_*} \tag{7}$$

We now have a relation between average length $\overline{L}$ and a kind of edge density $\hat{\delta}_*$. The measured edge density in our experiments $\hat{\delta}$ is related to $\hat{\delta}^*$ by $\hat{\delta}^* = \beta \cdot \hat{\delta}$ where the factor>1 accounts for the empty space between aggregates (not included in $\sum A$), as discussed earlier. Now, introduce the quantity $\tilde{\sigma}_L = \sigma_L / \overline{L}$, which is a kind of normalized standard deviation. Then, $\overline{L} + \sigma_L^2 / \overline{L} = \overline{L} + \tilde{\sigma}_L^2 \cdot \overline{L}$, leading to

$$\overline{L} = \frac{\overline{s}}{\beta \hat{\delta} \cdot (1 + \tilde{\sigma}^2_L)} \tag{8}$$

Of course, we should not expert to be able to calculate the average $r(\xi_1)$ and $r(\xi_2)$ exactly. An approximation $r_m \approx r(\xi_1)$, $r_m \approx r(\xi_2)$ may be calculated from crudely segmented data by using a kind of "equivalent ellipse" concept, yielding an estimate

$$\overline{s} = (4/\sqrt{2}) \cdot \sqrt{1 + r^2_m} / r_m \tag{9}$$

As the shape factor we use in the experiments.

4 Examples

Let's take two examples in the following. The first example is aggregate particles of sieving size between 32-64 mm. The images are shown in Fig. 4. The image sequence is used and Table 1 displays the results for the first 8 frames of that sequence. In Table 1 we can see that the estimate of N, i.e. $\hat{N}_e$, here only marginally differs from the "ground truth" (i.e. counting and segmentation by hand), $|\hat{N}_e - N| < 5$. The average percentage error $100 \cdot |\hat{N}_e - N|/N$ is about 7%. This demonstrates the utility of using edge density (together with the shape factor) for estimating number of aggregate particles and average size.

One may also note that average size estimates ($\hat{N}$-estimates) whether based on edges are quite stable. A fairly constant level of N in the sequence is reflected in just small fluctuations in $\hat{N}_e$ or $\hat{N}_i$ in Table 1.

Table 1. the number estimation of the eight images

Image	$\hat{\delta} = n_e/n_{tot}$	t_M^{new}	$\hat{N}_e$	$N \pm 2$
#1	0.1842	18.4	44.6	42
#2	0.1807	19.7	42.9	44
#3	0.1818	19.5	43.5	42
#4	0.1823	18.8	43.7	42
#5	0.1860	18.6	45.5	42
#6	0.1882	18.4	46.5	42
#7	0.1892	18.2	47.0	50
#8	0.1859	18.6	45.4	46

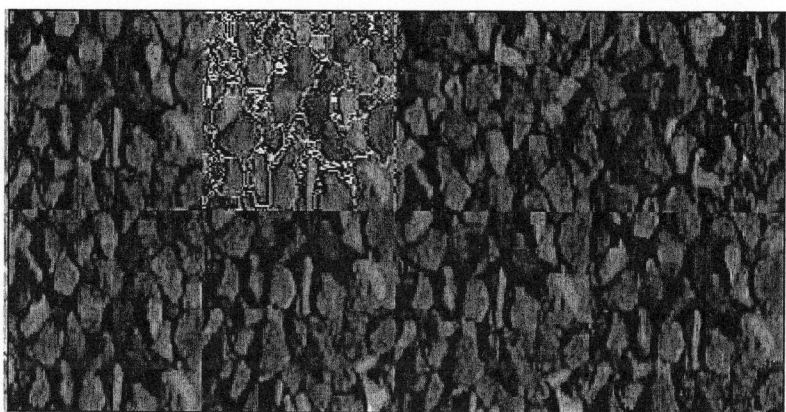

Fig. 4. The sequence of eight aggregate images. From top-left to the bottom-right, they are images #1, #2, ..., #8.

The second example of aggregates is of particle size between 0.1 and 1.5 mm. The original image is on the Figure 1a. In Figure 5, the top image is edge detection result by using the above described edge detection algorithm, and bottom image is a semi-automatic segmentation result which gives average size 0.45 mm (1992 particles), and the new method for average size estimation is 0.4396 mm. The two results are very close, say, difference is 2.3%.

For the two examples, we compared the processing speeds between the new method and watershed segmentation algorithm (even it doe not correctly delineates aggregate particles), the result is that the new method is 500-1000 times fast than ordinary segmentation method (image size 512x512 pixels) in a PC (2Ghz) environment (Windows 2000).

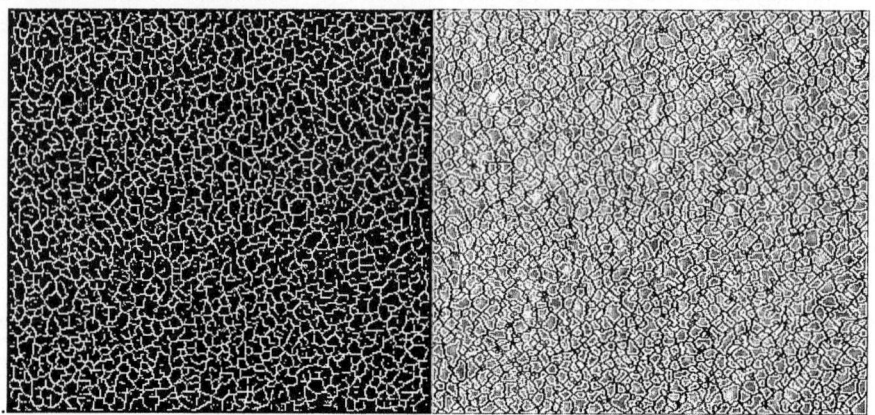

Fig. 5. Edge detection and image segmentation results on the image. Top image is edge detection result, and bottom image is segmentation result by a semi-automatic procedure.

5 Conclusions

We have presented a method for estimating average size of densely packed particles on a moving conveyor belt. The method mainly consists of one-pass valley edge detection (boundary detection) and estimation of particle size, and it is suitable for an online system. The algorithms can also be used separately. We have shown the results of experiments on image sequences of aggregate particles. For closely packed aggregate particles (difficult to delineate), the use of edge density to estimate the number of particles and or average size is a quite reasonable method. The new boundary detection algorithm detects edges in one-pass (without thresholding and labeling), and the algorithm is robust for the images of a mass of particles. Particle size estimation is carried out based on edge density and a shape factor. The proposed two algorithms can also be used in many other fields where multiple and complicated objects are densely packed.

References

1. Nyberg L, Carlsson O, Schmidtbauer B. Estimation of the size distribution of fragmented rock in ore mining through automatic image processing. Proc. IMEKO 9th World Congress, May, Vol. V/III (1982) 293 - 301.
2. Lin CL, Miller JD. The Development of a PC Image-Based On-line Particle Size Analyzer. Minerals & Metallurgical Processing, No. 2 (1993) 29-35.
3. Wang WX. Image analysis of aggregates. Computers & Geosciences (1999), No. 25, 71-81.
4. Schleifer J, Tessier B., Fragmentation Assessment using the FragScan System: Quality of a Blast, Fragblast, Vol. 6, No. 3-4 (2002), 321 – 331.
5. Kemeny J, Mofya E, Kaunda R, Lever P. Improvements in Blast Fragmentation Models Using Digital Image Processing, Fragblast, Vol. 6, No. 3-4 (2002) 311 – 320.
6. Norbert H Maerz, Tom W, Palangio. Post-Muckpile, Pre-Primary Crusher, Automated Optical Blast Fragmentation Sizing, Fragblast, Vol. 8, No. 2 (2004) 119 – 136.
7. Shou-Yi Tseng. Motion estimation using a frame-based adaptive thresholding approach. Real-Time Imaging 10 (2004) 1-7.
8. Yang JF, Chang YC, Chen CU. Computation reduction for motion search in low rate video codes. IEEE Transactions on Circuits System Video Technology (2002), 948-51.
9. Marr D. and E. Hildreth, Theory of Edge detection, Proc. Royal Society of London, vol. B-207 (1980), 187-217.
10. Haralik R., Digital Step Edges from zero Crossing of Second Directional Derivatives, IEEE Trans. Pattern Analysis and Machine Intelligence, vol. 6 (1984), 58-68.
11. Canny J., A computational Approach to Edge Detection, IEEE Trans. Pattern Analysis and Machine Intelligence, vol. 8, no. 6 (1986), 679-698.
12. Clark J.J., Authenticating Edges Produced by Zero Crossing Algorithms, IEEE Trans. Pattern Analysis and Machine Intelligence, vol. 11, no. 1 (1989), 43-57.
13. Bergholm F., Edge focusing, IEEE Trans. Pattern Analysis and Machine Intelligence, vol. 9 (1987), 726-741.
14. Elder J.H. and S.W. Zucker, Local Scale Control for Edge Detection and Blur Estimation, IEEE Trans. Pattern Analysis and Machine Intelligence, vol. 20, no. 7 (1998), 699-716.
15. Heath M.D., S. Sarkar, T. Sanocki, and K.W. Bowyer, A Robust Visual Method for Assessing the Relative Performance of Edge-Detection Algorithms, IEEE Trans. Pattern Analysis and Machine Intelligence, vol. 19, no. 12 (1997), 1338-1359.

A Statistical Image Fusion Scheme for Multi Focus Applications

Z.W. Liao[1,2], S.X. Hu[3], W.F. Chen[1], Y.Y. Tang[4], and T.Z. Huang[2]

[1] Key Lab of Medical Imaging, School of Biomedical Engineering,
Southern Medical University, Guangzhou, China
liaozhiwu@163.com, chenwf@fimmu.com
[2] School of Applied Mathematics,
University of Electronic Science and Technology of China,
Chengdu, Sichuan, China
[3] School of Physical Electronics,
University of Electronic Science and Technology of China,
Chengdu, Sichuan, China
hushaox@163.com
[4] Department of Computer Science, Hong Kong Baptist University,
Kowloon Tong, Hong Kong
yytang@comp.hkbu.edu.hk

Abstract. In this paper, we propose a statistical scheme to judge the activity level measurement (ALM) that is based on wavelet-domain hidden Markov model (WD-HMM) and maximum likelihood (MLK). The source images are firstly decomposed by the wavelets and only the coefficients in the high frequency (HH) are utilized. Considering the shift-variance of wavelets, the merged image is obtained from the source images directly. The regions of each source image are obtained by the Hough transform (HT) and their ALM are decided by the ALM of their coefficients in HH according to MLK. Finally, two multi focus images are merged by our new framework. The fusion results show the high ability of our scheme in preserving edge information and avoiding shift-variant.

1 Introduction

Multi focus is an important topic in image fusion, especially in improving the quality of images in digital camera [1] [5]. The term, image fusion, denotes a process generating a single image, which contains a more accurate description of the scene than any of the individual source image. This fused image should be more useful for human visual or machine perception. The source images in image fusion are perfectly registered in assumption. In this paper, the term, "the source images", denotes the original images that should be fused, and "the fused image" or "the composite image" denotes the fused image from the source images.

In multi focus fusion, there are several source images in which some regions are in focus while others are out of focus. These regions are related to the objects that are in focus or out of focus of the lens. The target of multi focus fusion is to choose the in focus regions from the source images and compose these regions to a fused image whose regions are all in focus [1] [9]. Since region is a more reasonable structure in multi focus fusion, the region based scheme is used in our new framework.

However, most image fusion schemes are based on pixel-level, which require more complex frameworks to ensure the consistency of fused images [1].

Recently, many researchers recognized that multiscale transforms (MSTs) are very useful for analyzing the information content of images for the purpose of fusion [1] [9] [5] [4] . Most Common MSTs include the pyramid transform (PT), the discrete wavelet transform (DWT) and the discrete wavelet frame (DWF). The basic idea is to perform a multiscale transform on each source image, and then constructs a composite multiscale representation from the source images. The fused image is obtained by taking an inverse multiscale transform. Thus how to overcome the shift-variance of the MSTs becomes a crucial problem. Although there are some shift-invariant MST techniques, the computation complexity hampers the applications of them [1].

In addition, traditional MST techniques measure the activity level (MAL) of an MST coefficient by the local energy in the space spanned by the term in the expansion corresponding to the coefficients. Although the local energy can partly show the nature of the coefficient in a simple way, constructing a unified theory of this measurement is still an unsolved problem. A more reasonable alternative is statistical techniques, which have not yet been found in literatures.

Most recently, WD-HMMs have been used widely in image processing and obtained good processing results because of their high ability to capture the structure information of images even on simple scalar transformation domain [7][3]. Besides this, WD-HMMs also allow us to utilize the prior information in a proper way. Therefore we try to set up a new framework based on WD-HMM to utilize the prior efficiently.

1.1 Some Discussions

The basic ideas to construct the new framework are as follows:

1. *The new framework should avoid the shift-variance of wavelets;*
2. *The new framework should utilize the prior in a proper way;*
3. *The ALM of coefficients should be decided by the statistical method;*
4. *The regions should be split according to the nature of the source images;*
5. *The ALM of regions should be decided on the ALM of the pixels in each region.*

These ideas combined with the nature of multi focus fusion help us to construct a completely different fusion scheme from others.

Although most fusion schemes did not consider the prior, it is fortunate that the prior can be extracted easily in multi focus applications. The prior can be obtained from training WD-HMMs. Therefore, two WD-HMMs related in focus images and out of focus images can be easily acquired.

Since there are only two types of region in the source images, the judgement of ALM becomes simple. Then we can obtain some conclusions about the problem:

1. The difference between two types of region is mainly on high frequency since out of focus regions are blurred while in focus are not [6] [9]. That is the reason why wavelets can help us improve the fusion results and why we only select coefficients of HH in judgement. The contextual HMM, which can efficiently group the high frequency coefficients, is selected [3] [7].

2. The source images can be split into different regions by HT since the digital camera can focus on different objects to obtain the source images [8] [11]. In our scheme, both the source images and HH bands are split to avoid the registration between wavelet coefficients and the source images.

3. In order to avoid the shift-variant of wavelets, only wavelet decomposition is used to decompose the source images into different wavelet subbands, while wavelet reconstruction is not used [9].

4. Since two trained HMMs are obtained previously, the ALM of each pixels can be determined by the HMMs and MLK; that is, compute the likelihood of each coefficient in the source image, and then compare the likelihoods of each coefficient: if the likelihood of out of focus is bigger than the in focus, the coefficients is out of focus; otherwise, it is in focus. Therefore, each coefficient of the source images are labelled by the label, whose value is out of focus or in focus [7].

5. Base on the results of discussion 4, the labels of the regions in the source images are decided in a simple way. Since the source images are also split into the same regions as in HH, the label of the region in HH can be given to the relative regions of the source images directly.

Based on the discussion, the basic issues of image fusion are solved completely and the new framework is set up. The contents of this paper are as follows: in the next section, we will introduce some backgrounds about our framework; then the structure of the scheme is discussed step by step; after that, experiment results will be given; some discussions about the experiments and future work will be presented finally.

2 Background

In this section, we will introduce some background about our scheme, including HT, contextual HMMs and likelihoods etc.

2.1 WD-HMM

To accomplish image fusion, we model each wavelet coefficient as a realization from mixture Gaussian model(MGM), whose parameters should be estimated using EM algorithm. The estimation of the parameters for a given coefficient is conditioned on a function of its neighboring coefficients, a method called context [3], which can group the high frequency coefficients efficiently. Now, given that one can estimate the parameters for each coefficient, the final step is to use them for image processing.

To each wavelet coefficient $W_{i,j}$, we associate a discrete hidden state $S_{i,j}$ that takes on values $m = 0, 1$, where 0 represents the small state and 1 represents the large state, with pmf $P_{S_{i,j}}(m)$. Conditioned on $S_{i,j} = m$, $W_{i,j}$ is Gaussian with mean $\mu_{i,j,m}$ and variance $\sigma_{i,j,m}$. Thus, overall pdf of the MGM is given by:

$$f_{W_{i,j}}(\omega_{i,j}) = \sum_{m=0}^{1} P_{S_{i,j}}(m) f_{W_{i,j}|S_{i,j}}(\omega_{i,j}|S_{i,j} = m) \qquad (1)$$

The context for $W_{i,j}$ is defined as a length P vector $V_{i,j} = [V_{i,j,1}, V_{i,j,2}, , V_{i,j,P}]$ formed as a function of the wavelet or scaling coefficients. We condition $S_{i,j}$ on $V_{i,j}$ to predict the parameters of $W_{i,j}$. The idea is for $V_{i,j}$ to provide supplementary information to the HMM, so that, given the context, we can treat the wavelet coefficients as independent. Therefore, the overall pdf of contextual HMM is:

$$f_{W_{i,j}}(\omega_{i,j}) = \sum_{m=0}^{1} P_{S_{i,j}|V_{i,j}}(m|v_{i,j}) f_{W_{i,j}|S_{i,j}}(\omega_{i,j}|S_{i,j} = m) \qquad (2)$$

In fact, there are several methods which condition $S_{i,j}$ on $V_{i,j}$. However, the idea of context modelling is the same. That is, clustering pixels with similar context for parameter estimation. The conditioning is based on the context, and each class is formed by clustering coefficients whose context falls within a specified range. The distribution parameter is estimated from the coefficients for each class, which is then used to fuse the image.

In order to clarify our explanation, we show a context parts wavelet coefficients into two groups in this paper. The context value for $W_{i,j}$ is defined as:

$$v_{i,j} = \begin{cases} \sum_{i-1,j-1}^{i+1,j+1} \omega_{i,j} > \delta_k & : \quad v_{i,j} = 1 \\ \text{otherwise} & : \quad v_{i,j} = 0 \end{cases}$$

where δ_k is the average energy of the scale.

This simplest context can cluster coefficients into two groups: one is with small local energy and the other is with large local energy. Since the high frequency is more useful in determining the quality of the source images, only the coefficients with large local energy are used in judgement. This will be discussed in detail in subsection 2.3.

In order to utilize the prior, two HMMs are trained using EM algorithm whose recursive formula are given in [3]. The aim of training is to obtain the parameters of the contextual HMMs and different observations will lead to different parameters. From pattern recognition review, the parameters can be considered as the features and the types of the new observations can be determined by the "distance" from different types.

In our context, the "distance" is defined as the function of likelihood and the type is determined as the type of HMM with large likelihood. The details about likelihood will be discussed in subsection 2.3.

In our applications, two images, one in focus and the other out of focus, are used to train two HMMs separately. Therefore, we can obtain two different sets of parameters and these parameters will be used in determining the types of the coefficients in the source images.

2.2 Hough Transform

The Hough transform is the most popular technique for digital straight line detection in a digital image. The form proposed by Duda and Hart [10] is

$$\rho = x \cos \theta + y \sin \theta \tag{3}$$

where ρ is the distance of the point of origin to the line and θ is the angle of the normal to the straight line with the x-axis.

The (ρ, θ) space is segmented into cells with length $\Delta\rho$ and width $\Delta\theta$. Each point in (x, y) space corresponds to a straight line in (ρ, θ) space. Therefore, all points on the same straight line in (x, y) space will intersect at the same point of space (ρ, θ) in theory.

Each point in (ρ, θ) space corresponds to a straight line in (x, y) space. The number of votes of a certain straight line (ρ_j, θ_j) is kept in the member of the accumulation matrix $C[i][j]$.

The initial values of all members of the accumulation matrix are set to zero. For each feature point (x, y) and for each θ_j, Equation 3 is used to calculate the corresponding $\rho(\theta_j, x, y)$. After the ρ_j, which is the member of the segmentation set along the ρ-direction that is closest to the calculated ρ, is found, the number of votes of the cell that corresponds to ρ_j, θ_j is incremented by one. A highly voted cell is an indication of the existence of a digital straight line segment.

2.3 Likelihood

Since the HMMs have been trained, we will discuss the classification method using the trained HMMs. This is the basic problem for HMMs [2]: Given the observation sequence $O = (o_1, o_2 \cdots o_T)$, and the model λ, how do we choose a corresponding state sequence $q = (q_1, q_2 \cdots q_T)$ that is optimal in some sense (i. e., best "explains" the observation)? This problem is the one in which we attempt to uncover the hidden part of the model- that is, to find the "correct" state sequence. In our paper, we used the max-likelihood as an optimality criterion. The parameter λ has been decided by the EM algorithm, where the likelihood function is defined as:

$$L(\lambda) = P(X|\lambda) = \prod_{k=1}^{N} P(x_k|\lambda) \tag{4}$$

As mentioned in subsection 2.1, the probability distribution function of each wavelet coefficient is Gaussian mixture distribution conditioned on a context, and λ is the trained parameters of in focus or out of focus image. The value of likelihood function of the wavelet coefficients in the source images is used to decide the quality of the coefficients.

In multi focus fusion, only the coefficients whose context value $V_{i,j} = 1$ is considered. Therefore all coefficients with large local energy in HH of a source image can be considered as observation sequence, and the state sequence is defined as a discrete random vector, whose elements are discrete random variable with the value: in focus or out of focus. The values of the hidden states are determined by MLK and the criterion is: if the likelihood of out of focus HMM is bigger than out of focus', the hidden state is in focus; otherwise, it is out of focus. Using this optimality criterion, the wavelet coefficients can be efficiently grouped to two groups: in focus coefficients and out of focus.

Since the coefficients in HH of the source images are split into mutually exclusive spatial connected regions using HT, each of the regions should be assigned a label: out of focus or in focus. The labels can be decided in a simple way, whose numbers of out of focus coefficients are bigger than the in focus are assigned as out of focus; while others are assigned as in focus. Therefore, all regions in HH of the source images are assigned with labels.

Note that the regions in the source images are split and each of them related to the regions of its HH. Thus, the labels of the regions in HH are assigned to the regions of the source images.

3 New Framework

In this section, we describe the new image fusion method in detail.

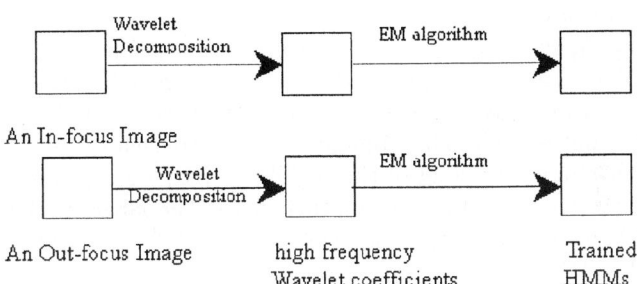

Fig. 1. Diagram on training HMMs

In our scheme, the WD-HMM is trained through EM algorithm in order to utilize the prior of multi focus fusion. Because there are two types of pixels, in focus and out of focus, the prior can be extracted easily.

The diagram of training HMM is presented in Fig 1. Two images, one is in focus and the other is out of focus, are decomposed by wavelets and two HMMs are trained by the coefficients in HH of two images. Thus, we can obtain two trained HMMs: one is in focus and the other is out of focus.

Since our scheme is region-based, the source images are split into several regions using HT. With the same reason, the HH of each source image is split into regions similar to the source image (Fig 2).

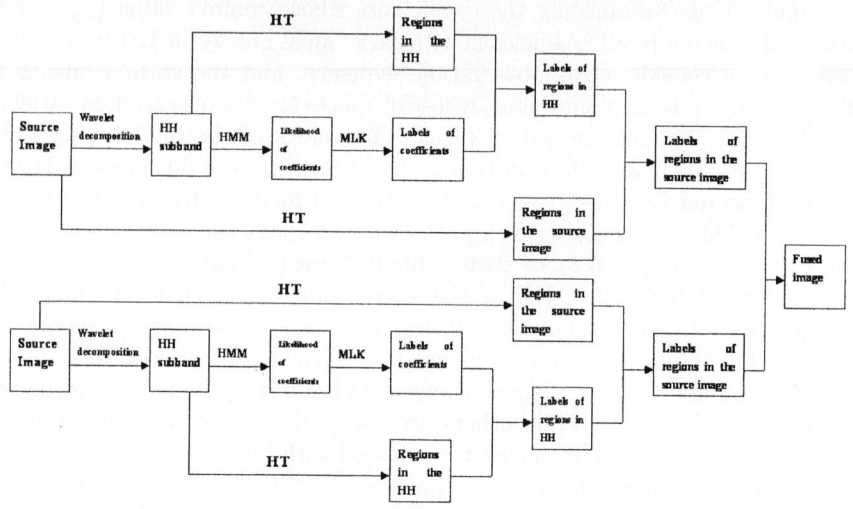

Fig. 2. Diagram on training HMMs

Then the quality of each coefficient with large local energy is determined by two trained HMMs, who will produce two likelihoods for a coefficient. According to MLK, the larger one is the quality of the coefficient, named the label, whose value is in focus or out of focus.

Combining the split regions in HH, we can obtain the labels of the regions in a simple way. The label of the region is determined by the labels of its coefficients. If the number of in focus is bigger than the out of focus, the label is in focus; otherwise, it is out of focus. This step gives a label to each region in HH.

After determining the label of the regions in HH, we can decide the labels of the regions in the source images by their map. The labels of the regions are assigned as the labels of related regions in HH. Therefore, the fused image can be composed to the in focus regions in the source images.

4 Experiment Results

In order to prove the power of our scheme, two 512 × 512 images, clockA and clockB are used. There are two clocks in each of them. In clockA the big clock is in focus and the small is out of focus while the small is in focus and the large is out of focus in clockB and they are shown in Fig 3.

Since HT is very complex in gray images, we compute the context of the source images and obtain two binary images. Then the HT can split the source images efficiently and the segmentation results are shown in Fig 4

The HMM is trained with two combined images from clockA and clockB: all pixels in one are in focus while in the other they are out of focus. Then the context in HH defined on subsection 2.1 is computed and two binary images are

A Statistical Image Fusion Scheme for Multi Focus Applications   1103

Fig. 3. Two resource images: the left is clockA while the right is clockB

Fig. 4. Two segmented resource images: the left is clockA while the right is clockB

Fig. 5. Two segmented contextual images in HH and their likelihoods: the right is likelihoods while the left is context

obtained. Based on these binary images, two images of segmented regions in HH using HT are represented in Fig 5. Then the likelihoods of coefficients with large local energy are computed and the results are in Fig 5(right). From the right of Fig 5, we can give an obvious conclusion that the right region in HH of clockA is in focus while the left is out of focus (Fig 4). The fused image is constructed from the in focus regions of two resource images and shown in Fig 6. It is clear the fused image is the best one in all of the multi focus fusion frameworks, especially in preserving edge and avoid shift variant.

Fig. 6. The fused image

5 Summary and Future Work

The new framework obviously has a better composite image than the traditional methods. Future works summary as follows:

First, we try to construct a new wavelet or new wavelet domain HMMs to obtain better results in deciding the quality of the wavelet coefficients in the source images.

Second, we attempt to use the new framework on another image-fused problem. Since the wavelet domain HMMs can efficiently decide the different quality of the wavelet coefficients, we can use the new framework for image-fused problem, which also needs to decide the quality of the wavelet coefficients.

Third, generalizing the HT to detect simple curves is still an open problem. We try to construct some new methods to partly resolve this problem, especially in image fusion.

Finally, we expect wavelet-domain HMMs to be more accurate and sophisticated, yet still tractable, robust, and efficient for image fusion.

References

1. Z. Zhang and R. S. Blum, "A Categorization of Multiscale-Dcomposition-Based Image Fusion Schemes with a Performance Study for a Digital Camera Application", Proc. of the IEEE, Vol. 87, No. 8, pp. 1315-1326, Aug. 1999.
2. L. Rabiner, "A Tutorial on Hidden Markov Models and Selected Applications in Speech Recognition", Proc. of IEEE Signal Processing, Vol. 77, PP. 257-285, Feb. 1999.
3. M. S. Crouse and R. G. Baraniuk, "Contextual Hidden Markov Models for Wavelet-domain Signal Processing", Proc. of 31st Asilomar Conf on Signals, Systems and Computers, Nov. 1997.
4. K. C. Chou, A. S. Willsky and A. Benveniste, "Multiscale Recursive Estimation, Data Fusion, and Regularization", IEEE Tran. Automat. Contr., vol. 39, PP. 464-478, Mar. 1994.
5. D. L. Hall and J. Llinas, "An Introduction to Multisensor Data Fusion", Proc. IEEE, vol. 85, PP. 6-23, Jan. 1997.

6. Yang Xuan, Yang Wan Hai and Pei Ji Hong, "Fusion Multifocus Image Using Wavelet Decomposition", ACTA Electronica Sinica, June 2001, vol. 29, No. 6, pp846-848.
7. Z. W. Liao, Y. Y. Tang, "Signal Denoising using Wavelet and Block Hidden Markov Model", International Journal of Pattern Recognition and Artificial Intelligence, Vol. 19, No. 5 (August 2005), pp 681-700.
8. Zhiwu Liao, Hu Shaoxiang and T. Z. Huang "Line Segments and Dominate Points Detection Based on Hough Transform", Accepted by International Conference on Computational Intelligence and Security 2005.
9. Hu Shaoxiang, Zhiwu Liao and Yuan Y. Tang, "Image Fusion for a Digital Camera Application Based on Wavelet Domain Hidden Markov Models", Proceeding of the 3rd International Conference on Machine Learning and Cybernetics 2004, Shanghai, China, pp. 4356-4361. (EI)
10. R O OUDA, and P E HART: Use of the Hough transformation to detect lines and curves in pictures. Commun. ACM, 1972, 15, VOL 1, (1972) 11-15
11. Nicolas Guil, Julio Villalba, and Emilio L. Zapata: A Fast Hough Transform for Segment Detection. IEEE TRANSACTIONS ON IMAGE PROCESSING, VOL. 4, NO. 1 1 , NOVEMBER (1995) 1541–1548

Author Index

Abidi, Syed Sibte Raza 219
Agogino, Alice M. 428
Albayrak, Sahin 30

Bai, Jie 1077
Bao, Lei 448
Budiarto, Rahmat 662

Cai, Wei-You 842
Cao, Mukun 53
Cao, Wenming 974
Chai, Bian-fang 711
Chai, Yu-hua 930
Chan, Aki P.F. 682, 851
Chang, Hong 721
Chang, Hong-jun 142
Chang, Jiang 133
Chang, Taihua 790
Chen, Degang 588, 918
Chen, Jian 624
Chen, Junfen 377, 871
Chen, Kuisheng 813
Chen, Ling 169
Chen, Qing-Cai 538
Chen, Tianhang 1033
Chen, W.F. 1096
Chen, Xiang 21
Chen, Xueguang 43
Chen, Yanju 377, 1014
Chen, Yao 965
Chen, Yixin 169
Cheng, Yuhu 780
Chi, Jiayu 43
Chi, Yu-Liang 295
Chu, Dian-Hui 278
Chung, C.Y. 908
Cooper, Leon N. 548
Cui, Pingyuan 81

Dai, Wei-Di 189
Deng, Yafeng 938
Do, Tien Dung 199
Dong, Chunru 918
Du, Ruizhong 70
Du, Xuan-Min 804

Du, Zhen-Long 249
Duan, Guang-Ren 338

Fan, Li 285
Fan, Tiegang 1014
Fang, Lijin 91
Feng, Hao 974
Feng, Huimin 1014
Feng, Yuqiang 53
Fong, Alvis C.M. 199
Fu, Bo 938
Fu, Xiang-jun 268
Fung, Chun Che 889

Gan, Min 159
Gao, Huijun 112
Gao, Ji 11
Gao, Li-qun 930
Gao, Wen 1033
Gu, Wen-Xiang 1
Guo, Hang 11
Guo, Mao-Zu 322
Guo, Peng 790
Guo, Ping 285
Guo, Qianjin 760
Guo, Yanying 1070

Ha, Ming-hu 517, 1005
Han, Yiqiu 209
He, Huacan 367
He, Hui 672
He, Liang 338
He, Pi-Lian 189
He, Qiang 871, 918
He, You 64
Heng, Pheng Ann 239
Hou, Yue-Xian 189
Hu, Jie 268
Hu, Jing-song 633
Hu, Mingzeng 672
Hu, S.X. 1096
Hu, Shan-li 21
Hua, Qiang 538
Huang, Dong-mei 517
Huang, Hao 813

Huang, T.Z.   1096
Huang, Yan   329
Huang, Yuan-sheng   397
Hui, Siu Cheung   199

Ivins, Jim   750

Ji, Qiao-ling   842
Ji, Zhicheng   387
Jian, Ming   407
Jiang, Lihui   1070
Jiang, Qingshuang   219
Jiang, Wei   948
Jiang, Yong   91
Jin, Shuyuan   691

Kamalian, Raffi   428
Kang, Xiao-Dong   189

Lai, L.L.   898
Lam, Wai   209, 477
Lang, Fenghua   642
Lao, Lan-Jun   605
Lao, Song-Yang   315
Lazarescu, Mihai   750
Lee, John W.T.   568, 578, 701
Lei, Quansheng   624
Lei, Zhao-ming   142
Li, Da-yong   268
Li, Fachao   347
Li, Fan   507
Li, Geng-yin   438
Li, Guo-Hui   984
Li, Haiming   407
Li, Huai-yang   614
Li, Jia-Bin   889
Li, Jian   642
Li, Jian-Fu   322
Li, Jian-qiang   149
Li, Jin-Chao   880
Li, Jinling   731
Li, Qi-Yuan   448
Li, Shou-tao   101
Li, Xiao-Li   249
Li, Xuefei   1014
Li, Ya-min   517
Li, Yan   53, 731
Li, Yuan-chun   101
Liao, Z.W.   1096

Liu, Bo   258
Liu, Feng   861
Liu, Fengqiu   81
Liu, Ji-zhen   149
Liu, Na   1077
Liu, Qi-He   507
Liu, Shaohui   1033
Liu, Wenju   965
Liu, Yan   614
Liu, Yan-Kui   377
Liu, Yi-xuan   652
Liu, Yu-Hong   804
Liu, Yuling   70
Liu, Zhen-peng   711
Liu, Zhi-Qiang   994
Liu, Zhi-qiang   558
Liu, Zhijun   1043
Liu, Zuo-jun   142
Lu, Ming   528
Lu, Qin   740
Luan, Xi-Dao   315
Luo, Shuxin   347
Luo, Yongqiang   467

Ma, Jian-wei   438
Ma, Jin   832, 958
Ma, Liangyu   832, 958
Ma, Yingcang   367
Ma, Yongguang   832, 958
Manderick, Bernard   861
Mao, Chi-Long   315
Meng, Guangwu   417
Meng, Shuanghui   750
Millot, Patrick   770
Milosevic, Dragan   30
Min, Fan   507
Myers, Douglas G.   889

Neskovic, Predrag   548
Ng, Wing W.Y.   682, 851
Niu, Cheng-lin   149
Niu, Dong-Xiao   880

Okazaki, Kozo   797

Pasha, Muhammad Fermi   662
Peng, Hong   633
Peng, Yan   133

Peng, Ying-hong   268
Pham, Tuan D.   595

Qi, Jian-xun   397
Qi, Wei-Min   842
Qin, Xiao-Lin   448
Qiu, Xiaoping   407

Ren, Danan   467
Ren, Jia-Dong   179
Ren, Ren   467
Ruan, Xiaogang   965

Sang, Hongshi   1043
Shen, Jun   459
Shen, Xubang   1043
Shen, Yanxia   387
Shi, Lin   239
Su, Guangda   938
Su, Lianqing   347
Sun, Hai-bin   652
Sun, Haojun   229
Sun, He-xu   142
Sun, Jianyong   948
Sun, Junwei   81
Sun, Ling   43
Sun, Mei   229
Sun, W.C.   898
Sun, Wei   780
Sun, Zhengxing   948
Syukur, Mohammad   662

Takagi, Hideyuki   428
Tang, Hui-Xuan   1051
Tang, Y.Y.   1096
Tian, Junfeng   70
Tian, Rui-Li   1077
Tian, Xue-dong   1005
Ting, T.O.   908
Tsang, Eric C.C.   517, 568, 588, 682, 691, 851
Tu, Li   169
Turpin, Andrew   750

Vanderhaegen, Frédéric   770
Vanschoenwinkel, Bram   861

Wang, Bai-ling   652
Wang, Bingshu   958
Wang, Changhong   112

Wang, Chunyan   53
Wang, Hongguang   91
Wang, Hongru   112
Wang, Jia   122
Wang, Jiabing   633
Wang, Jianwei   497
Wang, Jigang   548
Wang, Jinfeng   578
Wang, Jun   305
Wang, Li-Juan   538
Wang, Qiang   880
Wang, Rong   930
Wang, Rong Long   797
Wang, Shenwen   159
Wang, Shoujue   974
Wang, Wei-ming   268
Wang, Weixing   1086
Wang, Xi-Zhao   459
Wang, Xiao-Long   538
Wang, Xiaodong   1060
Wang, Xizhao   578, 691, 871, 918
Wang, Xuesong   780
Wang, Yi   558
Wang, Yingfeng   822
Wang, Yong-Jun   487
Wei, Hui   1051
Wei, Xiaopeng   497
Wong, Alex K.S.   701
Wong, K.P.   908
Wong, Tak-Lam   477
Wong, Tien-Tsin   239
Wu, Congxin   329, 358
Wu, Da-peng   528
Wu, Ling-Da   315
Wu, Xiaobei   122
Wu, Yanwen   731
Wu, Zhenghong   731

Xiao, Jitian   305
Xie, Chang-Sheng   614
Xie, Hong   438
Xie, Lei   994
Xie, Sheng-li   1025
Xie, Yu-Xiang   315
Xiong, Wei   64
Xu, Aidong   760
Xu, Jian-min   711
Xu, Jin   467
Xu, Li   1
Xu, Ping   11

Xu, Ruifeng 740
Xu, Yang 407
Xu, Zhiliang 122

Yamada, Masashi 662
Yan, Leifan 871
Yang, Guo-Wei 507
Yang, Shen-Hua 804
Yang, Shu 930
Yang, Xiaohui 70
Yang, Yao-Quan 1077
Yang, Yixian 642
Yao, Hongxun 1033
Ye, Lian 285
Yeung, Daniel S. 568, 682, 691, 701, 822, 851
Yeung, Dit-Yan 721
Yu, Ge 258
Yu, Haibin 760
Yuan, Fang 258
Yuan, Jian 984
Yun, Xiao-chun 652

Zeng, Liangcai 813
Zeng, Xiaoqin 822
Zhan, De-Chen 278
Zhang, Changjiang 1060
Zhang, Guo-li 438
Zhang, Haoran 1060
Zhang, Hongli 672
Zhang, Jian-ping 528
Zhang, Jiang-She 487
Zhang, Jianming 497
Zhang, Jing-wei 64
Zhang, Jinlong 43
Zhang, Jun 448
Zhang, Luan-ying 149
Zhang, Mingyi 159
Zhang, Q.P. 898
Zhang, Weizhe 672
Zhang, Xin-Mei 1
Zhang, Xingfang 417
Zhang, Ying 428
Zhang, Yu-Fen 487
Zhang, Zhicheng 770
Zhao, Liang 358
Zhao, Mingyang 91
Zhao, Shuang 711
Zhao, Suyun 568
Zhao, Zhen 614
Zheng, Hong-Zhen 278
Zhou, Fei 268
Zhou, Jun 938
Zhou, Jun-hua 397
Zhou, Li-zhu 558
Zhou, Xiao-Lei 179
Zhou, Zhi-heng 1025
Zhu, Rongjia 387
Zhu, Shihua 467
Zuo, Guoyu 965

Lecture Notes in Artificial Intelligence (LNAI)

Vol. 3946: T.R. Roth-Berghofer, S. Schulz, D.B. Leake (Eds.), Modeling and Retrieval of Context. XI, 149 pages. 2006.

Vol. 3930: D.S. Yeung, Z.-Q. Liu, X.-Z. Wang, H. Yan (Eds.), Advances in Machine Learning and Cybernetics. XXI, 1110 pages. 2006.

Vol. 3918: W.K. Ng, M. Kitsuregawa, J. Li, K. Chang (Eds.), Advances in Knowledge Discovery and Data Mining. XXIV, 879 pages. 2006.

Vol. 3910: S.A. Brueckner, G.D.M. Serugendo, D. Hales, F. Zambonelli (Eds.), Engineering Self-Organising Systems. XII, 245 pages. 2006.

Vol. 3904: M. Baldoni, U. Endriss, A. Omicini, P. Torroni (Eds.), Declarative Agent Languages and Technologies III. XII, 245 pages. 2006.

Vol. 3899: S. Frintrop, VOCUS: A Visual Attention System for Object Detection and Goal-Directed Search. XIV, 216 pages. 2006.

Vol. 3898: K. Tuyls, P.J. 't Hoen, K. Verbeeck, S. Sen (Eds.), Learning and Adaption in Multi-Agent Systems. X, 217 pages. 2006.

Vol. 3891: J.S. Sichman, L. Antunes (Eds.), Multi-Agent-Based Simulation VI. X, 191 pages. 2006.

Vol. 3890: S.G. Thompson, R. Ghanea-Hercock (Eds.), Defence Applications of Multi-Agent Systems. XII, 141 pages. 2006.

Vol. 3885: V. Torra, Y. Narukawa, A. Valls, J. Domingo-Ferrer (Eds.), Modeling Decisions for Artificial Intelligence. XII, 374 pages. 2006.

Vol. 3881: S. Gibet, N. Courty, J.-F. Kamp (Eds.), Gesture in Human-Computer Interaction and Simulation. XIII, 344 pages. 2006.

Vol. 3874: R. Missaoui, J. Schmidt (Eds.), Formal Concept Analysis. X, 309 pages. 2006.

Vol. 3873: L. Maicher, J. Park (Eds.), Charting the Topic Maps Research and Applications Landscape. VIII, 281 pages. 2006.

Vol. 3863: M. Kohlhase (Ed.), Mathematical Knowledge Management. XI, 405 pages. 2006.

Vol. 3862: R.H. Bordini, M. Dastani, J. Dix, A.E.F. Seghrouchni (Eds.), Programming Multi-Agent Systems. XIV, 267 pages. 2006.

Vol. 3849: I. Bloch, A. Petrosino, A.G.B. Tettamanzi (Eds.), Fuzzy Logic and Applications. XIV, 438 pages. 2006.

Vol. 3848: J.-F. Boulicaut, L. De Raedt, H. Mannila (Eds.), Constraint-Based Mining and Inductive Databases. X, 401 pages. 2006.

Vol. 3847: K.P. Jantke, A. Lunzer, N. Spyratos, Y. Tanaka (Eds.), Federation over the Web. X, 215 pages. 2006.

Vol. 3835: G. Sutcliffe, A. Voronkov (Eds.), Logic for Programming, Artificial Intelligence, and Reasoning. XIV, 744 pages. 2005.

Vol. 3830: D. Weyns, H. V.D. Parunak, F. Michel (Eds.), Environments for Multi-Agent Systems II. VIII, 291 pages. 2006.

Vol. 3817: M. Faundez-Zanuy, L. Janer, A. Esposito, A. Satue-Villar, J. Roure, V. Espinosa-Duro (Eds.), Nonlinear Analyses and Algorithms for Speech Processing. XII, 380 pages. 2006.

Vol. 3814: M. Maybury, O. Stock, W. Wahlster (Eds.), Intelligent Technologies for Interactive Entertainment. XV, 342 pages. 2005.

Vol. 3809: S. Zhang, R. Jarvis (Eds.), AI 2005: Advances in Artificial Intelligence. XXVII, 1344 pages. 2005.

Vol. 3808: C. Bento, A. Cardoso, G. Dias (Eds.), Progress in Artificial Intelligence. XVIII, 704 pages. 2005.

Vol. 3802: Y. Hao, J. Liu, Y.-P. Wang, Y.-m. Cheung, H. Yin, L. Jiao, J. Ma, Y.-C. Jiao (Eds.), Computational Intelligence and Security, Part II. XLII, 1166 pages. 2005.

Vol. 3801: Y. Hao, J. Liu, Y.-P. Wang, Y.-m. Cheung, H. Yin, L. Jiao, J. Ma, Y.-C. Jiao (Eds.), Computational Intelligence and Security, Part I. XLI, 1122 pages. 2005.

Vol. 3789: A. Gelbukh, Á. de Albornoz, H. Terashima-Marín (Eds.), MICAI 2005: Advances in Artificial Intelligence. XXVI, 1198 pages. 2005.

Vol. 3782: K.-D. Althoff, A. Dengel, R. Bergmann, M. Nick, T.R. Roth-Berghofer (Eds.), Professional Knowledge Management. XXIII, 739 pages. 2005.

Vol. 3763: H. Hong, D. Wang (Eds.), Automated Deduction in Geometry. X, 213 pages. 2006.

Vol. 3755: G.J. Williams, S.J. Simoff (Eds.), Data Mining. XI, 331 pages. 2006.

Vol. 3735: A. Hoffmann, H. Motoda, T. Scheffer (Eds.), Discovery Science. XVI, 400 pages. 2005.

Vol. 3734: S. Jain, H.U. Simon, E. Tomita (Eds.), Algorithmic Learning Theory. XII, 490 pages. 2005.

Vol. 3721: A.M. Jorge, L. Torgo, P.B. Brazdil, R. Camacho, J. Gama (Eds.), Knowledge Discovery in Databases: PKDD 2005. XXIII, 719 pages. 2005.

Vol. 3720: J. Gama, R. Camacho, P.B. Brazdil, A.M. Jorge, L. Torgo (Eds.), Machine Learning: ECML 2005. XXIII, 769 pages. 2005.

Vol. 3717: B. Gramlich (Ed.), Frontiers of Combining Systems. X, 321 pages. 2005.

Vol. 3702: B. Beckert (Ed.), Automated Reasoning with Analytic Tableaux and Related Methods. XIII, 343 pages. 2005.

Vol. 3698: U. Furbach (Ed.), KI 2005: Advances in Artificial Intelligence. XIII, 409 pages. 2005.

Vol. 3690: M. Pěchouček, P. Petta, L.Z. Varga (Eds.), Multi-Agent Systems and Applications IV. XVII, 667 pages. 2005.

Vol. 3684: R. Khosla, R.J. Howlett, L.C. Jain (Eds.), Knowledge-Based Intelligent Information and Engineering Systems, Part IV. LXXIX, 933 pages. 2005.

Vol. 3683: R. Khosla, R.J. Howlett, L.C. Jain (Eds.), Knowledge-Based Intelligent Information and Engineering Systems, Part III. LXXX, 1397 pages. 2005.

Vol. 3682: R. Khosla, R.J. Howlett, L.C. Jain (Eds.), Knowledge-Based Intelligent Information and Engineering Systems, Part II. LXXIX, 1371 pages. 2005.

Vol. 3681: R. Khosla, R.J. Howlett, L.C. Jain (Eds.), Knowledge-Based Intelligent Information and Engineering Systems, Part I. LXXX, 1319 pages. 2005.

Vol. 3673: S. Bandini, S. Manzoni (Eds.), AI*IA 2005: Advances in Artificial Intelligence. XIV, 614 pages. 2005.

Vol. 3662: C. Baral, G. Greco, N. Leone, G. Terracina (Eds.), Logic Programming and Nonmonotonic Reasoning. XIII, 454 pages. 2005.

Vol. 3661: T. Panayiotopoulos, J. Gratch, R.S. Aylett, D. Ballin, P. Olivier, T. Rist (Eds.), Intelligent Virtual Agents. XIII, 506 pages. 2005.

Vol. 3658: V. Matoušek, P. Mautner, T. Pavelka (Eds.), Text, Speech and Dialogue. XV, 460 pages. 2005.

Vol. 3651: R. Dale, K.-F. Wong, J. Su, O.Y. Kwong (Eds.), Natural Language Processing – IJCNLP 2005. XXI, 1031 pages. 2005.

Vol. 3642: D. Ślęzak, J. Yao, J.F. Peters, W. Ziarko, X. Hu (Eds.), Rough Sets, Fuzzy Sets, Data Mining, and Granular Computing, Part II. XXIII, 738 pages. 2005.

Vol. 3641: D. Ślęzak, G. Wang, M. Szczuka, I. Düntsch, Y. Yao (Eds.), Rough Sets, Fuzzy Sets, Data Mining, and Granular Computing, Part I. XXIV, 742 pages. 2005.

Vol. 3635: J.R. Winkler, M. Niranjan, N.D. Lawrence (Eds.), Deterministic and Statistical Methods in Machine Learning. VIII, 341 pages. 2005.

Vol. 3632: R. Nieuwenhuis (Ed.), Automated Deduction – CADE-20. XIII, 459 pages. 2005.

Vol. 3630: M.S. Capcarrère, A.A. Freitas, P.J. Bentley, C.G. Johnson, J. Timmis (Eds.), Advances in Artificial Life. XIX, 949 pages. 2005.

Vol. 3626: B. Ganter, G. Stumme, R. Wille (Eds.), Formal Concept Analysis. X, 349 pages. 2005.

Vol. 3625: S. Kramer, B. Pfahringer (Eds.), Inductive Logic Programming. XIII, 427 pages. 2005.

Vol. 3620: H. Muñoz-Ávila, F. Ricci (Eds.), Case-Based Reasoning Research and Development. XV, 654 pages. 2005.

Vol. 3614: L. Wang, Y. Jin (Eds.), Fuzzy Systems and Knowledge Discovery, Part II. XLI, 1314 pages. 2005.

Vol. 3613: L. Wang, Y. Jin (Eds.), Fuzzy Systems and Knowledge Discovery, Part I. XLI, 1334 pages. 2005.

Vol. 3607: J.-D. Zucker, L. Saitta (Eds.), Abstraction, Reformulation and Approximation. XII, 376 pages. 2005.

Vol. 3601: G. Moro, S. Bergamaschi, K. Aberer (Eds.), Agents and Peer-to-Peer Computing. XII, 245 pages. 2005.

Vol. 3600: F. Wiedijk (Ed.), The Seventeen Provers of the World. XVI, 159 pages. 2006.

Vol. 3596: F. Dau, M.-L. Mugnier, G. Stumme (Eds.), Conceptual Structures: Common Semantics for Sharing Knowledge. XI, 467 pages. 2005.

Vol. 3593: V. Mařík, R. W. Brennan, M. Pěchouček (Eds.), Holonic and Multi-Agent Systems for Manufacturing. XI, 269 pages. 2005.

Vol. 3587: P. Perner, A. Imiya (Eds.), Machine Learning and Data Mining in Pattern Recognition. XVII, 695 pages. 2005.

Vol. 3584: X. Li, S. Wang, Z.Y. Dong (Eds.), Advanced Data Mining and Applications. XIX, 835 pages. 2005.

Vol. 3581: S. Miksch, J. Hunter, E.T. Keravnou (Eds.), Artificial Intelligence in Medicine. XVII, 547 pages. 2005.

Vol. 3577: R. Falcone, S. Barber, J. Sabater-Mir, M.P. Singh (Eds.), Trusting Agents for Trusting Electronic Societies. VIII, 235 pages. 2005.

Vol. 3575: S. Wermter, G. Palm, M. Elshaw (Eds.), Biomimetic Neural Learning for Intelligent Robots. IX, 383 pages. 2005.

Vol. 3571: L. Godo (Ed.), Symbolic and Quantitative Approaches to Reasoning with Uncertainty. XVI, 1028 pages. 2005.

Vol. 3559: P. Auer, R. Meir (Eds.), Learning Theory. XI, 692 pages. 2005.

Vol. 3558: V. Torra, Y. Narukawa, S. Miyamoto (Eds.), Modeling Decisions for Artificial Intelligence. XII, 470 pages. 2005.

Vol. 3554: A.K. Dey, B. Kokinov, D.B. Leake, R. Turner (Eds.), Modeling and Using Context. XIV, 572 pages. 2005.

Vol. 3550: T. Eymann, F. Klügl, W. Lamersdorf, M. Klusch, M.N. Huhns (Eds.), Multiagent System Technologies. XI, 246 pages. 2005.

Vol. 3539: K. Morik, J.-F. Boulicaut, A. Siebes (Eds.), Local Pattern Detection. XI, 233 pages. 2005.

Vol. 3538: L. Ardissono, P. Brna, A. Mitrović (Eds.), User Modeling 2005. XVI, 533 pages. 2005.

Vol. 3533: M. Ali, F. Esposito (Eds.), Innovations in Applied Artificial Intelligence. XX, 858 pages. 2005.

Vol. 3528: P.S. Szczepaniak, J. Kacprzyk, A. Niewiadomski (Eds.), Advances in Web Intelligence. XVII, 513 pages. 2005.

Vol. 3518: T.-B. Ho, D. Cheung, H. Liu (Eds.), Advances in Knowledge Discovery and Data Mining. XXI, 864 pages. 2005.

Vol. 3508: P. Bresciani, P. Giorgini, B. Henderson-Sellers, G. Low, M. Winikoff (Eds.), Agent-Oriented Information Systems II. X, 227 pages. 2005.

Vol. 3505: V. Gorodetsky, J. Liu, V.A. Skormin (Eds.), Autonomous Intelligent Systems: Agents and Data Mining. XIII, 303 pages. 2005.

Vol. 3501: B. Kégl, G. Lapalme (Eds.), Advances in Artificial Intelligence. XV, 458 pages. 2005.